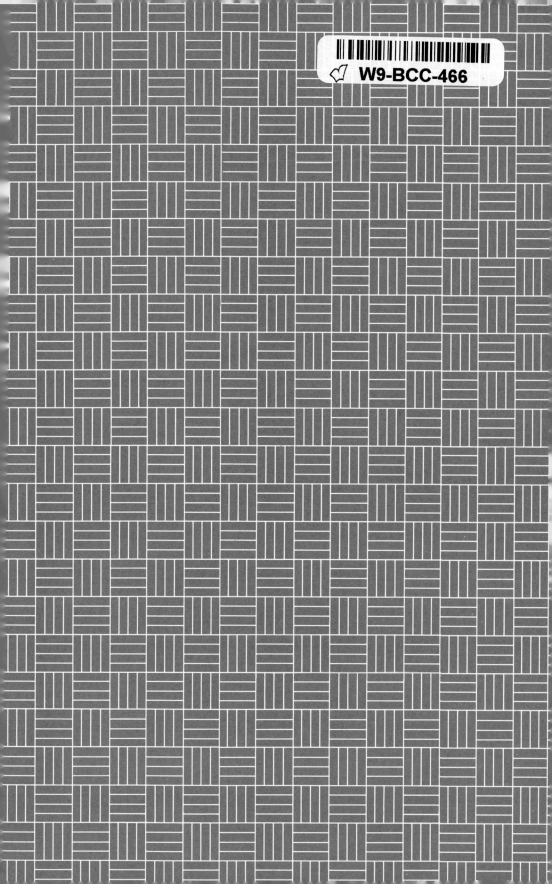

# AN ENCYCLOPAEDIA OF LANGUAGE

# AN
# ENCYCLOPAEDIA
# OF LANGUAGE

EDITED BY

## N. E. COLLINGE

**R**
## ROUTLEDGE
LONDON AND NEW YORK

First published 1990
by Routledge
11 New Fetter Lane, London EC4P 4EE
29 West 35th Street, New York, NY 10001

Typeset by Leaper & Gard Ltd, Bristol, England
Printed in Great Britain by
Richard Clay Ltd, Bungay, Suffolk

British Library Cataloguing in Publication Data

An Encyclopaedia of language.
1. Language
I. Collinge, N.E. *Neville Edgar,* 1921-
400

Library of Congress Cataloging in Publication Data

An Encyclopaedia of language / edited by N.E. Collinge.
p.      cm.
Includes indexes.
ISBN 0-415-02064-6
1. Language and languages.    2. Linguistics.    I. Collinge, N.E.
P106.A46 1989
410-dc20                    89-6203

# CONTENTS

# NOTES ON THE
# CONTRIBUTORS

*Jean Aitchison* is Senior Lecturer in Linguistics at the London School of Economics. She has two major interests within linguistics. The first is psycholinguistics, on which she has written two books: *The Articulate Mammal: an Introduction to Psycholinguistics* (3rd edition 1989) and *Words in the Mind: an Introduction to the Mental Lexicon* (1987). Her other interest is historical linguistics, on which she has published the book *Language Change: Progress or Decay?* (1981). She is also the author of *Linguistics* in the Teach Yourself' series (3rd edition 1987).

*D.J. Allerton* studied German and linguistics in Manchester, Heidelberg and Vienna. After eighteen years teaching at the University of Manchester he has since 1980 been Professor of English Linguistics at the University of Basle (Switzerland). He has over forty publications, mostly on grammatical topics but also on semantics and intonation; they include the books *Essentials of Grammatical Theory* (1979) and *Valency and the English Verb* (1982). He is currently working on various aspects of noun phrases in English and some other European languages.

*Christopher S. Butler* is Senior Lecturer and Head of the Department of Linguistics at the University of Nottingham. His first degree (from Oxford) was in biochemistry after teaching which for some years he turned to linguistics with a doctoral thesis (Nottingham) on the directive function of the English modals. As well as qualifications in music and French, he has research and teaching interests in semantics and pragmatics, systemic linguistics, computational linguistics and statistical methods. In 1985 he published three books: *Systemic Linguistics: Theory and Applications, Computers in Linguistics,* and *Statistics in Linguistics,* and has written many articles on related topics.

*Ronald Carter* is Senior Lecturer in English Studies and Director of the Centre for English Language Education at the University of Nottingham. He has published extensively in the fields of literary and linguistic stylistics, language and education, and second language teaching. His main recent publications are: *Vocabulary: Applied Linguistic Perspectives* (1987) and *Styles of English Writing* (with Walter Nash, 1988). He has edited *Language and Literature* (1982), *Literary Text and Language Study* (1982), *Linguistics and the Teacher* (1982), *Literature and Language Teaching* (1986) and *Language, Discourse and Literature* (1989). He is editor of the *Interface Series: Language in Literary Studies* published by Routledge.

*N.E. Collinge* is Professor Emeritus of Comparative Philology at the University of Manchester. A founder of the Linguistics Association of Great Britain, he has headed the linguistics departments in the universities of Toronto, Birmingham and Manchester. He has been president of the Societas Linguistica Europaea. He has published numerous articles on grammar and on historical linguistics, and books which include *Collectanea Linguistica* (1970) and *The Laws of Indo-European* (1985).

*Bernard Comrie* is Professor of Linguistics at the University of Southern California, Los Angeles. His publications include *Aspect* (1976), *The Russian Language since the Revolution* (with Gerald Stone, 1978), *Language Universals and Linguistic Typology* (1981), *Languages of the Soviet Union* (1981) and *Tense* (1985). He is the general editor of the Croom Helm series of Descriptive Grammars and edited *The World's Major Languages* (1987).

*A.P. Cowie* is Senior Lecturer in Modern English Language at the University of Leeds. He has published widely on lexicology, on the teaching and learning of vocabulary, and on the theory and practice of lexicography. He is joint compiler of the *Oxford Dictionary of Current Idiomatic English* (1975, 1983) and chief editor of the *Oxford Advanced Learner's Dictionary of Current English* (1989). He is also a member of the editorial board of the *New Oxford English Dictionary*.

*D.A. Cruse*, who has taught at the universities of Baghdad and the West Indies, has been since 1972 Lecturer in Linguistics at the University of Manchester. He has published the book *Lexical Semantics* (1986) and numerous articles on semantic and pragmatic topics. His main research interests lie in the field of lexical semantics.

*Martin Durrell* has been Lecturer in German at the University of Manchester and guest Professor at the University of Alberta. He is currently Professor of German Language and Literature at Royal Holloway and Bedford New College, University of London. His research interests comprise contrasting grammar and semantics (English-German), historical German phonology and the study of German dialects. His book *Die semantische Entwicklung der Synonymik für 'warten'* appeared in 1972 and his *A Guide to Contemporary German Usage* is due to be published in 1989.

*Paul Fletcher* is Reader in Linguistic Science at the University of Reading, having been a faculty member since 1975. His recent research has been on normal child language, and on the characterisation of language impairment. Until 1985 he was Associate Editor of the *Journal of Child Language*, and he has lectured widely in Britain and abroad on language acquisition and impairment. His recent books include *A Child's Learning of English* (1985) and *Language Acquisition: Studies in First Language Development* (with M. Garman, 1986).

*Erik Fudge* was a schoolteacher before embarking on linguistic research at the University of Indiana, USA. He became Lecturer in Linguistics at the Universities of Edinburgh and Cambridge and in 1974 was appointed to the Chair in the subject at the University of Hull. From 1988 he has been Professor of Linguistic Science at the University of Reading. He was the Editor of the *Journal of Linguistics* from 1979 to 1984; and his own major publications include *Phonology* (1973) and *English Word Stress* (1984).

*Vivien Law* was trained in classics and Germanic languages at McGill University, Montreal, and in Medieval Latin at the University of Cambridge. Now Lecturer at Cambridge in the history of linguistics, she has written one book and numerous articles on ancient and medieval linguistic thought. Her current projects include the first edition of a newly discovered late Latin grammar, a book on the discovery of form in Western linguistics, and collaborative work on linguistics in Islam and the medieval West.

*Donald C. Laycock*, a modern languages graduate of the University of New England (Newcastle, New South Wales), completed in 1962 a doctorate (ANU, Canberra) on the study of a group of Papuan languages. After teaching in North-Western and Indiana Universities, USA, he has since 1964 been a member – now Senior Fellow – of the Research School of Pacific Studies at the Australian National University. His principal interests are in Papuan and Austronesian languages, in pidgins and creoles of the Pacific region, and especially in sociolinguistics, semantics and language contact, as well as in invented languages and the legends of non-human speech.

*Geoffrey Leech* has been Professor of Linguistics and Modern English Language at the University of Lancaster since 1974, and is Chairman of the Institute of English Language Education and co-Director of the Unit for Computer Research on the English Language. He has been author, co-author, or editor of some sixteen books in the areas of grammar, semantics and pragmatics, including *Semantics* (1974, 2nd edition 1981), *Principles of Pragmatics* (1983) and *A Comprehensive Grammar of the English Language* (with R. Quirk, S. Greenbaum and J. Svartvik, 1985). Since 1987 he has been a Fellow of the British Academy.

*Ruth Lesser* is Head of the Department of Speech at the University of Newcastle upon Tyne. She graduated in English (University College, London, 1951) and Speech (Newcastle, 1971); and after three years as Ridley Fellow in Psychology she took her doctorate with a thesis in 'Verbal Comprehension in Aphasia'. Her best-known publication in that field is *Linguistic Investigations of Aphasia* (1978). Her current research includes a project funded by the Medical Research Council on the Psychological Assessment of Language Processing in Aphasia (PALPA).

*M.K.C. MacMahon* is Senior Lecturer in the Department of English Language at the University of Glasgow. He has taught in the fields of speech therapy, linguistics and phonetics, and medieval English language. His research covers aspects of speech pathology (his doctorate was on 19th century British neurolinguistics), English dialectology, and the history of phonetics. He is currently engaged in bibliographical studies in phonetics and on a biography of the English phonetician and philologist Henry Sweet.

*P.H. Matthews* has been since 1980 Professor of Linguistics at the University of Cambridge, having previously held appointments at the University College of North Wales and the University of Reading. He was an editor of the *Journal of Linguistics* from 1970-78. He has been active in discussions of the theory of grammar, and his publications include *Inflectional Morphology* (1972), *Morphology* (1974), *Generative Grammar and Linguistic Competence* (1979) and *Syntax* (1981). He is a Fellow of the British Academy.

*James Milroy* was until recently Professor of Linguistics at the University of Sheffield and is now engaged on full-time research. He has taught at the universities of Colorado, Leeds, Manchester and Belfast. He has published books on *The Language of Gerard Manley Hopkins* (1977), *Regional Accents of English (Belfast)* (1981) and *Authority in Language* (with Lesley Milroy, 1985). He is to publish a book entitled *Society and Language Change*; his current interest is in developing a social theory of language change.

*Lesley Milroy* is Professor of Sociolinguistics at the University of Newcastle upon Tyne, having previously taught at Ulster Polytechnic and having held a Senior Simon Research Fellowship at the University of Manchester (1982-83). She is the author of *Language and Social Networks* (1987), *Observing and Analysing Natural Language* (1987), and (with James Milroy) *Authority in Language* (1985). She is currently interested in applications of sociolinguistics to language problems, and sociolinguistic method and theory.

*John Mountford* taught classics before studying general and applied linguistics at the University of Edinburgh. Since 1968 he has published various articles on writing systems in the *Journal of Typographic Research* (= *Visible Language*), in the *Encyclopaedia of Linguistics, Information and Control* and in the *Information Design Journal.* He has more recently taught in the University of Southampton. He wishes to dedicate his chapter 'Language and writing systems' to the memory of Merald Wrolstad, founder and editor of the journal *Visible Language*, who died in 1987 while the chapter, in which he took a most friendly interest, was being written.

*Peter Mühlhäusler* has specialised in pidgin and creole languages since his first degree (in Afrikaans at the University of Stellenbosch). He later studied general linguistics at the University of Reading, his M.Phil thesis being on 'Pidginization and Simplification of Language', and also at the Australian National University where his doctoral dissertation was on the lexicon of Tok Pisin. He subsequently taught at the West Berlin Technische Universität, then went on to become Lecturer in General Linguistics at the University of Oxford, and is now Professor of Linguistics and Communication at the new Bond University.

*Marion Owen* took her first degree, in English language and literature, at the University of London (1975) and a doctorate in linguistics at the University of Cambridge (1980). Her thesis *Apologies and Remedial Interchanges: A Study of Language Use in Social Interaction* was subsequently published (1983). After a post-doctoral research appointment in the Department of Linguistics at Cambridge, she now works for Acorn Computers. She is currently engaged on a European Economic Community 'Esprit' project, in text-to-phoneme and phoneme-to-text conversion.

*John Payne*, having held an appointment at the University of Birmingham, has been since 1981 Lecturer in Linguistics at the University of Manchester. He has worked on the grammar of English, Russian, and the Iranian languages of the USSR, with respect of such problems as grammatical relations, sentence structure and negation. He has been a visiting faculty member at the

Australian National University. He is currently engaged on a linguistic survey of the Iranian family of languages.

*János Sándor Petöfi* is Professor of General Linguistics at the University of Bielefeld. After taking degrees in mathematics and physics at the University of Debrecen (Hungary) and in linguistics at the University of Umeå (Sweden), he has researched mainly in semantics, and text and interpretation theory. He is at present working on a monograph to provide a detailed description of his ideas on text theory. He has published, among others, the books *Transformationsgrammatiken und eine ko-textuelle Texttheorie* (1971), *Vers une théorie partielle du texte* (1974) and (with A. García Berrio) *Lingüística del texto y crítica literaria* (1978), as well as numerous articles. He is co-editor of the series *Papiere zur Textlinguistik/Papers in Textlinguistics* (1972-) and Editor of the series *Research in Text Theory/Untersuchungen zur Texttheorie* (1977-).

*Edgar C. Polomé*, a graduate in Germanic Philology from the universities of Brussels and Louvain (Ph.D 1949), was Professor of Dutch and of Linguistics and Germanic languages in Belgium, the Belgian Congo and Ruanda-Urundi. He has since 1961 been a professor at the University of Texas and since 1984 Christie and Stanley E. Adams Jr. Centennial Professor of Liberal Arts. His work has been divided between Indo-European (and especially Germanic) languages and cultures and sociolinguistic (as well as grammatical) research in East Africa and India. Among his recent books are *The Indo-Europeans in the Fourth and Third Millennia BC* (1982) and *Language, Society and Paleoculture* (1982). He is managing editor of the *Journal of Indo-European Studies* and co-editor of *The Mankind Quarterly*.

*Michael Stubbs* is Professor of English in Education at the University of London Institute of Education. A graduate of the universities of Cambridge and Edinburgh, he worked as a Research Associate at the University of Birmingham (1972-74) before becoming Lecturer in Linguistics at the University of Nottingham (1974-85). His publications include the books *Language, Schools and Classrooms* (1976), *Language and Literacy* (1980), *Discourse Analysis* (1983) and *Educational Linguistics* (1986). He has co-edited collections of articles on classroom research and on language in education, as well as publishing on teaching English as a mother tongue and as a foreign language, on stylistics, on the relations between spoken and written language, and other aspects of language in education.

*Jenny Thomas* has been Lecturer in Linguistics at the University of Lancaster since 1983. She has published widely in the areas of pragmatics, discourse analysis, and applied linguistics, in such journals as *Applied Linguistics* and the

*Journal of Pragmatics.* Two books are due to appear in 1989: *Speaker Meaning: an Introduction to Pragmatics* and *The Dynamics of Discourse.* She is particularly interested in the analysis of cross-cultural interaction, and in the language of 'unequal encounters'. She is currently undertaking research into the problems of communication among cancer patients and those who care for them.

*David Wilkins* began his career as a teacher of English as a foreign language in West and North Africa. In 1966 he was appointed to teach at the University of Reading, where he now occupies the Chair of Applied Linguistics. He has been Head of the Department of Linguistic Science, and is Director of the Centre for Applied Language Studies. His research has been in the application of linguistics to the study of second language learning and teaching. His major publications are *Linguistics in Language Teaching* (1972) and *Notional Syllabuses* (1976).

*Bencie Woll* is Research Fellow in the School of Education Research Unit at the University of Bristol, where she has been engaged since 1979 in teaching, and research on, sign languages. She has published over thirty articles in that field, and has co-authored or edited the books *Sign Language: the Study of Deaf People and their Language* (with J.G. Kyle, 1985) and *Perspectives on British Sign Language and Deafness* (with J.G. Kyle and M. Deuchar, 1981). Her current interests are in historical change and variation in British Sign Language, acquisition of sign language, and comparison between such languages.

# EDITOR'S INTRODUCTION

In the study of language the late 1980s may be seen in retrospect as an era of consolidation. No moderately aware eye will miss the epidemic of encyclopaedias of that time, their didactic sameness masked by a variety of style, even a desperate individuality. Some spread a single topic (say, dialectology) over an ample volume; some report on a kaleidoscope of topics under a summary, not always illuminating, heading (say, grammar). Some are terse and sober lexicons; some, like advertisers, seek their targets with a fine typographic frenzy. All suggest, no doubt involuntarily, that language and its study had for the moment stood still and might, while they caught their breath, conveniently sit for their portrait. And that is not a false picture.

It is not a true one, either. The truth is, as ever, muddy. Language is, after all, the medium of human interaction. Like humans, it is very rich in associations and enterprises and achievement, and fearfully complex in its own being. Neither it, nor its pursuit by scholars, ever stands still; even in apparently dormant parts lies a restless tic. At its heart are the sounds we use, the patterns we honour (however inadequately), the meanings we exploit; and phonology, grammar and semantics are their respective sciences. In the later 1980s phonology is perhaps not offering exciting new paths to the fuller understanding of how available sounds are organised. Phonetic facts, and products, are well known and documented; and hypotheses about systems have practically come to terms with one another. The domain of description (segment or sequence?) is still debated; and a novel conception of how syllables are sequenced and stress placed is being energetically 'sold'. But preclusive devotion to specific theories has faded. Grammarians still admit to different allegiances. But they take in one another's washing with surprising readiness: such a notion as 'case' is currently to be found, comfortably at home, in several apparently competing schools. Semantics concentrates on, and refines, its delineation of the manifold relations of word-meaning; but there is an air of prevailing orthodoxy.

But it must strike the objective observer, contemporary or later, how anxious grammarians now are to handle real sentences and to construe what may occur rather than simply prescribe what must; or again, how semantics has a brave and realistic special force of pragmaticists, happy only when accounting for actual effects of attested utterances in natural contexts. Grammar may worry that we might say what we cannot interpret, and semantics admit that we seem always to mean more than we say. Yet both betray an urge to confront reality; language, not theory, is once more the starting point of description. This mood of realism, and an accompanying unevenness in scholarly dynamism, is paralleled in the fields where language meets (or conveys) other activities of mind or behaviour. One thinks of the 'hyphenated' subdisciplines of 'psycho-' or 'neuro-' or 'socio-linguistics'; or of language in computation, in education, in the hands of the literary artist or critic. Where there is a will to encounter reality, there is ferment. Even where (at this volume's date) there is not much of either, there remains much solid old and recent progress to report and renewal of impetus to forecast. Still, what arrests the attention and quickens the pulses is (for example) the sheer fertility of inventive methods in neurological study of language in the brain, or the sociolinguists' empirical pursuit of facts of usage and mechanisms of change through recorded conversations within peer groups and social networks. Typology is pressed hard and rigorously verified; the problems of learners, or of the impaired, are precisely diagnosed; computation is applied to achievable ends; and a factual control on theoretical constructs is once again sought, without apology, in language history. Sign language, for a last example, is discovered to be no clumsy and threadbare substitute for speech but a natural language with a variety of forms and all the required design features (including its own evolution).

Such are the stances of the time, and such is this volume's background. Against that background, the lineaments of a serious survey must stand out pretty sharply. No longer does it do to pretend that the whole subject is quite unknown to, or misunderstood by, outsiders; interested and skilled practitioners of other sciences increasingly look to learn (and no doubt hope to criticise) what is at present merely unfamiliar to them in its ramifications. What has to be explained is just how the various branches of linguistics have arrived at their late 1980s position, just what past insights had better not be forgotten, just what are now the agreed aims and the respectable methods and the accepted results. Inanition and activity must equally be revealed; and what J. R. Firth somewhat archly desiderated of the most elegant hypotheses, a 'renewal of connection' with the data, must be constantly applied as a touchstone. This volume consists of attempts to offer that sort of testing review; acquainting with all that is valuable but selling nothing. It presupposes a reader's intelligent interest, successively, in the essential features of how language works, of how human experience and thought are mediated through it, of how it is learnt and taught, of how we express it and study it - and even itch to refashion it into shapes of our own desiring. The three parts, like the individual chapters, may each be taken on its own. But everything connects with everything else, and the inevitable linkage (if only with where a hinted aspect or an implied kindred topic may be pursued more fully) is clarified by the titles, the cross-references and the guides to further reading. The essays are meant to complement, rather than corroborate, one another; they seek to fit together to form a composite demonstration of how a trade of deep disagreements and recurrent crises of faith has already, nonetheless, produced an astonishingly consensual body of knowledge about the most characteristic of all human activities. I think they succeed.

Editorial toil on a multifarious typescript has been eased by the ready co-operation of all the contributors, who have often subordinated personal preferences to the common aim. The expert service and guidance of our publishers has been of great value; Jonathan Price especially deserves, and has, my gratitude for his considerable part in shaping this volume and for much prompt and percipient advice.

N. E. Collinge
Cambridge

# THE INNER NATURE OF LANGUAGE

# 1

# LANGUAGE AS AVAILABLE SOUND: PHONETICS

## M.K.C. MacMAHON

## 1. SOUND

Sound is the perception of the movement of air particles which causes a displacement of the ear-drum. The air particles are extremely small – about 400 billion billion per cubic inch – and when set in motion create patterns of sound-waves. Certain concepts in acoustics (frequency, amplitude, wave-form analysis and resonance) provide the bases for an understanding of the structure of these sound-waves. The subject is dealt with by Fry (1979).

## 2. PHONETICS

Phonetics (the scientific study of speech production) embraces not only the constituents and patterns of sound-waves (ACOUSTIC PHONETICS) but also the means by which the sound-waves are generated within the human vocal tract (ARTICULATORY PHONETICS). PHYSIOLOGICAL PHONETICS, which is sometimes distinguished from articulatory phonetics, is concerned specifi-cally with the nervous and muscular mechanisms of speech. The term GENERAL PHONETICS refers to a set of principles and techniques for the description of speech that can be applied to any language; it should be distin-guished from a more restricted type of phonetics concerned with those prin-ciples and techniques which are required for a phonetic statement of a specific language. Hence, for example, the phonetics of English will require some theoretical constructs which are not necessary for the phonetics of Swahili, and vice versa. In this article, the aim is to present the essential features of a general phonetic theory.

The discipline of phonetics has a long history. In India, it originated in the work of certain Sanskritic linguistic scholars between about 800 and 150 BC (see Allen 1953: 4-7 for details). In Europe, amongst the Classical Greek and

3

Roman linguists it did not achieve the same importance, although the phonetic descriptions of Aristotle, Dionysius Thrax, and Priscian merit attention (see e.g. Allen 1981). In the Middle Ages, a number of Arab and Muslim scholars showed considerable interest in phonetics (see Bakalla 1979 for a summary). From the sixteenth century onwards, especially in Britain and Western Europe, the subject attracted the attention of a number of scholars, but for a long time, until well into the nineteenth century, much of the work was carried out under the aegis of other subjects such as rhetoric, spelling reform, and language teaching. Starting in the second half of the nineteenth century and continuing into the present, the discipline has determined its own fields and methods of enquiry, building on concepts in anatomy, physiology, acoustics and psychology, and freed itself from its association with other disciplines – although its connection with linguistics remains a close one. (The articles in Asher and Henderson 1981 trace the historical development of particular aspects of phonetics.) At the present time, much of the research in phonetics is undertaken in departments and phonetic laboratories in Britain, Europe and Japan; the contribution from North America, although important, has been relatively small in relation to the number of institutions devoted to linguistics.

## 3. ORGANS OF SPEECH

The sound-waves of speech are created in the VOCAL TRACT by action of three parts of the upper half of the body: the RESPIRATORY MECHANISM, the voice-box (technically, the LARYNX), and the area of the tract above the larynx, namely the throat, the mouth, and the nose. They constitute what are known collectively as the *organs of speech*. For most sounds, air is stored in and transmitted from the LUNGS (see below under *Air-Stream Mechanisms* for the exceptions). It is forced out of the lungs by action of the rib-cage pressing down on the lungs, and of the diaphragm, a large dome-shaped muscle, which lies beneath the lungs, pressing upwards on them. Air passes then through a series of branching tubes (the bronchioles and bronchi) into the windpipe (technically, the TRACHEA). At the top of the trachea is the larynx. The front of the larynx, the ADAM'S APPLE (the front of the THYROID CARTILAGE), is fairly prominent in many people's necks, especially men's. Anatomically, the larynx is a complicated structure, but for articulatory phonetic purposes it is sufficient to take account of only two aspects of it. One is its potential for movement, the other is that it contains two pairs of structures, the VOCAL FOLDS and VENTRICULAR FOLDS. The latter lie above the former, separated by a small cavity on either side. The vocal folds are often called the vocal cords (or even vocal chords) cr vocal bands. They lie horizontally in the larynx, and their front ends are joined together at the back of

4

the Adam's Apple but the rear ends remain separated. However, because of their attachments, they can move into various positions: inwards, outwards, forwards, backwards and, tilting slightly, upwards or downwards. They are fairly thick, and when observed from the back are seen to bulge inwards and upwards within the larynx. The ventricular folds are capable of a similar, though less extensive, range of movements.

For most phonetic purposes, it is sufficient to be able to say that the vocal folds are either (i) apart – in which case the sound is said to be VOICELESS, (ii) close together and vibrating against each other – then the sound is VOICED, or (iii) totally together – in which case no air can pass between them. Further information about the action of the vocal and ventricular folds is given below in section 10.3 under *State of the Glottis and Phonation Types.*

Directly behind the larynx lies a tube running down into the stomach, the oesophagus. Both the oesophagus and the larynx open into the throat, the PHARYNX. This is a muscular tube, part of which can be seen in a mirror – the 'back of the throat' is the back wall of the central part of the pharynx. Out of sight, unless special instrumentation is available, are the lower and upper parts of the pharynx. The lower part connects to the larynx. The upper part, the NASO-PHARYNX, connects directly with the back of the NASAL CAVITIES. These are bony chambers through which air passes. At the front of the nasal cavities is the nose itself.

The contents of the mouth are critical for speech production. Starting with the upper part of the mouth, we can note the *upper lip*, the *upper teeth*, the ALVEOLAR RIDGE (a ridge of bone at the front of the upper jaw (the MAXILLA), which forms part of the sockets into which the teeth are set), the HARD PALATE and the SOFT PALATE. The soft palate (also called the VELUM because it 'veils' the nose – see below) finishes in the UVULA (Latin = 'little grape'). The soft palate, unlike the hard palate, can move, and when it is raised upwards it will make contact with the back wall of the pharynx and thereby prevent the movement of air either into the nasal cavities from the pharynx or vice versa. The movement of the soft palate can be observed by saying the vowel sound in the French word *blanc* and observing the back of the mouth in a mirror, and then saying the vowel sound in an English word like *pa*. For the French vowel, the soft palate will be lowered; for the English one, it will be raised.

The bottom part of the mouth contains the *lower lip*, the *tongue*, and the *lower jaw* (technically, the MANDIBLE), to which the tongue is partly attached. Although there is no obvious anatomical division of the tongue, in phonetics it is essential to have a method for referring to different parts of it. Hence it is traditionally divided into five parts: the TIP (or APEX), the BLADE, the FRONT (a better and more realistic term for this would be the middle), the BACK and the ROOT. An additional feature is the RIMS, the edges of the tongue. The boundaries between the five 'divisions' are established on the basis of where the tongue lies in relation to the roof of the mouth when it is at rest on the floor of the mouth. The tip lies underneath the upper central teeth, the blade under the alveolar ridge, the front underneath the hard palate, and the back underneath the soft palate. The root is the part of the tongue that faces towards the back wall of the pharynx. The reader should refer to Figure 1, which shows the outline of the organs of speech in a mid-line section of the head and neck, and should identify the position of as many as possible of the speech organs in his or her own vocal tract. A dentist will be able to show the actual shape and size of the hard palate from a plaster cast. A more detailed anatomical description of the organs of speech can be found in Hardcastle 1976.

X-ray studies of the organs of speech of different individuals show quite clearly that there can be noticeable differences – in the size of the tongue, the soft palate and the hard palate, for example – yet regardless of genetic type, all physically normal human beings have vocal tracts which are built to the same basic design. In phonetics, this assumption has to be taken as axiomatic, otherwise it would be impossible to describe different people's speech by means of the same theory. Only in the case of individuals with noticeable differences from this assumed norm (e.g. very young children or persons with structural abnormalities of the vocal tract such as a cleft of the roof of the mouth or the absence of the larynx because of surgery) is it impossible to apply articulatory phonetic theory to the description of the speech without major modifications to the theory.

## 4. INSTRUMENTAL PHONETICS

Information about the postures and movements of the vocal tract in speech comes from three sources: what the speaker can report as happening, what an observer can see to be happening, and what particular forms of instrumentation can reveal. Much phonetic theory is based on the first two sources; the sub-discipline of phonetics that considers objective data derived from instrumentation is known as INSTRUMENTAL PHONETICS or EXPERIMENTAL PHONETICS. In what follows, data from the latter source will be quoted and illustrated whenever appropriate. For a résumé of the range of instrumentation available to the phonetician, see Code and Ball 1984 and Painter 1979.

## 5. SEGMENTS AND SYLLABLES

Unless we are trained to listen to speech from a phonetic point of view, we will tend to believe that it consists of words, spoken as letters of the alphabet, and separated by pauses. This belief is deceptive. Speech consists of two simultaneous 'layers' of activity. One is sounds or SEGMENTS. The other is

6

*Figure 1.* The organs of speech.

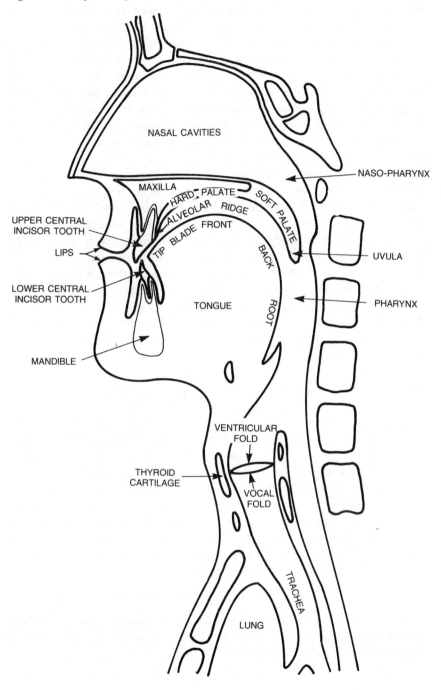

features of speech which extend usually over more than one segment: these are known variously as NON-SEGMENTAL, SUPRASEGMENTAL or PROSODIC features. For example, in the production of the word *above*, despite the spelling which suggests there are five sounds, there are in fact only four, comparable to the 'a', 'b', 'o' and 'v' of the spelling. But when the word is said fairly slowly, the speaker will feel that the word consists not only of four segments but also of two syllables, 'a' and '-bov'. Furthermore, the second syllable, consisting of three segments, is felt to be said more loudly or with more emphasis. (The subject of non-segmental features is dealt with below.)

The nature of the syllable has been, certainly in twentieth-century phonetics, a matter for considerable discussion and debate. Despite the fact that most native speakers of a language can recognise the syllables of their own language, there is no agreement within phonetic theory as to what constitutes the basis of a syllable. Various hypotheses have been suggested: that the syllable is either a unit which contains an auditorily prominent element, or a physiological unit based on respiratory activity, or a neuro-physiological unit in the speech programming mechanism. The concept of the syllable as a phonological, as distinct from a phonetic, unit is less controversial – see, for example, O'Connor and Trim 1953; and Chapter 2, section 7.2.

## 6. LINGUISTIC AND INDEXICAL INFORMATION IN SPEECH

It is necessary to draw a distinction between information in the stream of speech, both segmental and non-segmental, that is linguistic in nature and information that characterises the individual speaker. Thus, a sentence like 'When did she say she was coming?' must be articulated in such a way that the listener hears 'she', not 'he'; similarly, 'coming' not 'humming' – the pronunciation of the sentence has to be such that the necessary linguistic information can be extracted from it. But simultaneously, the speaker may wish to indicate by the pronunciation that certain words are more important linguistically than others: perhaps 'When', 'say' and 'coming', rather than 'When' and 'she'. Again, this can be seen as part of the linguistic structure of the sentence. However, the manner in which the speaker produces the sentence will provide the listener with other sorts of infor-mation: for example, about his or her sex, age, state of health, and perhaps the part of the English-speaking world he or she is from. Information of this sort about the speaker is known as INDEXICAL information. A phonetic (as distinct from a phonological) description will need to distinguish, then, between what is a linguistic and what is an indexical fact.

## 7. SEGMENT-BASED VERSUS PARAMETRIC PHONETICS

X-rays of speech show not only the considerable speed at which some of the speech organs move, but also the fact that in very few instances do the speech organs remain stationary during the production of a sound-segment. In other words, the reality of speech is usually one of near-constant movement. For descriptive purposes, though, it is necessary to assume that the speech organs adopt certain positions or postures for a brief time before adjusting to new ones. However, to avoid having to make such an assumption and to introduce greater realism into the description, speech can be viewed as the product of a series of simultaneous and mainly overlapping movements of the speech organs. Such an approach, which so far has never been fully worked out, although the principles of it have been well recognised for a long time, is known as a PARAMETRIC one, and can be distinguished from the traditional type of phonetics described here (see, for example, Catford 1977: 226-9). There are certain similarities between parametric phonetics and a type of phonological theory, namely prosodic (or Firthian) phonology.

## 8. PHONETIC NOTATION

The alphabetic writing system of many languages has not only conditioned us to think of speech as being made up of discrete sound-segments; it has also given us the terms 'consonant' and 'vowel'. But it must be stressed that although these two terms are used in phonetics, they are defined with reference to features of the sound-segments themselves, not, as in the writing system, with reference to letter-shapes. From the point of view of the writing system of English, the letter 'y' at the end of *happy* would be a consonant; but the sound at the end of the word is a vowel. The 'e' in *above* would be a written vowel, but in speech it has no value in this particular word since no sound is pronounced after the 'v'. A clear distinction must always be made, then, between sounds described informally in terms of letters of the alphabet and scientifically in terms of phonetics. It will be seen that a notation can be provided for sounds, and although this bears certain similarities to the orthographic letters of certain languages, the phonetic values are articulatory, not orthographic.

Writers on phonetic subjects have long been aware of the limitations of traditional orthographies in providing a means of symbolising unambiguously the articulatory features of sounds. In England in the sixteenth century, Sir Thomas Smith used a modified orthography to serve as a phonetic notation: for example, he wrote *charity* as 'carite' and *cheese* as 'cës'. It was only in the nineteenth century with the growth of interest in dialect research that the

9

general need arose for systems of considerable sophistication for the representation of speech. In Britain, the notational systems of Alexander Melville Bell, particularly his 'Visible Speech' (Bell 1867), provided the student of phonetics with detailed notational devices. Slightly earlier, in Europe, the work of the German scholar Richard Lepsius had led to the publication in 1855 of his *Standard Alphabet*, a system which was to be used by many descriptive linguists and phoneticians, especially those engaged in Christian missionary activities in Africa and the Far East. But the major phonetic alphabet in use today originated in the work of a group of language teachers and phoneticians in Western and Northern Europe. The alphabet of the International Phonetic Association (IPA) was developed from the late 1880s onwards, and is now regarded as the standard method of phonetic notation. Over the past century, it has undergone a number of revisions, the latest of which is 'Revised to 1979'.

In what follows, the terminology and notations of this alphabet will be used as far as possible. The use of square brackets [ ] indicates a phonetic transcription; oblique brackets / / are reserved for a phonological one (on which, see Chapter 2, section 2.1). When no ambiguity can result, some sounds will be referred to by orthographic letters.

## 9. DEFINING VOWELS AND CONSONANTS

Any segment must be either a vowel or a consonant. A vowel is a sound in which there is no narrowing or obstruction between the supralaryngeal articulators, and hence no turbulence or a total stopping of the air can be perceived. The vowel sounds in words such as *sing* or *pat* illustrate the principle; compare them with the consonants in each word. Any segment, then, which is not a vowel will be a consonant. There is, however, a problematical area. Native speakers of English 'feel' that the initial segments in the following word patterns in the same way – they are all felt to be consonants: *pat, mat, hat, yes* and *wet*. In the first two there is total stopping of the air, and hence the sounds are consonants. But in the case of *hat*, depending on how forcefully the first segment is said, the speaker may feel that there is no turbulence – so the sound would be a vowel – and certainly in *yes* and *wet* the segments are vowels. The native speaker's feeling that the sounds belong to the same sound-type derives from phonological rather than strictly phonetic considerations. For this reason it is useful to introduce two additional terms, VOCOID and CONTOID (Pike 1943: 78) into the discussion. These are defined in strictly articulatory/auditory terms, leaving vowel and consonant as phonological categories. The initial segments in *yes* and *wet* are vocoids, but function as consonants. The Sanskritic phoneticians, amongst many others, recognised the dual nature of segments of this sort (Allen 1953), and from this has arisen

# THE INTERNATIONAL PHONETIC ALPHABET

(Revised to 1979)

| | | *Bilabial* | *Labiodental* | *Dental, Alveolar, or Post-alveolar* | *Retroflex* | *Palato-alveolar* | *Palatal* | *Velar* | *Uvular* | *Labial-Palatal* | *Labial-Velar* | *Pharyngeal* | *Glottal* |
|---|---|---|---|---|---|---|---|---|---|---|---|---|---|
| CONSONANTS (*pulmonic air-stream mechanism*) | *Nasal* | m | ɱ | n | ɳ | | ɲ | ŋ | ɴ | | | | |
| | *Plosive* | p b | | t d | ʈ ɖ | | c ɟ | k g | q ɢ | | k͡p g͡b | | ʔ |
| | *(Median) Fricative* | ɸ β | f v | θ ð s z | ʂ ʐ | ʃ ʒ | ç ʝ | x ɣ | χ ʁ | | ʍ | ħ ʕ | h ɦ |
| | *(Median) Approximant* | | ʋ | ɹ | ɻ | | j | ɰ | | ɥ | w | | |
| | *Lateral Fricative* | | | ɬ ɮ | | | | | | | | | |
| | *Lateral (Approximant)* | | | l | ɭ | | ʎ | | | | | | |
| | *Trill* | | | r | | | | | ʀ | | | | |
| | *Tap or Flap* | | | ɾ | ɽ | | | | ʀ | | | | |
| (*non-pulmonic air-stream*) | *Ejective* | p' | | t' | | | | k' | | | | | |
| | *Implosive* | ɓ | | ɗ | | | | ɠ | | | | | |
| | *(Median) Click* | ʘ | | ʇ ʗ | | | | | | | | | |
| | *Lateral Click* | | | ʖ | | | | | | | | | |

DIACRITICS

- ̥ Voiceless n̥ d̥
- ̬ Voiced s̬ t̬
- ʰ Aspirated tʰ
- ̤ Breathy-voiced b̤ a̤
- ̪ Dental t̪
- ̼ Labialized t̼
- ʲ Palatalized tʲ
- ~ Velarized or Pharyngealized ɫ, ɫ
- ̩ Syllabic n̩ l̩
- ͡ or ͜ Simultaneous s͡f (but see also under the heading Affricates)
- ˔ or . Raised e˔, e̝, e̝ w
- ˕ or ˛ Lowered e˕, e̞, e̞ ʁ
- ̟ Advanced u+, u̟
- - or ̠ Retracted i̠, i-, t̠
- ̈ Centralized ë
- ~ Nasalized ã
- ˞, ʴ, ʶ r-coloured ɑ˞
- : Long ɑː
- ˑ Half-long ɑˑ
- ̆ Non-syllabic ŭ
- ̹ More rounded ɔ̹
- ̜ Less rounded y̜

OTHER SYMBOLS

- ɕ, ʑ Alveolo-palatal fricatives
- ʆ, ʓ Palatalized ʃ, ʒ
- ɼ Alveolar fricative trill
- ɺ Alveolar lateral flap
- ɧ Simultaneous ʃ and x
- ʃˢ Variety of ʃ resembling s, etc.
- ɪ = ι
- ʊ = ɷ
- ɜ = Variety of ə
- ɚ = r-coloured ə

VOWELS

*Unrounded*

| | *Front* | | *Back* |
|---|---|---|---|
| *Close* | i ɪ | ɨ | ɯ |
| *Half-close* | e | ə | ɤ |
| *Half-open* | ɛ æ | ɐ | ʌ |
| *Open* | a | | ɑ |

*Rounded*

| | *Front* | | *Back* |
|---|---|---|---|
| *Close* | y ʏ | ʉ ɷ | u |
| *Half-close* | ø | ɵ | o |
| *Half-open* | œ | | ɔ |
| *Open* | ɶ | | ɒ |

STRESS, TONE (PITCH)

ˈ stress, placed at beginning of stressed syllable: ˌ secondary stress: ¯ high level pitch, high tone: ˍ low level: ˊ high rising: ˏ low rising: ˋ high falling: ˎ low falling: ˆ rise-fall: ˇ fall-rise.

AFFRICATES can be written as digraphs, as ligatures, or with slur marks; thus ts, tʃ, dʒ: ʦ ʧ ʤ: t͡s t͡ʃ d͡ʒ.
c, ɟ may occasionally be used for tʃ, dʒ.

*(Reproduced by permission of the International Phonetic Association)*

the use for many centuries of the term 'semi-vowel'. In what follows, vowel and consonant will be retained (on the grounds of greater familiarity), although vocoid and contoid are the actual objects of the description.

## 10. CONSONANTS

In the production of any consonant at least two ARTICULATORS are used. For example, for the 'p' in *pat*, both lips; for the 't' in *ten* the blade (or, depending on the speaker, the tip) of the tongue and the alveolar ridge. (Some speakers of English use the back of the upper teeth, not the alveolar ridge.) Both sounds, then, will be consonants. Consonants which use two articulators are known as SINGLE ARTICULATIONS; those with four, DOUBLE ARTICULATIONS (examples of each are given below).

Different categories of consonant are established on the basis of (i) the actual relationship between the articulators and thus the way in which the air passes through certain parts of the tract, the MANNER OF ARTICULATION, (ii) where in the vocal tract there is approximation, narrowing or obstruction, the PLACE (or POINT) OF ARTICULATION, (iii) the activity of the vocal folds, the STATE OF THE GLOTTIS (or, more specifically, the PHONATION TYPE), and (iv) the type of mechanism used to move the column of air, the AIR-STREAM MECHANISM.

To facilitate the exposition, examples of consonant sounds will be drawn as far as possible from English. For details of these articulations in a range of other languages, see Pike 1943, Abercrombie 1967, Catford 1968, 1977 and Maddieson 1984.

### 10.1 Manner of articulation

(1) STOP The air-flow is prevented momentarily from leaving the tract by the articulators coming together. In the production of the initial sounds [p], [t], [k] in words such as *pin, tin* and *kin* the articulators (different ones in each case) come together and form an air-tight seal. Air, however, continues to leave the lungs, and as a result pressure builds up behind the articulators. After a short time, usually about 90 milliseconds, the articulators separate and the pressurised air leaves the mouth. The sound of a stop being released has sometimes been likened to a small 'explosion' – hence the use of the term *plosive* instead of stop. (The term 'stop' is sometimes distinguished from 'plosive': see section 10.6 below, under *Air-stream Mechanisms*.) The actual way in which the air is released requires further discussion – see section 10.5 below, under *Types of Stop Release*.

(2) FRICATIVE The articulators are positioned such that there is a small gap between them, and the air is forced through the gap with resulting turbulence

('friction'). The vocal tract can produce numerous fricatives. For example the initial consonant sounds [f], [θ], [s] and [ʃ] in the words *fin, thin, sin,* and *shin* involve setting the articulators to produce turbulence.

(3) AFFRICATE The sound consists of a stop followed immediately afterwards by a fricative at the same place of articulation. The initial sounds [tʃ] and [dʒ] and *check* and *just* are affricates. Using the term as a purely phonetic (rather than a phonological) category, it is possible to describe a number of other sounds as affricates: for example, the [ts] of *hits* (so long as the stop is made on the alveolar ridge or teeth and not in the larynx), the [dz] of *bids* and the [t̪θ] of *eighth.*

(4) NASAL The air is directed into the nasal cavities as a result of the soft palate being lowered away from the back wall of the pharynx. In addition, there must be a total obstruction at some point in the mouth. Examples in English are the initial consonants [m] and [n] of *man* and *net* and the final consonant [ŋ] of *hang.* (Some speakers of English have a nasal followed by a stop, i.e. [ŋg], after the vowel in this and similar words.)

(5) TAP An articulator touches another articulator very briefly and lightly so that there is a momentary interruption to the air-flow. In terms of its formation, the sound is similar to a stop, but does not last as long, nor is the contact between the articulators as firm as in a stop. Taps are used in many accents of English: for example, some speakers would use a tap [ɾ] for the 'r' sound in *merry,* others for the 'r' in *red,* others for the 'r' in *dry.* In Spanish, the 'r' of *pero* 'but' is a tap.

(6) FLAP This involves the same basic action as a tap except that the articulator that touches the other articulator then moves on to another position instead of returning, as in a tap, to its original position. A retroflex flap is used in languages of the Indian sub-continent such as Punjabi and Bengali, and may be heard in the English spoken by such speakers, in words such as *very* or *red.*

(7) TRILL A trill consists of at least two taps in quick succession. They are commonly heard in English, more from Scots than from Englishmen, in words such as *red* or *very.* The Spanish 'rr' of *perro* 'dog' is a trill [r].

(8) LATERAL An obstruction is formed between the median line of one articulator and the other articulator, but the articulators are set in such a way that air can still pass on either or both sides of the obstruction. In English the [l] sound in *land* is an alveolar (or dental) lateral: there is a median obstruction between (usually) the blade of the tongue and the alveolar ridge or the central incisor teeth, but the rims of the tongue are lowered on one or both sides, with the result that air can still pass out of the mouth.

(9) APPROXIMANT The gap between the articulators is larger than for a fricative, and no turbulence (friction) is generated. The 'r' sound in *red* is, for many speakers of English, particularly in the south of England, an

approximant [ɹ]. The 'y' and 'w' sounds ([j] and [w]) in *yes* and *wet* can be analysed as approximants; they can also be analysed as vowels – see section 9 above, under *Defining Vowels and Consonants*. This illustrates an important point: certainly in acoustic, but also to an extent in articulatory terms, the category of approximant overlaps with that of vowel. Other, older terms for approximant are FRICTIONLESS CONTINUANT and SEMI-VOWEL.

## 10.2 Place of articulation (or point of articulation)

Consonant sounds may be produced at practically any place between the lips and the vocal folds. Fifteen places are distinguished on the IPA chart.

(1) BILABIAL Both lips are used as the articulators. Examples in English are the initial consonants [p], [b] and [m] in *pin, bin* and *man*.

(2) LABIO-DENTAL The lower lip and the biting edge of the upper central incisor teeth act as the articulators. Two examples in English are the initial fricative consonants [f] and [v] in *fat* and *vat*. Other labio-dental sounds exist in English, depending on the accent and style of speech used by the speaker. For some speakers, the 'n' in *infant* or *fine fare* is a labio-dental nasal [ɱ]. Some speakers use a labio-dental approximant [ʋ] as the articulation of 'r' in words such as *roy* and *red*.

(3) DENTAL The back of the upper central incisors is one of the articulators. The other is usually the tip of the tongue; sometimes, depending on the accent or language, it may be the blade. Examples in English are the two 'th' sounds [θ] and [t̪ð] in the words *thigh* and *thy*; these are dental fricatives. Dental stops can be found in English in most speakers' pronunciations of the 'd' and 't' of *width* and *eighth*, [d̪] and [t̪]. Depending on the speaker, other manners of articulation, such as nasal and lateral, can be produced at the dental place of articulation.

(4) ALVEOLAR The alveolar ridge acts as one of the articulators; the other articulator is usually the blade of the tongue, or sometimes the tip. There are a number of alveolar consonants in English, for example the [t] and [d] in *ten* and *den*, the [n] and [l] in *knell* (no 'k' sound!), the [s] of *scenic*, the [z] of *busy*, and for some speakers the 'r' of *red* if it is pronounced as a tap or a trill. The Welsh 'll' in the word *llan* is an alveolar fricative [ɬ] in which the air-flow is lateral not median.

(5) POST-ALVEOLAR This refers to the area at the rear edge of the alveolar ridge. Productions of the 'tr' and 'dr' of *try* and *dry* often involve post-alveolar articulations. A common pronunciation of the 'r' in *red* is a post-alveolar approximant, [ɹ].

(6) PALATO-ALVEOLAR This may be regarded as an alveolar place in which there is simultaneous raising of the front (=middle) of the tongue towards the hard palate. (The technical term of this raising is *palatalisation* – see section

10.4 below, under *Secondary articulations.*) The [ʃ] and [ʒ] consonants in *sheep* and *vision* are palato-alveolar fricatives. The initial consonants in *check* and *judge* are palato-alveolar affricates. Many phoneticians do not use the term, however, perferring to describe 'palato-alveolar' sounds as variants of alveolars (or post-alveolars).

(7) ALVEOLO-PALATAL Similarly, this may be described as a place where the front of the tongue forms a manner of articulation with the hard palate and there is simultaneous raising of the blade of the tongue towards the alveolar ridge (*alveolarisation*). Adult speakers of English tend not to use this place, but alveolo-palatal consonants can be heard in the speech of young children (e.g. in *she* or *chin*) and in the normal, adult speech of other languages, for example Polish and Russian.

(8) RETROFLEX Strictly speaking, the term describes the shape of the upper surface of the tongue – i.e. the tongue is curled back or retroflexed. It is used, however, to designate a place, namely the hard palate, with which the under-side of the tip and blade forms a stricture. Examples in English, depending on the accent, are the 'r' of *red* (a retroflex approximant or a retroflex flap). Some Northern Scottish speakers use retroflex consonants in their pronunciation of the 'r', 's' and 't' in the word *first.*

(9) PALATAL The hard palate is one of the articulators; the other is normally the front of the tongue. The 'y' of *yes* [j] can be described as a palatal approximant – equally it can be described as a vowel sound. Many speakers use a palatal fricative [ç] for the 'h' at the beginning of *Hugh*. In other languages, e.g. French and Italian, other palatal manners of articulation can be found: cf the 'gne' [ɲ] of *Boulogne* and the 'gl' [ʎ] of *figli.*

(10) VELAR The soft palate (or velum) is one of the articulators. The other is usually the back of the tongue. Examples in English are the initial stop consonants [k] and [g] in *catch* and *get* and the nasal consonant [ŋ] in *hang.* The pronunciation of the Scots word *loch* contains (at least for native Scots) a velar fricative [x] after the vowel. If the tongue is set slightly further away from the soft palate than for a fricative – and therefore no turbulence results – a velar approximant will be made. A voiced velar approximant [ɰ] can be heard from some speakers of English as a production of the 'r' of e.g. *red.* The [w] sound of *wet* is also velar but it involves an additional place of articulation, and is discussed below (15).

(11) UVULAR The uvula is a relatively small object compared to the soft palate, and the production of 'uvular' sounds frequently involves not only the uvula but also the bottom half of the soft palate. The uvular fricatives [χ] and [ʁ] can occasionally be heard, for example, in certain rural Northern accents of English as realisations of the 'r' in *try* or *dry.* The sounds are standard, however, in accents of French and German and in the various accents of Arabic. A voiceless uvular stop [q] is used in, for example, Arabic. Its voiced

equivalent [θ] is much more restricted: it occurs in, for example, Somali. The uvular nasal [N], although easily pronounceable, is very restricted in the world's languages. Some accents of Eskimo use it.

(12) PHARYNGEAL (or *pharyngal*) There are few sounds at this place because of the physiological difficulty (or impossibility) of manœuvring the speech organs into the appropriate positions – a pharyngeal trill would seem to be out of the question for most vocal tracts. Arabic is a language which contains pharyngeal fricatives.

(13) GLOTTAL The vocal folds are usually employed to produce the difference between 'voiced' and 'voiceless' sounds (see also section 10.3, under *State of the glottis and phonation types*). However, they can be used as articulators to obstruct or narrow the air-flow from the lungs. The famous 'glottal stop' [ʔ] is produced with the vocal folds pushed together such that air-pressure builds up beneath the closure, which after a short time is released. The [h] in many productions of words such as *help* and *hat* can be described as a glottal fricative; an alternative, and sometimes more realistic, interpretation is that it is a type of vowel – see section 11 below, under *Vowels*.

(14) LABIAL-PALATAL This and the next place of articulation are so-called *double articulations* because they use two separate places or articulation. To make a labial-palatal approximant, for example, two simultaneous approximants must be created: one involving both lips (hence *labial*), the other the front of the tongue and the hard palate (*palatal*). Such a sound can be heard in young children's pronunciation of the 'w' of *wet* [ɥ], or in French in a normal, adult pronunciation of the consonant following the 'l' in *lui*.

(15) LABIAL-VELAR By analogy, this will be a double place of articulation involving the lips, the back of the tongue and the soft palate. The [w] in *wet* in English is a labial-velar approximant. The consonant 'wh' of *when* in many Scottish and American pronunciations of the word is a labial-velar fricative [ʍ].

## 10.3 State of the glottis and phonation types

The *glottis* is the space between the vocal folds. The term 'state of the glottis' is used more generally to refer, not to the actual space, but to the action of the folds. For simple descriptive purposes, two states are required: open (the resulting sound is voiceless) and vibrating (the sound is voiced). Sometimes the term *devoiced* is used to refer to a further state of the glottis in which there is no vibration of the folds but the volume-velocity of the air-flow is that of a voiced sound. The English word *big*, said with silence following it, will elicit a devoiced rather than a voiced [g]; compare this with the voiced [g] of *bigger*.

However, phoneticians have become increasingly aware, especially in the last 25 years, of the need for a much more rigorous descriptive and classificatory system, which will take account not only of the phonological facts of certain languages but also of the discoveries that have been made using either subjective introspective techniques of observation or instrumentation for the direct observation of the larynx (e.g. fibre-optic laryngoscopy and electromyography). Greater attention is now being paid in phonetics than previously to PHONATION TYPES, the characteristic sound-types associated with different settings of the vocal and ventricular folds. The system devised by Catford (see e.g. Catford 1977: 93-116) can be regarded as central in any discussion of the subject.

A distinction is made between the type of stricture (the actual physical relationship between the folds), and the location of the stricture: does it involve the entire length of the folds, or only part? Six categories of type of stricture are set up: CLOSED GLOTTIS (as for a glottal stop), WHISPER (a slight gap is created along at least part of the edges of the folds), BREATH (a wider gap is created, and the air-pressure is relatively high), NIL-PHONATION (the folds are set as for breath, but the air-pressure is lower), CREAK (slow irregular vibration of the front end of the folds) and VOICE (regular vibration of the folds). Combinations of these are possible: for example, breathy voice and whispery creak. Locations of stricture are less precise: the entire length of the folds, the anterior half, the posterior half, and the ventricular folds. Experience with Catford's system allows one to describe sounds such as the [b] in many pronunciations of the English word *hobby* not simply as a voiced bilabial stop, but as a whispery creaky voiced bilabial stop. A slightly different systematisation of phonation types can be found in the work of Laver (1981a). Further instrumental investigation, involving not only physiological but also aerodynamic techniques, should in due course refine the descriptive system even further.

## 10.4 Secondary articulations

In the production of the [s] of *see* the lips are unrounded, whereas in the [s] of *sue* they are rounded. Yet both fricatives are voiceless and alveolar. A further dimension of description is obviously required: SECONDARY ARTICULATIONS. These are settings of the articulators which produce a stricture no narrower than that of an approximant. In the case of [s] in *sue*, a bilabial approximant accompanies the alveolar fricative; the sound is said to be *labialised*, or *lip-rounded*. In the so-called 'dark l' of most English pronunciations of the 'l' of *help*, there is not only an alveolar (or dental) lateral, but also a velar approximant - the sound is VELARISED. Other categories of secondary articulation include PALATALISATION (raising the front of the tongue towards the hard palate) as in the 'clear l' of many Irish accents of English, and PHARYNGEAL-ISATION (retracting the root of the tongue into the pharynx) as in many Arabic consonant sounds. To the list can be added NASALISATION, in which there is simultaneous air-flow through the nose as well as through the mouth, as in the [l̃] of *tell me* (the nasalisation derives from anticipatory lowering of the soft palate for the [m]). If the nasalisation precedes the release of certain stops, the sounds are said to be PRENASALISED.

## 10.5 Types of stop release

The manner in which a stop sound is completed varies according to its context and, to to a lesser extent, according to the style of speaking. In English, for example, in the word *happy* the intervocalic [p] is released both orally and with the air flowing along an imaginary median line from the back to the front of the mouth (ORAL MEDIAN release). In *Atlantic*, if the first 't' is alveolar (or dental) and not glottal, the air will be released over the sides of the tongue in anticipation of the following lateral sound and without the median line of the tongue being removed from the alveolar ridge or the teeth (LATERAL release). The 'b' of *submerge* will, on account of the following nasal consonant, be released not through the mouth but through the nose (NASAL release). In the word *lecture* where 2 stop sounds are juxtaposed ([k] and [t]), the release of the first will be held back until it is practically simultaneous with the second (DELAYED release). Depending on the speaker, a stop such as the [t] of *tin* can be released at a slower rate, and the result will be the acoustic and auditory effect of a short fricative following the stop itself (AFFRICATED release). Finally, if a stop is released and is followed by an appreciable interval of voiceless air before the onset of the following segment, then it is said to be ASPIRATED, or more accurately POSTASPIRATED. If an interval precedes the formation of the entire stop, then that sound is said to be PREASPIRATED. Many speakers of Northern Scottish would postaspirate the [k] of *cat* and preaspirate the [t]. The duration of this interval (VOT or VOICE ONSET TIME) is critical in certain circumstances for the perception of the phonological distinction of 'voiced' and 'voiceless'.

It should be emphasized that different languages (and even accents of the same language) may contain patterns of stop releases which differ in some respects from those listed above. The subject is described in detail in Abercrombie 1967: 140-50.

## 10.6 Air-stream mechanisms

For sound-waves to be generated in the vocal tract there must obviously be motion of part of the tract. In most instances, it is the respiratory (PULMONIC) mechanism that sets an air-column in movement, and the direction of the air-flow is outwards or EGRESSIVE. (The term PLOSIVE is often reserved for a pulmonic egressive stop, leaving the term STOP as a general category for any consonant made with a total obstruction to the air-flow, or OBSTRUENT where there is some obstruction, regardless of the air-stream mechanism employed.) Consonant sounds can still be produced, albeit very quietly, if there is pulmonic INGRESSIVE air-flow: for example when counting to oneself.

A different mechanism entirely is the GLOTTALIC, in which the base of the air-column is formed at the level of the vocal folds. The folds are held together, a supralaryngeal consonantal type is made, and to force the air out egressively the larynx is moved upwards. If the sound is a stop, it is called an EJECTIVE. In many Northern and Scottish accents of English, an ejective realisation of word-final voiceless stops in certain contexts is not uncommon. In many African and North American languages, ejectives are phonologically contrastive with plosive sounds. If the larynx is lowered, rather than raised, the stop sound will be an IMPLOSIVE.

The back of the tongue moving against the soft palate can move a column of air. If it moves backwards whilst a more anterior stop is made, then the result will be a CLICK – a velaric ingressive stop. English *tut-tut*, if said as two consonants rather than two syllables, is a geminate (=repeated) alveolar click [ǁ]. The equivalent egressive sound-type is produceable but rarely used in any language.

## II. VOWELS

The notion that there are five vowels in English is quite erroneous, and derives from a confusion of letter-shapes and sounds. Most accents of English contain about 40 vowel phonemes, but the number of actual vowel sounds that can be delimited in any one accent runs into hundreds. Until the mid-nineteenth century the description of vowel sounds followed the long established tradition dating back to the Indians and the Greeks of describing vowels by means of selective consonantal terminology. Thus the vowel of *good* would be 'labial' because the lips played a part in the production of the sound; the vowel of *hit* would be 'palatine' or 'palatal' because the tongue was humped underneath the hard palate in its production; and the vowel of *far*, especially in a Southern English pronunciation, would be 'guttural' (=velar/uvular/pharyngeal) because the tongue was felt to be set well back in the mouth. It was the Scottish-American phonetician Alexander Melville Bell who was to devise a radically different and workable alternative to the older method (Bell 1867). With certain modifications, this is the method of vowel description and classification used today. The English phonetician Daniel Jones was responsible for refining some of the features of the Bell system, and it is Jones's vowel theory that will be described here.

In the production of practically all vowels, the surface of the tongue is convex when looked at in a mid-line section of the mouth, as in Figure 1. The highest point of the convex line is taken as the 'marker' of the vowel, and this marker is then plotted along two axes, horizontal and vertical. In addition, the position of the lips is noted - rounded or unrounded. (In most cases, vowels are voiced. The realisation of the 'h' of *help*, however, is best regarded as a voiceless vowel with the same tongue and lip position as the following voiced vowel.) In the mouth there is only a limited area within which vowels can be produced – in other words, the tongue's 'marker' is restricted in its move-ments, given the necessity for the tongue to retain a convex shape. This 'vowel area' or 'vowel space' lies beneath the hard and soft palates. One of Jones's contributions to the study of vowels was to define more accurately than Bell had done the shape of the vowel area. The realistic shape of the vowel area, when viewed two-dimensionally, is similar to an oval – more precisely, it is almost identical to two hysteresis curves in electro-magnetism. But for practical purposes, various deliberately distorted versions of the shape have been employed. Special terminology, some of it deriving from Bell, is used for the names of the lines. The trapezium shape of Figure 2 is the one to be encountered in most works on phonetics.

*Figure 2.* The Cardiunal Vowel chart. Symbols towards the inside are for *unrounded* vowels.

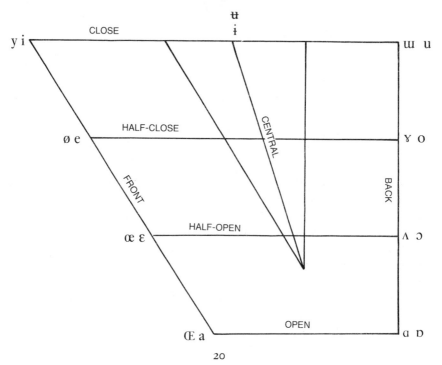

Jones's other, more famous contribution was to provide a set of reference points around the periphery of the area in relation to which any vowel sound of any language whatever could be plotted. These reference points are known as the Cardinal Vowels. Altogether there are 18 Cardinal Vowels, divided for reasons to do with the early history of the system into 2 sets, Primary and Secondary. (Some phoneticians have argued for the need for a further 4 central vowels; these were not included by Jones in his system.) The distance between adjacent Cardinal Vowels may not be physically the same, but there is, nevertheless, what Jones called 'auditory equidistance' between them – at least for the Primary set. It must be emphasised that the Cardinal Vowels are reference points: they are not to be seen as in any sense 'more important' than non-Cardinal vowels.

The qualities of the Cardinal Vowels cannot be learned from a verbal description. They must be acquired either from recordings, of which Daniel Jones made three, or, better still, from a phonetician who has been taught them. Ideally, there should be an unbroken 'line of descent' from Daniel Jones! With training, a student of phonetics will acquire a Jonesian pronunciation of the vowels and will then be able to apply the knowledge in the plotting on the vowel chart of any vowel sound of any language whatever.

The notation of vowel sounds which are not Cardinal in quality can be achieved by two methods. Special diacritics exist to indicate particular directions of movement away from a Cardinal Vowel. The notation of a Southern English pronunciation of *ah*, for example, could be [ɑ̟]. An alternative, but less accurate method for some vowel sounds is to employ a set of 'float' symbols. These refer to general areas within the vowel space, not to specific points. They are set out in Figure 3. When making a phonological transcription (see Chapter 2, section 4.1), the use of a particular Cardinal Vowel symbol does not necessarily mean that the phonological unit represented by that symbol is Cardinal in quality. The choice of a symbol for a vowel phoneme is dependent on a number of factors, including the proximity of the phoneme to a Cardinal Vowel and the availability of particular symbols on typewriter and computer keyboards.

Jones's vowels are MONOPHTHONGS, that is, sounds which do not vary in quality within a syllable. Most productions of the vowel of *good* will be of this type. If, however, there is an adjustment in the quality of a vowel, as a result of tongue or lip movement or both, the sound will be a DIPHTHONG. (Some earlier phonetic descriptions often used 'vowel' as equivalent to 'monophthong', leaving 'diphthong' as a separate category. That distinction is no longer followed.) Articulatorily, diphthongs can be classified in two ways: in terms of tongue movement across the vowel space, and secondly in terms of changing auditory prominence. In the production of the diphthong in the word *boy*, the tongue moves forwards and upwards in the mouth at the same

*Figure 3.* The 'float' vowel symbols and their approximate areas.

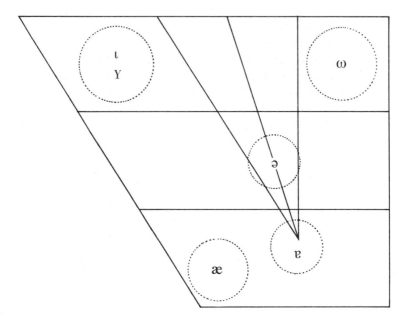

time as the lips unround; whereas in many English pronunciations of the word *hear* the tongue moves into the centre of the vowel space. These and other possible types of movement lead to the setting up of the following diphthong types: FRONT CLOSING, BACK CLOSING, FRONT OPENING, BACK OPENING, and CENTRING.

The second method of classification is quite different and relies on the auditory judgement of increasing or decreasing prominence during the diphthong. For example, in the word *boy* one senses a greater degree of prominence at the beginning rather than at the end of the diphthong; the diphthong is therefore described as *falling*. (The prominence falls away or decreases. It has nothing to do with pitch movement.) The reason for the change has, in this particular case, to do with the greater sonority of the first part of the diphthong compared with the second part. In the word *tide* as pronounced by a Scottish speaker, the second part of the diphthong is more prominent, due to the speed at which the tongue moves from a more open position to a closer one, and the diphthong is therefore described as *rising*.

Any vowel sound, whatever its type, may be accompanied by certain other features. For example, if the soft palate is in a lowered position, then the vowel will be nasalised. The French phrase *un bon vin blanc* illustrates 3 (and for some speakers, 4) nasalised vowels. In English, nasalisation of vowels is fairly common if the vowel occurs between nasal consonants. Compare the nasalised quality of the vowel in *man* with the non-nasalised quality in *bad*. See, however, section 12.4 below, on *Voice quality features* for a refinement of this statement.) Secondly, since only the front or back of the tongue forms the highest point of the tongue surface during the production of vowels, the tip and blade and/or root are able to take up specific positions if need be. Thus, a vowel may be, for example, a front vowel but be simultaneously 'coloured' by retroflexion of the tip and blade. Many vowels occurring before /r/ in South Western English and in many American accents of English have this 'r-coloured' or *retroflexed* quality.

## 12. NON-SEGMENTAL FEATURES

These can be divided into three sorts: first, those which involve the manipulation of the parameters of loudness, pitch and duration; second, those features which act more or less as a constant auditory background to everything a person says (voice quality), and third, those which are superimposed on the stream of speech for specific emotional reasons (voice qualifications).

### 12.1 Loudness

*Loudness* is the perceived correlate of an increase of energy in the outflow of air from the lungs. It can be measured as an acoustic phenomenon in decibels. Some accents of English, especially in the South of England, are noticeably louder than accents further north. A language like Arabic can sound louder – at least in some accents – than for example English or German.

The term STRESS is often used by describe the physical characteristics that underlie the creation of loudness. Stress depends on power, that is the power exerted by the respiratory system to move the column of air from the lungs, bearing in mind the obstructions that that column may meet on its path from the lungs to air at atmospheric pressure beyond the vocal tract (see Catford 1977: 80-5 for a discussion of the concept of stress). To say, however, that the second syllable in the word *ago* is 'stressed' – as many phonetics textbooks do – is to raise a further issue, namely the role played by other prosodic features in the creation of so-called stress. Certainly, in many (if not all) accents of English, the physical constituents of stress (in the sense in which we say that the second syllable of *ago* is stressed) embrace not only respiratory power but also pitch change and to a lesser extent the duration and the relative sonority of the syllable itself. For a discussion of some of the issues involved in 'stress' in English (or, to use a preferable term, ACCENT), see Gimson 1980: 221-6.

## 12.2 Pitch

The role that the vocal folds play in speech has already been mentioned in connection with the glottal place of articulation and phonation types. A further, and equally important, role is to mediate PITCH in speech. The subjective impression of pitch corresponds in most cases to the speed at which the vocal folds vibrate: a slow speed of movement correlates with a low pitch, a fast speed with a higher pitch. The actual physical values of the speeds associated with low and high pitches vary from individual to individual, but for an adult male the lowest pitch that might be used in normal, unemotional conservation might be c 70 Hz, and the highest might be c 120 Hz. For an adult female, the figures might be c 150 Hz and c 290 Hz respectively. From these figures can be established a range of pitch values within which the speaker will operate, the TESSITURA.

*Figure 4.* Pitch patterns in a pronunciation of 'When did she say she was coming?'.

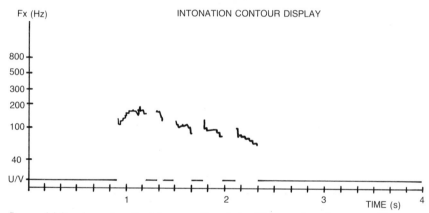

Source: Adult male speaker, English accent. Data derived from an electrolaryngographic analysis, Phonetics Laboratory, University of Glasgow. Gaps in the contour represent voiceless sounds.

A description of pitch changes in speech can be made either instrumentally (see Figure 4 for example) or subjectively. Working subjectively, the phonetician assesses the relative position in the tessitura of the individual syllables and the contour of the pitch – either level, falling or rising. The result is then plotted on a scale and an analysis is carried out of the patterns of pitch movements. The IPA alphabet provides certain diacritics to indicate the general pitch pattern of syllables or larger units, which can be incorporated into a transcription of the segments of speech; a tessitura-based diagram then becomes unnecessary.

In any discussion of pitch changes in speech, the terms TONE and

INTONATION require clarification. The former refers to the use of pitch to signal a lexical difference. In Mandarin Chinese, for example, the syllable [dʒi] will convey different meanings depending on the pitch with which it is said: *clothing, aunt, chair* or *easy*. See Figure 5 for instrumental traces of a slow pronunciation of the four words. The majority of the world's languages are *tonal.* The term *intonation* means the use of pitch fluctuation for exclusively non-lexical purposes. Languages such as English, French, German, Russian and Japanese are 'intonation languages'.

The analysis of intonation in English would involve establishing a domain or unit within which pitch fluctuation operates: usually it is taken to be the 'tone-unit', which may or may not correspond with the grammatical phrase or clause (see Chapter 2, sections 7.6, 9.5). Within the tone-unit, the pattern of pitch movement is analysed with reference to the 'accented' syllables; possible types of movement are then set up. Once the range of pitch movements has been established, attention is focused on the relation between the various movements and grammatical and attitudinal factors. For a description of English intonation within these terms, see Crystal 1969.

## 12.3 Duration

Segments are traditionally described subjectively as either short, half-long or long. Duration as a non-segmental feature is most relevant in the area of RHYTHM, the temporal organisation of stressed and unstressed syllables. The word *ago* will be felt by native speakers of English to contain a short syllable followed by a somewhat longer one. Measurements can be made of the duration of each syllable, either in milliseconds or in a musical notation (dotted crotchets etc). For most phonetic purposes, though, it is sufficient to provide a subjective assessment of the duration, using the terms 'short' and 'long', with for some languages an intermediate degree of 'medium' or 'half-long'. But the description of rhythm hinges as much on the relationship of syllables to stress as on the length of the individual syllables. One could, for example, relate the rhythm of a sentence such as 'When did she say she was coming' to the ISOCHRONOUS (equal-timed) pulsing of the stresses *when, say* and *com-*, and draw up a scheme of rhythm which emphasises the isochrony of the stresses and the effect that this has on the lengths of the individual syllables. An alternative, but related approach is to discuss the isochrony of the stressed syllables in relation to the grammatical structure of the sentence, and set up 'rhythm units' based on this. For English, at least, both approaches can be found. (See Chapter 2, section 7.5.)

*Figure 5.* The syllable [ɑ3i] in Mandarin Chinese said on four different tones.

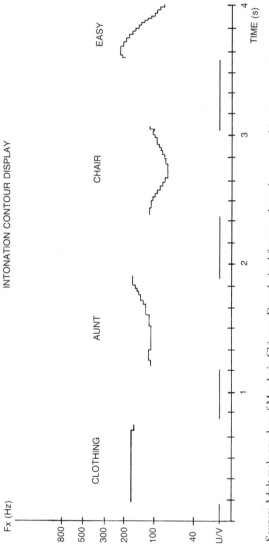

INTONATION CONTOUR DISPLAY

Source: Adult male speaker of Mandarin Chinese. Data derived from an electrolaryngographic analysis, Phonetics Laboratory, University of Glasgow.

## 12.4 Voice quality features

Listening to a speaker of any language, one is soon aware of a certain constant background colouring to everything that is said. It might be breathiness, or nasalisation, or a general 'dullness' or, conversely, strong resonance in the voice. The term *voice quality* has been given to this constant or near-constant background auditory effect. For many years, impressionistic labels have been used to try to capture the essence of the quality: for example, a 'silvery' voice, or a 'sepulchral' voice, or a 'sexy' voice (see Laver 1981). In recent years, however, attention has been focused on the phonetic constituents which together create the auditory impression of 'silveriness' etc. (The major study of the subject is Laver (1980).

Three factors can be isolated. One is the distance from the larynx to the lips, which can be shortened or extended by movement of the larynx and/or the lips. A particular length of tract, maintained by the speaker more or less all the time he or she is speaking, will give rise to acoustic effects which are then judged impressionistically to relate to a certain voice quality feature. A second factor is the arrangement within the mouth and pharynx of particular articulators: a constant forward setting of the tip and blade of the tongue and raising of the front of the tongue towards the hard palate will lend a certain 'effeminate' quality to a male speaker's voice; raising and backing of the tongue so that the centre of gravity is higher and further back in the mouth is characteristic of many Northern English pronunciations of English; and permanent slight lowering of the soft palate, even in so-called oral sounds, will introduce a degree of nasalisation into the voice. (For a historical survey of this topic see Laver 1978.) The third factor is the habitual use of phonation types: many male speakers of English have some creak and whisperiness in their voice quality. Studies of voice quality across different accents of languages are at a fairly early stage, but the main parameters of the descriptive system have already been established.

## 12.5 Voice qualifications

Finally, there are a number of voice qualification features. These differ from voice quality features in that they are not permanent, but are superimposed on speech according to specific emotional circumstances. The terms *laugh*, *cry, tremulousness* and *sob* will be self-evident. For further discussion of their place in the overall phonology of English, and indeed of non-segmental phonology generally, see Crystal 1969.

# REFERENCES

Abercrombie, D. (1967) *Elements of General Phonetics*, Edinburgh University Press, Edinburgh.

Allen, W.S. (1953) *Phonetics in Ancient India*, Oxford University Press, London.

Allen, W.S. (1981) 'The Greek Contribution to the History of Phonetics', in Asher, R.E. and Henderson, E.J.A. [eds]: 115-22.

Asher, R.E. and Henderson, E.J.A. [eds] (1981) *Towards a History of Phonetics*, Edinburgh University Press, Edinburgh.

Bakalla, M.H. (1979) 'Ancient Arab and Muslim Phoneticians: An Appraisal of Their Contribution to Phonetics', in Hollien, H and Hollien, P. [eds] *Current Issues in the Phonetic Sciences. Proceedings of the IPS-77 Congress, Miami Beach, Florida, 17–19th December 1977*. Benjamins, Amsterdam, Part 1:3-11.

Bell, A.M. (1867) *Visible Speech: the Science of Universal Alphabetics*, Simpkin & Marshall, London.

Catford, J.C. (1968) 'The Articulatory Possibilities of Man', in Malmberg, B. [ed.] *Manual of Phonetics*, North-Holland Publishing Company, Amsterdam: 309-33.

Catford, W.C. (1977) *Fundamental Problems in Phonetics*, Edinburgh University Press, Edinburgh.

Code, C and Ball, M.J. (1984) *Experimental Clinical Phonetics. Investigatory Techniques in Speech Pathology and Therapeutics*, Croom Helm, London.

Crystal, D. (1969) *Prosodic Systems and Intonation in English*, Cambridge University Press, Cambridge.

Fry, D.B. (1979) *The Physics of Speech*, Cambridge University Press, Cambridge.

Gimson, A.C. (1980) *An Introduction to the Pronunciation of English*, [3rd edn] Edward Arnold (Publishers) Ltd, London.

Hardcastle, W.J. (1976) *Physiology of Speech Production: An Introduction for Speech Scientists*, Academic Press, London.

Laver, J. (1978) 'The Concept of Articulatory Settings: an Historical Survey' *Historiographia Linguistica*, 5: 1-14.

Laver, J. (1980) *The Phonetic Description of Voice Quality*, Cambridge University Press, Cambridge.

Laver, J. (1981) 'The Analysis of Vocal Quality: from the Classical Period of the Twentieth Century', in Asher, R.E. and Henderson, E.J.A. [eds]: 79-99.

Lepsius, R. (1855; 2nd edn 1863) *Standard Alphabet for Reducing Unwritten Languages and Foreign Graphic Systems to a Uniform Orthography in European Letters*, Williams & Norgate, London: W Hertz, Berlin [Reprinted with an Introduction by J.A. Kemp, 1981, Benjamins, Amsterdam.]

Maddieson, I. (1984) *Patterns of Sounds*, Cambridge University Press, Cambridge.

O'Connor, J.D. and Trim, J.L.M. (1953) 'Vowel, Consonant, and Syllable - A Phonological Definition' *Word*, 9: 103-22.

Painter, C. (1979) *An Introduction to Instrumental Phonetics*, University Park Press, Baltimore.

Pike, K.L. (1943) *Phonetics. A Critical Analysis of Phonetic Theory and a Technic for the Practical Description of Sounds*. The University of Michigan Press, Ann Arbor.

## FURTHER READING

Abercrombie, D. (1967) *Elements of General Phonetics*, Edinburgh University Press, Edinburgh.

Catford, J.C. (1977) *Fundamental Problems in Phonetics*, Edinburgh University Press, Edinburgh.

Catford, J.C. (1988) *A Practical Introduction to Phonetics*, Oxford University Press, Oxford.

Ladefoged, P. (1975) *A Course in Phonetics*, Harcourt Brace Jovanovich, New York.

O'Connor, J.D. (1973) *Phonetics*, Penguin Books, Harmondsworth.

Pike, K.L. (1943) *Phonetics; A Critical Analysis of Phonetic Theory and Technic for the Practical Description of Sounds*, The University of Michigan Press, Ann Arbor.

# 2

# LANGUAGE AS ORGANISED SOUND: PHONOLOGY

## ERIK FUDGE

## 1. INTRODUCTION

General Phonetics, as described in Chapter 1, gives an account of the total resources of sound available to the human being who wishes to communicate by speech. In its essence it is thus independent of particular languages. Phonology gives an account of, among other things, the specific choices made by a particular speaker within this range of possibilities. In the first instance, therefore, phonology is concerned with a single language, or, to be more precise, a single variety of a language. General phonological theories can be built up only at one remove, i.e. on the basis of phonological facts established for particular languages. There are thus many fundamental differences between the two disciplines.

To begin with, the data of General Phonetics are, in principle if not in fact, just about all observable; the same is, however, not true of Phonology. This has consequences which are well expounded by Fischer-Jørgensen; observing that older theories of phonology are not totally out of date, she continues (1975: 2):

In this respect there is an important difference between phonology and phonetics. Phonetics is dependent on technical apparatus; rapid and continuous technical development, especially in recent years, has resulted in a steadily increasing growth of our phonetic knowledge. . . . Older phonetic studies . . . are therefore regarded by everybody as outdated and of historical interest only.

It is not quite the same with phonology. . . . phonological analysis does not produce new concrete facts which must be acknowledged by everybody in the same way as phonetics. . . . the phonological schools differ chiefly in having different general views due to the historical-philosophical context in which they are placed.

The advances in phonetic study to which Fischer-Jørgensen draws attention have proved that more and more detail is discoverable in the speech signal, and that it is very rare for two repetitions of an utterance to be exactly identical, even when spoken by the same person. At the same time, it is clear that for communicative purposes much of this detailed variation is quite irrelevant: the fundamental assumption of linguistic study is that many utterances, even if differing in detail, are taken by members of a speech-community as being alike in form and meaning, cf. Bloomfield (1933: 78).

Phonetic study also disproves a common fallacy about the nature of speech, i.e. the assumption that speech is made up of 'sounds' which are built up into a sequence like individual bricks into a wall (or letters in the printed form of a word), and which retain their discreteness and separate identity. One difficulty is that the various organs involved in the production of a particular sound move at different speeds: a slow-moving organ needs to be set in motion a fraction of a second before a quicker-moving one, or may go on moving after the quicker organ has stopped. Movements of the organs thus overlap in complicated ways, and this often makes it very difficult to say at what precise instant a sound actually begins or ends.

Again, particularly where vowel sounds (strictly VOCOIDS see Chapter 1, section 9) occur next to each other, the precise location of the boundary between them may be hard to establish. In the utterance *I see all that*, for example, the vocal tract moves from the position for [iː] in *see* to the position for [ɔː] in *all*, but does not move instantaneously: there is a brief phase during which the vocal tract in fact moves through all the positions between [iː] and [ɔː], and so makes all the sounds between [iː] and [ɔː] (note, furthermore, that there is not a finite number of positions or sounds between [iː] and [ɔː], but a continuum). Hence any decision to locate the boundary between [iː] and [ɔː] at a specific point on that journey would be entirely arbitrary, just as it would be arbitrary to attempt to locate the boundary between two neighbouring letters in a cursive script at a precise point on the pen-stroke joining them.

The human hearer, however, is not aware of such transitions: in perceiving speech the ear has been trained to ignore phonetic facts which are unavoidable, purely automatic, consequences of the way the vocal tract functions. We assume therefore that such transitions will not be among the phonologically relevant aspects of the signal. As a first approximation, then, we could say that the phonological representation of an utterance is obtained from the totality of phonetic properties of that utterance by discarding all phonetic properties which the speaker is 'forced' to produce and concentrating on the properties which he is able to control and alter at will. If this is the case, then it is much more reasonable to regard the phonological representation as being a string of individual, discrete elements much like letters in a printed word.

As a theory of phonology, the position just outlined is in fact deficient in two important respects:

(i)   A number of the properties which the speaker *can* control are also not relevant in a phonological sense (for further discussion see section 2 below);

(ii)  The notion that phonologically relevant properties connected with an utterance are necessarily *physically present in the utterance* is not in fact correct (see section 4 below).

For the present, however, this over-simple theory points us in the right direction in beginning to establish the difference between Phonology and Phonetics.

There are a number of general works on phonology which can be recommended. Hyman (1975) is a widely-used textbook, and is for the most part genuinely introductory. Lass (1984) is rather more advanced, but will prove stimulating to the reader who has a grasp of the basic concepts in phonology. Fischer-Jørgensen (1975) and Anderson (1985) aim at a detailed treatment of the historical development of the subject, and the philosophical issues it raises. Fudge (1973a) is an anthology of some of the key articles in the field. Works on more specific aspects of the field will be referred to at the appropriate points in the remainder of this chapter.

## 2. DISTINCTIVENESS

### 2.1 Phoneme and allophone

In Standard English as spoken in England, the *l* of *feel* is pronounced differently from the *l* of *feeling*: in the former, the body of the tongue is bunched up towards the soft palate (velum) (see Chapter 1, sections 10.1 and 10.4), while in the latter it is not. The technical term for the former articulation is 'velarised', though the usual term applied to the velarised *l* of *feel* is 'dark [l]' (from the sound effect of lowered pitch which velarisation causes); correspondingly the non-velarised *l* of *feeling* is referred to as 'clear [l]'. Other varieties of English do not exhibit this difference: many Scots and American varieties have dark [l] in both *feel* and *feeling*, while many Irish varieties have clear [l] in both words. This shows clearly that the difference between the two sounds is in principle under the control of the speaker.

Further investigation, however, will show that, for the Standard English speaker, the difference between clear [l] and dark [l] is completely predictable from the phonetic context in which the *l* appears: before a vowel the pronunciation is clear [l] (cf. *feeling, leaf, law*), while in all other contexts (i.e. before a consonant, as in *field, help*, and in word-final position, as in *feel, well*) *l* is always dark. When the difference between two similar sounds is completely predictable in this way from the phonetic context, we say that they are ALLOPHONES of the same PHONEME.

Some scholars have viewed the phoneme as a family of sounds (allophones) in which (i) the members of the family exhibit a certain family resemblance, and (ii) no member of the family ever occurs in a phonetic context where another member of the family could occur. The technical terms for these two properties of allophones of the same phoneme are (i) PHONETIC SIMILARITY and (ii) COMPLEMENTARY DISTRIBUTION.

In transcriptions, if the units being transcribed are phonemes rather than allophones, it is customary to enclose the symbols in slant lines: /l/. If, on the other hand, the transcription specifies allophones, square brackets are used: [ł]. There is a general tendency for phonetically-based writing systems to have separate symbols for distinct phonemes, while allophones of the same phoneme are not separately represented.

It is important to notice that sounds which are allophones of the same phoneme in one language may in other languages operate as distinct phonemes. In Russian, for example, sounds very similar to clear [l] and dark [l] can make a difference of meaning: /mɔl/ 'moth' v. /mɔł/ 'pier'. Such differences between allophonic status and phonemic status can cause difficulties for learners; English learners of Russian will have no trouble learning Russian /mɔł/ 'pier', with dark [ł] in the final position, but may be expected to find /mɔl/ 'moth' problematic because of the clear [l] in a position where it would not appear in English.

For the allophone v. phoneme distinction see Jones (1957), Jones (1950: chapters II-IX), Hyman (1975: 5-9).


## 2.2  Some allophones in English

Other examples of sets of English sounds which are allophones of one phoneme include the following:

(*a*) At the beginning of a stressed syllable, voiceless plosives are strongly aspirated (cf. Chapter 1, section 10.5); in other words, after the lip closure of /p/ is released, the vocal cords do not begin to vibrate for the vowel immediately, but only after a perceptible delay, giving rise to a puff of breath before the vowel proper begins. When preceded by /s/, on the other hand, these plosives are unaspirated; the vocal cords in this case begin to vibrate immediately after lip closure is released, and no puff of breath intervenes. Thus *pin* is pronounced [phɪn], whereas *spin* is [spɪn]. The strongly aspirated [ph] never occurs after /s/, and the unaspirated [p] never occurs at the very beginning of a syllable. Again, at the end of a syllable, /p/ may be slightly aspirated. However, if followed by a /t/ (as in *chapter*), the closure for the /p/ is very likely not to be released until the release of the /t/ closure occurs (cf. the [k] of *lecture* in the example cited in Chapter 1, section 10.5). Again, an utterance-final /p/ (as in *Come on up!*) is quite likely not to be released at all.

(*b*) Any vowel followed by a voiceless sound is shorter than the same vowel phoneme followed by a voiced sound. For example, the vowel of *beat* is shorter than that of *bead*, the vowel of *bit* is shorter than that of *bid*, and the vowel of *rice* is shorter than that of *rise*. 'Shorter vowels' of this kind are not to be confused with the 'short vowels' which *contrast* with 'long vowels' e.g. the vowel of *bid* in contrast with the vowel of *bead*. The difference between short and long in *bid/bead* is a difference between two distinct phonemes, whereas the difference between shorter and longer in *beat/bead*, *bit/bid*, and *rice/rise* is an allophonic one. We shall refer to the shorter vowels of the allophonic pairs as 'shortened', and to the longer members as 'non-shortened'; where necessary, the shortened allophone of /iː/ will be transcribed [i], without a length mark.

(*c*) English /r/ has at least four different allophones: it is voiceless after voiceless aspirated plosives (the delay in the onset of vocal cord vibration is likely to persist through most or all of the /r/ in such cases), and voiced elsewhere. After the alveolar plosives /t/ and /d/, the tongue tip is close enough to the alveolar ridge to set up turbulence in the air stream, giving a fricative sound (cf. Chapter 1, section 10.1(2); this fricative is voiceless after the aspirated /t/ and voiced after /d/. After sounds other than /t/ and /d/, or initially in a word, there is no turbulence, and the sound is an approximant (cf. Chapter 1, section 10.1(9)).

(*d*) For many speakers the 'long *o*' phoneme has a much more 'back' pronunciation before dark [l] than before other sounds: *coat* is pronounced [kəut] (where the vowel begins as a central vowel) while *coal* is [kɔuɫ] (in which the beginning of the vowel is fully back). For the terms 'central' and 'back', see Chapter 1. Section 11, Figure 2.

For some purposes, allophones of the same phoneme may need to be recognised as important – a beginner learning English as a foreign language, for example, may well have to practise making the difference between clear and dark [l], and that between 'shortened' [i] and 'non-shortened' [iː] etc., if his pronunciation is to sound right. For other purposes, however, these differences can safely be ignored: English spelling, for instance, loses nothing in clarity by noting both clear and dark [l] with the same letter *l*, 'shortened' [i] and 'non-shortened' [iː] with the same set of possibilities *e-e* (as in *concrete*), *ea* (as in *bead*), *ee* (as in *meet*), etc., all the allophones of /r/ with the same letter *r*, and central and back 'long *o*' *o-e* (as in *vote*), *oa* (as in *boat*), etc.

A fuller description of English allophones may be found in Gimson (1980: Part II), or O'Connor (1973: chapter 5).

## 2.3 Distinctive differences

Where a particular phonetic difference does not give rise to a corresponding phonemic difference, we say that this phonetic difference is NON-DISTINC-TIVE. Thus [fi:l] with a clear [l] will be perceived as an unusual pronunciation of *feel*, not as a word which is totally different from *feel*; the difference between [fi:l] and [fi:ɫ] is non-distinctive. On the other hand, differences which can give rise to a change of meaning, i.e. phonetic differences between phonemes, are referred to as DISTINCTIVE. The difference between [p] and [b] in English for example, is distinctive: *pit* and *bit*, *ample* and *amble*, *tap* and *tab*, are pairs of distinct words, not alternative pronunciations. Clearly, all distinctive differences within a language must be readily perceptible to native speakers of that language.

A few of the non-distinctive differences present in their language may also be perceptible to native speakers: thus, many native speakers of English find it reasonably easy to become aware of the difference between clear [l] and dark [l]. Most such differences, however, can be perceived by native speakers only after some degree of phonetic training. Speakers of another language, on the other hand, may readily perceive certain non-distinctive differences in English, especially where these differences are distinctive in their own language. Russian speakers, for instance, might be expected to have no difficulty whatever in hearing the difference between English clear [l] and dark [l].

Typically, distinctive differences recur in different parts of the inventory of phonemes. Whatever the difference is between English /b/ and /p/ (traditionally called 'voicing', though as we shall see in section 2.5, it is not always signalled by the presence of vocal cord vibration), the same difference is used to distinguish /d/ from /t/, and /g/ from /k/. A very similar difference distinguishes /v/ from /f/, and /z/ from /s/. Likewise the difference between /m/ and /b/ is the same as that between /n/ and /d/ ('nasality'), and the difference between /s/ and /t/ is the same as that between /z/ and /d/ ('continuance'). The net result of this situation is that the phonemes of English fall into classes for which the distinctive features form convenient labels: /p t tʃ k f θ s ʃ h/ are the class of 'voiceless' sounds in English, /t d s z θ ð l n tʃ dʒ ʃ ʒ r/ are the 'coronals' (sounds made with the tongue tip or blade raised – see Chapter 1, Figure 1), /m n ŋ/ are the 'nasals', /ɪ e æ ɒ ʊ ʌ/ are the 'short vowels', and so forth.

The symbols [ɪ] and [ɑ], for the vowel sounds in *big* and *good*, have the free variants [i] and [u].

For an account of distinctiveness and of phonological theories founded on that notion, see Hyman (1975: 5–9 and chapter 2), and Fischer-Jørgensen (1975: chapter 3).

## 2.4 Distinctive features and the phonological system

These classes of phonemes can be represented as being characterised by the presence or absence of certain properties: thus voiceless sounds will all be marked 'absence of the property "voicing"', coronal sounds 'presence of the property "tongue tip or blade raising"', nasal sounds 'presence of the property "nasality"', etc. This information may be displayed in a diagram like Table 1, which lists the properties or 'features' in the left hand column, and then shows for the sound at the head of each column whether the property is present (by inserting '+' in the appropriate cell), or absent (by inserting '−'). There is no one generally agreed assignment of feature values for English, nor even one generally agreed set of features; Table 1 represents just one possible way of analysing the English consonant system.

*Table 1*: One method of using distinctive features to set up natural classes of English consonant phonemes.

| | p | b | f | v | w | m | k | g | h | y | ŋ | t | d | s | z | θ | ð | l | n | ʧ | ʤ | ʃ | ʒ | r |
|---|---|---|---|---|---|---|---|---|---|---|---|---|---|---|---|---|---|---|---|---|---|---|---|---|
| Sonorant | − | − | − | − | + | + | − | − | − | + | + | − | − | − | − | − | − | + | + | − | − | − | − | + |
| Nasal | − | − | − | − | − | + | − | − | − | − | + | − | − | − | − | − | − | − | + | − | − | − | − | − |
| Coronal | − | − | − | − | − | − | − | − | − | − | − | + | + | + | + | + | + | + | + | + | + | + | + | + |
| Anterior | + | + | + | + | + | + | − | − | − | − | − | + | + | + | + | + | + | + | + | − | − | − | − | − |
| High | − | − | − | − | + | − | + | + | − | + | + | − | − | − | − | − | − | − | − | + | + | + | + | − |
| Continuant | − | − | + | + | + | − | − | − | + | + | − | − | − | + | + | + | + | + | − | − | − | + | + | + |
| Voiced | − | + | − | + | + | + | − | + | − | + | + | − | + | − | + | − | + | + | + | − | + | − | + | + |
| Strident | − | − | − | − | − | − | − | − | − | − | − | − | − | + | + | − | − | − | − | + | + | + | + | − |

Brief explanations of the features used:
[+ sonorant]:        Air flow not radically restricted.
[+ nasal]:            Velum lowered, allowing air through nasal passages.
[+ coronal]:        Tongue tip or blade raised.
[+ anterior]:       Constriction at alveolar ridge or further forward.
[+ high]:             Tongue body raised.
[+ continuant]:     Air flow through oral cavity not blocked.
[+ voiced]:          Vocal cords vibrate (but see section 2.5).
[+ strident]:        High level of noise ('sibilance').
Minus values of a feature mean the absence of the property.

By taking the intersections of these various classes, we obtain smaller classes: e.g. the 'voiceless fricatives' /f θ s ʃ/ are the class of English sounds which in feature terms are both [− voiced] and [+ continuant]; the 'coronal sonorants' / l n r/ are the class which are both [+ sonorant] and [+ coronal]; the 'alveolar plosives' /t d/ are the class which are [− sonorant], [+ coronal],

[− anterior] and [− continuant]; in the framework we have set up here, the 'labials' /p b f v w m/ are in fact the set of sounds which are both [− coronal] and [+ anterior].

For more detailed accounts of the theory of distinctive features, see Hyman (1975: chapter 2), Jakobson and Halle (1956), Fudge (1973b).

## 2.5 Distinctive features and acoustic cues

It appears plausible to assume that the distinctive features might be precisely the cues which enable hearers to distinguish the phonemes which, to express it in terms of the over-simplified theory put forward in section 1, occur in speech. In the past, several approaches to phonology actually made this assumption (see e.g. Jakobson and Halle 1956), but it now appears clear that the range of cues actually used by hearers is much wider than the range of distinctive features. The distinctive feature distinguishing /b/ from /p/, for example, (referred to as 'voicing' in section 2.3 above), may correspond to any of the following acoustic cues depending on the context (see Parker 1977):

(i) When preceding stressed vowels (e.g. *bat* vs. *pat*): the vocal cords begin to vibrate for /b/ significantly earlier than for /p/, aspiration (see Chapter 1 section 10.5) may occur with /p/ but not /b/, the pitch contour of the following vowel begins significantly lower for /b/ than for /p/, etc.;

(ii) When between two vowels, the second being unstressed (e.g. *ribbing* v. *ripping*): the silent interval between the vowels is significantly shorter for /b/ than for /p/, the vocal cords may begin to vibrate before the end of the silent interval for /b/ but not for /p/;

(iii) When word-final (e.g. *tab* v. *tap*): the preceding vowel is longer for /b/ than for /p/, and runs smoothly into the /b/, whereas it is terminated abruptly for /p/ by a closure of the vocal cords; if the plosive is released, the manner of release for /b/ is different from that for /p/.

Notice that some of these acoustic cues in fact refer to information which is *non-distinctive*: the shortening of vowels before voiceless consonants, for instance. This shows how important it is that foreign learners of a language acquire the correct ALLOPHONES of the phonemes of that language, in order to provide native hearers with the acoustic cues they expect.

# 3. ALTERNATIONS

## 3.1 Allophones and alternations

In the *feel/feeling* case which we considered earlier, the two words concerned are closely connected (being different forms of the root *feel*): the difference may be described as an ALTERNATION (the pronunciation of the root alternates between [fiːɬ] for the infinitive and [fiːl] with a clear [l] for the participle). Allophones of the same phoneme often participate in alternations in this way. However, it is not necessary to have an alternation in order for two sounds to be allophones of the same phoneme. Indeed, there are some languages, e.g. Vietnamese, in which morphological processes like suffixation and prefixation just do not occur, but which do have allophonic variation.

Conversely, the existence of an alternation does not necessarily indicate that the alternating sounds are allophones of the same phoneme. Consider, for example, *felt*, the past tense form of the verb *feel*: assuming the *-t* of *felt* represents the past tense suffix (cf. *learn/learnt*), we have an alternation between *feel* [fiːɬ] and *fel-* [feɬ]. This certainly does not mean that [iː] and [e] are allophones of the same phoneme: there are plenty of pairs of words like *beat/bet, sheaf/chef, reek/wreck* which use the difference between [iː] and [e] as a distinctive difference. Here, then, we have an alternation between distinct phonemes. Alternations of this kind are often termed MORPHOPHONEMIC alternations, because they are alternations between phonemes, with morphological relevance.

Certain morphophonemic alternations are more regular than others: the /iː/ v. /e/ of *feel/felt* recurs in *kneel/knelt* and *deal/dealt*, but is not the normal case for verbs in /-iːl/: *appeal, conceal, heal, heel, keel, peel, reel, repeal, reveal, seal, squeal, wheel* all have the same vowel /iː/ in their past tense as in their base form (*steal* is a different case again – see the next paragraph). On the other hand, the alternation between /s/ and /z/ in the regular plural suffix of English is just about totally predictable for all roots: when the immediately preceding phoneme is voiceless, the suffix has the form /s/, as in *cats* /kæts/, while if the immediately preceding phoneme is voiced, the suffix is pronounced /z/, as in *dogs* /dɒgz/ and *horses* /hɔːsɪz/ (note that in the last example it is the (voiced) vowel /ɪ/, not the voiceless consonant /s/, which immediately precedes the consonant of the plural suffix).

A third type of case is exemplified by the verb *steal*, with past tense *stole*. Here there is no suffix to signal the past tense; this is in fact signalled by the vowel change (ABLAUT, to give it its traditional name). Thus in this case the vowel change is not an alternation in the sense we are dealing with here.

The /s/ ~ /z/ alternation recurs in the pronunciation of the possessive ending (*cat's* /kæts/ v. *dog's* /dɒgz/), in the third person singular ending in the present of verbs (*looks* /lʊks/ v. *sees* /siːz/), and in the contracted forms of *is* and *has* (*it's arrived* /ɪts/ v. *he's arrived* /hiːz/).

Analogous to the /s/ ~ /z/ alternation is the /t/ ~ /d/ alternation shown by regular past tenses and past participles in English: /t/ after a voiceless sound, as in *stopped* /stɒpt/, but /d/ after a voiced sound, as in *stayed* /steɪd/ and *waited* /weɪtɪd/.

Accessible accounts of morphophonemic alternations may be found in Martinet (1973) and Lass (1984: 55–62).

### 3.2 Differences between varieties of the same language

So far we have been speaking of alternations between forms in the *same* variety of a language. However, as our remarks above on the pronunciation of *l* in different varieties of English begin to suggest, the situation becomes much more complex when we compare different regional or social accents. While not all speakers can consistently reproduce accents in their own speech, the overwhelming majority of speakers are able to understand a very wide range of regional and social varieties. Our understanding of other people's speech does not depend on their use of exactly the same sounds as we use in our own speech.

All this indicates clearly that it is not merely the *phonetic properties* of sounds which are important for the hearer, but also the *place* each sound holds *within the system* of sounds (see Sapir 1925). This is particularly true of vowel sounds; speakers appear to set up a series of correspondences between the differing vowel sounds of other varieties and their own vowel sounds. These correspondences, in fact, may cut clean across the correspondences which might be set up on phonetic grounds between the sounds of one variety and those of another. Thus, a Cockney's pronunciation of *know* might well be physically very similar to an RP speaker's pronunciation of *now*, while the RP speaker's *know* could be just like a Scotsman's *now*. Again a Yorkshire speaker's *know* might be almost identical with the RP *gnaw*.

A further complication arises from the observation that, across varieties, *the systems themselves* may differ from one another as well as the pronunciations of the vowels within the system. Thus many Northern English speakers have a system of five short vowels instead of the six in RP and other varieties: the vowels of *put* (RP [pʊt]) and *putt* (RP [pʌt]) are not distinguished (both pronounced by some Northerners as [pʊt] and by others as [pət]). Many Scots speakers have no distinction corresponding to /ʊ/ v. /uː/ in RP: for them, *soot* and *suit* are pronounced identically, as [sʉt].

We are still not at an end of the complicating factors. A major clue in the establishment of links across systems is of course the fact that the same words tend to have the same systematic units in them: the word *know* which was our example above, for instance, consists for all the speakers mentioned of a consonant /n/ (pronounced just about identically for everyone) followed by a vowel, which is pronounced very differently in each case, but corresponds to the same systematic unit for all speakers – a unit which we might term 'long *o*'. Many other words, e.g. *boat*, *home*, will likewise have 'long *o*' as their vowel for all the speakers.

Sometimes, however, a word may not have the (systematically) same vowel unit across all varieties: many people begin the word *economics* with 'long *e*' (the vowel of *beat*), while others, with an equal claim to be speaking Standard English, begin it with 'short *e*' (the vowel of *bet*). Some speakers say *neither* with 'long *e*', others with 'long *i*' (the vowel of *bite*). Situations of this kind may be referred to as LEXICAL-DISTRIBUTIONAL differences between the varieties concerned (Wells 1982: 78–9), or SELECTIONAL differences (O'Connor 1973: 182–4).

Finally, the relationship between a careful pronunciation of a particular phrase by a particular speaker and a colloquial pronunciation of the same phrase by the same speaker may be an extremely complicated one, and raises a whole range of further problems for the phonologist. The word *extra-ordinary*, for example, has a whole range of pronunciations, ranging for most British English speakers from the hyper-careful [ˈekstrəˈʔɔːdɪnərɪ] through the fairly careful [ɪkˈstrɔːdn̩rɪ] to the very colloquial [ˈstrɔːnrɪ].

O'Connor (1973; 152-75) gives a clear account of the range of vowel sounds which may represent particular systematic vowel units in different varieties of English. A thorough but readable account of the differences between the systems underlying different varieties is given by Wells (1982).

## 4. PHONOLOGICAL REPRESENTATIONS

### 4.1 Types of transcription

Types of speech may vary from one occasion of speaking to another, as we have seen in section 3. Different types of transcription must also be recognised: we have already encountered PHONEMIC and ALLOPHONIC transcriptions (section 2). Under the influence of tiredness, inebriation, or perhaps even the presence of food in the mouth, utterances can be distorted from the norm for the variety concerned. In that case we can distinguish between a transcription which represents that norm, and one which attempts to represent every detail of the utterance including any distortions from the norm. The former has been termed a SYSTEMATIC transcription and the latter an IMPRESSIONISTIC transcription.

In most cases, impressionistic transcriptions will be allophonic, and phonemic transcriptions will be systematic. Allophonic transcriptions, on the other hand, may be either systematic or impressionistic. Any transcription used in the task of transcribing speech in an unknown language is by definition impressionistic: the investigator has no basis for deciding that certain features of pronunciation are norm or distortion until he becomes familiar enough with the language.

Notice that the first paragraph of this section speaks of a transcription which '*attempts* to represent every detail of the utterance': the investigator making an impressionistic transcription can never be absolutely sure he has succeeded in including every single phonetic detail, however carefully he may be aiming at such an ideal. Modern phonetic instruments may be able to give extremely detailed measurements of many features of sounds, but even then we cannot know for certain whether they are measuring every phonetic detail which could possibly be of relevance.

A third pair of terms for types of transcriptions is BROAD v. NARROW. In the strict sense, these are synonymous with phonemic and allophonic respectively: a broad transcription is one which shows no detail which is contextually predictable, while a narrow transcription is one which shows some contextually predictable detail. It is thus possible to recognise degrees of narrowness in transcriptions: one which showed clear [l] and dark [l] for English, but no other allophonic detail, would be narrow, but not very narrow, whereas one which in addition showed minute allophonic detail of vowels, aspiration and non-aspiration for voiceless stops, and voiceless [l], [r], [w] and [j] where these occurred, would be very narrow. The term 'broad' is often used in a loose sense meaning 'not very narrow'.

Thus for some phoneticians, the term 'broad phonetic transcription' is synonymous with 'phonemic transcription', whereas for others it means an allophonic transcription in which comparatively little allophonic detail is shown.

For more detail on types of transcription see Abercrombie (1964: 16–24).

## 4.2 Morphophonemic transcription

A further type of transcription has sometimes been advocated: one which takes account of certain common morphophonemic alternations (see section 3.1 above) and in effect incorporates them into the transcription. This results in what is known as a MORPHOPHONEMIC transcription and is often indicated by the use of braces: { . . .}. For example, the verbs *feel, deal* and *kneel* contain an /i:/ which alternates with /e/ in the formation of the past tense and the past participle (see section 3 above), and might therefore be transcribed as {f i: ~ e l} and {d i: ~ e l} and {n i: ~ e l} respectively; the notation {i: ~ e} indicates that the vowel of the stem is sometimes /i:/ and sometimes /e/, depending on the context in which the stem finds itself. The past tenses *felt, dealt* and *knelt* would then be transcribed {f i: ~ e l + t}, {d i: ~ e l + t} and {n i: ~ e l + t} respectively, where '+' represents the boundary between the root and the suffix. (See Chapter 3 for these terms.)

The remaining verbs ending in /−i:l/. which form their pasts regularly (*peel* /pi:l/, *conceal* /kən'si:l/ etc.), would be transcribed with {i:}, and would therefore have a morphophonemic transcription identical with their phonemic transcription. Again, words ending in /-elt/ which were not pasts, e.g. *melt* /melt/, *felt* ('type of cloth') /felt/, would have morphophonemic transcriptions identical to the phonemic ones.

This would have the effect that the same sound in the same phonetic context might be transcribed in two different ways depending on the morphological properties of the word concerned. Thus /i:/ in *feel* would be {i: ~ e}, whereas the (phonetically identical) /i:/ of *peel* would be {i:}; the /e/ of *felt* (past of *feel*) would be {i: ~ e}, whereas the /e/ of *felt* ('type of cloth') would be {e}. In many approaches the notation {i: ~ e} represents a unit which is referred to as the MORPHOPHONEME.

It will be noticed that, for many segments in English, the morphophonemic transcription does not differ from the phonemic; indeed there are languages in which no differences at all between the two transcriptions will ever occur. This brings into question the need to have both transcriptions.

There are two ways of dealing with this situation. One is to say that morphophonemic transcriptions are on a different level from phonemic transcriptions, and that a truly phonological transcription does not take account of morphophonemic alternations; for those who espouse this view, the phonemic transcription is thus the only one which is of importance to phonology. The other possible approach is to say that a morphophonemic transcription is just a phonemic transcription with occasional excursions into regions beyond; *feel* and *felt* (past of *feel*) would then be transcribed /f {i: ~ e} l/ and /f {i: ~ e} l t/ respectively. In these transcriptions, /f/, /l/, and /t/ are phonemes, while {i: ~ e} would represent, not a different type of unit, but an instruction to choose /i:/ in one specifiable set of contexts and /e/ in another set of contexts; for *felt* this would be 'choose /e/ for past tense or past participle, and /i:/ in all other contexts': see Lass 1984: 57-8.

A modification of this second approach led in the 1950s and 1960s to the development of the theory known as 'generative phonology' (see section 5 below).

## 4.3 Informal speech and phonological representation

One approach to phonology takes it that the communicative essentials of an utterance may be extracted by throwing away the adventitious, purely automatic properties of the sound wave (cf. the position provisionally adopted in section 1 above). This view implies that the phonologically relevant units are in a real sense *in* the phonetic signal. This approach runs into difficulties with informal or colloquial speech, however: many of the properties which systematically are taken to be a part of the form of a word may in these contexts not be present within the speech signal at all (cf. the representations of the word *extraordinary* in section 3.2 above).

Take, for instance, the English word *seven* (phonetically [sevən] in careful speech). The fricativeness of the segment after the [e] vowel would certainly be taken as an essential property (the distinctive feature [+ continuant]) of that segment: in English the difference between [b] and [v] is distinctive, since e.g. *ban* and *van* are different words. In informal speech the word might be pronounced something like [sebm], where the segment after [e] is a plosive (and thus [− continuant]), not a fricative; the essential distinctive feature of fricativeness ([+ continuant]) can no longer be found in the speech signal at this point. Indeed, in very colloquial speech the pronunciation might well be simplified to something like [sem], in which what was originally the fricative has no separate existence of its own in the speech signal.

The view that the phonologically relevant properties are *in* the speech signal would in fact require that each word of the language had to have a different phonological form for each style of utterance. In our example *seven* would have the forms /sevən/ for careful speech, /sebm/ for informal speech, and /sem/ for fast colloquial speech. This would appear to be excessively complicated.

A more illuminating approach is to view the phonological representation of an utterance as a form of prescription or plan for the utterance (see e.g. Linell 1979: 47–69). The utterance might then follow the plan closely (as in careful speech) or depart from it in varying ways (as in informal or colloquial speech).

A helpful analogy here is with a yacht race. The race is defined by a series of marker buoys, which are the counterpart of the phonological representation. In the race itself, probably no two yachts steer exactly the same course, and yet every yacht's course is recognisably governed by the markers. The markers, like the elements of the phonological representation, are discrete; the courses steered are continuous, and any decision to split the course into sections which relate exclusively to one particular marker buoy will be arbitrary.

The analogy breaks down in two respects:

(*a*) In a race, the markers are the same for all yachts, whereas, as we have already seen (section 3.2 above), the phonological 'markers' for speech may be genuinely different across speakers.

(*b*) Yachts must pass outside the markers in every case, on pain of disqualification, whereas there is no such requirement in speech. In careful speech it is quite often the case that the prescription is followed closely, but, in informal and colloquial speech, the phonetic 'course steered' may often 'cut off corners', make merely token gestures towards the 'markers', or even ignore them completely. The only requirement is that, on the basis of the 'course steered' by the speaker, the hearer can guess what 'markers' the speaker has in mind. This is done on the basis of contextual information, such as the knowledge of what strings of phonemes actually form words.

## 5. PHONOLOGICAL RULES

### 5.1 Rules linking phonemes and allophones

Phonemic and allophonic transcriptions can be related to one another by statements which are often referred to as RULES. Thus the two types of [l] in English can be related to the phoneme /l/ by a rule like the following:

$$
/l/ \rightarrow \begin{cases} \text{[l] before a vowel} \\ \\ \text{[ł] elsewhere} \end{cases}
$$

This rule expresses the fact that English speakers consistently pronounce these two sounds differently, and yet at the same time treat them as if they were 'the same', finding it quite normal that one symbol in the spelling system can stand for either of the sounds. Since English speakers do not in normal circumstances produce [l]-sounds which 'break' the above rule (i.e. they do not produce dark [l] before vowels or clear [l] utterance-finally), they can be said to 'know' the rule, even though most of them will not be able to bring the contents of the rule to conscious awareness.

Other rules of English (implied by examples (*a*) to (*d*) in section 2.2 above) include the following:

$$
(a) \quad /p/ \rightarrow \begin{cases} \text{[p] after /s/ in syllable-initial position} \\ \text{[ph] initially in a stressed syllable} \\ \text{[p⹁] (unreleased) before another plosive} \end{cases}
$$

$$
(b) \quad /i:/ \rightarrow \begin{cases} \text{[i] (shortened) before a voiceless sound} \\ \text{[i:] elsewhere} \end{cases}
$$

$$
(c) \quad /r/ \rightarrow \begin{cases} \text{voiceless fricative after syllable-initial /t/} \\ \text{voiced fricative after syllable-initial /d/} \\ \text{voiceless approximant after syllable-initial /p/ or /k/} \\ \text{voiced approximant elsewhere} \end{cases}
$$

$$(d) \quad /\text{ou}/ \rightarrow \begin{cases} [\text{ɔu}] \text{ before dark [l]} \\ \\ [\text{əu}] \text{ elsewhere} \end{cases}$$

Notice that the processes stated in rule (a) apply to *all* voiceless plosives, and not merely to /p/. It is thus an advantage to use the distinctive feature notation introduced in section 2.4, so that /p/ to the left of the arrow is replaced by the notation for the class of voiceless plosives, i.e.:

$$\begin{bmatrix} - \text{ sonorant} \\ - \text{ continuant} \\ - \text{ voiced} \end{bmatrix}$$

Note too that rule (b) may be generalised to *all* vowels, a class which can be represented by the single feature [+ syllabic] ('has the property of forming the nucleus of a syllable').

Again, rule (c) can be restated more illuminatingly by using distinctive features, and by recognising first, that /r/ is basically a voiced approximant, and second, that two distinct processes operate on it: (i) fricativisation (when the /r/ is preceded by any alveolar plosive), and (ii) devoicing (when the /r/ is preceded by any voiceless plosive). Where the /r/ is preceded by /t/ (the voiceless alveolar plosive) both of these processes operate.

The first part of the restated rule (c) would then say something like:

(c) (i) The [+ sonorant] feature of /r/ becomes [− sonorant] after a sound which is [− sonorant], [+ coronal], [− anterior] and [− continuant]: informally 'approximant /r/ becomes a fricative after /t/ or /d/'.

The second part would say something like:

(c) (ii) The [ff voiced] feature of /r/ becomes [fl voiced] after a sound which is [− sonorant], [− continuant] and [− voiced]: informally, 'voiced /r/ (whether approximant or fricative) becomes voiceless after /p/, /t/ or /k/'.

As well as making it possible to refer to classes of phonemes, distinctive features can make explicit another frequently-occurring property of allophonic rules. In both (c)(i) and (c)(ii) above, the value of one feature of the segment concerned is altered to agree with the value of that same feature in the preceding segment: in (c)(i) the feature concerned is [sonorant] and its value changes from + to −, while in (c)(ii) it is [voiced] and its value again changes from + to −. Processes of this kind are cases of ASSIMILATION.

The revised form of rule (c) in fact comprises two rules; in the word *dry* only (c)(i) applies, in *cry* only (c)(ii), whereas in *try* both rules apply. In this particular instance, it does not matter whether (c)(i) applies to *try* before (c)(ii) or after it: the same result (a voiceless fricative pronunciation of /r/) obtains

45

in both cases. In other cases, things may turn out to be more complex: for a discussion of problems involving the order of application of rules see Hyman (1975: 125–31), Kenstowicz and Kisseberth (1979: chapter 8), Fischer-Jørgensen (1975: 257–61).

## 5.2 Rules handling morphophonemic alternations

We should also note that it is possible to use rules of a rather similar form to handle morphophonemic alternations (see section 3.2 above). Thus for English:

$(e)$ {i: ~ e} → 
- /e/ in a past tense or past participle
- /iː/ elsewhere

$(f)$ {s ~ z} → 
- /s/ after a voiceless sound
- /z/ elsewhere

$(g)$ {t ~ d] → 
- /t/ after a voiceless sound
- /d/ elsewhere

The major systematic difference between the two types of rule is that allophonic rules have phonemes as input and allophones as output, whereas morphophonemic rules have morphophonemes as input and phonemes as output. Note too that $(e)$, unlike $(f)$ and $(g)$, involves reference to information which is not phonological: not all phonologists are agreed that this is legitimate (see section 5.3 below).

An examination of rules $(e)$, $(f)$ and $(g)$ indicates that the morphophonemes {i: ~ e}, {s ~ z} and {t ~ d} are not strictly speaking necessary for the description of the phenomena concerned. If we took the phoneme specified by the 'elsewhere' line of the rule and assumed that this was the one which occurred as basic in all instances of the words concerned, we could specify that it changed into the other phoneme in the relevant context. Thus the plural suffix could be given the form /z/, and rule $(f)$ could be modified to say:

$(f')$ /z/ → /s/ after a voiceless sound

Of course, $(f')$ will have to be further restricted to prevent it from applying in utterances like *If Zoe comes*, in which /z/ occurs immediately after a voiceless phoneme /f/. In this particular case, all that is needed is to restrict the context to 'after a voiceless sound within the same word'.

Similarly, *felt* could be /fiːl + t/, but the rule would have to state $(e')$

(actually, (*e'*) applies in a number of other contexts, but this fact will be ignored for present purposes).

(*e'*) /iː/ → /e/ in past tenses of verbs like *feel*, but not of verbs like *peel*

This is not such a simple modification, chiefly because it introduces factors which are not phonological at all, i.e. the difference in morphological behaviour between two classes of verbs: for discussion of whether this kind of information can legitimately be referred to in phonological rules, see section 5.3.

This results in the simplification of the *transcription* of utterances, but on the other hand the *rules* have to be made more complex: the information implicit in the morphophonemic notation must be made explicit in the rules themselves.

Although morphophonemic units are no longer present in rules like (*e'*) and (*f'*), these rules are still normally referred to as morphophonemic rules, in that their function is very much the same as that of rules (*e*), (*f*) and (*g*). The situation now is that both types of rules have phonemes as input; morphophonemic rules have phonemes as output also, whereas allophonic rules have allophones as output.

It has been claimed that there are sometimes advantages in refusing to draw a strict distinction between the two types of rule. Consider, for instance, the following facts: In Russian, a voiceless obstruent (i.e. plosive, affricate or fricative: see Chapter 1, section 10.1.) becomes voiced when immediately followed by a voiced obstruent. In most cases, voicing a voiceless obstruent in Russian changes it into a distinct phoneme (/t/ becomes /d/, /k/ becomes /g/, etc.); in the cases of /ts/, /tʃ/ and velar fricative /x/, however, there is no corresponding voiced obstruent in the phonemic system. This means that the resulting sounds [dz], [dʒ] and [ɣ] occur *only* before voiced obstruents, while the sounds [ts], [tʃ] and [x] *never* occur in that context: the three voiced sounds are therefore allophones of the /ts/, /tʃ/ and /x/ phonemes respectively. Thus for these sounds the process of voicing will have to be an allophonic rule, while for all other obstruents the process of voicing will have to be a morphophonemic rule: the result of this is that one and the same phonological process (assimilatory voicing) has to be stated twice:

(i) A voiceless obstruent other than /ts/, /tʃ/, /x/ becomes the corresponding voiced obstruent phoneme before a voiced obstruent.

[A morphophonemic rule]

(ii) /ts/ → [dz]
/tʃ/ → [dʒ]   } before a voiced obstruent
/x/ → [ɣ]                          [An allophonic rule]

Furthermore, there is no simple way of specifying the class of phonemes

47

'/ts/, /tʃ/ and /x/' by using distinctive features, so that rule (ii) has to be stated in terms of individual cases; still less is it possible for the class of phonemes 'voiceless obstruents other than /ts/, /tʃ/, /x/' to be simply and naturally specified, which makes (i) above a very complex rule to state.

What happens if the process is stated as a single process of assimilation? In this case the rule we need is (iii):

(iii) A voiceless obstruent becomes voiced before another voiced obstruent.

This rule has much greater generality than (i) and (ii), and is much simpler to state. If we adopt it as preferable, however, an important consequence follows: the distinction between allophonic and morphophonemic rules is blurred. This in turn brings into question the status of the phonemic representation, and hence the status of the phoneme as defined in section 2 above.

On the grounds of the existence of situations like the voicing of obstruents in Russian, the 'generative phonologists' have fully accepted the consequence described in the previous paragraph, and have recognised just *two* significant levels of representation, neither of which corresponded exactly to the phonemic:

(*a*) A kind of morphophonemic representation which they term 'systematic phonemic representation'.

(*b*) A fully-specified allophonic representation which they refer to as 'systematic phonetic representation'. (Note that the general theoretical question of determining when a phonetic representation has become 'fully-specified' (cf. section 4.1 above) has not been treated by the generative phonologists.) No other kind of representation had any real significance, and in particular the 'pure phonemic' transcription (not taking account of alternations) was an artefact with no systematic status. For a full discussion see Fischer-Jørgensen (1975: 280–6), Halle (1959), Chomsky (1964): for an exhaustive application of the approach to English see Chomsky and Halle (1968).

## 5.3 The use of non-phonological information in rules

Phonologists have disagreed fundamentally on the question of how far it is legitimate for phonological rules to refer to facts other than those of pronunciation. The traditional linguistic description places phonology first, morphology second, and syntax third. There is some practical justification in doing this, as putting phonology first enables the reader to pronounce the words which are involved in the later sections. Similarly, putting morphology before syntax focuses attention on the words themselves before considering the constructions in which they are involved.

Some phonologists have taken this to imply that in stating the phonology of a language, it is illegitimate to call on information from the later sections of the description. This is also, of course, consistent with the view that 'phonological representation equals phonetic representation minus predictable phonetic features'. For phonologists who adopt this approach, the whole of morphophonemics, even if closely related to phonology, lies strictly outside it. Pike (1947) outlines this approach, and gives some reasons why other phonologists of the period do not entirely accept it.

The problem was given an entirely new dimension by the generativists in the 1960s. A generative grammar typically starts by stating the syntactic processes of a language (or even, in some cases, the semantic structure), and treats them as logically prior to the phonological rules; in this view, the phonology is purely a means of giving a phonological (and ultimately a phonetic) interpretation to the words of a language in their constructions with one another. Such an approach, far from using *none* of the information contained in the syntactic and other parts of a language description, can in fact legitimately use *any* of this information. For an indication of the kinds of information that have been used in such phonological descriptions, see Postal (1968: chapter 6).

The difficulty with treating phonology as purely interpretative in this way, however, is that it becomes impossible to account satisfactorily for the behaviour of the larger phonological units, which are essentially independent of syntax and morphology (see section 7 below).

## 6. UNDERLYING FORMS

### 6.1 The 'single base-form' principle

It is evident that one of the chief motivations for a morphophonemic transcription (see section 4.2 above) is to establish a single common base form from which all occurring forms of a morpheme may be derived. Thus the notation {i: ~ e} enables us to relate *feel* with /i:/ and *felt* with /e/ to a single representation {fi: ~ el}, on its own in the case of *feel*, and followed by a past tense suffix in *felt*. The notation {s ~ z} enables us to have a single representation for the plural suffix, even though it is sometimes pronounced /z/ and sometimes /s/.

If we adopt the approach which puts morphophonemic information within the rules rather than within the representations (see section 5.2 above), we can take it that the base form of the verb *feel* is /fi:l/, and that the form /fel-/ which occurs before the past ending is derived from it by changing the /i:/ to /e/. Base forms of this type are also referred to as UNDERLYING FORMS.

Many words and suffixes may be regarded as having a single underlying form from which all the actually occurring forms may be derived. This does not always hold, however; it would be surprising if, for instance, *go* and its past tense *went* could be derived in this fashion from the same base form. As far as possible, however, generative phonologists in particular have sought to establish a single underlying form for each root or affix, from which all the occurring forms may be derived.

The notion of an underlying form is further explored in Hyman (1975: 80–98), Kenstowicz and Kisseberth (1979: 140–4), and Lass (1984: 59–69).

## 6.2 Concrete v. abstract representations

The drive towards a single base form from which all occurring forms of a morpheme could be derived led to systematic phonemic representations which were increasingly ABSTRACT REPRESENTATIONS, i.e. increasingly remote from the pronunciation of some of those occurring forms. Thus Chomsky and Halle (1968: 201), for reasons they discuss fully in the pages preceding, assigned the word *satisfaction* (pronounced [sætɪsˈfækʃən]) the underlying form /sæt + is + fīk + ǣt + iVn/, where '⌐' represents a tense (long) vowel and V a vowel of unspecified quality.

In this situation, the phonologist has to face the question: how does a hearer recognise that he or she has to deal with the systematic phonemic form /. . . fīk +ǣt + iVn/ when a speaker produces an utterance of the systematic phonetic form [. . . fækʃən]? The answer which was given to this question by the generative phonologists made use of the well-known fact (see section 4.3 above) that perception always calls on contextual information (including knowledge of what strings of phonemes are actually used to form lexical items). Abstract underlying representations merely entail making more thoroughgoing use of this principle. On the other hand, against this generative approach, it could be argued that perception also needs to have recourse to phonetic information present in the signal, and in the case of a very abstract underlying form much of this information would have to be actively ignored in the perception process.

Arising from this, the crucial question to be faced is: how remote from the phonetic representation can we permit underlying forms to be? Some possible answers to this are examined in Kenstowicz and Kisseberth (1979: chapter 6).

## 7. UNITS LARGER THAN THE PHONEME

### 7.1 Linear and non-linear phonology

The notion that the phonological representation of an utterance consists of a string of discrete segments is not the whole truth. A number of other units, consisting of strings of segments of different sizes, need to be recognised for a variety of purposes. The units we shall consider here are the following:

(i)   Syllable;
(ii)  Word;
(iii) Stress-group;
(iv)  Foot;
(v)   Tone-group.

Units (i), (ii), (iii) and (v) form a hierarchy: a tone-group consists of an integral number of stress-groups, a stress-group of an integral number of words, a word of an integral number of syllables, and a syllable of an integral number of segments. These units have a particularly important role to play in connection with suprasegmentals (see sections 9 and 10 below). In addition, (i) and (ii) are the domains over which phonotactic constraints operate (see section 8 below).

Unit (iv), the foot, fits in in a rather different manner: a tone-group consists of an integral number of feet, and a foot of an integral number of syllables. However, the foot does not relate in a simple fashion to words and stress-groups (see section 7.5 below). The foot is an important unit in determining the rhythmic properties of utterances.

Every approach to phonology has paid some attention to these larger units, although in some theories this attention has been piecemeal, making no reference to the hierarchical relations between the units. In such theories the accent has been upon the study of linear strings of segments, and any larger units have been regarded as secondary. Such approaches may be referred to as LINEAR approaches to phonology. Views in which the larger units are a primary and integral part of the phonological theory are then referred to as NON-LINEAR. Van der Hulst and Smith (1982) and Durand (1986) contain some useful discussion of several approaches within non-linear phonology, while Hogg and McCully (1987) provide a clear introduction to many of the essential concepts.

### 7.2 The syllable

As implied in Chapter 1 (section 5), native speakers tend to recognise a unit intermediate between the segment and the word, i.e. the SYLLABLE. The functions of the syllable appear to be threefold:

(a) To carry the phonetic manifestations of the 'suprasegmentals' (see section 9 below) such as stress or tone;

(b) To be the chief domain of patterns of arrangement of phonemes, or 'phonotactics' (see section 8 below);

(c) To act as a unit of organisation in the process of speech production.

The exact physical or physiological basis of the syllable is still a matter of uncertainty. Perhaps the most likely theory is that the syllable arises from the alternating opening and closing of the vocal tract during speech, resulting in an alternation of vowel-like and consonant-like articulations. The consonantal articulations, especially plosives, are often signalled phonetically as modifications to the vowel-like ones, and this results in the typical structure of the syllable – consonants grouped around a vowel. All languages have syllables of the form CV (vowel preceded by consonant); in addition many languages have patterns of greater complexity, with CVC (vowel flanked by a consonant on each side) being the most frequent.

It is useful to have terms for the various positions within the syllable. The central position, occupied by the V element, is normally referred to as the PEAK (or sometimes the NUCLEUS, though this lends itself to confusion with the intonational unit described in section 9.5 below). The initial C element is called the ONSET, and the final C element the CODA.

The Onset position in the syllable is normally stronger than the Coda, in several respects. To begin with, syllables in normal speech show a decrease in loudness from Onset to Coda (thus, when tape-recorded speech is played backwards, the syllables show an increase in volume, which sounds unnatural). Again, consonants in an Onset position tend to show greater resistance to assimilation and to historical change than do those in Coda position. Most theorists recognise this greater strength by giving the Onset position more independence, and by recognising that Peak + Coda forms a further unit, usually referred to as the RHYME.

In certain languages, two or more classes of syllables must be recognised, on the grounds of the amount of material in the Rhyme of the syllable (a parameter known as SYLLABLE WEIGHT or SYLLABLE STRENGTH): the Onset of the syllable is normally of no relevance for this parameter. Syllables with comparatively little material in the Rhyme are called *light* or *weak* syllables, while those with significantly more material are referred to as *heavy* or *strong*. In Latin, for instance, (cf. Allen 1973), light syllables have a rhyme consisting of a short vowel and no coda; any syllable with a long vowel, or with a short vowel and one or more consonants in the coda, is a heavy syllable. The difference between light and heavy syllables in Latin may affect the placement of word-stress (see section 9.2 below). Other scholars have accounted for differences of syllable weight by postulating a unit called the MORA: a light syllable is said to have one mora, while heavy syllables may have two or more morae.

Further complexity arises in some languages from the fact that the C and V positions in syllabic structures may be occupied by more than one element: up to four in the case of the C in some languages. English, for instance, permits up to three elements in the Onset of the syllable (see section 8.1 below).

For the place of the syllable in phonology, see further Hyman (1975: 188–93), Lass (1984: chapter 10), Selkirk (1982).

## 7.3 The word

The word is one of the points at which grammar and phonology meet. Grammatically, words can be regarded as the units which enter into syntactic constructions, and which are made up of morphemes (roots, prefixes and suffixes) combined according to the rules of inflectional and derivational morphology: for more details of these constructions see Chapter 3 below. Phonologically, words can be characterised as the minimal forms which can be pronounced in isolation: thus, *happiness* is a word, and so is *happy*, whereas -*ness* is not a word because it is not normally pronounced on its own. The *happi-* of *happiness* is phonetically identical with *happy* (the difference of spelling is immaterial), but does not constitute a word in that context, since -*ness* cannot be split off as a separate word.

One consequence of being able to stand alone in this way is that words must consist of an integral number of syllables. Native speakers of a language can often say unequivocally how many syllables a word contains, and in a very large number of cases will agree among themselves how many. Some types of words may lead to doubt or disagreement, however: for example, some English speakers will say *fire* has one syllable, others will say it has two.

When words stand next to one another in connected speech, the syllabic organisation which they exhibit in isolation may sometimes be modified. The English word *but* is a good example of this. Basically this consists of a syllable /bʌt/, with the /t/ in Coda position and thus receiving a syllable-final pronunciation (slightly aspirated or unreleased, and accompanied by glottal closure: see section 2.5 above): *but never* is normally pronounced [bəʔt = . nev . ə]. When it occurs before a word beginning with a vowel, however, the /t/ may move over into the onset position of the syllable containing the vowel: *but always* is normally pronounced [bə . thɔːl . wɪz], with the /t/ receiving the stronger aspiration typical of Onset position. Such processes of resyllabification are more marked in some languages than in others. In French they are very pervasive; the 'linking' consonants in liaison are always phonologically a part of the following syllable, not the preceding one. The phrase *bons amis* 'good friends' is invariably syllabified /bɔ̃ . za . mi/, and never /bɔ̃z . a . mi/.

As implied in the first paragraph above, words can be broken down into morphemes as well as into syllables. It is important to note that the two types of subdivision do not lead to the same results. Even in English, where similar subdivisions may occur relatively frequently (e.g. *goodness* is *good-ness* from both points of view), significant differences occur. Some words can be split into syllables but not into morphemes, e.g. *window*, while others may be split into morphemes but not into syllables, e.g. *goes* (*go* + 3rd person singular suffix *-es*, but one single syllable /gouz/); still others show splits in different places on the two levels; e.g. *mistake* is morphologically *mis+take* (cf. past tense *mistook*) but syllabically *mi.stake* (since the /t/ is unaspirated: to divide after the /s/ would mean that the /t/ would be aspirated – see section 2.2 above).

In certain other languages, the principles for morphemic division differ from those for syllabic division even more strikingly than they do in English. Many major lexical items (nouns, verbs and adjectives) in Iraqi Arabic split morphemically into a root, consisting of the consonants, and affixes, one of which consists of a vowel pattern. Thus /keteb/ 'he wrote' is /k-t-b/ 'write' plus a vowel pattern /-e-e-/ signalling past tense; /jiktab/ 'he writes' is the same root, plus a prefix /ji-/ signalling 'he' in this form of the verb, and a vowel pattern /-o-a-/ signalling non-past tense (o indicates no vowel at this position). Syllabically, however, the words split into non-overlapping pieces, just as in English: /ke.teb/, /jik.tab/.

## 7.4 The stress-group

In many languages, not all words in an utterance receive a stress (for the term 'stress' see sections 9.2, 9.4 below). English is a case in point: in uttering the sentence *Bill was at a conference*, a speaker is very likely to leave the words *was*, *at*, and *a* unstressed (consequently giving them each the vowel quality [ə]). There will thus be two stresses in the sentence: on *Bill*, and on (the first syllable of) *conference*. The unstressed words can in this instance be associated with the stressed word that follows them (though sometimes such words may be associated with the stressed word that precedes them, as in *Mary looked at us*, where *at* and *us* are associated with *looked*). The string of words *was at a conference* (and likewise *looked at us*) then forms a further phonologically relevant unit, often referred to as a STRESS-GROUP (though sometimes, rather confusingly, as a 'phonological word' – Chomsky and Halle 1968: 367–9).

Sometimes, as in our two examples so far, division into stress-groups coincides with division into syntactic units: the stress-groups here coincide with the subjects and predicates of the two sentences. This, however, is not necessarily the case. Sometimes the division clearly differs from a syntactic one, as in Chomsky and Halle's example *The book was in an unlikely place*; here there are three stress-groups: *the book* (which happens to coincide with the subject), *place* (which happens to consist of a single word), and *was in an unlikely* (which corresponds to no syntactic unit in the sentence). Even more important, however, is the fact that one and the same sentence may be uttered with a varying number and composition of stress-groups. All of the following are possible utterances of our first example (with varying emphases or contrasts implied), but are to be divided quite differently (= here representing stress-group boundary):

(i)   Bill = *was* [wɒz] = at a conference (but he is no longer there)
(ii)  Bill = was *at* [æt] = a conference (not GOING to one, but actually AT one)
(iii) Bill = was at *a* [ei] = conference (but not the one you mentioned)
(iv)  Bill = *was* = at *a* = conference (but not the one you mentioned)

## 7.5 The foot

Like the stress-group, the FOOT is a unit consisting of a stressed syllable together with a number of unstressed syllables. While the stress-group relates to higher-level phonological structure, the foot relates to rhythmic organis-ation. Within the stress-group, the stressed syllable may be accompanied by unstressed syllables before and/or after it. The foot, however, is a rhythmic unit rather like the bar in music – just as the bar begins with an accented note, which may then be followed by unaccented ones, so a foot begins with a stressed syllable, which may be followed by unstressed syllables. Thus in English, stress-group divisions respect word-boundaries, and hence a stress-group consists of an integral number of words. Foot-divisions on the other hand, may cut across words, and a foot does not necessarily consist of an integral number of words.

We may illustrate this with the sentence used by Chomsky and Halle (1968: 367–8 – see section 7.4 above): *The book was in an unlikely place*. The stressed syllables here are *book*, *–like-*, and *place*, and these therefore begin the feet, which consist of *book was in an un-*, *-likely*, and *place*. The word *the* with which the sentence begins belongs in its own foot, which is incomplete, not having a stress within it.

One important role of the foot in English relates to a basic principle of English rhythm, i.e. that stresses tend to recur at approximately equal intervals of time (ISOCHRONOUS stress). In any utterance, then, the feet will be of approximately equal length: only 'approximately', because we need not expect phonologically relevant units to be physically locatable *in* the signal (see section 4.3 above). All we need is that the underlying representation should contain feet which are equal in length; the variations in length will then be accounted for by the influence of other factors. For example, a foot consisting of a stressed syllable plus three unstressed syllables is likely to be longer in duration than one consisting of a stressed syllable alone; again, the general speed of utterance is capable of being modified in the course of utterance.

## 7.6 The tone-group

The TONE-GROUP (O'Connor and Arnold 1973) is the largest unit directly relevant to phonological structure and organisation. A variety of other terms are used to denote this unit, notably 'breath-group' (Hyman 1975: 194), 'phonological phrase' (Chomsky and Halle 1968: 60) and 'intonation-group' (Cruttenden 1986: 35–6). It sometimes coincides with what from the point of view of syntax would be described as a clause. For instance, a normal way of uttering the sentence *When it stops raining, I'll go to town* would have tone-groups coinciding with clauses: in this kind of utterance one might expect a rising intonation on *raining* and a second, falling, intonation on *town* (for more detail on intonation, see section 9.5). It would, however, also be possible to utter the whole sentence in one tone-group, with no pitch-movement or slackening of speed on *raining*. Sometimes, too, clauses can be split into two or more tone-groups. Frequently an emphatic utterance may split off the subject of a clause and make it into a separate tone-group: *The capital of France(,) is Paris.*

The tone-group consists of an integral number of feet, an integral number of stress-groups and an integral number of words. Its importance as a maximal phonological structure is shown among other things by the fact that speech errors involving transposition of segments ('spoonerisms') always transpose between words in the same tone-group, never from one tone-group to another.

## 8. PHONOTACTICS

In section 7.2 it was stated that English allows up to three consonant segments to constitute a syllable onset. Not any three consonants, however, can combine in this way, and those that can are strictly limited as to the order in which they occur. The only possible combinations are /spl-/ as in *split,* /spr-/ as in *spring,* /str-/ as in *strong,* /skl-/ as in *exclaim* (syllabically /ek.skleim/), /skr-/ as in *scrap,* and /skw-/ as in *square.* (Perhaps /spj-/ as in *spew,* /stj-/ as in *stew,* and /skj-/ as in *skew* ought to be added to this list, though there are reasons in these cases for considering the /j/ to be part of the peak of the syllable). In each case, the first segment is /s/, the second is a voiceless plosive, and the third is a non-nasal sonorant (/l/, /r/, or semi-vowel).

These facts are just as much part of the phonology of English as is the inventory of phonemes. Although the average English speaker is unlikely to be able to state these possibilities without considerable reflection, it is probable that, as hearers, all English speakers make some use of these facts to help them perceive the message behind the physical signal. For example, once hearers have established that a syllable begins with three consonants, /s/ and /l/ separated by a phoneme they cannot recognise, knowledge of the possible combinations will enable them to restrict the choice of the middle consonant to /p/ or /k/. The study of the possibilities of phoneme combination in a language is called PHONOTACTICS. The units most frequently involved in stating the permissible phonotactic combinations in any language are the syllable and the word.

Two-consonant clusters in the onset of an English syllable have a rather wide range of possibilities, as shown in Table 2: significantly, all those clusters consisting of the second and third members of the three-consonant clusters listed above are among the two-consonant clusters permitted.

*Table 2*: Permitted two-consonant clusters in English onsets. Note that clusters with /j/ as the second member are not included in this list.

| 1st cons. | 2nd cons. | Example words |
|---|---|---|
| p, b, f | l | *plain, black, flat* |
|  | r | *print, bread, frame* |
| t, d, θ | r | *track, drag, throw* |
|  | w | *twin, dwarf, thwart* |
| k, g | l | *clap, glad* |
|  | r | *crack, great* |
|  | w | *quick, language* |
| s | p, t, k | *spade, stand, school* |
|  | f | *sphere* |
|  | l, w | *sleep, swan* |
|  | m, n | *smell, snow* |
| ʃ | r | *shrivel* |

One or two words are in use by English speakers in which the restrictions are broken, e.g. *pueblo* with /pw-/ and *bwana* with /bw-/, but these are in general recognisable as unassimilated loanwords from other languages.

There are also restrictions on the clusters that can occur in codas of English syllables, though these are rather less easy to state than the above.

For a full statement of the clustering possibilities of English consonants, and of the combinations of vowels and consonants that can occur in English syllables, see Gimson (1980: 237–54).

There appear to be other principles at work also governing the combination of phonemes in English words and syllables. If a syllable has an onset which is a cluster containing /l/, for example, it cannot also have a coda which is a cluster containing /l/: there are no words of English of the form */flɪlp/. A similar restriction holds for nasal consonants in clusters: thus there are no English words of the form */smænt/. For a more detailed account of such restrictions see Fudge (1969).

## 9. SUPRASEGMENTALS

### 9.1 Scope of the term 'suprasegmentals'

Of the three types of non-segmental features mentioned in Chapter 1 (section 12), only the first will be considered under this heading. This type involves 'the manipulation of the parameters of loudness, pitch and duration' (Chapter 1, sections 12.1–12.3). From the phonological point of view their description is complicated by the fact that the correspondence between the phonological categories and the phonetic parameters is not one-to-one. There are two aspects to this complication:

(*a*) A particular phonological category may not correlate exclusively with any one phonetic parameter, but involve a mixture of two or even three of the parameters; thus word-stress in English is manifested by longer duration of the syllable concerned, and by particular pitch patterns, as well as by additional loudness (see Gimson 1980: 222–6).

(*b*) Phonological categories of quite different scopes and implications may utilise the same parameter or combination of parameters; thus both word-stress and sentence-stress in English may be manifested by similar combinations of loudness, pitch and duration (for a fuller account see section 9.2 and 9.4 below).

The phonological categories we shall be dealing with are:

(i) Word-stress;
(ii) Tone;
(iii) Sentence-stress;
(iv) Intonation;
(v) Quantity.

For a general account of these properties, see Hyman (1975: chapter 6).

## 9.2 Word-stress

In most languages, words of more than one syllable are characterised by the fact that one of the syllables tends to be stronger than the others, and that for a particular word, the syllable concerned is always the same one. The English word *en.cyc.lo.'pe.di.a*, for example is always stressed on the last syllable but two; *pan.o.'ra.ma* on the last but one; and *kan.ga.'roo* on the final syllable. (Single dots indicate syllable divisions, and the stressed syllable is shown by a vertical mark standing before it.)

Languages differ as to the principles by which word-stress is placed within their words. Some languages place stress on a particular syllable of the word in all cases: Czech and Hungarian, for example, place stress on the initial syllable, Polish on the last syllable but one. Others pay attention to particular properties of syllables: thus Latin in words of three or more syllables stresses the last syllable but one (*a.'ma:.mus* 'we love', *a.'man.te.s* 'loving (plural)'), unless that syllable is light (i.e. ends in a short vowel with no consonant in the coda position: see section 7.2 above), in which case the last syllable but two is stressed: *'a.ni.mus* 'mind'.

All the languages cited in the previous paragraph pay attention solely to phonetic and phonological facts in determining where word-stress falls. Such languages are often referred to as FIXED-STRESS languages. In other languages, facts of morphology (i.e. the make-up of a word in terms of prefixes, roots and suffixes) may influence stress placement. Russian appears to work very much in this way (cf. Garde 1973: 315–6). Languages of this sort may be referred to as FREE-STRESS languages (a term not to be taken as implying that stress can fall on any syllable according to the speaker's whim, but merely that phonological facts are not sufficient to determine stress-placement).

A large number of languages combine both principles. Thus German is basically a language in which the initial syllable is stressed, but there is a class of prefixes which cannot take stress, as in *ver'stehen* 'to understand'. Arguably, English also combines the two principles (see Fudge 1984) – even where a basically fixed-stress approach is followed (see e.g. Chomsky and Halle 1968), reference has to be made to specific suffixes in order to arrive at correct results.

As stated in section 9.1 above, no single phonetic parameter correlates precisely with the presence of stress: for English, experiments (cf. Fry 1958) have shown that higher pitch is the most important cue for hearers, followed by increased duration, with increased loudness only in third place. Other languages may have a different balance between the three parameters, or even look for different pitch configurations; because of such differences, it is not unknown for a speaker of one language to hear a word of another language pronounced, and 'perceive' stress on a different syllable from the one on which a native speaker of that language will perceive it.

The classical treatment of word-stress placement in English is Chomsky and Halle (1968: chapters 2 and 3); a clear summary of this approach is to be found in Hogg and McCully (1987: chapter 1). Chapter 3 of this latter work introduces the rather different account given by the theory known as 'metrical phonology'.

## 9.3 Tone

TONE is the use of suprasegmental parameters to differentiate lexical items. The parameter most frequently in evidence is pitch (cf. Chapter 1, section 12.2), though the others may often play a part in the differentiation process (see Kratochvil 1968: 35–47 for a discussion of Mandarin Chinese). Normally each morpheme (root, prefix or suffix) has its own tonal pattern associated with the string of phonemes of which it is made up. Just as segmental elements may undergo processes of changes (often assimilation) because of neighbouring elements (cf. the alternations between voiced and voiceless sounds in English plurals and regular past tenses – see rules (*f*) and (*g*) in section 5.1 above), so tones may also be modified because of neighbouring tones.

Sometimes a morpheme may consist purely of a tonal pattern with no segmental material (phonemes) associated with it. Thus in many languages, different tenses of a verb may be differentiated by tonal means alone. Again, in some languages relative clauses are signalled by tonal differences rather than by the presence of relative pronouns realised by phonemes.

From the phonological point of view, word-stress and tone have a great deal of overlap: the interplay of tone and stress in Mandarin Chinese is discussed by Kratochvil (1968: 40–4). Norwegian and Swedish (though not Swedish as spoken in Finland) have two possible tonal patterns ('word-accents') associated with the stressed syllable in every word of more than one syllable.

The so-called 'pitch-accent' of languages like Japanese (see Hyman 1975: 231–2) is in many ways an intermediate case between word-stress and tone.

## 9.4 Sentence-stress

Where word-stress picks out one syllable within the word or similar stretch of speech, SENTENCE-STRESS picks out one word within the sentence or similar stretch of speech. The main functional difference between the two is that the function of word-stress is to determine the rhythm of the utterance, whereas the function of sentence-stress is to indicate which meaningful elements are of most importance. Sentence-stress does, however, interact with rhythm, as shown by Hogg and McCully (1987: chapters 4 to 6).

Word-stress does not move freely from one syllable of a word to another: as we have seen (section 9.2), the word *encyclopedia* always has stress on the syllable *-pe-*. Sentence-stress, on the other hand, is much more mobile; all of the following six stressings of the given sentence can occur, with different implications:

(i) I've never actually seen Edward playing *golf* (though I have seen him playing football)

(ii) I've never actually seen Edward *playing* golf (though he talks a lot about it)

(iii) I've never actually seen *Edward* playing golf (though I've seen a lot of other people doing so)

(iv) I've never actually *seen* Edward playing golf (though people have told me he does)

(v) I've *never* actually seen Edward playing golf (you're wrong if you say I have)

(vi) *I've* never actually seen Edward playing golf (though a lot of other people have)

In most of these cases, the operative factor is a contrast with some other element: golf v. football in (i), playing v. talking about it in (ii), Edward v. other people in (iii), etc. The contrast may be made explicit (as it would be if the parenthesised material in (i) to (vi) were actually spoken), or may be left implicit (if the parenthesised material is not spoken): in this latter case, the contrast is quite as clear to the hearer as in the former, and is signalled by the place of the sentence-stress. This particular type of sentence-stress is referred to as CONTRASTIVE STRESS.

Where there is no contrastive stress in a sentence, the sentence-stress usually falls on the last noun, verb or adjective in the sentence: *It was an unusually dark NIGHT* (where there is no implied contrast with *day, morning* etc.). Certain sentence-types, however, may be exceptions to this principle: *Somewhere a DOG barked.* For a fuller account see Cruttenden (1986: 80–95), Gussenhoven (1983).

The syllable bearing the main sentence-stress is often referred to as the NUCLEAR syllable, since it is the bearer of the intonation nucleus (see section 9.5 below). If the word on which the main sentence-stress falls is a mono-syllable, then clearly that single syllable is the nuclear one. If, however, the word bearing sentence-stress has more than one syllable, the place of the nuclear syllable within that word will have to be determined; it normally falls on that syllable of the word where word-stress is placed. Thus if *Edward* is the word picked out in (iii) above, then *Ed-* is the nuclear syllable.

## 9.5 Intonation

As stated in Chapter 1 (section 12.2), intonation is 'the use of pitch fluctuation for non-lexical purposes'. A good general account of intonation may be found in Cruttenden (1986). Just about all languages use intonation, including tone languages, though in these the range of possible distinctions is comparatively restricted, as might be expected given the simultaneous use of pitch for lexical purposes. For a clear account of how tone and intonation interact in Mandarin Chinese, see Kratochvil (1968: 39–40).

The most prominent feature of intonation, and the one which permits of the most variety, is the final pitch pattern, or NUCLEUS. In English, this normally affects the whole of the tone-group (see section 7.6 above) from the nuclear syllable onwards (see section 9.4). For standard British English (RP) the primary distinction is between rising nuclei and falling ones, with further differentiation within each type; other varieties of English, however, may show quite different patterns. It is often stated that falling nuclei correlate with statements and rising ones with questions, but this is in fact not at all the case: each pattern can co-occur with statements, with questions and with commands, as shown by O'Connor and Arnold (1973), and may convey a variety of attitudes in each context.

A certain amount of variety within the overall intonation pattern is also possible in the HEAD, i.e. that part of the tone-group beginning from the first stress and leading up to the nuclear syllable. A level pattern is the least emphatic, while other types of pattern may contrast with this; for fuller details see O'Connor and Arnold (1973: 18–22).

Other factors which can be used by the speaker to convey attitudes include pitch range (wide v. narrow), general pitch level, voice quality, and speed of utterance. Detailed accounts may be found in Crystal (1969) and Laver (1980).

## 9.6 Quantity

The term QUANTITY is applied to phonemic differences of duration (though once again pitch may also enter into the matter), such as that between English *bid* and *bead*; it is not used for allophonic differences of duration such as that between English *beat* and *bead* (see section 2.2 above). In many languages quantity is not a suprasegmental, but merely a distinctive feature of vowel segments: English is basically of this type, though there is some interaction with word-stress.

In some languages, however, there are restrictions on possible combinations of syllables containing long vowels. Slovak, for example, has a rule (the 'rhythmic law') which prevents consecutive syllables from containing long vowels: an accessible statement of the basic facts may be found in Kenstowicz and Kisseberth (1979: 99–109). In these cases, the occurrence of quantity is partly determined by rhythmic considerations operating over longer stretches, rather as stress in English and many other languages is governed by a principle of alternating weak and strong units. In these cases, quantity certainly operates like a suprasegmental element.

## 10. ILLUSTRATIVE EXAMPLES

Figures 6 and 7 illustrate the interaction of the various phonological units discussed in this chapter, and the way in which this interaction accounts for certain phonetic features of English utterances.

Figure 6 represents the unemphatic utterance of the sentence *John's driving to London* as a statement. The tone-group has no special marking, and this shows up phonetically as a falling nucleus. The stress-groups likewise have no special marking, since no element of the sentence is being emphasised or contrasted; in this situation, the falling nucleus is located on the last major lexical item, which is *London*. Notice that the stress-group boundaries do not follow syntactic divisions here: *John's* is a single stress-group (and a single word), even though the -*'s* represents *is*, which must be part of the predicate of the sentence, and *John* is the subject of the sentence. At word level, the zero on *to* specifies that this word loses its independence and forms a single stress-group with the word *London*. The phonetic consequence of this is that *to* is pronounced [tə] rather than [tu:].

The syllables marked with '/' are those which bear word-stress within their stress-groups. This means in particular that the nucleus will fall on the first syllable of *London*. The symbols O, P, and C within the syllables denote Onset, Peak and Coda respectively. The three stressed syllables give rise to three feet, the second of which will probably be slightly longer than the others because it will contain two unstressed syllables in addition to the stressed one. Stressed syllables are represented in the 'Pitch and rhythm' section by 'o', unstressed by '/'.

The phonological rules then operate on the vowel and consonant phonemes, including the following:

(i) The -*'s* of *John's* is pronounced [z] after the (voiced) /n/ (section 3.1, and rule (*f*), section 5.2);

(ii) The /r/ of *driving* is pronounced as a voiced fricative (rule (*c*), sections 2.2, 5.1);

(iii) The /l/ of *London* is a clear [l] since it is immediately followed by a vowel (sections 2.1, 5.1);

(iv) The /t/ of *to* is initial in an unstressed syllable, and is therefore slightly aspirated (rule (*a*), sections 2.2, 5.1).

*Figure 6.* Utterance of *John's driving to London* as an unemphatic statement.

| | | | | | | |
|---|---|---|---|---|---|---|
| **TONE-GROUP** | | | | | | |
| **STRESS-GROUPS** | | | | | | |
| **WORDS** | | | | Ø | | |
| **SYLLABLES** | / | / | | | / | |
| **SEGMENTS** | O P C<br>dʒ ɒ nz | O P<br>dr ai | O P C<br>v ɪ ŋ | O P<br>t uː | O P C<br>l ʌ n | O P C<br>d ə n |

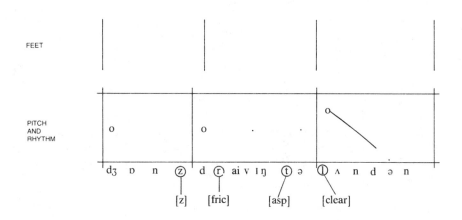

Figure 7 represents the utterance of the same sentence as an echo-question (implying 'Did you say that John's driving to London?'), with special emphasis on the element *driving*; the overall implication of this utterance is something like 'I know John's going to London, but do I understand you as saying that he's going by car?'

*Figure 7.* Utterance of *John's driving to London* as an echo-question, emphasising *driving.*

| | | | | | | | | | | | | | | | |
|---|---|---|---|---|---|---|---|---|---|---|---|---|---|---|---|
| **TONE-GROUP** | | | | | | HR | | | | | | | | | |
| **STRESS-GROUPS** | | | | | | | | | | | | | | | |
| **WORDS** | | | | | / / | | | | Ø | | | | | | |
| **SYLLABLES** | | / | | / | | | | | | | / | | | | |
| **SEGMENTS** | O<br>dʒ | P<br>ɒ | C<br>nz | O<br>dr | P<br>ai | O<br>v | P<br>ɪ | C<br>ŋ | O<br>t | P<br>uː | O<br>l | P<br>ʌ | C<br>n | O<br>d | P<br>ə | C<br>n |

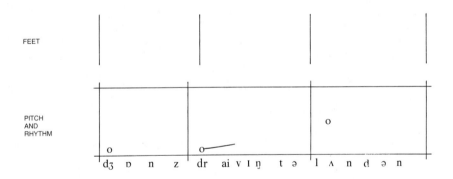

Echo-questions are normally accompanied by a high rising nucleus, and this is especially marked at tone-group level. Stress-groups, and the zero on the word *to*, are as in Figure 6. The double stress-mark '//' on *driving* indicates the emphasis on this word, which causes it to carry the nucleus. The word-stress in turn brings the nucleus on to the syllable *dri-*, and this is the beginning of the rising pitch, which spreads over the whole of the subsequent part of the utterance.

65

# REFERENCES

Abercrombie, D. (1964) *English phonetic texts*, Faber and Faber, London.

Allen, W.S. (1973) *Accent and rhythm*, Cambridge University Press, Cambridge.

*Anderson, S.R. (1985) *Phonology in the twentieth century*, University of Chicago Press, Chicago.

Bloomfield, L. (1933) *Language*, Holt, New York. (English edn 1935, George Allen & Unwin, London).

Chomsky, N. (1964) *Current issues in linguistic theory*, Mouton, The Hague. Reprinted in Fodor, J.A. and Katz, J.J. (eds) *The structure of language*, Prentice-Hall, Englewood Cliffs, New Jersey: chapter 3.

*Chomsky, N. and Halle, M. (1968) *The sound pattern of English*, MIT Press, Cambridge, Mass.

*Cruttenden, A. (1986) *Intonation*, Cambridge University Press, Cambridge.

Crystal, D. (1969) *Prosodic systems and intonation in English*, Cambridge University Press, Cambridge.

*Durand, J. (ed.) (1986) *Dependency and non-linear phonology*, Croom Helm, London.

Fischer-Jørgensen, E. (1975) *Trends in phonological theory*, Akademisk Forlag, Copenhagen.

Fry, D.B. (1958) 'Experiments in the perception of stress', *Language and Speech*, 1: 126-52.

Fudge, E.C. (1969) 'Syllables', *Journal of Linguistics*, 5: 253-86.

*Fudge, E.C. (ed.) (1973a) *Phonology* (Penguin Modern Linguistics Readings), Penguin Books, Harmondsworth, Middlesex.

Fudge, E.C. (1973b) 'On the notion "universal phonetic framework".' Reading 12 in Fudge (1973a).

Fudge, E.C. (1984) *English word-stress*, Allen & Unwin, London.

Garde, P. (1973) 'Principles of the synchronic description of stress', Reading 22 in Fudge (1973a).

Gimson, A.C. (1980) *An introduction to the pronunciation of English*, 3rd edn, Edward Arnold, London.

Gussenhoven, C. (1983) 'Focus, mode and the nucleus', *Journal of Linguistics*, 19: 377-417. Reprinted in Gussenhoven, C. *On the grammar and semantics of sentence accents*, Foris, Dordrecht: 11–62.

Halle, M. (1959) *The sound pattern of Russian*, Mouton, The Hague.

*Hogg, R. and McCully, C.B. (1987) *Metrical phonology: a coursebook*, Cambridge University Press, Cambridge.

*Hyman, L.M. (1975) *Phonology: theory and analysis*, Holt, Rinehart and Winston, New York.

Jakobson, R. and Halle, M. (1956) *Fundamentals of language*, Mouton, The Hague, Excerpts as Reading 10 in Fudge (1973a).

Jones, D. (1950) *The phoneme: its nature and use*, Heffer, Cambridge.

Jones, D. (1957) *History and meaning of the term 'phoneme'*, International Phonetic Association, London. Reprinted as Reading 1 in Fudge (1973a).

Kenstowicz, M. and Kisseberth, C.W. (1979) *Generative phonology: description and theory*, Academic Press, New York.

Kratochvil, P. (1968) *The Chinese language today*, Hutchinson, London. Relevant pages reprinted as Reading 26 in Fudge (1973a).

*Lass, R. (1984) *Phonology*, Cambridge University Press, Cambridge.

Laver, J. (1980) *The phonetic description of voice quality*, Cambridge University Press, Cambridge.

*Linell, P. (1979) *Psychological reality in phonology*, Cambridge University Press, Cambridge.

Martinet, A. (1973) 'Morphophonemics', Reading 6 in Fudge (1973a).

O'Connor, J.D. (1973) *Phonetics*, Penguin Books, Harmondsworth, Middlesex.

O'Connor, J.D. and Arnold, G.F. (1973) *Intonation of Colloquial English*, Longman, London.

Parker, F. (1977) 'Distinctive features and acoustic cues', *Journal of the Acoustical Society of America*, 62: 1051–4.

Pike, K.L. (1947) 'Grammatical prerequisites to phonemic analysis', *Word*, 3: 155-72. Reprinted as Reading 8 in Fudge (1973a).

Postal, P.M. (1968) *Aspects of phonological theory*, Harper and Row, New York. Excerpts reprinted as Reading 9 in Fudge (1973a).

Sapir, E. (1925) 'Sound patterns in Language', *Language*, 1: 37-51. Reprinted as Reading 7 in Fudge (1973a).

*Selkirk, E.O. (1982) 'The syllable', in Van der Hulst, H. and Smith, N. (eds) (1982): p. 337–83.

Van der Hulst, H. and Smith N. (eds) (1982) *The structure of phonological representations* (Parts I and II), Linguistic Models 2, 3, Foris, Dordrecht.

*Wells, J.C. (1982) *Accents of English*, Cambridge University Press, Cambridge.

## FURTHER READING

The items asterisked in the list above will be found especially helpful for wider reading on this topic.

# 3

# LANGUAGE AS FORM AND PATTERN: GRAMMAR AND ITS CATEGORIES

### D.J.ALLERTON

## 1. WHAT IS GRAMMAR?

A language is basically a system of signs, i.e. of institutionalised sensory patterns that 'stand for' something beyond themselves, so that they 'mean' something. Linguistic signs are arbitrary sound patterns (or, in the case of written language, visual patterns) which have a particular meaning in the language in question, for example:

(1)  (a)  Watch!
     (b)  Shall I cook this meal for you?

The word 'grammar' when applied to the study of these patterns is used in two slightly different ways: whereas 'a grammar' may cover a language in all its aspects, 'grammar' (without any article) covers only part of it. Let us try to specify which part.

Phonology studies the nature of the sound patterns used as linguistic signs – the kinds of sound, how they differ, how they combine, etc. Semantics studies the meanings that can be conveyed in this way – the kinds of meaning, how they differ, how they combine, etc. What then is left for grammar to study? Roughly, the signs themselves and their relationships to each other, particularly the relations between simple and complex signs, and between different kinds of complex sign. Hence, whereas phonology makes contact with the outside world in describing speech sounds, and semantics does so in describing meanings, grammar is more of a language-internal study. It studies form and pattern in a more abstract sense.

Let us look at the linguistic signs of (1)(a) and (b) a little more closely.

They are both potential utterances and would count as 'sentences'. The second is clearly a complex sign and can be broken down into a number of smaller signs. Each of the words, for instance, has a meaning of its own, even *this* (by contrast with *that* or *a*). We can also recognise *this meal, cook this meal, for you,* and possibly also *shall I*, as constituent signs; we can further appreciate that the relationship between *cook* and *this meal* is a special one that is retained if we change *this meal* to *this food* but lost if we change it to *this time*. Compared with this complexity *Watch!* seems a simple sign, but its apparent simplicity is deceptive. Firstly, there are two words *watch*, but we immediately recognise this one as the one meaning 'observe' (not the one meaning 'wrist-clock'), and as the one that could be used in place of *cook* in (1)(*b*), to give a slight change of meaning. Consequently we realise that, although no other words occur with *watch* in (1)(*a*), 'you' must be understood as part of its meaning, corresponding to the *I* that occurs with *cook* in (1)(*b*) (as its 'subject'), and additionally something must be reconstructed from the context as the thing that is to be watched (the 'object').

All sentences, even the simplest ones, therefore have a grammatical aspect, separate from their phonology and their semantics; but this does not mean that there is no connection between these aspects. Obviously grammatical units must be expressed in some way, and, although many of them can be described quite simply as sequences of phonemes, there are more problematic modes of expression. For instance, if we change our phrase *this meal* into the plural *these meals*, we are impelled to ask what common phonological element or elements express the shared meaning of *this* and *these*; and if we compare the plural *meals* with a plural like *dishes*, we have a phonological (and orthographic) disparity in the realisation of the word-ending to account for. Such problems can be considered as part of phonology, or as part of grammar, or as the bridge-subject 'morphophonology'.

The boundary between grammar and semantics is more difficult to draw. We have noted that grammar deals with meaningful units of different sizes right up to the level of the sentence (and perhaps beyond); but so does semantics. Both subject areas take as basic a minimal meaningful unit, or 'morpheme': a word like *meals* consists of two such units, *meal* and *-s*. Again, both grammar and semantics are concerned with the question of which combinations of meaningful units may occur, and which are excluded. Consider, for instance, whether (2) and (3) involve normal, doubtful (= ?) or impossible (= *) word sequences:

(2)  (*a*)  This reason is important.
    (*b*)  *This reason are important.
    (*c*)  *This reason is principal.

(3)  (*a*)  This water is (im)pure.

(b) ?This water is wet.
(c) ?This water is dry.
(d) ?This water is intelligent.

The first sentence, (2)(a), is unproblematic; but (2)(b) is unacceptable, and if, by any chance, it does occur, it will be assumed to be a mistaken version of (2)(a) and would be corrected to this (or just possibly to *These reasons* . . .). Similarly, (2)(c) must be corrected to . . . *is the/a principal one.* In both cases correction is possible, because we recognise what meaning was intended, and what grammatical rules have been transgressed: in the first case a singular subject requires a singular verb, and in the second case 'attributive-only' adjectives like *principal* (cf. also *main, only, utter*) can only occur as part of a noun phrase. Grammatical deviance is thus a matter of breaking generally valid rules.

The semantic oddity of the sequences of (3)(b), (c) and (d), compared with the normality of (3)(a), is different in nature. Here it is the meanings themselves that are deviant, not the manner of expressing them: (3)(b) is true by definition (tautologous), (3)(c) is false by definition (contradictory), and (3)(d) is nonsensical because of the inappropriacy of the notion of intelligence as applied in inanimate things or substances. Consequently it is not possible to propose a correct version of these hypothetical sentences. Indeed, they do not transgress a rule so much as go against a semantic tendency. It would even be possible to imagine contexts in which they might occur, albeit rarely.

The grammar-semantics dichotomy is related to a further distinction, between the grammatical and the lexical. Whereas the former is basically a distinction between formal patterns and patterns of meaning, the latter distinguishes different kinds of forms and meanings. In sentence (4), for instance:

(4) *Will the* new students aim *to* arrive *more* promptly *than* John *did*?

the main function of the non-italicised words is the lexical one of making direct reference to the shared world of speaker and listener, whereas the italicised words have a predominantly grammatical function, in that they indicate the structure of the speaker's sentence and the relations of its parts to each other. Lexical and grammatical functions are not mutually exclusive, and some words, such as prepositions like *in* and *before*, are equally important in their lexical function of referring to a particular spatio-temporal relation (and distinguishing it paradigmatically from other such relations) and in their grammatical function of marking a particular grammatical role, such as that of converting noun phrases to adverbials (and thus syntagmatically determining the nature of their neighbouring elements). Unequivocally lexical items (preeminently nouns, verbs and adjectives) typically belong to large substitution classes and can usually be replaced by hundreds with the same function: the word *new*, for instance, in (4) could have *old, rich, tall, French*, etc. substituted for it. Clearly grammatical items, on the other hand, are members of closed classes (or sets) and can therefore only be replaced by a limited number of alternative words (*the* with *some, my, many*, etc.), or just with one (*more* by *less*), or even by none at all (*than* is irreplaceable); these words act as markers of grammatical patterns, as we shall see. Open classes of words are also open in the sense that the class may be extended at any time by the addition of new words from various sources, such as *blasé, brattish* and *butch* as further replacements for *new* in (4), whereas the extension of closed grammatical classes in the same way is inconceivable.

While grammar studies grammatical words (and parts of words) and their associated patterns, the study of lexical items is called lexicology or lexis. This field is concerned not only with individual words, including unique context-bound items like *(to and) fro*, but also with idiosyncratic phrases like *(a) red herring* 'irrelevant issue' or *(to) beat about the bush* 'prevaricate', which, though superficially in line with standard grammatical patterns, have an unpredictable meaning. Words that lose their full semantic value in certain contexts only and are subject to arbitrary lexical restrictions (e.g. the prepositions of *comment on* beside *refer to*, or the 'empty' verbs of *have a try* beside *make an attempt*) belong to both lexis and grammar.

The field of grammar is generally divided into morphology, which covers patterns below the word level, and syntax, which deals with words within the sentence. Morphology thus studies the morphemes referred to above (*meal-s*, cf. also *un-cook-ed*) and their structures within words. Syntax studies the structures of words found in phrases, clauses and sentences. Some elements, such as the possessive (or 'genitive') -'s of *the professor of history's secretary*, or the *-ed* of *red-haired*, seem to straddle the border-line, and thus present problems.

Given that we know what aspects of a language constitute its grammar (in the narrower sense of the word), we must now ask what kind of grammatical study is required. The word 'grammar', for many educated language-users, is associated with authority and rules for correctness – notions that stem from the traditional grammar they may have had the (mis)fortune to learn about. In countries like France and Spain authority is provided in the form of a national Academy, which makes recommendations about linguistic usage, but in other countries it is simply the mass of educated speakers, who try to adhere to the rules they were taught (however inadequately) at school. This traditional grammar was largely codified for English and other modern European languages by grammarians of the eighteenth and nineteenth centuries (by Lowth, Campbell, Murray and Cobbett for English, cf. Dinneen 1967: 159–65, Robins 1967: 121–2) whose classical education made them see modern languages largely as inferior analogues of Greek and Latin. They were intent on prescribing a standard grammatical usage for educated

71

speakers and writers, but they based their prescriptions not only on what such people did say and write, but also on the forms they thought people really ought to use. This meant that grammarians based their prescriptions partly on the earlier history of the language, partly on logic, and, inevitably, partly on the model of the classical languages, especially Latin. Some of their prescriptions were inappropriate: for instance, the rules for the use of *will* and *shall* were an artificial construct, which few language-users were able to apply systematically; and their regulation of grammatical case for English (based on a Latin model, when English is closer to French in this respect) had English speakers saying not only *It was (John and) I* for the natural *It was (John and) me* but also, by false analogy, *It amused* (or *involved*, etc.) *John and I* for the approved and natural *It amused John and me.*

Modern linguistics aims to provide a descriptive grammar, not a prescriptive one. An exception has to be made in the case of bilingual grammars for foreign learners, who need to have the usage prescribed to them; even here, however, the prescriptions need to be based on a prior description of the linguistic system of native speakers. But how should the nature of this system be ascertained? And how should the facts about it be presented? Feeling that there was no possible justification for modelling one grammar on another in the manner of traditional grammarians, linguists in the forties and fifties, particularly Americans following Bloomfield (1935), declared that every language was unique. We can accept this as a global comment on each language, noting, for instance, that in French only pronouns show case yet in German nouns and adjectives do as well, while Chinese has no case at all. But we should not follow the Bloomfieldians in devoting all our energy to demonstrating the differentness of languages, because it is equally true that all languages share certain features. Some of these language 'universals' are quite abstract, such as those proposed by Chomsky (1965: 27–30; 1972: 124–7); but others are fairly concrete, for instance, that all languages have a word class that can suitably be termed 'noun' (though, of course, it differs from language to language). (Chapter 9, below, discusses such things.) It is essential, therefore, in describing languages, to achieve a balance between the language-specific and the language-universal.

If it is a mistake to remodel a language on the pattern of another language, it is equally unjustified to describe it as an aberration from some ideal earlier form of the same language. Nineteenth-century English for instance, may seem to us today to have venerable correctness about its grammar, but of course it was in some respects innovatory by comparison with the eighteenth and earlier centuries. Ferdinand de Saussure's distinction between synchronic studies of a language at a particular time and diachronic studies of linguistic change through time is as relevant in grammar as anywhere.

Assuming we wish to describe the grammar of a language as it is at a particular time, where do we find the entity 'grammar' that we want to describe? Grammar in this sense is obviously an abstraction based on observation by the grammarian, either of himself and what he thinks he would say (or write) or of other people actually talking (or writing) and understanding. These twin sources of information represent different aspects of the grammar distinguished by Saussure as *langue* and *parole*, which we might refer to, respectively, as the language-system itself and the use made of the language-system in the speech of individual language-users. Saussure's terms in fact quite unnecessarily link the basic distinction between the potential and the actual with the difference between the linguistic community and the individual speaker, though certainly this further variable of the language as a whole as against the dialects of individuals (so-called 'idiolects') is obviously an important one. Whether we look at our own intuitions about language or at the utterances of others, we are in either case dealing with individual human beings, with all their frailties. Chomsky's notion of 'competence' (1965: 8–10; see below Chapter 4 section 2), however, is intended to designate the system of an idealised language-user, free from all the imperfections of 'performance' that automatically arise whenever an individual speaks or listens to others speaking; what he has in mind as factors adversely affecting linguistic performance are faults such as hesitations, repetitions, grammatical inconsistencies and incoherence (= anacolutha) rather than failure to follow the prescriptions of traditional grammarians.

A further aspect of grammatical competence that Chomsky has always stressed is its immense potential, which encompasses a myriad of sentences that never have a chance to occur in actual performance, and which means that many of those that do occur are occurring for the first time (at least for the speaker in question). Whether they are 'new' sentences or not, the vast majority of utterances are 'generated' by the individual speaker, in the sense that he uses his unconscious knowledge of the grammar of the language and of its vocabulary to construct a sentence to suit his needs for a particular occasion. He does not simply recall a previously used sentence, except in the case of rote-learnt formulae, such as greetings and other ritualised speech acts, or proverbs (e.g. *(Good) morning, Cheers, Never say die*).

Chomsky's idea that a grammar should 'generate' sentences (which had been present in the notion of 'innere Sprachform' propounded by the early-nineteenth-century grammarian-philosopher Wilhelm von Humboldt, cf. Robins 1967: 175) is an important one, and grammars which merely give a rough indication of patterns with a few examples, are seriously inadequate. But as Chomsky himself has emphasised, the notion of generation is not so much intended to provide a psychological model for the speaker-writer (– the listener-reader is, after all, almost equally important); rather, our grammar should be able to 'generate' sentences in the sense that it is so explicit that in principle it could be asked to list all the sequences that accord with its rules (even though in practice these might be infinite in number) and to provide each with a description indicating its relationship to other sentences. At the outset, however, we should note that even this limited interpretation of generativity is put at risk by the existence, first, of strings that we are unsure whether to regard as grammatical or not (e.g. *?the too heavy suitcase*) and, second, by types of structure that seem to have more than one appropriate grammatical description (e.g. *wait for John*: verb plus prepositional object, or prepositional verb plus object).

Before we embark on our study of grammar, we should know what kind of units we are going to use as the basis of our description. We can provisionally take the sentence as our highest unit of description; but it is equally important to know what kind of smaller element is going to be the basis for our analysis of sentences. Traditionally, this smaller unit has been the 'word'. In fact both Greek and Latin had a word that had the two senses of 'sentence' and 'word' (Greek *lógos*, Latin *verbum*, the latter having the further sense of 'verb'). Interestingly the English word *word* (with cognates in other Germanic languages) and Latin *verbum* have a common Indo-European source, which suggests that our ancestors have had such a word for thousands of years, since before the time when European languages were first written down; admittedly, the meaning(s) of the word must have originally been very imprecise.

But words alone do not suffice as units of analysis. First, words must be structured to give grammatical patterns, and that means grouping them into phrases and other intermediate units, such as clause. Second, we have already seen the need for morphemes as minimum grammatical-semantic units in describing structures within the word. We shall now examine this question more closely.

## 2. MORPHOLOGY AND THE MORPHEME: PATTERNS OF REALISATION

We have noted that a language-system contains within it the potential for a vast range of different sentences. How is this possible? First and foremost because words can be combined in a variety of different ways, and some of these ways are in principle infinitely extendable (e.g. *bacon and eggs and sausages and tomatoes and . . ., the house behind the pub opposite the bank next to. . . .* These are a matter of syntactic structure.

A second reason for the vastness of a language is the fact that the vocabulary of most languages is extremely large. Large dictionaries of English, for example, have in excess of 100,000 entries, and there are many individual speakers who make use of over 10,000 words. The load on the memory would be too great if many of these items were not linked in some way. For instance, in any dictionary, besides the word *friend* we will also find *befriend, friendly, friendliness, friendship, boyfriend, girlfriend,* etc.; and these are all separate words, even though they share the element *friend.* Even *friends,* the plural form, is in one sense, a different word from *friend,* just as *befriended* is from *befriend.* It is the task of morphology to explain the precise nature of the connections between these related words. Our first step in this must be the recognition that words are ultimately constructed out of morphemes – these smaller meaningful units like *friend, be-, -ly, -ness, boy,* etc., some of which can occur elsewhere as words in their own right. These truly minimal grammatical units are the building blocks of morphology; in fact morphology can be defined as the study of morpheme patterning within the word.

How can we tell how many morphemes a word consists of? We need to look at the phonological segments that make up the word and ask if any of them can recur in some other word or on their own as a word, while making the same semantic contribution as they do in the word under scrutiny. If we consider the word *boyish,* for instance, we recognise the element *boy,* which we have already noted (in *boy* itself, and in *boyfriend*), and the remainder of the word *-ish* can be found with a similar meaning (roughly 'having some of the typical qualities of a . . .') in *girlish,* a word we could add to our list. If, on the other hand, we inspect words like *boil* or *boycott,* we find that *boi-/boy-* (phonetically representing the same phoneme sequence /bɔɪ-/) does not have the required meaning; and that the rest of the word in each case is a segment that in this context could either not have any meaning at all (like *-l*) or could only have an unrelated meaning (like *-cot(t)*).

Bloomfieldian structuralists were amongst the first to practise morphemic analysis systematically; but their approach was coloured by behaviourist psychologists' suspicion of meaning and all other mental phenomena. The result was that scholars like B. Bloch and G.L. Trager (1947), and especially Z.S. Harris (1951), preferred to place more reliance on the recurrence of formal patterns than on intuitions about meaning. For example, on the evidence of word sets like *receive, deceive, perceive; retain, detain, pertain; desist, persist* they were prepared to set up morphemes *re-, de-, per-* and *-ceive, -tain, -sist.* But if the morpheme is to have any serious semantic basis in the living language, such analyses must be rejected. Whereas the comparison of the pair *boys/girls* with the pair *boyish/girlish* (in a context like *I think of them as . . .*) reveals the same difference of meaning, there is no such parallel to be obtained by comparing, say, *receive/deceive* with *retain/detain.* Such word-parts have a purely historical status and are only relevant in etymological studies. Purely formal recurrence of a segment is not enough. In this connection it is interesting to compare the simple (i.e. unanalysable) word *recover* 'get back' (with the first syllable pronounced /rɪ-/ or /rə-/, just as in *receive, retain, resist*) with the analysable word *re-cover* 'cover again' (with initial /riː-/ as also in *re-build, re-enter, re-marry*), and to note that the opposite of *cover* is not the (unanalysable) *discover* but rather *uncover* with the prefix *un-*.

It is therefore essential for us to be clear about our semantic criteria for morphemic status. Ideally morphemes should always be 'semantic constituents' in the sense of Cruse (1986: 24f), i.e. they should be semantically identifiable on the basis of semantic parallelism (like *boys/girls* beside *boyish/girlish*). If, however, we compare the phrase *(a) black berry* with the word *(a) blackberry*, we find that, whereas the phrase passes the semantic test (cf. *(a) red berry, (a) black shoe*), the word *blackberry* does not correspond to a word *\*redberry* or *\*yellowberry*, and, although there is a contrast between *blackberry* and *black-currant*, both of them are equally entitled to be called 'berry'. Compound words like *blackberry* thus contain an element of the arbitrary and the idiosyncratic; but this should not blind us to the semantic contribution made by their components, which, though perhaps only 'semantic indicators' (to use Cruse's term) are still worth calling morphemes.

A more problematic case is illustrated by the now classic example *cranberry*. Comparing this word with *blackberry* (or *strawberry*) we find that the *-berry* element seems familiar enough and indeed seems to make the same contribution to the meaning of the compound in all cases. But what about *cran-*? Its only semantic contribution is that of distinguishing cranberries from other berries; it tells us nothing about the semantic features of the berries, because *cran-* fails to recur outside this combination. The element *cran-* and its like (the *dor-* of *dormouse*, the *bon-* of *bonfire*, etc.) are often referred to as 'unique morphemes'. These 'single context' morphemes are, however, exceptional; normally morphemes occur in a variety of contexts. Across these contexts they should have a consistent meaning. This means that cases of homonymy (see Chapter 5) such as *bank* 'company specialising in financial transactions; strip of (sloping) land acting as a border' must be regarded as representing two different morphemes, which just happen to be identical in form.

Ideally there should also be constancy in the form of a morpheme; but on this level, too, there are discrepancies. Take the case of the plural form of nouns in English, which usually seems to involve the addition of a morpheme, as exemplified by the following words for animals:

(5)  (a)  (i)  cheetah/cheetahs, dog/dogs, lion/lions, seal/seals, tiger/tigers;
       (ii)  cat/cats, duck/ducks, goat/goats, sloth/sloths;
      (iii)  giraffe/giraffes, snake/snakes;
      (iv)  horse/horses, tortoise/tortoises;
      (v)  bitch/bitches, fish/fishes [*alternatively*: fish], fox/foxes, walrus/walruses;
  (b)  wolf/wolves;

(c) goose/geese, mouse/mice;
(d) deer/deer, sheep/sheep.

The examples of (5)(a) represent the regular pattern for noun plural formation which is followed by new nouns entering the language (e.g. *yeti*); the examples of (5)(b), (c) and (d) therefore represent irregular or minor patterns. In terms of the written shape of the words, type (5)(a) appears in two forms, -*s* in (i) and (ii), and also (iii) and (iv) (where the singular already ends in -*e*) but -*es* in (v). It seems arbitrary to add -*es* only to words ending in -*ch*, -*sh*, -*x* and -*s* (also -*z*), while adding only -*s* to words ending in -*h* and -*th* (also -*ph*) – until we realise that -*ch*, -*sh*, -*x*, -*s* and -*z* represent similar final sounds, viz. sibilants (including sibilant affricates). Such a sound is also found in (iv), so that in the plural forms *horses* and *tortoises* the letter *e* represents an actual vowel that is not present in the singular form. The words of (iii), on the other hand, have a different kind of consonant, and their *e* is silent in both singular and plural. Phonetically, moreover, the words of (i) and (ii) differ from each other in having the -*s* pronounced as /-z/ and /-s/ respectively.

The patterns of (5)(a) for the pronunciation of regular plural -*(e)s* can thus be summarised as (6):

(6) /-ɪz/ after sibilant types of fricative and affricate, viz. /s, ʃ, tʃ/ also /z, ʒ, dʒ/ as in (iv) and (v).
   /-s/ after any other voiceless-fortis consonant, viz. /t, k, θ, f/ also /p/ as in (ii) and (iii).
   /-z/ after any other voiced-lenis consonant or any vowel, as in (i).

The choice between these variant pronunciations of the morpheme – so-called 'allomorphs' – is thus determined by the phonetic context. What is more, this variation is automatic and predictable if we regard /-z/ as the basic form of the morpheme and say that, for ease of pronunciation, the vowel /ɪ/ is inserted to prevent a sequence of two sibilants, and that in any other resulting consonant sequence fortis /s/ is preferred to lenis /z/ after a fortis consonant.

We can in fact regard this alternation of forms as a kind of phonological rule that applies not only to the regular noun plural morpheme but also to other morphemes with basically the same form, like possessive -*'s/-s'* (as in *the horse's/cat's/dog's eyes*) and unaccented *is* (as in *The horse's/cat's/dog's limping*). An analogous rule applies to the -*ed* of the regular English past tense suffix, distributing the allomorphs as follows:

(7) /-ɪd/ after /t, d/, e.g. *waited, wasted, waded*
   /-t/ after other fortis consonants, e.g. *whipped, whacked, washed, bewitched.*

/-d/ after other lenis consonants and vowels, e.g. *wagged, wailed, waned, weighed.*

In this case the vowel is inserted to prevent a sequence of two alveolar plosives (either /-td/ or /-dd/); and again a fortis consonant, in this case /t/, is required to follow another fortis in any permitted sequence of consonants.

Such general phonological rules, requiring morphemes of a language to adapt their shape according to the phonetic context in which they appear, are common in the world's languages. In Portuguese, for instance, every morpheme ending in written *-s* (e.g. *mais* 'more') has four variant pronunciations with final /ʃ/, /ʒ/, /z/ or with no final consonant, depending on the nature of the initial phoneme of the following word. Similarly in Turkish, a language with 'vowel harmony', nearly every suffix has a variable vowel, and some have a variable consonant as well.

Some cases of allomorphy are phonologically conditioned but cannot be subsumed under a general phonological rule. A well-known example is the English indefinite article, which has two forms *a* /ə/ and *an* /ən/. Their occurrence is clearly determined by the phonetic nature of the immediately following sound – whether it is a consonant (including /w/ and /j/, even in words like *onestep* and *use*!) or a vowel. On the other hand, English has no general rule for inserting /n/ between a final unstressed vowel and an initial vowel in a following word (– if anything /j/, /w/, /r/ or a glottal stop is inserted); and equally no rule exists for dropping /n/ before an initial consonant. This alternation, though phonologically conditioned, is therefore word-specific; it can be compared with the variation in Latin of *ā* (only before consonants) and *ab* (most commonly before vowels) for the preposition meaning 'away from', beside the invariability of prepositions like *infrā* 'below' and *sub* 'under'. Even generative grammarians, following Chomsky (1964) and Chomsky and Halle (1968), accept the need to specify such variations on a partly individual basis in what they call 'spelling rules' or 're-adjustment rules' (cf. Dell 1980: 62–3).

There is more disagreement, however, about cases of variation which affect several or many morphemes, but not all. Generative phonologists have made alternations like /t/ with /ʃ/ (*president — presidential*) or /k/ with /s/ (*elastic — elasticity*) the basis for wide-ranging phonological rules for English, but although these rules apply to many words, these are limited in number and also in origin – they are all of Latin-French origin and rely on the ortho-graphic-phonetic correspondences for such words. (Imagine a formation *Warwickism* ('following the cause of Warwick'): this would preserve its /k/, unlike *Gallicism*, which has the alternation to /s/.)

A similar case is the irregular plural of (5)(*b*) above, viz. *wolf/wolves*, in which addition of plural *-(e)s* necessitates a change in the stem. Although many nouns follow the same pattern, e.g. *thief, loaf,* others are perfectly regular, e.g. *chief, roof.*

A consideration of morphemes with variable shape leads naturally on to the question of just what shapes morphemes can take. Consider the verb past tense forms in English shown in Table 3 (including some given before under (7)).

*Table 3*

| Infinitive (stem) | Past tense | Change needed to form past tense |
|---|---|---|
| *wait* | *waited* | addition of /-ɪd/ |
| *whip* | *whipped* | addition of /-t/ |
| *wag* | *wagged* | addition of /-d/ |
| *weep* | *wept* | addition of /-t/ to modified stem |
| *go* | *went* | addition ot /-t/ to new stem |
| *be* | *was* | total replacement ('suppletion') |
| *bet* | *bet* | no change |
| *bend* | *bent* | replacement of (final) consonant |
| *win* | *won* | replacement of (medial) vowel |
| *bite* | *bit* | subtraction of vocalic segment [a]? |

The first three verbs, *wait, whip* and *wag* represent the regular pattern of phonological alternation that we have already discussed. The verb form *wept* shows the expected suffix /-t/, but it has an unpredictable vowel alternation in the basic 'stem' (/e/ beside /iː/); *went* is a similar case, except that the 'stem' has undergone a total change, and that the suffix is /-t/ rather than the expected /-d/. An even greater divergence is seen in *was*, which has no trace of either *be* or of a recognisable past tense allomorph; such cases are sometimes referred to as 'suppletion', and the problem they raise is that there are no criteria for making a phonological division of the supposedly complex form *was* (cf. French *au* /o/ beside *à la* /a la/). So does it represent two morphemes or one? If, following Lyons (1968: 183–4), we allow morphemes without a clear phonological realisation, we open the door to a totally abstract notion of morpheme, and we cannot then refuse to recognise a zero allomorph in the next example *bet* (N.B. a zero only in the past, not in the infinitive!); cf. also the noun plurals of (5)(*d*) above. Past tense forms like *bent* and *won* present the further problem that their pastness is manifested not in the simple addition of something but in a simultaneous addition and removal – in other words, in a replacement. If we have to identify a segment representing 'past' in *won*, this must be the vowel /ʌ/, but this has apparently been inserted in medial position into a sequence /w-n/ without a vowel, although the present *win* /wɪn/ clearly has one. The case of *bent* can be looked at similarly, but this time it involves the addition of final /-t/ to an allomorph

/ben-/ of the basic form /bend/. Both *win/won* and *bend/bent* (and many similar verbs) appear to involve replacement of part of the original morpheme rather than simply addition of a new morpheme. Verbs of this kind with their apparently replacive morphemes (whether medial or final) are often cited as evidence of the need for a non-segmentational approach to morphological analysis. In this approach addition and replacement are regarded as alternative 'processes' to which basic words or morphemes can be subjected. Particularly striking evidence is afforded by some cases of replacement that involve changing a single phonetic feature of the final consonant like *bend/bent* (= devoicing) (cf. also verbs formed from nouns, such as *shelf/shelves, sheath/sheathe*, etc. (= voicing), because if we insist that morphemes are segments, we overlook the importance of such features.

A further alternative process might be subtraction, as perhaps illustrated by *bit*, which has orthographically lost an *e* compared with *bite*, and phonologically has /ɪ/ in place of the diphthong (aɪ/, which superficially means loss of the phonetic segment [a]. In a similar vein Bloomfield (1935: 217) once suggested that the feminine forms of most French adjectives like *laide* /lɛd/, *grise* /griz/ could serve as the basis for deriving the masculine forms by a simple rule of subtraction of the final consonant (providing that every item spelt with *-e* in both forms, e.g. *riche*, is lexically recorded as an exception and thus distinguished from cases like *blanc(he)*.

But a model of morphological description (sometimes called the IP (= Item and Process) model) which uses the various processes we have discussed, addition, replacement and subtraction (and presumably also zero-change), while side-stepping some of the problems of segmentation, forces us to make a division between 'derived' forms (like the past tense) and 'basic forms' (like the infinitive) and often gives us insufficient guidance as to what the precise shape of the basic form should be.

Our different past tense formations raise a further point of interest: the difference between the regular and the irregular forms. Of our past tense forms the first three were regular, and, what is more, subsumable under a phonological rule. But in all the other cases the choice of past tense form is not even phonologically conditioned, because knowing the phonological structure of the verb does not enable us to predict the type of past tense formation, whereas such information for nouns enables us to predict the form of the indefinite article (despite the idiosyncratic forms this takes). We need to know the individual verb involved before we can say precisely what the past tense form is; this point is well demonstrated by the three past tenses that can be formed from verbs with the phonological structure /rɪŋ/, viz. *rang*, *wrung* and *ringed*. English past tense formation is this a blend of regular phonological rule (e.g. *ringed*) and morphologically-conditioned selection of (irregular) forms (e.g. *rang, wrung*).

Many inflecting languages have patterns of purely morphologically conditioned alternation. The formation of masculine noun plurals in German given in Table 4 is a good example of this.

*Table 4*

| (9) | Singular | Plural | Change needed for plural |
|---|---|---|---|
| 'dog(s)' | *Hund* | *Hunde* | addition of *-e* |
| 'spirit(s)' | *Geist* | *Geister* | addition of *-er* |
| 'federation(s)' | *Bund* | *Bünde* | addition of *-e* + vowel-change |
| 'man/men' | *Mann* | *Männer* | addition of *-er* + vowel-change |
| 'father(s)' | *Vater* | *Väter* | vowel-change |
| 'pain(s)' | *Schmerz* | *Schmerzen* | addition of *-en* |
| 'uncle(s)' | *Onkel* | *Onkel* | no change |

Once again there is no unequivocal way of predicting a plural form on the basis of the singular, and there are many cases of a single phonological sequence having more than one plural form corresponding to it, depending on which morpheme it represents, e.g. *Band/Bände* 'volume(s)', *Band/Bänder* 'ribbon(s)', *Band/Bande* 'bond(s)', the first being masculine, the other two neuter. Unlike the English past tense forms, however, the German noun plural (for masculine nouns) has no regular formation – everything is irregular! In other words, it is a case of purely morphologically-conditioned allomorphy.

Such allomorphy can affect the lexical part of a word just as well as the grammatical part. The French verb *aller*, for instance, has the different tense forms *v-ais, all-ais, i-rais* compared with a regular verb like *porter* with *porte, port-ais, porte-rais.*

Finally, on the question of the form morphemes take, what about morphemes that have allomorphs with no rules at all for their use, neither phonological nor morphological? Some morphemes have two (or more) pronunciations, such that the choice between them is left to the individual speaker (though doubtless it is determined by his/her personal linguistic history). Such monomorphemic words as *either* /ˈaɪðə, ˈiːðə/. *graph* /græf, grɑːf/, *scone* /skɒn, skəʊn/ each have two pronunciations that are acceptable within educated Southern British English. They are cases of free variation, in other words, of non-conditioned allomorphy.

## 3. MORPHOLOGY AND THE WORD: WORD STRUCTURE

Apart from the diversity and variability of form exhibited by morphemes, it is their contribution to the structure of words that constitutes the main task of morphology. Let us therefore return to a consideration of the words listed at the beginning of the last section (*befriend(ed)*, *boyfriend(s)*, *friendly*, *friendliness*, etc.) to see how they have been built up out of morphemes. If we look at their constituent morphemes, listed below under (8), we see that, while some are 'free' to occur as words in their own right, others are 'bound', in the sense that they only ever occur as part of a word and are thus dependent on other morphemes within the word:

(8)

| | |
|---|---|
| FREE (ROOTS): | *boy*, *friend*, *girl*, *berry (berri-)*, *currant*, *black*, *enter*, *marry (marri-)* |
| BOUND (AFFIXES): | *be-*, *re-*, *un-*, *-ly (-li-)*, *ish*, *-ness*, *-(e)s*, *-ed* |

As the use of the hyphen makes clear, bound morphemes need to be attached to something else inside a word. Free morphemes can occur as complete words, but they do not necessarily always do so: *boy*, for instance, occurs in the words *boyfriend*, *boyish* and *boys* merely as a constituent morpheme. Free morphemes are potential words, but not always actual ones.

The question of a morpheme's potentiality for occurrence alone as a word is sometimes complicated by allomorphic variation. Take the case of the word *blackberry*, which we analysed earlier as having two morphemes: the second one of these is usually pronounced /-bərɪ/ in the compound word but as /berɪ/ when it is an independent word; nevertheless, we can regard this as a case of one morpheme with two allomorphs (cf. also *enter/entr-ance*). If, however, we consider the word *friendless* (alongside *careless*, *cloudless*, etc.) we can certainly recognise a suffix *-less*, usually pronounced /-lɪs/ or (-ləs/, which often contrasts with *-ful* or *-y*; but the suffix *-less* has the meaning 'totally lacking in' by contrast with the meaning 'a smaller quantity of' exhibited by the free morpheme *less*, pronounced /les/.

All of the bound morphemes given in the list above have a further characteristic: they are 'affixes', in the sense that they have been added or attached as minor appendages to their partner (free) morphemes. Semantically speaking, the basic form or 'stem' (such as *boy*) carries the basic lexical meaning, and the added affix (such as *-ish*) then has the task of modifying or adjusting this. But what are these 'stem' elements to which affixes are added? In all our examples so far in which the affix has been attached to a single morpheme (e.g. *be-friend*, *re-build*, *friend-ly*, *enter-ed*) this has been a free morpheme. But now consider these examples of the suffix *-ist* 'practitioner concerned with':

(9)  (*a*)  artist, Marxist, violinist;
    (*b*)  scientist, dramatist, tobacconist;
    (*c*)  atheist, chemist, hypnotist.

In (9) (*a*) *-ist* has been added to a free morpheme; in (9)(*b*) *-ist* has been added to a bound allomorph of a free morpheme (*scient-* = *science, dramat-* = *drama, tobaccon-* = *tobacco*); but in (9)(*c*) *-ist* has been added to a morpheme that is totally bound. Yet *athe-, chem-* and *hypnot-* (which also appear in *atheism, chemical* and *hypnotism* respectively) are not affixes, because they provide the core lexical meaning of the word in question. We call such morphemes 'roots', and these are bound roots; but the other free morphemes we listed earlier (*boy, friend,* etc.) were also roots. Roots may thus be free or bound: in English they are mostly free, but in highly inflectional languages like Latin or Russian, they are mostly bound (like Latin *mēns-(a)* 'table'). Affixes are bound non-roots. Grammatical particles like *the, to, than* also have a primarily relational meaning, but they are independent words; they are therefore free non-roots. We have thus arrived at the scheme:

|  | Bound | Free |
| --- | --- | --- |
| Relational (Grammatical) elements | affixes | particles |
| Core (Lexical) elements | bound roots | free roots |

Affixes are added not only to single root morphemes, as is evident from some of our previous examples, e.g. *befriend-ed, boyfriend-s, friendli-ness*. The element, whether simple or composite, to which an affix is added is usually termed a 'stem'. Roots can therefore be defined alternatively as 'minimum stems'. A word can be built up step-by-step by successively adding affixes, as in:

| (10) | *friend* | =ROOT (i.e. minimum stem) | |
| | *friend-ly* | = (ROOT) STEM + AFFIX | producing STEM/WORD |
| | *un-friendly* | = AFFIX + STEM | producing STEM/WORD |
| | *unfriendli-ness* | = STEM + AFFIX | producing ?STEM/WORD |

In principle *unfriendliness* could also count as a stem, but it is doubtful whether it could actually form a part of some larger combination. In English most stems also qualify as words, but in languages like Latin and Russian, as we have already noted, this is not the case.

Affixes are far from being homogeneous; in fact they differ from each other in a number of different ways. Firstly, affixes differ in the position in which they are placed relative to their stem: prefixes, like *be-* and *un-*, precede the stem, and suffixes, like *-ed, -(e)s, -ly/-li-* and *-ness*, follow the stem; further, some languages have infixes, which interrupt the stem (e.g. Tagalog, Cambodian; or Semitic languages like Arabic and Hebrew, in which they are discontinuous); and some languages have what we might term 'circumfixes' (e.g. Malay, cf. also the German past participle *ge-hoff-t* 'hoped'). Even the replacive and feature realisations of morphemes we noted earlier must be placed somewhere: thus English, as we saw, has final replacives, while in Welsh initial consonant mutations have partly morphological value, e.g. *ei ben* 'his head' and *ei phen* 'her head', deriving from *pen* 'head'. Stress patterns with morphological function, such as English *insult*, with first or second syllable stress in the noun or verb respectively, could be said to involve 'superfixes' (or 'suprafixes').

A second point of difference amongst affixes can be exemplified with the English suffixes *-ness* and *-ity*, which both form nouns from adjectives. The difference lies in the ways in which they combine phonologically with their stems: whereas *-ness* /-nəs, nɪs/ is phonologically neutral in being simply added to stems like *opaque* /əʊˈpeɪk/, *rapid* /ˈræpɪd/, giving *opaqueness* /əʊˈpeɪknəs/, *rapidness* /ˈræpɪdnəs/, the suffix *-ity* /-əti/, on the other hand, can modify the final vowel and/or the final consonant and/or the stress pattern of its stem, as in *opacity* /əʊˈpæsəti/, *rapidity* /rəˈpɪdəti/. Non-neutral suffixes like *-ity* (cf. also *-ous*, *-ory*, *-(i)al* and various others of Latin origin) seem to form a close-knit combination with their stem; in fact the stems used with such suffixes are often bound, whereas neutral suffixes typically combine with free stems (cf. Selkirk 1982).

Probably the most important of all distinctions to be made amongst affixes is that between those that are inflectional and those that are derivational. These two affix-types differ in the role they play within the word and in relating different words and stems. We have already discussed the criteria by which a word is recognised as such, but we have not yet considered a related point that arose in our initial discussion of morphology: how can some different 'words' (e.g. *friend* and *friends*, or *befriend*, *befriending* and *befriended*) in some sense also be forms of the same 'word'? We are faced with two different senses of 'word' here. Members of such sets constitute the same word in the sense of 'vocabulary/dictionary item' – they are a single lexeme; but they are different 'word-forms' (or 'allolexes'), so that, for instance, *friend* is the singular, and *friends* is the plural of the lexeme FRIEND. We expect the same class of lexeme to have the same range of word-forms: thus an English noun has a singular and a plural, a verb has a gerund, a past tense, etc. We say that a word-form has been inflected (for a particular grammatical category), and the affixes used for this purpose (e.g. *-(e)s*, *-ing*, *-ed*) are inflectional affixes. These affixes are thus built into the very nature of the word-classes they are used with, so that in an inflectionally rich language each word-class has a range of different word-forms associated with it: Latin, for instance, has up to six different case forms for its nouns in the singular and another set of forms for the plural, with the further variable of three genders for adjectives and an even greater variety of verbal forms. Latin and English inflections are initially all suffixes, but in Arabic they are partly (discontinuous) infixes, and in Bantu languages like Swahili they are prefixes. Whatever their position, inflectional affixes have generality of application (despite their possible irregularities of form); this is the reason why the Roman grammarian Varro referred to them as involving 'declinatio naturalis' ('natural change in form') (cf. Robins 1967: 50).

Derivational affixes are different with regard to both these points: first, they indicate not different forms of one lexeme but different lexemes; and, second, their use is not regular but highly lexeme-specific – hence Varro's term 'declinatio voluntaria'. It is evident, for instance, that *friend* and *befriend* cannot be regarded as forms of the same lexeme; they are clearly separate lexical items, as are also such pairs as *kind* and *unkind*, or *friend* and *friendly*. Equally the affixes *be-*, *un-* and *-ly* have arbitrary lexical limitations on their use: so that while *befriend* exists as a word *beacquaintance* does not, while *unkind* exists *unnice* does not, and while *friendly* and *motherly* exist *relationly* and *auntly* do not; furthermore, while *befriend* has a fairly literal meaning 'make a friend of (by being friendly oneself)', *bewitch* means more like 'affect someone with witch-like or magical effects', so that each word has an individual specialisation of meaning.

Inflectional affixes like *-(e)s*, *-ed* and *-ing* mark a word with a particular grammatical feature like 'plural' or 'past', and this feature may play a wider role beyond the word in the phrase or sentence it is part of. As a result an inflected form of a word can often only be replaced with a similarly inflected word, as in:

(11)  Mary liked reading those books.

where the word *liked* can only be replaced by words like *loved*, *hated*, etc. or *likes*, *loves*, *hates*, etc., where *reading* needs a replacement like *selling*, *checking*, *using*, etc., and where only plural nouns can be substituted for *books*. Derivational affixes, on the other hand, form new lexical items, which, though morphologically complex, occur in precisely the same contexts as simple stems, with the result that *befriend* can be replaced by *accept*, *unkind* by *bad*, and *friendly* by *kind*. Not only do derivational affixes produce new lexemes, they are also capable of producing lexemes of a grammatical class different to that of the stem: *be-*, for instance, is added to noun stems to produce verbs (e.g. *befriend*, *bewitch*), and *-ly* is added to nouns to produce adjectives (e.g. *friendly*, *motherly*); on the other hand, some derivational affixes leave the stem class unaffected, for instance *re-* (as in *re-enter*), *un-* (as in *unkind*), *-ess* (as in *hostess*). Inflectional affixes are obviously incapable of changing the class of their stems, because they leave the lexeme intact; their role is to specify the particular word-form, whereas derivational affixes serve to produce a different lexeme.

Adding a derivational affix to a stem is not the only way of producing a composite lexeme. In the alternative process of 'compounding', two stems are added together. In the simplest case, it is a matter of adding together two roots, e.g. *boyfriend, girlfriend, blackberry, blackcurrant*. Ideally, such compounds are written as a single word, e.g. as a sequence of letters surrounded by spaces; but unfortunately languages are not always consistent about what they treat as a single word. (To make things worse, in English, authorities seem to differ in what they write as a single word, dictionaries seeming to be very fond of hyphens and newspapers averse to them.)

A majority of native speaker-writers of English would probably agree to the spellings *firewood, fire-engine* and *fire hazard*; and yet these are all basically the same kind of unitary element compounded of two morphemes, each of which makes a contribution to the meaning but not sufficient to predict the precise overall meaning of the whole. We know, for instance, that firewood is for keeping fires going, while fire-engines are not, but this is part of the idiosyncratic meaning of these lexical items, cf. our earlier example *blackberry* by contrast with the phrase *black berry*, the latter being a genuine sequence of independent words. In a technical linguistic sense, the 'word' can be defined as a 'minimum semantically and grammatically independent unit'; such units are usually spelt as one orthographic word, but English compound lexemes are frequently spelt with a space or hyphen in the middle, instead of having the natural spelling as a single written word, as such elements almost invariably have in German, cf. *Brennholz, Feuerwehrauto, Brandgefahr*. As we have seen, it is only the whole compound that has semantic independence. Grammatical independence is demonstrated by the tests of interruptibility and positional mobility (Lyons 1968: 202); applied to our example *fire hazard*, they show *\*fire serious hazard* and *\*hazard fire* to be impossible (without destroying the sense), whereas *fire hazard* as a unit may occur in a variety of sentence positions. The items *firewood, fire-engine* and *fire hazard* must therefore each be regarded as a single compound word.

We have seen that a compound can be formed by adding together two stems that are simply roots, cf. also *postmaster*; alternatively one or both of the items can itself be derived or compound, e.g. *postage stamp, post-office worker, post-office savings bank*. Furthermore, a compound stem can be used with an affix to form a derived word, as in *ex-boyfriend, blackberryade* (= 'blackberry-flavoured lemonade'), *schoolmasterly*.

It is not surprising that derivational formations and compounding should interact with each other in this way, because they are the two aspects of what is generally called 'word-formation', but might better be called 'lexeme-formation' or 'lexical morphology'. It is therefore only to be expected that the points that we listed as characteristic of derivational affixation (compared with inflection) should apply equally to compounding: compounds constitute different lexemes from their stems (e.g. *boyfriend* beside *boy* and *friend*); they are defective in their formation (e.g. *redcurrant* but not *\*redberry, playing field* but *playground*) and partly unpredictable in their individual semantic values (cf. *steamship, airship* and *cargo ship*). Finally, although most compound stems belong to the same class as one of their constituent stems (in English, usually the second, e.g. *boyfriend* (noun = noun + noun), *blackberry* (noun = adjective + noun), *seasick* (adjective = noun + adjective)), and thus have a clear nuclear element, this is not true of all: there are some that either have no nuclear element, e.g. *throwback* (noun = verb + adverb), or apparently have a missing one, e.g. *hothead* (noun = [adjective + noun] + Ø 'person'); there are also co-ordinative (or 'copulative') compounds with two heads of equal importance, e.g. *radio-recorder*.

As the two processes of word-formation, derivational affixation and compounding can clearly combine to form lexemes of different degrees of complexity, which can be displayed, as in (12), in the form of so-called 'tree-diagrams', e.g.:

(12)

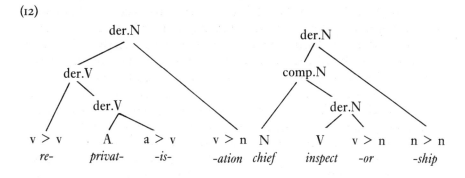

The possibility of such structures is simply the result of the rules of affixal and compound derivation: for instance, *re-* is regularly prefixed to verb stems to produce derived verbs; similarly, *-ise* is suffixed to adjective stems to produce verbs; while any two nouns can in principle be combined to produce a compound with the second one (the so-called 'head') providing the basic meaning of the compound.

Rules like these provide a framework for word-formation. But whereas syntactic rules for the construction of sentences are only limited by psychological complexity and semantic plausibility, morphological rules of word-formation merely specify a theoretical potential which is only realised to a limited degree. Lexemes are only required for certain recurrent concepts, and, as we have seen, this means that derived and compound words are often 'lexicalised' with a very particular meaning (cf. further *fireman* and *coalman*), and their choice amongst the competing patterns is in part arbitrary (cf. further *histor-ian, geograph-er, geolog-ist*). Such competing affixes and patterns are not all equally likely to be used when it comes to creating a new lexeme: say, for instance, we wish to form a new abstract noun to denote the quality of being Tamil, then the likelihood of our using any one of the different suffixes available might be assessed in a ranked order, as follows: *-ness* > *-ity* > *-hood* > *-cy*. This aspect of an affix is usually termed its 'productivity' and is a very complex matter, involving semantic and phonological factors as well as purely morphological ones, but it is undoubtedly important.

How does inflectional affixation relate to these patterns of derivational morphology? Inflectional affixes supply the lexeme as a whole with those grammatical meanings and syntactic features that it needs to qualify as a word fit for use in a sentence. An English noun lexeme like *chief inspectorship*, for instance, can be made plural, or a verb like *reprivatise* (or *denationalise*) can be given an appropriate inflectional affix out of the range *-(e)s, -ed, -ing*. These infectional affixes are thus added as an outermost layer, usually in an extreme position, either at the very end of the lexeme (as in English or Latin) or at the very beginning (as in Swahili). Because of their special status some authorities, for instance Bauer (1983), prefer to reserve the term 'stem' for the stem to which inflectional affixes are added, and otherwise to use the term 'base'.

In an inflectionally rich language, like Latin, Russian or Eskimo, many more inflections may be added to a stem than in English, and sequences of such affixes are common. They present a number of special problems of analysis: it is sometimes difficult to say how many morphemes are to be found in a given segment (e.g. the Latin nominative plural suffix in (*ūs)ūs* '(use)s'), or where their boundaries are (e.g. Latin *amās* 'you (sing.) love', *amăt* 'he/she loves'), or why there is such excessive allomorphy (e.g. the German plural affixes given in Table 4 above), cf. further Matthews 1970: 107–8. Inflectional morphology can therefore require a grammar of its own, and this is closely linked to syntax, because inflectional affixes make links with other words.

## 4. SYNTAX AND THE WORD: CLASSES AND CATEGORIES

Syntax is the (study of the) patterning of words within the sentence. Speakers of a language do not have total freedom in combining words to make sentences. They are obliged to follow certain rules or patterns of combination, which place limitations on the use of words, so that a sequence like:

(13) *You obligatory avoidance hesitant.

is unacceptable as a sentence on grammatical grounds. It is 'ungrammatical', even though it might be semantically interpretable. Words fall into different classes according to the grammatical limitations placed on their use, the members of each class having the same (or a similar) potential for occurrence. For instance, only nouns (e.g. *author, car, rowdiness, town, traffic, word*) can be substituted for the noun *hesitation* in:

(14) Any *hesitation* would be deplorable.

On the other hand, any word that can replace *hesitate* in:

(15) You must not *hesitate* at all.

is a verb (e.g. *abscond, live, misbehave, sit, speak, write*). Further, *hesitant*, or any possible substitution for it in:

(16) (*a*) You must not seem at all *hesitant.*
     (*b*) Quite *hesitant* officials can be a problem.

is an adjective (e.g. *angry, exhausted, good, lively, personal, sleepy, verbose*). (The difference between (16)(*a*) and (16)(*b*) will concern us later.)

Word classes can thus be seen as generalised sets of words that are mutually substitutable in particular grammatical contexts. The examples used in (14), (15) and (16), the noun *hesitation*, the verb *hesitate* and the adjective *hesitant* show clearly that different word classes can be endowed with the same basic meaning; and yet in traditional grammar we are given mainly semantic definitions of the 'parts of speech' (= Latin 'partes orationis', as word classes are usually termed). This is mainly due to the influence of the Roman grammarians Palaemon and Priscian, who (unlike their more enlightened predecessor Varro) not only insisted on finding eight word classes, just because Greek had eight (they had to recognise interjections as a class, because Latin had no equivalent to the Greek definite article, cf. Robins 1967: 52–3) but also defined their classes on a purely semantic basis. This is unfortunate, because, for instance, although verbs, e.g. *hesitate*, are meant to be the words that designate an activity, nouns like *hesitation* do so just as much, and even if the adjective *hesitant* does, as required, denote a quality, the derived noun *hesitancy* does so equally. It is true that prototypical nouns (such as *author, town, word*) designate a person, place or thing (or more generally an 'entity'), that verbs (like *abscond, write* and *sit*) designate an event, process or state, and that most adjectives denote qualities. The difficulty is with the large number of abstract nouns, verbs and adjectives. If there is a generally valid semantic difference, it is that while verbs are for asserting that events, etc. have taken place or are taking place, nouns look at these events, etc. as entities; similarly, while adjectives look at qualities as properties of things, nouns can consider the same properties as independent entities.

The grammatical basis of word classes must therefore remain paramount. Indeed whereas languages may all be similar in their semantic needs, they differ in important ways as far as the grammatical classes they distinguish are concerned. For instance, although all languages appear to have a word class that might reasonably be termed 'verb', only some languages have verbs that are characterised by tenses and/or aspects, and only some languages have a verb *be* (Spanish actually has two, and Japanese three) or a verb *have*. Moreover, whereas in some languages there is a clear distinction between verbs and adjectives, in others these seem to constitute subclasses of a single larger class (e.g. Mandarin Chinese, cf. Kratochvil 1968: 113–14).

In languages like English, it is worth distinguishing a class of 'determiners', embracing the articles and words such as *any* and its possible replacements in (14) above, i.e. words such as *the, a, any, some, all, my, your, this, that.* The words *my, your*, etc. are traditionally called either pronouns or adjectives: but they differ from true pronouns like *mine, yours* (which stand for a whole noun phrase) in that they occur with a noun; equally they differ from adjectives like those listed above as possible replacements for *hesitant.* An independent class of determiners is thus certainly justified in English, though not, for instance, in Chinese; by contrast in Chinese, but not in English, recognition is usually given to a separate class of 'classifiers' (or 'measures') which correspond roughly to the subset of English nouns that includes *piece, bar, pair* as in *piece of advice, bar of soap, pair of trousers* (cf. T'ung and Pollard 1982: 43–5).

In English it is probably also worth recognising (verbal) auxiliaries as a word class separate from lexical (or 'main') verbs. For one thing, in most English sentences – all except those with simple present or past tense verbs like (17)(*a*) – both an auxiliary and a lexical verb are present, as in (17)(*b*):

(17) (*a*)      You hesitate(d).
    (*b*) (i)    You must/will/may/should/*etc.* hesitate.
        (ii)   You have/had hesitated.
        (iii) You are/were hesitating.

Moreover an auxiliary is obligatory in negative and interrogative sentences (DO is supplied, where necessary), and indeed it is the auxiliary that appears before the subject in questions. Auxiliaries are therefore almost as different from lexical verbs as determiners (e.g. articles) are from nouns.

If auxiliaries were not a separate class, they would have to be an important subclass of verbs – which leads us on naturally to the general question of subclassification (or subcategorisation) of the parts of speech. The division of words into major classes accounts for the most important differences in their use in sentences, but there are other significant differences to be taken account of. For instance, we noted earlier that a wide range of nouns (probably the majority of all nouns that are not proper names) could replace *hesitation* in sentence (14). But if we change the preceding determiner *any* to *a (single)*, we find that of our sample words only *author, car, town* and *word* are possible, the sequences *\*a (single) rowdiness/traffic* being ungrammatical; we get similar results with the determiner *(too) many*, but this time the nouns *author*, etc. must appear in their plural form. If, on the other hand, we change the determiner to *(too) much*, we discover that only *rowdiness* and *traffic* (out of our set of words) are acceptable, and that *author*, etc. are impossible in singular and plural form alike. Words like *rowdiness* and *traffic* are termed 'mass' nouns, and they are uncountable in the sense that they are impossible not only with *a (single)* but also with *two, three*, etc. or *(too) many* and a number of other determiners. Countable nouns like *author*, etc., however, can occur with the indefinite article and with numerals but in the singular they are impossible with *(too) much, (too) little* and unstressed *some* (= /səm/, sometimes written *s'm* by linguists). Countable and mass nouns are not so much subclasses of nouns as of common nouns. Common nouns all occur with some determiners, as compared with proper nouns like *John (Smith), London, the Thames, England* or *the BBC*, which have either no determiner or a non-contrastive definite article as part of the name itself. The basic classification of nouns is thus:

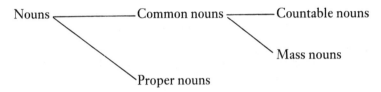

and the countable-mass distinction, strictly speaking, involves sub-subclasses.

Lexical verbs also need to be subclassified in most, if not all, languages. The subdivision into transitive and intransitive is well-known. Transitive verbs are verbs such as *like, watch, read, give, put*, which take an object, while intransitive verbs like *hesitate, drizzle, seem, rain, reside* do not. But this simple division is inadequate in a number of ways: firstly, although intransitive verbs all occur without an object, some of them require something else, such as a predicative complement (*seem (an) expert*) or a place adverbial (*reside in London*), while others are self-sufficient (*hesitate, drizzle*), some of the latter, however, only taking an empty subject *it* (e.g. *drizzle*); secondly, amongst the transitive verbs, although they all occur with an object, some require the object always to be present (*like, put*), while others allow the object to be left out when it is of no significance (*read*) or when it is clear from the context (*watch*), and some of them, furthermore, permit, or even require, a further element, such as a second (indirect) object (*give*) or a place adverbial (*put*). A partial representation of the required subclassification would look like the one given in Figure 8.

Both the major classification of words into parts of speech and the minor classification into subclasses is complicated by the fact that many words have

*Figure 8*

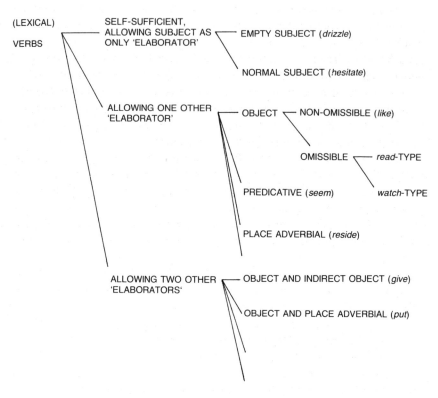

more than one use. For example, we noted the difference between the noun *hesitation* and the verb *hesitate*, but the word *pause* is used as both noun and verb; in a similar way, although *hesitate* and *hesitant* are clearly different, the verb *idle* and the adjective *idle* are identical in form. There are various ways of describing this state of affairs. We may simply say that words may belong to more than one class – that such words display multiple class membership (or 'class cleavage', as Bloomfield (1935: 204–6, 265–6) terms it). Alternatively we may say that there are two different words *pause* (NOUN) and *pause* (VERB), or *idle* (VERB) and *idle* (ADJECTIVE), which exhibit grammatical homonymy.

In some cases it may be worth grouping the two classes into a broader class, though not just for the sake of words like *pause* and *idle*: a super-class of 'nerbs' like *pause* or 'vadjectives' like *idle* would serve little purpose. But we do probably want to have a single comprehensive class of adjectives despite the fact that such words occur in two radically different positions (as illustrated in (16)(*a*) and (*b*) above), predicative (e.g. . . . *seem (at all) hesitant*) and attributive (e.g. *hesitant officials*), with some adjectives occurring in the one position but not the other, cf. . . . *seem (at all) awake*; \*. . . *seem (at all) principal*; \**awake officials, principal officials*. From the point of view of morphology, as we noted earlier, zero elements cannot be ruled out as allomorphs of an otherwise overt morpheme: it would therefore also be possible to say that *pause* and *idle* involve derivation with a zero affix, though it is less easy to say which word class has the plain form, and which the zero affix, the history of the words being irrelevant in a synchronic account. This problem applies equally to another mode of description popular in works on word-formation, namely, 'conversion', which again makes one use of the word primary and thus makes the description appear quasi-historical. Nevertheless a morphological mode of explanation (i.e. zero-derivation or conversion) would be more in line with the idiosyncratic way in which the meanings within each pair of uses are related: for instance, the verb *pause* and the noun *pause* are related in a quite different way compared with the verb *shade* and the noun *shade*.

The phenomenon of class cleavage (or whatever else we like to call it) also operates at the level of subclasses. The subclassification of common nouns into mass and countable, for example, is clear, but many nouns have both uses, e.g. *a stone, some stone*; *a glass, some glass*; *a hesitation, some hesitation*; and the members of each pair again display different kinds of semantic relationship. In some cases, one use is clearly secondary and limited in its use, e.g. the countable use of basically mass nouns in 'restaurantese', e.g. *an orange juice, two soups*; here it seems more natural to speak of '(*ad hoc*) conversion'. Proper nouns may be 'converted' to common nouns in this way, cf. *She sees herself as a female Churchill.*

Given that words can in principle belong to more than one class or subclass, how do we recognise the class or subclass being used in a particular sentence? Word classes are defined in terms of the syntactic potential of words; the syntactic context must therefore be our principal means of recognition. The word(s) *light*, for instance, in (18)(*a*), (*b*) and (*c*) appears as a noun, adjective and verb respectively:

(18) (*a*) The new light illuminates the room effectively.
　　 (*b*) The new lamp makes the room light.
　　 (*c*) The new lamps light the room effectively.

In (18)(*a*), for example, it is its position between the unequivocal adjective *new* and the verb *illuminates* that marks it out as a noun; there is similar syntactic marking in (18)(*b*) and (*c*) for the other two uses. But, in addition, morphological factors may help identify a word as a member of a particular class. The word *illumination*, for instance, is unmistakably a noun because of the derivational suffix *-ion*, while the derivational suffix *-en* clearly marks *brighten* as a verb (derived from an adjective). Inflectional affixes are equally important in this respect, at least in languages that have a significant number of inflectional affixes. In Latin or Russian it is nouns, pronouns and adjectives that have a marker of grammatical case, and it is only verbs that may take tense-marking suffixes. Similarly, although English is not so rich in inflections, we may observe that the noun *light* in (18)(*a*) may be given a suffix *-s* to mark plurality, the adjective *light* in (18)(*b*) may be given a suffix *-er* to mark the comparative, and that the verb *light* in (18)(*c*) may be given the suffix *-ed* (or in this case, more commonly accept a medial replacive affix to become *lit*) to mark the past tense.

Inflectional affixes, unlike derivational ones, are used regularly with the appropriate word-class (ignoring irregularities of form): virtually every noun has a plural form, every verb a past tense, etc. in so far as the language has these categories. Inflections characterise individual words, not lexemes; indeed, they form pan-lexeme categories like number and tense, which play a part beyond the boundaries of their particular word. Each category involves choosing one of a fixed range of options, depending on the required meaning and grammatical pattern, and the subcategory selected is indicated in the inflectional affixes of predetermined words in the given structure.

In Latin, for instance, every noun belongs to one of five or six declensional classes (with subvarieties), and this determines the form of the inflectional affixes of case and number, e.g. nominative singular and plural *mālus/mālī* 'mast' but *frūctus/frūctūs* 'fruit'; for adjectives there are two models of declension. This category of declensional class is perhaps the only one to have no significance outside the noun or adjective itself; but it has a close association with another category, gender, in that for most declensional classes there is a typical gender. For instance, most words of the declensional class of *mālus* 'mast' are masculine (e.g. *amīcus* 'friend', *hortus* 'garden'), but there are exceptions, including an absolute homonym of *mālus* with the meaning 'apple-tree', which is feminine; similarly most words with nominative forms like *mēnsa/mēnsae* 'table' are feminine, but some, like *poēta* 'poet' are masculine. Gender is thus an arbitrarily fixed characteristic of individual nouns but is not directly indicated in the noun itself; rather, it shows itself in the inflectional affixes of dependent adjectives which agree with it. Latin (like Russian, Sanskrit, etc.) has three genders, masculine, feminine and neuter; many languages have just two, usually dispensing with neuter (e.g. French, Hindi) but in some cases merging masculine and feminine to give a 'common' gender (as in Dutch). Some languages have more than three genders: Swahili, for instance, has six.

The grammatical category of case applies not only to nouns but to a whole noun phrase and may be shown by nouns, adjectives and determiners. Cases indicate the grammatical and/or semantic role of a noun phrase in a sentence. They are sometimes determined directly by the role: for example, a genitive case is often used to signal a noun being used to modify a higher noun phrase, just as the preposition *of* is; a special case, the nominative, is commonly used for the subject; the Russian instrumental (or Latin ablative) can mark an adverbial of instrument; there can be special cases for location and direction (Turkish has three, Finnish six). Otherwise the choice of case depends on the requirement of the individual verb or preposition: for instance, some German verbs take (or 'govern') an accusative object, others a dative; in Basque intransitive verb 'subjects' and transitive verb 'objects' have the absolutive (also called the 'nominative'), while transitive verb 'subjects' have the ergative (which makes identification of transitive clause functions problematic); in Russian prepositions can demand any one of five different cases (accusative, genitive, dative, instrumental or prepositional). A language may, like Chinese, lack case entirely, but to have a case system it needs more than one case. Swedish has two cases for nouns, Rumanian three, German four, Ancient Greek five, Russian six, Serbo-Croatian seven, Sanskrit eight, Basque twelve and Finnish fourteen.

Number is a primarily nominal category with a relatively clear semantic basis. But many languages have no such category, so that nouns are neutral between singular and plural. Many languages do have a singular-plural distinction, however, and a few distinguish a dual number (e.g. Arabic). Number is often multiply marked in a noun phrase, cf. Spanish *la(s) playa(s) español(es)* 'the Spanish beach(es)'. Furthermore, the number of the subject is often indicated in the verb (*It hurts/They hurt*), and in some languages the same applies to the object.

The remaining major inflectional categories, person, tense, aspect, mood and voice, belong primarily to the verb. The distinction of person, though, also characterises pronouns – ordinary noun phrases are normally third person – and, as with number, the subcategory of the subject (and sometimes the object) is indicated in the verbal inflection. Tense and aspect are chosen according to the time, timing, duration and stage-of-completion of the eventuality referred to by the verb. Mood involves a choice between indicative, imperative, subjunctive, etc. on the semantic basis of the factuality or otherwise of the eventuality, although it may partly be grammatically determined by the choice of subordinating conjunction.

Voice is a rather more complex matter than the others. Although it resides in the verb (morphologically speaking), it is intimately linked to the structure of its clause in terms of subject, object, etc. Languages which have a passive voice opposed to the active (e.g. Latin, English) use it in a sentence pattern with the active subject moved to another structural position, and possibly another element, for instance the active object 'promoted' to subject position. Ancient Greek had a third ('middle') voice which had a meaning that was indirectly reflexive (with the subject as agent as well as beneficiary or sufferer) or causative (with the subject as instigator of action by some other(s)). Languages like Basque that have an ergative-absolutive pattern (see above)

95

sometimes have a so-called 'anti-passive' which shifts the originally ergative noun phrase to a structural position in which it takes the absolutive case.

These inflectional categories are thus displayed by individual words; but the words of a phrase or sentence interact with each other in the selection of the value for each category. This subselection takes two forms, government and concord. In government, as when a verb or preposition selects a particular case, an inflectionally unmarked word selects a subcategory in another word or group of words; the gender of nouns is also usually a matter of government, since gender itself need not be not strictly indicated in the noun itself – only its declensional class.

In concord the selection of subcategory is made outside the structure in question, as in number or case in a noun phrase (in Latin or German, say) where it is either directly semantic or is controlled by something outside the phrase, but inside it all words are equally marked. Thus in German *mit den Büchern* 'with the books' (compared with *ohne die Bücher* 'without the books') the preposition *mit* governs the dative of *den Büchern* but *den* and *Büchern* are in concord for case and number. Concord implies a redundant use of inflectional affixes, but some languages use their affixes more sparingly: for instance, although both Finnish and Basque have similar case systems, Finnish makes adjective agree with nouns, whereas Basque has one case marker for the whole noun phrase; a rather different economy is seen in Welsh and Turkish, which both have plural suffixes for nouns but do not use one with a (plural) numeral, cf. Welsh *pum ci* 'five dogs' but *cwn* 'dogs'.

It frequently happens that the full range of grammatical distinctions made through inflectional means is reduced under certain conditions. When a theoretically possible inflectional subcategorisation is suspended, we speak of grammatical 'neutralisation'. It can come about in one of three ways. In system-determined neutralisation, a distinction systematically fails to apply in combination with another grammatical feature in a related paradigm, as when in German the gender distinction of singular noun phrases is non-applicable in the plural; this is also termed 'syncretism'. Context-determined neutralisation can be exemplified by the loss of the present-future tense contrast in French subordinate clauses: with reference to future eventualities only the present is permitted after *si* 'if', but only the future after *quand* 'when' etc. Finally, lexically-determined neutralisation applies by accident, so to speak, to certain lexical items that fail to make the expected inflectional distinctions, e.g. *sheep* (singular/plural), *hit* (present/past). Whatever the mechanism involved, neutralisation has the effects of reducing the number of grammatical distinctions made and of thereby complicating the system.

## 5. SYNTAX AND THE SENTENCE: STRUCTURES AND FUNCTIONAL RELATIONS

Syntax is in the main about putting words together to form phrases and sentences, with the right grammatical form for the required meaning. Let us imagine an impossibly bad learner of English who wants to say sentence (19)(*a*) but instead comes out with (19)(*b*):

(19) (*a*)   The head teacher does not treat my children well.

    (*b*)   *Head teacher treat not good mine childs.

Obviously our learner has not used the right grammatical form for his meaning, but his mistakes can be instructive. They can be classified under different headings, the first three of which we have already discussed:

(i) *Morpheme Realisation.* The word *children* has been given the wrong form (i.e. allomorph) for its inflectional morpheme.

(ii) *Morphological Structure (of Words).* The word *treat* (or whatever other verb is used) needs to have a third person singular suffix in the present after a singular subject.

(iii) *Syntactic Class of Word.* The adjective *good* has been wrongly substituted for the corresponding adverb *well*; and the pronoun *mine* has been wrongly used in place of the determiner *my*.

(iv) *Use of Grammatical Marker Words.* In the absence of any other determiners, English (unlike Russian, etc.) requires the use of an article (in this case a definite one) before a singular countable noun like *teacher*. Similarly sentence negation with *not* requires the presence of an auxiliary, and if none is present, the 'empty' verb DO must be used (here in the form *does*).

(v) *Word Order.* The word *not* needs to precede the verb *treat* (to give *does not treat*), and the word *well* (in place of *good*) needs to be placed in final position.

Leaving aside prosodic factors (such as selecting the correct element to stress in the compound *head teacher*, and choosing a suitable intonation pattern), the above points are the grammatical factors that a speaker needs to take account of and therefore that a grammarian needs to describe. The first two are morphological; so to describe the syntax of a sentence do we simply need to specify word classes, grammatical marker words and word order? In a sense, yes. But there is a danger of missing the wood for the trees, because these individual grammatical features combine to form part of an overall pattern for the sentence, and this may not be immediately obvious – indeed, we often meet pairs of sentences that in terms of superficial features (like those of (i) to (v) above) are identical but which nevertheless represent different structural patterns with different meanings. We have already seen that many words are

97

ambivalent as regards syntactic class, but a different kind of grammatical ambiguity is seen in (20)(*c*):

(20) (*a*)  The head teacher surprised the man with a limp.
    (*b*)  The head teacher surprised the man with a kick.
    (*c*)  The head teacher surprised the man with a cane.

In this case (20)(*a*) and (*b*) clearly have different grammatical structures, with the result that the semantic interpretation is different, whereas (20)(*c*) allows both structures and is therefore structurally ambiguous. This difference may be reflected in the rhythmical and intonational patterns used.

How are we to detect the syntactic structure that lies behind such sentences? Just as a chemist has tests for identifying a particular substance, so a syntactician needs operational tests (in addition to his own intutitions) to help establish the structure of a sentence. As in a scientist's test our assumption would be that sentences that respond to tests in the same way have the same structure. Taking sentence (21) as an example we can carry out a whole series of operational tests which give us different kinds of grammatical information:

(21) My father brought Swiss wine home at Christmas.

Substitution for single words is a test we have already considered: it tells us about the class of element under examination, and as we saw in the first section of this chapter, words belonging to small substitution sets, or having no possible substitution, are grammatical markers, e.g. *my*, *at* in (21). Substituting a single word for a whole phrase in effect reduces the size of an element, and this reduction test tells us which elements form a single construction (that acts as a constituent in a larger construction), e.g. *my father* (→ *he*), *Swiss wine* (→ *some*, *wine*), *at Christmas* (→ *later*, *then*). A special case of reduction is when we simply omit one of the existing words, thereby reducing to the other word, as when we reduce *Swiss wine* to *wine*; this omission test identifies the two parts of the construction as optional and obligatory, thus *(Swiss) wine*, although sometimes we know an element to be optional without being sure which element in the context is its (obligatory) partner. It frequently happens that neither of two elements may be omitted individually, but they can be omitted as a group, e.g. *at Christmas*; this joint omission test simultaneously establishes the group as a construction and shows that it is optional within a wider framework. A further test for construction status is that of joint permutation: for instance, *at Christmas* can be moved to initial position as a group, but neither of its constituent words can be moved alone. Permutation of a single word, such as moving *home* to the pre-object position (between *brought* and *Swiss*) demonstrates its relative independence, and perhaps its structural relations (*home* is just as closely related to *brought* as *Swiss wine* is, though the relationship is a different one). A final simple operational test is that of insertion: basically, insertions can be made at construction boundaries but not inside a construction, so that, for instance, an adverb like *occasionally* can be introduced into our sentence not only in initial and final positions but also between subject and predicate (= verb phrase, in this case) or between the place adverb *home* (which belongs to the verb phrase) and the more independent time adverbial *at Christmas* – but not in the middle of the verb phrase. We also need to consider more complex operational tests, but we shall do this later under the heading of 'transformations.'

What exactly do such tests tell us? If we indicate with brackets all the groupings into constructions that our test on sentence (21) has indicated, presupposing that the sentence as a whole is also a construction, we arrive at something like:

(21′) [[My father] [brought [Swiss wine] home] [at Christmas]]]

The only pair of brackets we have not so far justified is that grouping the whole predicate from *brought* to *Christmas* together as a unit; this can be defended on the grounds that the whole sequence can be reduced quite naturally to the auxiliary *did* in a context like (21″):

(21″) Who brought Swiss wine at Christmas? My father did.

The bracketing of (21′) thus represents the different degrees of 'togetherness' displayed by the words of sentence (21) with respect to each other.

An alternative representation to bracketing is the so-called 'tree diagram' (actually, it looks more like a root diagram). The bracketing of (21′) can be converted to the tree diagram of (21‴) by starting at the innermost bracketings (each pair of facing brackets) and drawing lines to a joint higher 'node', then proceeding in the same way until the 'top of the tree' has been reached:

(21‴)

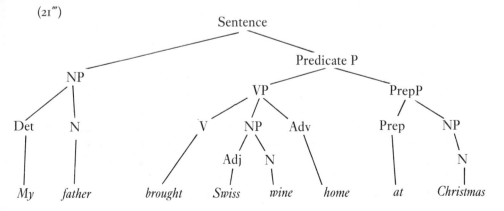

The tree diagram of (21‴) has had labels added to the nodes (and is thus equivalent to labelled bracketing). The word-class labels can be justified along the lines discussed earlier. The labels for the phrases here are based on the name given to the principal constituent (the Predicate Phrase could just as well be called the 'Higher Verb Phrase'). There are problems with this approach, and it certainly needs supplementation, as we shall see. There are equally problems with determining some constituent boundaries.

One such problem concerns word boundaries, and can be illustrated with the phrase *my father's Swiss wine*, in which it is clear that *father's* is not (like *Swiss*) a modifier of *wine*; rather, *my father's* is a construction equivalent to *his*, giving a structure [[[*my father*]'*s*] *Swiss wine*]. A second problem is whether we should be happy with constructions of three constituents. We can be happy with *brought + Swiss wine + home*, and we are forced to recognise three constitutents in coordinate patterns like *red and white*, but should we try to subdivide, for instance, *the Swiss watch* into *the + Swiss watch* or *the Swiss + watch*? There is even the further possibility of regarding *the . . . watch* as a construction, but are such discontinuous constituents permitted? Such problems were well-known to the Bloomfieldians, who studied distributional methods of Immediate Constituent (= I.C.) analysis in detail (cf. Wells 1947); exactly the same problems arise in the grammatical descriptions of Chomsky and his followers, but they are not always so willing to discuss them (for a notable exception, see Radford 1981: chapters 2 and 3).

In some cases the existence of discontinuous constructions seems undeniable – unless of course they are ruled out *a priori* by the theory. Consider the following adjective phrases, as candidates for appearing in a context like *Mary is . . .*:

(22) (*a*) helpful, quite helpful, very helpful; more helpful, less helpful; as helpful.

    (*b*) *helpful than John, *quite helpful than John, *very helpful than John; more helpful than John, less helpful than John; *as helpful than John.

    (*c*) *helpful as John, *quite helpful as John, *very helpful as John; *more helpful as John, *less helpful as John; as helpful as John.

It is clear that *than John* is dependent on *more/less* for its occurrence, and that it therefore forms a construction with it; the same applies to *as John* and *as*. But linking these elements in a tree diagram would mean a crossing of lines, something excluded by the conventional theory of tree diagrams. Transformational-generative grammarians got around such problems by positing a 'deep structure' (in the form of a tree) in which the linked elements were adjacent, and a transformational rule linking this to the 'surface structure', in which they are separated with the tree not showing the link. Such movement rules were said to be necessary anyway to link alternative structures like . . . *brought Swiss wine home* and . . . *brought home Swiss wine*; but in cases like *more/less . . . than* the transformational movements were said to be obligatory. Thus 'deep structure' representations were being proposed that never appeared at the surface.

Since the advent of transformational-generative grammar in the mid-fifties the role of transformations in this type of grammar has become progressively specialised, so that they are now no more than movement rules (cf. chapter 4). Yet Harris's (1952, 1957) and Chomsky's (1957) original transformations in the main corresponded to a set of relationships between grammatical structures which was recognised in traditional grammar and has remained in the armoury of many modern grammarians of different theoretical persuasions. To distinguish them from transformational-generative rules, we can refer to the traditional notion as 'transformational relation(ship)s'. They are well illustrated by the active-passive relationship, and also by what Jespersen (1969 [1937]: 73–4) called 'cleft' sentences. Take the following semantically similar sentences:

(23) (*a*)  The postman contacted the students yesterday in the lecture-room.
    (*b*)  The students were contacted by the postman yesterday in the lecture-room.
    (*c*)  It was the students that the postman contacted yesterday in the lecture-room.
    (*d*)  It was in the lecture-room that the postman contacted the students yesterday.

If we compare (23)(*a*), the basic sentence, with (23)(*b*), the passive one, we find only the slightest difference in meaning, but a whole series of differences in form: the originally initial subject has been shifted to final position and has gained a *by*, the original object has been moved to subject position, and the verb has been converted to a passive form. Elsewhere in grammar and in lexis we expect each difference in expression to correspond to a separate difference in meaning; but in these transformationally-related sets of sentences, a complex difference in expression corresponds to a simple (and often slight) difference in meaning. The same applies to our cleft sentence (23)(*c*) and (*d*), which differ only in emphasis from (23)(*a*): the emphasised element (which can be subject, object, place adverbial or time adverbial) is moved to initial position, and then has *it is/was* inserted before it and *that* inserted after it. Needless to say, passivisation and clefting are only two of a wide range of such transformational relationships.

Let us now look at a rather different phenomenon, which has some affinities with transformational relations, and might be regarded as a special case of them:

(24) (*a*)  The students were in the lecture–room (opposite the staircase (behind the toilets (next to the . . .))).

  (*b*)  The secretary encouraged the professor to help the porter to persuade the postman to contact the students.

The sentence (24)(*a*), like (23)(*a*), has the preposition phrase *in the lecture-room* as a direct constituent of the predicate phrase, and as a construction its constituents are the preposition *in* and the noun phrase *the lecture-room*; this noun phrase in turn can be modified by a preposition phrase (*opposite the staircase*), which only plays a role within the noun phrase, schematically:

(24)(*a′*)

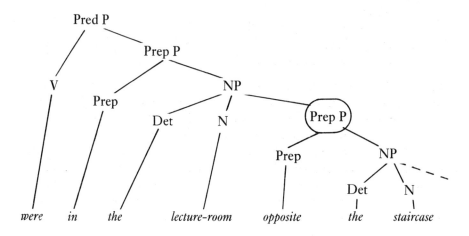

This lower preposition phrase (ringed in the tree diagram), though occurring in a position where a simple adverb like *nearby* could have occurred, is a structure that has the same potential as the higher one, and is thus a structure 'embedded' within a (similar) structure. It is clear that the phenomenon of 'embedding' has a capacity for recursion, as indicated by the further parentheses. This also applies to the structure of (24)(*b*), in which an infinitive clause-like element (= *to* + a verb phrase) has been successively embedded as a second 'elaborator' of a verb alongside its direct object, with the infinitival proclitic *to* acting as a marker of the embedding. Such differences between the embedded and non-embedded forms of the structure are akin to a transformational relationship, in that an indicative verb form corresponds to an infinitive (or a subjunctive in some languages), cf. also the Latin accusative-and-infinitive construction, in which the embedded subject has the accusative corresponding to the normal nominative.

In an embedding, one element is downgraded and used as a constituent (or constituent of a constituent) of a higher element, to which it is in principle equal, formulaically: $X_0 [= A + X_1]$, or $X_0 [= A + B [= C + X_1]]$. In co-ordination two similar elements are added together as equals in a combination which could have been represented by one of them alone, formulaically: $X_0 [= X_1 \ldots \& X_n]$, where $n \geqslant 1$. This normally means that each of the co-ordinated items is of the same class as the other(s) and of the whole. For instance, in the examples of (25)(a), (b) and (c) both the co-ordinated elements and the whole structure are (semantically related) nouns, noun phrases and verb phrases respectively:

(25) (a) my mother and father, those cups and saucers;
    (b) my mother and my headmaster, John's new cups and my German coffee;
    (c) I've dropped a cup and broken it.
    (d) [[[plaice and chips] and [strawberries and cream]] and [[goulash and rice] and [apple-pie and custard]]].

In co-ordinations, then, a compound element paradoxically consists of a series of elements equivalent to itself (just as a compound word is superficially often a sequence of potential words). This has the consequence that co-ordination within co-ordination is possible, as in (25)(d).

Both embedding and co-ordination involve combining constituents of the same size and class. We have already discussed the question of class, but how many different size-units are there? Clearly words are combined into phrases, but phrases of different size and class occur within each other without the need for any downgrading of the kind associated with embedding. For instance, in:

(26) . . . [might [live in [a [very poor] area]]]]

we might distinguish an adjective phrase inside a noun phrase inside a preposition phrase inside a verb phrase inside a predicate phrase. The term 'clause' is used to indicate an embedded or co-ordinated sentence like the inner elements of (27)(a) or (b) respectively:

(27) (a) [[Whoever arrives last] washes up].
    (b) [[John arrived last] and [he washed up]].

But we should beware of the idea that a sentence can be exhaustively divided into clauses. In (27)(a) the subordinate clause *Whoever arrives last* is a sentence embedded inside another sentence, not alongside another clause. Similarly we should be clear that the co-ordinate 'clauses' of the compound sentence (27)(b) are nothing more than co-ordinated sentences, just as a compound noun phrase like that of (25)(b) consists simply of co-ordinate noun phrases.

In the hierarchy of different size-units in syntax (sometimes referred to as 'rank' in 'systemic-functional grammar', cf. Halliday 1985: 25–6) we only need to have words, different levels of phrases and sentences; 'clauses' are just embedded or co-ordinated sentences.

In describing grammatical patterns, so far we have seen that the two main factors are the extent of each construction and the classes of its member constituents. Given the various complications involved, including transformations, are these factors enough to explain all the subtleties of grammatical patterning? Or is it also necessary to take account of the relations of the constituents to each other and their functions within the whole construction – in short, of functional relations? Chomsky (1965: 68–74) asserts that this information is redundant. Let us consider the evidence.

Looking at examples like those of (28)(*a*), (*b*) and (*c*), Bloomfield and his followers distinguished three main types of construction:

(28) (*a*)  netting, wire (that type of thing); netting and wire,
    (*b*)  thick wire,
    (*c*)  with wire.

In (28)(*a*) two nouns *netting* and *wire* occur, possibly linked by a conjunction, and either one of them could stand in place of the whole construction, which is a nominal element; in (28)(*b*) only *wire*, the noun, could replace the whole construction. Both constructions have (at least) one central element or 'head', and are therefore described as 'endocentric'; but whereas (28)(*a*) is co-ordinative, (28)(*b*) is subordinative, with the adjective *thick* acting as an optional modifier. In (28)(*c*), on the other hand, we have a combination made up of a preposition and a noun, but together they make an element of a further category, either adverbial (as in *(mend it) with wire*) or adnominal (= quasi-adjectival) (as in *(puppets) with wire*); this is therefore termed an 'exocentric' construction, consisting of a basic element and a relational element. But are these construction types and functional labels predictable on the basis of the classes involved? Is it not precisely the function of a preposition to convert a noun(phrase) into an adverbial or adnominal, and of an adjective to act as optional modifier of a noun? This is true; but then what about *wire netting*? In this phrase, which is not a compound noun but a regular syntactic pattern (cf. *gold watch*, *cotton shirt*, etc.), two nouns occur side by side but not as coordinates – rather with the first as 'modifier' and the second as 'head'.

Let us take a further example of the need for functional relations:

(29) (*a*)  (Mary) consulted/saw/interviewed an expert.
    (*b*)  (Mary) became/was/sounded an expert.

In each case the verb phrase (which is also the predicate phrase) consists of a verb followed by a noun phrase, but the function of the noun phrase differs: in

(29)(*a*) it is an object (and accepts subject position in a corresponding passive sentence), while in (29)(*b*) it is a predicative (complement) and has a similar function to that of an adjective phrase (cf. *very expert*). There are two ways in which we might make good this lack of a functional-relational specification: we might replace our constituent structures with a different model, or we might try supplementing them in some way. The more radical policy is to abandon constituent structure altogether, and this is done in the various versions of dependency grammar (cf. Hays 1964, Korhonen 1977). Dependency grammar takes as its basis the relations between lexical elements, and the dependency involved is not so much one of a unilateral requirement for occurrence (as in a subordinative endocentric construction) as a semantic dependency for interpretation. For instance in the predicate phrase (*Students* . . .):

(30)

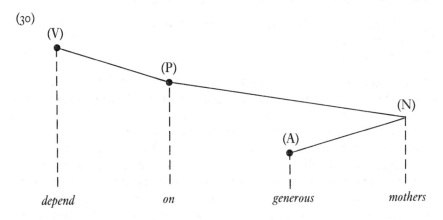

the word *generous* depends on *mothers*, which depends on *on*, which depends on *depend*. Only the first of these relations involves optionality, and in the case of *mothers* and *on*, it is difficult to see the latter as the dominating element. But, it is argued (with less than total conviction), in each case the 'dependent' relies on the 'governor' for its semantic interpretation.

Closely related to dependency grammar is valency grammar, which (following Tesnière 1959) emphasises that certain 'governors', especially verbs, have the power to require a particular number and particular types of 'dependent' (i.e. subject, object, adverbial, etc.), cf. for instance the different needs of the verbs in Figure 8 above. But dependency and valency grammar, if interpreted too narrowly, are in danger of failing to give sufficient attention to the structure of the superficial form of sentence, and a functionally-supplemented constituency grammar might be preferable. Candidates in this field include the rather programmatic Relational Grammar (cf. Johnson 1977, Perlmutter 1983: chapters 1–3) and Functional Grammar (cf. Dik 1978), in which functional notions like subject and object are basic but occur at different levels of description to allow for the different applications of the notions to cases like:

(31) (*a*)  Someone's broken a window, have they?
    (*b*)  A window's been broken (by someone), has it?
    (*c*)  There's been a window broken (by someone), has there?

In (31)(*a*) *someone* is clearly the subject and has the semantic role of agent, but it retains the role of agent and is in some sense still the underlying subject in (*b*) where superficially *a window* is the subject; and in (*c*) even the empty word *there* shows some sign of being at least a surface subject (by being echoed in the final tag question). Bresnan's lexical-functional grammar, on the other hand (cf. Bresnan 1982: chapter 4), has attempted to link active and passive forms lexically by giving each transitive verb a double syntactic potential.

In his 'case grammar' Fillmore (1968, 1977) tried to make a direct link between surface subjects, etc. and semantic roles like agent. The allied movement of 'generative semantics' (associated with the names of G. Lakoff, J.D. McCawley, P.M. Postal and J.R. Ross) aimed at a full integration of syntax and semantics (on which see Chapter 4). These projects now seem to have been abandoned; but we should note that recent work in Montague grammar/semantics has similar aims but works on a logical basis of truth conditions, 'possible worlds' and abstract mathematical models (cf. Dowty *et al.* 1981). An integration of syntax and semantics is also called for by the proponents of Generalized Phrase Structure Grammar (cf. Gazdar *et al.* 1985).

Chomsky has always maintained that syntax is autonomous of semantics, although in his recent work grammatical deep structures have given way to semantic rules (cf. Chapter 4). Whatever the theory to be adopted, syntax and semantics need to be brought together, because it is insufficient to establish grammatical patterns without being able to describe their meanings. The difficulty is that, whereas in syntax we try to work with discrete structures, in semantics we are faced with a multidimensional continuum of partly overlapping subtle distinctions. Consider, for a moment, the meanings of (32)(*a*) and (*b*) with their reflexive and reciprocal pronouns (which have been one of Chomsky's recurring themes in recent years, cf. Chomsky 1981):

(32) (*a*)  They liked themselves/each other.
    (*b*)  They said they liked themselves/each other.

Both versions of (32)(*a*) involve a kind of reflexiveness: assuming two people A and B, the *each other* version clearly has the meaning 'A liked B, and B liked A', while at first sight the *themselves* version means 'A liked A, and B liked B'; yet, on reflection, we realise that the version with *themselves* can also mean 'A liked A and B, and B liked A and B'. With (32)(*b*) the situation is more complex: in the *themselves* version did A, for instance, say that he liked B, or that he liked A and B, or that B liked A (and B), and did B say the same or something different? (We can leave aside here the question of whether the liking is present or past.) Needless to say, if more than two people are involved, the possibilities become even more complex, and the question naturally arises: how much such semantic detail can a grammar cope with?

There is a further question to be considered about the limits of a grammar in another direction: what are its upper limits in terms of the size of its units? The sentence was traditionally regarded as the upper limit of grammatical analysis, and this was re-affirmed by Bloomfield (1935: 170). But in recent years the developing fields of text-linguistics, discourse analysis and pragmatics (see Chapters 6, 7 and 8) have all given attention to the links between sentences, and some of these links are undoubtedly grammatical. 'Proforms', like pronouns (both 'pro-noun phrases' like *she, it,* and the pronoun in the narrower sense, *one* of *a big one*) and the pro-verb *do*, often rely on anaphoric reference to previous sentences for their interpretation. Equally the selection between sentence-types such as active vs. passive, cleft vs. non-cleft, is made on the basis of the wider text. Furthermore, a choice often available to the speaker is between articulating two sentences separately and combining them through embedding or coordination.

## 6. FORMALISATION IN GRAMMAR

At the beginning of this chapter it was suggested that full explicitness, possibly even generativity, was a desirable quality for a grammar. Various attempts have been made to achieve this in the history of modern linguistics. One of the first was Jespersen's *Analytic syntax* (1969 [1937]), which, although it presents mere 'formulas', does have a double system of description to refer to both functions (S(ubject), P(redicate), etc.) and to 'ranks' (1 = primary, etc.) of modification, as well as a system of brackets for representing subordination and embedding; but the system is not really fully explicit and only works through examples and intuition.

Harris's (1951) system was much more rigorous. Starting from a set of word classes (N, V, A, etc.) he attempted to relate these to word-sequence classes ($N^1$, $N^2$, etc.) through a series of equations, some of which were 'repeatable' (i.e. recursively applicable), others not. This came very close to the explicitness claimed for generative grammar by Chomsky, Harris's pupil. In later work (1952, 1957) Harris suggested transformations as a way of stating relations between different sentences and of accounting for similarities of lexical collocational restrictions between different structures (e.g. *write the poem/\*house, wire the house/\*poem* compared with *The \*house/poem is written,* etc.); these were also presented in the form of equations, which can, of course, be read in either direction.

Chomsky's rewrite rules, first presented in 1955-7, were, however, unidirectional (e.g. S → NP+VP, VP → V+NP, etc.) and were fundamentally different in that they were intended to specify (= 'generate') sentences and assign structural descriptions automatically in one fell swoop. From the beginning he argued that both context-free and context-sensitive rules were necessary; he also claimed that transformational rewrite rules were required not only to relate different sentences, but also to relate 'deep' and 'surface' forms of the same sentence. With the development of transformational grammar, it became apparent that the overall rewriting potential of the model was so powerful that restrictions came to be suggested.

The variant of generative grammar that has gone furthest in this direction is GPSG (Gazdar *et al.* 1985), which has abandoned context-sensitive rules and transformational rules, and redesigned context-free rules so that the constituency of constructions ('Immediate Dominance') and the sequence of constituents ('Linear Precedence') are stated separately; this gets around the problem of discontinuous constructions. Furthermore metarules are introduced to allow new rules to be based on existing rules, thus taking care of some transformational relations. Although this theory has some attractive features, it is apparently too concerned with the form grammar should take rather than with making it accurately reflect the structure of a language. The same criticism can be made of Montague grammar (Dowty *et al.* 1981), which seems more concerned with the niceties of mathematical logic than with the analysis of the language actually used by speakers.

There is no reason to suppose that natural language as a social or psychological reality comes close to either a computer program (often the inspiration of work in GSPG) or the formulae of mathematical logic. Nevertheless Chomsky made explicit rule-formulation fashionable, and even some already established grammatical theories suddenly found that (rather like Molière's Monsieur Jourdain) they had been practising generative grammar for years without realising it, for instance tagmemics (Cook 1969: 144, 158f) and systemic grammar (Hudson 1974).

One of the simplest and earliest mathematical modes of representation for grammar which was implicitly generative, actually came from a logician. The Pole Ajdukiewicz (1935; following Leśniewski, see Lyons 1968; 227-31) developed a 'categorial grammar', which, rather in the manner of Harris, related word categories and construction categories to the basic units 'sentence' and 'noun' through a series of equations involving fractions: for instance, a verb is something that when combined with, or 'multiplied by', a noun (phrase) gives a sentence, and therefore must be a sentence 'divided by' a noun (phrase). A verb is thus an element that converts nouns to sentences, and an adjective is an element that can be added to nominal elements without changing their category. There is no clear place for the articles in Ajdukiewicz's scheme, but then Polish has none!

'Categorial grammar' shares certain features with dependency and valency grammar. Tesnière, for instance, defines prepositions as convertors ('transla-tifs') of noun elements into adverbials or adjectivals. On the other hand, in dependency grammar the verb is not seen merely as a convertor but as the principal element in the sentence, which achieves sentence status with the aid of its dependent nominals and adverbials. A formalised system of dependency grammar must therefore make provision for verbs (at least) that 'govern' but also require certain 'complements'. Hays (1964) proposes a formalism for achieving this with rules of the form $V_a(N_1, *)$ for intransitive verbs and $V_b$ $(N_1, * N_2)$ for transitive ones, with the asterisk indicating the linear position of the 'governor' relative to its 'dependents'. But, as we have already seen, there are different kinds of relationship subsumed under 'dependency', and any formalism, however attractive, is likely to obscure this.

We need to ask ourselves why such a degree of formalism is required. Chomsky himself denied that his formalism was intended as a model for linguistic performance, either for speaking, or (still less) for understanding; he proposed it, rather, as a model for linguistic competence. But is the gram-mar of a language really like that? Is there a clearly defined list of sentences which are as grammatical in the language in question? For example, does the grammar of English allow sentences with phrases like *?the too heavy suitcases* (cited above) or sentences like those of (33)?

(33) (*a*)  John wasn't enjoying starting driving.

    (*b*)  Who did the students say the professor claimed he wanted to write a poem in honour of?

Equally, in view of the complex subtleties of structures like English prepositional verbs or indirect object constructions, can we be sure that one mode of analysis is ever going to give us a perfect description? If the answer to either of these questions is 'No', and language is not well-defined in the fullest sense, we are entitled to ask whether a closed system of fully-formalised rules can ever capture the natural elasticity of language. Certainly, though, we can accept the view expressed by Mephistopheles (in Goethe's *Faust Part I*), roughly:

    With words one can have a splendid fight,

    With words devise a system right.

or, as the original has it:

    Mit Worten läßt sich trefflich streiten,

    Mit Worten ein System bereiten.

# REFERENCES

Ajdukiewicz, K. (1935) 'Die syntaktische Konnexität, *Studia Philosophica (Warszawa)*, I: 1–28.

Bloch, B. and Trager, G.L. (1947) *Outline of linguistic analysis*, Linguistic Society of America, Baltimore, Md.

Bloomfield, L. (1935) *Language*, British edition (American edition: 1933), Allen & Unwin, London.

Bresnan, J. (ed.) (1982) *The mental representation of grammatical relations*, MIT Press, Cambridge, Mass.

Chomsky, N. (1964) 'Current issues in linguistic theory', Fodor and Katz (1964): 50–118.

Chomsky, N. (1965) *Aspects of the theory of syntax*, MIT Press, Cambridge, Mass.

Chomsky, N. (1972 (1968)) *Language and mind*, enlarged edition, Harcourt Brace, New York.

Chomsky, N. (1981) *Lectures on government and binding*, Foris, Dordrecht.

Chomsky, N. and Halle, M. (1968) *The sound pattern of English*, Harper & Row, New York.

Cole, P. and Sadock, J.M. (eds) (1977) *Syntax and semantics, volume 8: grammatical relations*, Academic Press, New York.

Cook, W.A. (1969) *Introduction to tagmemic analysis*, Holt Rinehart, New York.

Cruse, D.A. (1986) *Lexical semantics*, Cambridge University Press, Cambridge.

Dell, F. (1980) *Generative phonology*, Cambridge University Press, Cambridge, and Hermann, Paris.

Dik, S.C. (1978) *Functional grammar*, North Holland, Amsterdam.

Dinneen, F.P. (1967) *An introduction to general linguistics*, Holt Rinehart, New York.

Dowty, D.R., Wall, R.E., and Peters, S. (1981) *Introduction to Montague semantics*, Reidel, Dordrecht.

Fillmore, C.J. (1977) 'The case for case re-opened' in Cole and Sadock (1977): 59–81. *linguistic theory*, Holt Rinehart, New York: 1–88.

Fodor, J.A. and Katz, J.J. (1964) *The structure of language: readings in the philosophy of language*, Prentice-Hall, Englewood Cliffs, N.J.

Gazdar, G., Klein, E., Pullum, G and Sag, I. (1985) *Generalized phrase structure grammar*, Blackwell, Oxford.

Halliday, M.A.K. (1985) *An introduction to functional grammar*, Edward Arnold, London.

Harris, Z.S. (1951) *Methods in structural linguistics*, University of Chicago Press, Chicago (reprinted as *Structural linguistics*, (1955)).

Harris, Z.S. (1952) 'Discourse analysis', *Language*, 28: 1–30. (Reprinted in Fodor and Katz (1964): 355–83.)

Harris, Z.S. (1957) 'Cooccurrence and transformation in linguistic structure', *Language*, 33: 283–340. (Reprinted in Fodor and Katz (1964): 155–210.)

Hays, D.G. (1964) 'Dependency theory: a formalism and some observations', *Language*, 40: 511–25. (Reprinted in F.W. Householder, *Syntactic theory I: structuralist*, Penguin, Harmondsworth: 223–40.)

Hudson, R.A. (1974) 'Systemic generative grammar', *Linguistics*, 139: 5–42.

Jespersen, O. (1969) *Analytic syntax*, Holt Rinehart, New York. (First published 1937, Allen & Unwin, London.)

Johnson, D.E. (1977) 'On relational constraints on grammars' in Cole and Sadock (1977): 151–78.

Korhonen, J. (1977) *Studien zu Dependenz, Valenz und Satzmodell, Teil I*, Peter Lang, Berne.

Kratochvil, P. (1968) *The Chinese language today*, Hutchinson, London.

Lyons, J. (1968) *Introduction to theoretical linguistics*, Cambridge University Press, Cambridge.

Matthews, P.H. (1970) 'Recent developments in morphology', in J. Lyons (ed.) *New horizons in linguistics*, Penguin, Harmondsworth: 96–114.

Perlmutter, D.M. (ed.) (1983) *Studies in relational grammar 1*, University of Chicago Press, Chicago.

Radford, A. (1981) *Tranformational syntax: a student's guide to Chomsky's Extended Standard Theory*, Cambridge University Press, Cambridge.

Robins, R.H. (1967) *A short history of linguistics*, Longman, London.

Tesnière, L. (1959) *Eléments de syntaxe structurale*, Klincksieck, Paris.

T'ung, P.C. and Pollard, D.E. (1982) *Colloquial Chinese*, Routledge & Kegan Paul, London.

Wells, R.S. (1947) 'Immediate Constituents', *Language*, 23: 81–117. (Reprinted in M. Joos (ed.) (1957) *Readings in linguistics* I, University of Chicago, Chicago: 186–207.)

## FURTHER READING

Allerton, D.J. (1979) *Essentials of grammatical theory*, Routledge & Kegan Paul, London.

Bauer, L. (1983) *English word-formation*, Cambridge University Press, Cambridge.

Brown, E.K. and Miller, J.E. (1982) *Syntax: generative grammar*, Hutchinson, London.

Huddleston, R. (1984) *Introduction to the grammar of English*, Cambridge University Press, Cambridge.

Matthews, P.H. (1974) *Morphology: an introduction to the theory of word structure*, Cambridge University Press, Cambridge.

Matthews, P.H. (1981) *Syntax*, Cambridge University Press, Cambridge.

Sampson, G.R. (1980) *Schools of Linguistics*, Hutchinson, London.

# 4

# LANGUAGE AS A MENTAL FACULTY: CHOMSKY'S PROGRESS

## P.H. MATTHEWS

Noam Chomsky is at once a brilliant grammarian and an important philosopher of language. As a grammarian, he has had greater influence on our conception of English syntax, both of the nature of syntax and the nature of particular constructions, than any other scholar now living, and continues to display a remarkable ability to discover new problems and new generalisations that his predecessors had entirely failed to notice. As a philosopher of language, he is responsible above all for the belief that linguistics is, in his terms, a branch of cognitive psychology, and that human beings have a genetically inherited faculty of language which is independent of other faculties of the mind. If these contributions were separate, they might well be thought to merit two chapters in an encyclopaedia of this kind. But they are intimately related. Chomsky's philosophy of mind rests directly on a philosophy of grammar, in which the term 'grammar' was used, in the 1960s, to refer not simply to a linguist's description of a language, but to the basic knowledge of linguistic structures that every speaker of a language has acquired in infancy. The central issues of linguistic theory are then posed as follows. First, we must ask what grammars are like: what form does a speaker's basic knowledge of a language take? Second, we have to ask how speakers do in fact acquire this knowledge. Chomsky's answer to the second question largely reflects his answer to the first, and both are central to his view of mind in general. The term 'philosophy of grammar' will recall the title of a famous work by Otto Jespersen (1924), a scholar with whose interests Chomsky has himself expressed sympathy (1975, 1986: 21f.). The aim of this chapter is to examine the development of his own philosophy of grammar, from its beginning in the 1950s to the form in which we find it now, thirty years after the work which first made his reputation.

I have referred, in the singular, to Chomsky's 'philosophy' of grammar. Like that of any other major scholar, his work forms a historical unit. One can see the roots of things he says now in things that he said at the very outset of his career in the early 1950s. But one might also speak, in the plural, of Chomsky's 'philosophies'. His thought has never been static, and within this unity there have been many important shifts of emphasis, many innovations and much reshaping of old theory into new. On some central issues, notably on the place of semantics in grammar, his views have changed not once but twice. For a historian of linguistic theory it is fascinating to trace the continuities and discontinuities in Chomsky's ideas. But for a student of current theory it is the best and possibly the only way to understand him. He is not a systematiser, and attempts to impose a system on him are liable to be betrayed by the next book that he writes. For those who are maddened by such things, he can be maddeningly inconsistent. At present, as always, his theories are in transition. To appreciate why they are going where they are one must have a thorough critical appreciation of their background.

I have also referred to Chomsky in particular, and not, in general, to a Chomskyan school. For it is doubtful whether any permanent school can be identified. Since the early 1960s Chomsky has, at any time, had crowds of followers. Many pupils have clung to his coat tails and, after publishing a thesis which was proclaimed to be important, have done little or nothing thereafter. Others have been scholars of independent intellect whose work has then diverged so much from Chomsky's own that no community of interest has remained. The greatest number have been teachers; by the early 1970s there were classroom versions of what Chomsky and others were supposed to have established in the 1960s which, as the decade wore on, were increasingly enshrined in textbooks. But both teachers and textbooks were left stranded when it was clear that he had taken a fresh turn. In the 1980s there is a new wave of followers, and little dialogue between them and the best of the old. We will refer to some of these people as we go along. But in Chomskyan linguistics the only element of continuity is Chomsky himself.

His career may be divided into four periods. Externally it is one: he moved as a young man from the University of Pennsylvania, via Harvard, to the Massachusetts Institute of Technology, and has stayed there since. But the first stage of his intellectual history begins in the early 1950s and is centred on his first book, *Syntactic Structures* (1957). In this period he was still strongly influenced by older theorists in the United States, retaining many of their biases while, in other ways, reacting against them. The second period begins towards the middle 1960s. It was brief, but immensely productive: a space of three years saw two monographs on grammar (1965a, 1966a), a rash excursion into the history of linguistics (1966b), an important set of general lectures (1968), not to mention a joint work on phonology (Chomsky and Halle 1968).

For many commentators this is Chomsky's classic period, the period of what he himself has called the 'standard' theory of transformational grammar. But by the end of the 1960s we can already distinguish the beginnings of a period of groping and reorientation, which was to last through most of the 1970s. This is marked most clearly by a series of technical papers (collected in Chomsky 1972a and 1977a) and a further set of general lectures (1976). By the end of the decade the reorientation was complete, and we may therefore distinguish a fourth phase whose latest manifesto (1986) opens, in part, a new perspective.

I will take these periods in turn. But this is not a chronicle, and I will not hesitate to refer both backwards and forwards where connections can be drawn.

## 1. 'SYNTACTIC STRUCTURES'

One remark of Chomsky's that seemed provocative or puzzling at the end of the 1970s was his assertion that the notion of a grammar is more central than that of a language (1980: 126ff). Since then he has changed his terms: what was formerly a 'grammar', and had been called so for the previous twenty years, is renamed a 'language' or 'I-language' (1986: 21ff.). But, in ordinary parlance, a grammar is not a language. It is merely one of the means by which a language, as the primary object of study, is described. Nor would Chomsky have disagreed with this at the beginning. To understand why both his views and his terms have shifted, we have to go back to his first book, and in particular to ideas that he inherited from his teachers.

In the view that was dominant in America when he entered the subject, the first or only task of linguistics was to study the formal patterning of units. For example, there is a unit *hat* which is identified by the smaller units /h/, /a/ and /t/, in that order. Ignore its meaning; in this conception of linguistics it is not relevant. There is also a unit *coat* and, still ignoring meaning, these can generally be substituted one for the other: *I wear a hat/coat, Some hats/coats were on sale,* and so on. In the key term of this school, *hat* and *coat* have similar DISTRIBUTIONS. We can therefore class them together, and can then go on to class together larger units such as *a hat* or *a coat, these coats* or *that scarf,* still for no other reason than that, in such sentences as *A hat would look nice* or *These coats would look nice,* they can all be said – meaning once more apart – in the same context. The description of a language is complete when the distribution for all units has been stated in terms of classes which are ideally general.

This approach was developed most consistently by Zellig Harris, in a book (1951) with whose typescript Chomsky himself helped (preface, v). Chomsky said later that this was how he learned linguistics (reference in Newmeyer 1980: 33). His own work shows this very clearly. Critics of Harris and others had asked how a language could be described without appeal to meaning; but in Chomsky's view the implication that it could be done '*with* appeal to meaning' was 'totally unsupported' (1957: 93). He saw 'little evidence that "intuition about meaning" is at all useful in the actual investigation of linguistic form' (94). His own investigation of syntax was 'completely formal and non-semantic' (93), and linguistic theory in general, for him as for Harris, was a theory of distributional relations.

For Harris, a language was simply the collection of utterances whose formal structure one set out to describe. Similarly, for Chomsky, it was 'a set . . . of sentences' (1957: 13). In describing a language one must then do two things. Firstly, one must define the membership of this set. For example, the set 'English' has among its members *I wear a coat*, *That scarf would look nice*, and so on. In Chomsky's terms, these are GRAMMATICAL SEQUENCES of elements, whereas *Coat Wear I a* or *Would nice look that scarf* are sequences that are UNGRAMMATICAL. Secondly, one has to indicate the structure that each sentence has. For example, in *I wear a coat* the pronoun *I*, classed by Chomsky as a Noun Phrase, is followed by a Verb and a further Noun Phrase, which in turn consists of an Article plus a Noun. According to Chomsky, a *grammar* was a 'device' which performed both tasks. It contained a series of rules for the distribution of smaller and larger units. Thus, by one rule, a Noun Phrase can consist of an Article followed by a Noun. Unless there are other rules to the contrary, this excludes the possibility that successive Articles and Nouns might not form a Noun Phrase, or that, within such a phrase, the Noun might come first and the Article after it.

In this conception, a language is the primary object and a grammar is a set of statements about it. One standard way of putting this was to say that grammars were *theories* of languages. But let us now ask what it means to 'know a language'. As Chomsky saw it, speakers of English know what sequences of elements are grammatical sentences in English. But that is because they know the rules by which sentences are formed; to use a term which Chomsky popularised in the 1960s, it is because they have INTERNALISED (1965a: 8) the grammar of English. 'Knowing a grammar' is thus the primary concept, and 'knowing a language', in the technical and rather unnatural definition of a language with which he began, is at best derivative. It took several years for the implications of this shift to sink in. But once it had, it was obvious that this definition of a language made sense only when linguistics was restricted to the study of distributional relations. For these may indeed be seen as relations in a set of sentences. To 'study language' in a real sense is to study something else; and that might very appropriately be called an INTERNALISED LANGUAGE or 'I-LANGUAGE'.

In the rest of this section we will look further at Chomsky's thought as we find it in his first phase. As we have seen, he followed Harris in excluding meaning from the analysis of a language. The reason he gave was that there is no one-to-one relation between meaning and form. Forms can differ phonemically but mean the same; equally the same form can have different meanings. Not all morphemes have an independent meaning, and some forms that are not morphemes do. There is no coincidence between syntactic constructions such as Verb plus Object and constructional meanings such as Action-Goal (1957: 94ff.). Therefore a grammar had to treat forms on their own.

If a grammar was a theory of a particular language, a linguistic theory was in turn a general theory about grammars. But what can we expect of such a theory? The answer, in part, was that it had to specify the forms that grammars might take. They consisted of rules: thus, in Chomsky's formulation at that time, of phrase structure rules followed by transformational rules followed by morphophonemic rules. These rules were seen as *generating* the sentences of a language, in that, by following them through, it would be possible to produce any grammatical sequence of elements and none that were ungrammatical. Such rules had to be precise and had to conform to a format which the theory of grammar laid down. They also had to be as restrictive as possible. The main thrust of Chomsky's work in the 1950s was to demonstrate that some forms of grammar were too restrictive. With a finite state grammar (1957: Ch. 3) one could not generate the sentences of English. With a phrase structure grammar one might be able to generate them, but one could not describe their structure satisfactorily. With a transformational grammar one could do both. But one did not want to form a grammar which would also allow one to generate sets of sentences which were quite unlike any human language. Part of Chomsky's insight was to see this as a problem of mathematical formalisation. A grammar was a type of mathematical system. If the sets of sentences that can be generated by one type of system (A) include all those that can be generated by another type of system (B) but not vice versa, A is more POWERFUL than B. What was needed was a theory that had just the power – no more, no less – that was needed.

But a linguistic theory also had to provide what Chomsky called an EVALUATION MEASURE. Suppose that we have two grammars, both in the form that the theory prescribes and both generating the same language. But one may be simpler and, in that respect, better. According to Chomsky, the theory itself should then discriminate between them. Given a precise account of the forms of rule that it permits, including a detailed specification of the notation in which they are to be written, it should, in addition, prescribe a way of measuring the relative simplicity of alternative grammars for the same set of sentences. Now since these grammars are different they will in part describe the language differently. They might establish different units: for example, in *A hat would look nice*, one grammar might relate *would* to a Complement *look nice* while the other might say that *nice* was the Complement of a single Verb *would look*. If not, they would establish different classes. For example, one might class both *I* and *a hat* as Noun Phrases, while the other might deal with Pronouns separately. The evaluation measure will therefore tell us which analysis of the language a given theory favours.

This account of the aims of linguistic theory was new and brilliant. But, in retrospect, it seems clear that there were problems. Grammars, as we have seen, were theories of languages and, like many other theories, they were based on limited evidence. They therefore made predictions: in Chomsky's words, which echo those of Harris (1951: 13) or Hockett (1948), any grammar 'will *project* the finite and somewhat accidental corpus of observed utterances to a set (presumably infinite) of grammatical utterances' (1957: 15). It was then true to the extent that its predictions of what was and what was not grammatical were borne out. But then we have on top of that another theory which will take two grammars that are in this sense equally true, and literally calculate that one is, in some other sense, better. Does 'better' just mean 'simpler'? That is what Chomsky seemed to be saying, and still more his associate Morris Halle (1961). But simplicity is not itself a simple notion: how then could we decide what sort of simplicity should be measured? Or does 'better' again mean 'truer'? Then in what respect truer and why should these levels of truth be separated?

These questions were answered, as we will see, in Chomsky's next phase (see section 2). For the moment, however, a more obvious problem was whether the study of forms and meanings could sensibly be divorced. For although Harris and others had sought to base their analyses on purely distributional evidence, they did not, of course, maintain that meanings could not be investigated. Likewise, for Chomsky, 'the fact that correspondences between formal and semantic features exist . . . cannot be ignored' (1957: 102). All that was claimed was that the formal features had to be investigated first, that descriptive linguistics (Harris 1951: 5) was concerned with them alone, and that any study of meaning had to come later.

In Harris's terms, the meaning of utterances was, 'in the last analysis', their 'correlation . . . with the social situation in which they occur' (1951: 187). This had its roots in Leonard Bloomfield's theory (1933: Ch. 9). For Chomsky, 'the real question that should be asked' was: 'How are the . . . devices available in a given language put to work in the actual use of this language?' (1957: 93). A language could therefore be studied like an 'instrument or tool' (103). On the one hand, we can describe its formal devices without reference to their use. In the same way, to develop the analogy, one could in principle describe a knife – handle, blade, sharp edge and all – without knowing, or while pretending that one did not know, that it was used for cutting. However, these devices have a purpose. So, given this account of the handle, edge and so on, one could then go on to incorporate it in a wider form of description which would also explain what they are for. In the same way, we can envisage a 'more general theory of language' (102) of which a linguistic theory, in the sense already described, is only one part. The other part would be a separate 'theory of the use of language'.

In this light, both a grammar and a linguistic theory can be evaluated on two levels. Considered on its own, grammar A may be simpler than grammar B. This notion of simplicity may be given a precise sense, as we have seen, by an evaluation measure. In a looser sense, theory A may also permit a simpler form of grammar than theory B. Thus, in his first book, Chomsky argued that a theory which included transformational rules allowed a simpler grammar of English than one which included phrase structure and morphophonemic rules alone (1957: Chs. 5 and 7). But if we then go on to study meaning, simplicity is only one criterion. For we can also require of a grammar that it should 'provide explanations' (1957: 85) for semantic facts. The form /əneym/ has two meanings ('a name' and 'an aim'); this is explained, as Chomsky saw it, by a formal grammar in which it is divided into two different sequences of morphemes. In a passage that became famous, he argued that *the shooting of the hunters* could be used either of hunters shooting or of hunters being shot. That could be explained by a grammar in which, for reasons of pure simplicity, it is derived by different transformations (88f.). A theory which allows transformations is therefore better for another reason. Not only does it give a simpler description of the knife; but, if we may continue the analogy, a description which is simpler in terms of the proposed evaluation measure will also explain why the knife is held as it is and used to cut things.

What then was the real argument for transformations? For most of Chomsky's followers, it was precisely that they threw light on distinctions and similarities of meaning. On the one hand, forms which are ambiguous would have analyses to match, thus *the shooting of the hunters* and many other stock examples. On the other hand, a transformation could relate forms that were partly or wholly synonymous. For example, Actives were said to be synonyms or paraphrases of the corresponding Passives. Moreover, given that a linguistic theory allowed transformations, how did one decide in particular cases whether such a rule should be established? The sophisticated answer was that this should be decided by the evaluation measure; and, since the linguistic theory of which the measure was part could itself be seen as part of a more general theory which would also include a theory of use, it should ideally be so devised that a grammar whose formal descriptions contributed to the explanation of meanings would be simpler than one which did not. But in practice most of those who applied the model took what in an earlier phase of distributional linguistics might well have been disparaged as a 'short cut'. If there were semantic reasons for establishing a transformation they established it. The grammar might in an intuitive sense be simplified or it might not; but the appeal to meaning was overriding.

Now Chomsky's followers are not Chomsky himself, and by the end of the 1960s this had led to a remodelling of grammar under the name of generative semantics (see the beginning of section 3) which he rejected. But neither he nor anyone else made any serious attempt to justify a syntactic evaluation measure. A proposal was developed in morphophonemics or, as it was misnamed, generative phonology. But in that field meanings were irrelevant and, even then, it did not in the end work. In syntax, despite the great place that it had in Chomsky's initial programme, the evaluation measure was still-born. For, by relating theories of form to subsequent theories of meaning, he had ensured that it would be transcended.

## 2. THE 'CLASSIC' CHOMSKY

In his account of the battle of El Alamein, Liddell Hart (1970: 315) comments on Montgomery's 'adaptability and versatility' in devising a fresh plan when his initial thrust had failed. It was 'a better tribute to his generalship' than his own habit of talking as if everything had gone as he intended. One might say much the same about Chomsky, both in his next phase and in the long re-adjustment which followed. From his own accounts, one might suppose that his thought has been consistent from the beginning. But in this way his true genius has often been disguised from his own troops.

Of the changes that mark Chomsky's general thinking in the middle 1960s, the most straightforward, on the face of it, was his extension of the concept of a grammar to include a SEMANTIC COMPONENT. Its syntactic component, as before, said nothing about meanings. Syntactic rules continued to indicate which sequences of morphemes could and could not represent grammatical sentences. But each sentence was now interpreted semantically. A generative grammar, as Chomsky put it in a series of lectures delivered in the summer of 1964, became 'a system of rules that relate [phonetic] signals to semantic interpretations of these signals' (1966a: 12). The objects that it generated were sentences in the old sense. But they now had meanings attached. More precisely, therefore, they were pairings of a phonetic representation of a sentence and its SEMANTIC REPRESENTATION.

How does this relate to the earlier division between a theory of form and a theory of use? One might say simply that the term 'linguistic theory' had been redefined: whereas it was previously part of a 'more general theory of language' (Chomsky 1957: 102), it now *was* that theory. But then there is a problem as to what was meant by 'use'. In 1957 Chomsky had talked of the 'actual use' of the language; this could be taken to mean that semantic theory was concerned with the use made of a particular utterance, by a particular speaker, at a particular time, in a particular set of circumstances. But a generative grammar is a system of rules; particular uses vary indefinitely; there-fore, if a grammar was to assign semantic interpretations to sentences, these had to be something else. In Chomsky's formulation, they were 'intrinsic meanings' of sentences (1968 = 1972b: 71). In this context he no longer spoke of 'uses'. But, if we go back to the analogy of the knife, we might say that its intrinsic use is for cutting. I may then use it, on a particular occasion, to slice this particular cabbage which is in my kitchen. On another occasion I may use it in a non-intrinsic way, say as a makeshift screwdriver. In the same sense there was now a distinction that had not existed previously in Chomsky's thinking, between the meaning of a sentence as defined by rules and its actual meaning in a concrete utterance.

With that insight in mind, we can now turn to his general concept of 'knowing a language'. In his earliest publications Chomsky had said little about the psychological status of rules, his primary aim being to account for distributions. But at least one commentator had gone further. Towards the end of an enthusiastic review of Chomsky's first book, Robert Lees talked of the 'device' within the speaker's head which is used 'to generate the sentences of his language'. We cannot study it directly; but if our rules are adequate and general, then by the canons of science as Lees conceived them 'it is not too much to assume that human beings talk in the same way that our grammar "talks"' (Lees 1957: 406 ff.). In his own chapter on finite state grammars, Chomsky remarked that, if we accept that form of grammar, 'we can view the speaker as being essentially a machine of the type considered'. 'In producing a sentence', he too 'begins in the initial state, produces the first word of the sentence, thereby switching into a second state', and so on (1957: 20). Now Chomsky did not talk similarly about machines which included phrase struc-ture rules and transformational rules. But to Lees at least it seemed that a grammar was a literal model for the production of utterances.

Two years later Chomsky dismissed the suggestion (1959: 56). But at the same time he assumed, without argument, that a generative grammar could be said to 'characterise abstractly' what he later called the speaker's linguistic COMPETENCE. Speakers can, for example, 'distinguish sentences from non-sentences'; as Chomsky saw it, that ability is characterised by a grammar that gives rules for the distinction. It also characterises, 'in part', their ability to understand a sentence that they have not heard before. In his words they are 'somehow capable of determining the process by which this sentence is derived' in the grammar. Likewise it can characterise their ability to 'note certain ambiguities'. Now a language, as we have seen, was a set of sentences; and a speaker who knows the language can be said to know what these sentences are and to know their structure. Accordingly, he can be said to know a grammar: that is, he knows a set of rules which specify what the language is. In this light, Chomsky uses the term 'grammar' with what he later called a 'systematic ambiguity' (1965a: 25). 'Grammar$_1$', we might say, is a set of rules constructed by a grammarian. But in Chomsky's interpretation these are an attempt to characterise the competence of a speaker, and that is itself a grammar. 'Grammar$_2$' is thus the set of rules, that everyone who knows a language has also 'in some sense constructed' (1959: 57).

If linguistic competence is 'the speaker-hearer's knowledge of his language' (1965a: 4), 'the actual use of language in concrete situations' constitutes his PERFORMANCE. A generative grammar cannot account for this directly: thus, to return to semantics, it can account for intrinsic meanings but not actual, concrete meanings. Nor was it seen any longer as a projection from a set of 'observed utterances'. On the one hand, Chomsky remarked that 'a record of natural speech will show numerous false starts, deviations from rules, changes of plan in mid-course, and so on' (1965a: 4). A grammar was not concerned with these, but only with an ideal form of speech in which all sentences were correct. On the other hand, he proposed that certain sentences which were grammatical might, in performance, be unacceptable (10ff.). Again the grammar was concerned with grammaticality only. Nevertheless a speaker's performance rested on his underlying competence, and it was this competence that a grammar (grammar$_1$) described. Therefore, in any study of performance, the study of a grammar (grammar$_2$) had to be primary. As Chomsky had put it in his earliest formulation, any 'direct attempt to account for the actual behavior' of speakers or hearers, 'not based on a prior understanding of the structure of grammar', will have 'very limited success' (1959: 58).

All this was quite a mouthful, and it is remarkable, in retrospect, that Chomsky should have introduced it with so little argument. He seems genuinely to have believed that, if one was prepared to think about the psychology of language at all, what he had said was uncontroversial. But once a 'grammar$_1$' is reified as a 'grammar$_2$', the rest of Chomsky's mature theory follows without much difficulty. A speaker has as a child acquired, constructed or internalised grammar$_2$; to be able to do so, children must have in their heads a LANGUAGE-ACQUISITION DEVICE which takes 'primary linguistic data' (1965a: 25, 31) as input and yields a grammar as output. There is therefore a direct comparison, developing in effect a remark of Hockett's (1948), between the construction of a grammar$_2$ by a child and that of a grammar$_1$ by a linguist. In either case, grammar$_1$ or grammar$_2$, the set of rules is very complex. Moreover, in the child's case, its construction is 'accomplished in an astonishingly short time, to a large extent independently of intelligence, and in a comparable way by all children'. (See Chapter 10, below, section 4.) How can these 'facts' (1959: 58) be explained?

Chomsky's answer was to reify not just the concept of a grammar, but also that of a linguistic theory. As first envisaged, this was a second-order theory that restricted the forms that grammars might take and the class of languages that they might generate. A grammar was, in turn, a first-order theory about a language. But let us now suppose that such restrictions are known to children when they learn their native language. In that case, just as a grammar$_1$ is an attempt to describe a grammar$_2$, so a linguistic theory posited by a linguist – call it linguistic theory$_1$ – can be reinterpreted as a hypothesis about a linguistic theory$_2$ (Chomsky again makes clear that he is using terms with 'systematic ambiguity') that every child possesses. All children must possess it equally. It constitutes a faculty of the mind distinct from general intelligence, and therefore stupid children can acquire a grammar as quickly and successfully as bright children. By the same token, it cannot itself be learned. Instead it must be part of our genetic make-up; briefly, it must be *innate*.

The linguistic theory which was reified in this way was conceived in other respects exactly as in 1957. First, it specified the form that grammars might take. As Chomsky saw it, 'a child who is capable of language learning must have', among other things, 'some initial delimitation of a class of possible hypotheses about language structure' (1965a: 30). This was again seen as restricting the class of languages for which a grammar might be constructed. Accordingly, 'the child approaches the data with the presumption that they are drawn from a language of a certain antecedently well-defined type', and must then 'determine which of the . . . possible languages is that of the community in which he is placed' (27). In short, he already knows what human languages are like and what grammatical rules are like. 'Language learning would be impossible', Chomsky said, 'unless this were the case' (27). The passages cited make clear how complete the parallel was thought to be, not just between theory$_1$ and theory$_2$ or grammar$_1$ and grammar$_2$, but in the entire cognitive task that children and grammarians faced.

Second, the theory had to provide an evaluation measure. In Chomsky's words again, 'a child who is capable of language learning' must, in addition, have 'a method for selecting one of the (presumably, infinitely many) hypotheses that are allowed . . . and are compatible with the primary linguistic data' (30). In this light he was able to explain more clearly what a linguist's evaluation measure – evaluation measure$_1$ – was meant to assess. A grammar$_1$ is, once more, a hypothesis about a speaker-hearer's grammar$_2$. It is therefore *descriptively adequate* (1965a: 24) 'to the extent that it correctly describes' the competence that underlies his performance. But in developing their competence, or in constructing a grammar$_2$, children have 'a method of selecting' between hypotheses. Accordingly, the linguist's evaluation measure$_1$ may be interpreted as a theory about this method. In devising it, we again aim to select the simplest and most general set of rules; however, we do this not because we have an *a priori* concept of elegance, but because we assume that there is an innate evaluation measure – evaluation measure$_2$ – which selects a grammar in the same way. 'Simplicity' was therefore reinterpreted as an empirical concept (see, in particular, Chomsky and Halle 1965). The evaluation measure literally measured truth – that is, the descriptive adequacy of grammars$_1$.

The chapter in which these ideas are introduced is very loosely argued (see Matthews 1967: 121 ff.). The ideas have always been hard to expound, and I have therefore given quotations where possible. But it was clear at the time that their historical importance was much greater than the trains of thought by which they had been reached. For once we accept that a linguist's grammar$_1$ is a description of a speaker-hearer's grammar$_2$, and a linguist's linguistic theory$_1$ an account of a learner's innate linguistic theory$_2$, our subject is given a new purpose and a new standing in relation to other disciplines. In later years, Chomsky and his followers were to talk resoundingly of language as a window on the mind, of a linguistic faculty peculiar to human beings and unparalleled in other species, of the problems raised for human evolution, of linguistics in general as a science whose findings no other human science, from philosophy to biology, could ignore. But although these external prospects seemed to many to be very exciting, perhaps the most important implications bore directly on the discipline itself and the methods by which its findings could be reached.

Let us consider first the data on which our descriptions of languages are based. In Chomsky's earliest phase, a grammar (grammar$_1$) characterised a set of sentences. The data were therefore possible sentences, either observed utterances or sentences that could in principle be utterances. They formed a corpus or sample of the language, and the grammarian's task was to extrapolate from the part to the whole. Where there were alternative extrapolations he chose the simplest. If he was not sure whether a sentence was possible or not, he started from data that were certain and made whatever extrapolation offered simpler or else more general rules. In Chomsky's own words (1957: 14), he was 'prepared to let the grammar itself decide'.

But now a grammar$_1$ is a description of the speaker-hearer's competence (grammar$_2$). As such, it accounts for a variety of abilities: thus, as we have seen, the ability to 'distinguish sentences from non-sentences', to 'note certain ambiguities', and so on. Moreover, a person's competence is reflected only indirectly in performance. Suppose, for example, that a speaker of English is observed to say *I went to home.* It may be that the observation is misleading and that he really meant to say *I went home.* Or perhaps he was going to say *I went to the pub* but changed his plan too late. Or perhaps he really did say *I went to home*, but the preposition was used by mistake. The observation itself is unreliable, and a corpus which includes it may well be an inaccurate sample of the language whose grammar$_2$ has been internalised. We will therefore do better if we simply ask the speaker, or attempt to find out by some other direct experiment, whether *I went to home* is grammatical for him. Since he has internalised a grammar$_2$ he knows whether it is or not, and it is this knowledge, not his actual speech, that we are seeking to describe.

Now consider a sentence like *I watched the shooting of the hunters.* A speaker who has internalised a grammar$_2$ of English knows that this is ambiguous. He knows that it has two different semantic representations and, corresponding to these, two different syntactic structures. There is therefore no need to argue, as before, from distributional evidence. Nor is there any reason to appeal, in either the first or the second instance, to data bearing on the actual use of such a sentence. Nor does it make sense to ask whether our evidence is of form or of meaning. It is simply evidence of the speaker-hearer's inter-nalised knowledge of his grammar$_2$, and, in constructing our own grammar$_1$, we may rely directly on it.

In short, a grammarian's data are primarily the speaker's *intuitions.* That they were among his data was not new: Lees's review of Chomsky's first book is again more explicit than the book itself (Lees 1957: 376). But increasingly they became the only evidence that generative grammarians were to use. Nor were they got from what had earlier been called 'naïve informants'. A follower of Chomsky typically worked on his own language; he himself spoke it, and therefore had his own intuitions about what was grammatical and ungram-matical, which sentences were ambiguous, and so on. Therefore he could proceed by pure introspection, without appealing to observational evidence at all. By the end of the 1960s this method was employed with almost total confidence. When one grammarian's intuition clashed with that of another, either each said he was right and the other was wrong, or they agreed chari-tably that the 'dialects' which they had learned as children must be different. Scholars began to worry about the problems of investigating dead languages, for which such data could not be got. Others argued that only native speakers could describe a language safely, since only they had intuitions which were correct. In his review of 1957, Lees had distinguished carefully between this form of evidence and 'the intuitive or prescientific perceptions which the linguist, qua scientist, has about the data'. But, in practice, it became very hard to keep them apart.

A second important bearing was on the study of UNIVERSAL GRAMMAR. It had always been assumed that there were features common to all languages; we could therefore 'look forward', as Bloomfield (1934 = 1970: 285) had put it, 'to . . . a General Grammar, which will register similarities' between them. The term 'linguistic universal' or 'universal of language' was itself introduced by scholars who were not among Chomsky's followers (see especially Green-berg 1963; and, here, Chapter 9 below). But Chomsky's new interpretation of linguistic theory quite transformed this field of research.

A child, to recapitulate, constructs a grammar. This is very complex; so, to construct it as consistently and quickly as they do, children must already know in detail many features that a grammar has to contain. But they are not genetically equipped to learn particular languages. A baby born of parents who speak English can as readily internalise a grammar of Russian or Chinese or Quechua if that is spoken in the community in which it grows up. Therefore the features that are known innately must be common to all languages. At the same time they must be specific. If they were merely general indications – as, for example, that a sentence can be analysed into words, or that it has a deep structure and a surface structure – their value as a blueprint for constructing grammars would be slight. Therefore languages must be much more similar than Chomsky's predecessors had supposed. The diversity of their structures must be superficial. Behind it a rich and intricate set of universal principles must be waiting to be discovered.

This was a matter of faith and not an empirical finding. It simply followed from the logic of Chomsky's new conception of linguistic theory. Let us now consider how a universal feature may be discovered. The obvious method, if one was not a follower of Chomsky, was to look in general at the widest possible range of languages. This requires extensive knowledge and, to Bloomfield at least, it had seemed that 'lack of data' still forbade it. But in Chomsky's programme this form of study was in any case peripheral. For one cannot argue directly from universality to innateness. As critics pointed out, a feature may in fact be present in every language but may not be genetically inherited (thus, for instance, Matthews 1967: 122 ff.). But, conversely, if a feature is innate it has to be innate universally. To discover it we do not have to look all round the world. We must simply show that adult speakers of whatever language could not construct the grammars that, on the evidence of their abilities, they do construct unless, when they are learners, this feature is already fixed. Indeed the evidence of just one language may suffice. 'Paradoxical as it may seem at first glance', Chomsky remarks in a note to the next chapter (1965a: 209), 'considerations internal to a single language may provide significant support' not just for its own grammar but also for universal theory.

I recall that at least one reader flung the book down when he read the note which I have cited. But in retrospect its wording was cautious. For, in the years that followed, and for reasons that were perfectly legitimate if one accepted the logic of Chomsky's theory, the study of the universal properties of human language was to proceed almost wholly on the basis of a generative grammarian's intuitions about English.

## 3. THE PERIOD OF TRANSITION

Many years later, Chomsky said that if he had to rewrite the introductory chapter of *Aspects of the Theory of Syntax*, he would not change what he had written. It is indeed the pivot on which the 'generative enterprise' (Chomsky, Huybregts and van Riemsdijk 1982) was set in motion. But although the core of its interpretation of grammars remains, there are other things in it, perhaps less central to Chomsky's own evolving concerns, that he soon abandoned or qualified.

Let us begin once more with meaning. The semantic theory which Chomsky took as uncontroversial in the mid 1960s was not his invention. It was primarily that of Jerrold Katz (Katz and Fodor 1963, Katz and Postal 1964), and its central tenets, as we have seen, were that sentences have what Chomsky called intrinsic meanings, and that these are derived by rules interpreting syntactic structures. A more precise way of putting this was to say that each syntactic structure 'uniquely determines' (Chomsky 1966a: 13) a semantic representation. But such a theory must provide criteria for distinguishing intrinsic meaning from all other meanings that a sentence may have when it is uttered. Take once more our analogy of the knife. A knife that I have often used for chopping onions was used by my mother as a bread knife. Has it just one general use (cutting)? But surely there is some intrinsic difference between this knife, which is large, and one which I might use to peel an apple. Has it, alternatively, two intrinsic uses (chopping, slicing)? But how does one put a stop to the distinctions that might then be drawn? Thus peeling an apple is not the same as slicing a cucumber; yet I often do both with the same knife, which is still intrinsically unsuitable for slicing bread. Do we say that the large knife has intrinsically just one specific use (*either* chopping onions *or* slicing bread)? In that case either my mother has used it, or I have used it, in a deviant way. But which of us?

A theory of intrinsic meanings cannot avoid similar problems, and in the early 1970s they were beginning to cause theoretical anguish. One reason is that most of Chomsky's followers had adopted the theory of GENERATIVE SEMANTICS. According to this, a generative grammar began by characterising semantic representations. These were not determined by, or derived by the interpretation of, syntactic structures. Instead the latter were derived from them. Therefore, in dealing with any body of data, a grammarian's first task was to work out what the semantic representations should be. Was a sentence ambiguous, and if so how many meanings did it have? Answers were given which seemed at first sight to be ludicrous: for example (seriously), that any plural had an infinite set of semantic representations (*men* = 'two men', 'three men', 'four men' and so on); or, in parody, that *He stood on one leg* was ambiguous because it could have been his left leg or his right. Ludicrous such proposals may have been. But they rest on judgements that, at some level, we can recognise to be correct, and if they do not concern intrinsic meanings, one is forced to wonder how such meanings can be teased out.

Chomsky himself dismissed generative semantics. At the time many

followers were surprised. For he himself had said that semantic representations were determined by rules; in principle, there was no reason why they
should not be generated directly. He had also said that judgements of
ambiguity and so on were data that reflected a speaker's competence; and, as
we noted in section 1, semantic arguments had been increasingly used as a
primary ground for establishing transformations. The more that was done,
the more grammarians were led directly to meanings and not merely to a
deeper level of syntax. Finally, in the lectures of 1964 in which he had introduced the revision of his model of grammar, Chomsky had implied that the
reason for starting from syntax was simply that we did not know very much
about how meanings should be represented (1966a). That was a clear challenge
to find out more and start from them instead.

But Chomsky had originally taken a different view of the relation between
grammar and meaning and, although he had approved the concept of semantic representations, saying at one point that it was, 'Quite obvious that
sentences have an intrinsic meaning determined by linguistic rule' (1965b =
1972b: 115), his own interests have always centred on syntax and he has rarely
discussed a particular problem of meaning which did not have a syntactic
point to it. Where other aspects are concerned (for example, the meanings of
lexical units or the status of speech acts) he has said little and then mainly in
polemic (as in Chomsky 1976: ch. 2). Moreover, there are signs that, by the
end of the 1960s, he had himself begun to doubt that the intrinsic meanings of
sentences could be isolated. In a lecture in 1969, he remarked that 'the notion
"representation of meaning" or "semantic representation" is . . . highly
controversial'. 'It is not at all clear', he goes on, 'that it is possible to distinguish sharply between the contribution of grammar to the determination of
meaning, and the contribution of so-called "pragmatic considerations", questions of fact and belief and context of utterance' (1972b: 111). In short, it is not
clear whether semantic competence can be distinguished from performance.
At the time, he continued to posit semantic representations. But they were an
abstraction, and might prove invalid.

Seven years later, in a series of conversations that did not appear in
English until 1979, Chomsky effectively ditched Katz's theory. He points out,
correctly, that it is not what he had proposed in the 1950s. In addition, it
posits a semantic representation based on a 'universal system of semantic
categories' (1979: 141). But although some 'traditional notions' can be taken as
universal (for example, 'agent of action' or 'instrument'), and although some
other features of meaning (for instance, anaphora or the properties of quanti-
fiers) also belong to 'the system of rules that specifies our purely linguistic
knowledge', it is 'not at all clear' that a universal system, which he himself had
also taken as necessary (1965a, 1966a) could be defended. In the next paragraph he returns to the role of pragmatic factors. 'It is not at all clear', he says,

'that much will remain if we try to separate the purely linguistic components of what in informal usage or even in technical discussion we call "the meaning of linguistic expression"'. 'I doubt', he continues, 'that one can separate semantic representation from beliefs and knowledge about the world' (1979:142).

This was a major turn-around, as Katz (1980) at once recognised. But where exactly does it lead? A first possibility, which no one at the time appears to have spelled out in so many words, would have been a return to something like the view that Chomsky had held in the 1950s. A generative grammar would be concerned with syntax and phonology, and the primary aim of syntax would be to describe distributions. It would also assign to sentences structures which were suitable for semantic interpretation. But the interpretation itself would lie outside the grammar, and in it many different factors, some depending entirely on the state of a particular speaker or hearer on a specific occasion, would be mingled.

But it is easy to see why that would not do. For in the conversation cited Chomsky accepts that some semantic notions (anaphora, roles of participants and so on) are universal. If so, they are candidates for the innately determined universal grammar (section 2) and, if they are part of that, they must be part of the particular grammars that speakers construct. Alternatively, they are candidates for some other innate mental structure that is also specific to language, and it is hard to see why this should be separate.

A second possibility would have been to abandon the concept of an internalised grammar. According to Chomsky, a grammar was, by definition, a set of rules relating meanings to phonetic signals (see again Chomsky 1966a: 12). But meanings are only partly determined by grammatical rules; accordingly, such a grammar is a contradiction. Moreover, it is 'not at all clear' that the contribution of rules can be separated from that of other factors. If it cannot, there is no other way in which a grammar with semantic rules may be delimited. If we follow this argument through, a speaker's competence is simply the ability to speak and understand speech in specific contexts. There would be no delimitable aspect that a grammar could be said to describe.

Some proponents of generative semantics had already reached this conclusion. But it plainly strikes at the foundation of Chomsky's philosophy. For it is because speakers were believed to have internalised a grammar (the grammar$_2$ of section 2) that a linguist's grammar (grammar$_1$) could be interpreted psychologically. And it is because the linguist's rules were so complex, and the speaker's were assumed to be similar, that the ability to learn languages had to be explained by a prior knowledge of universal grammar. And it is because the knowledge of grammar was believed to be separate from the use that speakers made of it that one could posit a specific faculty of the mind to which this prior knowledge belonged. Abandon the basic concept and all that rests on it dissolves.

Such arguments are a reconstruction, since Chomsky did not debate the matter overtly. But the alternative that he adopted was in effect a compromise. On the one hand, it posited that some semantic rules – call them semantic rules$_1$ – do apply independently of the contexts in which sentences are used. They include, for example, rules for obligatory anaphora (in *Bill cut himself* the reflexive pronoun must be anaphoric to *Bill*), for obligatory non-anaphora (in *Bill cut him* the simple pronoun cannot be anaphoric to *Bill*), for the meanings of agent, goal or instrument (in Chomsky's terminology these are 'thematic' relations), and for other features of grammatical meaning that Chomsky took to be universal. Such rules form the semantic component of what was at this point called a 'sentence grammar' (1976: 105). But, on the other hand, there is another type of semantic rule – call them semantic rules$_2$ – which operates conjointly with other forms of knowledge. An example is the interpretation of *him*, in *Bill cut him*, as referring not just to a male individual, but to that particular individual who, on a particular occasion, is in question. Semantic rules$_2$ are also part of our linguistic knowledge. But they form a second semantic component that, in a narrow sense, is outside the grammar.

Having adopted this theory, Chomsky was then free to concentrate on sentence grammar. Within it a first set of rules – the rules of syntax –.derived a structure that (still on the model of the 1960s) must be interpreted by semantic rules$_1$. For example, in *Who did he say Mary kissed?*, which is a type of sentence that Chomsky discussed throughout the 1970s, the syntactic structure shows, among other things, that *who* is moved by transformation from an initial position after *kissed*. The semantic rules$_1$ will then derive what Chomsky called the LOGICAL FORM of the sentence. This term was defined by the general theory: it referred to 'those aspects of semantic representation that are strictly determined by grammar, abstracted from other cognitive systems' (Chomsky 1977a: 5). But, as the name implies, a logical form particularly represented what older grammarians would have described as logical relations. Thus *Who did he say Mary kissed?* had the logical form 'for which person $x$, he said Mary kissed $x$?' (Chomsky 1976: 99). Apart from marking *who* as personal, this is in particular designed to show that it is logically the object of *kissed*.

But where was the division between a syntactic structure that determines logical relations and a semantic structure that represents them? The semantic rule that links *who* to its position in the subordinate clause is of a type appropriately called a RULE OF CONSTRUAL (Chomsky 1977a: 6). But do not rules of syntax also show how sentences are construed? They operate differently; but, in the same example, there is a transformational link between *who* in its initial position in deep structure (. . . *kissed who?*) and the same word in its position in surface structure (*Who . . . kissed?*). By what criterion is a construction in part syntactic and in part semantic?

Now syntax had originally been distributional (section 1), and in the model adopted in the 1960s (section 2) it had continued to distinguish sentences from non-sentences. But by the mid 1970s this constraint had been dropped. Take, for example, the non-sentence *They said that Mary kissed each other*. At the beginning of the decade, the grammatical *They kissed each other* was usually derived, by a transformation, from the deep structure of *They each kissed the other*. The transformation could apply within a clause; but, given the deep structure of *They each said that Mary kissed the other*, it could not cross the boundary of a clause to attach *each* to the object of the subordinate verb. That is still the solution assumed by Chomsky 1973 (= 1977a: 89ff.).

But another solution is to say that such a sequence cannot be interpreted. In *They kissed each other*, the reciprocal phrase is linked anaphorically to *they*: that would again be effected by a rule of construal. But this semantic rule may likewise be said not to apply across clause boundaries. So, in *They said that Mary kissed each other*, there cannot be an anaphoric link between *each other* and *they*. But the reciprocal phrase cannot be linked to *Mary* either, since one is plural and the other singular. Nor, finally can it be understood without an antecedent. It follows that the sequence is unconstruable; but then, if its unacceptability can be explained at that level, there is no reason why the syntax should not permit it.

That is the solution adopted in Chomsky's next paper (1975 = 1977a: 178). It is merely one of many cases (some already in Chomsky 1973) where a sequence once excluded by the rules of syntax is instead rejected because no logical form can be assigned to it. Chomsky accordingly denied that there was any *a priori* difference between levels. A speaker knows, for example, that *The police think who the FBI discovered that Bill shot* is ungrammatical, whereas, if we replace *think* with *know*, it is grammatical. But, as we remarked in passing in section 2, he cannot say directly whether this intuition is about form or about meaning. Chomsky himself was 'not persuaded that the question makes very much sense, or that any reasonably clear criteria exist to settle it' (1976: 95). The same type of fact might in principle be explained in either way.

At the time this matter did not seem to be central. For most commentators, the issue of the day was whether semantics was 'generative' or 'interpretive'. Should a grammar start from semantic representations (as in the model of generative semantics) or should they be derived from representations of syntax? If one took the 'interpretive' view, a second question concerned the level of syntactic structure that they interpreted. Originally it had been, by definition, the deep structure; subsequently, it was a paired deep structure and surface structure (Chomsky 1972a); later still, just the surface structure (Chomsky 1976 and thereafter). Successive models of grammar were distinguished on that basis: a 'standard theory' of the mid 1960s; an 'extended standard theory'; finally a 'revised extended standard theory'.

But in retrospect it seems clear that, behind the façade of technical progress, we were in fact witnessing the death throes of distributionalism. In Chomsky's earliest phase, the whole grammar was concerned with distributional relations only; and, as we saw in section 1, the requirement that it should be formally simple was prior to the expectation that it might, in part, explain the uses of sentences. But in the 1960s the priorities were reversed. A measure of simplicity, if relevant at all, applied to the entire grammar, and this included a semantic component. The primary requirement was that grammars should at all levels be descriptively adequate. Moreover, this did not imply that they should deal with every fact of distribution. For among the sentences generated by the grammar there might be many that, for other reasons, could not serve as utterances (thus again Chomsky 1965a: 10ff.). Their unacceptability would be explained by the interaction of a grammar, as a theory of competence, with a theory of performance.

Distributionalism died hard. In the enlarged grammar of the mid 1960s, the syntactic component was effectively equated with that of the earlier distributional model. It continued to characterise 'all and only the sentences' that were deemed to be grammatical, and, in justifying the form that its rules took, Chomsky appealed directly to earlier arguments. The semantic component was correspondingly no more than an interpretative appendage. As late as the mid 1970s, at least one textbook still insisted that formal arguments were separate from semantic arguments, and that the latter should not be used to justify syntactic rules (Culicover 1976: 45 and elsewhere). But by that stage Chomsky himself had concluded that the separation was nonsense. The very basis for a distributional grammar, or for a purely formal theory within 'a more general theory of language' (Chomsky 1957: 102), had collapsed.

Where did that leave the criterion of generativity? In the beginning the first requirement for a generative grammar was that it should generate 'all and only the sentences'. As Chomsky put it in the 1960s, it had to be *observationally adequate*. As the primary criterion for grammars this was superseded, as we have seen, by that of *descriptive adequacy*. But a still more vital requirement was that a theory of grammar should be *explanatorily adequate*: it should explain how a child's construction or development of a grammar is possible. Let us suppose then that a particular aspect of a speaker's competence has to be ascribed to a universal principle. We say 'has to' because we have evidence that speakers have internalised a certain set of rules, and cannot explain how they could do so if the principle were not innate. Now there is no objection if these rules as such are not observationally adequate. For no particular set of rules, and no particular component of the grammar, has a privileged role in separating what is grammatical from what is ungrammatical. Suppose, for instance, that the principle determines a set of transformations. It might allow numerous constructions that seem wholly ungrammatical. But perhaps they are so because there are other rules and principles, perhaps unknown, which block the corresponding logical forms. Or perhaps they are excluded by the rules deriving phonetic forms. Or perhaps the explanation lies outside the grammar altogether. Just as we do not have to look at languages in general to propose that a feature is universal (end of section 2), so we do not have to be sure of every other aspect of the speaker's mind.

At the end of the 1970s Chomsky began to emphasise that the mind, as he saw it, had a *modular* structure. It should be seen not as an undifferentiated whole, but as a system of 'distinct though interacting' subsystems, each of which has its own properties and is 'organised along quite different principles' (1980: 40ff., 89). Our linguistic faculty had originally been conceived as one module; as such, it interacted with other modules, and it was only in that way that our actual use of language could be explained. But by the middle of the decade it too had a modular character. In the light of Chomsky's shifting view of meaning, it made sense, 'in particular, to distinguish what is sometimes called "grammatical competence" from "pragmatic competence"' (1980: 59). Within grammatical competence we can then conceive of further modules, distinguished not, as before, by *a priori* concepts of linguistic levels, but again by different organising principles. These too are 'distinct though interacting'. We cannot know in advance what they are, and we cannot expect of any one of them that it should characterise a language with observational accuracy.

The period of readjustment was then over. It had seen, in part, the rejection of ideas that had been innovations in the 1960s: in particular, Katz's notion of a semantic component. But it had also made clear the peripheral status of a set of notions that had been central in the 1950s. One was Chomsky's initial concept of a language: as we noted in section 1, it took time for the implication to work through, but once a grammar is reified as the speaker's competence or 'internalised language', the 'externalised language', as Chomsky now calls it, is 'an epiphenomenon at best' (Chomsky 1986: 25). In the 1960s Chomsky had reified the entire linguistic theory of his first phase. Thus, in addition, the sets of sentences called natural or human languages were of 'a certain antecedently well-defined type' (Chomsky 1965a: 27) and, in constructing rules that generated the one spoken in a particular community, a child made use of an evaluation procedure. One therefore had the illusion that the notation and the generative power of grammars were still important. But these too were relics of the earlier marriage between mathematics and descriptive linguistics. Fifteen years later they had in practice ceased to matter.

## 4. A NEW SYNTHESIS

The modular theory that has developed in the 1980s is essentially a theory of what Chomsky calls CORE LANGUAGE (or, in his earlier terminology, CORE GRAMMAR). This is one of a mass of burgeoning ideas that emerged obliquely in Chomsky's own work and which it is hard to separate and follow systematically. But, to put it briefly, a child has an innate universal grammar (section 2). This comprises a set of universal rules or principles, each of which allows an individual language – we are speaking again of the 'language' internalised by a speaker – to vary within limits. But let us now propose that, at a certain level of abstraction from the detailed facts of particular languages, the variation that the principles allow is finite. They will then constitute a set of PARAMETERS. Each parameter will have a fixed set of values; and, in developing his internalised language, a child will select, by experience, a particular value for each. The result is his core grammar (Chomsky 1981: 7) or core language (1986: 147): a central part of his knowledge that develops solely by a choice of values that are already innately given.

The term 'core grammar' had first been used in the later 1970s, when it referred in particular to an area of grammar delimited by certain specific principles (Chomsky 1977b). They included the principle by which, in a sequence like *They said that Mary kissed each other*, the rules of construal could not take *each other* as anaphoric to *they*. By 1980 this was part of what was called (temporarily) the 'opacity principle'. They also included a principle by which, for example, *Who did he believe the story that Bill kissed?* cannot be derived by transformation from an underlying *I believed the story that Bill kissed who*. From the early 1970s this had been known as the 'subjacency principle'. It thus united parts of what were technically semantic interpretation with other matters that were still conceived syntactically. In current versions, it includes 'such modules of grammar as X-bar theory, theta theory, binding theory, Case theory, control theory, and bounding theory' (Chomsky 1986: 155). Each 'theory' is highly abstract, and it is only by their interaction that the representations of a set of sentences within core language is determined. Within an internalised language, a core language is in turn no more than a fragment. There is therefore further interaction between this central set of subsystems and a PERIPHERY consisting of whatever else 'is added on in the system actually represented in the mind/brain of a speaker-hearer' (Chomsky 1986: 147). Finally there is a wider interaction, as before, between the systems that make up the speaker's internalised language, his pragmatic competence (see again Chomsky 1980), and other components of his mind. If we start from a common-sense notion of the speaker's knowledge of a language, core language is a very restricted and very abstract part.

The implications of this new approach were partly clear in 1981, when it first crystallised, and are in part still emerging. But, to begin with the simplest, a core grammar has no rules. In acquiring a language, children have to learn the properties of individual words, including those properties that relate to universal grammar. The various parameters must also be fixed. But within the core language that is all: any specific rule, for any specific construction that is not allowed directly by the universal principles, must by definition fall outside it. As Chomsky makes clear, a core language is in this respect unlike the generative grammars that he had conceived of earlier. Universal grammar is, as it were, a system that is 'only partially "wired up"' (Chomsky 1986: 146). As soon as a child has fully wired it up, 'the system functions' and a core language is in being.

If there are no rules, there can be no types of rules. So, in particular, there is no distinction between rules that can be labelled syntactic and others that can be labelled semantic. Now the universal principles will still distinguish different levels of representation, and in recent work these are still named in ways that recall the model of syntax and semantics current ten years earlier. But since 1981 they have all been of the same sort. A sentence such as *Who did you see?* has an initial structure (roughly) *you saw who*, and this is naturally represented in the same way as the structure which results when *who* is moved (*who you saw*). Since the late 1970s these have been known respectively as the 'D-structure' and the 'S-structure'. A third level is that of 'LF', a term intended to 'suggest' (Chomsky 1986: 67) logical form. But here too there is no fundamental difference. The 'LF representation', as it is called, is another object of precisely the same kind as the D-structure and the S-structure. Indeed it may on occasion be identical to either (see, for instance, Chomsky 1986: 75 ff.) or, for that matter, to both. The form of representation that was originally called a logical form (see again Chomsky 1976: 99) is now called an interpretation of the LF representation, or an 'LF interpretation' (Chomsky 1986: 76 and *passim*).

The drift of all this is perhaps not perfectly clear. But LF is itself described as a syntactic level (e.g. Chomsky 1986: 84) and, on the face of it, the whole of the core language is concerned with syntax in a traditional sense. It is not, of course, a distributional syntax, or the relic of distributional syntax that had survived in the 1960s. But a theory of core grammar allows certain sets of constructions, all of which are represented by an LF representation, a D-structure and an S-structure. The choice of parameters will select a particular set for any particular language. At the same time, individual words will have specific properties. For example, *each other* is a reciprocal pronoun: therefore it can only satisfy constructions where the universal principles allow it to be linked to a plural antecedent. Properties like 'reciprocal' are traditionally semantic, and Chomsky too describes the lexicon in terms of 'semantic selection' (1986: 86). Beyond this, and beyond the internalised language as a whole, semantics can be seen as a relation between language and the world (44) or between language and other cognitive systems (68). But within the language semantic construal is essential to syntax and not separate from it. That was the view before distributionalism, and for Chomsky too it now seems that it may be so.

Another implication, which was clear much earlier and has a far more central place in Chomsky's programme, concerns the extension of the theory of universal grammar to languages other than English. As we noted in section 2, the study of a single system can be instructive. In the middle 1970s Chomsky reaffirmed this point (1976: 118), and five years later saw its denial as 'irrational' (1981: 6). But by this stage proposals were becoming complex, and their limitation to English, which was virtually complete until the brink of the 1980s, was a 'serious limitation' (1976: 118). For suppose that we have developed a theory that, in the case of English, has a wide explanatory power. We then find that there are other languages for which a different theory is needed. Perhaps it will have partly similar principles or perhaps ones that are different altogether. We do not want to say that either theory is false, since our original data, which by the logic of the argument required us to posit that these structures were innate, are left unexplained. But if they are innate they must be innate universally. How then can both theories be true?

The concept of parameters provided an immediate answer. Suppose that principle A, which holds for one set of languages, differs in only one respect from principle B, which holds for another. We can then say that A and B are the same principle; but it incorporates a variable with two alternative values. In Chomsky's image, it can be 'wired up' in two ways and, in the light of different sets of forms to which they are exposed, some children wire it one way and some the other. Suppose that the differences between two languages are wider. Then it may be that the principles include more variables. In the extreme case, the application of a principle in any form may be a parameter. In core language A it is effective in one form. In core language B it is wired up differently in one or two or more places. In core language C it is not effective at all; but that too can be one of the several different wirings that the universal grammar allows. We may also posit what in another context are called implicated universals (see Chapter 9, below). If a core language is wired in one way at point A, it can only be wired in such and such a way at point B. If principle A holds, principle B cannot hold; or if it does, a parameter X must have a particular value $q$, and so on. A child might then begin by fixing the value of some very basic parameter. Perhaps this is determined by some obvious property of the sentences to which it is exposed. The values of many others might then follow automatically, some so subtle that it might be hard to fix them directly.

A theory of universal grammar can thus incorporate a typology of languages. In particular, Chomsky and his current wave of followers have talked of a 'configurational' and a 'non-configurational' type (traditionally, languages with fixed and free word order), or of 'pro-drop' languages (those in which a subject pronoun is used only for emphasis). But the motive is not to classify systems in a botanising fashion. Instead it is to explain how any internalised language, whatever its type, can develop. Once more, speakers can (according to Chomsky) make what, on the face of it, are inexplicable judgements. For example, he says that they can see 'with thought and preparation' that *John is too stubborn to expect anyone to talk to* is a sentence meaning that, because of his stubbornness, 'an arbitrary person would not expect' anyone to talk to John, whereas *\*John is too stubborn to visit anyone who talked to* is gibberish (Chomsky 1986: 11). They know such things 'without instruction or even direct evidence'; how then can they know them unless the relevant principles are innate? 'In many cases that have been carefully studied in recent work' (I am now citing Chomsky 1981: 3), 'it is a near certainty that fundamental properties of the attained grammars are radically underdetermined by evidence available to the language learner and must therefore be attributed to UG [universal grammar] itself'.

If one rejects this basic argument, the theory of core language will seem weak. On the one hand, a great deal of any internalised language lies outside it. The periphery will evidently include 'exceptions' such as irregular morphology or idioms (see again Chomsky 1986: 47). It will also include the idiosyncratic constructions taken by particular words. For example, *want* cannot take a *that-* clause (*\* The students want that Bill visit Paris*); however, 'we may assume' that this is 'an accidental gap reflecting properties that are not part of core grammar'. Although the construction is not 'idiomatic English', it is therefore 'fully grammatical at the relevant level of abstraction' (Chomsky 1981: 19). In this case, the counteraction of core grammar by the periphery may be trivial. But it is easy to imagine cases where it might be judged more serious. Suppose that a principle finds support over a wide range of languages; but, in just one, it does not hold. We could, of course, establish a parameter to cover this. But we might not wish to do so, since a universal grammar cannot be a mechanical accumulation of everything that we must posit in individual grammars. An alternative is to say that the principle does hold universally; but, outside the core, the speakers of this language must have internalised peripheral rules which (exceptionally) negate it.

On the other hand, the theory of core language can itself be weakened. Suppose that parameter A is, in general, set to $q$ if parameter B is set to $r$; but, once more, there is one language where it is not. We could, of course, say that the implication is not part of universal grammar. But we might be reluctant, since any implication simplifies the child's task. An alternative is to say that it is given innately as the normal or, in Chomsky's terms, the UNMARKED case.

The language which is an exception represents a MARKED case where, in wiring up a core language, children will be compelled by the facts to set parameter B to r but A to some other value. We thus have a theory which incorporates alternatives, and can accommodate at least two sorts of exception. If it is considered simply as a theory of linguistic universals, there is a risk that it will be immune to counter-evidence.

But if one accepts Chomsky's basic argument, none of this is crucial. For, yet again, we posit that something is innate not because we have found it to be universal, but because we see no way by which it can be learned. In this discussion I have continued to use the word 'learn', as Chomsky too does occasionally. But a child's learning of a language is not seen as learning in an ordinary sense. Nor is it like a scholar's construction of a theory, as Chomsky had first suggested. In the mid 1970s, he compared the acquisition of 'cognitive structures' to the development of bodily organs (thus, in particular, Chomsky 1976: 10f.). Language itself was thus described, at first in inverted commas, as a 'mental organ' (36). It is not learned, but grows in the child's head by a complex interaction between genetically-determined structures and the environmental input through the senses. As Chomsky remarked later, the assumption that the mind has 'a rich innate structure' sits naturally with the belief that it is modular (1980: 40 ff.). Each module has its own innately structured properties, like an arm, an organ of vision, and so on.

At the time, a theory of the language organ barely existed. Its empirical study, now restricted to core language, is still highly idealised. Many, including the present writer, are not convinced that it exists. But as the result of many successive shifts in Chomsky's thinking, in which he has abandoned most of the ideas that had been central in his first phase, and a great deal of what seemed to be crucial in his second, he at least has a conceptual model that is appropriate to his ends.

## REFERENCES

Bloomfield, L. (1933) *Language*, Holt, New York.

Bloomfield, L. (1934) Review of Havers, *Handbuch der erklärenden Syntax*, *Language*, 10: 32–9. Reprinted in Hockett 1970: 281–8.

Chomsky, N. (1957) *Syntactic Structures*, Mouton, The Hague.

Chomsky, N. (1959) Review of Skinner, *Verbal Behavior*, *Language*, 35: 26–58.

Chomsky, N. (1965a) *Aspects of the Theory of Syntax*, MIT Press, Cambridge, Mass.

Chomsky, N. (1965b) 'The formal nature of language', in Lenneberg, E., *Biological Foundations of Language*. Reprinted in Chomsky 1972a: 115–60.

Chomsky, N. (1966a) *Topics in the Theory of Generative Grammar*, Mouton, The Hague.

Chomsky, N. (1966b) *Cartesian Linguistics*, Harper & Row, New York.

Chomsky, N. (1968) *Language and Mind*, Harcourt Brace, New York.

Chomsky, N. (1972a) *Studies on Semantics in Generative Grammar*, Mouton, The Hague.

Chomsky, N. (1972b) *Language and Mind.* Enlarged edition (of Chomsky 1968), Harcourt Brace Jovanovich, New York.

Chomsky, N. (1973) 'Conditions on transformations', in Anderson, S and Kiparsky, P., *A Festschrift for Morris Halle.* Reprinted in Chomsky 1977a: 81–160.

Chomsky, N. (1975) 'Conditions on rules of grammar', in Cole, R., *Current Issues in Linguistic Theory.* Reprinted in Chomsky 1977a: 163–210.

Chomsky, N. (1976) *Reflections on Language,* Maurice Temple Smith, London.

Chomsky, N. (1977a) *Essays on Form and Interpretation,* North-Holland, New York.

Chomsky, N. (1977b) 'On wh-movement', in Culicover, P.W., Wasow, T. and Akmajian, A. (eds), *Formal Syntax,* Academic Press, New York: 71–132.

Chomsky, N. (1979) *Language and Responsibility,* based on conversation with Ronat, M., translated Viertel, J., Harvester Press, Hassocks, Sussex.

Chomsky, N. (1980) *Rules and Representations,* Blackwell, Oxford.

Chomsky, N. (1981) *Lectures on Government and Binding,* Foris, Dordrecht.

Chomsky, N. (1986) *Knowledge of Language,* Praeger, New York.

Chomsky, N. and Halle, M. (1965) 'Some controversial questions in phonological theory', *Journal of Linguistics* 1: 97–138.

Chomsky, N. and Halle, M. (1968) *The Sound Pattern of English,* Harper & Row, New York.

Chomsky, N., Huybregts, R. and van Riemsdijk, H. (1982) *The Generative Enterprise,* Foris, Dordrecht.

Culicover, P.W. (1976) *Syntax,* Academic Press, New York. (New edn 1982.)

Greenberg, J., (ed.) (1963), *Universals of Language,* MIT Press, Cambridge, Mass.

Halle, M. (1961) 'On the role of simplicity in linguistic descriptions', in Jakobson, R, (ed.), *Structure of Language and its Mathematical Aspects,* American Mathematical Society, Providence: 89–94.

Harris, Z.S. (1951) *Methods in Structural Linguistics,* University of Chicago Press, Chicago.

Hockett, C.F. (1948) 'A note on "structure"', *International Journal of American Linguistics,* 14: 269–71.

Hockett, C.F. (ed.) (1970) *A Leonard Bloomfield Anthology,* Indiana University Press, Bloomington.

Jespersen, O. (1924), *The Philosophy of Grammar.* Allen & Unwin, London.

Katz, J.J. (1980), 'Chomsky on meaning', *Language,* 56: 1–41.

Katz, J.J. and Fodor, J.A. (1963), 'The structure of a semantic theory', *Language,* 39: 170–210.

Katz, J.J. and Postal, P.M. (1964), *An Integrated Theory of Linguistic Descriptions,* MIT Press, Cambridge, Mass.

Lees, R.B. (1957) Review of Chomsky 1957, *Language,* 33: 375–408.

Liddell Hart, B.H. (1970), *History of the Second World War,* Cassell, London.

Matthews, P.H. (1967) Review of Chomsky 1965a, *Journal of Linguistics,* 3: 119–52.

Newmeyer, F.J. (1980) *Linguistic Theory in America: the First Quarter-century of Transformational Generative Grammar,* Academic Press, New York.

# 5

# LANGUAGE, MEANING AND SENSE: SEMANTICS

## D.A. CRUSE

## 1. PROLOGUE

One might have thought that since the role of language is primarily to convey meaning, the study of meaning would always have been a major focus of attention within the scientific study of language. Yet this is not so. Of course, philosophers (and others) have been preoccupied with questions of meaning for millennia; but of the major branches of modern linguistics, semantics is paradoxically the youngest and least evolved. In recent years, however, meaning has come to be taken much more seriously by linguists. It is probably true to say that the most influential work to date in semantics has been somewhat theoretical in orientation, and has been directed preponderantly towards elucidating and accounting for the logical properties of sentences within the framework of some system or other of formal logic. There has been relatively less in the way of descriptive work. However, systematic descriptive work is also important, and ideally engages in a continual dialogue with theory. This chapter looks at meaning primarily from the point of view of its embodiment in words, and is biased towards disciplined description rather than formalised theory.

## 2. LANGUAGE AND MEANING

### 2.1 Meaning, signs and sign systems

The ability to convey meaning is the distinctive property of signs. Any sign must be capable of manifesting itself in some way in the experience of an observer: usually it has a physical existence of some sort. To be considered a sign, such a manifestation must do more, for at least some observer, than merely call attention to its own occurrence or existence. This crucial 'something more' involves the *meaning* of the sign. Thus smoke is not just an opaque cloud of tiny particles suspended in the air: to a suitably experienced observer it betokens the existence of fire. In this sense, of course, most natural phenomena are capable of signalling something beyond themselves. It is useful to distinguish between natural signs and conventional signs. Natural signs derive their meanings from their normal antecedents and consequences as physical events; hence their interpretation requires only a knowledge of the natural world and will be similar for all observers. Conventional signs have meaning allotted to them by human custom; their interpretation requires special learning and skill, and may well be different for different users. To interpret smoke as a sign of fire one needs only to have experience of burning things; to interpret American Indian smoke signals (other, that is, than signs of fire, which, of course, they also are) requires knowledge of special conventions, which may differ from one group of users to another.

A language is a system of conventional signs all aspects of whose structure – phonology, morphology, syntax, or whatever – exist ultimately to serve the sovereign function of conveying meaning. Most sign systems have a limited expressive range – think, for instance, of mathematical symbols, or the conventions of cartography. Language is unique in being able to express virtually anything that is conceivable. This extraordinary expressive power depends heavily on certain crucial properties of its constitutive signs, notably their *arbitrariness* and their *discreteness*.

An important typological distinction among signs is that between arbitrary signs and *iconic* signs. An iconic sign is one that bears some resemblance, direct or analogical, to what it designates. A map is an iconic sign because its shape has a systematic relationship to what it depicts. The Roman numerals, I, II, and III are iconic, having in their forms a clear indication of unity, duality and triality, respectively. In contrast, the Arabic numerals 3, 4 and 5 are arbitrary, because one could not guess from their shape which numbers they stood for. Some traffic signs are iconic: those for 'road narrows' or 'hump-backed bridge', for example. But the use of a red circle for mandatory and a red triangle for warning signs is entirely arbitrary. As for linguistic signs, some, usually termed 'onomatopoeic', are iconic: they are the ones which either refer imitatively to sounds, like *thwack, splash, buzz, hum, click, fizzle, plop, whoosh*, and so on, or which imitate the characteristic sounds of their referents, like *cuckoo, peewit* or *drum*. However, the vast majority of linguistic signs are arbitrary, and give no hint in their form of the nature of their referents, witness the oft-quoted example of the equivalents for *dog* in different languages: *chien, Hund, perro, cane, kalb, it*, etc. It was Saussure who first drew attention to the fundamental importance for linguistic theory of the arbitrariness of the linguistic sign. This arbitrariness is no accident: it is a prerequisite of the semiotic efficiency of the medium. Only a tiny proportion of conceivable notions could be effectively portrayed in sound, so a limitation to iconic signs would seriously constrain the expressive range of language. It is possible that the earliest words to develop in the history of language were imitative; if so, then the break with iconicity, whenever it occurred, was a decisive step in the evolution of the language faculty.

The property of arbitrariness is intimately linked with another important property of linguistic signs, namely, their discreteness. This is a little more difficult to grasp. It means that two word forms are either identical (as far as the linguistic system is concerned), or they represent two completely different words. Except in rare instances, we find no continuum of form correlating with the continuum of meaning between any pair of words. A speaker, in forming an utterance, must choose from a finite set of discrete and distinct possibilities. If someone observes an animal intermediate in appearance between a dog and cat, he cannot describe it as a *dag* or a *dat*, in the hope that intermediate forms will convey intermediate meanings. Discrete signs are to be contrasted with continuously varying signs. Consider, again, a map. When we draw a map, we do not have to choose from a fixed and limited set of geometrical shapes to represent the shape of, say, an island. We can vary our representations with infinite subtlety and in imperceptible stages, and the representation of an island intermediate in shape between two others will be intermediate in form between their representations. The connection between arbitrariness and discreteness is this: only signs that are to some degree iconic can vary continuously, and only discrete signs can be wholly arbitrary.

## 2.2 Language and other channels of communication

Language is the prime vehicle for the conveyance of meaning; but it is not the only one, and it is illuminating to look at it in the context of the full repertoire of signs used in human communication. Confining our attention to a typical everyday manifestation of communicative activity – two or more people in face-to-face conversation – we may inquire into the range of sign-types that will typically be found to be operative. It is useful to distinguish three types of signs: *linguistic, paralinguistic* and *non-linguistic.*

The linguistic component of face-to-face communication can be further sub-divided into *verbal* and *non-verbal* sub-components. The former is principally a matter of the words used and their grammatical arrangement; the latter involves *prosodic* aspects of language, that is to say, *intonation* and *stress.* Our main concern in this chapter is of course with the verbal sub-component.

Paralinguistic signs are those which either manifest themselves through the voice, and are therefore inseparable from spoken language (voice colour, for instance), or which are interpreted primarily in conjunction with linguistic signs. (Some of the latter can function independently of language, so the border-line between paralinguistic and non-linguistic signs is not a rigid one.) Paralinguistic signs have one or both of two characteristic functions. First, there are those signs which impart an overall emotive or attitudinal colouring to the linguistic message which they accompany: these are said to have the function of 'modulation'. Here we may usefully distinguish between vocal and non-vocal signs. Among vocal modulatory signs are: the quality of voice, or 'timbre' – warm, cold, hoarse, breathy, or strangulated, for instance; the general tempo of speech – perhaps slow and emphatic, or rapid and excited; the overall pitch (as distinct from particular tunes imposed on the general level) – generally speaking, higher pitch indicates greater excitement or intensity of emotion. Non-vocal modulatory signs include such matters as: posture – someone who leans towards his interlocutor when speaking conveys a different impression from someone who leans backwards; facial expression – it makes a difference whether an utterance is executed with a smile or a scowl; gestures – imagine *You've found us!* delivered first with the hands extended and second with the hands clasping the head. The other main paralinguistic function is given the name 'punctuation', and it is the spoken analogue of punctuation in a written text. Signs whose main function is punctuation will indicate the placement of emphasis, and will assist the hearer to analyse the flow of speech into its proper constituents. This is accomplished partly by pausing, but also by head movements, eye contact, eyebrow raising, manual gestures, and so on.

In addition to linguistic and paralinguistic signs, there are various signs which are quite independent of the linguistic system, and which can function perfectly well on their own. Some are vocal: an admonitory cough; sighs of boredom, exasperation or relief; a gasp of astonishment; a deprecatory clicking of the tongue; a yelp of pain; a sceptical *Hmmm*. Others are non-vocal: smiles, frowns, winks, obscene gestures, wrinkling the nose as a sign of disapproval, and many more.

The linguistic component of communication, although it will be our main topic in this chapter, is thus only one of several. In some respects it is the most important. But this must not be exaggerated: for some types of meaning, language (particularly in its verbal aspect) is, if anything, the poor relation. Experiments have shown – and everyday experience confirms – that for the expression of attitude or emotion, non-verbal means (i.e. prosodic, paralinguistic or non-linguistic) are the most effective. If verbal and non-verbal expressions of feeling are in conflict, it is generally the non-verbal which will prevail. The language of words is, of course, sovereign in its own domain: it is the only channel of everyday communication through which a conceptual content of any complexity can be conveyed.

### 2.3 Semantics and pragmatics

Now that we have seen something of the position of language against the background of communication in general, we may now begin to focus our attention on those aspects of linguistic meaning which are the principal concern of this chapter. This would seem to be an appropriate place to introduce the distinction usually drawn nowadays, but whose exact placing is still a matter of controversy, between semantic meaning and pragmatic meaning (on which, see Chapter 6, below). It seems worthwhile to differentiate between meaning which an utterance possesses, as it were, inherently, by virtue of the words it contains and their grammatical arrangement – meaning which the same utterance might be expected to exhibit in any other context in which it might occur – and meaning which is either 'picked up' from the context (as, for instance, the identity of 'I', 'him' and 'it' in a normal occurrence of *I saw him take it*), or which arises as a result of interaction between inherent meaning and context (as when *I've cleared the table*, in answer to *Have you cleared the table and washed the dishes?* carries the implicature that the dishes remain unwashed). For present purposes, the inherent sort of meaning will be taken to be the concern of semantics, and meaning in which context plays an essential role will be considered to fall into the province of pragmatics. In this chapter we are concerned with semantic meaning.

## 3. APPROACHES TO WORD MEANING

### 3.1 Word and sentence

Perhaps because of the familiarity of dictionaries, and perhaps, too, because of a naïve conception of the way language is learnt, according to which we first learn single words, and only later learn how to string them together, we tend to think of word meaning as basic and sentence meaning as secondary. Of course, the meaning of a sentence is in some sense or other composite, and systematically related to the meanings of its constituent elements. But at the same time, sentence meanings are much more directly experienced as linguistic objects than words are, and are more accessible to reliable intuitive judgements. If we ask an ordinary educated speaker of English whether, say, *violin* and *fiddle* mean the same, he may well find it difficult to answer; on the other hand, if we ask him or her whether *Kyung Wa Chung is recording all the fiddle sonatas of Brahms* or *Kyung Wa Chung is recording all the violin sonatas of Brahms* is the more normal, he or she will not hesitate, and as we shall see later, this fact can be taken as evidence that *fiddle* and *violin* are not, in fact, absolutely synonymous. Furthermore, it is often extraordinarily difficult to say what words mean, even though actually using them appropriately in sentences presents no problem. (The reader is invited to try to explain the difference in meaning between *disease* and *illness,* or between *however* and *nevertheless.*) For reasons such as these, the study of a word's meaning is best grounded in the use of the word in sentences, and the meaning itself is best derived, directly or indirectly, from the meanings of sentences containing the word.

## 3.2 Lexical and grammatical meaning

The inherent meaning of a sentence may be carried by lexical elements proper, or it may be carried by elements or patterns of arrangement that are normally considered to be part of the grammatical system of a language. The basic grammatical building-blocks of language, the MORPHEMES, fall into two classes, namely, CLOSED-SET ELEMENTS and OPEN-SET ELEMENTS. More extensive discussion of these will be found in Chapter 3, but briefly, closed-set elements belong to grammatical classes which have few members and whose membership changes so slowly that for most purposes it can be regarded as fixed; open-set elements belong to classes with typically large numbers of members, and a relatively large turn-over (both gain and loss) in membership. In the following sentence the closed-set elements are italicised:

*The* boy-*s were* play-*ing* nois-*i-ly in the* garden

There is semantic significance in the distinction between closed-set and open-set elements. Most of what would normally be considered to be the meaning of a sentence is carried by its open-set elements. Indeed, this is their principal function, and they are commonly referred to as LEXICAL or CONTENT elements. The principal function of closed-set elements (also known as GRAMMATICAL ELEMENTS or STRUCTURE SIGNALS) is to articulate the grammatical structure of the sentence and thus to indicate how the meanings of the open-set items are to be combined. This is not to say that closed-set items never carry meaning; on the contrary, they often do. Consider, for example, the plural -*s,* the past tense -*ed,* the comparative -*er* and prepositions like *in, on* and *at.* Nor is it the case that grammatical elements carry a particular type of meaning, different from that carried by lexical elements. It is true, however, that meanings carried by grammatical elements tend to be of a very general, attenuated sort (this is because they need to be compatible with a wide range of lexical elements), whereas lexical meaning is typically richer and more complex.

The semantics of closed-set items is usually reckoned to be the business of the grammarian, and will therefore not be further pursued here. For the rest of this chapter, it will be the meanings of open-set items, or what comes to almost the same thing, the meanings of words, which will occupy our attention.

### 3.3 Word-meaning and reference

Since we use language to talk about things in the world around us, there is obviously a connection of some sort between words and expressions and the things they can be used to refer to. Equally obvious is the fact that we have some kind of mental conceptions of the things in our world and that these are linked both to the words in our language and to the things themselves. (Saying these matters are 'obvious' is not to minimise their philosophical complexity.) These relationships are represented in the famous 'triangle of reference' of Ogden and Richards (1923: II). Various versions of this can be found – the one illustrated here is adapted from that of Ogden and Richards:

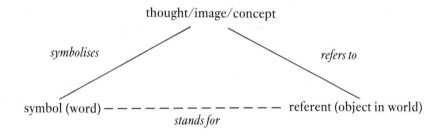

Notice that according to this view of signification, the relation between word and thing is indirect, being mediated by the concept. We commonly speak of words referring to things, but in this version of reference it is concepts which refer.

There is a question, here, of what we are to identify as the meaning of a word. According to Ullmann (1957: 72), what lies in the world outside of language is no concern of semantics. For him, the meaning of a word is the concept or image associated with it. His theory of meaning is thus one of those known as 'ideational'. A theory of meaning aims to account for all aspects of semantic functioning. Hence, ideational theories of meaning imply, first, that every meaningful expression has an image or concept associated with it, and second, that this image or concept is 'called forth' every time the expression is meaningfully employed (it is not enough for some words to evoke images some of the time). Sober reflection suggests that neither of these implications is true; there are grounds, therefore, for doubting whether any such account of meaning can be fully adequate.

Many scholars view any theory of meaning couched in mentalistic terms with deep scepticism. One way of getting rid of concepts is to picture the meaning of a word as being either constituted by, or at least directly related to, what the word refers to. To do this is to adopt a 'referential' theory of meaning. The simplest type of referential theory merely identifies the meaning of a word with its referents; a more sophisticated version identifies meaning with the relationship between word and referent. However, all versions take it for granted that all words refer to something. But there are considerable difficulties with this notion, too. We may accept, for instance, that the expression *Margaret Thatcher* refers to the person holding the office of British Prime Minister in 1987. But what does, say, *however* refer to, or *concerning*? It is not even clear what a concrete noun like *table* refers to. It obviously does not refer to some particular table. Nor does it refer to the class of tables: if we want to say something about the class of tables – for instance, that it has a lot of members – we cannot say *\* Table has a lot of members.* One way round this problem is to say that the meaning of *table* is not what it refers to, but what it denotes and/or what it connotes (this last to be understood in the logician's sense). The denotation of a word is the class of things to which it can be correctly applied; so the denotation of *table* is the class of things of which one can correctly say 'This is a table'. The connotation of a word is the property or set of properties the possession of which is a necessary and sufficient condition for the word to be correctly applied. So *table* connotes the set of properties which qualifies something to belong to the class of tables, and *happy* connotes the property which someone must possess for *happy* to furnish a correct description. This way of looking at meaning has a certain plausibility for certain types of word, but again we run into the problem of generality: it does not seem to be the case that all words have a denotation and/or a connotation. Here, too, the examples of *however* and *concerning* may be cited.

Another strategy for eliminating mental entities (one favoured by Bloomfield – see 1935: 23–33) is to attempt to account for meaning in behaviourist terms. Unfortunately, this approach fares no better than the referential or ideational approaches. It is very difficult – many would say impossible – to identify constant behavioural correlates of words. Even in the simplest cases this is so. Suppose A says to B 'Shut the door'. B might well feign deafness, or say 'Shut it yourself', or put his tongue out. (He might even shut the door!) To circumvent this rather obvious, but none the less telling objection, some adherents (for instance Morris 1946) have resorted to 'dispositions to act' to replace overt behaviour, in the hope that more constants will be found. However, not only is it doubtful whether this ploy does in fact achieve any more constancy, but dispositions suffer the additional drawback, in common mental entities, of being unobservable. (For more detailed discussion of theories of meaning, see Alston 1964: 10–30.)

Behind the ideational, referential and behaviourist theories of meaning lie some important truths – that language and thought are intimately connected; that language is used to say things about the world; and that language is an aspect of behaviour. But they all fail as general theories of linguistic meaning not only for the reasons outlined in this section, but also because none of them, on present evidence at any rate, has seemed to carry the seeds of fruitful research. Most progress seems to have been made by linguists who conceive the proper object of semantic study to be the sense of words, and to this notion we now turn.

## 3.4 Sense

The sense of a word reveals itself through the relations of meaning which the word contracts with other words in the language. Some of these semantic relations are well-defined and systematic – synonymy, antonymy, hyponymy (e.g. *dog:animal*), incompatibility (e.g. *dog:cat*), for instance. (Relations of this type are discussed in later sections of this chapter.) The sense of *dog* is thus (partly) revealed through (some would say 'constituted by') its semantic relations with such words as *animal, spaniel, bitch, puppy,* and so on. But the sense of a word cannot be treated purely in terms of systematic sense relations of this kind: a word has semantic relations, direct or indirect, with every other word in the language. A word may display semantic affinity or disaffinity with another word in one of two ways. The first is by normality or abnormality of co-occurrence in some grammatical construction. To take a very simple example, the patterns of normality and oddness in the following sentences show that *duck* and *quack*, and *sparrow* and *chirrup* have a greater affinity than *duck* and *chirrup*, or *sparrow* and *quack*:

> The duck quacked. (normal)
> The sparrow chirruped. (normal)
> The duck chirruped. (odd)
> The sparrow quacked. (odd)

The second indication of semantic affinity between two words is the degree to which they occur normally in the same contexts. For instance, *dog* and *cat* share a greater range of normal contexts than do *dog* and *whale*, and therefore have a greater semantic affinity. Using these notions, we may say that the sense of a word manifests itself through its contextual relations, that is to say, its total pattern of affinities and disaffinities with other words in the language (including indirect relations, which have not been illustrated). This is one form of 'contextual' theory of meaning, and is based on the ideas of Haas (for a more detailed exposition see Cruse 1986: 1–22). It should be noted that many linguists – see, for instance, Lyons (1977: 202) – conceive of sense purely in terms of descriptive meaning (this notion is explained in the following section): the definition presented here includes all kinds of meaning.

The notion of sense is thus a purely intra-linguistic one, and does not require us to take account either of things in the extra-linguistic world or of things in the mind. The restricted nature of sense has made it attractive to many linguistics who are daunted by the seemingly unmanageable chaos and complexity of extra-linguistic reality, and/or the inaccessibility to direct observation of mental entities. Some, however, (see, for instance, Palmer 1976: 33) find a restriction of semantics to sense unacceptable, on the grounds that this ignores the principal function of language, which is to communicate about things and events in the world around us. Be that as it may, most advances in understanding in linguistic semantics have been founded on the notion of sense, which must therefore be accorded a prominent place in the present chapter.

## 3.5 Kinds of meaning

There have been many attempts to sort meaning into different types, but, although it is undoubtedly a worthwhile enterprise, it has proved difficult to devise a proper classification with an exhaustive set of non-overlapping categories. For present purposes, a relatively simple three-way division into descriptive, expressive and evocative meaning will be adopted.

The descriptive meaning of a sentence (other names for essentially the same thing are: propositional meaning, ideational meaning, cognitive meaning, denotative meaning) is that part of its meaning which, if it has the force of a statement, determines whether it will be true or false in a particular situation; it also governs the logical relations between sentences. It is by virtue of their descriptive meaning that *It's a dog* entails *It's an animal*, for instance. The relevance of descriptive meaning is not restricted to statements: it is also important for questions and commands. It is by virtue of descriptive meaning that *Half-past ten* constitutes an answer to *What time is it?*, while *Two spoonfuls of treacle* does not, and that, if the time is actually 11.30, the answer is false. In the case of a command, descriptive meaning indicates the sorts of actions that will count as compliance with it. For many linguists, descriptive meaning is the only sort that matters. Since it is what governs truth and falsehood, it is obvious enough why those who wish to deal with meaning within the framework of logic have tended to concentrate on it to the exclusion of other types of meaning.

Expressive meaning is concerned with feelings and attitudes which are expressed rather than described. To understand this distinction think of the difference between *Ouch!*, which expresses pain, and *I felt a sudden sharp pain*, which describes it. Someone who produced the second utterance could, in theory, be accused of telling a lie; but not so the producer of the first example, since no statement would have been made. It is expressive meaning which differentiates the meaning of *Cedric has gone and eaten all the damn caviar* from that of *Cedric has eaten all the caviar*, and *She has spent the whole day weeping* from *She has spent the whole day blubbering.* Notice that the two sentences in each pair have the same truth conditions, so they are identical in respect of descriptive meaning. The meaning which differentiates *John is here* from *Is John here?* (this difference is often described as one of 'propositional attitude') is also expressive in nature. An important feature of expressive meaning is that it is valid only for the time and place of utterance; in this, it resembles the meaning carried by a gasp of surprise, or a dog's bark (descriptive meaning suffers no such restrictions). Expressive meaning commonly occurs blended together with descriptive meaning within the sense of a single word: the meaning of the verb *blubber*, for instance, can be roughly analysed as 'weep' (descriptive) + 'scorn' (expressive). Some words, however, (many expletives, for example) are wholly expressive in nature.

Many words have the power to evoke images and feelings in a hearer beyond what is directly sanctioned by their descriptive and/or expressive meaning. This evocative power is often deliberately made use of in, for instance, literature, advertising and propaganda. The associations aroused by a word may be highly personal, or they may be shared to a greater or lesser extent by other language users; but to be considered part of the evocative meaning of a word they need to be shared to a significant degree. Two types of lexical evocation can be distinguished. The first type are really properties of the referents of words and only secondarily properties of the words themselves. For instance, the phrase *angry bull* may well provoke an actual tingle of fear, even when encountered in the safety of a suburban living-room. Presumably the origins of a reaction like that would lie in real-life experiences with bulls. (Notice that we could not say that *angry bull* denoted fear, nor that it expressed it.) Other evocations are definitely linked to particular words rather than their referents. This would be the case with, for instance, *Ah yes, John — re your request for additional funding*, said by a father whose son has asked for more pocket money. In their natural habitat – perhaps some Civil Service department – such words would be relatively neutral; transposed to the domestic scene, however, they carry with them a penumbra of associations.

## 4. LEXICAL ITEMS

### 4.1 Syntagmatic aspects: how to divide a sentence into lexical units

The basic working unit of lexical semantics is the LEXICAL ITEM. This has a form and a meaning. We shall discuss the question of how many meanings a form has in the next section. Here we consider how to delimit the forms of lexical items. Generally speaking, lexical items are simply words, but there are interesting exceptions. Normally the meaning of a grammatically complex expression is built up, in conformity with the principle of compositionality, by combining the meaning of its parts. However, there are some complex expressions which do not behave in this way. Compare the sentences *John pulled Bill's arm* and *John pulled Bill's leg (about his hair-style)*. The first of these is straightforwardly compositional: *pull* means much the same as it does in *John pulled the rope*; -*ed* signals the past tense; -'*s* is an indicator of possession; *arm* denotes one of the upper appendages. All these meanings are combined – in a way dictated by the syntax – to form the global meaning of the sentence. The second sentence, however, is different. *John*, to be sure, has the same semantic significance as in the previous example (and *Bill*, too). So does the past tense affix. But what about *pull*? Obviously it does not mean the same as it does in *pull the rope*. Does it, in fact, have *any* individual meaning? Once this question is posed, the answer is plain – it does not, neither does *leg*, nor even -'*s*. Only a rather peculiar unit consisting of these three elements together, *pull —— 's leg*, can be said to carry a recognisable meaning. This unit cannot be broken down semantically any further: it is an elementary lexical unit which means something like 'tease'. Expressions of this sort, which are syntactically complex, but semantically simple, are called 'idioms'. Other examples are: *to paint the town red, to be up the creek, to get cold feet, to cook someone's goose*. Certain consequences follow naturally from the fact that the apparent constituents of idioms do not have independent meanings. For instance, since the *leg* in *to pull someone's leg* is not a 'normal' leg, it cannot be qualified as *right*, or *left*, or *wooden* or *injured*; nor can it be topicalised (i.e. made into the topic of the sentence) or even pluralised. Thus none of the following sentences has an idiomatic interpretation:

John pulled Bill's left leg.
It was Bill's leg that John pulled (not his arm).
As for Bill's leg, John pulled it.
John pulled Bill's legs.

Somewhat like idioms, but significantly different none the less, are 'frozen metaphors'. These are relatively fixed expressions (although usually not so rigidly as idioms) whose non-literal meanings can still be seen to be related to their literal meanings. Consider *She painted a glowing picture of her life in Wolverhampton*. Presumably the person in question did not actually put brush to canvas, but merely described her life in favourable terms. But the connection is obvious, unlike that between the literal and non-literal meanings of *We painted the town red*. Compare also *He has one foot in the grave*, which in one of its meanings is a frozen metaphor, and *He got cold feet*, which has an idiomatic interpretation. Frozen metaphors often translate fairly intelligibly into another language; literal translations of idioms hardly ever make any sense. An idiom is a single lexical item, at least from the semantic point of view. Frozen metaphors are less clear. They have a certain unity and integrity; on the other hand, their global meanings are related at least to some extent to the meanings of their parts. Which of these considerations is seen as the most significant will obviously vary with circumstances.

## 4.2 Lexical forms with more than one meaning

Many lexical forms clearly have more than one meaning: *boot* ('luggage space of car', 'item of footwear'); *rake* ('garden implement', 'dissolute fellow'); *tip* ('place for disposal of household refuse', 'piece of useful information or advice', 'pointed end of object'). Other lexical forms can be found, however, which although they can be used to refer to different types of thing, would not normally be felt to have multiple meanings. Take, for example, *book* (think of a paperback novel, a dictionary, a textbook); *horse* (a mare, a stallion, a foal, a race-horse, a cart-horse); or *red* (scarlet, crimson, maroon). We shall say that lexical forms like *boot, rake,* and *tip* are ambiguous, whereas *book, horse* and *red* are not ambiguous (at least with respect to the interpretations mentioned) but general or non-specific. An important difference between an ambiguous lexi-cal form and non-ambiguous one is that in using the former a speaker will usually (unless he is indulging in deliberate word-play) have one specific interpretation in mind, and the hearer will normally be expected to identify which it is. In ordinary conversation this usually presents no problems because of the abundance of contextual clues: *I'll just nip along to the bank to cash a cheque, John can't row for toffee — we kept bumping into the bank.* But if the hearer cannot identify the appropriate sense of an ambiguous item he cannot be said to have fully understood the utterance in which it appears (this could be the case with, for instance, *We finally reached the bank*). In the case of a word which is non-specific with regard to a particular distinction of meaning, neither the speaker's intentions nor the hearer's understanding is required to be more specific. If someone says *I understand my brother's new car is red,* he or she may not even know what shade of red it is. Generally speaking, at least for the quite unrelated choices of meaning illustrated so far, there is no inclusive meaning attributable to an ambiguous form of which the separate interpre-tations are more specific manifestations. There is no meaning of *rake,* for instance, which covers both its possible interpretations in the way that *fruit* subsumes *apple* and *banana.* A general word, however, has only the inclusive meaning, although particular contexts may narrow this down. In *Our teacher is expecting a baby,* for instance, although the word *teacher* applies indifferently to men and women, the teacher referred to is obviously a woman.

There are various ways of testing a word to see whether it is ambiguous or not. A full discussion of ambiguity tests is not possible here (for more detail see Cruse 1986: 54–66), but it is perhaps worth looking briefly at one example – the so-called 'identity test'. The way this works can be illustrated using the following two sentences:

John is wearing a light jacket; so is Bill
John is sponsoring a child; so is Bill

Consider the first sentence: *light* has two possible interpretations here – 'light in colour' or 'light in weight'. But notice that while we have a choice of readings for *light* in the first part of the sentence, in the second part (which of course has to be interpreted 'Bill is also wearing a light jacket') we must stay with the reading selected in the first part. That is to say, either John and Bill both have light-weight jackets, or they both have light-coloured jackets. The so-called 'crossed interpretation', where John has a light-weight jacket, and Bill a light-coloured one (or vice versa) is not available (except in word play). In contrast to this, there is no embargo on a crossed interpretation in the second sentence, at least in respect of the 'boy'/'girl' distinction: the two children referred to may be of the same sex, or of different sexes. The possibility of a crossed interpretation indicates generality; a restriction to identical interpretations in such circumstances indicates ambiguity.

When a word can be interpreted differently in different contexts (or even in the same context) it is useful to be able to classify the differences as either contextual variation, polysemy or homonymy. Contextual variation is variation within a single meaning, as with the two readings of *cousin* in *My cousin has just had a baby* and *John's cousin is married to my sister*. In such cases there is no ambiguity; in general, when ambiguity is present, we are dealing with either polysemy or homonymy. We would not expect a dictionary, even a very large one, to list the contextual variants for words – since these are not limited in number, that would be impossible anyway – but we would expect polysemous and homonymous variants to be listed, since they involve different meanings.

The primary unit of lexicography is the lexeme: generally speaking, each lexeme has a separate main entry in a dictionary. A lexeme is an abstract lexical unit which may be realised in a variety of forms. Thus, *walk*, *walks*, *walked*, and *walking* are all variant realisations of the lexeme *walk*. The variant forms of a single lexeme may differ only in respect of inflectional affixes. So, for instance, *obey* and *disobey* are different lexemes, as are *kind* and *kindness*, because they differ in respect of derivational affixes. (The distinction between inflection and derivation is discussed in Chapter 3.) A lexeme is said to be polysemous (or to exhibit polysemy) if it has more than one distinct meaning. A word-form is said to be homonymous (or to exhibit homonymy) if it functions as the phonetic realisation of more than one lexeme.

How do we know whether a word-form with several meanings is a case of polysemy or homonymy? In principle this depends on how closely related the meanings are: polysemous variants of a lexeme are relatively closely related; the meanings of homonyms are unrelated. But herein lies a problem: the scale of semantic closeness is a continuous one, so where do we draw the line between homonymy and polysemy? Extreme cases, of course, present no difficulty. Obviously the two senses – i.e. distinct meanings – of *lion* (*lion* v. *tiger*/ *lion* v. *lioness*) are polysemous variants, and while we would expect the distinction to be recognised in any reasonably comprehensive dictionary, we would not expect two main entries. In this case we have evidence that the relationship between the senses is a close one, namely, the fact that a parallel relationship exists between the senses of *dog*, *tiger*, and others. It is equally obvious that the word-form *boot*, with its quite unrelated meanings 'item of footwear' and 'luggage space of car', is homonymous, and represents (at least) two lexemes. In this case two main dictionary entries would be expected. But what about *expire* ('die') and *expire* ('come to the end of a period of validity')? Is this a matter of polysemy, or homonymy? Most lexicographers treat metaphorically related senses as polysemous variants and do not give them separate main entries, but there is much less agreement among linguists. There is simply no clear answer.

## 5. SENSE RELATIONS I: PARADIGMATIC

### 5.1 Introductory

At first sight the vocabulary of a language may appear to be fairly unstructured – some areas of meaning are more copiously supplied with lexical items than others, but there seems to be a more or less random scatter overall. However, there is more structure than initially meets the eye: certain meaning relationships between words crop up again and again, binding the words into recurrent semantic patterns. In this section and the next we shall be looking at the most important of these systematic relationships (a much more detailed treatment of sense relations will be found in Cruse 1986).

There are two fundamental kinds of semantic relationship between words. First, there are those which hold between words which can be chosen at particular structure points in a sentence: *Sarah stroked the cat/kitten/dog/squirrel/ horse/animal/cushion.* These are called paradigmatic relations; they represent systems of choices of conceptual categories provided by the language. Second, there are meaning relations which hold between the words of a particular sentence – between, for example, *kick* and *ball*, *kick* and *foot*, and *left* and *foot* in *John kicked the ball with his left foot.* Notice the oddness which results when these relations are not in order: *?John kicked the ball with his left shoulder, ?John kicked the smoke with his left foot, ?John kicked the ball with his left hand.* Semantic relations of this sort are known as syntagmatic relations; they add redundancy to messages and serve textual cohesion. Syntagmatic sense relations will be examined in the next section. First let us look at the paradigmatic variety in greater detail.

## 5.2 Synonymy

SYNONYMY amd OPPOSITENESS are the only sense-relations likely to be familiar to non-specialists. The study of both has a long history, but until the appearance of Lyons's *Structural Semantics* (1963) there was nothing of a systematic nature. Writings on synonymy, for instance, tended to give lists of permissible differences between synonyms, but these were not underpinned by a sound definition of the concept and the lists of differences were somewhat *ad hoc*. Superficially, the notion of synonymy is a straightforward one: two words are synonyms if they have the same meanings. However there is an inconsistency in the general use of expressions like 'mean the same as' which points to the existence of (at least) two competing conceptions. On the one hand, it is extremely difficult to find a pair of words that an average group of educated people would unanimously accept as being identical in meaning. Indeed, it is often laid down as a cardinal principle that perfect synonyms do not exist in real languages, and therefore a writer or a translator is always faced with real choices – it always makes *some* difference which word is chosen. On the other hand, we do find dictionaries of synonyms; and a child, or foreign learner, who asks what *repair, conceal* or *commence* means will be told unblushingly that it means the same as *mend, hide* or *begin,* as the case may be. The fact seems to be that there is an intuitively clear sense in which *begin* and *commence,* say, do not have the same meaning, and an equally clear sense in which they do.

Those who maintain that natural languages do not have perfect synonyms are applying very strict criteria, and their conception of synonymy is probably close to what will here be called absolute synonymy. This can be defined as follows: two words are absolutely synonymous if and only if they are inter-changeable in all contexts without any change in the degree of semantic normality. Thus, the fact that *Daddy, can you mend Teddy's arm?* is more normal than *Daddy, can you repair Teddy's arm?*, and that *The Company undertakes to reimburse the cost of repairing damaged items* is more normal than *The Company undertakes to reimburse the cost of mending damaged items,* is enough to show that *repair* and *mend* are not absolute synonyms. This definition does not rule out the possibility of such synonyms, but anyone who tries to find examples will soon become convinced that absolute synonyms are, at the very least, few and far between.

Synonymy can be defined in another way, and for this we shall adopt the expression 'descriptive synonymy'. As its name implies, descriptive synonymy means sameness of descriptive meaning. Descriptive meaning, as we have seen, is what determines the truth-conditions of sentences, so descriptive synonymy can be defined as follows: two lexical items are descriptive synonyms if and only if they can be substituted for one another in all declarative sentences without affecting their truth-conditions. By this definition, *begin* and *commence* are descriptive synonyms. This means that, for instance, *The recital began ten minutes ago* and *The recital commenced ten minutes ago* have identical truth-conditions, that is to say, in any situation in which one of them is true, the other must also be true, and in any situation in which one is false, the other is likewise necessarily false.

Since descriptive synonyms are required to be equivalent only in respect of descriptive meaning, and since few, if any, are absolute synonyms, it follows that in the vast majority of cases descriptive synonyms differ in meaning – perhaps in expressive meaning, or evocative meaning, or both. The members of a pair of descriptive synonyms therefore are likely to have different conditions of appropriacy, and must be used with care. Dictionaries commonly use descriptive synonymy (or something even weaker) as a criterion of equivalence, which is why a dictionary can be a dangerous weapon in the hands of a foreign learner. Multiplicity of synonyms is most striking in the so-called taboo areas: think of the range of descriptive equivalents, polite and not-so-polite, technical or colloquial, for *urinate* or *make love*, for example.

A glance through any dictionary of synonyms suggests that the compilers have not felt constrained by the strict definition of descriptive synonymy. In fact, probably only a minority of entries conform to this definition. Most are what might be termed 'near-synonyms'. Typical examples are *brave:fearless, strong:powerful* and *murder:kill.* A strict definition of this relation is not at present available – it may not, in fact, be well-defined. It will be enough for present purposes to say that near-synonyms are identical in the central aspects of their meanings, but differ in relatively peripheral aspects. So, for instance, *murder* and *kill* are both centrally concerned with the causing of death; *murder*, however, has additional features of illegality and intent.

## 5.3 Relations of inclusion and exclusion

There are two parallel but distinct sorts of exclusion and inclusion relation; one type is to do with classification, and the sub-division of larger categories into smaller ones; the other type is to do with dividing things into their constituent parts. Let us begin with the classificatory type.

Consider the relationship of inclusion between *tree* and *willow*. This can be viewed in two complementary ways. Either we can say that the class of trees includes the class of willows as a sub-class, so that any member of the class of willows is automatically and necessarily also a member of the class of trees (but not vice versa); or we can say that the meaning 'willow' incorporates the meaning 'tree'. In the former case we would be viewing the relationship from the standpoint of reference, while in the latter case we would be viewing it from the standpoint of sense. This very important semantic relation is called HYPONYMY: in a pair of words so related, the more specific term is called the hyponym, and the more general term the superordinate. Hence, in the pair *tree:willow*, *tree* is the superordinate, and *willow* the hyponym.

A useful test for hyponymy is based on the one-way entailment which holds between parallel sentences containing hyponym and superordinate. So, for instance, the relationship of hyponymy between *willow* and *tree* is reflected in the fact that *It's a willow* entails, but is not entailed by, *It's a tree*. (That is to say, if *It's a willow* is true, then the truth of *It's a tree* necessarily follows; but if it is known only that *It's a tree* is true, then nothing can be inferred about the truth of *It's a willow*.) Other examples of hyponymy are: *trout:fish, lion:animal, carnation:flower, lorry:vehicle, hammer:tool, cathedral:building, iron:metal, petrol:liquid.*

The relation of inclusion just described is partnered by an equally important relation of exclusion. Consider how *trout* and *pike*, or *willow* and *sycamore* are related. It may at first be thought that this is just difference of meaning. But there is more to it than that. *Plumber* and *golfer* are also different in meaning, but there is no reason why someone should not be both. In the case of *willow* and *sycamore*, however, while it is perfectly possible for a tree to be neither (if it is, say, a larch), it is not possible for it to be both. This relationship is called INCOMPATIBILITY. We can recognise it by the following entailment relations between sentences: *It's a willow* entails but is not entailed by *It's not a sycamore*; likewise, *It's a trout* entails but is not entailed by *It's not a pike*. Incompatibles frequently come in largish sets, all hyponyms of a single superordinate: *trout, salmon, pike, carp, cod, hake*, etc. (all hyponyms of *fish*). In this way, hyponymy and incompatibility are essential to the building up of classificatory schemes for objects and phenomena in the world.

Relations of inclusion and exclusion of the second type hold between the names of things and the names of their parts. The inclusion and exclusion are thus, at least in the central cases, spatial in nature. The name of this semantic relationship is MERONYMY; the term designating the whole is called the HOLONYM, and the term designating the part is called the MERONYM. Examples of meronymy are: *finger:hand, spoke:wheel, petal:flower, lens:telescope.*

The meronymic relation of exclusion holds between the different parts of a particular whole: properly constituted parts do not overlap. It will be clear that meronymy, like hyponymy, is an important cognitive structuring relationship. It is part of the human desire for order and intelligibility that names of objects, processes and so on are related in the ways detailed in this section; well-constructed naming schemes are powerful conceptual tools.

## 5.4 Opposites

Opposites have intrigued laymen and scholars alike from antiquity. They still present a nest of problems of analysis and description. The basic idea of oppositeness is apprehended at a very early age, so it must be cognitively simple, but a fully satisfactory characterisation of the notion has yet to be put forward. It seems likely, however, that at the heart of any opposition there are two component features: one is binarity – a quintessential two-ness; the other is some idea of confrontation – in the most elementary cases a purely spatial one, but in many cases an analogical extension of this. A number of distinct types of opposite can be defined, each with its own peculiar properties. Here we shall illustrate only the major varieties: complementaries, antonyms, reversives and converses (for the most part, the terminology established by Lyons (1963) will be used).

### 5.4.1 Complementaries

Examples of this type are: *dead:alive, true:false, open:shut*. The picture presented by a pair of complementaries is of a conceptual area exhaustively divided into two compartments in such a way that anything that does not fall under one of the terms must necessarily, under pain of unintelligibility, fall under the other term. Hence the denial of one term is tantamount to the assertion of the other. In other words, *It's not dead*, for example, entails and is entailed by *It's alive* (in the same way, *It's not alive* entails and is entailed by *It's dead*). Notice that *dead* and *alive* are also incompatibles (like, for example, *red* and *blue*) by our previous definition. However, in the case of 'mere' incompatibles, the denial of one term is not logically equivalent to the assertion of the other: *It's not red* does not entail *It's blue*.

### 5.4.2 Antonyms

(This term is often used to refer to opposites of any type; here it has a more specific meaning.) Typical members of this groups are: *large:small, long:short, fast:slow, strong:weak, heavy:light, hard:soft, difficult:easy*. Antonyms differ from complementaries in two fundamental ways. Firstly, denying one term is not tantamount to asserting the other: just because something is said to be 'not short', it does not follow that it is 'long'. Secondly, members of an antonym pair denote degrees of some variable property which are greater or lesser than some reference value, which itself varies from context to context. *It's long* and *It's short*, for instance, do not designate any particular lengths in absolute terms – think of the sort of lengths indicated by *long fingernails* and *long rivers*, for instance; rather, they designate values on the scale of length which are greater or less than some average or expected value. Antonyms exemplify to perfection the linguistic property of gradability: they can be freely modified, that is, by intensifying expressions such as *very*, *slightly*, *extremely*, *rather*, and so on, and they occur readily in the comparative and superlative degrees, whether these be marked inflectionally, as in *longer* or *slowest*, or formed periphrastically, as in *more intelligent*, *most polite*.

## 5.4.3 Reversives

Under this heading we find pairs such as *enter:leave*, *rise:fall*, *advance:retreat*, *ascend:descend*, *appear:disappear*, *tie:untie*, *dress:undress*. All of them denote changes of state of some sort, which are, in principle at least, reversible, and each verb in a pair refers to a process which, in principle, could undo the process indicated by its partner and restore the original state. Thus, if someone *advances* two steps, he can regain his original position by *retreating* two steps; if a suitcase gets *unpacked*, the original disposition of contents can be achieved by *packing* it again, and so on. Interestingly, although reversives refer to processes, it is not necessary for the processes denoted by the members of a pair to be strict reversals of one another: what is necessary is simply a reversal of the direction of change between terminal states. An example will make this clear. Take the pair *fasten:unfasten*: the action of fastening something may not be exactly the same as the action of unfastening executed backwards. But this does not affect the reversive relationship. What is important for this is simply that the object undergoing the process of fastening should start out unfastened and end up fastened, while something undergoing the process of unfastening should start out fastened and end up unfastened.

## 5.4.4 Converses

The pairs *above:below*, *before:after*, *precede:follow*, *buy:sell*, and *lend:borrow* exemplify this category. Converses are sometimes called relational opposites. They all express relationships between two (or more) people or things. Both members of a pair express what is essentially the same relationship, but viewed from the vantage point of different participants. Take, for instance, *buy* and *sell*: *Brian sold the car to Michael* and *Michael bought the car from Brian* both indicate that a particular transaction has taken place. But the first sentence highlights Brian's role in the proceedings, while the second focuses on Michael. These sentences express a relationship between three participants: Brian, Michael and the car (tacitly, there is a fourth, namely, a sum of money); for some converse pairs there are only two participants: *Brian preceded Michael, Michael followed Brian*. It is worth noting that the comparative forms of antonym pairs express a converse relationship: *Brian is taller than Michael, Michael is shorter than Brian*; so do the active and passive forms of transitive verbs: *England beat Austria, Austria was beaten by England*.

## 5.5 Markedness and polarity

Lexical opposites exhibit two very interesting and not yet fully understood properties, which are interlinked in complex ways: these are polarity, and markedness. We shall begin with polarity. There is a strong intuitive feeling in the case of most lexical oppositions that there is a positive term and a negative term, even when no negative prefix is present:

positive terms: *long, heavy, good, clean, alive, true, build, light*
negative terms: *short, light, bad, dirty, dead, false, demolish, dark*

It turns out to be extremely difficult to define exactly what is meant by 'positive' and 'negative': different criteria seem to operate in different instances. However, it can be said that positiveness is generally associated with a relatively high (as opposed to low) value of some scaled property such as length, speed or weight: *long*:(*short*), *fast*:(*slow*), *heavy*:(*light*); with a favourable (rather than unfavourable) evaluative attitude: *good*:(*bad*), *clean*:(*dirty*), *kind*:(*cruel*); and with constructive or ordering activity (as opposed to destructive or disordering activity): *build*:(*demolish*), *pack*:(*unpack*), *arrange*:(*disarrange*). Negative terms, in addition to being opposed to positive terms in the ways just mentioned, sometimes produce a reversal of polarity when applied to themselves, which does not occur with positive terms:

*It's false that it's false* entails *It's true*
*It's true that it's true* does not entail *It's false*

(This is analogous to the arithmetical $(-1) \times (-1) = (+1)$.) Another characteristic of negative terms is that they usually do not accept negative prefixes: compare *untrue*:(?*unfalse*), *unkind*:(?*uncruel*), *unclean*:(?*undirty*).

Markedness also shows itself in a number of different ways. The most interesting manifestations appear with antonyms. The terms of an antonym pair are typically strongly asymmetrical in their properties. For instance, only one term from a pair will yield a neutral question of the form *How X is Y?*:

someone who asks *How tall is John?* betrays no preconceptions concerning John's height; on the other hand, the somewhat less probable question *How short is John?* would indicate that the questioner was assuming that John was on the short side. The ability to form a neutral question is a characteristic of unmarked terms, so *tall* is the unmarked term and *short* the marked term of this particular opposition. The same criterion indicates that *big, much, many, fast, wide, deep* and *far* are the unmarked terms of their respective oppositions. Only one term of a pair of antonyms (again the unmarked one) is capable of yielding a name for the underlying dimension: we say *Its length is two metres* rather than *?Its shortness is two metres,* and *Its width is two metres* rather than *?Its narrowness is two metres.* We describe a person as *fifty years old,* and not, except jocularly, as *?fifty years young,* and as *two metres tall* rather than *two metres short.* As a final instance of asymmetry, we may note that unmarked terms are much more readily modified by such expressions as *twice as* and *half as:* compared *twice/half as many, twice/half as long, twice/half as big,* which are all normal, with *twice/half as few, twice/half as short,* and *twice/half as little,* which most people find a trifle odd.

There is a close association between markedness and polarity. The relationship is, in fact, quite complex, but briefly, there is a strong tendency for the positive term to be also the unmarked term.

## 6. SENSE RELATIONS II: SYNTAGMATIC

### 6.1 Semantic normality and abnormality

It is obvious that some combinations of words are normal in that they constitute a fully acceptable phrase or sentence for which it is easy to think of an occasion of use; other combinations are not normal in this sense. There are two principal dimensions of normality. To begin with, words must fit together grammatically: *When shall we leave?* is a grammatical sentence, *When the from why?* is not. But the rules of grammar do not guarantee a good semantic fit: *?The beans were too melodious for cream punishment* is perfectly grammatical, but is semantically very odd. (It is true that it is virtually impossible to construct a grammmatical sentence that defies all attempts at interpretation, but this is a reflection of the malleability of meaning, not of the sapience of syntax.) Our concern here is with the semantic dimension of normality.

We have seen that the patterns of normal and abnormal occurrence of a word are a reflection of its meaning. In a sense, there is only one kind of normality, but there are several types of abnormality, and this fact makes abnormality potentially more informative than normality as an indicator of a word's meaning. We may first of all divide semantic oddness into two broad types. On the one hand there is semantic clash – *?a radiant scowl, ?a whopping great terminological inexactitude, ?melodious beans* – and on the other hand, semantic redundancy – *?female aunts, ?Bite it with your teeth, ?a bad disaster*. Intuitively this division is fairly clear. It is a little more difficult, but still worthwhile, to distinguish varieties, or at least degrees, of semantic clash. The least serious degree of clash may be termed inappropriateness; here a wrong synonym or near-synonym is involved: *?I was sorry to hear that your father had kicked the bucket*. Among more serious clashes, we can distinguish contradiction – *?senile youngster, ?John blushed green* – and incongruity – *?melodious beans, ?hand-knitted scent*. The difference between these is mainly one of degree. Contradiction involves a clash of values along a particular dimension: for instance, blushing involves a change of colour, but green is the wrong colour. Incongruity arises when the incompatibility of meaning reaches up to the highest levels of abstraction, i.e. when whole dimensions are inappropriate. For instance, not only is melodiousness not a familiar property of beans, but beans do not make any characteristic noise at all, so the anomalousness of *melodious beans* is not merely a matter of choosing the wrong type of noise, but is more radical.

## 6.2 Sectional restrictions, collocational restrictions and presuppositions

Semantic oddness arises because of the semantic constraints lexical items impose on their companions in sentences. These constraints, called CO-OCCURRENCE RESTRICTIONS, are a necessary consequence of having meaning: we would be justified in describing a word as meaningless that showed no preferences at all with regard to its companions. Co-occurrence restrictions involving descriptive meaning are dependent on grammatical structure. For instance, a transitive verb will typically impose different constraints on its subject and object; *hear*, for instance, demands an animate subject, but not an animate object: *The cat/?chair heard the mouse/bell*. But the object of *hear* is required to be a sound (*John heard the scream*), a sound-producer (*John heard the cat*) or something abstract that can be embodied in the form of sound (*John heard the story*).

In principle, co-occurrence restrictions are multilateral; but in any pair of words which interact with one another semantically it is usually possible to identify a 'selector' and a 'selectee' – that is to say, the constraints operating in one direction are more easily definable and more stringent than those operating in the other direction. Consider the relationship between *John* and *drank* in *John drank the potion*. It is difficult to make any useful generalisation about the meanings of verbs which will accept *John* as subject, but it is relatively easy to say what sort of subjects *drank* requires; *drank* is thus the selector and *John* the selectee. The selector in *drank the potion* is again *drank*:

little meaningful generalisation is possible concerning what sort of things can be done to potions; on the other hand, we know that the objects of *drank* must normally refer to liquids.

Two sorts of co-occurrence restriction can be distinguished – SELECTIONAL RESTRICTIONS and COLLOCATIONAL RESTRICTIONS. The difference lies in whether the restrictions are an inescapable consequence of the meaning of a word (selectional restrictions), or whether they are, as it were, extraneous to the core meaning of the word (collocational restrictions). Consider, first, an example of selectional restrictions. It is obvious that to be normal the direct object of the verb *kill* must be capable of referring to something that is animate and alive at the time the action is carried out. It makes no sense to kill something that is already dead, or that is inanimate, like a table or a chair: hence both *?John killed the chair* and *?John killed the corpse of the pirate* violate the selectional restrictions of *kill*. Contrast this with the oddness of *The Vice-chancellor's wages are hardly enough to make ends meet* (as opposed to *The Vice-chancellor's salary is . . .*). The restriction which is violated here does not arise logically from the concept of 'earnings', which in any case is common to both *wages* and *salary*; rather, it is attached as a kind of peripheral extra. This is an example of collocational restriction. Roughly speaking, if a semantic oddness can be cured by replacing one or more items by their synonyms (or near-synonyms), then we are dealing with collocational restrictions. (Put another way: violating collocational restrictions leads to inappropriateness; violating selectional restrictions leads to contradiction or incongruity.)

Selectional restrictions are usually explained in terms of lexical presuppositions. These are a semantic property of selectors. Normally, when we use a word which exerts selectional restrictions, we presuppose, or take for granted, that those restrictions are satisfied; but this is not normally part of what is being stated, questioned, commanded or whatever in the utterance. It is necessary at this point to distinguish presupposition from entailment. Suppose someone says *John killed the curdgeon*. Even if we had never heard of a curdgeon before (and who has?), we would be justified in inferring both that a curdgeon was a living thing, and that the curdgeon in question was now dead. But these two inferences have different statuses. The fact that the curdgeon is dead is a logical entailment of *John killed the curdgeon*; it is part of what is being stated. The fact that a curdgeon is a living thing is presupposed by the use of *kill* but is not actually stated. Notice that neither *John didn't kill the curdgeon* nor *Did John kill the curdgeon?* entails *The curdgeon is dead*, but they both presuppose that a curdgeon is a living thing, and will engender an inference to that effect in a hearer. Constancy under negation and interrogation can be taken as diagnostic of presupposition as opposed to entailment. (The reader should be warned that the topic of presupposition is a complex and contentious one and should refer to Chapter 6; a fairly naïve position has been taken here, which should, however, be adequate to identify the phenomenon.)

## 7. LEXICAL FIELDS

### 7.1 Saussure and structuralism

The idea of a lexical field – a structured group of words with related meanings that perhaps has some sort of distinctive life of its own – has been around since the early days of modern linguistics. It still shows some vitality, although there are, and have been, a number of different versions of it. The development of what is now known as field-theory was strongly influenced by Saussurean structuralism, a few of the relevant concepts of which we now need to examine.

A convenient starting-point is Meillet's dictum that a language is a system 'où tout se tient' – that is to say, a relational structure in which everything hangs together with everything else. This principle applies throughout language, from phonology to semantics. For Saussure, a language system consisted, at every level, of sets of paradigmatic choices, arranged along the syntagmatic axis according to definite principles of combination. (Halliday succinctly summarised this picture as a union of 'chain and choice'.) There is a certain obviousness about this, at least once it has been pointed out. But Saussure's conception is more radical than it might appear at first sight. He held that linguistic units (of whatever sort) did not possess inherent significance in isolation, but acquired their 'valeur' – their linguistic value – only by virtue of their relationships, paradigmatic and syntagmatic, with other units in the system. Applied specifically to lexical semantics this principle means that it is useless to inquire into the meaning of warm, for instance, without at the same time examining its relations with *hot, cool, cold, scorching, freezing,* and so on. This is because the meaning of *warm* is basically a point in a network of contrasts. The same applies to concrete nouns like *cat*: we cannot say what *cat* means in isolation, because it, too, is a point in a system of contrasts, along with such other items as *animal, kitten* and *dog.* (The connection between these ideas and the definition given earlier of sense will be obvious.) As Lyons has pointed out, a consequence of this interdependence of word meanings is that it is impossible for a child (or anyone else) to learn the meaning of a single item out of a structured set without at the same time mastering the other members of the set: one does not know the meaning of *dog* until one can refrain from applying the label to foxes and wolves, for instance.

Each language, according to Saussure, is in principle a unique system, different from all others, and should be analysed in its own terms. This, too, has relevance for lexical semantics: an important consequence of a language's uniqueness is that there will inevitably be some lack of congruence between any two languages (and not just at the semantic level). Lexical incongruence – the lack of 'semantic fit' between words from two different languages – will be acutely obvious to anyone who has tried to translate a passage word-by-word from one language to another. The fact is that each language 'packages' its meanings differently, both syntagmatically (notice the different distribution of the elements of meaning in *John ran up the stairs* and *Jean monta l'escalier en courant*) and paradigmatically (both *watch* and *look at* are normally rendered into French as the unambiguous *regarder*; English does not distinguish between *fleuve* and *rivière*, and the distinction between *rivière* and *ruisseau* does not correspond exactly to that between *river* and *stream*).

## 7.2 Trier and the 'mosaic' model of a lexical field

For a long time the study of lexical semantics consisted mainly in tracing the history of the meanings of individual words – a study by no means without interest, but not lending itself to systematisation or abstraction. It was the work of Trier and his followers that initiated what has been called 'a new phase in the history of semantics' (Ullmann 1962: 7). Since Trier, a large body of descriptive and theoretical work has been carried out under the banner of field-theory (for a review, see Geckeler 1971). We shall illustrate the general approach by reference to Trier's work.

Trier's innovation was to adopt an out-and-out structuralist approach to word meaning. He viewed the entire vocabulary of a language as an integrated system, in which each lexical item was defined and delimited by its relations with its fellows in the system. He pictured the vocabulary of a language as forming a kind a mosaic, with individual words playing the part of tessellae. Individual words were grouped into larger units called lexical fields, which themselves formed mosaic-like elements of the whole vocabulary. These primary and intermediate units of the mosaic were held to cover completely, without gaps, all areas of meaning covered by the vocabulary. Trier saw the whole system as being in a state of flux. Hence, if a change occurred in any item, at whatever level, consequential changes in neighbouring items would inevitably follow.

This model of semantic structure led to a new way of studying word meanings. Tracing the changes occurring in the meanings of individual words, said Trier, was of limited interest; what was much more revealing was to look at changes in a whole system over time. Needless to say, the whole vocabulary of a language could not be studied in this way; what was feasible, however, was to study the more limited lexical fields, that is to say, sets of words covering a particular conceptual area. Trier's most famous example concerned the conceptual field of knowledge and understanding in Medieval German. According to Trier, a change occurred in the structure of the lexical field associated with this conceptual area during the course of the thirteenth century. At the beginning of the century the lexical field was structured as follows (after Lehrer 1974: 15–16):

| Wîsheit | |
|---------|---------|
| Kunst | List |

*Kunst* referred to 'courtly knowledge, including social behaviour' (Ullmann 1957: 166); *List* referred to technical knowledge and skill; *Wîsheit* was a general term, that is to say a superordinate, of which the other two were hyponyms. By the end of the century, the structure of the field had changed:

| Wîsheit | Kunst | Wizzen |
|---------|-------|--------|

*List* moved out of the conceptual field altogether: *Wîsheit* came to be used for religious, mystical knowledge only; *Kunst* lost its association with courtly knowledge and came to denote special technical skill or knowledge, not unlike the former meaning of *List*; at the same time, a new term, *Wizzen*, came into the field to designate the most ordinary, everyday type of knowledge.

Many criticisms were made of Trier's assumptions and methodology (none of which, however, diminish the importance of his influence on lexical studies). For instance, Trier's contention that the whole vocabulary of a language was structured as a single global field has not proved tenable. Likewise, his claim that the members of a field form a tightly-structured set leaving no gaps has not been possible to maintain (see Lehrer 1974: 97–102). Other problems have been the precise delimitation of conceptual areas, and the identification of the 'same' conceptual area at different periods of time – both essential to Trier's method. Trier has also been criticised for concentrating exclusively on paradigmatic relations; an alternative version of field-theory based on syntagmatic relations was advanced by Porzig (1950).

Recently, the appropriateness of the 'mosaic' metaphor, with its emphasis on the boundaries between concepts, has been called into question. Work by Berlin and Kay (1969) on colour vocabularies suggests that boundaries between meanings are less important than the locations of 'core' meanings. In particular, they found that while different languages located the boundaries between colours in unpredictable and idiosyncratic places, there was much greater agreement as to the location of the 'best' red, blues, greens, and so on.

## 8. SEMANTIC FEATURES

### 8.1 Some history

The basic idea of lexical decomposition – explaining the meanings of words in terms of simpler units of meaning (semantic features, or components) – is not, in essence, a difficult one. A lexicographer who gives the meaning of *stallion* as 'male horse' is doing just this. Hardly controversial, one might think. Yet there is still very little in the way of a consensus amongst linguists as to how far and in what way lexical decomposition should be carried out. The difficulties arise when we try to be precise about these simpler units of meaning: What is their nature? How do we detect their presence? How are they related to one another? Is there a finite number of them? Are they universal or language-specific? How much of the vocabulary can be decomposed?

Probably the first thorough-going attempt at a systematic componential approach to meaning was that of the philosopher Leibniz (see discussion in Wierzbicka 1980: 1–37). What he hoped to do was express complex meanings in terms of ever simpler meaning elements until he arrived at an inventory of unanalysable primitive semantic units. These, he thought, would constitute the 'alphabet of human thought'.

Leibniz's pioneering work was not taken up by any followers and it was not until the present century that interest in the problem revived. One of the first to pick up the trail was the Danish linguist Hjelmslev (1953). He started out from the Saussurean picture of the linguistic sign as an arbitrary association between a meaning and a phonetic form. He reasoned that since the phonetic form of the word could be analysed into simpler units (phonemes and, ultimately, distinctive features), the structure of language being essentially symmetrical (an article of faith with Hjelmslev), it must likewise be possible to analyse the meaning aspect of signs. Ultimately Hjelmslev envisaged an inventory of 'content figurae' (elements of meaning) in terms of which the meanings of all vocabulary items in the language could be expressed. The analysis of word meanings into content figurae would be a 'reduction', like the analysis of word-forms into phonemes, in the sense that the inventory of elements in terms of which an analysis could be expressed would be much smaller in number than the set of items being analysed. Unlike Leibniz, Hjelmslev considered that any inventory of content figurae would be specific to a particular language.

Independently, in America, a componential approach to meaning was developing by certain anthropologists with a strong interest in kinship terminologies (see Leech 1974, chapter II, for examples and discussion). A later more sophisticated version of componential theory was put forward by Katz and Fodor (1963) as part of a comprehensive theory of language structure, the syntactic part of which was being developed by Chomsky and his followers. Most recently, Wierzbicka, taking inspiration directly from Leibniz, has suggested a radically new version of lexical decomposition, using only thirteen primitive notions (1980).

## 8.2 Two examples of semantic feature analysis

In 1963 Katz and Fodor published 'The structure of a semantic theory', an article in which they attempted to sketch the outlines of the semantic component of a generative grammar. This was the part of the grammar that would assign a semantic interpretation to a string of words on the basis of its lexical content and its syntactic structure. The interpretation would indicate various semantic properties of the string, such as how many meanings it had, what its semantic relations (such as entailment) were with other strings, whether it was semantically anomalous, and so on. The semantic component envisaged by Katz and Fodor comprised a dictionary, in which the meaning of each lexical item was specified in a uniform way, and a set of rules for combining the separate word meanings, according to the syntactic structure, to give a global meaning. The following was offered as an example of a dictionary entry (slightly modified):

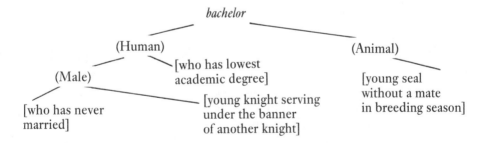

The items in parentheses indicate 'semantic markers'. These are features which have systematic patterning in the language; they are used in specifying the meanings of other words, and are therefore involved in semantic relations between words. For instance, it should be possible to gauge the closeness of two meanings by the number of semantic markers that they have in common. The items within square brackets are 'semantic distinguishers'. These take care of any idiosyncratic aspects of the meaning of a word – the residue not accounted for by the markers. This analysis is designed to give specific kinds of information about the meaning of a word. For instance, the number of branch-endings gives the number of ways in which the word is ambiguous. The analysis of each sense can be read off as the items traversed in going to the end of the branch, so the analysis of the most likely meaning of *bachelor* in *John is still a bachelor* is: (Human) (Male) [who has never married]. As we have noted, the degree of resemblance between senses can also be read off. (There is also provision in the system – but not illustrated in our example – for indicating selectional restrictions by means of markers.)

The second illustrative example of componential analysis is in the Continental tradition of structural semantics: Table 5 is adapted from Baldinger (1980: 67) (which in turn derives from Pottier). It presents a feature analysis of various types of furniture designed for sitting on:

*Table 5*

|  | with a back | raised above ground | for one person | to sit on | with arms | of solid material |
|---|---|---|---|---|---|---|
| chaise/chair | + | + | + | + | – | + |
| fauteuil/armchair | + | + | + | + | + | + |
| tabouret/stool | – | + | + | + | – | + |
| canapé/sofa | + | + | – | + | + | + |
| pouf/pouffe | – | + | + | + | – | – |

A plus sign in the table indicates the presence of a feature; a minus sign indicates its absence. Obviously the features which are possessed by all the items in the set cannot be used to distinguish members of the set from one another; they will serve, however, in an analysis of a wider range of items. For instance, the feature [to sit on] distinguishes members of this set from other types of furniture such as tables and beds. This analysis differs from the Katz and Fodor example in two important ways. First, it is not hierarchically organised; there are reasons for believing that insistence on hierarchical organisation makes things unnecessarily difficult. Second, there is nothing corresponding to Katz and Fodor's distinction between markers and distinguishers; the features here are more like markers, except that they are intended to give a full analysis, without residue, of the meanings of the lexical items.

## 8.3 Some issues in componential theory

This sort of analysis has an obvious intuitive appeal. Indeed, it seems likely that some kind of feature analysis is inescapable for any adequate semantics, whether theoretical or descriptive; it is certainly hard to see how the meanings of words could be specified without recourse to something of the sort. However, all concrete proposals to date have met with strong criticism, and there does not seem to be much agreement as to the best way forward. Obviously a full discussion of these complex matters is not possible here; but it is perhaps worth indicating briefly some of the more salient issues.

There are a number of related questions concerning the proper scope of componential analysis. Is it the case, for instance, that all or most lexical meanings should be considered complex and therefore susceptible of analysis into features? Or are a significant proportion of word meanings atomic in the sense that they cannot be broken down any further? Sampson (1979) believes that all word meanings are atomic, and thus rejects the whole basis of componential analysis. Wierzbicka (1980) treats all words denoting natural species, such as *cat, dog, crab, robin, oak, tulip*, as unanalysable. On the other hand, a Katz/Fodor-type analysis would presumably assign markers like (Animate) and (Insect), (Bird), (Tree), or whatever, to such items. Another question concerns how much of a word's meaning is to be accounted for by a feature analysis. Katz and Fodor, it will be remembered, allowed for an unanalysed residue. Their distinction between markers and distinguishers was severely criticised, but there is perhaps some advantage in allowing for a degree of indeterminacy in word meaning, and it is not obvious how to do this within a componential framework. A feature-analysis which aims to account for the whole of a word's meaning runs the risk of an infinite proliferation of features. Although few componentialists nowadays share Hjelmslev's desire for a reductive analysis (Wierzbicka is an exception), most would balk at the idea of an infinite inventory of features. Probably most componentialists (certainly those who are looking for the 'alphabet of human thought') would agree that semantic features are not to be seen merely as a convenient descriptive device, but correspond to something real in the minds of language users; they would also agree that we should not expect each language to yield a unique set of features. None the less, both topics – psychological reality and universality – have given rise to a great deal of discussion (see, for example, Leech 1974: 231–62; Lyons 1977: 331–3; Baldinger 1980: 93–109).

It is common practice to use ordinary words like *human, male* and *cause* to label semantic features, and an analysis often looks like a translation into some sort of Pidgin (scornfully referred to as 'Markerese' by critics); so *kill*, for instance, might be rendered as (Cause) (Become) (Not) (Alive). Such an analysis raises some serious theoretical problems. For instance, what exactly is the relationship between the word *cause*, say, and the semantic feature (Cause)? Are semantic feature synonymous with the words which label them? If they are, then one must somehow explain why it is that *John killed Bill on Thursday* is not exactly paraphrased by *John caused Bill to become not alive on Thursday* (if John had given Bill a slow-acting poison some time earlier the latter sentence, but not the former, would be applicable). One possible way of circumventing this problem is to say that semantic features are abstract entities, not necessarily synonymous with any concrete lexical items, and that in the case in question (Cause) has whatever meaning is necessary to account for the difference between the two sentences. But this only raises a further series of problems. If semantic features are purely abstract, how do we find out what features there are? How do we discover their meanings (do they indeed have the same kind of meaning as words)? How do we know whether they are present or not in particular cases? In short, how can we ensure that the facts of language exert strong enough constraints on the imaginations of linguists? At least one linguist committed to a componential approach, Wierzbicka, maintains that only features whose meanings are expressed in ordinary language can be brought under proper empirical control.

Problems of a different kind are posed by some recent work in cognitive psychology. In classical componential theory the meaning of a word is given by a list of features all of which are necessary and which collectively are all that is necessary. The semantic relation of hyponymy is represented by the inclusion of all the features defining the superordinate in the feature-specification of the hyponym. Thus if a lexical item X is defined by the set of features (A) (B) (C), and a second lexical item Y is defined by the set (A) (B), then X will be a hyponym of Y, and the class of Xs will be a sub-category of the class of Ys. This model of meaning would lead us to expect that all members of a category would have the same membership status, since they all must possess the same set of qualifying features; or, to put it in semantic terms, all immediate hyponyms of a superordinate would have the same relationship with the superordinate term. Take the category of birds: the classical componentialist picture would imply that ostriches, kiwis, turkeys, blackbirds and humming-birds were all on a par, since they all possess the defining characteristics of birds (whatever these are). However, psychological research has shown that not all sub-categories of a superordinate category have the same status within the category: some are judged by informants to be 'better' examples of their category than others. For instance, blackbirds are judged to be better examples of birds than are ostriches. The correlated semantic observation is that some hyponyms are judged – on various measures of semantic distance – to be closer in meaning to their super-ordinates than others. The best examples of a category are called the 'proto-typical' examples: componential theory has no obvious explanation of prototypicality. (For a thorough discussion of the semantic significance of psychological research on prototypicality see Pulman 1983.)

## EPILOGUE

This survey of descriptive and theoretical issues in the study of meaning has necessarily been extremely cursory. It is hoped, however, that it has succeeded in giving some idea of the scope, inherent interest and possibilities of semantic – especially lexical – studies. Although semantics was for many years the Cinderella among the core areas of language study, this is much less true today, and it is certain that we can look forward to considerable advances in understanding in the near future.

## REFERENCES

Alston, W.P. (1964) *Philosophy of Language*, Prentice-Hall, Englewood Cliffs, NJ.

Baldinger, K. (1980) *Semantic Theory: Towards a Modern Semantics*, translated by W.C. Brown and edited by R. Wright, Blackwell, Oxford.

Berlin, B. and Kay, P. (1969) *Basic Color Terms: Their Universality and Evolution*, University of California Press, Berkeley.

Bloomfield, L. (1935) *Language*, Allen & Unwin, London.

*Cruse, D.A. (1986) *Lexical Semantics*, Cambridge University Press, Cambridge.

Geckeler, H. (1971) *Strukturelle Semantik und Wortfeldtheorie*, Fink, München.

Hjelmslev, L. (1953) *Prolegomena to a Theory of Language*, translated from the Danish by F.J. Whitfield, Indiana University, Bloomington, Ind.

Katz, J.J. and Fodor, J.A. (1963) 'The Structure of a Semantic Theory', *Language*, 39: 170–210. Reprinted in Fodor, J.A. and Katz, J.J. (eds) (1964) *The Structure of Language: Readings in the Philosophy of Language*, Prentice-Hall, Englewood Cliffs, NJ: 479–518.

*Leech, G.N. (1974) *Semantics*, Penguin, Harmondsworth.

Lehrer, A.J. (1974) *Semantic Fields and Lexical Structure*, North Holland, Amsterdam.

Lyons, J. (1963) *Structural Semantics*, Blackwell, Oxford.

*Lyons, J. (1977) *Semantics* (2 vols), Cambridge University Press, Cambridge.

Morris, C.W. (1946) *Signs, Language and Behaviour*, Prentice-Hall, Englewood Cliffs, NJ.

Ogden, C.K. and Richards, I.A. (1923) *The Meaning of Meaning*, Routledge & Kegan Paul, London.

Palmer, F.R. (1976) *Semantics: A new Introduction*, Cambridge University Press, Cambridge.

Porzig, W. (1950) *Das Wunder der Sprache*, Franke, Berne.

*Pulman, S.G. (1983) *Word Meaning and Belief*, Croom Helm, London.

Sampson, G. (1979) 'The Indivisibility of Words', *Journal of Linguistics*, 15: 39-47.

*Ullmann, S. (1957) *The Principles of Semantics*, 2nd edn, Blackwell, Oxford.

Ullmann, S. (1962) *Semantics*, Blackwell, Oxford.

Wierzbicka, A. (1980) *Lingua Mentalis: The Semantics of Natural Language*, Academic Press, Sydney.

# FURTHER READING

The items marked with an asterisk in the list above will be found especially helpful for readers who wish to pursue these topics in greater depth.

# 6

## LANGUAGE, MEANING AND CONTEXT: PRAGMATICS

### GEOFFREY LEECH AND JENNY THOMAS

Compared with the branches of linguistics dealt with in earlier chapters, pragmatics has only recently come on to the linguistic map. Some may doubt, in fact, whether it has become a respectable branch of linguistics, or even if there is any legitimate field of study called 'pragmatics'. It nevertheless became a significant factor in linguistic thinking in the 1970s, and since then has developed as an important field of research. In this chapter, we trace the main trends in the modern development of pragmatics, from its beginning as a 'fringe subject' on the borders of philosophy and linguistics, to its present broad concern with linguistic communication in its social and cultural context. In the English-speaking world, pragmatics is more narrowly defined in its concerns than in continental Europe. We begin with the 'Anglo-American' tradition of pragmatics, and later make reference to a somewhat broader and distinct European tradition.

## 1. PRAGMATICS WITHIN THE ANGLO-AMERICAN TRADITION

We may roughly describe pragmatics as the study of the meaning of linguistic utterances for their users and interpreters. It is important, as far as its origin is concerned, to see pragmatics as part of a triad of studies distinguished by the American philosopher Charles Morris (1938), and later used by logicians such as Rudolf Carnap (1942, 1955). Pragmatics, according to this line of thought, is the study of signs (and sign systems) in relation to their users; whereas SEMANTICS is the study of signs in relation to their designata (what they refer to), and SYNTAX is the study of signs or expressions in relation to one another. The three fields are subdivisions of SEMIOTICS, the study of signs and sign systems, and may therefore be just as fittingly applied to the study (say) of artificial signs such as traffic lights, or of signs used in animal communication, as to human language. But, in practice, work in pragmatics has principally been carried out on human language, or 'natural language' as logicians are accustomed to call it.

Before we turn from non-human communication, however, let us use it to give a simplified illustration of the difference between syntax, semantics and pragmatics as components of semiotics. Our example, from the famous studies by von Frisch, is the 'linguistic' dance by which honey bees indicate the position of a source of pollen and nectar to other bees. The actual structure of the dance message – the sequence of movements – is a matter of syntax. The referential content of the dance – signalling the direction, distance, and so on, of the food source – is a matter of semantics. The way the dance functions as an aspect of bee behaviour – as a means of summoning bees to a food source – is a matter of pragmatics.

For philosophers and logicians like Carnap, pragmatics was the Cinderella of the three studies. It was important, in the empiricist and positivist thinking of the mid-twentieth century, to formalise precisely the relation between symbols and what they represented, so that conditions of truth and falsehood could be established or verified. For this enterprise, both syntax and semantics were important. But pragmatics introduced a messy, unformalisable element – the attitudes, behaviour and beliefs of symbol-users. Hence, for many philosophers and linguists, pragmatics became a convenient wastetip where one could dump (and frequently forget about) aspects of language and communication which were awkward, because they did not fit a nice neat world of syntactically well-formed sentences and their semantically wellbehaved truth conditions.

As the previous paragraphs suggest, pragmatics was born out of the abstractions of philosophy rather than of the descriptive needs of linguistics (and this, it will be argued below, accounts in part for the difficulties which were later experienced by linguists when they tried to apply pragmatic models to the analysis of stretches of naturally-occurring discourse). Even when pragmatics started to become important for linguistics, it was again, at least in the English-speaking world, informed by the work of philosophers. Three philosophers in particular – J.L. Austin, J.R. Searle and H.P. Grice – must be mentioned as the inspirational sources of linguistic pragmatics as it developed in the 1970s, although strangely enough, none of them adopted the term 'pragmatics' in their own work.

These three philosophers were closely associated with the Oxford philosophical tradition (although Searle and Grice ended up teaching in California). They all belonged to the 'ordinary language' school of philosophy, rather than the 'formal language' school represented by Carnap: this is, they were interested in the way natural human language conveys meaning, as a way of understanding the nature of thought, logic and communication. We may indeed call them 'philosophers of communication': for the term communication, associating language with its use to convey messages by users for interpreters, is at the heart of their work, and is at the heart of pragmatics. Yet, it is important to understand that in their own thinking, these philosophers were heavily influenced by the orthodox truth-based approach to meaning. In fact, their contribution was precisely in finding out and exploring problems, limitations and failures of the truth-based paradigm.

### 1.1 J.L. Austin

Austin's seminal book (a posthumous reworking of the notes he had prepared for a series of lectures delivered at Oxford and Harvard) was *How to Do things with Words* (1962). The emphasis which this title places on 'doing things' is shown in his exploration of PERFORMATIVE utterances, such as:

I resign.
I name this ship *Boniface*.
I bet you £1,000 you will be acquitted.
I hereby give you notice of dismissal.

Such utterances are problematic because, although they have all the outward signs of being declarative sentences, or statements, they do not appear to have a truth value. They thus seem to lack what is normally treated as a necessary property of statements. Austin denied that such sentences could be true or false in arguing that their nature was PERFORMATIVE rather than CONSTATIVE, in that their meaning was to be identified with the performance of an action. In saying 'I resign', a person does in fact resign; in saying 'I hereby give notice', a person actually performs the action of giving notice, etc. Conditions of the kind required to elucidate their meaning are not truth conditions, but rather 'felicity conditions', as Austin called them – or conditions of appropriateness.

In addition to their declarative form, performatives generally have well-recognised syntactic characteristics, such as a verb (of a particular kind) in the present tense, a first-person subject and the possibility of adding the adverb *hereby*. But Austin's investigation of them led him to conclude that not only performatives, but all utterances, partake of the nature of actions. Hence one could bring out the action-like qualities of a statement, a question, a request, etc. by prefixing to it an implicit performative:

You'll definitely get paid tomorrow.
   (i.e. *I promise you* that you'll definitely get paid tomorrow.)

What's the time?

(i.e. *I ask you* to tell me what the time is.)

Be quiet when I'm talking.

(i.e. *I order you* to be quiet when I'm talking).

Even a colourless statement of fact such as *Beavers build dams* arguably has an implied performative such as 'I state that . . .'.

The approach to meaning which says that linguistic phenomena are basically actions or deeds has an advantage over truth-based approaches, in that it invites us to go beyond the traditional logician's limited concern with declarative or PROPOSITIONAL meaning. Austin took this idea further, in claiming that the same utterance could at the same time constitute three kinds of act:

(1) a LOCUTIONARY ACT (or locution): the act of uttering some expression with a particular sense and reference.

(E.g. He said to me 'Shoot her!' meaning by 'shoot' shoot and by 'her' her.)

(2) an ILLOCUTIONARY ACT (or illocution): the act performed in, or by virtue of, the performance of the locution,

(E.g. he **urged**, or **requested**, or **invited** me to shoot her.)

– such that we may say that what was said had the FORCE of that illocution (e.g. of a request, or an invitation).

(3) a PERLOCUTIONARY ACT (or perlocution); the act performed by means of what is said:

(E.g. He **persuaded** me to shoot her).

Austin focused on the second of these. The locution (1) belongs to the traditional territory of truth-based semantics. The perlocution (3) belongs strictly beyond the investigation of language and meaning, since it deals with the effect, or result, of an utterance: whether my words *persuade* someone to lend me £10 depends on factors (psychological, social, or physical factors) beyond my control, and is only partly a matter of what I said. The illocution (2) occupies the middle ground between them: the ground now considered the territory of pragmatics, of meaning in context. The verbs used to describe illocutions – such as *claim, promise, beg, thank* and *declare* – can generally be used as performative verbs, and by this connection, Austin and his student Searle were able to think of the performative prefix (*I beg you* . . .) as an illocutionary force indicating device or IFID (a term now widely used to include not only explicit *linguistic* indicators of illocutionary intent, but also paralinguistic and non-linguistic indicators). In contrast, it is not possible to use a perlocutionary verb such as *persuade* or *incite* as a performative: *I (hereby) persuade/incite you to vote against the government* is a nonsensical utterance, implying as it does that the addressee is totally under the 'thought-control' of the speaker.

## 1.2 J.R. Searle and 'Classical Speech-Art Theory'

Austin's book was rambling, conversational, and (as books on philosophy go) entertaining. It was left to John Searle to bring greater systematicity to the ideas which Austin had so perceptively explored. In another surprisingly readable book *Speech Acts: An Introduction to the Philosophy of Language* (1969), Searle took even further than Austin the idea that meaning is a kind of doing: he went so far as to claim that the study of language is just a sub-part of the theory of action. Although Searle's method was still the informal method of ordinary language philosophy, he crystallised the concepts of illocutionary act and illocutionary force to the extent where one can reasonably speak of Searle's 'Speech-Act Theory' as the 'classical' account which subsequent work on speech acts treats as its point of departure. The interest of his work for pragmatics, like that of Austin, centres around illocutionary acts and illocutionary force (understood as the functions or meanings associated with illocutionary acts). Therefore, when we use the term 'Speech Act Theory' in pragmatics, we in practice refer to illocutionary acts.

Searle offered definitions of various speech acts in terms of the conditions which were required to be present if a given speech act was to be effectively performed. Comparable to Austin's 'felicity conditions', these were described as four kinds of rules:

(a) PROPOSITIONAL CONTENT rules specify the kind of meaning expressed by the propositional part of an utterance (for example, a *promise* necessarily refers to some future act by the speaker).

(b) PREPARATORY rules specify conditions which are prerequisites to the performance of the speech act (e.g., according to Searle, for an act of *thanking*, the speaker must be aware that the addressee has done something of benefit to the speaker).

(c) SINCERITY rules specify conditions which must obtain if the speech act is to be performed sincerely (e.g. for an *apology* to be sincere, the speaker must be sorry for what has been done. Other analysts, however, have argued that *I apologise* is a self-verifying performative, which is always felicitous, whether uttered sincerely or not).

(d) ESSENTIAL rules specify what the speech act must, conventionally, 'count as' (e.g. the essential rule for a *warning* is that it counts as an undertaking that some future event is not in the addressee's interest).

Searle argued that, on the basis of these four rule types, different speech acts can be easily distinguished (although more recent work in pragmatics – see section 5 below – indicates that the establishing of discrete categories of speech acts is far more problematical that Searle leads us to believe). Consider, for instance, the rules for *requesting* and *advising*:

[*Note*: These rules are taken from Searle (1969: 66–7): S = speaker; H = 'hearer' or addressee; A = act; E = event.]

(I) REQUEST
    Propositional content: Future act A of H
    Preparatory:
    1. H is able to do A, S believes H is able to do A.
    2. It is not obvious to both S and H that H will do A in the normal course of events of his own accord.
    Sincerity: S wants H to do A.
    Essential: Counts as an attempt to get H to do A.

(II) ADVICE
    Propositional content: Future act A of H.
    Preparatory:
    1. S has some reason to believe A will benefit H.
    2. It is not obvious to both S and H that H will do A in the normal course of events.
    Sincerity: S believes A will benefit H.
    Essential: Counts as an undertaking to the effect that A is in H's best interest.

To elucidate the differences between these definitions, Searle adds the comment:

Advising you is not trying to get you to do something in the sense that requesting is. Advising is more like telling you what is best for you.

The descriptive force of these rules or conditions, like that of Austin's 'felicity conditions', can best be appreciated by finding examples where they are violated. For example, a request would be 'infelicitous'

(*a*) if it did not refer to a future act:
    Could you please phone me by 5 o'clock last Tuesday?
(*b*) or if H were unable to do A:
    Would you mind translating this letter into Swahili?
    (spoken to someone who knows no Swahili).
(*c*) or if S did not want H to do A:
    Please phone me at the office tomorrow.
    (spoken by someone who does not want to be phoned, and indeed will not be at the office tomorrow; in this case the request would be effectively performed, but would not be sincere)
(*d*) or if the utterance did not count as an attempt to get H to do A:

Would you kindly refrain from laughter?
(spoken by a TV comic in a situation where there was a clear intention to provoke laughter).

We can all agree that there would be 'something odd' about the quoted utterances if they were spoken under the conditions described.

Speech-act theory lends itself to establishing systems of classification for illocutions. Austin proposed one such classification, in an attempt to reduce to some kind of order the multitude of different speech acts – which he estimated to number somewhere between 1,000 and 9,999. Searle improved on this classification, when he divided speech acts (Searle 1979) into five categories:

(i) ASSERTIVES commit S to the truth of some proposition (e.g. stating, claiming, reporting, announcing)
(ii) DIRECTIVES count as attempts to bring about some effect through the action of H (e.g. ordering, requesting, demanding, begging)
(iii) COMMISSIVES commit the speaker to some future action (e.g. promising, offering, swearing to do something)
(iv) EXPRESSIVES count as the expression of some psychological state (e.g. thanking, apologising, congratulating)
(v) DECLARATIONS are speech acts whose 'successful performance ... brings about the correspondence between the propositional content and reality' (e.g. naming a ship, resigning, sentencing, dismissing, excommunicating, christening).

### 1.3 H.P. Grice: Logic and conversation

The third of our trio of philosophers, H.P. Grice, like Searle attempted to face up to the problem of how meaning in ordinary human discourse differs from meaning in the precise but limited truth-conditional sense. Whereas Searle, however, proposed subsuming the truth-based paradigm in an action-based one, Grice was interested in explaining the difference between what is **said** and what is **meant**. 'What is said' is what the words mean at their face value, and can often be explained in truth-conditional terms. 'What is meant' is the effect that the speaker intends to produce on the addressee by virtue of the addressee's recognition of this intention (see Grice 1957). There can often be a considerable gap between these two types of message, one of which consists of only 'explicit meaning', while the other contains inexplicit meaning too. Consider an exchange between two people as follows:

A:  Where's Janet?
B:  Uh – she was walking in the direction of the post office five minutes ago.

B's reply simply reports the behaviour of Janet five minutes before the conversation. But actually it conveys, by implication, more than that: it implies that B thinks that, seeing that A wants to know where Janet is, the post office, or thereabouts, would be a good place to look for her. If we ask how that implication is conveyed, the answer must take account of such matters as 'general knowledge' and 'shared contextual knowledge'. Thus, the expression *the post office* implies that B expects A to share knowledge of the location of a particular post office (presumably the nearest one to where they are standing). Moreover, the implication that Janet may be at the post office *now* rests on common knowledge that the post office is the sort of place you might be expected to walk to in a few minutes. (There would be no comparable implication if B had said: '. . . she was walking in the direction of the setting sun . . .'!)

But even assumptions like these do not explain the process of inferring such conversational meanings entirely. To give a reasonable explanation, we have to assume that interactants in a conversation have regard to what Grice (1975) calls 'the *Co-operative Principle*' (CP):

Make your contribution such as is required, at the stage at which it occurs, by the accepted purpose of direction of the talk exchange in which you are engaged.

The Co-operative Principle (CP), stated in its most general terms above, can be expanded into four constituent maxims:

The maxim of Quality:
    Try to make your contribution one that is true, specifically:
(i)   do not say what you believe to be false
(ii)  do not say that for which you lack adequate evidence

The maxim of Quantity:
(i)   Make your contribution as informative as is required for the current purposes of the exchange
(ii)  Do not make your contribution more informative than is required

The maxim of Relation:
    Make your contribution relevant

The maxim of Manner:
    Be perspicuous and specifically:
(i)    avoid obscurity
(ii)   avoid ambiguity
(iii)  be brief
(iv)   be orderly.

If we now return to the example, we can explain the inference that Janet may be at or near the post office, in terms of the maxims, as follows:

(a) At face value, B's reply is not an answer to A's question. It therefore appears (at face value) to be irrelevant. But the maxim of Relation leads A to expect that B *is* being relevant, in spite of appearances. Hence, A looks for an interpretation whereby 'I saw her walking towards the post office about five minutes ago' can be relevant. The maxims of Quantity and Quality lead A to expect that what B says will give the right amount of information to answer the question, if B can truthfully give that information. But what if B doesn't know the answer to the question? Then B will give whatever information is truthfully possible, to help A find the answer.

(b) On the basis of the above argument, as well as from general and contextually shared knowledge, A can reasonably infer that B does not know where Janet is now, but has suggested, on the basis of what *is* known, that Janet may be at or near the post office. Moreover, by the Co-operative Principle, A can assume that it was B's intention to convey this implicit message.

This illustration shows how extra meaning can be 'read into' what people say, on the assumption that people not only know the meaning of expressions in their language, but have general knowledge and general human rationality at their command.

Like Austin, Grice writes in an informal, conversational style, and leaves a great deal of scope for subsequent interpreters and misinterpreters. For example, many commentators have assumed that Grice's Co-operative Principle is built on some *a priori* notion of human benevolence and co-operativeness; that Grice is therefore making some kind of ethical claim about human behaviour (see, for example, Apostel 1980, Kasher 1976, 1977 Kiefer 1979, Pratt 1977, 1981 and Sampson 1982). But nothing is further from the truth. The CP is simply a device to explain how people arrive at meanings. There is certainly no assumption that people are inevitably truthful, informative and relevant in what they say (for a full discussion of this, see Thomas 1986, Chapter 2). Hence, as Grice points out, we can simply 'OPT OUT' of the CP, in that, for example, we may decide to withhold whatever information we possess: 'No comment!' We may inadvertently *infringe* a maxim or we can secretly *violate* a maxim – e.g. A could maliciously and falsely tell B that Janet had walked in the opposite direction from the post office. Or – more importantly – we can make a blatant show of breaking one of the maxims (Grice terms this *flouting* a maxim), in order to lead the addressee to look for a covert, implied meaning. This last kind of exploitation of the CP is basic to what Grice called CONVERSATIONAL IMPLICATURES, i.e. pragmatic implications which the addressee figures out by assuming the speaker's underlying adherence to the CP. It is the very blatancy of the flouting of the maxims which leads to the generation of a conversational implicature in each of the following examples:

*Quantity*

At the time of recording, all the members of the cast were members of The BBC Players.
[Implicature: One or more of them are no longer members of The BBC Players.]

*Manner*

Interviewer:     Did the U.S. Government play any part in Duvalier's departure? Did they, for example, actively encourage him to leave?
Spokeswoman:     I would not try to steer you away from that conclusion.

[Implicature: The U.S. Government *did* play a role, although the speaker is not in a position to make a commitment to that effect.]

*Relation*

Female Guest:     Has the doctor been?
Basil Fawlty:     What can I get you to drink?
Female Guest:     Basil, has the doctor been?
Basil Fawlty:     Nuts?

[Implicature: Basil does not want to answer the question.]

Similarly, implicit meanings of irony or of metaphorical interpretation can be explained, at least in part, by reference to the CP. For instance, at its face value interpretation, the following example (taken from a 'Peanuts' cartoon) breaks the maxim of Quality; literally speaking, older siblings (of whatever sex) are not coarse grass:

Big sisters are the crab grass in the lawn of life.

The covert interpretation 'Big sisters are unpleasant and have a tendency to take over' depends on the assumption that what is intended is related to the face-value meaning, but is also relevant, truthful and informative.

Levinson, in his seminal article 'Activity types and language' (1979), suggests that interactants' expectations of the degree to which the maxims will be observed vary according to the type of interaction in which they are engaged:

'... there may in fact be some relation between Grice's maxims of conversation and particular expectations associated with particular activities. Grice's maxims of quality, quantity, relevance and manner are supposed to outline preconditions for the rational co-operative exchange of talk. But one thing we can observe is that not all activity types are deeply co-operative. Consider an interrogation: it is unlikely that either party assumes the other is fulfilling the maxims of quality, manner and especially quantity.

(Levinson 1979: 374)

Harnish (1979) and Holdcroft (1979) make similar observations:

There are ... many garden-variety counter-examples, social talk between enemies, diplomatic encounters, police interrogations of a reluctant suspect, most political speeches, and many presidential news conferences. These are just some of the cases in which the maxims ... are not in effect, *and are known not to be in effect by the participants.*

(Harnish 1979: 340 n. 29)
[Our emphasis]

The implications of the activity-type specificity of the maxims are taken further by Martinich (1984: 33), who argues that it is necessary to introduce a further category of non-observance of maxims, namely 'suspending' a maxim (see also Thomas 1986: 44–7):

'A person can *suspend* a maxim ... When a person opts out of a maxim, that maxim remains operative; but when a person suspends a maxim, that maxim becomes inoperative. Institutions that allow filibustering suspend the maxims "Be brief" and "Be relevant."'

Thus, if a speaker says: *Did you hear the one about . . .*, we may safely assume that the Maxim of Quality has been suspended.

### 1.3.1 Implicatures

The notion of implicature (or 'pragmatic implication') has been Grice's most important contribution to the development of pragmatics. Its significance is that it clearly marks a departure from the kinds of inferences allowable in the truth-based study of logic: notably, material implication and entailment. Unlike these, which are definable entirely in truth-conditional terms, implicature depends on, or refers to, factors of context. However, Grice recognises different kinds of implicature. *Conversational* implicatures (which depend on the assumption of the CP) are distinct from *conventional* implicatures, which are simply associated, by convention, with the meanings of particular words. For example, *but* carries the implicature, for any utterance X *but* Y, that Y is unexpected, given X:

She lives alone, but she has an active social life.

*But* here implicates that, given that she lives alone, it is not to be expected that she has an active social life. Without this implicature, *but* would have the same meaning as *and*. More recently it has been argued (cf. Morgan 1979) that the distinction between conversational and conventional implicatures is not wholly sustainable. Utterances such as the polite request formula *Can you X . . .?*, whose force can at first be calculated only by means of conversational implicature may, through repeated use, become conventionalised.

Another example of this passing from conversational to conventional implicature is provided by the expression 'to be economical with the truth'. When this was uttered by Sir Robert Armstrong in the High Court in Sydney during the *Spycatcher* case, a meaning could have been worked out by means of a conversational implicature generated by a flouting of the maxim of Manner. The saying was repeated so often that it rapidly became a 'frozen metaphor', even though he has since disavowed any intended implicature.

Grice makes another distinction between GENERALISED and PARTICULAR-ISED conversational implicatures. The former is a type of inference which is made generally, without reference to a specific situation. Thus 'not all X . . .' is generally taken to implicate 'At least some X'. Suppose, for example, that A is a famous author, whom B meets at a party. If B says 'I haven't read all your books', A can reasonably conclude that B intends to imply 'but at least I've read some of them': and can justifiably feel misled if it then turns out that B hasn't read any at all.

Cases like this contrast with particularised implicatures, which arise from specific utterances taking place in specific situations. For example:

A:  Who finished off the brandy?
B:  Geoff was using your room while you were away.

B's reply implicates that Geoff may have finished off the brandy, but this inference depends on a highly specific context, namely that provided (among other things) by A's question.

Even generalised conversational implicatures, however, are distinguished from cases of logical inference in that they can be cancelled out by a statement which is inconsistent with them. (To use the technical term, they are 'defeasible'.) For instance, in our 'famous author' example it would be possible for B, without self-contradiction, to add: '. . . In fact, I haven't read any of them', thus cancelling the implicature normally derived from 'not all'.

## 2. DEVELOPMENTS OF SPEECH ACT THEORY IN LINGUISTICS

In the preceding section, we have surveyed the philosophical underpinning of pragmatics as a branch of linguistics. Now, we consider what linguistic issues brought pragmatics into prominence in the 1970s. Our standpoint is still that of the 'Anglo-American tradition', but, as far as linguistics goes, a leading role is taken by the predominantly American paradigm of TRANSFORMATIONAL GENERATIVE GRAMMAR (TGG) – on which see Chapters 3 and 4.

The particular variant of TGG which was instrumental in developing linguistic pragmatics was the school of thought known as GENERATIVE SEMANTICS, led by Chomsky's disaffected former students Ross, McCawley and George Lakoff. The main tenet of the generative semantics school was that the base component of a generative grammar was to be associated with semantic structure. A corollary of this was that syntax and semantics were ultimately non-distinct: semantics was simply the 'deepest' level of syntax. But the same spirit of adventure which led to the placing of semantics at the heart of grammar also led to the inclusion of pragmatic concerns within semantics, and hence, by extension, as part of syntax. Thus the whole of meaning was to be dealt with in terms of the phrase structure formalism of 'deep syntax'.

### 2.1 The domain of linguistic pragmatics

To appreciate this better, let us try to define the domain of pragmatics, within linguistics, more carefully. In the introduction to this chapter, we defined pragmatics as accounting for the meaning which utterances have for their users and interpreters. A minimal way of distinguishing semantics from pragmatics is to say that semantics has to do with meaning as a dyadic relation between a form and its meaning: 'X means Y' (e.g. 'I'm feeling somewhat esurient' means 'I'm rather hungry'); whereas pragmatics has to do with meaning as a triadic relation between speaker, meaning and form/ utterance: 'S means Y by X' (e.g. The speaker, in uttering the words 'I'm rather hungry', is requesting something to eat).

However, once the speaker is introduced into the formula, it is difficult to exclude the addressee, since the utterance has meaning by virtue of the speaker's intention to produce some effect in some addressee. (In this sense, Grice's formulation of meaning as stated above, is fundamental to pragmatics.)

Moreover, the speaker's meaning (as we have seen in examples of implicature) cannot exclude reference to the context of knowledge, both general and specific, shared by the interactants. This must include knowledge of the time and place of the utterance; and hence the interpretation of deictic expressions such as verb tenses, demonstratives, and adverbs such as *here*, *there*, *now* and *then*. In all, the domain of pragmatics is to be identified with a SPEECH SITUATION including not only the utterance (what is said), the utterer (speaker) and utteree (addressee), but the shared knowledge of these inter-actants both particular (about the immediate situation) and general. This shared knowledge is often referred to as the CONTEXT of the utterance.

It is noticeable, even so, that the domain of pragmatics has been artificially limited above by the exclusion of the rest of the discourse of which an utterance is a part. Clearly, to be exhaustive, contextually shared knowledge must include whatever information has been derived, whether by inference or by direct decoding, from what has been said already. In this sense, pragmatics ultimately presupposes a discoursal setting.

So the pragmatic domain is potentially vast. At the same time, some pragmatic questions, such as the interpretation of tenses and deictic expressions like *this* and *that*, are integral to grammar and cannot easily be excluded from consideration by semanticists, whether of a generative or some other persuasion. We can appreciate, then, that in entering the domain of pragmatics, the generative semanticists were opening up a Pandora's box of potential problems for linguistics. The boundary between semantics and pragmatics is an unclear one. Should one draw a line between them, and if so, where? Both these questions were, and are, contentious.

The generative semantics school approached this problem by, in effect, assimilating pragmatics to the syntactic formalism they had already applied to semantics. The so-called PERFORMATIVE HYPOTHESIS, of which Ross (1970) was the major proponent, claimed that underlying each sentence (i.e. in the 'deep syntax' or semantic structure of each sentence) there is a clause, dominating everything else in the sentence, in which the subject represents the speaker, the verb is performative and the indirect object (if one is present) represents the hearer. The direct object corresponds to the sentence itself, as it manifests itself in speech or in writing. Thus the sentences labelled (*a*), (*b*) and (*c*) below are assumed to have underlying forms something like (*a'*), (*b'*) and (*c'*) respectively:

(*a*) Dinner is ready.            (*a'*) I assert [dinner is ready].
(*b*) What's the time?        (*b'*) I ask you [what is the time].
(*c*) Shut the door.           (*c'*) I order you [you shut the door].

To help explain how the surface forms (*a*)-(*c*) are derived from structures like (*a'*)-(*c'*), a special transformational rule, deleting the performative prefix 'I ask you . . .' etc. is postulated. Since sentences with the same deep structures are assumed, within generative semantics, to have the same meaning, this deletion rule provides a formal explanation for Austin's and Searle claim that performative utterances have the same meaning (or rather illocutionary force) as their non-performative analogues.

Other arguments in favour of the performative hypothesis were mainly those involving indicators of situational reference, such as first- and second-person pronouns. For example, Ross points out an apparent syntactic anomaly, namely that sentences containing an expression *as for X-self* are grammatical either if (*a*) X-self is a first-person reflexive (e.g. *as for myself*), or if (*b*) X-self is co-referential with the subject of a higher clause, but otherwise are ungrammatical (*c*). The three cases are illustrated below:

(*a*)  As for myself, I enjoyed the play.
(*b*)  James claims that, as for himself, he enjoyed the play.
(*c*)  *As for himself, James enjoyed the play.

This apparent anomaly is no longer anomalous if we assume, with Ross, that the underlying structure of (*a*) is:

(*a'*)  I claim that, [as for myself, I enjoyed the play.]

– since *myself* now co-refers, like *himself* in (*b*), to the subject of a higher clause.

Although they were ingenious and impressive, the arguments for the performative hypothesis invited a multitude of criticisms, including the following counterargument from Ross himself. Since the performative hypothesis claims that in *as for X-self*, X-self co-refers to a higher clause, what are we to make of an overt performative preceded by *as for myself*?

As for myself, I promise that the money will be repaid tomorrow.

This is grammatical, so there must be yet another higher clause (presumably a deleted performative) to which *myself* here co-refers:

I assert that, as for myself I promise that . . .

But once we accept more than one deleted performative, the performative deletion must be capable of iteration, and we have to entertain the possibility of multiple performatives allowing multiple deletions:

I assert that I assert that I assert that . . . .

This is one kind of *reductio ad absurdum* of the performative hypothesis, as an attempt to make illocutionary acts a part of grammar. Another is that, if every sentence has an underlying performative, a piece of informative prose, such as an encyclopaedia article, must contain the same performative repeated *ad nauseam* at the beginning of each of a long series of sentences. This is all the more ridiculous in that encyclopaedia articles belong to that genre of impersonal prose which avoids first person references.

As the performative hypothesis was clearly inspired, in part, by the thinking on performatives of Austin and Searle, it is perhaps surprising to find Searle himself (1979c) strongly opposed to it. The explanation, in simple terms, is that Searle's Speech-Act Theory was a bid to incorporate semantics into pragmatics, whereas the performative hypothesis was a bid to incorporate pragmatics into semantics (and hence into syntax). Thus, although superficially similar, Searle's and Ross's points of view were diametrically opposed.

We may distinguish these two opposite positions as 'pragmaticism' and 'semanticism' respectively. They both deny, for different reasons, that there is a valid division of labour between semantics and pragmatics. A third position, which we may call 'complementarism', acknowledges that such a division or labour is necessary, and hence regards semantics and pragmatics as distinguishable, but closely interrelated domains of inquiry. A 'complementarist' analysis of performatives is tenable (see, for example, Kempson 1975: 38–40), and has been given the name 'descriptive' (Harris 1978, Edmondson 1979). According to this position, performative utterances are exactly what they appear to be: they are declarative in form, and propositional in meaning. Thus, (despite Austin) it is argued that they can be assigned a truth value, but that value is always 'true'. Performative utterances are 'pragmatically reflexive': i.e. they refer to their own speech situation (see Leech 1980), and are hence self-verifying. Thus, if a defendant says *I plead not guilty* we must assign the utterance the value 'true' (she did so plead), even though we know her to be guilty. And similarly with utterances such as *I apologise, I object, I say he's a liar, I give you my word.* More problematic are 'ritual' performatives such as *I sentence you to ten years' hard labour, I name this ship . . . ., I baptise you . . . ., I pronounce you man and wife,* or what Hancher (1979) calls 'co-operative illocutionary acts', i.e. speech acts such as challenging, betting, appointing, which involve more than one consenting participant. According to one analysis a performance utterance such as: *I pronounce you man and wife* can be judged false if it turns out that the speaker has no authority to perform a marriage ceremony. This, in turn, means that opportunities for denying the truth of performatives are pragmatically very unlikely to occur: hence their truth is taken for granted. The alternative analysis is that such utterances are 'true' but 'unsuccessful'.

As the 1970s progressed, the generative semantics paradigm came under more criticism, and linguists became more willing to adopt a complementarist position. Grice's work on conversational implicature was a catalyst for this development: the Gricean treatment of the meaning of logical operators such as 'or' and 'if' enables linguists to see how a reasonable line could be drawn between logical semantics and pragmatics; also, the rule-governed domain of grammar could be contrasted with the freer organisation of pragmatic principles (such as the CP and its maxims) and pragmatic inference, based on commonsense reasoning rather than strict logical inference.

Two examples of this evolving 'division of labour' can be observed in the study of presupposition and of indirect speech acts. To these we now turn.

## 3. PRESUPPOSITION

The study of presupposition is another issue which was prominent in the early 1980s, when pragmatic explanations were beginning to be seriously considered as alternatives to semantic explanations in the study of meaning. Here we will merely touch on this somewhat complex subject.

The origin of the study of presupposition in recent years is often traced to yet another Oxford philosopher – Strawson (1952) – who reintroduced a concept which had already been raised by the German mathematician Frege (1892). Once again, the issue began as a problem of truth-based logical semantics. When we make a statement such as:

(1)  The King of France is wise

we seem to take for granted the truth of:

(2)  There is a present King of France.

But when we deny the truth of (1), we do not necessarily (or for that matter, normally) deny the truth of (2). That is, the chief defining characteristic of presuppositions, as illustrated by (2), is that they remain unaffected by the negation of the presupposing sentence. (2) is therefore a presupposition not only of (1), but of (1a):

(1a) The King of France is not wise.

In addition to definite descriptions such as *The King of France*, a wide range of other lexical or grammatical phenomena tend to have associated presuppositions:

(3)  What annoyed me about Jim was his hypocrisy.
(3a) PRESUPPOSES: Something annoyed me about Jim.
(4)  He was Arsenal's captain when it was the best team in the country.
(4a) PRESUPPOSES: Arsenal was the best team in the country.
(5)  Tom has a better stamp collection than I have.
(5a) PRESUPPOSES: I have a stamp collection.
(6)  Mary knows that the earth is a planet.
(6a) PRESUPPOSES: The earth is a planet.

During the ascendancy of generative semantics, the predominant assumption was that presupposition, like illocutionary force, could be dealt with in purely syntactico-semantic terms. As a starting point favourable to this assumption, it can be noted that presupposition can be partially assimilated to the relation of entailment. To say that one proposition $p$ entails another proposition $q$ is to say that if $p$ is true, then it is necessarily the case that $q$ is true. This certainly seems to apply to cases (3)-(6a) above. But presupposition is a stronger relation than entailment: the fact that presupposition remains unaffected by negation should enable us (following this line of thought) to claim that '$p$ presupposes $q$' is equivalent to:

if $p$ is true, then $q$ is necessarily true
if *not-p* is true, then $q$ is necessarily true.

Hence the claim, with respect to (6) and (6a) for example, is that

If (6) presupposes (6a), then

If 'Mary knows that the earth is a planet' is true, then
'The earth is a planet' is true, and
If 'Mary does not know that the earth is a planet' is true,
then 'The earth is a planet' is still true.

But this is both theoretically and observationally too strong a definition of presupposition. Since, at any given time, either $p$ or its negation *not-p* is true, this definition in fact implies that all presuppositions are always true! Moreover, it is clear that a presupposition can sometimes be cancelled when the negative sentence is uttered. E.g. it is not self-contradictory to say:

The King of France is not wise – for there is no King of France in existence.

or:

Tom doesn't have a better stamp collection than I have – in fact, I don't have a stamp collection at all.

The fact that, in negative propositions, presuppositions are defeasible (i.e. cancellable by contextual features) reminds us of the defeasibility of conversational implicatures (see above), and suggests that presupposition cannot be treated as a purely semantic phenomenon: that it shares some of the characteristics of implicatures.

Such a conclusion had been already suggested by Strawson's treatment of presupposition. He claimed that *a statement A presupposes a statement B if and only if B is a precondition of the truth or falsity of A*. Using the 'King of France' example again, we may illustrate this with the claim that 'There is a present King of France' is a precondition for the truth or falsity of 'The King of France is wise'. Pursuing this line of thought, let us assume, on a given occasion when

'The King of France is wise' is uttered, that there is no King of France in existence. Then the conclusion, according to the Strawson, is that the utterance is neither true nor false – it is not a statement at all. Since logic normally allows for two truth values only ('true' and 'false'), this can be made sense of in two ways. One – the logical way – is to assume that there is, in addition to 'true' and 'false', a third possible state of affairs where a proposition is neither true nor false, which applies to this case. (This means causing a major rethinking of logic in order to allow three truth values, or else 'truth value gaps'.) The second way of making sense of Strawson's position is to assume something like Austin's position on illocutionary acts: that a statement (or assertion) is a kind of illocutionary act, which can only be successfully performed subject to certain felicity conditions. On this assumption, which is more appealing than overhauling logic, Strawson's presupposition becomes a pragmatic condition on the performance of speech acts.

In the middle and later 1970s, a number of attempts were made to deal with presupposition within what we have called a 'complementarist' framework. Wilson (1975) and Kempson (1975) both rejected 'semanticist' and 'pragmaticist' attempts to give a unitary account of presupposition, arguing that some aspects of presuppositional phenomena need a semantic explanation, and others a pragmatic one. One thing that remained unclear was how presupposition was associated with particular grammatical or lexical forms: e.g. with definite noun phrases, and the complements of 'factive' verbs such as *know* and *realise*. It was also unclear how the presuppositions of a whole sentence or utterance could be derived from the presuppositions associated with its various parts. Gazdar's (1979) solution to these problems involved deriving from a sentence's form its *potential* presuppositions, and then deducing the *actual* presuppositions of the sentence in context with the help of pragmatic factors, including conversational implicatures. Here again, then, is an example of how the 'complementarist' position can be applied to a problem for which a semantic truth-based solution is clearly inadequate.

## 4. INDIRECT SPEECH ACTS

The study of INDIRECT SPEECH ACTS (or INDIRECT ILLOCUTIONS) brought a challenge both to the 'classical' speech act theory of Searle, and to the 'grammatical' version of speech acts attempted by means of the performative hypothesis.

Indirect speech acts are, in the words of Searle (1979) 'cases in which one illocutionary act is performed indirectly, by way of another'. Well-known examples are requests which are superficially questions:

(1)   Can you pass the salt?

(2)  Would you mind sitting down over there?
(3)  Could you please just sign this paper?

and the statements which are superficially questions (so-called rhetorical questions):

(4)  Who cares? (=No one cares)
(5)  Didn't I tell you to be careful? (= I told you . . .).

Sadock (1974), attempting an account of these from the point of view of generative semantics, gave them names like 'whimperatives' and 'queclaratives' to indicate their apparent hybrid status. This status is sometimes overtly signalled in the form of the sentence, e.g. in the occurrence of the request-marker *please* in (3) above. But the phenomenon of 'indirectness of illocutionary force' is much more varied and widespread than a few stereotyped examples suggest. A statement such as *This is thirsty work*, for example, may have the ulterior illocutionary force, in context, of requesting a drink. It is difficult to find a sentence which could *not* be used as an indirect speech act, given a suitable context.

A number of ways of accounting for the relation between the direct and indirect force of such utterances has been proposed. Gordon and Lakoff (1971), from a generative semantics point of view, proposed certain 'conversational postulates', or pragmatic rules, which would operate on the deep structures of sentences. Although essentially *ad hoc*, such rules sometimes captured useful generalisations. Here is one of the most useful:

One can convey a request by (a) asserting a speaker-based sincerity condition or (b) questioning a hearer-based sincerity condition.

(Part (a) applies to examples such as *I want you to pass the salt*, whereas Part (b) applies to examples such as *Can/Will you pass the salt?* These postulates obviously draw on the felicity conditions and sincerity conditions of Austin and Searle.)

A second approach was explored by Sadock (1974) and other (e.g. some contributors to Cole and Morgan (1975)). This was to extend the performative hypothesis to indirect speech acts, so that their underlying or covert illocutionary forces are represented by their 'deep syntax'. Thus underlying (1) above is a performative such as 'I request you [pass the salt]'. In this account, the relation between the indirect and direct illocution is accounted for by transformational rules, and is treated as an especially oblique example of the syntactic relation between deep structure and surface structure. However, there are both technical and theoretical problems with this account. Technically, it is very difficult to provide transformational derivations of a question structure like that of *Can you pass the salt* from an assertive performative like *I request*.... Theoretically, the problem with this account, like that of Gordon and Lakoff, is that it gives no explanation of why *Can you pass the salt?* is a reasonable form for a request: from the performative hypothesis point of view, this is purely an arbitrary and anomalous fact; whereas it is possible, from a Gricean point of view, to give reasons as to why, if you want someone to do something, it is appropriate to ask them whether it is possible for them to do it.

Searle (1979) gives an account of indirect speech acts which tries to overcome these deficiencies. His argument is that the relation between an indirect illocution and its face-value illocution is similar to that between Grice's 'what is said' and 'what is meant', and therefore that a similar explanation, in terms of the Co-operative Principle, as well as speech act rules, should be given.

An alternative, more Gricean approach to indirect speech acts is that of Leech (1980), who argues for a distinction to be drawn between the SENSE of an utterance (its semantic interpretation) and its FORCE (its pragmatic interpretation). As far as indirect speech acts are concerned, the sense is identified with the 'face value interpretation' and the force with 'indirect illocution'. According to this view, *Can you pass the salt* is interrogative in its sense, but directive in its force. Leech's account places emphasis on the fact that indirectness is a matter of degree, depending on the amount of inferencing that has to be undertaken to derive force from sense. To explain this inferencing process, not only the CP but other pragmatic principles – notably a Principle of Politeness – are invoked. In terms of the threefold distinction mentioned in section 2 above, Leech's explanation of indirect speech acts is 'complementarist', dividing the burden of explanation between semantics (sense) and pragmatics (forces). In contrast, Sadock's explanation in terms of the performative hypothesis is basically 'semanticist' (although he admits some cases have to be explained pragmatically), and Searle's is basically 'pragmaticist'.

In the mid-1970s, the focus of attention within pragmatics switched from attempts to explain **how** language-users interpret indirectness of pragmatic meaning towards an explanation of **why** speakers use indirectness at all. One explanation, of course, is that speakers sometimes *lack the ability* to express themselves directly (this could include the expression of complex or abstract concepts, such as 'infinity', or the expression of strong emotions, such as love or grief). In other cases it has to be assumed that speakers gain some social or communicative advantage by employing indirectness. An excellent summary of what pragmaticists have put forward as the motivations for indirectness in interaction can be found in Dascal 1983: 158–63. Among the most important are:

Speakers are frequently faced with a 'clash of goals' (e.g. a doctor may need to make absolutely clear to a patient the gravity of his illness, without appearing inhumane or uncaring).

'Instrumental rationality' (the speaker knows from experience that an indirect approach is likely to succeed and so uses it).

The speaker wishes 'to say and not say something simultaneously'. By using indirectness, the speaker can say one thing and imply another, leaving him/herself an 'out' in case of reprisals.

'Interestingness' (cf. Altieri 1978, who argues that speakers may use indirectness simply for the fun of it, or in order to appear more interesting).

But by far the most frequent explanation of indirectness is that speakers employ indirectness for reasons of 'politeness'. It is important to note, however, that not all writers are using the term 'politeness' in the same way. Grice and Searle (and subsequently Brown and Levinson (1978=1987) are principally concerned with 'politeness' as an *underlying motivation* for indirectness, whereas Leech (1983) is principally concerned with 'politeness' as a *surface-level adherence to social norms*. 'Politeness', according to this second definition, need have nothing to do with any genuine desire to be pleasant to one's interlocutor. Both Grice and Searle acknowledged in passing the importance of politeness, but by far the most significant study of politeness phenomena in the 1970s was that of Brown and Levinson (1978=1987), who proposed that politeness was a question of maintaining positive and negative 'face', and that the indirectness of examples such as (1)–(3) above can be explained by the fact that a request is essentially a 'face-threatening act' which, however, may be mitigated by various strategies of indirectness. According to Brown and Levinson, the degree of mitigation required depends on the three factors of social distance (a composite of psychologically real factors such as status, age, sex, degree of intimacy, etc. which together determine the 'overall degree of respectfulness' required in a given speech situation), relative power and size of imposition. For many analyses it is also necessary to introduce the additional parameter of rights and obligations (see Thomas 1981: 13–15). All these factors have to be weighted in relation to the cultural context and all should be considered as potentially negotiable within interactions, rather than as givens. For example, a speaker may choose to use first names in order to reduce the social distance between speaker and addressee or may employ various minimising tactics to reduce the perceived size of imposition: e.g. 'Could you *just pop* this in the letter box *as you go past?*'

## 5. INDETERMINACY OF MEANING

When Austin (1962) discussed the concept of the speech act, he initially

194

presented it as if a single force could be unproblematically assigned to any utterance. For many years it appeared that the pragmaticist's chief aim was to explain which features of context (such as the power relationship obtaining between speaker and hearer, how well the speaker knew the hearer, etc.) led to an utterance such as '*Is that you car?*' being interpreted as an expression of admiration on one occasion and as an order to move the car on another.

We noted in section 1 that many of the inadequacies of early pragmatic theory came about because practitioners were working with contrived or idealised examples of language and with isolated utterances or pairs of utterances. In the late 1970s and 1980s, attempts at a speech-act description of extended stretches of naturally-occurring language forced pragmaticists to confront the problems of the indeterminacy of speaker meaning. Pragmatic force, like 'social distance', 'size of imposition', etc., could no longer be thought of as *given*, but as something to be negotiated through interaction. Attention has thus switched from the rule-governed approaches of Lakoff, Sadock and Searle towards the development of models which are capable of handling the complexities of naturally-occurring language in a more adequate manner.

### 5.1 Pragmatic ambivalence

The work of Leech (1977) and Brown and Levinson (1978=1987) has meant that one form of indeterminacy, 'ambivalence', has become generally accepted within pragmatics. They noted that the intended force of an utterance such as: *Is that the 'phone?* may be quite deliberately indeterminate – it might be either a 'straight question' or a request to the hearer to answer the telephone. Where the relative rights and obligations of, or role relationships between, the participants are unclear (and, as we noted in section 4, they frequently are), it may be in the interests of both participants that the force of the utterance should be negotiable. The speaker thereby avoids any risk of a confrontation or of an embarrassing refusal, since the hearer is at liberty either to respond to the question by saying: *Yes, it is,* or alternatively, to interpret the utterance as an indirect request and to comply.

Ambivalence, then, occurs when the speaker does not make clear precisely which of a range of (generally *related*) illocutionary values is intended. For example, *I must have left it open*, could be situated anywhere on the cline between 'reluctant admission' and 'apology'.

### 5.2 Other forms of multiple meaning

The concept of ambivalence is now generally established within pragmatics (even though it is still rarely taken into consideration in, for example, discourse analysis – see section 6, below). Other forms of multiple meaning, including, 'bivalence' (see Thomas 1986), 'plurivalence', 'multivalence' have also been discussed, albeit not extensively, in the pragmatics literature cf Levinson (1981) and Thomas (1986) while Fotion (1981), Hancher (1979) and Ohmann (1972) have discussed the theoretical and descriptive problems presented by various forms of collaborative illocutionary acts.

The term 'bivalent' is applied to those instances where a single utterance performs two or more different illocutionary acts for the *same* addressee, whilst 'multivalence' refers to those instances where a single utterance performs different illocutionary acts for two (or more) different receivers. For example, at its most straightforward, the multivalent illocutionary act is a pleasing example of an economical use of language (the linguistic equivalent of killing two birds with one stone).

## 5.3 Indeterminacy and speech act theory

Assigning a single pragmatic force to an utterance can thus be seen to be anything but straightforward in the majority of cases, both for the analyst of discourse and for the participant in interaction. In a challenging article, Levinson (1981) argues that there are two major, and probably insuperable, problems for speech-act theory:

(i)  the impossibility of assigning a single force to an utterance;
(ii)  the *post hoc* assignment of illocutionary force.

It rapidly becomes apparent when one examines stretches of naturally-occurring discourse that indeterminacy of pragmatic force is, to a greater or lesser degree, the norm. Even in relation to an *isolated* utterance, it is rarely possible to say with absolute certainly which illocutionary act has been performed. For the majority of illocutionary acts it no longer seems plausible to argue that any *formal* linguistic criteria can be established to distinguish, say, 'order' from 'request' (although an understanding of social role relationships, together with other contextual and paralinguistic features, certainly helps to narrow the range of possible interpretations). Today few pragmaticists see speech act theory as anything other than a shorthand way of discussing speaker meaning: a helpful means of abstraction whose terminology lingers on because it is such common currency and useful for that reason alone.

Politeness is an example of a topic which brought pragmatics squarely into contact with issues from fields such as sociology and social anthropology, and therefore widened the range of factors requiring consideration in any pragmatic analysis. However, Brown and Levinson and Leech's work did not pay sufficient attention to the problems of CO-TEXT (i.e. to the stretch of discourse in which a particular utterance is embedded) and failed to take sufficient account of institutional and societal factors which crucially affect the production and interpretation of discourse. In relation to the latter problem, pragmatics could usefully draw on early sociolinguistic attempts (such as that of Labov and Fanshel (1977)) to embed linguistic descriptions firmly within given social and institutional settings. Examples of such attempts within pragmatics include the work of Mey (1985), Fairclough (1985) and Candlin and Lucas (1986). We now turn our attention to the question of co-text.

## 6. THE ANALYSIS OF PRAGMATIC FORCE IN SITUATED DISCOURSE

Two further and interrelated problems for traditional pragmatic theory surfaced when serious attempts were made to apply pragmatic theory to situated discourse. These problems, in turn, have major implications for neighbouring areas of linguistics, such as discourse analysis or the description of cross-cultural interaction, which draw upon pragmatic theory:

1.  Indeterminacy of meaning is not just an utterance-level phenomenon (see section 5), but also occurs at the level of discourse function;
2.  The assignment of pragmatic force to a particular utterance is crucially affected by utterances which precede it.

### 6.1 Indeterminacy of discourse function

An example taken from Milroy (1984: 25) illustrates well the difficulty *interactants* may experience in assigning discourse function even in very short stretches of discourse:

Wife:      Will you be home early today?
Husband:   When do you need the car?
Wife:      I don't, I just wondered if you'd be home early.

In Milroy's example, the husband quite reasonably (though, as it happens, wrongly) interpreted the wife's utterance as a preparatory illocutionary act (equivalent to the 'pre-request' in conversational analysis), probably designed to prepare the ground for a request to use the car. In fact, as the final utterance makes clear, it was simply a 'straight question'. What interests us here is the reason for the husband's mistake. As the following example shows, the discourse function of an utterance depends, at least in part, on the way in which the addressee responds to it:

A:  Are you going to be using the computer this afternoon?

B: No.

A: Is it OK if I use it, then?

In this case, B responds to *Are you going to be using the computer this afternoon?* as if it were a straight question. However, it could equally well have served as a request in its own right, if B had chosen to take it as such. B might very well have responded: *No, it's all yours.* Similarly, *Is that your coat on the floor?* very often serves as a 'scolding' in its own right.

In other words, the assigning of discourse function is not a problem for the interactant alone, but also for the analyst, who can only assign value *post hoc*. What we are dealing with is not only a multiplicity of illocutionary force, but also a multiplicity of *discourse* function – a form of **discoursal ambivalence** which is far from rare.

### 6.2 The pragmatic force of utterance in situated discourse

In section 5, we discussed the problems of the indeterminacy of pragmatic force in relation to isolated utterances. To some small degree, the problem of assigning pragmatic force becomes simpler with respect to situated discourse. The analyst is able to take into account not only the various pragmatic parameters (power, size of imposition, etc.) and the role of a speech event in a given institution, but also the situation of the utterance in the discourse. An interactant is often able to eliminate some potential interpretations, since interpretations of utterances later in the interaction are 'biased' – in the psycholinguistic sense (cf. Kess and Hoppe 1981) – by the force the hearer has assigned to earlier utterances. Take the final utterance in the example below: *perhaps you'd be good enough to move it?* This could, (in isolation from its co-text) be taken as an enquiry, a polite request, a sarcastic request, an order, etc. In the context of the whole exchange, however, the first two interpretations would have to be ruled out:

A: Is that your car?

B: Yes.

A: That's the third time this week you've taken my parking space. I don't pay fifteen quid a year for you to keep taking my place.

B: Sorry, I didn't know it was yours.

A: What the hell's that got to do with it? And now you do know, perhaps you'd be good enough to move it?

Pragmatic force, then, is CUMULATIVE, both in the way that Labov and Fanshel (1977: 95) have described (they point out, for example, that *repeated* requests, however indirect in themselves, are often heard as challenges to the addressee's competence) and in the sense that participants assign value to utterances in the light of what has gone before. It is important to take account of preceding utterances and of the cumulative effect of pragmatic force in assessing, say, the appropriateness of a given utterance. A speaker may well have used earlier utterances strategically in order to 'prepare the ground' for a particular speech act. To return to our earlier example of a request to use a computer: *Is it OK if I use the computer?* might well be judged impolite, if it were not assessed in conjunction with the first utterance, which established that B was not going to be using it (thereby reducing the size of imposition – cf. our discussion in section 4 of the negotiability of pragmatic parameters).

### 6.3 Implications for the practice of pragmatics

The existence of discoursal ambivalence and the difficulty of assigning a single illocutionary intent to an utterance pose major problems, not just for speech act theory. They also present insuperable problems for any descriptive framework (such as 'slot-and-filler' approaches to discourse analysis) premised on the assumption that the analyst can unproblematically identify a unitary discourse act, whether at the time of utterance or *post hoc.*

The cumulative nature of pragmatic force much signal the need for caution in two areas where traditional speech-act theory has been widely applied: the description of cross-cultural interaction and research into the acquisition of pragmatic competence in a second language (cf. Fraser 1978, Fraser, Rintell and Walters 1981, Rintell 1979, Walters 1979). The techniques employed to elicit data have rarely permitted the use of preparatory illocutionary acts or the negotiation of felicity conditions. Since there may be considerable cross-cultural variation in the directness with which illocutionary acts are approached, comparisons which take no account of co-text, and hence of the degree to which the speaker has 'prepared the ground' for an illocutionary act, may be seriously misleading.

Within the European tradition of pragmatics there has been a movement away from the application of rigid models or frameworks, which leads inevitably to a distortion of data, towards a dynamic system of utterance-interpretation which takes account of speaker goals and assigns to utterances not one single meaning but meaning *potential.* This has frequently involved borrowing insights from conversational analysis (cf. Levinson 1983, Chapter 6), in which tradition the uncertainties the analyst experiences in assigning pragmatic and discourse value to utterances are seen as mirroring the problems which participants experience in processing meaning in real-time. The problem confronting pragmaticists is how to incorporate the richness, complexity and multiplicity of pragmatic and discourse meaning which conversational analysis allows, whilst retaining the predictive and explanatory power of pragmatics.

## 7. REASSESSING GRICE'S CO-OPERATIVE PRINCIPLE

Attempts at applying pragmatic theory to stretches of naturally-occurring discourse have led to a general reassessment of Grice's account of conversation, and of the status of the maxims in particular. Many commentators have noted that Grice's maxims of Quality, Quantity, Relation and Manner frequently overlap and are certainly not all of the same order. Assessments of truth or falsity (the maxim of quality), for example, can only be made in relation to the real world, whereas the maxim of Manner is textual (judgements regarding its observance or non-observance are made on the basis of *linguistic* criteria). It relates, in Grice's terms:

'. . . not to what is said but, rather, to *how* what is said is to be said.'

Observance of the maxim of Quality is a yes/no proposition, whereas the observance of the maxims of Manner and Quantity is usually a matter of degree. How well-ordered is 'orderly'? How prolix is 'prolixity'? How much information is 'enough information'?

The ways in which a speaker can observe or fail to observe the CP ('infringing', 'flouting', 'violating', 'opting out', etc. – see section 1.3 above) vary greatly from maxim to maxim. The maxim of Manner, in particular, is frequently *infringed* unintentionally and (unlike the maxims of Quality and Quantity) it is difficult to *violate* it unobtrusively: speakers cannot disguise, for example, the fact that they are being muddled or repetitious (although an obscure or ambiguous expression may be used in order to mislead).

'Opting out' of the CP presents a particularly interesting case. When speakers explicitly opt out of observing a maxim, they provide privileged access to the way in which speakers *do*, as a rule, attend to the maxims. This in turn offers prima-facie evidence for Grice's contention that there exists on the part of interactants a strong expectation that, *ceteris paribus* and unless indication is given to the contrary, the CP and the maxims will be observed. The frequency with which speakers explicitly opt out of observance of the maxim of Relation, and the comparative infrequency with which they opt out of the other maxims, suggests that it is of a different order from (and more important than) the others.

But it is the status of the maxim of Relation which has excited most interest. Many writers (Bach and Harnish 1979, Bird 1979, Dascal 1977, Holdcroft 1979, Wilson and Sperber 1981) have commented on the over-arching importance of the maxim of Relation and several have gone on to argue that the CP itself should be replaced by a re-defined 'Principle of Relevance' (Dascal 1977, Holdcroft 1979, Swiggers 1981, Wilson and Sperber 1981):

'. . . Grice's maxims can be replaced by a single principle of relevance. In interpreting an utterance the hearer uses this principle as a guide, on the one hand towards correct disambiguation and assignment of reference, and on the other in deciding whether additional premises are needed, and if so what they are, or whether a figurative inter- pretation was intended. The principle of relevance on its own provides an adequate, and we think rather more explicit, account of all the implicatures which Grice's maxims were set up to describe.'

(Wilson and Sperber 1981: 171)

The arguments most frequently proposed in favour of replacing the CP are:

(1) that the CP already *is*, in essence, a Principle of Relevance. It is argued that it is not possible to find instances of implicatures being generated where the maxim of Relevance is *not* invoked;
(2) that a redefined Principle of Relevance, unlike the CP, is not trivially true: although relevance can be shown to be an extremely powerful factor in utterance-interpretation, in that hearers will look very hard for relevance, there *are* occasions on which interactants will conclude that an utterance is *not* relevant (e.g. that a speaker is 'talking past' them) and that no conversation is taking place;
(3) that forms of relevance (unlike 'co-operation') can, in principle, be specified and defined fairly precisely.

Dascal (1977), Sanders (1980) and Thomas (1986) argue that it is necessary to distinguish different *types* of relevance. Sanders (1980: 91–92) argues that there are at least four ways in which an expression can be relevant to an antecedent expression or expression-sequence (not counting word-play). Dascal argues that interactants operate with at least two quite distinct notions of relevance, including:

. . . a 'pragmatic' and a 'semantic' one. The former has to do with the relevance of speech acts to certain goals . . . the latter concerns the relevance of certain linguistic, logical, or cognitive entities, say, 'propositions' to others of the same type: its character- ization, . . . involves concepts such as reference 'aboutness', meaning relations, entailment, etc. . . .

(Dascal 1977: 311)

## 8. RELEVANCE THEORY: SPERBER AND WILSON

Perhaps the most significant development in pragmatics over the past few years has been the extensive treatment by Sperber and Wilson (1986) of relevance theory.

Their book *Relevance: Communication and Cognition* (1986), while drawing on earlier work by the same authors, presents in effect a new paradigm for pragmatics, and more ambitiously, a new theory of communication. Their relevance theory is meant to account not only for the interpretation of individual utterances in context, but for stylistic effects, including given and new information, and the 'special effects' of metaphor and irony. (One of the claims of the theory, however, is that metaphor is not 'special', but requires for its interpretation no more than is required for a general approach to communication.)

Communication is described as *ostensive-inferential*, since it is founded on the complementary concepts of *ostension* (the signal that the speaker has something to communicate) and *inference* (the logical process by which the addressee derives meaning). Grice's intentional theory of meaning (see section 1.3) is recast in terms of:

(*a*) *An informative intention*: the intention to make manifest or more manifest to the audience a certain set of assumptions.
(*b*) *A communicative intention*: the intention to make mutually manifest to audience and communicator the communicator's informative intention.

*Ostensive-inferential communication* is described as follows:

'. . . the communicator produces a stimulus which makes it mutually manifest to communicator and audience that the communicator intends, by means of this stimulus, to make manifest or more manifest to the audience a certain set of assumptions *[I].'*

(Sperber and Wilson 1986: 63)

It will be noticed that the theory makes use of the term 'manifestness' (rather than the stronger term 'knowledge') in referring to information processed in the course of communication. An assumption may be 'manifest' to a person to varying degrees, and hence by saying that differing assumptions are manifest of different degrees, one allows for the phenomenon of *ambivalence* in communication (see section 5).

Similarly, the term 'assumption' (rather than the term 'proposition') is used in referring to units of information. Assumptions, unlike propositions, allow for varying degrees of commitment to the truth.

This retreat towards a weaker theory of communication is welcome when one considers the importance of ambivalence in the process of communication, and the difficulties which philosophers and pragmaticists have found in the seeming circularity associated with the concept of 'mutual knowledge'. At the same time, Sperber and Wilson adhere to a rigorous conception of logical inference in explaining the 'inferential' aspect of communication. This means that they have the problem of explaining how, in spite of the recursive properties of logical inference, audiences in general are able to arrive at apt decisions about other meanings of utterances. The means of restricting the number of inferences drawn from an utterance, Sperber and Wilson argue, is the *Principle of Relevance*:

*Principle of Relevance*: Every act of ostensive communication communicates the presumption of its own optimal relevance.

The audience's *presumption of optimal relevance* is explained as follows:

(*a*) The set of assumptions *I* which the communicator intends to make manifest to the addressee is relevant enough to make it worth the addressee's while to process the ostensive stimulus.

(*b*) The ostensive stimulus is the most relevant one the communicator could have used to communicate *I*.

From this definition, it is clear that relevance is a matter of degree: a position which is clarified by Sperber and Wilson's 'extent conditions' on the nature and degree of relevance:

*Extent condition 1*: an assumption is relevant in a context to the extent that its contextual effects in that context are large.

*Extent conditions 2*: an assumption is relevant in a context to the extent that the effort required to process it in that context is small.

From these 'extent conditions', we learn that relevance is basically a trade-off between informativeness (cf. Grice's maxim of Quantity) and processibility (cf. Grice's maxim of Manner).

It is necessary, however, to grasp that 'contextual effects' are basic to Sperber and Wilson's theory of communication. If we think of contextual effects as information, we shall not go far wrong. More exactly, there are three types of contextual effects:

(*a*) new assumptions (contextual implications);

(*b*) strengthening of old assumptions;

(*c*) elimination of old assumptions in favour of new assumptions which contradict them.

Sperber and Wilson claim that 'the Principle of Relevance applies without exception' – which is to say that human nature abhors a vacuum of sense – and that the 'Principle of Relevance does all the work of Grice's maxims and more . . .'

It is too early for an evaluation of Sperber and Wilson's relevance theory, but we can perhaps hazard the assertion that Sperber and Wilson have made the grandest possible claim for pragmatics: that pragmatics is to be equated with the general theory of communication, in which linguistics, conceived of as a theory of linguistic code (semantics, syntax, phonology) plays a relatively minor part. As the title of their book announces, theirs is a 'cognitive' theory of communication, which gives prominence to the psychological, rather than the sociological, perspective on communication. This brings a certain return to rigour, at the same time as it largely disregards the advances and insights into social description which have characterised the development of pragmatics in other areas. Nevertheless, relevance theory as propounded by Sperber and Wilson will no doubt be a major focus for future investigations into the nature of pragmatic meaning. In pragmatics, as in semantics, we need to strike a balance between the psychological and the sociological perspectives on the meaning of human language. If one may hazard a guess about the future, it is that the struggle between the linguistic psychologist and the linguistic sociologist will continue here, as elsewhere in the study of linguistic meaning and language use.

## REFERENCES

Altieri, C. (1978) 'What Grice offers literary theory: a proposal for "expressive implicature",' *Centrum*, 6 (2): 90–103

Apostel, L. (1979) 'Persuasive communication as metaphorical discourse under the guidance of conversational maxims' in *Logique et Analyse* 22: 265–320.

Austin, J.L. (1962) *How To Do Things With Words*, Oxford University Press, Oxford.

Bach, K. and Harnish, R. (1979) *Linguistic Communication and Speech Acts*, MIT Press, Cambridge, Mass.

Baker, C. (1975) 'This is just a first approximation, but . . .', *Papers From the Chicago Linguistics Society*, 11: 37–47.

Bar-Hillel, Y. (1970) *Aspects of Language*, North-Holland, Amsterdam.

Bar-Hillel, Y. (1971) *Pragmatics of Natural Language*, Reidel, Dordrecht.

Bird, G. (1979) 'Speech acts and conversation – II' *Philosophical Quarterly*, 29: 142–52.

Brockway, D. (1981) 'Semantic constraints on relevance', in Parret, H. *et al.* (eds) 1981: 57–78.

*Brown, P. and Levinson, S. (1987) *Politeness: some universals in language usage*, Cambridge University Press, Cambridge. (Reissued and extended version of 1978 monograph.)

Candlin, C.N. and Lucas, J.L. (1986) 'Modes of counselling in family planning', in Ensink, T. *et al.* (eds) *Discourse in Public Life*, Foris, Dordrecht.

Carnap, R. (1942) *Introduction to Semantics*, MIT Press, Cambridge, Mass.

Carnap, R. (1955) 'On Some Concepts of Pragmatics', *Philosophical Studies*, 6: 89–91.

Cole, P. (ed.) (1978) *Syntax and Semantics, 9: Pragmatics*, Academic Press, New York.

Cole, P. and Morgan, J.L. (eds) (1975) *Syntax and Semantics, 3: Speech Acts*, Academic Press, New York.

Dascal, M. (1977) 'Conversational relevance', *Journal of Pragmatics*, 4: 309–28.

*Dascal, M. (1983) *Pragmatics and the Philosophy of Mind I: Thought in Language*, Benjamins, Amsterdam.

Edmondson, W.J. (1979) 'Harris on performatives', *Journal of Linguistics*, 15: 331–4.

Fairclough, N.L. (1985) 'Critical and descriptive goals in discourse analysis', *Journal of Pragmatics*, 9: 739–63.

Fotion, N. (1971) 'Master speech acts.' *Philosophical Quarterly*, 21: 232–43.

Fotion, N. (1981) 'I'll bet you $10 that betting is not a speech act.', in Parret, H. *et al.*: 211–23.

Fraser, B. (1978) 'Acquiring social competence in a second language' in *RELC Journal* 9 (2): 1–21

Fraser, B., Rintell, E. and Walters, J. (1981) 'An approach to conducting research on the acquisition of pragmatic competence in a second language', in Larsen-Freeman, D. (ed.), *Discourse Analysis*. Newbury House, Rowley, Mass.: 75–81.

Frege, G. (1952) 'On sense and reference', in Geach, P.T. and Black, M. (eds) *Translations from the Philosophical Writings of Gottlob Frege*, Blackwell, Oxford: 56–78. (Original 1892.)

Gazdar, G. (1979) *Pragmatics: Implicature, Presupposition and Logical Form*, Academic Press, New York.

Gordon, D. and Lakoff, G. (1975) 'Conversational postulates', in Cole, P. and Morgan, J.L. (eds): 83–106.

Grice, H.P. (1957) 'Meaning', *Philosophical Review*, 66: 377–88.

Grice, H.P. (1975) 'Logic and conversation', in Cole, P. and Morgan, J.L. (eds): 41–58.

Grice, H.P.(1978) 'Further notes on logic and conversation', in Cole, P. (ed.) 113–27.

Grice, H.P. (1981) 'Presupposition and conversational implicature', in Cole, P. (ed.) *Radical Pragmatics*, Academic Press, New York: 183–98.

Hancher, M. (1979) 'The classification of cooperative illocutionary acts', *Language in Society*, 8: 1–14.

Harris, R. (1979) 'The descriptive interpretation of performative utterances', *Journal of Linguistics*, 14, 331–4.

Harris, S.J. (1980) *Language Interaction in Magistrates' Courts*, unpublished Ph.D. thesis, University of Nottingham.

Holdcroft, D. (1979) 'Speech acts and conversation – 1', *Philosophical Quarterly*, 29: 125–41.

Hughes, J. (1984) 'Group speech acts', *Linguistics and Philosophy*, 7: 379–95.

Kasher, A. (1976) 'Conversational maxims and rationality', in A. Kasher (ed.) *Language in Focus*, Reidel, Dordrecht: 197–216.

Kasher, A. (1977a) 'Foundations of philosophical pragmatics' in R.E. Butts and J. Hintikka (eds) *Basic Problems in Methodology and Linguistics*: 225–42, Reidel, Dordrecht.

Kasher, A. (1977b) 'What is a theory of use?' *Journal of Pragmatics* 1 (2): 105–20.

Kempson, R.M. (1975) *Presupposition and the Delimitation of Semantics*, Cambridge University Press, Cambridge.

Kess, J.F. and Hoppe, R.A. (1981) *Ambiguity in Psycholinguistics*, Benjamins, Amsterdam.

Kiefer, F. (1979) 'What do the conversational maxims explain?' *Linguisticae Investigationes* 3 (1): 57–74.

Labov, W. and Fanshel, D. (1977) *Therapeutic Discourse*, Academic Press, New York.

Leech, G.N. (1977) 'Language and tact', *LAUT Series A* Paper 46, University of Trier.

Leech, G.N. (1980) *Explorations in Semantics and Pragmatics*, Benjamins, Amsterdam.

*Leech, G.N. (1983) *Principles of Pragmatics*, Longman, London.

Levinson, S. (1979) 'Activity types of language', *Linguistics* 17 (5/6): 365–99.

Levinson, S. (1981) 'The essential inadequacies of speech act models of dialogue', in Parret, H. *et al.* (eds): 473–89.

*Levinson, S. (1983) *Pragmatics*, Cambridge University Press, Cambridge.

Martinich, A.P. (1984) *Communication and Reference*, Walter de Gruyter, Berlin.

Mey, J.L. (1985) *Whose Language: A Study in the Pragmatics of Language Use*, Benjamins, Amsterdam.

Milroy, L. (1984) 'Comprehension and context: successful communication and communication breakdown', in Trudgill, P (ed.) *Applied Sociolinguistics*, Academic Press, London: 7–31.

Morgan, J. (ed.) (1979) *Syntax and Semantics*: Volume 9. Academic Press, London/New York.

Morris, C.W. (1938) *Foundations of the Theory of Signs*, Chicago University Press, Chicago.

*Nuyts, J. and Verschueren, J. (1987) *A Comprehensive Bibliography of Pragmatics*: 4 vols, Benjamins, Amsterdam.

Ohmann, R. (1972) 'Instrumental Style: notes on the theory of speech as action', in Kachru, B.B. and Stahlke, H.F.W. (eds). *Current Trends in Stylistics*. Linguistic Research, Edmonton, Illinois: 115–41.

Parret, H., Sbisa, M. and Verschueren, J. (eds) (1981) *Possibilities and Limitations of Pragmatics*, Benjamins, Amsterdam.

Pratt, M.L. (1977) *Toward a Speech Act Theory of Literary Discourse*, Indiana University Press, Bloomington.

Prastt, M.L. (1981) 'The ideology of speech-act theory', *Centrum* (New Series): 5–18.

Pyle, C. (1975) 'The function of indirectness', Paper read at N-WAVE IV. Georgetown University.

Rintell, E. (1979) 'Getting your speech act together: the pragmatic ability of second language learners' in *Working Papers in Bilingualism* 17: 97–106.

Ross, J.R. (1970) 'On declarative sentences', in Jacobs, R.A. and Rosenbaum, P.S. (eds) *Readings in English Transformational Grammar*, Blaisdell, Waltham, Mass.: 222–72.

Sadock, J.M. (1974) *Towards a Linguistic Theory of Speech Acts*, Academic Press, New York.

Sadock, J.M. (1978) 'On testing for conversational implicature', in Cole, P. (ed.): 281–98.

Sampson, G. (1982) 'The economics of conversation: comments on Joshi's paper', in Smith N.V. (ed.) (1982) 200–10.

Sanders, R.E. (1980) 'Principles of relevance: a theory of the relationship between language and communication', *Communication and Cognition*: 77–95.

Searle, J.R. (1969) *Speech Acts: An Essay in the Philosophy of Language*, Cambridge University Press, Cambridge.

Searle J.R. (1979a) *Expression and Meaning*, Cambridge University Press, Cambridge.

Searle, J.R. (1979b) 'A taxonomy of illocutionary acts', in Searle, J.R. 1979a: 1–29. (Original 1975.)

Searle, J.R. (1979c) 'Indirect speech acts', in Searle, J.R. 1979a: 30–57. (Original 1975.)

Searle, J.R. (1979d) 'Speech acts and recent linguistics', in Searle, J.R. 1970a: 162–79. (Original 1975.)

Searle, J.R., Keifer, F. and Bierwisch, M. (eds) (1980) *Speech Act Theory and Pragmatics*, Reidel, Dordrecht.

Smith, N.V. (ed.) (1982) *Mutual Knowledge*, Academic Press, London/New York.

*Sperber, D. and Wilson, D. (1986) *Relevance: Communication and Cognition*, Cambridge University Press, Cambridge.

Stampe, D.W. (1975) 'Meaning and truth in the theory of speech acts', in Cole, P. and Morgan, J.L. (eds): 1–39.

Strawson, P.F. (1952) *Introduction to Logical Theory*, Methuen, London.

Swiggers, P. (1981) 'The supermaxim of conversation', *Dialectica* 35: 303–6.

Thomas, J.A. (1981) 'Pragmatic Failure', unpublished M.A. thesis, University of Lancaster.

Thomas, J.A. (1983) 'Cross-cultural pragmatic failure', *Applied Linguistics*, 4: 91–112.

Thomas, J.A. (1984) 'Cross-cultural discourse as unequal encounter', *Applied Linguistics*, 5: 226–35.

Thomas, J.A. (1985) 'The language of power: towards a dynamic pragmatics', *Journal of Pragmatics*, 9: 765–83.

Thomas, J.A. (1986) *The Dynamics of Discourse: a pragmatic approach to the analysis of confrontational interaction*, unpublished Ph.D. thesis, Department of Linguistics, University of Lancaster.

Walters, J. (1979a) 'The perception of politeness in English and Spanish', in *On TESOL '79*: 289–96.

Walters, J. (1979b) 'Strategies for requesting in Spanish and English – structural similarities and pragmatic differences', *Language Learning* 9 (2): 277–94.

Wilson, D. (1975) *Presupposition and Non-Truth Conditional Semantics*, Academic Press, New York.

Wilson, D. and Sperber, D. (1981) 'On Grice's theory of conversation', in Werth, P. (ed.) *Conversation and Discourse — Structure and Interpretation.* Croom Helm, London: 155–78.

# FURTHER READING

The items marked with an asterisk in the list above will be found especially helpful for further exploration of the subject.

# 7

## LANGUAGE AS A WRITTEN MEDIUM: TEXT

### JÁNOS S. PETÖFI

### 1. WHAT IS A TEXT?

Anyone who can read and write also has an idea about what usually can be called a 'text'. If, however, we try to define (or at least explicate) the notion *text*, we are faced with the following questions: What should be called a 'text' (i) a physical semiotic object or a relational semiotic object (i.e. the manifestation of a signifier-signified relation)? (ii) a unimedial or a multimedial object? (iii) an object that is an element of a semiotic system or an object that belongs to the domain of applying such a system? (iv) only a totally autonomous or also a partially autonomous semiotic object? Finally, depending on the answers given to the questions (i)–(iv) what should be declared as criteria of textuality? – It is only possible to understand the history and the present state of text research if the problems involved in the questions formulated above are clearly recognised.

The first question is a specification of a more general question discussed in semiotics: What should be called a 'sign' or a 'sign-complex'? These terms are used inconsistently in the literature: sometimes they refer to the signifier itself (to a physical object or a state of affairs), sometimes to the relation between the signifier and the signified. Applied to texts, this question can be reformulated as follows: Do we call a hand-written or printed string of words that forms a physical object a 'text' or is it only a hand-written or printed object, together with a meaning assigned to it, that deserves the name *text*?

From a semiotic perspective the second question deals with two aspects. On one hand, with the text-constitutive role of verbal and non-verbal elements; on the other hand, with the relationship between hand-written or printed verbal objects and their possible acoustic manifestations. As to the verbal and non-verbal elements, the question arises to what extent illustrations, tables, diagrams, pictures etc. can be used in a semiotic object constructed out of lexical elements if one still wants to call this semiotic object a 'verbal text'. It would perhaps be more expedient to introduce a term like *dominantly-verbal text* and to investigate what criteria have to be fulfilled for dominantly-verbal textuality. (In the past two decades the term *text* has also been used for non-verbal or not dominantly-verbal semiotic objects; however, I do not want to deal with this question here.) As to the relationship between hand-written or printed verbal objects and their possible acoustic manifestations, we have to ask ourselves whether it is possible at all to disregard the acoustic manifestations. Does a reader or a theoretically-trained interpreter rely on the hand-written or printed text (as a physical object) during text processing or does the potential acoustic manifestation, even if it is not read aloud, also play any role? In *Alice's Adventures in Wonderland* by Lewis Carroll, for instance, on the one hand many of the illustrations form organic parts of the work; on the other hand, many language puns cannot be understood unless the acoustic manifestation of the words in question is realized.

In connection with the second question I would also like to make the following remarks: (i) In linguistics the term *written text* in many cases does not refer to a hand-written or printed text as a physical or relational semiotic object. What is really meant by this term is the way of producing a text, the fact that the text producer can correct, edit or revise his work before he declares it to be finished. In this sense the written text is the counterpart of the *impromptu speech* or *conversation*. (ii) In discussions about so-called 'concrete poetry' the term *visual text* is sometimes used to refer to hand-written or printed texts without linear order or to texts where the linear order is not the only rule for text organisation. Acoustic manifestations can be assigned to some visual texts but not to others. The description of Alice's idea about the mouse *tale/tail* in chapter III of *Alice's Adventures in Wonderland* is an example of a case where an acoustic manifestation can be assigned to a picture-like text part.

The third question listed above relates to the distinction between *langue* and *parole*, as introduced by Saussure, or *competence* and *performance*, as Chomsky called an analogous pair of notions. In principle, the question is whether we consider texts as elements of the language system (i.e. *langue* or *competence*) along with the elements morphemes, words, clauses, sentences, and sentence chains, or whether texts are to be regarded as elements of language use (i.e. *parole* or *performance*). As to Saussure, in his conception not even the sentence is an element of the language system (*langue*), while for Chomsky the sentence is the largest unit of *competence* (see chapter 4, above). (Later, other members of the Chomsky school made the sentence chain the largest unit of competence.) If we consider verbal (or dominantly-verbal) texts as units belonging to the domain of language use, the question of size becomes irrelevant because linguistic units of any size can function as texts.

The question of the autonomy of (dominantly-verbal) texts tackled in the fourth question above provokes considerations such as whether, for instance, *The Tales of The Thousand and One Nights* as a whole should be regarded as an autonomous text or whether the individual tales could be regarded as autonomous texts as well. Is a collection of sonnets such as Dante's *Vita nuova* an autonomous text or are the individual sonnets autonomous texts as well? Is the whole of *Alice's Adventures in Wonderland* an autonomous text, or can the Prefatory Poem or the passage 'You are old, Father William' in chapter V (together with its illustrations) be counted as autonomous texts? The problem arises how to explicate the terms *totally-autonomous text* or *partially-autonomous text*. The question of the interrelationship between texts of the same author with an identical main character like, for instance, Alice in *Alice's Adventures in Wonderland* and Alice in *Through the Looking Glass* is, to my mind, a question of intertextuality and not a question of text autonomy.

After discussing these questions we have arrived at the basic question of how the inherent and the external properties of (dominantly-verbal) texts can be defined, if it is possible to define them at all, or how we can arrive at a consensus about these properties. The formulation of this question implies that a certain subjectivity may be involved in the notions *text* and *textuality* apart from further interference from historical and socio-cultural considerations.

In concluding these introductory ideas I would like to point out that the term *text* is used in the following sense in this contribution: (i) a text is a dominantly-verbal relational semiotic-object with a hand-written or printed physical manifestation; (ii) in the dominantly-verbal relational semiotic-object *text* the lexical elements are the dominant meaning-bearing elements; even though the hand-written or printed physical manifestations are the primary objects of text processing, potential acoustic manifestations have to be considered as well; (iii) texts are elements of language use, not of the language system; (iv) there is a distinction between totally-autonomous texts and partially-autonomous texts; (v) a dominantly-verbal relational semiotic-object fulfils the criteria for textuality if the following expectations are met: in a given or assumed communication-situation this object expresses a connected (and complete) configuration of states of affairs and fulfils a given or assumed communicative function; it has a connected and complete verbal constitution, where the connectedness and completeness of the constitution can depend on the type of the given object.

## 2. ELEMENTS OF TEXT CONSTRUCTION

By the term *text*, as I explained it in the first section, I am referring to a dominantly-verbal relational-object, – in terms of semiotics, to a signifier-signified relation. In this relation the following four entities play a relevant role: (i) the configuration of the physical objects constituting the signifier and their mental image (called the *vehiculum* and the *mental image of the vehiculum*), (ii) the formal organisation of the vehiculum and of its mental image or, more precisely, the knowledge about this formal organisation (called the *formatio*), (iii) the sense-semantic organisation of the vehiculum and of its mental image or, more precisely, the knowledge about this sense-semantic organisation (called the *sensus*), and finally (iv) the state-of-affairs configuration constituting the text-external signification and its mental image (called the *relatum* and the *mental image of the relatum*). In the sign-model underlying this presentation, the vehiculum (plus the mental image of the vehiculum) and the formatio together are called the signifier (*significans*), while the sensus and the relatum (plus the mental image of the relatum) together are called the signified (*significatum*). The organisation of the vehiculum (and of its mental image) is indicated by the term *constitutio*, while the organisation of the significans-significatum relation is indicated by the term *constructio*. As to the organisation, it is necessary to distinguish between the inherent-organisation of the text assumed by us and the representation of this organisation produced by us. On the basis of the distinction between the static and the dynamic aspect of the organisation, we can call the theoretical construct produced as the representation of the static aspect of the organisation *structure*, and the theoretical construct produced as the representation of the dynamic aspect *procedure*. Only if we distinguish between the inherent-organisation and its representation is it possible to understand how different structural and procedural descriptions can be assigned to one and the same text. In particular, the structure and the procedure are entities which always depend on the interpreter and/or on the theory applied.

In addition, it is necessary to make a distinction between the two main aspects of text constitution: the textural aspect, in short the *texture*, and the compositional aspect, in short the *composition*. In metaphoric terms the texture is the horizontal aspect of text constitution, i.e. the pattern manifest/displayable in the text which is brought about by text constituents recurring on different compositional levels. The composition, on the other hand, is the vertical aspect of text constitution, i.e. the architecture manifest/displayable in the text which arises through the organisation of the text constituents into higher and higher hierarchic-units until the whole text results as the highest-grade hierarchic-unit. (This explication of course does not exclude the possibility that one single word – as an element of the language system – can constitute a text, i.e. can function as a unit of language use called 'text'; let us think for example of the exclamation 'Fire!' in a given context.)

The elements of text-construction and their aspects will be discussed under the headings of the terms for the four sign components, and illustrative material will be taken mainly from Lewis Carroll's *Alice's Adventures in Wonderland* (in the following: AAW) and also from Lewis Carroll's *Through the Looking-Glass* (in the following: TLG). Although both are literary works, the aspects demonstrated (or their analogues) can also be found in texts of other text types. (All references to AAW and TLG will be, for convenience's sake, to the recent (1982) Oxford publication; cf. References.)

### 2.1 Vehiculum: the physical manifestation of the text

In dealing with written media (hand-written or printed texts) the physical manifestation is the visual manifestation. The visual manifestation is characterized by the type of elements it consists of, by the form, the size, and perhaps the colour of these elements, and by the global arrangement of the manifestation.

In AAW in Carroll (1982) we encounter the following types of elements: words, punctuation marks, brackets, Roman numerals, configurations of asterisks, and pictures. Beyond these, TLG also contains the representation of a chess-configuration arranged on a chess-board, two adjoining lists (Carroll 1982: 114), and also a mathematical formula (Carroll 1982: 190). The Arabic numerals which in Carroll (1982) are used to refer to foot-notes are left out of consideration here.

The words are set partly in normal type, partly in italics, by using different types of letters. In TLG (Carroll 1982: 134) we also find a text-part set in mirror writing; the asterisk-configurations are always arranged in the same way; the pictures are partly vertically, partly horizontally arranged, of square form or L-shaped, partly with a frame, partly without, partly between text parts, partly between and beside text parts; only the frontispiece of Carroll (1982) is coloured.

As to the global organisation of AAW and TLG, the following can be said: both texts are divided into twelve well-distinguishable main-sections (disregarding here the text parts which are separate from the so-called 'chapters'); the word-strings are either arranged according to conventional prose-setting or conventional verse-setting, except for one place (in AAW Ch. III, Carroll 1982: 28) where the organisation of a word-string is different from both conventional setting forms; the text parts set in prose form and in verse form as well as the text parts and the pictures alternate with each other without any visually recognisable system.

Since the physical manifestation of the texts is in most cases meaning-constitutive and thus may facilitate or hinder the understanding of the texts, the physical manifestation is of interest both in itself and from the viewpoint of its perception (bringing about its mental image). (Let us think here not only of literary texts but also of texts in school-books and manuals.) To discuss questions of text perceptions in detail would go beyond the limits of my presentation; however, I want to point out that an explicit description of text processing (text analysis) also requires an explicit representation of the mental image arising in the interpreter. This especially applies to the acoustic mental-image assigned to written or printed texts. (This question will be handled in sections 2.2 and 2.3.)

## 2.2 Formatio: the formal organisation of the vehiculum

When we investigate the formal organisation, the vehiculum can, on the one hand, be considered as a *physical* object in the full sense of the word (a visual picture and/or an acoustic sound-configuration, concerning which it is not even necessary to know which semiotic system or which language supplies its/their elements); on the other hand, it can be considered as a *semiotic* object (a configuration consisting of elements of a known semiotic system). In the first case we concentrate on the organisation of the (visual and/or acoustic) physical manifestation-form of the vehiculum (the *figura*), while in the second case we concentrate on the formal semiotic-organisation of the vehiculum as a sign-configuration (the *notatio*). To indicate the formal organisation we use the terms *connexity* and *completeness* and distinguish, according to the notions introduced at the beginning of this chapter, textural and compositional connexity and completeness.

### 2.2.1 Figura: the formal organisation of the vehiculum as a physical object

The *visual figura* plays an especially relevant role in the calligrams and in the products called 'visual texts' in 'concrete poetry'; however, it also may have relevance in other types of texts. If we analyse the visual figura of AAW, we have to analyse the connexity and the completeness of the visual figura both in the text parts consisting of words and in the pictures, as well as in the entirety of the text constituted by words and pictures. In the text parts consisting of *words* the analysis of the textural connexity must register the recurrent application of the type-faces which are different from the basic type-face of the text (verse-insertions, italics, capitals) as well as the recurrence of certain elements (words, text parts, asterisk-configurations), since we assume (indeed expect) that they are meaning-constitutive. As we will see in 2.3, they are in fact to a great extent meaning-constitutive. Among the text parts consisting of words we find a text part which has a compositionally connex and complete visual figura: it is the *Mouse tail* (Carroll 1982: 28) referred to previously. When analysing the textural connexity of the pictures, it is important to recognise figures representing one and the same person and/or animal. In AAW in Carroll (1982) for example, there is on each of the pages 12, 13, 16, 18, 20, 22, 24, 33, 38, 40, 52, 56, 57, 61, 71, 74, 80, 85, 89, 103, and 109 a girl-figure representing Alice, even if these figures differ from one another both as to their internal proportions and as to their proportion with respect to one and the same objects/persons; another example may be the picture of the Cheshire Cat on pages 57, 59 and 77, the first picture showing the whole figure, the second one mainly its head, and the third one only its head. Limitations of space do not allow me to treat the compositional connexity of *pictures*, and the connexity and completeness of the visual figura of the full text consisting of *pictures and words*, but I wish to mention an example: the visual figura of the autonomous text-part '*You are old, Father William*' (Carroll 1982: 42–5) is a compositionally connex and complete picture-*and*-verse text-unit: it begins with a picture on the bottom of page 42, which is followed by four strophes and an adjoining picture on page 43, and then by a picture and four adjoining strophes on page 44, and finally closes with a picture at the top of page 45.

The *acoustic figura* plays an eminently relevant role in verse; however, like the visual figura, it may have a meaning-constitutive role and/or may facilitate understanding in other types of texts as well. The acoustic figura has a different status according to whether texts received by listening or text received by reading (seeing) are concerned. In the first case the acoustic figura is the object of the perception of the receiver, while in the second case the receiver must construct it. In the latter case the receiver, of course, must know the semiotic system (language), out of the elements of which the text has been brought about, because he can construct the acoustic figura only in interaction with the revelation of the syntactic and sense-semantic organisation of the text to be received.

After these remarks let me consider some examples in connection with the acoustic figura of AAW: (i) the acoustic figura (the metric-rhythmic and the rhyme pattern) of the verse-insertions in AAW will be constructed in the same way as is usual with verse; only one example should be mentioned here concerning the rhyme pattern: the second strophe of the song of the Mock Turtle (Carroll 1982: 95):

> '*Beautiful Soup! Who cares for fish,*
> *Game, or any other dish?*
> *Who would not give all else for two p*
> *ennyworth only of beautiful Soup?*
> *Pennyworth only of beautiful soup?*
> *Beau—ootiful Soo—oop!*

> *Beau—ootiful Soo—oop!*
> *Soo—oop of the e—e—evening,*
> *Beautiful, beauti—FUL SOUP!*

The organisation of the third and fourth line of this strophe (the way in which the word 'pennyworth' is printed in these lines) is a very unusual way of ensuring that the rhyme pattern of this strophe remains identical with that of the first strophe; and the visual image of the last four lines of the second strophe can be understood as a kind of score for the acoustic image to be produced; (ii) the dashes of different length in the verse-insertions and also in prose-parts indicate pauses of different length (and/or character); (iii) in the text-parts in prose the text-pieces in italics which are not between quotation marks always indicate stressed elements and thus they influence the production/construction of the acoustic figura; (iv) one part of the language puns (cf. the *tale/tail*-example already mentioned which can be explained by the homophonic nature of this non-homographic pair of words) can only be understood in the light of both the visual and the acoustic figura. To illustrate the connection of the visual and the acoustic figura, in TLG we find an even more complex example – an example of iconic character – (Carroll 1982: 150):

> Alice couldn't see who was sitting beyond the Beetle, but a hoarse voice spoke next. 'Change engines' it said, and there it choked and was obliged to leave off.
>
> 'It sounds like a horse,' Alice thought to herself. And an extremely small voice, close to her ear, said 'You might make a joke on that – something about "horse" and "hoarse," you know.'

(The petite setting always recurs when the 'extremely small voice' is speaking.)

### 2.2.2 *Notatio: the formal organisation of the vehiculum as a semiotic object*

When analysing the notatio, it has to be established first how many *notatio-systems* the elements of the text to be interpreted belong to, then the analysis of the connexity and the completeness of the element-configurations belonging to the individual systems should follow. There are notatio-systems which differ from each other also figurally, e.g. hand-written/printed text vs. pictures, sound-text vs. music, and, within the verbal written medium, writing in Latin vs. writing in Arabic letters. There are also notatio-systems which cannot – or not so easily – be differentiated from each other formally; these systems include all languages using Latin letters.

Let us see some examples from Carroll's works to illustrate the different verbal notatio-systems: in AAW we find a French utterance 'So she began again: "Où est ma chatte?", which was the first sentence in her French lesson-book' (Carroll 1982: 21). As a matter of fact, in the verse-insertion Jabber-

*wocky* in TLG, elements of two different notatio-systems have also been mixed: those of the real and those of a potential English language. Let me demonstrate this mixture by the first strophe (Carroll 1982: 134):

> 'Twas brillig, and the slithy toves
> Did gyre and gimble in the wabe:
> All mimsy were the borogoves,
> And the mome raths outgrabe.

It is to be mentioned that the setting-form in mirror characters of this strophe can again be considered as belonging to another notatio-system: 'she turned over the leaves, to find some part that she could read, "– for it's all in some language I don't know," she said to herself.' (Alice's comment on it in Carroll 1982: 133.)

The analysis of the connexity of the notatio is, as a matter of fact, the analysis of the syntactic organisation. With respect to the aspect of the composition, this means primarily the analysis of the syntactic organisation of the individual utterances/text-sentences, secondarily the investigation of what can be said about the syntactic organisation of the higher level hierarchic units (paragraphs and chapters) – if it is at all possible to tell anything about the syntactic organisation of these units without taking the sense-semantic aspect into consideration. With respect to the aspect of the texture, connexity is carried by the recurrence of units of the same syntactic organisation at any hierarchic level.

*Syntactic composition-units* are syntactically-connex word-configurations, syntactically-connex formulaic-patterns, and syntactically-connex configurations of syntactic categories. For example, the formulaic pattern of the strophe quoted from *Jabberwocky* is the following:

> Twas _____, and the _____y _____s
> Did _____ and _____ in the _____:
> All _____y were the _____s,
> And the _____ _____s _____.

In the strophe quoted the slots of this pattern are filled by potential English words. Hockett demonstrates the syntactic connexity (syntactic well-formedness) of this pattern by constructing sentences in real English fitting this pattern. One of these sentences is the following: '*Twas* morning, *and the* merry sunbeam*s did* glitter *and* dance *in the* snow; *all* tinsell*y were the* treetop*s, and the* happy fairie*s* frolicked.' (Hockett (1958: 262); the italics are mine; cf. also Sutherland (1972: 208ff.).)

Hockett's sentence is a syntactically-connex word-configuration, and thus we can also consider the original strophe as a syntactically-connex word-configuration, despite the fact that its lexical elements do not belong to one and the same notatio system. If we substitute the constituents of this word-configuration by functional syntactic-categories, we obtain a syntactically-connex configuration of syntactic categories. One can easily understand that syntactically-connex (syntactically well-formed) category-configurations of paragraphs (and chapters) cannot be defined in the same sense as they can be defined for clauses or for simple sentences. Consequently, it is reasonable to ask whether we can speak at all of text syntax, and if we can, in what sense. While it is obvious that pronominalisation, use of conjunctions, use of tenses – all relevant factors of the text organisation – also have a syntactic aspect, the crucial point remains that it is not the syntactic aspect which dominates in the organisation of texts.

However, in TLG we encounter a syntactic organisational factor (occurring twice) which should be mentioned. This factor is the chapter-connecting function of a text-sentence pattern: (i) the title of Chapter IV is an organic constituent of the closing sentence of Chapter III (Carroll 1982: 158–9):

> So she wandered on, talking to herself as she went, till, on turning a sharp corner, she came upon two fat little men, so suddenly that she could not help starting back, but in another moment she recovered herself, feeling sure that they must be

### [CHAPTER IV]
#### TWEEDLEDUM AND TWEEDLEDEE

(ii) even more radical is the connection between the chapters X and XI, also reinforced by the illustrations belonging to them (Carroll 1982: 240–1):

### CHAPTER X
#### SHAKING

SHE took her off the table as she spoke, and shook her backwards and forwards with all her might.

The Red Queen made no resistance whatever: only her face grew very small, and her eyes got large and green: and still, as Alice went on shaking her, she kept on growing shorter – and fatter – and softer – and rounder – and –

### CHAPTER XI
#### WAKING

– and it really *was* a kitten, after all.

The syntactic connexity of the *textural organisation* is ensured by the recurring word-configurations, formulaic patterns and, configurations of syntactic categories. Examples of the recurrence of word-configuration are the refrain of the first and third strophe of the verse-insertion (in Chapter X of AAW) *Will you walk a little faster* (Carroll 1982: 90), and the recurring expression 'and the moral of that is' in the statements of the Duchess in

Chapter IX (Carroll 1982: 79–81). The pattern 'I . . . what I . . .' in Chapter VII in AAW is an example of the recurrence of formulaic patterns where the pattern mentioned recurs in the text-sentences 'I mean what I say', 'I see what I eat', 'I eat what I see', 'I like what I get', 'I get what I like' (Carroll 1982: 61). It is primarily in verse that the recurrence of configurations of syntactic categories plays (or may play) a relevant role. A very simple example of this is the following nursery rhyme: 'Solomon Grundy,/ Born on a Monday,/ Christened on Tuesday,/ Married on Wednesday,/ Took ill on Thursday,/ Worse on Friday,/Died on Saturday,/Buried on Sunday./ This is the end/of Solomon Grundy.' In this nursery rhyme the recurring category configuration is Pred + Adv$_{temp}$. (Recurring configurations of syntactic categories may of course also be found in both AAW and TLG.) Without going into further details, I want to mention that the frequency of certain patterns/categories may be characteristic of the style of an author, even if the connexity-carrying role of a special configuration is of no particular relevance.

## 2.3 Sensus: the sense-semantic organisation of the vehiculum

The sense-semantic organisation of the vehiculum can/should be investigated from two points of view: from the aspect of the language, out of the elements of which the text is constructed (let us call this aspect '*language*-specific organisation'), and from the aspect of the world-fragment (presumably expressed in the text) indicated by the language-specific sense-semantic organisation of the text (let us call this aspect '*relatum*-specific organisation'). In order to characterise the sense-semantic organisation, we investigate its connectedness called '*cohesion*' and its *completeness*, differentiating between textural and compositional cohesion and completeness, respectively.

### *2.3.1 Sensus: the language-specific sense-semantic organisation of the vehiculum*

To illustrate the types of language-specific sensus let us take the following text-sentence from AAW (Carroll 1982: 26):

> This question the Dodo could not answer without a great deal of thought, and it stood for a long time with one finger pressed upon its forehead (the position in which you usually see Shakespeare, in the pictures of him), while the rest waited in silence.

This text-sentence – like text-sentences and texts in general – can be assigned the following types of sensus: (i) *conceptual verbal sensus* (the sensus we obtain by combining the verbal sensus which can be assigned to the individual words of the text-sentence in the given verbal context); (ii) *conceptual non-verbal sensus* (a picture-like mental-image which we create (which arises in us) during the reception of this text-sentence); (iii) *non-conceptual sensus* (the experience or feeling which we associate with the conceptual verbal and/or non-verbal sensus of this text-sentence). Let us investigate now some aspects of these three sensus-types.

### Conceptual verbal sensus.

Three aspects of the conceptual verbal sensus can be distinguished: the relational, the inferential and the configurational.

From the *relational aspect* the conceptual verbal sensus is an elementary proposition or a proposition-complex. An elementary proposition is, to put it simply, a relation expressed in the form *predicate + its arguments*; the relation indicated by the predicate exists among the entities represented as arguments. (In the frames of this presentation it is not possible to discuss questions concerning the propositions in detail. In what follows I will represent the units to be handled as propositions in a form which is near to the surface structure and will mark them off from other parts of the text by using another type of setting.) For example, in the part of the above-quoted text-sentence which precedes 'without', the following two propositions are manifested: (i) IT WAS NOT THE CASE, THAT DODO COULD DO SOMETHING, where this DO SOMETHING is (ii) DODO ANSWERS THIS QUESTION. In the given verbal context the reference of the expressions 'Dodo' and 'this question' are known. In a text, as in the text-sentence quoted, however, not only is the reference a relevant factor, but also the co-reference: we are to recognise that 'it/its' in 'it stood' and in 'its forehead' are co-referent with the expression 'Dodo'; further, to recognise that the expressions 'thought' and 'finger' are to be understood as the thought and the finger of *it* (namely the Dodo). One can easily see that for these recognitions language competence alone does not suffice. (I will return to the question of reference/co-reference later.)

The *inferential aspect* is a highly relevant aspect of verbal communication. It is the capacity to draw inferences which renders the economy of communication possible (among other topics, the understanding of a text without it being necessary for everything to be set forth in detail), even if on the other hand false inferences may cause confusion in the communication. There are numerous types of inferential conceptual verbal sensus, but I only want to illustrate four of them by examples. (i) In the verbal context in which the expression 'beautiful Soup!' has been repeated several times, it is not at all difficult to perceive (to create the acoustic figura of) the expressions 'Beau-ootiful Soo–oop' and 'beauti–FUL SOUP!' (in AAW Ch. X; Carroll 1982: 95) in the right way; similarly, after the expression 'and the moral of that is' has been repeated several times, it is easy to identify the expression-fragment 'and the m____' (AAW Ch. IX in (Carroll 1982: 81). This inference-type can be called morpho-syntactic inference. (ii) We understand an utterance/text-sentence in most cases in such a way that we assign to the individual words of the utterance/text-sentence our knowledge about the object/property/ . . . indicated by the word in question. (This knowledge is called, when represented in an explanatory dictionary, an '*explication*', and, when inferred, an '*implicature*'.) The assignment of the explications may, of course, also be carried out on the quoted text-part beginning with 'This question . . .'. We should also bear in mind that explications are not definitions – i.e. are not implications in both directions –, the *explicans* does not represent the necessary *and* sufficient condition of the *explicandum*. Thus it is often difficult to name an entity from the knowledge of certain properties of it. AAW offers examples illustrating this difficulty, e.g. the following one: in Ch. VI we can read that 'suddenly a footman in livery came running out of the wood' (Carroll 1982: 50); we can assign to the word 'footman' the following knowledge: 'liveried *servant* for . . .', where 'servant' is understood as a '*person* who has undertaken (. . .) to carry out the orders of an individual . . .', i.e. a footman is a liveried person. (As to both explications cf. *The Concise Oxford Dictionary*; the italics are mine.) Only if we are aware of the difficulties concerning the use of explications is it possible to understand the remark of the narrator standing in brackets after the expression quoted: '(she considered him to be a footman because he was in livery: otherwise, judging by his face only, she would have called him a fish)'. As a possible solution to this problem, in the text to follow the indication 'Fish-Footman' also occurs. (iii) Among the inferences there are some which emphasise the conceptual verbal sensus of the text-sentence in question by contrast. In Ch. XI of AAW we find an example which also contains the background of the contrast explicitly (Carroll 1982: 100): '"I am a poor man, your Majesty", he began. /"You're a *very* poor *speaker*," said the King.' The elements in italics in the text (on which in living speech an extra stress would be laid) can be assigned the following inferences: You are not only simply poor, but very poor, and not as a man, but as a speaker. The function of setting some elements in the text of AAW in italics – if they are not representations of titles – is to express differentiating semantic stress. (iv) The fourth inference-type to be mentioned here may be called syllogistic inference; such an inference can be found, for example, in AAW Ch. XII: 'At this moment the King (. . .) read out from his book, "Rule Forty-two. (. . .)" / (. . .) / "It's the oldest rule in the book," said the King. / "Then it ought to be Number One," said Alice,' (Carroll 1982: 105). Syllogistic inferences may often be applied in different ways to one and the same text-part. In AAW Ch. VII we can find an example to illustrate this: '"Take some more tea", the March Hare said to Alice, very earnestly. / "I've had nothing yet," Alice replied in an offended tone: "so I ca'n't take more." / "You mean you can'n't take *less*," said the Hatter: "It's very easy to take *more* than nothing."' (Carroll 1982: 65). The inferences explicitly contained in these text-parts are partly also implicatures since in the first inference the explication assignable to the expression 'oldest rule' plays a role and in the second one the explication assignable to the relation 'nothing' – 'more' – 'less'.

The *configurational aspect* is concerned with the arrangement of the individual pieces of information in the given text sentences. It depends on the individual characteristics of the given language which configuration is admissible and which is not, which one alters the conceptual sensus of the text sentence and which one does not. The text sentence 'This question . . .' (see above) might as well begin in the following way: 'The Dodo could not answer this question' – but it does not begin like this. Similarly we might also alter the order of the lexical elements in other parts of this text sentence. Further, one might also change the order of the lexical elements in more than one text sentence at the same time. The questions are: What is being changed, if the alteration of an arrangement does not alter the relational and the inferential sensus? When is changing the order of merely stylistic nature, when is it of another nature and what is characteristic of it? In AAW we find examples both for changing the order which alters the relational sensus and for changing the order which leaves the relational sensus unchanged. In Ch. VII, for instance, the text part

> 'Then you should say what you mean,' the March Hare went on.
> 'I do,' Alice hastily replied; 'at least – at least I mean what I say – that's the same thing, you know.'
> 'Not the same thing a bit!' said the Hatter. 'Why, you might just as well say that "I see what I eat" is the same thing as "I eat what I see"!'

(Carroll 1982: 61), and in Ch. VI the text part

> The Fish-Footman began by producing from under his arm a great letter, nearly as large as himself, and this he handed over to the other, saying, in a solemn tone, 'For the Duchess.
> An invitation from the Queen to play croquet.' The Frog-Footman repeated, in the same solemn tone, only changing the order of the words a little, 'From the Queen. An invitation for the Duchess to play croquet.'

(Carroll 1982: 51).


*Conceptual non-verbal sensus.*

It is a well-known fact that in many cases we not only understand the received text but we can also imagine the states of affairs expressed in it. It is also well-known that the understanding of a text is often disturbed, if we cannot imagine what the text is about. Both facts hold, of course, only for texts for which it is possible to construct pictorial mental images; the conceptual non-verbal sensus only plays a role in connection with such texts.

The conceptual non-verbal sensus, too, has a relational, an inferential and a configurational aspect. The constituent 'and it stood for a long time with one finger pressed upon its forehead' of the text-sentence analysed above will serve as an example to shed light on some questions concerning these aspects. This constituent can be assigned the following two propositions: (i) IT WAS THE CASE THAT DODO STOOD FOR A LONG TIME, and (ii) (AT THE SAME TIME) IT WAS THE CASE THAT DODO PRESSED ONE (OF ITS) FINGER(S) UPON ITS FOREHEAD. These two propositions can be considered as the conceptual verbal representation of the *relational* aspect of the conceptual non-verbal sensus. It is obvious that the relation expressed in these propositions (a state – we know that the state of thinking is meant) can be imagined in different ways. The question of whether the comment in brackets in the analysed text part '(the position in which you usually see Shakespeare, in the pictures of him)' provides any help for imagining this state can only be investigated if the text-constitutive role of irony is accounted for, as well. The pictorial mental image of a relation/state – thus also the pictorial mental image of the above propositions – is the *configurational* mental representation of this relation/state. Repetition-tests or narrative texts show that the majority of readers assign *inferences* to the mental images in the same way as to the conceptual verbal sensus.

In a dominantly-verbal text furnished with illustrations, the *illustrations* have the role of fixing in some way the pictorial manifestation of a character/situation. This function can also be well recognised in AAW, where certain characters could hardly be imagined by the reader without illustrations. In some places there is an explicit reference to this assistance, cf. in Ch. IX the following text part (Carroll 1982: 83): 'They very soon came upon a Gryphon, lying fast asleep in the sun. (If you don't know what a Gryphon is, look at the picture.)'

To conclude my comments on conceptual non-verbal sensus I wish to emphasise that while I was only concerned here with the pictorial mental images, the role of the non-pictorial images (acoustic or other images accessible to other sense-organs) may also be (and to the same degree) relevant, and a text theory aiming at an all-embracing approach to text should investigate their function and organisation, too.

*Non-conceptual sensus.*

During the process of understanding a text we not only understand its (conceptually verbal) lexical material and create a conceptual non-verbal mental image assignable to it; we also very often reactivate the experience we have had concerning the state-of-affairs configuration we think to be expressed in the text. (For example, we were also in a situation where we could not answer a question immediately and had to think a lot, and in this situation we might also have stood in a similar posture to the Dodo.) This experience we call 'non-conceptual sensus'.

The three types of language-specific sensus discussed above are also different from the aspect of intersubjectivity: we can consider the conceptual verbal sensus to be the most intersubjective, while the least intersubjective is probably the non-conceptual sensus.

*Textural and compositional cohesion.*

In this subsection I will deal exclusively with some aspects of the cohesion of the conceptual verbal sensus.

The carriers of *textural cohesion* are (i) recurring verbal units of the same order (as sense-semantic units), (ii) recurring co-referential sense-semantic units, and (iii) recurring units belonging to one and the same semantic field. Since group (i) of the cohesion-carriers does not need any special analysis, I will concentrate on examples of cohesion carriers belonging to groups (ii) and (iii). As to group (ii), in Ch. VI of AAW we find, among others, the following chains of co-referential units: 'a footman' – 'the Fish-Footman', 'another footman' – 'the Frog-Footman' – 'the Footman'; 'a baby' – 'her child' – 'the poor little thing' – 'this child' – 'the little thing' – 'the thing' – 'this creature' – 'the little creature'. These chains of course have to be complemented by the pronouns which are co-referent with the elements of the chains; I have left these out of consideration here for the sake of simplicity. What is to be mentioned here, however, is that the co-referential pronominal chains can be of different complexity. In a descriptive text the co-referential pronominal chains generally consist of pronouns of the third person; in a dialogue text a 'you' and an 'I' can also be co-referential if they occur in different speech-contributions. Since Alice often talks to herself and the narrator also comments on her soliloquies, we find in AAW co-referential chains concerning Alice in which a pronoun occurs in all the three persons as e.g. in Ch. II (Carroll 1982: 17): '"*You* ought to be ashamed of *yourself*," said Alice, "a great girl like *you*," (*she* might well say this), "to go on crying in this way! Stop this moment, *I* tell *you*!" But *she* went on . . .' (the italics are mine). As far as (iii) is concerned, the following example may be mentioned: in Ch. III of AAW the characters are different living creatures. The text classifies them as 'birds' and 'animals' and the names of these living creatures are used as quasi-Christian names: Lory, Duck, Dodo, Eaglet, Magpie and Canary as birds, while Mouse, Crab (and Dinah – Alice's cat) are animals. Also mice, frogs, worms and oysters are mentioned, but are used as common nouns.

When *compositional* cohesion is being investigated, the main questions are the following: (i) what is to be considered as the basic unit of the compositional sense-semantic organisation? and (ii) how are the higher-grade composition-units constructed from these basic units?

To the first question it is expedient to provide a deep-structure-specific and a surface-structure-specific answer. In the deep structure the basic unit is the so-called elementary proposition (cf. the examples of propositions discussed previously); in the surface structure the basic units are the text units declared by the author himself as text sentences (and indicated by a full stop, an exclamation mark or a question mark) – to be called further on 'first-grade composition-units'. It should be mentioned that paragraphs, sub-chapters and chapters are (formal) composition units belonging to the *formatio*; they may – but they do not necessarily – coincide with sense-semantic composition-units.

A proposition net which contains all those propositions, an argument or the predicate of which is identical, can be called a deep-structure-specific (higher-grade) cohesional composition-unit. AAW may, for example, be assigned nets which contain the propositions concerning the Rabbit, the Rabbit-hole, Alice, Dinah, etc.

In investigating the compositional cohesion of the surface structure, we have to examine the compositional organisation of both the first-grade and the higher-grade composition-units. For the analysis of some aspects of compositional cohesion let us consider the paragraphs 2–4 in Ch. XI of AAW (Carroll 1982: 96):

2.  Alice had never been in a court of justice before, but she had read about them in books, and she was quite pleased to find that she knew the name of nearly everything there. 'That's the judge,' she said to herself, 'because of his great wig.'

3.  The judge, by the way, was the King; and, as he wore his crown over the wig (look at the frontispiece if you want to see how he did it), he did not look at all comfortable, and it was certainly not becoming.

4.  'And that's the jury-box,' thought Alice; 'and those twelve creatures,' (she was obliged to say 'creatures,' you see, because some of them were animals, and some were birds,) 'I suppose they are the jurors.' She said this last word two or three times over to herself, being rather proud of it: for she thought, and

223

rightly too, that very few little girls of her age knew the meaning of it at all. However, 'jurymen' would have done just as well.

Let us call the independent sense-semantic basic-units of the first-grade composition-units 'communicates'. The first first-grade composition-unit of the fourth paragraph can be broken down into communicates as follows: 'And /1/ that's the jury-box,' /2/ thought Alice; 'and /3a/ those twelve creatures,' (/4.1*/ she was obliged /4.1/ to say 'creatures,' /4.2/ you see, because /4.3/ some of them were animals, and /4.4/ some were birds,) '/3*/ I suppose /3b/ they are the jurors.' This first-grade composition-unit contains 9 communicates (/1/, /2/, /3*/, /3a+3b/, /4.1*/, /4.1/, /4.2/, /4.3/, /4.4/). From among these communicates five are connected by brackets to form a constituent of this composition unit, thus the remaining four communicates form another constituent. /4.3/ and /4.4/ are connected by *and*; /4.1/ is dominated by /4.1*/, and the two form together the syntactic unit [/4.1*/::/4.1/] (where '::' stands for syntactic embedding); [/4.1*/::/4.1/] and [/4.3/ *and* /4.4/] are connected by *because*; /3*/ is the comment of Alice on /3a+3b/ (cf. the use of 'I' and of the quotation marks); /4.2/ connects [[/4.1*/::/4.1/] *because* [/4.3/ *and* /4.4/]] to /3a/ metalinguistically-deictically; [/3*/ + /3a+3b/] is connected to /1/ by *and*; /2/ is the communicative comment of the narrator on [/1/ *and* [/3'/ + /3a+3b/]]; in addition, cf. the co-reference of 'Alice' and 'she' in /2/ and /4.1*/, respectively.

The 'And' introducing the fourth paragraph connects the above analysed first-grade composition-unit of this paragraph with the last first-grade composition-unit ('"That's the judge," . . .') of the second paragraph; in this latter first-grade composition-unit in the first communicate 'the judge' is the comment part which will be converted into the topic part by the first communicate of the third paragraph ('The judge, by the way, . . .'); 'that', 'that' and 'those' are deictic expressions, the extra-textual context to which they refer is described in the first paragraph of Ch. XI. Chapter XI forms a thematic unit, which is *a trial in the court of justice*. The events taking place there have a special local and temporal scheme, The investigation of the compositional cohesion between the chapters of AAW can be carried out analogously to the way in which it was done in the case involving the communicates, first-grade composition units and chains of first-grade composition-units (paragraphs, chains of paragraphs) etc.

A longer text-part or a text can also be assigned a so-called 'abstract' which provides a summing up of this text-part/text. These abstracts are also called 'macro-structures' in the literature. Since making an abstract always involves some idiosyncratic point of view, one and the same text-part/text can be assigned more than one different abstract/macro-structure.

The example treated in this section shows almost all relevant manifestations of compositional cohesion: communicational cohesion, thematic cohesion, conjunctional cohesion, co-referential cohesion and cohesion by topicalisation. Two remarks appear to be appropriate here: (i) many of the schemata underlying the thematic organisation (and their recognition) are socio-culturally determined; their typical manifestations are called story scheme (story grammar), expository scheme, etc; (ii) in the analysis and description of the semantic function of the conjunctions, the relevance-relations between the states of affairs (the verbal description of which is connected (or can be connected) by the particular conjunctions) do, in fact, play important roles. To discover and classify these relevance-relations with respect to conjunctions such as 'but' or 'because', is as important as it is with respect to 'and' and to the colon or the semicolon which are capable of fulfilling the function of all conjunctions.

To conclude this section, I want to make a remark on the completeness of the (language-specific) sense-semantic compositional-organisation. There are different ways for a text to indicate that the (sense-semantic) composition is accomplished: the end of a theoretical proving can be referred to by the conclusion sign QED (=*quod erat demonstrandum* [=which was to be demonstrated]); or – as it is the case in AAW – the expression 'THE END' can appear at the end of the last chapter of a text. However, judging whether the sense-semantic composition is really complete is only possible by also analysing/interpreting the state-of-affairs configuration expressed in the text.

### 2.3.2 *Sensus; the relatum-specific sense-semantic organisation of the vehiculum*

To discover the relatum-specific sense-semantic organisation of the vehiculum means to discover that world-fragment which, according to the assumption of the interpreter, finds an expression in the text. The main questions concerning this world-fragment are the following: (i) is this world-fragment a fictive one or a non-fictive one, and if it is fictive, in what way; (ii) of what subworlds does this world-fragment consist; what is the relational organisation of the individual subworlds and the whole world-fragment like; what inferences can be assigned to the individual subworlds and to the whole world-fragment; (iii) what is the vehiculum-specific configurational arrangement of the verbal manifestation of the objects/events of this world-fragment like? Let us clarify these questions by examples taken again from Carroll (1982).

(i) The *world* of AAW is a fictive world embedded into the real world or, more exactly, a fictive world created by a created dream. We also find explicit hints in AAW of the fact that we are faced with a (created) dream: in the

Prefatory Poem and in the last two paragraphs preceding the concluding part of Ch. XII. This fictive world is fictive in that its organisation partly conforms to and partly does not conform to the regularities according to which the world we consider as the real world is organised.

(ii) Within a world-fragment we can demarcate *subworlds* in different ways; we may consider some places (and/or times) world-constitutive but we may also consider individual characters as being world-constitutive. Thus in AAW we can refer to the world of the Rabbit, the Duchess, the March Hare, the Hatter and the Dormouse, as well as to the world of the King and of the Queen, etc., as *subworlds*. In these subworlds there are animals which can speak (and which are dressed and behave like human beings), as well as figures of playing cards acting like human beings. The relational organisation of the individual subworlds can be represented, for example, by constructing sets/nets of those propositions, the arguments of which are names (definite descriptions) of the persons constituting the respective subworld. These subworlds are connected with one another in various ways; Alice gets in touch with all of them, while also preserving the memory of her own world. The local dimensions of these subworlds are different from the real world, and Alice, when contacting them, is capable of changing her own size by different means (in general by eating and/or drinking something). The asterisk configurations as elements of the composition always indicate such a change. Through her person and through the events taking place with her or around her one can well illustrate the problem which is, under the influence of certain philosophical logics, called the problem of trans-world identity. An example of the problem of transworld identity in a normal context is the connection between the physically existing person of a friend of ours, his person reconstructed in our imagination, and his person appearing in our dream, etc. Alice often expresses that she is aware of the problems concerning her identity: in Ch. II (Carroll 1982: 18) she reflects:

> Let me think: *was* I the same when I got up this morning? I almost think I can remember feeling a little different. But if I'm not the same, the next question is "Who in the world am I?" Ah, *that's* the great puzzle!' And she began thinking over all the children she knew that were of the same age as herself, to see if she could have been changed for any of them.

in Ch. V she answers the questions of the Caterpillar concerning who she is, as follows (Carroll 1982: 41):

> Alice replied, rather shyly, 'I – I hardly know, Sir, just at present – at least I know who I *was* when I got up this morning, but I think I must have been changed several times since then.'

> 'What do you mean by that?' said the Caterpillar, sternly.
> 'Explain yourself!' .
>    'I ca'n't explain *myself*, I'm afraid, Sir,' said Alice, 'because I'm not myself, you see.'

and these answers are followed by some dialogue-parts of similar character.

We can, in addition, also speak of subworlds within the individual subworlds, if we consider, for example, those states of affairs as individual (sub-) subworlds which are experienced by a subworld-constitutive person, i.e. those which he knows, believes, imagines, etc. (These (sub-)subworld-constitutive expressions – somebody experiences, knows, believes, etc., – are called 'propositional attitudes' in the literature.) In the individual subworlds the inferences are also different. The constitutive-rules of a subworld generate inferences of their own and/or they fulfil the role of a filter, i.e. they select from among the real-world-specific inferences the subworld-specific ones. For example in the real world the expression 'something appears' can be assigned completely different inferences from the examples seen in certain subworlds in AAW; the Cheshire Cat can, for example, appear and disappear in parts. In AAW Ch. VIII, we can read the following about this (Carroll 1982: 75):

> 'How are you getting on?' said the Cat, as soon as there was mouth enough for it to speak with.
>    Alice waited till the eyes appeared, and then nodded. 'It's no use speaking to it,' she thought, 'till its ears have come, or at least one of them.' In another minute the whole head appeared, and then Alice put down her flamingo, and began an account of the game, feeling very glad she had some one to listen to her. The Cat seemed to think that there was enough of it now in sight, and no more of it appeared.

(Cf. also the concluding part of this chapter.)

(iii) When the system of the subworlds (and (sub-)subworlds) of the world fragment assignable to a text are being established, the *surface structure* of the text can also be investigated from the point of view of how the events of the individual subworlds alternate in it. While Alice, for instance, (in her altered size) actively takes part in some events of some subworld, she sometimes also dwells in thought in her own real world.

The aspects of the relatum-specific sense-semantic organisation treated earlier are (relationally, inferentially, configurationally) analogous to the aspects of the sensus called the 'conceptual verbal-sensus' of the language-specific sense-semantic organisation. In addition, we can also find the analogue (analogues) of the conceptual non-verbal sensus. An explicit example of this, in the concluding part of Ch. XII of AAW (Carroll; 1982: 110) is:

> and still as she listened, or seemed to listen, the whole place around her became alive with the strange creatures of her little sister's dream.
>
> The long grass rustled at her feet as the White Rabbit hurried by – the frightened Mouse splashed his way through the neighbouring pool – she could hear the rattle of the tea-cups as the March Hare and his friends shared their never-ending meal,

The question of whether the non-conceptual sensus also has an analogue in the relatum-specific sense-semantic organisation cannot be investigated here.

The relatum-specific relational sensus is also called the '*discourse world*' in the literature. The connectedness and completeness of a discourse world (or discourse subworld) is guaranteed by those relations existing among its states-of-affairs which are considered as relevant by the interpreter. Concerning the relatum-specific configurational sensus we can speak about cohesion and completeness in the same way as we do concerning the language-specific configurational sensus.

### 2.4 Relatum: what a text is about

Concerning the (re) constructed *relatum-specifically organised sensus* two further questions arise: (i) is the text only about the thing the interpreter believes manifests itself in the text according to this sensus, or is it (also) about something else?; (ii) is the thing the interpreter believes that the text is about compatible with his knowledge concerning the world, and does it meet his expectations concerning verbal communication? Let us investigate these questions with reference to Carroll's texts.

(i) The opinion of the reader about AAW may be that it is nothing but the description of a fictive dream; however, he also may be of another opinion. If he thinks that it is a description of a fictive dream, then it is this fictive dream which for him is what AAW is about, which is the extra-textural relatum of AAW. If, however, the interpreter thinks that AAW is (also) about another thing, he has to (re)construct this other thing. (It is well-known that AAW can also be interpreted as a caricature of the Victorian epoch in England.) When this other thing is being (re)constructed, the dominating operation is the *symbolic reinterpretation* of the language specific sensus and of the relatum-specific sensus implied by it in order to construct the mental image of a *new* (extra-textual) *relatum* . In this symbolic reinterpretation the referents of the expression 'the King and the Queen of Hearts' will not be picture-card figures capable of acting like human beings, but they will be Prince Albert and Queen Victoria, and Ch. XI will not be the description of a trial in a court of justice in a dream, but it will be a caricature of English jurisdiction of that epoch, etc. Symbolic (re)interpretation has two conditions: on one hand we must know how the mechanism operates which controls the symbolic (re)interpretation, on the other hand we have to be in the position to estimate adequately the measure and consistency of the symbolisation we may expect from a text-producer when creating a symbolic text. A symbolic text is, after all, not a message in cipher of which all elements must (and can) be translated into another language.

(ii) When judging whether the relatum assigned to AAW is *compatible* with the knowledge of the interpreter about the world and whether it meets his expectations concerning the assumed communication-situation or not, the interpreter proceeds one way if he considers AAW as the description of a fictive dream in the form of a book for children, and another way if he considers it as a caricature of England in the Victorian epoch. In the first case the question of compatibility arises in the form of whether the events described in AAW are accessible to the fantasy of a child or not, while the expectation concerns the connectedness of the events described in the individual chapters and of the chain of these events in the whole of AAW, and whether these events or chains of events can be considered as in some way complete or closed. (Of course, the expectation also comprises the intelligibility of the language puns and the intelligibility of at least one part of the intertextual references.) In the second case AAW will be compatible with the knowledge of the interpreter about the world, if he himself thinks that the caricature corresponds to the state of that epoch, or he can at least imagine that some people might think that it does. The expectation of the interpreter concerns the events to which the texts of the individual chapter symbolically refer, and it also concerns whether the chain of the events as presented in the whole of AAW can be considered as in some way complete and closed. (Of course, in this case the expectation also comprises the question of whether the language puns and the intertextual references fulfil an appropriate function in the mental image of the extra-textual relatum, (re)constructed by symbolic interpretation.)

In order to form a judgement about the connectedness and completeness of state-of-affairs configurations we only have intersubjective knowledge about those configurations which are institutionalised in some socio-cultural context. Such configurations are, for instance, a cricket-match, a tea-party, a legal trial, etc. Other configurations and the knowledge applied when compatibility is being judged are, in general, idiosyncratic.

Recent literature provides the following, more or less generally accepted, conception of *text coherence*: Speaking about text coherence we refer to (the mental image of) an extra-linguistic relatum. If the interpreter is capable of assigning a sensus to the text to be interpreted which enables him to (re)construct the mental image of a connected and complete state-of-affairs configuration, this text qualifies for him, with reference to this mental image, as coherent. Since the significans of a text almost never contains the description of all those events the knowledge of which is inevitably necessary for constructing the (connected and complete) mental image mentioned here, the inferences leading to the missing events play a relevant role in the (re-) construction of both the sensus and the mental image of the extra-linguistic relatum.

## 3. TEXT PROCESSING – TEXTOLOGICAL RESEARCH.

In the second section the most relevant constituents of text construction were discussed. When I used expressions like 'the interpreter is doing now this and now that', I did it for the sake of comprehension; the second section does not provide the description of either a structural or a procedural interpretation process. In the present section I will first briefly treat some aspects of text processing, primarily of the various types of interpretation, then I will outline the main aspects of textological research.

### 3.1 Some aspects of text processing

The term *text processing* is used to indicate all operations carried out upon texts and with texts, from the compilation of an automatic index to translation by means of computer or to the computerised simulation of human text understanding. The *interpretation processes* form the central subset of text processes. The possible objects and types of interpretation are represented by Figure 9.

In the interpretation processes one usually investigates what are called the '*system-specific (system-immanent) construction of a text*' and the '*functional settings of a text*'. By the investigation of the system-specific (system-immanent) construction of a text we understand the investigation of the text constituents discussed in the second section and the relations existing between them by means of explicitly-formulated rules and knowledge- and belief-systems; the investigation may only reach as far as the explicitly-represented systems permit. When investigating the functional settings of a text, we are concerned with the following questions: what was the motivation of the text-producer for producing the text to be investigated?; what are the characteristics (what is the process) of production of the text in question?; what are the characteristics (what is the process) of reception of the text in question?; what kind of effect does (might) the text in question have on which receivers and under which circumstances?

Both the system-specific construction and the functional settings (or any aspect/factor of them) can be investigated as a *static* or as a *dynamic* entity. In

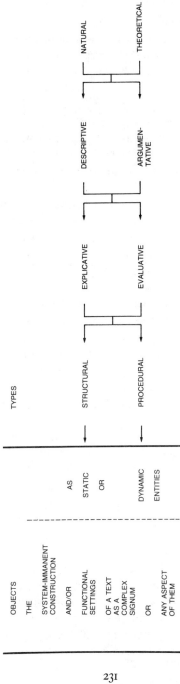

*Figure 9* Objects and types of interpretation

the first case we may speak about *structural* interpretation, in the second case about *procedural* interpretation. It should be emphasised again that in my conception a *structure* (that is a constructum) is intended to be an approximation of the assumed inherent static organisation, while a *procedure* (that is again a constructum) is intended to be an approximation of the assumed inherent dynamic organisation of the object to be interpreted.

We may differentiate further on between *explicative* and *evaluative, descriptive* and *argumentative, natural* and *theoretical* interpretation. The aim of the *explicative* interpretation is to produce a structure and/or procedure; the *evaluative* interpretation evaluates a produced structure and/or procedure from a historical, aesthetic, ideological, moral, etc. point of view. The aim of the *descriptive* interpretation is the description of a produced structure and/or procedure or the description of the evaluation of a produced structure and/or procedure; the *argumentative* interpretation presents arguments for the validity of these descriptions. We speak about *natural* interpretation when an average reader/hearer performs the interpretative operations in a normal communication situation; we speak about *theoretical* interpretation when a theoretically trained interpreter performs the interpretative operations according to the requirements of a theory. Let us comment on some types of interpretations.

When interpreting the *system-specific construction,* (i) the descriptive explicative *structural*-interpretation (as a product) is a static net of the elements taking part in the organisation of the interpreted object (i.e. a net which does not contain any information about the way it came into being); (ii) the descriptive explicative *procedural*-interpretation (as a product) is a dynamic net of the elements taking part in the organisation of the interpreted object (i.e. a net which also contains information about the way it came into being).

The decision of which elements to consider when constructing these nets depends solely on the system-immanent set of knowledge and/or beliefs and the rule system of the theoretical apparatus chosen as the device of the interpretations; no psychological/perceptional or other kind of production- and/or reception-specific viewpoints play a role here. In general, the interpretation of the system-specific construction does not supply a full interpretation of the construction and, even if it were capable of doing so, this interpretation could not be adequate because of the disregarded aspects of the functional setting.

When interpreting the *functional settings,* (i) the descriptive explicative *structural*-interpretation (as a product) is an interpretation representing the result of an accomplished interpretation-process; it does not contain any reference to the way the process has been carried out; (ii) the descriptive explicative *procedural*-interpretation (as a product) is an interpretation representing the process of the interpretation carried out; it does contain information about the way this process has been carried out.

The choice of the elements and the way to take them into consideration when interpreting the functional settings depends on the properties of the real or assumed producer/receiver (the set of his knowledge/beliefs, his psychological state, his social status, etc.) and on the parameters of the real or assumed communication-situation.


### 3.2 Textological research. Some methodological questions

The term *textological research* should be understood as the generalisation of the term *text-linguistic research*. This generalisation is in my opinion necessary and expedient for two reasons: On one hand, because the term *textology* neither implies a linguistic extension of the domain of (text) linguistics which could no longer be accepted as a linguistic domain by some (text) linguists, nor does it require narrowing the research field to an extent that would make an adequate investigation of the research objects in a homogeneous frame unrealistic. On the other hand, because of the different explications of the term *text linguistics*, to use the term 'text-linguistic research' would not be unambiguous.

Textological research may be focused on various objects and can be pursued with various goals applying various methods.

The *object* of this research may be any type, factor and/or aspect of text processing, more exactly any of the interpretation types listed in Figure 9.

As to the motivation of the possible goals of this research, there are some distinctions which have to be taken into consideration. Let us consider the two most relevant ones.

(i) Textological research can be competence-orientated or corpus-orientated. Let us call 'textological competence' the knowledge a language community possesses concerning texts, communication, and the different relations between texts and communication. I am aware of the difficulty of explicating the term *textological competence* sufficiently. However, from the angle of the distinction to be treated here, it suffices to assign an intuitive meaning to this term. (It must be pointed out that the term 'textological competence' cannot be considered as a generalisation of the term *competence* introduced by Chomsky, since textological competence also refers to knowledge concerning performance in Chomsky's sense.) In connection with the use of the term *corpus* it suffices to know that we may call any set of texts a 'corpus'. The compilation of corpus can be controlled by various points of view. The oeuvre of an author can be considered a corpus in just the same way as the economic news published during a given period in a given newspaper. As to the aim of verbal textological research, we can distinguish between textological research, the aim of which is a fundamental analysis and an explicit description of textological competence, and textological research the aim of which is the interpretation of a corpus defined in some specific way.

(ii) Textological research can be orientated either towards *theoretical knowledge* or towards *practice*. Although this distinction is not independent of the distinction treated in (i), it is still different from it. We are speaking of theoretical-knowledge-orientated research if the aim of the research is to enlarge *either* theoretical knowledge concerning textological competence in general *or* theoretical knowledge concerning a text type or a text corpus. (The final aim of this kind of research is the construction of a theory.) Textological research is practice-orientated if the aim of research is to contribute to the solution of a given practical task. Such practical tasks might be the following: to extend language teaching to the textual level; to render translation more effective; to restore the communicative ability of persons suffering from organic or psychic language disorders; to abolish or at least to reduce communication barriers, etc. However, one must not consider this distinction as a rigid either/or distinction. There is no doubt that the better our theoretical knowledge in the field of textological research becomes, the more effective our contribution to the solution of practical textological problems will be. Some practical textological problems can, however, be so important that the endeavour to solve them cannot be postponed until our theoretical textological knowledge reaches its maximum and optimum development.

As to the *methods* applied/applicable in textological research, one should bear in mind that textological research is – regarded in its entirety – an interdisciplinary branch of research. There does not yet exist a single academic discipline which could consider the investigation of the construction and the functional settings of texts as its own special task even if one single interpretation type is concerned.

By the term *textology*, I intended to refer to a discipline which considers all objects and goals of text research as *its own* research objects and goals. In textological research rhetorics, traditional philology, philosophy of interpretation, linguistics, cognitive psychology and sociology of verbal communication (ethnomethodology) – to mention just the most important disciplines – play an equally relevant role; thus its methods involve all traditional, formal, empirical and technical-modelling methods which we encounter in the disciplines listed above. It is widely known that research can more easily yield acceptable results if its object and/or aim remains within certain limits of complexity. This is the reason why individual disciplines investigate so-called idealised objects (cf. the notion of *ideal speaker/hearer* in Chomsky's theory) and/or are confined only to certain special aspects of a research object (e.g. system-linguistics to the language-system specific aspects of text construc-

234

tion, psychology to the psychological conditions of text understanding, etc.) Even if the methodological questions are not simple in this case either, they are certainly much simpler than in the case of research which is persued with constant regard to the aim of a later integration of the results yielded in the individual disciplines which are, from the point of view of the spectrum and integrity of the research object, partial results. This fact must not be disregarded if we examine the question of the autonomy of so-called 'text linguistics'. Even if it is legitimate to consider text linguistics as an autonomous discipline, as to both its historical development and its methods, this autonomy can, in a rational light, only be a partial autonomy defined within a textological framework.

Any research, thus also textological research, is determined by the hierarchic configuration of the object to be analysed and described, the goal and the methodology applied. In this configuration, the object, the goal or the methodology may play the dominating role. From among the possible configurations, some configurations in which the methodology is dominant may in some cases turn out to be problematic. It can, for instance, happen that allowing a methodology to become dominant will to some extent determine the possible choice of the goal and the object to be analysed, so that one should rather speak of extending the domain of a methodology than of genuine object-orientated research.

In textological research, in my opinion, it is *the goal and the object* which should be the dominant elements, and the main task in the present stage of research should be to elaborate an adequate (interdisciplinary) methodology. I want to point out here only one aspect of an adequate methodology: the objects of textological research are dominantly-verbal semiotic-objects; however, at the same time the representations of the rule- and knowledge-systems applied in the research and the representations of the research results are also dominantly-verbal semiotic-objects. From this specific feature of textology, it follows that one of the basic tasks in the elaboration of an adequate methodology of textology is to construct representation languages which can explicitly be marked off from the language of the research object.

## 4. TEXT AS A MULTI-FACETED RESEARCH OBJECT. A SHORT THEMATIC BIBLIOGRAPHICAL GUIDE

As we have seen in the preceding sections, the investigation of texts (of text construction and the functional settings of texts) as a research object pertains to the research fields of different disciplines at the same time. Considering *textology* as a discipline the task of which is to investigate texts as multi-faceted research objects in an *integrative theoretical framework*, the construction of a textological framework can be approached from each of these disciplines. In fact, in the past two or three decades in many disciplines (in semiotics, in the philologies, in linguistics, rhetoric, cognitive psychology, communication sociology, artificial intelligence research, etc.) attempts have been made at the construction of such an (integrative) textological framework, with of course the dominance of the given discipline. It is true that text research looks back upon a tradition more than a thousand years old (e.g. in rhetoric); the development of textology as a discipline of its own with a balanced inter-disciplinary methodology is, however, just beginning.

Within *linguistics*, the way leading towards a textological theoretical-framework can be described briefly as follows.

Whatever one's personal attitude towards the generative transformational theory of language may be (See Chapter 3, above), one has to admit that it initiated a methodological discussion which has had a considerable influence on the further development of the whole discipline of linguistics. It is instructive to study both the development of the generative transformational paradigm itself and the development of linguistic thinking since 1957 (when Chomsky's *Syntactic Structures* appeared). This is the subject of Chapter 4, above. Within the framework of the generative transformational sentence-grammatical theory, syntax was soon complemented by a sense-semantic component; however, even the theory extended in this way proved to be inappropriate for many researchers as a theory of the description of linguistic reality. The importance of pragmatic factors was increasingly pointed out, so-called 'pragma-linguistic research' initiated, phenomena belonging to the domain of speech-act theory were considered with ever greater interest, and the theory of Montague, a logical theory also accounting for the extra-linguistic relatum (i.e. also having an extensional-semantic component), gained ground. This development can also be characterised as the way towards constructing an *integrative* (i.e. syntactic, semantic and pragmatic) *theory of the sentence*.

Partly parallel to the development described above, partly closely corre-lated with it, text-linguistic research has gradually taken shape. The goal of this research was, to formulate it globally, to elaborate a text-grammatical and/or text-linguistic framework which would make possible the analysis and description of all phenomena which could not be analysed adequately and described in a sentence-grammatical/sentence-linguistic framework. However, text grammarians and text linguists soon had to realise that the analysis and description of texts also required consideration of several factors which can hardly (or not at all) be classified as objects of the domain of grammar/linguistics, even if grammar and linguistics are interpreted as broadly as possible. To be able to describe the construction and/or the functional settings of texts, one necessarily has to transgress the boundaries of grammar/linguistics in whatever way laid out, and to employ the methods/ results of disciplines which deal with texts and/or various aspects of natural-language communication, even if not primarily linguistically initiated. Thus, it seems to be not only justifiable, but also necessary to see the goal of this development as the attempt to set up an *integrative textological theoretical-framework*.

To form an adequate picture of the methods of a *textology dominated by linguistics* is difficult because linguistics is not a homogeneous discipline. Even within grammar in its narrower sense there are a number of directions or schools using basically different methods, and almost every one of them has attempted to widen its object domain so as also to cover the objects that can be called 'sentence-chains'/'texts'.

*Note*: In my presentation I have aimed at providing a survey of the *main question of textological research*, without characterising the way in which text research is done by particular linguistic schools. That is why I have used Latin terms which are neutral and which are not connected to any of these schools.

## REFERENCES

It may be helpful to point out in which of the references given below the following specific topics are discussed:

**The notion of text**: Petöfi (ed.) (1979) and (1981); **Text types, text sorts**: (Genot (1979), Gutwinsky (1976), Jakobson (1981), Jones (1977), Kinneavy (1980), Korpimies (1983), Meyer (1983), Propp (1968).

**Vehiculum** (aspects of the physical manifestation): Cooper and Greenbaum (eds) (1986), Coulthard, Brazil and Johns (eds) (1979), Enkvist (ed.) (1982), Gibbon and Richter (eds) (1984), Nystrand (ed.) (1982), Nystrand (1986), Sebeok (1978), Tannen (ed.) (1982), Tannen (ed.) (1984); **Formatio** (formal constitution, aspects of connexity): Enkvist and Kohonen (eds) (1976), Givón (ed.) (1979), Harris (1963), Jakobson (1981), Werth (1976); **Sensus** (sense-semantic constitution, aspects of cohesion): Crothers (1979), van Dijk (1977), (1979) and (1981), Daneš (ed.) (1974), Eikmeyer and Rieser (eds) (1981), Gazdar (1979), Givón (ed.) (1983), Grimes (1975), Gutwinsky (1976),. Halliday and Hasan (1976), Hinds (ed.) (1978), Hopper (1982), Jones (1977), Li (ed.) (1976), Longacre (ed.) (1970) and (1984), Ortony (ed.) (1979), Östman (ed.) (1978), Prince (1973), Propp (1968), van de Velde (1984), Werth (1984); **Extra-textual relatum** (what a text is about, aspects of world-knowledge): Fahlmann (1979), Goodman (1978), Metzing (ed.) (1979), Schank and Abelson (1977); **Connectedness** (connexity, cohesion, coherence): Coulthard and Montgomery (eds) (1981), Enkvist (1985), Kinneavy (1980), Neubauer (ed.) (1983), Petöfi (ed.) (1985) and (1987), Petöfi and Sözer (eds) (1983), Tannen (ed.) (1984).

**Text processing**: Allén (ed.) (1982), Ballmer (ed.) (1985), Petöfi (ed.) (1983); **Text production, text composition**: Beach and Bridwell (eds) (1984), de Beaugrande (1984), Cooper and Greenbaum (eds) (1986), Dillon (1981), Enkvist (ed.) (1985), Freedle (ed.) (1977), Scinto (1982); **Reading, Interpretation**: Eco (1979), Fish (1980), Iser (1978), Meyer (1983), Spiro, Bruce and Brewer (eds) (1980).

**Aspects of the construction and the functional settings of texts in different disciplines**: in *Semiotics*: Eco (1976) and (1979); in *Linguistics*: de Beaugrande (ed.) (1980), Daneš (ed.) (1974), van Dijk (1972), van Dijk and Petöfi (eds) (1977), Harris (1963), Hawkes (1977), Longacre (ed.) (1970) and (1984), Petöfi and Rieser (eds) (1973), Pike (1967); in *Rhetorics*: Gray (1977), Kinneavy (1980), Valesio (1980); in *Poetics and Stylistics*: van Dijk (1972), Dillon (1981), Jakobson (1981), Ringbom (ed.) (1975); in *Cognitive Psychology*: van Dijk and Kintsch (1983), Freedle (ed.) (1977), Johnson-Laird (1983), Spiro, Bruce and Brewer (eds) (1980); in *Sociology of Communication*: Sanches and Blount (eds) (1975), Saville-Troike (1982), Whiteman (ed.) (1981); in *Artificial Intelligence Research*: Charniak and Wilks (eds) (1976), Metzing (ed.) (1979), Spiro, Bruce and Brewer (eds) (1980).
**Textology and Teaching**: Coulthard, Brazil and John (eds) (1979), Kinneavy (1980), Kohonen and Enkvist (eds) (1978).

*The text analysed and literature on it.*

Carroll, Lewis (1982) *Alice's Adventures in Wonderland* and *Through the Looking-Glass and What Alice Found There*, Oxford University Press, Oxford.
Hockett, C.F. (1958) *A Course in Modern Linguistics*, Macmillan, New York, especially 262 ff.
Sutherland, R.D. (1970) *Language and Lewis Carroll*, Mouton, The Hague.

# BIBLIOGRAPHIES

*Linguistic Bibliography/Bibliographie Linguistiques*, (1939–) Comité International Permanent des Linguistes, Nijhoff, The Hague; since 1976 with section 2.3 'Text linguistics (Discourse Analysis)'.
Tannacito, D.J. (1981) *Discourse Studies: A Multidisciplinary Bibliography of Research on Text, Discourse, and Prose Writing*, Imprint Series, Indiana University Press, Ind.
Thorndyke, P.W. (1978) *Research on Connected Discourse: Structure, Comprehension and Memory. A General Bibliography: 1900–1977*, P–6131, Stanford University, Stanford.

*Surveys*

Charolles, J., Petöfi, J.S. and Sözer, E. (eds) (1986) *Research in Text Connexity and Text Coherence. A Survey*, Buske, Hamburg.
Dressler, W. (ed.) (1978) *Current Trends in Textlinguistics*, W. de Gruyter, Berlin.
Freedle, R.O. (ed.) (1979) *New Directions in Discourse Processing*, Ablex, Norwood, N.J.
Petöfi, J.S. (1986a) 'Text, Discourse', in Sebeok, Th.A., (ed.) *Encyclopedic Dictionary of Semiotics*, Mouton de Gruyter, Berlin, 1080–87 (+ Bibliography).
Petöfi, J.S. (1986b) 'Report: European Research in Semiotic Textology. A historical, thematic, and bibliographical guide', *Folia Linguistica 20*: 545–71.
Rieser, H. (1981) 'On the development of text grammar', in Dorfmüller-Karpusa, K. and Petöfi, J.S. (eds) *Text, Kontext, Interpretation. Einige Aspekte der texttheoretischen Forschung*, Buske, Hamburg: 317–54.

## Periodicals and series

*Advances in Discourse Processes*, (1977–) ed. by Freedle, R.O., Ablex, Norwood, NJ.

*Discourse Processes. A Multidisciplinary Journal*, (1978–) ed. by Freedle, R.O., Ablex, Norwood, NJ.

*Discourse analysis monographs*, (1979–), University of Birmingham, English Language Research/ELR/, Birmingham.

*Papiere zur Textlinguistik/Papers in Textlinguistics*, (1972-) ed. by Ihwe, J., Petöfi, J.S. and Rieser, H., Buske, Hamburg.

*Research in Text Theory/Untersuchungen zur Texttheorie*, (1977–) ed. by Petöfi, J.S., W. de Gruyter, Berlin.

*Text. An Interdisciplinary Journal for the Study of Discourse*, (1980–) ed. by van Dijk, T.A., Mouton, The Hague.

*Written Communication: A Quarterly Journal of Research, Theory, and Application*, (1984–) ed. by Daly, J. and Witte, S., Sage, Beverly Hills.

*Written Communication Annual. An International Survey of Research and Theory*, (1986–) ed. by Cooper, C.R. and Greenbaum, S. Sage, Beverly Hills.

## Introductions

de Beaugrande, R. (1980) *Text, Discourse, and Process. Toward a Multidisciplinary Science of Texts*, Ablex, Norwood, NJ.

de Beaugrande, R.-A. and Dressler, W.U. (1981) *Introduction to Text Linguistics*, Longman, London.

Brown, G. and Yule, G. (1983) *Discourse Analysis*, Cambridge University Press, Cambridge.

van Dijk, T.A. (ed.) (1985) *Handbook of Discourse Analysis*, 1–4, Academic Press, London.

Hartmann, R.R.K. (1980) *Contrastive Textology. Comparative discourse analysis in applied linguistics*, Julius Groos, Heidelberg.

Hoey, M. (1983) *On the Surface of Discourse*, George Allen & Unwin, London.

## Readers and Monographs

Allén, S. (ed.) (1982) *Text Processing. Test Analysis and Generation, Text Typology and Attribution. Proceedings of Nobel Symposium*, 51, Almqvist & Wiksell International, Stockholm.

Ballmer, T. (ed.) (1985) *Linguistic Dynamics. Discourses, Procedures and Evolution*, W. de Gruyter, Berlin.

Beach, R. and L. Bridwell (eds) (1984) *New Directions in Composition Research*, Guilford, New York.

de Beaugrande, R. (ed.) (1980) *European Approaches to the Study of Text and Discourse* (= *Discourse Processes*, Vol. 3. Number 4), Ablex, Norwood, NJ.

de Beaugrande, R. (1984) *Text Production. Towards a Science of Composition*, Ablex, Norwood, NJ.

Charniak, E. and Wilks, Y. (eds) (1976) *Computational Semantics: An Introduction to Artificial Intelligence and Natural Language Communication*, North Holland, Amsterdam.

Cooper, C.R. and Greenbaum, S., (eds) (1986) *Studying Writing: Linguistic Approaches*, Sage, Beverly Hills.

Coulthard, M., Brazil, D. and Johns, C., (eds) (1979) *Discourse, Intonation and Language Teaching*, Longman, London.

Coulthard, R.M. and Montgomery, M.M., (eds) (1981) *Studies in Discourse Analysis*, Routledge & Kegan Paul, London.

Crothers, E.J. (1979) *Paragraph Structure Inference*, Ablex, Norwood, NJ.

Daneš, F. (ed.) (1974) *Papers on Functional Sentence Perspective*, Academie, Prague.

van Dijk, T.A. (1972) *Some Aspects of Text Grammars: A Study in Theoretical Linguistics and Poetics*, Mouton, The Hague.

van Dijk, T.A. (1977) *Text and Context. Explorations in the Semantics and Pragmatics of Discourse*, Longman, London.

van Dijk, T.A. (1979) *Macro-Structures*, Erlbaum, Hillsdale, NJ.

van Dijk, T.A. (1981) *Studies in the Pragmatics of Discourse*, Mouton, The Hague.

van Dijk, T.A. and Kintsch, W. (1983) *Strategies of Discourse Comprehension*, Academic Press, New York.

van Dijk, T.A. and Petöfi, J.S., (eds) (1977) *Grammars and Descriptions (Studies in Text Theory and Text Analysis)*, W. de Gruyter, Berlin.

Dillon, G.L. (1981) *Constructing Texts, Elements of a Theory of Composition and Style*, Indiana University Press, Bloomington, Ind.

Eco, U. (1976) *A Theory of Semiotics*, Indiana University Press, Bloomington, Ind.

Eco, U. (1979) *The Role of the Reader. Explorations in the Semiotics of Texts*, Indiana University Press, Bloomington. Ind.

Eikmeyer, H.-J. and Rieser, H., (eds) (1981) *Words, Worlds, and Contexts. New Approaches in Word Semantics*, W. de Gruyter, Berlin.

Enkvist, N.E. (ed.) (1982) *Impromptu Speech: A Symposium*, Akademi, Åbo.

—— (ed.) (1985) *Coherence and Composition: A Symposium*, Akademi, Åbo.

Enkvist, N.E. and Kohonen, V. (eds) (1976). *Reports in Text Linguistics: Approaches to Word Order*, Akademi, Åbo.

Fahlmann, S. (1979) *A System for Representing and Using Real-World Knowledge*, MIT Press, Boston.

Fish, S. (1980) *Is There a Text in This Class?* Harvard University Press, Cambridge, Mass.

Freedle, R.O. (ed.) (1977) *Discourse Production and Comprehension*, Ablex, Norwood, NJ.

Gazdar, G. (1979) *Pragmatics: Implicature, Presupposition and Logical Form*, Academic Press, New York.

Genot, G. (1979) *Elements of Narrativics. Grammar in Narrative, Narrative in Grammar*, Buske, Hamburg.

Gibbon, D. and Richter, H., (eds) (1984) *Intonation, Accent and Rhythm. Studies in Discourse Phonology*, W. de Gruyter, Berlin.

Givón, T. (ed.) (1983) *Topic Continuity in Discourse: A quantitative cross-language study*, New York.

Givón, T. (ed.) (1983) *Topic Continuity in Discourse: A quantitative cross-language study*, Benjamins, Amsterdam.

Goodman, N. (1978) *Ways of Worldmaking*, Harvester Press, Hassocks, Sussex.

Gray, G. (1977) *The Grammatical Foundations of Rhetoric. Discourse Analysis*, Mouton , The Hague.

Grimes, J.E. (1975) *The Thread of Discourse*, Mouton, The Hague.

Gutwinsky, W. (1976) *Cohesion in Literary Texts*, Mouton, The Hague.

Halliday, M.A.K. and Hasan, R. (1976) *Cohesion in English*, Longman, London.

Harris, Z.S. (1963) *Discourse Analysis Reprints*, Mouton, The Hague.

Hawkes, T. (1977) *Structuralism and Semiotics*, Methuen, London.

Hinds, J. (ed.) (1978) *Anaphora in Discourse*, Linguistic Research Inc., Edmonton.

Hopper, P.J. (1982) *Tense-Aspect: Between Semantics and Pragmatics*, Benjamins, Amsterdam.

Iser, W. (1978) *The Act of Reading*, Johns Hopkins University Press, Baltimore, Md.

Jakobson, R. (1981) *Roman Jakobson Selected Writings III. Poetry of Grammar and Grammar of Poetry*. ed. with a preface by S. Rudy, Mouton, The Hague.

Johnson-Laird, P.N. (1983) *Mental Models. Towards a Cognitive Science of Language Inference and Consciousness*, Cambridge University Press, Cambridge.

Jones, L.K. (1977) *Theme in Expository Discourse*, Jupiter Press, Lake Bluff.

Kinneavy, J.L. (1980) *A Theory of Discourse* (2nd edn), Norton, New York.

Kohonen, V. and Enkvist, N.-E. (eds) (1978) *Text Linguistics, Cognitive Learning and Language Teaching*, Akademi, Åbo.

Korpimies, L. (1983) *A Linguistic Approach to the Analysis of a Dramatic Text*, University of Jyväskylä, Jyväskylä.

Li, C.N. (ed.) (1976) *Subject and Topic*, Academic Press, New York.

Longacre, R.E. (ed.) (1970) *Discourse, Paragraph, and Sentence Structure in Selected Philippine Languages* 3 vols, the Summer Institute of Linguistics, Santa Ana, Calif.

Longacre, R.E. (ed.) (1984) *Theory and Application in Processing Texts in non-Indo-European Languages*, Buske, Hamburg.

Metzing, D. (ed.) (1979) *Frame Conceptions and Text Understanding*, W. de Gruyter, Berlin.

Meyer, M. (1983) *Meaning and Reading. A Philosophical Essay on Language and Literature*, Benjamins, Amsterdam.

Neubauer, F. (ed.) (1983) *Coherence in Natural Language Texts*, Buske, Hamburg.

Nystrand, M. (ed.) (1982) *What Writers Know: The Language, Process, and Structure of Written Discourse*, Academic Press, London.

Nystrand, M. (1986) *The Structure of Written Communication. Studies in Reciprocity between Writers and Readers*, Academic Press, London.

Ortony, A. (ed.) (1979) *Metaphor and Thought*, Cambridge University Press, Cambridge.

Östman, J.-O. (ed.) (1978) *Cohesion and Semantics*, Akademi, Åbo.

Petöfi, J.S. (ed.) (1979) *Text vs. Sentence. Basic Questions of Text Linguistics* 2 vols., Buske, Hamburg.

Petöfi, J.S. (ed.) (1981) *Text vs. Sentence, Continued*, Buske, Hamburg.

Petöfi, J.S. (ed.) (1983) *Methodological aspects of discourse processing* (= *Text 3—1*), Mouton, Berlin.

Petöfi, J.S. (ed.) (1985) *Text Connectedness from Psychological Point of View*, Buske, Hamburg.

Petöfi, J.S. (ed.) (1987) *Text and Discourse Constitution. Empirical Aspects, Theoretical Approaches*, W. de Gruyter, Berlin.

Petöfi, J.S. and Rieser, H. (eds) (1973) *Studies in Text Grammar*, Riedel, Dordrecht.

Petöfi, J.S. and Sözer, E., (eds) (1983) *Micro and Macro Connexity of Texts*, Buske, Hamburg.

Pike, K.L. (1967) *Language in Relation to a Unified Theory of Human Behavior*, Mouton, The Hague.

Prince, A. (1973) *A Grammar of Stories*, Mouton, The Hague.

Propp, V. (1968) *Morphology of the Folktale*, Texas University Press, Austin.

Ringbom, H. (ed.) (1975) *Style and Text: Studies Presented to Nils Enkvist*, Skriptor, Stockholm.

Sanches, M. and Blount, B.G., (eds) (1975) *Sociocultural Dimension of Language Use*, Academic Press, New York.

Saville-Troike, M. (1982) *The Ethnography of Communication: An Introduction*, Blackwell, Oxford.

Schank, R.C. and Abelson, R.P., (1977) *Scripts, Plans, Goals, and Understanding: An Inquiry into Human Knowledge Structures*, Erlbaum, Hillsdale, NJ.

Scinto, L.F.M. (1982) *The Acquisition of Functional Composition Strategies for Text*, Buske, Hamburg.

Sebeok, T.A. (ed.) (1978) *Sight, Sound and Sense*, Indiana University Press, Bloomington, Ind.

Sözer, E. (ed.) (1985) *Text Connexity, Text Coherence. Aspects, Methods, Results* Buske, Hamburg.

Spiro, R.J., Bruce, B.C. and Brewer, W.F. (eds) (1980) *Theoretical Issues in Reading Comprehension: Perspectives from Cognitive Psychology, Linguistics, Artificial Intelligence, and Education*, Erlbaum, Hillsdale, NJ.

Tannen, D. (ed.) (1982) *Spoken and Written Language: Exploring Orality and Literacy*, Ablex, Norwood, NJ.

Tannen, D. (ed.) (1984) *Coherence in Spoken and Written Discourse*, Ablex, Norwood, NJ.

Valesio, P. (1980) *Novantiqua. Rhetorics as a Contemporary Theory*, Indiana University Press, Bloomington, Ind.

Velde, R.G. van de (1984) *Prolegomena to Inferential Discourse Processing*, Benjamins, Amsterdam.

Werth, P. (1976) 'Roman Jakobson's Verbal Analysis of Poetry', *Journal of Linguistics*, 12,: 21–73.

Werth, P. (1984) *Focus, Coherence and Emphasis*, Croom Helm, London.

Whiteman, M.F. (ed.) (1981) *Writing: The Nature, Development, and Teaching of Written Communication. Volume 1. Variation in Writing: Functional and Linguistic-Cultural Differences*, Erlbaum, Hillsdale, NJ.

## SOME SUGGESTIONS FOR FURTHER READING

The following works are suggested as a reasonably immediate continuation for enlarging the picture the reader has received from the present article:

The second volume of the *Handbook of Discourse Analysis* (in the subsection 'Introductions' in the References), *Dimensions of Discourse*, provides a rather detailed survey of the aspects of the research object 'text'. The first volume of this Handbook (*Disciplines of Discourse*) presents a good survey of the text-specific problems/methods of the disciplines involved in text research. What the reader will not find in this Handbook is a presentation of text-construction and the functional settings of texts which could serve as a common basis for the individual studies. Thus an integration of the partial pictures has to be attempted by the reader himself.

Concerning the aspects of *written communication* in its narrower sense the following books are useful surveys: Cooper and Greenbaum (eds) (1986), Kinneavy (1980), Nystrand (ed.) (1982), in the subsection 'Readers and Monographs' in the References.

The following two bibliographical surveys provide detailed information about textological research reaching beyond literature written in English: Petöfi (1986a), (1986b), in the subsection 'Surveys' in the references.

# 8

---

# LANGUAGE AS A SPOKEN MEDIUM: CONVERSATION AND INTERACTION

## MARION OWEN

## 1. INTRODUCTION

Spontaneous, spoken interaction is of interest to a wide range of disciplines. From a linguistic point of view it is the archetypal use of language, in which all of us acquire our first language, and many properties of language must be accounted for with reference to it. Sociologists, similarly, are interested in conversation simply because so much of our everyday lives is conducted through the medium of speech. Computational linguists use machines to model language understanding and production. We shall be examining in detail all these three perspectives in the course of this chapter. Others who have taken a more specialised interest in conversation include social and clinical psychologists, psychotherapists, educationalists and teacher trainers. It is therefore only to be expected that there is no unified theory of conversation that can be put together from these varied approaches, and this chapter reflects that diversity. We begin, however, with some general observations.

### 1.1. Spoken and written language use

Let us begin by stepping back temporarily from consideration of spoken interaction, and look at the ways in which spoken and written language differ.

(1) Speech is ephemeral. The fact that when processing speech the hearer cannot whenever he chooses stop the flow of production and search the records to check on some interpretation, and that participants have no record of conversations to take away with them means that speakers have to monitor hearers' understanding as they go along, and that hearers

provide evidence not just that they have heard, but that they have understood. Like some of the other generalisations I am making here, this is not true in all possible circumstances – speech is not ephemeral if it is tape-recorded – but it remains true in 'normal' circumstances.

(2) Speech is planned over units of less than a sentence in length. Speakers do not always produce complete grammatical sentences that would look acceptable if written down in every detail; as part of the monitoring process just mentioned, for example, a speaker may detect a failure to understand on the part of his addressee, and may therefore break off and rephrase his utterance, or offer additional explanatory material. Production failures – an inability to 'find the right word', or to remember a name – may result in hesitations or 'filled pauses' (ums and ers). The boundaries of planning units may be indicated by pauses, though not always in obvious ways (Butterworth 1980). It should not be taken for granted that apparent 'failures' in fluency or 'correctness' are all in fact errors. In the first place, we should not allow conscious criteria of what is correct for written usage to be carried over without modification to our consideration of spoken language. And secondly, apparent failures may turn out to be produced deliberately, or exploited for certain conversational effects. Albert (1972) describes how, among the Burundi of Central Africa, the appropriate form of speech for a peasant speaking to his caste superior is 'haltingly delivered [and] uncontrolled, [his] words and sentences clumsy' (1972: 78).

(3) Speech relies heavily on the context of utterance for its interpretation. Indeed, it is not so much that speakers *may* rely on the context, to save effort, as it were, but rather that they *must* rely on it, if unwanted implicatures are not to be generated. The context of utterance includes knowledge already known to be shared by speaker and hearer; if A wishes to refer to his sister, Jane, and B is a friend of Jane, were A to refer to *my sister*, and not to *Jane*, B would probably conclude that A has another sister, or that A does not know that B knows Jane. Also part of the context of utterance, of course, are objects in the surroundings, which are typically referred to by pronouns rather than descriptive expressions. The reader may discover for himself that this is so by noting how in radio drama, the playwright has to identify something the characters are looking at in a way that sounds natural, but is sufficiently informative to the listener at home; this is extremely difficult to do, and often results in unnatural modes of expression.

(4) Less complex syntactic structures are used in speech than in writing. This relates to the second point, since speakers have to express their thoughts as they produce them and in such a way that will be reasonably easy for the addressee to process. Concepts that in writing would be

expressed by passive sentences and relative clauses tend to be 'unpacked' and conveyed bit by bit in a more linear fashion. Crystal (1980) and Brown and Yule (1983: 14–19) enumerate the syntactic features of spontaneous speech and provide further references. These last two points taken together – the reliance on context and the use of linear rather than hierarchical sentence structures – mean that we could describe speech as making heavier use of the pragmatic aspects of language, rather than the syntactic.

It has been pointed out (by Givón, 1979) that these differences correlate with each other and with other contrasts in language and language use, giving the following set of dichotomies:

| | |
|---|---|
| unplanned $<->$ planned | (Ochs 1979) |
| child language $<->$ adult language | (Ochs 1979) |
| pidgins $<->$ creoles | (Sankoff & Brown 1976) |
| pragmatic organisation $<->$ syntactic organisation | (Sankoff & Brown 1976) |
| informal styles $<->$ formal styles | |

Many scholars have pointed to additional differences between spoken and written language (recent treatments include Givón 1979, Tannen 1982, and Redeker 1984), but many of these can be regarded as contingent rather than necessary. Most of them can ultimately be derived from the ephemerality of the speech signal and the rapidity of speech production, which give rise to demands on both speaker and hearer. Speakers generally produce their utterances in such a way that the hearer will be able to process them in 'real time'; and speakers know what the demands on hearers are, since they themselves are hearers too.

## 1.2 How to approach the study of conversation

The following remarks are intended to warn the reader against a very natural inclination, that of looking at a transcription of a conversation as if it were some kind of object, jointly produced by the participants; an object that can be inspected, turned around and examined from different angles. Brown and Yule (1983: 23–5) describe this as the 'product', as opposed to the 'process' view of discourse and conversation.

It is the 'product' view of conversation that leads some scholars to treat conversations in exactly the same way as monologues, even written monologues. Van Dijk, for example, writes:

Those utterances that can be assigned textual structure are thus acceptable discourses of the languages . . . In this way we disregard the possibility of dialogue-discourse, i.e.

a sequence of utterances by different speakers, but it may be assumed that such a sequence also may have textual structure similar to that of (monologue-)discourse. (1977: 3)

It is to contrast with this perspective that I have stressed the ephemerality of speech: when people converse, they talk, and then they part company: they do not have a transcription to take away with them. They are, we assume, changed: they have learnt things about their co-participant or the world in general; they may have succeeded in all or some of their goals. They may have made arrangements to go to the cinema or to get a divorce, or one participant may have bought a box of matches from the other. Even if every word spoken or heard is forgotten, something has been achieved, but that achievement is not the manufacture of an object: most transcriptions of conversation that linguists or sociologists study would look bizarre to the participants. This fact should be borne in mind whenever one studies a transcription.

## 1.3 Perspectives

In this chapter we shall be examining three different perspectives on spoken interaction. The first of these, conversation analysis, is the chief method of a school of sociology – ethnomethodology – which is rather different from mainstream sociology. Whereas linguistic discourse analysis is usually concerned to *assign* labels to stretches of speech, and then to write rules combining the labelled units into larger, hierarchical structures, conversation analysts do not make it a priority to assign structure to the whole of a piece of data in this way, though they are interested in large-scale organising principles such as topics, and large-scale conversational units such as stories. Those who work from this point of view study only spontaneous spoken dialogue – hence the use of the term 'conversation' – and pay particularly close attention to details of speech production and timing, which, for them, provide the underpinning for an account of conversational structure.

The second approach, discourse analysis, is the one that has arisen most directly from linguistics, and whose methods therefore most closely resemble those of theoretical syntax and phonology. This resemblance lies in the search for a *grammar* of conversation and in a reliance, for those whose work lies closest to linguistic pragmatics, on intuitions as a source of data. Some discourse analysts advocate a unified approach – at least at the most abstract level – to the study of both literary texts and transcriptions of spontaneous conversation, and the choice of the term 'discourse' is intended to reflect this neutrality. Fillmore, for example, adopts the term 'text'

to designate any whole product of human linguistic capacity, including . . . words and tone groups at the narrow end of its scope, novels and bodies of law at the wide end (1985: 11).

Chapter 7, above, describes this approach.

The third approach, the computational modelling of conversation, is motivated for some researchers by the practical requirements of computer systems that are designed to stimulate an interaction in natural language, rather than some computer programming language, and which may be entered at a keyboard or some other input device, and not spoken. Nevertheless, as in computational linguistics generally, a serious attempt to formalise the procedures and knowledge utilised by a computer model of speakers and hearers raises important theoretical issues, but issues that are often rather different from those encountered when discourse is viewed either from a more conventionally linguistic or from a sociological viewpoint.

It is important to remember that although for most of this chapter we shall be concerned with spoken language, it is quite possible for spontaneous interaction to take place without speech. One medium for non-spoken face-to-face interaction is genuinely 'conversational', in the sense that it is used in a wide range of contexts and for the normal range of conversational purposes, and that is the sign-language used by the deaf. This has the special feature that the production of signs by one signer does not 'blot out' the reception of signs produced by another person in the way that speaking, to a large extent, prevents the simultaneous reception of speech. There will be, nevertheless, psychological limits on how much can be processed and understood during production, and for this reason alone, as well as in its own right, sign language conversation would be worthy of study. However, it falls outside the scope of this chapter (as well as presenting special transcription problems), and the reader is referred to the works mentioned in the Further Reading section and to Chapter 21, below.

Dialogues with computers may also not involve speech. There are so many aspects to the complex problem of man-machine dialogue that for research purposes these have to be treated separately, and the interpretation of conversational contributions is usually based on written input from a keyboard. As research in this field matures, however, it will become necessary to consider seriously in what ways the properties of spontaneous dialogue derive from the fact that until very recently, and for all but a minority of speakers, conversation is conducted through the medium of speech.

## 2. CONVERSATION ANALYSIS

### 2.1 The origins of conversation analysis

Conversation analysis – the detailed analysis of conversational data, usually in the form of written transcriptions – is one of the chief techniques used in a school of sociology known as ethnomethodology. To understand why this is so it is necessary to look briefly at the motivations that led to the foundation of this way of looking at society.

Ethnomethodology owes its origins to the insights of one person, the American sociologist Harold Garfinkel, who in the early 1950s was studying tape recordings of discussions in jury rooms, during which jurors attempted to reach their decisions. He began to focus on issues that had until then been taken for granted by participants and sociologists alike: common-sense questions such as what is taken to be true as opposed to matters of opinion, what is relevant evidence, and so on. Garfinkel realised that these matters amount to a substantial body of knowledge which can be thought of as a set of interpretive strategies used by individuals in order not only to structure and make sense of their world but also actually to create it. Garfinkel saw the sociologist's task as the making explicit of these strategies. Hence the use of the term ethnomethodology – the *methods* used by *people* to build the social world in which they live. The methods used by the sociologist should then merely be explicit versions of the methods used by ordinary people. Ethnomethodology is an approach to sociology which sees power and control in social life as devolved, in the sense that individuals are not seen as merely observing rules or fitting into categories that are imposed on them by 'society' from without or above, but as building their own rules and categories as they go along. Broad-scale sociological categories such as class, education, and religion must be reinterpreted as created by the members of a society, and if they are valid categories, then evidence for their existence must be sought in the minutiae of everyday life.

Since most of the interaction we have with others is conducted through speech, attention came to be focused on conversation, especially ordinary everyday conversation. The pioneers in this work were Harvey Sacks and Emmanuel Schegloff, joined a little later by Gail Jefferson. Many of the classic papers in conversation analysis were written by one or more of these three collaborators, though Sack's major contribution is under-represented in print owing to his tragic early death in a car accident in 1975. The lectures he gave at the University of California from the late 1960s until his death were, fortunately, tape-recorded and subsequently transcribed by Gail Jefferson. Although they have remained unpublished, copies have been quite widely circulated around sympathetic sociology and linguistics departments in Europe as well as North America, and single lectures have been edited for publication.

## 2.2 The significance of structure

### 2.2.1 'Orderliness'

The approach taken by conversation analysis to spoken interaction is distinguished by a close attention to certain aspects of conversation often left unattended by other scholars. Ethnomethodologists like to refer to the *orderliness* of conversation: as Schegloff and Sacks put it,

If the materials (records of natural conversations) were orderly, they were so because they had been methodically produced by members of the society for one another . . . our analysis has sought to explicate the ways in which the materials are produced by members in orderly ways that exhibit their orderliness and have their orderliness appreciated and used. (1973; 290)

In other words, orderliness is not something to be imposed by the analyst, like a grid through which the data is viewed, rather, the orderliness is produced by the participants themselves, and is the essence of conversational interaction. Conversation analysts thus replace our conscious intuition that conversation – especially 'casual chat' – is a random, unstructured kind of activity, with the view that in the course of co-ordinating their contributions, speakers collaborate to produce something which can be seen to be highly structured. It is also central to the ethnomethodological point of view that that structure cannot be discovered by introspection or controlled experimentation, but only through the close study of spontaneous – in their terminology, 'naturally-occurring' – conversation. In addition, although it is often argued, by linguistically-orientated discourse analysts in particular, that the place to start is with the more highly organised talk (in the sense that its order is imposed partly by formal rules) to be found in classrooms, interviews and law-courts, ethnomethodologists have worked primarily with informal, unplanned data. 'Classic' and widely used collections, examples from which turn up in many published papers, include group therapy sessions for teenagers in California, and a series of telephone conversations between members of a group of women friends in Northern England. Nevertheless, some conversation analysts have turned to more overtly constrained data such as that used in courts and tribunals (see, especially, Atkinson and Drew 1979).

### 2.2.2 Data collection and transcription

Before we pursue the question of orderliness in more detail, it is appropriate to look at the methodology of conversational analysis, particularly the policies adopted for representing data. As we have just said, most of the data consists of informal conversation, and much of it comes from telephone conversations:

this has the advantage that an audio tape-recording preserves all the signals that were available to the participants at the time. It is also technically easy, by attaching a microphone to the receiver, to record a telephone conversation, and the participants do not move away, whereas for face-to-face recording, both the positioning of the microphone and controlling the tape are problematic. More recently, some conversation analysts, notably Charles Goodwin (e.g. Goodwin 1981), have used video recordings, but gestures, facial expressions and body movements are much harder to represent as discrete units for notation than speech, even when, as in the case of deaf sign language, they actually *are* discrete units. Video-recorded data presents such daunting problems of categorisation and description that most analysts have continued to work on the vocal output only.

Linguists have often been critical of the notation used in conversational analysis, and some of their criticisms are justified. In particular, intonation is not represented in systematic detail: no distinction is made between rising and falling-rising nuclei and both are indicated by a question mark at the end of the phrase. (We have chosen, for the sake of readability, to adopt a very simple notation in this chapter.) It is of course true that notations such as that used by O'Connor and Arnold (1973) have been devised for a particular accent of English, Received Pronunciation, and would not be appropriate for the American varieties of English that form much of the data used by conversational analysis. But it is fair to say that in conversational analysis, no systematic attention is paid to accent or dialect differences: major collections of data such as those I have mentioned come from both sides of the Atlantic and are used freely by analysts from both communities. In their defence, conversation analysts would argue that since they are looking for the structure that is actually displayed in the data itself, it is therefore not necessary to be a member of the community to which the participants belong. Conversation analysts have also pointed out that few linguists (there are exceptions, of course) have taken the trouble to show how what they wish to represent can be adapted to the needs of conversational analysis. Nevertheless, as Eleanor Ochs has remarked: 'transcription is a selective process reflecting theoretical goals and decisions' (1979: 44). The debate is thus not so much about techniques for representation as about underlying, often not fully articulated, theories of conversation and discourse.

## 2.2.3 *Utterance sequencing and turn-taking*

Apart from its data-centred approach, the most distinctive feature of conversational analysis is the way the interpretation of utterances, their sequencing, and the demands of the turn-taking system are all integrated into a single perspective. This is in contrast to linguistic speech-act theory, which starts by attempting to define criteria for assigning act-descriptions to utterances, and regards the building of utterances into sequences as – analytically speaking – a separate task for description.

In spite of a general lack of interest on the part of linguists in conversational analysis, the seminal paper on turn-taking (Sacks, Schegloff and Jefferson 1974) was published in the journal *Language*. It starts from the observation that turn-taking systems operate in many contexts, not just in conversation, and all involve the co-ordination of some activity which requires, ideally, that only one person engages in it at a time. This is clearly true of speaking, since if two people speak at once, it is hard for each to hear and understand what the other is saying (that simultaneous speech occurs much more than usual in heated arguments is only to be expected, since a desire to listen and understand is not characteristic of such interactions). Whereas some turn-taking systems – card games, for example, and the alternation between the members of each pair in table tennis doubles – depend on overt rules, no such rules appear to exist for conversation, and yet the amount of overlapping talk is very little indeed; speaker-change regularly occurs with startling precision. How, then, is this done?

Crucial to the functioning of conversational turn-taking is what Sacks, Schegloff and Jefferson call the 'turn-constructional component'. This is a unit that is quite easy to get a feel for intuitively, but hard to define: Sacks, Schegloff and Jefferson state that:

There are various unit-types with which a speaker may set out to construct a turn. Unit-types for English include sentential, clausal, phrasal, and lexical constructions. (Sacks, Schegloff and Jefferson 1974: 702)

It has been proposed recently (Power and Dal Martello 1985) that Sperber and Wilson's Relevance Theory (see Chapter 6, section 8) could provide a basis for identifying what Sachs, Schegloff and Jefferson call 'transition relevance places':

It seems quite likely that the duration of the speaking turn is governed by the requirement that the speaker must be permitted to establish the relevance of what he is saying. In terms of Sperber and Wilson's definition, this would mean that transition-relevance places would occur at points where the hearer was able to derive pragmatic implications from the semantic content that had so far been presented.

The details of how Relevance Theory might be applied to conversation analysis remain to be worked out, though an explanation along these lines has an attractive generality. It is enough for us, here, to say that when a speaker starts his turn, hearers are given some idea, which becomes clearer as the turn proceeds, of what kind of contribution is being made, and of what it will take to complete the turn. A hearer thus knows when it will be appropriate for him to take the floor. The following extract shows how this can contribute to an instance of overlap, where the turn-taking system briefly breaks down:

(1)  1    B:  Sorry I didn't make it on Friday: I was

                                    [

      2    A:                       It's a shame!

      3         (0.7)

      4    B:  absolutely stricken down with food poisoning!

Assuming A's intention in line 2 is not to take the floor from B and hold it in order to make a longer contribution of her own, we can account for the interruption which nevertheless does take place by recognising the first part of line 1 as constituting an apology which could well have stood as a complete utterance. By its commencing with a highly conventionalised opening for an apology, A can reasonably expect B's turn to be complete when the apology is complete. However, many apologies consist only of the word *sorry*, so how is it that A does not commence her response at that point? The Relevance Theory explanation would suggest that until B has stated what he is apologising for, the relevance of his utterance is not evident to B. Once the relevance of the apology *is* established, A produces a sympathetic response; B, however, continues simultaneously with an account for his absence, with the result that the two utterances overlap. Note also how quickly B abandons his hold on the floor, until A's contribution is recognisably complete, only resuming – continuing the sentence he had begun in 1 – after a pause has indicated that A does not intend to continue speaking.

### 2.2.4 Adjacency pairs

There are many regularly-occurring conversational contexts in which the perception of transition-relevance places is straightforward, and it is on these that most analysis has concentrated. In this way the other problematic analytic step, that of how utterance units are identified and interpreted as performing one speech act rather than another, is also, even if only temporarily, avoided. These relatively straightforward chunks of conversation are referred to as *adjacency pairs* by conversation analysts. Adjacency pairs are discussed in the turn-taking paper (Sacks, Schegloff and Jefferson 1974), and in greater detail in another important paper by Schegloff and Sacks (1973). There, they define adjacency pairs as sequences of two utterances, produced by two different speakers, in which

given the recognizable production of a first pair part, on its first possible completion its speaker should stop and a next speaker should start and produce a second pair part from the pair type of which the first is recognizably a member. (1973: 296)

Thus, for example, if A speaks to B and produces what is recognisably an invitation, B should speak and produce a recognisable acception or rejection.

It is important to appreciate what is being said here, since Schegloff and Sacks's statement suggests a grammatical model according to which failure to produce a second pair part, or the production of an inappropriate second part, will result in an 'ill-formed' sequence. What they have in fact in mind is the powerful inference-generating capacity of the slot following a first pair part. Almost anything B says in the slot following A's invitation will be interpreted by A as a response of some sort to that invitation. Only as a last resort will A conclude, perhaps, that B misheard or misunderstood. Conversation analysts call this sequential property 'conditional relevance' (Schegloff 1972: 363–9). The following example shows this inference-generation in action:

(2a) 1    A: I wonder if you can charge it to my department,
    2      at the university, who will pay for it
    3      (0.2)
    4      If you can't I'll write you a cheque
    5    B: yeah, well, they're extremely good discount prices

In lines 1 and 2, A makes a request. The short pause in 3 already implicates a refusal by B, and A offers to retreat. Given A's production of a request, an acceptance or rejection – the appropriate alternative second pair-parts – remain conditionally relevant: that is, anything heard in the appropriate slot will be interpreted as a second pair-part if at all possible. Only in these sequential terms can we account for the relevance of B's utterance 5, which is interpretable as implying rejection. That this is so is confirmed by the way the conversation develops: it continues for a few turns with the participants discussing the price. Eventually, A makes a direct offer:

(2b) 11    A: would you rather I wrote a cheque?
    12    B: yeah. You got a card I suppose, a banker's card?
    13    A: yes, I have, yes.
    14    B: yes, I think so in this case.

B accepts the offer, in line 14 (after a 'side'-sequence: see below for discussion of these) following a brief indication of acceptance in line 12.

Extract (2b) illustrates another feature of adjacency pairs: it is not essential for the two parts to be adjacent. Line 11 expresses an offer, to which there is a provisional response in line 12, but to which the main response occurs in line 14. After 11, the conditional relevance of the offer remains in force while another pair – question and answer – the content of which bears on the response B will give to the offer, is completed. Once A has answered B's question, an answer to the offer becomes immediately relevant again, though there is no limit, in principle, to the number of pairs that can be inserted in this way, and indeed, pairs can be inserted into pairs that are themselves inserted. Sequences of such complexity are, however, rare. Jefferson calls these insertions 'side-sequences' (1972), and describes many types, including those dealing with mishearings and misunderstandings, requests for clarification, repeats expressing surprise, and correction sequences.

As we have seen, there are many distinct adjacency pairs that can be recognised in conversation: questions and answers, offers and acceptances/rejections, apologies and their responses, compliments and acknowledgements. It is true that conversations do not consist simply of chains of adjacency pairs, but 'conversation' is something on which it is very difficult to gain an analytical handle; discourse analysts do this by starting with the more overtly constrained types of discourse: conversation analysts achieve a similar end by starting at the points in their data where utterances can most easily be identified as performing specific acts, and working 'out' from there.

It is in their accounts of adjacency pairs that conversation analysts offer their best challenge, though a limited challenge, to speech-act theory. Speech-act theory (on which see Chapter 6, above) demands that it must be possible to specify rules relating utterances to contexts so that, for example, we can (informally) identify an utterance as an invitation if the speaker proposes that the hearer do something which is assumed to be something the hearer would like to do and which involves some effort on the part of the speaker. This we can identify – even out of context – utterances such as 'Would you like to come round for dinner?' as invitations. Of course, claiming that we can interpret such an utterance 'out of context' is misleading, since what is happening here is that, firstly, the utterance itself contains deictic clues to its interpretation (it explicitly mentions the addressee(s) – *you* – and uses the verb *come*), and secondly, we can supply the necessary knowledge that going to dinner with someone is generally taken to be an enjoyable experience. Nevertheless, given this information, speech act theory seems to be capable of handling such utterances. But what can it do with the response? Not much help will be given by its form: 'Yes, please', for instance. Clearly, it is the conversational positioning of the utterance that is the strongest factor in its interpretation. Now there is no reason why speech act theory should not permit the act-status of the prior utterance to be specified as one of the conditions for interpretation, though in fact this will not work in all cases, since if a side-sequence intervenes, the invitation to which the utterance is a response may not have occurred in the immediately prior turn.

Even if we could successfully 'bolt on' some conditions concerning sequencing to the rules by which speech-act theory constrains the assignment of acts to utterances, this would still be, from the ethnomethodological point of view, to look at the problem from entirely the wrong direction. Speech act approaches to the contextualised interpretation of utterances proceed by first imagining a decontextualised utterance and only then considering what remaining ambiguities may be cleared up by supplying a context. As Schegloff puts it:

> Taking sentences in isolation is not just a matter of taking such sentences that might appear *in* a context *out* of the context; but that the very composition, construction, assemblage of the sentences is predicated by their speakers on the place in which it is being produced, and it is through *that* that a sentence is context-bound, rather than possibly independent sentences being different intact objects in or out of context. (1984: 52)

However, it can then be argued that although it makes sense to identify a second pair-part such as a response to an invitation by its occurrence following a first pair-part, this only postpones the problem, since we are left with the problem of identifying the first pair-part itself. Some are relatively easy, since as we have already pointed out, certain acts carry their identity on their sleeve, and most can be performed using conventionalised expressions that identify the intended function. An inspection of any more extended stretch of conversation, however, will reveal how difficult it is, first to break up the talk into units, and then to assign each of these to some speech act. This is the 'utterance-to-act' assignment problem described by Levinson (1983) and Gazdar (1981).

### 2.2.5 *Breakdowns in turn-taking, and their conversational consequences.*

We have already seen how overlap may occur between turns when the second speaker perceives the first as having completed his contribution, and especially when, as in example (1), the first speaker has produced the first pair-part of an adjacency pair. Overlap may also occur even when a speaker intends only a single conversational move, but when he uses an address term, as in (3), or a tag, as in (4):

(3)  1   A:   well then it was *her* fault Claire
                          [
    2   B:                             Yeah she said one
    3        no trump
                              (Sacks, Schegloff and Jefferson 1974: 704)

(4)  1   A:   well I guess she's been working pretty steadily,
    2        hasn't she
               [
    3   B:   Yeah, she's been working pretty steady
                            (Sacks, Schegloff and Jefferson 1974: 722)

What these turn-final elements achieve, Sacks, Schegloff and Jefferson point out, is a recycling of the turn-allocation rules, producing two transition-relevance places, the second of which unequivocally marks the end of a turn: consider how awkward it is for the current speaker to continue if no response is produced after one of these items. Frequently, however, as in the above examples, the addressee recognises the first transition-relevance place and enters at that point.

In addition to overlaps, pauses may occur between turns. If a pause occurs immediately after a clear transition-relevance place – if B, for example, fails to produce a response when A's invitation is complete – the silence that ensues is not just 'silence'; it is 'B's silence'. To illustrate the conversational implications of this, consider the following data:

(5)  1   C:   well you can both stay
     2        (0.4)
     3   C:   got plenty of room
          [
     4   B:   oh I . . .

(6)  1   A:   come on down here, it's okay
     2        (0.2)
     3   A:   I got lotta stuff, I got beer an' stuff

(Davidson 1984: 105)

In each of these examples, the first turn contains an invitation; a pause then ensues and the first speaker continues, giving supporting reasons for the recipient to accept the invitation. In other words, a brief breakdown in the smooth transition between speakers results in a recognisable pattern:

A:   INVITATION
     PAUSE
A:   REASONS FOR RECIPIENT TO ACCEPT INVITATION

where the pause is attributable to B, given a strong transition-relevance place at the end of the invitation. Such a pattern will surely strike a familiar note, but why should it re-occur in this way? Conversation analysis often has the interesting effect of making something routine into a curiosity demanding explanation. In this case, why is it that a failure to respond promptly is taken to imply a rejection, leading to the first speaker offering additional reasons for acceptance? Conversation analysts, especially Davidson, in the paper from which these examples are taken, and Pomerantz (1978, 1984), have called this phenomenon 'preference', arguing that for the slot following, in this instance, an invitation, there are only two broad alternatives – acceptance and rejection – and that there is a 'preference' for acceptance. Acceptances are typically produced as soon as the invitation is complete, so that failure to produce the acceptance immediately is taken to imply rejection. Thus a silence is not only attributable to a particular speaker, but also implies one conversational act rather than another. The next example shows a similar pattern:

(7) 1   A:  I don't know whether it makes for happiness to join,
   2         belong to a union, but I think you've got more say
   3         in what goes on
   4         (2.4)
   5   A:  I don't know really
   6   B:  I don't really know, no
   7   A:  it's a debatable point

In this example, A presents an opinion in lines 1–3, creating a slot for an agreement or a disagreement. For this slot, agreement is the preferred alternative; the long pause in 4 indicates a withholding of agreement by B, leading to a withdrawal by A from her earlier position: this withdrawal is the counterpart of the renewed invitation in examples (5) and (6). In line 6 B is able to show agreement with A's second, neutral, point of view.

It is stressed by writers who have proposed the notion of preference that an actual mental disposition in, say, the recipient of an invitation, is not what they intend by their use of the term. Clearly we do not always 'prefer' to accept. The observation that is being made is that, regardless of our actual inclinations, we 'do' acceptance and rejection in different ways: whereas acceptances follow immediately on the completion of the invitation, rejections occur after a pause (or after other hesitation phenomenon such as 'filled pauses'). Conversation analysts attempt to avoid any speculation into what is 'really' going on in participants' minds, and shun explanations that go beyond purely structural observations: in this case, having identified certain types of acts in a given sequence, we can observe pauses between one pair of acts and not between another.

However, it is not essential to draw the analytical boundary at this point. That would be to propose that the set of dispreferred second pair-parts had nothing in common other than their distribution. But why do they share the same distribution? A general account can in fact be offered that does not require us to make a psychological speculation into the state of mind of an individual at a particular time. This account rests on the notion of 'face', originally proposed by the sociologist Erving Goffman and developed in detail, in its linguistic manifestations, by Brown and Levinson (1987). Briefly, face is a property possessed by each of us which can only be fully maintained by the actions of others (though it is also essential to maintain our own face by behaving with appropriate decorum). It is therefore in everyone's interest to act so as to maintain the face of others, in the knowledge that he is dependent on those others to maintain his own. Face is thus a property of people living together in society, rather than something about their own personal make-up;

even the least altruistic individuals generally act so as to preserve and enhance others' face.

Now, it is not hard to see why accepting an invitation rather than rejecting it preserves the face of the inviter, and thus why, whether we are obliged to reject or whether we simply wish to do so for our own 'selfish' reasons, we go about doing rejections in ways that enact reluctance. Such ways naturally include not rejecting instantly, but displaying evidence of reflection, and thus pausing before rejecting.

### 2.2.6 Openings and closings

Much of our social life, then, consists of spoken interaction with others. Conversational analysis focuses on the turn-taking system used by speakers to control this process. It remains to consider how it is that this usually very smooth sequencing of utterances is initiated, and how it is closed down, since the condition of talking to person A about topic B is not something that can merely be started 'out of the blue', nor can it simply stop. Like much work in conversational analysis, most work on openings and closings, including the classic papers by Schegloff (1968) and Schegloff and Sacks (1973), is concerned with telephone conversations. Apart from the advantages already mentioned, these have the property that the duration of talk is the same as the duration of 'co-presence': the channel is only opened, and kept open, when there is talk to be done.

Schegloff (1968) begins with an apparent puzzle: at the opening of telephone calls, the 'answerer' speaks first. This is less of a puzzle when we realise that the initiating contribution is non-linguistic: it is the ring of the bell. The bell and the answerer's words are merely a special case of an adjacency pair – summons/answer – in which both parts are normally spoken. Schegloff then notes that having completed a summons/answer pair, the ball is back in the caller's park and it is required that he speak next: he cannot remain silent. Furthermore, he has established his own obligation to listen to what the answerer has to say, and in this way, a 'state of talk' has been established, and the turn-taking system set up, simply through the ring of the telephone bell and the answerer's response. What happens next allows for some variation: by some means, the caller has to identify himself, and introduce his main reason for calling (telephone calls require such a reason, and if one does not really exist, the caller needs to account for this by saying, for example, 'I just rang for a chat'). Before the introduction of this topic, other routine enquiries may be made – about the health of the speakers, very commmonly – which may themselves develop into full topics, displacing the 'reason for calling'. Nevertheless, however successful the participants may be at discovering such unplanned-for topics, it is still incumbent upon the caller to produce the 'official' reason for the call. Otherwise, even though a half-hour conversation may have been enjoyed, the recipient will put the phone down wondering 'why did he call?'.

The following extract illustrates some of these features:

(8)  1  A:  double six two five eight
     2  B:  Marina, hello, it's Paul
                       [
     3  A:            oh hi Paul
                       [
     4  B:               hi
     5  A:  how did the, er, thing with the solicitor go
     6  B:  it went fine (I I)
                     [
     7  A:            oh good
     8  B:  thanks. I'll tell you about it (in fact)
                              [
     9  A:                      yes
    10  B:  er I was ringing for two things
    11  A:  yes
            [
    12  B:  one to say er I hear we've got a very generous
    13      invitation

The recognition and greeting sequence in lines 2–4 is worthy of discussion in its own right, but for reasons of space we must refer the reader to Schegloff (1979). In line 5 the recipient of the call produces the first topic, initiating a four-part exchange: Query – Response (with good news) – Response to news – Thanks. B could at this point allow this topic to develop, but he explicitly postpones it in order to state his 'official' reason for calling. In fact, there are two such reasons in this case, and it is noteworthy that when a caller has more than one reason, he will state this at the beginning, since otherwise the assumption is that there is only one, and introducing the second topic becomes difficult.

Once the opening section, typically including identifications, greetings and routine health enquiries, is complete, then, the caller moves on to the reason for calling. This topic may provide the basis for the main 'body' of the call, but somehow, 'topic talk' has to be brought to an end and the conversation closed. This is particularly crucial in the case of telephone conversation since once the channel is closed, the whole procedure has to be gone through again. It is simply not open to speakers to stop talking and hang up. This much may seem obvious, but what is less obvious is that it is equally impossible to come to the end of a topic, exchange farewells, and then hang up. A proper closing sequence has to take place, the purpose of which appears to be for both speakers to establish that the other has no new topics to introduce. Only then can the farewell sequence take place. The following example runs from the closure of the last topic in a conversation to its end:

(9) 1 A: how did your rowing go?
2 B all right. it's er (.) good having (.) not
3 having done anything for a week it's quite
4 energetic hhh
5 A: yes.
6 B: still, anyway, never mind
7 A: yes
8 B: OK
9 A: OK. I'll ring you at the weekend.
10 B: right, yes, have a nice week then.
11 A: OK Anne
12 B: right. see you.
13 A: see you
      [
14 B:   bye mum
        [
15 A:     bye
16 B: bye bye
17 A: bye

In line 1 A introduces what will turn out to be the last topic in the conversation. After B's response, A responds in turn with a move that acknowledges what B has said but adds nothing new. Such utterances effectively propose topic closure; B continues with an utterance which in turn adds little that is new, thereby accepting A's proposal, and in line 7 the topic is finally closed. Lines 8 and 9 contain a pre-closing pair – more strictly, a 'possible' pre-closing, since such pairs, whose function is to say 'I have no more new topics and will close the conversation if you have nothing new', frequently lead to further topic talk – which lead on to a common feature of closing sections, a mention of the next meeting. After conventional good wishes, the goodbye sequence – a four-part one in this example – is reached. The very sketchy analysis will be sufficient, I hope, to indicate that closings are done in such a way as to bring topic talk – the 'body' of the conversation – to an end while providing a slot for further topics to be introduced, if there are any.

### 2.3 Conclusions

Conversation analysis offers a way of looking at conversation that, while strongly motivated by the view that talk is structured, does not impose any overall categorisation on it. 'Accounting for all the data', something which is, as we have seen, important to many linguistic discourse analysts, is not a high priority for conversation analysis. Rather, the strategy has been to examine closely certain act-types that are readily identifiable, or certain conversational phases such as openings, and to explore the orderliness that is revealed by careful analysis. An overriding concern is to approach the data with as few preconceptions as possible, and certainly to avoid imposing external categorisation, for fear of becoming blind to the richness of the data.

## 3. DISCOURSE ANALYSIS

### 3.1 Discourse structure and 'well-formedness'

It is not controversial to claim that one of the central aims of the linguistic description of a language is to account for

(1) Which sequences of words are well-formed.
(2) How well-formed sentences can be analysed into chunks, with the largest chunks further segmentable into smaller units, and so on until the word level is reached.
(3) How words fall into distinct classes, each class having different formal and distributional properties.
(4) The distributional potential within a sentence of each phrase-type.

Many, perhaps most, linguists regard the sentence as the upper limit for analysis of this type. However, the aim of syntactic and semantic description is, in principle at least, to account for the distribution and interpretation of each word in the language, and therefore, some would argue, it is essential to extend linguistic analysis 'above' the sentence level. Those who claim that larger units are amenable to linguistic description in exactly the same way as sentences hold what we shall call the 'strong' version of the linguistic approach to discourse. Others see linguistic ideas and methodology as transferable into the domain of discourse and conversation, and this we call the 'weak' version of the linguistic approach. But for those who hold these assumptions, whether in their strong or weak form, three questions arise:

(1) What are the units of conversation and discourse? That is, what are the counterparts of syntactic word classes such as nouns and verbs to which we must refer in our explanation?
(2) What are the rules for combining these units into larger structures? Are they purely linear or do they form a hierarchy?
(3) Do speakers have similar intuitions about the well-formedness of

discourses that they do about sentences? For all the difficulties associated with the notion of grammaticality, it is easy to find strings that are syntactically ill-formed, even if they 'make sense'; can ill-formed discourses or conversations be similarly identified?

## 3.2 A 'linguistic' approach to discourse

The previous chapter, on text grammar, described the work of those who support the grammatical view of discourse and conversation most strongly. Van Dijk, for example, has said that 'those utterances which can be assigned textual structure are thus acceptable discourses of the language' (1977: 3). The text grammarians are, however, predominantly concerned with written texts; written language certainly forms the basis for their theories. Some have argued that discourse is a genuinely *linguistic* level of description analogous to phonology and syntax, but this strict view is not shared by those whose views we describe in more detail in this chapter, nor by Petöfi (see Chapter 7, above), who makes it clear that a description of text structure must incorporate non-linguistic information.

Many linguists working within the tagmemic tradition (see Chafe (1965) for an outline) also share the view that discourse should be studied in ways essentially the same as those used for syntax, especially Grimes (1975) and Longacre, who states (writing of extended monologues, especially folk tales):

discourse has grammatical structure [which] is partially expressed in the hierarchical breakdown of discourses into constituent embedded discourses and paragraphs and in the breakdown of paragraphs into constituent embedded paragraphs and sentences. (1979: 115)

Longacre is speaking of oral monologue, and goes on to make it clear that he is not thinking of paragraphs as orthographic units, though it is no doubt the case that when such monologues are written down, the writer may make orthographic paragraph divisions that parallel the spoken structure. Longacre and his colleagues have studied traditional monologues in a great variety of languages, and find that there are frequently conventionalised words and expressions used to demarcate thematically distinct discourse segments. For their full linguistic description, therefore, reference must be made to units larger than sentences. For Longacre, this is sufficient evidence that grammar itself extends beyond the sentence.

## 3.3 Discourse rules

Another American linguist, best known for his work on sociolinguistic variables, who also proposes the strong 'grammatical' view of discourse, is

William Labov (1972, 1977), on whom see Chapter 14, below. Labov was initially motivated by a desire to portray the verbal skills of black adolescents, who in the formal school context appeared almost tongue-tied but in their own social groups turned out to display great expertise in ritual verbal games known as 'sounding' and 'playing the dozens'. (In the years since Labov published this work, the value placed on verbal performance in the black communities in North America and elsewhere has become much more generally recognised through the popularity of 'rapping' disc jockeys who use the same rhyming, rhythmic patterns as the boys on the New York streets.)

In his 1972 paper 'Rules for Ritual Insults' Labov states the fundamental principle of his approach to discourse analysis:

There is a small number of sentence types from a grammatical viewpoint . . . and these must be related by discourse rules to the much larger set of actions done with words . . . [These rules] are complex; the major task of discourse analysis is to analyze them, and thus to show that one sentence follows another in a coherent way. (1972: 121)

Labov is thus claiming that *acts*, not *sentences*, are the units in terms of which discourse structure must be described: a sequence of sentences can only be seen as coherent once the mapping from sentences into acts is carried out. Labov believes (Labov and Fanshel 1977: 110) that having constructed such a set of rules relating utterances to actions, the task of writing sequencing rules is relatively simple.

A major component in Labov's interpretive rules is the distinction between A-events, B-events, and AB-events. In a two-party conversation, A-events are those that A has particular knowledge of; B-events are those that B has particular knowledge of and AB-events are known to both. (It is not essential, for an event to be an A-event, that B is entirely ignorant of it.) As an example of a rule of interpretation, Labov proposes that 'If A makes a statement about a B-event, it is heard as a request for confirmation' (1972: 124). Thus if A is interviewing B for a job, and remarks 'You are 38 years old', he is requesting B to confirm that he is indeed 38 years old. On the other hand, if A says 'We are looking for an experienced sales manager', he is making a statement about an A event, and is therefore performing some other act. In the context of 'sounding', however, the rule is different. Labov's rules for the interpretation of insults as *ritual* insults, which should then be responded to using the special forms appropriate to the insult exchange and not as if they were intended literally, include the knowledge that the content of the insult cannot in fact be true. An insult such as 'Your mother a duck!', for example, must be interpreted by the addressee as an invitation to play the game and produce a counter-insult displaying greater virtuosity; if he responds otherwise, by denying the charge, he will be regarded as a less than fully competent member of the peer group. In such situations, therefore, A makes a statement about a B-event, but the appropriate response is not a confirmation of the truth of the claim.

Labov elaborated his framework for discourse analysis in a later work with David Fanshel (Labov and Fanshel 1977), in which a highly detailed analysis of the opening minutes of a therapy interview is presented. The aim was to get behind the surface form of utterances to the level of *action*, to describe 'what is really going on'. Consistent with his belief that what the discourse analyst has to specify is the *knowledge* employed by speakers that enables them to recover what is meant from what is said, Labov specifies not only a set of interpretive rules, but also a substantial amount of background knowledge about the participants (especially the client). The conversation is then studied in depth, a fragment at a time, each utterance being glossed and expanded as exhaustively as possible. This method requires that the analysis of data can be undertaken only if, as far as possible, all the background knowledge available to the participants at the time is also available to the analyst: a condition that is impossible to meet in full. Contrast with this the ethnomethodological approach in which appeals to intuitions about 'what is really going on' are regarded as illegitimate, and in which only those features of the conversation that participants 'orientate to' can be brought into the analysis. So, for example, speakers can be shown to 'orientate to' the asymmetry between preferred and dispreferred alternatives by the different ways in which they produce them – with or without pauses, hesitation phenomena, and so on. Maintaining this stance strictly is extremely difficult, but if it can be achieved it legitimises analysis of data the only knowledge of which the analyst has is the tape-recording.

Another major difference between discourse and conversation analysis is that the former appeals to a notion of discourse well-formedness (though many working within this framework recognise the problems with this, cf. Stubbs (1981)). If there are recognisable discourse acts which may be combined only in certain ways, then combining acts in other ways will result in an 'ungrammatical' discourse. Examples of these are hard to construct; Labov and Fanshel, however, propose that the following actually-occurring dialogue, from a psychiatric interview, is an instance:

(10) Doctor:  What is your name?
     Patient:  Well, let's say you might have thought you had something from before, but you haven't got it anymore.
     Doctor:  I'm going to call you Don.

(Labov and Fanshel 1977: 2)

The patient's response is certainly difficult to read as a meaningful response to the doctor's question. However, its oddity is not so much that it is, in conversation-analytical terms, the 'wrong' second pair-part – as if, for example, it were a greeting – but that it conveys no information that would enable the questioner either to infer an answer or to infer that the patient is declining to answer. It is not so much that the patient's utterance is the wrong type of act, since it could function as an answer in another context but rather that it could only be an answer to a different question. The notion of discourse well-formedness seems suspect if we have to look at the productions of a mentally sick speaker to find an example. All normal individuals regularly produce syntactically ill-formed utterances, but if a conversational contribution seems not to be appropriately addressed to the prior utterance, we place an interpretation on it if we possibly can, and only as a last resort conclude that the speaker misheard, not that he has an imperfect command of conversational practices.

Levinson (1983) provides an example (taken from a lecture given by Sacks in 1968) of an exchange which seems equally ill-formed.

(11)  A:  I have a fourteen year old son
      B:  Well that's all right
      A:  I also have a dog
      B:  Oh I'm sorry

(Levinson 1983: 292)

This is hard to make sense of – why should B apparently apologise, or express regret that A has a dog? – until we learn that it forms part of a conversation in which A is enquiring about her eligibility to rent a flat; in this context, a fourteen-year-old boy and a dog can be understood as members of a relevant set: possible disqualifications as a tenant. One lesson to be learnt from such examples is that while it may not be necessary to have a lot of background knowledge in order to study a conversation, it is advisable to have the complete conversation.

The issue of well-formedness for discourses does not arise within ethno-methodological discourse analysis, since so much more emphasis is placed on the contribution that the positioning of utterances makes to their interpretation; it therefore makes no sense to talk of conversational acts out of context, since a fragment of language use is not an act unless it has a context. This is in strong contrast to Labov's view that once the rules mapping utterances into acts have been constructed, little is left for the analyst to do.

## 3.4 Coverage and levels of description in discourse

Discourse analysis also differs from conversation analysis in that – as with the grammatical description of a sentence – an account is considered inadequate if it does not 'cover all the data'. That is, given a framework – a set of acts to which utterances must be assigned, and some sequencing rules for those acts – and a piece of data, it must be possible to fit the data into the framework without anything left unaccounted for and without stretching the interpretive rules too much. Coverage in this sense has never been a priority for conversation analysts, who prefer to focus on just those sections of dialogue that display the features they are currently interested in.

Coverage, or comprehensiveness, is one of the criteria for a system of discourse analysis set out by John Sinclair and his colleagues from Birmingham University in the UK. He sets out four criteria (1973; also Sinclair and Coulthard 1975: 15–17):

(1) the descriptive system should be finite (a limited vocabulary of acts or other higher-level units),
(2) the terms in the system should be precisely relatable to their exponents in the data (cf. Labov's interpretive rules),
(3) the descriptive system should be comprehensive, and
(4) there must be at least one impossible combination of symbols.

It is the last criterion that places Sinclair and his colleagues firmly in the 'linguistic' camp; they explicitly ally themselves with Halliday's (1961) type of analysis which rests on the notions of a *rank scale*, in which units at one rank of analysis are *realised* by units at the next rank down (Sinclair and Coulthard 1975: 20). Thus, on the broadest level, units of syntax are realised by morphological units. (Halliday's analysis does not go 'below' this level, but in principle there is no reason why it should not be extended to a phonological level, which in turn can be related to the physical reality of utterances.) Just as in syntax, however, the difficulties lie in the relation between the second and fourth criteria; it is one thing to say that a question may not be followed by a greeting, but people are adept at somehow placing interpretations on responses which allow them to be heard as coherent. A further problem arises from the fact that utterances do not necessarily perform only one act at a time; this idea is familiar from speech act theory – one act may be performed 'indirectly' via the performance of another – but a single level of acts is generally assumed not only by discourse analysts but by conversation analysts too.

The analytic system proposed by Sinclair and his colleagues (notably Coulthard and Brazil) has, naturally enough, been modified since it was first set out in 1975. Then, some of the analysis was tailored to the type of data – classroom interaction – being studied at the time. In particular, 'lesson' was proposed as the largest unit, though a lesson was not necessarily regarded as filling the entire period during which the teacher was with the pupils. In the following extract, for example, the teacher spends some ten minutes at the beginning of the period finding out from pupils where they have been for university interviews: he speaks to each pupil individually, though not privately. When the lesson itself begins, the boundary is very clearly marked:

(12)  1  T:  Alison?
      2  P1:  erm, I've been to Birmingham for an interview
      3      [inaudible exchange between teacher and pupil]
      4  T:  [louder] right (2.5) your (1.0) complete undivided
      5      attention.
      6      (9.0)
      7  T:  right.
      8  T:  these questions. erm, first question. explain
      9      why an experiment to determine acceleration
     10      due to gravity . . .

The teacher indicates by speaking louder that he is now addressing the whole class, and by the use of a marker (*right*) and an explicit demand for their attention, followed by a long pause until he obtains it, demarcates the start of the 'lesson' very clearly. Other types of interaction may be marked in similar ways: doctor-patient consultations, for example, may open with a greeting sequence in which the doctor may enquire about the patient's health in the way that any acquainted individuals do, and receive the answer 'Fine', since for this type of enquiry, a detailed and accurate description of the speaker's health is not expected. When the consultation begins, however, this is exactly what is required. Though the label 'lesson' may therefore not be appropriate for a linguistic level, it represents a unit which may occur in a variety of types of interaction.

'Lessons' are realised at the next level down by a series of 'transactions', which can more or less be regarded as topic units. Speakers characteristically demarcate the boundaries of transactions, like units at other levels, with intonational cues; although news broadcasts are not spontaneously produced, it may be observed that the reader typically marks a new item by raised pitch, the pitch then falling steadily through the item. It should be noted that this fall is superimposed on the intonation of individual sentences, and that intonation (studied especially by David Brazil) is regarded as crucial to the model proposed by Sinclair and his colleagues; here, however, limitations of space preclude discussion of it (see Coulthard 1977: Ch. 6; Brazil 1981).

Below 'transaction' is the level within which most analysis has been done, that of 'exchange'. In classroom discourse, distinctions may be made between *boundary* exchanges and *teaching* exchanges. These two types are then realised at the next level by sequences of *moves*: in the case of boundary exchanges, by two moves, *framing* and *focusing*, and in the case of teaching exchanges, by three moves, *opening*, *answering*, and *follow-up*. Moves are not, however, the smallest unit: they may be seen as structural slots defined largely by their position in the sequence, rather as the 'subject' slot, say, in an English active declarative sentence is typically the first position in the sentence. At the lowest level is the *act*, a unit similar to the speech act and including such examples as elicit, prompt, react, acknowledge, and evaluate. The following exchange illustrates the basic pattern:

|        |    |                          | Move       | Act      |
|--------|----|--------------------------|------------|----------|
| (13) 1 | T: | do you know what we mean | opening    | elicit   |
| 2      |    | by accent?               |            |          |
| 3      | P: | it's the way you talk.   | answering  | reply    |
| 4      | T: | the way we talk.         | follow-up  | accept   |
| 5      |    | this is a very broad     |            | evaluate |
| 6      |    | comment.                 |            |          |

(Sinclair and Coulthard 1975: 48)

The first two moves in this exchange are each realised by a single act, but the third, follow-up, is realised by two. In the publications of discourse analysts, many such perfectly plausible analyses are presented. However, the virtue of a well-defined system should be that it can be taken over and applied to new data without too many uncertainties, and all too often alternative analyses can be produced, with little seeming to hinge on the selection. The next example illustrates some of the problems. Here we attempt to apply the framework of Sinclair and Coulthard's discourse analysis to a new piece of data, using the vocabulary of acts in Burton (1981) and the exchange structure proposed by Stubbs (1981), in which *opening* has been replaced by *initiate*, *answering* by *respond*, and *follow-up* by *feedback*.

|        |    |                            | Move     | Act         |
|--------|----|----------------------------|----------|-------------|
| (14) 1 | A: | you've sold out of Listeners, | initiate | elicit   |
| 2      |    | have you?                  |          |             |
| 3      | B: | yes,                       | respond  | reply       |
| 4      |    | I'm terribly sorry, dear   |          | excuse      |
| 5      |    | we have.                   |          | reply       |
| 6      |    | Is there something special | initiate | elicit      |
| 7      |    | in it this week?           |          |             |
| 8      | A: | it's the Reith lectures    | respond  | informative |
| 9      | B: | oh, so that's it           | feedback | acknowledge |

We will begin by examining the exchange structure of the extract and the move status of each utterance. The analysis given above proposes that this extract contains two exchanges, the first consisting only of an initiating move and a responding move, the second containing, in addition, a feedback move.

However, Stubbs's (1981) proposals for exchange structure allow a contribution to be both predicted by the prior move, and predictive of the next one: he calls such moves *initiate/respond*. Lines 6–7 are clearly predictive, and this is why we have labelled them as *initiate*, but this does not capture the link between the two exchanges, so perhaps we should identify the item as an instance of *initiate/respond*. Perhaps lines 6–7 can then be regarded as belonging simultaneously to two exchanges, as part of the *reply* move in the first exchange, and as the *initiate* move of the second. My point is that an analysis is not forced by the data; more than one competing description can quite easily be found, and this serves to illustrate some of the descriptive problems that arise when this system is applied. It is perhaps unfair to use as an example a piece of non-classroom data, but this passage is quite tightly organised: it contains no very long turns, and is basically concerned with exchanging information.

The assignment of act labels to the utterances is equally uncertain. First, line 8 could be either an *informative* or a *reply*; indeed, the inclusion of *reply* in Burton's set of acts seems strange, since in general it is the purpose of the *move* level of description to capture the positional aspects of the unit, whereas on the act level, units should be capable of appearing in a variety of slots. Second, the sequence *reply — excuse — reply* also seems unsatisfactory, since it does not indicate that the reply to lines 1–2 is spread over lines 3 and 5, with the apology intervening.

For the four criteria of adequacy to be met, there should be a limited number of moves and acts which are combinable in a limited number of ways, and the process of utterance-to-act assignment should be straightforward, in most cases. Current sets of units have few members at the level of moves but very little restriction on how they may be combined. On the level of acts there are larger numbers, but even then it is not hard to find utterances for which no label, especially no *single* label, seems appropriate. Partly this is because in many cases utterances perform more than one act simultaneously, whereas for this type of analysis, we are forced to choose one.

Most of these problems arise from the belief that assigning act-labels to utterances can be performed, from the analyst's point of view at least, as a logically separate step, prior to the combination of acts into sequences. But as the ethnomethodologists have shown, real utterances cannot be extracted from their context, labelled, and then slotted back again. In addition, the labelling process seems to be regarded as an end in itself, as though, once one plausible analysis has been completed, with no part of any utterance unlabelled, with acts assigned to moves, and with moves combined into a valid sequence, the work of the discourse analyst has been done.

In conclusion, it cannot be maintained that discourse analysts have provided anything that approximates to a theory comparable in explicitness and predictive power to those that have been developed – at least in recent years – by syntacticians. Perhaps such a theory cannot exist (though we shall see in the next section that something like one is urgently needed), and it could therefore be argued that the function of discourse analysis is to generate insights that cannot be reached without a framework to guide description. I believe that the comparison of discourse analysis with conversation analysis shows that for the description of interaction between human beings (as opposed to man-machine interaction) the attempts to formalise described in this section tend more to obscure than to illuminate.

## 4. THE COMPUTATIONAL MODELLING OF DIALOGUE

At the time of writing, in the late 1980s, computer design is making major advances in both speed and memory capacity. As computers become capable of displaying human-like intelligence, their users, especially those who are not themselves computer professionals, expect to be able to communicate with machines in ways that are similar to those they use for communicating with their fellow human beings. Crucially, these modes of communication involve both speech and natural language.

However, it is unlikely that humans will ever want or expect to be able to engage computers in the full range of conversational behaviour. Until recently, the naïve image of a robot included a fully human appearance, but now that 'robots' are actually in use it is clear that mimicking human shape is only necessary to the extent that the task to be performed demands it. Grasping objects, for example, requires some kind of hand-like grasp, but fingernails are not called for. Similarly in the case of speech and language; if all we want a system to be able to do is to take in and give out factual information, some features of normal dialogue, such as what Brown and Levinson (1987) would call 'positive politeness', may be unnecessary. Indeed, on the assumption that the user knows it is a machine he is dealing with, and therefore also knows that at some stage its capacity to respond was determined by another human being, the user may regard apparent courtesy as contrived and ultimately irritating, reducing his inclination to use the system.

The term 'computational modelling of dialogue' (here, CMD) can refer to two things: the construction of models that will enable man-machine interaction in natural language, and the study of ordinary human interaction from a computational perspective, that is, making explicit statements about structures and realisation. In this section we shall not consider *spoken* man-machine dialogue, for two reasons: first, so much work has yet to be done for computer use of both speech and language that for research purposes these two domains are at present treated separately, and second, speech synthesis and recognition are substantial research fields in their own right and there is not space to do them justice here; but readers may consult Chapter 18, below.

### 4.1 What is required

Just as linguists and programmers need to provide the computer with models of syntax and semantics, so, one would suppose, it is also necessary to supply models of discourse and dialogue in order to account for the situated interpretation of utterances in conversational contexts. However, it will be evident to the reader from what has been presented so far in this chapter that discourse analysis, whether approached from the direction of sociology or linguistics, has not, as yet, delivered the sort of results required for computational modelling. In the first place, as those who engage in syntactic and semantic analysis would agree, it is one thing to produce a plausible description of a piece of data, and quite another to use that description as a basis for generating new data. Even a generative model is not necessarily a model of production, and indeed, most generative linguistics has stood well clear of what would be classed as 'performance'; it has frequently been argued that linguistic productions do not provide the right evidence for linguistic theories. In the second place, as we have seen, it is by no means clear that a well-defined 'grammar' of discourse can be constructed, since the notion of well-formedness may simply not apply in this domain.

It is striking how few references to the work of linguists or sociologists are made by those concerned with CMD. Perhaps the only body of linguistically-orientated work recognised extensively is the speech-act theory of Austin and Searle, and this can be regarded as philosophy, not linguistics as such. Reichman (1985: 9–10, and Ch. 9) makes reference both to the ethnomethodologists and to Halliday and Hasan's work (1976) on surface cohesion, and though in the case of ethnomethodology she recognises some common ground with her own 'context space' model, she claims that it is inadequate because it cannot handle hierarchical discourse structures; she rejects the cohesion approach on the grounds that it is restricted to surface linguistic phenomena. Reichman may overstate her case, but it remains true that CMD has not found from sociologists or linguists the kind of input it requires. To some extent this is only to be expected, since as the next section will argue, among the first things one discovers when attempting CMD is that large amounts of groundwork have to be done that are not genuinely linguistic at all.

### 4.2 Knowledge representation

The long-running debate about the boundaries between linguistic knowledge and knowledge of the world cannot be put aside if a machine is to be enabled to 'understand' an utterance. In the analysis of a conversation, a great deal of knowledge held by the analyst as well as the participants, even when they come from different cultures, will be used in the interpretation of utterances. All this knowledge has to be explicitly represented in the machine; one cannot therefore concentrate on the more strictly linguistic aspects of the model until this knowledge-base exists. Indeed, some (notably Morgan and Sellner 1980) argue that discourse structure is epiphenomenal: that apparent structure in discourse is merely a reflection of structure in the world or in the domain of conversation. Some work that is presented as concerned with discourse structure does seem to support this claim: Linde (1979), for example, shows how speakers' descriptions of their apartments correspond to the path that would be taken in showing a visitor round, and Grosz (1977, 1981) demonstrates that task-orientated dialogues display a structure that reflects the structure of the task itself.

The problem of knowledge representation can be made manageable for research purposes, and for some restricted applications by simplifying either the range of material to be interpreted (travel time-tables (Waltz and Goodman 1977), geological samples (Wood, Kaplan and Nash-Webber 1972), or an artificially-constructed 'blocks world' (Winograd 1973)), or the range of speech acts to be used (typically questions, answers and commands). For these restricted domains a grammatical model for conversation is all that can be currently conceived.

## 4.3  Recognising speech acts

A model of conversation that is impoverished by human standards may in fact be appropriate even in the long term for human-machine interaction. Politeness, interpreted narrowly as the use (by the system) of surface markers such as 'please', may not be required. Even in the light of Brown and Levinson's (1987) broader notion of politeness, a machine has no 'face' to be maintained, and it is probably irrelevant to demand that the machine contribute to maintaining the user's face.

Nevertheless, concern for 'face' extends beyond the surface forms of politeness, so that many face-preserving ways of performing acts such as requests are automatically done (by humans) 'off-record' (Brown and Levinson 1987: 69), that is, indirectly or by means of hints. If users expect or want to interact with machines in this way, we have to ensure that the machine has the resources for understanding their contributions: we must specify how utterances are to be related to acts. In addition, just because people are so accustomed to the use of 'indirect' speech acts (see Chapter 6, above) – to the extent that they are hardly regarded as indirect at all – it is important that the machine's responses are expressed in a similar way. Therefore, even if we can show that a complete account of discourse interpretation is impossible along these lines, explicit rules – very similar to the felicity conditions of speech act theory – must be written to express the relation between 'surface' and 'underlying' or 'indirect' acts. Cohen and Perrault (1979), for example, regard speech acts as part of a plan-based theory of action, and propose a formal interpretation of felicity conditions in the following format:

*REQUEST (SPEAKER, HEARER, ACT)*
CANDO. PR:    SPEAKER BELIEVE HEARER CANDO ACT AND
                     SPEAKER BELIEVE HEARER BELIEVE HEARER
                     CANDO ACT
WANT. PR:     SPEAKER BELIEVE SPEAKER WANT request-instance
EFFECT:        HEARER BELIEVE SPEAKER BELIEVE SPEAKER
                     WANT ACT

Cohen and Perrault then suggest that:

the relation between direct and indirect readings can be largely accounted for by considering the relationship between actions, their preconditions, effect, and bodies, and by modelling how language users can recognise plans, which may include speech acts, being executed by others.

Given a representation of each speech act, as above, there is no need, they suggest, for special 'conversational postulates' (Gordon and Lakoff 1975) to explain the interpretation of indirect speech acts. That is, it is not necessary to state that a question about the hearer's ability to perform an act may be intended as a request to perform that act, since such connections can be inferred on a more general basis. We need a theory of plans anyway, for non-linguistic inferencing, and that will do the work for us. Furthermore, as Allen and Perrault (1980) argue, it will do more than this: given the ability to recognise an interlocutor's plan, a speaker may offer additional information if he believes this will help the interlocutor in the execution of his plan. So, for example, if a traveller asks at the information booth in a station: 'When does the Montreal train leave?', the clerk may reply: '3.15 at gate 7' (Allen and Perrault 1980: 441); given what the traveller has revealed about his plans, the clerk has inferred that there may be other obstacles to the traveller achieving his goals, such as not knowing the gate number. The clerk then provides this information without being asked. Clearly there is a need to ensure that too much information is not given under such conditions, since this will then impose a tedious task of selection on the requester. This is a problem for the knowledge-base of the system: in particular, items must not be represented at too specific a level.

## 4.4 Interpreting referring expressions

A second, largely independent, problem in CMD is that of the assignment of referents to referring expressions such as pronouns and noun phrases. Some help with pronouns may be provided by number and gender, but even in a language such as German in which gender is not semantically-based, whether or not it helps in disambiguating a particular instance is purely contingent. Nevertheless, Hobbs (1978) shows that this approach can be surprisingly effective.

Grosz (1977: 2) presents the following dialogue:

(15)  1  A:  I'm going camping next weekend. Do you have a
      2      two-person tent I could borrow?
      3  B:  Sure. I have a two-person backpacking tent.
      4  A:  The last trip I was on there was a huge storm. It
      5      poured for two hours. I had a tent, but I got
      6      soaked anyway.
      7  B:  What kind of tent was it?
      8  A:  A tube tent.
      9  B:  Tube tents don't stand up well in a real storm.
     10  A:  True.
     11  B:  Where are you going on this trip?
     12  A:  Up in the Minarets.
     13  B:  Do you need any other equipment?
     14  A:  No.
     15  B:  OK. I'll bring the tent in tomorrow.

What has to be explained is how we know that the tent referred to in line 15 is the same as that of line 3, and distinct from that referred to in lines 5–8. How can this intuition be made explicit enough for machine representation? Grosz argues that in this dialogue there are two 'focus spaces', one embedded in the other, and that the 'discourse entities' referred to in these two spaces are stored in a type of stack. When the second space is activated in line 4, the focus space in which the first tent is referred to is 'pushed down' in the stack, and the new one stacked on top.

Any reference to a tent will now be taken as belonging to the new focus space. Mention of 'this trip' in line 11 'pops' the second focus space off the stack, reactivating the old one, so the tent mentioned in line 15 is taken to be B's tent, not the tube tent.

## 4.5 Using surface features

If we can make use of some of the surface features of what is said in conversation, it may enable us to reduce the amount of knowledge that has to be represented. Some resources, such as a user's inclusion of forms such as *please*, may mark a move as a request for action or information.

Kaplan (1981) has argued that more work than one might at first sight imagine can be done using what he calls *language-driven inference* rather than *domain-driven inference*. He illustrates this claim in his discussion of database queries such as

How many students got a grade F in CIS500 in Spring '77?
If, in fact, no students took course CIS500 in spring '77, or if the course was not even given in that term, the response 'None' would be strictly true, but very misleading. It is even more important than in the examples given by Allen and Perrault – in which the user knows he lacks some information, and can ask for it – that the system does not allow the user to go away with misconceptions. Kaplan argues that 'the linguistic structure of questions encodes considerable information about the presumptions that the questioner has made' (1981: 130); in the above example, the questioner presumes that some students did in fact take CIS500 in Spring '77, and in addition, therefore, that the course was given. If either of these presumptions fails, the system can answer appropriately by correcting the false presumption and saying, for example. 'No students took CIS500 that term'. Kaplan calls the inferences that can be drawn from the linguistic form of such a question 'language-driven', since, in his view, the lexical representation of the expression 'x get a grade y on course z' includes the information 'x took course z'. Work of this kind amounts to an attempt to formulate linguistic and philosophical theories of presupposition and implicature (Levinson 1983, Chs 3 and 4; cf. also Chapter 6 above).

## 5. FUTURE DEVELOPMENTS

It is to be hoped that in the near future ways will be found to derive properties of dialogue from general principles, as Brown and Levinson (1987) have done for politeness. They argue, for example, that we do not need to specify particular rules for individual speech acts if, on the basis of some property of speakers (in their case, 'face') we can predict the forms speech acts will take. Similarly, if a principle such as 'relevance' can be used to account for conversational coherence, then we need fewer specific rules, each of which would wastefully incorporate general principles. Whereas at present accounts of conversational structure and interpretation, and their machine implementations, tend to be tied to particular applications or types of dialogue, in the long term more general theories of conversation will be both more explanatory and more economical to implement as computer systems.

# REFERENCES

Albert, E.M. (1972) 'Cultural Patterning of Speech Behaviour in Burundi', in Gumperz and Hymes (eds) *Directions in Sociolinguistics*, Holt, Rinehart, New York: 72–105.

Allen, J.F. and Perrault, C.R. (1980) 'Analysing Intention in Utterances', *Artificial Intelligence*, 15: 143–78. Reprinted in Grosz, B.J. *et al.* (eds) (1986).

Atkinson, J.M. and Drew, P. (1979) *Order in Court*, Macmillan, London.

Atkinson, J.M. and Heritage, J. (1984) *Structures of Social Action: Studies in Conversational Analysis*, Cambridge University Press, Cambridge.

Brazil, D. (1981) 'The Place of Intonation in a Discourse Model', in Coulthard and Montgomery (eds): 146–57.

Brown, G. and Yule, G. (1983) *Discourse Analysis*, Cambridge University Press, Cambridge.

Brown, P. and Levinson, S.C. (1987) *Politeness: Some Universals in Language Usage*, Cambridge University Press, Cambridge.

Burton, D. (1981) 'Analysing Spoken Discourse', in Coulthard and Montgomery (eds): 61–81.

Butterworth, B. (1980) 'Evidence from Pauses in Speech', in Butterworth, B. (ed.) (1980) *Language Production: Speech and Talk*, Academic Press, New York: 155–76.

Chafe, W. (1965) Review of Longacre, R.E. (1964), *Grammar Discovery Procedures*, *Language*, 41: 640–7.

Cohen, P. and Perrault, C.R. (1979) 'Elements of a Plan-Based Theory of Speech Acts', *Cognitive Science*, 3 (3): 177–212. Reprinted in Grosz *et al.*, (eds) (1986): 423–40.

Coulthard, M. (1977) *An Introduction to Discourse Analysis*, Longman, London.

Coulthard, M. and Montgomery, M. (eds) (1981) *Studies in Discourse Analysis*, Routledge & Kegan Paul, London.

Crystal, D. (1980) 'Neglected grammatical factors in conversational English', in Greenbaum, S. *et al.*, (eds) *Studies in English Linguistics for Randolph Quirk*, Longman, London: 153–66.

Davidson, J. (1984) 'Subsequent versions of invitations, offers, requests, and proposals dealing with potential or actual rejection', in Atkinson, J.M. and Heritage, J. (eds): 102–28.

van Dijk, T. (1977) *Text and Context*, Longman, London.

van Dijk, T. (ed.) (1985) *Handbook of Discourse Analysis*, (four volumes), Academic Press, New York.

Fillmore, C. (1985) 'Linguistics as a Tool for Discourse Analysis', in van Dijk (ed.), Volume I: 11–40.

Gazdar, G. (1981) 'Speech Act Assignment', in Joshi, A.K., Webber, B.L. and Sag, I.A. (eds): 64–83.

Givón, T. (ed.) (1979b) *Syntax and Semantics Vol 12, Discourse and Syntax*, Academic Press, New York.

Givón, T. (ed.) (1979b) *Syntax and Semantics Vol 12, Discourse and Syntax*, Academic Press, New York.

Goodwin, C. (1981) *Conversational Organisation: Interaction between Speakers and Hearers*, Academic Press, New York.

Gordon, D. and Lakoff, G. (1975) 'Conversational Postulates', in Cole, P. and Morgan, J.L. (eds) *Syntax and Semantics Volume 3: Speech Acts*, Academic Press, New York: 83–106.

Grimes, J. (1975) *The Thread of Discourse*, Mouton, The Hague.

Grosz, B.J. (1977) *The Representation and Use of Focus in Dialogue Understanding*, Technical Note 151, SRI International, Menlo Park.

Grosz, B.J. (1981) 'Focus and Description in Natural Language Dialogues', in Joshi, A.K. *et al.*, (eds) (1981): 84–105.

Grosz, B.J., Sparck Jones, K. and Webber, B.L. (eds) (1986) *Readings in Natural Language Processing*, Kaufmann, Los Altos, Calif.

Halliday, M.A.K. (1961) 'Categories of the Theory of Grammar', *Word*, 17: 241–92.

Halliday, M.A.K. and Hasan, R. (1976) *Cohesion in English*, Longman, London.

Hobbs, J. (1978) 'Resolving Pronoun References', *Lingua*, 44: 311–38. Reprinted in Grosz B. *et al.*, (eds) (1986): 338–52.

Jefferson, G. (1972) 'Side Sequences', in Sudnow, D. (ed.); 294–338.

Joshi, A.K. Webber, B.L. and Sag, I.A. (eds) (1981) *Elements of Discourse Understanding*, Cambridge University Press, Cambridge.

Kaplan, S.J. (1981) 'Appropriate Responses to Inappropriate Questions', in Joshi, A.K. *et al.*, (eds) (1981): 127–44.

Labov, W. (1972) 'Rules for Ritual Insults', in Sudnow, D. (ed.): 120–69.

Labov, W and Fanshel, D. (1977) *Therapeutic Discourse: Psychotherapy as Conversation*, Academic Press, New York.

Levinson, S.C. (1979) 'Activity Types and Language', *Linguistics* 17, 5/6: 356–99.

Levinson, S.C. (1983) *Pragmatics*, Cambridge University Press, Cambridge.

Linde, C. (1979) 'Focus of Attention and the Choice of Pronouns in Discourse', in Givón T. (ed.) (1979b): 337–54.

Longacre, R.E. (1979) 'The Paragraph as a Grammatical Unit', in Givón, T. (ed.): 115–34.

Morgan, J. and Sellner, M. (1980) 'Discourse and Linguistic Theory', in Spiro, R., Bruce, B., and Brewer, W. (eds) *Theoretical Issues in Reading Comprehension*, Erlbaum, Hillsdale, NJ: 165–200.

O'Connor, J.D. and Arnold, G.F. (1973) *Intonation of Colloquial English*, Longman, London.

Ochs, E. (1979a) 'Transcription as Theory', in Ochs, E. and Schieffelin, B. (eds) (1979) *Developmental Pragmatics*, Academic Press, New York: 43–72.

Ochs, E. (1979b) 'Planned and Unplanned Discourse', in Givón, T. (ed.): 51–80.

Pomerantz, A.M. (1984) 'Agreeing and Disagreeing with Assessments: Some Features of Preferred/Dispreferred Turn Shapes', in Atkinson, J.M. and Heritage, J. (eds): 57–101.

—— (1984) 'Agreeing and Disagreeing with Assessments: Some Features of Preferred/Dispreferred Turn Shapes', in Atkinson, J.M. and Heritage, J. (eds): 57–101.

Power, R.J.D. and Dal Martello, M.F. (1985) 'Methods of Investigating Conversation', *Semiotica* 53, 1/3: 237–57.

Psathas, G. (ed.) (1979) *Everyday Language: Studies in Ethnomethodology*, Irvington, New York.

Redeker, G. (1984) 'On Differences between Spoken and Written Language', *Discourse Processes* 7: 43–55.

Reichman, R. (1985) *Getting Computers to Talk Like You and Me*, MIT Press, Cambridge, Mass.

Sacks, H., Schegloff, E.A. and Jefferson, G. (1974) 'A Simplest Systematics for the Organisation of Turn-Taking for Conversation', *Language*, 50: 696–735.

Schegloff, E.A. (1972) 'Sequencing in Conversational Openings', in Gumperz, J.J. and Hymes, D. (eds) *Directions in Sociolinguistics: The Ethnography of Communication*, Holt, Rinehart & Winston, New York: 346–80.

Schegloff, E.A. (1979) 'Identification and Recognition in Telephone Conversation Openings', in Psathas, G. (ed.): 23–78.

Schegloff, E.A. (1984) 'On Some Questions and Ambiguities in Conversation', in Atkinson, J.M. & Heritage, J. (eds): 28–52.

Schegloff, E.A. and Sacks, H. (1973) 'Opening up Closings', *Semiotica* 8: 289–327.

Schenkein, J.N. (ed.) (1978) *Studies in the Organisation of Conversational Interaction*, Academic Press, New York.

Schiffrin, D (1987) *Discourse Markers*, Cambridge University Press, Cambridge.

Sinclair, J. McH. (1973) 'Linguistics in Colleges of Education', *Dudley Journal of Education*: 17–25.

Sinclair, J. McH. and Coulthard, R.M. (1975) *Towards an Analysis of Discourse: The English Used by Teachers and Pupils*, Oxford University Press, Oxford.

Sperber, D. and Wilson, D. (1986) *Relevance*, Blackwell, Oxford.

Stubbs, M. (1981) 'Motivating Analyses of Exchange Structure', in Coulthard and Montgomery (eds) (1981): 107–19.

Stubbs, M. (1983) *Discourse Analysis: The Sociolinguistic Analysis of Natural Language*, Blackwell, Oxford.

Sudnow, D. (ed.) (1972) *Studies in Social Interaction*, Free Press, New York.

Tannen, D. (ed.) (1982) *Spoken and Written Language: Exploring Orality and Literacy*, Ablex, Norwood, NJ.

Waltz, D.L. and Goodman, B.A. (1977) 'Writing a Natural Language Data Base System', in *Proceedings of the International Joint Conference on Artificial Intelligence*, MIT Press, Cambridge, Mass: 144–50.

Winograd, T. (1973) 'A Procedural Model of Language Understanding', in Schank, R. and Colby, K. (eds) *Computer Models of Thought and Language*, Freeman, San Francisco: 152–86.

Woods, W.A., Kaplan, R.M. and Nash-Webber, B. (1972) *The Lunar Sciences Natural Language Information System: Final Report*, Bolt, Beranek and Newman Report No 2378, Cambridge, Mass.

## FURTHER READING

The best sources for further reading of a general nature in both conversation and discourse analysis are Brown and Yule (1983) and Stubbs (1983). Chapter 7 of the latter is concerned with discourse from Sinclair's perspective. Schiffrin (1987) presents a sensitive analysis of 'discourse markers' – expressions such as *well* and *you know* – which takes a broadly linguistic stance but is not tied to any specific formal model of discourse.

Levinson (1983: ch. 6) compares discourse analysis and conversation analysis – to the detriment of the former – and the chapter contains a valuable summary of ethnomethodological work on conversation. Partly because of its interdisciplinary nature, conversation analysis has never found a natural home in scholarly journals, and for this reason, several collections of papers have been published in which most of the seminal papers appear. The most recent of these collections is Atkinson and Heritage (1984), in which Schegloff's paper on questions (Schegloff 1984) is particularly valuable. The volume also contains two classic papers by Harvey Sacks, as well as the most complete statement of current transcription practices and notation. Other valuable collections are Schenkein (1978), which includes a reprint of Sacks, Schegloff and Jefferson's (1974) turn-taking paper, Psathas (1979), Sudnow (1972), which contains Labov's paper on ritual insults and Jefferson's on side-sequences, and van Dijk (1985: Vol 3).

From the discourse point of view, Coulthard and Montgomery (1981: ch 1) contains a recent overview by some of this method's chief practitioners, and a very readable though much earlier version is presented by Coulthard (1977), where a comparison is drawn with conversation analysis.

Several important papers on the computational modelling of dialogue are contained in Grosz et al. (1986). Hobbs (1978) and a shorter version of Grosz (1977) are both included, and the volume most conveniently includes papers on other aspects of natural language processing using computers, including Cohen and Perrault (1979) and Allen and Perrault (1980).

# 9

# LANGUAGE UNIVERSALS AND LANGUAGE TYPES

## J.R. PAYNE

## 1. LANGUAGE UNIVERSALS

### 1.1 Introduction

A general way of describing research into language universals is to say that it aims to characterise the notion 'possible human language' through an examination of the properties which actually occurring human languages have in common.

By the term 'actually occurring human language', we mean those human languages which are in principle amenable to description; these would include not only the languages spoken around the world at the present time, but also any languages spoken in the past for which the relevant documentation is available. A first assumption that is made in language universals research is therefore the assumption that the actually-occurring human languages in general represent a common stage of evolution: the earliest documented languages like Sumerian and Akkadian (c. 3000 BC) are reasonably claimed to be fundamentally no different from any language spoken today.

The number of languages that must be taken into account in language universals research is not entirely clear. The most recent attempt at a listing of the world's languages (Ruhlen 1987), including those which are extinct, has about 5,000 entries. On the other hand, the most extensive list of all names ever attributed to language groups, individual languages and dialects (Jarceva 1982) has approximately 30,000 entries. Of these, one half are estimated to be doublets referring to the same entity, leaving the number of distinct entries still around 15,000. This figure is significantly higher than Ruhlen's 5,000, but the discrepancy can be at least partially explained by the fact that many entries in Jarceva's list refer to what might be considered dialect forms of a single language. In principle, however, the properties of individual dialects are no less relevant than those of individual languages, no matter how the distinction between language and dialect is defined. The notion of 'actually occurring human language' must be sufficiently broad to include both. Chapter 26, below, is informative on this matter.

In the face of such a large number of languages and dialects, the majority of which lack detailed description, the language universals researcher is compelled in practical terms to establish a reasonably representative sample on which to base his conclusions. The sample should, as far as possible, be free of bias towards any particular genetic grouping of languages, or towards languages spoken in any particular geographic area. It would not be satisfactory, for example, to select a sample solely from the Indo-European languages, or from the languages of Western Europe, since such a sample would be unlikely to be representative. But how many languages should be chosen, and from which genetic groups and geographical areas?

A practical solution to the problem of genetic bias has been proposed by Bell (1978). It involves estimating the number of language groups in the world which are separated by at least 3,500 years of divergence. This is an arbitrary figure, which could be amended upwards or downwards, but gives a working list of 478 groups. A sample of 478 languages can then be created from the descriptions available, with one language drawn at random from each group, or smaller samples can be created in a similar manner, with no more than one language from each group. For the purpose of illustration, the 478 groups are arranged by Bell into larger stocks which represent definite or claimed genetic affiliations (some of which are very doubtful, but nothing much hinges on whether they are correct). The number of languages which should be chosen from each stock is then proportional to the number of groups in each stock, as shown in Table 6 for samples of 30, 100 and 300 languages.

Viewed in this light, not all the samples which have actually been used in language universals research can be seen to be free of genetic bias. Greenberg's (1963a) famous sample of 30 languages which initiated research into universals of constituent order over-represents the Indo-European and Nilo-Saharan stocks, and under-represents Amerindian and Indo-Pacific. Nevertheless, as an exploratory survey it was of inestimable value. More recently, large samples (for example, Tomlin 1986) have been created on Bell's principles, sometimes with additional corrections for areal bias.

## 1.2 Cross-linguistic definitions

Implicit in all language universals research is the idea that linguistic

*Table 6:* Representative samples of the world's languages

| Stock | Estimated number of groups | Number of languages in sample of: | | |
|---|---|---|---|---|
| | | 30 | 100 | 300 |
| Dravidian | 1 | 0 | 0 | 1 |
| Eurasiatic | 13 | 1 | 3 | 8 |
| Indo-European | 12 | 1 | 3 | 8 |
| Nil-Saharan | 18 | 1 | 4 | 11 |
| Niger-Kordofanian | 44 | 3 | 9 | 28 |
| Afroasiatic | 23 | 2 | 5 | 14 |
| Khoisan | 5 | 0 | 1 | 3 |
| Amerindian | est. 150 | 9 | 31 | 94 |
| Na-Dene | 4 | 0 | 1 | 2 |
| Austric | ca. 55 | 4 | 11 | 34 |
| Indo-Pacific | est. 100 | 6 | 21 | 63 |
| Australian | ca. 27 | 2 | 6 | 17 |
| Sino-Tibetan | ca. 20 | 1 | 4 | 13 |
| Ibero-Caucasian | 4 | 0 | 1 | 2 |
| Ket | 1 | 0 | 0 | 1 |
| Burushaski | 1 | 0 | 0 | 1 |

categories, rules and constraints are capable of cross-linguistic definition. Of course, in the initial stages of such research, these definitions are bound to be limited by what we know about restricted subsets of languages within particular linguistic areas. But as we proceed, new evidence can cause us to revise our definitions, or even abandon the theories on which they were based. Indeed, evidence from language universals research is the strongest evidence we possess for discriminating between competing linguistic theories.

As an illustration of these points, let us consider whether it is possible to give a cross-linguistic definition of the notions 'subject' and 'object'. Our notions of what 'subjects' and 'objects' are have largely evolved within grammatical theories based on the major European languages, but many problems have arisen in applying these notions to other languages. The problems have been severe enough to cause some linguists to argue that 'subject' and 'object' must be abandoned as valid cross-linguistic categories. We hope to demonstrate, however, that such pessimism is at least premature. (Chapter 3, above, may usefully be consulted.)

Perhaps the key idea behind the traditional notion 'subject' is that there is a set of properties linking the single noun phrase in a basic intransitive sentence with the more active of the two noun phrases in a basic transitive sentence. The single noun phrase in a basic intransitive sentence can be given the mnemonic S, since most linguists seem to agree that if anything can be called a 'subject', it is this noun phrase, while the more active noun phrase in a basic transitive sentence can be given the mnemonic A for 'agent' or 'actor'. For the notion of 'subject' to be a valid one, the properties which link S and A must be absent in all other noun phrases, including the less active of the two noun phrases in the basic intransitive sentence, which following Dixon (1979) we can give the mnemonic O for 'object'.

This idea seems to present no difficulties for a language like English, where many properties of S are easily seen to extend to A but not O. These include obvious surface coding properties like case-marking and verb agreement, as well as deeper syntactic properties. In the basic intransitive sentence (1), S (the pronoun *he*) is nominative and triggers the agreement *-s* on the verb. Correspondingly, in the basic transitive sentence (2), A (the pronoun *he*) is nominative and triggers the agreement *-s*, but O (the pronoun *us*) is accusative and triggers no agreement:

(1)  He sing-s
(2)  He visit-s us

Surface case and verb agreement patterns are examples of surface coding, but it is also possible in English to see deeper syntactic properties linking S and A to the exclusion of O: for example, if we co-ordinate two basic intransitive sentences with identical Ss like (3) and (4), we can delete the identical S in the second sentence to give (5):

(3)  The dog went downhill
(4)  The dog barked
(5)  The dog went downhill, and barked

If however we co-ordinate a basic intransitive sentence like (3) with a basic transitive sentence like (6), it is A which is deleted and not O:

(6)  The dog chased the man
(7)  The dog went downhill, and chased the man

If we co-ordinate (3) and (6) in the reverse order to form a sentence like (8), it is always understood by speakers of English that the dog went downhill, and not the man:

(8)  The dog chased the man, and went downhill

The evidence from English linking S and A is very clear, but on *a priori* grounds, it is not immediately obvious why that link should exist to the exclusion of O. If we consider the semantic roles (agent, experiencer, etc.) which are typical for S, these include both roles that are more closely associated with A and roles that are more closely associated with O. The semantic role of S is determined partially by the choice of verb phrase, and partially by whether S can be considered in control of the state or event described by the verb phrase. In English, for example, we could distinguish in the first instance between the following roles:

(9)  John fell (deliberately)
(10) John fell (accidentally)
(11) The water boiled
(12) John was warm
(13) John was rich

The first three sentences denote events. In (9) John is an animate entity in control of the event, whereas in (10) he is an animate entity controlled by outside forces. In (11), which seems similar to (10), the water could also be regarded as an entity controlled by outside forces, but (11) differs from (10) in that the water is inanimate and therefore incapable of being considered as a controlling entity. By contrast, the final two sentences denote states. In (12) the state seems to be one that John experiences, whereas in (13) all that is required is that John be a member of a certain set (the set of rich people): he need not even know that he is rich.

It does not matter what names we associate with the various semantic roles illustrated above. The name 'agent' would certainly be associated with the role in (9), and might perhaps be extended to include (10). It probably would not be applicable to the role in (11), which is the typical role of the inanimate affected object, and it certainly could not include the typical 'experiencer' role in (12), or the role in (13) which one might give the neutral name 'theme'. The point is simply that while the more active roles of S link Ss with typical As, the less active roles link Ss with typical Os. This is illustrated in sentences (9')–(13') where the bold noun-phrase has a similar role to the single noun phrase in (9)–(13):

(9')  **John** dented his car (deliberately)
(10') **John** dented his car (accidentally)
(11') John boiled the **water**
(12') The sun warmed **John**
(13') The bequest enriched **John**

If all the Ss in (9)–(13) are indeed to be linked with As as 'subjects', as seems to be appropriate in English, the notion of 'subject' must be based on some other property than semantic role. There is no single semantic role x of which we can say: all 'subjects' have semantic role x. In particular, we cannot say that all 'subjects' are 'agents'.

Closely dependent on the notion of semantic role is the ability of Ss to be deleted in the formation of imperative sentences. We can certainly delete agent Ss as in (9) to form an imperative sentence like *fall!* (deliberately), but it is not obvious that this can naturally be done with the Ss in (10)–(13). Imperatives like *fall!* (accidentally), *boil!*, *be cold!*, and *be rich!*, while one can invent contexts in which they might be used, seem to imply that control of the event or state by the addressee is possible, counter to the semantic role which would normally be attributed. Similarly, therefore, if all the Ss in (9)–(13) are to be linked with As as 'subjects', we cannot insist that all 'subjects' are deletable to form the addressee in imperatives.

Given the semantic heterogeneity of the category S, and the semantic parallels between S and O as well as between S and A, we should not be surprised that in many languages surface coding properties and deeper syntactic properties fail to conform to the pattern of English where Ss and As are treated alike. It is possible for different Ss to be treated differently, and for some properties of Ss to extend to As while others extend to Os.

In English, the Ss in sentences (9)–(13) could be considered either to be unmarked for case, inasmuch as nouns in English show no surface case distinctions, or to be in a single 'nominative' case, inasmuch as the pronominal forms like *he/him, she/her* show distinctions of surface case. We might hope that universally it would be possible to state that languages which have case marking for S present all semantic roles of S in the same case. However this is incorrect.

In the Caucasian language Tsova-Tush (Batsbi), third person Ss are invariably nominative, but first and second person Ss can be either nominative or ergative depending on the choice of verb and the semantic role (Holisky 1987). The ergative is typically the case of the animate agent, but some event verbs permit the nominative when the event happens outside the agent's control. The verb *dobžar* 'fall over (from a standing position)' always takes an ergative S, but the verb *gareḳa(d)dalar* 'run', though normally used with an ergative S, could acquire a nominative subject in the situation where S doesn't want to run, but finds himself running while walking down a steep hill. Verbs like *gexkar* 'boil', *mildar* 'be cold' and *da* 'be' essentially take nominative Ss.

Examples of this kind are easily multiplied. In Colloquial Sinhala (Sinhalese), three cases are possible for S (Gair 1976). The use of nominative versus accusative case can distinguish between deliberate and accidental events: *mamə waeTennan* (I(nom.) fall) I'll fall (purposefully)', *maawə wae-Teewi* (me(acc.) fall) 'I slip and fall'. Dative Ss express a further refinement: the role is one of 'internally powered' but externally induced action: whereas *mamə na Tənəwa* (I(nom.) dance) means 'I dance', *maTə nae Tenəwa* (me(dat.) dance) means 'I get to dancing' (for example, when I hear music). In the Papuan language Waris, the dative case is used for Ss when there is an uncontrolled change of state, as with the verb 'die': *he-m daha-v* (he-dat. die-pres.) 'he is dying' (Foley 1986: 109). We can note also that in some European languages experiencer Ss can be accusative or dative, rather than nominative: examples are German *mich friert* (me(acc.) cold(pres.3s)) and Russian *mne xolodno* (me(dat.) cold(neut.s)) 'I am cold'.

The question then arises as to whether all of these Ss should be considered as 'subjects', regardless of surface case. If they are so considered, then there will be insuperable problems in identifying S uniquely with either A or O on the basis of surface case, since the cases of S will typically distribute between A and O. In Tsova-Tush, for example, the ergative is the case of A and the nominative the case of O. On the other hand, if we attempt to exclude certain Ss from the category of 'subject' on the basis of surface case, it is not obvious what non-arbitrary principles could guide us. Using semantic roles as a criterion would simply reduce the notion of 'subject' to notions like 'agent'.

The surface coding property of verb-agreement essentially presents the same problems for the definition of 'subject' as case-marking. Not all languages show verb-agreement with S, but even in those that do, it is not necessarily true that all Ss trigger agreement, or that all Ss trigger the same forms of agreement. In the Nepalese language Newari, only agent Ss (and As) trigger agreement (Gair 1976, citing Hale and Watters 1973: 186). In the Muskogean language Chickasaw, agent Ss trigger one form of agreement and non-agent Ss another (Payne, D. 1982): *sa-chokma* (Is-good) means 'I am good' and *chokma-li* (good-Is) means 'I act good'. These two forms of agreement then distribute like the case-markers in Tsova-Tush to O and A respectively. The question then arises whether only agent Ss and As are 'subjects': as before, the notion of 'subject' would then essentially reduce to that of 'agent'.

Equally problematic for the notion of 'subject' are cases where a uniform property of S extends to O rather than A. This is shown in the Kurmanji Kurdish examples (14) and (15):

(14) ez     ket –im
     I(abs.) fell –1s
     'I fell'

(15) jin   -ê   ez    dît – im
     woman- obl. I(abs.) saw – 1s
     'The woman saw me'

The general case for S is absolutive, as in (14), and this case extends to O in (15). The case of A is oblique. This pattern, called the 'ergative' pattern, is seen also in the verb agreement marker -*im*, which agrees with S in (14) and O in (15). It is distinct from the so-called 'active' pattern of Tsova-Tush or Chickasaw, where only non-active Ss are linked to Os.

There are therefore extreme difficulties in trying to base the notion of 'subject' either on semantic roles or on surface coding properties. Unfortunately, however, deep syntactic properties fare little better. It is probably true that deep syntactic properties, like deletability in co-ordinate sentences, are more general properties of Ss than particular surface coding properties, like particular cases or particular forms of verb-agreement. It is also true that in a large number of languages we see ergative surface coding patterns combined with deep syntactic patterns which link S and A (Kurdish is an example). However, deep syntactic properties can in some languages extend not from S to A, but from S to O. The classic example is the Australian language Dyirbal.

In Dyirbal, there is no verb agreement, but the categories of pronoun, determiner and noun are marked for case. The pronoun system works as in English, with nominative case for S and A and accusative case for O, but the determiner and noun system works on the ergative principle, with one case for S and O (called the 'absolutive') and a separate case for A (called the 'ergative'). Examples from Dixon (1980: 439, 461) are:

(16) ŋana       nyurra- na bura - n
     we all(nom.) you all-(acc.) see - past
     'We all saw you all'

(17) nyurra - na    yara -ŋgu bura - n
     you all-(acc.) man-(erg.) see - past
     'The man saw you all'

(18) balan     guda      baŋgul yara -ŋgu      bura-n
     she(abs.) dog(abs.) he(erg.) man-(erg.)    see -past
     'The man saw the dog'

(19) balan     guda      buŋa    - n
     she(abs.) dog(abs.) descend-past
     'The dog went downhill'

On the basis of the surface coding we evidently have grounds for linking both A and O with S, and therefore it is difficult to see how we might say that either A or O is a 'subject' to the exclusion of the other. With respect to the deeper syntactic properties, however, S is linked with O to the exclusion of A: if we attempt to co-ordinate sentences (18) and (19), we derive the acceptable sentences (20) and (21):

(20) balan     guda      buŋa    -n     baŋgul yara -ŋgu bura-n
     she(abs.) dog(abs.) descend-past he(erg.) man-(erg.) see -past
     'The dog went downhill and the man saw (it)'

(21) balan     guda      baŋgul yara -ŋgu bura-n     buŋa    -n
     she(abs.) dog(abs.) he(erg.) man-(erg,) see -past descend-past
     'The man saw the dog, and (it) went downhill'

In both (20) and (21), it is the noun phrase in the absolutive case which is deleted from the second clause, i.e. O in (20) and S in (21). A speaker of Dyirbal always understands in a sentence like (21) that it is the dog which went downhill, and not the man.

What should a linguist say about the notion of 'subject' in basic transitive sentences in Dyirbal? The evidence from surface case-marking is contradictory: neither A nor O is exclusively identifiable with S. The evidence from deeper syntactic processes points towards an identification of O with S, but this seems to contradict our original expectation that the notion 'subject' should link the more active A with S.

Perhaps we should try a structural definition of 'subject', as suggested for example by Chomsky (1965). A 'subject' would be a noun phrase (NP) which was immediately dominated by the sentence node in a tree diagram, and sister of a verb phrase (VP). An 'object', on the other hand, would be immediately dominated by VP, and be sister of a verb (V). This is illustrated in (22) for the basic intransitive sentence in English and (23) for the basic transitive sentence:

(22) $[_S [_{NP} John ] [_{VP} [_V sings ] ] ]$
(23) $[_S [_{NP} John ] [_{VP} [_V speaks ] [_{NP} French ] ] ]$

S and A would then be linked by their identical structural position.

This definition also runs into difficulties. Keenan (1988) surveys the numerous languages for which it can be argued that there is no observable VP linking V and O into a single constituent, but rather A and O are equal daughters of the sentence. An example would be the Australian language Warlpiri, as discussed by Hale (1983). Word order in Warlpiri is exceptionally free, and S, A and O are identified primarily by surface case. A typical transitive sentence is shown in (24):

(24) $(_S[_{NP}$ karnta-ngku] $[_{AUX}$ ka   -ø   -ø] $[_{NP}$ ngarrka-ø]   $[_V$ nya-nyi     ] ]
     woman      -erg.        pres.-she-him   man      -abs.     see-non past
     'The woman sees the man'

Simply exchanging the ergative and absolutive suffixes in (24), with no change in order, gives the reading 'the man sees the woman'. Languages like Warlpiri, which lack a VP, have been styled 'non-configurational'.

Even more problematic for the configurational definition of 'subject', however, are the languages which Keenan cites as possessing 'VP-nominative' sentences, i.e. sentences grouping V and A into a single constituent rather than O. One of the languages he gives as an example is (Tamazight) Berber, the other Toba Batak. Transitive sentences in Toba Batak, for instance, have the structure $[_S [ x - V NP] NP]$, where x begins with *M-* or *D-*:

(25) [$_S$ [Mang  -ida si  Ria ] si  Torus ]
　　　imperf.-see art.Ria  art.Torus
　　　'Torus sees Ria'

(26) [$_S$ [ Di  - ida si  Ria ] si  Torus ]
　　　perf. - see art.Ria  art.Torus
　　　'Ria saw Torus'

Following Schachter (1984), Keenan argues that in both aspects, imperfective and perfective, the noun phrase immediately following the verb forms a constituent with the verb. For instance, no adverbial can be inserted between it and the verb, nor can it be moved away from the verb under any circumstances. In the case of *M-* sentences, this gives an English style 'accusative VP' in which V is grouped with O, and A is immediately dominated by the sentence node, in conformity with the configurational definition of 'subject'. But in the *D-* sentences it is A which is grouped with V, forming a 'nominative VP', and the NP immediately dominated by the sentence node is O. If in an intransitive sentence S is considered to be the NP immediately dominated by the sentence node, this might be argued to be an instance of configurational ergativity.

Evidently none of the properties we have surveyed so far universally provides a unique identification of S and A to the exclusion of O. There is however one further property which *might* serve: this is essentially the autonomous reference property suggested by Keenan (1976a: 313–15 and reformulated in Keenan 1988). It seems to be a property of Ss that they cannot be anaphoric expressions (pronouns, reflexives and reciprocals) whose interpretation depends on the interpretation of other NPs in the same clause. For instance, the interpretation of the English pronoun *his* in (27) depends on the interpretation of *everyone* (this can be symbolised by assigning *everyone* and *his* the same subscript letter):

(27) Everyone$_i$ went to his$_i$ bed

In this case, *his$_i$* is said to be 'bound' by *everyone$_i$*. Note, however, that reversing the positions of the two expressions is not possible with the same meaning:

(28) *He$_i$ went to everyone's$_i$ bed

An interpretation of (28) is only available when *he* refers autonomously of *everyone*, as in (29):

(29) He$_j$ went to everyone's$_i$ bed

　　Interestingly, this property extends to many cases of what might be thought of as 'unusual' Ss, like the dative Ss of Russian. We can say (30), where the reflexive pronoun *sebja* is bound by the dative S *vsem*, but not (31), where the reflexive *sebe* itself is the dative S:

(30) Vse      -m$_i$ xorošo u sebja$_i$ doma
     everyone-dat. fine    at self's at home
     'Everyone feels fine in his own home'

(31) *Seb - e$_i$ xorošo u vsex$_i$    doma
     self - dat. fine   at everyone's at home
     *'Heself feels fine in everyone's home'

The attempted English translation of (31) captures the feel of why the Russian is unacceptable, but it should be noted that although there is no nominative reflexive pronoun *heself*, the Russian dative reflexive pronoun *sebe* does exist (as in *on kupil sebe knigu* (he bought self book) 'He bought himself a book'). It simply cannot be used as a bound form in the dative S position.

Surprisingly, as far as is definitely known, this property of Ss extends to As and not to Os. In English, for example, sentence (32) is unacceptable with *he* bound in A position, but (33) is acceptable with *himself* bound in O position:

(32) *He$_i$ likes everyone$_i$
(33) Everyone$_i$ likes himself$_i$

More significantly, in languages like Toba Batak which display the rather rare property of configurational ergativity, bound anaphoric expressions are excluded in A position and not O position, irrespective of the structural configuration. There is no corresponding 'anaphoric ergativity':

(34) [ Mang  - ida dirina ] si  Torus
     imperf. - see self    art.Torus
     'Torus sees himself'

(35) *[ Mang  - ida si  Torus ] dirina
      imperf. - see art.Torus  self
     *'Heself sees Torus'

(36) [ Di  - ida si  Torus ] dirina
     perf – art.Torus     self
     'Torus saw himself'

(37) * [ Di  - ida dirina ] si  Torus
      perf. - see self    art.Torus
     *'Heself saw Torus'

The unacceptable examples are (35) and (37), where the anaphoric expression is A. The crucial example is (36), which is configurationally ergative, but not anaphorically ergative.

The notion of 'subject' we have been developing is one in which certain properties of the single noun phrase S in a basic intransitive sentence extend preferentially to one of the two noun phrases in a basic transitive sentence, namely A: there is a fundamental asymmetry between A and O. In the case of surface coding properties, this preference is less marked but nevertheless seems to exist: there are probably more languages which show verb agreement with S and A exclusively than with S and O exclusively, and there are probably more languages which extend the surface case of S to A than extend the surface case of S to O. The preference for linking S and A is however especially clear in the case of deep syntactic properties and configurationality; and in the case of the autonomous reference property it may even be universal: there may be no anaphorically ergative languages.

In some languages, therefore, the properties of S and A may essentially coincide. Such languages are said by Shibatani (1987) to possess 'prototypical' subjects. In other languages, the properties of S may be split between A and O, but here there are clear preferences as to how the properties should be split: even if surface coding properties link S and O, we still expect the autonomous reference property, configurationality (if present) and perhaps some deep syntactic properties to link S and A.

The fact that properties of S sometimes extend to O gives us a clue as to how to think of O. As we have seen, O bears a fundamentally asymmetric relation to A, particularly with respect to the autonomous reference property. Even though it is possible to imagine a language which is anaphorically ergative, it is difficult to imagine a language in which neither A nor O could be a bound anaphoric expression, i.e. in which the autonomous reference property of S extended to both A and O. But with properties such as surface coding and deep syntactic relations, we see that properties of S may extend either to O alone, or to both A and O to the exclusion of other noun phrases. Verb agreement, for example, may be a phenomenon common to S and A (as in English), S and O (as in Kurmanji Kurdish) or all of S, A and O (as in Hungarian) to the exclusion of indirect and other oblique noun phrases. To the extent that Os share properties with Ss and As, they can perhaps be thought of as 'non-prototypical subjects', but we would still like to maintain that it is premature to abandon the definition of 'subject' as the linking of S with A.

In this case study, we have seen that the definition of linguistic concepts which have cross-linguistic validity is far from simple, and leads to results which are far from our initial conceptions based on the analysis of a limited sample of languages. There are of course many aspects of the problem of 'subjects' and 'objects' that we have not been able to touch on, for example the properties of these categories in non-basic sentences like passives, or the properties distinguishing 'direct objects' from 'indirect' and other 'oblique' objects. The problems here are real, but we trust not insoluble.

### 1.3 Greenbergian universals

The term 'language universal' itself can be given various interpretations within this general framework. One set of interpretations, which are stated most clearly in the well-known 'Memorandum Concerning Language Universals' written by Joseph. H. Greenberg, Charles Osgood and James Jenkins as an introduction to the report (Greenberg 1963b) on the Dobbs Ferry conference on language universals held in 1961, treats language universals as *statements* about (possible human) languages which take the form (i):

(i)  For all x, if x is a language, then . . .

The simplest form such a statement can take is (i'):

(i')  For all x, if x is a language, x has property P

Such a universal is called by Greenberg, Osgood and Jenkins an *unrestricted universal*, and by Comrie (1981: 19) an *absolute non-implicational universal*. The property P must of course be capable of cross-linguistic definition. Typical examples of this type of universal within the Greenbergian framework concern the status of basic categories as universally present properties of language.

A relatively uncontroversial example from phonology would be the statement: for all x, if x is a language, x has vowels (i.e. all languages have vowels). This universal can in fact be attributed to Jakobson (1941), who regarded the consonant-vowel opposition as the basic phonological opposition. Such a universal would of course be falsified if we found any (actually occurring) languages which lacked vowels. In fact, the minimal attested vowel systems seem to consist of two vowel phonemes: Arandic languages such as Kaititj from Central Australian have two vowels /ə/ and /a/ (Dixon 1980: 131). As predicted by Jakobson, also, the distinction between the two vowels is essentially one of height: high /ə/ has front, central and back allophones [i], [ə] and [u].

There is indeed a claim in the literature that the North-West Caucasian language Kabardian lacks phonological vowels (Kuipers 1960). The North-West Caucasian languages in general have large consonant inventories (from 48 in Kabardian to perhaps 83 in Ubykh), and phonetic vowels (which certainly do exist) show many differences in timbre according to the consonant they are adjacent to. Phonetically, there seem to be twelve short vowels which can be reduced straightforwardly to two short phonological vowels /ə/ and /a/ with six allophones each. In addition, there are five phonetically long vowels [ī], [ē], [ū], [ō] and [ā]. Depending on one's view of the abstractness of phonological representation, the first four of these could be regarded as deriving from the vowel-glide sequences /əj/, /aj/, /əw,/ aw/. Pushing phonological abstractness a bit further, the vowel [ā], which contrasts with /ə/ in such examples as *jə-tx'ə-ns* 'he is to write it' and *jā-tx'ə-ns* 'they are to write it', can be derived from the sequence /ha/, the plural marker. This requires a metathesis rule: *jə-ha-tx'əns* = > *jə-ah-tx'ə-ns* = > *j-ah-tx'ə-ns* = > *j-ā-tx'ə-ns*. Plausibly, then, we have an underlying two vowel system of /ə/ and /a/ in Kabardian.

Kuipers's strategy then consists of two controversial moves which centre on stressed syllables, where /ə/ and /a/ indeed seem to contrast. One is to say that in stressed syllables the absence of /a/ implies the occurrence of /ə/, and therefore the occurrence of /ə/ is predictable. The second is to treat the 'remaining' vowel /a/ as a consonantal feature of openness. As Halle (1970) points out, these two strategies seems to be notational tricks: one could equally well have chosen /a/ as the predictable vowel and /ə/ as the 'remaining' vowel in stressed syllables, and treating stressed vocalic elements as consonantal features strains the principles of phonological analysis to the limit. Kuipers's arguments are now generally rejected in favour of assuming either two vowel phonemes /a/ and /ə/ for Kabardian, or three including /ā/. Hewitt (1981: 205–7) provides a discussion and bibliography. This example, however, well illustrates the point that even apparently innocuous language universals must be based on an agreement about how languages are to be analysed.

Grammatical unrestricted universals tend to be rather more controversial, because of the abstractness of the definitions that are involved even with the most basic grammatical categories. One example (adapted from Bolinger 1968) would be the claim: all languages use nominal phrases and verbal phrases, corresponding to the two major classes of noun and verb. In order to make sense of this claim, we would first have to decide how to define the basic categories of noun, verb, nominal phrase and verbal phrase in a manner which had some cross-linguistic validity. This is far from being a simple task, since the distinction between noun and verb in languages like Nootka, although it probably exists, is much less clearly marked than in a language like English where lexical verbs are marked for the category of tense and nouns are not (Schachter 1985: 11–13).

In Nootka, notionally noun-like roots like *qu.ʔas* 'man' can be used both as arguments and as predicates, without any accompanying copula. Similarly, notionally verbal roots like *mamu.k* 'work' can be used not only as predicates, but also as arguments, i.e. 'working one':

(40) Mamu.k - ma    qu.ʔas - ʔi
    work    - pres. man    - def.
    'The man is working'

(41) Qu.ʔas - ma    mamu.k    - ʔi
    man    - pres. working one - def.
    'The working one is a man'

It appears in (41) that the 'noun' man has a tense suffix -*ma*, but as Schachter points out, this is misleading, since the tense particles attach to the clause initial word, whatever its category. In addition, verbal roots like *mamu.k* can never be used on their own as arguments: they must always be suffixed as in (41), while nominal roots can occur on their own:

(42) Mamu.k - ma    qu.ʔas
    work    - pres. man
    'A man is working'

(43) *Qu.ʔas - ma    mamu.k
    man    - pres. working one
    'A working one is a man'

More damaging to Bolinger's claim, though, is the accumulating evidence that, although nominal phrases may well be a universally present category, verbal phrases are not, at least not when they are defined as a syntactic constituent consisting of the verb and an argument which is interpreted like an object. As we have seen in the analysis of the notion 'subject', while it can be argued that English does have such a constitutent, it can be argued equally convincingly that Tamazight Berber and Toba Batak group together the verb and an argument which is interpreted like a subject, and that languages like Warlpiri and Malayalam fail to group the verb with any particular argument (Keenan 1988).

Another category which fails to be universal is the category of 'adjective'. This category is discussed by Dixon (1982) and Schachter (1985), who come to the conclusion that there are some languages in which a separate class of adjectives does exist, but that it is a 'closed' class, consisting of a restricted number of members. A paradigm example is Igbo, which has eight adjectives covering the basic dimensions of size (*ukwu* 'large', *nta* 'small'), colour (*ojii* 'black, dark', *ọca* 'white, light'), age (*ọhuru* 'new', *ocye* 'old') and value (*ọma* 'good', *ọjọọ* 'bad'). In other languages there are no adjectives at all, the concepts we think of as adjectival in English being expressed by either nouns or verbs.

Many properties of language, while not being universally present, are nevertheless found with a greater than chance frequency. It is a feature of the definition of language universal embodied in schema (i) above that statements about such properties can be considered as language universals (although the properties themselves are not universal). Such statements, called *statistical universals* by Greenberg, Osgood and Jenkins, and *non-implicational tendencies* by Comrie, take the form (i''):

(i'') For all x, if x is a language, then the probability that x has property P is greater than the probability that x has property Q

A phonological instantiation of (i'') would be the statement (taking Q as not-P): for all x, if x is a language, then the probability that x has at least one nasal stop (i.e. a segment like /m/, /n/ or /ŋ/ as in English 'rum', 'run' and 'rung') is greater than the probability that x has no nasal stops. In fact, complete absence of nasal stops is quite rare. Their absence in three Salish languages was the reason Ferguson (1963: 44) originally proposed this universal as a statistical universal, and only a few others have since been discovered (Thompson and Thompson 1972).

A grammatical example (with Q not simply the negation of P) would be the claim that for all x, if x is a language, then the probability that x exclusively uses suffixes is greater than the probability that x exclusively uses prefixes. In the English word *pre-fix-es*, *pre-* is a prefix and *-es* is a suffix, so English is neither exclusively prefixing nor exclusively suffixing. In Greenberg's 30 language sample (Greenberg 1963a), 12 languages are claimed to be exclusively suffixing and only one (Thai) to be exclusively prefixing. Even Thai may not be *exclusively* prefixing: it can be argued that the comparative -*kwa* and the classifiers are suffixes (Kazevič and Jaxontov 1982: 65).

A combination of statements of the form (i'') can be used to state the relative probabilities of occurrence of properties which represent a multi-valued choice, i.e. property P occurs with greater probability than property Q, which in its turn occurs with greater probability than property R. For instance, given a definition of the categories 'subject' (S), 'object' (O) and 'verb' (V), as well as a notion of what constitutes the basic word order of a language, it is easy to see that there are six possible basic word orders that can be attributed to the world's languages. English for example has the basic word order SVO, as in (44), and Japanese the basic word order SOV, as in (45):

(44) John(S)       saw(V)      Mary(O)

(45) Taroo-ga(S)     Hanako-o(O)     nagutta(V)
     Taroo-nom       Hanako-acc     hit
     'Taroo hit Hanako'

As was first observed by Greenberg (1963a), these possible orders do not seem to occur with the same frequency. A recent sample of 402 languages (Tomlin 1986) gives the results shown in Table 7.

*Table 7*

| Order | Number of languages | Frequency |
|-------|---------------------|-----------|
| SOV | 180 | 44.78 |
| SVO | 168 | 41.79 |
| VSO | 37 | 9.20 |
| VOS | 12 | 2.99 |
| OVS | 5 | 1.24 |
| OSV | 0 | 0.00 |

It appears that the orders SOV and SVO, with S in initial position, are overwhelmingly the most frequent orders. The difference between the frequency of SOV and SVO is not statistically significant. Of the remaining orders, VSO is the most frequent, followed by the three orders which place O before S. Although Tomlin's sample is carefully selected to minimise any genetic or areal bias, it is risky, on the basis of a single sample and given the small numbers involved, to attribute any significance to the differences between VOS and OVS, or between OVS and OSV. While VOS has been a well-documented order for some time, from relatively well-known language stocks like Austronesian and Penutian, the two object-initial orders OVS and OSV have become documented relatively recently, starting in about 1978, from the rather less well-known stocks of Amazonia. The recent survey by Derbyshire and Pullum of Amazonian languages (1986: 18) now claims 8 certain cases (Apalai, Arecuna, Asurini, Barasanasos (Southern), Hianacoto, Hixkaryana, Teribi, Urarina) and 6 probable cases (Amahuaca, Bacairi, Macushi, Oiampí, Panare, Wayana) of the order OVS, and 4 certain cases (Apurinã, Hupda, Nadëb, Xavante) and 2 probable cases (Jamamadí, Urubù) of the order OSV.

As Hockett (1963: 3) points out, statistical universals are no less important than unrestricted universals. One fundamental assumption of language universals research has to be the assumption that the actually occurring human languages are representative qualitatively and quantitatively of what is possible in human language. On the other hand, it is dangerous in many cases to assume that because a particular property has not been observed in an actually occurring human language, then it is in principle impossible. Many of the rarer properties that we now know about are apparently found in geographically-restricted areas, rather than as isolated occurrences spread randomly across the world. An excellent example is the restriction of object-initial languages (in our present knowledge) to Amazonia. Let us suppose that these languages had never been discovered (perhaps the tribes which spoke them might have died out in the last century); what therefore might have been our conclusions about the possible basic word orders of human languages? It would have been tempting to suggest as an unrestricted universal that no languages have object-initial basic word order. Indeed, before the object-initial languages were discovered, many linguists did indeed posit such an unrestricted universal. But the known existence of the other orders SOV, SVO, VSO and VOS should have made us wary: these orders tell us that in principle (*a*) languages can operate with differing orders of constituents, (*b*) the position of the verb is not fixed, (*c*) subjects can appear both before and after objects. These principles of course also admit the possibility of OSV and OVS orders. In such cases, we should have done better to make the statistical claim.

The general point seems to be that if it is possible to describe the observed properties of actually-occurring human languages in terms of a set of principles which also permit non-observed properties, we should not base unrestricted universals on the simple fact that these properties have not been observed. Rather, we should say that the probability of a language possessing them is low. Many unrestricted universals might better be reframed as statistical ones without their significance being thereby diminished: ultimately it must be hoped that the preponderance of one property over another can be shown not to be an accident of world-history, but correlated in a significant number of cases with such factors as the nature of the human cognitive system, the nature of language as a communicative system, or the principles which govern linguistic change.

The same criticisms which apply to unrestricted universals can also be levelled against the third kind of universal proposed in Greenberg, Osgood and Jenkins's schema. These take the form:

(i''') For all x, if x is a language, then if x has property P, x has property Q

Such a statement is called a *universal implication* by Greenberg, Osgood, and Jenkins, and an *absolute implicational universal* by Comrie (1981: 19). It allows for the existence of three classes of language: (*a*) languages which have both P and Q, (*b*) languages which have neither P nor Q, and (*c*) languages which have Q but not P. It would be falsified only by the discovery of a language which had P but not Q. Such universals have played a major role in recent language universals research.

As a phonological example of a universal implication, we can cite Ferguson's (1963: 46) claim that in a given language the number of nasal vowel phonemes is never greater than the number of non-nasal vowel phonemes. In the form (i'''), this would read: for all x, if x is a language, than if x has n nasal vowel phonemes, x has m non-nasal vowel phonemes (where m ≥ n). An example of a nasal vowel phoneme would be the segment /ã/ in the French word *dent* /dã/ 'tooth'/. Two recent samples have not disconfirmed this universal. Crother's (1978) survey of vowel systems, based on the Stanford Phonology Archive, worked with a sample of 209 languages of which 50 (24%) had nasal vowel systems. Of these 50, 22 had the same number of non-nasal vowels as nasal vowels (m=n) and 28 had more non-nasal vowels than nasal vowels (m > n). Ruhlen's (1978) sample of approximately 700 languages contained 155 (22%) with nasal vowel systems, of which 83 had the same number of non-nasal vowels as nasal vowels and 72 had more non-nasal vowels than nasal vowels. No languages in either sample had more nasal vowels than non-nasal vowels (n > m).

A grammatical example of a claimed absolute implicational universal is Greenberg's (1963: 88) word order universal: languages with dominant VSO order are always prepositional. Prepositions are words like English *in*: they precede the noun phrases which they govern as in *in Tokyo*. Postpositions, on the other hand follow the noun phrase they govern, as in Japanese *Tokyo ni* 'in Tokyo'. In Greenberg's 30 language sample there are 6 languages with dominant VSO order (Berber, Hebrew, Maori, Masai, Welsh and Zapotec), and all of these have prepositions and not postpositions. On the other hand the 13 SVO languages divide into 10 with prepositions, as in English, and 3 with postpositions (Finnish, Guarani and Songhai), while the 11 SOV languages are exclusively postpositional. In fact, however, Greenberg learnt of a possible exception to his universal after the Dobbs Ferry conference and just in time to be included in an additional note to his paper. The language in question was the Uto-Aztecan language Papago, which was thought to be VSO and postpositional. The status of Papago both as a postpositional language and as a VSO language has since been questioned (see Comrie 1981: 28 and the reference in Payne, D. 1986: 462), but was included as such in the major survey of word order universals by Hawkins (1983) which used a sample of 336 languages. In this sample there were a total of 52 VSO and VOS languages, which Hawkins groups together as V–1 (Verb First). Papago is the only one claimed to have postpositions: the remaining 51 are all prepositional.

Is it possible to maintain that there are any genuine universal implications? As Smith (1981) points out, one has the strong impression that exceptions to them will not be a great surprise. Given that a language can in principle use dominant word order VSO, and given that a language can in principle use postpositions, the combination of the two in a single language might in principle be expected to occur. In fact, regardless of the status of Papago, the combination of V–1 and postpositions has recently been argued to occur in a number of Amazonian languages, namely Yagua, Caquinte, Amuesha, Taushiro and Guajajara (Payne, D. 1986; Derbyshire 1987). What is significant is the preponderance of V–1 and prepositional languages over V–1 and post-positional languages.

We need therefore to reformulate this particular universal implication, and probably many others, in statistical terms. This lead us to the fourth instantiation of schema (i), called a *statistical correlation* by Greenberg, Osgood and Jenkins, and an *implicational tendency* by Comrie. Such universals take the form (i''''):

(i'''') For all x, if x is a language, then if x has property P, the probability that it has property Q is greater than the probability that it has property R

In our example, the property P is the property of being dominantly V–1, the property Q is the property of using prepositions, and the property R is the property of using postpositions.

The four instantiations of schema (i) given above are the main framework within which research into Greenbergian universals takes place. Greenberg, Osgood and Jenkins do however also suggest two more types of synchronic universal, as well as the general form which must be taken by universal statements of linguistic change (diachronic universals).

The first of the two types of synchronic universal is called a *restricted equivalence*. It takes the form (i'''''):

(i''''') For all x, if x is a language, then if x has property P, it has property Q, and vice versa

Such a statement is easily seen to be equivalent to two statements of type (i'''). The example given is that if a language has a lateral click, it always has a dental click, and vice versa. Since clicks are known only in a very restricted set of languages in southern Africa, this statement has limited import. The difficulty in finding genuine cases of restricted equivalence is probably insurmountable: even in the case of the statement about clicks we ought to be wary, since there is no obvious reason why a language should not have one type of click without the other.

On the other hand, there might be grounds for postulating a statistical version of (i'''''), which would be equivalent to two statements of type (i''''), if we could find two properties which mutually implicated each other to a significant extent. Note that we could not use the properties V–1 and prepositional, since although the majority of V–1 languages are prepositional, the majority of prepositional languages are not V–1 (they are SVO). But the property of having dominant SOV order and the property of using postpositions rather than prepositions do seem to provide an example. Out of 174 SOV languages in Hawkins's (1983) sample, 162 are postpositional and only 12 are prepositional. Out of the 188 postpositional languages in the same sample, 162 have dominant order SOV and 25 have other orders. Following Comrie's lead in calling non-absolute universals *tendencies*, we might call such a universal a *mutual implicational tendency*. The logical type of such a universal is clear, however: it is simply a combination of two implicational tendencies (which incidentally need not involve the same numerical probabilities).

The second extra type of synchronic universal is what Greenberg, Osgood and Jenkins call a *universal frequency distribution*. What they seem to have in mind are universals in which it is possible to make a measurement of a certain property across all languages (for example, the degree of redundancy in the information theory sense) and get a result which shows a statistical distribution around a mean. The statement of the statistical properties of the distribution (its mean, standard deviations etc.) would then be a valid universal fact. Comrie (1981: 22), having avoided the use of the term *statistical* for universals of types (i″) and (i″″), is able to call such a universal a *statistical universal*.

Finally, Greenberg, Osgood and Jenkins's general formula for diachronic universals is given as (ii):

(ii)  For all x and all y where x is an earlier and y a later stage of the same language, then . . .

An example of such a universal would be Ferguson's (1963: 46) claim that nasal vowel phonemes, except in cases of borrowing and analogy, always result from the loss of a nasal consonant phoneme. This can be illustrated by the development of the nasal vowel phoneme /ɛ̃/ in French (Harris 1987: 216): Latin *fin-em* (end-acc.s) developed first into [fin] with the loss of the accusative singular ending, then the vowel was allophonically nasalised to give [fĩn] and lowered to give [fɛ̃n]. Subsequently the loss of the nasal consonant, giving modern French [fɛ̃] (spelt *fin*), led to the creation of a nasal vowel phoneme.

One feature of diachronic universals stressed by Greenberg, Osgood and Jenkins is that, apart from generalities like 'all languages change', they are invariably probabilistic. No-one can say with certainty that a particular property of an earlier stage x of a language will definitely change into another property at a later stage y, or even say retrospectively that a particular property at a later stage y must have arisen from another property at an earlier stage x. Although the majority of nasal vowel phonemes do indeed seem to have arisen through the kind of mechanism illustrated above (Ruhlen 1978: 230), one cannot predict that a sequence of oral vowel and nasal consonant will invariably be converted into a nasal vowel phoneme within a given time span: the Old English dative masculine pronoun *him* has survived in modern English unchanged, and not resulted in a form like /hɪ̃/. Nor can one say that all existing nasal vowel phonemes have arisen from a sequence of oral vowel and nasal consonant in a given language: other mechanisms include borrowing from one language into another via loan-words, as in French loans like *Restaurant* /restorã/ 'restaurant' in German, the emergence of nasalisation in the environment of glottalic sounds (Ruhlen 1978: 231–2), and spreading as an areal feature. For instance, nasalised vowels are a characteristic areal feature of northern India, found in a wide range of languages from the Indo-Aryan family (except Sinhalese and Romani, which are outside the area, and some dialects of Marathi), in the isolate Burushaski, and in many languages from the Tibeto-Burman, Dardic and Munda families. Interestingly, some neighbouring Iranian dialects belong to the area, including eastern dialects of Pashto and Balochi, as does the northern Dravidian language, Kurukh, although the majority of both Iranian and Dravidian languages lack nasal vowels (Edel'man 1968: 77, Masica 1976: 88).

### 1.4 Explanation of Greenbergian universals

Given that Greenbergian universals are valid statements about the nature of the set of possible human languages, how can their validity be explained? The problem is an acute one, since an explanation based on the behaviour or knowledge of individual speakers of a language appears at first sight to be excluded. How can an individual speaker of a particular language conceivably have any knowledge of the distribution of basic word order patterns in the world's languages, or the distribution of oral and nasal vowels? A child faced with learning an OVS language with nasal vowels, like the Amazonian language Apalai (Koehn and Koehn 1986), learns it just as naturally as a child learns an SVO language without nasal vowels, like English. Why then are there many more languages which resemble English with respect to these features than languages which resemble Apalai?

Of particular interest in answering this kind of question is the relationship between diachronic and synchronic universals. Since diachronic universals are inevitably probabilistic in nature, nothing can be predicted with absolute certainty about the presence or absence of a given property in any individual language on the basis of a diachronic universal. On the other hand, individual synchronic universals, in particular the statistical ones ('tendencies' in Comrie's terminology), may be at least partially accounted for in terms of the probabilities of language change.

Greenberg (1966) states the idea that Ferguson's (1963) synchronic universal concerning the relationship between the number of nasal and non-nasal vowel phonemes in a language, viz. that there are never more nasal than non-nasal vowel phonemes, is a straightforward consequence of Ferguson's (1963) diachronic universal concerning the development of nasal vowel phonemes from oral vowel and nasal consonant sequences: if there are five oral vowels in a language, then a maximum of five vowels are available for nasalisation in the environment of a nasal consonant. Of course, this cannot be the whole explanation: once the language has developed a symmetric system with five oral and five nasal vowels, what is to prevent a subsequent merger of one or more of the oral vowel phonemes leading to a state of affairs in which there are more nasal vowels than oral vowels? The fact that this development is conceivable ought to make us wary of thinking about the synchronic universal as an absolute one. However, the apparent rarity of the development can be formulated as another diachronic universal: in languages with both oral and nasal vowel systems, merger is at least as probable in the nasal vowel system as in the oral vowel system. In French, for example, the nasal vowel phoneme /œ̃/ is in the process of being absorbed by /ɛ̃/, whereas the oral vowel phoneme /œ/ (or /œ = ø/ for those speakers who do not distinguish between /œ/ and /ø/) is not being absorbed by /ɛ/ (Harris 1987: 217).

Such a diachronic account of the synchronic universal seems preferable to the notion that the class of nasal vowels is in some sense 'unnatural' or 'marked' with respect to the class of oral vowels, as is implied in classical generative phonology (Chomsky and Halle 1968: 402–19). Indeed, to the extent that the notion of 'unnaturalness' or 'markedness' is merely a restatement of the synchronic universal governing the distribution of nasal and oral vowel phonemes across the world's languages, it suffers from the same problems of explanation.

Of course, accounting for the synchronic universal in terms of the diachronic universal simply throws the problem of explanation one stage back; but explanation of linguistic change *can* eventually be based on the behaviour of individual speakers. In this particular example the development of nasal vowels from a sequence of oral vowel and nasal consonant eventually results from the anticipatory articulation of the nasality inherent in the nasal consonant, for which a psycholinguistic explanation seems plausible. The tendency for nasal vowels to merge more than oral vowels may be explicable if it can be demonstrated that nasal vowels possess a lesser degree of perceptual differentiation than the corresponding oral vowels. Much work remains to be done in this area, but ultimately we might hope that the explanation for the synchronic universal would reduce to factors which are involved in the pressure on individual speakers for linguistic change. These factors are essentially psycholinguistic in nature, relating to processes of production and perception.

Similar issues arise in the attempt to explain the non-absolute grammatical universals. Why, for instance, is there a correlation between basic word order and the use of prepositions or postpositions? Attempts to explain this phenomenon in purely synchronic terms essentially rely on the idea of natural serialisation introduced by Vennemann (1973): it is claimed that the relationship between a verb and its object is similar to the relationship between an adposition (preposition or postposition) and its object, and that therefore languages will naturally express this relationship linearly in the same order. A language with Verb-Object order will tend to have Preposition-Object order, and a language with Object-Verb order will tend to have Object-Postposition order. The similarity can be stated in semantic terms, based on notions like operator and operand or function and argument (Keenan 1979), or in syntactic terms, based on the notion of government or case-assignment (Haider 1986). In languages with overt case systems, for example, the range of cases which can be assigned to objects by verbs is essentially the same as the range of cases governed by prepositions. However, we might be suspicious of such explanations on the grounds that a natural serialisation principle, like a markedness principle in phonology, does not seem to be something that an individual speaker of a language, or a child learning a language, in principle needs to know or indeed can know. For example, there seems to be no evidence that a child has any more difficulty in learning a language which fails to conform to the natural serialisation principle than learning one which does. In addition, even if the explanation is accepted, there remains the problem of explaining just why the principles of linguistic change act in such a way that the majority of languages conform to the principle (Mallinson and Blake 1981: 393).

An alternative explanation of the correlation between basic word order and adposition type is therefore the diachronic one, likewise first proposed by Vennemann (1973), that verbs are a major historical source for adpositions. This can be seen for example in the development of the English preposition *regarding* from the verb *regard*: in a sentence like *he made a speech regarding the new proposal*, the form *regarding* seems to act as a high style replacement for the preposition *about*. It cannot be treated synchronically as a participial form of the verb *regard*, since sentences like *\*his speech regarded the new proposal* are unacceptable. If a language has verbs preceding objects, therefore, an automatic consequence of the development of adpositions from verbs will be that these adpositions will be prepositions. Of course, this cannot be the whole story, since prepositions can arise historically from other sources than verbs. Nevertheless, the diachronic explanation seems promising.

There are grounds for thinking that many of the functional explanations for grammatical universals are also best thought of in this diachronic sense. A functional explanation for a grammatical universal essentially aims to demonstrate that a system which observes that universal increases the ease with which the semantic content of an utterance can be recovered from its syntactic structure. Why should languages develop in such a way as to conform, in the majority, to a particular functional principle, unless it is the functional principle itself which motivates the change?

As an illustration of this point, let us consider one of best known functional explanations in syntax. This is Anderson's (1976) and Comrie's (1978, 1981) explanation for the distribution of case marking in simple intransitive and transitive sentences. Reverting to the use of S (=Subject) as a mnemonic for the single argument in intransitive sentences, and A (= Agent), and O (=Object) for the two arguments in a typical transitive sentence with an active verb, we have the following two basic sentence patterns (abstracting from considerations of word order):

(46)    S        $V_{intransitive}$

(47) A       O   $V_{transitive}$

In the intransitive construction, there is only a single argument, S, so this argument does not need to be distinguished in any way from the others. However the two arguments A and O in the transitive sentence do need to be distinguished, otherwise ambiguity will result. Case marking is one way of achieving this, hence we would expect the most frequent case marking systems to be those in which A and O are assigned distinct cases: the case marking of S can then be identified either with A, giving the nominative-accusative system, or with O, giving the ergative-absolutive system. Examples of these two systems are given in (48)–(51), from Russian and Kurdish (Kurmanji dialect) respectively:

(48) on        pad – ët
     he(nom.) fall - 3s
     'He is falling'

(49) on        sestr - u    ljub - it
     he(nom.) sister – (acc.) love – 3s
     'He loves his sister'

(50) ew       ket
     he(abs.) fell
     'He fell'

(51) jin    ê    ew      dît
     woman – (obl.) he(abs.) saw
     'The woman saw him'

We can indeed formulate a Greenbergian universal to the effect that if a language has a case-marking system, the probability that it has distinct cases for A and O is greater than that it has the same case for A and O. This is not an absolute universal, since the system in which A and O have the same case, as opposed to S, is attested in the Iranian Pamir language Roshani (Payne, J. 1980). Roshani exhibits this system (the double-oblique system) in past tenses only:

(52) az     - um    pa Xaraɣ   sut
     I(abs.) - ıs     to Xorog went
     'I went to Xorog'

(53) mu    tā       wunt
     I(obl.) you(obl.) saw
     'I saw you'

(In the present tense, the system is nominative-accusative, in that the absolutive case is used for S and A, and the oblique case for O:

(54) čāy       sā - t
     who(abs.) go - 3s
     'who is going?'

(55) az    tā       wun - um
     I(abs.) you(obl.) see - ıs
     'I see you'

The historical origin of the double-oblique system can be easily reconstructed: the transitive past with its characteristic double-oblique form as shown in (53) was originally ergative, with an oblique A and an absolutive O. The absolutive case of O in the past tenses at this stage contrasted with the oblique case of O in the present tense: this dysfunctionality of the system was resolved by the development of the use of the oblique case for O in past tenses, thereby however creating another dysfunctionality: the double-oblique construction. At this stage, we might expect the functional principle to come into force as a pressure on individual speakers of Roshani to find a way of again differentiating A and O in transitive past sentences. Indeed, this seems to be happening: younger speakers of Roshani use forms like (56), in which A is absolutive, or (57), in which O is additionally marked by the preposition *az* (literally 'from'):

(56) az     - um tā       wunt
     I(abs.) - ıs   you(obl.) saw
     'I saw you'

(57) mu    az    taw      wunt
     I(obl.) from you(obl.) saw
     'I saw you'

In this case, the functional principle in question is clearly seen as a force behind the historical change. It remains to be seen whether other functional principles can be considered in this way, but the line of enquiry is a promising one. The diachronic dimension in explanation is fully discussed by Bybee (1988).

## 1.5 Chomskyan universals

The Chomskyan view of language universals differs in important respects from the Greenbergian view. At the heart of the difference lies Chomsky's notion that the goal of linguistic theory is to characterise I-language, which is language viewed as the internalised knowledge incorporated in the brain of a particular speaker, rather than E-language, which is language viewed as a shared social phenomenon external to the mind.

The important questions to which Chomsky attempts to provide an answer are (Chomsky 1988: 3):

(*a*) What is the system of knowledge? What is in the mind/brain of the speaker of a language?
(*b*) How does this system of knowledge arise in the mind/brain?

The answer to question (*a*) is logically prior: it consists firstly in the construction of a grammatical description which is the theory of a particular language, and secondly in the construction of a theory of universal grammar (UG), whose role is to determine which principles of the grammatical description of the particular language are language universals, i.e. invariant and fixed principles of the language faculty of mankind. The construction of UG contributes to the solution of question (*b*), inasmuch as the principles of UG can be considered as innate and not part of what must be discovered by the language learner. (See Chapter 4, above.)

As will be evident from the above, Chomskyan universals are universal principles of grammar which are incorporated in the grammar of a particular language. The explanation for them is that they are innate. As we have seen, Greenbergian probabilistic universals cannot sensibily be incorporated in the grammars of particular languages, since they are statements about how languages *tend* to be rather than how they *must* be. The explanation for them may be reducible to principles of linguistic change, but in any event, innateness does not seem to be involved in their explanation, since all languages seem to be learned with equal facility. Clearly only absolute Greenbergian universals are candidates for incorporation into Chomsky's UG.

The development of ideas about UG within the Chomskyan framework can be divided into two phases. In the early phase, it was thought that the principles of UG could be incorporated as such in the grammars of individual languages. As Katz (1966: 109) puts it: 'each linguistic description has a common part consisting of the set of linguistic universals and a variable part consisting of the generalisations that hold only for the given language.' Such a view leads immediately to the 'Chomskyan syllogism' (Haider 1986):

(A) The principles of UG hold for any natural language
(B) Language x is a natural language

Hence: The principles of UG hold for x
Hence: A detailed analysis of x will lead to the principles of UG

In fact, as demonstrated by Keenan (1976b), this view of the principles of UG, and the research strategy based on it, is untenable. It is untenable because any particular language x greatly under-realises what is universally possible: the constraints on the forms of its structures are generally much stronger than the constraints that are universally valid. As a simple illustration of this point, Keenan considers the notion of 'promotion rule': many languages, including English, have rules whose effect is to form complex structures from simpler ones by assigning the properties of one NP to another. The English passive, no matter how it is formally defined, has the effect of assigning subject properties, such as initial position in the sentence, to an underlying object: from *John gave the book to Mary* we can derive *The book was given to Mary by John.* It turns out, however, that many languages have no promotion rules of this kind: examples are Hausa, Urhobo and Arosi. If the principles of UG were based on these languages, we would be motivated to exclude promotion rules from the set of possible rules permitted by UG.

Since Chomsky (1981), the theory of UG has been modified to include principles which are 'parametrised', i.e. principles which include variables which may have different values in different languages. Different settings of these values then account for the observed diversity of languages. Although there are strong arguments to the contrary (see especially Bowerman 1988), it is often argued that this conception of UG simplifies the problem of accounting for the acquisition of language, since the task of the language learner can be thought of in part as establishing the values of the parameters, and this can be done on the basis of relatively simple sentences. A change in the value of even one parameter can have radical consequences as it works its way through the whole system of grammar.

As a simple example of a parameter we can cite the 'head parameter', which fixes the order of heads and complements. UG permits basically four lexical categories: V (verb), N (noun), A (adjective) and P (preposition). These four lexical categories occur as the 'head' in the corresponding phrasal categories: VP (verb phrase), NP (noun phrase), AP (adjective phrase) and PP (prepositional phrase). Letting X and Y be variables for any of the lexical categories V, N, A or P, the general structure of a phrase can be expressed in the formula (58):

(5) $XP = X - YP$

This is understood to mean that a phrase of a certain category, say VP, will consist of a V which is its head and a complement which can be a phrase of any category, say NP. The English VP in (59) is an instantiation of these choices:

(59) [$_{VP}$ [$_V$ speak ]   [$_{NP}$ English] ]

The principle in (58) is an invariant principle of UG, but several parameter values have to be fixed before it can yield actual phrases in a particular language. In particular, one set of parameters fixes the choices of X and Y, and another fixes the order of the head and complement in each case. In English, the general rule is that the head precedes the complement, while in Japanese it follows.

It is an interesting question whether principle (58) does account for all the variety of phrasal types across the world's languages. There are at least three prima facie objections. Languages with VSO and OSV orders are potential candidates for counter-examples, since V is not adjacent to O. In the case of VSO languages, Chomsky argues for an abstract analysis in which the under-lying structure is SVO and the verb is moved to the front of the clause. Non-configurational languages like Warlpiri are another potential objection, since in these languages it can be argued that V and O do not form a phrase: here Chomsky again has to postulate an abstract structure. Finally, languages with VP-nominative structures like Toba Batak seem difficult to fit into the schema, since the subject would not normally be thought of in the Chomskyan framework as a complement of the verb. Here however the principle (58) might be maintained if the structural definition of subject as a sister of VP were abandoned, with considerable consequences for many other principles of grammar.

One of the consequences of the adoption of the principles and parameters model of UG is that the Chomskyan syllogism now fails. It is impossible to deduce the principles of UG by detailed study of a single language. Another consequence, as pointed out by Keenan (1982), is that it becomes possible to state Greenbergian absolute implicational universals as constraints on the choice of parameters.

For instance, Keenan's view of passivisation in UG is that it is a rule which derives n-place predicates from n + 1—place predicates, a process often described as a reduction of valency (see Chapter 3, above). In English, the one-place predicate *is seen* (which is intransitive and takes a single obligatory subject NP) is derived from the two-place predicate *see* (which is transitive and requires both object and subject NPs). In English we cannot form a zero place predicate from a one-place predicate: there are no passives of intransitive verbs. But such passives do exist in languages like German: from the verb *tanzen* 'dance' it is possible to form a passive *es wird getanzt* (it is danced, i.e. there is dancing) with dummy *es*, which is not a subject. Keenan's preliminary formulation of the Passive in UG is therefore as follows:

(60) a.  Rule: Pn $->$ {Pass,Pn+1}, all n $\geq$ 0
    b.  Parameter Conditions
        (i) if $n_L$ is not zero, then 1 $\epsilon$ $n_L$

English just has one instantiation of the rule, with n = 1, i.e. P1 $->$ {Pass,P2}. The P1 *is seen* can be formed by adding passive morphology and the auxiliary *be* to the P2 *see*. German has two instantiations of the rule: we can not only form the P1 *wird gesehen* from the P2 sehen, but also the P0 *wird getantzt* from the P1 *tanzen*. The Greenbergian implicational universal that if a language forms passives from intransitive verbs, it will also form passives from transitive verbs follows from the parameter condition that if a language forms passives at all, it forms passives from transitive verbs.

We can perhaps see here a move towards a successful synthesis of work within the Chomskyan and Greenbergian paradigms. However a word of caution is in order: we have argued that many implicational universals may simply be tendencies, and if they are, it is inappropriate to include them within a characterisation of innate knowledge. Regardless of the problem of explanation, however, generalisations like (60) based on a principles and parameters approach within an adequate sample of languages seem a promising way forward.

## 1.6 Hierarchies

One of the most successful notions to emerge from language universals research is the notion of 'hierarchy'. Linguistic categories can be ordered hierarchically according to which rules apply to them. Hierarchies therefore follow from the statement of implicational universals and tendencies.

One example is the Keenan-Comrie hierarchy of grammatical relations known as the Accessibility Hierarchy (Keenan and Comrie 1977, Comrie 1981). Essentially, the hierarchy is as follows:

subject > direct object > non-direct object > possessor

The hierarchy plays a role in numerous grammatical processes, but was originally proposed as a statement of the different accessibility of these noun phrase positions to relativisation. English provides essentially no evidence for the existence of the hierarchy, since the method of forming relative clauses in English with the relative pronouns *who* and *which* (the wh-strategy) permits all four of the positions to be relativised:

(61) the man [ *who* bought a book for the girl ]
(62) the book [ *which* the man bought for the girl ]
(63) the girl [ *for whom* the man bought a book ]
(64) the girl [ *whose book* was a success ]

In (61), for example, the head noun *man* plays the role of subject within the relative clause, and in (64) the head noun *girl* plays the role of possessor. As predicted by the hierarchy, the two intermediate positions of direct object in (62) and non-direct object in (63) are also relativisable.

However, there are languages like Malagasy which permit only the subject position to be relativised. Keenan (1985: 157) provides some examples.

(65)  Manasa ny lamba  ny vehivavy
      wash    the clothes the woman
      'The woman is washing the clothes'

(66)  ny vehivavy [ (izay) manasa ny  lamba ]
      the woman      that wash    the clothes
      'The woman that is washing the clothes'

(67)  *ny lamba   [ (izay) manasa ny vehivavy ]
       the clothes    that wash    the woman
      'The clothes that the woman is washing'

Sentence (65) illustrates the basic word order VOS in Malagasy. While the relative clause construction in (66) is acceptable, where the head noun *vehivavy* plays the subject role in the relative clause, the relative clause in (67) is not permitted. Neither are relative clauses based on the oblique object or possessor positions. In order to express the meaning in (67), Malagasy is forced to promote the direct object, by passivisation, into the subject position, where it can be relativised:

(68)  Ny lamba  [ (izay) sasan'ny      vehivavy ]
      the clothes   that washed by the woman
      'The clothes that are washed by the woman'

The hierarchy also states that there are languages in which the subject and direct object positions are relativisable, but not the oblique object and possessor positions: Bantu languages like Luganda seem to fall into this category. And we can also expect languages in which subject, direct object and oblique objects are relativisable, but not possessors: an example is the Fering dialect of North Frisian.

As we begin to expect of generalisations based on implicational statements, there are counter-examples to the hierarchy as presented. Ergativity presents an initial problem, forcing us to distinguish between intransitive subjects (Ss) and transitive subjects (As): the syntactically ergative Dyirbal for example permits relativisation on Ss and Os, but not As. Interestingly, it has a process (called the 'anti-passive') which has the effect of converting As into Ss, just as the passive in Malagasy converts Os into Ss. They can then be relativised.

Other problems are presented by West Indonesian languages like Malay, which permit relativisation of subjects and possessors, but not of direct objects or most non-direct objects (Comrie 1981: 150). Keenan and Comrie (1977) attempt to preserve the hierarchy as an absolute universal by distinguishing between different strategies for forming relative clauses within the same language (for example, the expression of the role of the head noun within the relative clause by the use of case-marked pronouns like English *who/whom/whose*, as opposed to the use of forms which lack case, like English *that*). Each strategy must then operate on contiguous elements of the hierarchy, and one strategy must operate on at least some subjects. Significantly, however, even with this hedging, there still remain recalcitrant counterexamples like Tongan, which has a [+case] strategy for (some) subjects, non-direct objects and possessors, but a [−case] strategy for direct objects (Comrie 1981: 151).

A second hierarchy which seems to have quite a pervasive role in language is the animacy hierarchy of Silverstein (1976). This has the form:

| | | | | | | | | |
|---|---|---|---|---|---|---|---|---|
| 1st & 2nd person non-singular pronouns | > | 1st & 2nd person singular pronouns | > | 3rd person pronouns | > | proper nouns | > | human common nouns | > |
| animate common nouns | > | inanimate common nouns | | | | | | |

This hierarchy was originally proposed as a statement of the distribution of case-marking systems in languages which show 'split' ergativity, i.e. where some nominals work according to an ergative-absolutive system, but others work according to a nominative-accusative system. We have already seen one example of this in the case-marking of nominals in Dyirbal, where all 1st and 2nd person pronouns and proper nouns are nominative-accusative, and all common nouns (and determiners) are ergative-absolutive. There are no 3rd person pronouns distinct from the determiners. The general principle is that ergative marking extends from the right of the hierarchy, and accusative marking from the left. Dixon (1980: 290) gives a plausible functional reason for this: things which are high on the animacy hierarchy are typically instigators of actions and therefore more likely to be As than are things which are low on the hierarchy. It therefore makes sense that things which are low on the hierarchy should have a special marking (the ergative) when untypically they occur as As. The reverse argument applies for the accusative marking of things which are high on the hierarchy.

The animacy hierarchy has since been refined and extended in various ways. The relative ordering of the persons is thoroughly reviewed by Plank (1985). Lazard (1984) incorporates into the hierarchy such notions as definiteness versus indefiniteness and genericity versus non-genericity in a wide-ranging account of the ways Os can differ: in Persian, for example, all definite Os are marked by the postposition -rā, but some indefinite Os may or may not take -rā, according to whether they are human or not. Lazard's combined scale resembles Table 8.

*Table 8*

| 1st & 2nd | 3rd person pronouns | Definite | Indefinite | Mass | Generic |
|---|---|---|---|---|---|
| person | | | | | |
| | Proper | Human | Non-human | | |
| pronouns | names | | | | |

Ultimately, we seem to see a scale running from maximal individualisation on the one hand to maximal generalisation on the other hand. Such notions also play a fundamental role in Seiler's (1986) attempt to relate a wide body of linguistic phenomena involving nominals to a single scale.

## 2. LANGUAGE TYPES

### 2.1 Introduction

The aim of linguistic typology is to categorise actually-occurring languages according to their properties. It is essentially an application of work in language universals research to the question of how similar particular languages are to each other, or how different.

There are essentially two ways in which languages can be categorised. The first is to partition the set of actually-occurring languages into subsets which share a particular property P. Such a partitioning is usually called a 'classificatory' typology, and the individual subsets are called 'classificatory' types. We can then say of any particular language x which possesses the relevant property P that it 'belongs to' the (classificatory) type T.

Which property we choose as the basis of a classificatory typology is completely open, and depends on the purpose for which we wish to use the typology. There is of course little point in choosing a property which is genuinely universal (like the use of vowels), since then every language would belong to the same type with respect to that property. But any other property might be of interest for some purpose: we could for example classify languages into those which use clicks ('click languages') and those which do not, or those which use distinctive tone ('tone languages') and those which do not. Such classifications are typically used by one linguist describing to another the salient feature(s) of a particular language.

Many linguists have felt, however, that there should be more significance to the notion of 'language type' than simple classification. A first move that is often made is to suggest that the property which is chosen as the basis of classification should be a property on which other properties depend, i.e. a property which is the antecedent of a Greenbergian universal. We could for example choose basic word orders (in terms of the elements, S, O and V), which serve as the antecedents for such further properties as prepositional versus postpositional. If yet more properties could be found which were dependent on the basic word order, we might form a 'general' or 'holistic' typology which classified languages not on the basis of a single property, but on the basis of whole systems of properties.

Unfortunately, such general or holistic typologies seem to be illusory (for discussion see Vennemann 1981 and Ramat 1986). One reason is that not enough properties seem to depend on each other, but more seriously, even those implications which do hold invariably turn out to be tendencies rather than absolute universals.

A possible solution to this problem is the notion of 'ideal' (or 'consistent') type: this is an abstraction based on the most frequently observed co-occurrences, or deduced *a priori* from abstract principles. We then have a second way of classifying languages, namely, in relation to an abstraction which may or may not be represented in actually-occurring languages. We can say such things as: language x belongs to the (ideal) type T except for property P, or, in numerical terms, language x belongs to the (ideal) type T to the extent e. Ideal types therefore provide a convenient way for linguists to talk about particular languages in global terms: they have no other status than this.

It is important to distinguish between classificatory and ideal types when making statements to the effect that a particular language belongs to a particular type. Japanese might be said to be an 'SOV language' in both senses: it has basic word order SOV and a number of related properties like the use of postpositions. But Persian is an 'SOV language' only in the classificatory sense that it has SOV basic word order: it differs from the ideal type in many respects, including the use of prepositions.

In the sections which follow, we shall concentrate on examples of ideal types from phonology, morphology and syntax respectively.

## 2.2 Phonological types

The most intriguing ideal types of phonology are Gil's (1986) 'iambic' and 'trochaic' types. Iambic metres, which are based on the principle weak-strong, tend to contain more syllables than trochaic metres, which are based on the principle strong-weak. Iambic metres are more suited to be spoken, while trochaic metres are more suited to be sung. Starting from these metrical notions, Gil establishes the two ideal types: (*a*) iambic languages have more syllables than trochaic languages, (*b*) iambic languages have simpler syllable structures than trochaic languages, (*c*) iambic languages are stress-timed while trochaic languages are syllable-timed, (*d*) iambic languages have more obstruent segments than sonorant segments in their phonemic inventories, while trochaic languages have more sonorant segments than obstruent segments, (*e*) iambic languages have more level intonation contours, and trochaic languages have more variable intonation contours, (*f*) iambic languages are tonal while trochaic languages are non-tonal.

English is closer to the trochaic ideal, with a very complex syllable template of up to three segments before the syllable peak (as in *strengths* /s-t-r-e-ŋ-θ-s/) and up to four segments after the syllable peak (as in *sixths* /s-i-k-s-θ-s/. It is of course not tonal, but does possess a rich variety of intonation contours and a relatively low consonant/vowel ratio of 2.08: the number of consonants in the phonemic inventory is 27 and the number of vowels 13.

By contrast, Turkish is closer to the iambic ideal, with a very simple syllable structure template (C)V(C)(C), no tone, and a higher consonant/vowel ratio of 3 (24 consonants and 8 vowels). Gil even has statistical evidence that word order may be related: SVO languages like English are more likely to be trochaic, and SOV languages like Turkish are more likely to be iambic.

## 2.3 Morphological types

Morphological typologies attempt to characterise languages according to:

(i)   the extent to which linguistic concepts are expressed by morphological (i.e. word-internal) modification, rather than by the use of separate words

(ii)  the morphological techniques employed

The foundations of morphological typology were laid primarily at the beginning of the nineteenth century, although, as Frans Plank pointed out in a recent lecture to the Linguistics Association of Great Britain, eighteenth-century precursors like Beauzée are known. In these early typologies, however, the two factors mentioned above are typically conflated into a simple tripartite or quadripartite classification of languages. August Wilhelm von Schlegel (1818), developing the work of his brother, Friedrich, proposed a tripartite division into the classificatory types:

(*a*)  languages without any grammatical structure

(*b*) languages which employ affixes
(*c*) languages with inflection

In the first type were placed languages like Chinese, where roots are in general not modified by affixation or internal change and where words therefore appear to lack any 'grammatical' structure. From a modern description (Li and Thompson (1987: 825), we can cite a typical Chinese sentence illustrating this property:

(69) tā   qù zhōngguó xué   zhōngguó huà
    s/he go China    learn China    painting
    'S/he went to China to learn Chinese painting.'

The pronoun *tā* has one invariant form: it does not change according to gender (*he* vs. *she* vs. *it*), nor does it have any case ending to show its role in the sentence (this is shown instead by its initial position before the verb). The verb *qù* shows no distinction of tense (e.g. past vs. present), nor does it change to show agreement with the third-person pronoun *tā*. Equally the verb *xué* has no special infinitive form to indicate its relation to the verb *qù* (this must be inferred from the context). Finally, the noun *zhōngguó* does not vary according to whether it is the object of the verb *qù* (as in its first occurrence) or an attributive modifier of the noun *huà* (where it corresponds to the English adjective *Chinese*).

By contrast, the languages in types (*b*) and (*c*) are said to permit their roots to undergo modification, differing solely in whether the technique of modification consists simply of affixation of elements to an invariant root, or whether the root itself can be internally modified.

As examples of type (*b*), Schlegel cites the American-Indian languages and Basque. Basque, for instance, is commonly thought of as having a complex system of cases which are expressed as endings. It also possesses a three-term category of number: singular, plural and indeterminate. The paradigm can be presented as in Table 9 (adapted from Iturrioz 1982).

Despite the apparent complexity of this paradigm, the endings which represent the individual cases are for the most part invariant and easily recognisable. With the exception of the absolutive plural, the final element in each column has essentially the same form for each case (e.g. *-(r)ekin* for the comitative, *-tik* for the ablative). The representation of number by elements preceding the case endings is certainly more complex, but it can be seen that the plural is always represented by *-e-* (except in the absolutive, or when the following element itself begins with *-e*). Otherwise, the invariant elements *-a-* and *-ta-* seem to be for the most part in complementary distribution: either the presence of *-a-*, which Iturrioz (1982) suggests is a marker of individualisation, or the absence of *-ta-*, which might be analysed as a marker of

*Table 9*

| Case | Indeterminate | Singular | Plural |
|------|---------------|----------|--------|
| Absolutive | -Ø | -a-Ø | -ak |
| Ergative | -k | -a-k | -e-k |
| Dative | -(r)i | -a-ri | -e-i |
| Genitive | -(r)en | -a-ren | -en |
| Destinative | -(r)entzat | -a-rentzat | -entzat |
| Causative | -(r)engatik | -a-rengatik | -engatik |
| Comitative | -(r)ekin | -a-rekin | -ekin |
| Instrumental | -z | -a-z | -e-z |
| Deliminative | -ta-ko | -ko | -e-ta-ko |
| Inessive | -ta-n | -a-n | -e-ta-n |
| Allative | -ta-ra | -ra | -e-ta-ra |
| Tendentional Allative | -ta-rantz | -rantz | -e-ta-rantz |
| Terminative Allative | -ta-raino | -raino | -e-ta-raino |
| Ablative | -ta-tik | -tik | -e-ta-tik |
| Partitive | -(r)ik | | |
| Prolative | -tzat | | |

generalisation, sets the singular paradigm apart from the indeterminate and plural. Most importantly for Schlegel's classification, however, these endings are simply attached to any root noun without any change in the noun itself (apart from stress). The indeterminate 'with bridges' is *zubí-ekin*, the singular 'with the bridge' is *zubi-a-rekin*, and the plural 'with the bridges' is *zubi-ékin* (with different stress to the indeterminate).

Schlegel's type (*c*), the inflectional languages, contains both the classical Indo-European languages such as Greek, Latin and Sanskrit, and modern Indo-European languages such as the languages of the Romance group. Characteristic of the type for Schlegel is the fact that roots themselves can be modified in the expression of grammatical categories, with or without the concomitant presence of affixes. One example would be the Greek verb forms *leíp-ō* 'I leave', *lé-loip-a* 'I left' (perfect), *é-lip-on* 'I left' (aorist), where the root shows three distinct forms *leip*, *loip*, and *lip*. Here the alternation in the root is the vocalic alternation known as 'ablaut', the vowels *e, o* or zero being inserted into a basic form *l-ip*. Consonantal alternations are equally possible, as in the declension of a Latin noun like *pecus* 'head of cattle':

| Case | Singular | Plural |
|------|----------|--------|
| Nominative | pecus | pecud-es |
| Accusative | pecud-em | pecud-es |
| Genitive | pecud-is | pecud-um |
| Dative | pecud-i | pecud-ibus |
| Ablative | pecud-e | pecud-ibus |

Here the form *pecus* of the nominative singular alternates with the form *pecud* of the rest of the paradigm.

Nevertheless, it was clear to Schlegel that a modern Indo-European language like French differed substantially from a classical Indo-European language like Latin. French was obliged to use articles before nouns and personal pronouns before verbs; it also used a greater number of auxiliary verbs in its system of conjugation, and resorted to the combination of preposition and noun where in Latin a case ending on the noun would suffice. In order to distinguish the languages which made extensive use of such categories as article, personal pronoun, auxiliary verb and preposition, and the languages which did not, Schlegel further divided the inflexional languages in type (*c*) into:

(*c*1) analytic languages
(*c*2) synthetic languages

An analytic language like French would use a combination of words like *sur la terre* 'on the ground' to express what in a synthetic language like Latin might be said in a single word, *humi*. Nevertheless, the presence in French of alternating verb-roots like *vien-s* (come-1s) and *ven-ons* (come-1p) would in principle keep French in the inflectional class.

The tripartite classificatory typology of Schlegel was expanded into a quadripartite typology by Wilhelm von Humboldt (1822, 1836), who added the type of 'incorporating' languages. Realising that many languages would not fit neatly into Schlegel's classificatory types, Humboldt conceived of his types as ideal. The names Humboldt assigned to Schlegel's types are the names with which they are very often associated to this day:

(a) isolating languages
(b) agglutinating languages
(c) flectional languages
(d) incorporating languages

An 'isolating' language like Chinese would present its roots in isolation, without any grammatical modification. An 'agglutinating' language like Basque (the term derives from Latin *gluten* 'glue') would glue any number of invariant endings, each with its own meaning, on to an invariant root, while a 'flectional' language like Greek or Latin would permit the roots themselves to undergo modification. The 'incorporating' class was added to cover American-Indian languages which showed a verbal morphology so complex that one word could stand for a whole sentence, even incorporating concepts which in other languages would be expressed by separate objects and adverbial modifiers. The Hokan language Yana, for example, has verbal suffixes such as *ʔai* 'in the fire', *-xui* 'in(to) the water, *-sgin* 'early in the morning', -ca(a) 'at night', -xkid 'slowly' and -ya(a)gal 'quickly' (see Schachter 1985: 23). The Yana word ya-ba-hau-si (burn-pl-east-3) means 'they burn in the east' (Sapir 1921: 105).

Many attempts have been made to improve the classical nineteenth-century typologies, both throughout the nineteenth and into the twentieth century. Nineteenth-century typologies are reviewed by Horne (1966). In the twentieth century, the most notable attempts are undoubtedly those of Sapir (1921), Skalička, whose works on morphological typology were issued in one volume as Skalička (1979), and Sgall (1986).

Sapir clearly distinguishes between factors (i) and (ii), the extent to which word-internal modification is used in a language, and its technique. Initially, he suggests four fundamental types based on the types of concept a language uses:

(a) Simple Pure-relational
(b) Complex Pure-relational
(c) Simple Mixed-relational
(d) Complex Mixed-relational

Simple pure-relational languages have ways of expressing concepts of Group I (these are basic concepts normally expressed by independent words or lexical roots), and ways of expressing concepts of Group IV (these are pure-relational concepts which indicate the relation of the basic concepts in the proposition to each other, such as subject-object relations). They lack concepts of Group II (derivational concepts which enable the formation of new concepts of Group I from other concepts of Group I, e.g. the formation of the concept *depth* from the concept *deep* in English), and concepts of Group III (concrete relational concepts like number, tense and definiteness). Complex pure-relational languages express concepts of Groups I, II and IV, simple mixed-relational languages express concepts of Groups I, III and IV, and complex mixed-relational languages express concepts of all four Groups.

Within this framework, it is then possible to talk of the techniques which can be used to express the concepts of Groups II, III and IV. These are (a) isolation (defined as the use of position in the sentence rather than morpho-logical modification), (b) agglutination (with the notion of invariance of affixes defined very strictly: the English plural affix -s as in *book-s* is for Sapir not agglutinative on account of the existence of the plural affix -en in *ox-en*), (c) fusion (the use of affixes with variance either in the affix or the root or both), and (d) symbolism (variance of the root without affixation). The classical notion of '(in)flection' is abandoned, the term 'inflection' being used more specially for fused affixes representing relational concepts of Groups III and IV. Confusingly there is yet a third sense of the term 'inflection', which is a general term for all bound affixes which are not derivational, whether they are fusional or agglutinating.

The extent to which a language chooses to use word-internal modification at all is expressed by Sapir quantitatively in the scale analytic-synthetic-polysynthetic. Analytic languages are simply those which have the least word-internal modification, while polysynthetic languages have the most. It should be noted that Sapir's use of the term 'analytic' is not exactly the same as Schlegel's. In Sapir's terms, a simple pure-relational language like Chinese which uses isolation as its main technique can be analytic, whereas for Schlegel the essence of analyticity seems to be the use of grammatical words.

As an illustration of Sapir's typology, English can be described as a complex mixed-relational language, using all four Groups of concepts. To express concepts of Group II (derivation), it uses primarily the technique of fusion (as in *deep/depth*). To express concepts of Group III (concrete-relational) it uses the techniques of fusion (as in *walk/walk-ed*) or symbolism (as in *run/ran*). To express concepts of Group IV (pure-relational), it uses primarily position (i.e. isolation). On the scale of degree of synthesis, English is analytic.

One of the main worries linguists have had about morphological typologies is that they do not seem to be based on any implicational tendencies (Anderson 1985: 9–11). Sapir's work suggests how this might be remedied: it is an interesting question whether languages which use one kind of technique to express one Group of concepts also use the same technique to express another, or whether a mixture of techniques is more typical. Skalička's and Sgall's ideal types are types in which the same technique extends to derivational and relational concepts across all the different lexical and phrasal categories. An ideal agglutinating language would use the agglutinating technique in noun phrases as in verb phrases, and for the expression of derivational as well as relational concepts. Unfortunately, little work seems to have been done on large samples to see whether real languages do show any significant correlations.

Instead, it is possible to discern two main directions in which morphological typology has developed in recent years. The first is in the direction of giving a numerical basis to the extent a language belongs to a type. The second is the attempt by Nichols (1986) to determine a pattern in the placement of morphological marking across a wide range of constructions within a given language.

Just as the degree of synthesis in a language can be conceived of as a quantitative measure, so can the degree to which particular morphological techniques are used. Even Chinese is not totally isolating: it possesses a number of grammatical suffixes, for example aspectival suffixes -*le* (perfective) and -*zhe* (durative) which are attached agglutinatively to verbal roots (Li and Thompson 1987: 822–4).

The quantitative approach to morphological typology was started by

Greenberg (1960), and has been followed up by Cowgill (1963), Mejlax (1973), and Kasevič and Jaxontov (1982). The technique is to take sample texts from a range of languages and segment them into words, morphs and morph boundaries of various kinds. For each text it is then possible to give a precise number for such quantities as: W (number of words), M (number of morphs), J (number of morph junctures), A (number of agglutinating morph junctures), R (number of root morphs), D (number of bound derivational morphs), I (number of bound inflectional (i.e. non-derivational) morphs, Aux (number of word-like grammatical morphs), and many others.

Of course, it is imperative in calculating such numbers that consistent cross-linguistic definitions are available for notions such as 'word' and 'agglutinating'. Kasevič and Jaxontov for example take the English plural in -s to be agglutinating (on the grounds that plurals like *ox-en* are a very restricted class of exception), whereas Greenberg follows Sapir in treating -s as fusional. Even more refined decisions are needed, as pointed out by Plank (1986): do we treat as agglutinative morphs like the English third-person singular affix -s as in *sing-s*, which are cumulative (i.e. contain more than one distinction) but not sensitive (i.e. do not show or cause any unpredictable variation)?

Given consistency of analysis, it is then possible to compare indices across languages. For instance, the index M/W (morphs per word) is a count of the degree of analyticity (or rather syntheticity) in a language in Sapir's sense. The index Aux/W (grammatical words per word) is a measure of the degree of analyticity in a language in Schlegel's sense. The index A/J (agglutinating morph juncture per morph juncture) is a measure of the extent to which a language is agglutinating rather than fusional. The index D/W is a measure of the extent to which a language expresses concepts of Sapir's Group II by bound morphs. The index I/W is a measure of the extent to which a language expresses concepts of Sapir's Groups III and IV by bound morphs. More complex indices are possible: the index (R-Aux)/M (number of lexical roots per morph) is a measure of the degree of lexicality versus grammaticality in a language.

Specimen values of these indices for five well-known languages (from Kasevič and Jaxontov) are as follows:

|          | M/W  | Aux/W | A/J  | D/W  | I/W  | R-Aux/M |
|----------|------|-------|------|------|------|---------|
| Tagalog  | 1.43 | 0.51  | 1.00 | 0.12 | 0.22 | 0.35    |
| Vietnamese | 1.47 | 0.14 | 1.00 | 0.03 | 0.10 | 0.82    |
| Persian  | 1.67 | 0.30  | 0.83 | 0.04 | 0.53 | 0.42    |
| Turkish  | 2.15 | 0.01  | 0.93 | 0.13 | 1.01 | 0.47    |
| Arabic   | 3.14 | 0.26  | 0.50 | 0.20 | 1.94 | 0.23    |

Of these five languages, Tagalog is the most analytic in both senses of the term (it has the lowest M/W index and the highest Aux/W index), whereas Arabic is the most synthetic in Sapir's sense (highest M/W) and Turkish is the most synthetic in the sense of having least auxiliary grammatical words. The classic agglutinating language Turkish certainly has a higher A/J index than the fusional Arabic, but to the extent that Tagalog and Vietnamese use bound morphs, as shown by the D/W and I/W indices, the technique of juncture is agglutinating. Arabic has the highest derivational and inflectional indices and the classic isolating language Vietnamese the lowest. Similarly, Vietnamese emerges with the highest lexicality index and Arabic the lowest.

It is an interesting question whether there are any statistical correlations between the above scales. The existing samples of languages are unfortunately not free of bias and not sufficiently large. However as an indication of the kind of results which might emerge, we give in Figure 10 a plot of the two indices analyticity (Aux/W) and lexicality for the sample of twenty-six languages studied by Kasevič and Jaxontov. Some clustering seems to be observable, with languages like Turkish, Tagalog, Arabic and Vietnamese at opposite poles, and Persian in the middle.

Nichols's (1986) morphological typology is based on the placement of morphological marking in different construction types within a sample of sixty languages. The key to the typology is the notion of head versus dependent item in a construction. For some constructions the notion of what the head might be is relatively uncontroversial: for instance the verb can be taken as the head of the clause, the noun can be taken as the head in a noun-adjective construction and the preposition/postposition can be taken as the head in a prepositional/postpositional phrase construction. For other constructions like auxiliary verb-lexical verb, it is far from being uncontroversial which constituent is the head (cf. Zwicky (1985) and Hudson (1987) for comment). However, on the basis of the relatively uncontroversial cases, Nichols is able to show a clustering of languages at the consistently head-marking or consistently dependent-marking ends of the scale, with a smaller cluster of languages with split or double marking in the middle.

At the clausal level, the distinction between head-marking and dependent marking is essentially whether the relationship of the verb to its arguments is shown by verbal affixes or by case-marking on the nouns. A consistent head-marking language would be Abkhaz (Hewitt 1979), with for example clauses like (70) and postpositional phrases like (71), and a consistent dependent marking language would be Chechen, with clauses (like (72) and post-positional phrases like (73):

(70) a -xàc'a a  -pħỳs  a  - š̥°q°'àØ-  là -y -te-yt'
    the - man  the - woman the - book  it - to her - he - gave
    'The man gave the woman the book'

*Figure 10*

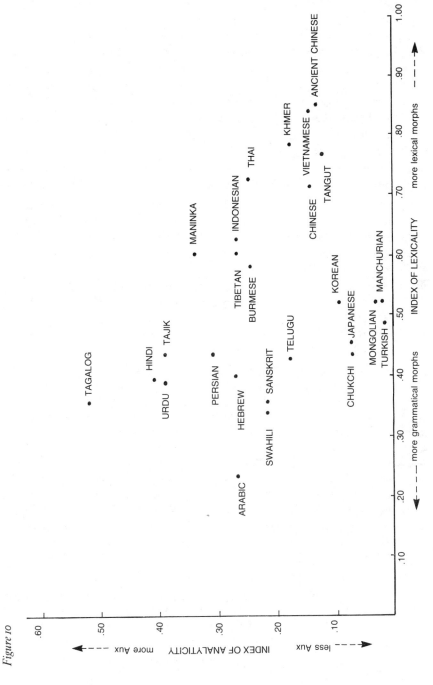

(71) a - jàyas a - q'nà
the - river its - at
'at the river'

(72) da:  - s  woʕa - na  urs  - Ø  tö:xira
father – erg. son  - dat. knife - nom. struck
'The father struck the son with a knife'

(73) be:ra - na  t'e
child - dat.on
'on the child'

## 2.4. Syntactic Types

There are of course many classificatory types in syntax. Taking basic sentence structure as a starting point, one important distinction has been between languages in which the relation subject-predicate plays a major role ('subject-prominent' languages) and languages in which the relation topic-comment plays a major role ('topic-prominent' languages) (Li and Thompson 1976). English is a clear example of a subject-prominent language, while Lahu is a clear example of a topic-prominent language:

(74) Elephant's noses are long

(75) hɔ    ɔ̄    na-quô yɨ  ve  yò
elephant topic nose  long part decl.
'Elephants (topic), noses are long'

The English subject *elephant's noses* is internal to its clause and bears a selectional relation to the predicate in its clause, while the Lahu topic *elephants* is external to the clause and does not bear any selectional relation to the predicate. Topics are also invariably definite, whereas subjects need not be.

A second classificatory typology based on basic sentence structure is the case-marking/verb-agreement typology which considers the ways in which S, A, and O are marked (typically according to the nominative-accusative principle, ergative-absolutive principle, or active principle (as in Tsova-Tush)). An attempt has been made by Klimov (e.g. Klimov 1977) to convert this typology into a more holistic typology, but Lazard (1986) argues very convincingly against the correlations suggested by Klimov.

Undoubtedly the most successful ideal syntactic typology is the basic word-order typology based on the Greenbergian implicational universals of word-order. Table 10, from Hawkins (1983), illustrates the correlations which are found in a sample of 336 languages between the basic order of the elements S, V, and O, the type of adposition (preposition or postposition), the order of genitive expression and head noun, and the order of adjective and head noun.

*Table 10*

| Type | Basic Order | Pr/Po | NG/GN | NA/AN | Languages in sample |
|------|-------------|-------|-------|-------|---------------------|
| 1 | V–1 | Pr | NG | NA | 38 |
| 2 | V–1 | Pr | NG | AN | 13 |
| 3 | V–1 | Pr | GN | AN | 1 |
| 4 | V–1 | Pr | GN | NA | 0 |
| 5 | V–1 | Po | NG | NA | 0 |
| 6 | V–1 | Po | NG | AN | 0 |
| 7 | V–1 | Po | GN | AN | 1 |
| 8 | V–1 | Po | GN | NA | 0 |
| 9 | SVO | Pr | NG | NA | 56 |
| 10 | SVO | Pr | NG | AN | 17 |
| 11 | SVO | Pr | GN | AN | 7 |
| 12 | SVO | Pr | GN | NA | 4 |
| 13 | SVO | Po | NG | NA | 0 |
| 14 | SVO | Po | NG | AN | 0 |
| 15 | SVO | Po | GN | AN | 12 |
| 16 | SVO | Po | GN | NA | 13 |
| 17 | SOV | Pr | NG | NA | 10 |
| 18 | SOV | Pr | NG | AN | 0 |
| 19 | SOV | Pr | GN | AN | 2 |
| 20 | SOV | Pr | GN | NA | 0 |
| 21 | SOV | Po | NG | NA | 11 |
| 22 | SOV | Po | NG | AN | 0 |
| 23 | SOV | Po | GN | AN | 96 |
| 24 | SOV | Po | GN | NA | 55 |

Counter to Hawkins, we do not believe that the zeroes in this table are significant: they represent rare combinations rather than absolute impossibilities. Indeed, languages in some of the unattested types are now coming to light. For example, Payne, D. (1986) cites the Amazonian language Yagua as belonging to Type 8, and the northern or Jewish dialect of the Iranian language Tati seems, according to the description of Grjunberg and Davydova (1982), to belong to type 18.

Rather, the significance of the table lies in the strong tendencies which can be observed. Particularly striking is the correlation between Pr and NG on the one hand, and Po and GN on the other, irrespective of basic word order. Out of 145 languages with the order NG, 134 are prepositional and only 11 postpositional. Out of 191 languages with the order GN, 177 are postpositional and only 14 prepositional. Evidently the historical explanation is the strongest one here: a major historical source for adpositions is the genitive-noun or noun-genitive construction: a form like *top (of) table* (NG) can frequently develop into a form like *top table* (Pr N), with the noun *top* becoming a preposition meaning 'on'. Such developments are seen for example in Persian with the noun *sar* 'head'.

Other strong correlations can of course be observed in the table, the tendency for V–1 and SVO languages to be prepositional and for SOV languages to be postpositional in particular. The correlation with adjectival order seems less strong, but also significant. Looking at the table from a typological point of view, however, the most important type is type 23, the SOV language with Po, GN and AN. The sheer numbers of languages in this type have led to the identification of these properties as an ideal type to which real languages can approximate very closely. Examples from Turkish are:

(76) Bu    çiçek-ler-i    siz - e   al  - dı   - m (SOV)
     these flower-p-obj. you - for buy - past - is
     'I bought these flowers for you'

(77) bu   adam gibi (Po)
     this man   like
     'like this man'

(78) ev     - im - in   kapı - sı  (GN)
     house - my - gen door - its
     'the door of my house'

(79) büyük bir ev     (AN)
     big    a   house
     'a big house'

Other properties are very often attributed to the ideal SOV type: for example, other word order tendencies, with all modifying expressions preceding the constituents they modify. Properties of a different nature may also be linked, for example non-configurationality (the lack of a VP constituent), and even ergativity. These wider correlations are for the time being speculative, but intriguing.

## REFERENCES

Anderson, S.R. (1976) 'On the Notion of Subject in Ergative Languages', in Li 1976 (ed.): 3–23.

Anderson, S.R. (1985) 'Typological Distinctions in Word Formation', in Shopen 1985, vol 3: 3–56.

Bell, A. (1978) 'Language Samples', in Greenberg 1978, vol 1: 123–56.

Bolinger, D.L. (1968) *Aspects of Language*, Harcourt, Brace and World, New York.

Bowerman, M. (1988) 'The "No Negative Evidence" Problem: How Do Children Avoid Constructing an Overly General Grammar?', in Hawkins 1988: 73–101.

Bybee, J.L. (1988) 'The Diachronic Dimension in Explanation', in Hawkins 1988: 350–79.

Chomsky, N. (1965) *Aspects of the Theory of Syntax*, MIT Press, Cambridge, Mass.

Chomsky, N. and Halle, M. (1968) *The Sound Pattern of English*, Harper & Row, New York.

Chomsky, N. (1981) *Lectures on Government and Binding*, Foris, Dordrecht.

Chomsky, N. (1988) *Language and Problems of Knowledge. The Managua Lectures*, MIT Press, Cambridge, Mass.

Comrie, B. (1978) 'Ergativity', in Lehmann, W.P. (ed.) *Syntactic Typology: Studies in the Phenomenology of Language*, University of Texas Press, Austin: 329–94.

Comrie, B. (1981) *Language Universals and Linguistic Typology*, Blackwell, Oxford.

Comrie, B. (1984) 'Language Universals and Linguistic Argumentation: a Reply to Coopmans', *Journal of Linguistics*, 20: 155–63.

Coopmans, P. (1983) 'Review of Comrie (1981)', *Journal of Linguistics*, 19: 455–73.

Cowgill, W. (1963) 'A Search for Universals in Indo-European Diachronic Morphology', in Greenberg 1963: 91–113.

Crothers, J. (1978) 'Typology and Universals of Vowel Systems', in Greenberg 1978 vol 2: 93–152.

Derbyshire, D.C. (1987) 'Areal Characteristics of Amazonian Languages', *International Journal of American Linguistics*, 53: 311–26.

Derbyshire, D.C. and Pullum, G.K. (eds) (1986) *Handbook of Amazonian Languages: Volume 1*, Mouton de Gruyter, Berlin.

Dixon, R.M.W. (1979) 'Ergativity', *Language*, 55: 59–138.

Dixon, R.M.W. (1980) *The Languages of Australia*, Cambridge University Press, Cambridge.

Dixon, R.M.W. (1982) *Where have all the Adjectives Gone? And other Essays in Syntax and Semantics*, Mouton, The Hague.

Edel'man, D.I. (1968) *Osnovnye Voprosy Lingvisticeskoj Geografii*, Nauka, Moscow.

Ferguson, C.A. (1963) 'Assumptions about Nasals', in Greenberg 1963: 42–7.

Foley, W.A. (1986) *The Papuan Languages of New Guinea*, Cambridge University Press, Cambridge.

Gair, J.W. (1976) 'Is Sinhala a Subject Language? (or, How Restricted is Your PNP)', in Verma, M.K. (ed.) *The Notion of Subject in South Asian Languages*, South Asian Studies, Publication #2, University of Wisconsin, Madison: 39–64.

Gil, D. (1986) 'A Prosodic Typology of Language'. *Folia Linguistica*, 20: 165–231.

Greenberg, J.H. (1960) 'A Quantitative Approach to the Morphological Typology of Language', *International Journal of American Linguistics*, 26: 178–94.

Greenberg, J.H. (1963a) 'Some Universals of Grammar with Particular Reference to the Order of Meaningful Elements', in Greenberg 1963b: 58–90.

Greenberg, J.H. (ed.) (1963b) *Universals of Language. Report of a Conference Held at Dobbs Ferry, New York, April 13–15, 1961*, MIT Press, Cambridge, Mass. (2nd. ed. 1966; references are to 1st ed.)

Greenberg, J.H. (1966) 'Synchronic and Diachronic Universals in Phonology', *Language*, 42: 508–18.

Greenberg, J.H. (ed.) (1978) *Universals of Human Language* (4 volumes), Stanford University Press, Stanford.

Grjunberg, A.L. and Davydova, L.X. (1982) 'Tatskij Jazyk', in Rastorgueva, V.S. (ed.) *Osnovy Iranskogo Jazykoznanija. Novoiranskie Jazyki: Zapadnaja Gruppa, Prikaspijskie Jazyki*, Nauka, Moscow: 231–86.

Haider, H. (1986) 'Who's Afraid of Typology?', *Folia Linguistica*, 20: 109–45.

Hale, A. and Watters, D. (1973) 'A Survey of Clause Patterns', in *Clause, Sentence and Discourse Patterns in Selected Languages of Nepal*, Part II, Summer Institute of Linguistics, Norman, Oklahoma: 178–249.

Hale, K. (1983) 'Warlpiri and the Grammar of Non-Configurational Languages', *Natural Language and Linguistic Theory*, 1.1: 5–49.

Halle, M. (1970) 'Is Kabardian a Vowel-less Language?', *Foundations of Language*, 6; 95–103.

Harris, M. (1987) 'French', in Comrie, B. (ed.) *The World's Major Languages*, Croom Helm, London: 210–35.

Hawkins, J.A. (1983) *Word Order Universals*, Academic Press, New York.

Hawkins, J.A. (ed.) (1988) *Explaining Language Universals*, Blackwell, Oxford.

Hewitt, B.G. (1979) *Abkhaz, Lingua* Descriptive Series 2, North-Holland, Amsterdam.

Hewitt, B.G. (1981) 'Caucasian Languages', in B. Comrie *The Languages of the Soviet Union*, Cambridge University Press, Cambridge: 196–237.

Hockett, C.F. (1963) 'The Problem of Universals in Language', in Greenberg 1963b: 1–22.

Holisky, D.A. (1983) 'The Case of the Intransitive Subject in Tsova-Tush (Batsbi)'. *Lingua*, 71: 103–22.

Horne, K.M. (1966) *Language Typology: 19th and 20th Century Views*, Georgetown University Press, Washington, D.C.

Hudson, R.A. (1987) 'Zwicky on Heads', *Journal of Linguistics*, 23: 109–32.

Humboldt, W. von (1822) *Über das Entstehen der grammatischen Formen, und ihren Einfluss auf die Ideenentwicklung*, Königliche Akademie der Wissenschaften, Berlin. Reprinted in A. Flitner and K. Giel (eds) (1963) *Wilhelm von Humboldt: Werke*, J.G. Cotta'sche Buchhandlung, Stuttgart, III: 31–63.

Humboldt, W. von (1836) *Über die Verschiedenheit des menschlichen Sprachbaues und ihren Einfluss auf die geistige Entwicklung des Menschengeschlechts*, Königliche Akademie der Wissenschaften, Berlin. Reprinted in A. Flitner and K. Giel, (eds) (1963) III; 368–756. Translated by Heath, P. (1988) as *On Language: the diversity of human language structure and its influence on the mental development of mankind*, Cambridge University Press, Cambridge.

Iturrioz, J-L. (1982) 'Apprehension im Baskischen' in H. Seiler and F.J. Stachowiak (eds) *Apprehension: Das Sprachliche Erfassen von Gegenständen. Teil II: Die Techniken und ihr Zusammenhang in Einzelsprachen*, Gunter Narr, Tübingen: 1–43.

Jakobson, R. (1941) *Kindersprache, Aphasie und Allgemeine Lautgesetze*, Uppsala. (Reprinted in R. Jakobson (1962) *Selected Writings I: Phonological Studies* (Mouton, The Hague: 328–401.))

Jarceva V.N. (ed.) (1982) *Jazyki i Dialekty Mira: Prospekt i Slovnik*, Nauka, Moscow.

Kasevič, B.V. and Jaxontov, S.E. (eds) (1982) *Kvantitativnaja Tipologija Jazykov Azii i Afriki*, Izdatel'stvo Leningradskogo Universiteta, Leningrad.

Keenan, E.L. (1976a) 'Towards a Universal Definition of Subject', in 1976: 303–33.

Keenan, E.L. (1976b) 'The Logical Diversity of Natural Languages', in Harnad, S., Steklis, H. and Lancaster, J. (eds) *Origins and Evolution of Language and Speech*, New York Academy of Sciences Volume 280, New York. (Reprinted in Keenan 1987: 429–55.)

Keenan, E.L. (1979) 'On Surface Form and Logical Form', *Studies in the Linguistic Sciences*, Volume 8, Number 2. (Reprinted in Keenan 1987: 375–428.)

Keenan, E.L. (1982) 'Parametric Variation and Universal Grammar', in Dirven, R. and Radden, G. (eds) *Issues in the Theory of Universal Grammar*, Gunter Narr, Tübingen.

(Reprinted in Keenan 1987: 245–315.)

Keenan, E.L. (1985) 'Relative Clauses', in Shopen 1985, vol. 2: 141–70.

Keenan, E.L. (1987) *Universal Grammar: 15 Essays*, Croom Helm, London.

Keenan, E.L. (1988) 'On Semantics and the Binding Theory', in Hawkins 1988: 105–44.

Keenan, E.L. and Comrie, B. (1977) 'Noun Phrase Accessibility and Universal Grammar', *Linguistic Inquiry*, 8, 1. (Reprinted in Keenan 1987: 3–45.)

Klimov, G.A. (1977) *Tipologija Jazykov Aktivnogo Stroja*, Nauka, Moscow.

Koehn, E. and Koehn, S. (1986) 'Apalai', in Derbyshire, D.C. and Pullum, G.K. (eds) *Handbook of Amazonian Languages. Volume 1*, Mouton de Gruyter, Berlin.: 33–127.

Kuipers, A.H. (1960) *Phoneme and Morpheme in Kabardian*. Mouton, The Hague.

Lazard, G. (1984) 'Actance Variations and Categories of the Object', in Plank 1984: 269–92.

Lazard, G. (1986) 'Le Type Linguistique Dit "Actif": Réflexions sur une Typologie Globale'. *Folia Linguistica*, 20: 87–108.

Lehmann, W.P. (ed.) (1986) *Language Typology 1985*. Papers from the Moscow Symposium, 1985. *CILT* 47. Benjamins, Amsterdam.

Li, C.N. (ed.) (1976) *Subject and Topic*, Academic Press, New York.

Li, C.N. and Thompson, S.A. (1976) 'Subject and Topic: A New Typology of Language', in Li 1976: 457–89.

Li, C.N. and Thompson, S.A. (1987) 'Chinese', in Comrie, B. (ed.) *The World's Major Languages*, Croom Helm, London: 811–33.

Mallinson, G. and Blake, B.J. (1981) *Language Typology*, North-Holland Linguistic Series 46. North-Holland, Amsterdam.

Masica, C.P. (1976) *Defining a Linguistic Area: South Asia*, University of Chicago Press, Chicago.

Mejlax, M. (1973) 'Indesky Morfologičeskoj Tipologii', in Zaliznjak, A.A. (ed.) *Problemy Grammatičeskoj Modelirovanija*, Nauka, Moscow; 155–70.

Nichols, J. (1986) 'Head-marking and Dependent-marking Grammar'. *Language*, 62: 56–119.

Payne, D.L. (1982) 'Chickasaw Agreement Morphology: A Functional Explanation', in Hopper, P.J. and Thompson, S.A. (eds) *Studies in Transitivity*, Syntax and Semantics 15, Academic Press, New York: 351–78.

Payne, D.L. (1986) 'Basic Constituent Order in Yagua Clauses: Implications for Word Order Universals', in Derbyshire and Pullum 1986: 440–65.

Payne, J.R. (1980) 'The Decay of Ergativity in Pamir Languages', *Lingua*, 51: 147–86.

Plank, F. (ed.) (1979) *Ergativity: Towards a Theory of Grammatical Relations*, Academic Press, London.

Plank, F. (ed.) (1984) *Objects: Towards a Theory of Grammatical Relations*, Academic Press, London.

Plank, F. (1985) 'Die Ordung der Personen', *Folia Linguistica*, 19: 111–76.

Plank, F. (1986) 'Paradigm Size, Morphological Typology, and Universal Economy', *Folia Linguistica*, 20: 29–48.

Ramat, P. (1986) 'Is a Holistic Typology Possible?', *Folia Linguistica*, 20: 3–14.

Ruhlen, M. (1978) 'Nasal Vowels', in Greenberg 1978, vol 2: 203–41.

Ruhlen, M. (1987) *A Guide to the World's Languages. Volume 1: Classification*, Edward Arnold, London.

Sapir, E. (1921) *Language: An Introduction to the Study of Speech*, Harcourt, Brace & World, Inc., New York.

329

Schachter, P. (1984) 'Semantic Role Based Syntax in Toba Batak', in Schachter, P. (ed.) *Studies in the Structure of Toba Batak*, UCLA Occasional Papers in Linguistics 5, Department of Linguistics, UCLA, Los Angeles.

Schachter, P. (1985) 'Parts-of-Speech Systems', in Shopen 1985, vol 1: 3–61.

Schlegel, A.W. von. (1818) *Observations sur la langue et la littérature provençales*, Librairie grecque-latine-allemande, Paris.

Seiler, H. (1986) *Apprehension: Language, Object and Order. Part III: The Universal Dimension of Apprehension*, Gunter Narr Verlag, Tübingen.

Shibatani, M. (1987) 'Some Empirical Issues in Linguistic Typology', to appear in *Linguistics in the Morning Calm 2*, Linguistic Society of Korea, Seoul.

Shopen, T. (ed.) 1985 *Language Typology and Syntactic Description*, 3 Volumes, Cambridge University Press, Cambridge.

Silverstein, M. (1976) 'Hierarchy of Features and Ergativity', in Dixon, R.M.W. (ed.) *Grammatical Categories in Australian Languages*, Linguistic Series Number 22, Australian Institute of Aboriginal Studies, Canberra. (Reprinted in Muysken, P. and van Riemsdijk, H. (eds) *Features and Projections*, Foris, Dordrecht: 163–232.)

Skalička, V. (1979) *Typologische Studien*, Vieweg, Braunschweig.

Sgall, P. (1986) 'Classical Typology and Modern Linguistics', *Folia Linguistica*, 20: 15–28.

Smith, N.V. (1981) 'Consistency, Markedness and Language Change: On the Notion "Consistent Language"', *Journal of Linguistics*, 17: 39–54.

Thompson, L.C. and Thompson M.T. (1972) 'Language Universals, Nasals, and the Northwest Coast', in Smith, M.E. (ed.) *Studies in Linguistics in Honor of George L. Trager*, Mouton, The Hague: 441–56.

Tomlin, R.S. (1986) *Basic Word Order: Functional Principles*, Croom Helm, London.

Vennemann, T. (1973) 'Explanation in Syntax', in Kimball, J.P. (ed.) *Syntax and Semantics, Volume 2*, Seminar Press, New York: 1–50.

Vennemann, T. (1981) 'Typology, Universals and Change of Language, in Fisiak, J. (ed.) *Historical Syntax*, Trends in Linguistics, Studies and Monographs 23, Mouton, Berlin, New York, Amsterdam: 593–612.

Zwicky, A. (1985) 'Heads', *Journal of Linguistics*, 21: 1–30.

# FURTHER READING

There are two excellent text-books on language universals and typology (Comrie 1981 and Mallinson and Blake 1981). Full collections of articles on a wide range of topics can be found in the four-volume set on universals edited by Greenberg (1978), the three-volume set on typology edited by Shopen (1985), and also Lehmann (1986). Chomsky's views on language universals are very clearly explained in Chomsky (1988). The debate between the Greenbergian and Chomskyan traditions is found in Coopmans (1983) and Comrie (1984). Keenan's important works on universals are collected in Keenan (1987). Valuable collections on particular topics are: Li (1976) on subjects and topics, Plank (1979) on ergativity, Plank (1984) on objects, and Hawkins (1988) on explanation.

# THE LARGER PROVINCE
# OF LANGUAGE

# 10

# LANGUAGE AND MIND: PSYCHOLINGUISTICS

## JEAN AITCHISON

## 1. INTRODUCTION

The study of 'language and mind' aims to model the workings of the mind in relation to language, but, unlike the study of 'language and the brain' (see Chapter 11 below), does not attempt to relate its findings to physical reality. A person working on 'language and mind' is trying to produce a map of the mind which works in somewhat the same way as a plan of the London Underground. The latter provides an elegant summary of the connections in the system but makes no attempt to specify the exact distance between stations or the physical make-up of the trains. Since structures and connections in the mind are inevitably unobservable, researchers put forward hypotheses based on fragmentary clues. This accounts for the high degree of controversy which surrounds almost all areas of the subject. The label most usually given to the study of 'language and mind' is **psycholinguistics**, a term which is often perceived as being trendy. It has therefore been somewhat overused in recent years, and can be found applied to just about any linguistic topic. Psycholinguistics 'proper' can perhaps be glossed as the storage, comprehension, production and acquisition of language in any medium (spoken, written, signed, tactile). It is perhaps useful to distinguish it from a somewhat wider field, 'the psychology of language', which deals with more general topics such as the extent to which language shapes thought, and from a wider field still, 'the psychology of communication', which includes non-verbal communication such as gestures and facial expressions.

A possible divide within psycholinguistics is of those who style themselves 'cognitive psycholinguists' as opposed to 'behavioural psycholinguists'. The former are concerned above all with making inferences about the content of the human mind, whereas the latter are somewhat more concerned with empirical matters, such as speed of response to a particular word. In practice the two schools of thought often overlap, but extreme supporters of each way of thinking sometimes perceive the gap as being a large one.

## 1.1 Evidence

Psycholinguistics attracts adherents from both linguistics and psychology, though these often have somewhat different approaches, particularly with regard to methodology. Linguists tend to favour descriptions of spontaneous speech as their main source of evidence, whereas psychologists mostly prefer experimental studies. This divide highlights the fact that investigators face an unsolvable paradox: the more naturalistic a study, the greater the number of uncontrolled variables; the more rigidly the situation is controlled, the greater the likelihood that the responses obtained will be untypical of real speech situations. Care must therefore be taken to approach topics from different angles, in the hope that the results will coincide.

The subjects of psycholinguistic investigation are normal adults and children on the one hand, and aphasics – people with speech disorders – on the other, the primary assumption with regard to aphasics being that a break-down in some part of language could lead to an understanding of which components might be independent of others.

## 1.2 History of psycholinguistics

Sporadic useful work on how the mind copes with language is recorded from at least the end of the eighteenth century. In 1787, for example, the German philosopher Dietrich Tiedemann published a careful record of the develop-ment of his son, including observations about his language. From the experi-mental viewpoint, the British psychologist Francis Galton (1822–1911) is usually credited with being the first person to devise psycholinguistic experi-ments. The field was slow to expand, however, and most early work dealt with words and their relationship to one another. For example, word association experiments tested which word first sprang to mind when another was spoken (e.g. 'Tell me the first word you think of when I say "night"'). Perhaps because of its early limited approach, psycholinguistics remained a small and minor area within psychology until around halfway through the twentieth century.

The field expanded into a sub-discipline in its own right as a direct result of the work of the linguist Noam Chomsky. He inspired work primarily in two directions. On the one hand, he proposed a new type of grammar, a transfor-mational grammar, which he claimed encapsulated a human's linguistic knowledge: this triggered an immediate search into the possibility that a transformational grammar might reflect the way humans comprehend, produce or remember sentences. On the other hand, Chomsky argued that a considerable amount of language might be innately programmed: this stimulated research into child language acquisition.

The 1960s tidal wave of Chomsky-inspired work (much of which was somewhat naïve in its conception) failed to find any conclusive evidence for Chomsky's proposals. Partly because of this, and partly because of the speed with which Chomsky revised his ideas, a number of psychologists became disillusioned with the notion that the primary task of psycholinguistics was to test hypotheses advanced by theoretical linguists, and many branched off and initiated their own research. In recent years, therefore, the field has been characterised by a certain amount of splintering, as different people work within different traditions on different topics, without any common overall paradigm.

## 1.3 Current issues

In spite of the varied approaches found in modern psycholinguistics, a number of general trends and crucial issues can be identified. A major point of agreement among various researchers is that the human language system is likely to be 'modular', in the sense of being constituted out of a number of separate but interacting components. A considerable amount of recent work has attempted to elucidate this possible insight, although the number and nature of these modules is far from clear.

The realisation that language organisation is likely to be modular has, however, led to a major controversy concerning the integration of the modules, as to whether they remain separate with links between them, or lead to an overall central organiser which contains more abstract representations. For example, it is clear that at some level written and spoken representations of words must be kept separate. One can therefore argue for an approach which contains two separate lexicons, one for written speech, the other for spoken, with links between them. On the other hand, one could suggest that these separate lexicons lead ultimately to an abstract 'master-lexicon' in which differences between the various outputs are conflated. The issue is still undecided. More recently, the question of 'encapsulation' has become dominant, the extent to which each module works automatically and independently, with its content sealed off from that of other modules (Fodor 1983, 1985).

A further problem is the relationship between 'structure' and 'process'. It is generally agreed that the mind is likely to contain certain linguistic structures which are utilised in the course of various 'processes', such as comprehending or producing speech. Some researchers have argued that structures and processes are linked only indirectly, others that the connection is a close one. This debate is often phrased in terms of the relationship between a linguist's grammar and a human 'grammar', and the extent to which the former has 'psychological reality'. Those who believe that the relationship between structure and process is weak tend to accept the idea that a linguist's grammar may have 'psychological reality' even though there is no way in which it seems to be directly used in the processing of speech. Chomsky (1980) for example, has argued that any model which represents the 'best guess' as to the linguistic structures in the mind must be regarded as 'psychologically real' until superseded by a better model, even though it has no relevance for comprehension or production. Other researchers, however, have argued for a closer relationship between structure and process, suggesting that linguists' grammars ought to have a clear relationship to linguistic processing (e.g. Bresnan 1982). This controversy is unlikely to be solved in the near future.

The three major strands of research which can be identified in the literature are the comprehension, production, and acquisition of language (the storage of language, though important, is inferred partly through consideration of these). These are the three topics dealt with below. Owing to reasons of space, most work discussed relates to spoken language rather than signed or written (on which see Klima and Bellugi 1979, Ellis 1984, and Wilbur 1987), though in a number of areas (e.g. comprehension) the research has tended to conflate the results obtained from the different media, which may (or may not) be justified.

## 2. SPEECH COMPREHENSION

Speech comprehension can be divided into **speech recognition**, **parsing**, and **interpretation**. Speech recognition deals with the identification of sounds and words. Parsing involves the assignment of structure to the various words, and the analysis of the functional relationships between them. Interpretation covers the recognition of semantic relationships, and the linking up of the utterance with the 'real world'. This threefold division corresponds roughly to the linguistic levels of phonetics/phonology, syntax, and semantics/pragmatics. It is, however, purely one of methodological convenience, and is not meant to imply any ordering of priority, since in practice all processes are probably proceeding simultaneously, even though comprehension mechanisms are usually triggered by the recognition of at least some sounds.

### 2.1 Speech recognition

There are a number of basic problems involved in speech recognition. A naïve observer might assume that the process was simply one of identifying sounds one by one, then stringing them together. This simple scenario is quite unrealistic, for several reasons. Above all, it is physically impossible to identify each sound separately, due to the speed of speech: humans can identify fewer than 10 separate sounds per second, whereas speech involves around twice this number. Furthermore, sounds cannot be unambiguously identified, as they do not have clear invariant properties, but overlap in two ways: on the one hand, there is no clear break between adjacent segments (e.g. in *bed*, [b] and [e] cannot be separated, neither can [e] and [d]), and on the other hand, there is no rigid boundary between auditorily similar sounds: in a classic experiment, a synthesised (i.e. artificially produced) consonant was heard as [p], [t], or [k], depending on the vowel following (Liberman *et al.* 1957). In addition, sounds vary not only from speaker to speaker, but also within the speech of the same speakers, who alter them (mostly sub-consciously) in accordance with the formality of the occasion and their emotional state.

In view of the impossibility of identifying sounds accurately, speech recognition therefore consists of imposing expectations on to an incomplete acoustic signal. Hearers choose a 'best-fit' solution on the basis of partial evidence, selecting the word which seems most plausible in the circumstances, as shown by numerous observations and experiments, for example:

(1) The 'kiss' experiment: subjects were played a synthesised sound which was intermediate between [k] and [g]. When this was followed by [ɪs] (-*iss*), the word was reported as *kiss*. When followed by [ɪft] (-*ift*), it was reported as *gift* (Ganong 1980).

(2) The 'legislature' experiment: subjects were asked to listen to a sentence, which included the word *legislature*, part of which was masked by a cough. The hearers accurately reported the word, and denied hearing any interruption (Warren 1970).

(3) Shadowing: in 'shadowing' experiments, subjects are instructed to repeat back speech as it is played into their ears through headphones. They tend to alter what they hear slightly, including correcting mistakes, such as changing *tomorrance* to *tomorrow* (Marslen-Wilson and Tyler 1980).

(4) Slips of the ear: mishearings (known as 'slips of the ear') reveal the imposition of lexical expectations on to incompletely perceived fragments, as in *chocolate* for 'chalk-dust' (Garnes and Bond 1980).

(5) No clues situation: when deprived of clues, hearers suggest transcriptions which may be far from the original. Subjects who were asked to transcribe an unlikely sequence of English words beginning 'In mud eels are . . .' produced quite varied and inaccurate transcriptions (Cole and Jakimik 1980).

The possible intermediate stages involved in the process of speech recognition are disputed. Some researchers have argued that acoustic clues are mapped directly on to words, whereas others have claimed that there is an intermediate stage in which a sequence of phonemes or syllables is set up. One intriguing possibility is that the route taken varies, both from situation to situation and from language to language (Frauenfelder 1985).

There is also considerable disagreement as to how speakers select the 'best fit', since there may be several words roughly consistent with the outline clues heard. There is a basic divide between those who argue for a **serial** model of word recognition, in which candidate words are examined one after the other, and those who propose a **parallel processing** model, in which numerous words are considered simultaneously.

The main evidence in favour of a serial model is the fact that frequently used words are recognised more quickly in lexical decision tasks (a task in which subjects are asked to assess whether a sequence of sounds is a word or not). Proponents of serial models argue that this shows that humans try to match frequent words against the auditory fragments before they move on to testing less common ones. For example, Forster (1976) argues that words are kept in 'bins', based on the initial sequence (e.g. all words beginning with [p] would be in the same bin), and that within bins the words are organised in order of frequency, so that the search for a word goes from top to bottom of a bin. A word such as *pithy* might be recognised slowly because the hearer had first checked the more usual word *pity* against the acoustic stimulus. However, the fast recognition of frequent words is not necessarily due to order of matching (it might alternatively be due to the greater strength of the stored representation), so cannot be taken as proof of serial processing.

Recently, support for serial models has been dwindling, and parallel processing models now seem a stronger possibility. This is to a large extent due to recent work on ambiguous words (i.e. words such as *bank* which have more than one meaning). It now seems likely that hearers consider all possible meanings of such words, including inappropriate ones. In a much-quoted experiment, Swinney (1979) found evidence that hearers activated both the 'insect' meaning of *bug* and the 'electronic listening device' one in a context which clearly related only to insects, and other more recent researchers have confirmed his findings.

The 'cohort' model is perhaps the best-known parallel processing model of word recognition. A cohort was a division of the Roman army: use of this name is meant to indicate the parallel consideration of a 'cohort' of words (Marslen-Wilson and Tyler 1980). Its proponents suggest that on hearing the first section of a word, a hearer activates simultaneously all words which begin with this sequence, which is known as the 'word initial cohort' (e.g. the sequence *sta-* would activate *stack, stagger, stand,* etc . . .). The hearer then uses other available syntactic, semantic, and contextual information in order to narrow this cohort down to the most appropriate word.

The cohort model is probably correct to assume that all aspects of the word need to be taken into consideration in word recognition, but in its original version it also contained certain weaknesses. Above all, it assumed that the hearer had accurately heard the beginning of the word, which is not necessarily the case. If the wrong cohort was activated, there was no way in which a hearer might make a correct interpretation, whereas it is fairly clear that humans can interpret words in which they have failed to hear the initial sound (as has been demonstrated experimentally, when subjects interpreted an indistinct sound followed by -*ate* as *date, gate* or *bait* depending on the context; Garnes and Bond 1980). The original cohort model further wrongly assumed that recognition proceeded word by word. However, it now seems likely that many words, particularly short ones, are given a definitive inter-pretation only in the course of the next word (Grosjean 1985): for example, the next word is likely to signal that the sequence *ham* is a complete word, since it might have continued as *hamper* or *hamstring*. A further problem with the original cohort model was that non-selected words were eliminated from the cohort one by one, leaving only the final 'winner': it did not allow for provisional hunches about the word being spoken, which may have to be altered.

There has therefore been a search for a more flexible model, which could deal with these problems (as well as proposals for updating the cohort model). A 'spreading activation model' (also known as an 'interactivation model') has received a considerable amount of attention (Elman and McClelland 1984). As the name suggests, this model proposes that any perceived portion of a word immediately activates all words containing similar sequences, which in turn activate all words similar to them, with excitation spreading outwards somewhat like waves on a pond. Activated words are compared with the perceived sequence, and also assessed for semantic probability. Likely candidates get progressively more excited, and unlikely ones fade away or are suppressed. Eventually, the most probable candidate 'wins out' over the others.

This model is superior to the cohort model, in that it allows words to be activated which differ in their initial consonant. For example, if *plays* was misheard as *prays*, the initial sequence [pl] would be sufficiently close to [pr] to be activated. It also allows for fluctuation in levels of excitation, so a word which is initially considered to be a highly probable candidate can later lose out to another which, on further consideration, is more plausible. Further-more, there is no essential necessity for recognition to have occurred by the end of the word.

The main problem with spreading activation models is their amazing power: if everything activates everything else all the time, then have we said anything useful about the process of word recognition? Such models, if they are to be retained, probably need to incorporate a device which assesses how near a particular word is to 'winning out'. This concept was a prominent feature of an early influential model of word recognition, the 'logogen' model (Morton 1979), meaning 'giving birth to a word'. In this model, a device collected up information about each candidate word until a critical threshold was reached. Different types of information counterbalanced one another, so that more phonological information could be traded against less semantic information, and frequent words had a lower threshold than infrequent ones. A similar notion is incorporated in a type of scoring system proposed by Norris (1986), who suggests that at each moment a word is scored for nearness of match to the perceived sequence, for contextual probability, and for frequency. The exact mechanisms of such devices are still a matter of debate. A current central topic, then, is specification of the ongoing computations and decision processes involved in word recognition.

In word recognition, then, a number of different pieces of information must be kept in the mind at the same time. Each piece interacts with the others: it constrains them and is constrained by them (McClelland and Elman 1986). This interaction happens in other psychological processes as well, such as visual perception. A class of models, known as 'parallel distributed processing' (PDP) models, are currently being developed in an attempt to simulate this computationally (Rumelhart and McClelland 1986; McClelland and Rumelhart 1986). In such models, simple processing units both excite and inhibit other units. Their essential claim is that humans process a considerable amount in parallel, and possibly in scattered locations.

## 2.2 Parsing

Most researchers agree that parsing involves two intertwined processes: on the one hand, the identification of linguistic structures by assigning words to phrases, and phrases to clauses; on the other hand, the specification of the relationship between the various phrases. But here agreement ceases.

Over the last quarter century, the topic of parsing has been 'paradigm dominated' to some extent, in the sense that different theories have held sway at different times, and have tended to guide the bulk of the research. Broadly speaking, three eras can be identified: a **transformational era** (1960s), a **perceptual strategy era** (early 1970s), and a **computational era** (late 1970s and early 1980s), each of which has contributed in some way to our current understanding.

In the **transformational era** of the 1960s, the field of parsing was dominated by attempts to assess the 'theory of derivational complexity'. This theory suggested that processing difficulty was related to transformational complexity: a sentence which had few transformations (according to an early version of transformational grammar), such as *The woman did not see the dog* would be easier to comprehend than one with several, such as *Was the dog not seen by the woman?* This theory proved to be unfounded: in cases where the predictions were borne out (e.g. Miller 1962), there were several other equally plausible explanations. For example, the sentences with multiple transformations were in many cases simply longer than those with fewer. And in numerous other cases, the predictions were not borne out. For example, *There is an oak tree in the garden* with the so-called 'there insertion' transformation was processed more quickly than the less-transformed *An oak tree is in the garden.* Another major problem was that this theory assumed that a whole sentence had to be heard before parsing could begin, which is clearly unrealistic. Furthermore, the version of transformational grammar on which the experiments were performed soon became outmoded.

A few researchers (e.g. Fodor, Bever and Garrett 1974) tried to maintain the claim that transformational grammar (as it was then formulated) was important for sentence processing by proposing a somewhat weaker theory, known as the 'deep structure hypothesis': they suggested that, even though the transformations themselves might be irrelevant, parsing nevertheless involved recovering a 'deep structure' which was isomorphic to the deep structure proposed by Chomsky in the so-called Standard theory of transformational grammar (Chomsky 1965). Most of the experiments which purported to support this theory were somewhat problematical, since they tested not comprehension itself but memory for sections of the sentence after comprehension had occurred. One possible much-discussed exception was a 'click experiment' (Bever, Lackner, and Kirk 1969): subjects who were played a 'click' (a burst of 'white noise') into one ear and a sentence into the other ear tended to move the click to a point where a transformational grammar would propose a structural break. For example, in the sentence *The corrupt police can't bear criminals to confess quickly,* a click played during the word *criminals* tended to be heard before it. However, in another superficially similar sentence. *The corrupt police can't force criminals to confess quickly,* the click remained on *criminals,* supposedly because in the deep structure, the word *criminals* occurred twice, once before the structural break, and once after it.

The deep structure hypothesis gradually fell from popularity, partly because the relatively few experiments which seemed to support the notion were consistent with other explanations, and partly because transformational grammar was again radically revised. The ambiguity of the evidence, and the impossibility of keeping up with the fast-moving theories of linguists, eventually led to an abandonment of this type of research by many psychologists.

The importance of the transformational era lay in the emphasis it laid on syntax, which had been virtually ignored in previous work on psycholinguistics. It therefore laid the essential groundwork for more sophisticated work on sentence parsing.

The **perceptual strategy era** can be said to date from 1970, initiated by the publication of an important article by Bever (1970). This seminal paper utilised insights which were commonplace in theories of speech recognition, but had not yet been applied to syntax. This was the notion that people do not process the syntax in full, but, on the basis of outline clues, use their expectations to jump to conclusions about what they are hearing.

The best-founded of the strategies proposed by Bever came to be known as the 'canonical sentoid' strategy. This encapsulates the expectation that English sentences will follow a noun – main verb – (noun) pattern which is functionally associated with subject – verb – (object). Expectation of this pattern explains the slow processing of a sentence such as: *The horse raced past the barn fell*, where the hearer initially assumes that *raced* constitutes the main verb, rather than the past participle (i.e. 'The horse which was raced . . . .') which is the only interpretation consistent with the rest of the sentence. Such misleading sentences are often known as 'garden path' sentences, since hearers are initially led astray, 'up the garden path'.

The strength of the canonical sentoid strategy led to a proliferation of attempts to identify further strategies which might be utilised in speech processing, including a search for universal principles (e.g. Kimball 1973). A typical example of a possible strategy was the 'parallel function strategy' (Gruber *et al.* 1978): hearers, it was claimed, expected the subject of the first of two clauses also to be the subject of the second. Therefore, in a sentence such as *Annabel phoned Veronica as soon as she returned from Australia*, Annabel rather than Veronica is presumed to have been in Australia.

But strategies proved to be too vague and too powerful: they seemed to be numerous, heterogeneous and unordered. The notion of strategies was by no means abandoned (as shown by some recent insightful proposals, e.g. Frazier 1988), but many researchers felt that a more constrained and ordered approach to comprehension was required and that the strategies identified needed to be integrated into a more orderly overall model.

The **computational era** (c. 1975 onwards) was due to the convergence of two groups of researchers: at a time when psycholinguists were looking for more constrained models of comprehension, computational linguists became attracted to the idea of simulating parsers.

ATNs ('augmented transition networks') were the first serious computational candidates to be proposed as parsing models (e.g. Woods 1973). These were essentially models in which the hearer started with certain outline expectations about structure, in particular, the notion of a canonical sentoid, and the composition of its phrases. The hearer then worked through the sentence from left-to-right, building up words into phrases, and phrases into clauses, and assigning each phrase a function (subject, object, etc). For example, in a sentence such as *The small boy ate a large apple*, *The small boy* would be assembled as a noun phrase, and assigned the functional label 'subject', *ate* would be labelled verb, then *a large apple* would be assembled as a noun phrase and labelled 'object'. Any words which could not immediately be assigned a place in the structure were placed in a 'hold' mechanism until a slot could be found for them as the parser worked through the sentence. For example, a phrase such as *Which boy . . .?* might fit into several possible 'slots': *Which boy will come?* (subject); *Which boy shall I send?* (object); *Which boy shall I give these apples to?* (indirect object). Some initial experiments provided a measure of support for this theory (Wanner and Maratsos 1978), though they were not conclusive as the sentences were both written and somewhat unusual ones.

There are a number of obvious problems with ATNs. Above all, they are serial models, which test out one structure at a time. They have to back-track if a wrong category label or function has been assigned. For example, in the sentence *The old train the young*, the first three words might initially have been wrongly identified as a noun phrase. Or in the sentence *The small boy was punished by his mother*, the phrase *the small boy* turns out not to be the logical subject of the sentence, a role which would have to be reassigned to the phrase *his mother*. The time taken to parse a complicated sentence might therefore be lengthy if several false paths were taken. In addition, ATNs cannot cope with non-sentences, even if they are easily intelligible: a sentence such as *Many difficulties there are to see in the dark* would be rejected as being unparsable, which is clearly unrealistic. Furthermore, they deal only with syntax, and do not take lexical probability or context into consideration: in the sentences *Max comforted the boy with a chocolate bar* and *Max comforted the boy with a wounded foot*, humans would instinctively parse the first as: *Max comforted [the boy] [with a chocolate bar]*, and the second as *Max comforted [the boy with a wounded foot]*. Yet an ATN could not assess which was the most likely.

PARSIFAL is a more recent, and more sophisticated computational model which has been claimed to eliminate some of the problems inherent in ATNs (Marcus 1980). PARSIFAL has certain similarities to ATNs, in that it also is a left-to-right model which 'holds' items in abeyance until it finds their position in the structure. Its major advantage, however, is that it eliminates much of the back-tracking inherent in ATNs. It is therefore claimed to be 'deterministic', in the sense that it always goes down the right path. This is accomplished by means of a limited 'look-ahead' facility, which allows a certain number of items to be collected into a buffer store before being assigned. In addition, it combines being a top-down model (i.e. one in which a parser sets up an expected structure) with being a bottom-up model (i.e. one in which a parser collects up items, and then tries to decide how they should be assembled): it contains both an 'active node stack' – structures looking for constituents, and also a 'buffer', containing constituents looking for structures. PARSIFAL, like ATNs, cannot cope with intelligible non-sentences. Furthermore, again like ATNs, it is purely syntactic, and there is increasing evidence that humans utilise context and lexical probability in order to decide between competing structural possibilities.

Lexical functional grammar (Bresnan 1982) is one of several linguistic models which has been realised computationally, but differs from others in that it builds lexical probability into the structure, so that the sentences *Mary wanted the dress on the rack* and *Mary placed the dress on the rack* would be assigned different structures, since verbs would be marked with the constructions preferentially associated with them (Ford, Bresnan, and Kaplan 1982). However, the detailed implementation of these preferences has yet to be worked out, and this model (in common with all other computational models) has not yet solved the problem of coping with the multiple choices routinely made instantaneously by humans as they parse sentences.

Overall, computational models have played a role in demonstrating clearly the multiplicity of choices available to humans, but they have not succeeded in showing that the parsing process is anything like that which can be simulated on a digital computer.

As can be seen from the above discussion, there is much that remains obscure about parsing. Perhaps the most obvious result so far is the realisation that the human mind is enormously powerful, and that there may be no one route by which humans parse sentences. The primary task for psycholinguists, therefore, may be one of working out 'trading relationships' between different but simultaneous processes. Some of the current issues are: (1) Strategies versus algorithms. (An algorithm is a systematic procedure for solving a problem with a definite answer.) Both probably need to be incorporated into a successful parsing model, though the relationship between them is far from clear.

(2) Top-down processes versus bottom-up processes. The human parser appears both to set up expectations and check them out (top-down processing), and simultaneously to gather up information, and work out how the pieces might be assembled (bottom-up processing). The integration of these two processes needs to be clarified.

(3) Syntactic knowledge versus lexical knowledge. The human parser appears to utilise both syntactic knowledge (i.e. the overall structure of sentences in general) and local lexical knowledge (i.e. knowledge of particular constructions likely to be associated with individual lexical items, particularly verbs). The relationship between these two needs to be elucidated, so as to find out under which circumstances each has priority.

(4) Syntactic knowledge versus semantic and extralinguistic knowledge. Syntactic knowledge has to be integrated with other types of knowledge, but it is unclear how this is done.

## 2.3 Interpretation

Interpretation can be divided roughly into **semantics**, which deals with the meaning of words and their relationship to one another, and **pragmatics**, which deals with those aspects of meaning not predictable from the strict literal sense.

Most psycholinguistic studies of semantics have concentrated on word meaning, which, like parsing, has tended to be paradigm dominated: **feature theories**, **network theories**, and **prototype theories** have each been prominent. Feature theories suggest that words can be split up into smaller, and more basic components or 'features' of meaning. Network theories suggest that words are dealt with as wholes, which are linked to one another in a complex network. Prototype theories suggest that humans deal with word meaning in terms of prototypical instances, which provide a rough pattern against which less typical instances are matched. These theories have not necessarily taken comprehension as their central interest, but they all have important implications for the way in which words might be understood.

Feature theories were prominent in the 1960s, once again partly as a result of Chomsky's influence. In 1965 he explicitly suggested that the phonological and semantic components of transformational grammar might have certain parallels. Just as the sounds utilised by any one language can be further analysed into a more basic set of phonetic features which are selected from an apparently universal pool, the same, he suggested, might be true of word meaning: there might be a set of universal features of meaning, which different languages assemble in various ways.

The feature-theory view of comprehension suggests that words are stored in a disassembled state. Therefore, the hearer has to analyse a word into its basic components in order to comprehend it. To test this hypothesis, researchers tried to check whether words which had apparently fewer meaning components took less time to comprehend than words with a greater number, as one might predict if words had to be disassembled. For example, *kill* might take longer to comprehend than *die*, on the grounds that it had to be analysed into the components CAUSE DIE. Extensive investigations, however, failed to find any effect on comprehension (e.g. Kintsch 1974), which threw doubt not only on to the 'disassemblage' hypothesis as a mechanism of word comprehension, but (alongside other problems raised) on the whole notion of universal fragments of meaning.

Feature theories are important in that they encapsulate the insight that human beings are able to analyse words in various ways. In particular, they suggest a plausible way in which humans might cope with words with over-lapping meanings (such as *kill* and *die* which both involve the notion of death). However, in a number of cases these overlaps could be equally well explained by assuming that people treat words as wholes, with logical relationships holding between them.

Network theories therefore succeeded feature theories as the dominant viewpoint in the 1970s. According to this view, words are comprehended as wholes, but these wholes are linked to one another in a complex network (e.g. Fodor, Fodor and Garrett 1975). Psycholinguists therefore attempted to specify the details of this network, whose structure, it was assumed, would directly affect comprehension. One widely-held viewpoint was that words might be organised in hierarchical structures: a canary might be classified as a bird, which in turn might be classified as an animal. Therefore, it should be easier to verify a sentence such as *A canary is a bird*, which requires moving up one step of the hierarchy than *A canary is an animal*, which requires two. Although some initial experiments appeared to support this idea (e.g. Collins and Quillian 1969) later ones failed to replicate these results (e.g. Johnson-Laird 1983), and detailed network proposals were never made.

Most people assume that at least some words are linked in networks, but that the network is by no means as extensive or rigid as network theories suggest. Network theories mostly fail to take ongoing computation into consideration: they assume that humans in the course of comprehension navigate along existing pathways, when in fact a considerable amount of comprehension might involve computing new connections. They are also unable to cope with the problem of damaged exemplars: how can someone comprehend an unstriped three-legged tiger as a tiger, as people often seem able to do?

Prototype theory is the most recent paradigm (Rosch 1975). This takes into account the fact that words do not, and cannot, have fixed meanings: when asked to judge whether something is, say, a plate or a saucer, people make graded judgements. They are sure that certain things are plates, and others saucers, but there is a grey area in between where judgements made by a single person may vary depending both on the shape of the item and also on what it is used for. In other cases, a name may cover a whole class of items, but there may be no set of characteristics which describes them all, even though they may all overlap, as in the case of games, or furniture.

Prototype theory suggests that when people comprehend the meaning of a word, they do so by matching it against a prototype. A bird, for example would be assumed to have the characteristics of a prototypical bird such as a robin, with feathers, wings, a beak, and an ability to fly. Even if the bird in question was unable to fly, it could still be comprehended as a bird; it would just not be a prototypical bird. Prototype theory as the basis for comprehension lays stress on the active computation being carried out: a particular word might elicit a prototypical instance, but there has to be perpetual adjustment in order to match the item being described against the prototype.

There is considerable uncertainty as to the composition of prototypes, which seem to be an amalgam of features required for identification combined with linguistic knowledge (for example, bulls are known to be male, but may be identified in England by rings through their noses). This confusion has led some people to doubt the value of prototypes, and the identification-knowledge issue is still unsettled (e.g. Armstrong, Gleitman and Gleitman 1983). Prototype theory does, however, seem to have considerable value as a model of how people comprehend words, and recent developments of the theory are likely to shed new light on mental processes in general (e.g. Lakoff 1987).

As with parsing, there has in recent years been a greater realisation of the complexity of word comprehension, and current issues involve the 'trading relationships' between various factors:

(1) Fixed network vs. active computation. Certain word links are long-lasting in the mind, whereas others are possibly computed afresh in the course of comprehension. The trading relationship between using existing pathways and computing new connections needs to be clarified.

(2) Analysis vs. *Gestalt*. Words can, if necessary, be analysed into sets of characteristics. But it is not clear how much analysis (if any) is routinely carried out in the course of comprehension, or whether words are dealt with as wholes.

(3) Internal linguistic meaning vs. links with the external world. Words have meanings which (to some extent) exist independently of the external world, yet must also be integrated with items and events in the world outside. How this linking occurs is still unclear. However, on this point, some recent advances in pragmatics have influenced psycholinguistics, as will be outlined below.

Pragmatics is a relatively new field. It was initially inspired by philosophers, and has now spilled over into numerous areas of linguistics. The essential problem for psycholinguists is a threefold one:

(1) To explain how humans make decisions about the meaning of utterances when (in theory) there may be several possible interpretations. For example, in *Sid discovered the star with a telescope*, how do people know that Sid, not the star, has the telescope?

(2) To explain how humans cope with speech which goes against the literal meaning. For example, in *Fred's car is a converted wheelbarrow*, how do people know that this is unlikely to be literally true?

(3) To explain how people cope with inexplicit utterances. For example, in answer to the question: *Why are there so many dirty dishes?*, how did the hearer comprehend the seemingly unrelated answer: *The sink's blocked up?*

At the moment, there is no general agreement as to how humans cope with these, and work is somewhat splintered. Many people take the work of the

347

philosopher H.P. Grice as a starting point (Grice 1975). He suggested that humans by nature co-operate with one another, and they assume that this co-operation is taking place even when it is blatantly not. To say *Fred's car is a converted wheelbarrow* is, on the face of it, an example of non-co-operation, since the speaker is telling an untruth. However, a hearer would comprehend this by assuming that, contrary to appearances, the speaker *is* being co-operative, and would therefore attempt to compute the significance of this (perhaps by analysing the possible similarities between an ordinary car and a wheelbarrow). As yet, however, there is no general agreement as to how such computations are made, though various proposals are under discussion (e.g. Sperber and Wilson 1986, Horn 1988). (See Chapter 6, above.)

A possible approach to inexplicit utterances (which may also be useful for the notion of co-operation) has been the development of 'frame theory', which was initially inspired by work on AI (artificial intelligence) (Minsky 1975). This proposes that we set up in our minds stereotypical 'frames', outline pictures of typical scenes. In a kitchen frame, for example, there would be unfilled 'slots' for a sink, taps, dishes, and so on, into which we would slot items as required in order to understand the reply *The sink's blocked* in relation to the query about dirty dishes. The notion of stereotypical frames is a useful one, though no one has yet sorted out how various frames are combined: in *Jamie's playing cricket in the kitchen*, for example, a cricket frame and a kitchen frame would somehow have to be superimposed on one another.

Overall, however, this whole area is one about which we know least, and which is likely to be the source of considerable work in the near future.

## 3. SPEECH PRODUCTION

On the face of it, speech production and speech comprehension are mirror images of one another: meaning gets converted into sound in production, and sound gets converted into meaning in comprehension. However, articulatory and auditory mechanisms behave somewhat differently, and there may be equivalent differences in the unobservable mental correlates of these. We cannot therefore extrapolate production processes from knowledge of comprehension, and the two must be examined independently.

Speech production has received somewhat less attention than speech comprehension, probably because it is not so easy to test experimentally, and researchers are more dependent on the evidence available in spontaneous speech. There are two main sources of evidence: slips of the tongue, and pauses.

Pauses have turned out to be somewhat difficult to interpret. Although pauses can be experimentally manipulated (e.g. the effect of drugs on pauses occurring in the descriptions of particular scenes can be measured), it is unclear which pauses should be assigned to syntactic planning, and which to lexical choice – even though lexical searches undoubtedly account for some, as there is clear evidence for slower production of unpredictable words (Butterworth 1980a).

Slips of the tongue have proved somewhat more fruitful (Fromkin 1973, 1980, Cutler 1982). These are involuntary deviations from the speaker's intention, or 'target', as when someone accidentally says *left* instead of 'right', or *par cark* instead of 'car park'. Such slips follow predictable patterns, so much so that some researchers have claimed to be able to set up tongue slip 'laws' – even though these are not 'laws' in any literal sense, simply probability statements. The recurring patterns found can reveal information about the way speakers prepare sentences for utterance.

Speech errors can be divided into two main categories: selection errors, in which a wrong lexical item has been selected (e.g. *yesterday* for 'tomorrow'), and assemblage errors, in which correctly selected items are misassembled (e.g. *leak wink* instead of 'weak link'). This division provides evidence for at least two processes in production: the selection of relevant words and constructions on the one hand, and the organisation of those selected on the other. The account below, therefore, is divided into two main sections: the lexical selection process, and the assemblage process.

### 3.1 Lexical selection

Selection errors may be errors of meaning as in *nephew* for 'uncle', sound as in *confusion* for 'conclusion' (often referred to as 'malapropisms' from the fictional character Mrs Malaprop who repeatedly made such errors), or both meaning and sound as in *hydrangea* for 'geranium'. A further common category is that of blends, in which two words have coalesced into one, as in *tummach ache*, where *tummy* and *stomach* have been combined.

Such errors can be supplemented by 'tip of the tongue' phenomena. A 'tip of the tongue' state is the situation in which speakers feel that they are on the verge of finding a particular word, but cannot quite grasp it, since it remains elusively 'on the tip of their tongue'. In this situation, they often make a number of provisional attempts at the word, which are similar in kind to selection errors (Brown and McNeill 1966; Browman 1978).

Because a number of errors are 'pure', in the sense that they are either 'pure' meaning errors, or a 'pure' sound errors, these two aspects of the word can be regarded as separable, and these pure errors can provide some information about storage and/or retrieval procedures of each part of the word. The relationship between storage and retrieval is somewhat unclear, since tongue slips may reflect either facts about storage, or retrieval mechanisms.

349

For example, if someone picks *daffodil* instead of 'tulip', one might assume that all flower words are literally stored in the same location, so that it is fairly easy to accidentally select a near neighbour of the target. Alternatively, one might assume that a search for any one kind of flower immediately excites all the others to some extent, even though they may be widely distributed.

As the example above suggests, words from the same semantic field tend to get confused, both by normal speakers, and by aphasics (people with speech disorders), who may have genuine difficulty in assigning the correct names to words within a topic area. In particular, co-ordinates may get confounded, that is, words which form part of a natural clump in which they are all on an equal footing, such as different colours (*red, blue, yellow,* etc.) or different family relations (*brother, cousin,* etc.) or different pieces of fruit (*orange, lemon*) (Hotopf 1980).

These clumps of words may be to some extent independent of one another. Some recent studies have suggested that aphasics may have deficits in some semantic areas, but not others. In one much publicised case, a stroke victim recovered his vocabulary entirely except for fruit and vegetables: he could name a rare object such as an *abacus* with no hesitation, but items such as *orange, apple* or *carrot* were liable to cause him considerable difficulty (Hart, Berndt, and Caramazza 1985).

Traditionally, an error in which a word such as *orange* has been selected for 'lemon' has been regarded as a case of mis-selection of a neighbour, as if an adjacent book has been taken from a library shelf instead of the intended one. However, some recent work suggests that multiple activation of words may be a normal procedure. Instead of hunting down one particular word, speakers may activate a number of relevant or partially relevant words, and then select from them. This is suggested by blends, where the words concerned are often (though not inevitably) equally appropriate, as in *sleast* ('slightest/least'). Further evidence are cases in which a word intrudes either from within one's thoughts, or from the surrounding context, as when a woman cutting bread said: 'Yes, you can take the *bread* out', meaning 'dog'. Such examples suggest that the mind readily and subconsciously activates large numbers of words, the majority of which will not in the end be selected. This has led to the suggestion that in selecting words, suppression of unwanted extra ones may be an important factor: aphasics and language learners who flounder around searching for a word may not simply be having trouble pinpointing the word they want, they may also be having problems suppressing those they do not want. One might therefore interpret an error such as *fork* for 'knife' not as simply picking an adjacent word in error, but as a failure to suppress the unwanted cutlery words (Aitchison 1987).

From the point of view of sound, similar sounding words fall into certain patterns, suggesting that some aspects of a word are more salient than others:

if a word is picked in error for another, it is liable to have a similar beginning (Fay and Cutler 1977), and (slightly less often) a similar ending. In addition, it is likely to have a similar stress pattern, and a similar stressed vowel. If two words share all these characteristics, they are particularly likely to be confused, as with *antidote* for 'anecdote', *computer* for 'commuter', *masturbate* for 'masticate', all widely attested errors. There is some evidence for an ordering of these characteristics: adults are more likely to pay attention to the initial consonant than to any other feature, and children are more likely to pay attention to the stress pattern (Aitchison and Straf 1982).

If the multiple activation viewpoint is correct, all similar-sounding words are activated, then the speaker suppresses those which are irrelevant, with a malapropism resulting if this process is carried out erroneously.

The process of uniting the meaning and sound has been explained by some researchers by means of a serial model, in which the two aspects of the word get picked one after the other, and by others via a parallel processing model, in which the two aspects are processed simultaneously. Words which contain 'pure errors' (i.e. semantic errors only, or sound errors only) could be explained by a model in which the selection of the meaning and the sound occurred independently and serially (meaning first, then sound). However, such a model cannot account for the fact that numerous 'tip of the tongue' examples and selection errors share both a meaning, and a sound similarity with the target, as in *train component* for 'train compartment'. Furthermore, the presence of a meaning and sound similarity appears to make the occurrence of a slip more probable. This suggests that the selection of meaning and sound overlap, so that knowledge of the approximate meaning influences the choice of the sounds: perhaps all words that fulfil certain outline meaning and sound specifications are activated, then those which are not required are suppressed.

As with speech recognition, the notion of an interactive activation model seems a useful one, in which activation fans out and arouses all similar words (Stemberger 1985, Aitchison 1987). Words that fulfil certain specifications get extra-activated, and, if more than one share the same outline characteristics, then the wrong one can easily get selected.

However, as with word recognition, the problem with interactive activation models is their power. If every word activates every other word in a never-ending succession of waves, then we have said very little about the exact processes by which a word is finally selected. The assumption that a required word get progressively more excited, and that those which are unsatisfactory get suppressed tells us virtually nothing about how this activation and suppression takes place. As with word recognition, a considerable amount of parallel processing seems to be involved, and suppression appears to be as important as selection, though the precise mechanisms involved are still unclear.

A further characteristic of selection errors is that they almost invariably preserve the word class of the target, whether they are sound or meaning errors: nouns exchange with nouns as in *salt* for 'pepper', verbs with verbs as in *discard* for 'discuss', and adjectives with adjectives as in *cyclonic* for 'syphonic'. This suggests that the word class is not an optional extra attached at a later stage, but is firmly fastened to each part of the word at all times, and is therefore important in syntactic planning.

It has also been observed that verbs are found less often in selection errors than might be expected, even allowing for the fact that there are fewer nouns than verbs in the English language (Hotopf 1980). One possibility is that there are fewer errors involving verbs because they are selected first, and so set up the syntactic frame for the sentence.

A further important and controversial question is the extent to which words are selected as words, or as pieces of words (Butterworth 1983). Complex forms such as *compensation* might, in theory, either be selected as wholes, or they might have to be assembled in the course of production: words could be listed under their stems (e.g. *-pens-* might be a basic entry, with prefixes *dis-*, *con-* and suffixes *-ate*, *-ation*, listed as sub-entries).

Owing to the irregularity of the composition processes (e.g. we get *dispense, dispensation,* but *compensate, compensation*), there are very few rules which could guide speakers in assembling words in spoken speech if they were split up. It is therefore more likely that English derivational affixes are firmly attached to the words involved. And indeed, apparent examples of 'pure' affix attachment, cases in which an affix has been apparently put on to the wrong stem, often turn out to be blends, as in 'At the moment of *compact*' for 'collision/impact' (Aitchison 1987). One reason for the continuing controversy may be differing treatments by different languages. In addition, many of the studies have involved written language, and reading and writing strategies may well differ from those involved in spoken speech.

English speakers can, however, segment words if they need to, and may do so to provide a word if an existing one cannot be found, as in 'Children use *deduceful* rules', where the word *deductive* was apparently unavailable. Such examples indicate that humans have a seemingly limitless ability to perform computations involving existing vocabulary items.

The examples discussed above involve derivational affixes (as in *compensation*). Inflectional suffixes, however (as in *he eat-s bun-s*) are often added in the course of speech. The evidence for this comes particularly from phrasal verbs (verbs which consist of more than one word, as in *pick up, point out*). These are intermittently found with the inflection added at the end of the whole phrase, as in *she pick ups, he point outed.* Furthermore, jargon aphasics (aphasics who use nonsense words in place of real lexical items) are often able to inflect these correctly (e.g. *She wikses a zen from me,* Butterworth 1983). These examples suggest that attachment of inflections may be part of the normal assemblage procedure.

### 3.2 Assemblage

The slips of the tongue which give clues about assemblage involve words, morphemes, syllables, or sounds, though sound segments (phonemes) are by far the commonest. They can be categorised primarily into:

1. Anticipations, when an item comes in earlier than it should: It's more than your *wife's worth* (life's worth).
*Unwieldy* people. . . unscrupulous people can wield . . .
2. Perseverations, when an item is wrongly repeated:
Beef *needle* (noodle) soup.
The trains were disrupted and *dislayed* (delayed).
3. Transpositions, when items change places:
The shoes were *holed* and *sealed* (soled and heeled).
He put all the *bags* in a *wind* (winds in a bag).

As noted earlier, these errors do not occur randomly, and the following tendencies have been widely observed:

1. Anticipations outnumber perseverations (and also transpositions, though some anticipations may be unfinished transpositions).
2. Errors normally occur within the tone-group, and they do not usually disrupt the intonation pattern. (Tone-group or 'phonemic clause' is a somewhat vague term, and is normally defined as a stretch of speech bounded by a single intonation contour.)
3. Units confused tend to be of equal size, and metrically similar.
4. Sound slips obey a structural law of syllable place: initial consonants change place with initial consonants, finals with finals, vowels with vowels.
5. Slips normally obey the rules of English syllable structure.
6. Slips tend to form words to a greater extent than could be due to chance.

From these recurring observations, it is possible to draw certain inferences about the way humans assemble speech. The predominance of anticipations (1) suggests that humans do not simply chain words together, one at a time, but plan utterances in chunks. The extent to which an item can occur in advance indicates the size of the planning chunk, which is likely to be the tone-group (2). Key words, particularly verbs, are possibly used to set up a syntactic and prosodic framework for the tone group, then the details are gradually filled in, with inflections and negatives added at a later stage.

The metrical similarity of transposed items (3) and the similarity of placement within the syllable of sound segment slips (4) indicate that speakers work in accordance with a rhythmic principle, which appears to be hierarchically organised: phrases appear to be subdivided into 'feet', and feet

353

into syllables. Following this principle, speakers may have a 'scan-copying' mechanism (Shattuck-Hufnagel 1979), in which an internal 'slate' is scanned, and the contents 'copied over' into the form in which they can be pronounced. Any misordering in this system (such as copying off a sound too soon) would result in an anticipation or a transposition, whereas a failure to wipe an uttered sound off the slate would result in a perseveration.

The fact that errors normally obey the rules of syllable structure (5), and also form words to a greater extent than could be due to chance (6), suggests that humans have an efficient 'monitoring device', a checking mechanism which confirms that what is being said is both a possible sequence of sounds, and a possible word. Evidence for an additional 'post-utterance' check is also provided by the fact that people quite often correct themselves after making an error.

As with other aspects of psycholinguistics, there is still considerable discussion concerning the trading relationships between different aspects of the process. Two in particular are unclear:
(1) Metrical structure vs. syntactic structure. It is uncertain how these two factors are integrated, since they do not necessarily correlate.
(2) Syntax vs. lexicon. The relationship between word selection and choice of syntax needs to be clarified.

## 4. ACQUISITION

The study of child language has expanded enormously in recent years, though there is still considerable controversy over the fundamental principles underlying acquisition. There are perhaps two points only on which everyone agrees:
(1) Children have their own system. They are not simply imitating adults, nor just putting words together at random. At every point, they have internal rules which differ from those of adults, and which seem to be more important to them than the 'correct' form which they hear around them, as when (for example) they consistently regularise past tenses, as in *singed, breaked.*
(2) Similarity of development. There is considerable similarity in development among children who could not possibly be acquainted.

The basic questions which recur are, first, what impels children onwards in the task of language acquisition? And second, what accounts for the similarities between unrelated children? Innate programming, cognitive development, and parental guidance have all been proposed in turn as the major factor. All of these, it transpires, are to some extent relevant, and the crucial matter is the trading relationship between them, which is far from clear.

## 4.1 Biological foundations

The fact that language has biological foundations has gradually become accepted in recent years. There are signs of structural adaptation (mobile and muscular tongue and lips, even teeth, streamlined larynx, left hemisphere localisation within the brain), and also physiological adaptation (alteration of breathing patterns to cope with speech). Furthermore, language shows many characteristics of maturationally-controlled behaviour (Lenneberg 1967). No external event triggers it, or can significantly speed up its development. Speech emerges before it is crucially needed, and the acquisition period is roughly the same everywhere: children the world over start to combine words at around the age of two. By the age of five they can talk fluently, and by the age of around ten syntactic and phonological development is virtually complete, though acquisiton of vocabulary continues throughout life.

There is less agreement over whether the acquisition years (from approximately the age of eighteen months to adolescence) constitute a 'critical period', the only time in life during which language can be acquired. Lenneberg (1967), who first proposed this theory, attempt to link the critical period to the notion of lateralisation, the specialisation of language to the left hemisphere of the brain. He claimed that injuries sustained by a child prior to the onset of language learning would not significantly affect language ability, and that after language onset, the older the child, the more likely a left hemisphere injury was to leave permanent damage. He further claimed that the language of Down's syndrome cases failed to progress after adolescence, and pointed out that adult language learners have a considerable struggle, compared with children.

Lenneberg's critical period hypothesis was given apparent support by the case of Genie, a teenager found in California without language at the age of 13. In spite of intensive therapy, she has never acquired normal language (Curtiss 1977). However, Genie was so severely deprived, both physically and emotionally, that this deprivation could have altered her developmental possibilities, especially as she appears to be learning language with her right hemisphere. And Lenneberg's other arguments have all been queried: children suffering severe left hemisphere damage before the age of two have been found to have serious language deficits, the lateralisation period has been questioned (most people assume it is shorter than Lenneberg and some researchers believe that lateralisation is present from birth or even earlier), Down's syndrome children can and do progress in language after adolescence, and there are numerous documented cases of apparently perfect language-learning by adults. In brief, many people would agree that young brains tend to have greater plasticity than older brains, but few would accept that language acquisition is an ability which ceases at some arbitrary point.

Although the biological foundations of language appear to have been firmly established, there is considerably less agreement over the extent to which its details are preprogrammed and separate from other cognitive abilities. It is widely accepted that without some preprogrammed knowledge or constraints, children would never acquire language; there are too many possibilities to be considered: they would never succeed in cracking the code, just as humans cannot crack the dolphin code. The question of learnability, therefore, is a crucial one. However, there is considerable disagreement as to how much specific linguistic knowledge is 'wired into' infants.

The most extreme proponents of specific innate linguistic knowledge are Noam Chomsky and his followers, though their proposals have been modified over the years. In 1965 Chomsky suggested that children might be equipped with an innate Language Acquisition Device (LAD) which was wired with language universals, and contained in addition an evaluation mechanism which caused children to automatically select the most efficient grammar (Chomsky 1965).

More recently, Chomsky's suggestions have taken a somewhat different form (Chomsky 1986). He has proposed the notion of a genetically-inbuilt 'core grammar'. This contains a number of fixed principles, in addition to several crucial option points of which humans are instinctively aware. The task of children acquiring language is to discover which options have been selected in the language they are exposed to. In this way they 'fix the parameters' of UG (Universal Grammar), and set their language learning to go along certain pathways. Each option has multiple repercussions through-out the grammar, so an error in fixing one parameter might result in numerous different mistakes. In this situation, children might initially make a mistake about the option chosen by their language, and mistakenly assign it to a wrong type, which could account for a number of child language errors. For example, it had been suggested that some of the mistakes made by English children could be due to their mistakenly assuming that English is a 'pro-drop language', one which drops initial pronouns (Hyams 1986). These ideas are still fairly new, and have not yet been fully assessed (Roeper and Williams, 1987, discuss various facets).

## 4.2 The Role of cognition

Language development and general cognitive development proceed in parallel in normal children, though the exact relationship between the two is unclear.

In the early 1970s, partly as a reaction against the dominant innatist theories of the 1960s, a group of psychologists claimed that cognitive develop-ment was the major guiding force behind language. The research had several strands, though the overall aim was to link linguistic stages to prior stages of cognitive development. This overall notion came to be known as the 'cognitive hypothesis'.

Two-word utterances provide a typical example of this work. Children, it was observed, talk about very similar things at an early stage of language development: the same concepts recur in widely separated languages, such as 'possession' (e.g. *Mommy sock* 'That's mummy's sock'), location (e.g. *Kitty bed* 'The cat's on the bed'). A number of researchers therefore attempted to specify a universal order for the development of early concepts, which, it was suggested, might be guiding the acquisition of language. However, these attempts failed, as there turned out to be considerable variation from child to child, often as a result of environmental factors: for example, the concept of possession appeared to develop early among children with siblings.

The assumption that stages of language could be definitively linked to cognitive stages ran into a number of difficulties. A major problem was that even if such a correlation was established (which it was not), this did not entail a causal connection. As one researcher noted, hair growth might be positively correlated with language development, but there is not necessarily an interesting link between the two (Curtiss 1981).

Further evidence that the cognitive hypothesis cannot be upheld in its extreme form comes from accounts of a number of children who can speak fluently, but whose general intelligence is so low that they perform at below the two year-old level on a number of tasks that are sometimes regarded as relevant for language, such as classification, or hierarchical organisation (Curtiss 1981, 1988). Such children often talk nonsense but use sophisticated linguistic structures to do this (e.g. 16 year-old Marta: 'It was no ordinary school, it was just good old no buses', Yamada 1988). There are also children such as Genie, mentioned above, who exhibit high levels in various intelligence tests, but who cannot speak normally.

It is, of course, a truism that children do not talk about those things which they are not yet capable of thinking about. And the relatively early or late development of some structures may well be a reflection of this. For example, in one extensive cross-linguistic study, prepositions meaning 'front' and 'back' were acquired in a wide range of languages before those meaning 'between' (Slobin 1982). However, evidence of this type has on the whole proved to be scanty and elusive.

Although the 'cognitive hypothesis' cannot be supported in its extreme form, most researchers have come to realise that linguistic development cannot be studied detached from cognition, since they are likely to influence one another in normal children.

A variant of the cognitive hypothesis is a 'semantic matching' hypothesis. According to this theory, children learn language by matching words against the world: nouns are matched with people and objects, verbs with actions, and adjectives with states. This has turned out to be an oversimplification: although some matching is probably inevitable in the early stages, the lack of a one-to-one correspondence between syntax and the world is quickly apparent in child speech. Adjectives may express activities (e.g. *noisy*), and verbs may express states (e.g. *to sleep*). If children were working from a semantic basis, therefore, one would expect them to regularise these forms to fit in with their assumptions about basic semantic divisions, and to say (perhaps): 'I'm noisying' and 'He is sleep'. In fact, such errors are rare. Children seem to be tuned in to noticing syntactic co-restrictions, and there is some evidence that they give them priority over semantic matching. For example, a French-speaking child preferred to provide a boy with the feminine article *la* rather than associate masculine *le* with an ending typically connected with *la* (Karmiloff-Smith 1979).

### 4.3 Caregiver language

Another strand in the reaction against the 1960s obsession with innateness was a search for the possible environmental factors which might influence language, and in particular the role of parental language, often known as 'motherese', though now more usually referred to as 'caretaker language', or 'caregiver language'. The term 'baby talk' is also found occasionally, though tends to be avoided, as some people use it in a more restricted sense, that of uttering nonsense syllables to the child, such as *gee gee* 'horse'.

Speech addressed to children turned out to have certain predictable characteristics, compared to speech addressed to adults (Snow and Ferguson 1977, Ferguson 1978): the sentences tended to be shorter, well-formed, repetitive in subject-matter, slower, with fewer junctural deformations and of higher pitch. The question then arose as to whether these features merely facilitated acquisition for the child, or whether they actually guided the child's progress.

There are three possible points of view:

(1) Direct influence: caregiver language might directly influence the child (via imitation, etc).

(2) Indirect influence: features in the mother's speech might indirectly guide the child (for example, by providing a pattern of frequency of usage which the child might follow).

(3) Facilitation: parental speech simply provides clear input from which the child extracts what it considers relevant.

There appear to be no direct and overt links between caregiver language and child speech. Correction is generally ignored by the child. Furthermore, most corrections made by adults are fairly unhelpful for language development (Brown, Cazden and Bellugi 1968). Above all, parents tend to correct etiquette ('Say please',) and false statements ('No, we give the rabbit dandelions, not cabbage'), supplemented by sporadic comments on prononiciation ('Her name's Trisha, not Twisha') and word forms ('It's held, not holded'). Indeed, in some cases correction was found to hinder children's progress: the child became aware that its utterances were disapproved of, and consequently talked less (Nelson 1973).

Furthermore, direct teaching does not significantly speed acquisition, nor is any lasting effect produced by imitation of the mother by the child, as in 'Put on your coat', imitated by the child as 'Put coat', or expansion of the child's utterance by the caregiver, as in 'Doggy sleep' expanded by the mother into 'Yes, the dog's asleep' (Brown, Cazden and Bellugi 1968). More recently, 'repairs' by the mother, as in 'Put on your coat: I said your coat' have been found to account for such a small proportion of utterances, they also are unlikely to have an significant direct effect (Shatz 1982).

The direct effect hypothesis, therefore, cannot provide an explanation for child language acquisition. Frequency of usage is perhaps the most straightforward proposal that has been made about direct influence: the child might simply absorb the most consistently-used words and constructions it is exposed to. This is true in outline, in the sense that children do not acquire usages they hear only rarely. But there is no consistent correlation between frequency of usage and child language. Furthermore, in some cases, children are found to abandon frequently-heard forms, such as the irregular verb forms *went, took,* and replace them with their own over-regularised forms, such as *goed, tooked.*

A possible more subtle source of influence is known as the 'fine-tuning' hypothesis. This suggests that mothers might 'fine-tune' their speech to the syntactic needs of the child, subconsciously progressing from simple to more complex constructions as the child's language develops. It turns out, however, that mothers do not grade their speech syntactically to the requirements of their children. All types of constructions are found intermingled in speech addressed to the child, with no detectable order of presentation. In one well-known study, a group of mothers was recorded speaking to their children before and after a six-month interval – and the early recordings contained a greater admixture of constructions than the later ones (Newport, Gleitman and Gleitman 1977).

The facilitation hypothesis appears to be the most plausible. Furthermore, certain types of caregiver speech facilitate acquisition more than others: parents who engage in and talk about joint enterprises with their children appear to speed their progress. Many mothers, it has been claimed, engage in joint activities with girls ('Alice, help me peel the potatoes'), more often than with boys ('Bobby, go outside and play with your football'). This observed tendency might account for the finding that girls are usually minimally in advance of boys in their language development.

Children, then, seem to be geared to extracting language from the speech that is addressed to them. They are likely to proceed well if the input is copious, clear, varied and interesting. But in the long run, the children's 'uptake' out of this input is the most important factor. Parents can help their children, but they cannot lead them.

It seems, therefore, that in language acquisition, there is continuous interplay between innate linguistic capacity and general cognitive abilities, and that the whole process can be facilitated by exposure to sensitive and helpful caregivers – though the exact nature of the interaction involved has still not been fully elucidated.

### 4.4 Syntax

The various levels of language have on the whole been worked on separately, and the bulk of work has related to syntax.

'Mean length of utterance' (MLU) (estimated by counting morphemes) has traditionally been regarded as a rough measure of progress (Brown 1973), since as a child gets older its utterances get longer, even though longer utterances are not necessarily more complex than shorter ones (Bates *et al.* 1988).

Most people commence the study of child syntax at the so-called 'two-word stage), which normally occurs around the age of eighteen months. Early (1960s) work on the topic coincided with concentration on the notion of language universals. Psycholinguists attempted to identify similarities between different children, in the hope that these might reflect universal patterns, which in some cases could be innate.

One early proposal which evoked widespread interest was that a 'pivot grammar' might be a universal early language stage (Braine 1963). This suggested that child grammars at the two-word stage consisted of two word classes, a 'pivot' class, containing a small number of words which recurred frequently in a fixed position, such as *more, allgone, bye-bye*, and an 'open' class containing many more items, often nouns, which recurred less often. All utterances therefore were assumed to be of the type *More milk, Allgone juice, Bye-bye daddy*, in which a pivot word was placed alongside an open class word.

It turned out that such a grammar seriously undercharacterised the speech of numerous children. In particular, it failed to deal satisfactorily with utterances such as *Mummy banana*, which could have several possible meanings: 'Mummy's eating a banana', 'Mummy slipped on a banana skin', 'That's mummy's banana', 'Please mummy give me a banana'. This type of observation showed that child language could not be adequately described without an account of the context in which an utterance occurred. It also suggested that two-word utterances could be most easily described in terms of the semantic relationships they encode (e.g. *Sand eye* 'I've got sand in my eye' – location; *Penny doll* 'That's Penny's doll' – possession).

A major issue, therefore, is the point at which a child may be said to be using syntactic rules. If these early utterances are perceived as semantically based, the question arises as to when and how the switchover to syntax occurs. If, on the other hand, they are perceived as syntactic, then it is difficult to know how to characterise them: it may be wishful thinking to attribute adult-type syntactic relationships to them.

One useful approach to two-word utterances has been to regard them as 'limited-scope formulae', i.e. formulae for the utterance of a particular relationship, but formulae of a very limited scope (Braine 1976). In a possession formula, for example, perhaps only members of the family may be possessors: *Mummy shoe* 'That's mummy's shoe', *Daddy car* 'That's daddy's car'. As formulae widen out to include more lexical items, they may get combined in two ways: *red car* and *Daddy car* might get subsumed together under a wider relationship of qualifier-noun, and they may get combined together in an utterance such as *Daddy red car* 'That's daddy's red car'. It is possible that this coalescence of formulae represents the first real 'syntax', which may be triggered by the discovery that language and the world do not map neatly on to one another (Pinker 1984).

The development of inflections such as past tense and plural has raised considerable interest, mainly because there seems to be a relatively predictable order of acquisition (Brown 1973). One suggestion is that the various endings might be acquired in an order based on linguistic complexity (Slobin 1977): children might have certain expectations about language, that it will be 'regular; and 'transparent' in the sense of having one morpheme per unit of meaning. They will therefore be baffled by exceptions and discontinuous constructions (such as *is walking*, where *is* and *-ing* have been separated).

This theory has been examined by an investigation of the speech of bilingual children. These often acquire the same construction at different times in their two languages (e.g. children who are bilingual in Turkish and Serbo-Croatian tend to acquire the respective passives in these languages several years apart). This cannot be due to cognitive development, and so is likely to be due to the linguistic complexity of the construction in the language in which its onset is delayed. In this way, it has proved possible to build up a set of factors which make constructions easy for the child to learn, and others which make it difficult (Slobin 1977). A gradual accumulation of cross-linguistic studies has added considerably to our knowledge in this area (Slobin 1985).

There has been a change of emphasis in recent years: whereas early work looked at similarities between different children, more recent work has stressed the role of the child as an active puzzle-solver, and has looked for individual differences among language learners (e.g. Peters 1983, Bates *et al.* 1988). This has focused attention on the process by which constructions emerge. At one time, it was suggested that the acquisition of a particular construction might be 'across-the-board', in that once a child had acquired a particular rule in one place (e.g. use of inversion in questions, as in *Can kitty go?*, or correct past tense forms as in *melted, wanted*), the rule was automatically generalised to all similar instances. However, it transpires that although the final result of a rule may be across-the-board, its emergence takes place slowly, and partially piecemeal. A new form or construction first gets used in a particular place, where it may not at first be productive (e.g. use of *do* may first occur in questions with a particular verb, as in 'Do you know ..?'). The child is then likely to experiment with occasional extensions of this rule. Eventually, the rule will become general by a process of diffusion, progressively moving through the lexicon and being added to more and more instances.

A recent concern has been to discover how children manage to abandon their early errors. Since they do not pay attention to 'negative evidence' (i.e. overt correction), some subtler mechanism must be involved, though precisely what this is, is still a matter of speculation (Bowerman 1988).

## 4.5 Semantics

The main body of work on the acquisition of semantics has looked at word meaning. It is generally agreed that early word meanings are characterised both by underextension (e.g. *duck* might be applied only to white ducks, and not to brown ones) and overextension (e.g. *duck* may be applied to turkeys, hens, and geese as well as ducks).

Underextension is less contentious: it possibly occurs when a child has learnt a word in a particular context (Carey 1978). For example, *fluffy* may be applied only to a kitten, and the child might not realise that the word could be applied to mohair wool as well.

Overextension, on the other hand, has been the subject of considerable controversy. Several theories have been put forward to explain it, of which three – chain complexes, feature theory and prototype theory – are possibly the best known.

The notion of chain complexes was proposed by the psychologist Vygotsky (1934/1962). It attempts to account for cases where the child has overextended words in an idiosyncratic way, as when the same word *qua* was applied to a duck on a pond and a mug of milk. Vygotsky suggests that children may pay attention to one or two aspects only of an object, and may therefore reapply a word to another item which has some feature in common with the previous application: in the *qua* example, the liquid element of a duckpond has apparently been transferred to milk in a mug. Since the child continually reapplies words which share some feature with the previous application, they are all linked together in a chain, hence a 'chain complex'.

Perhaps feature theory has been the most widespread hypothesis put forward to account for overextensions in recent years (Clark 1973). According to this, the child has not yet analysed the item in question sufficiently, but has merely perceived a few outline characteristics. Originally, for example, any type of largish non-flying bird might be labelled *duck*. Then, as time goes by the child discriminates more, and adds extra features to its stored representation, so distinguishing ducks from other types of farmyard birds.

Although this may be a useful way of explaining cases in which the child appears to have underdifferentiated by adult standards, it cannot account for idiosyncratic overextensions, such as the *qua* example above, where some additional explanation is needed beyond failure to fill in the details.

A more recent view appeals to prototype theory: the child is working from a prototype, which it might analyse rather differently from the way an adult might have done (Bowerman 1980). For example, a prototypical moon might be perceived as crescent-shaped, shiny, and seen from below, against a broad backdrop. The child might then reapply the word *moon* to anything which was crescent-shaped and shared some other characteristic with the prototypical moon, such as a shiny green leaf, or a pair of animal horns on a wall. This promising theory is still being evaluated.

It has become clear that vocabulary acquisition proceeds fairly slowly, as does the integration of words into an overall semantic network. Some attempts have been made to predict the order in which words are acquired, though this turns out to be somewhat more complex than was once hoped. In particular, it is difficult to distinguish natural developments from environmental causes; distinctions acquired early by the child may simply be those it is most often exposed to, for example, children seem to be able to cope with the word *big* before *small*, but the word *big* is used more often by adults.

In general, however, there is relatively little information on how words are integrated into a semantic network. This is perhaps an important field for the future.

## 4.6 Phonology

In the first month of their life, children produce various cries (hunger, anger, pain), whose characteristics may be universal. At around six weeks, children begin to 'coo', producing vowel-like murmurs. At around six months, most children begin to babble, alternating consonant and vowel sequences, such as *bababa, mamama*. There is some evidence of a 'babbling drift', in which the sounds babbled approximate gradually to those of the language being acquired.

When children produce their first words, at around the age of a year, their approximations are still a long way from the adult form – though the sound substitutions found are rule-governed, so that if a child produces [w] in place of [f] in one word, it is likely to do this in other words also (e.g. *winger* for 'finger', *woot* for 'foot').

The substitution processes found may be universal. For example, consonant harmony is widely attested (in which consonants either side of a vowel tend to 'harmonise' in voicing or place of articulation, as in *tat* for 'cat', *quck* for duck), and so is fronting (in which velars tend to be moved further forward in the mouth, as in *ta* for 'car').

The possible mechanisms underlying the substitutions have been widely discussed. They cannot be solely due to immaturity of the auditory or articulatory organs, since the child can usually both discriminate and pronounce more contrasts than he or she regularly produces.

Roman Jakobson, a pioneer in child language development, suggested that children were following a universal pattern, arguing that there are fixed implicational relationships between sounds (Jakobson 1941/1968). He claimed for example, that a stop-fricative contrast must emerge later than one between front and back stops. However, Jakobson's proposals turn out to be statistical tendencies rather than strict laws, so cannot be regarded as true universals.

A more recent proposal suggests that children are under the influence of universal natural tendencies (Stampe 1979). Certain sounds are more 'natural' than others, and the child has to learn to implement the sounds used by his or her particular language by gradually suppressing the natural tendencies. For example, it may be natural to devoice sounds at the ends of words, so children would 'naturally' say *dok* rather than *dog* until they learn to overcome this preference. But there turn out to be so many proposed tendencies, and such variation between children, that only a few natural tendencies seem to be indisputable.

More recent theories have stressed the role of the child in actively working out the puzzle presented by the phonology of their language. In particular, children need to discover the articulatory movements required in order to produce a particular auditory effect: [kw], for example, as in *quick*, involves complex neuro-muscular skills, and requires considerable experimentation and practice before it can be routinely produced. Children appear to develop strategies for themselves, acquiring certain routines which they then utilise even in cases in which they may be aware that this is incorrect, such as using the same sequence [ebenin] for the words *ambulance* and *elephant* (Vihmann 1981).

Overall, then, in the acquisition of phonology, as in other aspects of child language, attention has to some extent shifted from looking for universal programmes, in which the child is a fairly passive participant in the learning process. Instead, the child is perceived as an active puzzle-solver, utilising individual strategies – though possibly guided in outline by universal constraints.

## REFERENCES

Aitchison, J. (1983) *The Articulate Mammal: An Introduction to Psycholinguistics*, 3rd edition 1989, Unwin Hyman.

Aitchison, J. (1987) *Words in the Mind: An Introduction to the Mental Lexicon*, Basil Blackwell, Oxford.

Aitchison, J. and Straf, M. (1982) 'Lexical storage and retrieval: A developing skill?; in A. Cutler (ed.), *Slips of the Tongue and Language Production*, Mouton, Berlin: 197–242.

Allport, A. MacKay, D., Prinz, W. and Scherer, E. (1987) *Language Perception and Production*, Academic Press, New York.

Armstrong, S.L., Gleitman, L.R. and Gleitman, H. (1983) 'What some concepts might not be', *Cognition*, 13: 263–308.

Bates, E., Bretherton, I., and Snyder, L. (1988) *From First Words to Grammar: Individual Differences and Dissociable Mechanisms*, Cambridge, Cambridge University Press.

Bever, T.G. (1970) 'The cognitive basis for linguistic structures', in Hayes, J.R. (ed.), *Cognition and the Development of Language*, Wiley, New York: 279–352.

Bever, T.G., Lackner, J.R. and Kirk, R. (1969) 'The underlying structures of sentences are the primary units of immediate speech processing', *Perception and Psychophysics*, 5: 225–31.

Bowerman, M. (1980) 'The structure and origin of semantic categories in the language learning child', in Foster, D. and Brandes, S. (eds), *Symbol as sense: New approaches to the Analysis of Meaning*. Academic Press, New York: 277–99.

Bowerman, M. (1988) 'The "no negative evidence" problem: how do children avoid constructing an overly general grammar', in Hawkins, J.A. (ed.), *Explaining Language Universals*, Basil Blackwell, Oxford: 73–101.

Braine, M.D.S. (1963) 'The ontogeny of English phrase structure: the first phase', *Language*, 39: 1–14.

Braine, M.D.S. (1976) *Children's First Word Combinations*, Monograph of the Society for Research in Child Development: 41.1

Bresnan, J. (1982) *The Mental Representation of Grammatical Relations*, MIT Press, Cambridge, Mass.

Browman, C. (1978) *Tip of the Tongue and Slip of the Ear: Implications for Language Processing, UCLA Working Papers in Phonetics*, 42.

Brown, R (1973). *A First Language*, Allen & Unwin, London.

Brown, R., Cazden, C. and Bellugi, U. (1968) 'The child's grammar from I to III'. Reprinted (1973) in Ferguson, C.A. and Slobin, D.I. (eds), *Studies of Child Language Development*, Holt, Rinehart, and Winston, New York: 295–333.

Brown, R. and McNeill, D. (1966) 'The "tip of the tongue" phenomenon', *Journal of Verbal Learning and Verbal Behaviour*, 5: 325–37.

Butterworth, B. (1980a) *Speech Production*, vol.1. Academic Press, New York.

Butterworth, B. (1980b). 'Evidence from pauses in speech', in Butterworth (1980a): 155–76.

Butterworth, B. (1983a) *Speech Production*, vol. 2. Academic Press, New York.

Butterworth, B. (1983b) 'Lexical representation', in Butterworth (1983a); 257–94.

Carey, S. (1978) 'The child as word learner', in Halle, Bresnan and Miller (1978): 264–93.

Chomsky, N. (1965) *Aspects of the Theory of Syntax*, MIT Press, Cambridge, Mass.

Chomsky, N. (1980) *Rules and Representations*, Basil Blackwell, Oxford.

Chomsky, N. (1986) *Knowledge of Language: Its Nature, Origin and Use*, Praeger, New York.

Clark, E.V. (1973). 'What's in a word? On the child's acquisition of semantics in his first language', in Moore, T.E. (ed.), *Cognitive Development and the Acquisition of Language*. Academic Press, New York: 65–110.

Clark, H.H. and Clark, E.V. (1977) *Psychology and Language*, Harcourt, Brace, Jovanovich, New York.

Cole, R.A. (1980) *Perception and Production of Fluent Speech*, Lawrence Erlbaum Associates, Hillsdale, NJ.

Cole, R.A. and Jakimik, J. (1980) 'A model of speech perception', in Cole (1980): 133–63.

Collins, A.M. and Quillian, M.R. (1969) 'Retrieval time from semantic memory', *Journal of Verbal Learning and Verbal Behaviour*, 8: 240–47.

Cooper, W. and Walker, E.C.T. (1979) *Sentence Processing*, Lawrence Erlbaum Associates, Hillsdale, NJ.

Cruttenden, A. (1979) *Language in Infancy and Childhood*, Manchester University Press, Manchester.

Curtiss, S. (1977) *Genie: A psycholinguistic study of a modern-day 'wild child'*, Academic Press, New York.

Curtiss, S. (1981) 'Dissociations between language and cognition: cases and implications', *Journal of Autism and Developmental Disorders*, 11: 15–30.

Curtiss, S. (1988) 'Abnormal language acquisition and grammar: Evidence for the modularity of language', in Hyman and Li (1988), 81–102.

Cutler, A. (1982) *Slips of the tongue and language production*, Mouton de Gruyter, Berlin. Also published as *Linguistics* 19. 7–8 (1982).

De Villiers, J.G. and De Villiers, P.A. (1978) *Language Acquisition*, Harvard University Press, Cambridge, Mass.

Dowty, D.R., Karttunen, L., and Zwicky, A.M. (1985) *Natural Language Parsing*, Cambridge University Press, Cambridge.

Elliot, A.J. (1981) *Child Language*, Cambridge University Press, Cambridge.

Ellis, A.W. (1984) *Reading, Writing and Dyslexia*, Lawrence Erlbaum Associates, London.

Elman, J. and McClelland, J.L. (1984) 'Speech perception as a cognitive process: The interactive activation model', in Lass, N. (ed.), *Speech and Language*, vol. 10, Academic Press, New York: 337–74.

Fay, D. and Cutler, A. (1977) 'Malapropisms and the structure of the mental lexicon', *Linguistic Inquiry*, 8: 505–20.

Ferguson, C.A. (1978) 'Talking to children: a search for universals', in Greenberg, J.H.,

Ferguson, C.A., and Moravcsik, E. (eds), *Universals of Human Language*, vol. 1, Stanford University Press, Stanford, California: 203–224.

Fletcher, P. and Garman, M. (1986) *Language Acquisition*, (2nd edn) Cambridge University Press, Cambridge.

Flores D'Arcais, G.B. and Jarvella, R.J. (1983) *The Process of Language Understanding*, Wiley, New York.

Fodor, J.A. (1983) *The modularity of mind*, MIT Press, Cambridge, Mass.

Fodor, J.A. (1985) Precis of *The modularity of mind* and peer commentary, *The Behavioral and Brain Sciences* 8, 1–42.

Fodor, J.A. Bever, T.G. and Garrett, M.F. (1974) *The Psychology of Language*, McGraw-Hill, New York.

Fodor, J.D., Fodor, J.A., and Garrett, M.F. (1975) 'The psychological unreality of semantic representations', *Linguistic Inquiry*, 6: 515–31.

Ford, M., Bresnan, J., and Kaplan, R.M. (1982) 'A competence-based theory of syntactic closure', in Bresnan (1982): 727–96.

Forster, K. (1976) 'Accessing the mental lexicon', in Wales, R.J., and Walker, E. (eds), *New Approaches to Language Mechanisms.* North-Holland, Amsterdam: 257–87.

Frauenfelder, U.H. (1985) 'Cross-linguistic approaches to lexical segmentation', *Linguistics* 23: 669–88.

Frauenfelder, U.H. and Tyler, L.K. (1987) *Spoken word recognition*, MIT Press, Cambridge, Mass. Also published as *Cognition*, 25. 1. (1987).

Frazier, L. (1988) 'Grammar and language processing', in Newmeyer (1988), vol: 2, 15–34.

Fromkin, V.A. (1973) *Speech Errors as Linguistic Evidence*, Mouton, The Hague.

Fromkin, V.A. (1980) *Errors in Linguistic Performance: Slips of the Tongue, Ear, Pen and Hand*, Academic Press, New York.

Ganong, W.F. (1980) 'Phonetic categorization in auditory word perception', *Journal of Experimental Psychology: Human Perception and Performance*, 6: 110–25

Garnes, S. and Bond, Z. (1980) 'A slip of the ear: A snip of the ear? A slip of the year?' in Fromkin (1980): 231–9.

Garnham, A. (1985) *Psycholinguistics: Crucial Topics*, Methuen, London.

Grice, H.P. (1975) 'Logic and conversation', in Cole, P. and Morgan, J. (eds), *Syntax and Semantics 3: Speech Acts*, Academic Press, New York: 41–58.

Grosjean, F. (1985) 'The recognition of words after their acoustic offset: Evidence and implications', *Perception and Psychophysics*, 38: 299–310.

Gruber, E.H., Beardsley, W. and Caramazza, A. (1978) 'Parallel function strategy in pronoun assignment'. *Cognition*, 6: 117–33.

Halle, M., Bresnan, J. and Miller, G.A. (1978) *Linguistic Theory and Psychological Reality*, MIT Press, Cambridge, Mass.

Harris, M. and Coltheart, M. (1986) *Language Processing in Children and Adults*, Routledge & Kegan Paul, London.

Hart, J., Berndt, R.S. and Caramazza, A. (1985) 'Category-specific naming deficit following cerebral infarction', *Nature*, 316: 439–40.

Horn, L.R. (1988) 'Pragmatic theory', in Newmeyer (1988), vol: 1, 113–145.

Hotopf, W.H.N. (1980) 'Semantic similarity as a factor in whole word slips of the tongue', In Fromkin (1980): 97–109.

Hyams, N. (1986) *Language Acquisition and the Theory of Parameters*, Reidel, Dordrecht.

Hyman, L.M. and Li, C.N. (1988) *Language, Speech and Mind*, Routledge, New York.

Jakobson, R. (1941/1964) *Child Language, Aphasia and Phonological Universals*, Mouton, The Hague.

Johnson-Laird, P.N. *Mental Models*, Cambridge University Press, Cambridge.

Karmiloff-Smith, A. (1979) *A Functional Approach to Child Language: A Study of Determiners and Reference*, Cambridge University Press, Cambridge.

Kimball, J. (1973) 'Seven principles of surface structure parsing in natural language', *Cognition*, 2: 15–47.

Kintsch, W. (1974). *The Representation of Meaning in Memory*, Lawrence Erlbaum Associates, Hillsdale, NJ.

Klima, E. and Bellugi, U. (1979) *The Signs of Language*, Harvard University Press, Cambridge, Mass.

Lakoff, G. (1987), *Women, Fire and Dangerous Things*, Chicago University Press, Chicago, Ill.

Lenneberg, E.H. (1967) *Biological Foundations of Language*, Wiley, New York.

Liberman, A.M., Harris, K.S., Hoffman, H.S. and Griffith, B.C. (1957) 'The discrimination of speech sounds within and across phoneme boundaries'. *Journal of Experimental Psychology*, 54: 358–68.

McClelland, J.L. and Elman, J.E. (1986) 'The TRACE model of speech perception', *Cognitive Psychology*, 18: 1–86. Condensed version in McClelland and Rumelhart (1986): 58–121.

McClelland, J.L. and Rumelhart, D.E. (1986) *Parallel distributed processing*, vol. 2, MIT Press, Cambridge, Mass.

MacWhinney, B. (1987), *Mechanisms of Language Acquisition*, Lawrence Erlbaum Associates, Hillsdale, NJ.

Marcus, M.P. (1980) *A Theory of Syntactic Recognition for Natural Language*, MIT Press, Cambridge, Mass.

Marslen-Wilson, W.D. and Tyler, L.K. (1980) 'The temporal structure of spoken language understanding', *Cognition*, 8: 1–71.

Matthei, E. and Roeper, T. (1983) *Understanding and Producing Speech*, Fontana, London.

Miller, G.A. (1962) 'Some psychological studies of grammar', *American Psychologist*, 1: 748–62.

Minsky, M. (1975) 'A framework for representing knowledge', in Winston, P.H. (ed.) *The Psychology of Computer Vision*, McGraw-Hill, New York: 211–77.

Morton, J. (1979) 'Word recognition', in Morton, J. and Marshall, J.C. (eds) *Psycholinguistics 2: Structures and Processes* Elek, London: 107–56.

Nelson, K. (1973) *Structure and Strategy in Learning to Talk*, Monograph for the Society for Research in Child Development 38.

Newmeyer, F. (1988) *Linguistics: the Cambridge Survey*, vols. 1–4, Cambridge University Press, Cambridge.

Newport, E.L., Gleitman, H. and Gleitman, L.R. (1977) 'Mother, I'd rather do it myself: some effects and non-effects of maternal speech style', in Snow and Ferguson (1977): 109–49.

Norris, D. (1986) 'Word recognition: Context effects without priming', *Cognition*, 22: 93–136.

Peters, A.M. (1983) *The Units of Language Acquisition*, Cambridge, Cambridge University Press.

Pinker, S. (1984) *Language Learnability and Language Development*, Harvard University Press, Cambridge, Mass.

Reich, P. (1986) *Language Development*, Prentice-Hall, Englewood Cliffs, NJ.

Roeper, T. and Williams, E. (1987) *Parameter Setting*, D. Reidel, Dordrecht.

Rosch, E. (1975) 'Cognitive representations of semantic categories', *Journal of Experimental Psychology*: General 104: 192–233.

Rumelhart, D.E. and McClelland, J.L. (1986) *Parallel distributed processing*, vol. 1., MIT Press, Cambridge, Mass.

Shattuck-Hufnagel, S. (1979) 'Speech errors as evidence for a serial-ordering mechanism in sentence production', in Cooper and Walker (1979): 295–342.

Shatz, M. (1982) 'On mechanisms of language acquisition; Can features of the communicative environment account for development?; in Wanner and Gleitman (1982); 102–27.

Slobin, D.I. (1977) 'Language learning in childhood and in history', in Macnamara, J. (ed.), *Language Learning and Thought*, Academic Press, New York: 185–214.

Slobin, D.I. (1982) 'Universal and particular in the acquisition of language', in Wanner and Gleitman (1982): 128–70.

Slobin, D.I. (1985) *The Cross-linguistic Study of Language Acquisition*, Vols. 1 and 2., Lawrence Erlbaum Associates, Hillsdale, NJ.

Snow, C.E. and Ferguson, C.A. (1977) *Talking to Children: Language Input and Acquisition*, Cambridge University Press, Cambridge.

Sperber, D. and Wilson, D. (1986) *Relevance: Communication and Cognition*, Basil Blackwell, Oxford.

Stampe, D. (1979) *A Dissertation on Natural Phonology*, Garland Press, New York.

Stemberger, N. (1985) *The Lexicon in a Model of Speech Production*, Garland, New York.

Swinney, D. (1979) 'Lexical access during sentence comprehension: (Re)consideration of context effects', *Journal of Verbal Learning and Verbal Behavior*, 18: 645–59.

Vihmann, M.M. (1981) 'Phonology and the development of the lexicon: Evidence from children's errors', *Journal of Child Language*, 8: 239–64.

Vygotsky, L.S. (1934/1962) *Thought and Language*, MIT Press, Cambridge, Mass.

Wanner, E. and Gleitman, L.R. (1982) *Language Acquisition: The State of the Art*, Cambridge University Press, Cambridge.

Wanner, E. and Maratsos, M. (1978) 'An ATN approach to comprehension', in Halle, Bresnan and Miller (1978): 119–59.

Warren, R.M. (1970) 'Perceptual restoration and missing speech sounds', *Science*, 167: 393–5.

Wilbur, R.B. (1987) *American Sign Language: Linguistics and Applied Dimensions*, Little Brown, Boston.

Woods, W. (1973) 'An experimental parsing system for transition network grammars', in R. Rustin (ed.), in *Natural Language Processing*, Prentice-Hall, Englewood Cliffs, NJ: 112–54.

Yamada, J. (1988), 'The independence of language: evidence from a retarded hyper-linguistic individual, in Hyman and Li (1988): 175–206.

# FURTHER READING

*General Surveys.* Aitchison (1983/89, 1987); Clark and Clark (1977); Cruttenden (1979); De Villiers and De Villiers (1978); Elliot (1981); Garnham (1985); Harris and Coltheart (1986); Matthei and Roeper (1983); Reich (1986).

*Books of Readings.* Allport, Mackay, Prinz and Scherer (1987); Butterworth (1980, 1983); Cole (1980); Cooper and Walker (1979); Cutler (1982); Dowty, Karttunen and Zwicky (1985); Fletcher and Garman (1986); Flores D'Arcais and Jarvella, (1983); Frauenfelder and Tyler (1987); Fromkin (1973, 1980); Hyman and Li (1988); MacWhinney (1987); Slobin (1985); Wanner and Maratsos (1982).

# 11

# LANGUAGE IN THE BRAIN: NEUROLINGUISTICS

## RUTH LESSER

## 1. INTRODUCTION

The history of studying how language is organised in the brain goes back about 5,000 years. Howard and Hatfield (1987) cite observations made in an Egyptian papyrus of around 3,000 BC on how severe injury to the temple (such that fragments of bone could be seen in the interior of the ear) resulted in speechlessness. The surgeon, Imhotep, who describes these sad cases in the papyrus also commented on the importance of noting which side of the body had been injured, an observation which was not taken up with enthusiasm until the late nineteenth century AD, and the beginning of the systematic clinical study of language disorders after brain damage, aphasiology.

The newer discipline of neurolinguistics which is developing, however, has additional roots to those it has derived from clinical aphasiology. Its multidisciplinary supports include the neurosciences, biology and anthropology, on the one hand (Thatcher 1980), and artificial intelligence and philosophy, on the other (Arbib, Caplan and Marshall 1982; Churchland 1986). The approach to be taken in this chapter, however, will largely be one which reviews the limitations of present methods available to neurolinguists, and touches on the prospects for the development of a neuropsychology of language which may move towards realistic models of brain function.

Neurolinguistics is defined by a modern dictionary (Hanks 1986) as 'the branch of linguistics that deals with the encoding of the language faculty in the brain', and the major emphasis in it on the study of language after brain damage has been a matter of pragmatic convenience. As will be discussed below it is becoming easier now to study some aspects of language functioning in intact brains, but neurolinguistics has had to draw substantially on the accidents of strokes and head injuries in human brains for its searchings as to where language may be neurally located, as neuroscience draws on stimulation or controlled lesions inflicted on non-human brains for its study of how neuronal function is related to behaviour. Indeed one of the concerns of neurolinguists is to justify extrapolation from the behaviour of brain-damaged people to that of non-brain-damaged people, so that evidence from pathology can be used to make generalisable statements about how language is encoded in the brain *per se*. The extent to which this can be done depends on the level of abstraction of the statements. Since Jackson in the last century, students of aphasia have cautioned about the inferences that can be made from damaged brains about localisation of language functions to anatomical centres; the behaviour observed is necessarily controlled by the surviving areas in the brain rather than the dead ones, and symptom localisation must not be confused with function localisation (see Caplan 1981, for a review of the issues). The detailed structural and physiological mapping of language on to brain has, therefore, yet to be achieved.

The level of abstraction used in neuropsycholinguistic modelling, however, lacks this constraint. The models originate from studies of how normal subjects process language and are tested and refined from observations from brain-damaged subjects. It is inherent in this approach that there is no sharp dichotomy between 'pathological' and 'normal' language, but that aphasic speakers are experiencing to a greater degree the performance disruptions of all other speakers (see for example Butterworth and Howard's (1987) account of paragrammatisms). The guiding principle employed in many models is that the mental structure of language is composed of separable components or modules. What may occur in aphasia are selectively greater disruptions of some components than of others, and the language behaviour of aphasic people, therefore, can be used to dissect out these language subsystems. This is essentially quite independent of attempts to map these subsystems on to neural subsystems, and cognitive neuropsychologists have emphasised that their 'fractionation' models of boxes and arrows are not meant to represent neural systems.

The present state of play, therefore, is one of increasing sophistication in neuropsychological models of language, on the one hand, and of techniques for examining brain function, on the other, but still a yawning gap between them. Cognitive neuropsychological studies are at present undertaken with a principled resistance to translation into brain studies; brain studies are undertaken with generally only the most elementary notions of the structure of language. Later in this chapter, some of these current neuropsychological models of language subsystems will be reviewed. Before we reach this point, however, studies will be discussed which have attempted to explore in a somewhat crude way the neurological substrate of language considered as an ill-defined entity, in respect of its cerebral lateralisation and localisation to cortical and subcortical zones. To understand why knowledge of the neurology of language is at present so limited, we need first to consider what techniques are currently available to study the neurology of living human brains, and the problems of interpretation which arise in respect of individual differences.

## 2. BRAIN INVESTIGATION TECHNIQUES

Figure 11 shows the major landmarks on the left cerebral hemisphere, which will be referred to in this section.

*Figure 11* Main regions associated with language in the left cerebral hemisphere.

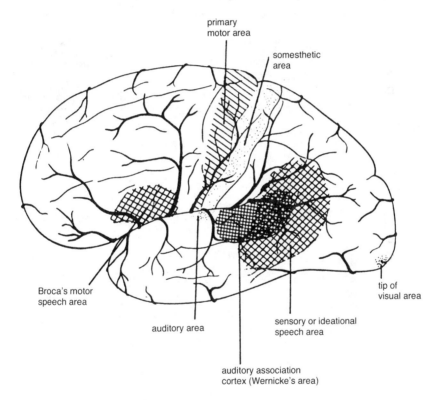

From G.A. Davis (1983) *A Survey of Adult Aphasia*, Prentice-Hall, Englewood Cliffs, NJ: 30

Reference to defined cerebral areas is now necessary. Readers unfamiliar with neuroanatomical terms are referred to the following book: Mitchell and Mayor 1983: 48–85.

## 2.1 Pharmacological and surgical

Because of their inherent dangers, these techniques are only used with people for whom some clinical intervention is essential. The conclusions that can be drawn from them are therefore clouded by the knowledge that they have been applied to people whose brains are functioning in a severely abnormal way.

The Wada Test, sometimes known as the Amytal Aphasia Test, was developed by Wada in the 1940s. Sodium amytal is injected into either the left or right carotid artery in the neck, so that either the left or right cerebral hemisphere is temporarily inactivated. If the left cerebral hemisphere is dominant for language, the patient, who has been asked to perform a verbal task such as counting backward in threes from a hundred, will cease speaking. During the recovery period which lasts for up to six minutes or so, the patient's speech is aphasic during the language tasks which are presented, such as naming, reading aloud, and rehearsing sequences like days of the week. A protocol for language and memory testing through the Wada technique is given by Blume, Grabow, Darley and Aronson (1973). Although there may be some leakage of amytal to the opposite hemisphere, the technique is a much more reliable way of establishing language dominance than noting handedness, and is used prior to neurosurgery to guide the surgeon as to the likely consequence of extirpating tissue from that side of the brain. Its particular relevance to the study of aphasia lies in Kinsbourne's (1971) demonstration that what speech is recovered after severe aphasia may be supported entirely by the right hemisphere. Wada tests were given to three such aphasic patients; right-sided injections arrested speech completely, but not left-sided injections.

Surgical techniques include hemispherectomy, hemidecortication (in which all subcortical structures are spared), lobectomy and section of the corpus callosum which links the two cerebral hemispheres. Such drastic measures are only taken to preserve life in the case of tumours, or the quality of life in the case of medically intractable epilepsy or infantile hemiplegia. There are obvious problems in drawing conclusions about the normal lateralisation or intracerebral localisation of language from patients who have experienced such surgery. Not only is there a probability that such patients will have an abnormal brain organisation, but the operations themselves induce some additional damage to the remaining structures through handling of the brain and cutting of arterial supplies (Millar and Whitaker 1983). A considerable literature has discussed what evidence such patients can provide about the role of the right hemisphere in the neural organisation of language (see section 3 in this chapter).

An innovatory surgical technique, which may in due course reveal something about recovery from speech and language impairment caused by degenerative diseases which affect both hemispheres, is the implantation of foetal tissue. It is likely that the first applications will be with people who have Parkinson's disease or Alzheimer's disease.

## 2.2 Electrophysiological

The electroencephalograph (EEG), first used in 1929, is still in common use both in clinics and research laboratories today, despite the difficulty of interpretation of its readings. Matched pairs of silver or gold cup electrodes are placed on the scalp, on either side of the head, and referenced to an electrode placed elsewhere on the head, such as the mastoid, with a ground electrode on the forehead. Typically electrodes are placed on the frontal, central, temporal, parietal and occipital areas of the skull. The recordings from each pair of electrodes are amplified (to the order of some 400,000 times) and outputted to an X-Y plotter or chart-recorder, oscilloscope and/or computer display. Although the usual display is of lines of waves, responses can also be further processed by a computer to produce tomographic maps showing how different areas of the cortex of the brain respond to different tasks (see, for example, Breitling, Guenther and Rondot 1986). The EEG records ongoing brain activity, and waves of different frequencies (Delta, 1.5–3.5 hz; Theta, 3.5–7.0 hz; Alpha, 7–13 hz; and Beta, 13–25 hz) have been found to occur under different conditions. Characteristic patterns are used for the diagnosis or investigation of epilepsy, brain death and sleep disorders associated with psychiatric problems. There appears also to be a systematic relationship between the development of alpha wave activity and presumptive brain growth spurts in children, particularly in the parietal-occipital regions of the brain (Thatcher 1980).

There are many difficulties, however, associated with interpretation of what the wave patterns indicate from the EEG, which make for caution in using it to dissect cognitive processes such as those involved in language. It cannot be assumed that each electrode is recording the summation of action potentials of a functional neuronal assembly. The method is too crude for this, and the electrodes, placed on the scalp rather than on or in the brain itself, are probably recording a mass of cellular and extracellular activities.

Nevertheless, because EEG is a non-invasive and readily available technique, there have been several studies of aphasic people using EEG (reviewed by Brown 1985). Aphasics may have abnormal EEG patterns, and slowing of waves from the anterior part of the left cerebral hemisphere appears to be associated with difficulties in expressive language. Moreover there is a relationship between degree of slowing and the potential for recovery from aphasia (Tikovsky, Kooi and Thames 1960).

Since the EEG is recording a diffuse mass of events during spontaneous activity, an attempt to improve its usefulness has been made by introducing stimuli to the subject, in order to establish to what extent the recordings are influenced by the brain's reaction to external events. This technique is known as the use of averaged evoked or event-related potentials (variously abbreviated to ERP, EP or AEP). In this method a series of tactile, auditory or visual stimuli are given and the consequent long series of EEG recordings (at least 60) are cumulatively averaged by a computer. In this way a clearer wave form pattern can be extracted of the significant changes in the waves, supposedly free from extraneous factors or 'noise'. Eye movements, which could produce artefacts, are also recorded from an additional electrode placed close to an eye, and then filtered out. The peaks and troughs of the wave forms which emerge from such an analysis are labelled according to the time in milliseconds of peak latency from the stimulus and whether they are negative (i.e. peaks) or positive (i.e. troughs) e.g. N100, P300 (sometimes abbreviated to N1 or P3). The components can be distinguished according to whether they occur early (exogenous components which occur even when the subject is anaesthetised) or late (endogenous components, which appear to be related to cognitive processing). The late components, which occur between 300 and 600 msecs or longer after the stimulus, have been described as the contingent negative variation (CNV) waveform. The early components have been sub-divided according to whether they are fast (1–10 msec), middle (10–60 msec) or slow (60–300 msec).

Detailed examination of the fast early components has been used productively in electrocochleography (ECoG) and auditory brainstem responses (ABR) to detect the early stages of processing of auditory signals. ABR is used to test hearing in young infants and other subjects who cannot reliably be tested by behavioural audiometry. It is hypothesised that the wave components reflect anatomically-distinct activity beginning with the cochlea in the ear, through the various subcortical stations (the olive, lateral lemniscus, inferior colliculus and medial geniculate) to the primary auditory cortex (Seitz, Weber, Jacobson and Morehouse 1980). Brown (1985), however, reviews some studies which come to the conclusion that auditory ERPs are not necessarily altered by lesions of the primary auditory cortex. He concludes that loss of auditory ERP is likely to be linked only to the extent of subcortical pathology.

ERP techniques using auditory stimuli have been used in the examination of the lateralisation of speech and language perception e.g. in bilinguals (Seitz *et al.* 1980). But ERP suffers from the same problems of interpretation as EEG, while making even greater claims as to precision. The longer the latency of the wave, the more variability is included in its timing, and the more hazardous does it become to relate it to stages of information-processing (see Churchland 1986: 213–17). Molfese's (1983) review, however, offers evidence that, despite the methodological flaws of many studies, ERPs are sensitive to phonological cues (voicing and place of articulation contrasts) and to syntactic, denotative and connotative manipulations. He concludes that 'the time is indeed ripe to make significant inroads into our understanding of brain-language relationships using ERP techniques' (367). A recent study is an example of such an application. Herning, Jones, and Hunt (1987) claim that different ERP components can be distinguished according to whether hearers are making decisions about whether four-word computer-synthesised sentences are correct (e.g. 'The sea flows in'), semantically anomalous (e.g. 'The sea points low') or grammatically incorrect (e.g. 'The peas again case'). A P250 component was observed after the onset of each word, and this was significantly larger when subjects were judging ungrammatical sentences. An N480 component was observed when the critical third word was heard, followed by a P780 component; this latter was significantly greater from electrodes placed on the central and parietal areas than the frontal area. A slow positive wave developed in the parietal region up to 1400 msec after the onset of the fourth word, which completed the sentence. Herning *et al.* interpret the P250 component as reflecting the amount of mental effort required to evaluate each word, regardless of whether the sentence is meaningful. They suggest that the N480 reflects the mismatch when an unexpected word is heard, and that the P780 represents the reprocessing forced by such a mismatch, while the slow positive wave reflects the processing of the entire sentence as a semantic unit. This study is particularly interesting for its implication of a greater role in semantic processing in the central and parietal brain regions.

It is the examination of the fast components by ARB which has most applications in diagnosing neurological disorders. The stimuli used in ARB, however, are generally non-meaningful clicks or tones. Speech stimuli using phrases come into the CNV waveform range, and studies using these in language pathology have so far restricted the analysis to presence, absence or reduction of CNV. Brown (1985) reviews a few studies which suggest that presence of CNV to heard sentences is associated with improvement of comprehension in aphasia, and that CNV asymmetry occurs significantly less often in stutterers than in normal speakers. Not all studies using CNV have supported the latter claim: e.g. Pinsky and McAdam (1980).

Visual stimuli provide an alternative input. Samar and Berent (1986) have used this technique with normal subjects to test between psycholinguistic models which claim that there is a degree of syntactic processing before lexical retrieval and ones which claim that syntactic processing is postlexical. This subtle experiment used a lexical decision task (deciding whether a string of letters is a real word or not) amd assessed the effect of priming with a syntactically appropriate or inappropriate word presented on a screen 400 msecs before a target word. Both nouns and verbs were used as target words, as well as words of ambiguous grammatical class. Examples of the paired primes and targets are: the job; we bring; the cut; we cut; the bring; we job. Measuring the visual ERP after the onset of the target word, Samar and Berent found that a P140 component was responsive to whether the priming words had ben syntactically appropriate or not, and that this was independent of the syntactic class of the target word as noun or verb. This component appeared to be widely distributed over the cortex. It seems to be related to an early syntactic process in comprehension which primes selective access to those words within the mental lexicon which possess the appropriate syntactic features to fit the slot which the prime has provided. A later component, P220, was also found which was sensitive to the syntactic class of the target word, but was independent of the appropriacy of the priming word. A hemispheric difference was noticed with this component, favouring left hemisphere processing. There is an interesting correspondence between these results and those of Herning *et al.* just discussed in respect of the P250 component in a not dissimilar task, although using auditory stimulation.

Visual ERP studies of language-disordered populations have not yet reached this degree of sophistication. Neville (1980) has reported studies which compared hearing and congenitally deaf children's visual ERPs to line drawings; opposite patterns of cerebral asymmetry were found in the two groups. She has also examined the ERPs of alexic patients to visual presentation of words and drawings. N100 responses in the right occipital area to stimuli presented to the left visual field (and therefore transmitted to the right hemisphere) were evoked for drawings but not for words in these patients who had a pure alexia after left posterior brain damage; more anteriorly-placed electrodes (right parietal and right central) showed normal responses. Neville suggests that visual language information may be relayed anteriorly for transfer to the intact central zones of the left hemisphere, or that perhaps it is processd by the right hemisphere.

A further, if restricted, application of electrophysiological techniques to neurolinguistics is electrical stimulation of the brain (ESB). This involves the placing of silver ball electrodes on the exposed brain. It is undertaken when an area of skull has been removed during the course of surgical operations, so as to expose the brain; patients are given only a local anaesthetic so that they are able to respond to instructions. The majority of the patients studied are suffering from intractable epilepsy, although the technique is also used on subcortical sites with patients who are having stereotaxic operations for the relief of chronic pain or movement disorders, as in Parkinsonism. Since the 1950s (see Penfield and Roberts 1959), cortical electrical stimulation has been used to guide the surgeon as to the extent of brain which may be excised without significant interference to language functions. Although the operations last for hours, electrical stimulation can only be applied continuously to one point on the brain with safety for a maximum of fifteen seconds (Ojemann 1983); moreover, measures of baseline performance must be repeated during the operation. Thus the amount of language which can be examined is restricted. Ojemann (1983) has given a detailed description of the technique used in Seattle. Patients are shown slides of objects, and are asked to read out the carrier phrase 'this is a . . .' and complete it with the object's name. This is followed by a series of slides with 8–10 word incomplete sentences (e.g. 'If my son is late for class again. . . .') which the patient is asked to read out and complete. After this a slide appears with the instruction 'Recall', which cues the patient to speak the name of the first object he or she saw. Next, slides are shown of oro-facial postures such as pursing the lips, which the patient has to imitate, both as single actions and in series. Finally a tape is played in which stop consonants are embedded in a carrier non-word (/a . . . ma/) and the patient has to name the embedded phoneme. All tasks therefore involve speech production or movements of the articulators, although Ojemann critically distinguishes them as predominantly involving naming, reading (including syntax), phonemic perception, memory storage, memory retrieval and single and sequential motor organisation.

ESB has also been used with subdural electrode plates left inserted on the surface of the brain, embedded in 1.5mm thick silastic rubber, so that epileptic seizures can be monitored; again these are used to identify where stimulation interferes with speech, as a guideline for the surgeon, but their longer period of placement potentially allows for a more extended examination of speech in conditions outside the operating theatre (Lesser, Leuders, Hahn, Dinner, Hanson, Rothner and Erenberg 1982).

The results of ESB studies have several interesting implications for the localisation of language in the brain, which will be discused in later relevant sections. It should be noted, however, that there are limitations to such studies, to which Ojemann himself draws attention. They are undertaken on a highly selected population (mostly people in their twenties) who have abnormal brains and who are generally on medication. All the patients are shown on Wada testing to be left-hemisphere dominant for language. Only one side of the brain is examined, and only on that portion which the surgeon has laid open, generally centring on the upper portion of the temporal lobe. The language testing is limited and is based on a small number of samples from each site. Moreover stimulation generates both excitatory and inhibitory effects which cannot be distinguished, and which may spread to unknown distances. Nevertheless ESB seems to produce results which show discrete and local effects, and suggest that the association areas of the brain are not organised diffusely but in specific macrocolumnar or mosaic systems as is primary cortex.

Another electrophysiological technique which has sometimes been applied in the study of the lateralisation of language is that of electroconvulsive therapy (ECT). This method is used in the control of schizophrenia and depression and in the relief of Parkinsonism; it involves the induction of seizures through electric shocks applied to one side of the head. For a few minutes after the seizure there is general depression of brain activity, from which the unshocked side recovers quickly. The stimulated hemisphere generally takes up to an hour to recover, during which time tests can be given to establish the effect on language (or other cognitive functions) of the temporary suppression of one hemisphere (Warrington and Pratt 1973; Chernigovskaya and Deglin 1976).

The use of magnetic fields is an alternative to electrophysiological measurements which is just being developed. Magnetic stimulation of the motor cortex has been used in the monitoring of motor disorders. It promises to have advantages over electrical stimulation, since it requires no physical contact or attachments to the scalp; a flat coil can be passed over the skull, which presents less of a barrier to magnetic fields than it does to electrical forces (Barker, Jalinous and Freeston 1985). Another use of magnetic fields parallels the ERP studies. Evoked cortical magnetic fields to auditory stimuli can be recorded by means of a SQUID gradiometer in magnetoencephalography (MEG). Contralateral responses are larger and shorter in latency than ipsilateral responses, and the left hemisphere appears to have a current dipole which is stronger than the right to auditory stimulation, and which is situated some 14mm more posteriorly. Evoked magnetic fields (EF) to auditory probes have been used to explore hemispheric asymmetries in phonetic processing (i.e. detecting the occurrences of the CV syllable /na/ in a recorded passage in an unfamiliar language) (Papanicolaou *et al.* 1987). They provide a better localisation of the origin of the brain's response than do ERPs.

## 2.3 Brain imaging

A number of methods now exist whereby images can be obtained of brain tissue inside a living skull. The least invasive method is by ultrasound examination of sonography. This draws on the fact that sound waves have different lengths and frequencies when they pass through biological tissues which depend on the acoustic 'density' of the tissue. A piezo-electric transducer is used as a source of ultrasonic waves with a reflecting interface as echo detector. The signals are converted by a computer to black and white pictures, which may be static or real-time if successive images are rapidly replaced as the tissue moves. This technique is thought to be so safe that it has become an almost routine procedure for examining the brains of babies in neonatal intensive care units (Levene, Williams and Fawer 1985). Coronal, sagittal and parasagittal scans can be obtained using the anterior fontanelle as an acoustic window, and haemorrhages, enlarged ventricles, cysts and other brain abnormalities can be detected. With real-time sonography, arteries appear as bright pulsatile reflections, and in adults the technique has principally been used to investigate carotid artery functioning. For pictures of the brain, sonography is limited in its resolution power, however, and in the extent to which the frontal and occipital poles can be visualised. For more detailed pictures, and where more invasive methods are clinically acceptable to adults, other imaging techniques are used.

These are basically of two kinds: transmission and emission (Metter 1987). X-rays measure the absorption or transmission of different kinds of tissues, and are the means whereby computerised axial tomography (CT or CAT scanning) derives its pictures. A narrow-beam X-ray source is rotated around the patient's head in synchrony with an X-ray detector on the other side. As the scanner rotates, the lines pick out different amounts of absorption at their points of juncture, and a cross-sectional image of the differential absorption is calculated from the pattern of transmission (in 'pixels' or picture cells) in one plane or 'slice'. The procedure is repeated for other parallel slices, usually about eight, each 10 mm thick. Generally the planes are not horizontal but are angled so as to take in the maximum amount of brain tissue. In aphasia research, most attention has been given to three cuts, that which takes in the frontal zone of the brain known as Broca's area, that which takes in both this and the posterior third of the superior temporal lobe or Wernicke's area, and that which takes in Wernicke's area while passing above Broca's area (Naeser, Hayward, Laughlin, and Zatz 1981). Most regional neurological centres now have CT scanners for the diagnosis of tumours, abscesses, demyelinating diseases etc, despite the limitations of their resolution and their dependence on differential absorption factors of tissues. Though CT scans may be sufficient in some cases to confirm the presence of a space-occupying lesion or area of infarct, the information they provide is static, and they offer frustratingly limited insight into dynamic aspects of language in aphasia and make no contribution to the study of language in normal speakers.

Of more potential interest to neurolinguistics is the use of emission techniques. The technique of measuring regional cerebral blood flow (rCBF) is based on the assumption that blood flow within regions of the brain varies according to the metabolic needs of that part of the brain. This was first postulated in 1890 by Roy and Sherrington who noticed a swelling of the brain within seconds after the onset of an epilectic seizure (Lassen, Ingvar, and Skinhoj (1978). Shifts of blood flow, it is argued, should therefore correspond to different cognitive, motor, and perceptual tasks, if these do indeed selectively activate different zones in the brain. These shifts are detected by tagging the blood with a radioactive tracer, the radiation from which can be detected by scintillators cupped below the head which are connected with a computer. The most commonly-used tracer is 133 xenon, which can be inhaled. This presents less risk to the subject than arterial injection, and in some countries ethical permission can be obtained to use it with normal subjects as well as most patients. Risberg's (1980, 1986) descriptions of the technique draw attention to its limitations. Since only the average blood-flow level can be calculated, a series of similar items has to be presented continuously for at least the five minutes which it takes for the flow of blood through grey matter to be determined. The subject is supine, wears a face mask and has to remain still, all of which limits the tasks which can be used, and the number of measurements which can be taken of mentally disturbed or confused patients. Due to the absorption of the emitted photons by the brain tissue, two-dimensional rCBF systems are essentially only recording differential patterns of radiation from the superficial cortical layers, obscured by a factor of two by the diffuse radiation from deeper, including contralateral, structures. Nonetheless, Meyer, Sakai, Yamaguchi, Yamamoto, and Shaw (1980) report that rCBF distinguishes well between demented and aphasic people, the latter group showing a local failure of blood flow to increase in Broca's area. Gur, Gur, Silver *et al.* (1987) demonstrated different flow patterns between verbal and spatial tasks in right- and left-brain-damaged people; the right-brain-damaged had normal responses for verbal tasks, but lower activation than expected for spatial tasks, while the left-brain-damaged showed reduced activation for both tasks. In normal subjects also, rCBF has been shown to discriminate between verbal and spatial tasks (Gur *et al.* 1987) and between tasks which involve episodic memory (recalling whether a word had previously been heard in a list) and semantic memory (deciding whether each word in the list belonged to a semantic category) (Wood, Taylor, Penny, and Stump 1980). These early studies were achieved with arrays of 16 or 32 scintillator detectors; a finer resolution is now available with 254 mini-detector arrays.

Three dimensional recordings of rCBF can also be made, using tomographic equipment, and this technique is known as single photon emission computerised tomography (SPECT). In SPECT the emission of the radionuclide is detected by a camera which takes pictures around the head. This technique is now beginning to be used in neurolinguistics (Tikofsky, Collier, Hellman, Saxena, Krohn, and Gresch 1986; Goldenberg, Podreka, Suess, Steiner, Deecke, and Willmes 1987). 133 xenon, however, as a tracer provides poor spatial resolution, and newer tracers like iodoamphetamine bring better resolution at the cost of higher radiation exposure. At the time of going to press, a new machine developed in Copenhagen (the Tomomatic 232) has become available for routine clinical use, with a scan time of six minutes or less. It gives a resolution better than 12 mm using Tc99 HMPAO injected intravenously, and can reveal areas of reduced blood flow which appear to be normal on transmission CT scanning. Due to the length of time taken for a scan, even on these faster machines, SPECT is not suitable for real-time investigation of cognitive processing, but is used to detect 'functional' lesion sites.

A further development has been positron emission tomography (PET). This is one of the most expensive procedures, and can only be undertaken in places geographically near to cyclotrons, which produce the short-lived positron-emitting radionuclides which are used, such as 18F in fluorodeoxy-glucose (FDG). If glucose is tagged with such a radionuclide, injected intravenously, its metabolism in the cell can be followed. As the radioactive fluorine decays, it emits positrons, which in turn collide with electrons in such a way that their mass is annihilated and two gamma rays are emitted in exactly opposite directions. A fan-like array of detectors can therefore catch these decay events, which are in effect drawing a multiplicity of straight lines through the head. From the many individual events, a computer draws tomographic images in slices in a similar way to the X-ray CT scanning described earlier, although, as with rCBF imaging, these use colour to show the different relative shifts of metabolic activity from one part of the brain to another. These images at present have achieved a resolution of 7–10 mm (Heiss, Herholz, Pawlik, Wagner, and Wiehard 1986). PET provides more accurate diagnosis of tumours, infarcts etc. than does X-ray CT scanning; metabolic disorders have been shown to extend far beyond the site of lesion and to exist where no CT lesion is shown, particularly in aphasia (Metter 1987). PET is valuable in the early detection of dementia, since cerebral glucose consumption is depleted, and this can be demonstrated in subcortical sites (as in Huntington's disease) as well as in cortical. In normal subjects distinctive patterns of glucose uptake have been correlated with different psychological states such as doing mental arithmetic, recalling a story and analysing musical chords, and with the particular strategies individuals use with such tasks. In subjects in a resting state (i.e. with ears plugged and eyes covered), the left hemisphere remains more active than the right (Metter 1987). Raichle and his team at Washington University, St. Louis, have pioneered a new application of PET scanning in the exploration of the neural basis of language (Petersen, Fox, Posner, Mintun, and Raichle 1988, Posner, Petersen, Fox, and Raichle 1988, Petersen, Fox, Posner, Mintun, and Raichle in press). By giving subjects staged tasks requiring increasing processing of words, they have been able to subtract the PET scan images of a simpler task from a more complex one, thus showing what brain regions are called on specifically for each task. For example the simplest task, looking at a fixation point, could be subtracted from the next stage of looking passively at a series of words. According to these studies, the coding of visual word forms appears to take place entirely within the occipital lobe, while the presentation of auditory words does not produce any activation in this area. When the scans obtained during repeating nouns were subtracted from those obtained during generating verbs associated with those nouns, an area in the left frontal lobe was activated. The same area was activated by a task in which subjects had to estimate what proportion of the sequence of animal names they were shown were the names of dangerous animals, suggesting that this area of the brain is involved when semantic processing is required. The researchers conclude that their PET data provide strong support for the localisation of operations performed on visual, phonological, and semantic codes. These PET activiation techniques provide a promising means of relating cognitive and neural processes. As a research instrument PET has exciting applications, although its expense and dependency on a cyclotron limit its routine clinical usefulness in its current state of development. The subtraction technique used by Raichle's team also at present relies on group data, or repeated trials with the same subject, which makes for caution in its application to brain-damaged individuals.

Another imaging technique which is developing is that of proton nuclear magnetic reasonance imaging (NMR or MRI). Since it requires no moving parts to produce a scan, unlike CT scanners, slices can be produced easily in any plane, transverse, coronal or sagittal (Holland, Hawkes, and Moore 1980). More significantly, however, there is no known hazard attached to it (if used within the prescribed limits), and the technique does not require the use of radioactive substances or ionising radiation. It exploits the phenomenon that the nuclei of some atoms have an uneven number of particles, which cause them to spin and behave like a magnet. Hydrogen and phosphorus, plentiful in the brain (and elsewhere in the body), are such atoms. When such nuclei are placed in a magnetic field, they orientate themselves in line with the magnetic lines of force. If these lines are switched on and off in pulses, the nuclei are repeatedly 'flipped back', releasing energy. It is this emission which is picked up by detectors and converted into an image by a computer. Different sequences of pulses can be manipulated to pick up different features (saturation recovery, inversion recovery and spin echo: Bydder 1984), and thus detect more sensitively responses from grey or white cerebral matter, blood, cerebrospinal fluid or oedema. Bone does not produce signals, which allows for the detection of soft-matter signals in parts of the brain which are obscure to X-ray CT scanning e.g. from acoustic neuromas on the eighth cranial nerve in the petrous temporal bone. As well as detecting tissue type and structure through the use of responses from the hydrogen atoms which are plentiful in the water and lipids that the brain contains, metabolic portraits can also be achieved from phosphorus atoms, since these form part of the energy-storing molecule, adenosine triphosphate (ATP). ATP is concentrated in regions of greatest metabolic activity, and NMR techniques can therefore detect functional activities in the brain, like rCBF and PET techniques.

Although still at an early stage of development, NMR with all its advantages is likely to play a major role in neuroradiological practice in the future. Particularly when lacunar stroke is suspected (i.e. where damage in the small penetrating branch arteries has left lacunae, as may occur with diabetes) NMR provides a clearer diagnosis than CT (Rothrock, Lyden, Hesselink, Brown and Healy 1987). NMR has already been applied to the study of aphasia (DeWitt, Grek, Buonanno, Levine, and Kistler 1985). DeWitt *et al*.'s study has demonstrated, for example, that what a CT scan, in a young woman with a non-fluent aphasia, suggested was a restricted subcortical lesion extended widely into the fronto-temporal cortex.


## 2.4 Behavioural

Behavioural methods, requiring less expensive equipment than the electro-physiological and imaging methods just described, have been used exten-sively by neuropsychologists to study differences between the hemispheres.

The technique of dichotic listening was extended to neuropsychological research by Kimura in the early 1960s. The method involves presenting messages simultaneously to the subject's ears through stereophonic head-phones in such a way that the right ear and left ear hear different items. In general, verbal stimuli are identified more accurately when they are delivered to the right ear, under such competing conditions, than when they are delivered to the left. The theory is that, although both ears have ipsilateral and contralateral connections to the cerebral cortex, the contralateral connections dominate, and, if signals conflict, inhibit the ipsilateral message. To be sure of eliminating timing discrepancies, the exact co-occurrence of the signals must be ensured, making recordings using natural speech elaborate. Many studies have therefore used computer generated stimuli, which can also be selectively manipulated for experimental variables such as formant transitions and duration. Dichotic listening therefore lends itself best to the study of phonetic, phonemic, and lexical semantic processing rather than to that of other domains of language. The main interest has been in attempting to establish the degree of lateralisation of these facets of auditory perception. Individual variability appears to be great, however, and test-retest reliability is limited.

Some use of this technique has been made with brain-damaged patients, in attempts to discover whether aphasics have shifted dominance for language to the right hemisphere. Some studies have claimed that the shift in dominance occurs as the patient recovers language (Pettit and Noll 1979) and that left anterior lesions result in a transfer of dominance rather than left posterior regions (Castro-Caldas and Botelho 1980). Since aphasics with posterior damage increase their right ear scores as they recover, rather than their left ear scores, there may be functional recovery of the auditory pathways which had been lesioned, and which had been making any decisions about auditory verbal input difficult. It is not clear, however, why non-fluent patients with anterior damage (and presumably intact auditory pathways) should show the dominance shift. Not all studies, however, report a shift of ear advantage in dichotic listening with aphasic patients. Niccum (1986; Niccum, Selnes, Speaks, Risse and Rubens 1986) monitored 27 aphasic patients monthly for six months with this technique, using digits and nouns, and found no overall change in ear preference. Individual differences were the most noticeable: although four patients showed a shift to a left ear advantage, three patients showed a shift in the opposite direction. Niccum *et al.* found that right ear scores were related to the presence of lesions in Heschl's gyrus, and concluded that ear preference reflects intactness of the auditory system, not hemispheric dominance for language.

Another technique which presents information preferentially to one hemisphere is that of hemifield (or divided field) viewing. Visual input from the nasal hemifield of the left eye and the temporal hemifield of the right eye (together making up the right hemifield of viewing) is projected on to the left occipital cortex, and, similarly, the left hemifield is projected on to the right occipital cortex. The separation of routes between hemispheres seems to be more distinct than that of the auditory routes. This means that it is more feasible to use single input to one hemisphere, without the need for introducing competing bilateral stimuli, although this latter technique has been used in dichoptic viewing as in dichotic listening. With use of a tachistoscope or computer for fast presentation of visual displays (usually less than 200 msecs), information can be presented in one visual field while the subject fixates on a central point. The use of half-occluded contact lenses (when these can be individually made) allows for longer presentation of stimuli without fixation (Zaidel 1975). The need for ensuring that fixation is maintained in most studies, by asking the subjects to report on a central signal, has been found to affect whether the predicted right visual field advantage for verbal material occurs; if the central stimulus is verbal, a priming effect occurs which enhances this advantage.

Amongst supplementary techniques which have been used to examine the lateralisation of language in normal subjects is time-sharing, or competing activities. The subject is required to tap with the right hand while performing some verbal task; if there is interference it is assumed that the left hemisphere (with dominant control over the right hand) is also dominant for the language task (Kinsbourne and Cook 1971). The potential for using this simple task to explore differences of lateralisation of different types of verbal task or in different types of brain damage has been little explored, possibly because of the compounding factors of coincident hemiparesis or limb apraxia.

Other behavioural techniques have been used with normal and aphasic subjects to examine different components in language, although not necessarily related to lateralisation. In the technique of eye movement tracking, a videotape recorder monitors the corneal reflections as the eye moves, referenced to the centre of the pupil, and position co-ordinates are calculated by computer (Young and Sheena 1975). Huber, Luer and Lass (1983) have used this technique with aphasic subjects while they looked at a circular array of unordered words from sentences. They demonstrated that these subjects fixed on content words rather than function words, and that their processing of the sentences did not appear to be related to their linear syntactic structure. Another technique is pupillometry, which uses change in pupil size as a sentence is being listened to as an index of the amount of mental processing. A movie camera close to the eye takes frames at about every half-second interval, while the subject hears a sentence. Ben-Nun (1986) used his technique with normal subjects who were listening to ambiguous sentences, and showed a rise in pupil size as ambiguous words were reached, compatible with the notion that such words require extra lexical search.

An important behavioural measure which has been widely used is that of reaction time. This underpins many psycholinguistic processing models, as well as hemifield viewing experiments. Its use presents some problems in aphasia research, since reaction times are often so slow that they must span over several cognitive activities, and error counts are generally preferred. Because of the increasing interest in neuropsycholinguistics in interactive processing as an alternative way of conceptualising language operations as distinct from the modular box-and-arrow models, reaction time studies which attempt to measure on-line processing are now beginning to be applied in aphasia research. Blumstein, Milberg and Shrier (1982) used reaction times in a lexical decision task with aphasics. They compared the effect of semantic priming (i.e. preparing the subject with a semantically associated word) in Broca's and Wernicke's aphasics, and showed, contrary to prediction, that Wernicke's aphasics were influenced by such automatic priming of semantics. Tyler (1987) has used reaction time to develop an individual 'processing profile' for a few aphasic patients, by measuring reactions to probe words while they were listening to different types of sentences, e.g. normal prose, semantically anomalous prose, pragmatically implausible prose and scrambled strings. Data from one young agrammatic patient, DE, for example, showed that his reaction times were normal except in respect of the pragmatically-anomalous materials, as he appeared to rely particularly on pragmatic information.

Having looked at some of the principal techniques which have been used to explore the gross neurological correlates of language, let us consider how far these techniques have been able to throw light on this difficult problem. One of the major emphases has been, unsurprisingly, on individual variation. This includes the examination of how the neural organisation of language changes as the brain develops during childhood, and how much the number and type of languages an individual speaks (or writes or signs) may affect this neural organisation. Other emphases have been on the role played by sub-cortical and right hemisphere structures in the neural organisation of language. After looking at these issues we shall return to a discussion of how far current neuropsychological models of language may pave the way for the eventual marriage of neuroscience and neuropsychology.

## 3. INDIVIDUAL DIFFERENCES

### 3.1 The standard model

The late nineteenth- and early twentieth-century investigators of aphasia were predominantly neurologists whose concern was to make sense out of individual observations and derive from it common patterns for identifying aphasia or variants of it which could be associated with site of lesion. Arbib, Caplan, and Marshall (1982) describe how Wernicke and Lichtheim attempted to integrate into a single model the concepts of computational centres and associational links for language (Figure 12). Lesions to Centre A (the centre for auditory word memories) produced sensory, or Wernicke's, aphasia; to Centre M (the centre for motor word memories) motor, or Broca's, aphasia; and to Centre B (the centre for concepts) anomic aphasia. (The linguistic effects of these types of aphasia are discussed in Chapter 12, section 2.) These centres were located respectively in the posterior third of the superior temporal gyrus, the anterior part of the third frontal gyrus, and the lower parietal lobe. Lesions to the connecting tracts between these centres resulted in, for pathway 1, subcortical motor aphasia; for pathway 2, subcortical sensory aphasia; for pathway 3, transcortical sensory aphasia; for pathway 4, transcortical motor aphasia; and for pathway 5, conduction aphasia. The model was therefore a simple proposal in which psychological functions were presented as having a one-to-one mapping on to the anatomy of the brain – and specifically on to the left cerebral hemisphere, not the right.

In clinical practice, blessed by its ease of learning for medical students, this is still the dominant model. With some additions and modifications, it underlies what is internationally the best-known classification system for

*Figure 12* Lichtheim-Wernicke model of language processes.

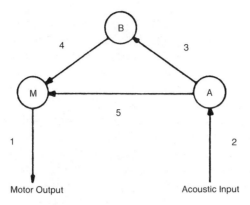

From M.A. Arbib, D. Caplan and J.C. Marshall (1982) *Neural Models of Language Processes*
Academic Press, New York: 11

*Table 11* Distinctions amongst the classical aphasia syndromes. From J.C.
Marshall (1986) 'The description and interpretation of aphasic language
disorder', *Neuropsychologia*, 24: 5–24.

|  | Speech | Repetition | Comprehension | Naming |
|---|---|---|---|---|
| Global aphasia | non-fluent | − | − | − |
| Broca's aphasia | non-fluent | − | + | − |
| Transcortical motor aphasia | non-fluent | + | + | − |
| Wernicke's aphasia | fluent | − | − | − |
| Transcortical sensory aphasia | fluent | + | − | − |
| Conduction aphasia | fluent | − | + | − |
| Anomic aphasia | fluent | + | + | − |

aphasia, with its attendant assessment method, the Boston Diagnostic
Aphasia Examination (Goodglass and Kaplan 1972, 1983). The additions made
include global aphasia, mixed transcortical aphasia (or isolation of the speech
area), pure word deafness, aphemia, jargon aphasia and the alexias (with and
without agraphia). The dimensions on which they are distinguished are
linguistically crude. They comprise auditory comprehension, reading aloud,
repetition of heard language, naming, fluency in speech, articulation of
speech and intelligibility of speech (see Table 11 for the main distinctions).
On the basis of lesion sites some of these aphasias have been mapped on to
locations in the left cerebral hemisphere, in a very similar way to the
Wernicke-Lichtheim model (see Figure 13). The architectonics of the
classical Broca's area, Wernicke's area and supplementary motor area are
summarised by Galaburda (1982).

389

*Figure 13* Maximum overlap of lesion sites corresponding to types of asphasia.

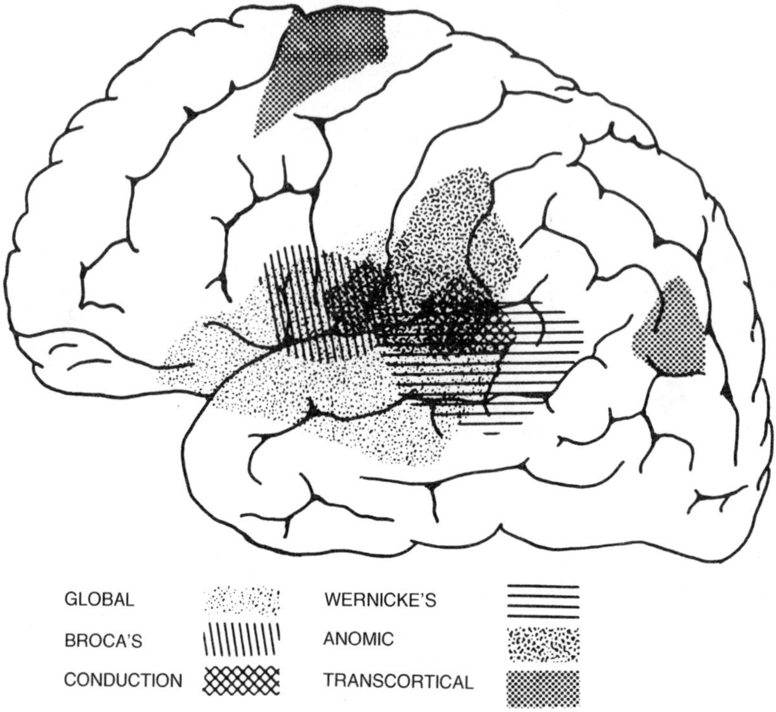

| | | | | | |
|---|---|---|---|---|---|
| GLOBAL | | WERNICKE'S | | | |
| BROCA'S | | ANOMIC | | | |
| CONDUCTION | | TRANSCORTICAL | | | |

From A. Kertesz, D. Lesk, and P. McCabe (1977) 'Isotope localization of infarcts in aphasia'. *Archives of Neurology* 34: 590–601 (600).

Even in Boston, however, and even with this extended possibility of using the additional syndromes, a classification of individuals was only possible for 59 per cent out of 444 cases (Benson 1979) or as few as 20 per cent (Albert, Goodglass, Helm, Rubens, and Alexander 1981). Such problems reinforce criticisms of the classical syndrome classification. This presupposes the homogeneity of essential features in members of each syndrome, a homogeneity which can only be achieved if the model on which the classification is based has indeed been able to specify psychologically real essential features. Luria's (1976) classification, which has applied linguistic distinctions such as minimal pair discrimination and grammatical operations, and is based on the notion of extended functional brain circuits rather than centres, has come much closer to offering a principled basis for identifying syndromes than has the Boston classification. The developments in brain imaging, described above, however, are lessening the need for using language behaviour to predict site of lesion, and are prompting aphasiologists to consider abstract psycholinguistic models independently of neuroanatomical correlates. Such models attempt to 'fractionate' the language process on dimensions which linguistics and psycholinguistics can justify from normal users of language. For them the language of aphasia provides confirmatory or refining evidence regardless of the site and type of damage. The classical syndromes may then seem to be patterns which occur, not because language is organised in brain centres and linking tracts, but because the blood supply of the brain is organised in such a way that blockage or haemorrhage in one zone will interfere with what Marshall has called 'disparate fragments of behaviour that are not related to any meaningful cluster of processing mechanisms' (1986: 8).

The classical model also rests on the assumption that the brain is essentially anatomically and functionally organised in the same way in every individual. That this is not necessarily so can be discussed in respect of gross structural variation, gender, age, and other factors.

## 3.2 Anatomical variation

Ojemann (1983), in his review of ESB, found considerable variability in individuals in the cortical locations which evoked changes in naming, with some sites extending into middle and superior parts of the frontal lobe, the parieto-occipital junction and the anterior part of the temporal lobe, all well outside the 'classical' language zone. One explanation he suggests is that the anatomic organisation in this area is quite different from person to person, and he cites studies which show that the gyral and cytoarchitectonic patterns at the end of the Sylvian fissure in the left hemisphere are highly variable from individual to individual. The same has also been reported of primary visual cortex. Indeed, many students of anatomy will recall having had considerable difficulty identifying amongst different brains what their teachers assured them was the Rolandic fissure along which the sensorimotor cortex is aligned.

Whitaker and Selnes (1975) reported on studies of individual variation in the brain. Brain weights differ considerably: the range can be as much as from 1938 grams to 680. The patterns of gyri and sulci are also extremely variable, as are cytoarchitectural features. For example, in a study described by Whitaker and Selnes in which the striate cortex was examined in 52 hemispheres to test the feasibility of implanting electrode arrays to act as visual protheses for the blind, a fourfold difference was found in the area of this cortex, from 359 to 1308 mm$^2$. Stimulation with electrodes in the striate cortex produces phosphenes, or sensations of spots of light. It was found, in a study of 15 volunteer patients, that the phosphene map produced by electrode arrays varied considerably from subject to subject, although it was consistent over time within the subjects. Whitaker and Selnes conclude that 'These data clearly show that a physiological variability from person to person exists concomitantly with the anatomic variation'. This variation is probably even greater in the auditory and surrounding cortex than in the visual cortex. Brain arteries also have a very individual pattern, in terms both of number of branches and of branching patterns. Since the predominant aetiology in most aphasics studied has been cerebrovascular lesion, patterns of interruption of blood supply must also be inconsistent from patient to patient, further compounding the general conclusions that can be drawn about the localisation of language from this source. There is some variation also in the overall comparative shape and size of the two hemispheres as shown on CT scans (Naeser, Hayward, Laughlin, and Zatz 1981). Some people have larger posterior extension of the brain on the left side and larger frontal extension of the brain on the right side. Post-mortem studies of men with developmental dyslexia have been undertaken also by Galaburda, Sherman, Rosen, Aboitiz, and Geschwind (1985). Despite there being no evidence of neurological abnormality during life, these brains all showed distortions affecting the lamination and columnar organisation of the brain and abnormal clusters of neurons. The authors believe that these and other brain anomalies were acquired before birth. Given the parallel problems in classifying the language features of aphasia, it is surprising that there has been so much agreement as to the prototypical model of localisation within the left hemisphere around which individuals differ.

## 3.3 Handedness

Due to the techniques available which have been described above, it has been easier for psychological studies of individual differences to examine inter-hemispheric distinctions than intrahemispheric. Handedness has been a prime candidate, because of a speculation that speech may be an overlaid function on other motor activities and that control of speech has developed in most people in the left cerebral hemisphere because it is this hemisphere which controls the dominant right hand (Kimura and Archibald 1974). In its simplest form this is refuted by the observation that the actual articulation of speech requires bilateral and subcortical co-ordination. Hardyk (1977) reviewed a large number of studies which examined hemispheric functions associated with handedness, and postulated that there were two types of human cerebral organisation, representing extremes of a continuum. In the first there is strong specialisation of the hemispheres, with language and semantic memory in the left hemisphere, and spatial abilities and pattern recognition in the right hemisphere. In the second, rarer, type, each hemisphere duplicates most functions. He links these patterns with handedness; the right-handed individual with no familial history of left-handedness is strongly lateralised for language, and the familial left-hander has bilateral representation of language. A corollary to this is that right hemisphere damage should result in aphasia more frequently in left-handers than in right-handers. Segalowitz and Bryden (1983), however, have calculated from published studies of the incidence of aphasia after unilateral damage that only 19.8 per cent of left handers have bilateral representation of language, with 61.4 per cent having left-hemisphere representation and 18.8 per cent right representation. In contrast 95.5 per cent of right handers have left hemisphere representation and 4.5 per cent right, with virtually none having bilateral representation. It should be noted that these figures are based on clinical observations of aphasia with frank disturbances of spoken language, and do not take cognisance of the more subtle disturbances of language which may occur after 'non-dominant' right-hemisphere damage (see below). Dichotic listening and hemifield viewing studies (also reviewed by Segalowitz and Bryden) have tended to support a distinction between left- and right-handers, though the evidence concerning familiality remains equivocal.

Those right-handers who have right-hemisphere dominance for language, and who become aphasic, are described as having 'crossed aphasia'. From the few cases reported in the literature it appears that they tend to show similar patterns of disorder as do left hemisphere dominant right-handers (see e.g. Carr, Jacobson, and Boller 1981).

## 3.4 Gender

Studies of normal and brain-damaged subjects generally converge in their support for a sex difference in hemispheric organisation. Language seems to be more bilaterally represented in female brains (Segalowitz and Bryden 1983). The study of sex differences in aphasia is relatively recent, possibly due to the fact that the majority of aphasic people studied in the classical literature have been men – head-injured soldiers (Luria 1970) or stroke patients receiving treatment in American Veterans' Administration Hospitals. McGlone's studies (1978, 1983) found that right-handed women who had suffered unilateral brain damage (but without severe aphasia) did not show the clear patterns of verbal or performance deficits, according to side of lesion, that men did. Pizzamiglio, Mammucari, and Razzano (1985) monitored the recovery of aphasics with global aphasia and found that women with this severe aphasia showed greater improvement than men on tests of phonemic, semantic, and syntactic comprehension, in agreement with McGlone's suggestion that it is particularly in respect of verbal comprehension that women have more bilateral language representation than men. In contrast Basso, Capitani, and Moraschini's (1982) study of recovery in 264 aphasic men and 121 aphasic women found that women recovered in spoken language abilities (but not in verbal comprehension) more than men did. Segalowitz and Bryden (1983) argue for some caution in the interpretation of such results, suggesting that women may use different strategies from men to achieve the same behavioural results e.g. in using visuospatial strategies in 'verbal' tasks. In dichotic listening experiments with normal men and women, they suggest that it is differences in the deployment of attention rather than hemispheric specialisation which accounts for significant differences in scores. Sarno, Buonaguro and Levita (1985) have failed to find significant differences between 37 men and 23 women in recovery from aphasia after stroke.

### 3.5 Cognitive style, education, literacy

As Segalowitz and Bryden's comments above indicate, what have been called neurosociologic variables have been invoked to account for individual differences. A theory of 'hemisphericity' has been proposed (Bogen and Bogen 1983) which suggests that each individual tends towards a preferred type of cognitive processing which might predominantly involve left- or right-hemisphere functioning. This has also been associated with the educational habits which are imposed on children, which have in the past been thought to emphasise verbal skills strongly. Beaumont, Young, and McManus (1984) have critically reviewed the EEG, lateral eye movement, and other studies which underpin this proposal, and conclude that the notion of hemisphericity cannot be supported, at least in so far as it refers to lateralisation of hemispheric function.

There is a more robust basis for believing that environmental and learning experiences have a considerable influence on the cerebral organisation of language in individuals. Ojemann's (1983) ESB investigations showed that two groups of patients could be distinguished according to their verbal IQs in the pattern of localisation of sites with naming changes in the posterior language areas. Patients with lower IQs demonstrated naming changes with stimulation in the parietal zones, while patients with higher IQs were more likely to show naming changes with stimulation of the superior temporal gyrus. Deprivation of language experience, in the tragic cases of 'wild children' such as Genie (Curtiss 1976), suggests that the left cerebral hemisphere loses its ability to support language, and that any such gains are achieved by the right hemisphere. Measures of language, including many aphasia batteries, correlate with educational level (Borod, Goodglass, and Kaplan 1980). The degree to which achievement in literacy in English, Portuguese, and Brazilian influences results on aphasia tests, in normal and aphasic subjects, is currently the subject of an extensive study (Lecours, Mehler, Parente, Caldeira *et al.* 1987, in press). This may throw some light on a claim made by Damasio, Castro-Caldas, Grosso, and Ferro (1976). Using a threefold division of aphasia types into fluent, Broca's, and global, these clinicians concluded that the incidence and proportions of type of aphasia were the same in illiterate patients as literate, and that the development of neural structures for language does not depend on the acquisition of reading and writing skills.

## 3.6 Age

Compounded with the factors of environmental experience, degree of learning, and educational skill is the factor of age. The relationship between age and cerebral organisation has been the subject of study both in respect of the acquisition of language by children and changes in language functions with increasing age in adult life. As with other aspects of individuality, evidence has been drawn from examination of what happens when the brain is damaged.

If a child's brain is damaged at birth, or at any time up to the development of speech, language acquisition can be unaffected. This may be so even if the damage has been the extreme one of hemidecortication (Bishop 1988), and is thus evidence that the right hemisphere can fully support language under these circumstances. Acquisition of language may be slower, however, as a detailed study of the cognitive development of one boy has shown, observed from his radical hemispherectomy (excluding only the thalamus and basal ganglia), until the age of 5 (Byrne and Gates 1987). Damage which occurs after a child has learned to talk, however, has different consequences. Lenneberg (1967) noted that the younger the child at the time of the damage, the better the prospect for a complete recovery, with children over age 10 or so showing the adult picture of aphasia; he suggested that this age marked the end of the critical period for acquiring language. More recent studies have shown, however, that children who have apparently recovered from aphasia can be impaired on language tests (Woods and Carey 1979; Hécaen 1983; Vargha-Khadem, O'Gorman, and Watters 1985; Cooper and Flowers 1987). A longitudinal study of children with unilateral brain damage by Aram and Ekelman (1987) indicates persisting mild language deficits in verbal memory, comprehension, spoken syntax, and word retrieval, which were not related to the age at which the lesion occurred (i.e. over or under 1 year). Deficits in the use of pronouns in discourse cohesion in two adolescents after left hemidecortication before 5 months of age have been reported by Lovett, Dennis, and Newman (1986). It has been proposed, in fact, that the left hemisphere is already specialised for language at birth (Woods 1983). It is only recently that the examination of children who might be aphasic has been undertaken in the same detail as is that of adult aphasics, and most studies so far have applied psycholinguistic modelling only to selective aspects of children's language, reading, and writing (e.g. Sawyer 1987). It has proved even more difficult to slot individual children into the classical syndromes than individual adults

(Van Hout, Evrard, and Lyon 1985). Even more speculative are attempts to associate children with reading and other language difficulties without a history of brain damage with patterns of dysfunctioning anatomical areas, as has been essayed by Sawyer (1987). One of the few studies to discriminate amongst the domains of language in considering childhood acquisition of language is by Seron (1981). He comments on the role played by the right hemisphere in semantics and pragmatics, and suggests that left hemisphere damage only has an obvious effect on a child's language when acquisition has reached the stage when grammatical aspects of language should be as developed as semantic and pragmatic.

The theory that the plasticity of the brain (which Lenneberg proposed lasts till puberty) in fact extends over the whole life span has been proposed by Brown and Jaffe (1975; Brown and Grober 1983). What begins as a process of specialisation between hemispheres continues as a process of specialisation within the left hemisphere. There is substantial evidence that aphasia type is correlated with age, with Wernicke's aphasics being significantly older than Broca's aphasics (see Obler and Alber 1981 for a review). Brown and Jaffe explain this as due to the earlier lateralisation of expressive speech processes, and its gradual focusing to the anterior region, preceding a slower lateralisation and focusing of verbal comprehension. Obler and Albert (1981), however, consider that the evidence can be accounted for by a higher incidence of strokes to the posterior region of the brain in older men. It is also likely that strokes in older people will occur in brains which have some degree of widespread deterioration bilaterally. If comprehension draws on the right hemisphere as well as the left, this would account for the greater occurrence of comprehension disorders in the elderly aphasic patient, even if obvious confounding factors like deteriorating hearing and eyesight are controlled.

### 3.7 Type and number of languages

Since interactive exposure to language is an essential part of language acquisition, the question has been asked whether the type of language used has an effect on the way it becomes organised in the brain. One indirect way to study this is to compare aphasic phenomena in several languages (e.g. the international study of agrammatism by Menn and Obler and their colleagues, which has just been completed) on the presumption that if different languages require different accommodations in the brain, this would be revealed by different patterns in brain damage. Most studies of aphasia have been in the most spoken European languages, which have a common ancestry. Eastern languages which use tone phonemically and have ideographic writing systems open up other possibilities for the test of the universality of aphasic symptoms, as do those European languages which have complex morphology, such as Finnish. They provide additional possibilities through which the fractionation of language can be examined (e.g. Sasanuma's 1986 process model of writing ideographic kanji or phonic kana words to dictation in Japanese – on which see Chapter 20, below). Although different languages bring different problems into focus, the evidence predominantly favours the universality of language dissolution (Peuser and Fittschan 1977). Studies which have correlated to site of lesion different patterns of reading and writing difficulties in Japanese are comprehensively reviewed by Paradis, Hagiwara, and Hildebrandt (1985), with the conclusion that the commonly-held view that kanji symbols are processed by the right hemisphere is wrong; the evidence from alexia supports rather a left parieto-occipital basis. More-over, another putative candidate for differences in the neural bases of language related to the specific language spoken, tone production deficit in Chinese aphasics with left-hemisphere damage, does not seem to provide evidence of a hemispheric difference. Such deficits are qualitatively and quantitatively equivalent to consonant production deficits, giving no support to a right hemisphere basis for the phonemic use of tone (Packard 1986).

The same holds for another form of language which has a visuospatial medium, sign language (see Chapter 21, below). Two studies have indepen-dently reported on the effect of Wada tests in hearing women who also used American Sign Language (ASL). The right-handed patient studied by Damasio, Bellugi, Damasio, Poizner, and Van Gilder (1986) had left-hemisphere dominance for both oral and sign language, both of which remained intact after right temporal lobectomy. Mateer, Rapport, and Kettrick's (1984) patient, left-handed after a presumptive stroke at the age of 2, showed a mixed lateralisation, but one which was the same in both oral and signed expression i.e. showing motor disruption from right-sided perfusion of sodium amytal, and grammatical and semantic disruption after left-sided perfusion. This was corroborated by ESB before surgery. Lebrun (1985) has reviewed a dozen or so reported cases of deaf signers who have become aphasic. Parallels occur between the speech errors of oral aphasics and the sign errors of deaf aphasics: sign substitutions resemble verbal paraphasias, formational errors phonemic paraphasias, and nonsense signs neologisms. Dissociations between writing and other means of language expression have been reported in sign aphasia as in oral language aphasia. This is particularly interesting when the non-preferred hand is used for both, since it has been suggested that use of the non-preferred hand may be a substantial element in the production of aphasic writing disorders (Brown, Leader, and Blum 1983). Dissociations have also been reported (see Ross's 1983 review) between finger-spelling and the production of signs, which could be interpreted either in terms of the closeness to the oral language system or of the different demands on skilled movement. Despite the distinctive quality of sign as a visual-gestural language not dependent on auditory input (Bellugi, Poizner, and Zurif 1982), the limited evidence available so far points to the use of the same cerebral hemisphere for both. It seems that 'normal auditory experience is not necessary for the development of cerebral specialization' (Ross 1983: 309). There is some qualification in this conclusion, however; the educational experiences of deaf individuals are influential on whether they show left-hemisphere dominance; according to Ross, deaf children who attend signing schools or who are not grammatically skilled in English do not show the degree of hemispheric asymmmetry found in other deaf children.

With other forms of non-vocal communication, used by all communicators, deaf or oral, controversy continues as to whether they are mediated by the same cerebral structures as verbal communication or not. These issues have been reviewed in respect both of comprehension and expression by Feyereisen and Seron (1982a, b), and since they are not central to neurolinguistics will not be further discussed here.

People who use both oral language and sign language are only a somewhat special type of bilinguals. The relationship of bilingualism to aphasia is being extensively explored by Paradis (1987) in respect of several combinations of languages. Paradis and Lecours (1983) have reviewed the evidence for the dissociations of recovery from aphasia in the different languages of bilinguals or polyglot speakers. Six patterns have been reported, the most common by far being parallel recovery of both languages. In differential recovery, one language is not recovered to the same extent as another, or is recovered more slowly. In successive recovery, recovery in one language precedes that in another. In selective recovery, one language is not regained (or may be regained in only one modality). An interesting pattern is when recovery is antagonistic, such that one language appears to regress while another progresses, and this can happen alternately with the patient swinging back from one language to another (Paradis, Goldblum, and Abidi 1982). Recovery may also be mixed, when bilinguals systematically mingle the two languages in their speech. These different patterns of recovery are not mutually exclusive. The fact that languages are not necessarily recovered in parallel does suggest that there may be different neural substrates for each language. As with sign language in the deaf the proposal has been considered that the second language may use the right hemisphere (Albert and Obler 1978). Dichotic listening studies with Spanish-English (Galloway and Scarcella 1982), Wada and ESB studies with Chinese-English (Rapport, Tan, and Whitaker 1983) and concurrent activities studies with Portuguese-English (Soares 1984) have failed to find any supporting evidence for this. Nor does there seem to be the higher incidence of aphasia in bilinguals that such a hypothesis would predict (Green and Newman 1985). Again individual variability confuses the picture and this is particularly so in the case of bilinguals, who may learn their languages at different times and by different means. Vaid (1983) suggests that right-hemisphere participation is more likely the later the second language is acquired relative to the first, and that the pattern of hemispheric involvement only differs between languages when they have been acquired differently. The existence of antagonistic recovery has prompted speculation by Paradis and Lecours (1983) that there may be a switching mechanism (possibly in the supramarginal gyrus) which controls the selection of one language or the other. Paradis and Lecours point out that the decision to speak in one language or another is only an extreme case of the decision to use a different register when addressing different individuals, which is part of normal communication. Some sort of decision-making mechanism is therefore essential in the microgenesis of language. However it is unlikely that such a mechanism, or switch, could have an all-or-none nature, since both language systems in bilinguals can be active at the same time (Green and Newman 1985). Green and Newman prefer the analogy of a tag to that of a switch for selection of one language schema rather than another, and explain the different patterns of recovery in bilingual aphasia in terms of limits in resources for activation rather than damage to the structural processes in the languages themselves.

In summary this survey of individual differences would seem to suggest that the claims made so far about the localisation of language are essentially presupposing male, right-handed, well-educated, monolingual adults. Even in respect of such cases, however, doubt has been cast on the precise localisation claims made by the classical model, and these are due to the impossibility of a clear specification of what the essential disorders are if patients are grouped by syndrome rather than symptoms. For example, Mohr (1976) showed that a lesion in Broca's area results in an articulatory difficulty, not in agrammatism, for which the lesion needs to be both more extensive and more posterior in the brain.

## 4. RIGHT-HEMISPHERE LANGUAGE

The studies of language lateralisation in the different types of individuals described above seem to leave little role for language to the right hemisphere, except in exceptional people. Yet there is a growing body of evidence which points to the involvement of the right hemisphere in some aspects of language. The reason that most of the studies just reported have not detected this is that they have regarded language as being largely a single entity, or as being divisible only in terms of the medium through which it is used, speaking, listening, reading, or writing. In fact, even in the rare case of adult hemispherectomy, it has been recognised that comprehension of speech and some limited production of it are not abolished (Smith 1966), and examination of the isolated right hemispheres in a few patients with severed corpus callosum has suggested that some of these hemispheres retain a degree of comprehension of single words (Zaidel 1976). It has also been suggested that, in the normal brain, the right hemisphere is involved in the processing of words which have referents which are highly imageable, and that in reading, while the left hemisphere accesses abstract words through a phonological route, the right hemisphere accesses concrete words directly through imagery (see, for example, Ellis and Sheppard 1974). Deloche, Seron, Scius and Segui (1987) from the results of semantic priming of homographs biased towards their high or low imagery meaning conclude that high imagery words are represented bilaterally in the brain, and low imagery words only in the left hemisphere. It is number of letters in a word for reading, moreover, not phonological length, which influences the right hemisphere, and this is interpreted as meaning that the right hemisphere achieves lexical access in reading through the short-term storage of graphemic information, the method used by the left hemisphere only when it is confronted with unusual rather than familiar words (Young and Ellis 1985).

Inferences about the role of the right hemisphere have been made through observations both of people with unilateral right-brain damage and with unilateral left-brain damage. In the first case it is to see what impairment is produced to language, in the second case it is to see what abilities are retained. Reviews of both these methods can be found in Millar and Whitaker (1983), Perecman (1983), and Code (1987).

Lund, Spliid, Andersen, and Bojsen-Moller's (1986) study, using CT scan localising information, found no impairment of the ability to identify unrounded front vowels after right-brain damage (or after anterior left-brain damage), but a significant impairment in aphasic patients who had damage to a zone centring on Wernicke's area (interpreted in this study as comprising a wider area than in the classical model). These authors argue that this vowel perception is dependent on this area of the left hemisphere. In contrast, a number of studies have suggested that many patients with right-brain damage show a degree of specifically semantic impairment in comprehension tests, despite the preservation of phonological discrimination (Lesser 1974; Gainotti, Caltagirone, and Miceli 1983). Lesser's patients performed well on standard vocabulary tests (as well as on measures of syntactic and phonological comprehension), and the impairment was only displayed when the patients were required to make close discriminations within a semantic field; the impairment also occurred in the sorting of written words into ones which were close or distant semantic associates, and could, therefore, not be explained as due to the use of pictorial material in a group which might have visuospatial problems.

These tests were concerned with the denotative aspect of reference, but there is also a substantial body of evidence in support of the notion that connotative aspects of lexical semantics are disturbed by right-brain damage. Brownell, Potter, Michelgow, and Gardner (1984) have demonstrated that right-brain-damaged patients who retain general denotative comprehension are insensitive to connotative facets of meaning. The task was to pair adjectives from a set of eight (warm, cold, deep, shallow, loving, hateful, wise, foolish) which could be categorised denotatively as antonyms or by their connotations e.g. metaphorically. A further experiment (Brownell, Simpson, Bihrie, Potter, and Gardner 1986) confirmed the finding that right-brain-damaged patients showed a selective impairment in appreciation of metaphoric meanings. Brownell and his colleagues infer a special role for the right hemisphere in lexical-semantic processes related to metaphor comprehension.

Such findings have raised the question of whether right-brain damage impairs the ability to process emotion in language, not only lexically in connotation but in prosody, both in respect of lexical stress and sentence intonation. Bowers, Coslett, Bauer, Speedie, and Heilman (1987) have recently examined this question, considering in particular whether any such disability could be explained in terms of distraction effects in right-brain damage rather than processing defects. They used a method in which subjects heard recorded sentences spoken in different emotional tones (happy, sad, angry, or indifferent). For half of the sentences the semantic content was incongruous with the emotional tone, a condition which would be expected to distract listeners from decisions about the emotion (indicated by pointing to drawings of faces). Although the right-brain damaged did show such a distraction effect, they were also impaired on making decisions when the prosody was congruent with the semantics. They were also impaired on making decisions when sentences were used in which the semantic content had been filterd out, although left-brain-damaged patients performed as well as the normal controls under this condition. Bowers *et al.* conclude that processing deficits for emotional prosody do occur after right-brain damage which cannot be explained in terms of distraction effects.

Ross (1981, 1983) has advanced the proposal that damage to the right hemisphere results in patterns of aprosody which mirror some of the patterns of aphasia in the left hemisphere in classical localisation theory i.e. motor, sensory, global, transcortical sensory, and mixed transcortical aprosodias. Ross's proposal was based on a superficial examination of a few patients, and there is as yet no detailed evidence in support of it. A study by Bryan (1986) comparing left- and right-brain-damaged patients on a battery of language measures, including measures of prosody, found no clear correspondence between lesion sites in the right hemisphere, as ascertained by CT scans, and impairment in prosody. The study, however, added further evidence that deficits in the comprehension of prosody do occur after unilateral right-hemisphere damage, and that this extends beyond the emotive use of prosody to its propositional use. The right-brain-damaged had difficulty in distin-guishing between words in which placement of lexical stress changes gram-matical class, structure and/or meaning ('present/pre'sent: green'house/'greenhouse) or in which intonation distinguishes the speech act of a sentence as a question, a statement, or a request. Left-brain-damaged aphasic people also have difficulty in such distinctions (Blumstein and Goodglass 1972; Lonie and Lesser 1983; Emmorey 1987); but Bryan was able to show that the right-hemisphere-damaged were impaired on a task which the aphasics could do well i.e. detecting whether the intonation pattern of filtered speech was Chinese or English. The relative roles of left and right hemisphere in non-emotional prosody are still not established, however, and some studies (e.g. Emmorey's) have reported no disturbance of prosody in their samples of right-brain-damaged subjects.

The pragmatic aspects of language after right-brain damage have been investigated from a number of perspectives by Gardner and his colleagues (reviewed by Wapner, Hamby, and Gardner 1981 and Gardner, Brownell, Wapner, and Michelow 1983). A battery of tests showed that right-brain-damaged patients had difficulty in organising sentences into coherent narratives, missed the nicety of linguistic humour and accepted bizarre endings to stories as plausible. Gardner describes such behaviour as 'missing the point'. Anteriorly-damaged patients contrasted with posteriorly-damaged patients in having an extreme rather than flat response to humour. Wapner *et al.* suggest that such results indicate that a distinction must be made between the core aspects of language – phonology, syntax, referential semantics – and the pragmatic aspects which involve more complex linguistic entities depen-dent on contextual information. It is proposed that the latter are the domain of the right hemisphere. This suggests that it is particularly in the integration of complex information in language and its contexts that the right-brain-damaged should have difficulty. Such a hypothesis has recently been investigated by McDonald and Wales (1987). They predicted that right-brain-damaged people would store the information they had heard in its literal form without making inferences about it, as do normal people. The hypothesis was not supported, but another problem was revealed i.e. that the right-brain-damaged were willing to accept incorrect statements and inferences as having been heard before. Foldi (1987) did find, however, that right-brain-damaged patients prefer literal to pragmatically appropriate responses when asked to choose an appropriate picture to illustrate the consequences of certain situ-ations e.g. what happens after a father has said to his son, who is idly leaning against his dirty car, 'Do you have everything to clean the car?'

Some studies have already attempted to correlate pragmatic disorders with localisation of function in the right hemisphere. Grossman and Haberman (1987) found that it was anterior right-brain damage that resulted in most difficulty, within the right-brain-damaged group, in judging the correctness of causal conjunctions ('although', 'because', 'so') linking statements such as 'Gloria cleaned the room. The room was dusty'. The impairment of these patients was most marked in judging sentences which required a rearrangement of the order of the propositions so as to be plausible. Comparing their results with others which have also contrasted sentence comprehension in left- and right-brain damage, Grossman and Haberman conclude that 'the role played by the right hemisphere in sentence processing does not replicate the contribution of the left hemisphere' (171).

In studies of retained abilities after left-brain damage which attempt to make inferences about the capacity of an undamaged right brain, it has to be borne in mind that the language which is produced may be as much the product of the left hemisphere, or of interference from the left hemisphere, as of the right. A dissociation between propositional language and emotive language in aphasia after left-brain damage is well documented (see, for example, Code's 1987 review), and it has been proposed that this speech arises from the right hemisphere. The implications of this have been applied in aphasia therapy in several ways e.g. in the use of Melodic Intonation Therapy to stimulate speech in patients who have good comprehension (and therefore are presumed to have intact right hemispheres) but difficulty organising phonological output (Helm-Estabrooks 1983). The Lateral Shift Hypothesis, that recovery from aphasia is mediated by the right hemisphere in some patients, also postulates that the right hemisphere has the potential for serving the production of speech.

It has also been proposed that it is the right hemisphere which is mediating reading in a type of acquired reading disorder, deep dyslexia (Coltheart 1980; Saffran, Bogyo, Schwartz, and Marin 1980; Landis, Regard, Graves, and Goodglass 1983). This is based on the analysis of the semantic paralexias in the reading aloud of such patients (e.g. 'sepulchre' read as 'tomb'), which seem to reflect the limited semantic abilities of the right hemisphere uncorrected by the phonological-orthographic abilities of the left hemisphere. Landis et al. demonstrated that the occurrence of semantic paralexia increased with lesion size in the left hemisphere. This position has been questioned by Patterson and Besner (1984) (but see further discussions by Jones and Martin 1985 and Marshall and Patterson 1985). One query is as to why, if the right hemisphere can support reading after left-brain damage, it does not do so in patients who have a pure alexia. In fact it has been demonstrated that some such patients are not only able to decide whether fast-presented items are real words or not but also have some knowledge of the meaning of words they do not read aloud (Shallice and Saffran 1986: Coslett and Saffran in press). It has been argued that, if the left hemisphere's attempt to read aloud through letter-by-letter reading could be inhibited, functional reading for meaning could eventually be achieved. Since such patients generally deny that they can understand printed words, and can make accurate decisions about their meaning only when they are using a strategy of fast impressionistic responding, this is further evidence of a dissociation of controlled from automatic processing – the latter in this case, it is argued, being the function of the right hemisphere.

Confusing and contradictory though this evidence is, it points to the existence, even in people with recognised dominance for language in the left hemisphere, of a substantial role for the right hemisphere in many aspects of language, in particular in lexical semantics, prosody and pragmatics.

## 5. SUBCORTICAL STRUCTURES AND LANGUAGE

Since the right hemisphere seems to have a role to play in language, it has also been asked whether the same may be so for the clusters of nuclei which underlie the white matter below the cortex and act as way-stages between cortex and brain stem. These comprise the thalamus and the basal ganglia. The thalamus is the most central of these, with wedge-shaped left and right masses (sometimes linked) on the edge of the ventricle. The left and right thalamuses incorporate a number of neclei, including the pulvinar posteriorly. The basal ganglia within each hemisphere are lateral to the thalamus, The two main ganglia are the lenticular ('lens-shaped') nucleus and the caudate nucleus. The latter is a C-shaped structure which loops around the lenticular nucleus and is separated from it by bands of white fibre tracts known as the internal capsule. The lenticular nucleus itself has two parts, the globus pallidus and the putamen lateral to it. Bridges of grey cells pass through the internal capsule and link the putamen with the caudate; this produces a striped appearance under the microscope, and has led to these structures becoming known as the striatum. More laterally another fan of white fibres is called the external capsule, with alongside it a thin sheet of grey matter, the claustrum. These are all behind the folded-in part of the cortex behind the temporal lobe which is called the insula. Of all these structures the ones which have been most studied in respect of language are the thalamus and the lenticular nucleus.

All the evidence concerning the role of these structures in language inevitably comes from brain-damaged patients including ones undergoing electrophysiological stimulation prior to surgery. That some of these structures play a role in the motor production of speech has been known for some time, but the idea that damage to them might produce aphasia (although milder and less longer-lasting than cortical aphasias) has been revived relatively recently. Studies have generally distinguished between damage to the basal ganglia and damage to the thalamus (Wallesch and Wyke 1983).

Damage to the basal ganglia accompanying Parkinson's disease has been reported to result in language difficulties as well as motor speech disorders. Lees and Smith (1983) describe naming difficulties in this condition. Tanridag and Kirshner (1987) have reviewed a number of studies which describe language disorders after strokes in the left internal capsule and striatal regions. Particular attention has been paid to the lenticular nucleus, and aphasic symptoms have been described after either putamenal lesions or lesions to the globus pallidus. Haemorrhage frequently occurs in the region of the putamen, and Nauser, Alexander, Helm-Estabrooks, Levin, Laughlin, and Geschwind (1982) have suggested that the pattern of aphasia differs according to whether the damage is anterior or posterior. Although these subcortical aphasias are most commonly linked in type with the transcortical aphasias (Wallesch 1985), since the ability to repeat is generally preserved, patterns distinct from those of cortical aphasias have been described e.g. the occurrence of articulatory difficulty with jargon.

Aphasia after damage to the thalamus has been studied in rather more detail (Ojemann 1982; Mateer and Ojemann 1983; Mohr 1983; Lhermitte 1984). Word-finding difficulties are greater and may be accompanied by perseveration and lack of insight. Language difficulties, however, fluctuate, a feature not seen in cortical aphasias, and the perseverations may be intrusions of irrelevant words. ESB, instead of blocking language, may result in the production of these perseverative words. Perseveration seems to be associated particularly with the medial central portion of the ventral lateral thalamus, which Ojemann interprets as a site of interaction between language and motor speech functions. The ventrolateral part of the thalamus is said to include alerting circuits which are involved in short-term memory as well as in naming. Stimulation here can have an effect on word retrieval which may last as long as a week, suggesting that it participates in long-term memory as well. Crosson, Parker, Kim, Warren, Kepes, and Tully (1986), however, consider that that part of the thalamus known as the pulvinar is the critical zone, as deduced from a post-mortem study of an 82-year-old man, whose thalamic lesion had resulted in a fluent aphasia with semantic paraphasias. These authors hold that the thalamus maintains the tone of cortical language mechanisms and releases monitored language for its motor programming. Bechtereva, Bundzen, Gogolitsin, Malyshev, and Perepelkin (1979) have also suggested that subcortical structures have a pace-maker mechanism which controls and reorganises the brain for the maintenance of mental activity.

Specifying in more detail what role subcortical structures play in language will require the tracing of cortical-subcortical circuits, such as those proposed by Lamendella (1977). Wallesch and Wyke (1983) have proposed three parallel anatomical pathways: firstly a cortical-subcortical (basal ganglia and thalamus) loop; secondly reciprocal cortical-thalamic-cortical connections and thirdly the ascending reticular-thalamic-cortical activation system. Crosson (1985) has advanced a more elaborate model in which he has incorporated some features of the classical cortical model (e.g. that the posterior zone performs phonological verification and the anterior zone motor programming) with inhibitory circuitry through the caudate nucleus from the anterior zone, and inhibitory links with the posterior zone through the lenticular nucleus and thalamus. In this model subcortical structures inhibit motor output, while the cortex exercises an editing and checking function on the planned language. This could perhaps account for the reportedly frequent occurrence of semantic paraphasias after subcortical damage. Crosson's model is reviewed by Murdoch (in press).

A scheme of subcortical aphasias has been set out by Alexander, Naeser and Palumbo (1987), based empirically on the profiles of 19 patients who had subcortical damage and showed language disturbances of varying types and degrees. This model suggests that 'white matter pathways are the critical structures in the language disorders' (984), and proposes that the patterns of the disorders can be mapped specifically on to the combinations of subcortical lesions. For example two cases had lesions in the putamen, posterior limb of the internal capsule and/or posterior periventricular white matter; their language disorder was like that of Wernicke's aphasia, without dysarthria but with hemiparesis.

A question mark hangs over any model based on subcortical aphasias, however, and that is the uncertainty as to whether such patients do not also have cortical damage due to secondary degeneration of cortical neurones. The rCBF and other imaging studies described earlier have indeed suggested that such distance effects may occur. Weinrich, Ricaurte, Kowall, Weinstein, and Lane (1987) have acknowledged this difficulty of interpretation in the patient they examined; rCBF study showed that cortical hypoperfusion might be a possible cause of the 'subcortical' aphasia. Intuitively plausible though it is that the neural substrate of language in the brain involves a synergism of cortical and subcortical activity, the extent to which the damage is limited to subcortical structures in 'subcortical aphasias' is controversial.

## 6. NEUROPSYCHOLOGICAL MODELS

It is clear that much is yet to be learned even about the gross neuroanatomy of language, in respect of subcortical involvement, right-hemisphere involvement and intrahemisphere localisation. The advances in techniques of brain imaging described earlier will play some part in clarifying a very obscure picture, but until large numbers can be studied the problems of individual differences will dominate. Developing as rapidly on the psychological front, in parallel with the anatomo-physiological, are models which interpret language disorders as malfunctions of abstract language structures and processes, and which may eventually lend themselves to the embrace of mind and brain, although at present they resist such an extrapolation.

For an introductory review of such models in the context of aphasia and alexia, see Coltheart (1987). Two such 'box and arrow' models are shown in Figures 14 and 15. Figure 14 shows a cross-modality model indicating stages and routes in reading aloud, writing to dictation, repeating heard words and copying writing. The dissociations which have been found in language disorders after brain damage have been instrumental in developing such a model and in fostering the modular approach in the analysis of the mental representations of language. From such a model patients have been identified who have selective disturbances in repetition, reading, or writing which can be related to dysfunctioning semantic, lexical or non-lexical routes. The number of psycholinguistically-motivated symptom profiles (e.g. through subdivisions of the main features previously noted in deep, surface, phonological, and letter-by-letter dyslexias) multiplies (Ellis 1987). Despite their authors' intentions, these psycholinguistically-motivated symptom profiles are already being related to anatomical locations. Rapcsak, Rothi, and Heilman (1987) studied a man with a transient phonological alexia (i.e. who could not read non-words successfully) and spelling difficulties, but with no other problem except some mild naming difficulties. His lexical route was apparently intact for reading, although the grapheme-phoneme conversion route was non-functional. He attempted to use a phonic system in spelling, however, as evidenced by such errors as 'ritchewal' for 'ritual'. CT scans indicated a small infarct at the temporo-occipital junction, which involved only the posterior part of the middle and inferior temporal gyri and their underlying white matter, but not Wernicke's area. The authors postulate that 'a ventral pathway from inferior occipital association cortex to Wernicke's area via the posterior-inferior portion of the left temporal lobe may be involved in mediating reading by the non-lexical phonological route' (120).

This model in Figure 14 is restricted to single words. The model in Figure 15, taken from Butterworth and Howard (1987), incorporates some aspects of the lexical model and extends it to sentence production. Here five distinct systems are identified: semantic (which encodes thought into a semantic specification), lexical (which selects words from an inventory on the basis first of semantic identity and then on the basis of phonological form), prosodic (which chooses the appropriate intonation contour for the semantics and pragmatics of the utterance), phonological assembly (which merges the

*Figure 14* A simple process model for the recognition, comprehension and production of spoken and written words and non-words.

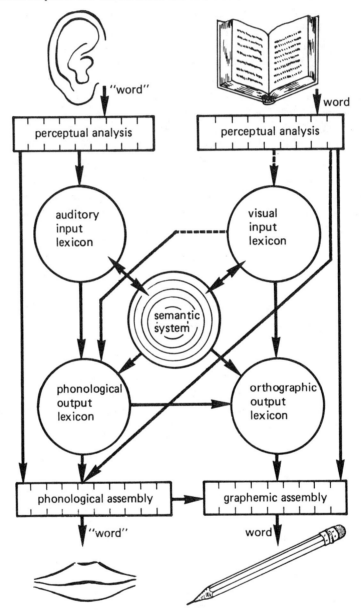

From M. Coltheart, G. Sartori, and R. Job (1987) *The Cognitive Neuropsychology of Language.* Lawrence Erlbaum: London: 6. (The dotted lines indicate three hypothesised routes in reading aloud.)

*Figure 15* A model of the production of sentences.

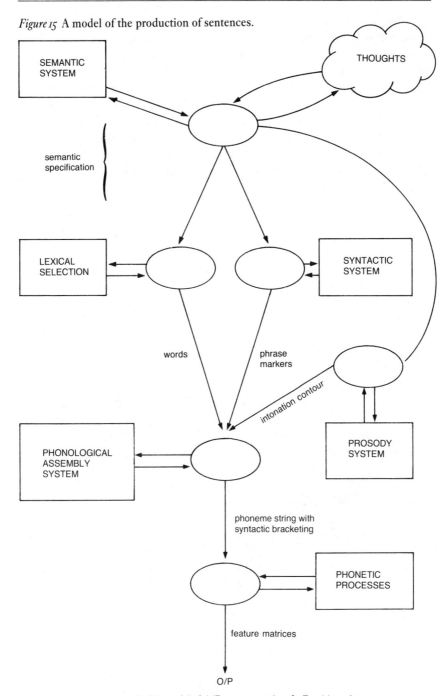

From B. Butterworth and D. Howard (1987) 'Paragrammatisms', *Cognition*, 26: 1–37: 32

outputs from the last three systems) and the phonetic (which specifies the phonetic parameters needed for programming articulation). Butterworth and Howard drew up their model partly on the basis of observations of five patients who had paragrammatic speech (i.e. who produced fluent but grammatically incorrect utterances). They made no attempt to draw localisation inferences about such language symptoms, but report incidentally that the three who had had CT scans had signs of bilateral damage, in two cases in the temporal lobes and in one case in the parieto-occipital region of the left hemisphere with extensive right hemisphere damage. Again, speculations have been made about localisation in respect of aphasic problems with grammar. Zurif (1980) optimistically stated that computational units in language 'have been pinpointed neuroanatomically' (311) through the investigation of aphasia, and proposed that processing of functors in their syntactic role (but not their semantic) is discretely localised in the anterior part of the left hemisphere.

The ultimate question is whether it will ever be possible to find neural systems which correspond to components such as these models define. The models bear resemblances to the processing models which have been used in artificial intelligence. For this reason, Arbib et al. (1982) have urged that neurolinguistics should be computational. An intermediate step between mapping such models on to brain function is to test them by setting up a computer model which can then be 'lesioned', to see if its output follows the predicted pattern. Attempts to do this have been made by Marcus (1982) and Lavorel (1982). Marcus used a computer parser, PARSIFAL, to predict what would happen if a selective difficulty in comprehension of closed-class words (functors) was introduced; the resulting comprehension was similar in some (not all) respects to that associated with Broca's aphasia. Lavorel applied a computer model of the (denotative) lexicon, JARGONAUT, to the study of lexical retrieval for speech in Wernicke's aphasia, specifying 'lesions' such as semantic fuzzing, paraphasia applied to lexical selection and blends applied to parallel selection.

As Lavorel's use of adaptive network theory in many-layered intelligent machines indicates, not all psychological models applied to aphasia postulate a box-and-arrow separation of components. We have already referred to models of interactive processing in the section concerned with behavioural measures of reaction time. Allport (1983) applies a distributed memory (or adaptive network) model to an analysis of naming disorders in aphasia. Allport proposes that we need a model of functionally separable components which also has some meaning at the neural level, and offers the distributed memory model as an example of this. In this, single elements participate in higher level patterns according to a particular set of on/off states. The same elements can therefore simultaneously participate in a vast number of patterns, which are maintained through recurrent activity. Retrieval from this memory system consists, not of fetching from a distinct store, but of selection of a particular pattern for heightened activation. There is thus no difference between 'store' and 'processor'. In such a model behavioural deficits can be consistent with complete anatomical overlap in the underlying representations. Allport argues that the behaviour of anomic speakers supports such a model, particularly in respect of semantic paraphasias. For a simple introduction to how associative network theory has been applied to neural networks, see Ferry (1987).

The modelling of cognitive processing by computers linked in parallel and using interactive networks of neuron-like units has been given the label of 'connectionism' (see Schneider 1987 for a review). The ability of such systems to make inferences, categorise semantic information, and to learn how to associate English text with English phonology has close similarities to human behaviour (Sejnowski and Rosenberg 1987). A connectionist system can also cope with a differentiation between controlled and automatic processing, a distinction which is noticeable in many aspects of behaviour in aphasic individuals, and which may be related to physiological and anatomical differences between cortex and subcortical structures like the thalamus.

Churchland (1986) has sought a similar rapport between neurophysiology and neuropsychology by application of tensor network theory to the control of movement in the cerebellum. As with Allport's proposal, it is the connectivity of arrays of neurons which is important. These arrays can be considered to form mathematical matrices, in which vectors on one co-ordinate system can be transformed into other vectors in another co-ordinate system by means of tensors (generalised mathematical functions). Churchland speculates as to how the brain might make adjustments to the reach of an arm for a seen object on the basis of a neural grid which has become adapted to transforming visual space to the required motor space of the arm. Neuronal activity, in fact, may be able to pattern itself so as to constitute an analogy map of the relevant space. This may even provide an explanation for the laminar, columnar, and mosaic patterns that have been noted in the structure of the cortex. Churchland suggests that tensor network theory may eventually help to explain even more complicated activities than moving an arm e.g. how a phonemic string might be recognised as a word. For further discussion of how neuropsychology and neurophysiology may meet, see Caplan (1987).

From this chapter it will have become clear how rudimentary is present knowledge of the relationship between brain and language. These pages have set out some of the problems, and described how limited our tools are for attempting to answer them. Nevertheless, mathematical modelling of neural network functions, computational representations of language, the refinement of neuropsycholinguistic models, the more accurate analysis of linguistic and psycholinguistic dimensions of language disorders after brain damage of various kinds, the further development of electrophysiological techniques and of imaging of localised metabolic changes, all these hold out promise in nibbling away at this challenging question. In many ways we are at the threshold of new perspectives and in the next decade a chapter on neurolinguistics might have much more to add.

## ACKNOWLEDGEMENT

The author is grateful to Dr Vic McAllister, Consultant Neuroradiologist, Newcastle General Hospital, for comments on an earlier version of a section of this chapter.

## REFERENCES

Albert, M.L., Goodglass, H., Helm, N.A., Rubens, A.B., and Alexander, M.P. (1981) *Clinical Aspects of Dysphasia*, Springer, Vienna.

Albert, M.L. and Obler, L.K. (1978) *The Bilingual Brain: Neuropsychological and Neurolinguistic Aspects of Bilingualism*, Academic Press, London.

Alexander, M.P., Naeser, M.A., and Palumbo, C.L. (1987) 'Correlations of subcortical CT lesion sites and aphasia profiles', *Brain*, 110: 961–991.

Allport, D.A. (1985) 'Distributed memory, modular subsystems and dysphasia', in Newman, S. and Epstein, R., (eds) *Current Perspectives in Dysphasia*, Churchill Livingstone, Edinburgh: 32–60.

Aram, D.M. and Ekelman, B.L. (1987) 'Language and learning sequelae following left or right unilateral brain lesions in children'. Paper presented at International Neuropsychological Society conference, Barcelona.

Arbib, M.A., Caplan, D., and Marshall, J.C. (1982) *Neural Models of Language Processes*, Academic Press, New York.

Barker, A.T., Jalinous, R., and Freeston, I.L. (1985) 'Non-invasive magnetic stimulation of human motor cortex', *Lancet*, 1: 1106-7.

Basso, A., Capitani, E., and Moraschini, S. (1982) 'Sex differences in recovery from aphasia', *Cortex*, 18: 469–75.

Beaumont, J.G., Young, A.W., and McManus, I.C. (1984) 'Hemisphericity: a critical review', *Cognitive Neuropsychology*, 1: 191–212.

Bechtereva, N.P., Bundzen, P.V., Gogolitsin, Y.L., Malyshev, V.N., and Perepelkin, P.D. (1979) 'Neurophysiological codes of words in subcortical structures of the human brain', *Brain and Language*, 7: 145–63.

Bellugi, U., Poizner, H., and Zurif, E. (1982) 'Prospects for the study of aphasia in a visual-gestural language', in Arbib, M.A., Caplan, D., and Marshall J.C. (eds) *Neural Models of Language Processs*, Academic Press, New York: 271–92.

Benson, D.F. (1979) *Aphasia, Alexia, Agraphia*, Churchill Livingstone, Edinburgh.

Ben-Yun, Y. (1986) 'The use of pupillometry in the study of on-line verbal processing: evidence for depths of processing', *Brain and Language*, 28: 1–11.

Bishop, D.V.M. (1988) 'Language development after focal brain damage', in Bishop, D.V.M. and Mogford, K. (eds) *Language Development in Exceptional Circumstances*,

Churchill Livingstone, Edinburgh.

Blumstein, S. and Goodglass, H. (1972) 'The perception of stress as a semantic cue in aphasia', *Journal of Speech and Hearing Research*, 15: 800–6.

Blumstein, S., Milberg, W., and Shrier, R. (1982) 'Semantic processing in aphasia: evidence from an auditory lexical decision task', *Brain and Language*, 17: 301–15.

Blume, W.T., Grabow, J.D., Darley, F.L., and Aronson, A.E. (1973) 'Intracarotid amobarbitol test of language and memory before temporal lobectomy for seizure control', *Neurology*, 23: 812–19.

Bogen, J.E. and Bogen, G.M. (1983). 'Hemispheric Specialization and cerebral duality', *The Behavioural and Brain Sciences*, 3: 517–20.

Borod, J., Goodglass, H., and Kaplan, E. (1980) 'Normative data on the Boston Diagnostic Aphasia Examination, Parietal Lobe Battery and Boston Naming Test', *Journal of Clinical Neuropsychology*, 2: 209–16.

Bowers, D., Coslett, H.B., Bauer, R.M., Speedie, L.J., and Heilman, K.M. (1987) 'Comprehension of emotional prosody following unilateral hemispheric lesions: processing defect versus distraction defect', *Neuropsychologia*, 25: 317–28.

Breitling, D., Guenther, W., and Rondot, P. (1986) 'Motor responses measured by brain electrical activity mapping', *Behavioral Neuroscience*, 100: 104–16.

Brown, J.W. (1985) 'Electrophysiological studies of aphasia: review and prospects', *Language Sciences*, 7: 131–42.

Brown, J.W. and Grober, E. (1983) 'Age, sex and aphasia type: evidence for a regional cerebral growth process underlying lateralization', *Journal of Nervous and Mental Disease*, 171: 431–4.

Brown, J.W., Leader, B.J., and Blum, C.S. (1983) 'Hemiplegic writing in severe aphasia', *Brain and Language*, 19: 204–15.

Brown, J.W. and Jaffe, J. (1975) 'Hypothesis on cerebral dominance', *Neuropsychologia*, 13: 107–10.

Brownell, H.H., Potter, H.H., and Michelow, D. (1984) 'Sensitivity to lexical denotation and connotation in brain-damaged patients: a double dissociation?' *Brain and Language*, 22: 253–65.

Brownell, H.H., Simpson, T.L., Bihrle, A.M., Potter, H.H., and Gardner, H. (1986) 'Appreciation of metaphoric alternative word meanings by right or left brain-damaged patients'. Paper presented at International Neuropsychological Society meeting, Veldhoven.

Bryan, K. (1986) 'Prosodic and other language deficits after right cerebral hemisphere damage'. Ph.D. Thesis, University of Newcastle upon Tyne.

Butterworth, B. and Howard, D. (1987) 'Paragrammatisms', *Cognition*, 26: 1–37.

Bydder, G.M. (1984) 'Nuclear Magnetic Resonance imaging of the brain', *British Medical Bulletin*, 40: 170–4.

Byrne, J.M. and Gates, R.D. (1987) 'Single-case study of left cerebral hemispherectomy: development in the first five years of life', *Journal of Clinical and Experimental Neuropsychology*, 9: 423–34.

Caplan, D. (1981) 'On the cerebral localization of linguistic functions: logical and empirical issues surrounding deficit analysis and functional localization', *Brain and Language*, 14: 120–37.

Caplan, D. (1987) *Neurolinguistics and Linguistic Aphasiology*, Cambridge University Press, Cambridge.

Carpenter, M.B. (1976) 'Anatomical organization of the corpus striatum and related nuclei', in Yahr, M.D. (ed.) *The Basal Ganglia*, Raven Press, New York: 1–35.

Carr, M.S., Jacobson, T., and Boller, F. (1981) 'Crossed aphasia: an analysis of four cases', *Brain and Language*, 14: 190–202.

Castro-Caldas, A. and Botelho, M.A.S. (1980) 'Dichotic listening in the recovery of aphasia after stroke', *Brain and Language* 10: 145–51.

Chernigovskaya, T.V. and Deglin, V.L. (1986) 'Brain functional asymmetry and neural organization of linguistic competence', *Brain and Language*, 29: 141–53.

Churchland, P.S. (1986) *Neurophilosophy: Toward a Unified Science of the Mind-Brain*, Bradford Books, Cambridge, Mass.

Code, C. (1987) *Language, Aphasia and the Right Hemisphere*, Wiley, Chichester.

Coltheart, M. (1980) 'Deep dyslexia: a right hemisphere hypothesis', in Coltheart, M., Patterson, K., and Marshall, J.C. (eds) *Deep Dyslexia*, Routledge & Kegan Paul, London: 326–80.

—— (1987) 'Functional architecture of the language-processing system', in Coltheart, M., Sartori, G., and Job, R. (eds) *The Cognitive Neuropsychology of Language*, Lawrence Erlbaum, London: 1–25.

Cooper, J.A. and Flowers, C.R. (1987) 'Children with a history of acquired aphasia: residual language and academic impairments', *Journal of Speech and Hearing Disorders*, 52: 251–62.

Coslett, H.B. and Saffran, E.M. (in press) 'Evidence for preserved reading in "pure alexia"', *Brain*.

Crosson, B. (1985) Subcortical functions in language: a working model, *Brain and Language*, 25: 257–92.

Crosson, B., Parker, J., Kim, A.K., Warren, R.L., Kepes, J.J., and Tully, R. (1986) 'A case of thalamic aphasia with postmortem verification', *Brain and Language*, 29: 301–14.

Curtiss, S. (1976) *Genie: a psycholinguistic study of a modern-day 'wild child'*, Academic Press, New York.

Damasio, A., Bellugi, U., Damasio, H., Poizner, and Van Gilder, J. (1986) 'Sign language aphasia during left-hemisphere amytal injection', *Nature*, 322: 363–5.

Damasio, A.R., Castro-Caldas, A., Grosso, J.T., and Ferro, J.M. (1976) 'Brain specialization for language does not depend on literacy', *Archives of Neurology*, 23: 300–1.

Deloche, G., Seron, X., Scius, G., and Segui, J. (1987) 'Right hemisphere language processing: lateral difference with imageable and nonimageable ambiguous words', *Brain and Language*, 30: 197–205.

DeWitt, L.D., Grek, A.J., Buonanno, F.S., Levine, D.N., and Kistler, J.P. (1985) 'MRI and the study of aphasia', *Neurology*, 35: 861–5.

Ellis, A.W. (1987) 'Intimations of modularity, or, the modularity of mind: doing cognitive neuropsychology without syndromes', in Coltheart, M., Sartori, G., and Job, R. (eds) *The Cognitive Neuropsychology of Language*, Lawrence Erlbaum, London: 397–408.

Ellis, H.D. and Shepherd, J.W. (1974) 'Recognition of abstract and concrete words presented in left and right visual fields', *Journal of Experimental Psychology*, 103: 1035–6.

Emmorey, M.D. (1987) 'The neurological substrates for prosodic aspects of speech', *Brain and Language*, 30: 305–20.

Ferry, G. (1987) 'Networks on the brain', *New Scientist*, 115 (1569): 54–8.

Feyereisen, P. and Seron, X. (1982a) 'Non-verbal communication and aphasia: a review. I Comprehension', *Brain and Language*, 16: 191–212.

Feyereisen, P. and Seron, X. (1982b) 'Non-verbal communication and aphasia: a review. II Expression', *Brain and Language*, 16: 213–36.

Foldi, N.S. (1987) 'Appreciation of pragmatic interpretations of indirect commands: comparison of right and left hemisphere brain-damaged patients, *Brain and Language*, 31: 88–108.

Gainotti, G., Caltagirone, C., and Miceli, G. (1983) 'Selective impairment of semantic-lexical discrimination in right-brain-damaged patients', in Perecman, E. (ed.) *Cognitive Processing in the Right Hemisphere*, Academic Press, New York: 149–67.

Galaburda, A.M. (1982) 'Histology, architectonics and aysmmetry of language areas', in Arbib, M.A., Caplan, D., and Marshall, J.C. (eds) *Neural Models of Language Processes*, Academic Press, New York: 435–45.

Galaburda, A.M., Sherman, G.F., Rose, G.D., Aboitiz, F., and Geschwind, N. (1985) 'Developmental dyslexia: four consecutive patients with cortical anomalies', *Annals of Neurology*, 18: 222–33.

Galloway, L.M. and Scarcella, R. (1982) 'Cerebral organization in adult second language acquisition: is the right hemisphere more involved? *Brain and Language*, 16: 56–60.

Gardner, H., Brownell, H.H., Wapner, W., and Michelow, D. (1983) 'Missing the point', in Perecman, E. (ed.) *Cognitive Processing in the Right Hemisphere*, Academic Press, New York: 169–91.

Goldenberg, G., Podreka, I., Suess, E., Steiner, M., Deecke, L., and Willmes, K. (1987) 'Regional cerebral blood flow patterns in verbal and visuospatial imagery tasks: results of single photon emission computer tomography (SPECT)', *Journal of Clinical and Experimental Neuropsychology*, 9: 284 (abstract).

Goodglass, H. and Kaplan, E. (1972, 1983) *The Assessment of Aphasia and Related Disorders*, Lea and Febiger, Philadelphia.

Green, D. and Newman, S. (1985) 'Bilingualism and dysphasia: process and resource', in Newman, S. and Epstein, R. (eds) *Current Perspectives in Dysphasia*, Churchill Livingstone, Edinburgh: 155–81.

Grossman, M. and Haberman, S. (1987) 'The detection of errors in sentences after right brain damage', *Neuropsychologia*, 25: 163–72.

Gur, R.C., Gur, R.E., Silver, F.L., Obrist, W.D., Skolnick, B.E., Kushner, M., Hurtig, H.I., and Rewich, M. (1987) 'Regional cerebral blood flow in stroke: hemisphere effects of cognitive activity', *Stroke*, 18: 776–80.

Hanks, P. (ed.) (1986) *Collins Dictionary of the English Language* (2nd edition), Collins, London.

Hardyk, C. (1977) 'A model of individual differences in hemispheric functioning', in Whitaker, H. and Whitaker, H.A. (eds) *Studies in Neurolinguistics, Vol. 3.* Academic Press, New York: 223–55.

Hécaen, H. (1983) 'Acquired aphasia in children revisited', *Neuropsychologia*, 21: 581–7.

Helm-Estabrooks, N. (1983) 'Exploiting the right hemisphere for language rehabilitation: Melodic Intonation Therapy', in Perecman, E. (ed.) *Cognitive Processing in the Right Hemisphere.* Academic Press, New York: 229–40.

Heiss, W.-D., Herholz, K., Pawlik, G., Wagner, R., and Wienhard, K. (1986) 'Positron

Emission Tomography in neuropsychology', *Neuropsychologia*, 24: 141–9.

Herning, R.I., Jones, R.T., and Hunt, J.S. (1987) 'Speech event related potentials reflect linguistic content and processing level', *Brain and Language*, 30: 116–29.

Holland, G.N., Hawkes, R.C., and Moore, W.S. (1980) 'Nuclear Magnetic Resonance (NMR) tomography of the brain: coronal and sagittal sections', *Journal of Computer Assisted Tomography*, 4: 429–33.

Howard, D. and Hatfield, F.M. (1987) *Aphasia Therapy: Historical and Contemporary Issues*, Lawrence Erlbaum, London.

Huber, W., Luer, G., and Lass, U. (1983) 'Processing of sentences in conditions of aphasia as assessed by recording eye movements', in Groner, R., Menz, C., Fisher, D.F., and Monty, R.A. (eds) *Eye Movements and Psychological Functions*, Lawrence Erlbaum, Hillsdale, NJ: 315–44.

Jones, G.V. and Martin, M. (1985) Deep dyslexia and the right hemisphere hypothesis for semantic paralexia: a reply to Marshall and Patterson', *Neuropsychologia*, 23: 685–8.

Kimura, D. and Archibald, Y. (1974) 'Motor functions of the left hemisphere', *Brain*, 97: 337–50.

Kinsbourne, M. (1971) 'The minor cerebral hemisphere as a source of aphasic speech', *Archives of Neurology*. 25: 302–6.

Kinsbourne, M. and Cook, J. (1971) 'Generalized and lateralized effects of concurrent verbalization on a unimanual task', *Quarterly Journal of Experimental Psychology* 23: 341–5.

Lamendella, J.T. (1977) 'The limbic system in human communication', in Whitaker, H. and Whitaker, H.A. (eds) *Studies in Neurolinguistics, Vol. 3*, Academic Press, New York: 157–222.

Landis, T., Regard, M., Graves, R., and Goodglass, H. (1983) 'Semantic paralexia: a release of right hemisphere function from left hemisphere inhibition', *Neuropsychologia*, 21: 359–64.

Lassen, N.A., Ingvar, D.H., and Skinhoj, E. (1978) 'Brain function and blood flow', *Scientific American*, October: 50–9.

Lavorel, P.M. (1982) 'Production strategies: a systems approach to Wernicke's aphasia', in Arbib, M.A., Caplan, D., and Marshall, J.C. (eds) *Neural Models of Language Processes*. Academic Press, New York, 135–64.

Lebrun, Y. (1985) 'Sign aphasia', *Language Sciences*, 7: 143–54.

Lecours, A.R., Mehler, J., Parente, M.A., Caldeira, A. *et al.* (1987). 'Illiteracy and brain damage: 1: Aphasia testing in culturally contrasted populations (control subjects)', *Neuropsychologia*, 25: 231–46.

Lecours, A.R. (in press) 'Illiteracy and brain damage: 3: A contribution to the study of speech and language disorders in illiterates with unilateral brain damage', *Neuropsychologia*.

Lees, A. and Smith, E. (1983) 'Cognitive defects in the early stages of Parkinson's Disease', *Brain*, 106: 257–70.

Lenneberg, E. (1967) *The Biological Foundations of Language*, Wiley, New York.

Lesser, R. (1974) 'Verbal comprehension in aphasia: an English version of three Italian tests', *Cortex*, 10: 247–63.

Lesser, R.P., Lueders, H., Hahn, J., Dinner, D.S., Hanson, M., Rothner, A.D., and Erenberg, G. (1982) 'Location of the speech area in candidates for temporal lobectomy: results of extraoperative studies', *Neurology*, 32: A91.

Levene, M.I., Williams, J.L., and Fawer, C.-L. (1985) *Ultrasound of the Infant Brain*, Blackwell, Oxford.

Lhermitte, F. (1984) 'Language disorders and their relationship to thalamic lesions', in Rose, F.C. (ed.) *Advances in Neurology. Vol. 42. Progress in Aphasiology*, Raven Press, New York: 99–113.

Lonie, J. and Lesser, R. (1983) 'Intonation as a cue to speech act identification in aphasic and other brain-damaged patients', *International Journal of Rehabilitation Research*, 6: 512–13.

Lovett, M.W., Dennis, M. and Newman, J.E. (1986) 'Making reference: the cohesive use of pronouns in the narrative discourse of hemidecorticate adolescents', *Brain and Language*, 29: 224–51.

Lund, E., Spliid, P.E., Andersen, E., and Bojsen-Moller, M. (1986) 'A neuroradiological localization of the perception of vowels in the human cortex', *Brain and Language*, 29: 191–211.

Luria, A.R. (1970) *Traumatic Aphasia*, Mouton, The Hague.

Luria, A.R. (1976) *Basic Problems of Neurolinguistics*, Mouton, The Hague.

McDonald, S. and Wales, R. (1986) 'An investigation of the ability to process inferences in language following right hemisphere damage', *Brain and Language*, 29: 68–80.

McGlone, J. (1978) 'Sex differences in functional brain asymmetry', *Cortex*, 14: 122–8.

McGlone, J. (1983) 'Sex differences in human brain organization: a critical survey', *The Behavioural and Brain Sciences*, 3: 215–27.

Marcus, M.P. (1982) 'Consequences of functional deficits in a parsing model: implications for Broca's aphasia', in Arbib, M.A., Caplan, D. and Marshall, J.C. (eds) *Neural Models of Language Processes*, Academic Press, New York: 115–33.

Marshall, J.C. (1986) 'The description and interpretation of aphasic language disorder', *Neuropsychologia*, 24: 5–24.

Marshall, J.C. and Patterson, K.E. (1985) 'Left is still left for semantic paralexias: a reply to Jones and Martin (1985)', *Neuropsychologia*, 23: 689–90.

Mateer, C.A. and Ojemann, G.A. (1983) 'Thalamic mechanisms in language and memory', in Segalowitz, S. (ed.) *Language Functions and Brain Organization*, Academic Press, New York: 171–91.

Mateer, C.A., Rapport, R.L., and Kettrick, C. (1984) 'Cerebral organization of oral and signed language responses: case study evidence from amytal and cortical stimulation studies', *Brain and Language*, 21: 123–35.

Metter, E.J. (1987) 'Neuroanatomy and physiology of aphasia: evidence from positron emission tomography', *Aphasiology*, 1: 3–33.

Meyer, J.S., Sakai, F., Yamaguchi, F., Yamamoto, M., and Shaw, T. (1980) 'Regional changes in cerebral blood flow during standard behavioral activation in patients with disorders of speech and mentation compared to normal volunteers', *Brain and Language*, 9: 61–77.

Millar, J. and Whitaker, H.A. (1983) 'The right hemisphere's contribution to language: a review of the evidence from brain-damaged subjects', in Segalowitz, S. (ed.) *Language Functions and Brain Organization*, Academic Press, New York: 87–113.

Mitchell, G.A.G. and Mayor, D. (1983) *The Essentials of Neuroanatomy* (4th edn), Longman, (Churchill Livingstone), London, New York.

Mohr, J.P. (1976) 'Broca's area and Broca's aphasia', in Whitaker, H. and Whitaker, H.A. (eds) *Studies in Neurolinguistics. Vol. 1*, Academic Press, New York: 201–35.

—— (1983) 'Thalamic lesions and syndromes', in Kertesz, A. (ed.) *Localization in Neuropsychology*, Academic Press, New York: 269–93.

Molfese, D.L. (1983) 'Event related potentials and language processes', in Gaillard, A.W. and Ritter, W. (eds) *Tutorials in ERP Research: Endogenous Components*, North-Holland, Amsterdam: 345–68.

Murdoch, B.E. (in press) 'Subcortical aphasia syndromes: a review', *British Journal of Disorders of Communication.*

Naeser, M.A., Alexander, M.P., Helm-Estabrooks, N., Levine, H.L., Laughlin, S.A., and Geschwind, N. (1982) 'Aphasia with predominantly subcortical lesion sites: description of three capsular/putaminal aphasia syndromes', *Archives of Neurology*, 39: 2–14.

Naeser, M.A., Hayward, R.W., Laughlin, S., and Zatz, L.M. (1981) 'Quantitative CT scan studies in aphasia. I: Infarct size and CT numbers', *Brain and Language*, 12: 140–64.

Neville, H.J. (1980) 'Event-related potentials in neuropsychological studies of language', *Brain and Language*, 11: 300–18.

Niccum, N. (1986) 'Longitudinal dichotic listening patterns for aphasic patients. 1: Description of recovery curves', *Brain and Language*, 28: 273–88.

Niccum, N., Selnes, O.A., Speaks, C., Risse, G.L., and Rubens, A.B. (1986) 'Longitudinal dichotic listening patterns for aphasic patients. 3: Relationship to language and memory variables', *Brain and Language*, 28: 303–17.

Obler, L. and Albert, M. (1981) Language in the elderly aphasic and in the dementing patient', in Sarno, M.T. (ed.) *Acquired Aphasia*, Academic Press, New York: 385–98.

Ojemann, G.A. (1982) 'Subcortical aphasias', in Kirshner, H.S. and Freeman, F.R. (eds) *The Neurology of Aphasia*, Swets and Zeitlinger, Lisse: 127–37.

Ojemann, G.A. (1983) 'Brain organization for language from the perspective of electrical stimulation mapping', *The Behavioral and Brain Sciences*, 2: 189–230.

Oxbury, S.M. and Oxbury, J.M. (1984) 'Intracarotid amytal test in the assessment of language', in Rose, F.C. (ed.) *Advances in Neurology, Vol. 42: Progress in Aphasiology*, Raven Press, New York: 115–23.

Packard, J.L. (1986) 'Tone production deficits in nonfluent aphasic Chinese speech, *Brain and Language*, 29: 212–23.

Papanicolaou, A.C., Wilson, G.F., Busch, C., De Rego, P., Orr, C., Davis, I., and Eisenber, H.M. (1987) 'Hemispheric asymmetries in phonetic processing assessed with probe evoked magnetic fields', Paper presented at International Neuropsychological Society Conference, Barcelona.

Paradis, M. (1985) 'On the representation of two languages in one brain', *Language Sciences*, 7: 1–39.

Paradis, M. (1987) *The Assessment of Bilingual Aphasia*, Lawrence Erlbaum, Hillsdale, NJ.

Paradis, M., Goldblum, M.-C., and Abidi, R. (1982) 'Alternate antagonism with paradoxical translation behavior in two bilingual aphasic patients, *Brain and Language*, 15: 55–69.

Paradis, M., Hagiwara, H., and Hildebrandt, N. (1985) *Neurolinguistic Aspects of the Japanese Writing System*, Academic Press, New York.

Paradis, M. and Lecours, A.R. (1983) 'Aphasia in bilinguals and polyglots', in Lecours,

A.R., Lhermitte, F., and Bryans, B. (eds) *Aphasiology*, Baillière Tindall, London: 455–64.

Patterson, K. and Besner, D. (1984) 'Is the right hemisphere literate?' *Cognitive Neuropsychology*, 1: 315–41.

Penfield, W. and Roberts, L. (1959) *Speech and Brain Mechanisms*, Princeton University Press, Princeton.

Perecman, E. (ed.) (1983) *Cognitive Processing in the Right Hemisphere*, Academic Press, New York.

Petersen, S.E., Fox, P.T., Posner, M.I., Mintun, M., and Raichle, M.E. (1988) 'Positron emission tomographic studies of the cortical anatomy of single-word processing', *Nature*, 331: 585–8.

— (in press) 'Positron emission tomographic studies of the processing of single words', *Journal of Cognitive Neuroscience*.

Pettit, J.M. and Noll, J.D. (1979) 'Cerebral dominance in aphasia recovery', *Brain and Language*, 7: 191–200.

Peuser, G. and Fittschan, M. (1977) 'On the universality of language dissolution: the case of a Turkish aphasic', *Brain and Language*, 4: 196–207.

Pinsky, S.D. and McAdam, D.W. (1980) 'Electroencephalographic and dichotic indices of cerebral laterality in stutterers', *Brain and Language*, 11: 374–97.

Pizzamiglio, L., Mammucari, A., and Razzano, C. (1985) 'Evidence for sex differences in brain organization in recovery from aphasia', *Brain and Language*, 25: 213–23.

Posner, M.I., Petersen, S.E., Fox, P.T., and Raichle, M.E. (1988) 'Localization of cognitive operations in the human brain', *Science*, 240: 1627–31.

Rapcsak, S.Z., Rothi, L.J.G. and Heilman, K.M. (1987) 'Phonological alexia with optic and tactile anomia: a neuropsychological and anatomical study', *Brain and Language*, 31: 109–21.

Rapport, R.L., Tan, C.T., and Whitaker, H.A. (1983) 'Language function and dysfunction among Chinese- and English-speaking polyglots: cortical stimulation, Wada testing and clinical studies', *Brain and Language*, 18: 342–66.

Risberg, J. (1980) 'Regional cerebral blood flow measurements by 133 xenon inhalation: methodology and applications in neuropsychology and psychiatry', *Brain and Language*, 9: 9–34.

— (1986) 'Regional cerebral blood flow in neuropsychology', *Neuropsychologia*, 24: 135–40.

Rothrock, J.F., Lyden, P.D., Hesselink, J.R., Brown, J.J., and Healy, M.E. (1987) 'Brain magnetic resonance imaging in the evaluation of lacunar stroke', *Stroke*, 18: 781–6.

Ross, E.D. (1981) 'The aprosodias: functional-anatomic organization of the affective components of language in the right hemisphere', *Archives of Neurology (Chicago)*, 38: 561–9.

Ross, P. (1983) 'Cerebral specialization in deaf individuals', in Segalowitz , S. (ed.) 287–313.

Saffran, E.M., Bogyo, L.C., Schwartz, M.F. and Marin, O.S.M. (1980) 'Does deep dyslexia reflect right-hemisphere reading?', in Coltheart, M., Patterson, K., and Marshall J.C. (eds) *Deep Dyslexia*, Routledge & Kegan Paul, London: 381–406.

Samar, V.J. and Berent, G.P. (1986) 'The syntactic priming effect: evoked response evidence for a prelexical locus', *Brain and Language*, 28: 250–72.

Sarno, M.T., Buonaguro, A., and Levita, E. (1985) 'Gender and recovery from aphasia after stroke', *Journal of Nervous and Mental Disease*, 173: 605–9.

Sasanuma, S. (1986) 'Universal and language-specific symptomatology and treatment of aphasia', *Folio Phoniatrica*, 38: 121–75.

Sawyer, D.J. (1987) 'The brain in language and reading: research application and interpretation', *Folia Phoniatrica*, 39: 38–50.

Schneider, W. (1987) 'Connectionism: is it a paradigm shift for psychology?', *Behavior Research Methods, Instruments and Computers*, 19: 73–83.

Segalowitz, S. (ed.) (1983) *Language Functions and Brain Organization*, Academic Press, New York.

Segalowitz, S.J. and Bryden, M.P. (1983) 'Individual differences in hemispheric representation of language', in Segalowitz, S. (ed.) *Language Functions and Brain Organization*, Academic Press, New York: 341–72.

Seitz, M.R., Weber, B.A., Jacobson, J.T., and Morehouse, R. (1980) 'The use of averaged electroencephalic response techniques in the study of auditory processing related to speech and language', *Brain and Language* 11: 261–84.

Sejnowski, T.J. and Rosenberg, C.R. (1987) 'Learning and representation in connectionist models.' *Report No. 31 of the Cognitive Neuropsychology Laboratory*, Johns Hopkins University, Baltimore.

Seron, X. (1981) 'Children's acquired aphasia: is the initial equipotentiality theory still tenable?', in Lebrun, Y. and Zangwill, O. (eds) *Lateralisation of Language in the Child*, Swets and Zeitlinger, Lisse: 82–90.

Shallice, T. and Saffran, E.M. (1986) 'Lexical processing in the absence of explicit word identification: evidence from a letter-by-letter reader', *Cognitive Neuropsychology*, 3: 429–58.

Smith, A. (1966) 'Speech and other functions after left (dominant) hemispherectomy', *Journal of Neurology, Neurosurgery and Psychiatry*, 29: 467–71.

Soares, C. (1984) 'Left hemisphere language lateralization in bilinguals', *Brain and Language*, 23: 86–96.

Tanridag, O. and Kirshner, H.S. (1987) 'Language disorders in stroke syndromes of the dominant capsulostriatum – a clinical review', *Aphasiology*, 1: 107–17.

Thatcher, R.W. (1980) 'Neurolinguistics: theoretical and evolutionary perspectives', *Brain and Language*, 11: 235–60.

Tikovsky, R.S., Kooi, K.A., and Thames, M.H. (1960) 'Electroencephalographic findings and recovery from aphasia', *Neurology*, 10: 154–6.

Tikovsky, R.S., Collier, B.D., Hellman, R.S., Saxena, V.K., Krohn, L., and Gresch, A. (1986) 'Reduction of chronic aphasia and regional cerebral perfusion imaging by single photon emission computed tomography (SPECT)'. Paper presented at International Neuropsychological Society Conference, Veldhoven.

Tyler, L.K. (1987) 'Spoken language comprehension in aphasia: a real-time processing perspective', in Coltheart, M., Sartori, G., and Job, R. (eds): 145–62.

Vaid, J. (1983) 'Bilingualism and brain lateralization', in Segalowitz, S. (ed.): 315–39.

Van Hout, A., Evrard, P., and Lyon, G. (1985) 'On the positive semiology of acquired aphasia in children', *Developmental Medicine and Child Neurology*, 27: 231–41.

Vargha-Khadem, F., O'Gorman, A.M., and Watters, G.V. (1985) 'Aphasia and handedness in relation to hemispheric side, age at injury and severity of cerebral lesion during childhood', *Brain*, 108: 677–96.

Wallesch, C.-W. (1985) 'Two syndromes of aphasia occurring with ischemic lesions involving the left basal ganglia', *Brain and Language*, 25: 357–61.

Wallesch, C.-W. and Wyke, M. (1985) 'Language and the subcortical nuclei', in Newman, S., and Epstein, R. (eds) *Current Perspectives in Dysphasia*, Churchill Livingstone, Edinburgh: 182–97.

Wapner, W., Hamby, S., and Gardner, H. (1981) 'The role of the right hemisphere in the apprehension of complex linguistic materials', *Brain and Language*, 14: 15–33.

Warrington, E.K. and Pratt, R.T.C. (1973) 'Language laterality in left-handers assessed by unilateral ECT', *Neuropsychologia*, 11: 423–8.

Weinrich, M., Ricaurte, G., Kowall, J., Weinstein, S.L., and Lane, B. (1987) 'Subcortical aphasia revisited', *Aphasiology*, 1: 119–26.

Whitaker, H. and Whitaker, H.A. (eds) (1976, 1977) *Studies in Neurolinguistics*, Academic Press, New York.

Whitaker, H.A. and Selnes, O.A. (1975) 'Anatomic variations in the cortex: individual differences and the problem of the localization of language functions'. Paper presented to the Conference on Origins and Evolution of Language and Speech.

Wood, F., Taylor, B., Penny, R., and Stump, D. (1980) 'Regional cerebral blood flow response to recognition memory versus semantic classification tasks', *Brain and Language*, 9: 113–21.

Woods, B.T. (1983) 'Is the left hemisphere specialized for language at birth?' *Trends in Neurosciences*, 6: 115–17.

Woods, B.T. and Carey, S. (1979) 'Language deficits after apparent clinical recovery from childhood aphasia', *Annals of Neurology*, 6: 405–9.

Young, A.W. and Ellis, A.W. (1985) 'Different methods of lexical access for words presented in the left and right visual hemifields', *Brain and Language*, 24: 326–58.

Young, L.R. and Sheena, D. (1975) 'Survey of eye movement recording methods', *Behavioral Research Methods and Instrumentation*, 7: 397–429.

Zaidel, E. (1975) 'A technique for presenting lateralized visual input with prolonged exposure', *Vision Research*, 15: 282–9.

—— (1976) 'Auditory vocabulary of the right hemisphere following brain bisection and hemidecortication', *Cortex*, 12: 191–211.

Zurif, E.B.(1980) 'Language mechanisms: a neuropsychological perspective', *American Scientist*, 68: 305–11.

# 12

## THE BREAKDOWN OF LANGUAGE: LANGUAGE PATHOLOGY AND THERAPY

### PAUL FLETCHER

### 1. INTRODUCTION

Most children learn language successfully and most adults find no difficulty in maintaining the language they have learned. But any speech community (at least in the developed world, which is as far as our knowledge extends) will contain a small proportion of children for whom language learning is considered to present particular problems. And it seems reasonable to suppose that adults in any speech community are prone to the cerebrovascular accidents, or stroke, which we know result in the disruption of language. Because language is so intimately concerned with other areas of intellectual functioning in both development and breakdown, and because many of the identifiable causes of language impairment are medical, language pathology cannot be the sole province of the linguist or phonetician. Nevertheless, recent years have seen a steady infiltration of linguists and phoneticians into the field of speech and language disorders. Of course an interest by linguists into this area is not new: Jakobson's hypothesis concerning phonological breakdown in aphasia is over forty years old (Jakobson 1968 (1941)). But in the last decade we have seen much more than the occasional foray. There is, particularly in the English-speaking world, a quite widespread application of phonetics (including instrumental techniques) and phonology, of descriptive grammatical frameworks, of grammatical theory, and of concepts from semantics and pragmatics, to a variety of disorders and their remediation, and an extensive literature is developing. The term 'clinical linguistics' is often now used to refer to this new field (see Crystal 1981), suggesting an emerging identity. In this chapter we will illustrate how the main areas of linguistics are applied across a varied range of impairments. Before considering the application of linguistics to language disorders in any detail, however, we need to examine the contexts in which this application is made, so as to assess how the contribution from linguistics fits into the overall framework of language disorder.

## 2. LANGUAGE DISORDER: BACKGROUND

We will use the term *language disorder* to refer to any persistent non-normal language behaviour in children or adults. For convenience, the label is taken to include those disorders which are primarily problems of speech, as well as those that concern the language faculty more generally. We will concentrate here on disorders to do with spoken language; it should be remembered, though, that some affected individuals may have reading and/or writing disorders in addition to whatever spoken language problems they show (Snowling 1987). We will also restrict our focus to those cases where the linguistic problem is primary, and not a concomitant of a more general intellectual deficit such as mental handicap (Rondal 1987), or of some abnormal psychological condition such as schizophrenia or autism. Chapter 11, above, discusses the neurological aspects of these various conditions.

### 2.1 Adult aphasia

The area of language disorder which has the longest history of systematic study in modern times is adult *aphasia*. The present-day field of research into this problem, known as *aphasiology*, brings together the medical tradition, and more recent linguistic investigations, in an inquiry into the relationship between brain injury and language behaviour.

One of the most common causes of brain damage is cerebral vascular accident (CVA) or 'stroke', as it is usually known. There are several types of CVA (see Garman 1989), but all involve interruptions to the blood supply to an area of the brain, and consequential effects on the tissue surrounding the site of the CVA. If the area damaged is in that part of the left hemisphere of the brain which controls language functions, then the affected individual will, depending upon the location and extent of the CVA, experience difficulties in understanding, or expression, or both. A good deal of aphasiological research has been devoted to determining correlations between focal brain injury and the nature of the concomitant disturbances in linguistic behaviour, even though the 'localisationist' hypothesis, as this line of research is referred to, is not uncontroversial (Garman 1989). It will be helpful to examine this correlation in some more detail, not in order to address the complexities of brain-behaviour relationship (for which see Chapter 11), but to illustrate one important type of language disorder, in which there is an identifiable cause and more or less specific linguistic consequences. As we shall see, in many instances of linguistic disorder, particularly in children, cause-effect linkages are not so readily available.

### 2.1.1 Broca's aphasia

An illustration of the source of a particular adult aphasic syndrome appears in Figure 16.

*Figure 16* Lesion site for Broca's aphasia

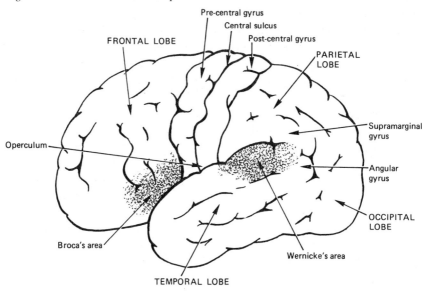

The figure is a schematic representation of the surface (the cerebral cortex) of the left hemisphere of the brain, with a number of salient features marked. The forward shaded area indicates a focus of damage often associated with what is known as *Broca's aphasia,* after the French neurologist Paul Broca, who first described it in 1861. The site of the lesion with which this type of aphasia is associated tends to be in the anterior portion of the left hemisphere, just in front of or involving the primary motor strip for muscles involved in speech (Cooper and Zurif 1983). The major clinical symptoms of this syndrome so far as oral language is concerned centre round the effortful and non-fluent utterances that are produced, and their syntactic form. Output rate is low, and utterances tend to be short. The utterances also show what is referred to as an *agrammatic* character. This term refers to the tendency of sufferers from this type of aphasia to omit grammatical morphemes in their spontaneous speech. A grammatical morpheme is either a member of a grammatical category with a limited number of items, such as determiner, preposition, or auxiliary, or an inflection such as third person present tense, past tense, or progressive, in English. It is not the case that all grammatical morphemes are always omitted: there are reliable differences in the rates of omission of different types of function words (e.g. determiners are more readily omissible than connectives) and of different inflectional markers (e.g. in English -*ing* is retained much more frequently than past tense). (See Caramazza and Berndt 1978, Garman 1989, Cooper and Zurif 1983, Goodglass and Menn 1985, for more detailed information on the nature of agrammatism.) However the frequent omissions of function words and inflections, in relatively short utterances, with often quite effortful articulation, give the speech of these aphasics the telegrammatic character on which its label is based.

It would appear from this outline of agrammatism that in one kind of aphasia, at least, a rather basic linguistic description of the utterances of a patient's spontaneous speech can be helpful in delineating symptoms of a particular type of brain damage. Is such an approach possible for other types of aphasia?

### 2.1.2 Other types of aphasia

In a study of the incidence of aphasic syndromes, Kertesz (1979, reported in Garman 1989) found that in a sample of 365 patients, Broca's aphasics comprised 17 per cent of the total – the second most common type. Over three-quarters of the sample fell into either this category, or one of three others: anomic (29 per cent of the total), global (16 per cent), or Wernicke's (15 per cent). Each of these syndromes can be associated with different lesion sites. To characterise the linguistic behaviour associated with them, however, we may need to go beyond the grammatical form of spontaneous speech utterances. Anomic aphasia, for example, is the term applied when the major symptom is a general word-finding difficulty. Sometimes the word that the speaker is searching for as he is producing an utterance is substituted by a word that seems inappropriate but is somehow linked in meaning to the assumed target word, e.g. *chair* for 'table', *knee* for 'elbow', or *hair* for 'comb' (Gardner 1974, quoted in Aitchison 1987: 21). In this type of aphasia, then, the focus of interest will be the nature of these difficulties of lexical access. The inquiry will be considerably assisted by an appropriate model of how the lexicon is represented and accessed in the course of speech recognition and production. The investigation of anomic aphasia will thus go beyond formal linguistic frameworks. Explicit attention to the processes which are assumed to be involved in language use may be termed the psycholinguistic approach to language disorders. Such processes (or 'computations') happen in real

time, and as Caramazza and Berndt put it (1985: 28): 'although these computations will bear some relationship to the formal, linguistic description of a
language (the grammar), they are not isomorphic with such descriptions'.
Linguistic frameworks are still essential to the characterisation of aphasic
language impairments. In the view of a number of investigators, however, a
psycholinguistic approach which incorporates linguistic descriptions but
takes proper account of the language-processing abilities in normals and their
impairment in brain-injured adults, is essential.

Wernicke's aphasia, which occurs with similar frequency to Broca's in the
Kertesz sample, is characterised by fluent (sometimes over-fluent) spontaneous speech, with generally good grammatical structure (at least for simple
declarative utterances – Gleason *et al.* 1980). There may however be inappropriate stem/affix formations such as *is louding* for *is loud/is talking loudly*
(Garman 1989: Chap. 10). There are lexical problems also. Utterances are
lacking in specific content words, and there are errors in word usage. Some of
these are of the semantic type exemplified above for anomics; others result
from sound substitutions, such as *plick* for 'clip'; yet others are neologisms,
such as *lungfab* for 'window' (Benson 1979, quoted in Aitchison 1987: 22; see
also Edwards 1987: 272). Perhaps the most crucial feature of Wernicke's
aphasia, though, is a severe loss in auditory comprehension:

> Several studies are in agreement in concluding that, although Wenicke's [aphasics] can
> use order information in the service of assigning meaning to sentences, they do not
> have the normal capacity to compute algorithmically full structural descriptions –
> either for complex sentences featuring discontinuous constituents . . . or for simpler
> sentences in which relations are signalled morphologically. (Cooper and Zurif 1983:
> 235)

Comprehension, unlike production, cannot be reliably investigated by observation in naturalistic contexts. The studies referred to used sentence-picture
matching tasks, in which the patient has to select from a pair or set of pictures
the matching item for a stimulus sentence. A classic grammatical contrast
(used also in comprehension tests for children) is active-passive.

The study of auditory comprehension abilities in this way is necessarily
time-consuming and somewhat limited. Certain areas of the grammar are
difficult if not impossible to represent pictorially – temporal contrasts, for
example, or modality, or even the declarative-interrogative contrast. It is also
not clear how performance on grammatically-based picture-matching tasks
relates to the normal processes of impaired individuals. Nevertheless the
study of auditory comprehension is clearly of at least equal relevance to that
of production in Wernicke's aphasia, and by extension in other syndromes as
well. We will wish to determine, for example, whether the problems with
grammatical morphemes, which are apparent in production for Broca's
aphasics, are paralleled in comprehension (Cooper and Zurif 1983: 228ff.).

This brief consideration of some well-known syndromes underlines some important points about the role of linguistics in aphasiological research. The study of language disorders needs to be concerned with both expressive and receptive language. Linguistic descriptions and theories use as data the language output of normal individuals. The study of language disorder requires, in addition to the analysis of output patterns, the use of techniques for investigating how impaired individuals comprehend language input. And as speaking and understanding are real-time processes which involve the interaction of the linguistic system with attentional and memory mechanisms, the interpretation of linguistic descriptions of aphasic language should be set in a framework that takes this into account.

## 2.2 Child language disorders

While the localisationist hypothesis for aphasic impairments may still continue to be a matter of controversy in aphasiology, disagreement centres on the relative ease with which different syndromes can be localised, or on techniques for identifying and delimiting the site of the lesion. (Garman 1989: Chap. 10). That the brain insult is the cause of the observable cluster of symptoms of language disruption is not at issue. The role of aetiological factors in children's language disorders is much less clear. There are of course some obvious cause-effect relationships. A severe hearing-loss is likely to have marked effects on the pronunciation of an individual and later on his written language abilities (Crystal 1980: 137). A cleft palate, a congenital malformation which can involve the hard and soft palates, and the upper lip, will have obvious effects on speech if it is not repaired (see below). A very small percentage of young children have strokes or other brain injuries with consequent effects on the language they have acquired up to the point of the injury (Miller *et al.* 1984). There is however a large proportion of children who present as language-impaired to speech therapists, but who do not have a hearing loss, any identifiable neurological disorder, or any intellectual deficit. The (rather unwieldly) term used to refer to the class of problems manifested by these children is *Specific speech and language disorder in children*, henceforth abbreviated to SSLDC.

### 2.2.1 SSLDC: aetiology

The absence of any clear aetiology, and the lack of delineation of predictable clusters of linguistic symptoms, make this a very imprecise term. A good deal of effort has been applied in the last decade to make good the shortfall in linguistic characterisations of language-impaired children in this category, which we will deal with in more detail in the later part of this chapter.

Research into the causes of SSLDC has been more limited, but there are available both large-sample studies of correlations between possible aetiological factors and clinical features (e.g. Rapin and Allen 1987, Sonksen 1979, Shriberg *et al.* 1986, Robinson 1987), and smaller-scale experimental tests of specific neuropsychological or cognitive hypotheses (Tallal *et al.* 1985a, Johnston and Weismer 1983).

### 2.2.2 *Correlational studies*

There is at present no clear indication of a neurological basis for any of the sub-syndromes of SSLDC (Rapin and Allen 1987: 21). By contrast with adult aphasia, the aetiological picture is diffuse. There are a number of well-known facts established about language-disordered children, and a range of independent variables that can be associated to a greater or lesser degree with the clinical symptoms. Robinson (1987), in a study of 82 language-disordered children, examined a range of correlations between aetiological factors and clinical features. Table 12 summarises his conclusions from his own work and others he reviewed.

*Table 12* Possible aetiological factors in SSLDC
(adapted from Robinson 1987: 13)

---

1. There is a high proportion of boys, and there is an important genetic or familial component, which appears to be stronger in boys.
2. About a quarter of the affected children have a plausible medical 'cause', but these causes are very varied, and they are rarely sufficient in themselves to account for the SSLD, since none of these 'causes' invariably leads to such a disorder.
3. A number of other associated anomalies are found more commonly in these children than in the general population. These include: seizures, left handedness, late walking, and clumsiness. However, none of these factors except clumsiness is found in more than 30 per cent of children with SSLD.

---

1. In his own study and in ten others reviewed, Robinson found a much higher proportion of boys than girls. The sex ratio is, overall, in these studies 2.82 to 1. (See also Shriberg *et al.* 1986: 143).
2. Medical causes include definite factors – those that have a recognised link with language disorders such as a major neurological illness, as well as other problems less certainly associated with subsequent language problems, such as low birth weight. None of the 'causes' represented in the Robinson study, however, leads inevitably to a language disorder.
3. The 'associated anomalies', while more frequent in the SSLD children than in the general populatoin, are found in a minority of them, except for

clumsiness: 90 per cent of the children in Robinson's studies had 'significant motor impairment'.

Robinson's (entirely reasonable) conclusion from the correlations found is that SSLDC children are a heterogeneous group, and that 'in most of them causation must be multifactorial' (1987: 13; see also Rutter 1987: 52).

### 2.2.3 Experimental studies

The most extensive experimental work is that of Tallal and her associates (see Tallal 1987). This has been devoted to experimental studies of the possible neuropsychological basis of language disorders, in deficits in the speed of processing of temporally-ordered information. Initially deficits in SSLD children were identified in auditorily processed material. Tallal and Piercy (1973) found that, in order to discriminate successive non-verbal tones as same of different successfully SSLD children required a 300 msec pause between the tones, whereas normals only required 75 msec. Later studies have identified a relationship between such temporal-processing deficits and the pattern of speech perception and production deficits, and the degree of receptive language impairment in language-impaired children (Tallal 1987).

The other prominent area in which deficits have been documented is in cognition, specifically with reference to symbolic function or representational thought. As Miller (1987) notes in discussing this, for neither the auditory processing nor cognitive deficits have central nervous system deficits been identified which would help to explain the deficits or at least provide a neural basis for them, though this may simply be a result of limitations on investigative methods currently available.

It is reasonable to conclude, with respect to aetiological factors in SSLD, that no clear picture emerges at present. It is also true that in terms of clinical symptoms also, there is as yet no agreed syndrome delineation. As with adult disorders, research into child disorders has to consider receptive as well as expressive language (see Bishop 1987), and speaking and understanding as real-time processes (Chiat and Hirson 1987, Fletcher 1987). To date, however, most progress has been made in the detailed description of linguistic output which, carefully analysed, can lead us towards the delineation of symptom-complexes. It may then be possible, (particularly in phonological disorders – see below) to link clinical symptoms to potential causes.

With this brief account of some of the background to language disorders, we can now turn to examples of the linguistic contribution to language pathology, using the major headings of linguistics dealt with in Part A of this book – mainly phonetics, phonology, and grammar, with some reference to semantics and pragmatics.

## 3. PHONETICS, PHONOLOGY, AND LANGUAGE DISORDERS

Pronunciation problems (other than those associated with stuttering) which affect intelligibility are estimated to be present in 10 per cent of the pre-school-age and early school-age population (Enderby and Philipp 1986: 155 ff.). Some of these problems can be traced to an obvious cause. For example, cleft lip and/or palate, which occurs in one of every 700 live births in the U.K. (Enderby and Philipp 1986), is associated in a significant number of cases with speech problems. In many cases though there may not be such an obvious physical cause which can be directly linked to the pronunciation difficulties. Both types of disorder require detailed descriptions, so that the therapist can assess the nature of the problem, plan a therapeutic programme, and evaluate the success of this programme over time. To enable speech therapists to characterise pronunciation disorders, phonetic ear-training, and transcription have long been part of speech therapy training. In Britain, phonetics has been part of the syllabus in training establishments since the mid-1940s (Quirk Report 1972: 9). More recently however, while phonetic transcription of samples of speech continues to be the initial data for assessment in most instances, this data serves as the starting-point for a phonological analysis. An early example of this approach is Haas (1963), a case study of a six-year-old boy. Despite being written a quarter of a century ago, this analysis has most of the features that form part of today's assessments:

1.  An initial description using a broad phonetic transcription, in the symbols of the International Phonetic Alphabet (IPA) (to be found in Chapter 1), with some special symbols added for particular features of the child's speech.
2.  A phonological analysis based on a phonetic inventory organised according to place, manner, and voicing features of segments identified in the transcription. The analysis considers the functional (contrastive) value of the child's restricted system, and also makes an explicit comparison with the adult phonological system.
3.  Therapeutic implications. What advice to the speech therapist for planning a remediation programme seems to emerge out of the analysis?

### 3.1 Transcription

The starting-point for a description and analysis of a pronunciation disorder remains an auditory impressionistic transcription using the IPA, together with a set of symbols specifically designed for some of the commonly-occurring immature or deviant pronunciations of children. An extract from a recent set of conventions suggested for additional symbols for clinical transcription appears in Fig. 17.

The first set of symbols, under A, relate to place of articulation; there are other symbols relating to manner of articulation, vocal fold activity, co-articulation and so on. The second set of symbols in Fig. 17, under G, are provided to assist the transcriber by allowing for underspecified segments of various types. It is in the nature of transcription of disordered speech that certain segments will resist full identification. Such modifications are necessary because the IPA symbols (segmental and diacritic) are devised to deal with the range of sounds possible in the languages of the world as used by adult speakers. The articulation of both normal and disordered children may (and does) deviate considerably from such 'normal' adult speech sounds. Without specific transcriptional features to capture the idiosyncratic character of the pronunciations of impaired individuals in particular, there is a considerable risk of data distortion.

As Carney (1979) points out, however, the limitations of standard transcription systems for dealing with disordered speech are often not acknowledged. The drawbacks are most obvious when a transcription of speech amounting to a phonemic representation is used. In normal circumstances such a transcription allows the inference of a considerable amount of phonetic detail, since the range of allophonic variation, for most accents of English, is well-known. Thus (to take one of Carney's examples) in RP the transcription of a lateral in different contexts using the same symbol will not mislead: in [klei], [lei] and [eil], we are able to predict the phonetic variation in *clay, lay* and *ale* from the position in which the lateral appears. Following the voiceless velar stop, it is likely to be devoiced, while pre-vocalically so-called 'clear' [l] has what Gimson (1970: 201) describes as a relatively front-vowel resonance, as opposed to the back-vowel resonance of the post-vocalic 'dark' l. (For these differences, see Chapter 2, above.) There is no guarantee however that a child with speech problems will respect the allophonic variation of the adult language. It is not uncommon for example for such children to produce 'clear' l in both pre-vocalic and post-vocalic positions. A transcription which assumed adult allophonic variation would miss this information which is potentially valuable for remediation, and so constitute what Carney (op. cit.) would refer to as 'inappropriate abstraction'. Careful and detailed transcription by well-trained individuals, using where relevant the recommended symbols of Figure 2, will overcome most of the problems of too abstract a transcription, and in most instances furnish the speech therapist with the information needed.

*Figure 17* Extracts from suggested transcriptional conventions for disordered speech (reprinted with permission from Grunwell 1987)

**PRDS — Recommended additional phonetic symbols**

For the representation of segmental aspects of disordered speech

A. *Relating mainly to place of articulation*

| | | |
|---|---|---|
| 1. Bilabial trills | | ppp b̑b̑b̑ |
| 2. Lingualabials | plosives, nasal | P̼ B̼ M̼ |
| (tongue tip/blade | fricatives | θ̼8 |
| to upper lip) | lateral | L̼ |
| 3. Labiodental plosives and nasal | | p̪ b̪ m̪ |
| (m̪ is an alternative to the usual ɱ) | | |
| 4. Reverse labiodentals | plosives, nasal | p̯ b̯ m̯ |
| (lower teeth to | fricatives | f̯ v̯ |
| upper lip) | | |
| 5. Interdentals | plosives, nasal | t̪̟ d̪̟ n̪̟ (or t̟ etc.) |
| (using existing IPA | | |
| convention for advancement) | | |
| 6. Bidental | fricatives | h̪ ɦ̪ (or ə̯ etc.) |
| (lower teeth to | percussive | ʮ |
| upper teeth) | | |
| 7. Voiced palatal fricative | | ʝ |
| (reserving j for palatal approximant) | | |
| 8. Voiced velar lateral | | ʟ̠ |
| (using existing IPA | | |
| convention for retraction) | | |
| 9. Pharyngeal plosives | | q̠ G̠ |
| (using existing IPA | | |
| convention for retraction) | | |

G. *Relating to inadequacy of data or transcriptional confidence*

31. 'Not sure'                                          Ring doubtful symbols
                                                        or cover symbols, thus:

Ο            entirely unspecified articulatory segment
Ⓒ            unspecified consonant
Ⓥ            unspecified vowel
Ⓢ            unspecified stop
Ⓕ            unspecified fricative
Ⓐ            unspecified approximant
⟨NAS⟩        unspecified nasal
⟨AFF⟩        unspecified affricate
⟨LAT⟩        unspecified lateral
⟨PAL⟩        probably palatal, unspecified manner (etc.)
ⓘ            probably [ɨ] but not sure (etc.)
mɪ Ⓥ Ⓚ       probably [ɤk], but not sure (etc.)

*Note:* A voiced, but otherwise unspecified, fricative may be shown as Ⓕ ; similarly, a voiceless, but otherwise unspecified, stop as Ⓢ ; and so on.

32. Speech sound(s) masked by                               (( ))
    extraneous noise                          thus    bɪg ((bæd wʊl))f
                                              or      bɪg ((2 sylls))

33. *The asterisk.* It is recommended that free use be made of asterisks (indexed, if necessary) and footnotes where it is desired to record some segment or feature for which no symbol is provided.

## 3.2 Instrumental supplementation

It has been argued however that the procedure of phonetic transcription can be unreliable, because the child (normal or disordered) may be making distinctions, or using articulatory postures that the transcriber cannot hear, however skilled. Since this information may be relevant to the characterisation and/or remediation of the child's problem, it may be necessary in certain areas to supplement an auditory impressionistic transcription with information from instrumental phonetic techniques. We will consider one example which uses acoustic data from spectrograms, and one from speech production data, using the electropalatograph.

It has been a general observation of young normal children's developing speech that the voicing distinction in initial English stops is neutralised at a certain, quite early stage in their acquisition. An instrumental analysis of the speech development of normal children (Macken and Barton 1980) revealed that one stage of development, for some children producing their versions of voiced and voiceless stop targets, involved a consistent but sub-phonemic difference in voice onset time, a crucial cue for voicing in English and other languages. In distinguishing /p/ and /b/ in English, described respectively as *voiceless* and *voiced* labial stops, the point at which voicing begins, after the release of the stop is crucial. If voicing begins at the time of release or up to about 30 milliseconds after, then the sound will be interpreted as /b/. But if voice onset is delayed until after this 30 msec cross-over point, then the sound will be heard as /p/. The VOT range for /b/ (and other voiced plosives) is referred to as the 'short lag' range, and the values for /p/ as the 'long lag' range.

The children in the Macken and Barton study, in their early pronunciations (and the age of the children in this longitudinal study was from about 18 months to 2 years) showed no consistency in their use of short lag and long lag for labial stop targets. But then for a period before they gave evidence of having controlled adult parameters, they made a consistent VOT distinction, but *within* the adult short lag category. This distinction was not one that a transcriber would reliably pick up, and it required spectrographic analysis to be detected. Similar data for VOT in labial stops (but using pneumotachography as the instrumental technique) is reported for one of the disordered child subjects considered in detail by Hardcastle and Morgan (1982). They also considered other aspects of their subjects' pronunciation instrumentally, with some interesting results. One technique they used was electropalatography, in which a real-time analysis of tongue dynamics can be made by fitting the patient with an artificial palate, in which a number of small electrodes are embedded. As the patient speaks, the tongue contacts he makes are recorded by the electrodes and transmitted to a computer, which records them. Comparisons were made between contact patterns of the impaired subjects and those of normal children, in the pronunciation of single words. For one impaired child, for example, it was apparent from the pattern of contacts that for initial alveolar or alveolopalatal sounds such as the [t] in *tent*, or [ʃ] in *sheep*, there was considerable velar contact as well as the more forward contact necessary for the alveolar obstruents. The velarisation would not have been picked up by a transcriber, but is obviously important for a speech therapist concerned to have detailed information on articulation available for planning remediation.

In the remainder of our discussion of phonetics and phonological disability we will for the most part be concerned with data analyses that rely on auditory impressionistic transcriptions. It should be clear however even from this brief excursus on instrumental analyses that auditory transcriptions will not always be reliable. In particular, explanations of phonological disability which rely on such transcriptions need to be evaluated carefully. (See Hardcastle *et al.* 1987. A detailed review of supplementary instrumental analyses appears in Weismer 1984.)

## 3.3 Analysis

The introduction of phonological concepts into speech pathology in the 1960s led to a re-interpretation of the data of 'articulation disorder' and 'misarticulations' (Grunwell 1985a). The initial analyses of available phonetic transcriptions were within the framework of phonemic theory (e.g. Haas 1963). More recently a variety of generative frameworks has been applied. The most widely used has been some form of *process analysis*, particularly in North America (Shriberg and Kwiatowski 1980, Ingram 1981). Some researchers in Britain (e.g. Crystal 1982, Grunwell 1985b) have argued for and exemplified a more eclectic approach to analysis, which combines insights from phonemic theory and process analysis, in an initial description of a disorder. We will accept this approach in providing illustrations of children's pronunciation problems in English.

## 3.4 The phonetic inventory and systems of contrast

The majority of approaches to the assessment of pronunciation problems in English have concentrated on consonants. It used to be generally accepted that vowels did not present problems to children acquiring the sound system normally (although Haas 1963 does mention vowel problems in his case study, and Crystal 1982 allows for the analysis of vowels). More recently problems with vowel acquisition (which, however, probably seem to occur only in a small percentage of cases) have been reported (Stoel-Gammon and Harrington 1987). However, the data to be reviewed here will refer only to consonants.

Most recent approaches to assessment, following the normal phonological acquisition literature, accept that procedures need to be sensitive to distributional differences in the availability of phones for contrastive use. The system of contrastive phones that a child might be able to use in initial position in a monosyllable is usually different from (most commonly, more extensive than) the system in final position. To provide a full description, then, it is necessary to examine separately phones in different positions in syllable or word structure. A clear illustration of this appears in Figures 18 and 19.

Figure 18, adapted from Grunwell 1988, shows the inventory of phones available to two children. Figure 18(a) is a consonant chart for Simon, aged 4 years 7 months (4;7), while Figure 18(b) shows the range of consonant sounds available to Graham, aged 9;0. It is clear that Graham has a greater range of sounds available to him, overall. He has the full range of plosives (p/b, t/d, k/g, plus a glottal stop), fricatives in two places of articulation (f/v, s) and the alveolopalatal affricate /tʃ/. Simon has no velar sounds, no fricatives, and no glottal stop or affricate sound. Despite Graham's wider articulatory repertoire, an analysis of how this repertoire is deployed can reveal limitations on Graham which Simon does not have.

The consonant chart reveals the extent of the child's articulatory abilities (or limitations). Further analysis is required to determine how these abilities are employed at different positions in word and syllable structure. Figure 19, again adapted from Grunwell 1988, reveals how the two children use their articulatory potential in making meaning distinctions, in one position, syllable final/word final.

If we consider the structure of the word *piglet*, in terms of its consonant and vowel structure, we can represent it as:

$$c\ v\ c\ c\ v\ c$$
$$p\ i\ g\ l\ e\ t$$

The word consists of two syllables, and, without considering here exactly where the syllable boundary is, we can safely say that *p* is a syllable initial/word initial sound (SIWI) and *t* is syllable final/word final (SFWF). These labels are also used for monosyllabic words: in *pet*, *p* and *t* would still be referred to as SIWI and SFWF respectively.

It has long been an observation in the literature on normal language development that children's phonological systems are not monosystemic.

*Figure 18* Phonetic inventories for Simon (a) and Graham (b)
(adapted from Grunwell 1988)

Name: Simon (4; 7)                          **Phonetic inventory (a)**

|  | Labial | Dental | Alveolar | Post-Alveolar | Palatal | Velar | Glottal | Other |
|---|---|---|---|---|---|---|---|---|
| Nasal | m |  | n |  |  |  |  |  |
| Plosive | p b |  | t d |  |  |  | ? |  |
| Fricative |  |  |  |  |  |  |  |  |
| Affricate |  |  |  |  |  |  |  |  |
| Approximant | w |  | l |  | j |  |  |  |
| Other |  |  |  |  |  |  |  |  |

Marginal Phones: ɬ        ʋ

Name: Graham (9; 0)                         **Phonetic inventory (b)**

|  | Labial | Dental | Alveolar | Post-Alveolar | Palatal | Velar | Glottal | Other |
|---|---|---|---|---|---|---|---|---|
| Nasal | m |  | n |  |  |  |  |  |
| Plosive | p b |  | t d | ʧ |  | k g | ? |  |
| Fricative | f v |  | s |  |  |  | h |  |
| Affricate |  |  |  |  |  |  |  |  |
| Approximant | w |  | l |  |  |  |  |  |
| Other |  |  |  |  |  |  |  |  |

Marginal Phones: ɬ        ɣ        ʋ

436

*Figure 19* Contrastive possibilities for Simon(a) and Graham (b), SFWF position (adapted from Grunwell 1988)

(a) Simon
Syllable Final Word Final

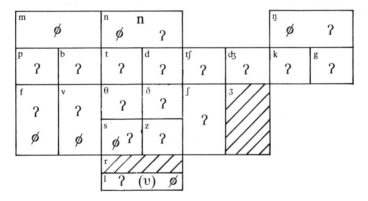

(b) Graham
Syllable Final Word Final

Phonological development is not simply a matter of developing phonemic contrasts which are then immediately generalisable to all places in word and syllable structure; different systems develop in different positions. In English it is in general the case that a wider range of contrasts develop earlier in SIWI position than in SFWF. This generalisation does not however rule out the existence of children who run counter to this tendency or particular contrasts, e.g. fricatives (Shriberg and Kwiatowski 1980: 135), being more readily developed in SFWF.

Since assessment procedures in child language disorders are referenced to normal development, a number of them, including Grunwell (1985b) and Crystal (1982) examine the child's use of the phonetic inventory at different positions in word structure. The charts for Simon and Graham in Figure 19 show only SFWF position (from Grunwell's procedure). Each chart shows the range of phonetic realisations for target adult phonemes. Thus the top left hand cell of Simon's chart (Figure 19a) indicates that for all adult target words ending in *m*, Simon produced *m*. Graham however (Figure 19b) failed to produce any realisation at all for a final *m* target (Ø indicates a zero realisation). A cell by cell comparison shows very obviously that despite having the more restricted phonetic inventory, Simon has a more extensive range than Graham of potentially contrastive elements. Pronunciation problems seem to require for their full characterisation not simply an account of phonetic limitations but also details of the distributional patterning of the segments that are available to the child.

## 3.5 Process analysis

The phonemic approach embodied within the description of pronunciation problems so far described has either been supplemented (Grunwell 1985, Crystal 1982) or supplanted by some form of phonological process analysis (Ingram 1981, Shriberg and Kwiatowski 1980). This is now widely used in assessment procedures, particularly in the United States.

The term 'phonological process' derives from Stampe, who sees the phonological system of a language as 'the residue of an innate system of phonological processes, revised in certain ways by linguistic experiences' (Stape 1969: 443). The processes were seen as innate, and acquisition was a matter, in part, of inhibiting those processes not relevant for the language of the child's environment. Processes have been commonly observed in sound changes in the world's languages. A commonly cited example of such a process is devoicing of word-final obstruents, which synchronically is a feature of German but not English. Stampe's account of the English child's acquisition would require that an innately-present devoicing tendency was eventually inhibited, to allow for voicing, which is phonemically relevant in English, to occur word-finally; on the route to mastery we would expect a stage in which all final obstruents were devoiced. The German child on the other hand, will devoice from the beginning.

It is not necessary to subscribe to Stampe's views on the innateness of processes to find them useful in characterising impairment. Processes can be viewed as strategies adopted by the child in the face of the complex task of learning how to pronounce, and related to structural and physiological aspects of speech production (Shriberg and Kwiatowski 1980: 4). We can illustrate some of these features with examples from V., a Southern English girl of 4;8 with a history of pronunciation difficulties:

(*a*)  cluster reduction

initial: [t] for /tr/ in *train*

/st/ in *stamps*

/kw/ in *queen*

/cl/ in *clouds*

/kr/ in *Christmas*

Any consonant cluster target containing a voiceless stop is substituted in V.'s output by a singleton voiceless alveolar stop. The obvious outcome of this will be considerable homonymy in her vocabulary. The following words, for instance, would all be pronounced as [teɪ]: *tray, clay, stay*. Cluster reduction is a widely attested phenomenon in normal and impaired child phonologies in English and related languages (see for example Magnusson 1983 on Swedish).

(*b*)  assimilation

A commonly reported assimilatory process is consonant harmony, in which for a CVC monosyllable target the child produces the second consonant at the same place of articulation as the first (there may also be manner assimilation). Examples from V.:

[ti:d]  *lip*

*cheese*

*queen*

Both stop consonants in V.'s production are alveolar. Of course the relationship between her segments and the targets is quite complex, showing the simultaneous application of a number of processes, with resultant homonymy. Initially the lateral, voiceless affricate and cluster are all substituted for by [t]; finally a labial stop, voiceless alveolar fricative, and alveolar nasal, have [d] substituted. The influence of the [tVd] word-shape on V.'s output at this stage of her development can be gauged by her production of CV target monosyllables at this point:

[ti:d]  *key*

[tɜ:d]  *cow*

In both cases open syllable targets have a closed syllable representation for V. (We will deal with vowel problems separately below.) This is an unusual phenomenon in normal developmental terms.

(*c*)  stopping

[ti:d]  *cheese*

[pɔ:]  *four*

In these examples from V. fricative targets are represented by stops at the same place of articulation. Like cluster reduction and consonant harmony, this is well-attested.

The process approach to the description of pronunciation difficulties collapses the separate stages of phonetic inventory and contrastive analysis seen in the examples above from Grunwell 1985. Its essentially rule-based approach however does make comparisons across language-disordered children, and between normal and language-disordered, more straight-forward. Shriberg *et al.* (1986) in a comparison of the characteristics of children with 'phonological disorders of unknown origin' and normals, find that there are eight processes (which they refer to as 'natural sound changes') which 'capture over 90 per cent of the deletion and substitution errors made by normally developing and speech-delayed children above age 3' (1986: 145). Three of these processes, cluster reduction, assimilation and stopping, are present in V.'s output, above. All are listed, with examples where necessary, in Figure 20.

But what is it that distinguishes the 'phonologically disordered' children from normal children? In the Shriberg *et al.* large sample comparison, it is the different proportion of errors that is most striking. The highest proportion of errors in the normal group is 15 per cent, while in the disordered group it is 75 per cent. More generally, the current view taken of what constitutes a phonological disorder is that it consists in the non-elimination by the children involved of processes regularly found in normal development. There is some data available (reviewed in Leonard 1985) which goes against this generalisation. However, for most of the current literature it seems reasonable to assert that the child referred to as phonologically disordered is one whose development of pronunciation skills is delayed or 'frozen' relative to other aspects of his language development, particularly vocabulary size (Ingram 1987).

It has become common in the speech therapy field to refer to a child who shows up pronunciation problems on one of the assessment procedures we have described as 'phonologically disordered', and we have used this term

*Figure 20* Common natural processes

| | |
|---|---|
| 1. cluster reduction | |
| 2. final consonant deletion | |
| 3. unstressed syllable deletion | (e.g. *tomato* — ['maːtoʊ] ) |
| 4. stopping | |
| 5. liquid simplification | (e.g. *lay* — [peɪ] ) |
| 6. palatal fronting | (e.g. *shoe* — [ðuː] ) |
| 7. velar fronting | (e.g. *good* — [dʊd] ) |

(from Shriberg *et al.* 1986)

above. The practice is a reaction to the historical tendency to assume that all pronunciation problems were a matter of articulatory skills (or lack of them), and uses the label 'phonological' to emphasise the linguistic nature of the disorder. However while modern assessment procedures all use phonological frameworks (features, phonemes, rule statements, phonotactics, etc.) in order to arrive at a descriptin of the data, analysts have not rested there. There has been an unfortunate tendency to take such descriptions as explanations, rather than as a set of phenomena to be explained (Grunwell 1987, Locke 1983). The assessment procedures we have used as examples are neutral concerning the sources of the problem they represent (in the terms of Hewlett 1985, they are *data-oriented* rather than *speaker-oriented*). One example will perhaps suffice to emphasise the need to search beyond the descriptions for the basis of a problem. The instance cited comes from normal development.

Smith (1973) in his detailed longitudinal account of the sound system development of an individual child notes a point at which cluster reduction in SFWF positions occurs. Final nasal + stop clusters (e.g. *nt, nd*) are reduced to singletons ([t], [n] respectively). In Smith's analysis, this difference is dealt with solely in terms of realisation rules – i.e. in production terms. The child's lexical representation is assumed to be the same as the adult from the beginning – i.e. the child's phonological perception is perfect; errors in pronunciation and their elimination depend upon production rules and developmental changes in them. However, as Braine (1976) pointed out, this particular type of cluster reduction may have an auditory basis. Vocalic elements in English (including vowels and nasals) are appreciably longer before voiced stops than before voiceless stops. The representations chosen by the child in this instance for *nt* and *nd* clusters may then reflect the relative salience of the nasal consonants auditorily in these sequences. The assessment procedures that we have considered can only consider production data. The example from Smith shows that at least some instances of cluster reduction in the production data may have a perceptual basis. Other data which indicates a perceptual basis for some pronunciation difficulties is reviewed by Locke (1980).

The descriptive approaches to so-called phonological disorder have provided useful guidelines for remediation by speech therapists, as well as a wide range of information on error types among children with pronunciation problems. It is clear however that a new phase of research has begun in which the descriptive status of current procedures is recognised, and the search for explanations of the patterns recognised is on (see Grunwell 1987, Menn 1987, Ingram 1987).

## 4. GRAMMAR AND LANGUAGE DISORDERS

While the study of disorders of pronunciation has the longest history, the influence of transformational generative grammar brought applications in the field of language disorders from the early 1970s, and from that time a variety of grammatical approaches have been developed, particularly in the English-speaking world. The recognition that a child's grammatical system could be impaired – or at least that a language disorder could be characterised in terms of deficits in the grammatical system – has generated research which has yielded useful information. This phase of research has been (properly) descriptive, and has provided (*a*) useful frameworks for assessment and thus therapeutic application and (*b*) identification, usually in surface terms, of the grammatical system deficits (most often with respect to English) that children classed as SSLD tend to have. In this phase of research whatever repertoire of deficits emerged were labelled as grammatical problems, and it is only now that a new research thrust is developing, which looks beyond the level at which the problems are identified, and asks what the basis for these disorders is, and how they can be explained. The remainder of this section reviews the historical development of research into grammatical disorders, and considers current trends.

### 4.1 Rule-based analyses

The most careful early investigation of the grammatical differences between normal and SSLD children is reported in Morehead and Ingram (1973). They attempted to resolve the issue of whether SSLD children had qualitatively-distinct linguistic systems by taking considerable care in subject matching for their samples. In addition to the usual IQ and socio-economic criteria that had been applied, they also used a measure of sentence length (mean utterance length in morphemes) as a more reliable indicator of relative linguistic development than age.

Morehead and Ingram compared the grammatical abilities of the two groups of children, using the components of a standard theory model transformational grammar. They found that the phrase structure rules needed to account for the children's utterances in the samples they collected were 'nearly identical' for the two groups. A comparison of transformations used by the two groups showed that, with certain exceptions, the majority of transformations used were similar across the two groups. Where then does the difference between the two groups lie?

The most obvious difference between the groups is the age at which particular linguistic milestones are achieved. The normal and language-impaired groups were matched for mean length of utterance, as we have pointed out. The age-ranges of the two groups are however dramatically different. The span for the normal group was 1 year, 7 months to 3 years, 1 month. The impaired group ranged in age from 3 years, 6 months to 9 years, 6 months. So for any particular linguistic level, the impaired group show a marked chronological delay:

'Given that normal children initiate and acquire base syntax between approximately 18 and 40 months, it appears that deviant children take on the average three times as long to initiate and to acquire base syntax.' (Morehead and Ingram 1973: 216).

As with phonological disorder, at least some of the problem for children whose language impairment is revealed by grammatical analysis is that they are not able, for whatever reason, to make the transition from one stage to another of the acquisition process. This chronological mismatch, which goes far beyond the variability found in large-sample studies of normal development (e.g. Wells 1986), has been a consistent finding of subsequent studies.

While the Morehead and Ingram study indicates that, so far as syntactic structure is concerned, SSLD children do not develop 'bizarre linguistic systems', there was one point of difference that did emerge when the analysis went beyond a comparison of phrase structure and transformational rules. A significant difference was found in the number of major lexical categories (N, V, A) used by the two groups. This is interpreted as a restriction on the variety of construction types available to the language-impaired group, where these types are seen simply as strings of category labels.

## 4.2 Surface structure approaches

Since the Morehead and Ingram study the points of contact between language impairment and generative theory, as it has developed, have been slight. There are several reasons why this should be so. One of them is the finding that, viewed from the perspective of syntactic rules, language-impaired children have 'normal' systems, even though these may take an inordinately long time to develop, or, for some of the children, may be only partial systems 'frozen' at a particular stage of acquisition. Another reason concerns the tendency of studies in non-normal language development to follow trends in the study of normal language acquisition. In the 1970s this research was much less dependent on current trends in linguistic theory than was earlier the case; it is only recently, in a period of relative stability in linguistic theory that acquisition researchers have once again turned to the dominant linguistic model for insights (e.g. Atkinson 1986, Goodluck 1986). Research on language disorders similarly departed from a reliance on transformational generative theory, but has still to reconnect so far as grammar is concerned. Clinical approaches to grammatical problems since the late 1970s have tended to rely on surface structure descriptive frameworks, and it is to one of these that we now turn.

## 4.3 LARSP

A grammatical profiling procedure widely used in the UK and elsewhere is the Language Assessment, Remediation, and Screening Procedure (LARSP; for details see Crystal *et al.* 1989). This has been applied to child disorders and to adult disordered data (e.g. Penn and Behrmann 1986), and versions of it have been applied to data from other languages (Feilberg 1987 – Norwegian; Bol and Kuiken 1987 – Dutch). Figure 21 shows a part of the profile which will illustrate the general principles on which it is based.

In the figure, a section across the profile shows what is referred to as Stage III of grammatical development. The framework used for the categories represented in the profile was based on that used in Quirk *et al.* 1972, for their grammar of contemporary English. This is emphatically a surface structure approach, in which clause structure is represented at three separate levels:

1.  *clause*: major clause constituents are labelled as S, V, C, O, or A.
2.  *phrase*: here category labels such as Det, N, V, Aux, Adj, Prep are used to label members of noun, verb or prepositional phrases.
3.  *word*: at this level of analysis morphological processes are recognised.

Stage III of the LARSP profiling approach reflects the clause/phrase/word division, with cols. 2, 3 and 6 representing clauses (commands, questions, and statements respectively), while col. 7 lists noun and prepositional phrase types, together with pronouns and auxiliary premodification. The final column shows some morphological features (past participle, third person plural, and possessive). This approach, carried through the developmental range from the beginnings of syntax at about eighteen months to the point at about five years of age when the child has acquired most of the major syntactic structures, provides a template against which those structures actually occurring in a child's language sample can be checked. The LARSP profile, systematically applied to individual cases or groups, can provide a picture of the strengths and weaknesses of the grammatical repertoire. The profile can be used either as the basis for further enquiry, or, for the clinician, as the starting-point for remediation.

As a format for preliminary data-organisation then, the profiling approach has advantages. It is perhaps best viewed as a (partial) analogue, at the grammatical level, of the transcription that is the initial representation of the data for phonological analysis (Garman 1989). It is not based on a coherent theoretical framework, and does not of itself admit any conclusions about the status of the child's grammatical system. It will however identify categories

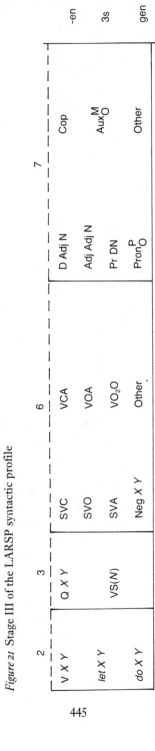

*Figure 21* Stage III of the LARSP syntactic profile

or construction types which are consistently lacking in a child's repertoire, and thus direct more detailed and principled enquiry into the precise nature and bases of these problems. The areas of difficulty identified for the SSLD child tend to be consistent, though they differ for younger and older groups of children. In younger SSLD children it is possible to locate obvious areas of structural deficit, whereas in the older children the identification of such gaps is not so straightforward. In the remainder of this section we will consider some of the deficits that have been identified in SSLD children and the possible bases for them.

### 4.4 The English auxiliary

It is a general clinical finding, well-supported in the research literature, that language-impaired children have problems with verb-forms in English, particularly auxiliaries (Fletcher and Peters 1984, Ingram 1972, Johnson and Kamhi 1984, Johnson and Schery 1976, Steckol and Leonard 1979). By comparison with normal children of the same age, SSLD children will have a less developed auxiliary system, and when normal and SSLD children are matched in terms of mean length of utterance (MLU), the SSLD children are found to have a more restricted range of auxiliaries and to use them less frequently. To identify a consistent gap in a grammatical profile is however merely to identify a problem which requires an explanation. Why should the language-impaired child find the English auxiliary system problematical? There are a range of possible factors that are relevant, which may operate either singly or in conjunction.

For some areas of the auxiliary system, which in normal development takes a considerable time to be acquired, cognitive explanations have been preferred. One example of an attempt at this type of explanation was the claim by Cromer (1974) that the late acquisition of the present perfect (as in *I've finished, have you seen her*) relative to past tense, in the children studied by Brown and his associates at Harvard, was because of its relative cognitive difficulty. The present perfect form, in its relation of a past action to the time of speaking (the so-called 'current relevance' meaning), was argued by Crome to present a cognitive complexity over and above the simple past (which locates an action at some time prior to the moment of speaking). Subsequent research has made it clear that Cromer's explanation for the late acquisition of the present perfect (at up to five years of age, in his sample) was a consequence of his studying American children. One of the dialectal differences between American and British English is that the former has a much lower frequency of occurrence of present perfect, and when we examine British children's acquisition, we find that they develop present perfect much earlier than the American children (see Wells 1979, Fletcher 1981, 1985: 33ff;

and particularly Gathercole 1986). The alternative (and simpler) environmental explanation rules out the semantic-cognitive one in this particular case.

This does not mean that in certain areas of normal language development generally, and verb-form use in particular, we will not want to appeal to the child's conceptual abilities to account for the nature of change, or lack of it. As Johnston points out,

'if children learn language by analysing context, and mapping form to meaning, then their conceptual and factual resources should constrain the acquisition process' (1985: 48).

One of the pieces of linguistic evidence claimed by Johnston in support of this view is the acquisition of members of some form classes in a predictable order over a protracted course despite their formal similarity. In the area of verb-forms, the obvious example of this in English is the lengthy development of modal auxiliaries, which begins in the third year and continues into the primary school (Stephany 1986). If it is appropriate to ground aspects of the course of normal language development in the child's conceptual abilities, then there is every reason to consider the possible involvement of these abilities in the same aspects of the linguistic behaviour of some language-impaired children.

That said, grammar, as Bruner (1983: 169) reminds us, still 'constitutes its own problem space'. Each child has to determine which meanings are coded, and how, in the particular language he is trying to learn. Auxiliaries in English present the following features which may affect the child's establishment of a linguistic representation:

(i)  Two auxiliaries are in construction with non-continuous morphemes (*have* + past participle, *be* + ing). All other auxiliaries are not.
(ii)  *Have* and *be* have a range of variant forms, contractible and non-contractible; for contracted third person, the *have* and *be* form is the same (*'s*).
(iii) All auxiliaries (including a number of modals) tend to be phonetically brief, reduced forms in input language, particularly in initial position. This might present a particular problem to language-impaired children. (Fletcher 1983; see also Leonard *et al.* 1987).

So either the constituent structure of the verb-form (i), or the paradigms associated with particular auxiliaries (ii), or their particular realisations (iii) could affect, independently or interactively, the (normal or non-normal) child's learning.

A structural deficit for auxiliaries, identified on the grammatical profile of a language-impaired child, may therefore have a *variety* of possible sources. It

447

may have a cognitive basis, it may be at root a grammatical problem, or it may have its basis in the problems in interpretation of input, or some combination of these factors. Future research will require the testing of hypotheses which relate to the basis of the problem.

Surface-structure approaches of the LARSP type will isolate broad areas of difficulty such as the auxiliary system, or complex sentences, another widely recognised problem area for SSLD children (Crystal 1984). There may be deficits however which relate to the grammatical system, construed more broadly, but which a profile of the LARSP type will not locate. We will look briefly at two of these: adverbials, which while structurally simple have functional differentiation; and processing constraints.

## 4.5 Adverbials

Fletcher and Garman (1988) report on a comparison between a group of older language-impaired children in residential schools in the UK, and matched normals. On a variety of syntactic measures (including noun and pre-positional phrase structure, verb phrase structure, and availability of complex sentences) the groups are not significantly different. When adverbials – words, phrases, or clauses that serve as adjuncts in clause structure – are examined in terms of their function rather than their structural properties, differences emerge, particularly in the use of time adverbials. Time adverbials are involved in a complex system of specification of tense and aspect choices on the main verb and reflect in their lexical realisations both calendric (day, month, hour, etc.) and non-calendric (seasons, festivals, holidays) temporal reference points. To use these adverbials successfully, the child has to learn the relationship between particular tense/aspect choices and the forms, the semantics of time, and when it is appropriate to use temporal adverbials in discourse. Fletcher and Garman (1988) report that the SSLD children used fewer time adverbials than their age-matched normal peers, and that they had a very limited grasp of calendric time, as revealed both in their infrequent use of the relevant lexical items, and errors such as:

I do go home on the weekend on Fridays and Wednesdays.

They also showed uncertainty, as a group, over the appropriate provision of temporal specification. Speakers provide an overt time reference for their hearers unless one can be construed from the context. Fletcher and Garman (1988) examined the use of past tense by normal and SSLD children, and identified instances where the reference time could not be determined from context, and asked whether an appropriate time adverbial was provided by the speaker. Normal five and seven-year-olds provide the time adverbial on the majority of occasions, but the SSLD group supply fewer than a third of the necessary time references.

It might be argued that these rather subtle limitations do not merit inclusion under the heading of grammatical disorders, but rather represent the two aspects of what has been referred to as a 'semantic-pragmatic' disorder (Rapin 1982). The semantic aspect of the disability could be said to be revealed in the problems found by the SSLD group in structuring the lexical information that relates to conventional time organisation, while the pragmatics of temporal deixis and the requirements of conversational behaviour are apparently violated by the non-provision of temporal adverbials. It is true that in using the 'semantic-pragmatic' label writers have tended to highlight problems of word-finding (semantic) and problems of conversational structure and inference (pragmatic) (Rapin 1982, McTear 1985, Conti-Ramsden and Gunn 1986), but the term is so vague that it is not easy to see how the temporal problems identified can be excluded. The general point is, of course, that once we take a broader interpretation of grammar than possible structural types and/or the categories represented in them, and consider the functions of adverbials (and determiners, pronouns, modal auxiliaries, etc.) then we have a much wider range of deficit phenomena which could be included under the heading of 'grammatical disorders'. The availability of a single coherent theory within which the phenomena of disability could be interpreted would avoid current problems of demarcation. In the absence of such a theory, it is perhaps sensible to avoid labels, and to adopt a heuristic strategy which combines syntactic profiles and a functional perspective, to develop a typology of linguistic deficits.

Implicit in this strategy is the assumption that even if we do not yet know the full range of possibilities for grammatical impairment, broadly construed, sub-types with consistent linguistic profiles will emerge. Some recent work by Chiat and Hirson (1987) suggests that in certain cases a quite heterogeneous grammatical profile will be found, which may not be explicable as, at base, a grammatical disorder at all.

## 4.6 Processing constraints: children

In their analysis in detail of a girl of 10, Ruth, Chiat and Hirson explore the data from a perspective that considers the processing of individual utterances, and ask whether the perturbations found in this individual's output can be explained in terms of processing limitations – consistent and specifiable constraints on the real-time production of utterances. The analysis works within a psycholinguistic framework that conceives of the production of an utterance beginning with a 'conceptual intention', and then proceeding through various stages of 'mapping', including a final phonological stage which structures the output that we hear and record.

The account of Ruth's problems considers first of all the range of conceptual intentions that she wishes to communicate. Chiat and Hirson are satisfied that her intended meanings, identifiable in the structures she produces in relation to their context, cover a wide variety of the types of conceptual relations expressed by language. These include basic propositional structure (verb + arguments), embedded propositions as arguments, adverbials of various structural types as modifiers of propositions, negation, and interrogation. Despite this relative richness of conceptual intentions, Ruth's output shows many deviations from normal language. There is often unintelligibility, and when her utterances can be understood, she omits words or parts of words, and uses inappropriate substitutions. Some examples of Ruth's output are listed on the right hand side of Table 13. It can be seen even from the few examples quoted under (b) that many of her utterances are ungrammatical, in various ways. Chiat and Hirson however argue that the omissions and substitutions we record are not governed by syntactic factors. Rather, the reasons for the disordered output are phonological. The affected elements within her utterances (i.e. those items omitted), are words or parts of words which are unstressed and which 'precede word or sentence stress'. Thus in Table 13a we find that the pre-stress syllable of *disgusting* is omitted, while in Table 13b relatively unstressed parts of sentence structure disappear. On the basis of a detailed analysis of an extensive corpus of Ruth's output, it is claimed that a phonological description can 'provide a unified account of a wide range of limitations'.

*Table 13* Examples of Ruth's output (from Chiat and Hirson 1987)

| | | |
|---|---|---|
| **(a)** | **Phonological omissions in words and stereotyped phrases** | |
| | disgusting | [ˈgʌstɪn] |
| | invisible | [ˈvɪgzɪl, ˈvivible, ˈvɪdəbəl] |
| | look after | [ˈkaftə] |
| **(b)** | **Omissions in sentences** | |
| | get the stuff out | *the stuff out* |
| | put the puppets on here | *[də] the puppets on here* |
| | what's the matter with you | *[du] matter with you* |
| | I'm not going to be a teacher | *[amɒʔ] go [ə] teacher* |
| | you go to my school | *you my school* |
| **(c)** | **Lexical substitutions** | |
| | he'll help me | *he'll help with me* |

If this is the case, and if there is a significant proportion of SSLD children who behave in a similar way (see Fletcher 1987 for some discussion), then analyses which assume a purely grammatical basis for this type of disorder are likely to be misleading. The Ruth case-study demonstrates that a serious and careful appraisal of a corpus of accurately transcribed output is still the best source of information about a language-impaired child. It does indicate the value of a dynamic perspective on children's speech production in analysing this data and interpreting the analysis. The output we transcribe is the product of a complex of interacting sub-systems; any one of these, or some combination, may be the source of the problem.

### 4.7 Processing constraints: adults

A similar perspective to that adopted by Chiat and Hirson for their child data has been put forward by Kean (e.g. 1977) to account for production data from Broca's aphasics.

Descriptions of Broca's aphasia (summarised above, section 2.1.1) refer to the agrammatic character of the output. The relatively short utterances of those affected by this type of aphasia tend to lack 'function' words (members of closed grammatical classes such as pronoun, article, auxiliary verb, preposition) and inflections (e.g. possessive, present tense *s*, past tense, plural). The term *agrammatism*, and the description of the surface character of the output in terms of syntactic categories, reinforces the historical view that this is primarily a grammatical disorder, though with associated phonological and even semantic problems. In a very similar way to Chiat and Hirson, Kean's approach to characterising Broca's aphasia is to provide a unified explanation for the heterogeneous surface phenomena that occur within the syndrome, in terms of 'an interaction between an impaired phonological capacity and otherwise intact linguistic capacities' (Kean 1977: 10).

Kean's analysis is formalised within the phonological model provided by Chomsky and Halle (1968). She exploits within this model a parallelism between inflectional morphemes (e.g. *ing*, *ed*) and cliticised auxiliary verb forms (e.g. the *'s* of *the boy's playing*), in terms of their phonological representation, to explain the similarity of their behaviour in the output of Broca's patients. Though superficially distinct, with quite distinct distributional characteristics grammatically, they can be shown to be formally similar in the role they play within the phonological component: briefly, inflections and clitics (under which heading Kean argues we should include articles and prepositions as well as contracted auxiliaries) are those affixed components of phonological words (see Chapter 2, section 9.2, above) which do *not* play a role in the assignment of stress. They are also the items which Broca's aphasics tend to omit. So if we take a phonological perspective on this type of aphasia we can capture both the formal similarity of the items which, looked at grammatically, are disparate, and the fact that Broca's aphasics omit these affixes, rather than other affixes which do play a role in stress assignments. (But see Garman 1982 for a critique of this view.)

## 5. CONCLUSIONS

A major impetus for the forays by linguists into the field of language disorders has been the desire to provide speech therapists with guidelines for remediation arising out of detailed characterisations of the language behaviour of disordered individuals. This was apparent even in the earliest contributions (e.g. Haas 1963). It seems obvious that a detailed account of an individual's phonetic repertoire, for example, and of the systemic use to which that repertoire is put, will be of assistance to a speech therapist who wishes to identify problems in order to conduct a rational remediation programme. There is no doubt that the last decade has seen real progress in the contribution of descriptive linguistics, broadly understood, to the assessment of speech and language disorder.

There are however two caveats to be entered. First, while there has undoubtedly been progress in assessment, there has not been a comparable effort in the development and evaluation of linguistically principled remediation programmes in child or adult disorders. Second, the search for explanation (a recent concern in child disorders, of longer standing in adult research), indicates that product descriptions which insist on a strict demarcation of linguistic levels, and the isolating of a disorder at one of these levels, may well be misleading about the source of the disorder (Crystal 1987, Feilberg 1987). The next decade will see the extension of research which seeks better models and explanations of language disorders. One consequence of such research should be better targeted and adapted remediation.

## REFERENCES

Parts of the research referred to in this chapter were supported by MRC Grant No. 68306114N and NATO Collaborative Research Grant No. RG84/0135. I am grateful to Susan Edwards and Michael Garman for helpful comments on an earlier draft.

Aitchison, J. (1987) *Words in the Mind: an Introduction to the Mental Lexicon*, Basil Blackwell, Oxford.
Atkinson, M. (1986) 'Learnability', in Fletcher, P. and Garman, M. (1986): 90–108.
Benson, D.F. (1979) 'Neurologic correlates of anomia', in Whitaker, H. and Whitaker, A.H. (eds) *Studies in Neurolinguistics*, 4, Academic Press, New York.
Bishop, D. (1987) 'The concept of comprehension in language disorder', in *Proceedings of the First International Symposium on Specific Speech and Language Disorders in Children*, AFASIC, London: 75–81.
Bol, G. and Kuiken, F. (1987) 'Morphosyntactic analysis of specific language disorders'. Paper presented at the First International Symposium on Specific Speech and Language Disorders in Children, Reading, April.

Braine, M. (1976) Review of N.V. Smith, *The Acquisition of Phonology, Language*, 52: 489–98.

Bruner, J. (1983) *In Search of Mind: Essays in Autobiography*, Harper & Row, New York.

Caramazza, A. and Berndt, R. (1978) 'Semantic and syntactic processes in aphasia: a review of the literature', *Psychological Bulletin*, 85: 898–918.

Caramazza. A. and Berndt, R. (1985) 'A multicomponent deficit view of agrammatic Broca's aphasia', in Kean, M-L. (ed.) *Agrammatism*. Academic Press, New York: 27–63.

Carney, E. (1979) 'Inappropriate abstraction in speech assessment procedures', *British Journal of Disorders of Communication*, 14: 123–35.

Chiat, S. and Hirson, A. (1987) 'From conceptual intention to utterance: a study of impaired language output in a child with developmental dysphasia', *British Journal of Disorders of Communication*, 22: 37–64.

Chomsky, N. and Halle, M. (1968) *The Sound Pattern of English*, Harper & Row, New York.

Conti-Ramsden, G. and Gunn, M. (1986) 'The development of conversational disability: a case study', *British Journal of Disorders of Communication*, 21: 339–51.

Cooper, W. and Zurif, E. (1983) 'Aphasia: information processing in language production and reception', in Butterworth, B. (ed.) *Language Production* vol. 2. Academic Press, New York & London: 225–56.

Cromer, R. (1974) 'The development of language and cognition: the cognition hypothesis', in Foss, B. (ed.) *New Perspectives in Child Development*. Penguin Books, Harmondsworth: 184–242.

Crystal, D. (1980) *An Introduction to Language Pathology*, Edward Arnold, London.

Crystal, D. (1981) *Clinical Linguistics*, Springer, Vienna & New York.

Crystal, D. (1982) *Profiling Language Disability*, Edward Arnold, London.

Crystal, D. (1984) *Linguistic Encounters with Language Handicap*, Basil Blackwell, Oxford.

Crystal, D. (1987) 'Towards a "bucket" theory of language disability: taking account of interaction between linguistic levels', *Clinical Linguistics and Phonetics*, 1: 7–22.

Crystal, D., Fletcher, P., and Garman, M. (1981) *The Grammatical Analysis of Language Disability*, Edward Arnold, London. (Revised edition).

Crystal, D., Fletcher, P., and Garman, M. (1989) *The Grammatical Analysis of Language Disability* (second edition), Cole and Whurr, London.

Edwards, S. (1987) 'Assessment and therapeutic intervention in a case of Wernicke's aphasia', *Aphasiology*, 1: 271–6.

Enderby, P. and Philipp, R. (1986) 'Speech and language handicap: towards knowing the size of the problem', *British Journal of Disorders of Communication*, 21: 151–65.

Feilberg, J. (1987) 'Pragmatic assessment of children's communication'. Paper prepared for the Workshop on Communicative Disorders, Fourth International Congress for the Study of Child Language, Lund, July.

Fletcher, P. (1981) 'Description and explanation in the acquisition of verb-forms', *Journal of Child Language*, 8: 93–108.

Fletcher, P. (1983) 'From sound to syntax: a learner's guide', in *Proceedings of the Fourth Annual Wisconsin Symposium on Research in Child Language Disorders*, University of Wisconsin, Madison: 1–29.

Fletcher, P. (1985) *A Child's Learning of English*, Basil Blackwell/André Deutsch, Oxford.

Fletcher, P. (1987) 'The basis of language impairment: a comment on Chiat and Hirson', *British Journal of Disorders of Communication*, 22: 65–72.

Fletcher, P. and Garman, M. (eds) (1986) *Language Acquisition: Studies in First Language Development*, Cambridge University Press, Cambridge.

Fletcher, P. and Garman, M. (1988) 'Normal language development and language impairment: syntax and beyond', in *Clinical Linguistics and Phonetics*, 2: 97–114.

Fletcher, P. and Peters, J. (1984) 'Characterising language impairment in children: an exploratory study', *Language Testing*, 1: 33–49.

Gardner, H. (1974) *The Shattered Mind*, Random House, New York.

Garman, M. (1982) 'Is Broca's aphasia a phonological deficit?', in Crystal D. (ed.) *Linguistic Controversies*, Edward Arnold, London: 152–71.

Garman, M. (1989) *Psycholinguistics*, Cambridge University Press, Cambridge.

Gathercole, V. (1986) 'The acquisition of the present perfect: explaining differences in the speech of Scottish and American children', *Journal of Child Language*, 13: 537–60.

Gimson, A. (1970) *An Introduction to the Pronunciation of English*, Edward Arnold, London.

Gleason, J.B., Goodglass, H., Obler, L., Hyde, M., and Weintraub, S. (1977) 'Narrative strategies of aphasic and normal-speaking subjects', *Journal of Speech & Hearing Research*, 23: 370–82.

Goodglass, H. and Menn, L. (1985) 'Is agrammatism a unitary phenomenon?', in Kean, M-L. (ed.) *Agrammatism*. Academic Press, New York: 1–26.

Goodluck, H. (1986) 'Language acquisition and linguistic theory', in Fletcher, P. and Garman, M. (1986): 49–68.

Grunwell, P. (1987) *Clinical Phonology*, Croom Helm, London. (1st edn 1982.)

Grunwell, P. (1985a) 'Comments on the terms "phonetics" and "phonology" as applied in the investigation of speech disorders', *British Journal of Disorders of Communication*, 20: 165–70.

Grunwell, P. (1985b) *Phonological Assessment of Child Speech (PACS)*, NFER-Nelson, Windsor.

Grunwell, P. (1988) 'Phonological assessment, evaluation and explanation of speech disorders in children', *Clinical Linguistics and Phonetics*, 2: 221–52.

Haas, W. (1963) 'Phonological analysis of a case of dyslalia', *Journal of Speech & Hearing Disorders*, 28: 239–46.

Hardcastle, W., Morgan Barry, R., and Clark, C. (1987) 'An instrumental phonetic study of lingual activity in articulation-disordered children', *Journal of Speech & Hearing Research*, 30: 171–84.

Hardcastle, W. and Morgan, R. (1982) 'Experimental investigation of articulatory disorders in children', *British Journal of Disorders of Communication*, 17: 47–65.

Hewlett, N. (1985) 'Phonological versus phonetic disorders: some suggested modification to the current use of the distinction', *British Journal of Disorders of Communication*, 20: 61–74.

Ingram, D. (1972) 'The acquisition of the English verbal auxiliary and the copula in normal and linguistically deviant children', *Papers and Reports on Child Language Development*, 4: 79–91.

Ingram, D. (1981) *Procedures for the Phonological Analysis of Children's Language*, University Park Press, Baltimore, Md.

Ingram, D. (1987) 'Categories of phonological disorder', in *Proceedings of the First*

*International Symposium on Specific Speech and Language Disorders in Children*, AFASIC, London.

Jakobson, R. (1968) *Child Language, Aphasia and Phonological Universals*, (trans. A. Keiler), Mouton, The Hague. First published 1941 as *Kindersprache, Aphasie und Allgemeine Lautgesetze.*

Johnston, J. (1985) 'Cognitive prerequisities: the evidence from children learning English', in Slobin, D.I. (ed.) *The Crosslinguistic Study of Language Acquisition*, vol. 2, Erlbaum, Hillsdale, NJ: 961–1004.

Johnston, J. and Kamhi, A. (1984) 'Syntactic and semantic aspects of the utterances of language-impaired children: the same can be less', *Merill-Palmer Quarterly*, 30: 65–85.

Johnston, J. and Schery, T. (1976) 'The use of grammatical morphemes by children with communication disorders', in Morehead, D. and Morehead, A. (eds) *Normal and Deficient Child Language*, University Park Press, Baltimore: 239–58.

Johnston, J. and Weismer, S. (1983) 'Mental rotation abilities in language-disordered children', *Journal of Speech & Hearing Research*, 26: 397–403.

Kean, M-L. (1977) 'The linguistic interpretation of aphasic syndromes: agrammatism in Broca's aphasia, an example', *Cognition*, 5: 9–46.

Kertesz, A. (1979) *Aphasia and Associated Disorders: Taxonomy, Localisation and Recovery.* Grune & Stratton, New York.

Leonard, L. (1985) 'Unusual and subtle phonological behaviour in the speech of phonologically disordered children', *Journal of Speech and Hearing Disorders*, 50: 4–13.

Leonard, L., Sabbadini, L., Volterra, A., and Leonard, J. (1987) 'Influences on the sentence use of English- and Italian-speaking children with specific language impairment'. Paper presented at the Fourth International Congress for the Study of Child Language, Lund, July.

Locke, J. (1980) 'The inference of speech perception in the phonologically disordered child. Part 1: a rationale, some criteria, the conventional tests. Part 2: some clinically novel procedures, their use, some findings', *Journal of Speech & Hearing Disorders*, 45, 431–68.

Locke, J. (1983) 'Clinical phonology: the explanation and treatment of sound disorders', *Journal of Speech and Hearing Disorders*, 48: 339–41.

McTear, M. (1985) 'Pragmatic disorders: a case study of conversational disability', *British Journal of Disorders of Communication*, 20: 129–42.

Macken, M. and Barton, D. (1980) 'A longitudinal study of the acquisition of the voicing contrast in American English word-initial stops, as measured by voice onset time', *Journal of Child Language*, 7: 41–74.

Magnusson, E. (1983) *The Phonology of Language Disordered Children: Production, Perception and Awareness*, CWK Gleerup, Lund.

Menn, L. (1987) 'Theoretical issues in phonological development'. Paper presented at the Symposium on Research in Child Language Disorders, University of Wisconsin-Madison, May.

Miller, J. (1985) 'Language and communication characteristics of children with Down's Syndrome'. Paper prepared for *Down's Syndrome: State of the Art Conference*, Boston, April. (To appear in Crocker, A. *et al.* (eds) *Down's Syndrome: State of the Art*, Brooks Publishing Co, Baltimore, Md.)

Miller, J. (1987) 'A grammatical characterisation of language disorder', in *Proceedings of the First International Symposium on Specific Speech and Language Disorders in Children*, AFASIC, London: 100–13.

Miller, J., Campbell, T., Chapman, R. and Weismer, S. (1984) 'Language behavior in acquired childhood aphasia', in Holland, A. (ed.) *Language Disorders in Children*, NFER-Nelson, Windsor: 56–99.

Morehead, D. and Ingram, D. (1973) 'The development of base syntax in normal and linguistically deviant children', *Journal of Speech and Hearing Research*, 16: 330–52. Reprinted in Morehead, D.M. and Morehead, A.E. (eds) (1976) *Normal and Deficient Child Language*, University Park Press, Baltimore: 209–38.

Penn, C. and Behrmann, M. (1986) 'Towards a classification scheme for aphasic syntax', *British Journal of Disorders of Communication*, 21: 21–38.

Quirk Report (1972) *Speech Therapy Services*, HMSO, London.

Quirk, R., Greenbaum, S., Leech, G. and Svartvik, J. (1972) *A Grammar of Contemporary English*, Longman, London.

Rapin, I, (1982) *Children with Brain Dysfunction*, Raven Press, New York.

Rapin, I, and Allen, D. (1987) 'Developmental dysphasia and autism in pre-school children: characteristics and sub-types', in *Proceedings of the First International Symposium on Specific Speech and Language Disorders in Children*, AFASIC, London: 20–35.

Robinson, R. (1987) 'Introduction and overview', in *Proceedings of the First International Symposium on Specific Speech and Language Disorders in Children*, AFASIC, London: 1–19.

Rondal, J. (1987) 'Language development and mental retardation', in Yule, W. and Rutter, M. (eds) *Language Development and Disorders*, Clinics in Developmental Medicine no. 101/102 (Blackwell Scientific Publications), Mackeith Press, Oxford.

Rutter, M. (1987) 'Developmental language disorders: some thoughts on causes and correlates', in *Proceedings of the First International Symposium on Specific Speech and Language Disorders in Children*, AFASIC, London: 48–53.

Shriberg, L. and Kwiatowski, J. (1980) *Natural Process Analysis: a Procedure for Phonological Analysis of Continuous Speech Samples*, John Wiley & Sons, New York.

Shriberg, L., Kwiatowski, J., Best, S., Hengst, J., and Terselic-Weber, B. (1986) 'Characteristics of children with phonologic disorders of unknown origin', *Journal of Speech and Hearing Disorders*, 51: 140–61.

Smith, N. (1973) *The Acquisition of Phonology: a Case Study*, Cambridge University Press, Cambridge.

Snowling, M. (1987) 'The assessment of reading problems in specific language impairment, in *Proceedings of the First International Symposium on Specific Speech and Language Disorders in Children*, AFASIC, London: 148–61.

Sinksen, P. (1979) 'The neurodevelopmental and paediatric findings associated with significant disabilities of language development in pre-school children'. MD dissertation, London University.

Stampe, D. (1969) 'The acquisition of phonetic representation'. *Papers from the Fifth Regional Meeting of the Chicago Linguistic Society*: 443–54.

Steckol, K. and Leonard, L. (1979) 'The use of grammatical morphemes by normal and language-impaired children', *Journal of Communication Disorders*, 12: 291–301.

Stephany, M. (1986) 'Modality', in Fletcher and Garman (1986): 375–400.

Stoel-Gammon, C. and Harrington, P. (1987) 'Vowel productions of normally developing and phonologically disordered children'. Paper presented at the Symposium on Research in Child Language Disorders, University of Wisconsin-Madison, May.

Tallal, P. (1987) 'The neuropsychology of developmental language disorders' in *Proceedings of the First International Symposium on Specific Speech and Language Disorders in Children*. AFASIC, London: 36–47.

Tallal, P. and Piercy, M. (1973) 'Defects of non-verbal auditory perception in children with developmental aphasia', *Nature*, 241: 468–9.

Tallal, P., Stark, R., and Mellits, D. (1985) 'The relationship between auditory temporal analysis and receptive language development: evidence from studies of developmental language disorder', *Neuropsychologia*, 23: 314–22.

Weismer, G. (1984) 'Acoustic analysis strategies for the refinement of phonologic analysis', in Elbert, M., Dinnsen, D. and Weismer, G. (eds) *Phonological Theory and the Misarticulating Child*, ASHA Monographs 22: 30–52.

Wells, G. (1979) 'Learning and using the auxiliary verb in English', in Lee, V. (ed.) *Language Development*, Croom Helm, London: 250–70.

Wells, G. (1986) 'Variation in child language', in Fletcher and Garman (1986): 109–39.

## FURTHER READING

Davis, Albyn G. (1983) *A survey of adult aphasia*, Prentice-Hall, Englewood Cliffs, NJ.

Yule, W. and Rutter, M. (eds) (1987) *Language development and disorders*, Clinics in Developmental Medicine no. 101/102. (Blackwell Scientific Publications.) Mackeith Press, Oxford.

and various papers, widely noted above, in:

*Proceedings of the First International Symposium on Specific Speech and Language Disorders in Children*, AFASIC, London (347 Central Market, Smithfield, London ECIA 9NH).

# 13

# LANGUAGE AND BEHAVIOUR: ANTHROPOLOGICAL LINGUISTICS

### EDGAR C. POLOMÉ

As students of man in his individual and social behavioural patterns, anthropologists have always considered linguistics as an important subfield of their discipline, and such prominent anthropologists as Boas, Sapir or Kroeber have been pioneers in linguistic research in specific areas. For three decades now, scholars concerned with language from an anthropological perspective have found an appropriate outlet for their views and discussions in the journal *Anthropological Linguistics*, published by the Anthropology Department of Indiana University at Bloomington, and papers on kinship systems, speech styles and registers, conversational analysis, semantic anthropology, the ethnography of speech, language and culture and related topics have appeared in *American Anthropologist*, the *International Journal of American Linguistics, Language in Society* and even the standard strictly linguistic journals. Quoting Malinowski and Sapir, Michael Silverstein (1975: 157) defined anthropological linguistics as the study of speech behaviour as it is recognised in society. To account for social behaviour, anthropologists resort to a conceptual system labelled 'culture', whereas linguists refer to a conceptual system called 'grammar'. Both have an, as yet, not quite thoroughly explored psychological foundation, but, as Silverstein points out, 'both grammar and culture are manifested only in society'. This implies that the anthropological linguist needs to associate the ways of speaking of definite groups with the corresponding cultural factors to get the full meaning of the messages they convey. It also entails the necessity for the linguist to understand fully the 'function' of the speech forms whose grammatical patterns he analyses.

Except for the 'semanticists', concerned, for example, with 'conversational implicature', modern linguistic theory has paid little attention to the contextual aspect of language use which is the central concern of the anthropo-logical linguist. A survey of linguistic science like W.O. Dingwall's (1970) leaves it out completely, and an extensive handbook like the *Lexikon der Germanistischen Linguistik* allocates 7 pages out of 870 (in its second edition (1980) to 'ethnolinguistics', more than half of them being actually devoted to the Neo-Humboldtian concept of *inhaltsbezogene Grammatik*, as elaborated by Leo Weisgerber in the successive editions of *Von den Kräften der deutschen Sprache* (1949–1954, 1957–1962). More interested in the relation between language and culture are the linguists working in the applied field of language teaching, but the kind of *Linguistics across cultures* described, e.g. by Robert Lado (1957) is strictly pedagogically orientated and of rather limited relevance to anthro-pological linguistics proper. They have, however, paved the way for very important investigations in the methods to cope with cultural diversity in education (cf. e.g. Abrahams-Troike 1972).

Language, culture and society are approached in different ways by the anthropologists. There is language and culture *per se*, and here the discussion may focus on the function of language as a way of defining experience for its speakers along the lines of the 'Sapir-Whorfian' hypothesis, or on the comparability of specific features of society like kinship systems to linguistic structures as Lévi-Strauss (1963: 54–96) suggested, or on 'ethnoscience' and the folk–taxonomies in (ethno)botany, (ethno)zoology and the like. Then, there is language in society where the details of the role of language in social interaction will be analysed (see Chapter 14, below), but the proper domain of the ethnography of speaking will then have to be defined versus the area of sociolinguistics.

The label 'Sapir-Whorfian hypothesis' has often been rejected as a misnomer because of the divergent views Sapir and Whorf held about the relationship of language to culture, as Landar (1966: 216–224) indicates. However, in his 1928 paper on 'The Status of Linguistics as a Science,' Sapir proclaimed:

'In a sense, the network of cultural patterns of a civilization is indexed in the language which expresses that civilization. It is an illusion to think that we can understand the significant outlines of a culture through sheer observation and without the guide of the linguistic symbolism which makes these outlines significant and intelligible to society . . . Language is a guide to 'social reality' . . . it powerfully conditions all our thinking about social problems and processes. Human beings do not live in the objective world alone, nor alone in the world of social activity as ordinarily understood, but are very much at the mercy of the particular language which has become the means of expres-sion for their society . . . The fact of the matter is that the 'real world' is to a large extent unconsciously built up on the language habits of the group. No two languages are ever sufficiently similar to be considered as representing the same social reality. The worlds in which different societies live are distinct worlds, not merely the same world with different labels attached.' (Mandelbaum 1960: 68–9)

On this foundation, Benjamin Lee Whorf elaborated his theory of 'linguistic relativity' which states that 'the automatic, involuntary patterns of language are not the same for all men, but are specific of each language and constitute the formalized side of the language, or its "grammar,"' and that 'users of markedly different grammars are pointed by their grammars toward different types of observations and different evaluations of externally similar acts of observation, and hence are not equivalent as observers, but must arrive at somewhat different views of the world'. (Carroll 1956: 221)

The principle that not all observers 'are led by the same physical evidence to the same picture of the universe, unless their linguistic backgrounds are similar, or can in some way be calibrated' (Carroll 1956:214) was a source of considerable debate: no fewer than two major conferences (Hoijer 1954, Pinxten 1976) were devoted to the examination of all the implications of the hypothesis with regard to language, logic and thinking, and with reference to the views of Piaget and Schaff on the relation between language and thought. 'Relativists' were confronted with 'universalists' which led to a greater awareness of the narrowness of exclusively universalistic or relativistic approaches and to a clearer formulation of the extent to which the concept of 'linguistic relativity' could be applied. Actually, in 1960, Joshua Fishman had already defined a set of levels on which the Whorfian hypothesis applied to illustrate how language codifies experience:

(*a*) vocabularies reflect culturally relevant categories: one does not expect Eskimos to have a wide variety of terms for trees, nor is one surprised if hunter-gatherer tribes possess a wide variety of terms to designate very specifically the different ways they catch their game. This is obviously the reason why linguists, operating with Swadesh's original lexicostatistic list of allegedly not-culture-bound terms, run into problems when inquiring about lexical items like 'hunt' in the equatorial rain forest, not to mention 'ice' or 'snow'.

This feature of linguistic codification is particularly evident in translation, where one is concerned with finding an adequate language-to-language correspondence: a French *bistro* is not an English *pub*, which partly accounts for such pervasive loanwords as *le drugstore* or for hybrid derivations like *disco-thèque*. Similarly, the translators of Chairman Mao's 'Little Red Book' into Swahili had to coin a whole set of new terms to render the political jargon of Chinese communism, and rather unexpected innovations became popular, e.g. *wabenzi* for 'capitalists', i.e. the elite group that rides in Mercedes-*Benz* cars. This latter case links up with Fishman's second level, implying namely:

(*b*) a definite correspondence between linguistic phenomena and specific non-linguistic responses. Howell and Vetter (1976: 361) discuss this point further with relation to colour names: it has long been noted that individuals presented with a range of colours will readily label sections of this range with single terms, lumping together, e.g. various shades of grey simply under 'grey', and a Japanese, for example, will label *aoi* what we describe as 'blue' (e.g. the sky) or as 'green' (e.g. edible seaweed). Does that mean the subjects *see* the colours as they label them? Apparently, the colour spectrum is segmented differently according to cultural conventions, and the members of specific cultures are assumed to perceive and label colours according to the relevant segmentation of the spectrum. However, cross-cultural examination of the perception of colour location on the spectrum indicates substantial agreement between cultures, i.e. they recognise the yellowest yellow in the same place, but disagree on the limits of the domain of each colour they perceive. That these boundaries also vary through time within one culture has been shown by the diachronic investigation of colour names in the Indo-European languages, especially in Latin (cf. André 1949, Vermeer 1963).

Whereas Fishman's first two levels dealt with the lexicon, examining the correlation between the linguistic code and the cultural data, his further ones examine:

(*c*) the relationship between language structure and cultural behaviour – a point that Whorf emphasised by showing that English segments an utterance in lexemes which isolate part of the experience, whereas a Nootka 'sentence' would encompass the whole event-complex in a single verbal sequence, e.g. *tl'imshya'isita'itlma*, corresponding to English *he invites people to a feast*, but meaning actually: 'he (= someone) goes for (= invites) eaters of cooked food,' on the basis of the following analysis: *tl'imsh* 'boiling, cooking' + the resultative *-ya* (= cooked) + *-'is* 'eating' + *ita* 'those who do' (= eaters of [cooked food]) + *-'itl* 'going for' + *ma* (= 3rd person singular indicative) (Carroll 1956: 240–3).

Referring to the findings of Kluckhohn about Navaho culture, Hoijer (1954: 100–2) stressed that the Navaho lives 'in a universe of eternal and unchanging forces with which he attempts to maintain an equilibrium', and some aspects of the verbal structure of his language seem to reflect his concern about disturbing the delicate balance of the powers in the activities of daily life, e.g. by contrasting the two forms of the second person of the perfective: *nínłį* 'you have lain down' versus *nišíłłį* 'you have put me down.' In the second case, the causative *-ł-* and the first person object *-ší-* are incorporated in the verbal form. The first form actually means: 'one animate being moves to a position of rest', whereas the second specifies that the agent 'causes movement of one animate being to end at a given point' – the persons involved being conceived as members of certain classes of beings rather than as mere 'actors' and 'goals'. The behaviour of human beings thus appears to be reported under reference to their assignment to the established division of nature into classes of entities in action or movement.

Commenting on these views, Howell and Vetter (1976: 363) point to the experiment Carroll and Casagrande conducted with Navaho children and Boston middle-class white children of the same age group: taking two sets of Navahos, one speaking primarily their native tongue, and the other using English as their first language, they submitted them to shape/colour-association tests geared to find out whether they would group the objects according to shape, as the Navaho verb forms would suggest, or according to colour. The Navaho-speaking children prevalently chose according to shape, as predicted by the Whorfian hypothesis, but the Bostonian control group did it even more! The explanation lay in the early exposure of the white middle-class children to toys focusing on shape recognition, as was confirmed by testing New York black children from Harlem, who responded like the Navaho children with English as their first language, choosing prevalently according to colour. As Howell and Vetter (1976: 364) remark, even in the grimiest slums, children are exposed to a variety of shapes, so that what seems determining is 'the extent to which they are encouraged to manipulate them'. Therefore, Fishman (1960) points out that there are degrees of *linguistic relativity*, and what is important is to find out to what extent the Whorfian hypothesis applies effectively to the relations between language structure and non-linguistic behaviour.

In certain respects, the matter is crucial for the historico-comparative linguist: the reconstruction of the social institutions of prehistoric linguistic communities like the Indo-Europeans rests indeed on the assumption that their language reflects the essential concepts on the basis of which the whole network of socio-economic relations operated, as well as the ideology underlying the internal structure of the society, motivating (at least partly) the elaboration of their pantheon. The patient and detailed analysis of the lexicon by Emile Benveniste (1960, 1973) has indeed enabled him to describe the whole system of personal relations within the family and the clanic and tribal society of the Indo-Europeans, defining their kinship system, specifying the contractual obligations involved in the exchange of services and goods, stipulating the rights and duties pertaining to the ruler, besides distinguishing the various ways to honour the deities and providing valuable information on animal husbandry. The hierarchisation of society in three functional levels which he and Georges Dumézil proposed, became the foundation for the latter's new analysis of the Indo-European mythological tradition (Littleton 1982). While discussing the basic Indo-European 'tripartite' ideology, Georges Dumézil frequently pointed to the close linkage of definite lexical items with the level of society which he has defined, e.g. the words for 'man' *(H,)ner-* and *w̆īro-*, which he related respectively with the 'second' (= warrior) function and the 'third' (= fertility/production) (Dumézil 1969: 225–41). More recently Thomas V. Gamkrelidze and Vjačeslav V. Ivanov (1984) stressed the binarism characteristic of various aspects of Indo-European life and culture and saw a reflection of this original binary conceptualisation of the cosmos in such features as the opposition between 'animate' and 'inanimate' which predates the traditional gender distinction in masculine, feminine and neuter. Such simple patterns can obviously not account for the complexity of Indo-European culture and the language that carried it (cf. Polomé 1988), although the study of preliterate societies demonstrates how their world view and basic ideology may affect every aspect of their material civilisation and socio-cultural life as well as the way they express them, as has been shown, e.g. for the Dogon of West Africa by Geneviève Calame-Griaule (1965).

The Lévi-Straussian paradigm has proved particularly challenging in the study of myth (Lévi-Strauss 1955), even if it required some reformulation, as has been suggested, e.g. by Willis (1967), and semanticists like Greimas (1963) have shown how it can apply to the structural analysis of the complex mythological patterns described by Georges Dumézil. The structural interdependence between kinship systems and the relevant nomenclature, stressed by Lévi-Strauss (1963: 29–52), is illustrated, e.g. by the case of the Indo-European *avunculate*, as described by Benveniste (1969: 223–35, 1973: 182–90): cross-cousin marriage accounts for the fact that the same person can be the paternal grandfather and the brother of the mother's mother; therefore, in Latin, the maternal uncle is called *avunculus*, literally 'little grandfather' ('grandfather' = *avus*), and *nepōs* designates both the nephew and the grandson. However, Lévi-Strauss was apparently more interested in the cultural patterning that accounts for the high valuation of the maternal uncle, as in the case of the ancient Germanic people according to Tacitus (*Germania*, chap. 20: 'The sons of sisters are shown as much regard by their uncles as by their own fathers. Some tribes even consider the former tie as closer and more sacred . . .'), and he accounted for it within the unity of the system where the bond between maternal uncle and nephew seems reinforced when the bond between father and son is weakened, and where a strong tabuisation of the father figure may entail extreme familiarity in relation to the uncle.

Anthropologists are indeed interested in the organising principles underlying behavioural patterns, and assuming, with Ward H. Goodenough (1957), that every society has its own system for perceiving and organising phenomena such as kinship type, or material things, events, behaviour and emotions, they try to determine *which* phenomena are significant for the people of a definite culture and *how* these people organise them according to distinctive principles of classification. Goodenough (1971) pointed out that behaviour is 'purposive', and for their most recurring purposes, people develop recipes – recipes for all kinds of behaviour, from setting the table for a family meal to wooing a person of the opposite sex. Recipes differ from routines and customs, in so far as they refer to the ideas presiding over the ways to do things, whereas routines and customs relate only to the execution of the relevant behaviour, e.g. the specific way to put the dishes, glasses and silverware on the table. If one 'routine' is deliberately chosen in preference to others and regularly applied, it becomes a 'custom'. Thus, Goodenough establishes a 'grammar of culture' providing rules for the generation of patterns of behaviour (Howell and Vetter 1976:376–7).

To apply the methodology of grammatical analysis to cultural patterns, the anthropologist has to proceed to a componential analysis of the cognitive structure he examines (cf. Goodenough 1956). Aware of the fact that the phenomena of the perceptual world can be grouped subjectively into classes, which, in turn, can be organised into larger – hierarchically arranged – groupings to form a *taxonomy*, he will focus on significant taxonomies, constituting a semantic domain, as, for example, 'animals' in American English (Tyler 1969: 7–10) according to the table of Sydney Lamb (1964: 68):

|  |  |  |  |
| --- | --- | --- | --- |
| ANIMAL Livestock | | | |
| cattle | horse | sheep | swine |
| cow | mare | ewe | sow |
| bull | stallion | ram | boar |
| steer | gelding | wether | barrow |
| heifer | filly | | gilt |
| calf | colt | lamb | shoat |
| | foal | | piglet |

It is obvious that the sequence in each column (representing one of the major categories of livestock) is the same: generic term, female, male, neutered male, 'adolescent' female, immature animal, new-born animal. This can be expressed in features as follows:

| | | | |
| --- | --- | --- | --- |
| stallion | H ♂ M–1 | boar | P ♂ M–1 |
| mare | H ♀ M–1 | sow | P ♀ M–1 |
| gelding | H ø M–1 M–2 | barrow | P ø M–1 M–2 |
| filly | H ♀ M–2 | gilt | P ♀ M–2 |
| colt | H ♂ M–3 | shoat | P ♂ M–3 |
| foal | H ♂♀ M–4 | piglet | P ♂♀ M–4 |

(♂ = male; ♀ = female; M–1 = adult; M–2 = adolescent; M–3 = child; M–4 = child; H = horse; P = swine; C would be 'cattle', and S 'sheep')

This paradigm can also be organised in a matrix pattern or under the form of a tree. Each semantic domain of a culture can be organised in a similar way:

the main problem for the anthropologist is to discover the semantic domains and their features. In almost Whorfian terms, Tyler (1969: 11) defines the goal of the researcher as the discovery of the order underlying the apparent chaos of the alien world he is confronted with. *Cognitive anthropology* provides him with a methodology to discover and describe these principles of organisation.

Kinship terminology has been one of the major paradigms analysed structurally according to these principles: a model was proposed by Floyd G. Lounsbury (1964), and componential analysis was widely applied to kin relationships, e.g. by Ward H. Goodenough, whose seminal papers (such as Goodenough 1965a) led to further deepening of the analytic procedure as well as to rethinking and critique of some aspects and implications of the method (the papers collected by Tyler (1969) abundantly illustrate this, e.g. Romney and D'Andrade 1964; Burling 1964; Schneider 1965; Wallace 1960, 1965; etc.). Goodenough (1969) even went a step further, suggesting another analytical method aimed at a 'grammatical aspect' of normative behaviour in a systematic and exhaustive description of the cultural domain of 'status' and 'role' in social relationships. But leaving aside the idiom of kinship whose privileged position in structural-functional analysis of cultural anthropologists was perhaps overstated in the recent past (cf. Schneider 1984), a further investigation of the wider field of language and ethnography, as defined, e.g. by Charles O. Frake (1962, 1964), and avoiding the pitfalls of cognitive anthropology (Frake 1977), is definitely appropriate to our theme.

The study of a culture's 'technical' terminology will not reveal all the aspects of its cognitive world, but it will indicate its significant features communicable in the standard symbolic system of the culture: categories of objects will be 'segregated', and within these categories, contrasting sets will be identified, which will then be organised into a *taxonomy*, based on the 'attributes' of the members of the sets, e.g. the Subanum of Mindanao (Philippines) will classify plants as follows (Frake 1980: 12):

| Contrast Set | Dimension of Contrast | |
| --- | --- | --- |
| | Woodiness | Rigidity |
| *gavu* 'woody plants' | + | − |
| *sigbet* 'herbaceous plants' | − | + |
| *belagen* 'vines' | − | − |

Complex taxonomies can be elaborated in this way: having determined the levels of contrast in 'skin disease' among the Subanum, Frake (1980: 111–26) goes on to examine the criterial contrasts in the subgroup of 'sores', which will motivate the diagnostic questions and trigger a range of contrasting answers: there are levels of 'depth', 'distality', 'severity', and 'spread'. Thus, a *telemaw glai* will be a 'shallow distal ulcer', single and severe, like the *baga'* which is a 'shallow proximal ulcer'; if the sore is mild, it is simply called *beldut* which is the generic term for 'sore', but if there are several of them, their name becomes *selimbunut*. If the patient wants to indicate that the ulceration is deep, he will resort to *telemaw glibun* for a 'distal' one, and to *begwak* for a 'proximal' one. Of course, since the real world of disease does not provide such neat distinctions, there may be some argument as to whether an ulcer is a *baga'* or a *begwak*, which is why the Subanum usually consult several people for diagnostics. The fact remains that, as Frake stresses (1980: 128), the conceptual world of disease is exhaustively divided into a set of mutually exclusive categories.

The importance of classificatory categorisations in the study of language has been enhanced by the analysis of the classifiers occurring in a number of languages in South-East Asia as well as in several American Indian languages: thus, Mary A. Haas (1967) shows that the basic covert Yurok dichotomy of the world into 'living beings' (= animate) and 'objects' (= inanimate) is evidenced by the classifiers of that language. Only humans and animals are included in the categorisation by 'animate' classifiers, whereas the plants are not: among the 'inanimate' classifiers, a distinction is made between 'bushlike' objects and 'sticklike' or straight objects, which corresponded to the Yurok division of the plant kingdom into (*a*) plants and bushes, and (*b*) trees and ferns. Furthermore, there are categories of round, ropelike, flat, pointed, amorphous objects, which enable the Yurok to classify rocks, silver dollars, drums, hats, flowers, berries, nuts, necks, etc. under the label 'round' objects, etc. For specific things, there are special categories, e.g. for houses, for boats and boat-shaped objects, etc. Thus, the system is strongly, although not exclusively, orientated towards shape-differentiation. In other languages, like Hupa, this classificatory system manifests itself in special sets of verb-stems rather than suffixes, which explains what was stated above about Navaho-speaking children.

Underlying semantic taxonomies also account for peculiarities in the class system of the Bantu languages: in the basic system that we can reconstruct (Polomé 1967: 16), mass nouns are apparently separated from individualised items, and the latter can be described as to their size, location, or some distinctive feature, or considered as separate entities or part of groups of two or more. Separate entities are divided into animate and inanimate, but the animate are subcategorised into those that act autonomously and those which do not. Although part of the system may have been lost or blurred in the individual languages, the underlying structure is still widely recognisable, e.g. in Swahili, where the *ma*-class still expresses the idea of totality and serves therefore as pluraliser for the *ji*-class which indicates specifically one object of a set of two, e.g. *jicho* 'eye', plural *macho*. The *n(i)*-class still defines entities by their most characteristic feature, e.g. animals like *mbega* 'colobus,' a monkey whose typical feature is his white shoulders (*mabega*), or *nyuki* 'bee', an insect whose main activity is to produce 'honey' (= [archaic] *uki*, now replaced by the Arabic loanword *asali*). There are two *m(u)*-classes: one, with a corresponding *wa*-plural, designates exclusively human beings; the other, with a *mi*-plural, provides some insight on the animistic world view of the Bantu, as it contains characteristically animated parts of the body like the heart (*moyo*), the limbs (*mkono* 'arm, hand,' *mguu* 'leg, foot'), the tail (of an animal) (*mkia*), etc.; plants and trees (e.g. *mnazi* 'coconut-tree'); natural phenomena (e.g. *moto* 'fire,' *mto* 'river,' *mwezi* 'moon,' etc.); a few names of animals (e.g. *mjusi* 'lizard') – but most striking is the fact that the term for 'prophet, apostle,' *mtume*, plural *mitume*, belongs here, as it designates him as a (non-autonomous) person acting as the instrument of a higher power. Inanimate objects belong generally to the *ki*-class (plural *vi*): thus, *mti*, plural *miti*, is a 'tree,' but a 'stool' – the object made of its wood – is called *kiti*; noticeable is the fact that the terms designating persons with physical defects which deprive them of any personal status in the society, are marked by the prefix for things, in a derogatory sense, e.g. *kilema* 'cripple,' *kipofu* 'blind,' etc.

Although semantic theory as initially treated by Katz and Fodor (1963) analyses the lexicon according to a model close to the anthropologists' componential analysis (cf. Eastman 1975: 111–12), the Chomskyan revolution had an essentially dampening influence on anthropological linguistic research as it was carried on in the sixties (Haas 1978), as the interest in doing field work waned and research was focused on English and the theoretical issues relating to its syntactically orientated investigation (cf. Davis 1973: 337–80; Sampson 1980: 130–65; Newmeyer 1986: 17–196, 227–9). Nevertheless, as Landar (1966: 107–14) indicated, the efforts of Chomsky towards axiomatisation of language could have an important impact on anthropology: the Peircean vision of the cognisable universe – the 'universe of signs' – is described in what Morris (1946) would call 'the syntactic part of semiotic theory', which 'coordinates formal signs, as facts in the real world, with strings, which are logical entities'. If the specifications of the formalism appear to be inadequate, they – and not the facts – are to be modified (hence, the constant revisions of the theory!). From the very start generative grammarians have been 'anti-taxonomic' because they felt that the post-Bloomfieldian phrase constituent syntactic analysis did not cover a sufficient range of phenomena. They stressed the importance of analysing data in relation to systems, e.g. the systematic relations of distinctive features in generative phonology. One danger of the method is, however, too much reliance on too simple theorems of decomposition – a danger anthropology also needs to overcome to reach its goals in analysing cultural systems. Moreover, as Landar (1966: 114) points out, one of the results of generative theory was 'the discovery of systems for breaking rules', i.e. bases for the production of ungrammatical utterances, which indicate that 'the problems inherent in co-ordinating strings of symbols with facts of experience are not insoluble'.

It is, however, in the *ethnography of speaking* that anthropological linguistics seems to have been most productive and innovative in recent years. Attention has been focused on the communicative competence and performance of individuals and on forms of talk in social interaction. Interested in the essence of communicative behaviour, anthropologists probed into the nature and definition of language: they examined the display repertoires by which non-human species encoded messages and behavioural information, and compared their increasingly formalised signal acts to assess the proper position of human language in the evolutionary scale (Smith 1977). For Greenberg (1971: 271), three characteristics are unique to the latter: multi-modality, duality and semantic universality. The multimodality of language need hardly be emphasised in view of the multiplicity of the world's languages (cf. Voegelin 1977, Ruhlen 1987); besides the primacy of the spoken word, phonological symbols can be translated into written signs, gestures (namely, in sign language), electrical impulses (namely, in the Morse code), etc.; moreover, human communication can be either declarative or refer-ential. The duality of human language is reflected by its two levels of func-tioning: a 'phonological' level, with a limited set of distinct sound units or inherently meaningless phonemes, and a 'grammatical' level, where the phonemes are clustered into meaningful larger units involved in syntactic constructions. Grammaticity is not, however, exclusively human: bee communication, for example, involves a complex signalling system analysable in terms of a combination of meaningful units, but bee communication is unimodal (Greenberg 1971: 267–8). Moreover, the bee's 'dance' only contains *two* meaningful components referring to the distance of the source of honey by the speed at which it 'draws' its 8-shaped figures, and to the direction by the angle of those figures; its mapping of distance and direction are accord-ingly *iconic*, whereas human language is *symbolic*, i.e. the sounds are arbitrary and, as a rule, not predictable from the meaning.

Communication theory has examined the various aspects of human verbal activity on the level of personal interaction: what devices does the individual resort to to achieve communication? How does the recipient react to the message? The dialectics of oral communicative exchange are analysed in detail (cf. Michel 1986): what is the conscious purpose of the speech act? Does it entail a change in situation? Is that change conditioned by socio-cultural factors? Is there a choice between various means to attain the goal pursued? Is an ethical connotation attached to the action? And so forth. If a three-year-old child asks her mother for a glass of milk, she will expect an immediate response, but if she wants a piece of chocolate, she may go through a whole scenario, identifying herself with a doll that has behaved very well all morning and deserves a reward. Volker Heeschen (1980) aptly compares these behaviours with those of natives of New Guinea or the South American rainforest: a Gururumba (in Papua New Guinea) who wants someone to give him a sweet or something similar, merely says: 'Give me!' The response can be a simple refusal, or the claim by the other person that he does not have the requested object, while he goes through the motion of allegedly looking for it, or the granting of the request when the thing is tossed with scorn to the asker, with the words: 'Take!' Another sociologically motivated behaviour is illustrated by the case of a Waika girl eating berries, when another girl wants to grab some of the fruit. The first girl prevents the other from taking the berries, but as soon as the latter signifies by turning her head and body that she has given up her claim, the first girl gladly shares the fruit with her.

This last example brings us into the domain of non-verbal communication where culturally conditioned behaviours prevail. A considerable amount of work has been done in this field since E.T. Hall (1959) focused attention on the 'silent language' of facial expressions, eye movements, gestures, postures and body movements. Where more traditionally-orientated researchers like Sainsbury (1955), Dittman (1962), Ekman (1964, 1985, and Friesen and Ellsworth 1971) and others concentrated on specific elements of behaviour, especially during psychotherapeutic interviews, and devised procedures to measure them, others, like Scheflen (1964, 1965), applied the *kinesic* method of Birdwhistell (1955) which stresses the independent communicative value of body movements, to analyse and interpret the non-verbal behaviour in its full structural context (cf. Howell and Vetter 1976: 62–86). Various models for non-verbal communication have been proposed, defining

(*a*) the 'parasyntactic' functions involved, namely the segmentation of the flow of speech by non-vocal acts, and the synchronisation of the various patterns of communicative behaviour;

(*b*) the 'parapragmatic' functions, such as the expressions of personal emotions and the reactions to the utterances and behaviour of the other speaker;

(*c*) the 'dialogue' functions, including the regulation of the flow of conversation and the relation with the other speaker (namely: immediacy, relaxation, responsivity; Helfrich and Wallbott 1980).

Gestures are an important part of oral communication: they help people formulate their thoughts (Calame-Griaule 1965: 72). In Africa, gestures have to be learned together with the language: some are obligatory substitutes for words or complement them (Claessen 1985). Thus, in southern Cameroon, one cannot utter a number right out in some circumstances; as a substitute, one uses an appropriate gesture and interjection, and the other speaker says the

number. Thus a Bulu would say: /mebilí bɔ́n hŋ́/ 'I have children ...'
(showing the little finger, the ring finger, and third finger), triggering the
reaction: /béláa/ 'three' (Alexandre 1972: 105).

As Goffman (1981) points out, there is an interplay of three themes in any
verbal exchange:
(*a*) 'ritualisation', reflecting the gestural conventions of the community;
(*b*) 'participation framework', providing the essential background for interaction analysis, as it specifies the (codified) position of those within perceptual range of the speech event and the norm for their appropriate conduct;
(*c*) 'embedding', referring to our linguistic capability to talk about events
remote in time and space and to make utterances whose subject is not
(directly) related to the present occurrence.
Whatever the form of talk, individuals responding to events in the presence of
others will have their glances, body postures and gestures carry all kinds of
implication and meaning, but the human voice in particular lends itself
through tone, pitch, variously positioned pauses and other discourse theatrics
to producing all the desired effects, which can be best illustrated in the technique of an accomplished lecturer or a successful radio-announcer.

Ritualisation is particularly evident in speech events involving interactional strategies in which the actors manœuvre for position: the structure of
greetings in some societies can demonstrate this, as it is determined by the
social distance separating the individuals involved. Examining how status
manipulation affects greetings among the Wolof of Senegal, Irvine (1974)
distinguishes 'self-lowering' and 'self-elevating' procedures based on the
manipulation of a sequence of utterances, each of which is an irreducible unit
within the routine, e.g.

> *Salaam alikum*
> *Malikum salaam*
> > *Ndiaye*      (Exchange of names)
> > *Diop*

The initiator, in a self-deprecatory sequence, starts a line of questioning:

> *Na ngga def?* 'How do you do?'

The respondent can ignore this question and repeat the same to the questioner, who then answers: *Maanggi fi rek* 'I am here only.' This would reverse
the situation, and it occurs therefore in service situations, e.g. when a
customer approaches a shopkeeper and greets him, but the shopkeeper turns
things around in the hope of making a profitable sale. Normally, the pattern
of the exchange calls for questions about the whereabouts and/or health of
the other person's family and friends, and ends with praising God, e.g.

470

*Ana sa dyabar?* 'Where (how) is your wife?'
*Mu-ngga fa.* 'She is there.'
*H'mdillay.* 'Thanks to God.'

If this is followed by *Tubarkalla* 'Blessed be God,' the questioning can start again, and go on for quite a while, according to a set of well established rules: as Sherzer and Bauman (1974: 164) put it, the invariant basic greeting exchange is represented by 'phrase structure rules', and the strategic manipulations, such as occur, by 'transformational rules'.

Communities tend to establish ground rules for oral 'performance'. A whole ritual grammar has codified encounters among the Maori of New Zealand where oratory has attained the status of verbal art (Salmond 1974); pattern of speaking, speech play and verbal art dominate the way of life of the Central American Kuna Indians, providing an organised means of handling problems and of channelling conflicts – both personal and social – into 'carefully controlled talk, in which decorum replaces the open expression of disagreement' (Sherzer 1983: 134). Among the manipulative uses of language, 'speech play' occupies a special position: more than the referential function of language, it stresses its stylistic or 'socio-expressive' function. Whereas in the continuum of verbal communication purely instrumental talk, like the exchanges between an airport controller and a jetliner pilot, maximises efficiency and focuses on the outcome of the communication process (= the safe landing of the plane), in speech play the process has priority over the outcome (Kirshenblatt-Gimblett and Sherzer 1976: 9). The motivation can be merely play, as with the Kuna children (Sherzer 1983), or disguise, as with 'secret' forms of the Caribbean Creole Saramaka (Price 1976). Psychologically as well as ethnically important is the use of wordplay in joking strategies, described by Bricker (1976) for the Zinacantecan Mayan community in the highlands of Chiapas (Mexico), which cleverly makes use of the lack of congruence between the reference and address systems of kinship terms to play the two systems off against each other (their strategies mainly employ the brothers-in-law relationship, as the reference system treats all brothers-in-law as equals, whereas the address system discriminates between those married to older siblings and the spouses of younger siblings).

Anthropological linguistics will investigate the forms of speech that are relevant to each pattern of behaviour – be it verbal duelling (= 'truly frivolous talk', linked with asocial behaviour, among the Chamulas; cf. Gossen 1976), or speaking in riddles, or using the proper canon of style or speech genre in definite contexts, etc. Numerous examples are to be found in such collections of papers on the socio-cultural dimensions of language use and the ethnography of speaking such as Gumperz and Hymes 1972, Sudnow 1972, Bauman and Sherzer 1974, Sanches and Blount 1975.

A special area where anthropological linguistics has opened new perspectives is the field of language and politics: traditionally, the works dealing with that theme (e.g. Edelman 1977, Shapiro 1984, Dallmayr 1984) have focused on the relationship between the political structure and the specific aspects of the contents of the speeches and other linguistic documents pertaining to political life, whether they belong to emerging Third World nations (cf. e.g. O'Barr 1976) or to an advanced western society (cf. e.g. Heringer 1982). More recently, the interest has been more concentrated on *talk as action*, exploring how language works politically in actually creating, rather than merely reflecting, political relationships, and examining in particular the contexts of language use. This has been illustrated, for instance, in a series of papers devoted to the situation in a number of societies in Oceania (Brenneis and Myers 1984), in which the authors study the individual strategies used by the speakers to influence and modify the socio-political context they speak about. Rosaldo (1984) exemplifies this approach by focusing on the relation between the Ilongot oratory (= *purung*) in the Philippines and their cultural view of the 'self' in terms of 'knowledge' and 'anger': *purung* contrasts with ordinary speech by not going directly to the point; it is punctuated by repetitions, flourishes, obscure phrases, metaphors and puns, comparable to a duel or contest, where the speaker skilfully 'circles around' his antagonist with a *liget* ('passion') in order to bring out his 'hidden feelings', which can be allayed, once their source is known!

Referring to the suggestion of Maurice Bloch (1985) that 'formalised language' might have coercive uses in traditional political orders, Atkinson (1984) shows how the Wana farming population of eastern Central Sulawesi in Indonesia uses two-line stanzas called *kiyori*, which can allegedly also come from the spirit world, as elegant disguises or persuasive strategies. Resisting governmental pressure from the 'coastal people', a Wana expressed his refusal to participate in the vote for the national elections in these terms (Atkinson 1984: 43):

| | |
|---|---|
| rani kupansoe witi ri pana nu eo mpili | I want to swing my feet in the rays of the afternoon sun. |
| ndate tondosi nruring pasi ngoyu taa nairi | Up at the perch of the *ruring* bird even the wind does not chill. |

The imagery of the pleasant late afternoon, indicating freedom from heat and cold, symbolises freedom from the Indonesian government and the elections it imposes (*eo mpili* possibly plays upon the Indonesian term for 'election': *pemilihan*). The refuge near the *ruring* bird refers to the mythical bird of the Wana in the magical past, and *ndate* 'up there' points to the contrast between the 'up country' Wana and the *lo'u tasi* ('down at the sea') Indonesian power structure. The implications of the poem are clear: the author prefers the old traditional order to the new rule imposed from the outside!

Central to the ethnography of speaking is a focus on the variety of speech events that occur in a community and a concern with the artistic and symbolic properties of verbal patterns, in particular formal and ritual speech, as well as with the strategies resorted to in face-to-face communicative behaviour. Speech styles, norms and strategies may vary considerably in actual performance, depending on the relevant social and cultural themes. This is illustrated for the Malagasy oratory by Ochs (1973) when she discusses the *kabary* or ceremonial speech used in marriage requests: although there is a basic structure to the scenario, accepted by all members of the community, involving preliminary discussions and an argumentation according to a set of ground rules, with possible adherence to contrastive approaches by the two parties negotiating, there is ample room for variability in the strategy of this verbal match of wits: as the tension between the two families relaxes, there is a 'sliding sense of obligatoriness' to adhering strictly to one way or another, and tolerance and acceptance of many approaches lead ultimately to a successful alliance. The procedure does not progress smoothly; there are emotional peaks in the discussion, but it is this very unpredictability that stimulates the oratory and ultimately brings the performance to a successful conclusion!

Defining the tasks of the ethnography of speaking, Dell Hymes (1974) mentions a fourth important factor, besides (*a*) the 'semantics' of social relationships and verbal forms, (*b*) the detailed study of the handling and function of speech acts within the community, and (*c*) the role of language in the study of kinship, myth, religion, etc., namely (*d*) the linguistic marking of social status and other features of anthropological interest. As a typical example, he contrasts the personal names on Truk, which emphasise the individuality of the person amidst pressing social obligations, with those on Nakani, which 'remind ambitious individuals of social obligations' (cf. Goodenough 1965b). The Italian ethnolinguist G.R. Cardona (1976: 133–55) stresses the importance of name-giving even more, pointing to the social and religious meaning of anthroponyms in various cultures, past and present. A typical example is provided by the individual names in Burundi (Ntahombaye 1983): traditionally, a man would have three names: (*a*) *izina* 'personal name,' often also with a nickname (*itâzirano*); (*b*) a name indicating his belonging to a *urugó* 'enclosure' > 'family group'; (*c*) a name denoting his clanic descent. The personal names may be descriptive, relating to physical or psychological features – with emphasis, in the traditional culture, on the courage and boldness of the warrior – or referential, reminding people of events taking place at the time of birth of the individual, e.g. *inzara*, if there was a famine, or *urwîno*, if there was trouble in the land. Names are also connected with social relations at the level of the family and of the neighbourhood and may refer to the system of reciprocal obligations prevailing in the tribal context, e.g. *ntiruâguma* 'it is not yet securely established' (a reference to the fact that the relations between husband and wife were still somewhat shaky at the time the baby was born); *baranshinyurira* 'they show me their teeth' (from -*shinyura* 'quickly show one's teeth' – pointing to a mocking, hypocritical smile of the neighbours!); *bankwûnguka* 'they hate him who wins' (alluding to the fact that the neighbours are jealous of the prosperity of the family), etc. Particularly interesting is the case of twins in the Bantu context: for most Central African tribes, their birth is a blessing, and their names are therefore predetermined by custom. Thus, in traditional Kongo society, the first-born was called *Nsimba* (from *simba* 'grasp'), and the other *Nzuzi*, but if one of them died, the surviving one would be called *Bole* 'both' instead (the dead one would be symbolically represented by a stick which the mother would wash, put to her breast, lay down to sleep at the same time as the still living baby). If there are triplets, the third is especially sacred: the baKongo call him *Katumwa* 'who cannot be sent away,' because he embodies the good fortune of the tribe; similarly, the baLuba of Kasayi (South Central Zaire) call him *Shikutumwe.* Among the latter, the bena Luluwa had specific names referring to important aspects of clanic life, e.g. *Kapajika* (a syncopated form of the 'constatative' of *kujika* 'be finished,' with the meaning: 'the lineage has not yet completely died out'), to mark the birth of a boy who will ensure the survival of the clan, or *Kalala* (from a verb *kulala* 'have one's turn,' when his clan will obtain the (rotating) chiefdom according to customary law – no longer understood today and connected with *kulala* 'sleep,' as if it meant 'who sleeps, while the others take the decisions'; cf. Polomé 1961).

Language is essential to social interaction, and speech cues provide important information about the speakers (Scherer and Giles 1979), some of them more relevant to other fields of linguistics, e.g. geographical origin, which would relate more closely to dialectology and linguistic geography; age, sex, occupational role, group membership and social status, which would rather belong to the domain of sociolinguistics, although such problems as those of language, gender and society are also germane to the field of investigation of the behavioural scientist (cf. Thorne and Henley 1975, Berryman and Eman 1980, Thorne *et al.* 1983, Smith 1985). Similarly, the features that reveal personal attitudes will interest both the psychologist and the social anthropologist, but lexical labelling reflecting some aspects of ethnic interaction and conflict can also be most instructive for the linguist. Allen (1983) has collected an impressive amount of data illustrating how the vocabulary of ethnic abuse is a response to social diversity, and how its elaboration and expansion is affected by population size and density. Proximity and visibility stimulate prejudice against particular groups of disliked cultural aliens and intensify ethnocentrically motivated social distance. Thus, deprecating terms for

Mexicans in Texas would include *wetbacks*, alluding to the illegal crossing of the border by wading through the Rio Grande, *chilibellies* (*chili* being one of the mainstays of Texan Mexican cuisine), *spicks* (a term applying elsewhere to Latin-Americans in general); white 'Anglos' are called *gringos* by Spanish-speaking Americans, whereas the derogatory term used by blacks for 'whites' is *honkeys*. A large variety of ethnic epithets apply to blacks, from the infamous mispronunciation of *negro* with a slur as [*nigɔ(r)*] to *jiggerboo* (of unknown origin) or *coon* (from *raccoon*, originally a symbol of cleverness; cf. Allen 1983: 19).

But if names can be used as insults, they can also be social markers of ethnic identity: if one examines the ancient tribal names of the Germanic peoples, for example, it appears that, while some merely point to some object that characterises the group, like its 'national' weapon, e.g. for the Saxons, their one-edged sword, called *sahs*, or a physical feature, e.g. the long beards of the *Langobardi*, others bear names that refer to their social status or their personality, e.g. the Franks, presumably 'the free (ones)' (in contrast to their kin under Roman tutelage?), unless the name is related to ON *frakkr* 'courageous'; the *Suebi* (later Swabians), literally 'those of our own people' – a name given in a typical act of ethnocentric identification; the *Ubii* (in the Rhineland) apparently the 'exuberant' ones, and the *Quadi* (living between the Danube and the western Carpathians), apparently a nickname, meaning 'odious, depraved,' given them by the *Suebi* who ill-treated them.

When two cultures come in contact, conflicts triggered by the language loyalty of their members are likely to result if the latter feel their social and linguistic identity threatened by the other culture (Hartig 1984). In many cases, there are indeed potent forces involved in promoting linguistic acculturation (Markey 1978). To react against this, speakers of threatened languages may resort to what Mackey (1979) calls 'linguistic irredentism', referring to the claims of minorities like the Basques or the Frisians to a degree of regional autonomy that would ensure the survival of their language and culture. But there is more to the problem than the political issues involved, as Mackey illustrates with the case of Irish: national sovereignty outside the Commonwealth, with Irish constitutionally recognised as the official language, has not prevented the continuous decline of the use of the language in spite of governmental support, as economic and demographic factors prevailed over the efforts to 'revitalize' Irish. Careful attitudinal research has shown that, while people value Irish quite highly as a foremost element of their national and ethnic identity, their linguistic behaviour contradicts their statements in favour of its use when it comes to such practical matters as education and personal interaction. This situation strongly reminds one of the trenchant remarks of Khubchandani (1983: 48) about language allegiance and actual use in India:

An individual's identification through a particular language label is a categorically-determined institutional attribute and does not necessarily have an exact parallel with the structural characteristics in his speech matrix. Mother-tongue identity is a discrete alignment by an individual or a group with certain cultural or formal attributes. whereas speech behavior is not necessarily so.

Le Page and Tabouret Keller (1985) have shown how people in Belize have been able to change their linguistic behaviour to accommodate themselves to changes in the socio-cultural context. In the days of British rule, people had mostly close access simply to their own highly-focused group and only slight contact with others in the villages where they lived by subsistence farming. Thus, most of the inhabitants of Succotz would claim a 'Mayan' identity and actually speak Mayan. Nowadays, as transportation has improved with independence, and as people go out looking for work, since mahogany and chiche are no longer producing earnings locally, their attitude has changed, and they have become Spanish-speaking, claiming 'Spanish' identity as well (Le Page and Tabouret 1985: 183). A Belizean tongue has even developed, and although many speak Spanish, Creole is widely claimed as the language identifying people ethnically as Belizeans (ibid. 215).

A holocultural study of language would include many more aspects of linguistic communication, but much in the field of language and communication (cf. e.g. Myers 1975, Esau 1980) lies outside the proper domain of the anthropological linguist: sociolinguistics will often claim as its own such fields like language and social identity (cf. Gumperz 1982a) or language as social semiotic, focusing on the social interpretation of meaning (cf. Halliday 1979). Nevertheless, the logic by which signs are connected (cf. Leach 1976) is certainly as relevant to the inquiries of anthropology as to dialectical sociology and semiotics (cf. Rossi 1983) or linguistics (cf. Rauch and Carr 1980): thus, the study of the Warlpiri sign language by Kendon (1986), although it stresses its iconicity in a semiotic context, is typical of linguistic anthropology. Indicating that the 'sign language' is not strictly a back formation from the spoken language, the author shows how the base of the sign *wanakiji* for an edible solanum fruit is a small wooden tool, called *kajalarra*, used to clean the fruit. The sign, then, is a kind of enactment of the process of preparing the *wanakiji* for eating. Similarly, for a *wati* 'fully initiated man,' the base are the scars left on his chest by cutting it with a knife during the initiation process: drawing the tips of his fingers over these cicatricial ridges to form the sign also communicates the implications of his social position as 'fully initiated man'.

One could also look into variation in speech communities (Romaine 1982), discourse strategies (Gumperz 1982b), attitudes towards language variation (Ryan and Giles 1982), language and milieu (Venaä 1982) and the like, but such topics rather belong to sociolinguistics. However, the linguistic

476

component of transactions whose study has become prominent in social anthropology (cf. Kapferer 1976), falls within the range of anthropological linguistics, as does the study of language and myth (cf. Cook 1980). Thus the study of the poetic formulas applying to the Homeric heroes (Nagy 1979) has provided a new insight into the world of values of ancient Greek epic poetry. But perhaps the field of language universals has proved the most promising for linguistic anthropology as it attempts to flesh out, through cross-cultural studies, the cognitive framework which humankind innately shares, and to determine how the systems of the individual languages are ultimately all built upon its base. This brings us back full circle to such problems as ethnobiology and colour classification: all humans classify plants and animals into labelled categories, and the use of *generic* and *specific* categories appears to be a cross-language universal; they always have a core classificatory system in which specific classes are always marked relative to unmarked generic categories in which they are immediately included. Moreover, folk biological taxonomies follow an invariant encoding sequence (Brown and Witkowski 1980):

[no life-forms] → ['trees'] → ['grerb'] → ['bush/vine/grass']

in which the critical features are:
(*a*)   tree = large plant, whose parts are chiefly ligneous;
(*b*)   grerb = small plant, whose parts are chiefly herbaceous;
(*c*)   bush = plant of intermediate size (between 'tree' and 'grerb');
(*d*)   grass = herbaceous plant with narrow (bladelike) leaves;
(*e*)   vine = plant with a creeping, twining, climbing habit.

The case is somewhat more complex for colour terms, but Berlin and Kay (1969) have gathered enough evidence to show that they can also be encoded in a marking sequence:

[red] → [yellow &/or green/blue] → [brown] → [pink/purple/orange/grey]

(See, e.g., *Language*, 49 (1973), 245).

However, the design principles underlying these models remain rather general, and with the limitations of our information processing model we can not yet capture all the variety and complexity of the human language faculty, but anthropological linguistics provides us at least with a rich cognitive model to deal adequately with the evidence at hand.

# REFERENCES

Abrahams, Richard D. and Troike, Rudolph C. (eds) (1972) *Language and Cultural Diversity in American Education*, Prentice-Hall, Englewood Cliffs NJ.

Alexandre, Pierre (1972) *Languages and Language in Black Africa*, translated by F.A. Leary, Northwestern University Press, Evanston.

Allen, Irving Lewis (1983) *The Language of Ethnic Conflict: Social Organization and Lexical Culture*, Columbia University Press, New York.

Althaus, Hans Peter, Henne, Helmut, and Wiegand, Herbert Ernst (eds) (1980) *Lexikon der Germanistischen Linguistik*, 2nd (thoroughly revised) edition, Max Niemeyer, Tübingen. [Pp. 501–8: Johann Knobloch, 'Ethnolinguistik.']

André, Jacques (1949) *Les termes de couleur dans la langue latine* (Etudes et Commentaires, vol. 7), C. Klincksieck, Paris.

Atkinson, Jane Monnig (1984) '"Wrapped Words": Poetry and Politics among the Wana of Central Sulawesi, Indonesia', in Brenneis and Myers (1984) 33-68.

Baugh, John and Sherzer, Joel (eds) (1984) *Language in Use: Readings in Sociolinguistics*, Prentice-Hall, Englewood Cliffs, NJ.

Bauman, Richard and Sherzer, Joel (eds) (1974) *Explorations in the Ethnography of Speaking*, Cambridge University Press, Cambridge.

Benveniste, Emile (1969) *Le vocabulaire des institutions indo-européennes 1. économie, parenté, société 2. pouvoir, droit, religion*, Editions de Minuit, Paris.

Berryman, Cynthia L. and Eman, Virginia A. (eds) (1980) *Communication, Language and Sex. Proceedings of the First Annual Conference*, Newbury House, Rowley, Mass.

Birdwhistell, R.L. (1955) 'Background to kinesics', *ETC Review of General Semantics*, 13: 10–15.

Bloch, Maurice (ed.) (1975) *Political Language and Oratory in Traditional Society*, Academic Press, New York (the reference in Atkinson [1984: 34] is to the 'Introduction').

Blount, Ben G. (1974) *Language, Culture and Society: A Book of Readings*, Winthrop, Cambridge, Mass.

Blount, Ben G. and Sanches, Mary (1977) *Socio-Cultural Dimensions of Language Change*, Academic Press, New York.

Bouissac, Paul, Herzfeld, Michael, and Posner, Roland (eds) (1986) *Iconicity. Essays on the Nature of Culture. Festschrift for Thomas E. Sebeok on his 65th birthday*, Stauffenburg Verlag, Tübingen.

Brenneis, Donald Lawrence and Myers, Fred R. (eds) (1984) *Dangerous Words: Language and Politics in the Pacific*, New York University Press, New York.

Bricker, Victoria Reifler (1976) 'Some Zinacanteco Joking Strategies', in Kirshenblatt-Gimblett 1976: 51–62.

Brown, Cecil H. and Witkowski, Stanley R. (1980) 'Language Universals', in Levison and Malone 1980: 359–84.

Burling, Robbins (1964) 'Cognition and Componential Analysis: God's Truth or Hocus Pocus?', *American Anthropologist*, 66: 20–8 [reprinted in Tyler 1969: 419–28].

Calame-Griaule, Geneviève (1965) *Ethnologie et langage. La parole chez les Dogon* (Bibliothèque des Sciences Humaines), NRF-Gallimard, Paris.

Cardona, Giorgio Raimondo (1976) *Introduzione all'etnolinguistica*, Il Mulino, Bologna.

Carroll, John B. (ed.) (1956) *Language, Thought and Reality: Selected Writings of Benjamin Lee Whorf*, The MIT Press, Cambridge, Mass.

Claessen, A. (1985) 'An Investigation into the Patterns of Non-Verbal Communication

Behaviour Related to Conversational Interaction between Mother Tongue Speakers of Swahili', in Maw, J. and Parkin, D. (eds), *Swahili Language and Society* (Veröffentlichungen der Institut für Afrikanistik und Ägyptologie der Universität Wien, vol. 33; Beiträge zur Afrikanistik, Nr. 23), Vienna: 159–93.

Cook, Albert (1980) *Myth and Language*, Indiana University Press, Bloomington, Ind.

Dallmayr, Fred A. (1984) *Language and Politics. Why Does Language Matter to Political Philosophy?*, University of Notre Dame Press, Notre Dame.

Davis, Philip (1973) *Modern Theories of Language*, Prentice-Hall, Englewood Cliffs, NJ.

Dingwall, William Orr (1970) *A Survey of Linguistic Science*, University of Maryland, Linguistics Program.

Dittman, A.T. (1962) 'Relationship between body movement and moods in interviews', *Journal of Consulting Psychology*, 26: 480.

Dumézil, Georges (1969) *Idées romaines*, NRF-Gallimard, Paris. (The chapter: 'L'homme: *ner-* et *uiro-*': 225–41, first appeared under the title: '*ner-* et *uiro-* dans les langues italiques' in *Revue des Etudes Latines*, 31 (1953): 175–89.)

Eastman, Carol M. (1975) *Aspects of Language and Culture*, Chandler and Sharp, Novato, Cal.

Edelman, Murray (1977) *Political Language. Words That Succeed and Policies That Fail*, Academic Press, Harcourt Brace Jovanovich, New York.

Ekman, P. (1964) 'Body positions, facial expression and verbal behavior during interviews', *Journal of Abnormal and Social Psychology*, 68: 295–301.

Ekman, P. (1965) 'Differential communication of effect by head and body cues', *Journal of Personality and Social Psychology*, 2: 726–35.

Ekman, P., Friesen, W., and Ellsworth, P. (1971) *Emotion in the Human Face*, Pergamon Press, New York.

Esau, Helmut (1980) *Language and Communication*, Hornbeam Press, Columbia, SC.

Fishman, Joshua (1960) 'A systematization of the Whorfian hypothesis', *Behavioral Science*, 5: 323–39.

Frake, Charles O. (1962) 'The Ethnographic Study of Cognitive Systems', in Gladwin, T. and Sturtevant, W. (eds), *Anthropology and Human Behavior*, Anthropological Society of America, Washington: 72–85 (reprinted in Frake 1980: 1–17).

Frake, Charles O. (1964) 'Notes on Queries in Ethnography', in *American Anthropologist* 66 (No. 3, Part 2): 132–45 (reprinted in Frake 1980: 26–44).

Frake, Charles O. (1977) 'Plying Frames Can Be Dangerous: An Assessment on Methodology in Cognitive Anthropology', in *The Quarterly Newsletter of the Institute for Comparative Human Development* (The Rockefeller Foundation) 1 (No. 3), 1–7 (reprinted in Frake 1980: 45–60).

Frake, Charles O. (1980) *Language and Cultural Description* (Essays Selected and Introduced by Anwar S. Dil), Stanford University Press, Stanford.

Gamkrelidze, Thomas V. and Ivanov, Vjačeslav V. (1984) *Indoevropejskij jazyk i indoevropejcy. Reconstrukcija i istoriko-tipologičeskij analiz prajazyka i protokul'tury* (Indo-European and Indo-Europeans. A Reconstruction and Historical Typological Analysis of a Protolanguage and a Proto-Culture), 2 volumes, Publishing House of the Tbilisi State University, Tbilisi.

Goffman, Erving (1981) *Forms of Talk*, University of Pennsylvania Press, Philadelphia.

Goodenough, Ward (1956) 'Componential analysis and the study of meaning', *Language*, 32: 195–212.

Goodenough, Ward (1957) 'Cultural anthropology and linguistics', in Paul Garvin (ed.), *Report of the Seventh Annual Round Table Meeting on Linguistics and Language Study* (Georgetown University Monograph Series on Language and Linguistics, vol. 9), Institute of Languages and Linguistics, Georgetown University, Washington: 167–73.

Goodenough, Ward (1965a) 'Yankee Kinship Terminology: A Problem in Componential Analysis', *American Anthropologist* 67 (No. 5, Part 2): 259–87.

Goodenough, Ward (1965b) 'Personal names and modes of address in two Oceanic societies', in Spiro, M.E. (ed.), *Context and Meaning in Cultural Anthropology*, Free Press, New York: 265–76.

Goodenough, Ward (1969) 'Rethinking "Status" and "Role": Toward a General Model of the Cultural Organization of Social Relationships', in Tyler(1969): 311–30.

Goodenough, Ward (1971) *Culture, Language and Society* (An Addison-Wesley Module in Anthropology), Addison-Wesley, Reading, Mass.

Gossen, Gary H. (1976) 'Verbal Dueling in Chamula', in Krishenblatt-Gimblett 1976: 121–46.

Greenberg, Joseph H. (1971) 'The Nature and Definition of Language', in Dil, Anwar S. (ed.), *Language, Culture, and Communication: Essays by Joseph H. Greenberg*, Stanford University Press, Stanford: 260–73 (first published in Greenberg, J.H., *Anthropological Linguistics: An Introduction*, Random House, New York, 1968: 3–17).

Greimas, Algirdas Julien (1963) 'La description de la signification et la mythologie comparée', *L'homme* 3, 3: 51–66.

Gumperz, John J. (1982a) *Language and social identity*, Cambridge University Press, Cambridge.

Gumperz, John J. (1982b) *Discourse Strategies*, Cambridge University Press, Cambridge.

Gumperz, John J. and Hymes, Dell (1972) *Directions in Sociolinguistics: The Ethnography of Communication*, Holt, Rinehart and Winston, New York.

Haas, Mary R. (1967) 'Language and Taxonomy in Northwestern California', *American Anthropologist*, 69: 358–62.

Haas, Mary R. (1978) 'The Study of American Indian Languages: A Brief Historical Sketch', in Dil, Anwar S. (ed.), *Language, Culture, and History: Essays by Mary R. Haas*, Stanford University Press, Stanford: 110–29 (first published as 'Anthropological Linguistics: History' in Wallace, Anthony F.C. *et al.* (eds) *Perspectives in Anthropology* (A Special Publication of the American Anthropological Association, No. 10, 1977): 33–47).

Hall, E.T. (1959) *The Silent Language*, Doubleday & Co., Garden City, New York.

Halliday, M.A.K. (1978) *Language as social semiotic. The social interpretation of language and meaning*, Edward Arnold, London.

Hartig, Matthias (1984) 'Sprachkontakt und Kulturkonflikt aus soziolinguistischer Perspektive', in Kühlwein 1984: 49–50.

Heeschen, Volker (1980) 'Theorie des sprachlichen Handelns', in Althaus *et al.* 1980: 259–67.

Helfrisch, H. and Wallbott, H.G. (1980) 'Theorie der nonverbalen Kommunikation', in Althaus *et al.* 1980: 267–75.

Heringer, Hans Jürgen (ed.) (1982) *Holzfeuer im hölzernen Ofen. Aufsätze zur politischen Sprachkritik*, Gunter Narr, Tübingen.

Hoijer, Harry (ed.) (1954) *Language in Culture. Conference in the Interrelations of Language and Other Aspects of Culture*, The University of Chicago Press, Chicago.

Howell, Richard W. and Vetter, Harold J. (1976) *Language in Behavior*, Human Sciences Press, New York.

Hymes, Dell H. (1974) 'Sociolinguistics and the Ethnography of Speaking', in Blount 1974: 335–69.

Irvine, Judith T. (1974) 'Strategies of Status Manipulation in the Wolof Greeting', in Bauman and Sherzer 1974: 167–91.

Kapferer, Bruce (ed.) (1976) *Transaction and Meaning. Directions in the Anthropology of Exchange and Symbolic Behavior*, Institute for the Study of Human Issues, Philadelphia.

Katz, J.J. and Fodor (1963) 'The Structure of a Semantic Theory', *Language* 39: 170-210.

Kendon, Adam (1986) 'Iconicity in Warlpiri Sign Language', in Bouissac *et al.* 1986: 437–46.

Kirshenblatt-Gimblett, Barbara (1976) *Speech Play: Research and Resources for Studying Linguistic Creativity*, University of Pennsylvania Press, Philadelphia.

Kirshenblatt-Gimblett, Barbara and Sherzer, Joel (1976) 'Introduction', in Kirshenblatt-Gimblett 1976: 1–16.

Khubchandani, Lachman M. (1983) *Plural Languages, Plural Cultures. Communication, Identity, and Sociological Change in Contemporary India*, East West Center, University of Hawaii Press.

Kühlwein, Wollfgang (1984) *Sprache, Kultur, Gesellschaft (Kongreßberichte der 14. Jahrestagung der Gesellschaft für Angewandte Linguistik, Duisburg 1983*, Gunter Narr, Tübingen.

Lado, Robert (1957) *Linguistics across cultures. Applied Linguistics for Language Teachers*, The University of Michigan Press, Ann Arbor.

Lamb, Sydney M. (1964) 'The sememic approach to structural semantics', *American Anthropologist*, 66 (Part 2, No. 3): 57–76.

Landar, Herbert (1966) *Language and Culture*, Oxford University Press, New York.

Leach, Edmund (1976) *Culture and Communication. The logic by which symbols are connected. An introduction to the use of structuralist analysis in social anthropology*, Cambridge University Press, Cambridge.

Le Page, R.B. and Taubouret-Keller, Andrée (1985) *Acts of Identity. Creole-based approaches to language and ethnicity*, Cambridge University Press, Cambridge.

Lévi-Strauss, Claude (1955) 'The Structural Study of Myth', *Journal of American Folklore*, 67; 428–44 (reprinted in *Myth: A Symposium*, edited by Sebeok, Thomas A. (Midland Books, vol. 83), Indiana University Press, Bloomington: 81–106).

Lévi-Strauss, Claude (1963) *Structural Anthropology*, translated from the French by Claire Jacobson and Brooke Grundfest Schoepf, Basic Books Inc., New York (quoted from the Anchor Books edition, Doubleday, New York, 1967).

Levinson, David and Malone, Martin J. (1980) *Toward Explaining Human Culture. A Critical Review of the Findings of Worldwide Cross-Cultural Research*, Human Research Area Files Press.

Littleton, C. Scott (1982) *The New Comparative Mythology: An Anthropological Assessment of the Theories of Georges Dumézil*, 3rd ed., University of California Press, Berkeley.

Lounsbury, Floyd G. (1964) 'The Structural Analysis of Kinship Semantics', in Lunt, Horace G. (ed.), *Proceedings of the Ninth International Congress of Linguists, Cambridge, Mass., August 1962*, Mouton, The Hague: 1073–90.

Mackey, William F. (1979) 'L'irrédentisme linguistique: une enquête témoin', in Wald and Manessy 1979: 257–84.

Mandelbaum, David G. (ed.) (1960) *Edward Sapir: Culture, Language and Personality —
Selected Essays*, University of California Press, Berkeley/Los Angeles. ('The Status
of Linguistics as a Science': 65–77; first published in *Language*, vol. 5 (1929): 207–14).

Markey, Thomas L. (1978) 'Linguistic Acculturation: Coalescence vs. Conservation',
in Paradis 1979: 202–10 (reprinted from di Pietro, Robert J. and Blansitt, Edward I.
Jr. (eds), *The Third LACUS Forum*, Hornbeam Press, Columbia, SC, 1977).

Michel, Georg (ed.) (1986) *Sprachliche Kommunikation. Einführung und Übungen*,
Bibliographisches Institut, Leipzig.

Myers, Gail E. and Myers, Michele Tolela (1975) *Communicating When We Speak*,
McGraw-Hill, New York.

Nagy, Gregory (1979) *The Best of the Achaeans. Concepts of the Hero in Archaic Greek Poetry*,
The Johns Hopkins University Press, Baltimore.

Newmeyer, Frederick J. (1986) *Linguistic Theory in America*, 2nd ed., Academic Press,
Harcourt Brace Jovanovich, New York/London.

Ntahombaye, Philippe (1983) *Des noms et des hommes. Aspects psychologiques et sociologiques
du nom au Burundi*, Karthala, Paris.

O'Barr, William M.O. and O'Barr, Jean F. (eds) (1976) *Language and Politics* (Contributions to the Sociology of Language, vol. 10), Mouton, The Hague.

Ochs, Elinor (1973) 'A Sliding Sense of Obligatoriness: The Poly-Structure of
Malagasy Oratory', *Language in Society*, 2: 225–43 (reprinted in Baugh and Sherzer
1984: 167–82).

Paradis, Michel (ed.) (1978) *Aspects of Bilingualism*, Hornbeam Press, Columbia, SC.

Pinxten, Rik (ed.)(1976) *Universalism versus Relativism in Language and Thought.
Proceedings of a Colloquium on the Sapir-Whorf Hypothesis*, Mouton, The Hague.

Polomé, Edgar C. (1961) 'Personennamen bei einigen Stämmen in Belgisch-Kongo', in
Puchner, Karl (ed.), *Reports of the VIth International Congress of Onomastic Sciences.
Munich, 24–28 August 1958. III. Section Meetings* (Studia Onomastica Monacensia,
vol. 4), C.H. Beck, Munich: 615–21.

Polomé, Edgar C. (1967) *Swahili Language Handbook*, Center for Applied Linguistics,
Washington.

Polomé, Edgar C. (1988) 'Comparative Linguistics and the Reconstruction of Indo-
European Culture' (to appear in the *Proceedings of the IREX Conference on Comparative
Linguistics: Indo-European Symposium, held in Austin, Texas (November 1986) in honor of
W.P. Lehmann*, ed. E.C. Polomé (to be published by Mouton/de Gruyter, Berlin)).

Price, Richard and Price, Sally (1976) 'Secret Play Languages in Saramaka: Linguistic
Disguise in a Caribbean Creole', in Krishenblatt-Gimblett 1976: 37–50.

Rauch, Irmengard and Carr, Gerald F. (eds) (1980) *The Signifying Animal. The Grammar
of Language and Experience*, Indiana University Press, Bloomington.

Romaine, Suzanne (ed.) (1982) *Sociolinguistic Variation in Speech Communities*, Edward
Arnold, London.

Romney, A. Kimball and D'Andrade, Roy G. (1964) 'Cognitive Aspects of English Kin
Terms', *American Anthropologist*, 66 (No. 3, Part 2): 146–79 (reprinted in Tyler 1969:
369–96).

Rosaldo, Michelle Z. (1984) 'Words That Are Moving: The Social Meanings of Ilongot
Verbal Art', in Brenneis and Myers 1984: 131–60.

Rossi, Ino (1983) *From the Sociology of Symbols to the Sociology of Signs. Toward a Dialectical
Sociology*, Columbia University Press, New York.

Ruhlen, Merritt (1987) *A Guide to the World's Languages, 1: Classification*, Stanford University Press, Stanford.

Ryan, Ellen Bouchard, and Giles, Howard (eds) (1982) *Attitudes towards Language Variation: Social and Applied Contexts*, Edward Arnold, London.

Sainsbury, P. (1955) 'Gestural movements during psychiatric interview', *Psychosomatic Medicine*, 17: 458–69.

Salmond, Anne (1974) 'Rituals of Encounter among the Maori: Sociolinguistic Study of a Scene', in Bauman and Sherzer 1980: 192–212.

Sampson, Geoffrey (1980) *Schools of Linguistics*, Stanford University Press, Stanford.

Sanches, Mary and Blount, Ben G. (1975) *Sociocultural Dimensions of Language Use*, Academic Press, New York.

Scheflen, A.E. (1964) 'The significance of posture in communication systems', *Psychiatry*, 27: 316–31.

Scheflen, A.E. (1965) 'Quasi-courtship behavior in psychotherapy', *Psychiatry*, 28: 245–57.

Scherer, Klaus R. and Giles, Howard (eds) (1979) *Social Markers in Speech*, Cambridge University Press, Cambridge. Editions de la Maison des Sciences de l'Homme, Paris.

Schneider, David M. (1965) 'American Kin Terms and Terms for Kinsmen: A Critique of Goodenough's Componential Analysis of Yankee Kinship Terminology', *American Anthropologist* 67 (No. 5, Part 2): 288–308 (reprinted in Tyler 1969: 288–311).

Schneider, David M. (1984) *A Critique of the Study of Kinship*, University of Michigan Press, Ann Arbor.

Shapiro, Michael J. (ed.) (1984) *Language and Politics (Readings in Social and Political Theory)*, New York University Press, New York.

Sherzer, Joel (1983) *Kuna Ways of Speaking: An Ethnographic Perspective*, University of Texas Press, Austin.

Silverstein, Michael (1975) 'Linguistics and anthropology' in Bartsch, Renate and Vennemann, Theo (ed.), *Linguistics and neighboring disciplines*, North-Holland, Amsterdam: 157–70.

Smith, Philip M. (1985) *Language, the Sexes and Society*, Basil Blackwell, Oxford.

Smith, William John (1977) *The Behavior of Comunicating: An Ethological Approach*, Harvard University Press, Cambridge, Mass.

Sudnow, David (ed.) (1972) *Studies in Social Interaction*, The Free Press, New York/Collier-Macmillan, London.

Thompson, D.F. (1964) 'Communication of emotional intent by facial expression', *Journal of Abnormal and Social Psychology*, 68: 129–35.

Thorne, Barrie and Henley, Nancy (eds) (1975) *Language and Sex: Difference and Dominance*, Newbury House, Rowley, Mass.

Thorne, Barrie, Kramarae, Cheris, and Henley, Nancy (eds) (1983) *Language, Gender and Society*, Newbury House, Rowley, Mass.

Tyler, Stephen A. (ed.) (1969) *Cognitive Anthropology*, Holt, Rinehart & Winston, New York.

Venaà, Kjell (1982) *Mål og miljø 'Innføring i sosiolingvistikk eller språksosiologi*, Novus forlag, Oslo.

Vermeer, Hans Josef (1963) *Adjektivische und verbale Farbausdrücke in den indogermanischen Sprachen mit -ē- Verben* (Ein Beitrag zur Frage der Wortarten und zum Problem der

Übersetzbarkeit), Julius Groos, Heidelberg.

Voegelin, C.F. and Voegelin, F.M. (1977) *Classification and Index of the World's Languages*, Elsevier, New York.

Wald, Paul and Manessy, Gabriel (eds) (1979) *Plurilinguisme: normes, situations, stratégies*, L'Harmattan, Paris.

Wallace, Anthony F.C. (1965) 'The Problem of the Psychological Validity of Componential Analyses', *American Anthropologist*, 67 (No. 5, Part 2): 229–48 (reprinted in Tyler 1969: 396–418).

Weisgerber, Leo (1949–1962) *Von den Kräftern der deutschen Sprache*: (1957–1962) 1. *Grundzüge der inhaltbezogenen Grammatik* (1949; 2nd ed. 1962) 2. *Die sprachliche Gestaltung der Welt* (1954; 2nd ed. 1962) 3. *Die Muttersprache im Aufbau unserer Kultur* (1949; 2nd ed. 1957) 4. *Die geschichtliche Kraft der deutschen Sprache* (1950; 2nd ed. 1959) Schwann, Düsseldorf.

Wertsch, James V. (1985) *Culture, Communication and Cognition. Vygotskian Perspectives*, Cambridge University Press, Cambridge.

Willis, R.G. (1967) 'The Head and the Loins: Lévi-Strauss and beyond', *Man* 2, 519–34 (reprinted in Lessa, William A. and Vogt, Evon Z. (eds), *Reader in Comparative Religion: An Anthropological Approach*, 4th ed., Harper & Row, New York: 197–206).

# 14

## LANGUAGE IN SOCIETY: SOCIOLINGUISTICS

### JAMES MILROY AND LESLEY MILROY

### 1. INTRODUCTION

In the last two to three decades there has been rapid development in the branch of linguistics now known as *sociolinguistics*, i.e. the study of language as it is used by real speakers in social and situational contexts of use. These developments have been accelerated by technological advances, the first of these being the tape-recorder. Since the 1950s, it has become much more feasible than it formerly was to collect very large samples of speech in naturalistic contexts and to develop sophisticated methods of analysis of the corpora collected at all linguistic levels – from phonology to discourse and conversational structure. Before that time, those who were interested in language in social contexts were much more dependent for their data on either formal questionnaire techniques (which tend to encourage rather formal or brief responses from informants) or on relatively unsystematic observation of language in use. One obvious disadvantage of reliance on these methods was that, because of the limitations of human memory, it was difficult to study empirically linguistic organisation at any level above that of the *sentence*. Through advances in field techniques, including access to a much greater range of the speech behaviour of live speakers, sociolinguistics has opened up a number of questions of research interest – such as attitudes to language, the relation of the speaker to the language, the role of the speaker in linguistic change – that can now be investigated empirically much more fully than formerly.

For the purpose of the present chapter, we shall regard *sociolinguistics* as a wide-ranging subject that includes a number of more specific interests – some of which overlap with other areas that are treated in this volume: examples of these are *historical linguistics* (Chapter 24) and *pragmatics* (Chapter

6). One important branch is the study of language variation in speech communities. The most important underlying concern of this branch (which is sometimes called *social dialectology*) is to contribute to our understanding of the nature of linguistic change: within this area there have been several important contributions – notably the work of C-J. Bailey, which has shown the manner in which changes are diffused through successive phonological environments in 'waves' (Bailey 1973), and which has particularly influenced those sociolinguists who are interested in describing the precise phonological details of systematic change. The most influential research paradigm, however, is the *quantitative* paradigm developed by William Labov in New York City (Labov 1966, 1972). This approach is largely concerned with revealing patterns of variation in speech-communities by demonstrating co-variation of language use with social differences – typically socio-economic class, age and sex of speaker (Labov 1966, 1972b; Trudgill 1974; Macaulay 1977), and social network (L. Milroy 1987a; Bortoni Ricardo 1985). One of the most important findings of these studies (including those of Bailey) is that, despite traditional views to the contrary, linguistic change can be observed and documented while it is in progress. As a result of close analytic work within this paradigm, there have been advances in our understanding of how linguistic changes are socially diffused within communities, and how they spread geographically across communities (see particularly Trudgill 1986, etc). These studies have also made a significant contribution to the study of *why* languages change, using models based on social class or status (Labov 1972, 1980), accommodation theory (Trudgill 1986) and social network (Milroy and Milroy 1985b).

Whereas the main concerns of Labov's quantitative paradigm are to throw light on the nature of change and variation in language *systems*, other approaches to sociolinguistics are more directly concerned with the capacities of *speakers*: they overlap with psychological, sociological, anthropological and philosophical interests and draw insights from these disciplines. The focus here is generally on language in face-to-face interaction, and the questions that these approaches attempt to answer include: 'what kind of strategies do speakers use to sustain conversations?', 'what is the function of code-switching in bidialectal or bilingual communities?', and 'how is politeness encoded in language use?'. Much work in these areas has been carried out by John Gumperz (1982), and from different points of view, by P. Brown and Levinson (1987) (politeness), R. Brown and Gilman (1960) (terms of address) and Sacks, Schegloff and Jefferson (1974) (conversational structure – on which see Chapter 8 in this volume). Whereas work in the quantitative paradigm overlaps with dialectology, historical linguistics and the 'core' areas of phonology and syntax, the interest in speaker-strategies overlaps with *pragmatics* (on which see Chapter 6). Research into language in society is seen therefore to be very wide-ranging.

In what follows, we shall first attempt to place the developments outlined above in a historical perspective; we shall then pass on to an account of the interests and findings of *social dialectology* and related areas; in sections 5 and 6, we shall proceed to developments in the study of linguistic choice by *speakers* in face-to-face interaction, dealing separately with *monolingual* and *bi-* or *multi-lingual communities.*

## 2. HISTORICAL BACKGROUND

As Sapir commented (1921: 147): 'Everyone knows that language is variable'. Although ordinary people have always been interested in language variation, the systematic study of variation in social contexts can be seen as a 'new' subject. Yet, although older schools of linguistics and dialectological research were much less concerned with the social meaning of language variation than recent research has been, some of their methods and goals are nevertheless relevant to understanding the aims of present research. Similarly, some traditional research into historical language change has been able to speculate on the social causes of change and to foreshadow certain character-istics of present-day socially-based theories of change. As a background to the quantitative paradigm, therefore, we now briefly review the work of descriptivists and dialectologists, and relevant aspects of the historical linguistic tradition.

From the early nineteenth century onward in the wake of the Romantic movement, one important strand in linguistic research was the study and description of 'exotic' languages and dialects of known languages (such as English) that were remote from the literary standard languages. These interests are clearly stated by (amongst others) Max Müller, who considered 'literary' languages to be 'artificial' and claimed that 'the real and natural life of language is in its dialects' (1861: 47). Similarly he asserts that 'dialects which have never produced any literature at all, the jargons of savage tribes, the clicks of the Hottentots, the vocal modulations of the Indo-Chinese' are more important than literary languages for solving our problems in investigating the origin, nature and 'laws' of language (1861: 23). Such comments illustrate clearly that the emphasis on empirical investigation, which is characteristic of American structuralism (Bloomfield 1933, etc), of regional dialectology, and of the Labov paradigm, is not new in itself. However, the 'laws' that Müller refers to were, in the nineteenth century, very much historical laws – laws of linguistic change as codified from the study of past states of language – and for about a century after Müller's comments *dialectological* research turned out to be largely antiquarian in nature. It was inspired by the belief that remote dialects could preserve 'older' and hence more 'genuine' forms of a language, and that they could assist us in reconstructing the past.

This traditional interest in non-standard dialects has thus continued in an unbroken line in the study of *regional dialectology*; it is exemplified in the *Survey of English Dialects* (Orton *et al.*, 1962 *et seq.*), and in studies such as that of Wakelin (1972); in the social dialectological paradigm, however, this interest has re-surfaced in a new form. Whereas traditional approaches sought to discover the linguistic forms of remote rural dialects which were believed to be relatively 'pure' and 'uncontaminated', social dialectology has turned its attention to mixed and changing states of language – urban dialects, bi-dialectal and multilingual situations – and has studied the range of choices exploited by individual speakers and groups. It is argued that the seeds of linguistic change will be more readily found in these heterogeneous situations than in relatively uniform ones. Whereas traditional dialectology has attempted to discover relatively uniform language states and establish canonical forms for particular regions (often displaying the regional distri-butions on maps), social dialectology has explicitly focused on linguistic *he-terogeneity* (following the precepts of Weinreich, Labov and Herzog 1968) and has sought to establish the ways in which speakers *within communities* use the variable resources of language, in a structured way, for social purposes. Despite this important difference, however, one of the main interests of social dialectology is in principle the same as that of the tradition. This is the concern with reconstructing past language states on the basis of the study of present-day states, as in Labov's seminal paper 'On the use of the present to explain the past' (1975). Sociolinguistics, however, with its rich data-base and its emphasis on language variability at all times, has given us the possibility of new insights into these traditional questions. Furthermore, the methodology has enabled investigators to focus, at an abstract level, on general processes of linguistic change (in addition to merely documenting changes), and to ask why particular configurations of change come about; they are thus concerned with general issues in the theory of change rather than with the specific examples they use as evidence or attempt to reconstruct. Historical socio-linguistic research has included contributions to the theory of *syntactic* change (Romaine 1982), the relative chronology of linguistic changes (J. Milroy 1983) and the nature of *merger* – a process whereby distinctions that are present in a system are lost in the course of time (Labov (1974), Nunberg (1980), J. Milroy and Harris (1980), Harris (1985), Trudgill (1986), J. Milroy (forthcoming)). The application of social dialectology to historical issues has loomed very large, and it should not be forgotten that, although the perspective is wider, this is a continuation of traditional historical concerns.

Social dialectology differs from post-Chomskyan generative linguistics and continues the descriptivist tradition (e.g. that of American structuralism) in that it does not depend primarily on the analyst's intuitive judgement to decide what is, or is not, a 'well-formed' sequence in a language: it is empirically-based and depends on collection and analysis of data following a specified set of procedures. In this respect, it can be said to continue the tradition that Max Müller believed in and, more immediately, the American anthropological tradition of Boas and Sapir. The emphasis here was on the exploration and description of 'exotic' languages – for example, those of North American Indian tribes. Under the influence of Christian missions, American linguists additionally worked in various countries in order to introduce writing systems for previously unwritten languages and hence promote literacy.

The main difference between this descriptivist tradition and that of the Labov paradigm lies in the different goals of the two kinds of research. It would appear in general that American structuralism in the 1930s and 1940s did not place primary emphasis on exploring attitudes to language in the societies studied, nor on discovering patterns of language variation within such communities, but rather sought to establish uniformly correct and grammatical forms for particular languages by using sophisticated elicitation techniques. Thus, the emphasis was on exploring and describing linguistic *systems*, with relatively little attention to how speakers make functional use of these systems. However, since the 1950s, American anthropologists, further developing these empirical traditions, have turned their attention to language in social contexts and have made considerable contributions to our understanding of socially significant language patterns in different societies. Examples are the different ways that *silence* is used in different societies, code-switching and language repertoires of speakers, and the relation of language choice to social structure (such as the use of 'polite', humble and honorific linguistic forms in particular societies). For a representative selection of such work, (which is sometimes referred to as research in *ethnography of speaking*), see Bauman and Sherzer (1974) (and see further section 5 below, and Chapter 13 above).

A third area in which the social correlates of change and variation have been touched on in the tradition is in documentary histories of modern languages. Social interests, however, have usually been secondary in this historical work, the establishment of linguistic forms at different times in the past having been its primary concern. Thus, although standard histories (of English, for example) often attempt to distinguish between the 'internal' (linguistic) history of the language and the 'external' (social) history, the latter is generally secondary and social 'explanations' for particular changes are often *ad hoc*, and not based on any comprehensive theory of sociolinguistic variation. In this tradition, a notable contribution to the external history of English is McKnight (1928, 1956), who collects and discusses documentary evidence of the history of attitudes to usage, but the most important traditional scholar with these social interests is H.C. Wyld. In the first place, Wyld was reacting against the emphasis of some of his predecessors on rural dialectology (or, as he put it, on the language of 'illiterate peasants') and wished to document the history of the 'Received Standard' language. However, two of his books (*A Short History of English* (1914) and *A History of Modern Colloquial English* (1920)) are still very valuable sources for the study of variability in English from 1100 onward. Wyld uses these materials to document the sources of present-day *standard* English only, and his interpretation of data betrays many of the characteristic attitudes of an upper-class (or upper middle-class) person of his generation; for example, he is inclined to stop short of allowing what he calls 'vulgarisms' (e.g. 'aitch-dropping') a place in the history of the language. However, he was clearly interested in the fact that seventeenth-century dramatists and others could represent upper-class persons as using forms that would be considered non-standard today (e.g. *you was, he don't*), and it can be said that Wyld was the first to propose a theory (however shadowy) of sociolinguistic variation and change: this was, in effect, a theory that *social class* differences are fundamental in sustaining variation and promoting change. Amongst other things, Wyld notes that the anxious middle ranges of society attempt to adopt the forms of the class above them in the hierarchy – a point that is developed more systematically by Labov (1972b).

It was Wyld also (to our knowledge) who first proposed that certain vocabulary choices in English were markers of social class. Thus, whereas the upper and upper middle classes were alleged to speak of *napkins* and *boots* and *shoes*, the lower middle class (according to Wyld) preferred *serviettes* and *footwear*, and so revealed their lower status by using these markers. A generation later (Ross 1954), the distinction between 'U' and 'non-U' usage (based on these perceptions) was popularised and became a favourite topic of discussion at cocktail parties and the like. Wyld's emphasis on social class, class dialects, and class as a primary motivation for change no doubt seemed very persuasive in a highly class-conscious era in which the British class-system was rather rigid and seemingly permanent; yet, although there is no reason to assume that the relation between language use and the social structure of early-twentieth-century England is a universal state of affairs, class is still often assumed to be primary in linguistic variation and change, other social variables being given a secondary place and discussed in relation to social class. This applies to a greater or lesser extent to many popular accounts and textbooks (e.g. Quirk 1968), but the idea of class differences in language is subsumed also in the most important innovative research in quantitative sociolinguistics (that of Labov (1966) on the social stratification of language in New York City). This uses socio-economic class as the primary social variable (we shall discuss this further below). The main point here is that linguists still have a strong inclination to assume (as Wyld did) that social class differences are fundamental in providing social explanations for linguistic changes.

Even though social class arguments have usually been dominant, sex/ gender differences in language have also been commented on by traditional scholars, such as Jespersen (1922). Jespersen (like Sturtevant 1917) discusses many possible 'causes' of change, including errors and slips of the tongue, but also children's language and *women's language*. It is worth mentioning this here: as we shall see, there has been a good deal of interest in gender differences in recent sociolinguistic research (see especially Coates 1986): this can again be seen as a traditional interest resurfacing in a new methodological and theoretical perspective.

## 3. QUANTITATIVE SOCIOLINGUISTICS

Whereas traditional approaches have tended to focus on absolute, or categorical, differences in an attempt to characterise genuine forms belonging to relatively discrete varieties of language, the principal advantage of a quantitative method is that it enables us to compare populations who use the *same* linguistic variants but in *different quantities* (i.e. the differences between these sets of speakers are not absolute). Using the quantitative method, we can now detect patterns of distribution in a community in terms of greater or lesser preferences for particular realisations of items (e.g. percentage preferences for front /a/ as against back – i.e. 'broad' – /a/, or for presence v. absence of initial /h/ in *hat, home* etc.). Characteristically, these quantitative preferences have been shown to have varying social distributions.

The quantitative paradigm was developed by William Labov (1966) in order to account in a systematic way for the social correlates of linguistic variation and change. Reacting against the reliance on introspection characteristic of much linguistic theorising (Labov 1972a: 292), he developed an empirical methodology, involving careful sampling of populations to ensure representativeness, fieldwork methods designed to elicit a range of styles from the most casual to the most formal, and analytic techniques based on the notion of the *linguistic variable*. In order to draw confident conclusions about variation in speech-communities, the number of persons sampled in surveys is quite large and the number of speech-tokens analysed for any variable is also large (often in the thousands). In quantifying realisations of the *variable*, we have to be sure that the *meaning* of the variants remains constant. Thus, in practice, the variables chosen for quantification are often phonological, as we can be reasonably confident in phonological variation that two phonetic realisations (such as *horse* and *'orse*, for 'horse') have the same meaning. However, although phonological variation is less problematic in this way than (for example) syntactic variation (in which meanings may not be constant), the analyst may still face other difficulties as to which *tokens* from his/her data should be included in the quantification of phonological variables (for a discussion see J. Milroy 1982, L. Milroy 1987b).

The types of variable that have been studied can be tentatively classified into different types. For the first type of phonological variable, the tokens counted are more or less co-extensive with a phoneme class (e.g. New York (eh) which measures variation in /æ/ in words like *bad, cat, man*); another type is restricted to tokens representing a fairly narrow range of phonological environments (e.g. post-vocalic /r/ in New York); yet another type covers a particular phonological process affecting a number of different phonemes (e.g. the glottalisation of the voiceless stops /p, t, k/ in Newcastle upon Tyne, which is so characteristic of that urban dialect). A somewhat different type is the lexically alternating variable, typified by the (*pull*) variable in Belfast (J. and L. Milroy 1978, etc.), in which (for every instance of the class quantified) the alternative realisations can be said to belong to different phonemes (in this case /u/ and /ʌ/, rhyming with *book* and *dull*). *Morphological* variables have often in practice measured variation in the realisation of verbal inflexions, such as *he goes/he go* in Norwich (Trudgill 1974); for further morphological variables see Cheshire 1982; Kerswill 1987.

Once the variables to be quantified have been selected, a number of variants is distinguished for each variable; the differential incidence of the variants is then counted (for different individuals and groups) and related to speaker (or social) variables, such as age, sex, and socio-economic class. The variation revealed by these methods is then usually displayed in graphs, histograms or other diagrams, and can be further described in terms of *variable rules* (developed by Labov (1972a) and further by Cedergren and D. Sankoff (1974), D. Sankoff (1978)). In these ways we can show consistent socially-marked patterns (e.g. as between males and females in a community), and when there is an irregularity in the pattern, we may be able to locate a sound-change proceeding in a particular direction. These patterns are exemplified in Figures 22 and 23 below.

Figure 22, which measures deletion of intervocalic /ð/ in Belfast (the voiced *th* sound in words of the type: *mother, bother, gather*) shows a stable pattern of difference between the sexes: it is important to understand that a stable speech community is not viewed as one in which everyone speaks the same way, but one in which regular patterns of differentiation (in terms of co-variation with speaker variables) are well established (as in Figure 22, for sex-differentiation); Figure 23, on the other hand, which measures presence or absence of post-vocalic /r/ in New York in words of the type: *car, card*, shows a crossover pattern, in which the lower middle class use higher values of /r/ in formal style than the class immediately above them. This type of pattern shows an instability and can be interpreted as showing that the lower middle class are carrying a linguistic change (towards higher amounts of /r/-

*Figure 22* The distribution of (th) by age and sex in Belfast. Graph shows percentage of tokens in which [ð] is deleted in such words as *mother, bother.*

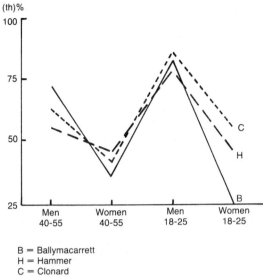

B = Ballymacarrett
H = Hammer
C = Clonard

*Figure 23* Class stratification of (r) in New York City. Classes range from 9 (Upper Middle Class) to 0 (Lower Class). The horizontal axis A–D represents an increasing line of formality. (Adapted from Labov 1980:125.)

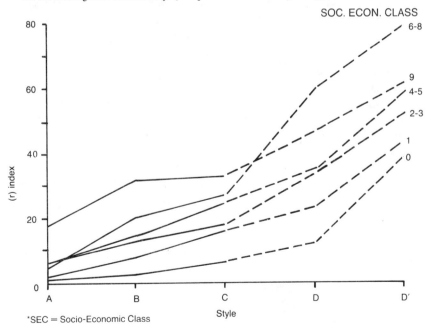

*SEC = Socio-Economic Class

493

insertion) downwards in the hierarchy. Using additional information about the history of /r/ in New York City, Labov has further shown that restoration of post-vocalic /r/ is generally in progress in the city and that the change has been continuing since the Second World War.

The historical aims of this type of research are set out by Weinreich, Labov and Herzog (1968), who distinguish five problems that have to be tackled by those who are interested in the empirical investigation of linguistic change. Amongst these, the problems of *transition, evaluation* and *actuation* are relevant here. Figure 23 can be interpreted as representing a stage in the transition from a language state in which there was no post-vocalic /r/ to one in which the /r/ is restored: the quantitative method helps us to understand the manner in which the change is diffused in the community. Ultimately it can be expected to throw light on *how* languages pass from one state to another and hence also on traditional questions, such as what it means to say that a sound-change is gradual or sudden.

A second problem to be considered is that of *evaluation*, which pertains principally to social responses 'at all levels of awareness, from overt discussion to reactions that are quite inaccessible to introspection', (Labov 1982: 28). It is well known that people can have very strong social attitudes to particular linguistic variants ('aitch-dropping' in British English, for example, has been overtly and publicly stigmatised), even though the favouring or disfavouring of a particular variant is, in linguistic terms, quite arbitrary: it is also known that other significant patterns of variation may be less consciously noticed, or evaluated in different ways (for example, as regional rather than social markers). Similarly, to the extent that phonetic/phonological variation is linguistically arbitrary, it follows that evaluation of variants can differ at different times and places. In Southern Britain, for example, absence of post-vocalic /r/ (in *car, card,* etc) is characteristic of the high-prestige dialect and is socially favoured: in the USA, however, there has been a reversal of evaluation here. Figure 23 demonstrates that in New York City, high status is accorded now to the presence of post-vocalic /r/ and low status to its absence. We can additionally suggest, however, that Figure 22 also can be interpreted as displaying attitudes – in this case towards the differentiation of male and female speech. Recurrent gender differences displaying a similar pattern (with males favouring local vernacular stereotypes) have led to a great deal of interest in male/female speech-differences. In general terms, of course, it is entirely reasonable to suggest that patterns of evaluation as studied by quantitative methods may help us to understand the social motivations of change.

Progress in the empirical study of *transition* and *evaluation* may be seen as giving access to the *actuation* problem, which according to Weinreich, Labov and Herzog, is 'the very heart of the matter' (in understanding linguistic change). It is formulated thus:

Why do changes in a structural feature take place in a particular language at a given time, but not in other languages with the same feature, or in the same language at other times? (Weinreich *et al.* 1968: 102)

With this formidable task in mind, a goal of quantitative sociolinguistics is to throw light on the ultimate causation of linguistic change by using an empirical methodology to investigate in a socially sensitive way particular cases of sound-change in progress. We shall return to this below.

It is important to understand that the aims of the quantitative method are not restricted to simply documenting variation in a community, and this is why we have emphasised the fact that its aims are ultimately historical. Criticisms of the method have sometimes been made on the grounds that the linguistic analysis involved is not detailed enough (Knowles 1978) for accurate phonetic description, or that the variables quantified in Labov's survey are relatively few and so cannot give a full picture of variation in a community (Jones-Sargent 1983). While these criticisms have some force in them, they do not alter the fact that work in this paradigm has been highly successful, since the 1960s, in studying the social embedding of variation and change, and illuminating traditional problems in a new perspective. See, for example, the essays collected in Labov (1980).

### 3.1 After New York City

Following the success of Labov's New York City survey, a number of large-scale studies of a similar kind were carried out in other urban locations. We notice here Shuy, Wolfram and Riley in Detroit (1968), Macaulay in Glasgow (1977), Trudgill in Norwich (1974), and J. and L. Milroy in Belfast (1978). A number of quantitative studies were also carried out by a group of scholars based in Montreal (for examples see G. Sankoff 1980), and it was in association with these scholars that Labov later developed the *variable rule paradigm* mentioned above. All of these studies sought to test, and if necessary extend and adapt, the methodology. Besides these, there have been many smaller-scale studies which have contributed greatly to our understanding, for example those of Romaine (1978) in Edinburgh and Kerswill (1987) in Durham.

A general problem with urban surveys is that of the representativeness of the language samples used to make generalisations about social patterns of variation and change. It is clearly not possible to generalise about the language of a city on the basis (for example) of the language of a few speakers already known to the investigator. Shuy *et al.* were therefore greatly concerned with the use of rigorous sampling techniques. The emphasis on scientific sampling together with the generally ambitious scope of this survey seems to have carried with it a corresponding risk that the language collected in interview situations would be relatively formal (or 'careful'); thus, the survey did not succeed in identifying a *casual* as against *careful* conversational style. The general importance of differentiating styles is clear in Figure 23 above, in which the detection of change in progress depends on being able to differentiate casual and careful styles.

Macaulay's work in Glasgow is a rigorous attempt to transfer the Labov methodology to a (Northern) British location. Macaulay's work is very clearly presented, and co-variation of the linguistic variables with occupational class, age and sex of speaker is documented in great detail. This, together with an extensive discussion of attitudes to language (especially amongst educators), is the main contribution of this study. Again, there is a difficulty in obtaining stylistic differentiation in field interviews, and the value of the Glasgow study for the investigation of linguistic change is to that extent lessened.

The most successful adaptation of the New York methodology to Britain is Trudgill's Norwich study, which was carried out in the late 1960s and published in 1974. Trudgill, like other investigators, is concerned with representativeness, but he also succeeds in obtaining the range of styles required by using interview techniques similar to Labov's. Like Labov, Trudgill uses a socio-economic class index as his main social variable, and additionally discusses age and sex differentiation. He gives very full attention to the historical and regional *embedding* of the linguistic forms occurring in the Norwich data (using, *inter alia*, the findings of the *Survey of English Dialects*) and is thus able to discern clear patterns of change in progress. The number of variables quantified is also much greater than in the New York study, ranging from nationally salient stereotypes like (h) (i.e. 'aitch-dropping') to localised variables that have social significance in the Norwich community and not necessarily outside. Trudgill, in a discussion of Gregg's work in the Larne area of Northern Ireland (1964, 1972), additionally calls attention to potential problems in transferring the Labov methodology to British locations: these arise from the fact that many British locations are 'dialect-divergent' – i.e. there is a wide and not necessarily continuous range of variation within speech communities. More recently, Johnston (1985) has discussed the patterns arising from this in his Edinburgh work, and this perception also underlies the work of J. and L. Milroy in Belfast – to which we now turn.

The New York method was very successful in demonstrating patterns of variation in a socio-economic continuum, which could often be shown to co-vary with a phonetic continuum, as in Figure 24 below. The Belfast methodology attempted to use quantification in a community in which the phonetic distribution of variants between social groups was not necessarily unidirectional or continuous. For example, at lower levels in the community, it was discovered that /a/ (as in *man, hat*) was changing towards back values

*Figure 24* Class and style stratification of (ing) in *working, living*, etc. For white New York City adults. Classes range from 9 (Upper Middle Class) to 0 (Lower Class). A = Casual speech; B = Careful speech; C = Reading style. The graph shows percentage of tokens in which (ing) is reduced to [in] (as in *workin*, etc.: adapted from Labov 1980:133).

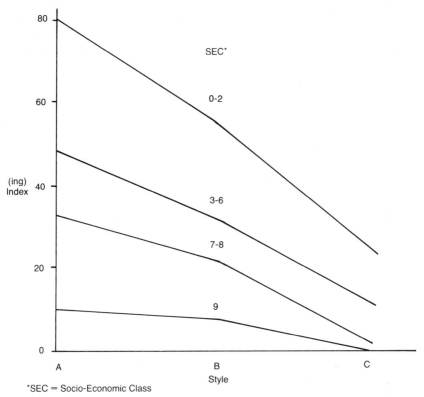

*SEC = Socio-Economic Class

of /a/ (so-called 'broad' /a/), whereas at higher levels the trend was towards fronting. Thus, paradoxically, some back-vowel pronunciations (e.g. of *grass, bath,* etc.) that happen to coincide with 'Received Pronunciation' are (variably) used at lower social levels and avoided at higher ones. It was this perception of divergent evaluation patterns in the community – and a desire to investigate the social correlates of these complex patterns – that motivated the Belfast research.

The Belfast work broke with the Labov paradigm (as used before 1974) to the extent that socio-economic class (the main New York social variable) was not used in the first place. The work was carried out as a series of community studies, backed up by a later random sampling of households throughout the city. The first step, however, was a study of three poor inner-city communities, in which clear patterns of differentiation according to age, sex, and region were demonstrated (J. and L. Milroy 1978). Additionally, as there was an interest in how relatively stable patterns of non-standard usage are maintained (despite social pressures to adopt higher status language), the investigators adopted from anthropological research the notion of *social network* (Bott 1971; Boissevain 1974), which, amongst other things, predicts that strong ('dense' and 'multiplex') social ties within small communities will function as norm-enforcement mechanisms. This was adapted successfully to quantitative use (L. Milroy 1987a), and it has important implications for the notion of speech community (which according to Labov is defined as one in which the variants used are evaluated in the same way throughout), for the interpretation of variation revealed within communities, and for our under- standing of the manner in which linguistic change is implemented and diffused. In particular, it has been argued (on the basis of social network) that the speech community is not organised primarily on a single dimension of *status* or of socio-economic class, but on interaction between the dimensions of *solidarity* (accessed by study of social network pressures) and *status* (L. Milroy 1987a; J. Milroy 1982). More recently, it has been further proposed that linguistic change is slow to the extent that communities are solidary, and rapid to the extent that 'weak ties' (Granovetter 1973, 1982) develop in communities (J. and L. Milroy 1985b). In effect, this is a theory of linguistic change which, although based on the empirical foundations of Weinreich, Labov and Herzog, does not accept as a prime the Labov notion of speech community, in which the underlying model is a unidimensional socio-economic class continuum. It accepts, amongst other things, that there may be *conflict* of values within speech communities, and further suggests that if this were not so, linguistic change could not take place.

Further research using a social network approach has been carried out successfully by a number of scholars, particularly Bortoni Ricardo (1985) in Brazil. In recent years, Labov himself has carried out an extensive study of Philadelphia by means of 'neighborhood studies', in which the methodology is very similar to that of the 'community studies' in Belfast. The findings of the Philadelphia studies are reported in several papers published in D. Sankoff (1986); it should be noted that Labov and his colleagues do not use social network as an *interpretative* category, and consider it to be chiefly a methodological tool.

Even though the quantitative methods pioneered by Labov (and discussed here) have led to new insights and have contributed greatly to our under- standing, the question of ultimate social motivations for the actuation and diffusion of linguistic change still remains controversial; this is an area of research in which further activity is likely to refine our understanding and (in our view) contribute to linguistic theory in general. However, work arising from the quantitative paradigm has also made significant contributions to areas of interest quite separate from the study of linguistic change, in particular the question of attitudes to language variation (e.g. in the educational system) and the practical consequences arising. Therefore, having reviewed some of the quantitative work that has been carried out in major urban research projects, we now turn to an account of some of the practical applications of such work.

## 3.2 Practical issues

Although the theoretical goals of the quantitative paradigm are ultimately to explain the *how* and *why* of linguistic change, Labov and his school have also been deeply involved in controversies about practical social and educational issues. This has arisen from their concern with *non-standard* language and its relationship to standard forms of language.

The question of language disadvantage (and 'language deficit') has been prominent and controversial for about thirty years. In Britain, for example, Bernstein (see Bernstein, 1971–5) proposed that the relative failure at school of working-class children might be explained on linguistic grounds – i.e. their relative lack of access to what he called the *elaborated code*. We can characterise this as the kind of language in which ideas can be expressed independently of immediate situational contexts – and this involves skills of context-free expression that are highly valued in the education system. The point here, however, is that some educational psychologists (and others) seized upon this alleged linguistic difficulty as a satisfactory explanation for failure in school, and further postulated that working-class children often suffered from *verbal deprivation* or *language deficit*. It was even suggested that some children started their schooling with no language at all. As many working-class children in the USA are black, this became a highly sensitive social and political issue in the late 1960s. See Chapter 16, section 8, below.

Using careful participant observation methods, Labov set out to investigate this alleged deficit empirically, and in several important essays arising from his work in Harlem, New York (1972a), he established that black children and adolescents belonged to a highly verbal culture in which verbal skills were greatly admired. The alleged deficit, he claimed, was in fact only a language *difference*: the black children were speakers of non-standard English ('Black English Vernacular'). Furthermore, their difficulties in the educational system arose from differences in cultural and social values. Their language, although of low social status, was as regular and rule-governed as standard English.

Labov's Harlem research further explored language in the community – outside of institutional settings – by looking at adolescent peer-group behaviour. This involves an aspect of co-variation of language and social

499

group which is different from the large-scale urban surveys discussed above, and in which socio-economic class is not an immediate methodological issue (the persons studied are of roughly equal social class). In his study of the Harlem gangs, Labov shows how group dynamics in some sense govern language use. Using quantitative methods, he shows that non-standard forms are used most frequently by 'core' members of the group – i.e. those who unquestionably have the highest status in the group – and least frequently by the 'lames' – those who, for various reasons participate only marginally in the group's activities. The core members, of course, are admired for various activities generally regarded as anti-social – including truancy – and are the most backward at school. Failure at school thus becomes a general social issue (involving a clash of values between the adolescent culture and the general social norms) and is no longer a matter of verbal deficit.

In Britain, the most substantial piece of work on peer-group language is Cheshire's (1982) study of Reading adolescents. This supports Labov's thesis that group dynamics dominate peer-group language and behaviour in contradistinction to the wider social norms, and further establishes significant differences between males and females. Work on non-indigenous groups has been carried out in Britain by Sutcliffe (1982), Edwards (1986), and the Linguistic Minorities project (1985), amongst others. These studies are plainly relevant to understanding educational, social and cultural differences between groups.

The educational issues involved here have been debated in Britain and the USA for many years. In general, they have focused on the place of the standard language in the educational system. Whereas many sociolinguists (Stubbs 1976, Trudgill 1975) have appealed for greater tolerance for non-standard varieties, others (notably Honey 1983) have argued that to focus on dialects may be to deny children access to standard English and so deprive them of a social and economic asset. The issue is a sensitive one, and it tends to become clouded by polemics. However, the study of language standardisation and prescription is, in itself, a matter of great importance, as standardisation of important modern languages in recent centuries has had a number of practical consequences. These are explored by J. and L. Milroy (1985a). Among them is the important question of language testing and assessment in education and speech therapy; it seems that many established tests of general linguistic competence do not take account of language variation, but assume (wrongly) that testees have equal access to standard English (which is taken as the norm). Lower scores on such tests may thus arise, not from language deficit, but merely from language *difference*.

We end this section by noticing briefly certain other matters that have arisen from quantitative sociolinguistic investigations. One recurrent finding is that there is a consistent difference between male and female usage, with females tending rather more to what is usually considered to be higher status forms and males favouring local vernaculars (as in Figure 22, above). There is, however, considerable dispute as to whether it is correct to generalise from this that females are more status-conscious in their speech. Male/female speech-differences are now discussed by Coates (1986).

A further important issue arising is the question of *communicative competence*, as proposed by Hymes (1967). This introduces a new perspective on many matters, including the educational issues discussed above, as it becomes possible to show that persons who do badly in education and in public uses of language may nevertheless have considerable verbal ability in everyday language use. Often, for example, they may control two or more dialects or languages, and so their competence may be in some senses wider than that of a monolingual standard speaker. In short, it seems that competence should be judged, not in terms of command of one dialect or restricted variety of *language*, but in terms of the *speaker's* repertoire (J. and L. Milroy 1985a). In sections 4 and 5, the issue of communicative competence is further discussed.

## 4. STYLISTIC VARIATION

In section 3 we discussed quantiative linguistic studies chiefly in terms of their ability to illuminate (with reference to such speaker characteristics as age, sex, ethnicity, and personal network structure) the nature of linguistic variation *between* speakers. The methods and results of such quantitative studies have theoretical implications in granting insight into the way languages change through time, but also are relevant to practical issues (for example, in education). However, just as quantitative sociolinguistic methods allow the language of two or more speakers to be viewed in terms of *greater* or *lesser use* (of an element like, for example, initial /h/) rather than in terms of *absolute* use or non-use, they can be used to compare the language styles used by *the same* speaker on different occasions. We turn for the remainder of the chapter to examine various traditions of sociolinguistic research which have focused on this dimension of language variation in such a way as to bring out the relationship between a number of social variables and a speaker's choice of language on *different occasions.* The approach associated with Labov's quantitative sociolinguistics may be exemplified by patterns of stylistic variation in the city of Norwich between *-in'* and *-ing* in the present participle form of the verb (as, for example, in *jumping, shooting*).

Table 14 shows the incidence of the *in'* variant according to whether (a) the speaker is reading words from a list presented to him and might therefore be expected to pay careful attention to each word; (b) reading a passage of connected prose – a slightly less careful style; (c) responding to direct

*Table 14* Percentage of *in'* in Norwich, shown according to style and class

|  | WLS | RPS | FS | CS |
|---|---|---|---|---|
| Middle middle class | 0 | 0 | 3 | 28 |
| Lower middle class | 0 | 10 | 15 | 42 |
| Upper working class | 5 | 15 | 74 | 87 |
| Middle working class | 23 | 44 | 88 | 95 |
| Lower working class | 29 | 66 | 98 | 100 |

(Adapted from Chambers and Trudgill 1980: 71)

questions in a tape recorded interview and therefore speaking fairly self-consciously but paying less attention to his speech than he would to a reading task; or (d) talking relatively casually when his attention has been diverted away from the fact that his speech is being tape-recorded. Thus, it is argued, the four styles WLS (Word List Style), RPS (Reading Passage Style), FS (Formal Style) and CS (Casual Style) may be interpreted as a continuum along which speakers move as they pay progressively less attention to producing careful speech.

Table 14, like many other similar sets of data reported in the literature, shows patterns similar to those first clearly identified by Labov in New York City. Its most striking feature is the consistency of the relationship between the large-scale social dimension of class and the small-scale personal dimension of style, the sensitivity of speakers to class-related pronunciations being revealed by differences in their use of these same variables according to style. Frequencies of *in'* regularly increase across rows and down columns, showing that although social groups characteristically use different frequencies, they all agree in style-shifting in the same direction as their speech style alters on the dimension of formality. One question of particular interest to (for example) teachers who want their pupils to be able to control the standard form of the language, is *why* people in the lowest status group continue to use stigmatised elements like *in'* when it is clear from information such as that presented in Table 14 that they are in fact sensitive to the variable and are moreover perfectly able to adjust its frequency quite considerably in formal contexts. In fact, the usage of the lowest status groups in formal contexts approximates quantitatively to the casual norm of the *highest* social group, a relationship between the personal and larger scale inter-personal dimensions of variation which has led Labov to suggest in a memorable phrase that it might be difficult to distinguish 'a casual salesman from a careful plumber' (Labov 1972b: 240).

An explanation of why individual speakers continue to use stigmatised forms in this consistent way should help us to understand why adverse comments on language patterns of low-status groups (by teachers and employers, amongst others) seem not to influence behaviour. However, as we noted in section 3, quantitative sociolinguistics was originally developed to offer explanations of large-scale, long-term patterns of variation and change; characteristically it starts by examining the way linguistic elements pattern in the community, rather than the use made by individual speakers of the linguistic resources available to them. If on the other hand we are interested primarily in the behaviour of individual speakers rather than long-term language changes and large-scale patterns of variation such as are revealed in Table 14 and Figures 22 and 23, we can learn more from approaches to stylistic variation which begin by examining speaker behaviour, as opposed to linguistic elements like /r/, /h/ and -*in*'. We shall focus for the remainder of this chapter on what might be described as the *speaker-orientated* tradition of sociolinguistic research (cf. the discussion on p. 486 above of the speaker/ system distinction).

It is a matter of commonplace observation that all normal speakers vary their language quite extensively according to situation. There are, as Labov has pointed out, no single-style speakers, and this ability to vary styles is often particularly difficult for foreign language learners to acquire. The capacity of persons to select and recognise the type of language appropriate to the occasion (a matter which involves much more than adjusting frequencies of linguistic elements in the manner illustrated by Table 14) is known as their *communicative competence.* This notion was introduced by Dell Hymes, whose interest is primarily in the behaviour of speakers rather than in more abstract patterns of language variation and change. He comments:

No normal person and no normal community is limited in repertoire to a single variety or code, to an unchanging monotony which would preclude the possibility of indicating respect, insolence, mock seriousness, role distance etc. by switching from one variety to another. (1967: 8)

The totality of styles (both spoken and written) available to a community is known as its *linguistic repertoire,* and speakers learn to select from this repertoire in order to fulfil various communicative needs. Thus, part of the communicative competence of a British school teacher might be command of the styles needed for the following purposes: addressing a formal meeting; teaching a class; writing a formal report; writing an informal letter; addressing his baby daughter; telling a joke; and chatting to his friends in the pub over a beer. Some styles in a community's repertoire are rather specialised, with quite clear linguistic characteristics; most people for example can recognise the styles of a racing commentary or a sermon, and are aware very early in the proceedings if they are being told a joke, as opposed to some other kind of narrative or descriptive account of events.

In fact, linguists who share Hymes's primary interest in this socially conditioned aspect of speakers' variable linguistic behaviour have adopted a great many approaches to the study of communicative competence. One very successful way of examining the way in which meanings of (for example) irony, hostility, deference and intimacy are indicated is to begin by examining a speaker's psycho-social orientation to his or her conversational partner on the dimensions of *social distance* and *solidarity* (or intimacy). Some languages have grammatical systems which allow speakers to mark these relationships to interlocutors in a formal way. Obvious examples are the various European languages such as French, German and Italian where choice of intimate or polite second person pronoun (*tu* versus *vous* in French for singular address) has been analysed as being conditioned specifically by these two variables. Furthermore, their conditioning effect differs subtly at different times and in different countries according to larger-scale social and political attitudes; one consequence of this is that in most European countries pronoun usage is now for the most part reciprocal, whereas it was once used to code *power* asymmetries between interlocutors (Brown and Gilman 1960).

Other languages (like Javanese, for example) encode similar social relationships by means of a different and highly complicated range of lexical and syntactic choices (Geertz 1960), while English speakers use a wide range of strategies, one of the most obvious of which is choice of first name or nickname (as opposed to title and last name). One rather complex area of English syntax which is strongly implicated in conveying this kind of social meaning is the *modal verb* system. As part of a much wider cross-cultural study of *politeness strategies*, which is concerned not only with expressions of politeness but its underlying motivations, Brown and Levinson (1987) have examined the way speakers use verbs like *can* and *might*, in conjunction with certain other choices, to indicate their orientation to each other. Consider for example the rather different speaker/addressee relationships implied in choosing each one of the following alternative ways of making a request, each of which a single speaker might select on an appropriate occasion:

Can you shut the window, please?
Could you shut the window, please?
Would you like to shut the window, please?
Would you mind very much if I asked you to shut the window, please?

Using the thorough and influential work of Brown and Levinson as a general background, Laver (1981) has looked in detail at *linguistic routines*, those highly ritualised, formally conventional exchanges such as greetings, partings and small-talk which occur at the fringes of conversation. Although one might think that such routines were unlikely to be subject to much variation in the usage of a single speaker, Laver shows that their form and structure in different conversations are also strongly constrained by the mutual orientation of speaker and addressee on the dimensions of status and solidarity. (See Chapter 6, section 4, above.)

It is plain then that when speakers shift styles they are selecting from a range of choices at several linguistic levels. Although this process certainly involves adjusting the frequency of key phonological elements in different situations in the manner revealed by Table 14, analyses such as those of Laver and of Brown and Levinson show that they are doing something rather more subtle with a clearer social motivation; they are adjusting their language to reflect social orientation to different *addressees*. For this reason, Bell (1984: 197) has suggested that it is misleading to analyse such patterns in terms of greater or less 'attention to speech', a variable controlled by the formality of the situation; a better generalisation is that 'at all levels of language variability, people are responding primarily to other people. Speakers are designing their style for their audience.' This view of *audience design* rather than *attention to speech* as the critical variable in accounting for stylistic variation allows us to address the problem raised at the beginning of this section: why do speakers continue to use low status, stigmatised language forms when they are capable of adjusting their speech substantially in the direction of higher status norms?

The answer which now suggests itself is as follows. We know from the findings of quantitative sociolinguistics that particular pronunciations are, in the sense that they are used at different frequencies, associated with particular groups of speakers; hence the relationship between language use on the one hand and the social variables of social class and social network on the other. These variables are associated respectively with the inter-personal dimensions of status and solidarity discussed above. Furthermore, in real-life situations different addressees are associated not only with different status and solidarity values, but with different contexts. High-status addressees are associated with formal situations, and solidary or intimate addressees with informal situations. Different pronunciations to which different social values are assigned are thus associated with different addressees, as are different styles of address and politeness routines. This association explains the relationship between the social and the stylistic dimensions of linguistic variation.

To illustrate the value of an audience design analysis of stylistic variation, Bell cites some interesting quantitative studies of the language of broadcasting. The phenomenon under investigation is variation in amount of intervocalic /t/ voicing in the speech of four newscasters broadcasting from two different stations, A and B; A is of higher status than B, and /t/ voicing shows patterns of social and stylistic stratification in New Zealand, similar in structure to those shown for *in'* in Table 14 above. Since a considerable amount of attention is necessarily paid to speech by *all* newscasters, it does

*Figure 25* Patterns of intervocalic (t) voicing by four newscasters each speaking from two New Zealand radio stations, A and B (adapted from Bell 1984:171).

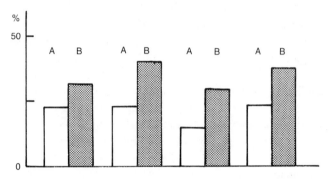

not seem plausible to suggest that the exact amount depends on the station from which the news is being broadcast. However, as Figure 25 shows, the style adopted by each of the four strikingly corresponds with the language patterns of the target audience, for whom they might be said to be *designing a speech style* (Bell 1984: 171). As we shall see in section 5, the concept of audience design can also be used to account for patterns of language choice by *bilingual* speakers.

## 5. TYPES OF LINGUISTIC REPERTOIRE

We have looked so far only at linguistic repertoires (see above) available to *monolingual* speakers. But there are throughout the world many communities, perhaps indeed a majority, whose speakers have access to linguistic repertoires which allow them to switch between codes which they (or others) define as different languages, or different dialects of the same language. We choose our words carefully here, since it is quite common for speakers to have a *consciousness* of two or more named components in their repertoires which may in fact be structurally almost indistinguishable. A well-known pair of examples is Punjabi and Urdu, which are structurally very close, but are, primarily because of their connection with different national and ethnic identities, defined as 'different languages'. The two languages in the repertoire might on the other hand be typologically quite different (like Irish and English). In any event, each code is usually associated with different sets of social values (often particularly strongly with ethnicity) and so is appropriate for use with different interlocutors. It is only where it does not seem feasible to separate out components in a repertoire in this way, that speakers are said to shift between *styles*, and it is generally accepted that although bilingual or bidialectal switching is a more visible process than monolingual style shifting,

*Figure 26* Factors affecting code choice (adapted from Rubin 1968:109).

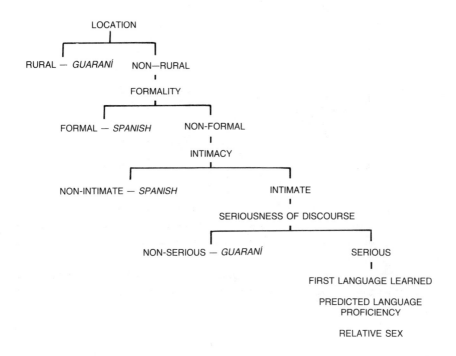

the psycho-social dynamics underlying these different kinds of *code-switching* are similar (see section 4, above; see also Le Page and Tabouret-Keller (1985) for an explicitly psycho-social account of code variation).

One interesting bilingual study (Rubin 1968) reports that 92 per cent of the population of Paraguay were bilingual in Guaraní and Spanish, with both languages having an official status. There was little sign that this bilingualism was a temporary phenomenon which would disappear as the population became monolingual in Spanish. Factors such as whether the conversation was taking place in an urban or rural setting, the sex of the interlocutors, their social orientation to each other and the topic of conversation all influenced language choice in much the same way as they would be likely to influence stylistic choice in a monolingual community. These social and contextual factors are presented in Figure 26 in the form of a tree diagram, which lays out decision on the appropriate code as a set of ordered, binary choices.

There have been a great many large-scale surveys of language use in bilingual and multilingual communities, which are typically concerned with 'who speaks what language to whom, and when and to what end'. Figure 27,

*Figure 27* Use ratings by 350 educated Indians for mother tongues in seven different social contexts. The vertical scale indicates ratings of relative frequency of use of mother tongue.

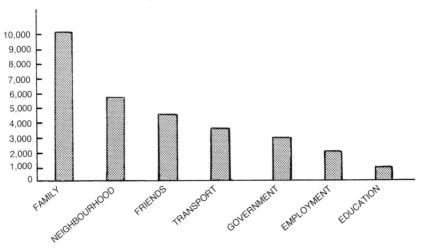

for example, presents information gathered by Parasher (1980) from 350 speakers in two Indian cities on their language use in a number of different *domains* (or sets of similar situations). The methods used by Parasher and others who have carried out similar studies of language use in bi- or multilingual communities are discussed in detail by Fasold (1984: chapter 7).

A number of these studies have focused in a more detailed way than have those of Rubin or Parasher on the circumstances in which speakers shift between different elements in their repertoire. For example, Denison (1972) reported his observations made in 1960 in the village of Sauris, in the Italian Alps, of how speakers switched between Italian, Friulian, and German. The main factors which determined language choice seemed to be the setting of the interaction (German was usually confined to domestic contexts), the participants and the topic. Friulian was usually used in interaction with other local residents outside the home, and Denison showed how persons could manipulate their repertoires for social and personal purposes. He described, for example, how one woman used German in an attempt to compel her husband to leave the bar where he was drinking, where Friulian would be the usual choice. Thus, consciously or unconsciously, she seems to select German, the language of domesticity, for clearly manipulative purposes. (The situation in Sauris in the 1980s is that German is no longer used; the repertoire now consists of Friulian and Italian.)

Perhaps the most detailed and influential study of all which focuses on speakers' use of their repertoire is the one carried out by Blom and Gumperz (1972) in Hemnesberget, a small town in Northern Norway, where the manner in which speakers alternate between standard Norwegian (Bokmål) and Norwegian dialect was carefully analysed. The difference between dialect and standard in Norway is comparable to the difference in central and southern Scotland between Lowland Scots and standard English, and like Scots speakers (who differ from most speakers of urban dialects in English cities in this respect), Hemnesberget people perceive the two codes as distinct elements in their repertoire. The fact that they can be better analysed at a structural level as overlapping on a continuum (much as Labov analysed the various accents found in New York City) is beside the point, since Blom and Gumperz are concerned chiefly with the strategies and behaviour of *speakers*. However, as we suggested earlier, the psycho-social principles underlying dialect-shifting are similar to those underlying style-shifting and language switching. One particular group of speakers with strong feelings of local loyalty, who were aptly described by Blom and Gumperz as members of the 'local team', use the dialect at all times with other locals, and are restricted in their use of the standard to contexts where it conveys 'meanings of officiality, expertise and politeness to strangers who are clearly segmented from their personal life' (1972: 434). In complete contrast, the local elite view the standard as their normal code, resorting to the dialect only for some special effect such as adding local colour to an anecdote.

Blom and Gumperz focus in their analysis on an issue which we have not yet made explicit here, although it underlies much of our discussion of style-shifting and code-switching: that is the *socially functional* nature of a varied repertoire. Since speakers can express important social meanings by manipu-lating elements in that repertoire, the two codes can be said to be *maintained* by a social system which distinguishes sharply between local and non-local norms and values. This leads to a broader understanding of why communities maintain distinctive codes, even when one of them is publicly regarded as being of low status (a matter parallel to the persistence in monolingual communities of stigmatised language forms). The local or 'insider' value assigned to the low-status code is likely to be quite positive, so that although it might seem in some sense simpler for speakers in Sauris or Norway or Paraguay to use a single code, the repertoires in these communities can be seen as extremely functional. By the same token, if as a consequence of social change the social values associated with 'insider' or local codes cease to be relevant, we might expect them to disappear from the repertoire. This is exactly what happens in the process of *language shift* from bilingualism in Hungarian and German to German monolingualism documented by Gal (1979) in the Austrian village of Oberwart; prior to the shift in the years following the Second World War the community had been bilingual for a thousand years. Similarly, Dorian (1981) describes the disappearance of Gaelic from a Sutherland community, after a long period of bilingualism.

Bidialectal and bilingual repertoires are by no means confined to the geographically remote rural communities which we have discussed here. There are many bilingual communities of immigrant origin in, for example, Australian and American cities, and recent research in Britain has documented similar code-switching patterns in a large number of immigrant communities, many of whom continue to use their mother tongues alongside English (Linguistic Minorities Project, 1985). Some recent work in London on children from communities of West Indian origin shows in detail how young speakers manipulate the available linguistic resources. Although West Indian creole is rather generally stigmatised (and creole-speaking communities will themselves express negative attitudes) it is not disappearing from the repertoires of children born and educated in Britain who now have a perfect command of English. Not only do black youngsters use creole increasingly as an insider code as they emerge from childhood to adolescence, but even white adolescents, under certain specifiable conditions, use creole with black friends (Hewitt 1982). (For explanation of the terms 'lingua franca', 'pidgin' and 'creole' see the note under the References to Chapter 26, below.)

## 6. CODE-MIXING AND CONVERSATIONAL CODE-SWITCHING

So far, we have treated code-switching as if it always involves a clear choice between two distinguishable parts of a linguistic repertoire. Although this is sometimes the case, we also find *mixed codes* in bilingual communities, where speakers alternate between one language and the other within the same conversation, and even within the same utterance. Mixed codes are particularly stigmatised, even by their users (see the comments of the Punjabi/English bilingual quoted below), and derogatory terms descriptive of such codes are very widespread. Examples are 'Tex-Mex' for the mixed code used by Spanish/English bilinguals in California; 'tuti futi' (Punjabi and English); 'Joual' (Canadian French and English) and 'verbal salad' (Yoruba and English; reported by Amuda 1986). However, as sociolinguists have observed, it is very common for low-status speakers to stigmatise their own dialects and languages, mixed or otherwise, and to report inaccurately on their own language use. These comments usually reflect widespread public stereotyping of the speakers' social group rather than the facts of their own language behaviour which, itself, does not appear to be accessible to conscious reflection. The following example of a mixed Punjabi/English code, recorded in Birmingham, illustrates vividly both the nature of code-mixing and this characteristic mismatch between attitudes and behaviour:

I mean . . . I'm guilty in that sense ke zIada əsī English i bolde ɛ̃ fer ode nal edā honda

ke tʊ hadi jeɽi zʊban ϵ, na? odec hər Ik sentence Ic je do tIn English de word hʊnde ϵ
... but I think that's wrong, I mean, mē̃ khʊd canā ke mē̃, na, jədo Panjabi bolda ϵ,
pure Panjabi bolā əsī mix kərde rϵne a, I mean, unconsciously, subconsciously, kəri
jane ϵ, you know, pər I wish you know ke mē̃ pure Panjabi bol səkā.

Translation

I mean . . . I'm guilty as well in the sense that we speak English more and then what
happens is that when you speak your own language you get two or three English words
in each sentence . . . but I think that's wrong, I mean, I myself would like to speak *pure*
Panjabi whenever I speak Panjabi. We keep mixing (Panjabi and English) I mean
unconsciously, subconsciously, we keep doing it, you know, but I wish, you know, that
I could speak *pure* Panjhabi. (Chana and Romaine 1984: 450)

In view of the particularly negative attitudes generally expressed to mixed
codes such as these, and the unconscious nature of code-mixing behaviour, it
is reasonable to ask what function such behaviour might have; we have
already seen that *different* codes in a repertoire may be said to be functional in
that they encode contrasting sets of social values. John Gumperz (1982) has
argued that conversational code-switching (or code-mixing) has a specific
rhetorical or communicative function which he has studied as part of a larger
field of investigation known as *interactional sociolinguistics*. Gumperz's interest,
like that of Hymes, is explicitly in the way the *speaker* uses available linguistic
resources for communicative purposes, rather than in patterns in an abstract
linguistic system which are then related to patterns in an equally abstract
social system. He therefore begins not by identifying variable elements in a
linguistic system as Labov does, but by looking directly at interactions
between speakers. Sometimes asking the participants themselves for interpretations of recorded conversations, he examines the use to which they put
various available linguistic resources, and the inferences which their conversational partners are able to draw from these 'discourse strategies';
conversational code-switching is seen as just one such strategy.

Gumperz gives numerous examples of the insights into conversational
interaction provided by his methods. In the first of the two cited below,
communication appears to be successful in that the addressee draws the
intended inferences from a particular code-switching routine; in the second
something has gone wrong. The first example involves a switch from English
to Spanish in the conversation of two bilingual businessmen. Apart from the
function of the shared ('insider') code in marking a solidary relationship, the
rhetorical function of this mixing is to reiterate and emphasise a portion of
the utterance. In the second example the conversation runs into trouble after
an initial choice of American Black English by the first speaker. He is a black
householder opening the door to a black interviewer who had made an
appointment to interview the woman of the house:

(1)  A: The three old ones spoke nothing but Spanish, nothing but Spanish.

*No hablaban inglés* (they did not speak English).

[Later in the same conversation]

A: I was . . . I got to thinking *vacilando el punto* (mulling over that point) you know?

(Gumperz 1982: 78)

(2) Husband: So y're gonna check out ma ol lady, hah?

Interviewer: Ah, no. I only came to get some information. They called from the office.

(Husband, dropping his smile, disappears without a word and calls his wife.)

(Gumperz 1982: 133)

Gumperz explains the linguistic source of the misunderstanding in (2) as follows:

The student reports that the interview that followed was stiff and quite unsatisfactory. Being black himself, he knew that he had 'blown it' by failing to recognize the significance of the husband's speech style in this particular case. The style is that of a formulaic opening gambit used to 'check out' strangers, to see whether or not they can come up with the appropriate formulaic reply. Intent on following the instructions he had received in his methodological training and doing well in what he saw as a formal interview, the interviewer failed to notice the husband's stylistic cues. Reflecting on the incident, he himself states that, in order to show that he was on the husband's wave-length, he should have replied with a typically black response like 'Yea, I'ma git some info' (I'm going to get some information) to prove his familiarity with and his ability to understand local verbal etiquette and values. Instead, his Standard English reply was taken by the husband as an indication that the interviewer was not one of them and, perhaps, not to be trusted.

(ibid. 133)

Analyses similar to (1) and (2) have been carried out by others who have studied conversational code-switching. For example, Gal cites a fairly lengthy extract which demonstrates the way a German/Hungarian bilingual participating in a mealtime dispute (carried out mainly in Hungarian) signals increasing anger by repeating a final, last word comment in German; this comment effectively ends the conversation and is, rhetorically, extremely effective (1979: 117).

Although Gumperz appears to have developed his approach initially by examining the communicative functions of code-switching, the field of study which he describes as interactional sociolinguistics is somewhat broader than these examples imply. Treating code-mixing as only one of several communicative resources, he examines various others such as prosody, use of politeness and emphasis routines, and types of discourse pattern which speakers use to signal their orientation to each other (see Brown and Levinson 1987 for a recent review of such work). Since these communicative resources are, like (2) above, often group specific and so not interpretable by outsiders, this approach can be used effectively to examine situations of inter-ethnic communicative breakdown in industrial and other workplace settings, and indeed, Gumperz and his colleagues have produced both a film and an associated book, *Crosstalk*, precisely for this practical purpose.

## 7. CONCLUSION

We noted in the Introduction to this chapter that the field of study described by the term 'sociolinguistics' covers a wide area. In fact, it partially overlaps at least four other fields covered in this volume. Perhaps the largest such overlap is with *Anthropological Linguistics* (here, Chapter 13), since (as we noted in section 1) modern sociolinguists owe a great intellectual debt to the anthropological linguistics which flourished in the early years of this century, and scholars like Gumperz, Hymes and Brown and Levinson continue to straddle both fields. Second, some of the issues treated in section 4 on style-shifting are closely connected with the areas covered by the chapters on Pragmatics (Chapter 6) and Interaction and Conversation (Chapter 8), in so far as they are concerned with a context-sensitive analysis of interaction between speakers. Third, our discussion of the practical issues arising from recent sociolinguistic work is likely to overlap to some extent with Chapter 16 on Language in Education. Finally, readers who are interested in bilingual and multilingual communities of the kind discussed in sections 5 and 6 are likely to find the subject matter of the last Chapter, 26, 'Languages of the world; who speaks what?' particularly relevant.

In this summary account of present-day sociolinguistics, we have tried to show how contemporary methods and interests have evolved from more traditional kinds of study. Subsequently, we devoted a large part of the chapter to the influential paradigm established by William Labov, which has dominated modern sociolinguistics. However, Labov's methods were designed principally to provide answers to questions on the nature of language change and variation, starting from an analysis of *linguistic forms*. Scholars who are attempting to focus on the nature of a *speaker's* abilities and behaviour are more likely to start from an examination of the speaker and the social context, before moving on to examine the relationship of the speaker's linguistic behaviour to that context. The work reviewed in this chapter shows that these different goals and methods are producing interesting insights into the nature of the relationship between language and society.

# REFERENCES

Amuda, A. (1986) 'Language mixing by Yoruba speakers of English', unpublished Ph.D. thesis, University of Reading.

Bailey, C.-J. (1973) *Variation and linguistic theory*, Center for Applied Linguistics, Washington DC.

Bauman, R. and Sherzer, J. (1974) *Explorations in the ethnography of speaking*, Cambridge University Press, Cambridge.

Bell, A. (1984) 'Language style as audience design', *Language in Society*, 13,2: 145–204.

Bernstein, B.B. (1971–5) *Class, codes and control*, Routledge & Kegan Paul, London.

Blom, J-P, and Gumperz, J. (1972) 'Social meaning in linguistic structures: code switching in Norway', in Gumperz, J. and Hymes, D. (eds), *Directions in sociolinguistics*, Holt, Rinehart & Winston, New York: 407–34.

Bloomfield, L. (1933) *Language*, Holt, Rinehart & Winston, New York.

Boissevain, J. (1974) *Friends of friends: networks, manipulators and coalitions*, Blackwell, Oxford.

Bortoni-Ricardo, S.M. (1985) *The urbanisation of rural dialect speakers: a sociolinguistic study in Brazil*, Cambridge University Press, Cambridge.

Bott, E. (1971) *Family and social network* (rev. ed.), Tavistock, London.

Brown, P. and Levinson, S.C. (1987) *Politeness*, Cambridge University Press, Cambridge.

Brown, R. and Gilman, A. (1960) 'Pronouns of power and solidarity' in Sebeok, T.A. (ed.) *Style in language*, MIT Press, Boston: 253–76.

Cedergren, H. and Sankoff, D. (1974) 'Variable rules: performance as a statistical reflection of competence', *Language*, 50: 333–55.

Chambers, J. and Trudgill, P. (1980) *Dialectology*, Cambridge University Press, Cambridge.

Chana, V. and Romaine, S., (1984) 'Evaluative reactions to Panjabi/English codeswitching', *Journal of Multilingual and Multicultural Development*, 5: 447–53.

Cheshire, J. (1982) *Variation in an English dialect: a sociolinguistic study*, Cambridge University Press, Cambridge.

Coates, J. (1986) *Women, men and language*, Longman, London.

Denison, N. (1972) 'Some observations on language variety and plurilingualism', in Pride, J.B. and Holmes, J. (eds) *Sociolinguistics*, Penguin, Harmondsworth: 65–77.

Dorian, N., (1981) *Language death*, University of Pennsylvania Press, Philadelphia.

Edwards, V. (1986) *Language in a black community*, Multilingual Matters, Clevedon, Avon.

Fasold, R. (1984) *The sociolinguistics of society*, Blackwell, Oxford.

Gal, S. (1979) *Language shift: social determinants of linguistic change in bilingual Austria*, Academic Press, New York.

Geertz, C. (1960) *The religion of Java*, Glencoe, Illinois.

Granovetter, M. (1973) 'The strength of weak ties', *American Journal of Sociology*, 78: 1360–80.

Granovetter, M. (1982) 'The strength of weak ties: a network theory revisited', in Marsden, P.V. and Lin, N. (eds) *Social structure and network analysis*, Sage, London.

Gregg, R. (1964) 'Scotch-Irish urban speech in Ulster', in Adams, G.B. (ed.), *Ulster dialect symposium*, Ulster Folk Museum, Holywood, Co. Down: 163–91.

Gregg, R. (1972) 'The Scotch-Irish dialect boundaries of Ulster', in Wakelin (ed.): 109–39.

Gumperz, J. (1982) *Discourse strategies*, Cambridge University Press, Cambridge.

Gumperz, J.J., Jupp, T.C. and Roberts, C. (1979) *Crosstalk: a study of cross-cultural communication*, National Centre for Industrial Language Training, Southall.

Harris, J. (1985) *Phonological variation and change*, Cambridge University Press, Cambridge.

Hewitt, R. (1982) 'White adolescent creole users and the politics of friendship', *Journal of Multilingual and Multicultural Development*, 3: 217–32.

Honey, J. (1983) *The language trap; race, class and the 'standard English' issue in British schools*, Kenton, Middlesex, National Council for Educational Standards.

Jespersen, O. (1922), *Language, its nature, development and origin*, George Allen & Unwin, London.

Johnston, P. (1985) 'Irregular style variation patterns in Edinburgh speech', *Scottish Language*, 2: 1–19.

Jones-Sargent, V. (1983) *Tyne bytes*, Peter Lang, Frankfurt am Main.

Kerswill, P. (1987) 'Levels of linguistic variation in Durham', *Journal of Linguistics*, 23, 1: 25–50.

Knowles, G. (1978) 'The nature of phonological variables in Scouse', in Trudgill (ed.): 80–90.

Labov, W. (1966) *The social stratification of English in New York City*, Center for Applied Linguistics, Washington DC.

Labov, W. (1972a) *Language in the inner city*, University of Pennsylvania Press, Philadelphia

Labov, W. (1972b) *Sociolinguistic patterns*, University of Pennsylvania Press, Philadelphia.

Labov, W. (1975) 'On the use of the present to explain the past', *Proceedings of the eleventh international congress of linguists*, Mulino, Bologna.

Labov, W. (ed.) (1980) *Locating language in time and space*, Academic Press, New York.

Labov, W. (1982) 'Building on empirical foundations', in Lehmann, W.P. and Malkiel, Y. (eds) *Perspectives on historical linguistics*, Benjamins, Amsterdam and Philadelphia: 17–92.

Laver, J. (1981) 'Linguistic routines and politeness in greeting and parting', in Coulmas, F. (ed.) *Conversational routines*, Mouton, The Hague.

Le Page, R. and Tabouret-Keller, A. (1985) *Acts of Identity*, Cambridge University Press, Cambridge.

Linguistic Minorities Project (1985) *The other languages of England*, Routledge & Kegan Paul, London.

Macaulay, R.K.S. (1977) *Language, social class and education: a Glasgow study*, Edinburgh University Press, Edinburgh.

McKnight, G. ((1928) 1956) *The evolution of the English language*, Dover, New York.

Milroy, J. (1982) 'Probing under the tip of the iceberg: phonological normalization and the shape of speech communities', in Romaine, S. (ed.) *Sociolinguistic variation in speech communities*, Edward Arnold, London.

Milroy, J. (1983) 'On the sociolinguistic history of /h/-dropping in English', in Davenport, M. *et al.*, *Current topics in English historical linguistics*, Odense University Press, Odense.

Milroy, J. (forthcoming) *Society and language change*, Basil Blackwell, Oxford.

Milroy, J. and Harris, J. (1980) 'When is a merger not a merger? The MEAT/MATE problem in a present-day English vernacular', *English world-wide*, 1, 2: 199–210.

Milroy, J. and Milroy, L. (1978) 'Belfast: change and variation in an urban vernacular', in Trudgill, P. (ed.): 19–36.

Milroy, J and Milroy, L. (1985a) *Authority in language*, Routledge & Kegan Paul, London.

Milroy, J. and Milroy, L. (1985b) 'Linguistic change, social network and speaker innovation', *Journal of Linguistics*, 21: 339–84.

Milroy, L. (1987a) *Language and social networks*, 2nd ed, Blackwell, Oxford.

Milroy, L. (1987b) *Observing and analysing natural language*, Blackwell, Oxford.

Müller, F. Max (1861) *Lectures on the science of language: first series*, London.

Nunberg, G. (1980) 'A falsely reported merger in eighteenth-century English: a study in diachronic variation' in W. Labov (ed.): 221–50.

Orton, H. *et al.* (1962 *et seq.*) *Survey of English dialects*, E.J. Arnold, Leeds.

Parasher, S.N. (1980) 'Mother-tongue-English diglossia: a case-study of educated Indian bilinguals' language use', *Anthropological Linguistics*, 22, 4: 151–68.

Quirk, R. (1968) *The use of English*, 2nd ed, Longman, London.

Romaine, S. (1978) 'Post-vocalic /r/ in Scottish English: sound-change in progress?', in Trudgill, P. (ed.): 144–58.

Romaine, S. (1982) *Socio-historical linguistics*, Cambridge University Press, Cambridge.

Ross, A.S.C. (1954) 'Linguistic class-indicators in present-day English', *Neuphilologische Mitteilungen*, lv; 20–56.

Rubin, J. (1968) *National bilingualism in Paraguay*, Mouton, The Hague.

Sacks, H., Schegloff, E. and Jefferson, G. (1974) 'A simplest systematics for the organisation of turn-taking in conversation', *Language*, 50: 696–735.

Sankoff, D. (ed.) (1978) *Linguistic variation: models and methods*, Academic Press, New York.

Sankoff, D. (1986) *Diversity and diachrony*, Benjamins, Amsterdam/Philadelphia.

Sankoff, G. (1980) *The social life of language*, University of Pennsylvania Press, Philadelphia.

Sapir, E. (1921) *Language*, Macmillan, New York.

Shuy, R.W., Wolfram, W. and Riley, W.K. (1968) *Field techniques in an urban language study*, Center for Applied Linguistics, Arlington, Va.

Stubbs, M. (1976) *Language, schools and classrooms*, Methuen, London.

Sturtevant, E. (1917) *Linguistic change*, University of Chicago Press, Chicago.

Sutcliffe, D. (1982) *British Black English*, Blackwell, Oxford.

Trudgill, P. (1974) *The social differentiation of English in Norwich*, Cambridge University Press, Cambridge.

Trudgill, P. (1975) *Accent, dialect and the school*, Edward Arnold, London.

Trudgill, P. (ed.) (1978) *Sociolinguistic patterns in British English*, Edward Arnold, London.

Trudgill, P. (1986) *Dialects in contact*, Blackwell, Oxford.

Wakelin, M. (1972) *Patterns in the folk speech of the British Isles*, Athlone Press, London.

Weinreich, U., Labov, W. and Herzog, M. (1968) 'Empirical foundations for a theory of language change', in Lehmann, W. and Malkiel, Y., *Directions for historical linguistics*, University of Texas Press, Austin: 95–195.

Wyld, H.C. (1914) *Short history of English*, J. Murray, London.

Wyld, H.C. (1920) *History of modern colloquial English*, Fisher Unwin, London.

# FURTHER READING

Chambers, J. and Trudgill, P. (1980) *Dialectology*, Cambridge University Press, Cambridge.

Fasold, R. (1984) *The sociolinguistics of society*, Blackwell, Oxford.

Gumperz, J. (1982) *Discourse strategies*, Cambridge University Press, Cambridge.

Trudgill, P. (1983) *Sociolinguistics* (2nd ed.), Penguin, Harmondsworth.

Wardhaugh, R. (1986) *An introduction to sociolinguistics*, Blackwell, Oxford.

# 15

## SECOND LANGUAGES: HOW THEY ARE LEARNED AND TAUGHT

### DAVID WILKINS

### 1. INTRODUCTION

There are two situations in which the learning of a second or foreign language typically takes place. The first is where the individual, usually but not inevitably a child, lives in an environment in which more than one language is used under conditions which lead to that individual becoming in some degree *bilingual.* The ensuing bilingualism is often referred to as *natural* since, given appropriate conditions, failure to learn the language would be the exception. It is also natural in the sense that the social and linguistic environment is not being manipulated in any way so as to promote the learning of one or both of the languages. In contrast, the other situation is one in which the learning is tutored, typically as part of the curriculum of an educational establishment. This is the typical foreign language learning of schools and colleges. While natural bilingualism is far more common world-wide than is apparent to those living in largely monolingual communities, it is tutored language learning which is the object of substantial educational planning and research and to which the greater human and economic resources are devoted. For this reason it is such language learning which primarily concerns us here, although we cannot ignore what is known about natural bilingualism, since people's views of how languages are learned 'naturally' have always influenced their views of the ways in which they should be taught.

### 2. THE BASES OF CHANGE IN LANGUAGE TEACHING

Information about what needs to be done to improve the quality of language teaching is likely to come from any one of three sources. First and ideally, the question of which is the best method of teaching a language or of whether one technique is better than another would be investigated directly by means of empirical research in which one variable is compared with the other. Unfortunately, there is such a multiplicity of factors that influence learning on any specific occasion that objective research of this kind faces immense problems. The variables that operate are so difficult to control that the interpretation of results is often open to challenge. The results of large-scale projects, which set out to compare whole methodologies of language teaching have been so disappointing that such research is now rarely attempted. A surprisingly small proportion of innovation in language teaching has resulted from empirical research of this kind.

A second and altogether more potent source of change has been the continuing re-conceptualisation of language learning and teaching. Our view of what a language is and what it is to learn a language is under constant review, frequently in the light of new and evolving theories in adjacent disciplines. Thus we look to psychology for what we can discover about learning in general and language learning in particular. For a model of language we look to linguistics and, to ensure that our approaches are in keeping with sound educational practice, we look to educational theory. Although the relationship with these and other disciplines is far from straightforward and, indeed, controversial, their impact on the historical development of language teaching has been very significant. Directly and indirectly they have affected everything from the most global decisions about our approach to teaching a language to the rationale behind a very specific classroom activity. On this topic much is said in Chapter 16, below. The history of language teaching is largely the history of successive redefinitions of the nature of the task facing language learners and of the conditions and linguistic experience that we have to create to help them master the task. Wherever possible empirical evidence in support of any new theorising should be sought but in reality the impact of a given theoretical perspective has often been determined more by its convincingness than by any out-and-out empirical proof of its validity. Discussion of change in language teaching therefore frequently takes the form of debate in which one theoretically-derived view confronts another and subsequently holds sway until it in turn is overthrown.

The difficulties facing empirical research and the powerful impact often made by theoretical developments do not mean, however, that pragmatic experience has played no part in the development of language teaching. On the contrary, a third source of change is to be found in the response of practising teachers to the experience of teaching a language. They and their pupils have first-hand and continuing experience of the actual effects of their approach to language teaching. That experience is rarely subjected to systematic evaluation but it leads to the common small-scale innovation that is characteristic of most teaching and is the basis for much of the most imaginative and creative thinking that comes in due course to have a wide impact on language teaching. Teachers are also likely to be the first to become aware of any change in the nature of the demand for the language, arising perhaps from different perceptions on the part of learners of the nature of the language skills that they need or from general social pressures. Historically the major contributions in the development of language teaching methodology have usually been made by gifted and insightful teachers who were responding to their experience of teaching and to observation of their pupils. It should be added that such people have rarely been unaware of the need for a coherent rationale and have often conceived their own approach in the light of current theoretical convictions. Similarly the evident success of some of the procedures initiated by language teachers has often prompted a reconsideration of the theoretical bases of language teaching. Theory has benefited from practice just as much as practice has benefited from theory.

## 3. LANGUAGE TEACHING IN THE TWENTIETH CENTURY: A HISTORICAL SKETCH

To a large extent the history of language teaching has to be first and foremost the history of ideas about language teaching. This is because the actual practice of language teaching around the world is so diverse that no single history can hope to provide an accurate description either of the ways in which language teaching has developed in the past or of how languages are taught at present. The pace of change is not everywhere the same, nor does change take place within a uniform cultural and educational tradition. This means that although at a given time a certain method or theory of language teaching may appear to be dominant, it is by no means certain that this dominance is true of all countries nor that actual practice in schools and elsewhere is in line with what current theory would suggest. The ideas that are described here have emerged largely from continental Europe, Britain and North America. However, we should not assume that language teaching practice has exactly matched the evolution of ideas nor, indeed, that this evolution has been identical across even these related cultures.

The recent history of language teaching is most easily understood if a broad distinction is first made between what might be termed *traditionalist* and *modernist* methods. In traditionalist methods we are assumed to possess knowledge of the facts and rules of language. The task of language teaching is then to find effective ways of transmitting this knowledge to learners so that they can make use of it. The basis of modernist methods, by contrast, is that language is *immanent* in the individual, that it is not so much conscious knowledge of facts and rules that renders learning effective as the quality of the linguistic experience that the learner undergoes. Traditionalist teaching tends to conclude that the existence of systematic knowledge about the language system requires that conscious attention should be given to the rules and that these rules should be mastered prior to the attempt to apply them. Such methods are therefore often referred to as *deductive* or, to use a label which captures both the nature of the mental operations involved and the focus on the language system, *cognitive-code* (Carroll 1966). In most modernist teaching it is accepted that the language system has to be mastered, but little importance is attached to the role of conscious learning in this process. Such approaches are therefore often called *inductive*. By contrast, great importance is attached to the learner's own language performance, so that modernist methods can also be characterised as *behavioural*.

The methodological options open to the strict traditionalist seem to be more limited than those available to the modernist. Our knowledge of the rule system of a language does not change dramatically over the years (although the theoretical framework within which that knowledge can be set out has changed). The 'facts' of language can be learned as rules, as paradigms or in some other form. The use of these facts can then be practised or, more accurately, tested through exercises. These may require the learner to follow a grammatical instruction, carry out a mechanical grammatical manipulation or translate a phrase or sentence which poses a particular grammatical problem. A correct performance confirms that the learner has the necessary knowledge of that part of the language system. Translation is a widespread feature of traditionalist teaching. The foreign language is approached through the mother-tongue (which is almost inevitably the language through which teaching takes place). The translation of texts is an activity which demands close attention to similarities and differences between the foreign language and the mother-tongue. It is probably particularly valuable in focusing the learner's attention on the many details of syntax, style and vocabulary which are not subject to rules that are sufficiently generalisable to be taught in their own right. New vocabulary is also usually presented through translation.

It is, of course, perfectly possible to combine elements from the different methodological traditions and, no doubt, this is what often happens in practice. Traditionalist approaches are likely to place high value on accuracy. They could readily incorporate other types of activity designed to increase fluency in use of the language. Conceptually, however, their rationale is as a kind of information-processing which makes substantial cognitive (academic) demands on the learner, as do other knowledge-based disciplines. It is against this view of what it means to know a language that modernist methods were initially a reaction.

The first major, though ultimately largely ineffective, assault on the dominance of traditionalist methods in the twentieth century was made by *direct method* language teaching. As usual, the case for change was based both on arguments against the existing traditionalist approach and on arguments for a new conception of language learning. Traditionalist teaching did not seem to be very effective in enabling learners to use the language that they had so painstakingly studied. Two elements seemed to make fluent use particularly difficult. First, the learners' high level of consciousness about the language rules and the high priority attached to accuracy made it extremely difficult to attain any degree of spontaneity in language use. Secondly, the mediation of the mother-tongue throughout the learning process made it difficult for the learners to operate directly in the foreign language.

A rationale which would solve these problems would be to make language learning a more *natural* process. That is to say, the way in which languages should be taught in schools should be based on the way in which natural language learning took place (or, at least, as it was perceived at the time to take place). The key elements of this were that there was no place for the mother-tongue (children learning their first language did not need another language through which to understand it), nor for explicit rules (children had no consciousness of the language system when learning a language naturally), and that the learning should be of the spoken language first (the child learning naturally had no need of written forms of language as a basis for speech). The teacher would introduce the language through speech (i.e. initially with a substantial emphasis on listening) and would make the language (vocabulary) comprehensible to the learners by associating it directly with experience (realia, activities, pictures etc.). Hence the term *direct* method. Nothing mediated between the forms of the language being learned and the experience that they referred or related to. The pupils' own language would be modelled on that provided by the teacher. The overall aim, then, was to make the learner's experience of the language conform to the experience of learning a first (or second) language naturally.

Direct method teaching was introduced by enthusiasts in many countries and officially adopted in some (e.g. France). Yet it never gained the general acceptance that its historical significance would seem to suggest. Before long the experiments in its use were abandoned and with a few exceptions (e.g. Germany) traditionalist teaching re-asserted itself. The reason probably lay in the demands which the new method placed on the teachers. Being based on the spoken language, it required a high level of language skill on the part of the teacher. More to the point, the method offered no guidance in the choice of language to be introduced. There was no suggestion that this should be controlled according to some predetermined principles (natural language use is not controlled) nor was there any systematic basis for the content or situations being presented. It required a teacher of great pedagogical insight and skill to make the language accessible to learners in these circumstances.

The aims of direct method language teaching were widely judged to be too ambitious to be reached under the normal conditions of school education. One result was that in the United States, for example, a public report (the Coleman Report 1929) concluded that language teaching should be directed to the more limited but realistic goal of establishing a reading knowledge of the foreign language only.

Although in Europe and North America traditionalist language teaching remained dominant in the period up to the Second World War, there was one domain from which the influence of the direct method did not disappear. This was the teaching of English as a foreign language (EFL). (See Howatt 1984 for a more detailed account.) Among the first of a growing number of native speakers of English to establish themselves abroad as teachers of their own language was H.E. Palmer. Palmer had begun his career as a teacher of English in Belgium but spent most of his working life in Japan. As well as being a creative and innovative methodologist he made an important contribution to English linguistics. The influence of Palmer and colleagues who worked in Japan at the same time (for example, A.S. Hornby) was such that EFL teaching has remained in the modernist camp ever since. Palmer did not so much abandon direct method teaching, as others had done, as reform it so as to overcome some of its shortcomings. His attitudes to language were those of early structural linguistics and he perceived language learning as the acquisition of a skill, although this did not emerge as a fully articulated theory. There were two main effects of this on the oral, structural methodology of language teaching that Palmer developed. First, the forms of language were to be introduced, not in random fashion, but with careful structural control (*gradation*), so that the new language to which the learner was being exposed at any one time was limited to that which could be assimilated. Secondly, a technique of structural drills was developed so that the learner was engaged in intensive production of sentences representing the given structure. The linguistic experience was thus constrained and focused according to systematic linguistic principles and specific pedagogic procedures were introduced. Apart from this the elements of direct method teaching remained largely as before. The mother-tongue was not used. Language was made meaningful by being directly associated with elements of the situation and with actions. Grammatical explanations were not given so that structure learning was inductive. The oral language was paramount, although the role of productive practice was increased over listening (Palmer 1921).

The work of Palmer, Hornby and others was the major influence on EFL teaching into the 1960s and 70s and, indirectly, on the teaching of other foreign languages, in Britain at least, from the 1960s. The principal further development was in the elaboration of the (pedagogic) principles according to which the grammatical and lexical content was organised. The task of selecting and grading vocabulary and structures was performed with increasing linguistic sophistication. Linguistic control became stricter until the generally accepted principle was that a unit would contain one new structure (or a limited set of new lexical items), and that the new would be presented through and in the context of the familiar, would be practised through intensive oral techniques and would then be integrated into the whole. Unfamiliar items of language would be eliminated from the language to which the learner was exposed until they had been properly presented and practised. The outcome was commonly a three-phase structure for teaching, consisting of *presentation, practice* and *exploitation.* The linguistic target was seen as mastery of a specified set of structures and a limited vocabulary within the context of the four language skills of speaking, listening, writing and reading. The same broad approach underlay a number of other methods, variously referred to as oral, structural, situational and audio-visual according to where the emphasis lay. The chain of development leads from the EFL work of Palmer in the early years of the century to such projects as the Nuffield and Schools Council schemes for teaching foreign languages in British primary and secondary schools in the 1960s.

If the Palmer-inspired oral approach represents one widely influential stream of modernism, another flows from the dissatisfaction that emerged during the Second World War in the United States with the results of a largely traditionalist methodology applied to limited learning objectives (reading comprehension). The war-time need for linguists showed that demand could not be met without special training and that the existing methods would not produce what was needed. Academic linguists were engaged to devise and supervise the Army Specialised Training Program (ASTP). Given the interests of those responsible for the programme, it is perhaps not surprising that the methodological solution adopted involved using native speakers of the target language as informants who would provide model sentences which the learners would imitate and on the basis of which they would be drilled under the supervision of a trained linguist. The work was very intensive, was almost always oral and contained only a minimum of explicit grammar. The approach was a direct reflection of that adopted by field linguists studying unfamiliar languages. The approach was considered successful, but the training took place under conditions that could not easily be reproduced elsewhere and as a result the same approach could not be taken over wholesale in ordinary learning situations. Nonetheless there were certain features of the approach that were characteristic of the developments that ensued. There was heavy emphasis on oral language; the approach was largely inductive; there was intensive, active participation (repetition) by the learners. It is worth noting that there was also a strong linguistic awareness on the part of those responsible.

For general purposes the most significant outcome of the ASTP approach was its influence on Fries's proposals for an approach to EFL teaching (Fries 1945). Fries's work had its impact on the teaching of languages in general in the United States and elsewhere and led fairly directly to the audio-lingual approach of the 1960s. What is striking about Fries's proposals is their similarity to the ideas found in the work of Palmer and Hornby. Learning is seen as the acquisition of a skill necessitating intensive repetition through drills. The spoken language is paramount. Explicit grammar is avoided and learning is inductive. The mother-tongue is banished. The linguistic focus of language learning is seen as the mastery of grammatical structures, with the consequence that the input of vocabulary is not only controlled but strictly limited. As in Palmer and Hornby the materials used are very largely sentence-based. The use of minimal contrast is important in the learning of both pronunciation and grammar, again reflecting the methods of structural linguistics. There is perhaps not a great deal that is highly innovative in language teaching technique. Best known is probably the development by Lado and Fries (Lado and Fries 1954–58) of the technique of *pattern practice*, a type of mechanical drill that permitted highly intensive repetition and manipulation of model sentences. As linguists, Fries and his colleagues held strongly the view that any approach should have a sound foundation in the linguistics. Apart from the attachment to the notion of structure and the use of descriptions derived from structural linguistics, the most obvious manifestation of this was the importance attached to the role of the mother-tongue in inhibiting (or sometimes facilitating) the learning of the foreign language. It was held that decisions on selection and grading of content should be based on predictions of the level of difficulty likely to be encountered. This in turn required contrastive studies of the two languages to be undertaken. This was a major linguistic research exercise in connection with which the term *applied linguistics* was first used.

The notion of *skill* or *habit* that underlies the approaches of both Fries and Palmer is relatively informal. In contrast, as the Friesian structural approach evolved into the *audio-lingual* method, the psychological basis became much more fully worked out and explicit (Brooks 1964). The skill element was now elaborated as an application of a behaviourist learning theory. The principles that determine the learning of a second language were seen as the same as those that operate in the learning of the first language and these in turn are no different from those that determine all forms of learning. In broad terms the child produces language by processes of imitation and analogy, based on what is heard, and learns by being *reinforced* for successful performance. Utterances

525

are conditioned responses to stimuli. No mental apparatus is postulated to account for either language learning or language use. Learning a language is learning to respond accurately and appropriately to stimuli. Various factors in the way in which the learner performs and in which reinforcement is provided affect the rate at which learning takes place. Language behaviour can be reinforced only when it is observed. It must therefore be active (productive). Previously acquired skills may affect the acquisition of new skills either as facilitating factors or as interference factors. Hence the already noted role of the mother-tongue.

Generally, the difference between audio-lingualism and other skill-based approaches is less in the nature of the methodological techniques used than in the elimination of any degree of eclecticism. New language is carefully graded and is usually introduced in the stimulus-response context of a minimal dialogue. This is rehearsed, memorised and manipulated. What follows is repeated drilling of structures, constituting the major part of the learning experience (up to 80 per cent of the learning time). There is, however, one way in which audio-lingualism contrasts sharply with the EFL tradition stemming from Palmer and this is in the handling of meaning. The direct method and other techniques for teaching the meaning of words and categories remained a central element in the work of Palmer, Hornby and their successors. The theoretical bases of audio-lingualism in structural linguistics and behaviourist psychology resulted in meaning receiving very little attention. The method is a highly mechanical one. It is probably for this reason that although its theoretical consistency gave it an important place in the history of language teaching concepts, it was never at all widely adopted outside the United States and countries influenced by American thinking. What audio-lingualism shows is how far a strict skills-based approach can be pushed.

What has been described in this brief and selective historical account is the progress and diffusion of modernist ideas in the first half of the century. It brings us towards the end of the 1960s and shows that there is a degree of common thinking at this time in Europe and America about foreign language teaching with the stimulus for change arising more from methodological innovation in the former case and from theoretical input in the latter. It is not possible to say at all precisely just how far practice had followed new principles. They had probably been most widely adopted in the teaching of English as a foreign language outside Europe and North America, but were coming to have considerable influence on the teaching of English and other languages in Britain, continental Europe and America. Traditionalist approaches had certainly not been wholly abandoned and were probably often being mixed with modernist techniques in a somewhat *ad hoc* way. We can say therefore that there existed a certain climate of opinion in the context of which new debates arose which are still very much with us. Since the issues of the last two decades have not yet been fully resolved, it is necessary at this point to abandon the historical perspective that we have followed so far.

## 4. THE CONCEPTUAL BASES OF LANGUAGE TEACHING

There are two major questions to which we need answers if we are to establish a well-reasoned and effective approach to teaching languages. First, what is the nature of the thing (language) that the students have to learn? Secondly, what is it that determines whether they *will* learn it (efficiently)? More briefly, what is language and how do people learn languages? Although answers to these questions are logically implicit in any approach to language teaching, they have not always been posed as openly and as directly as this. The body of knowledge about language that was transmitted in traditionalist teaching was relatively uncontroversial. Grammatical facts were the central concern. These, supported by a selected vocabulary together with appropriate pronunciations and spellings, were the focus of teaching. This is what language descriptions (*grammars*) were devoted to and there was no particular reason to think that this was inadequate. Learning in this case was a matter of the operation of the learner's intelligence, in effect an inaccessible black box, which was seen as largely unaffected by external (i.e. methodological) factors.

Our account of the modernist trend in language teaching suggests why the level of awareness of these issues could not long remain low. First, the desire to control more carefully the linguistic input forced more and more attention upon the nature of linguistic structure and of the relation between different parts of the grammatical system. Secondly, languages which are to be exercised as skills must be learned as skills and this suggests a learning process different from the acquisition of knowledge. Curiously the logic of this was not really pushed right the way through. It is true that the structural linguistics that became the basis of much modernist language teaching had some strikingly different features from the traditional grammars that had preceded them, but the essential preoccupations remained the grammar, lexicon and phonology (and, indeed, the units of content were not so much different as presented by means of a different metalanguage). The changes in classroom methods were far more radical, but, in spite of a recognition of the key importance of the learner's engagement in learning activities, these were actually discussed largely in terms of the *teacher's* control, and manipulation of the variables (see Chapter 16, below).

The receptiveness of language teachers to further change stemmed in part from a growing consciousness of the need for a sound conceptual foundation for their teaching and an openness to the contribution that relevant theory can make to this. It probably also stemmed from a degree of disappointment at the results achieved so far by modernist teaching. Given the difficulty of obtaining objective evidence about the effectiveness of methods, any evaluation must be substantially subjective. A cautious interpretation might be that practitioners were generally satisfied that oral, situational, structural etc., methods were an improvement on traditionalist approaches, but that the results still fell short of what was expected or hoped for.

## 4.1 Language

In the search for an explanation for this, the first thing to investigate is whether the view of language that underlies language teaching is an adequate one. In fact a number of new perspectives have emerged which have given language teachers and applied linguists cause for thought. First, the ideas about linguistic structure of post-Bloomfieldian structuralism have been overthrown in the Chomskyan revolution (together with the behaviourist account of language that was often associated with them) (Lyons 1970). Secondly, the notion of *linguistic* competence has been placed within the context of a wider *communicative* competence, suggesting that there is more to the knowledge underlying use of language than the triumvirate of syntax, vocabulary and phonology (Hymes 1971). Thirdly, through the notion of *speech acts* it has been shown that what speakers *do* with utterances is an important aspect of their intention in communicating and that it is no straightforward matter to extend the study of semantics to deal with this (Searle 1969). Fourthly, the study of actual discourse, particularly stretches of discourse longer than sentences, shows regularities and features of organisation that do not emerge through the study of individual sentences or sentence grammar (Brown and Yule 1983). The potential implication of these developments is that for language teaching to be fully effective it needs to extend the model of language that it uses as the basis for determining its linguistic strategy.

We should not necessarily expect to find that each of these specific developments in linguistics will have its own implications for language teaching. For the moment we will content ourselves with saying that an individual with a fully established linguistic/communicative competence is capable of using the rule system of language to construct novel sentences spontaneously and fluently. The sentences will express desired meanings and will be appropriate to the social purpose that the speaker has in uttering them. The form of the sentence will be determined not only by the meaning that it is intended to express but by the relations between it and the rest of the text (spoken or written) in which it occurs, by the emphasis that the producer chooses to give to the different parts of the sentence, and, where there is systematic variation in the language system, by the choices made according to social context. Where the sentence, as is normally the case, combines with other sentences to form part of a longer sequence (text), the arrangement of those sentences will not be a random matter. The producer will organise the content according to general principles which ensure that the text is coherent. In determining the overall form of the text, as in deciding the form of individual sentences within the text, the speaker will take into account what assumptions can be made about the persons to whom the text is being transmitted and what those persons can be expected to contribute to the interpretation themselves.

It is worth bearing in mind that competence cannot be observed directly and that the only valid evidence for the existence of competence is successful performance in a language. Obviously speakers of a foreign language rarely attain a full competence in that language if full competence is defined as native-speaker competence. However, a less than full competence is a wholly acceptable target for a second language learner. What is important is that speakers may fall short of full competence in at least two different ways. They may possess some of the components of competence to a high degree and others (virtually) not at all. An individual who had learned a large number of words, but had no syntax, would be a case in point. So too would someone who had internalised a considerable proportion of the syntax of a language and a substantial vocabulary but had no competence in applying this knowledge in meeting social needs in communication. Alternatively, speakers may possess a partial competence in *all* aspects of language. They may have some competence across the whole range of syntax and phonology without being able to produce any of it with complete accuracy, but they also have a similarly partial competence in aspects of language use. It is arguable that the concentration of language teaching on the core aspects of language (grammar, vocabulary and phonology) creates the former kind of incomplete competence and that an alternative would be to set out to create the second kind instead. It seems to hold out the hope of a quicker return in terms of performance than the former.

## 4.2 Language learning

As it happens, recent research into second language learning throws some light on this issue. We have noted that the views of language learning that have been dominant in language teaching have derived from a number of sources. Traditionalist language teaching is based on a view of knowledge acquisition and processing that does not see second language learning as in any way a special case. Behaviourist and other skill-based approaches are an extension of general learning theories that have their source in the obser-vation of general, non-linguistic skills. Even those methods which, like the direct method, are supposedly founded on notions of how languages are learned naturally, in practice identify natural language learning with (beliefs about) first rather than second language acquisition. The striking development of the last two decades has been that for the first time attention has been focused on second language learning itself.

The origins of this change of focus are in contrastive analysis (Lado 1957). The aim of contrastive analysis was to identify differences between the learner's source language and the target language in order to predict where difficulties would be likely to occur. The use of structuralist methods of linguistic analysis made it feasible for quite sophisticated linguistic predictions to be made. However, they were predictions and not descriptions of actual learner behaviour. Both the theory and the practice of contrastive analysis came under fire. Its roots in structuralist linguistics and behaviourist learning theory were undermined by the Chomskyan revolution in linguistics. More pragmatically, people began to question whether it could perform the predictive task adequately, whether what was predicted actually took place and whether interference was the major systematic explanation for learner error and difficulty that had been claimed. The evidence was to be found in the close observation of the learners' language behaviour.

Even within the behaviourist paradigm it had been recognised that transfer could take place not only between the mother-tongue and the target language but between different parts of the target language itself. A pattern that had been established in the target language could interfere with the later learning of a different aspect of the same language. Research carried out by Dulay and Burt was claimed to show that as many as 80 per cent of the errors committed by language learners could be accounted for without recourse to the notion of mother-tongue interference (Dulay and Burt 1974). Instead they proposed that the major process involved was one of 'creative construction' whereby learners generalise on the basis of learned forms to create forms that they have not actually experienced in the target language and which may actually be errors judged in terms of the eventual target. The resemblance of this process and the similarity of the actual errors to those made by learners of (English as) a first language led quickly to the idea that the linguistic process of learning a second language was in fact little different from that of learning a first language. It might well be the case that the innate language learning capacity which had long been assumed to be lost at puberty was in fact still operative.

The research of Dulay and Burt stimulated a number of other studies involving observation of the learning by both language students and 'natural' learners of different aspects of the syntactic system. The outcome of research into morpheme acquisition, and into the learning of negation and interrogation for example, was that there was evidence of intrinsic learning sequences which were followed by learners of different language backgrounds and by learners with different kinds of learning experience (Dulay, Burt and Krashen 1982). This learning was apparently relatively unaffected by the sequence or content of the linguistic input. What the research also showed, and this is hardly surprising, was that the accuracy of learners' performance in the second language varied according to the type of activity in which they were engaged (spontaneous conversation, multiple-choice test, written composition etc.) and the conditions under which it took place. If there was indeed some kind of developmental process involved in learning a second language, then the evidence for it was most likely to appear when the learner was engaged in genuinely communicative tasks. On this basis it became possible to hypothesise that there are in fact two distinct language learning processes.

The most extreme and fully articulated expression of this view is found in Krashen's monitor theory (Krashen 1982). According to this, learners develop two language systems. One, the *acquired* system, is established through the operation of inherent language learning capacities on language experienced through the process of communication, this being an almost wholly unconscious process; the other, the *learned* system, is established in an instructional environment in which attention is drawn to the regularities of the language system and the learners remain conscious of the language system in both learning and using the language. A crucial feature of Krashen's theory is that the two systems are held to remain apart. The learned system is used by the individual to monitor performance. What is learned does not get transferred into the acquired system. While it may not be unhelpful for a learner to have opportunities for (conscious) learning, since monitoring is feasible and useful in some kinds of language performance, it is the quality and quantity of the language that is *acquired* that eventually determines the potential of the individual's competence. Language performance that provides opportunities for monitoring and therefore is influenced by the learned system may show fairly direct effects of the (pedagogically structured) input that the learner has received. In fully communicative, spontaneous use of language, i.e. language that is supposedly unmonitored, the learner's language shows characteristic features of the developmental stage of language acquisition at which he or she has arrived rather than the direct effect of any pedagogic input.

There is of course nothing novel in the observation that there exist both formal and informal environments for the learning of languages, nor in the idea that we may not be able to make unconscious use of something that we know consciously. These distinctions have long been recognised and are important to all involved in the study of second language learning even if they do not put the same interpretation on them as does Krashen. An alternative

531

interpretation of the evidence from second language acquisition studies is that at any given moment a learner's *interlanguage* (Selinker 1972) will be made up of correct target language forms, borrowings from the mother-tongue and forms coming directly from neither source but nonetheless based upon them by some analogising process. The argument for a certain systematicity in this otherwise transitory language is that learners will show similarities in the pattern and sequence of forms, both correct and incorrect, over a period in which they are learning and using the language. However, it is unlikely at any point to be a stable and uniform system. There will indeed be the difference in the distribution of the forms used that Krashen noted. But, rather than hypothesise that this is the product of two distinct linguistic systems, many researchers see this as the differential output of a single system responding to the demands and stresses of different types of communicative situation. The passage from the consciously known to the unconsciously controlled is best represented as a continuum. There are many different points on this continuum reflecting the extent of the opportunity for use of conscious knowledge and there will be as many forms of interlanguage that the learners use. The monitoring process exists but more as a matter of degree than as an all-or-nothing process.

The close observation of learners' language behaviour has generated a great deal of interest in the mental processes involved in learning a second language. In spite of some differences in the theoretical accounts offered, there are two things on which most researchers would agree. First, the learner does not approach the task of learning a language *tabula rasa*. On the contrary, learners have complex cognitive attributes which enable them to interact very positively with their language environment. The learner's role is, in this rather than in the behaviourist sense, a very active one. Secondly, the situation which places the greatest demands on the learner's language system is that of attempting to use the spoken language for spontaneous communication. Effective and efficient language use in this situation requires that as much of the language as possible should have been internalised, i.e. that the learner should have an unconscious mastery of as much of the mechanics of the language as possible so that conscious attention can be given almost wholly to the content of the communication rather than to its form. To put it in slightly different, but perhaps more familiar terms, the learner needs to be fluent as well as accurate in use of the language. For this to be the case the learner will need to have had extensive experience of attempting to use the language under the normal constraints of (spoken) communication. Learning activities that are focused wholly on familiarising the learner with the language system will not be sufficient to provide the communicative competence that is needed.

## 5. THE EDUCATIONAL CONTEXT

We shall see that one of the features of approaches to language teaching in the last two decades has been a greater concern with the learner. This is partly explained by the closer attention to characteristics of the learner's language performance that we have just discussed, but there are other reasons, notably certain aspects of educational thinking and demand, that have probably been more important.

In our earlier discussion of methods of language teaching an underlying assumption went unchallenged. In spite of the sharp contrast of methods represented by traditionalist and modernist approaches, they were predicated upon the belief that there was either a certain body of linguistic knowledge or a certain set of basic linguistic skills that anyone learning a foreign language would have to master. Debate over methods of teaching was more often than not part of a search for the best approach. The context which was assumed in this debate was the teaching of languages in (secondary) schools as part of the general curriculum. The approaches which were applied to learners of different ages (primary, secondary, adult), for example, were more striking for their similarities than for their differences. In the same way, learners attending language courses outside the regular public institutions and probably for specific purposes followed a largely similar syllabus taught by largely similar methods to those used for general language learning.

The abandonment of this assumption resulted from two kinds of pressure. The first was purely pragmatic. From the 1960s onwards there was a sharp growth in the teaching of languages, especially English as a foreign language, within the context of specialised needs. Usually the students in question were adults. It was apparent to them and to their teachers that ordinary, generalised language courses were not what they needed and that account should be taken of their individual or group needs. The second was more philosophical. Education in general was becoming more child-centred. Previously teachers had been considered authoritative sources of information about their subjects. Their task was to transmit this knowledge to their pupils. Their success in doing so would be determined in large part by how well they taught. In this, teachers of languages were much like teachers of any other subject. A change came throughout education with acceptance of the idea that children differed substantially from one another in their learning abilities, that they could contribute more fully to their own learning by having a more active, participative role and that fuller educational benefit could be gained if children's acquisition of knowledge and skills was more under their own control. The conditions now existed for language teaching, like the teaching of other subjects, to become less subject-centred and more learner-centred.

## 5.1. Implications for the approach to language teaching: aims

Language teaching methodology in the broadest sense is concerned with *what* it is that learners have to learn and with *how* they will learn it. In fact, however, questions of methodology are logically secondary to or dependent on some prior agreement as to what the *aims* of language teaching are, either in general or in a specific situation. In practice, discussion of aims was often neglected and confusion or differences of opinion over methodology could often be traced back to a failure to agree initially on what we were attempting to achieve by teaching a foreign language. There is probably now a broad measure of agreement on what the aims of language teaching are and what, in a general sense at least, the implications of those aims are. Languages are learned primarily for the purpose of communication, although the types of communication in which learners might expect to engage using the foreign language will certainly not always be the same, as we shall see. Nonetheless some degree of communicative capacity over some domain of possible uses of language is the expected outcome and language teaching that did not achieve this would be considered a failure. The term *communication* here refers to any language activity in which a message composed by one person can be received and understood by another and encompasses, for example, reading and writing as well as spoken interaction. Consideration of more general educational aims for language learning tends to have been neglected or to be regarded as secondary. Given acceptance of this very general characterisation of aims, there is also a widespread commitment to basing language teaching on our understanding of what the key characteristics of linguistic communication are and on our knowledge of how a communicative competence (in a second language) is acquired. It is this general commitment that has led much modern language teaching to be called *communicative*. However, when it comes to considering what the practical implications of this general commitment are, we discover that people have approached the issue in very different ways and that substantial differences of view or of emphasis exist.

Central to the discussion is the role that is assigned to the language *syllabus*. Certain approaches have been based upon progressive revision of the syllabus as a means of instituting change. Others have seen matters of syllabus as largely irrelevant or ineffective and have seen the achievement of communicative aims as depending much more on the nature or quality of the linguistic experience that the learner undergoes. Viewed in conventional terms these are matters of method and technique, not content.

## 5.2 Developments in syllabus design

In many countries and in many educational institutions, the syllabus is a key instrument of educational planning. Although the elements found in syllabuses are not everywhere the same (some may state aims and give considerable methodological guidance, others may do neither), most syllabuses are centred on a detailed specification of the linguistic content to be covered in each of the stages of the course. The position reached at the zenith of skills and structure-based teaching in the 1960s was that a syllabus had two major components. First, it contained a selection of so-called grammatical structures usually arranged into what was regarded as an effective pedagogic sequence accpording to criteria that had evolved over thirty years or so. Secondly, it identified a limited vocabulary as a potentially attainable target for each stage of learning. Phonological and orthographic features of languages were, of course, unavoidable in any actual teaching, but were not usually specified in the same way. The syllabus broke the global language down into digestible quantities in a process of staging and sequencing which was generally referred to as *grading*. Although in the 1930s, when the first attempts were being made to control the introduction of new language according to systematic principles, it was vocabulary that had been taken as the central problem, by the 1960s there was widespread acceptance of the view that the essential task in learning a foreign language was to master the system of grammatical structure and that vocabulary should be limited to that which was necessary to 'service' the acquisition of grammatical structure. A syllabus covering the full programme of a school system, for example, would probably attempt to cover virtually the entire grammatical system in step-by-step fashion, but would limit the vocabulary to only a small proportion of the full lexicon of the language, say, 2,000 or 3,000 words. In short, syllabuses embodied the view of language as grammar, vocabulary and phonology (/orthography). A sentence had a meaning built cumulatively from individual word meanings and from grammatical meaning. By implication, this meaning was what we would communicate if we actually used the sentence.

One reaction to the perceived shortcomings of language teaching was to argue that improvement depended on bringing the conception of language underlying syllabus construction into line with the changing view of the nature of language outlined above. To put it another way, it was argued that the units of content should be identified in different terms. The need was to reflect more fully what had been learned about the use of language. It was felt that the structural syllabus presented language largely abstracted from its uses and that if students were to be able to make use of the systems that they were learning, then the planning of language teaching, through the syllabus, needed to find means of giving greater priority to the ways in which people choose and form utterances to meet social needs.

The most widely known of the new initiatives in syllabus-design and the one that has probably had the widest impact is that taken by the Council of

Europe's Modern Languages Project. The original thinking behind what came to be known as the *notional-functional* approach was provided by Wilkins (1972 and more fully 1976), but it is through the worked-out specification of what was called The Threshold Level (van Ek 1975) that the approach has become best known. The Threshold Level attempts to define the detailed objectives of an initial target level for language learning using categories which draw in part on those used by sociolinguists in accounting for language variation, in part on the categories of speech act proposed in the linguistic literature and in part on semantic categories largely developed for the purpose. The actual specification is presented under three headings. First there are *language functions*, for example, *identifying, denying, inviting, sympathising, apologising* and *greeting* which are grouped together into broader functional categories such as *imparting* and *seeking factual information, expressing* and *finding out intellectual attitudes, getting things done (suasion)* and *socialising.* Secondly there are what are called *general notions.* These provide the occasion for identification of the conceptual fields that can be expressed and cover such things as spatial, temporal, quantificatory and relational concepts (e.g. action/event relations). In the third section more *specific notions* are identified. These are derived from a set of topics or domains of language use. They include travel, relations with other people, services, personal identification and education. Actual linguistic forms (phrases, structures and lexical items) through which the functions and notions can be expressed are suggested. For reference purposes the syntactic and lexical content can be extracted from these specifications and inventorised, so that, although the planning units are socio-semantic, monitoring of the formal linguistic content need not be lost. The whole attempts to specify the nature of the target performance. It offers no guidance on pedagogic organisation nor on methodology. Although the original T-level specification was done for English, comparable versions have subsequently been prepared for many European languages.

The aim of the notion-functional syllabus is to conceptualise and plan the content of language teaching in terms of the meanings that we need to convey through language and the uses to which we wish to put it. In this way what is learned is expected to be more immediately usable and priority can be given to that which has the highest utility. An inevitable consequence is that the carefully graded exposure to the linguistic environment that was the keynote of the structural syllabus is abandoned. The intention is that communicative objectives (at least in so far as these categories do indeed capture possible communicative objectives) will be established and then the forms necessary to realise these objectives will be taught, whereas the structural syllabus tends to build up the language system first and then provide opportunities for learning how to use it.

The approach of the Council of Europe project has probably been the most widely promoted syllabus initiative, but it has not been the only one, nor has reaction to it always been one of wholesale acceptance. An independent development in Britain was the move in school language teaching towards what have been slightly misleadingly called *graded objectives* (Harding *et al.* 1980). Whereas the Council of Europe project was very much the product of applied linguists, the graded objectives schemes have emerged from local initiatives undertaken by practising modern-language teachers working within the school system. Their conceptual basis is perhaps less fully worked out, but the aim has been to introduce language teaching orientated towards meeting limited functional or situational objectives. The syllabuses list every-day concrete situations of language use and provide for learners to learn phrases of restricted productivity to meet the demands of these situations. The objectives are graded in the sense that limited but attainable communi-cative targets are set. The functional nature of the aim is very similar to that adopted by notional-functional teaching. However, at least in the early stages, graded objectives schemes were often introduced alongside more conven-tional approaches to language teaching and were seen as a solution to the problem of setting worthwhile objectives for pupils who were unlikely to be successful within the framework of the existing examination system. They were therefore not formulated as general solutions to determining an approach to language teaching. Subsequently a number of schemes have been developed or extended to incorporate the wider thinking typical of the notion-functional approach and the recently published national criteria for language learning, which are the basis for new national examinations in Britain, are closely modelled on the framework first put forward by the Council of Europe project.

A common reaction of those familiar with a structural approach to syllabus design is likely to be that these more functional approaches cannot ensure the learning of the grammatical system of the language. Certainly a wholly functional approach does nothing specifically intended to facilitate the internalisation of the language system. Many have seen this as a serious potential weakness. As a result, a number of people have made proposals for some kind of compromise between a structural and a functional syllabus. It is not difficult to find a rationale for such a compromise, particularly if one is not convinced by the Krashen argument that learning and acquisition are distinct processes. Language teaching will be expected to reflect the different features of language and linguistic communication. Learners will be exposed to language in such a way as to provide an adequate, focused opportunity to concentrate on each aspect and not exclusively on the structural or the functional aspect. Accordingly, in this view, there needs to be room in the syllabus for both the structural and the functional, as indeed for other aspects of the language system. This could be achieved through a syllabus which is initially structural and subsequently functional, one which has a structural core but which has functional exploitations continuously associated with this core (Brumfit 1980) or one in which both structural and functional are always present but in changing proportions as the syllabus progresses (Yalden 1983). An attempt to develop the notional syllabus further by applying more systematically recent work in the semantics of discourse has been made by Crombie (1985).

### 5.3 Needs analysis

Functional approaches to language teaching are inevitably associated with a concept of the *utility* of the language being learned. In order to identify which aspects of language have utility we have to know what possible *needs* for the language a learner may have. The generally functional orientation of the Council of Europe work generated an interest within the project in *needs analysis*. The value of precise analysis of needs was even more apparent in those situations where languages were being taught for specific purposes. A major contribution to syllabus design and needs analysis in the latter case was made by Munby (1978). Drawing on the early Council of Europe work and on an explicitly sociolinguistic model of language, Munby offers a set of procedures to be followed in working from identification of needs to specification of language content, i.e. the syllabus. Munby puts forward the categories of a *communicative needs processor* which can be used to describe in detail the needs of a given learner or learner-type. The learner's needs are elaborated in terms of the *purposive domain, setting, interaction, instrumentality, dialect, communicative event* and *communicative key*. A target level is established for the anticipated language behaviour. The output of this analysis is a profile of the learner. Operating on this profile are a *language skills selector* for which a detailed breakdown of potentially needed language skills (sub-skills) is provided and a *meaning processor* which offers an inventory of semantic categories like that found in Wilkins (1976). This provides the input to the *linguistic encoder* which actually specifies the linguistic forms (structures, phrases, lexical items) that form the language content of the syllabus. The output of the linguistic encoder is put together with that of the language skills selector to provide the *communicative competence specification* which is the total output of the whole procedure. The approach is founded on the belief that the need to learn specific linguistic forms can be established from a detailed and largely socially orientated analysis of language need. It is also committed to the view that a highly specified syllabus is an essential tool in the planning of language teaching.

The needs analysis work associated with the Council of Europe project has a similar starting-point, but eventually takes a rather different direction. In his initial study, Richterich (1972) also puts forward a sociolinguistically-influenced model of learner need which operates through categories which are very similar to those that are actually used in the syllabus specification. This similarity in the categories used also implies a certain redundancy since what is stated in the analysis of needs may simply be repeated in the syllabus itself. However, in his 1977 and 1985 publications (Richterich and Chancerel 1977, Richterich 1985) Richterich develops needs analysis as a process in which the learner, the teaching institution and the eventual consumer (e.g. employer) are involved. In general the analysis sets out to match needs, in the specification of which there is a role for each party, with resources, which, in turn, are not exclusively a matter for the teaching institution. Given the differing interests represented, the analysis is not something to be carried out and applied by the expert (by the applied linguist, for example), but for *negotiation* between the parties. Equally, the whole procedure is not an initial, once-and-for-all process, but something which operates continuously as the programme proceeds. The aims, content and form of the learning programme are subject to continuous renegotiation. There is therefore no single syllabus as the outcome.

We can now see that although both sorts of approach have the interests of the learner very much in mind and, in that sense, are learner-centred, in one case the conventional professional role of the teacher in identifying the objectives and determining by what sort of programme the objectives can be reached is unchanged, whereas in the other there are quite radical changes envisaged in the relationship of teachers to their clients. It is not difficult to see that one approach might find more favour where comparability of programmes across large numbers of institutions is important, whereas the other might be appropriate for an individual institution or programme where decisions are related only to specific identifiable groups.

## 6. COMMUNICATIVE METHODOLOGY

So far we have been looking at attempts to bring about reform through redefinition of the content and the appropriate units of language teaching. There are probably few who believe that this is sufficient and certainly some who believe that reform of this kind is altogether misguided. The arguments used by the latter would derive partly from linguistics and partly from second language acquisition. Functional approaches to language teaching are based on the assumption that relationships can be established between uses of language and the forms used to perform those uses, i.e. that there are ways of expressing individual functions which permit generalisability from one situation to another. As against this it can be argued that every utterance is a unique event, that communication is always achieved by a combination of linguistic and non-linguistic means and that therefore there is no direct, form-function relationship. In summary, it can be argued, the evidence from the analysis of real discourse challenges the assumptions behind the notional-functional and similar approaches. It could be concluded from this either that the syllabus should remain largely syntactic in its orientation or that there is no place at all for any kind of syllabus based on units of language or linguistic communication.

The evidence from second language acquisition has been taken by some to support the second of these conclusions. We have already seen that Krashen finds evidence of the continuing operation of innate language acquisition processes on an input consisting of natural communicative language. Corder postulates that within each learner there is a *built-in syllabus* which largely determines the progression in which the language is learned (Corder 1973). In order to operate effectively, the syllabus, being in-built, needs only a relatively balanced linguistic input, such as would be provided by normal communicative language behaviour, but which might not be provided by a tightly controlled, but skewed, linguistic syllabus.

The emphasis on negotiation that we have already noted in the work on needs analysis of Richterich is echoed in the views put forward by Breen and Candlin. Taking both the act and the acquisition of communication to be a negotiable process at all levels, they argue for a learner-centred approach which seeks not merely to take decisions on behalf of learners that are held to be beneficial to them, but to involve the learner personally in these decisions. The teacher is seen as having no special authority in this process and therefore no role in setting up a predetermined syllabus. Their theoretical position inevitably leads them towards the creation of communicative opportunities as the basis for accelerating language learning.

Finally, we might remember that probably the biggest deficiency felt in structure-based language teaching has been the difficulty of bridging the divide between a knowledge of how the language system works and a skill in actually exploiting the system in communication. This is a deficiency of which practising teachers have certainly been aware. All in all, what these pressures from different directions have meant is that there has been a much greater concern with the quality of the linguistic experience that learners undergo. It is argued that the syllabus designers have it wrong because they concentrate attention on the linguistic *product*, whereas what they should be doing is ensuring that learners experience the right sort of *process*. The result has been that for both pragmatic and theoretical reasons the search has been on for ways of achieving greater communicative authenticity in the language classroom. This has led to imaginative and exciting developments in language teaching methodology.

## 6.1 Communicative techniques

It does not follow because people have set themselves communicative targets or used communicative categories that any profound methodological innovation is involved. There are many functional language courses which still use what is essentially a behaviourist method. If learners are expected to memorise dialogues and to reproduce them or to follow with minimal modification patterns of interaction that have been set up through models, as can be the case with some of the more restricted kinds of role-play, they may well be doing no more than undergoing a process of linguistic conditioning little different from that associated with pattern practice. Any such activity lacks many of the crucial features of real communication and cannot really be regarded as communicative. In the teaching of languages for communication, such activities can at best be regarded as having some specific but restricted purpose within the wider aim, though the value of even this would be denied by some.

Generally speaking the language classroom is an artificial environment and one in which opportunities for genuine communication in a second language rarely occur. Whatever takes place there is intended to promote language learning and as such is unlikely to be something that is undertaken for its real communicative value to the individual. This is the dilemma. How can purposes for communicating in a foreign language be created where none exist?

One answer, but one that for reasons of administration and policy is not available in all situations, is to make the second language a medium of instruction for other subjects. Thus science, geography or any other subject on the curriculum might be taught through the foreign language. Because the learners will be concentrating on the subject content and not on the form of language used, it is argued, the natural processes of acquisition will be able to operate. The case for this approach has been made by Widdowson (1978). Probably the best known example of this strategy is found in the immersion programmes of Canada. Under these programmes anglophone children attending certain primary and/or secondary schools are taught virtually the entire curriculum in French. (It should be noted that these are not the schools provided for the francophone population.) It is claimed that these programmes are usually successful in getting children to a high level of proficiency in the language without adversely affecting their general level of educational attainment. (For a selective review see Swain and Lapkin undated.) At the same time, in other parts of the world, concern is expressed that the use of a medium other than the mother-tongue results in lower educational achievement which is not compensated by particularly high standards in command of the second language. No doubt the value of such an educational policy is dependent on the precise conditions under which it would operate.

Generally speaking, language teaching is confined to certain hours of the week which are timetabled for foreign language teaching. Communicative needs are not things that can be timetabled. The intention therefore must be to create opportunities for the use of the foreign language which capture as many features of real communication as possible. Viewed from the point of view of the speaker (writer) this means that there must be some intention to communicate, that the speaker has to convert this intention into a set of meanings for which he (she) has to select an appropriate linguistic form (from the total linguistic repertoire that is possessed at that stage), which in turn has to be produced with reasonable spontaneity and fluency. It may well not be necessary for the utterance to be wholly accurate for it to achieve its communicative effect, although the more complex the intention, the more likely it is that it will require elaborate language to achieve it. The receiver must be able to interpret or recognise the speaker's intention using a combination of linguistic and non-linguistic knowledge. Viewed from the point of view of the interaction, the very notion of communication implies that there must be some resolution of uncertainty. An interaction which is wholly predictable communicates nothing. To put it another way, there must be some information gap (Johnson 1979) which is closed by the communicative act which the speaker performs.

The essence of a communicative activity, as opposed to what often takes place in a 'conversation class', for example, or what is involved in writing an essay, is that it is purposive. Creating a purpose means motivating pupils to suspend the disbelief that the artificial environment of the classroom normally generates. The activity needs to be of sufficient interest for the learners to become preoccupied by the outcome of the activity rather than by the means that they use in the course of the activity. One approach has been to introduce into foreign-language teaching activities that are more commonly associated with first-language learning. Teaching units can be grouped around themes (unemployment, sport, the generation gap) which might be expected to be of intrinsic interest to adolescent pupils. Projects might be undertaken (preparing a newspaper, producing a television programme) which require material to be collected or produced, which in turn brings the learners into contact with the foreign language. It has been suggested that it is not essential that learners should always use the foreign language in the course of these activities given that they have intrinsic educational value for the pupils. However, in the sense that *communicative* is used here, it is clear that they achieve full communicative value only when it is the foreign language that is the vehicle of communication.

A more innovatory approach to the problem of making the language behaviour more purposive and one with which the communicative language teaching movement is usually identified is to introduce problem-solving or competitive activities (Littlewood 1981). For the former, language teaching has borrowed from business training the use of *simulations*. A group of learners may be asked to take the roles of executives required to take a business decision. They will either be given the information on which to base their decision or be expected to obtain it. The need to arrive at a decision provokes communicative interaction between the learners which must be carried out in the foreign language. The simulation technique can be applied to a great variety of situations. One particular variant is known as *jigsaw* listening or reading (e.g. as in Geddes and Sturtridge 1978). In this activity each individual participant is given different information, either spoken or written, which must be pooled with the information available to other members of the group for the problem to be solved. It thus provokes learners to read or listen for information before entering into oral interaction.

These activities stimulate co-operative language behaviour between members of the group, but a competitive element can be added by having groups compete with each other to find the right or the best solution to the problem. The competitive element is a key feature in the use of language games. In this context language games are not games that focus on language but games that require use of language and, specifically, in this context, use of the foreign language. The theory behind use of games is that the learners become so preoccupied with the desire to win the game that they will be stimulated to attempt the real use of the foreign language without too great a preoccupation with correctness. The games can be anything from familiar panel games like Twenty Questions or What's My Line to board games like Trivial Pursuit or Diplomacy. The only requirement is that they should provide reasonable opportunity for use of language. Games as conceived in the context of communicative language teaching are not amusing extras in the process of language teaching but have a wholly serious linguistic purpose.

The sort of activities referred to so far might well seem more appropriate to relatively advanced learners. To the extent that this is so, communicative language teaching could readily be seen as a suitable strategy to adopt for the later stages of a language course that has initially had a largely structural orientation or has otherwise been very controlled. However, it should not be concluded from this that communicative activities have no place in the earlier stages of language learning. In the first place, some games require only a very limited linguistic competence and would be suitable for beginners or near-beginners. Secondly, there are also types of communicative task, which may not resemble authentic communicative tasks, but which by their nature demand the use of a limited set of linguistic structures while requiring the speaker to process the language in a way that captures all the normal stages of communicative production. For example, young beginners can work in pairs so that one pupil has to colour a picture the original of which is only visible to the other pupil. The activity demands that the first pupil request the information he needs and that the second provide the necessary descriptive information using the appropriate vocabulary. Activities of this kind were originally proposed in *Concept 7—9*, a set of materials intended to improve the effectiveness of language use by speakers of non-standard dialects (Schools Council 1972).

Another activity that can make demands at different levels is *role-play*. As we have already noted, role-play can be a wholly mechanical activity and as such is not communicative at all. In fact we can trace what is virtually a continuum. A learner may start with dialogues that are to be memorised and acted out. Subsequently, the elements of the dialogue might be recombined in different ways. From here the pupils can move to making simple substitutions within the established dialogue frame. Next, dialogues can offer genuine choice so that one pupil has to respond to the choice made at a particular point by the other without having any advance knowledge of what that choice may be. At this point the learner has passed from being able to respond mechanically without regard to what the other pupil has said to having to process what he hears before knowing how to respond. At some point in the role-play the pupils can respond not as if they were someone else but as themselves expressing their own feelings or wishes. Finally the notion of any precise model for the role-play may be abandoned altogether and we reach what is in effect a simulation rather than a role-play and have thereby progressed by a series of stages from a wholly controlled to a largely communicative activity. Given the popularity of functionally-orientated objectives in much current language teaching, it would appear that some such progression should be aimed at if the teaching is to become truly communicative.

If one holds to the view that the necessary, sufficient and efficient conditions for the acquisition of a foreign language are assured through communicative experience alone, then a language course made up entirely from the kinds of activities just described could be seen as an adequate basis for language teaching. If, on the other hand, one believes that activities with specific linguistic foci are still needed (either because the classroom contact is too sparse to allow acquisition to proceed or because one does not hold to the sharp distinction between learning and acquisition), then one could see communicative activities as something to be used in conjunction with more conventional forms of language practice. In the former case, as already suggested, a syllabus that specified the linguistic content would be superfluous. This does not necessarily mean that there would be no kind of syllabus. It is most unlikely that anyone would be satisfied with a wholly random exposure to language and language activities. In any case selection of some kind is inevitably involved. If language teaching is organised around topical themes, a *thematic* syllabus could be envisaged. Prabhu has proposed that task-based language teaching could be planned through what he calls a *procedural syllabus* (Prabhu 1987).

## 7. TESTING AND EVALUATION

Testing is usually seen as being intended to evaluate and grade pupils. Certainly language tests will have as their primary purpose an assessment of the extent to which individual pupils have met the aims. However, tests should also be seen as intrinsic to the role of the teacher since it is only through some kind of objective procedure, such as language tests should provide, that the teacher can get the formal feedback which is essential to the continuing modification and improvement of the approach that he actually adopts in his teaching. For the teacher, testing is a tool through which he monitors his own success. It might be added that the form of tests often also has an important washback effect on the practice of language teaching. A reform of testing procedures can often be a more effective mechanism for achieving change in method than persuasion or the simple propagation of new ideas.

The form of language tests is likely to reflect an underlying conceptualisation of language and language learning in just the same way as teaching itself does. One would normally expect to find that teaching and testing in any one situation are based on the same conceptual framework. It should be said that this is not inevitably the case. Nonetheless it is not surprising to discover that the development of testing in recent years follows a path very similar to that which we have identified for language teaching itself. The period of structure and skill-orientated teaching coincides with the growth of approaches to testing which showed similar characteristics. The linguistic focus was on individual items of grammatical and phonological structure and on vocabulary. High priority was placed on the need to achieve objectivity and reliability in testing. This meant that more expressive and creative aspects of language use were neglected and that testing techniques such as the use of multiple-choice items came to predominate. Only the receptive skills (reading and listening) can be easily tested by multiple-choice techniques. Spoken and written discourse skills were often ignored altogether or given low priority. Performance on such tests provides a certain amount of information on which grammatical and lexical items are known, but overall performance is represented by a numerical score, usually a percentage. Such scores provide an indication of how one learner performs as compared with another or in relation to norms that can be established for the population as a whole, but they reveal very little about the level of communication that can be expected of a given learner. Such tests are commonly referred to as *norm-referenced* for this reason.

In recent years there has been a search for ways of testing that provide a more valid indication of a person's communicative skill. There has been a preference for basing evaluation on integrated language performance rather than on isolated linguistic sub-skills (syntactic structures etc.), since this should establish directly the level or extent of communicative competence. Specific criteria of successful communicative performance are set up so that the learner's success is measured against these criteria rather than against the performance of others (hence the term *criterion-referenced*). Since it is no longer a generalised linguistic competence that is being evaluated, communicative tests will have varied forms according to the type of communicative performance that is being assessed, for example, according to the different situations for which the language is needed, the different skills that are to be exercised, the different functions that are to be performed. The graded objectives schemes referred to above are strictly not syllabuses but specifications of types of target performance that can be used for criterion-referenced testing. A frequent feature of communicative tests is that degrees of success are indicated by scales which are defined, not in terms of percentage scores but of skill criteria. The difficulty faced by those preparing communicative tests is that they tend to be more elaborate and cumbersome than multiple-choice tests and as a consequence are more difficult to administer. They also depend on assessments of performance that are partly subjective and therefore may not reach the levels of scorer reliability that characterise more objective tests. In general in language testing greater validity has to be traded against a loss of reliability.

## 8. THE WORLD OF LANGUAGE TEACHING

So far in this discussion little reference has been made to the fact that the contexts in which people are taught a second language are widely varied. Indeed one of the basic distinctions that is made by the language teaching profession is between what are termed *foreign* language and *second* language situations (e.g. English as a foreign language (EFL) and English as a second language (ESL)). No neutral term is conventionally used to cover the two, although reference is sometimes made to teaching English to speakers of other languages (TESOL). Any foreign language is likely in reality to be a second (or occasionally third or fourth) language for the individual learner and no particular confusion arises from using the two terms interchangeably as in most of this article. However, although the general factors affecting language learning must be broadly the same everywhere, the strength of individual factors may vary substantially and will have an important influence on decisions concerning language teaching strategy. It is this that is the basis of the distinction between foreign and second language learning (FLL and SLL).

Broadly, in FLL the language in question has no social or educational function in the society in which it is being taught. For reasons of educational policy it forms part of the curriculum but the learners will have no contact with the language outside the timetabled hours. This is probably the typical situation for foreign languages in most school systems. The approach to language teaching would have to take account of the lack of external support for the language. This could affect the definition of aims as well as the methods adopted. By contrast, in SLL, use of the language is not confined to the language classroom. It may be the (partial) medium of instruction for other parts of the curriculum, may be used in the media, may have specialised functions within the society or may actually be the normal language of communication. The teaching of English in Nigeria, French in the Ivory Coast or either language to minority language groups respectively in Britain or France would be examples. As this suggests, there are wide differences in the extent of the external contact with the language, but any approach to teaching in these situations must take account of the extent to which language learning can be expected to take place outside the language classroom and of the exact role of language teaching in the given circumstances. At the extremes the differences between the two situations are so great that even within the same society teachers of foreign languages and teachers of second languages have very little professional contact with each other. They may well have quite different conceptions of their educational role. On the other hand the division between foreign and second language teaching can become very blurred. In the Netherlands all the normal social functions are performed through Dutch, but English is so widely available through radio, television and film that it has virtually the status of a second language.

In the situations referred to so far it is likely that the language needs being catered for are either so wide or so unpredictable that the overall aim will be to establish a fairly generalised linguistic and communicative competence in the learners. In recent years there has been a very rapid expansion in the teaching of languages for specific purposes (LSP). The demand has been most striking in the case of English (ESP). This stems from the growing use of English as an international language. English is seen as the language which gives access to education and technology, which serves as a common means of communication in international trade and commerce and is used as a lingua franca by people who otherwise do not share a language. As a result, competence in the language is sought by people who need it for instrumental reasons and are not primarily interested in language learning as an educational experience. This means in turn that they are likely to want the language for restricted domains of use only. While the learners are most likely to be adults whose needs are related to their employment, a special sub-category are those who need English for academic purposes (EAP).

The essence of LSP is to match the language training provided to the need of the learner. In a sense this is no different from what is attempted in general language learning except that in the case of LSP the desired language behaviour is, by definition, much more predictable. Indeed it may actually be possible to observe instances of the target behaviour, and describe in detail the language and the language skills involved. The ability to analyse relevant discourse, to produce detailed needs analyses and on this basis to design appropriate language learning programmes is generally considered to be the mark of professionalism in LSP. It is indicative of the increasing sophisti-cation of LSP activity in recent years that whereas in the past the learner's need was assumed to be for no more than a specialist terminology, which together with suitable formulae (as in commercial correspondence, for example) could be added to an existing basic linguistic competence, now the variability and restriction of language need is seen to cover all aspects of language, (syntax, phonology and discourse features included), the levels and types of skills to be exercised, the functional and semantic relations to be expressed, the channels of communication to be employed, the domain or field of activity and the situational and social contexts of language use. It is these factors that enter into the approach to needs analysis proposed by Munby (see section 5.3, above). It should finally be said that the issue of the relationship between a generalised competence on the one hand and a specialised and restricted competence on the other hand has not really been resolved. Although transfer of linguistic knowledge and skills across modal-ities and from one situation to another inevitably takes place to a degree, the rationale behind any LSP teaching is that it caters for the predictable, not the unpredictable. If transfer takes place more readily than most people believe, there is less justification for LSP programmes.

## REFERENCES

Breen, M.P. and Candlin, C.N. (1980) 'The essentials of a communicative curriculum in language teaching', *Applied Linguistics*, 1/2: 89–112.

Brooks, N. (1964) *Language and Language Learning. Theory and Practice*, 2nd ed., Harcourt, Brace & World, New York.

Brown, G. and Yule, G. (1983) *Discourse Analysis*, Cambridge University Press, Cambridge.

Brumfit, C.J. (1980) 'From defining to designing: communicative specifications versus communicative methodology in foreign language teaching', *Studies in Second Language Acquisition*, 3/1: 1–9.

Carroll, J.B. (1966) 'The contribution of psychological theory and educational research to the teaching of foreign languages', in Valdman A. (ed.) *Trends in Language Teaching*, McGraw-Hill, New York: 93–106.

Coleman, A. (1929) *The Teaching of Modern Foreign Languages in the United States*, American and Canadian Committee on Modern Languages, New York.

Corder, S.P. (1973) *Introducing Applied Linguistics*, Penguin, London.

Crombie, W. (1985) *Discourse and Language Learning: a Relational Approach to Syllabus Design*, Oxford University Press, Oxford.

Dulay, H. and Burt, M. (1974) 'Natural sequences in child second language acquisition', *Language Learning*, 24: 37–53.

Dulay, H., Burt, M., and Krashen, S.D. (1982) *Language Two*, Oxford University Press, New York.

Fries, C.C. (1945) *Teaching and Learning English as a Foreign Language*, University of Michigan Press, Ann Arbor.

Geddes, M. and Sturtridge, G. (1978) 'Jigsaw listening: integrating listening and oral skills', *Englisch*, 3: 90–2.

Harding, A., Page, B., and Rowell, S. (1980) *Graded Objectives in Modern Languages*, Centre for Information on Language Teaching and Research, London.

Howatt, A.P.R. (1984) *A History of English Language Teaching*, Oxford University Press, Oxford.

Hymes, D. (1971) 'On communicative competence'. Excerpts reprinted in Pride, J.B. and Holmes, J. (eds) (1972) *Sociolinguistics*, Penguin, London: 269–93.

Johnson, K. (1981) *Communicative Syllabus Design and Methodology*, Pergamon, Oxford.

Johnson, K. (1979) 'Communicative approaches and communicative processes', in Brumfit C.J. and Johnson K. (eds) *The Communicative Approach to Language Teaching*, Oxford University Press, Oxford: 192–205.

Krashen, S.D. (1982) *Principles and Practice in Second Language Acquisition*, Pergamon, Oxford.

Lado, R. (1957) *Linguistics Across Cultures*, University of Michigan Press, Ann Arbor.

Lado, R. and Fries, C.C. (1954–58) *An Intensive Course in English*, University of Michigan Press, Ann Arbor.

Littlewood, W.G. (1981) *Communicative Language Teaching*, Cambridge University Press, Cambridge.

Lyons, J. (1970) *Chomsky*, Fontana, London.

Munby, J. (1978) *Communicative Syllabus Design*, Cambridge University Press, Cambridge.

Palmer, H.E. (1921) *The Principles of Language Study*, Harrap, London.

Prabhu, N.S. (1987) *Second Language Pedagogy*, Oxford University Press, Oxford.

Richterich, R. (1972) 'A model for the definition of adult language needs'. Reprinted in Trim J.L.M. *et al.* (1973) *Systems Development in Adult Language Learning*, Council of Europe, Strasbourg: 29–88.

Richterich, R. and Chancerel, J.-L. (1977) *The Identification of Adult Language Learning Needs*, Council of Europe, Strasbourg.

Richterich, R. (1985) *Besoins Langagiers et Objectifs d'Apprentissage*, Hachette, Paris.

Schools Council (1972) *Concept 7–9*, Schools Council, London.

Searle, J. (1969) *Speech Acts*, Cambridge University Press, Cambridge.

Selinker, L. (1972) 'Interlanguage', *International Review of Applied Linguistics*, 10: 209–31.

Swain, M. and Lapkin, S. (undated) *Evaluating Bilingual Education: a Canadian Case Study*, Multilingual Matters, Clevedon.

van Ek, J.A. (1975) *The Threshold Level in a European Unit/Credit System for Modern Language Learning by Adults*, Council of Europe, Strasbourg.

Widdowson, H.G. (1978) *Teaching Language as Communication*, Oxford University Press, Oxford.

Wilkins, D.A. (1972) 'The linguistic and situational content of the common core in a unit/credit system'. Reprinted in Trim J.L.M. *et al.* (1973) *Systems Development in Adult Language Learning*, Council of Europe, Strasbourg: 129–46.

Wilkins, D.A. (1976) *Notional Syllabuses*, Oxford University Press, Oxford.

Yalden, J. (1983) *The Communicative Syllabus*, Pergamon, Oxford.

## FURTHER READING

In addition to books and articles already referred to, the following titles will provide useful further reading:

Brumfit, C.J. (1984) *Communicative Methodology in Language Teaching*, Cambridge University Press, Cambridge.

Ellis, R. (1986) *Understanding Second Language Acquisition*, Oxford University Press, Oxford.

Stern, H.H. (1983) *Fundamental Concepts of Language Teaching*, Oxford University Press, Oxford.

# 16

---

# LANGUAGE IN EDUCATION

## MICHAEL STUBBS

The title of this chapter is very general, and I will attempt a broad historical discussion of language in education, though concentrating on work after 1960. However, I will also focus on the relation between knowledge drawn from academic linguistics and the transformation of this knowledge (along with insights from elsewhere) into a form which can be of value to educational theory and practice. A brief summary of this question is: does it make sense to talk of *an educational theory of language*? I will argue that it does.

## 1. LANGUAGE, EDUCATION, AND CULTURAL VALUES

The field of language in education is enormous. Topics include: how children learn to read and write; why levels of adult illiteracy seem to remain high in many Western countries; how people learn English or other languages; how language is related to learning, or to a child's success or failure at school; and the place of languages other than English in schools – there are large numbers of languages spoken by children in Britain and other Western countries, due to a centuries-long pattern of migration, but particularly due to large-scale movements of labour forces since 1945.

All such questions are of great social importance, and issues of language in education have been debated over hundreds of years and are deeply embedded in cultural life and attitudes. One has only to think of the medieval concept of the trivium, which combined studies of grammar, rhetoric and dialectic; the decline of Latin as the language of educated people throughout Europe, and its replacement by English for many purposes; the consequent shift in English-speaking countries from a school curriculum based on classical languages to one based on English, 'modern' languages (in fact, a highly restricted set of such languages) and science; the fact that English has been recognised as an academic discipline with a place in universities only in the last hundred years; the fact that universal literacy has been a compulsory aim of schools in Britain only since the education acts of the 1870s; and the way in which the British concept of 'grammar' schools points to an assumed relation between language study and prestigious education. The inseparability of linguistic issues from assumptions about what it is socially and culturally valuable to know can be seen particularly clearly in historically changing views on the appropriate languages to be used in the British education system. (Perren 1983 discusses this in detail; and it is a major theme of Lawson and Silver's 1973 social history of education.)

This brief list collapses a thousand years of history into a few references. But it shows immediately that issues of language, education, curriculum, cultural prestige and social power are inseparable, and that the field of language in education requires not only a linguistic analysis, but a broad historical and cultural analysis. This article can only sketch the outlines of such a study.

## 2. A FRAMEWORK FOR LINGUISTIC AND CULTURAL ANALYSIS

Some aspects of language in education are dealt with elsewhere in this book: teaching English as a second or foreign language (Chapter 15); language variation (Chapter 25 considers the importance of dialectal and other linguistic diversity in schools); language planning (Chapters 14 and 23 consider the importance of policy decisions about what languages should be taught to whom, how bilingualism should be catered for in schools, etc); language and literature (Chapter 17 considers the relationship between language and literature in school and university syllabuses: long a matter for fierce debate). Even so, the areas remaining to the topic 'language in education' are vast, and need some *organising framework*.

I will propose a way of categorising work done in this area, particularly since the 1960s. I hope that my categorisation is at least helpful and rational, but it is certainly not neutral. Categorisations never are: in fact, one of their merits is that they expose their biases more clearly than a less structured discursive treatment might. This should be remembered by anyone who designs, writes or reads encyclopaedias, which almost inevitably divide knowledge according to some elaborate Baconian taxonomy, which implies in turn some particular theory of knowledge: what is known and what can in principle be known. Furthermore, such taxonomies are characteristic of some academic disciplines rather than others: for example, notably linguistics rather than literary studies. Summaries and surveys of knowledge are always interpretations, and as such, they involve distortion. But such distortions are inevitable – and are more visible when the basis of the categorisation is explicit.

These are not mere introductory points, but already the beginning of a central topic of language in education: the relation between forms of discourse and authoritative forms of knowledge. Techniques for naming the world can focus critical attention on the ways in which knowledge is constructed, and can therefore become tools for changing the world.

The categorisation will deliberately emphasise certain features of language in education: social, cultural, institutional and ideological. It clearly cannot ingore others: teaching and learning involve, by definition, children's psychology and individual cognitive development. However, cognitive styles, and views about child development are, in turn, irremediably imbued with social, cultural and political beliefs. For example, there are widespread folk beliefs about 'good English' and its relation to education; there are confusions between the concepts of 'literate' and 'educated'; conversely, 'illiterate' has connotations of poverty, crime and disease; whereas the spread of literacy is related in many people's minds to concepts of democracy, social development and the quality of life. However justified or unjustified such beliefs may be, they are very widely held, and show that a concept such as 'educated' or 'literate' has to do not only with the psychology of the individual, but with deeply-rooted assumptions about the nature of society. No-one has ever managed to formulate a definition of literacy which does not implicitly refer to purposes, and therefore to particular social circumstances, and therefore to the value of literacy for an individual or for a society. Literacy is therefore always related to the cognitive development of an individual or to the socio-economic development of a society. And development, whether of individual children or of whole societies, involves questions of value.

Educational theory as a whole is necessarily prescriptive: it is a theory about how children develop, about the aims of education, and about the value of certain kinds of knowledge over others (Lawton 1977: 171). It is therefore virtually impossible to write an article such as this without making policy recommendations in areas which are hotly contested by many people.

None of this means that we can ignore social and linguistic description. On the contrary, we must avoid social and political speculation which is not grounded in evidence about how language is actually used in homes and schools. One of my main arguments will be that we need a balance between linguistic and social analysis.

A historical perspective is particularly valuable for a discussion of language in education, because we then see that many things which are now widely taken for granted in education are in fact products of particular social, cultural and historical circumstances. For example, the view that children are essentially different from adults, with different modes of thinking, is a relatively recent one in Britain. Primary and secondary schools typically make

553

quite different assumptions about how children learn, and about relations between different subjects on the curriculum. Many notions about the education appropriate for young children were formulated in the Plowden Report (HMSO 1963), which was extremely influential in the late 1960s and early 1970s. It enshrined the concept of a 'progressive' child-centred curriculum, in which children are seen as naturally curious and able to discover for themselves, and in which the teacher is seen as a facilitator. In many ways, this was simply a straightforward rejection of a *tabula rasa* view of the mind. This 'child-centred' view has since been the quasi-official view of teacher training, however much actual practice preserves a more traditional model of children.

Medieval society had no concept that childhood was a particular state separate from adult society. And up until the seventeenth and eighteenth centuries in Britain, children were treated more or less like small adults and not as requiring any special treatment, linguistically or educationally. Paintings of the time, for example, show them dressed much more like adults than is now customary. Age groups were mixed in school classes, and the notion of a school class, as a group of children of the same age and level of education, and possibly also of the same ability or sex, is a relatively recent concept too (Aries 1962). It follows that different countries hold different assumptions again about the relations between children, education, formality and discipline (in both senses). And views about the relations between the child, the family and the state – who has responsibility for which aspects of children's education and welfare? – change significantly over time.

These general points are related to specific debates over contrasting concepts of acquisition versus learning, and of the contribution of home versus school to children's language development. Is it the case that children acquire all linguistic abilities 'naturally' as they do (under some interpretations) their native language? Is the teacher a mere facilitator? Or do children have to learn, and therefore be taught things, under artificial circumstances?

My main point so far is that such questions about language in education are embedded in broader sets of social beliefs about the nature of children and learning. A discussion of language in education must therefore relate language learning, in a relatively narrow sense, to issues of culture and society. Education is necessarily a process of social control and social engineering. Such concepts are inimical to many teachers, but it is naïve to think that it could be otherwise. This is all the more reason to understand the relations between language and development, learning and teaching, individual rights and social obligations.

## 3. LANGUAGE AND SOCIAL JUSTICE: 1960s TO 1980s

I will now restrict most of this article to the period 1960s to 1980s. The main rationale behind such a severe restriction is that it is from the 1960s that language in education was seen very explicitly as an area of academic study and social action, and developed around a particular problem of education failure. Particularly after 1945, considerable efforts were made by many Western countries to modernise their education systems. But by the 1960s it was realised that working-class and ethnic minority children were nevertheless still greatly overrepresented in school failures. Institutional reforms were seen to have failed and a great deal of academic attention was given to looking for explanations of such failure in the background of the children.

A major recent theme in British education has been social justice (Lawton 1977). The optimism of the 1940s and 1950s, riding on the back of the education act of 1944 (which established free secondary education for all children), assumed that if more money was spent on schools, teachers and materials, then all would be well. By the 1960s, this optimism had been badly shaken. One origin of this academic focusing was therefore the *specific and practical* one of demographic research, which showed inequalities in educational provision and success.

Another origin was the *general and theoretical* problem of classical sociology: 'how does the outside become the inside and how does the inside reveal itself and shape the outside?' (Bernstein 1987). What is the relation between the individual and society? And between what a child learns in school and in the wider society?

Changes in academic perceptions have variously tried to explain educational failure with reference to IQ (from the 1920s to the 1940s), social class and home background (in the 1950s and 1960s), and language (in the 1960s and 1970s). I think there is now a widespread recognition of the danger of looking for single causes which reside in children or in their families. In any case, across *groups* of children, social class, language and measured IQ are all interrelated. In addition, attributing the blame to children or their families may ignore institutional causes of injustice. And people are now aware of the 'extraordinary tendency . . . to blame what happens to people on the way they speak' (Cameron 1985: 170). At the very least, the problem of differential educational failure is caused by other people's *perceptions* of language, not directly or exclusively by language itself.

A key stage in the social justice debate was an article by Labov (1969). In this highly influential and highly polemical article, Labov argued against the tendency to condemn children as illogical simply because they speak a non-standard variety of English. The article was written in response to interventionist programmes (mainly in the USA) which held the view that if children are taught standard varieties of English, then this will solve their educational problems. Labov showed that this view was based on a severe muddle over the concept of 'good' English. His article then triggered, in turn, a flood of supporting articles purporting to show that concepts of linguistic and cultural deprivation were faulty. The deprivation debate rapidly became large and heated, and I have no space to review it directly here, though there are references to it in other sections of this chapter. (For reviews see Trudgill 1975, Edwards, J, 1979, Stubbs 1980, Gordon 1981; see also Chapter 14, section 3.3, above.)

## 4. THE QUESTION OF 'STANDARDS'

In many discussions about language in education, especially in the popular press, the concern is with 'standards' and it is generally assumed that standards are falling.

Such discussions usually take it for granted what standards we should be aiming at. Yet the standards referred to are often standards of spelling or punctuation, or other rather superficial aspects of writing, or are aspects of reading which are narrowly defined and are measurable only for this reason. In other words, such discussion takes for granted precisely what should be at issue: namely whether such relatively superficial aspects of language should be our central educational aims. (See Williams 1976 for a discussion of the changing meanings of the term *standard*.)

In addition, such discussions about falling standards seem to be a perpetual feature of the human condition. The French poet François Villon was already asking plaintively in 1460, 'Where are the snows of yesteryear?' More prosaically, the Bullock Report (HMSO 1975) points out that complaints about falling standards are a constant feature of discussion of language in education. But, logically speaking, standards cannot always have been falling.

I should make it clear (*a*) that I do think that spelling and other aspects of language development are interesting and important, and (*b*) that I do think that the issue of 'maintaining standards' is also important. My point is (*a*) that there is no real evidence that standards are declining, even in relatively measurable areas such as spelling, and (*b*) that the concept of 'standards' is extremely complex, that much discussion ignores this complexity and therefore ignores much more fundamental discussion of the aims of education.

These points – concern over standards and the socio-cultural values attached to all educational discussion – come clearly together in contemporary concern over standards of literacy. First, in Western countries literacy rates have really been recorded only for a hundred years. The demand for universal literacy and therefore the attempt to extend literacy from an elite to the whole population dates only from the late nineteenth century, and it is not surprising if this attempt is not yet successful, or that there is debate over appropriate standards. Second, it is commonly assumed nowadays that such literacy for the whole population is a good thing. But again, this is a relatively recent consensus. In the nineteenth century, many people argued that it was too dangerous to extend literacy to the working classes: it could lead to a shortage of manual labour and to social unrest if the working classes had access to seditious literature. In other words, the equation between schooling and literacy is not a self-evident one, but based on an evaluation of the dangers and usefulness of literacy. The argument that literacy (at least of a restricted kind) is necessary for socio-economic development has won, at least for the present. And most people would now argue that basic literacy is a right: it is simply unethical to give working- and middle-class children access to different educations. Third, however, there is still a great deal of dispute over the kind of literacy being taught. Before the twentieth century there were multiple forms of literacy, learned variously at home and in the community. What has developed more recently is a new notion that schooled literacy is self-evidently a single skill, which can be measured according to a single standard. And, fourth, the goalposts keep being moved. If standards of literacy are declining in any sense, it may be because the demands are rising. It is probably more serious for an individual to be illiterate nowadays than a hundred years ago, since a wider range of material must be read for a wider range of jobs. And the relative importance of writing (versus reading) has increased, if individuals are to have access to those with institutional power.

In so far as nation-wide evidence about standards of literacy is available, it is provided by the Assessment of Performance Unit. (The APU was set up by the Department of Education and Science in 1974 to monitor standards in schools.) Their findings, based on the monitoring of thousands of children, is that standards of literacy have risen slightly over the last twenty years: but that standards are still too low, given that demands are constantly rising.

## 5. 'EDUCATIONAL FAILURE IS LINGUISTIC FAILURE'?

If we look at how academics have defined such issues since the mid 1960s, the following main questions have been posed. How are language, social class and educational failure related? Why are middle-class children more success-ful *on average* at school than working-class children? In brief, what relations are there between

the language of the child (and his/her home)
the language of the school,

and the child's educational success or failure?

These questions could then be expanded. For example, we could, logically, look at *the language of the school* in only a restricted number of places. We might mean the language of school textbooks: does their style cause problems for children? Or the language of school subjects more generally: does academic jargon serve a genuinely intellectual or cognitive function? Is learning a school subject equivalent to learning the language of that subject? Or we might mean *the language of teachers*: do they talk in particular ways to pupils? Or *the language of pupils*: are they allowed to talk to each other at all in class? If they are, does this help their learning? Is their written language restricted in particular ways? How does this relate to their learning? Again, at least for the purposes of a reasonably comprehensive outline, there are only a restricted number of perspectives on pupils' language. The key relation is likely to be the relation between language at home and language at school.

However, note again that any categorisation is inherently ideological. We will almost inevitably be looking for differences and transitions between home and school, with an underlying assumption that homogeneity is normal and that diversity is problematic.

A widely-quoted notion, arising from the academic work of the 1960s and 1970s is that 'educational failure is linguistic failure'. This slogan sounds like an explanation, but it may simply be a tautology, true by definition. Schools place particular linguistic demands on their pupils, and if they fail those demands, then of course they fail altogether. The Western education system is thoroughly verbal and textual. The place of written texts, writing and literacy have always been central, and in some contexts 'literate' and 'educated' are synonymous. But the high value placed on written language is a view with its roots in middle-class Western culture: it is not universal. More specifically, a particular cluster of language characteristics – standard, written, formal – is fundamental to the British education system. For historical and social reasons, in Britain these three things are intimately related to each other, and an educational theory of language must involve a thorough analysis of their relations.

The education system and Standard English are mutually defining: SE is the expected and appropriate variety in the British education system; conversely, the education system has been a major standardising force and a major source of the institutional authority of SE. SE cannot really be defined independently of its functions in schools and other central institutions. (Milroy and Milroy 1985, Stubbs 1986, Chapter 5.)

# 6. THE CONSTITUENTS OF AN EDUCATIONAL THEORY OF LANGUAGE

In order to systematise further the discussion, we now require an organising framework: what I will call the constituents of *an educational theory of language*. As is obvious from other contributions to this book, there are many theories of language which have been developed for different purposes. What we are concerned with here is a way of organising a large and otherwise very disparate body of work on language in a way which is of help to teachers and other educationalists.

We cannot avoid studying *language in institutions*: in schools obviously; but, historically, we see a long-term and continuing battle over the place of language in religious and secular, private and state institutions. We are dealing therefore with *a theory of language variation*: how language use varies in different institutions, in pupils' homes and at school, in different academic disciplines, and in different social groups. And we are also inevitably dealing with the *language planning and policy* carried out by institutions: schools have long been central in such policy making and have themselves contributed to the creation and maintenance of Standard English; but other institutions concerned are printers and publishers, and the government committees who formulate educational and linguistic policy. We must deal with *pedagogy and classroom practice*: how notions of language policy and language variation are actually put into practice in classrooms. And in order to discuss all these issues, we have to have *linguistic descriptions* of how language is used by pupils and teachers, at home, in schools, in books, and so on. Figure 28 sets out these distinctions schematically, with reference to some topics for an educational theory of language discussed below. My claim is that any topic in language in education must be studied from all five of these points of view. The social must not be privileged at the expense of the linguistic or vice versa. In Figure 28, headings 1–5 along the top refer to the points of view from which topics in language in education require to be approached if the discussion is to maintain a balance between linguistic and social theory. The topics down the left refer to main sections in the rest of this chapter.

The rest of this article attempts to classify and integrate the wide range of things which are known about language in education, and to identify areas where basic knowledge is missing. I will not go mechanically through each subheading, but under each of the main headings below there are comments on the description of language varieties, on the nature of the language variation, on the place of language in institutions, on language policy and on pedagogical practice. All of these approaches must be given a cognitive dimension to relate them to children's language development.

The problem is not only what we know, but whether this knowledge can be coherently organised in educationally useful ways.

559

*Figure 28*

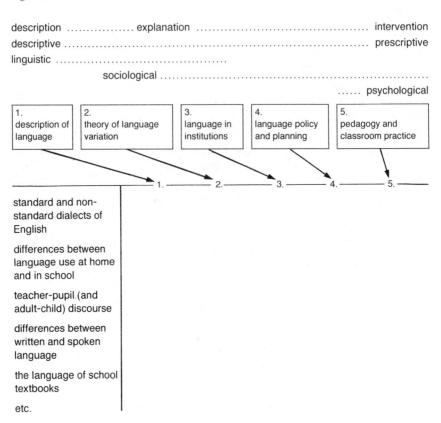

# 7. THE STANDARD ENGLISH ISSUE

Some of these points about the way in which language lies at the centre of the British education system, and the need for an integrated linguistic, cultural and pedagogical analysis, become clearer if we look in more detail at the concept of Standard English.

There are, first, very widespread conceptual confusions between Standard English and notions of good, proper, effective, appropriate, grammatical, academic, etc., English. Such topics are the subject of constant letters to newspapers and the BBC, and clearly strike at something deeply symbolic in British cultural life. As G.B. Shaw said: 'Every time an Englishman opens his mouth, he makes another Englishman despise him.' The sexist and geographical bias in this statement could be removed by talk of a British person. But Shaw's observation, on the evaluative class-based perceptions which underlie our reaction to accent and dialect, is accurate. Speaking 'properly' is often taken *in itself* as proof that someone is well educated: evaluative judgements are often based on the vocal sounds that people make.

It is clear, therefore, that SE cannot be defined in purely descriptive terms. Prescription has been involved in its history. Its current forms and functions are social-class based and concerned with the high prestige activities of mainstream culture. Nevertheless, it is possible to describe what has previously been prescribed. And some people do now speak SE as their native language: their usage can be described.

It is not difficult to define Standard English, but the definition is complicated by different factors. First, people think they know what it is, and they do in the sense that they can usually recognise it; though they may confuse it with 'correct' English and similar notions. And second, its definition relies on several logically-prior concepts. It is neither a dialect nor a style, but an intersection of dialectal and functional usages. Its definition depends on a theory of linguistic variation, and it is therefore not a first-order descriptive concept, but a higher order theoretical concept.

It is a set of particular lexical and syntactic forms (such as *child* rather than *bairn*, and *we were* rather than *we was*). These forms show considerably stylistic variation: speakers of SE can be just as formal, casual, polite or rude as anyone else. (The forms concerned are described in detail by Trudgill 1984.) Historically, SE derives from a prestigious dialect spoken in south-east England, but it is no longer geographically restricted: with relatively minor variation it is spoken all over Britain and in many other countries. SE is therefore not a geographical dialect (as non-standard dialects of English are), but a social dialect. It is the native language of a social class group: essentially educated middle-class speakers, though other speakers use it for some purposes. But neither is it just a dialect: it has particular functions, in particular activities (such as education), in writing (whereas non-standard dialects are largely restricted to spoken forms), and in formal usage.

Clearly a great deal of descriptive work has been done, but a great deal remains. We still have only very scanty descriptions of non-standard dialects of British English, and certainly these descriptions are not in an appropriate form for teachers and other educationalists.

There is a logical relation between standardisation and language variation. There are variant forms in language, though people think there should not be, and select between them. SE is the product of selections and decisions taken by men and women, sometimes individuals such as Samuel Johnson and Noah Webster, and sometimes groups such as teachers, publishers and printers. Most people have, however, lost sight of the means by which SE has been produced and is maintained. People treat SE as though it were a natural product, and forget the ideological basis of its authority, though the spread of international English is obviously related to historical and economic movements, and to colonisation. Standard languages do not reproduce themselves, though it is part of their ideology that they tend to deceive people into believing that they do; and this in turn is an essential part of their ability to operate as means of social control. The actual production of SE is made mysterious, ignored or suppressed, and it is seen as a finished commodity.

This large body of linguistic and sociological work has important pedagogical implications: unfortunately, it has often been unclear exactly what these implications are. Classroom practice seldom follows in a transparent way from sociolinguistic research. There are many studies, for example, which show that non-standard dialects of English are complex, systematic varieties. (See Chapter 14, above.) But this large body of work has not been able to generate coherent and specific pedagogical principles which can give teachers clear guidance on the place of standard and non-standard varieties in the classroom.

Some classroom practices have failed, although they seemed to follow logically from sociolinguistic research. For example, there were attempts (largely in the United States) in the 1970s to provide initial reading books for young children in non-standard dialects of English. The superficial rationale seemed very plausible. The argument was that children should not be taught two things at once: it should be easier to learn to read in a native dialect, than in a foreign dialect. But the attempt failed, broadly speaking, and has largely been abandoned. Essentially, it was perceived by children and parents as being artificial. 'Real books' are not written in non-standard dialect, and there is a strong perception that standard dialect is the appropriate language for formal written books in the school system.

Richmond (1986) usefully identifies various positions which have been adopted, and also some of the confusions: people have proposed apparently the same classroom practices with different underlying motives, and different practices with the same motives. (1) One might argue that non-standard dialect should not be used in the classroom at all: children need to spend as much time as possible mastering SE in order to maximise their chances in examinations and in their later careers. This view is essentially optimistic about the possibility of social mobility for children from working-class or ethnic minority backgrounds. (2) One might argue for the same classroom practice, but for a very different socio-political motive. Children must learn SE if they are not to suffer from a divide and rule policy. (Extreme versions of this situation are more easy to see in South Africa: the Soweto riots in 1976 were sparked off by a demand from parents that their children should learn English rather than Afrikaans, since only by learning English would they have access to international channels of communication.) (3) One might argue that SE is itself a form of oppression, and should not be adopted. Children should be taught to have pride and confidence in their own home language. This position has much the same intention as (2), but very different classroom effects. (4) One might take an essentially relativist, liberal humanist position that all groups of people have the right to use their own languages and dialects. It is not clear what follows from this position in terms of classroom practice.

My own view is as follows. Position (1) is linguistically unrealistic: you cannot prevent children from talking in their native dialect. And it is psychologically damaging: if you try to, you are denigrating their home language. It is also unrealistic about the possibility of easy social change. Position (2) suffers by definition from some, but not all of the same objections. Position (3) is socially unrealistic in a different way: if children are not given access to the mainstream language, they may be condemned to a permanent position of powerlessness. Position (4) is, as stated, just vague.

A balance is required which both recognises the educational and social importance of SE, and also respects the language background of the children. Berry (1986: 96) attempts to formulate this balance as follows. He is a black poet, born in Jamaica, who has lived in the UK since 1948 and has been actively involved in questions of language in education. He is talking specifically about Afro-Caribbean children, but the same point could be formulated to apply to all children who speak non-standard dialects of English or other community languages:

Conditioned to believe that their own language is 'bush talk' and 'bad' and 'downgrading', the parents want their children to use the language that will bring them qualifications and achievements. These should not be denied them, surely, but the children do not want to be denied their balance. For that Afro-Caribbean spirit that desires full expression of both identity and culture style maintains an increased and intensified momentum.

The pupil must adapt to the school, but the school must also adapt to the pupil. A balanced position argues that the pupil has to accept the social reality of the school language, and the school has to respect the language(s) of the pupil.

A coherent pedagogical position would seem to be as follows: Teachers have a responsibility to teach SE, given its place as the dominant language without which many careers are closed to children. However, it must be taught in ways which do not denigrate their home language. There is little point in correcting the spoken language of children. First, it is very unlikely to have much effect: teachers cannot change how children speak, against the pressure of home and peer group. And second, criticism of children's spoken language will inevitably be interpreted as criticism and rejection of their families and friends. SE has particular functions as a formal written language, and it is these written forms which must be taught. They must in any case be taught to children whose native spoken language is SE, since spoken and written SE differ quite considerably in some respects. But nor should children be asked to produce such standard written forms too early: otherwise children are being taught a foreign dialect at the same time as they are still learning some basic aspects of reading and writing. They will in any case constantly come across standard forms in what they read. They can be taught actively to produce standard written forms in explicit connection with formal public examinations. Just how soon is early enough in this respect is a matter of debate and probably for the individual judgement of teachers. Children do not acquire standard written forms suddenly: it is a process of learning which continues over years. If at some stage, children are sufficiently motivated to learn *spoken* standard forms, because they wish to join some social group (probably because they want to look for a particular kind of job), then they will acquire spoken SE without explicit teaching.

As should be obvious from this section, the issue of SE is a very complex one. Teaching of standard written forms should be combined with a sophisticated understanding of their history, functions and forms. This theme is taken up again in the section below on language study in schools.

## 8. HOME-SCHOOL TRANSITIONS

Much work has been concerned with whether there is a discontinuity or mismatch between children's language experiences at home and at school. It is possible to lay the blame on pupils and their background, and to argue that they have some kind of deficit: they lack something vital to success in schools. But it is also possible to attribute the failure to schools, and to argue (e.g. with Halliday 1978) that there is a sociolinguistic background to everything that happens in classrooms, and that educational failure is not a linguistic but a semiotic problem. Schools are to blame in their lack of understanding of language-society relations, and of the semiotic mismatches between pupils and teachers: that is, the two sides interpret the same events in symbolically different ways.

One of the most substantial bodies of work in this area is Bernstein's (1971, 1975, 1987). Bernstein's work is not just a sociolinguistic theory about language varieties. (Atkinson 1985 warns against such an interpretation.) And there is no doubt that his work has been subjected to trivial misinterpretations. It is difficult to summarise briefly Bernstein's work, precisely because it is so open to misinterpretation and so abstract: it is a theory of ways in which language transmits, maintains and modifies the social order. Bernstein talks of sociolinguistic coding orientations: there are subcultural differences in the communicative practices and semantic style of groups. Culture is seen as a system of meanings at the deepest level: systematic tendencies in the selection of meanings. He is not talking merely of varieties of language, but of principles of semiotic organisation. These principles are codes: and codes transmit culture. There is a tendency, for example, to associate different kinds of meaning with different contexts, and to form different interpretations of how much explicitness situations demand.

No-one would deny that there are differences in behaviour and language use across social groups: language is itself a major way of maintaining social group identity. The debate is over whether such differences cause educational problems. However, it is also important to realise that the academic interpretation of such differences does not lead automatically to equitable ways of treating such children in the education system. This is an instance of the classic philosophers' dictum that one cannot derive values from facts.

Suppose, for the sake of argument, that working-class and middle-class children differ in their use of language in ways that are significant to their educational success. It does not follow either that they should be kept different, or that they should be made the same. If you believe that the differences are irreconcilable, then you might argue that the two groups should have appropriately different educations. But you might equally argue that large sums of taxpayers' money should be spent in trying nevertheless to compensate for the difference. Facts about people's natures do not determine what education they should have. Beliefs about that depend on our beliefs about social equality and justice. And in any case, one can imagine many different routes towards the educational goals. (Radcliffe Richards 1982: 63 puts forward a very clear version of this argument in her discussion of male-female differences, and whether men and women should be treated differently on the basis of such differences in their natures – supposing such differences do exist.)

The concept of a home-school opposition is deeply embedded in cultural beliefs about education: in assumptions, for example, about oppositions between everyday and academic knowledge, and therefore about the valuing of some kinds of knowledge over others. This is not to imply that all kinds of knowledge are equally worthwhile: this would be absurd. But there are also absurdities in an educational system which attempts, not always successfully, to teach pupils French or German, but which gives no credit to (or does not even know about) pupils who speak an Indian language fluently, or who read Chinese or Greek, because these are their home languages. On the one hand, there are some languages which are high in social prestige in Western education systems. On the other hand, there is a deep-rooted belief in the value of knowledge acquired with difficulty under artificial circumstances, rather than acquired naturally at home.

It is important to realise that for very many children – a large majority of the school population in some areas – the language of the home is a non-standard dialect of British English, a creole variety of English, or a community language such as Welsh or Punjabi.

The basic statistics on languages other than English in Britain have not (writing in 1987) been collected by central government in the ten-yearly national censuses. This has been regarded as too sensitive for census forms, although it is difficult to see how any rational planning about language provision in the education system is possible without such statistics. The statistics which are available are either from academic research (Rosen and Burgess 1980, Linguistic Minorities Project 1985) or from LEA censuses in particular areas of Britain.

The most widely-spoken languages amongst ethnic minority communities are Punjabi, Urdu, Bengali, Gujarati (i.e. languages from the north of the Indian sub-continent), Polish, Italian, Greek, Spanish, and Cantonese or Hakka (the last two being southern Chinese varieties). Overall in Britain, the distribution of such languages is very uneven. By the mid 1980s, over 50,000 children in inner London schools spoke between them over 150 languages. However, London and some other large urban centres are much more linguistically diverse than other areas of Britain. And of these 150 languages, the majority of children speak one of a relatively small number: over 80 per cent of the children involved speak one of only 12 languages. In addition, some areas of London are much more linguistically diverse than others: there are schools where 40 different languages are spoken, but others are virtually all English or English and Bengali, for example. And different areas of London have very different concentrations of speakers of different languages, so that Greek and Turkish might be very common amongst children in some areas, whereas Gujarati might be very common in another. Education authorities often argue (quite correctly) that they cannot possibly be expected to make provisions for 150 different languages. But this is not really the point. In any given area, provision for two or three languages may well cover the majority of the children. The issues of policy and planning involved in a socially-just multilingual society are too large to discuss thoroughly here. They involve questions of whether community languages should be taught within state schools or in schools organised by the communities themselves, and questions of how English as a second language should be taught. These questions in turn involve what is known about bilingual education programmes from other countries in the world, and large-scale issues of social justice and human rights, and therefore differing views of multicultural education and of assimilationist versus cultural pluralist views of society. (For clear discussions of language and cultural identity see Edwards, J. 1985, of multicultural education see Lynch 1986, for an official view see HMSO 1985, and for statistics on ethnic groups and community languages in the UK see Printon (ed.) 1986: 19–46.)

The basic principles derivable from elsewhere in this chapter are that language diversity, including bilingualism, is the norm, not some deviation from monolingual normality; that children have the right both to have their home language respected by the school and to be taught the prestige language of standard international English; and that children's bilingualism can be a resource, not a problem – often children know, quite literally, more about language than their teachers.

## 9. TEACHER-PUPIL (AND PARENT-CHILD) DISCOURSE

There is a constant tendency to try to explain children's success or failure in schools with reference to external determinants, such as the child's social background or individual intelligence. However, children may succeed or fail due to features of the school system itself, such as the language used in schools and classrooms.

One very familiar formulation is: 'All teachers are teachers of English'. Language is not restricted to English or modern language lessons: it is something which concerns all teachers *across the curriculum.* Is there any difference, therefore, between (*a*) a good subject teacher, and (*b*) a good language teacher? Is (*a*) automatically (intuitively, unconsciously) (*b*)? Do good subject teachers teach their pupils about the language of their subject, how to express themselves effectively, and so on? Is teaching the language of chemistry just an inherent part of teaching chemistry? Is learning chemistry just learning to talk and write like a chemist?

Such a notion has considerable plausibility. Learning in any school subject must have to do with comprehension and interpretation, with the relation between academic and real-world knowledge, and with the ability to understand the kind of discourse of academic discussion in general and of particular subjects. For example, the English teacher is obviously concerned with narrative versus report writing. But then so is the history teacher. History books may be organised chronologically into a narrative, though they may also have other discourse organisation. But what is the difference between fictional and allegedly factual reporting? There are no such things as unproblematic 'facts' to which the historian can appeal: historical facts are the product of selection and editing, they are expressed in language and open to different interpretations. Historical accounts, just like fictional narratives, are constructed by authors. What, then, are the logical relations between everyday and academic English and the language of particular subjects? Learning a subject clearly relies on communicative competence to interpret how language, spoken and written, is conventionally used in that subject.

Classroom discourse is now a central area of educational research, though almost no work published before the mid-1960s discussed actual examples of teacher-pupil talk. Amongst the earliest work in the United States was Bellack *et al.* (1966), and in the United Kingdom Barnes *et al.* (1969).

Barnes's work was crucial for British teachers. He showed very clearly how many teachers regularly ask closed pseudo-questions to which they already know the answer: guess-what-I'm-thinking questions, as they have been called. And he therefore showed that the opportunity for pupils to participate linguistically and intellectually in lessons is often very restricted. These perceptive observations led to fundamental discussions about the nature of education, since they led to an altered perception of appropriate teacher-pupil relations, and to a view of collaborative learning within a classroom which is less teacher-dominated. They led therefore to a profoundly altered perception of authority relations in the classroom. If one accepts Barnes's version of the common observation that people learn through exploratory talk – that is, they learn by talking things through and putting things in their own words – then one is led to a view of classroom organisation which encourages pupils to talk to each other in small groups, and which does not put a unique premium on the teacher as the sole authority (intellectual and disciplinary) in the classroom.

This work of Barnes came at approximately the same time as developments within anthropology and linguistics were encouraging the study of communicative competence. Some of this work was explicitly concerned with classroom discourse, such as Cazden *et al.*'s (1972) studies of language use in American classrooms, or Sinclair and Coulthard's (1975) study of relatively formal talk in British classrooms. But there were also background developments in the associated academic disciplines, including ethnographic work in anthropology and sociology, micro-sociological work on everyday interaction, speech-act theory on the functions of language in use, and a shift in linguistics from the structure of sentences to the organisation of larger units of text and discourse.

There are several related reasons why a study of how teachers and pupils talk to each other is important. In many ways, teacher-pupil talk is the major educational fact: all over the world, throughout history, and with surprisingly (depressingly?) little variation in the general form of what goes on, teachers have talked and pupils have learned. At least that is what is supposed to have happened. In fact, the relation between what teachers teach and what learners learn is deeply problematic. An input-output model (in which what teachers say is directly related to what pupils learn) is now widely regarded as unsound. People still talk of transmitting or handing down the culture from generation to generation. But teachers know that pupils do not passively receive transmitted knowledge: they actively transform it and create their own relations to what they already know. This is also admitted in everyday expressions: there is generally deep suspicion of students who simply parrot what they have been told. To demonstrate real understanding, students have to be able to transform it and express it in their own words. One basic aim of work on classroom discourse is therefore to study the ways in which knowledge is negotiated and transformed between teacher and learner.

Ultimately, it is the pupil's individual ability which matters: some children are more intelligent than others. However, this ability is not absolute; and furthermore, it cannot be assessed in the abstract, but only in an interactive situation. What is important is not just what abilities a child has but how they are displayed in interaction, spoken or written. And there are different cultural styles and conventions for displaying knowledge which may be social-class based or school-based.

In brief language is not a transparent medium. Language, learning and knowledge are unavoidably related. And students therefore have to co-ordinate two forms of knowledge: the academic content of lessons, and their inter-actional form. As Willes (1983) shows, children have to learn to become pupils.

A description of classroom discourse is part of a theory of language variation: what is particular about the language used in the social institution of the classroom? It is also inseparable from a study of pedagogy. Teachers cannot just *be* teachers: they have to perform certain speech acts, such as lecturing, explaining, asking questions, and controlling pupils in various ways. But neither can a pupil just *be* a pupil. Pupils who are judged to be bored, bad readers, underachievers, slow learners or whatever, have such labels put on them as a result of teachers' interpretations of their verbal interaction under different circumstances, and possibly under communicative stress. These kinds of labels, which are familiar to all teachers, are abstract concepts which attempt to organise large amounts of observation.

Teacher-pupil talk, as Edwards and Westgate (1987: 27) put it, runs along deep grooves. Many researchers have identified a basic teaching exchange of: teacher question – pupil answer – teacher evaluation. (A detailed study is by Sinclair and Coulthard 1975.) This is the kind of exchange caricatured by Peter Ustinov (cited by Edwards and Westgate 1987: 98):

T. Who is the greatest composer?
P. Beethoven.
T. Wrong, Bach.

T. Name me one Russian composer.
P. Tchaikovsky.
T. Wrong, Rimsky-Korsakov.

It is also caricatured by Dickens in Mr Gradgrind, and by Joyce Grenfell in her monologues.

Such exchanges have been found to be very frequent over long periods of history in many countries. The teacher questions are not genuine requests for information: otherwise the teacher could not evaluate the answer. They are asked from a position of knowledge, from which the teacher can maintain linguistic, pedagogic and disciplinary control. Work by those such as Barnes can be seen as an attempt to redefine the characteristic high-power and low-solidarity of such teacher-pupil relations.

From the mid 1960s, observational work was done on mainly traditional chalk-and-talk classroom lessons, using coding schedules. (The best known work is by Flanders 1970.) In such work, an observer sits in a classroom coding teacher and pupil utterances, usually every few seconds, into relatively few (say a dozen) predetermined categories, such as

> teacher presents information
> teacher gives direction
> pupil responds to teacher
> pupil initiates talk to teacher.

Such work is open to severe interpretative problems, and no details of the actual language used are available for analysis. But such work can usefully reveal broad patterns of teacher style: whether a teacher asks large numbers of factual questions requiring brief answers, or is more problem- or pupil-centred. Flanders (1970) formulated the 70 per cent rule: for about 70 per cent of classroom time, someone is talking; for about 70 per cent of this time, it is the teacher who is talking. If a child spends 10 years at school, they might spend 10,000 hours in classrooms: and for most of this time, the teacher may be talking! This shows up the culture-specific assumption that education is verbal: rather than based on practical demonstrations, supervised participation, observation, trial and error.

The major British work which allows a comparison of discourse at home and at school was begun in 1972 by Wells (1981, 1985) in Bristol. The value of this work lies in its systematic linguistic analysis of naturalistic data. A group of 128 working-class and middle-class children were audio-recorded at home over 2½ years, and a sub-group of 32 were followed through their primary schools. The work found no absolute differences between language use in homes and schools. This is not surprising, since schools must after all be based on general conversational strategies. But there were considerable distributional differences. Question-answer-evaluation exchanges were found between child and parent at home. But the main finding was the child's freedom, at home, to initiate and negotiate with an interested adult. The child at home had more chances of learning through talk. In comparison, teacher-pupil talk was impoverished. In the classroom, children produced fewer utterances, received fewer utterances from adults, produced and received syntactically less-complex sentences, and initiated less exchanges.

This work is pessimistic about schools, in which teachers' practice is seen to be at odds with their often-expressed aims. And it turns on its head the stereotype of the impoverished linguistic environment of many homes. Tizard and Hughes (1984), in a much smaller but comparable study, recorded working-class and middle-class girls at home with their mothers. They also found extended child-initiated 'passages of intellectual search'. (Brice Heath 1983 is a major ethnographic study of black and white working-class communities in the southern USA from comparable points of view.)

## 10. READING, WRITING, AND LITERACY

Reading, writing and literacy are huge specialist areas, each with a large associated literature, and I cannot summarise a fair selection of this work here. I can only relate a few of the main arguments to my main theme.

To give an immediate indication of the range of literature involved: Brice-Heath (1983), Cook-Gumperz (ed. 1986), Levine (1986), Street (1985) and Stubbs (1980) give social and sociolinguistic accounts of how literacy is interpreted in different times and places. Goody (1977) and Scribner and Cole (1981) give important accounts of the relations between literacy and cognitive development. Freire (1972a,b) provides a powerful critique of various concepts of literacy in the context of his work with adult illiteracy in third world countries. Goodman (1982) and Smith (1985) provide influential accounts of the psycholinguistic processes involved in reading. And in addition to all such work, there is a large literature of methods of teaching reading: phonics, whole-word, etc. A flood of work on writing processes in schools was started by Britton *et al.* (1975); influential following items include Graves (1983), Kress (1982), Smith (1982), Wilkinson (ed. 1986) and many others.

A discussion should probably start from the realisation that the terms *reading, writing* and *literacy* can mean all things to all people. There is a basic ambiguity with the term *read*. A sentence such as *He read the sentence* might mean that he read it out loud, or that he read and understood it. I might read a legal document to my solicitor over the telephone: but it might be only my solicitor who can understand, interpret and translate it, so that I, in turn, can understand it. The notions of translation and interpretation seem to apply both to different languages, and to different varieties of a single language. Reading is hardly taught beyond the initial years of primary school; and if reading means interpretation and understanding of more than a superficial kind, then it is often hardly taught at all.

Freire provides a characterisation and critique of several different concepts of literacy (Freire and Macedo in press). An *academic* approach is based on a view of an elite class of educated men and women (often just men) who are able to study a society's accepted canon of literature. It is inherently concerned with reproducing this dominant canon of values. A *utilitarian* approach sees literacy as serving the needs of society. It is a socioeconomic view, that literacy is required so that people can better fulfil their role of good citizens. (See Levine's 1986 critique of the concept of functional literacy used by Unesco.) A *cognitive development* approach emphasises the way in which readers construct meanings. It sees reading as an intellectual process, and is rarely concerned with issues of cultural reproduction. A *romantic* approach is concerned with reading as a personal, affective, enjoyable process of individual development. It therefore ignores the social implications of literacy. Freire argues that all these approaches fail to tackle the ways in which literacy may give readers power (or may cut them off from power by restricting their literacy in certain ways). His view of *emancipatory* literacy is one which encourages readers' critical reflection on the social order.

Written language makes a radical difference to the complexity of organisation that humans can manage, since it changes the relation between memory and classification, and allows many forms of organising (referencing, cataloguing, indexing, recording) and transmitting information. Bureaucratic institutions, from small businesses to modern states, depend on written records. However, an educational theory of writing must recognise that the term writing is also ambiguous. It applies to a *product* (cf. *there is some writing on the wall*; the writings of Shakespeare) with particular functions and forms, and some of these forms have high prestige in the education system. But the term also applies to a *process* (cf. *children are taught writing in school*). Texts are the *products* of drafting and editing *processes*. Furthermore, as both process and product, writing has both social and personal functions. It has the social function of being able to communicate across time and space. But it also has the personal, cognitive and reflective function of organising and structuring one's ideas: it facilitates certain kinds of thinking and learning. It is evident in looking at both children's and adults' views of written language that there is often a preference for surface features such as neatness and spelling, over the ability to use written language to help formulate ideas.

A competence in written language is clearly a key to success in the educational and social system. As I pointed out briefly above, it is writing (rather than reading) which can give people power. It is the ability to write formal Standard English which allows people to initiate action (e.g. complaining against injustice) or to respond to a bureaucracy.

There is a strong tendency in recent work to emphasise the relations between reading and writing. For example, Tierney and Pearson (1983) argue that both reading and writing are concerned with creating meaning; both are interactive, collaborative processes. Writers obviously compose, but so do readers: readers may revise their interpretations of a text, just as writers may redraft a text. Both are processes of refining meaning.

It is also common to point out nowadays that *literate* and *illiterate* are not two discrete categories. They refer to a continuum of abilities which are dependent on context. (Even highly literate academics may still need to consult their solicitor for some tasks of reading and interpretation.) For example, I cannot read a book or newspaper in Chinese, but I can read (though not always write) a useful number of characters for words such as *exit* and *toilets*, plus numbers, some place names and some political slogans.

It is important to remember that many children in British schools are biliterate in, for example, Chinese, Greek or Urdu, and may have different abilities in English and in a community language.

## 11. WRITTEN AND SPOKEN LANGUAGE

A great deal of descriptive work has been done recently, particularly on the syntactic differences between written and spoken English. They clearly share the same basic lexis and grammar, but differ quite sharply in many details. Much work concerns the motivation for such differences in the psycho-linguistic processing required by written and spoken language. Written language can be re-read at leisure, but spoken language requires an organis-ation in which one thing is said and understood about one thing at a time. This leads to topic-comment structures which typify spoken rather than written English. (Brown 1978; Tannen and Chafe in Olson *et al.* (eds) 1985.)

Much descriptive work requires to be done, however. The English ortho-graphic system is discussed elsewhere in this book (Chapter 20, below). But in addition to descriptions of the organisation of English spelling, there is work on how young children learn to re-invent spelling for themselves: how they acquire the regularities in ways comparable to their acquisition of their native spoken language (Bissex 1980, Read 1987).

In some areas, there is still rather elementary descriptive work to be done. One cliché about spoken and written language is that speech is transitory, whereas writing is permanent. With the arrival of word-processing, this cliché (never entirely true in any case) is clearly untrue. The relative stability of a traditional written record gives way to a dynamic screen display, where written text can be edited, redrafted, reformatted or deleted, with great ease, leaving no trace of any change. The concept of a written text becomes profoundly different: it is just one of a series of transformations, some of which can be carried out automatically by repetitive edits, or by spelling checkers. Detailed descriptive studies require to be done on how such changes in technology affect the forms and uses of written texts, and also on what implications this has for learners. The main implication for learners is probably that it can take the pressure off the physical act of writing: hand-writing, redrafting, checking spelling and so on are no longer tedious chores, and attention can be given to the main intellectual task of creating meaningful texts.

An analysis of written language requires to be placed within an analysis of signifying systems. The mere fact *that* something is written conveys its own message, for example of permanence and authority. Certain people write and certain things get written (though this is changing fast with access to word-processors). Written language itself represents an orientation to the dominant mainstream culture, and this is doubtless one reason why it is rejected by many pupils in their more general rejection of dominant modes of education and culture.

The pedagogical implications of this huge body of work, which I have only referred to very sketchily, are enormous. I think we might expect wide agreement with Halliday's (1978: 234) view that education involves learning new registers, and that written language represents an extension of the pupil's functional meaning potential. Written language extends pupils' ability to express meanings and communicate them to others, and new forms of technology (such as word processing) extend this ability yet further. This implies that written language involves not only linguistic forms, functions and meanings, but also new forms of social relations, with teachers and other pupils, and also with distant anonymous or hypothetical audiences. Much of the work on children's acquisition of writing processes discusses both the cognitive development involved, and also the new forms of authority relations in schools when children are encouraged to write for real purposes and real audiences.

Contemporary views on reading and writing emphasise their relations to listening and speaking. For example, successful readers at school are often children who have had the experience of frequent story-reading at home. Wells (1981: 262), in the Bristol study referred to above, found that the best single predictor of attainment in literacy after two years schooling was the child's understanding of the functions and mechanics of literacy when they started school. The importance of early encounters with print seems to lie in the encouragement of positive attitudes to written language, in situations in which it has real, meaningful, communicative purposes.

In addition, once the relations between reading, writing, listening and speaking are seen, it is also seen that when children acquire competence in written language, they are not making a single transition from speech to writing. They are making a whole series of related transitions, which will therefore not all take place at once: for example, from casual to formal, from spontaneous to edited, from private to public, and possibly from non-standard to standard, and from first to second language. This rather simple

574

observation requires to be related to the debate on home-school transitions, and on how such language shifts may relate to educational success or failure.

## 12. THE LANGUAGE OF SCHOOL TEXTBOOKS

An important topic for an educational theory of language must be books which are used in schools. Written language, standard language, textbooks, teachers and the school as an institution all have perceived authority (Luke *et al.* 1983). We therefore require an analysis of the ways in which this authority is expressed in language, and therefore of the relation between linguistic usages and the authority of curricular knowledge. It seems evident that there are relations between forms of language in school textbooks, the institutions in which they are used, the social and intellectual control which they support, and the pedagogical practices which they assume. Such an analysis would be part of a wider analysis of the relations between written language, knowledge and power (Foucault 1980).

This relates again to the transition between the language of home and school. Walkerdine and Sinha (1981), for example, discuss the confusions caused by the use of everyday words in new senses in school subjects. For example, words such as *odd* and *even* in mathematics, or *man* and *behaviour* in social studies, have to be de- or re-contextualised. They are members of very different category systems, and very different contexts of discourse. (Pimm 1987 is a detailed study of the relations between everyday and specialist usages of language in mathematics teaching.)

Perera (1984) has made detailed studies of the discourse organisation, syntax and lexis of school textbooks and examination questions. She points to examples such as: *penitents, or people who were sorry for doing wrong* (from a history book). In everyday English, the construction *A or B* means: *if A not B*. But in this academic prose, *A or B* means: *A, that is to say B*; *both A and B*. The word *or* signals quite different relations in two styles of language. Furthermore, a reader can really only tell which interpretation is to be given to *or* if the meaning of *penitents* is already known. But such readers are precisely those who do not need the definition!

A great deal of work concerns the concept of the 'readability' of texts, that is, estimations of their difficulty for children of different ages and abilities. Much of this work is rather narrow in conception. It concerns, for example, the fact that long words (measured by number of letters or syllables) or long sentences tend to correlate with difficulty in comprehension. And such measures can relatively easily be combined into 'readability formulae' (which may be calculable by computational analyses of texts). Such formulae certainly have their uses for teachers wanting an estimate of the average difficulty of books for class use, but correlations of this kind have severe limitations. It is quite easy to construct passages with short words and short sentences which are difficult to understand. (Harrison 1980 provides an excellent review of the pros and cons of such analyses.) The discourse organisation of texts also affects readability, and this is much less easily measured in automatic ways (Lunzer and Gardner 1984).

It is also clear, however, that readability is not a feature which is found 'in' texts alone. Comprehensibility depends on the balance between old and new information: what a text assumes that the reader knows. But this clearly depends on the reader as much as on the text.

A fundamental topic is 'how effects of truth are produced within discourses' (Foucault 1980: 118, cf. 131). School textbooks often present information as objective and neutral. Authors are assumed to be corporate or anonymous. There is a lack of an explicitly personal, fallible world-view. This may be a feature of the books themselves or of the way in which they are used by teachers, but authorship is often irrelevant to teachers and pupils (Luke *et al.* 1983). However, writing always expresses propositions from a certain point of view. We require therefore detailed linguistic descriptions and theory which shows how language is used to convey a writer's attitude to propositions: whether they are taken to be the expression of true, certain authoritative statements, or are hypothetical and tentative, neutral and objective, personal and subjective, and so on. For example, I was once castigated by the editor of a book on classroom research for using too many first person pronouns. He altered several sentences such as *I will argue that* . . . to *It will be argued that* . . . In one sense, the meaning remained the same. However, he changed the relation between the author and the claims in the article, he hid a personal viewpoint and emphasised an objective inter- pretation of knowledge, and he implied that the views had more authority than they in fact did. Both teachers and pupils require ways of focusing critically on such usages, which concern the relation between linguistic forms, academic stylistic conventions and claimed curricular authority.

School texts are highly selected and controlled by institutions, such as examination boards. Texts may be selected by the teacher, distributed for the lesson, interpreted by the teacher or via another text (e.g. study notes), and then withdrawn. The amount of control over school textbooks, whether this control is central or local, differs greatly in different countries: compare for example the central control in France or Germany versus the teacher's autonomy in Britain. And in Britain, the control differs between private and state schools, and between different LEAs. The existence of books as material objects is also controlled by publishing houses: they exercise control over content, form, dissemination and reproduction. We are dealing with officially and commercially sanctioned versions of knowledge.

An educational theory of school textbooks is therefore concerned with the form, production, distribution and use of texts in Western education. Each historical genre of written text has served particular cultural functions: translations of the Bible, novels, newspapers, reading primers and textbooks. As new forms of written language, such as computer files and electronic mail, become available, they too come to be used to create new forms of social relations.

The authority of textbooks as a source of curricular knowledge is related to the view that the meaning of a book is 'in' the text. But students' interpretations of texts can be widely different under different classroom practices. Quite different views of knowledge are transmitted by the hidden curriculum of, say, dictation, rote memorisation, oral recitation, study notes, explication de texte, silent reading, small group discussion, and the like. A basic distinction is between a student's unmediated reading versus a use of a text which is mediated by the teacher's 'expert' interpretation or by study notes. Again, the use and interpretation of texts in the classroom is inseparable from social relations.

Forms and uses of language are related to theories of knowledge (beware readers of encyclopaedias!), and to concepts of literacy: instrumental and passive, or critical and active.

## 13. LANGUAGE STUDY IN TEACHER TRAINING

Knowledge about language (amongst both teachers and pupils) has declined in Britain since the 1960s for several reasons. There has been a decline in the teaching of Latin and Greek, and a consequent decline in the particularly explicit and analytic methods of teaching about grammar which had characterised this language teaching for hundreds of years. Latin and Greek were taught as dead classical languages, in which an active communicative competence was not required. Hence a grammar-translation method was not necessarily illogical: it could lead to a satisfactory reading competence for literary and historical texts, at least for the relatively small elite who were taught such competence. When people complain that the decline in Latin has led to a decline in logical and analytic thinking amongst pupils, what they probably mean is that the teaching *method* led to a particular kind of consciousness of surface linguistic organisation, with a concomitant ability in certain kinds of logico-linguistic analysis. Within modern language teaching, there was a shift away from the grammar-translation method: the argument here being that this was inappropriate for teaching active communicative competence, especially in spoken language. In other words, this shift accompanied the view that languages might be taught by different methods for different purposes. And in teaching English as a mother tongue, there was also a shift away from teaching explicitly about grammar and language

577

structures, to encouraging children's creativity and use of language. The shift from structure to use had the effect of making many teachers abandon all explicit teaching about language.

Twenty years of these various trends was enough to set up a vicious circle. A generation of pupils learned nothing explicitly about language: they became, in turn, teachers who could not pass such knowledge on to their pupils. It is ironic that such shifts happened at precisely the same time that academic linguistics was becoming prestigious in Britain. But this development did nothing to mend an often severe split between teaching about language and literature at university level. And in addition, much of the academic linguistic work was not at all in the appropriate form to be adopted for educational ends, either in teacher-training or in the classroom.

In 1975 the Bullock Report (HMSO 1975) recommended that:

> A substantial course on language in education (including reading) should be part of every primary and secondary school teacher's training, whatever the teacher's subject or the age of the children with whom he or she will be working.

However, this recommendation has never been systematically implemented in teacher training courses in Britain. Many teachers simply do not know enough about language, however one might define this. And, as Thornton (1986) argues, teachers and those administering the system lack a theoretical framework for evaluating knowledge and claims about language in education.

Several reasons why teachers should have a systematic knowledge of language have been discussed or implied above. They need to know about children's language development, normal and abnormal. They need to be prepared for the linguistic diversity they will find amongst their pupils; and for collaboration between different language departments in schools, and indeed for collaboration across a whole school, given that language is a medium of learning in all subjects.

There is a genuine problem in designing short simple courses about language, because the major argument must concern the complexity of knowledge about language. And there is a logical problem in trying to demonstrate the nature of this complexity in a simple course. Furthermore, much of the debate is essentially over the relation between everyday and specialist knowledge, and an important argument is that everyday stereotypes about language grossly underestimate the complexities involved. Because speakers' knowledge of their native language is so deeply ingrained, they *are* experts in their own language in one sense, yet can fail to see the need for explanations precisely because of this competence. The depth of this competence provides an enormous resource for teaching about language: but language can also be too close to the speaker's individual and social identity to be objectively observed.

578

Initial discussion therefore must distinguish clearly between different kinds of knowledge, for example: prescriptive versus descriptive; implicit versus explicit; unconscious versus conscious; everyday folk stereotypes versus contemporary scholarship; monolingual versus bilingual competence, and knowledge appropriate for teachers versus pupils.

When linguists emphasise the vast complexity of knowledge *of* a language, they are talking of the unconscious competence which speakers have in their native language – and therefore of the consequent complexity of descriptions and explanations of this competence. Teachers require a set of consistent principles which will ensure that they do not trivialise this competence. And, as this article has shown in detail, a problem here is the breadth of widely different kinds of knowledge which are required, from the narrowly linguistic to the broadly social.

It is important to realise that the framework above shows schematically the logical organisation of a body of knowledge: it implies nothing at all about how it should be conveyed to teachers. The intellectual framework underlying a course is not at all the same thing as actually organising the material into a teachable or learnable sequence. Apart from anything else, the language component would be very different on a one-year postgraduate certificate of education, on a four year B.Ed., or on a one-year MA for experienced teachers. I assume that presentational principles would include the need to start from the students' own experience in schools, and that topics would need to be tackled from professionally relevant viewpoints. For example, linguists might tend to start from notions of *products* such as spoken and written language, whereas teachers would tend to start from *processes* such as reading and writing.

## 14. LANGUAGE STUDY AS A SCHOOL SUBJECT

Much current educational wisdom holds that knowing-*that* is less important than knowing-*how*, and even that the former can interfere with the latter. However, there are two powerful arguments for the value of explicit *knowledge about* language, in addition to competence in the *use of* language.

The first is that human beings are creatures who know that they know: and it is precisely this which assures that their knowledge has a critical dimension. Language must be brought to attention as an object of conscious and critical inquiry. This is simply to say that theory is essential. The second is that formal education in the West requires that language be de- or re-contextualised. All language use is context-bound, but there are degrees. And the ability to focus critically on language itself allows the distinction between what people mean and what words mean. The ability to turn language upon itself is required for success in education: children have to learn how to conceptualise language as a partly autonomous system which is both subjective and objective. The first more overtly political point is argued by Freire and Macedo (in press). The second more psychological phrasing is argued by Donaldson (1978).

One rather obvious question, which has nevertheless been typically avoided in any direct way in British schools, is what should be taught *about language* to pupils? There are several traditional and less traditional categories in which pupils are taught about language, but as Hawkins (1984) points out, they derive from very different traditions, they have different views of their aims, and of the relations between language, literature and culture. And although several different teachers in a school may be teaching a language, it may be that no teacher is teaching about language itself. More generally, there may be quite different concepts of reading and writing being conveyed by teachers of different subjects, or different views of the appropriate way in which pupils should respond to teachers' questions. From many points of view, the organisation of schools may be quite incoherent from a pupil's point of view. This is not necessarily a bad thing: no-one has the whole truth about language. But one should at least ask whether it is possible to design an interesting and coherent syllabus about language itself.

I referred above to the related decline in teaching *about* language in classical and modern languages and English, and to shifting views of language-teaching purposes and methods. The decisions taken depend partly on the cultural value placed on different languages, and this depends on centuries of educational attitudes, and ultimately on how a society perceives itself in relation to other languages and cultures. Decisions depend also on changing views of valid knowledge. It was felt that grammar teaching was often narrow and meaningless to many children, and that it should be abandoned in favour of more concentration on children's own developing linguistic competence. But by the 1980s it was widely being asked if something valuable was lost when this grammar teaching was abandoned, and whether it is possible to develop more acceptable teaching about linguistic rules and patterns.

'Modern' languages means in effect a very narrow range of West European languages: often just French, sometimes also German, Spanish, Italian or Russian. Again the choice of such languages depends on centuries of tradition, and bears little relation to a logical selection of languages currently of economic or cultural value to Britain, such as Arabic, Chinese or Japanese. There is a vicious circle involved here. Since French has long been the main foreign language taught in British schools, there are many French teachers, and therefore French continues to be taught, irrespective of its genuine value to British school pupils or to British society.

An increasing number of schools now offer 'language awareness' courses, often in the early secondary school where there is no pressure from external examinations (but there are also related new A-levels which are more language- than literature-based). The term is an odd one, which might imply that it is enough to be 'aware' of aspects of language without either having competence in them, or being able to analyse them systematically. (Imagine the absurdity, in mathematics, of arguing that it is enough if children are 'aware' of processes such as addition and multiplication, without either being able to add or multiply, or understand what they were doing.) Nevertheless, whatever the subject is called, we are dealing with a form of language study, which is distinctly different from learning particular languages.

The language awareness movement grew up originally, in the early 1980s, amongst modern language teachers. They recognised a frequent lack of genuine motivation for children to learn French or German. But if they learn about language in general, this might, for example, put them in a better position later in life to learn a language which they really need for their careers. In addition, they would be learning about a central aspect of society. English teachers also recognised the potential of such study. And there is a further potential link to community languages. Many teachers have realised the potential of knowledge about language in a multicultural society, where more understanding of language should lead to more tolerance of linguistic and cultural diversity.

There are many different sub-motivations for such a course. Children might have 'taster' courses in different languages: say six weeks each of French, German, Arabic, Urdu. They would learn about language learning itself, and be in a better position to choose one language for detailed study. An explicit discussion of language forms and functions might have spin-off in developing study skills, such as the ability to read different kinds of material with critical understanding.

However, the real issue is whether it is possible to design a coherent course about language itself: not just a few lessons about dialect, slang or language varieties, but a conceptually coherent and cumulative course, developed over a child's whole school career. I think it is possible to develop such a course, and the general framework for language study proposed earlier in this article could, in appropriate form (see Stubbs 1986, Chapter 4), be a basis for a systematic study of language in society.

Such a course would have to start from children's own linguistic competence. It would aim to make explicit the large implicit linguistic competence which any normal user of a language has. It would be based on the children's own fieldwork, collecting and classifying language data, and thereby learning about principles of scientific method. Such language study must be based on a wide range of facts and also on coherent concepts.

The essential link between children's explicit knowledge about, and their developing competence in, a range of varieties is evident in the issue of Standard English. As I argue above, all pupils have the right to expect schools to develop their competence in the standard prestige language of the wider community. But if this teaching is not to be of an apparently arbitrary variety, different from the language of their families and friends, they need to know a great deal about SE: its forms, functions, status and uses in institutions in Britain and around the world. This cannot be dealt with in a few lessons: it is a substantial topic with historical, geographical, political and linguistic dimensions. Children have the right to know a great deal about SE. Teaching facts and concepts is unfashionable in some quarters, but it is impossible to see how children could discover for themselves many aspects about SE as an institutional and international language. In general, children have the right to have explained to them why their curriculum is worthwhile. School is compulsory, and pupils therefore have the right to have a worthwhile curriculum and not to have their time wasted in school (Lawton 1981: 130).

Many people regret the passing of teaching about formal grammar (parsing sentences and so on) on the grounds that it helped children to write better, more precisely, and so on. The research evidence is difficult to interpret. However, it is doubtful if such learning ever helped many people to write better, and it is clear that it put a large number of people off. The relation between analysis and understanding, and between conscious understanding and the production of effective language, is difficult to demonstrate. It is plausible, however, that if children have a wider understanding of the forms and functions of language in society, then they will have more understanding and control over the language they hear and read; and that their understanding will have a less direct but pervasive effect on the language they produce. In this sense, it is plausible that *knowledge about* language will improve children's *use of* language.

## 15. CURRENT ISSUES AND CONCLUSIONS

At the end of a long article, one should ask whether it is possible to predict the major issues which are likely in future debates. This list may look embarrassingly naïve and wide of the mark in ten or twenty years: but that in itself would be interesting, as it would reveal what seem now to be major issues as passing obsessions; and this would make visible some of the assumptions underlying the present article.

1. The centuries-long debate over the appropriate balance between individual rights and social responsibilities in education is still hotly debated and is unlikely to be resolved in the near future. (See Williams 1965 and Hargreaves 1982 for substantial accounts.)

2. Similarly, the centuries-long debate over appropriate languages in the curriculum is unlikely to be resolved. Its current focus is on the appropriate balance between traditional and other foreign languages. Within this is the debate over the place of language study. And within this again, the ebb and flow of the debate over the value of formal language study is unlikely to falter.

3. Attempts to find linguistic explanations of educational success and failure have essentially failed, despite twenty years research and a residual common-sense belief that the way you speak reveals how educated you really are. Although explanations have become more and more sophisticated, nothing has been found 'in' the language to explain the educational failure of various social groups. People's perceptions of language seem much more important. But there is likely still to be much debate over whether this formulation is accurate. It seems very difficult to shift people away from the view that there are single, simple causes of educational failure.

4. There is also continuous debate over reductionist versus holistic conceptions of literacy. There is an apparently unshakeable common-sense belief that reading and writing are 'basic skills', reducible to techniques which can be taught in straightforward ways. Against this runs the view, held by many professional educationalists, that reading and writing essentially involve comprehension, and that children's success often depends on cultural attitudes to literacy. This debate, about narrower or broader concepts of literacy, is related to the debate about changing concepts of print, media and computer literacy. These notions lead in turn to a notion of basic, instrumental or functional literacy versus a notion of critical literacy as part of children's competence in understanding the culture in which they live.

It may turn out (as Brumfit discusses, 1985: 148–9) that such concerns are the product of contemporary imagery in the social sciences, which are concerned with the construction and negotiation of meaning, and with the autonomy of the individual (and therefore learner-centred education), but also with the value of diversity and of cultural plurality. But it does seem that they reflect large-scale changes in society's attitude to knowledge, authority and social cohesion, and to the relation between the freedom of the individual and the control of the state. Such issues are unlikely to go away, since they concern what we mean by education.

There are two related underlying themes of this chapter, which are both central to teacher-pupil communication in the classroom: (a) the concept of language varieties, and (b) the question of sub-cultural differences in how the relations between language varieties and social contexts are interpreted. The education system is the main point of contact between people who do not share the same language or dialect. Since education is compulsory, and since the linguistic and cultural mix of British society has greatly increased since the 1960s, this is inevitable. (Gumperz 1982 has provided detailed case studies of some of the misunderstandings which arise between people in institutional settings, including education. And Halliday (1978) has discussed the kinds of semiotic mismatches which arise in modern societies, where large towns and cities are no longer speech communities.) For such reasons, Halliday places 'a deep study of language variation and varieties' at the centre of a study of education, and he places the ability to control varieties of language as fundamental to pupils' developing language education. Modern Western education systems are increasingly faced with linguistic and cultural diversity. If such diversity is perceived as a problem, then this perception itself becomes part of the problem. If it is perceived as a resource of competence amongst pupils, then it becomes an opportunity.

The whole area of language in education is riddled with folk knowledge, myths and stereotypes, many of which have persisted for centuries, and sometimes with deliberate distortions of linguistic and educational facts in the media. As Thornton (1986) has argued, linguists' ideas have penetrated the general cultural consciousness in Britain only in a very shallow way, and there is a strongly anti-intellectual streak in much of British cultural life. There is a widespread inability to perceive language as an object of critical reflection: it is often regarded as too obvious to be worth studying, or too mysterious to be explained. Prescriptive views about 'standards' just seem obvious, and language 'problems' seem amenable to easy and superficial treatment.

Nevertheless, since the 1960s, our knowledge about language in education has grown considerably. Much more is now known about the linguistic, cognitive and social processes involved when people construct meaning in spoken and written language. And to pursue educational debate and social action in ignorance of this knowledge is irresponsible.

## 16. APPENDIX: LANGUAGE PLANNING IN THE NATIONAL CURRICULUM

Since the main part of this article was written (in 1987), major changes have taken place in the education system of England and Wales. In July 1987, a consultative document was published on a proposed national curriculum for England and Wales (DES & Welsh Office 1987). Only a year later, and for the first time ever in the UK, a national curriculum was a legal requirement in state schools, to be taught from 1989. These requirements are part of the Education Reform Act, which became law in July 1988. This is the most far-reaching educational legislation since the Education Act of 1944, and makes many other fundamental changes in primary, secondary and tertiary education. It is clear that educational planning is moving very quickly in Britain in the late 1980s.

In a long term perspective, these changes simply mark a stage in the perennial debate over literacy and standard language, and over the nature of education: a vocational training for the adult world or a development of the spiritual being of the individual. Nevertheless, the debate has been sharpened in ways previously unknown in the UK, and a new style of language planning and policy is underway.

In the 1970s and 1980s, English teaching was subject to more official inquiries, reports and personal ministerial interest than any other school subject. Major documents, which relate specifically to the national curriculum, and which give a good idea of the way policy has been shaped, include: DES 1984, 1986; HMSO 1988; DES & Welsh Office 1988, in prep 1989; Welsh Office 1988. These reports have to do with the teaching of English, Welsh, and, to some extent, with bilingualism more generally, though this aspect of the reports is arguably not well developed. They have to do with language policy: the range of language and languages which is considered appropriate in British schools. This language planning is a highly symbolic part of the very detailed government intervention in education which is represented by the Education Reform Act.

The publication of the reports on the teaching of English was accompanied by very widespread, sometimes almost hysterical, press coverage, which demonstrated the deep-seated and emotive responses which language questions seem always to evoke in discussions of British education. It is a striking fact, for example, that the Kingman Report (HMSO 1988) was commented on in the editorial leading articles in the main British national daily newspapers. But it is disappointing that much of the press commentary was ill-informed.

The most disagreement centred on what children should know explicitly about language. As DES (1986) puts it: there are 'deep divisions upon matters of principle, practice and content'. And as the Cox Report (DES & Welsh Office 1988: 10) puts it:

Language enters individual and social life at many points, but the public is often not sufficiently well-informed for enlightened discussion to take place. This may be the strongest rationale for knowledge about language in schools. Difficult issues of language in an increasingly multi-cultural society require informed citizens.

## ACKNOWLEDGEMENTS

Eve Bearne, Tony Burgess, Henrietta Dombey and Gabi Keck all provided valuable critical comments on previous drafts of this paper or on related papers. I have also gained much from discussing with Tony Burgess the concept of an educational theory of language.

## REFERENCES

Aries, P. (1962) *Centuries of Childhood*, Penguin, Harmondsworth.

Atkinson, P. (1985) *Language, Structure and Reproduction*, Methuen, London.

Barnes, D., Britton, J. and Rosen, H. (1969) *Language, the Learner and the School*, Penguin, Harmondsworth.

Bellack, A., Kliebard, H.M., Hyman, R.T. and Smith, F.L. (1966) *The Language of the Classroom*, Teachers College Press, New York.

Bernstein, B.B. (1971, 1975) *Class, Codes and Control*, vols 1 & 2, Routledge & Kegan Paul, London.

Bernstein, B.B. (1987) 'Elaborated and restricted codes: an overview 1958–1985', in Ammon, U., Dittmar, N. and Mattheier, K. (eds) *Sociolinguistics: an International Handbook of the Science of Language and Society*, Walter de Gruyter, Berlin.

Berry, J. (1986) 'The literature of the Black experience', in Sutcliffe and Wong (eds): 69–106.

Bissex, G.L. (1980) *Gnys at Wrk*, Harvard University Press, Cambridge, Mass.

Brice Heath, S. (1983) *Ways with Words*, Cambridge University Press, Cambridge.

Britton, J., Burgess, T., Martin, N., McLeod, A. and Rosen, H. (1975) *The Development of Writing Abilities (11—18)*, Macmillan, London.

Brown, G. (1978) 'Understanding spoken language', *TESOL Quarterly*, 12, 3: 271–83.

Brumfit, C. (1985) 'Creativity and constraint in the language classroom', in Quirk, R. and Widdowson, H.G. (eds) *English in the World*, Cambridge University Press, Cambridge: 148–57.

Cameron, D. (1985) *Feminism and Linguistic Theory*, Macmillan, London.

Cazden, C.B., John, V. and Hymes, D. (ed.) (1972) *Functions of Language in the Classroom*, Teachers College Press, New York.

Cook-Gumperz, J. (ed.) (1986) *The Social Construction of Literacy*, Cambridge University Press, Cambridge.

DES (1984) *English from 5 to 16: Curriculum Matters 1*, London.

DES (1986) *English from 5 to 16: The Responses to Curriculum Matters 1*, London.

DES & Welsh Office (1988) *English for Ages 5 to 11* (The Cox Report), London.

DES & Welsh Office (1989, in prep.) *English for Ages 11 to 16* (The Cox Report), London.

DES & Welsh Office (1987) *The National Curriculum 5 to 16: a Consultation Document*, London.

Donaldson, M. (1978) *Children's Minds*, Fontana, London.

Edwards, A.D. and Westgate, D.P.G. (1987) *Investigating Classroom Talk*, Falmer, London.

Edwards, J. (1979) *Language and Disadvantage*, Edward Arnold, London.

Edwards, J. (1985) *Language, Society and Identity*. Blackwell, Oxford.

Flanders, N.A. (1970) *Analysing Teaching Behavior*, Addison Wesley, London.

Freire, P. (1972a) *Cultural Action for Freedom*, Penguin, Harmondsworth.

Freire, P. (1972b) *Pedagogy of the Oppressed*, Penguin, Harmondsworth.

Freire, P. and Macedo, D. (in press) *Literacy: Reading the Word and the World*, Routledge & Kegan Paul, London.

Goodman, K. (1982) *Language and Literacy*, 2 vols, Routledge & Kegan Paul, London.

Goody, J. (1977) *The Domestication of the Savage Mind*, Cambridge University Press, London.

Gordon, J.C.B. (1981) *Verbal Deficit: a Critique*, Croom Helm, London.

Graves, D. (1983) *Writing: Teachers and Children at Work*, Heinemann, London.

Gumperz, J.J. (1982) *Discourse Strategies*, Cambridge University Press, Cambridge.

Halliday, M.A.K. (1978) *Language as Social Semiotic*, Edward Arnold, London.

Hargreaves, D. (1982) *The Challenge for the Comprehensive School*, Routledge & Kegan Paul, London.

Harrison, C. (1980) *Readability in the Classroom*, Cambridge University Press, Cambridge.

Hawkins, E. (1984) *Awareness of Language*, Cambridge University Press, Cambridge.

HMSO (1963) *Children and their Primary Schools* (The Plowden Report), Central Advisory Council for Education, London.

HMSO (1975) *A Language for Life* (The Bullock Report), London.

HMSO (1983) *Education for Equality* (The Swann Report), London.

HMSO (1988) *Report of the Committee of Inquiry into the Teaching of English Language* (The Kingman Report), London.

Kress, G. (1982) *Learning to Write*, Routledge & Kegan Paul, London.

Labov, W. (1969) *The Logic of non-standard English*, Centre for Applied Linguistics, Washington, DC.

Lawson, J. and Silver, H. (1973) *A Social History of Education in England*, Methuen, London.

Lawton, D. (1977) *Education and Social Justice*, Sage, London.

Lawton, D. (1981) *An Introduction to Teaching and Learning*, Hodder & Stoughton, London.

Lawton, D. (1983) *Curriculum Studies and Educational Planning*, Hodder & Stoughton, London.

Levine, K. (1986) *The Social Context of Literacy*, Routledge & Kegan Paul, London.

Linguistic Minorities Project (1985) *The Other Languages of England*, Routledge & Kegan Paul, London.

Luke, C., de Castell, S. and Luke, A. (1983) 'Beyond criticism: the authority of the school text', *Curriculum Inquiry*, 13, 2: 111–27.

Lunzer, E. and Gardner, K. (1984) *Learning from the Written Word*, Oliver & Boyd, London.

Lynch, J. (1986) *Multicultural Education*, Routledge & Kegan Paul, London.

Milroy, J. and Milroy, L. (1985) *Authority in Language*, Routledge & Kegan Paul, London.

Olson, D., Torrance, N. and Hildyard, A. (eds) (1985) *Literacy, Language and Learning*, Cambridge University Press, Cambridge.

Perera, K. (1984) *Children's Writing and Reading*, Blackwell, Oxford.

Perren, G. (1983) 'English and other languages in English schools', in Stubbs, M. and Hillier, H. (eds) *Readings on Language, Schools and Classrooms*, Methuen, London: 39–49.

Pimm, D. (1987) *Speaking Mathematically*, Routledge & Kegan Paul, London.

Printon, V. (ed.) (1986) *Facts and Figures: Languages in Education*, Centre for Information on Language Teaching and Research, London.

Radcliffe Richards, J. (1982) *The Sceptical Feminist*, Penguin, Harmondsworth.

Read, C. (1987) *Children's Creative Spelling*, Routledge & Kegan Paul, London.

Richmond, J. (1986) 'The language of Black children and the language debate in schools', in Sutcliffe and Wong (eds): 123–35.

Rosen, H. and Burgess, T. (1980) *Languages and Dialects of London Schoolchildren*, Ward Lock, London.

Scribner, S. and Cole, M. (1981) *The Psychology of Literacy*, Harvard University Press, Cambridge, Mass.

Sinclair, J.M. and Coulthard, R.M. (1975) *Towards an Analysis of Discourse*, Oxford University Press, London.

Smith, F. (1982) *Writing and the Writer*, Heinemann, London.

Smith, F. (1985) *Reading*, 2nd edn., Cambridge University Press, Cambridge.

Street, B. (1985) *Literacy in Theory and Practice*, Cambridge University Press, Cambridge.

Stubbs, M. (1980) *Language and Literacy*, Routledge & Kegan Paul, London.

Stubbs, M. (1986) *Educational Linguistics*, Blackwell, Oxford.

Sutcliffe, D. and Wong, A. (eds) *The Language of the Black Experience*, Blackwell, Oxford.

Thornton, G. (1986) *Language, Ignorance and Education*, Edward Arnold, London.

Tierney, R.J. and Pearson, P.D. (1983) 'Toward a composing model of reading', *Language Arts*, 60, 5: 568–80.

Tizard, B. and Hughes, M. (1984) *Young Children Learning*, Fontana, London.

Trudgill, P. (1975) *Accent, Dialect and the School*, Edward Arnold, London.

Trudgill, P. (1984) 'Standard English in England', in Trudgill, P. (ed.) *Language in the British Isles*, Cambridge University Press, Cambridge.

Walkerdine, V. and Sinha, C. (1981) 'Developing linguistic strategies in young school children', in Wells 1981: 182–204.

Wells, G. (1981) *Learning through Interaction*, Cambridge University Press, Cambridge.

Wells, G. (1985) *Language, Learning and Education*, NFER-Nelson, Slough.

Welsh Office (1988) *National Curriculum Welsh Working Group: Interim Report*, Cardiff.

Wilkinson, A. (ed.) (1986) *The Writing of Writing*, Open University Press, Milton Keynes.

Willes, M. (1983) *Children into Pupils*, Routledge & Kegan Paul, London.

Williams, R. (1965) *The Long Revolution*, Penguin, Harmondsworth.

Williams, R. (1976) *Keywords*, Fontana, London.

# FURTHER READING

This list provides three general references which are closely related to the main theme of the chapter, then just one reference each on the main topics of classroom discourse, language and learning, language study in schools, community languages, Standard English, written language in schools, reading, literacy, and language at home and at school.

Lawson, J. and Silver, H. (1973) *A Social History of Education in England*, Methuen, London.

Stubbs, M. and Hillier, H. (ed.) (1983) *Readings on Language, Schools and Classrooms*, Methuen, London.

Stubbs, M. (1986) *Educational Linguistics*, Blackwell, Oxford.

Edwards, A.D. and Westgate, D.P.G. (1987) *Investigating Classroom Language*, Falmer, London.

Donaldson, M. (1978) *Children's Minds*, Fontana, London.

Hawkins, E. (1984) *Awareness of Language*, Cambridge University Press, Cambridge.

Linguistic Minorities Project (1985) *The Other Languages of England*, Routledge & Kegan Paul, London.

Milroy, J. and Milroy, L. (1985) *Authority in Language*, Routledge & Kegan Paul, London.

Perera, K. (1984) *Children's Writing and Reading*, Blackwell, Oxford.

Smith, F. (1985) *Reading*, 2nd ed., Cambridge University Press, Cambridge.

Street, B. (1985) *Literacy in Theory and Practice*, Cambridge University Press, Cambridge.

Tizard, B. and Hughes, M. (1984) *Young Children Learning*, Fontana, London.

# 17

# LANGUAGE AND LITERATURE

## RONALD CARTER

### 1. LANGUAGE, LITERATURE, AND THE STUDY OF STYLE: A HISTORICAL PERSPECTIVE

The history of work in stylistics and in contingent areas of language and literature has, during the past fifty years, been characterised by attempts to locate common territory, to find a middle ground in which the interests of both 'parties' can be accommodated. The attempt has not been a wholly successful one.

Occupying the 'middle-ground' involves us in making some careful distinctions in our understanding of the terms language, style and literature. Above all, the middle-ground must have its own territory and position clearly marked. In fact, military analogies are those most frequently used during the past years in discussions of the relationship between linguistics and literature. There is not the space here to rehearse in detail the specific arguments produced, but their general nature can be summarised by the following quotations:

> . . . the horse of poetry will be led into the stable of Parnassus not by a 'New Critic' and not at all by a traditional literary scholar, but by a linguist.
>
> (Whitehall 1957)

A year earlier the same writer produced a statement that has been much quoted since as a focus of antagonism for the respective camps:

> As no science can go beyond mathematics, no criticism can go beyond its linguistics.
>
> (Whitehall 1956)

From the other side, Bateson has asserted that:

> . . . it is . . . because of [the linguist's] failure to recognise that in literature language is for the reader a mere preliminary to style – as style itself is a preliminary to the literary

response in its fullest sense – that the critic finds so little nourishment in modern linguistics in any of its forms.

(Bateson 1968)

The positions adopted here are extreme and clearly many more conciliatory views exist. The fact remains, however, that considerable rigidity has characterised the respective arguments. Linguistics is seen as an *objective* science and thus disabled from revealing anything significant about such areas of interest to the literary critic as the nature of the literary response, the role of verbal art in culture or the operation of creativity; literary discussions of language are seen by linguists as *subjective*, impressionistic, inattentive to the structure and organisation of language and prone to draw on vague extra-linguistic categories such as 'life experience' in order to substantiate points made. On the one hand, rigidly postulated models have been constructed to account for the nature of literary communication; on the other hand, it is claimed that verbal art cannot by its very nature be made subject to rules. However, a common meeting point can be found in the appeal made to language by many literary critics as evidence to substantiate intuitions concerning the workings of the text. Here are two representative extracts from books organised on such principles:

In considering the language of poetry, it is prudent to begin with what is 'there' in the poem – 'there' in the sense that it can be described and referred to as unarguably given by the words.

(Nowottny 1962: 1)

The novelist's medium is language: whatever he does, *qua* novelist, he does in and through language.

(Lodge 1966: ix)

But a fundamental problem underlying this kind of statement and its ensuing literary critical application is that awareness of 'language' in an *ad hoc*, personal and arbitrarily selective way is an entirely different matter from an analysis founded on general linguistic theory and descriptive linguistics.

In a related way, too, if the linguist simply scrutinises the text, comes up with scientifically controlled and verifiable facts and passes them on to a literary critic for a literary interpretation, then in an important respect linguistic analysis becomes no more than an ancillary to literary study. For some this is indeed the status it should occupy. As Ruwet puts it:

. . . it seems to me that the status of linguistics, in relation to poetics and literary studies in general, can only be that of an auxiliary discipline, whose role is roughly analogous to that played by phonetics with respect to the whole of linguistics. In other words, linguistics can bring a great body of materials to poetics, but it is incapable,

591

working alone, of determining how pertinent these materials are from an aesthetic or poetic point of view.

(Ruwet 1970)

Conversely, as Crystal puts it, a middle-ground can be occupied if there is some appreciation of areas of mutual concern:

One reason why much linguistic analysis of literature has not been well received is that linguists take texts which seem interesting and problematic to them; they often forget that the text, or the problems, may not be of comparable interest to the critic. The stylistician must thoroughly appreciate the literary critics' problems and position.

(Crystal 1972)

One reason why stylistics has been parasitic on or, at the least, has sought to accommodate itself to, literary approaches to texts may have to do with the special place accorded to literary criticism as a humanist discipline. More or less from the time of Matthew Arnold the study of, and writing about, literature has been regarded as a singular repository for distinctions regarding authentic feeling (Trilling 1972), moral vision and true judgement (Leavis 1948, 1952), the awareness of human complexity (Crane 1953) – that is, its value lay and still does lie in the preservation and transmission of human, cultural values. Even criticism which purports to be linguistic in orientation does not move far without apologising for straying from the Arnoldian tradition (e.g. Lodge 1977: xii). The challenge to this view of literature from alternative perspectives has in recent years become a relatively sustained one (cf. Gibb 1976; Schilf 1977; Hawkes 1977), but its legacy is considerable. A natural concomitant of this view is that the fabric from which literature is made should be accorded a similarly elevated status. The language of literature could in several instances be said to have attracted stylisticians because of its 'uniqueness'.

If literary language is felt to be special or unique, then one of the main tasks of stylistics and one which might prove especially acceptable to traditional literary critical methodology, would be to demonstrate how the use of language in a literary text differs from uses of language outside a literary context. In fact, a considerable proportion of research and investigation in stylistics has been devoted to the question of the deviation of literary language from the normal or standard language. The general approach has been to consider those types of language to which literary or aesthetic value is attached as 'marked' or 'foregrounded' over against 'unmarked' language.

Let us begin by citing a much-adduced definition of style:

The message carried by the frequency distributions and transition probabilities of linguistic features, especially as they differ from those of the same features in the language as a whole.

(Bloch 1953)

Here we can infer that there are certain statistically determinable facts about language use which will enable stylisticians to measure the degree of deviation and hence the poeticalness of poetic utterances. This notion has received considerable support in influential papers by Levin (1962, 1963, 1965), and Hill (1967), and from several contributors, notably Stankiewicz and Saporta, to the Indiana Style Conference (see Sebeok (ed.) *Style in Language* 1960). Normal has the meaning here of most frequent in the statistical sense. The most frequently-used language will be usages that are the most expected: literary language will therefore either involve many unexpected, abnormal elements or unexpectedness will result from the 'periodic organisation of the message', Stankiewicz (1960: 77) where normal usages are made to be deviant through such devices as 'coupling' (Levin 1962) or 'parallelism' (Jakobson, 1960: 368).

Such a conception of style has its roots in theories of Russian (particularly Shklovsky) and Czech formalists (particularly Mukařovský and Havranek). Central to many formalists' views of how style works is the process of what has been termed 'automatisation' and 'foregrounding':

By *automatisation* we thus mean such a use of the devices of language, in isolation or in combination with each other, as is useful for a certain expressive purpose, that is, such a use that the expression itself does not attract any attention . . . By *foregrounding*, on the other hand, we mean the use of the devices of the language in such a way that this use itself attracts attention and is perceived as uncommon, as deprived of automatisation, as deautomatised . . .

(Havranek 1932)

In his classic paper Mukařovský (1932) argues that poetic language aims at 'the maximum of foregrounding' that is,

the aesthetically intentional distortion of linguistic components.

For him:

The distortion of the norm of the standard is . . . of the very essence of poetry.

The same notion has received detailed and unchallenged explication by Leech (1969). Furthermore, Mukařovský extends Havranek's inference that foregrounded usages attract attention to themselves by arguing that this special, 'poetic' language does not communicate in a way which is comparable with the normative, standard language. In fact, its main function is to be self-referring and to communicate about itself:

In poetic language foregrounding achieves maximum intensity to the extent of pushing communication into the background as the objective of expression, and of being used for its own sake; it is not used in the services of communication, but in order to place in the foreground the act of expression, the act of speech itself.

593

There is little doubt that foregrounding takes place or that degrees of expectation in literary usages play a significant part in determining particular effects. But a major difficulty with the notion concerns the problems encountered in attempting to measure what is expected or normal and thus how foregrounding actually takes place. A person doing stylistic analysis is hardly likely to have time enough to carry out statistical analysis for every example of deviation that he perceives. The likelihood is therefore that his view of the 'norm' will be impressionistic. Other perspectives on the question of norms have been offered, however. For example, Cluysenaar (1976) equates foregrounding with models for perceptual psychology while Crystal and Davy (1969) use 'casual conversation' as a norm because, they argue, of its neutrality, frequency of usage and predictability; other 'norms' include Esau's (1974) notion of 'casual speech' and Cohen's (1968) 'language of science'. Such propositions are all subjectively perceptible and theoretically interesting but, lacking any explicit substantiation, remain as yet dubious in application. Although more detailed work has been undertaken in defining grammatical norms, this too runs into problems associated with the impracticability of determining relative frequencies of occurrence. To be certain, grammatical norms can be established in terms of particular syntactic patterns but, as Short (1973) has shown, in the area of lexico-grammatical relations the predictability of co-occurrences is less certain. There is also the problem of what to do with a sentence, or sentence set, which may be grammatically normal but is felt to be lexically deviant. Areas of deviational overlap in different levels of language organisation need to be explained.

The transformational-generative approach to stylistic description adopted by Thorne (1970), Ohmann (1964, 1966) and, less explicitly, by Levin (1971) concentrates similarly on the establishment of grammatical norms. Stylisticians within this tradition argue that there is a difference between a poem's grammar and the underlying grammatical norm which is usually seen as a simple declarative base or kernel sentence. In an attempt to draw a direct and causative line from structural features to aesthetic effects, critics working within this system tend to define style in terms of particular choices or transformational options from these base sentence norms. (The 'history' of this whole approach to style has been well charted by Messing (1971).) Of transformational-generative stylisticians Thorne, in particular, posits the need to set up a separate grammar for each poem or text studied. Although, as Levin (above) has shown, the problem of constructing a grammar which generates the poetic line is a complex one, Thorne seeks to explain a writer's unique style in terms of measurable choices or transformations. At least in Thorne's work stylistic effects are seen to be structurally related to the internal language system. But, significantly perhaps, analysts such as Thorne tend to concentrate on poetry rather than prose and to be concerned primarily with texts which are by most intuitive criteria maximally deviant, devoting only minimal attention to texts where there appears to be a close approximation of 'poetic' language to a norm. After all, if it is accepted that there is more to literary language than linguistic oddity, may it not be the case that 'style' is characterisable not so much by deviation but also by achievement of or positive appeal to a norm? Furthermore, as Widdowson (1972) points out, what *kind* of departure from the norm constitutes a deviation? What about 'deflections' (Sinclair, 1966 i.e. his notions of 'arrest' and 'release'; Halliday, 1971) which remain grammatically impeccable in structure but which contain elements not quite in their usual order? It could be argued that many stylistic effects work in this way. It thus seems probable that style involves the totality of a writer's use of language and cannot be limited to isolated deviations. Indeed, if we are unable adequately to account for the background, how is it that so many writers on the subject speak so confidently of foregrounding?

As pointed out, one of the main assumptions underlying the application of deviation theory to literary texts is that literary language is distinguished by being set over against other uses as more 'poetic', 'complex', 'self-referring' or 'less automatised'. In certain respects this over-concentration on deviation might stem from a presupposition that if literature is special then its language *must* differ. In many formalistic definitions literary language is seen as existing for its own sake and as being somehow autonomous and, therefore, differentiable as communication from ordinary, or 'non-literary' usage. This assumption of its superiority can be measured by the descriptive terms applied by Russian, Czech and American New Critical Formalists to language which does not appear in literature: that is, for example, 'ordinary', 'non-poetic', 'practical', 'scientific', 'everyday', 'pragmatic', etc. Normal communication is thus devalued and literature absolved from being subject to ordinary communication processes. As a result, in several senses language which cannot be seen to be doing a literary job is put in the background. Until the late 1970s, norm and deviation constituted the sole descriptive vocabulary for stylistics.

In the last decade or so, several writers at the interface of language and literature have postulated that it is only by recognising the particular and context-specific conventions of discourse that description of style becomes possible. Instead of being regarded as differentiable by exclusive reference to linguistic factors, it is argued that style should be defined by reference to the interpenetration of discourse conventions with linguistic form and function. It follows from this position that there are as many styles as discourse types. A change or deviation in discourse type produces a change in style and changes in style should be seen in relation to the discourse which frames it.

In the description of literary meaning it would seem helpful therefore not to attempt to describe effects in terms of absolute rules or a system of solidified norms but with reference to a text-specific dynamic of relations inclusive of norms within which the set of conventions appropriate to the text or discourse in question would assume a significant pattern. It is not that the literary artist or any other writer in other contexts does not have the choice of making his own meanings, but that the constitutive conventions funda- mentally restrict the set of elements available for combination in specific utterances. And, of course, the constraints vary according to the type of discourse involved. In fact, when seen in the context of conventions and textual norms Todorov's (1973) essay devoted to a definition of literature and style comes to offer a sharp theoretical prime:

A particular type of discourse is in turn defined by the list of rules which it must obey. The sonnet, for example, is characterized by extra limitations on its meter and rhyme. Scientific discourse in principle excludes any reference to the first or second person of the verb, as well as to any but the present tense . . . It has become equally obvious that there is no common denominator for all 'literary' productions . . . each type of discourse usually referred to as literary has nonliterary relatives which resemble it more than do other types of literary discourse.

The main inference that can be drawn from this is that the danger inherent in opposing literary and other uses of language can be extended into setting literary discourse apart from other modes of communication. As Todorov states, the opposition between literature and non-literature can be replaced by a 'typology of the various types of discourse'.

A significant attempt to develop this line of investigation of language and literature is made by Mary Louise Pratt in *Toward a Speech Act Theory of Literary Discourse* (1977). Pratt argues against the notion that literature is formally or functionally distinct from our other verbal activities, and in a thorough and devastating attack on Russian and Czech literary formalism, asks that the traditional assumption that literature exists by opposition to other uses of language be abandoned and replaced by a view of literature as a linguistic activity which cannot be understood apart from the context in which it occurs, and the people who participate in it. Her theory of language use is based exclusively on the linguistic model of speech act theory, but, within these limits, she adduces numerous examples, mainly from Labov's (1972) studies of non-literary narrative, to demonstrate that so-called literary uses of language have their counterparts in everyday usage, e.g. in advertising, the telling of jokes, teasing, playing devil's advocate, speculative assumptions, persuasion, etc. etc. In fact, the framework Pratt develops is intended to elucidate literary phenomena in terms of general communicative practices not confined to literature. Like Fish (1980) she contends that definitions of literature have to be made with due recognition of language use which is related to the language we ordinarily speak and to the conventions governing that speech. As we shall see, Pratt's book and its underlying theoretical and analytical presuppositions, have been an influence on work in this field during the 1980s. There is still a concern to occupy the middle-ground, but that ground is now a somewhat different territory.

## 2. DISCOURSE-BASED STYLISTICS

The 1980s have witnessed progressively sophisticated attempts to describe the stylistic properties of 'literary' discourses, and, in terms of linguistic descriptive frameworks, this has been facilitated by developing work in sociolinguistics, text linguistics, and discourse analysis. Thus, larger units of text are dealt with and insights generated at suprasentential levels. The general trend is towards a view of style less as text-immanent, but as existing more within a dynamic domain of social discourse processes. An introductory textbook (Traugott and Pratt 1980) clearly illustrates this direction. Recent articles on politeness phenomena (Wadman 1983), on literary text as *process* (Lindemann 1983), and on interactive and discoursal semantics in novels by Raymond Chandler (Crombie 1983) reflect such a trend.

Two of the most prominent recent examples of discourse-based stylistics are Burton's study of drama dialogue (Burton 1980), and Banfield's study of narrative discourse (Banfield 1982). Banfield's book is an ambitious attempt to undermine much current narrative theory and to resettle it on the foundations provided by a generative grammar of narrative sentences. Banfield categorises and catalogues the communicative and expressive functions of language in narrative and then argues that narrative sentences are those which are neither communicative nor expressive, and which are therefore, by virtue of excluding the subjective and discoursal acts of the narrator, those sentences which signal the 'true' unmarked propositions of the narrative. There is not space to discuss Banfield's proposals in detail here (though see McHale, 1983, for an extensive critique) but her efforts to provide the reader of her study with detailed, explicit recognition criteria for the narrative language phenomena she discerns should be noted alongside a rather more extravagant claim that a universal grammar of linguistic representation in narration can be set up.

Burton's study likewise proposes models of analysis which aim to be as finite as possible to the available data. Here Burton offers a modified version of Sinclair and Coulthard's (1975) model for the analysis of classroom discourse applying it to examples of modern drama dialogue, mostly from the plays of Harold Pinter. The textual analysis she undertakes – in an area of language use not traditionally covered in stylistics – goes some considerable way towards systematically accounting for the 'alienated' structure of the dialogues in which numerous silences, non-sequiturs, breaking of rules for turn-taking, etc. serve to underscore the kinds of power relations which obtain in the dramatised conversations.

The studies of both Banfield and Burton serve to highlight the strengths and weaknesses inherent in recent work in stylistics. The strengths are that, first, a descriptive framework is supplied which is sufficiently detailed to allow the analyst's decisions to be retrieved and checked against our own analysis. There is thus a systematic basis provided for agreement and disagreement. Very few stylisticians meet such standards of explicitness or provide such clear criteria for their descriptive decisions. Second, in a related way, the use of models enables work to proceed in a suitably 'scientific' manner. In Popperian terms at least, we can take Burton's model as a hypothesis concerning key structural features of conversational interaction, apply it to data, examine the implications for the model of confirmatory or counter-examples and revise or extend the model as necessary. And it has sufficient predictive power to accommodate this. Third, the model also allows naturally-occurring conversation to be studied alongside drama dialogue and can thus serve pedagogically to demonstrate the kinds of patterning characteristic of dialogue in literary discourse. (The same can also be said of the studies by Banfield and Pratt cited above.) Fourth, there is no compromise made in the goals of linguistic descriptive adequacy in order to accommodate a dominant literary paradigm of analysis. Such studies make contributions to *linguistic* theory and *linguistic* description and imply that there should be no reason why literary texts cannot be 'used' for purposes of extending and refining models of linguistic description. Although these stylisticians have to recognise that literary critics may want to do different things with their models, such a methodology can ensure that identity is preserved for the linguistic side to stylistics and that due caution is exercised in terms of the sometimes undue semanticisation of linguistic features for literary interpretative purposes pointed out by Pearce (1977).

But it is in this kind of conjunction that some problems of explicit stylistic models become manifest. Disadvantages, both potential and actual, must be recognised accordingly. It is, in fact, in the area of *interpretation* that problems appear to surface most markedly.

First, it is naïve to pretend that any application of linguistic knowledge, whether modelled or otherwise and however dedicatedly and rigorously formalised the model, can result in an 'objective', value-free interpretation of data. The system will inevitably be partial (in both senses of the word) and so accordingly will be the interpretation.

Second, as Taylor and Toolan (1984) point out, models such as those described here do not of themselves indicate what in the language of the interaction or the narrative is relevant to an interpretation of the text, but only how this *might* be textually realised. The assignment of meaning or stylistic function to a formal category in the language remains an interpretive act, and thus cannot transcend the individual human subject who originates the inter-

598

pretation. Thus, while the recognition of specific formal features can in most cases be attested within the terms of the system, the analyst has to be taken on trust in his or her interpretive assignment. It is a perennial problem, or even dilemma in stylistics, that no reliable criteria can be generated whereby specific functions or effects can be unambiguously attributed to specific formal features of the language system. In this respect, stylisticians have still to answer satisfactorily charges made by Fish (1980) and, more recently, Thurley (1983).

Third, any description is only as good as the model or system of analysis used. And there is always a related danger that the analyst will reduce everything to the terms supplied by that system. Consistency might thus be achieved but interpretation will again be revealed as partial. The partiality of Banfield's model has, for example, been strongly criticised by McHale (1983) in that it operates with what is for McHale a static, decontextualised and essentialist model of language (the fate to some extent of most models) and does not therefore take sufficient account of either textual or, more seriously for literary study, historical context. Even the decision to formalise on the part of linguistic stylisticians and the extent to which many do proceed with formalisation, commits them to a belief that literary language use can be formalised in linguistic terms (a position to which many literary critics feel compelled to address themselves, and in stronger and more explicit terms than most linguists).

Finally, but perhaps less obviously, any resolution to describe the data rather than interpret it constitutes an interpretation. It is an interpretation of the way literary study can or should be approached, and analyses of it conducted. Moving 'beyond interpretation' as Jonathan Culler progressively advocates (see Culler 1982, Chapter 2) is only a substitution of one kind of interpretive activity by another, albeit less traditional, less institutionally authorised kind.

As far as interpretation is concerned, stylisticians have proceeded along the kinds of lines advocated by practical or New Criticism, and have provided mostly only pedagogical defences for their implicit 'interpretation' or theory of language, arguing particularly for the basis of familiarity to literature students which such modes of operation provide (see, particularly, Carter (ed.) 1982). Some, such as Leech and Short (1981) have proceeded cautiously, modestly and eclectically: others, such as Cluysenaar (1976) and Cummins and Simmons (1983), rather more incautiously, the latter being particularly insistent in their view of the transparency of language, and in an equation between linguistic forms and literary meanings which is predicated on an assumption of the kind of one-for-one correlation or iconicity between words and meanings to which 'neutral' and 'objective' linguistic description can 'attest'.

Burton (1982), implicitly recognising some limitations in her earlier position, explicitly politicises this failure on the part of stylisticians to interpret their own interpretations, and is one of very few to attempt answers to charges of theoretical shortsightedness. For Burton, no analysis can be anything other than ideologically committed. Stylistic analysis is a political activity. Neutrality and objectivity are not possible in a language game in which how we interpret the data of a literary work is inextricably connected with our beliefs. A goal of neutral, value-free literary-stylistic analysis embodies an ideologically reactionary adherence to keeping things the way they are.

## 3. AFFECTIVE STYLISTICS

Space only allows for a brief acknowledgement here of the significance of work in affective stylistics for pointing out, both directly and indirectly, issues of interpretation in the way responses to language in literature are organised (for a fuller review see Pratt 1982). Only one representative example of recent publications in this field will be discussed.

Work in affective stylistics confronts most directly the issues of interpretation raised thus far as well as some new ones, and foregrounds in particular the question of how different readers who are native speakers of the same language can make a text in that language mean differently. It is a question which returns us to the dilemma posed by Charles Bally, one of the originators of stylistics as a discipline (for a lucid recent discussion of Bally's relation to twentieth century stylistics, see Taylor 1980):

Thought tends towards personal, affective integral expression: *la langue* can only render the most general traits of thought by depersonalizing and objectifying it.

(Bally 1925)

On the one hand, therefore, style is linguistic and should be subject to generalisable, consensual description: on the other hand, it is individual and can only be inter-subjectively verifiable by recourse to potentially reductionist models (though I have argued that much depends on how models are used and for what purposes). This lends some support even to those literary critics who argue that it will only be works whose effects are limited, uniform and essentially non-creative which can be accounted for in terms of linguistic descriptive frameworks (see Knight 1982).

Stanley Fish's *Is There A Text In This Class?* (1980) contains an overview of developments in affective stylistics (mostly in relation to Fish's own work) during the seventies. In its earliest forms, it was developed by Fish to counter the theoretical dilemmas of text-immanence, form-function relations and intersubjectively attestable interpretation. Fish sought to locate 'meaning' not as a static, language-internal codified property in the text, but rather as a dynamic, sequential 'affective' response by the reader who processes the text. Meaning was thus seen to be in the reader and created by the reader rather than in the text itself.

In the essays published in the 1980 volume Fish reviews his position in the light of the numerous questions generated by affective stylistics. For example, who is the reader? How do we know what readers do when they process a text? What kind of reading qualifies as productive of meaning? What if, as seems likely, readers process the language of a text in similar ways, but still interpret it differently? How is one interpretation superior to another, and how are these interpretations legitimated and authorised? In other words, when is an interpretation not an interpretation and what is the relevance of all this to stylisticians anyway?

The clue to Fish's changed situation is in the subtitle to his book: 'the authority of interpretative communities' – which explains to some extent why the only reader Fish ever studied was himself. Fish acknowledges the partiality of his own earlier readings by recognising that they were controlled by a set of interpretative assumptions and competences, which he authoritatively took to be the procedures shared by other 'right-minded' readers, but which in fact, are the norms of sense-making authorised by an interpretative community of professional literary critics and stylisticians. Despite the claims for linguistic analogies made by authoritative figures such as Jonathan Culler, literary 'competence' is, unlike linguistic competence, taught not caught (see also Chilton 1983) and so the academy maintains the appearance of stable and consensual interpretations and of the interpretative procedures which underlie them by teaching (i.e. limiting and controlling – often by examination) the ways in which individuals in that community can interpret. Fish argues now that those working in the area of language and literature should adopt the somewhat more modest aim of persuading readers that the interpretation they offer, and the tools they use to attest it, are reasonable. This means that their procedures cannot but be tinged with prescriptivism. It also means that it would be naïve to conceal that they might represent a specialised and narrow community of readers with a specific ideology and an accompanying set of beliefs about the world.

## 4. LANGUAGE, LITERARINESS, AND RHETORIC

Another question opened up by Fish's studies in reader-response stylistics, though one not addressed by Fish himself, is the extent to which the kind of interpretative strategies and aims outlined so far are generalisable beyond the kind of canonical 'literary' texts authorised as worthy of attention by the professional academy. There is a hidden ideology at work here, too, making prior selections and interpretations of texts for analysis. It also carries with it a presupposition that not only do we know what are 'good' examples of literary language use, but that we also know what literary language is. Both the diversity of positions and awkward silences – which range from literary language being 'deautomatised' language (Russian formalists) through something you 'feel on the pulses' (Leavisean School – very much an awkward silence!), timeless and universal (New Criticism), the product of ever-changing historically-determined readings (some Marxists) – all these demonstrate, however, that such is not the case. In fact, one of the more theoretically-informed and productive of recent directions in stylistics has been that which has pursued the question of the differentiation of literary language from non-literary language, see section 5 below. It is a question of considerable pedagogical relevance and one closely connected with the kind of view of literature as social discourse, and of the need to develop a 'linguistic criticism' advocated by Roger Fowler (see below).

Recent work in this area has included individual papers and collections of articles addressed to the following issues (see Herman in Herman and Dodd (eds) 1983, for a clear and ground-clearing theoretical introduction). Is there such a thing as literary language or can the same patternings of language be found across a range of discourse types? (Candlin and Short 1986, and for an earlier formulation, Posner 1976.) Is it preferable to refer to a cline of literariness in language use? (Carter and Nash 1983); should stylistic analysis itself be seen as a form of discourse analysis studying the stylistic and textual patterns of different modes of discourse organisation? (Leech 1983): what is the nature and function of established literary tropes such as irony and metaphor, and to what extent are they exclusively literary phenomena? (Amante 1980; Pulman 1982, as well as pioneering work by Lakoff and Johnson 1980); what is the precise linguistic basis of literary competence? (Reeves 1983). Most of these studies and the many detailed suggestions which accompany them derive in one way or another from the position articulated by Todorov (1981):

. . . there is no longer any reason to confine to literature alone the type of studies crystallised in poetics: we must know 'as such' not only literary texts but all texts, not only verbal production, but all symbolism.

A footnote to Todorov's statement reads:

Our teaching still privileges literature to the detriment of all other types of discourse. We must be aware that such a choice is purely ideological and has no justification in the phenomena themselves. Literature is inconceivable outside a typology of discourses.

The extension to this work leads in two main directions. One, which is as yet underdeveloped, is towards analysis of stylistic features of texts not considered to be within the institutionalised canon of 'literary' texts. Such analysis can be text-specific or comparative in so far as established judge-ments of literary quality are explored through an examination of, for example, Mills and Boon 'romance', Western, action adventure, and other instances of 'popular' fiction.

Another dimension to this issue would be stylistic analysis of literature in English as opposed to English literature. The term 'contact literatures' has been used to refer to creative writing by non-Western bilingual users of English in typical non-Western settings, where English is primarily used as an institutionalised second language. Such literatures exhibit stylistic, ideological and discoursal characteristics which differ markedly from the traditional 'canons' of English literature. (See Kachru 1983.)

The other direction, which is in a generally stronger tradition in the United States than in Europe, can be broadly defined as a 'rhetorical' direction. Two recent full-length studies of the stylistic-rhetorical character of texts with particular attention to compositional processes, and the inter-active role of the reader, are Nash (1980) and Dillon (1981) (though see also Mailloux 1982: appendix, as well as Leech and Short 1981, Chapter 7). Such studies attempt to account for the designs texts have on readers and for how such rhetorics can be traced back to the stylistic design features which constitute individual phrases, clause structures, intersentential relations, and textual cohesion and coherence. Implicit in such studies is the notion that elements of literariness inhere in the patterning of almost all constructed texts. The detail supplied in these studies provides students with a kind of map by which they might trace patterning in poetry alongside, for example, the rhetorical patterning of different newspaper editorials or political speeches.

The most natural partner to such stylistic investigation would be the extensive studies of the relationship of language, style and ideology founded at the University of East Anglia by Professor Roger Fowler and his colleagues. Paralleling Burton's (1982) argument, Fowler points to the impossibility of attaining neutrality in linguistic description because 'linguistic meaning is inseparable from ideology and both depend on social structures', (Fowler et al. 1979: 2). It is naïve to suppose that literature is any different from any other language use in this respect, and linguistic criticism might thus serve continually to unmask ideologies, analyse critically the causes and consequences of the ways in which 'reality' is socially contained and politically reproduced, and offer linguistic tools for exploring the possibilities for alternative representations. Fowler et al.'s work is to be seen both as an example of socially-realistic linguistics attentive to language functions, and the systems which realise them – concerned, in other words, with what people do to each other (and how) with language and also within the framework of specific investigation and interpretation of literature and literary language as institutional sites.

This is not, of course, to suggest that the study of language and ideology can proceed unencumbered by theoretical or practical analytical problems. First, on linguistic grounds, Fowler *et al.* and subsequently Kress and Hodge (1981) do not claim any full or definitive model of systematic analysis. A number of valuable suggestions are made in these books about the consequences of linguistic phenomena such as the uses of passives to invert the order of *actor* and *affected*, the uses of nominalisations to 'simplify' or mask the complexity of causal relations, and about the ways in which agents and processes can be lexicalised to distort or direct emphasis away from real-world events and towards an expression of a writer's ideological viewpoint. But the linguistic detail of their arguments is, though always insightful, not always replicable and certainly limited in both scope and levels of analysis. Second, as Taylor and Toolan (1984) point out, this is connected with the fact, recorded above, that there appear to be no rules for relating specific surface linguistic features to specific ideological functions. Until such equations can be more explicitly formulated or, more probably, modes of analysis from non-linguistic disciplines conjoined, there will still be a necessary reliance on the intuitions of the analysts who, incidentally, will have their own interpretative assumptions and cannot help but reflect their own ideological position. Third, as more empirical studies of reader processing strategies demonstrate (e.g. Kintgen 1984), the assumption that all readers process and then interpret texts in uniform ways, and thus derive their analysis from the same linguistic, cognitive or attitudinal vantage point, is as yet not tested in socio-psychological or affective stylistic research. There are once again basic difficulties in the relation of structural operations to processing constraints.

## 5. PEDAGOGICAL STYLISTICS

The last ten years have seen the extensive application of stylistic work, particularly in the area of second-language teaching and development. This emergence of a new field of pedagogical stylistics is part of the growth of the teaching of English as a second or foreign language, a growth which is fed by a variety of determinants ranging from the rise of English as a world language to the increasing numbers of non-native speakers in British universities.

Pedagogical stylistics applies the 'convenience' argument outlined above, working from the practical justification of descriptive usefulness. Pedagogical stylisticians have been criticised for methodological and theoretical naïvety, but the overall strategy has proved successful in meeting the goals set. Readers have intuitions about texts; stylistic analysis enables these to be formalised and tested, and so refined or modified. In this way, students are encouraged to produce interpretive hypotheses for themselves, and to conduct their own experiments on texts; such activity, and the groupwork and discussion through which it takes place, develops analytic and interpretive skills.

One of the most influential books in pedagogical stylistics, H.G. Widdowson's *Stylistics and the Teaching of Literature* (1975), lays the basis for such activity and makes a strong argument for the re-insertion of literature into a second and foreign language curriculum, which has been dominated by communicative and functional goals, and alongside which the teaching of literary texts was seen as either irrelevant or, at best, a luxury. Widdowson's study examines how making sense of literary texts requires a more self-conscious and reflexive approach. The lack of situational context in literary texts means that the reader has only the text to go on, and has therefore to develop heightened procedural activities to read between the lines, to infer meanings, to work out its status as a communication. Such activities develop interpretive skills, Widdowson argues, in a more concentrated and intense way than is likely with non-literature material. Literary texts can, therefore, assist in the development of crucial language-learning capacities. A further implication of Widdowson's work (1975; ch. 6) is that literary and non-literary discourse should be studied alongside in a mutually supporting way, comparing and contrasting how they 'come to mean' in their different ways. Such work parallels that in mother-tongue stylistics on literariness, and the teaching of rhetoric. A recent collection of essays which addresses these and related questions in literature and language teaching is Brumfit and Carter (eds) 1986.

## 6. CONCLUSION: THEORIES AND PRACTICES IN LANGUAGE AND LITERATURE STUDIES

In the last decade work in stylistics has been increasingly influenced by developments in modern literary theory, as well as by advances in theoretical and descriptive linguistics. It is likely that the growth in courses in literary theory within English Studies will continue to influence language and literature studies during the next decade. The range of literary theoretical work is, however, vast, and it is difficult to envisage which of the current trends will be most relevant to stylistics, but among the most predominant issues are:

1. *Post-structuralist theories of language.* These derive from a discovery by literary critics of Saussure's notion of the arbitrariness of the sign, and stress the essentially polysemic, multi-accentual nature of the relationship between signifier and signified. Such theories stress the dangers of closure in interpretation which can result from more referentially-based theories. (See Norris 1982.)

2. *Socially-based theories of interpretation.* These underline how the interpretative

community into which each individual is inserted is not natural or value-free, but constituted by socio-political and ideological determinants. Any tendency by stylisticians to claim universalist readings of text, will be seen as tendentious. All interpretative activity is partial and provisional. (See here increasingly influential work by Michel Pêcheux and Michel Foucault.)

3. *The selection of texts for analysis.* Texts for stylistic analysis have tended to be canonical texts. The replacement of these canonical texts, by a wider range of 'literary' and 'non-literary' texts is a major preoccupation at present; but the ideological roots in the constitution of a canon are likely to be re-set in a range of popular and non-Eurocentric texts. There is increasing interest in the linguistic issues raised by the role of English as an international language in relation to literatures in English.

4. *Structuralist analyses of texts, especially narrative.* The range and depth of this enterprise continues to reveal continually newer descriptive frameworks. (See Toolan 1988.)

5. *Developments in reader-response criticism and affective stylistics.* The increasingly empirical nature of investigations in this domain is likely to reveal much about the way in which different kinds of text 'come to mean' for different individuals with different degrees of 'literary' competence.

Language is the medium of literature, but literature signifies in ways which depend on more than just linguistic organisation. Consequently, there is a need for continual refinement of the descriptive models appropriate to the analysis of the language of literary and non-literary texts. This applies particularly at the level of discourse, and will continue to lead away from the necessary focus on short, 'deviant' lyric poems and extracts from novels which has been the domain of much stylistic investigation during the past sixty years, towards the signifying practices of texts in relation to a range of sociolinguistic and socio-cultural factors. (See Carter and Simpson (eds) 1989.) Such developments will, it is to be hoped, work towards fuller integration of language and literature, both in terms of pedagogical and critical-interpretative practice. The relationship will, however, only be strengthened if partners show mutual respect and continue to heed Roman Jakobson's famous call made at the Indiana Style Conference:

A linguist deaf to the poetic function of language and a literary scholar indifferent to linguistic problems and unconversant with linguistic methods, are equally flagrant anachronisms.

(Jakobson 1960: 377)

# REFERENCES

Amante, D.J. (1980) 'Ironic language: a structuralist approach', *Language and Style*, 13: 15–26.

Bally, C. (1925) *La Langue et la Vie* (3rd ed.), Geneva.

Banfield, A. (1982) *Unspeakable Sentences: Narration and Representation in the Language of Fiction*, Routledge & Kegan Paul, London.

Bateson, F.W. (1968) 'Argument II (continued): language and literature', *Essays in Criticism*, 18, ii: 176–82.

Bloch, B. (1953) 'Linguistic structure and linguistic analysis', *Georgetown University Monograph Series on Language and Linguistics*, 4: 40–4.

Brumfit, C. and Carter, R.A. (eds) (1986) *Literature and Language Teaching*, Oxford University Press, Oxford.

Burton, D. (1980) *Dialogue and Discourse: A Sociolinguistic Approach to Modern Drama Dialogue and Naturally Occurring Conversation*, Routledge & Kegan Paul, London.

Burton, D. (1982) 'Through glass darkly: through dark glasses', in R.A. Carter (ed.) *Language and Literature*, Allen & Unwin, London: 195–214.

Candlin, C. and Short, M.H. (1986) 'Teaching study skills for English literature', in Brumfit, C.J. and Carter, R.A. (eds) *Literature and Language Teaching*, Oxford University Press, Oxford: 89–109.

*Carter, R.A. (ed.) (1982) *Language and Literature: An Introductory Reader in Stylistics*, Allen & Unwin, London.

Carter, R.A. and Nash, W. (1983) 'Language and literariness', *Prose Studies*, 6: 123–41.

Carter, R.A. and Simpson, P. (eds) (1989) *Language, Discourse and Literature: An Introductory Reader in Discourse Stylistics*, Unwin Hyman, London.

Chilton, P. (1983) 'Autonomy and paradox in literary theory', *Journal of Literary Semantics*, 12: 73–91.

*Cluysenaar, A. (1976) *Introduction to Literary Stylistics*, Batsford, London.

Cohen, J. (1968) *Structure du Language Poétique*, Flammarion, Paris.

Crane, R.S. (1953) *The Language of Criticism and the Structure of Poetry*, University of Toronto Press, Toronto.

Crombie, W. (1983) 'Raymond Chandler: Burlesque, Parody, Paradox', *Language and Style*, 16: 151–68.

Crystal, D. (1972) 'Objective and subjective in stylistic analysis', in Kachru, B. and Stahlke, N. (eds) *Current Trends in Stylistics*, Linguistic Research Inc., Edmonton: 103–13.

*Crystal, D. and Davy, D. (1969) *Investigating English Style*, Longman, London.

Culler, J. (1981) *The Pursuit of Signs*, Routledge & Kegan Paul, London.

Cummins, M. and Simmons, R. (1983) *The Language of Literature*, Pergamon Press, London.

Dillon G. (1981) *Constructing Texts: Elements of a Theory of Composition and Style*, Indiana University Press, Bloomington.

Esau, H. (1974) 'Literary style and the linguistic approach', *Journal of Literary Semantics*, 3: 57–65.

Fish, S. (1980) 'What is stylistics and why are they saying such terrible things about it?' in *Is There A Text in This Class?* Harvard Univ. Press, Cambridge, Mass.

Fowler, R. (1979) 'Linguistics *and*, and *versus* Poetics', *Journal of Literary Semantics*, 8: 3–21.

Gibb, F. (1976) 'Great tradition's end is near', *Times Higher Education Supplement*, March 5: 228.

Halliday, M.A.K. (1971) 'Linguistic function and literary style', in Chatman, S. (ed.) *Literary Style: A Symposium*, Oxford University Press, London: 330–65.

Havranek, B. (1932) 'The functional differentiation of standard language', in Garvin, P. (ed.) *Prague School Reader in Esthetics, Literary Structure and Style*, Georgetown, Georgetown University Press: 3–16.

Hawkes, T. (1977) *Structuralism and Semiotics*, Methuen, London.

Herman, V. and Dodd, P. (eds) (1983) *Prose Studies*, 6:2. Special issue on Linguistics and Literariness.

Hill, A.A. (1967) 'Some further thoughts on grammaticality and poetic language', *Style* 1, 2: 81-91.

Jakobson, R. (1960) 'Linguistics and poetics' in Sebeok, T. (ed.) *Style in Language*, MIT, Cambridge, Mass.: 350–77.

Kachru, B. (1983) 'The bilinguals' creativity: discoursal and stylistic strategies in contact literatures in English', *Studies in the Linguistic Sciences*, 13: 37–55.

Kintgen, E. (1984) *The Perception of Poetry*, Indiana University Press, Bloomington, Ind.

Knight, R. (1982) 'Literature and the language of linguists' *The Use of English*, 33: 58–67.

Kress, G. and Hodge R. (1981) *Language as Ideology*, Routledge & Kegan Paul, London.

Labov, W. (1972) 'The transformation of experience in narrative syntax', *Language in the Inner City*, University of Pennsylvania Press: 354–96.

Lakoff, R. and Johnson, M. (1980) *Metaphors We Live By*, Chicago University Press, Chicago and London.

Leavis, F.R. (1948) *The Great Tradition*, Penguin, Harmondsworth.

Leavis, F.R. (1952) *The Common Pursuit*, Penguin, Harmondsworth.

*Leech, G.N. (1969) *A Linguistic Guide to English Poetry*, Longman, London.

Leech, G.N. (1983) 'Pragmatics, discourse analysis, stylistics and the "Celebrated Letter"', *Prose Studies*, 6, 2: 142–59.

Leech, G.N. and Short, M.H. (1981) *Style in Fiction*, Longman, London.

Levin, S. (1962) *Linguistic Structures in Poetry*, Mouton, The Hague.

Levin, S. (1963) 'Deviation – statistical and determinate – in poetic language', *Lingua*, 12: 276–90.

Levin, S. (1965) 'Internal and external deviation in poetry', *Word*, 21: 225–37.

Levin, S. (1971) 'The analysis of compression in poetry', *Foundations of Language*, 7: 38–55.

Lindemann, B. (1983) 'Text as process: an integrated view of a science of texts', *Journal of Literary Semantics*, 12: 5–37.

Lodge, D. (1966) *Language of Fiction: Essays in Criticism and Verbal Analysis of the English Novel*, Routledge & Kegan Paul, London.

Lodge, D. (1977) *The Modes of Modern Writing: Metaphor, Metonymy and the Typology of Modern Literature*, Edward Arnold, London.

Mailloux, S. (1982) *Interpretive Conventions: The Reader in the Study of American Fiction*, Cornell University Press, Ithaca.

McHale, B. (1983) 'Unspeakable sentences, unnatural acts: linguistics and poetics revisited', *Poetics Today*, 4: 17–45.

Messing, G.M. (1971) 'The impact of transformational grammar upon stylistics and literary analysis', *Linguistics*, 66: 56–73.

Mukarovský, J. (1932) 'Standard language and poetic language', in Garvin, P. (ed.) *Prague School Reader in Esthetics, Literary Structure and Style*, University of Georgetown Press, Georgetown: 19–35.

Nash, W. (1980) *Designs in Prose*, Longman, London.

*Nowottny, W. (1962) *The Language Poets Use*, Athlone Press, London.

Norris, C. (1982) *Deconstruction: Theory and Practice*, Methuen, London.

Ohmann, R. (1964) 'Generative grammars and the concept of literary style', *Word*, 20: 423–39.

Ohmann, R. (1966) 'Literature as sentences', *College English*, 27, 4: 261–7.

Pearce, R. (1977) 'Literary texts: the application of linguistic theory to literary discourse', *Discourse Analysis Monographs*, 3, ELR, University of Birmingham.

Posner, R. (1976) 'Poetic communication versus literary language or: the linguistic fallacy in poetics', *PTL*, 1: 1–10.

Pratt, M.L. (1977) *Toward a Speech Act Theory of Literary Discourse* Indiana University Press, Bloomington.

Pratt, M.L. (1982) 'Interpretive strategies/strategic interpretations: on Anglo-American reader response criticism', *Boundary* II, 1/2: 201–31.

Pulman, S.G. (1982) 'Are metaphors "creative"?', *Journal of Literary Semantics*, 11, 2: 78–89.

Reeves, C.E. (1983) 'Literary competence and the linguistic model', *Journal of Literary Semantics*, 12, 1: 30–72.

Ruwet, N. (1970) 'Linguistics and poetics' in Macksey, R. and Donato, E. (eds) *The Structuralist Controversy: The Language of Criticism and the Sciences of Man*, Johns Hopkins Press, Baltimore: 296–313.

Schilf, H. (ed.) (1977) *Contemporary Approaches to English Studies*, Heinemann, London.

*Sebeok, T.A. (ed.) (1960) *Style in Language*, MIT, Cambridge, Mass.

Short, M.H. (1973) '"Prelude I" to a literary linguistic-stylistics', *Style*, 6, 2: 149–57.

Sinclair, J.M. (1966) 'Taking a poem to pieces', in Fowler, R. (ed.) *Essays on Style and Language*, Routledge & Kegan Paul, London: 68–81.

Sinclair, J.M. and Coulthard, R.M. (1975) *Towards an Analysis of Discourse: The English Used by Teachers and Pupils*, Oxford University Press, London.

Stankiewicz, E. (1960) 'Linguistics and the study of poetic language', in Sebeok, T. (ed.) *Style in Language*, MIT, Cambridge Mass.: 69–81.

Taylor, T.J. (1980) *Linguistic Theory and Structural Stylistics*, Pergamon Press, Oxford.

Taylor, T.J. and Toolan, M. (1984) 'Recent trends in stylistics,' *Journal of Literary Semantics*, 13, 1: 57–79.

Thorne, J.P. (1970) 'Generative grammar and stylistic analysis', in Lyons, J. (ed.) *New Horizons in Linguistics*, Penguin, Harmondsworth: 185–97.

Thurley, G. (1983) *Counter-Modernism in Current Critical Theory*, Macmillan, London.

Todorov, T. (1973) 'The notion of literature', *New Literary History*, 5: 5–16.

Todorov, T. (1981) *Introduction to Poetics*, Harvester Press, Brighton.

Toolan, M. (1988) *Narrative: A Critical Linguistic Introduction*, Routledge, London.

Traugott, E. and Pratt, M.L. (1980) *Linguistics for Students of Literature*, Harcourt Brace Jovanovich, New York.

Trilling, L. (1972) *Sincerity and Authenticity*, Oxford University Press, London.

Wadman, K.L. (1983) 'Private ejaculations: politeness strategies in George Herbert's poems directed to God', *Language and Style*, 16, 1: 87–105.

Whitehall, H. (1956) 'From linguistics to criticism', *The Kenyon Review*, 18: 411–21.

Whitehall, H. (1957) 'From linguistics to poetry', in Frye, N. (ed.) *Sound and Poetry: English Institute Essays*, Columbia University Press, New York: 134–45.

Widdowson, H.G. (1972) 'On the deviance of literary discourse', *Style* 6, 3: 294–306.

*Widdowson, H.G. (1975) *Stylistics and the Teaching of Literature*, Longman, London.

# FURTHER READING

The items asterisked in the list above are suggested as particularly suitable for reading further into this whole topic.

# 18

# LANGUAGE AND COMPUTATION

## CHRISTOPHER S. BUTLER

## 1. COMPUTERS, NUMBERS AND LANGUAGE

Although the computer has its origins in the 'Analytical Engine' conceived by Charles Babbage in the 1830s, it was not until 1946 that the first electronic computing machine was built, in the United States, as a result of the need to carry out large numbers of mathematical calculations at high speed in connection with weapons systems in the Second World War. The term 'computer' thus describes accurately the main use of the earliest machines. Today, numerical applications continue to be important in scientific and technological areas; however, a vast amount of computer power is expended on problems which, although often involving a quantitative dimension, do not use numbers as their primary source of data. Among these applications are a large and increasingly important range of uses which are concerned with work on natural languages, and it is with these that we shall be concerned in the present chapter. As will quickly become apparent, the scope and complexity of such applications is considerable, so that this survey can do no more than provide a summary and selected examples, together with references in which readers can follow up areas of particular interest to them.

### 1.1 Computer hardware

Usually, when the term 'computer' is used, it refers to a 'digital' machine, which uses counting as its basic mechanism, rather than the 'analogue' type, which operates by measuring quantities related to whatever is being investigated. Computers are also classified according to their size and power: many homes, as well as educational establishments and businesses, now have a

**microcomputer** (often called a 'personal computer'), with relatively limited power and storage capacities; in the middle of the range are the **mini-computers** now found throughout industry and academic institutions; most powerful of all are the **mainframe** machines, often costing millions of pounds, and capable of dealing with very large-scale analyses. Many of the applications to be discussed in this chapter were originally implemented on mainframes. However, because of the rapidly increasing power and storage capabilities of even the smallest computers, it is now possible to carry out quite sophisticated work of certain kinds on the domestic microcomputer.

Whatever the size of the computer system, its basic architecture varies very little. Only a brief summary of computer 'hardware' (that is, the actual equipment, as opposed to the 'software' or programs which it uses) can be given here: for further details see, for example, Hunt and Shelley (1983). The 'central processing unit' at the heart of the system consists of an arithmetic and logic unit which carries out computations and comparisons; a main memory which stores data and instructions relevant to particular stages in the computing process, and which usually consists physically of microscopic electronic circuits embedded in a silicon chip; and a control unit which coordinates the flow of information between the memory and the arithmetic and logic unit.

Although the main memory of a computer system can be quite sizeable, it is often not sufficient to hold at once all the data needed for the solution of a problem. Furthermore, once the information in the main memory has been used, it is replaced by further information, so that some other form of storage is required if, as is usually the case, we wish to keep a permanent record of the data. For these reasons, **secondary** or **backing storage** is required in the form of magnetic tapes and discs, on which information is coded in the form of patterns of magnetised spots arranged in tracks. Microcomputers make use of small 'floppy discs' for storage purposes, but high-capacity 'hard discs' are also common. Facilities are now available for the transfer of files from one kind of computer system to another, for instance from a mainframe to a microcomputer system or vice versa.

A number of types of device are available for the input of data to computer systems. The punched card system which used to be employed with the larger computers is now virtually obsolete, though punched paper tape is still in limited use. The most common means of input to a large multi-user system is a terminal with a keyboard, on which the information can be typed. Micro-computers are equipped with such a keyboard, and indeed are themselves often used as terminals for remote access to larger computers. Such terminals are usually provided either with a visual display unit (VDU), which shows the information on the screen as it is typed, or a teletypewriter, which prints out the information on paper.

Typing natural language texts at a terminal is a very time-consuming and hence costly activity, and until recently this has acted as a bottleneck in the preparation of texts for computer analysis. This problem can now be alleviated by means of Optical Character Recognition (OCR) devices, such as the Kurzweill KDEM machine, which can 'read' a number of standard type fonts, and can be trained to read others. The machine converts the text into a representation which is stored on tape or disc. If a clearly printed copy of the text is available, the machine can process it at the rate of about 250–300 words per minute, so that, for example, a fairly long novel can be read in about 10 hours. The pattern recognition process is by no means totally accurate, but this technique does offer a partial answer to the problem of text input. For a review of the KDEM machine's capabilities see Hockey (1986).

Hard copy output from computational analyses can be obtained using various types of printer. The **lineprinters** connected to mainframe computers produce low quality output, usually on fan-fold paper. Other printers now commonly available are the high quality **laser printers** and the smaller **daisy wheel** and **dot matrix printers**. The smaller printers are often attached to terminals, so that output can be obtained quickly and easily. Computer output microfilm is sometimes a useful form of output where linguistic analysis generates a large volume of material. Microfilm and microfiche readers are standardly available, and hard copy can be obtained by means of a printing attachment.


## 1.2 What computers can do

Basically, a computer is a highly sophisticated *sorting* and *counting* device. It can compare items stored in memory, in terms of numerical value or alphabetical sequence, and it can perform arithmetical calculations. The fact that all these operations are carried out at extremely high speeds, and with a high degree of accuracy, primarily accounts for why human beings find computers so useful. The sorting function is of great importance in linguistic applications, where we often want, for example, to arrange items alphabetically or investigate their relative frequency. The counting function, of paramount importance in the physical sciences, is relevant also in linguistics, since there is very often a quantitative aspect to computational linguistic studies. Furthermore, even where the results of a linguistic investigation are not themselves derived computationally, they may well require statistical analysis. As we shall see in section 2, programs are available for the performance of a large range of statistical tests; indeed, some of these tests require such complex calculations that a computer is an essential tool in the analysis.

Programs using the sorting and counting functions in a rather straightforward manner account for a large body of work in computational text analysis. Increasingly, however, computers are being used in linguistics for other functions which trade on the basic sorting and counting capacities of the machine. The most exciting and far-reaching function of the computer in language studies is as a device for *simulating* various linguistically-related activities of human beings. Computers are being used for translation, for the automatic synthesis and recognition of speech, for the generation and analysis of discourse, for the retrieval of information from large data bases, and for aiding writers by means of word processing systems, often combined with spelling checkers, style assessment programs and the like.

## 1.3 Computer software

In order to communicate with the computer, the user must present it with a set of instructions, or **program** (note that the American spelling is standard). The only kinds of instruction that the machine 'understands' are those written in a system-dependent **machine code**. Such programs, however, are tedious and difficult for the average user to write. A slightly more condensed form of program, written in a so-called **assembly language**, may be useful for some applications. Most programs are written in a **high-level language** which, like a natural language, has a vocabulary of words linked in syntactic constructions, and enables the programmer to present instructions in a more compact form than machine code or assembly language. Instructions in such a language are translated into machine code by a program inside the computer system, known either as a 'compiler' or an 'interpreter', depending on the mechanism involved.

Many high level languages are available, differing in their strengths and weaknesses for particular kinds of application, and also in their learnability. BASIC, originally intended for teaching programming, is universally available on microcomputers and also on most mainframes, and is, as we shall see, used in certain areas such as computer-assisted language learning (see section 4.7). PASCAL was also developed for teaching the principles of programming, but is now widely used for work in scientific disciplines, and is also in use for humanities applications. FORTRAN is often used in the numerical applications common in mathematics and the physical sciences. Although each of the languages mentioned above is capable of handling strings of characters as well as numbers, the facilities for such manipulations are often rather unwieldy and tedious to use. However, SNOBOL, and the later and more versatile version SPITBOL, have very powerful and easy-to-use mechanisms for constructing, and searching for, patterns of characters, such as are involved in the isolation of particular types of words, sentences, etc. Thorough introductions to the language may be found in Butler (1985a) and Hockey (1985). Recently, a language known as ICON, which is claimed to remedy some of the deficiencies of SNOBOL while retaining the advantages, has been developed (see Griswold and Griswold 1983).

For work in those areas of computational linguistics which are closely related to artificial intelligence (AI) (see section 4.5), a rather different class of programming languages may be more appropriate. LISP (a name derived from the LISt Processing facilities which constitute its main feature), and PROLOG (which enables the programmer to formulate his needs in a manner closely related to logical representations) are the most widely used AI languages. For a gentle introduction to LISP see Hasemer (1984) and for PROLOG Clocksin (1984).

For many linguists, interest in computational analysis does not extend beyond the requirement for a tool which will enable them to perform certain specific and limited forms of analysis. Such people are often, quite under-standably, reluctant to invest the considerable amount of time and energy needed to learn a programming language. To cater for the needs of such users, **package programs** have been developed for a number of commonly required functions such as performing statistical tests (see section 2), or producing information on the words present in a text (see section 3.2.1). Such packages are written by professional programmers in a high level language, but the user needs to know only a relatively simple, fairly English-like set of commands in order to instruct the computer to perform the analysis required. Since such packages will carry out only the analyses they were designed for, they clearly have important limitations, and some users may well find themselves learning a high level language in order to extend the range of problems they can solve computationally.

All the high-level languages mentioned in this section, and a number of package programs for text analysis, are available in versions for personal computers as well as for mainframes.

## 2. THE COMPUTER IN STATISTICAL WORK

Space permits only a very brief summary of this area here: for an account of simple but fundamental statistical techniques of relevance to language studies see Butler (1985b), and for a more comprehensive but rather more difficult treatment Woods *et al.* (1986).

Statistics is important to students of language for two reasons. First, faced with a mass of raw numerical data, we are often unable to understand what it means or to perceive trends in it. It is here that the techniques of **descriptive statistics** can help, by providing methods for summarising the properties of the data. For instance, we can calculate one or more measures of the most typical value of a particular variable: the most familiar is the arithmetical average or mean, but for certain types of data the median (the value above which and below which equal numbers of observations lie) or the mode (the most frequently-found value) may be more appropriate. We may also want to know about the extent of variability within the data: here, the simplest measure is the range between highest and lowest values for a particular variable, but since this is subject to distortion by single maverick values, a more reliable measure taking account of all the data is often obtained, in the form of the standard deviation, or its square, the variance.

A second reason for the importance of statistics in language studies is that such studies are often comparative: rather than wanting to describe only the properties of a single set of data, we are often interested in assessing differences between data sets. In such cases, statistical tests are often required in order to ascertain whether the observed differences between samples are big enough to allow us to conclude that the parent populations also differed significantly. We can never actually prove that our samples came from different populations: because of sampling variability there is always a margin of error, and it is up to the researcher to decide what constitutes an acceptable value of this error. Tests for significant differences are the domain of **inferential statistics**, and are of two types, **parametric** and **non-parametric**. The validity of *parametric* tests depends on the satisfaction of certain conditions relating to the data; *non-parametric* tests, on the other hand, impose fewer restrictions on the type of data which can be handled, and are particularly appropriate for many situations in language work. A particularly useful non-parametric test for linguists is the chi-square test, which assesses the independence (or, looking at it the other way round, association) of variables. Both parametric and non-parametric tests are available for assessing the significance of the correlation between variables, that is, the extent to which high scores on one variable tend to be associated with high (or low) scores on a second variable.

Of increasing importance in linguistic studies are **multivariate** methods, which allow the simultaneous investigation of a number of variables, so exploring the structure of the data without initially singling any variable out for special treatment. Such methods normally require, as input, a matrix showing how similar (or, more usually, how dissimilar) each experimental subject or observation is from all the others. A particularly useful set of techniques is cluster analysis, which isolates clusters of observations or experimental subjects in which the members are more like each other than they are like members of other clusters. In some types of cluster analysis, a tree-like representation shows how tighter clusters combine to form looser aggregates, until at the topmost level all the observations belong to a single cluster. A further useful technique is **multidimensional scaling**, which aims to produce a pictorial representation of the relationships implicit in the (dis)similarity matrix. In **factor analysis**, a large number of variables can be reduced to just a few composite variables or 'factors'. Discussion of various types of multivariate analysis, together with accounts of linguistic studies involving the use of such techniques, can be found in Woods *et al.* (1986). The rather complex mathematics required by multivariate analysis means that such work is heavily dependent on the computer.

A number of package programs are available for statistical analysis. Of these, almost certainly the most widely used is SPSS (Statistical Package for the Social Sciences), an extremely comprehensive suite of programs available, in various forms, for both mainframe and personal computers. An introductory guide to the system can be found in Norušis (1982), and a description of a version for the IBM PC in Frude (1987). The package will produce graphical representations of frequency distributions (the number of cases with particular values of certain variables), and a wide range of descriptive statistics. It will cross-tabulate data according to the values of particular variables, and perform chi-square tests of independence or association. A range of other non-parametric and parametric tests can also be requested, and multivariate analyses can be performed. Another statistical package which is useful for linguists is MINITAB (Ryan, Joiner and Ryan 1976). Although not as comprehensive as SPSS, MINITAB is rather easier to use, and the most recent version offers a range of basic statistical facilities which is likely to meet the requirements of much linguistic research. Examples of SPSS and MINITAB analyses of linguistic data can be found in Butler (1985b: 155–65) and MINITAB examples also in Woods *et al.* (1986: 309–13). Specific packages for multivariate analysis, such as MDS(X) and CLUSTAN, are also available.

## 3. THE COMPUTATIONAL ANALYSIS OF NATURAL LANGUAGE: METHODS AND PROBLEMS

### 3.1 The textual material

Text for analysis by the computer may be of various kinds, according to the application concerned. For an artificial intelligence researcher building a system which will allow users to interrogate a database, the text for analysis will consist only of questions typed in by the user. Stylisticians and lexicographers, however, may wish to analyse large bodies of literary or non-literary text, and those involved in machine translation are often concerned with the processing of scientific, legal or other technical material, again often in large quantities. For these and other applications the problem of getting large amounts of text into a form suitable for computational analysis is a very real one.

As was pointed out in section 1.1, most textual materials have been prepared for automatic analysis by typing them in at a keyboard linked to a VDU. It is advisable to include as much information as is practically possible when encoding texts: arbitrary symbols can be used to indicate, for example, various functions of capitalisation, changes of typeface and layout, and foreign words. To facilitate retrieval of locational information during later processing, references to important units (pages, chapters, acts and scenes of a play, and so on) should be included. Many word processing programs now allow the direct entry of characters with accents and other diacritics, in languages such as French or Italian. Languages written in non-Roman scripts may need to be transliterated before coding. Increasingly, use is being made of OCR machines such as the KDEM (see section 1.1), which will incorporate markers for font changes, though text references must be edited in during or after the input phase.

Archives of textual materials are kept at various centres, and many of the texts can be made available to researchers at minimal cost. A number of important corpora of English texts have been assembled: the Brown Corpus (Kucera and Francis 1967) consists of approximately 1 million words of written American English made up of 500 text samples from a wide range of material published in 1961; the Lancaster-Oslo-Bergen (LOB) Corpus (see e.g. Johansson 1980) was designed as a British English near-equivalent of the Brown Corpus, again consisting of 500 2000-word texts written in 1961; the London-Lund Corpus (LLC) is based on the Survey of English Usage conducted under the direction of Quirk (see Quirk and Svartvik 1978). These corpora are available, in various forms, from the International Computer Archive of Modern English (ICAME) in Bergen. Parts of the London-Lund corpus are available in book form (Svartvik and Quirk 1980). A very large corpus of English is being built up at the University of Birmingham for use in lexicography (see section 4.3) and other areas. The main corpus consists of 7.3 million words (6 million from a wide range of written varieties, plus 1.3 million words of non-spontaneous educated spoken English), and a supplementary corpus is also available, taking the total to some 20 million words. A 1 million word corpus of materials for the teaching of English as a Foreign Language is also available. For a description of the philosophy behind the collection of the Birmingham Corpus see Renouf (1984, 1987). Descriptive work on these corpora will be outlined in section 4.1. Collections of texts are also available at the Oxford University Computing Service and at a number of other centres.

3.2 Computational analysis in relation to linguistic levels

Problems of linguistic analysis must ultimately be solved in terms of the machine's ability to recognise a 'character set' which will include not only the upper and lower case letters of the Roman alphabet, punctuation marks and numbers, but also a variety of other symbols such as asterisks, percentage signs, etc. (see Chapter 20 below). It is therefore obvious that the difficulty of various kinds of analysis will depend on the ease with which the problems involved can be translated into terms of character sequences.

### 3.2.1 Graphological analysis

Graphological analyses, such as the production of punctuation counts, word-length and sentence length profiles, and lists of word forms (i.e. items distinguished by their spelling) are obviously the easiest to obtain. Word forms may be presented as a simple *list* with frequencies, arranged in ascending or descending frequency order, or by alphabetical order starting from the beginning or end of the word. Alternatively, an *index*, giving locational information as well as frequency for each chosen word, can be obtained. More information still is given by a *concordance*, which gives not only the location of each occurrence of a word in the text, but also a certain amount of context for each citation. Packages are available for the production of such output, the most versatile being the Oxford Concordance Program (OCP) (see Hockey and Marriott 1980), which runs on a wide range of mainframe computers and on the IBM PC and compatible machines. The CLOC program (see Reed 1977), developed at the University of Birmingham, also allows the user to obtain word lists, indexes and concordances, but is most useful for the production of lists of *collocations*, or co-occurrences of word forms. For a survey of both OCP and CLOC, with sample output, see Butler (1985a). Neither package produces word-length or sentence-length profiles, but these are easily programmed using a language such as SNOBOL.

### 3.2.2 Lexical analysis

So far, we have considered only the isolation of word forms, distinguished by consisting of unique sequences of characters. Often, however, the linguist is interested in the occurrence and frequency of lexemes, or 'dictionary words', (e.g. RUN) rather than of the different forms which such lexemes can take (e.g. *run, runs, ran, running*). Computational linguists refer to lexemes as **lemmata**, and the process of combining morphologically-related word forms into a lemma is known as **lemmatisation**. Lemmatisation is one of the major problems of computational text analysis, since it requires detailed specification of morphological and spelling rules; nevertheless, substantial progress has been made for a number of languages (see also section 3.2.4). A related problem is that of homography, the existence of words which belong to different lemmata but are spelt in the same way. These problems will be discussed further in relation to lexicography in section 4.3.

### 3.2.3 Phonological analysis

The degree of success achievable in the automatic segmental phonological analysis of texts depends on the ability of linguists to formulate explicitly the correspondences between functional sound units (phonemes) and letter units (graphemes) – on which see Chapter 20 below. Some languages, such as Spanish and Czech, have rather simple phoneme-grapheme relationships; others, including English, present more difficulties because of the many-to-many relationships between sounds and letters. Some success is being achieved, as the feasibility of systems for the conversion of written text to synthetic speech is investigated (see section 4.5.5). For a brief non-technical account see Knowles (1986).

Work on the automatic assignment of intonation contours while processing written-to-be-spoken text is currently in progress in Lund and in Lancaster. The TESS (Text Segmentation for Speech) project in Lund (Altenberg 1986, 1987; Stenström 1986) aims to describe the rules which govern the prosodic segmentation of continuous English speech. The analysis is based on the London-Lund Corpus of Spoken English (see section 4.1), in which tone units are marked. The automatic intonation assignment project in Lancaster (Knowles and Taylor 1986) has similar aims, but is based on a collection of BBC sound broadcasts. Work on the automatic assignment of stress patterns will be discussed in relation to stylistic analysis in section 4.2.1.

### 3.2.4 Syntactic analysis

A brief review of syntactic parsing can be found in de Roeck (1983), and more detailed accounts in Winograd (1983), Harris (1985) and Grishman (1986); particular issues are addressed in more detail in various contributions to King (1983a), Sparck Jones and Wilks (1983) and Dowty et al. (1985). The short account of natural language processing by Gazdar and Mellish (1987) is also useful.

The first stage in parsing a sentence is a combination of morphological analysis (to distinguish the roots of the word forms from any affixes which may be present) and the looking up of the roots in a machine dictionary. An attempt is then made to assign one or more syntactic structures to the sentence on the basis of a grammar. The earliest parsers, developed in the late 1950s and early 1960s, were based on context-free phrase structure grammars, consisting of sets of rules in which 'non-terminal' symbols representing particular categories are rewritten in terms of other categories, and eventually in terms of 'terminal' symbols for actual linguistic items, with no restriction on the syntactic environment in which the reformulation can occur. For instance, a simple (indeed, over-simplified) context-free grammar for a fragment of English might include the following rewrite rules:

S    → NP   VP
NP   → Art   N
VP   → V   NP
VP   → V
V    → *broke*
N    → *boy*
N    → *window*
Art  → *the*

where S is a 'start symbol' representing a sentence, NP a noun phrase, VP a verb phrase, N a noun, V a verb, Art an article. Such a grammar could be used to assign structures to sentences such as *The boy broke the window* or *The window broke*, these structures commonly being represented in tree form as illustrated below.

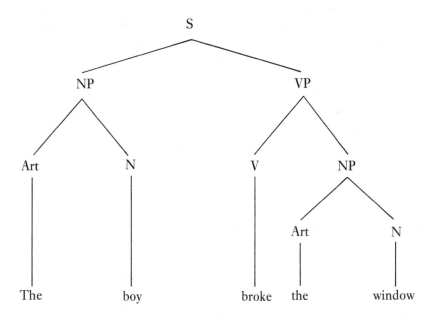

We may use this tree to illustrate the distinction between 'top-down' or 'hypothesis-driven' parsers and 'bottom-up' or 'data-driven' parsers. A top-down parser starts with the hypothesis that we have an S, then moves through the set of rules, using them to expand one constituent at a time until a terminal symbol is reached, then checking whether the data string matches this symbol. In the case of the above sentence, the NP symbol would be expanded as Art N, and Art as *the*, which does match the first word of the string, so allowing the part of the tree corresponding to this word to be constructed. If N is expanded as *boy* this also matches, so that the parser can now go onto the VP constituent, and so on. A bottom-up parser, on the other hand, starts with the terminal symbols and attempts to combine them. It may start from the left (finding that the Art *the* and the N *boy* combine to give a NP, and so on), or from the right. Some parsers use a combination of approaches, in which the bottom-up method is modified by reference to pre-computed sets of tables showing combinations of symbols which can never lead to useful higher constituents, and which can therefore be blocked at an early stage.

A further important distinction is that between non-deterministic and deterministic parsing. Consider the sentence *Steel bars reinforce the structure*. Since *bars* can be either a noun or a verb, the computer must make a decision at this point. A non-deterministic parser accepts that multiple analyses may be needed in order to resolve such problems, and may tackle the situation in either of two basic ways. In a 'depth-first' search, one path is pursued first, and if this meets with failure, backtracking occurs to the point where a wrong choice was made, in order to pursue a second path. Such backtracking involves the undoing of any structures which have been built up while the incorrect path was being followed, and this means that correct partial structures may be lost and built up again later. To prevent this, well-formed partial structures may be stored in a 'chart' for use when required. An alternative to depth-first parsing is the 'breadth-first' method, in which all possible paths are pursued in parallel, so obviating the need for backtracking. If, however, the number of paths is considerable, this method may lead to a 'combinatorial explosion' which makes it uneconomic; furthermore, many of the constituents built will prove useless. Deterministic parsers (see Sampson 1983a) attempt to ensure that only the correct analysis for a given string is undertaken. This is achieved by allowing the parser to look ahead by storing information on a small number of constituents beyond the one currently being analysed. (See Chapter 10, section 2.1, above.)

Let us now return to the use of particular kinds of grammar in parsing. Difficulties with context-free parsers led the computational linguists of the mid and late 1960s to turn to Chomsky's transformational generative (TG) grammar (see Chomsky 1965), which had a context-free phrase structure 'base' component, plus a set of rules for transforming base ('deep structure') trees into other trees, and ultimately into trees representing the 'surface' structures of sentences. The basic task of a transformational parser is to undo the transformations which have operated in the generation of a sentence. This is by no means a trivial job: since transformational rules interact, it cannot be assumed that the rules for generation can simply be reversed for analysis; furthermore, deletion rules in the forward direction cause problems, since in the reverse direction there is no indication of what should be inserted (see King 1983b for further discussion).

Faced with the problems of transformational parsing, the computational linguists of the 1970s began to examine the possibility of returning to context-free grammars, but augmenting them to overcome some of their short-comings. The most influential of these types of grammar was the Augmented Transition Network (ATN) framework developed by Woods (1970). An ATN consists of a set of 'nodes' representing the states in which the system can be, linked by 'arcs' representing transitions between the states, and leading ultimately to a 'final state'. A brief, clear and non-technical account of ATNs can be found in Ritchie and Thompson (1984), from which source the following example is taken.

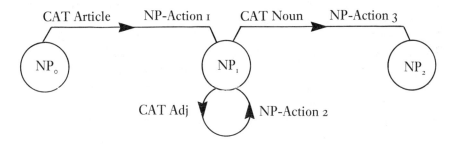

The label on each arc consists of a test and an action to be taken if that test is passed: for instance, the arc leading from NPo specifies that if the next word to be analysed is a member of the Article category, NP-Action 1 is to be performed, and a move to state $NP_1$ is to be made. The tests and actions can be much more complicated than these examples suggest: for instance, a match for a phrasal category (e.g. NP) can be specified, in which case the current state of the network is 'pushed' on to a data structure known as a 'stack', and a subnetwork for that particular type of phrase is activated. When the subnetwork reaches its final state, a return is made to the main network. Values relevant to the analysis (for instance, yes/no values reflecting the presence or absence of particular features, or partial structures) may be stored in a set of 'registers' associated with the network, and the actions specified on arcs may relate to the changing of these values. ATNs have formed the basis of many of the syntactic parsers developed in recent years, and may also be used in semantic analysis (see section 3.2.5).

Recently, context-free grammars have attracted attention again within linguistics, largely due to the work of Gazdar and his colleagues on a model known as Generalised Phrase Structure Grammar (GPSG) (see Gazdar *et al.* 1985). Unlike Chomsky, Gazdar believes that context-free grammars are adequate as models of human language. This claim, and its relevance to parsing, is discussed by Sampson (1983b). A parser which will analyse text using a user-supplied GPSG and a dictionary has been described by Phillips and Thompson (1985).

### 3.2.5 Semantic analysis

For certain kinds of application (e.g. for some studies in stylistics) a semantic analysis of a text may consist simply of isolating words from particular semantic fields. This can be done by manual scanning of a word list for appropriate items, perhaps followed by the production of a concordance. In other work, use has been made of computerised dictionaries and thesauri for sorting word lists into semantically based groupings. More will be said about these analyses in section 4.2. For many applications, however, a highly selective semantic analysis is insufficient. This is particularly true of work in artificial intelligence, where an attempt is made to produce computer programs which will 'understand' natural language, and which therefore need to perform detailed and comprehensive semantic analysis. Three approaches to the relationship between syntactic and semantic analysis can be recognised.

One approach is to perform syntactic analysis first, followed by a second pass which converts the syntactic tree to a semantic representation. The main advantage of this approach is that the program can be written as separate modules for the two kinds of analysis, with no need for a complex control structure to integrate them. On the negative side, however, this is implausible as a model of human processing. Furthermore, it denies the possibility of using semantic information to guide syntactic analysis where the latter could give rise to more than one interpretation.

A second approach is to minimise syntactic parsing and to emphasise semantic analysis. This approach can be seen in some of the parsers of the late 1960s and 1970s, which make no distinction between the two types of analysis. One form of knowledge representation which proved useful in these 'homogeneous' systems is the conceptual dependency framework of Schank (1972). This formalism uses a set of putatively universal semantic primitives, including a set of actions, such as transfer of physical location, transfer of a more abstract kind, movement of a body part by its owner, and so on, out of which representations of more complex actions can be constructed. Actions, objects and their modifiers can also be related by a set of dependencies. Conceptualisations of events can be modified by information relating to tense, mood, negativity, etc. A further type of homogeneous analyser is based on the 'preference semantics' of Wilks (1975), in which semantic restrictions between items are treated not as absolute, but in terms of preference. For instance, although the verb *eat* preferentially takes an animate subject, inanimate ones are not ruled out (e.g. as in *My printer just eats paper*). Wilks's system, like Schank's, uses a set of semantic primitives. These are grouped into trees, giving a formula for each word sense. Sentences for analysis are fragmented into phrases, which are then matched against a set of templates made up of the semantic primitives. When a match is obtained, the template is filled, and links are then sought between these filled templates in order to construct a semantic representation for the whole sentence. Burton (1976), also Woods *et al.* (1976), proposed the use of Augmented Transition Networks for semantic analysis. In such systems, the arcs and nodes of an ATN can be labelled with semantic as well as syntactic categories, and thus represent a kind of 'semantic grammar' in which the two types of patterning are mixed.

A third approach is to interleave semantic analysis with syntactic parsing. The aim of such systems is to prevent the fruitless building of structures which would prove semantically unacceptable, by allowing some form of semantic feedback to the parsing process.

### 3.2.6 From sentence analysis to text analysis

So far, we have dealt only with the analysis of sentences. Clearly, however, the meaning of a text is more than the sum of the meanings of its individual sentences. To understand a text, we must be able to make links between sentence meanings, often over a considerable distance. This involves the resolution of anaphora (for instance, the determination of the correct referent for a pronoun), a problem which can occur even in the analysis of individual sentences, and which is discussed from a computational perspective by Grishman (1988: 124–34). It also involves a good deal of inferencing, during which human beings call upon their knowledge of the world. One of the most difficult problems in the computational processing of natural language texts is how to represent this knowledge in such a way that it will be useful for analysis. We have already met two kinds of knowledge representation formalism: conceptual dependency and semantic ATNs. In recent years, other types of representation have become increasingly important; some of these are discussed below.

A knowledge representation structure known as the frame, introduced by Minsky (1975), makes use of the fact that human beings normally assimilate information in terms of a prototype with which they are familiar. For instance, we have internalised representations of what for us is a prototypical car, house, chair, room, and so forth. We also have prototypes for situations, such as buying a newspaper. Even in cases where a particular object or situation does not exactly fit our prototype (e.g. perhaps a car with three wheels instead of four), we are still able to conceptualise it in terms of deviations from the norm. Each frame has a set of slots which specify properties, constituents, participants, etc., whose values may be numbers, character strings or other frames. The slots may be associated with constraints on what type of value may occur there, and there may be a default value which is assigned when no value is provided by the input data. This means that a frame can provide information which is not actually present in the text to be analysed, just as a human processor can assume, for example, that a particular car will have a steering wheel, even though (s)he may not be able to see it from where (s)he is standing. Analysis of a text using frames requires that a semantic analysis be performed in order to extract actions, participants, and the like, which can then be matched against the stored frame properties. If a frame appears to be only partially applicable, those parts which do match can be saved, and stored links between frames may suggest new directions to be explored.

Scripts, developed by Schank and his colleagues at Yale (see Schank and Abelson 1975, 1977) are in some ways similar to frames, but are intended to model stereotyped sequences of events in narratives. For instance, when we go to a restaurant, there is a typical sequence of events, involving entering the restaurant, being seated, ordering, getting the food, eating it, paying the bill and leaving. As with frames, the presence of particular types of people and objects, and the occurrence of certain events, can be predicted even if not explicitly mentioned in the text. Like frames, scripts consist of a set of slots for which values are sought, default values being available for at least some slots. The components of a script are of several kinds: a set of entry conditions which must be satisfied if the script is to be activated; a result which will normally ensue; a set of props representing objects typically involved; a set of roles for the participants in the sequence of events. The script describes the sequence of events in terms of 'scenes' which, in Schank's scheme, are specified in conceptual dependency formalism. The scenes are organised into 'tracks', representing subtypes of the general type of script (e.g. going to a coffee bar as opposed to an expensive restaurant). There may be a number of alternative paths through such a track.

Scripts are useful only in situations where the sequence of events is predictable from a stereotype. For the analysis of novel situations, Schank and Abelson (1977) proposed the use of 'plans' involving means-ends chains. A plan consists of an overall goal, alternative sequences of actions for achieving it, and preconditions for applying the particular types of sequence. More recently, Schank has proposed that scripts should be broken down into smaller units (memory organisation packets, or MOPs) in such a way that similarities between different scripts can be recognised. Other developments include the work of Lehnert (1982) on plot units, and of Sager (1978) on a columnar 'information format' formalism for representing the properties of texts in particular fields (such as subfields of medicine or biochemistry) where the range of semantic relations is often rather restricted.

So far, we have concentrated on the analysis of language produced by a single communicator. Obviously, however, it is important for natural language understanding systems to be able to deal with dialogue, since many applications involve the asking of questions and the giving of replies. As Grishman (1986: 154) points out, the easiest such systems to implement are those in which either the computer or the user has unilateral control over the flow of the discourse. For instance, the computer may ask the user to supply information which is then added to a data base; or the user may interrogate a data base held in the computer system. In such situations, the computer can be programmed to know what to expect. The more serious problems arise when the machine has to be able to adapt to a variety of linguistic tactics on the part of the user, such as answering one question with another. Some 'mixed-initiative' systems of this kind have been developed, and one will be mentioned in section 4.5.3. One difficult aspect of dialogue analysis is the indirect expression of communicative intent, and it is likely that work by linguists and philosophers on indirect speech acts (see Grice 1975, Searle 1975, and Chapter 6 above) will become increasingly important in computational systems (Allen and Perrault 1980).


## 4. USES OF COMPUTATIONAL LINGUISTICS

### 4.1 Corpus linguistics

There is a considerable and fast growing body of work in which text corpora are being used in order to find out more about language itself. For a long time linguistics has been under the influence of a school of thought which arose in connection with the 'Chomskyan revolution' and which regards corpora as inappropriate sources of data, because of their finiteness and degeneracy. However, as Aarts and van den Heuvel (1985) have persuasively argued, the standard arguments against corpus linguistics rest on a misunderstanding of the nature and current use of corpus studies. Present-day corpus linguists proceed in the same manner as other linguists in that they use intuition, as well as the knowledge about the language which has been accumulated in prior studies, in order to formulate hypotheses about language; but they go beyond what many others attempt, in testing the validity of their hypotheses on a body of attested linguistic data.

The production of descriptions of English has been furthered recently by the automatic tagging of the large corpora mentioned in section 3.1 with syntactic labels for each word. The Brown corpus, tagged using a system known as TAGGIT, was later used as a basis for the tagging of the LOB corpus. The LOB tagging programs (see Garside and Leech 1982; Leech, Garside and Atwell 1983; Garside 1987) use a combination of wordlists, suffix removal and special routines for numbers, hyphenated words and idioms, in order to assign a set of possible grammatical tags to each word. Selection of the 'correct' tag from this set is made by means of a 'constituent likelihood grammar' (Atwell 1983, 1987), based on information, derived from the Brown Corpus, on the transitional probabilities of all possible pairs of successive tags. A success rate of 96.5–97 per cent has been claimed. Possible future developments include the use of tag probabilities calculated for particular types of text, and the manual tagging of the corpus with sense numbers from the *Longman Dictionary of Contemporary English* is already under way.

The suite of programs used for the tagging of the London-Lund Corpus of Spoken English (Svartvik and Eeg-Olofsson 1982, Eeg-Olofsson and Svartvik 1984, Eeg-Olofsson 1987, Altenberg 1987, Svartvik 1987) first splits the material up into tone units, then analyses these at word, phrase, clause and discourse levels. Word class tags are assigned by means of an interactive program using lists of high-frequency words and of suffixes, together with probabilities of tag sequences. A set of ordered, cyclical rules assign phrase tags, and these are then given clause function labels (Subject, Complement, etc.). Discourse markers, after marking at word level, are treated separately.

These tagged corpora have been used for a wide variety of analyses, including work on relative clauses, verb-particle combinations, ellipsis, genitives in -*s*, modals, connectives in object noun clauses, negation, causal relations and contrast, topicalisation, discourse markers, etc. Accounts of these and other studies can be found in Johansson 1982, Aarts and Meijs 1984, 1986, Meijs 1987 and various volumes of *ICAME News*, produced by the International Computer Archive of Modern English in Bergen.

## 4.2 Stylistics

Enkvist (1964) has highlighted the essentially quantitative nature of style, regarding it as a function of the ratios between the frequencies of linguistic phenomena in a particular text or text type and their frequencies in some contextually related norm. Critics have at times been rather sceptical of statistical studies of literary style, on the grounds that simply counting linguistic items can never capture the essence of literature in all its creativity. Certainly the ability of the computer to process vast amounts of data and produce simple or sophisticated statistical analyses can be a danger if such analyses are viewed as an end in themselves. If, however, we insist that quantitative studies should be closely linked with literary interpretation, then automated analysis can be a most useful tool in obtaining evidence to reject or support the stylistician's subjective impressions, and may even reveal patterns which were not previously recognised and which may have some literary validity, permitting an enhanced rereading of the text. Since the style of a text can be influenced by many factors, the choice of appropriate text samples for study is crucial, especially in comparative studies. For an admirably sane treatment of the issue of quantitation in the study of style see Leech and Short (1981), and for a discussion of difficulties in achieving a synthesis of literary criticism and computing see Potter (1988).

Computational stylistics can conveniently be discussed under two headings: firstly 'pure' studies, in which the object is simply to investigate the stylistic traits of a text, an author or a genre; and secondly 'applied' studies, in which similar techniques are used with the aim of resolving problems of authorship, chronology or textual integrity. The literature on this field is very extensive, and only the principles, together with a few selected examples, are discussed below.

### 4.2.1 'Pure' computational stylistics

Many studies in 'pure' computational stylistics have employed word lists, indexes or concordances, with or without lemmatisation. Typical examples are: Adamson's (1977, 1979) study of the relationship of colour terms to characterisation and psychological factors in Camus's *L'Etranger*; Burrows's (1986) extremely interesting and persuasive analysis of modal verb forms in relation to characterisation, the distinction between narrative and dialogue, and different types of narrative, in the novels of Jane Austen; and also Burrows's later (1987) wide-ranging computational and statistical study of Austen's style. Word lists have also been used to investigate the type-token ratio (the ratio of the number of different words to the total number of running words), which can be valuable as an indicator of the vocabulary richness of texts (that is, the extent to which an author uses new words rather than repeating ones which have already been used). Word and sentence length profiles have also been found useful in stylistics, and punctuation analysis can also provide valuable information, provided that the possible effects of editorial changes are borne in mind. For an example of the use of a number of these techniques see Butler (1979) on the evolution of Sylvia Plath's poetic style.

Computational analysis of style at the phonological level is well illustrated by Logan's work on English poetry. Logan (1982) built up a phonemic dictionary by entering transcriptions manually for one text, then using the results to process a further text, adding any additional codings which were necessary, and so on. The transcriptions so produced acted as a basis for automatic scansion. Logan (1976, 1985) has also studied the 'sound texture' of poetry by classifying each phoneme with a set of binary distinctive features. These detailed transcriptions were then analysed to give frequency lists of sounds, lists of lines with repeated sounds, percentages of the various distinctive features in each line of poetry, and so on. Sounds were also placed on a number of scales of 'sound colour', such as hardness vs. softness, sonority vs. thinness, openness vs. closeness, backness vs. frontness, (on which see Chapters 1 and 2 above), and lines of poetry, as well as whole poems, were then assigned overall values for each scale, which were correlated with literary interpretations. Alliteration and stress assignment programs have been developed for Old English by Hidley (1986).

Much computational stylistic analysis involving syntactic patterns has employed manual coding of syntactic categories, the computer being used merely for the production of statistical information. A recent example is Birch's (1985) study of the works of Thomas More, in which it was shown that scores on a battery of syntactic variables correlated with classifications based on contextual and bibliographical criteria. Other studies have used the EYEBALL syntactic analysis package written by Ross and Rasche (see Ross and Rasche 1972), which produces information on word classes and functions, attempts to parse sentences, and gives tables showing the number of syllables per word, words per sentence, type/token ratio, etc. Jaynes (1980) used EYEBALL to produce word class data on samples from the early, middle and late output of Yeats, and to show that, contrary to much critical comment, the evolution in Yeats's style seems to be more lexical than syntactic. Increasingly, computational stylistics is making use of recent developments in interactive syntactic tagging and parsing techniques. For instance, the very impressive work of Hidley (1986), mentioned earlier in relation to phonological analysis of Old English texts, builds in a system which suggests to the user tags based on a number of phonological, morphological and syntactic rules. Hidley's suite of programs also generates a database containing the information gained from the lexical, phonological and syntactic analysis of the text, and allows the exploration of this database in a flexible way, to isolate combinations of features and plot the correlations between them.

Although, as we have seen, much work on semantic patterns in literary texts has used simple graphologically-based tools such as word lists and concordances, more ambitious studies can also be found. A recent example is Martindale's (1984) work on poetic texts, which makes use of a semantically-based dictionary for the analysis of thematic patterns. In such work, as in, for instance, the programs devised by Hidley, the influence of artificial intelligence techniques begins to emerge. Further developments in this area will be outlined in section 4.5.4.

*4.2.2 'Applied' computational stylistics*

The ability of the computer to produce detailed statistical analyses of texts is an obvious attraction for those interested in solving problems of disputed authorship and chronology in literary works. The aim in such studies is to isolate textual features which are characteristic of an author (or, in the case of chronology, particular periods in the author's output), and then to apply these 'fingerprints' to the disputed text(s). Techniques of this kind, though potentially very powerful, are, as we shall see, fraught with pitfalls for the unwary, since an author's style may be influenced by a large number of factors other than his or her own individuality. Two basic approaches to authorship studies can be discerned: tests based on word and/or sentence length, and those concerned with word frequency. Some studies have combined the two types of approach.

Methods based on word and sentence length have been reviewed by Smith (1983), who concludes that word length is an unreliable predictor of authorship, but that sentence length, although not a strong measure, can be a useful adjunct to other methods, provided that the punctuation of the text can safely be assumed to be original, or that all the texts under comparison have been prepared by the same editor. The issue of punctuation has been one source of controversy in the work of Morton (1965), who used differences in sentence length distribution as part of the evidence for his claim that only four of the fourteen 'Pauline' epistles in the New Testament were probably written by Paul, the other ten being the work of at least six other authors. It was pointed out by critics, however, that it is difficult to know what should be taken as constituting a sentence in Greek prose. Morton (1978: 99–100) has countered this criticism by claiming that editorial variations cause no statistically significant differences which would lead to the drawing of incorrect conclusions. Morton's early work on Greek has been criticised on other grounds too: he attempts to explain away exceptions by means of the kinds of subjective argument which his method is meant to make unnecessary; and it is claimed that the application of his techniques to certain other groups of texts can be shown to give results which are contrary to the historical and theological evidence.

Let us turn now to studies in which word frequency is used as evidence for authorship. The simplest case is where one of the writers in a pair of possible candidates can be shown to use a certain word, whereas the other does not. For instance, Mosteller and Wallace (1964), in their study of *The Federalist* papers, a set of eighteenth-century propaganda documents, showed that certain words, such as *enough, upon* and *while*, occurred quite frequently in undisputed works by one of the possible authors, Hamilton, but were rare or non-existent in the work of the other contender, Madison. Investigation of the disputed papers revealed Madison as the more likely author on these grounds.

It might be thought that the idiosyncrasies of individual writers would be best studied in the 'lexical' or 'content' words they use. Such an approach, however, holds a number of difficulties for the computational stylistician. Individual lexical items often occur with frequencies which are too low for reliable statistical analysis. Furthermore, the content vocabulary is obviously strongly conditioned by the subject matter of the writing. In view of these difficulties, much recent work has concentrated on the high-frequency grammatical words, on the grounds that these are not only more amenable to statistical treatment, but are also less dependent on subject matter and less under the conscious control of the writer than the lexical words.

Morton has also argued for the study of high-frequency individual items, as well as word classes, in developing techniques of 'positional stylometry', in which the frequencies of words are investigated, not simply for texts as wholes, but for particular positions in defined units within the text. A detailed account of Morton's methods and their applicability can be found in Morton (1978), in which, in addition to examining word frequencies at particular positions in sentences (typically the first and last positions), he claims discriminatory power for 'proportional pairs' of words (e.g. the frequency of *no* divided by the total frequency for *no* and *not*, or *that* divided by *that* plus *this*), and also collocations of contiguous words or word classes, such as *as if*, *and the* or *a* plus adjective. Comparisons between texts are made by means of the chi-square test. Morton applies these techniques to the Elizabethan drama *Pericles*, providing evidence against the critical view that only part of it is by Shakespeare. Morton also discusses the use of positional stylometry to aid in the assessment of whether a statement made by a defendant in a legal case was actually made in his or her own words. Morton's methods have been taken up by others, principally in the area of Elizabethan authorship: for instance, a lively and inconclusive debate has recently taken place between Merriam (1986, 1987) and Smith (1986, 1987) on the authorship of *Henry VIII* and of *Sir Thomas More*. Despite Smith's reservations about the applicability of the techniques as used by Morton and Merriam, he does believe that an expansion of these methods to include a wider range of tests could be a valuable preliminary step to a detailed study of authorship. Recently, Morton (1986) has claimed that the number of words occurring only once in a text (the 'hapax legomena') is also useful in authorship determination.

So far, we have examined the use of words at the two ends of the frequency spectrum. Ule (1983) has developed methods for authorship study which make use of the wider vocabulary structure of texts. One useful measure is the 'relative vocabulary overlap' between texts, defined as the ratio of the actual number of words the texts have in common to the number which would be expected if the texts had been composed by drawing words at random from the whole of the author's published work (or some equivalent corpus of material). A second technique is concerned with the distribution of words which appear in only one of a set of texts, and a further method is based on a procedure which allows the calculation of the expected number of word types for texts of given length, given a reference corpus of the author's works. These methods proved useful in certain cases of disputed Elizabethan authorship.

As a final example of authorship attribution, we shall examine briefly an extremely detailed and meticulous study, by Kjetsaa and his colleagues, of the charge of plagiarism levelled at Sholokhov by a Soviet critic calling himself D*. A detailed account of this work can be found in Kjetsaa *et al.* (1984). D*'s claim, which was supported in a preface by Solzhenitsyn and had a mixed critical reaction, was that the acclaimed novel *The Quiet Don* was largely written not by Sholokhov but by a Cossack writer, Fedor Kryukov. Kjetsaa's group set out to provide stylometric evidence which might shed light on the matter. Two pilot studies on restricted samples, suggested that stylometric techniques would indeed differentiate between the two contenders, and that *The Quiet Don* was much more likely to be by Sholokhov than by Kryukov. The main study, using much larger amounts of the disputed and reference texts, bore out the predictions of the pilot work, by demonstrating that *The Quiet Don* differed significantly from Kryukov's writings, but not from those of Sholokhov, with respect to sentence length profile, lexical profile, type-token ratio (on both lemmatised and unlemmatised text, very similar results being obtained in each case), and word class sequences, with additional suggestive evidence from collocations.

### 4.3 Lexicography and lexicology

In recent years, the image of the traditional lexicographer, poring over thousands of slips of paper neatly arranged in seemingly countless boxes, has receded, to be replaced by that of the 'new lexicographer', making full use of computer technology. We shall see, however, that the skills of the human expert are by no means redundant, and Chapter 19, below, should be read in this connection. The theories which lexicographers make use of in solving their problems are sometimes said to belong to the related field of lexicology, and here too the computer has had a considerable impact.

The first task in dictionary compilation is obviously to decide on the scope of the enterprise, and this involves a number of interrelated questions. Some dictionaries aim at a representative coverage of the language as a whole; others (e.g. the *Dictionary of American Regional English*) are concerned only with non-standard dialectal varieties, and still others with particular diatypic varieties (e.g. dictionaries of German or Russian for chemists or physicists). Some are intended for native speakers or very advanced students of a language; others, such as the *Oxford Advanced Learner's Dictionary of English* and the new Collins *COBUILD* English Language Dictionary produced by the Birmingham team, are designed specifically for foreign learners. Some are monolingual, others bilingual. These factors will clearly influence the nature of the materials upon which the dictionary is based.

As has been pointed out by Sinclair (1985), the sources of information for dictionary compilation are of three main types. First, it would be folly to ignore the large amount of descriptive information which is already available and organised in the form of existing dictionaries, thesauri, grammars, and so on. Though useful, such sources suffer from several disadvantages: certain words or usages may have disappeared and others may have appeared; and because existing materials may be based on particular ways of looking at language, it may be difficult simply to incorporate into them new insights derived from rapidly developing branches of linguistics such as pragmatics and discourse analysis. A second source of information for lexicography, as for other kinds of descriptive linguistic activity, is the introspective judgements of informants, including the lexicographer himself. It is well known, however, that introspection is often a poor guide to actual usage. Sinclair therefore concludes that the main body of evidence, at least in the initial stages of dictionary making, should come from the analysis of authentic texts. The use of textual material for citation purposes has, of course, been standard practice in lexicography for a very long time. Large dictionaries such as the *Oxford English Dictionary* relied on the amassing of enormous numbers of instances sent in by an army of voluntary readers. Such a procedure, however, is necessarily unsystematic. Fortunately, the revolution in computer technology which we are now witnessing is, as we have already seen, making the compilation and exhaustive lexical analysis of textual corpora a practical possibility. Corpora such as the LOB, London-Lund and Birmingham collections provide a rich source which is already being exploited for lexicographical purposes. Although most work in computational lexicography to date has used mainframe computers, developments in microcomputer technology mean that work of considerable sophistication is now possible on smaller machines (see Paikeday 1985, Brandon 1985).

The most useful informational tools for computational lexicography are word lists and concordances, arranged in alphabetical order of the beginnings or ends of words, in frequency order, or in the order of appearance in texts. Both lemmatised and unlemmatised listings are useful, since the relationship between the lemma and its variant forms is of considerable potential interest. For the recently published *COBUILD* dictionary, for instance, a decision was made to treat the most frequently occurring form of a lemma as the headword for the dictionary entry. Clearly, such a decision relies on the availability of detailed information on the frequencies of word forms in large amounts of text, which only a computational analysis can provide (see Sinclair 1985). The *COBUILD* dictionary project worked with a corpus of some 7.3 million words; even this, however, is a small figure when compared with the vast output produced by the speakers and writers of a language, and it has been argued that a truly representative and comprehensive dictionary would have to use a database of much greater size still, perhaps as large as 500 million words. For a comprehensive account of the *COBUILD* project, see Sinclair (1987).

The lemmatisation problem has been tackled in various ways in different dictionary projects. Lexicographers on the *Dictionary of Old English* project in Toronto (Cameron 1977) lemmatised one text manually, then used this to lemmatise a second text, adding new lemmata for any word forms which had not been present in the first text. In this way, an ever more comprehensive machine dictionary was built up, and the automatic lemmatisation of texts became increasingly efficient. Another technique was used in the production of a historical dictionary of Italian at the Accademia della Crusca in Florence: a number was assigned to each successive word form in the texts, and the machine was then instructed to allocate particular word numbers to particular lemmata. A further method, used in the *Trésor de la Langue Française (TLF)* project in Nancy and Chicago, is to use a machine dictionary of the most common forms, with their lemmata.

Associated with lemmatisation are the problems of homography (the existence of words with the same spellings but quite different meanings) and polysemy (the possession of a range of meanings which are to some extent related). In some such cases (e.g. *bank*, meaning a financial institution or the edge of a river), it is clear that we have homography, and that two quite separate lemmata are therefore involved; in many instances, however, the distinction between homography and polysemy is not obvious, and the lexicographer must make a decision about the number of separate lemmata to be used (see Moon 1987).

Although the computer cannot take over such decisions from the lexicographer, it can provide a wealth of information which, together with other considerations such as etymology, can be used as the basis for decision. Concordances are clearly useful here, since they can provide the context needed for the disambiguation of word senses. Decisions must be made concerning the minimum amount of context which will be useful: for discussion see de Tollenaere (1973). A second very powerful tool for exploring the linguistic context, or 'co-text', of lexical items is automated collocational analysis. The use of this technique in lexicography is still in its infancy (see Martin, Al and van Sterkenburg 1983): some collocational information was gathered in the *TLF* and *COBUILD* projects.

We have seen that at present an important role of the computer is the presentation of material in a form which will aid the lexicographer in the task of deciding on lemmata, definitions, citations, etc. However, as Martin, Al and van Sterkenberg (1983) point out, advances in artificial intelligence techniques could well make the automated semantic analysis of text routinely available, if methods for the solution of problems of ambiguity can be improved.

The final stage of dictionary production, in which the headwords, pronunciations, senses, citations and possibly other information (syntactic, collocational, etc.) are printed according to a specified format, is again one in which computational techniques are important (see e.g. Clear 1987). The lexicographer can type, at a terminal, codes referring to particular citations, typefaces, layouts, and the like, which will then be translated into the desired format by suitable software. The output from such programs, after proofreading, can then be sent directly to a computer-controlled photocomposition device. Such machines are capable of giving a finished product of very high quality, and coping with a wide variety of alphabetic and other symbols.

The availability of major dictionaries in computer-readable form offers an extremely valuable resource which can be tapped for a wide variety of purposes, from computer-assisted language teaching (see section 4.7) to work on natural language processing (sections 3, 4.5) and machine translation (section 4.6). Computerisation of the *Oxford English Dictionary* and its supplement is complete, and has led to the setting up of a database which will be constantly updated and frequently revised (see Weiner 1985). The *Longman Dictionary of Contemporary English (LDOCE)* is available in a machine-readable version with semantic feature codings. Other computer-readable dictionaries include the *Oxford Advanced Learner's Dictionary of Current English (OALDCE)* and an important Dutch dictionary, the *van Dale Groot Woordenboek der Nederlandse Taal.* Further information can be found in Amsler (1984).

Computer-readable commercially produced dictionaries are also being used as source materials for the construction of lexical databases for use in other applications. For instance, a machine dictionary of about 38000 entries has been prepared from the *OALDCE* in a form especially suitable for accessing by computer programs (Mitton 1986). Scholars working on the ASCOT project in the Netherlands (Akkerman, Masereeuw, and Meijs 1985; Meijs 1985; Akkerman, Meijs, and Voogt-van Zutphen 1987) are extracting information from existing dictionaries which, together with morphological analysis routines, will form a lexical database and analysis system capable of coding words in hitherto uncoded corpora, and can be used in association with a system such as Nijmegen TOSCA parser (see Aarts and van den Heuvel 1984) to analyse texts. A related project (Meijs 1986) aims to construct a system of meaning characterisations (the LINKS system) for a computerised lexicon such as is found in ASCOT.

For further information on computational lexicography readers are referred to Goetschalckx and Rolling (1982), Sedelow (1985), and the bibliography in Kipfer (1982). For lexicography in general, see Chapter 19 below.

## 4.4 Textual criticism and editing

The preparation of a critical edition of a text, like the compilation of a dictionary, involves several stages, each of which can benefit in some degree from the use of computers. The initial stage is, of course, the collection of a corpus of texts upon which the final edition will be based. The location of appropriate text versions will be facilitated by the increasing number of bibliographies and library stocks held in machine-readable form.

The first stage of the analysis proper is the isolation of variant readings from the texts under study. Since this is essentially a mechanical task involving the comparison of sequences of characters, it would seem to be a process which is well suited to the capabilities of the computer. There are, however, a number of problems. The editor must decide what is to be taken as constituting a variant: variations between texts may range from capitalisation and punctuation differences, through spelling changes and the substitution of formally similar but semantically different words, to the omission or insertion of quite lengthy sections of text. A further problem is to establish where a particular variant ends. This is a relatively simple matter for the human editor, who can scan sections of text to determine where they fall into alignment again; it is, however, much more difficult for the computer, which must be given a set of rules for carrying out the task. A technique used, in various forms, by a number of editing projects is to look first for local variations of limited extent, then to widen gradually the scope of the scan until the texts eventually match up again. Once variants have been isolated, they must be printed for inspection by the editor. One way of doing this is to choose one text as a base, printing each line (or other appropriate unit) from this text in full, then listing below it the variant parts of the line in other texts. For summaries of problems and methods in the isolation and printing of variants, see Hockey (1980) and Oakman (1980).

The second stage in editing is the establishment of the relationships between manuscripts. Traditionally, attempts are made to reconstruct the 'stemmatic' relationships between texts, by building a genealogical tree on the basis of similarities and differences between variants, together with historical and other evidence. Mathematical models of manuscript traditions have been proposed, and procedures for the establishment of stemmata have been computerised. It has, however, been pointed out that the construction of a genealogy for manuscripts can be vitiated by a number of factors such as the lack of accurate dating, the uncertainty as to what constitutes an 'error' in the transmission of a text, the often dubious assumption that the author's text was definitive, and the existence of contaminating material. For these reasons, some scholars have abandoned the attempt to reconstruct genealogies, in favour of methods which claim only to assess the degree of similarity between texts. Here, multivariate statistical techniques (see section 2) such as cluster analysis and principal components analysis are useful. A number of papers relating to manuscript grouping can be found in Irigoin and Zarri (1979).

The central activity in textual editing is the attempted reconstruction of the 'original' text by the selection of appropriate variants, and the preparation of an apparatus criticus containing other variants and notes. Although the burden of this task falls squarely on the shoulders of the editor, computer-generated concordances of variant readings can be of great mechanical help in the selection process.

As with dictionary production, the printing of the final text and apparatus criticus is increasingly being given over to the computer. Particularly important here is the suite of programs, known as TUSTEP (Tübingen System of Text Processing Programs), developed at the University of Tübingen under the direction of Dr Wilhelm Ott. This allows a considerable range of operations to be carried out on texts, from lemmatisation to the production of indexes and the printing of the final product by computer-controlled photocomposition. Reports on many interesting projects using TUSTEP can be found in issues of the *ALLC Bulletin* and *ALLC Journal* and in their recent replacement, *Literary and Linguistic Computing*.

A bibliography of works on textual editing can be found in Ott (1974), updated in Volume 2 of *Sprache und Datenverarbeitung*, published in 1980.

### 4.5 Natural language and artificial intelligence: understanding and producing texts

In the last 25 years or so, a considerable amount of effort has gone into the attempt to develop computer programs which can 'understand' natural language input and/or produce output which resembles that of a human being. Since natural languages (together with other codes associated with spoken language, such as gesture) are overwhelmingly the most frequent vehicles for communication between human beings, programs of this kind would give the computer a more natural place in everyday life. Furthermore, in trying to build systems which simulate human linguistic activities, we shall inevitably learn a great deal about language itself, and about the workings of the mind. Projects of this kind are an important part of the field of 'artificial intelligence', which also covers areas such as the simulation of human visual activities, robotics, and so on. For excellent guides to artificial intelligence as a whole, see Barr and Feigenbaum (1981, 1982), Cohen and Feigenbaum (1982), Rich (1983) and O'Shea and Eisenstadt (1984); for surveys of natural language processing, see Sparck Jones and Wilks (1983), Harris (1985), Grishman (1986) and McTear (1987). In what follows, we shall first examine systems whose main aim is the understanding of natural language, then move on to consider those geared mainly to the computational generation of language, and those which bring understanding and generation together in an attempt to model conversational interaction. Where references to individual projects are not given, they can be found in the works cited above.

### 4.5.1 Natural language understanding systems

Early natural language understanding systems simplified the enormous problems involved, by restricting the range of applicability of the programs to a narrow domain, and also limiting the complexity of the language input the system was designed to cope with. Among the earliest systems were: SAD-SAM (Syntactic Appraiser and Diagrammer–Semantic Analysing Machine), which used a context-free grammar to parse sentences about kinship relations, phrased in a restricted vocabulary of about 1700 words, and used the information to generate a database, which could be used to answer questions; BASEBALL, which could answer questions about a year's American baseball games; SIR (Semantic Information Retrieval), which built a database around certain semantic relations and used it to answer questions; STUDENT, which could solve school algebra problems expressed as stories.

The most famous of the early natural language systems was ELIZA (Weizenbaum 1966), a program which, in its various forms, could hold a 'conversation' with the user about a number of topics. In its best known form, ELIZA simulates a Rogerian psychotherapist in a dialogue with the user/'patient'. Like other early programs, ELIZA uses a pattern-matching technique to generate appropriate replies. The program looks for particular keywords in the input, and uses these to trigger transformations leading to an acceptable reply. Some of these transformations are extremely simple: for instance, the replacement of *I/me/my* by *you/your* can lead to 'echoing' replies which serve merely to return the dialogic initiative to the 'patient':

Well, my boyfriend made me come here.
YOUR BOYFRIEND MADE YOU COME HERE.
The keywords are allocated priority codings which determine the outcome in cases where more than one keyword appears in the input sentence. The program can also make links between more specific and more general items (e.g. *father, family*) in order to introduce some variety and thus naturalness into the dialogue. If the program fails to achieve a match with anything in the input, it will generate a filler such as *Please go on.*

The output of these early programs can be quite impressive: indeed, Weizenbaum was surprised and concerned at the way in which some people using the ELIZA program began to become emotionally involved with it, and to treat it as if it really was a human psychotherapist, despite the author's careful statements about just what the program could and could not do. The success of these programs is, however, heavily dependent on the choice of a suitably delimited domain. They could not cope with an unrestricted range of English input, since they all operate either by means of procedures which match the input against a set of pre-stored patterns or keywords, or (in the case of SAD-SAM) by fairly rudimentary parsing operating on a small range of vocabulary. Even ELIZA, impressive as it is in being able to produce seemingly sensible output from a wide range of inputs, reveals its weaknesses when it is shown to treat nonsense words just like real English words: the program has nothing which could remotely be called an understanding of human language.

The second generation of natural language processing systems had an added power deriving from the greater sophistication of parsing routines which began to emerge in the 1970s (see section 3.2.4). A good example is LUNAR, an information retrieval system enabling geologists to obtain information from a database containing data on the analysis of moon rock samples from the Apollo II mission. LUNAR uses an ATN parser guided by semantic interpretation rules, and a 3500-word dictionary. The user's query is translated into a 'query language' based on predicate calculus, which allows the retrieval of the required information from the database in order to provide an answer to the user.

Winograd's (1972) SHRDLU system (named after the last half of the 12 most frequent letters of the English alphabet), like previous systems, dealt with a highly restricted world, in this case one involving the manipulation of toy blocks on a table, by means of a simulated robot arm. The system is truly interactive, in that it accepts typed instructions as input and can itself ask questions and request clarification, as well as executing commands by means of a screen representation of the robot arm. One of the innovative features of SHRDLU is that knowledge about syntax and semantics (based on the 'systemic' grammar of Halliday), and also about reasoning, is represented, not in a static form, but dynamically as 'procedures' consisting of sections of the computer program itself. Because one procedure can call upon the services of another, complex interactions are possible, not only between different procedures operating at, say, the syntactic level, but also between different levels, such as syntax and semantics. It is generally accepted that SHRDLU marked an important step forward in natural language processing. Previous work had adopted an 'engineering' approach to language analysis: the aim was to simulate human linguistic behaviour by any technique which worked, and no claim was made that these systems actually mirrored human language processing activities in any significant way. SHRDLU, on the other hand, could actually claim to model human linguistic activity. This was made possible partly by the sophistication of its mechanisms for integrating syntactic and semantic processing with each other and with inferential reasoning, and partly by its use of knowledge about the blocks world within which it operated. As with previous systems, however, it is unlikely that Winograd would have achieved such remarkable success if he had not restricted himself to a small, well-bounded domain. Furthermore, the use of inference and of heuristic devices, though important, is somewhat limited.

As was mentioned in section 3.2.5, the computational linguists of the 1970s began to explore the possibility that semantic analysis, rather than being secondary to syntactic parsing, should be regarded as the central activity in natural language processing. Typical of the first language understanding systems embodying this approach is MARGIE (Meaning Analysis, Response Generation, and Inference in English), which analyses input to give a conceptual dependency representation, and uses this to make inferences and to produce paraphrases. Later developments built in Schank's concepts (again discussed in section 3.2.5) of scripts and plans. SAM (Script Applier Mechanism) accepts a story as input, first converting it to a conceptual dependency representation as in MARGIE, then attempting to fit this into one or more of a stored set of scripts, and filling in information which, though not present in the story as presented, can be inferred by reference to the script. The system can then give a paraphrase or summary of the story, answer questions about it, and even provide a translation into other languages. PAM (Plan Applier Mechanism) operates on the principle that story understanding requires the tracking of the participants' goals and the interpretation of their actions in terms of the satisfaction of those goals. PAM, like SAM, converts the story input into conceptual dependency structures, but then uses plans to enable it to summarise the story from the viewpoints of particular participants or to answer questions about the participants' goals and actions. Mention should also be made of the POLITICS program, which uses plans and scripts in order to represent different political beliefs, and to produce interpretations of events consistent with these various ideologies.

Any language understanding system which attempts to go beyond the interpretation of single, simple sentences must face the problem of how to keep track of what entities are being picked out by means of referring expressions. This problem has been tackled in terms of the concept of 'focus', the idea being that particular items within the text are the focus of attention at any one point in a text, this focus changing as the text unfolds, with concomitant shifts in local or even global topic (see Grosz 1977, Sidner 1983).

### 4.5.2 *Language generation*

Although some of the systems reviewed above do incorporate an element of text generation, they are all largely geared towards the understanding of natural language. Generation has received much less attention from computational linguists than language understanding; paradoxically, this is partly because it presents fewer problems. The problem of building a language understanding system is to provide the ability to analyse the vast variety of structures and lexical items which can occur in a naturally occurring text; in generation, on the other hand, the system can often be constructed around a simplified, though still quite large, subset of the language. The process of generation starts from a representation of the meanings to be expressed, and then translates these meanings into syntactic forms in a manner which depends on the theoretical basis of the system (e.g. via deep structures in a transformationally-based model). If the output is to consist of more than just single sentences or even fragments of sentences, the problem of textual cohesion must also be addressed, by building in conjunctive devices, rules for anaphora, and the like, and making sure that the flow of information is orderly and easily understood. Clearly, similar types of information are needed in generation as in analysis, though we cannot simply assume that precisely the same rules will apply in reverse.

One of the most influential early attempts to generate coherent text computationally was Davey's (1978) noughts and crosses program. The program accepts as input a set of legal moves in a complete or incomplete game of noughts and crosses (tic-tac-toe), and produces a description of the game in continuous prose, including an account of any mistakes made. It can also play a game with the user, and remember the sequences of moves by both players, in order to generate a description of the game. The program (which, like Winograd's, is based on a systematic grammar) is impressive in its ability to deal with matters such as relationships between clauses (sequential, contrastive, etc.), the choice of appropriate tense and aspect forms, and the selection of pronouns. It is not, however interactive, so that the user cannot ask for clarification of points in the description. Furthermore, like SHRDLU, it deals only with a very restricted domain.

Davey's work did, however, point towards the future in that it was concerned not only with the translation of 'messages' into English text but also with the planning of what was to be said and what was best left unsaid. This is also an important aspect of the work of McKeown (1985), whose TEXT system was developed to generate responses to questions about the structure of a military database. In TEXT, discourse patterns are represented as 'schemata', such as the 'identification' schema used in the provision of definitions, which encode the rhetorical techniques which can be used for particular discourse purposes, as determined by a prior linguistic analysis. When the user asks a question about the structure of the database, a set of possible schemata is selected on the basis of the discourse purpose reflected in the type of question asked. The set of schemata is then narrowed to just one by examination of the information available to answer the question. Once a schema has been selected, it is filled out by matching the rhetorical devices it contains against information from the database, making use of stored information about the kinds of information which are relevant to particular types of rhetorical device. An important aspect of McKeown's work is the demonstration that focusing, developed by Grosz and Sidner in relation to language understanding (see section 4.5.1), can be applied in a very detailed manner in generation to relate what is said next to what is the current focus of attention, and to make choices about the syntactic structure of what is said (e.g. active versus passive) in the light of local information structuring.

As a final example of text generation systems, we shall consider the ongoing PENMAN project of Mann and Matthiessen (see Mann 1985). The aims of this work are to identify the characteristics which fit a text for the needs it fulfils, and to develop computer programs which generate texts in response to particular needs. Like Winograd and Davey before them, Mann and Matthiessen use a systemic model of grammar in their work, arguing that the functional nature of this model makes it especially suitable for work on the relationship between text form and function (for further discussion of the usefulness of systemic grammars in computational linguistics see Butler 1985c). The grammar is based on the notion of choice in language, and one particularly interesting feature of Mann and Matthiessen's system is that it builds in constraints on the circumstances under which particular grammatical choices can be made. These conditions make reference to the knowledge base which existed prior to the need to create the text, and also to a 'text plan' generated in response to the text need, as well as a set of generally available 'text services'. The recent work of Patten (1988) also makes use of systemic grammar in text generation. A useful overview of automatic text generation can be found in Douglas (1987, Chapter 2).

### 4.5.3 *Bringing understanding and generation together: conversing with the computer*

Although some of the systems reviewed so far (e.g. ELIZA, SHRDLU) are able to interact with the user in a pseudo-conversational way, they do not build in any sophisticated knowledge of the structure of human conversational interaction. In this section, we shall examine briefly some attempts to model interactional discourse; for a detailed account of this area see McTear (1987).

Most dialogue systems model the fairly straightforward human discourse patterns which occur within particular restricted domains. A typical example is GUS (Genial Understander System), which acts as a travel agent able to book air passages from Palo Alto to cities in California. GUS conducts a dialogue with the user, and is a 'mixed initiative' system, in that it will allow the user to take control by asking a question of his or her own in response to a question put by the system. GUS is based on the concept of frames (see section 3.2.6). Some of the frames are concerned with the overall structure of dialogue in the travel booking domain; other frames represent particular kinds of knowledge about dates, the trip itself, and the traveller. The system asks questions designed to elicit the information required to fill in values for the slots in the various frames. It can also use any unsolicited but relevant information provided by the user, automatically suppressing any questions which would have been asked later to elicit this additional information.

One of the most important characteristics of human conversation is that it is, in general, co-operative: as Grice (1975) has observed, there seems to be a general expectation that conversationalists will try to make their contributions as informative as required (but no more), true, relevant and clear. Even where people appear to contravene these principles, we tend to assume that they are being co-operative at some deeper level. Some recent computational systems have attempted to build in an element of co-operativeness. Examples include the CO-OP program, which can correct false assumptions underlying users' questions; and a system which uses the 'plan' concept to answer, in a helpful way, questions about meeting and boarding trains.

The goal of providing responses from the system which will be helpful to the user is complicated by the fact that what is useful for one kind of user may not be so for another. An important feature in recent dialogue systems is 'user modelling', the attempt to build in alternative strategies according to the characteristics of the user. For instance, the GRUNDY program builds (and if necessary modifies) a user profile on the basis of stereotypes invoked by a set of characteristics supplied by the user, and uses the profile to recommend appropriate library books. A more recent user modelling system is HAM-ANS (HAMburg Application-oriented Natural language System) which includes a component for the reservation of a hotel room by means of a simulated telephone call. The system models the user's characteristics by building up a stock of information about value judgements relating to good and bad features of the room. It is also able to gather and process data which allow it to make recommendations about the type and price of room which might suit the user.

If computers are to be able to simulate human dialogue in a natural way, they must also be made capable of dealing with the failures which inevitably arise in human communication. A clear discussion of this area can be found in McTear (1987, Chapter 9), on which the following brief summary is based.

644

Various aspects of the user's input may make it difficult for the system to respond appropriately: words may be misspelt or mistyped; the syntactic structure may be ill-formed or may simply contain constructions which are not built into the system's grammar; semantic selection restrictions may be violated; referential relationships may be unclear; user presuppositions may be unjustified. In such cases, the system can respond by reporting the problem as accurately as possible and asking the user to try again; it can attempt to obtain clarification by means of a dialogue with the user; or it can make an informed guess about what the user meant. Until recently, most systems used the first approach, which is, of course, the one which least resembles the human behaviour the system is set up to simulate. Clarification dialogues interrupt the flow of discourse, and are normally initiated in human interaction only where intelligent guesswork fails to provide a solution. Attempts are now being made, therefore, to build into natural language processing systems the ability to cope with ill-formed or otherwise difficult input by making an assessment of the most likely user intention.

The most usual way of dealing with misspellings and mistypings is to use a 'fuzzy matching' procedure, which looks for partial similarity between the typed word and those available in the system's dictionary, and which can be aided by knowledge about what words can be expected in texts of particular types. Ungrammatical input can be dealt with by appealing to the semantics to see if the partially parsed sentence makes sense; or metarules can be added to the grammar, informing the system of ways in which the syntactic rules can be relaxed if necessary. The relaxation of the normal rules is also useful as a technique for resolving problems concerned with semantic selection restriction violations and in clarity of reference. A rather different type of problem arises when the system detects errors in the user's presuppositions; here, the co-operative mechanisms outlined earlier are useful. If, despite attempts at intelligent guesswork, the system is still unable to resolve a communication failure, clarification dialogues may be the only answer. It will be remembered that even the early SHRDLU system was able to request clarification of instructions it did not fully understand. A number of papers dealing with the remedying of communication failure in natural language processing systems can be found in Reilly (1986).

### 4.5.4 Using natural language processing in the real world

Many of the programs discussed in the previous section are 'toy' systems, built with the aim of developing the methodology of natural language processing and discovering ways in which human linguistic behaviour can be simulated. Some such systems, however, have been designed with a view to their implementation in practical real-world situations.

One practical area in which natural language processing is important is the design of man-machine interfaces for the manipulation of databases. Special database query languages are available, but it is clearly more desirable for users to be able to interact with the database via their natural language. Two natural language 'front ends' to databases (LUNAR and TEXT) have already been discussed. Others include LADDER, designed to interrogate a naval database, and INTELLECT, a front end for commercial databases.

Databases represent stores of knowledge, often in great quantity, and organised in complex ways. Ultimately, of course, this knowledge derives from that of human beings. An extremely important area of artificial intelligence is the development of **expert systems**, which use large bodies of knowledge concerned with particular domains, acquired from human experts, to solve problems within those domains. Such systems will undoubtedly have very powerful social and economic effects. Detailed discussions of expert systems can be found in, for example, Jackson (1986) and Black (1986).

The designing of an expert system involves the answering of a number of questions: how the system can acquire the knowledge base from human experts; how that knowledge can be represented in order to allow the system to operate efficiently; how the system can best use its knowledge to make the kinds of decisions that human experts make; how it can best communicate with non-experts in order to help solve their problems. Clearly, natural language processing is an important aspect of many such systems. Ideally, an expert system should be able to acquire knowledge by natural language interaction with the human experts, and to update this knowledge as necessary; to perform inferencing and other language-related tasks which a human being would need to perform, often on the basis of hunches and incomplete information; and to use natural language for communication of findings, and also its own modes of reasoning, to the users.

Perhaps the best-known expert systems are those which act as consultants in medical diagnosis, such as MYCIN, which is intended to aid doctors in the diagnosis and treatment of certain types of bacterial disease. The system conducts a dialogue with the user to establish the patient's symptoms and history, and the results of medical tests. It is capable of prompting the user with a list of expected alternative answers to questions. As the dialogue proceeds, the system makes inferences according to its rule base. It then presents its conclusions concerning the possible organisms present, and recommends treatments. The user can request the probabilities of alternative diagnoses, and can also ascertain the reasoning which led to the system's decisions.

Some expert systems act as 'intelligent tutors', which conduct a tutorial with the user, and can modify their activities according to the responses given. SOPHIE (SOPHisticated Instructional Environment) teaches students to debug circuits in a simulated electronics laboratory; SCHOLAR was originally set up to tutor in South American geography, and was later extended to other domains; WHY gives tutorials on the causes of rainfall. Detailed discussion can be found in Sleeman and Brown (1982) and O'Shea (1983). The application of the expert systems concept to computer-assisted language learning will be discussed in section 4.7.

A further possibility of particular interest in the study of natural language texts is discussed by Cercone and Murchison (1985), who envisage expert systems for literary research, consisting of a database, user interface, statistical analysis routines, and a results output database which would accumulate the products of previous researches.

### 4.5.5 Spoken language input and output

It has so far been assumed that the input to, and output from, the computer is in the written mode. Since, however, a major objective of work in artificial intelligence is to provide a natural and convenient means for human beings to interact with computer systems, it is not surprising that considerable effort has been and is being expended on the possibility of using ordinary human speech as input to machine systems, and synthesising human-like 'speech' as output. The advantages of spoken language as input and/or output are clear: the use of speech as input strongly reduces the need to train users before interacting with the system; communication is much faster in the spoken than in the written mode; the user's hands and eyes are left free to attend to other tasks (a particularly important feature in such systems as car telephone systems, intelligent tutors helping a trainee with a physical task, aircraft or space flight operations, etc.).

Unfortunately, the problems of speech recognition are considerable (for a low-level overview see Levinson and Liberman 1981). The exact sound representing a given sound unit or phoneme (for instance a 't sound') depends on the linguistic environment in which the sound occurs and the speed of utterance. Different accents will require different speech recognition rules. There is also considerable variation in the way the 'same' sound, in the same environment, is pronounced by men and women, adults and children, and even by different individuals.

Early work on speech analysis concentrated on the recognition of isolated words, so circumventing the thorny problems caused by modifications of pronunciation in connected speech. Systems of this kind attempted to match the incoming speech signal against a set of stored representations of a fairly small vocabulary (several hundred words for a single speaker on whose voice the system was trained, far fewer words if the system was to be speaker-independent). A rather more flexible technique is to attempt to recognise certain key words in the input, ignoring the 'noise' in between; this allows rather more natural input, without gaps, but can still only cope with a limited vocabulary.

In later work the problem of analysing connected speech has been tackled in a rather different way: the higher-level (syntactic, semantic, pragmatic) properties of the language input are used in order to restrict the possibilities the machine must consider in trying to establish the identity of a word. Speech *recognition* systems are thus giving way to integrated systems which, with varying degrees of success, could be said to show speech *understanding*. These principles were the basis of the Speech Understanding Research programme at the Advanced Research Products Agency of the U.S. Department of Defense, undertaken in the 1970s (see Lea 1980). One project, HEARSAY, was initially concerned with playing a chess game with an opponent who spoke his or her moves into a microphone. The system was able to use its knowledge of the rules of chess in order to predict the correct interpretation of words which it could not identify from the sound alone.

Let us turn now to speech output from computers, which has a number of important applications in such areas as 'talking books' and typewriters for the blind, automatic telephone enquiry and answering systems, devices for giving warnings and other information to car drivers, office systems for the conversion of printed text to spoken form, and intelligent tutors for tasks where the tutee needs to keep his or her hands and eyes free. Although not presenting quite as many difficult problems as speech understanding, speech synthesis is still by no means a trivial task, because of the complex effects of linguistic context on the phonetic form in which sound units must be manifested, and also because of the need to incorporate appropriate stress and intonation patterns into the output.

One important variable in speech synthesis systems is the size of the unit which is taken as the basic 'atom' out of which utterances are constructed. The simplest systems store representations of whole performed utterances spoken by human beings; other systems store representations of individual words, again derived from recordings of human speech. Even with this second method the number of units which must be stored is quite large if the system is intended for a range of uses. Furthermore, attention must be given to the modifications to the basic forms which take place when words are used in connected human speech, and also the superimposition of stress and intonation patterns on the output. A variant of this technique is to store word systems and inflections separately.

In an attempt to reduce the number of units which must be stored, systems have been developed which take smaller units as their building blocks. Some use syllables derived by accurate editing of taped speech; for English 4000–10,000 such units are needed to take account of the variations in different environments. Other systems use combinations of two sounds: for example, a set of 1000–2000 pairs representing consonant-vowel and vowel-consonant transitions, which may be derived from human speech or generated artificially. With this system, the word *cat* could be synthesised from zero + /k/, /kæ/, /æt/ /t/ + zero. Still other systems use phoneme-sized units (about 40 for English), generated artificially in such a way that generalisations are made from the various allophonic variants. Such systems face very severe problems in ensuring appropriate modifications at transitions between sound units, and these can be only partly alleviated by storing allophonic units (50–100 for English) instead.

Because of the large amounts of data which must be stored, and the fast responses required for speech synthesis in real time, the information is normally coded in a compact form. This may be a digital representation of the properties of waveforms corresponding to sounds or sound sequences, or of the properties of the filters which can be used to model the production of particular sounds by the vocal tract; the term 'formant coding' is often used in connection with such techniques. The mathematical technique known as 'linear prediction' is also of considerable interest here, since it allows the separation of segmental information from the prosodic (stress, intonation) properties of the speech signal, so that stored segmentals can be used together with synthetic prosodies if desired. Details of the techniques used for speech synthesis can be found in Witten (1982), Cater (1983) and Sclater (1983).

Further problems must be faced in the automated conversion of written texts into a spoken form. This involves two stages in addition to those discussed above: the prediction, from the text, of intonational and rhythmic patterns; and conversion to a phonetic transcription corresponding to the 'atomic' units used for synthesis. These processes were discussed briefly in section 3.2.3. For an account of the MITalk text-to-speech system, see Allen, Hunnicutt and Klatt (1987).

## 4.6 Machine translation

The concept of machine translation (hereafter MT) arose in the late 1940s, soon after the birth of modern computing. In a memorandum of 1949, Warren Weaver, then vice president of the Rockefeller Foundation, suggested that translation could be handled by computers as a kind of coding task. In the years which followed, projects were initiated at Georgetown University, Harvard and Cambridge, and MT research began to attract large grants from government, military and private sources. By the mid-1960s, however, fully operative large-scale systems were still a future dream, and in 1966 the Automatic Language Processing Advisory Committee (ALPAC) recommended severely reduced funding for MT, and this led to a decline in activity in the United States, though work continued to some extent in Europe, Canada and the Soviet Union. Gradually, momentum began to be generated once more, as the needs of the scientific, technological, governmental and business communities for information dissemination became ever more pressing, and as new techniques became available in both linguistics and computing. In the late 1980s there is again very lively interest in MT. A short but very useful review of the area can be found in Lewis (1985), and a much more detailed account in Hutchins (1986), on which much of the following is based, and from which references to individual projects can be obtained. Nirenburg (1987) contains a useful collection of papers covering various aspects of machine translation.

The process of MT consists basically of an analysis of the source language (SL) text to give a representation which will allow synthesis of a corresponding text in the target language (TL). The procedures and problems involved in analysis and synthesis are, of course, largely those we have already discussed in relation to the analysis and generation of single languages. In general, as we might expect from previous discussion, the analysis of the SL is a rather harder task than the generation of the TL text. The words of the SL text must be identified by morphological analysis and dictionary look-up, and problems of multiple word meaning must be resolved. Enough of the syntactic structure of the SL text must be analysed so that transfer into the appropriate structures of the TL can be effected. In most systems, at least some semantic analysis is also performed. For anything except very low quality translation, it will also be necessary to take account of the macrostructure of the text, including anaphoric and other cohesive devices. Systems vary widely in the attention they give to these various types of phenomena.

**Direct** MT systems, which include most of those developed in the 1950s and 1960s, are set up for one language pair at a time, and have generally been favoured by groups whose aim is to construct a practical, workable system, rather than to concentrate on the application of theoretical insights from linguistics. They rely on a single SL-TL dictionary, and some perform no more analysis of the SL than is necessary for the resolution of ambiguities and the changing of those grammatical sequences which are very different in the two languages, while others carry out a more thorough syntactic analysis. Most of the early systems show no clear distinction between the parts concerned with SL analysis and those concerned with TL synthesis, though more modern direct systems are often built on more modular lines. Typical of early direct systems is that developed at Georgetown University in the period 1952–63 for translation from Russian to English, using only rather rudimentary syntactic and semantic analysis. This system was the forerunner of SYSTRAN, which has features of both direct and transfer approaches (see below), and has been used for Russian-English translation by the US Air Force, by the National Aeronautic and Space Administration, and by EURATOM in Italy. Versions of SYSTRAN for other language pairs, including English-French, French-English, English-Italian, are also available.

**Interlingual** systems arose out of the emphasis on language universals and on the logical properties of natural language which came about, largely as the result of Chomskyan linguistics, in the mid-1960s. They tend to be favoured by those whose interests in MT are at least partly theoretical rather than essentially practical. The interlingual approach assumes that SL texts can be converted to some intermediate representation which is common to a number of languages (and possibly all), so facilitating synthesis of the TL text. Such a system would clearly be more economical than a series of direct systems in an environment, such as the administrative organs of the European Economic Community, where there is a need to translate from and into a number of languages. Various interlinguas have been suggested: deep structure representations of the type used in transformational generative grammars, artificial languages based on logical systems, even a 'natural' auxiliary language such as Esperanto. In a truly interlingual system, SL analysis procedures are entirely specific to that language, and need have no regard for the eventual TL; similarly, TL synthesis routines are again specific to the language concerned. Typical of the interlingual approach was the early (1970–75) work at the Linguistic Research Center at the University of Texas, on the German-English system METAL (Mechanical Translation and Analysis of Languages), which converted the input, through a number of stages, into 'deep structure' representations which then formed the basis for synthesis of the TL sentences. This design proved too complex for use as the basis of a working system, and METAL was later redeveloped using a transfer approach. Also based on the interlingual approach was the CETA (Centre d'Etudes pour la Traduction Automatique) project at the University of Grenoble (1961–71), which used what was effectively a semantic representation as its 'pivot' language in translating, mainly between Russian and French. The rigidity of design and the inefficiency of the parser used caused the abandonment of the interlingual approach in favour of a transfer type of design.

**Transfer** systems differ from interlingual systems in interposing separate SL and TL transfer representations, rather than a language-independent interlingua, between SL analysis and TL synthesis. These representations are specific to the languages concerned, and are designed to permit efficient transfer between languages. It has nevertheless been claimed that only one program for analysis and one for synthesis is required for each language. Thus transfer systems, like interlingual systems, use separate SL and TL dictionaries and grammars. An important transfer system is GETA (Groupe d'Etudes pour la Traduction Automatique), developed mainly for Russian-French translation at the University of Grenoble since 1971 as the successor to CETA. A second transfer system being developed at the present time is EUROTRA (see Arnold and das Tombe 1987), which is intended to translate between the various languages of the European Economic Community. Originally, the EEC had used SYSTRAN, but it was recognised that the potential of this system in a multilingual environment was severely limited, and in 1978 the decision was made to set up a project, involving groups from a number of member countries, to create an operational prototype for a system which would be capable of translating limited quantities of text in restricted fields, to and from all the languages of the Community. In 1982 EUROTRA gained independent funding from the Commission of the EEC, and work is now well under way. Groups working on particular languages are able to develop their own procedures, provided that these conform to certain basic design features of the system.

A further important dimension of variation in MT systems is the extent to which they are independent of human aid. After the initial optimism following Weaver's memorandum it soon became clear that MT is a far more complex task than had been envisaged at first. Indeed, fully automatic high quality translation of even a full range of non-literary texts is still a goal for the future. However, the practical need for the rapid translation of technical and economic material continues to grow, and various practical compromises must be reached. The aim of providing a translation which is satisfactory for the end user (often one of rather lower quality than would be tolerated by a professional translator) can be pursued in any of three ways.

Firstly, the input may be restricted in a way which makes it easier for the computer to handle. This may involve a restriction to particular fields of discourse: for instance, the CULT (Chinese University Language Translator) system developed since 1969 at the Chinese University of Hong Kong is concerned with the translation of mathematics and physics articles from Chinese to English; the METEO system developed by the TAUM (Traduction Automatique de l'Université de Montréal) group is concerned only with the translation of weather reports from English into French. Restricted input may also involve the use of only a subset of a language in the text to be translated. For instance, the TITUS system introduced at the Institut Textile de France in 1970, for the translation of abstracts from and into French, English, German and Spanish, requires the abstracts to consist only of a set of key lexical terms plus a fixed set of function words (prepositions, conjunctions, etc.).

Secondly, the computer may be used to produce an imperfect translation which, although it may be acceptable as it stands for certain purposes, may require revision by human translators for other uses. It has been shown that such a system can compete well with fully manual translation in economic terms. Even in EUROTRA, one of the more linguistically sophisticated systems, there is no pretence that the products will be of a quality which would satisfy a professional translator.

Thirdly, man-machine co-operation may occur during the translation process itself. At the lowest level of machine involvement, human translators can now call upon on-line dictionaries and terminological data banks such as EURODICAUTOM, associated with the EEC in Brussels, or LEXIS in Bonn. In order to be maximally useful, these tools should provide information about precise meanings, connotative properties, ranges of applicability, and preferably also examples of attested usage. At a greater level of sophistication, translation may be an interactive process in which the user is always required to provide certain kinds of information, or in which the machine stops on encountering problems, and requires the user to provide information to resolve the block. In the CULT system, for instance, the machine performs a partial translation of each sentence, but the user is required to insert articles, choose verb tenses, and resolve ambiguities.

Looking towards the future, there seems little doubt that MT is here to stay. Considerable amounts of material are already translated by machine: for instance, over 400,000 pages of material were translated by computer in the EEC Commission during 1983. There seems to be a movement towards the integration of MT with other facilities such as word processing, term banks, etc. MT systems are also becoming available on microcomputers: for example, the Weidner Communications Corporation has produced a system, MicroCAT, which runs on the IBM PC machine, as well as a more powerful MacroCAT version which runs on larger machines such as the VAX and PDP11. It is likely that artificial intelligence techniques will become increasingly important in MT, though it is a moot point whether the full range of language understanding is required, especially for restricted text types. The idea that a translator's expert system might increase the effectiveness of MT systems by simulating human translation more closely is certainly attractive, but there are considerable problems in describing all the different techniques and types of knowledge used by a human translator and incorporating them into such a system. Nevertheless, AI-related MT is a major goal of the so-called 'fifth generation' project in Japan, which aims at a multilingual MT system with a 100,000-word vocabulary, capable of translating with 90 per cent accuracy at a cost of 30 per cent lower than that of human translation.

## 4.7 Computers in the teaching and learning of languages

Over the past few years there has been a considerable upsurge of interest in the benefits which computers might bring to the educational process, and some of the most interesting work has been in the teaching and learning of languages. The potential role of the computer in language teaching is twofold: as a tool in the construction of materials, however those materials might be presented; and in the actual presentation of materials to the learner.

The power of the computer as an aid in materials development derives from the ease with which data on the frequency and range of occurrence of linguistic items can be obtained from texts, and from the possibility of extracting large numbers of attested examples of particular linguistic phenomena. For example, word lists and concordances derived from an appropriate corpus were found extremely useful in the selection of teaching points and exemplificatory material for a short course designed to enable university students of chemistry to read articles in German chemistry journals for comprehension and limited translation (Butler 1974). We shall see later that the computer can also be used to generate exercises from a body of materials.

Although the importance of computational analysis in revealing the properties of the language to be taught should not be underestimated, it is perhaps understandable that more attention should have been paid in recent years to the involvement of the computer in the actual process of language teaching and learning. Despite a good deal of scepticism (some of it quite understandable) on the part of language teachers, there can be little doubt that computer-assisted language learning (CALL) will continue to gain in importance in the coming years. A number of introductions to this area are now available: Davies and Higgins (1985) is an excellent first-level teacher's guide; Higgins and Johns (1984) is again a highly practical introduction, with many detailed examples of programs for the teaching of English as a foreign language; Kenning and Kenning (1983) gives a thorough grounding in the writing of CALL programs in BASIC; Ahmad *et al.* (1985) provides a rather more academic, but clear and comprehensive, treatment which includes an extended example from the teaching of German; Last (1984) includes accounts of the author's own progress and problems in the area; and Leech and Candlin (1986) and Fox (1986) contain a number of articles on various aspects of CALL.

CALL can offer substantial advantages over more traditional audio-visual technology, for both learners and teachers. Like the language laboratory workstation, the computer can offer access for students at times when teachers are not available, and can allow the student a choice of learning materials which can be used at his or her own pace. But unlike the tape-recorded lesson, a CALL session can offer interactive learning, with immediate assessment of the student's answers and a variety of error correction devices. The computer can thus provide a very concentrated one-to-one learning environment, with a high rate of feedback. Furthermore, within its limitations (which will be discussed below), a CALL program will give feedback which is objective, consistent and error-free. These factors, together with the novelty of working with the computer, and the competitive element which is built into many computer-based exercises, no doubt contribute substantially to the motivational effect which CALL programs seem to have on many learners. A computer program can also provide a great deal of flexibility: for instance, it is possible to construct programs which will automatically offer remedial back-up for areas in which the student makes errors, and also to offer the student a certain amount of choice in such matters as the level of difficulty of the learning task, the presentation format, and so on.

From the teacher's point of view, the computer's flexibility is again of paramount importance: CALL can offer a range of exercise types; it can be used as an 'electronic blackboard' for class use, or with groups or individual students; the materials can be modified to suit the needs of particular learners. The machine can also be programmed to store the scores of students on particular exercises, the times spent on each task, and the incorrect answers given by students. Such information not only enables the teacher to monitor students' progress, but also provides information which will aid in the improvement of the CALL program. Finally, the computer can free the teacher for other tasks, in two ways: firstly, groups or individual students can work at the computer on their own while the teacher works with other members of the class; and secondly, the computer can be used for those tasks which it performs best, leaving the teacher to deal with aspects where the machine is less useful.

Much of the CALL material which has been written so far is of the 'drill and practice' type. This is understandable, since drill programs are the easiest to write; it is also unfortunate, in that drills have become somewhat unfashionable in language teaching. However, to deny completely the relevance of such work, even in the general framework of a communicatively-orientated approach to language teaching and learning, would be to take an unjustifiably narrow view. There are certain types of grammatical and lexical skill, usually involving regular rules operating in a closed system, which do lend themselves to a drill approach, and for which the computer can provide the kind of intensive practice for which the teacher may not be able to find time. Furthermore, drills are not necessarily entirely mechanical exercises, but can be made meaningful through contextualisation.

Usually, CALL drills are written as quizzes, in which a task or question is selected and displayed on the screen, and the student is asked for an answer, which is then matched against a stored set of acceptable answers. The student is then given feedback on the success or failure of the answer, perhaps with some explanation, and his or her score updated if appropriate. A further task or question is then set, and the cycle repeats.

There are decisions to be made and problems to be solved by the programmer at each stage of a CALL drill: questions may be selected randomly from a database, or graded according to difficulty, or adjusted to the student's score; various devices (e.g. animation, colour) may be chosen to aid presentation of the question; the instructions to the student must be made absolutely clear; in matching the student's answer against the stored set of acceptable replies, the computer should be able to anticipate all the incorrect answers which may be given, and to simulate the ability of the human teacher to distinguish between errors which reflect real misunderstanding and those, such as spelling errors, which are more trivial; when the student makes an error, decisions must be made about whether (s)he will simply be given the right answer or asked to try again, whether information will be given about the error made, and whether the program should branch to a section providing further practice on that point. For examples of drill-type programs illustrating these points, readers are referred to the multiple-choice quiz on English prepositions discussed by Higgins and Johns (1984: 105–20), and the account by Ahmad *et al.* (1985: 64–76) of their GERAD program which trains students in the forms of the German adjective.

The increasing power of even the small, relatively cheap computers found in schools, and the development of new techniques in computing and linguistics, are now beginning to extend the scope of CALL far beyond the drill program. The computer's ability to produce static and moving images on the monitor screen can be used for demonstration purposes (for instance, animation is useful in illustrating changes in word order). The machine can also be used as a source of information about a language: the S-ENDING program discussed by Higgins and Johns allows students to test the computer's knowledge of spelling rules for the formation of English noun plurals and 3rd person singular verb forms: and several of the papers in Leech and Candlin (1986) discuss ways in which more advanced text analysis techniques could be used to provide resources for language learning. Also of considerable interest for language learning are simulation programs, in which the outcome of a situation (for instance, running the economy, fighting a fire, or searching for hidden treasure) depends on decisions taken by the student. Such activities may involve role play, and can be used to stimulate talk in the target language if organised on a group basis. Games can also be valuable, especially if constructed around language itself.

So far, we have discussed only the type of program in which the computer simply presents material which has been totally predetermined by the writer, except perhaps for a certain degree of randomness in, for instance, simulations. The computer can, however, also be used to generate exercises, and to do this in such a way that a different exercise is produced each time the program is run. One valuable generative use of the machine is in the scrambling of texts, in random or partially controlled ways, for presentation to the student, whose task is to reconstitute the original text. In a rather different type of exercise, TEXTBAG, which is a variant of the cloze technique, a text is reduced to just a series of dashes representing the letters in words, together with punctuation marks, and the student has to put back the words, either by guessing them or by 'buying' them and so depleting his or her stock of points. For details of these and other generative CALL programs see Higgins and Johns (1984: 53–62).

The potential of generative CALL programs could, of course, be increased considerably by incorporating an 'intelligent' element, such that the computer could 'understand' the language it received and/or generated. Recently, attempts have indeed been made to apply to CALL the artificial intelligence techniques used in the intelligent tutoring systems mentioned in section 4.5.4. A major problem is that most CALL activity so far has been directed towards the requirements of language teachers in schools, where the computers are normally somewhat restricted in their memory capacity. There are, however, indications that even within the limitations imposed by the hardware available, simple artificial intelligence techniques can profitably be used. Higgins's (1985, 1986) GRAMMARLAND programs, for example, create a micro-world on the screen (rather similar to Winograd's blocks world), which students can explore by asking questions and giving commands. Other examples include: Emanuelli's (1986) vocabulary trainer, which can learn the properties of new words and conduct a dialogue game in which it tries to guess what word the student is thinking of; Farrington's (1986) LITTRE, which acts as an intelligent tutor in French translation; drill-and-practice software developed by Bailin and Thomson (1988), which uses natural language processing techniques for instruction in English grammar; and a system developed by Last (1986), which learns about the structures of simple declarative German sentences, and can conduct a tutorial with the student, presenting sentences for translation, testing vocabulary, asking comprehension questions, and so on.

Clearly, the writing of even the simpler drill type of CALL program makes substantial demands on the programmer in terms of both expertise and time, and the creation of programs which incorporate artificial intelligence techniques is an even more difficult task. Some material is available commercially, but language teachers who are convinced of the potential of CALL often want to move beyond this to try out their own ideas, and there is a small but growing band of linguists who have taught themselves the required computational techniques. The most powerful tool in such a linguist's armoury is certainly a high level computer language, and since most CALL programs need to be implemented on fairly modest microcomputers the most popular language for this type of work is BASIC. The availability of introductions to BASIC concerned specifically with CALL applications (Kenning and Kenning 1983, Higgins and Johns 1984) should mean that more language teachers will have the courage to take up this challenge.

For those who do not wish to invest time and energy in learning a high level computer language, and subsequently in putting that knowledge to use in writing programs from scratch, it may be more appropriate to learn one of the **authoring languages** in which the instructions to the computer are constructed around the kinds of category (questions, acceptable answers, feedback, etc.) which are relevant to computer-assisted instruction. The most popular general purpose authoring languages for microcomputers are probably PILOT and MICROTEXT (for discussion and examples see Davies and Higgins 1985: 72–4). EXTOL (East Anglia and Essex Teaching Oriented Language) is an authoring language written specially for CALL applications (see Kenning and Kenning 1982).

For those who find even the simplified requirements of an authoring language rather daunting, a third possibility is available. *Authoring packages* or *authoring systems* present the user with menus of choices at each point in the development of a lesson, or simply require the typing of the CALL dialogue into frames, the construction of the CALL program itself being handled automatically. For reviews of available packages see Davies and Higgins (1985: 62–71) and Davies (1986).

In our discussion so far, it has been assumed that input to, and output from, a CALL program will be in typed form. We saw in section 4.5.5 that speech recognition is still a very hard task even for powerful computers; furthermore, although speech synthesis can now produce intelligible output, this is not of the quality we should expect as a model for the language learner. There are ways in which this disadvantage can be lessened: for instance, Tandberg have marketed a system, AECAL (Audio Enhanced Computer Assisted Learning) which allows control, by the computer program, of a tape recorder with high speed forward and backward winding, so facilitating the automation of, for example, dictation and aural comprehension exercises. It is likely that in the future the combination of computers with interactive video-discs will become increasingly important (see, for instance, Schneider and Bennion 1983, Heather 1987). As technological advances are made in these areas, and as techniques for speech synthesis and recognition become more refined, it is likely that the major obstacle of speech input and output in CALL will be at least partially removed. We should not, however, be misled by the present limitations into thinking that CALL is of little value in a teaching situation which increasingly emphasises the spoken language. The principal value of CALL is in doing the jobs it can already do well, so freeing the teacher for tasks, including those concerned specifically with spoken language, at which he or she overwhelmingly outperforms the computer, and is likely to do so for some time to come. Despite the fears of some, the computer is merely a useful adjunct, and not a replacement for human language teachers.

## 4.8 Computers as an aid in writing

An area which is related to CALL, but which also has much wider implications, is the use of computers to help in the process of writing. Word processing programs are available for a wide range of microcomputers, as well as for larger machines. Many are now of the type where the text is formatted on the screen as it will be in the finished product; some also incorporate facilities such as spelling checkers and word counters. Word processing software is extremely useful, not only to business and home computer users, but also to the language learner, in that it can lead to an improvement in general literacy skills, stimulate class discussion, and raise motivational levels by permitting the stepwise conversion of the student's own drafts into a polished final copy (see Piper 1986).

The new generation of writing aids can, however, offer far more than just text formatting, spelling checks and word counting, although they do at present require rather more powerful computers than the simpler word processing packages we are familiar with in our homes. For example, the WRITER'S WORKBENCH system developed at Bell Laboratories (Macdonald *et al.* 1982) consists of a suite of programs which explain certain rules of English punctuation and grammar, provide a glossary of frequently confused words, and carry out a number of analyses of the user's style, directing attention to awkward phrases, sexist language, split infinitives, word repetitions, the overuse of abstract terms, and so on. The system will also suggest alternative formulations. These programs have been modified and supplemented at Colorado State University, where they are used in the teaching of composition (Smith *et al.* 1984). Another system, CRITIQUE (Richardson, forthcoming), is claimed to achieve even more impressive results, by the incorporation of an advanced parsing routine.

Whereas WRITER'S WORKBENCH and CRITIQUE provide stylistic information on texts which have already been constructed, systems at present being developed focus on giving help during the actual process of writing, and make use of the latest techniques in artificial intelligence. Such systems will incorporate a model of what writers do when they construct texts, and will offer access to a number of modes of writing, such as developing a network of ideas, or jotting down notes, as well as producing a finished formatted version (see O'Malley and Sharples 1986).

For a recent discussion of possible explorations in the area of computers and writing, see Selfe and Wahlstrom (1988).

## 5. COMPUTERS AND LANGUAGE: AN INFLUENCE ON ALL

This review will, it is hoped, have shown that no serious student of language today can afford to ignore the immense impact made by the computer in a wide range of linguistic areas. Computational linguistics is of direct relevance to stylisticians, textual critics, translators, lexicographers and language teachers. But through the techniques of natural language processing which are being developed at an ever-increasing pace in the artificial intelligence community, and the refinement of methods for speech recognition and synthesis, the computational handling of language is beginning to make its influence felt far beyond these specific areas. Linguistic communication is without doubt one of the most important features of human life, and as we get better at inducing computers to simulate it, the effects on our everyday living are bound to multiply.

## REFERENCES

Aarts, J. and Meijs, W. (eds) (1984) *Corpus Linguistics: Recent Developments in the Use of Computer Corpora in English Language Research*, Rodopi, Amsterdam.

Aarts, J. and Meijs, W. (eds) (1986) *Corpus Linguistics II: New Studies in the Analysis and Exploitation of Computer Corpora*, Rodopi, Amsterdam.

Aarts, J. and van den Heuvel, T. (1984) 'Linguistic and computational aspects of corpus research', in Aarts and Meijs (eds) 1984: 83–94.

Aarts, J. and van den Heuvel, T. (1985) 'Computational tools for the syntactic analysis of corpora', *Linguistics*, 23: 303–35.

Adamson, R. (1977) 'The style of *L'Etranger*', *ALLC Bulletin*, 5: 233–6.

Adamson, R. (1979) 'The colour vocabulary of *L'Etranger*', *ALLC Bulletin*, 7: 221–30.

Ahmad, K., Corbett, G., Rogers, M. and Sussex, R. (1985) *Computers, Language Learning and Language Teaching*, Cambridge University Press, Cambridge.

Akkerman, E., Masereeuw, P. and Meijs, W.J. (1985) *Designing a Computerized Lexicon for Linguistic Purposes, ASCOT Report No. 1*, Rodopi, Amsterdam.

Akkerman, E., Meijs, W. and Voogt-van Zutphen, H. (1987) 'Grammatical tagging in ASCOT', in Meijs (ed.) 1987, 181–93.

Allen, J.F. and Perrault, C.R. (1980) 'Analyzing intention in utterances', *Artificial Intelligence*, 15: 143–78.

Allen, J., Hunnicutt, M.S. and Klatt, D., with Armstrong, R.C. and Pisoni, D.B. (1987) *From Text to Speech: The MITalk System*, Cambridge University Press, Cambridge.

Altenberg, B. (1986) 'Speech segmentation in a scripted monolgoue', *ICAME News*, 10: 37–8.

Altenberg, B. (1987) 'Predicting text segmentation into tone units' in Meijs (ed.) 1987, 49–60.

Amsler, R.A. (1984) 'Machine-readable dictionaries', in Williams, M.E. (ed.) 1984, *Annual Review of Information Science and Technology*, 19: 161–209.

Arnold, D. and des Tombe, L. (1987) 'Basic theory and methodology in EUROTRA', in Nirenburg (ed.) 1987, 114–35.

Atwell, E. (1983) 'Constitutent-likelihood grammar', *ICAME News*, 7: 34–67.

Atwell, E. (1987) 'Constituent-likelihood grammar', in Garside, Leech and Sampson (eds) 1987, 57–65.

Bailin, A. and Thomson, P. (1988) 'The use of natural language processing in computer-aided language instruction', *Computers and the Humanities*, 22: 99–110.

Barr, A. and Feigenbaum, E.A. (eds) (1981) *The Handbook of Artificial Intelligence*, Vol. I, William Kaufmann Inc., Los Altos, California.

Barr, A. and Feigenbaum, E.A. (eds) (1982) *The Handbook of Artificial Intelligence*, Vol. II, William Kaufmann Inc., Los Altos, California.

Birch, D. (1985) 'The stylistic analysis of large corpora of literary texts', *ALLC Journal*, 6: 33–8.

Black, W.J. (1986) *Intelligent Knowledge-Based Systems*, van Nostrand Reinhold, Wokingham.

Brandon, F.R. (1985) 'Microcomputer software tools for a bilingual dictionary and an automatic bilingual dictionary', *ALLC Journal*, 6: 11–13.

Burrows, J.F. (1986) 'Modal verbs and moral principles: an aspect of Jane Austen's style', *Literary and Linguistic Computing*, 1: 9–23.

Burrows, J.F. (1987) *Computation into Criticism: A Study of Jane Austen's Novels and an Experiment in Method*, Clarendon Press, Oxford.

Burton, R. (1976) *Semantic Grammar: An Engineering Technique for Constructing Natural Language Understanding Systems*, BBN Report no. 3453, Bolt Beranek and Newman, Cambridge, Mass.

Butler, C.S. (1974) 'German for chemists', *CILT Reports and Papers 11*, CILT, London: 50–3.

Butler, C.S. (1979) 'Poetry and the computer: some quantitative aspects of the style of Sylvia Plath', *Proceedings of the British Academy*, LXV: 291–312.

Butler, C.S. (1985a) *Computers in Linguistics*, Blackwell, Oxford.

Butler, C.S. (1985b) *Statistics in Linguistics*, Blackwell, Oxford.

Butler, C.S. (1985c) *Systemic Linguistics: Theory and Applications*, Batsford, London.

Cameron, A. (1977) 'The Dictionary of Old English and the computer', in Lusignan, S. and North, J.S. (eds) 1977 *Computing in the Humanities*, University of Waterloo Press, Waterloo, Ontario: 101–6.

Cater, J.P. (1983) *Electronically Speaking: Computer Speech Generation*, Howard W. Sams, Indianapolis.

Cercone, N. and Murchison, C. (1985) 'Integrating Artificial Intelligence into literary research: an invitation to discuss design specifications', *Computers and the Humanities*, 19: 235–43.

Chomsky, N. (1965) *Aspects of the Theory of Syntax*, MIT Press, Cambridge, Mass.

Clear, J. (1987) 'Computing', in Sinclair (ed.) 1987, 41–61.

Clocksin, W.F. (1984) 'An introduction to PROLOG', in O'Shea and Eisenstadt (eds) 1984: 1–21.

Cohen, P.R. and Feigenbaum, E.A. (eds) (1983) *The Handbook of Artificial Intelligence*, Vol. III, William Kaufmann, Inc., Los Altos, California.

Cole, P. and Morgan, J.L. (eds) (1975) *Syntax and Semantics Vol. 3: Speech Acts*, Academic Press, New York.

Danlos, L. (1987) *The Linguistic Basis of Text Generation*, Cambridge University Press, Cambridge.

Davey, A. (1978) *Discourse Production*, Edinburgh University Press, Edinburgh.

Davies, G. (1986) 'Authoring CALL software', in Leech and Candlin (eds) 1986: 12–29.

Davies, G. and Higgins, J. (1985) *Using Computers in Language Learning: A Teacher's Guide*. 2nd edn, CILT, London.

de Roeck, A. (1983) 'An underview of parsing', in King (ed.) 1983: 3–17.

de Tollenaere, F. (1973) 'The problem of context in computer-aided lexicography', in Aitken, A.J., Bailey, R.W. and Hamilton-Smith, N. (eds) 1973 *The Computer and Literary Studies*, Edinburgh University Press, Edinburgh: 25–35.

Dowty, D.R., Karttunen, L. and Zwicky, A.M. (eds) (1985) *Natural Language Parsing: Psychological, Computational and Theoretical Perspectives*, Cambridge University Press, Cambridge.

Eeg-Olofsson, M. (1987) 'Assigning new types to old texts – an experiment in automatic word class tagging', in Meijs (ed) 1987, 45–7.

Eeg-Olofsson, M. and Svartvik, J. (1984) 'Four-level tagging of spoken English', in Aarts and Meijs (eds) 1984: 53–64.

Emanuelli, A.J. (1986) 'Artificial intelligence and computer assisted language learning', in Fox (ed.) 1986: 43–56.

Enkvist, N.E. (1964) 'On defining style: an essay in applied linguistics', in Spencer, J. (ed.) *Linguistics and Style*, Oxford University Press, London: 1–56.

Farrington, B. (1986) 'LITTRE: an expert system for checking translation at sentence level', in Fox (ed.) 1986: 57–74.

Fox, J. (1986) *Computer Assisted Language Learning*, special issue of *UEA Papers in Linguistics*, University of East Anglia, Norwich.

Frude, N. (1987) *A Guide to SPSS/PC+*, Macmillan, London.

Garside, R. (1987) 'The CLAWS work-tagging system', in Garside, Leech and Sampson (eds) 1987: 30–41.

Garside, R. and Leech, G. (1982) 'Grammatical tagging of the LOB Corpus: general survey', in Johansson, S. (ed.) 1982: 110–17.

Garside, R., Leech, G. and Sampson, G. (eds) (1987) *The Computational Analysis of English: A Corpus-based Approach*, Longman, London and New York.

Gazdar, G., Klein, E., Pullum, G.K. and Sag, I. (1985) *Generalised Phrase Structure Grammar*, Blackwell, Oxford.

Gazdar, G. and Mellish, C. (1987) 'Computational Linguistics', in Lyons, J., Coates, R., Deuchar, M. and Gazdar, G. (eds) *New Horizons in Linguistics, 2*, Penguin, Harmondsworth, 1987: 225–48.

Goetschalckx, J. and Rolling, L. (eds) (1982) *Lexicography in the Electronic Age*, Proceedings of a symposium held in Luxembourg, 7–9 July, 1981, North Holland, Amsterdam.

Grice, H.P. (1975) 'Logic and conversation', in Cole and Morgan (eds) 1975: 41–58.

Grishman, R. (1986) *Computational Linguistics: An Introduction*, Cambridge University Press, Cambridge.

Griswold, R.E. and Griswold, M.T. (1983) *The Icon Programming Language*, Prentice-Hall, Englewood Cliffs, NJ.

Grosz, B.J. (1977) *The Representation and Use of Focus in Dialogue Understanding*, Technical Note 151, Stanford Research Institute, Menlo Park, California.

Harris, M.D. (1985) *Introduction to Natural Language Processing*, Reston Publishing Company, Reston, Virginia.

Hasemer, T. (1984) 'An introduction to LISP', in O'Shea and Eisenstadt (eds) 1984: 22–62.

Heather, N. (1987) 'New technological aids for CAL', in Rahtz, S. (ed.) *Information Technology in the Humanities: Tools, Techniques and Applications*, Ellis Horwood Ltd, Chichester.

Hidley, G.R. (1986) 'Some thoughts concerning the application of software tools in support of Old English poetic studies', *Literary and Linguistic Computing*, 1: 156–62.

Higgins, J. (1985) 'GRAMMARLAND: a non-directive use of the computer in language learning', *ELT Journal*, 39/3: 167–73.

Higgins, J. (1986) 'The GRAMMARLAND parser: a progress report', in Fox (ed.) 1986: 105–15.

Higgins, J. and Johns, T. (1984) *Computers in Language Learning*, Collins ELT, London and Glasgow.

Hockey, S.M. (1980) *A Guide to Computer Applications in the Humanities*, Duckworth, London.

Hockey, S. (1985) *SNOBOL Programming for the Humanities*, Clarendon Press, Oxford.

Hockey, S. (1986) 'OCR: The Kurzweill Data Entry Machine', *Literary and Linguistic Computing*, 1: 63–7.

Hockey, S. and Marriott, I. (1980) *Oxford Concordance Program: Users' Manual*, Oxford University Computing Service, Oxford.

Hunt, R. and Shelley, J. (1983) *Computers and Commonsense*, 3rd ed., Prentice-Hall International, London.

Hutchins, W.J. (1986) *Machine Translation: Past, Present, Future*, Ellis Horwood, Chichester.

Irigoin, J. and Zarri, G.P. (1979) *La Pratique des Ordinateurs dans la Critique des Textes*, Colloques Internationaux du Centre National de la Recherche Scientifique, No. 579, Paris, 29–31 mars 1978, Editions du Centre National de la Recherche Scientifique, Paris.

Jackson, P. (1986) *Introduction to Expert Systems*, Addison-Wesley, Wokingham.

Jaynes, J.T. (1980) 'A search for trends in the poetic style of W.B. Yeats', *ALLC Journal*, 1: 11–18.

Johansson, S. (1980) 'The LOB Corpus of British English texts; presentation and comments', *ALLC Journal*, 1: 25–36.

Johansson, S, (ed.) (1982) *Computer corpora in English Language Research*, Norwegian Computing Centre for the Humanities, Bergen.

Kenning, M.J. and Kenning, M.-M. (1982) 'EXTOL: an approach to computer assisted language teaching', *ALLC Bulletin*, 10: 8–18.

Kenning, M.J. and Kenning, M.-M. (1983) *An Introduction to Computer Assisted Language Teaching*, Oxford University Press, Oxford.

King, M. (ed.) (1983) *Parsing Natural Language*, Academic Press, London.

Kipfer, B.A. (1982) 'Computer applications in lexicography: a bibliography', *Dictionnaires*, 4: 202–37.

Kjetsaa, G., Gustavsson, S., Beckman, B. and Gil, S. (1984) *The Authorship of 'The Quiet Don'*, Solum Forlag A.S., Oslo/Humanities Pres, NJ.

Knowles, G. (1986) 'The role of the computer in the teaching of phonetics', in Leech and Candlin (eds) 1986: 133–48.

663

Knowles, G. and Taylor, L. (1986) 'Automatic intonation assignment', *ICAME News*, 10: 18–19.

Kučera, H. and Francis, W.N. (1967) *Computational Analysis of Present-Day American English*, Brown University Press, Providence, RI.

Last, R. (1984) *Language Teaching and the Microcomputer*, Blackwell, Oxford.

Last, R. (1986) 'The potential of Artificial Intelligence-related CALL at the sentence level', *Literary and Linguistic Computing*, 1: 197–201.

Lea, W. (ed.) (1980) *Trends in Speech Recognition*, Prentice-Hall, Englewood Cliffs, NJ.

Leech, G.N. and Candlin, C.N. (eds) (1986) *Computers in English Language Teaching and Research*, Longman, London.

Leech, G., Garside, R. and Atwell, E. (1983) 'Recent developments in the use of computer corpora in English language research', *Transactions of the Philological Society*: 32–40.

Leech, G.N. and Short, M.H. (1981) *Style in Fiction: A Linguistic Introduction to English Fictional Prose*, Longman, London.

Lehnert, W.G. (1982) 'Plot units: a narrative summarization strategy', in Lehnert, W.G. and Ringle, M.H. (eds) *Strategies in Natural Language Processing*, Lawrence Erlbaum Associates, Hillsdale, NJ.

Levinson, S.E. and Libermann, M.Y. (1981) 'Speech recognition by computer', *Scientific American*, 244/4: 40–52.

Lewis, D. (1985) 'The development and progress of machine translation systems', *ALLC Journal*, 5: 40–52.

Logan, H.M. (1976) 'The computer and the sound texture of poetry', *Language and Style*, 9: 260–79.

Logan, H.M. (1982) 'The computer and metrical scansion', *ALLC Journal*, 3: 9–14.

Logan, H.M. (1985) 'Most by numbers judge a poet's song: measuring sound effects in poetry', *Computers and the Humanities*, 19: 213–20.

Macdonald, N.H., Frase, L.T., Gingrich, P. and Keenan, S.A. (1982) 'The WRITER'S WORKBENCH: computer aids for text analysis', *IEEE Transactions on Communication* (Special Issue on Communication in the Automated Office), 30: 105–10.

McKeown, K.R. (1985) *Text Generation: Using Discourse Strategies and Focus Constraints to Generate Natural Language Text*, Cambridge University Press, Cambridge.

McTear, M. (1987) *The Articulate Computer*, Blackwell, Oxford.

Mann, W.C. (1985) 'An introduction to the Nigel text generation grammar', in Benson, J.D. and Greaves, W.S. (eds) *Systemic Perspectives on Discourse, Volume I: Selected Theoretical Papers from the 9th International Systemic Workshop*, Ablex Publishing Corporation, Norwood, NJ: 84–95.

Martin, W.J.R., Al, B.P.F. and van Sterkenburg, P.J.G. (1983) 'On the processing of a text corpus', in Hartmann, R.R.K. (ed.) 1983, *Lexicography: Principle and Practice*, Academic Press, London and New York: 77–87.

Martindale, C. (1984) 'Evolutionary trends in poetic style: the case of English metaphysical poetry', *Computers and the Humanities*, 18: 3–21.

Meijs, W. (1985) 'Lexical organization from three different angles', *ALLC Journal*, 6: 1–10.

Meijs, W. (1986) 'Links in the lexicon: the dictionary as a corpus', *ICAME News*, 10: 26–8.

Meijs, W. (ed.) (1987) *Corpus Linguistics and Beyond: Proceedings of the Seventh International*

Conference on English Language Research on Computerized Corpora, Rodopi, Amsterdam.

Merriam, T. (1986) 'The authorship controversy of Sir Thomas More: Smith on Morton', *Literary and Linguistic Computing*, 1: 104–8.

Merriam, T. (1987) 'An investigation of Morton's method: a reply', *Computers and the Humanities*, 21: 57–8.

Minsky, M. (1975) 'A framework for representing knowledge', in Winston, P. (ed.) 1975, *The Psychology of Computer Vision*, McGraw-Hill, New York.

Mitton, R. (1986) 'A partial dictionary of English in computer-usable form', *Literary and Linguistic Computing*, 1: 214–5.

Moon, R. (1987) 'The analysis of meaning', in Sinclair (ed.) 1987, 86–103.

Morton, A.Q. (1965) 'The authorship of Greek prose', *Journal of the Royal Statistical Society, Series A*, 128: 169–224.

Morton, A.Q. (1978) *Literary Detection: How to Prove Authorship and Fraud in Literature and Documents*, Bowker, New York.

Morton, A.Q. (1986) 'Once. A test of authorship based on words which are not repeated in the sample', *Literary and Linguistic Computing*, 1: 1–8.

Mosteller, F. and Wallace, D.L. (1964) *Inference and Disputed Authorship: The Federalist*, Addison-Wesley, Reading, Mass.

Nirenburg, S. (ed.) (1987) *Machine Translation: Theoretical and Methodological Issues*, Cambridge University Press, Cambridge.

Norušis, M.J. (1982) *SPSS Introductory Guide: Basic Statistics and Operations*, McGraw-Hill, New York.

Oakman, R.L. (1980) *Computer Methods for Literary Research*, University of S. Carolina Press, Columbia, SC.

O'Malley, C. and Sharples, M. (1986) 'Tools for arrangement and support of multiple constraints in a writer's assistant', in Harrison, M.D. and Monk. A.F. (eds) 1986 *People and Computers: Designing for Usability*, Proceedings of the 2nd Conference of the British Computer Society Human Computer Interaction Specialist Group, University of York, 23–26 September 1986, Cambridge University Press, Cambridge: 115–31.

O'Shea, T. and Eisenstadt, M. (eds) (1984) *Artificial Intelligence: Tools, Techniques and Applications*, Harper & Row, New York.

O'Shea, T. and Self, J. (1983) *Learning and Teaching with Computers: Artificial Intelligence in Education*, Harvester Press, Brighton.

Ott, W. (1974) 'Bibliographie: Computer in der Editionstechnik', *ALLC Bulletin*, 2: 73–80.

Paikeday, T.M. (1985) 'Text analysis by microcomputer', *ALLC Journal*, 6: 29–32.

Patten, T. (1988) *Systemic Text Generation as Problem Solving*, Cambridge University Press, Cambridge.

Phillips, J.D. and Thompson, H.S. (1985) 'GPSGP – a parser for generalized phrase structure grammars', *Linguistics*, 23: 245–61.

Piper, A. (1986) 'Computers and the literacy of the foreign language learner: a report on EFL learners using the word-processor to develop writing skills', in Fox (ed.) 1986: 145–61.

Potter, R.G. (1988) 'Literary criticism and literary computing: the difficulties of a synthesis', *Computers and the Humanities* 22, 91–97.

Quirk, R. and Svartvik, J. (1978) 'A corpus of Modern English', in Bergenholtz, H. and

Schaeder, B. (eds) 1978, *Empirische Textwissenschaft: Aufbau und Auswertung von Text-Corpora*, Scriptor Verlag, Königstein: 204–18.

Reed, A. (1977) 'CLOC: A Collocation Package', *ALLC Bulletin*, 5: 168–83.

Reilly, R. (1986) *Communication Failure in Dialogue and Discourse*, North-Holland, Amsterdam.

Renouf, A. (1984) 'Corpus development at Birmingham University', in Aarts and Meijs (eds) 1984: 3–39.

Renouf, A. (1987) 'Corpus development', in Sinclair (ed.) 1987, 1–40.

Rich, E. (1983) *Artificial Intelligence*, McGraw-Hill, Auckland and London.

Richardson, S.D. (forthcoming) 'Enhanced text critiquing using a natural language parser', to appear in Jones, R.L. (ed.) *Computing in the Humanities* 7, Paradigm Press, Osprey, Florida.

Ritchie, G. and Thompson, H. (1984) 'Natural language processing', in O'Shea and Eisenstadt (eds) 1984: 358–88.

Ross, D. Jr and Rasche, R.H. (1972) 'EYEBALL: a computer program for description of style', *Computers and the Humanities*, 6: 213–21.

Ryan, T.A. Jr., Joiner, B.L. and Ryan, B.F. (1976) *Minitab Student Handbook*, Duxbury Press, Boston, Mass.

Sager, N. (1978) 'Natural language information formatting: the automatic conversion of texts to a structured data base', in Yovits, M.C. (ed.) 1978, *Advances in Computers* 17, Academic Press, New York.

Sampson, G.R. (1983a) 'Deterministic parsing', in King (ed.) 1983: 91–116.

Sampson, G.R. (1983b) 'Context free parsing and the adequacy of context-free grammars', in Kind (ed.) 1983: 151–70.

Schank, R.C. (1972) 'Conceptual dependency: a theory of natural language understanding', *Cognitive Psychology*, 3/4: 552–630.

Schank, R.C. and Abelson, R.P. (1975) 'Scripts, plans and knowledge', in *Proceedings of the Fourth Joint International Conference on Artificial Intelligence*, Tbilisi: 151–7.

Schank, R.C. and Abelson, R.P. (1977) *Scripts, Plans, Goals and Understanding*, Lawrence Erlbaum Associates, Hillsdale, NJ.

Schneider, E.W. and Bennion, J.L. (1983) 'Veni, vidi, vici via videodisc: a simulator for instructional conversations', *System*, 11: 41–6.

Sclater, N. (1983) *Introduction to Electronic Speech Synthesis*, Howard W. Sams, Indianapolis.

Searle, J.R. (1975) 'Indirect speech acts', in Cole and Morgan (eds) 1975: 59–82.

Sedelow, S.Y. (1985) 'Computational lexicography', *Computers and the Humanities*, 19: 97–101.

Selfe, C.L. and Wahlstrom, B.J. (1988) 'Computers and writing: casting a broader net with theory and research', *Computers and the Humanities*, 22: 57–66.

Sidner, C.J. (1983) 'Focusing in the comprehension of definite anaphora', in Brady and Berwick (eds) 1983, *Computational Models of Discourse*, MIT Press, Cambridge, Mass: 267–330.

Sinclair, J. McH. (1985) 'Lexicographic evidence', in Ilson, R. (ed.) 1985, *Dictionaries, Lexicography and Language Learning*, ELT Documents 120, Pergamon Press, Oxford: 81–94.

Sinclair, J. McH. (ed.) (1987) *Looking Up: An Account of the COBUILD project in Lexical Computing*, London and Glasgow: Collins ELT.

Sleeman, D. and Brown, J.S. (eds) (1982) *Intelligent Tutoring Systems*, Academic Press, New York.

Smith, C.R., Kiefer, K.E. and Gingrich, P.S. (1984) 'Computers come of age in writing instruction', *Computers and the Humanities*, 18: 215–24.

Smith, M.W.A. (1983) 'Recent experience and new developments of methods for the determination of authorship', *ALLC Bulletin*, 11: 73–82.

Smith, M.W.A. (1986) 'The authorship controversy of Sir Thomas More: an analysis of the arguments', *Literary and Linguistic Computing*, 1: 106–8.

Sparck Jones, K. and Wilks, Y. (eds) (1983) *Automatic Natural Language Parsing*, reprinted 1985, Ellis Horwood, Chichester.

Stenström, A.-B. (1986) 'Pauses in discourse and syntax', *ICAME News*, 10: 39.

Svartvik, J. (1987) 'Taking a new look at word class tags', in Meijs (ed.) 1987: 33–43.

Svartvik, J. and Eeg-Olofsson, M. (1982) 'Tagging the London-Lund corpus of spoken English', in Johansson, S. (ed.) 1982: 85–109.

Svartvik, J. and Quirk, R. (eds) (1980) *A Corpus of English Conversation*, Lund Studies in English 56, Gleerup/Liber, Lund.

Tallentire, D.R. (1976) 'Confirming intuitions about style, using concordances', in Jones, A. and Churchhouse, R.F. (eds) 1976, *The Computer in Literary and Linguistic Studies: Proceedings of the Third International Symposium*, University of Wales Press, Cardiff: 309–38.

Ule, L. (1983) 'Recent progress in computer methods of authorship determination', *ALLC Bulletin*, 10: 73–89.

Weiner, E. (1985) 'The New Oxford English Dictionary', *ALLC Bulletin*, 13: 8–10.

Weizenbaum, J. (1966) 'ELIZA – a computer program for the study of natural language communication between man and machine', *Communications of the Association for Computing Machinery*, 9: 36–45.

Wilks, Y. (1975) 'Preference semantics', in Keenan, E.L. (ed.) 1975, *Formal Semantics of Natural Language*, Cambridge University Press, Cambridge: 329–48.

Winograd, T. (1972) *Understanding Natural Language*, Academic Press, New York.

Winograd, T. (1983) *Language as a Cognitive Process, Vol. 1: Syntax*, Addison-Wesley, Reading, Mass.

Witten, I.H. (1982) *Principles of Computer Speech*, Academic Press, London.

Woods, A., Fletcher, P. and Hughes, A. (1986) *Statistics in Language Studies*, Cambridge University Press, Cambridge.

Woods, W.A. (1970) 'Transition network grammars for natural language analysis', *Comunications of the Association for Computing Machinery*, 13: 591–606.

Woods, W.A. *et al.* (1976) *Speech Understanding Systems* – Final Report, Vol. IV, Technical report no. 2378, Bolt Beranek and Newman, Cambridge, Mass.

PART C

---

# SPECIAL ASPECTS OF LANGUAGE

# 19

# LANGUAGE AS WORDS: LEXICOGRAPHY

## A.P. COWIE

## 1. HISTORY OF THE ENGLISH DICTIONARY

The past decade has seen a meteoric rise in the production of new dictionaries in Britain, accompanied by substantial if less spectacular progress in France and Germany (Stein 1979, Hausmann 1985). The phenomenon is remarkable not only for the number of new dictionaries published but also for their diversity and quality. Certainly in the case of English, growth has been greatly stimulated by its position as the leading language of international communication (Benson, Benson and Ilson 1986), and the opportunities of an expanding overseas market have sharpened competition between major publishers (Cowie 1981a). To some extent, however, the appeal of the dictionary remains traditional and emblematic. 'The Dictionary' shares with 'the Bible' the grammatical distinction of the definite article; both occupy space on the same shelf in the home; both are turned to as repositories of truth and wisdom (Quirk 1973, McDavid 1979). The recent surge of buying is at least partly explained by the assumed soundness and authority of dictionaries as compared with much present-day language teaching in schools (Hausmann 1985).

However, it is chastening to recall that in England the dictionary has evolved in a slow and largely unsystematic way over the past twelve centuries; that it has developed largely by a process of accretion; that, before about 1750, no theoretical basis existed for lexicographical practice; that for long periods plagiarism was commonplace and hardly remarked upon (Starnes and Noyes 1946).

The elaborate compilations of today evolved by stages from simple beginnings. From before the Norman Conquest (in the seventh and eighth centuries) the practice had developed in religious communities of inserting in Latin manuscripts, in a smaller hand, 'glosses' of difficult words, first in easier Latin, and later in the vernacular. The next stage, still in pre-Conquest times, was to write out a list of the difficult terms and their English equivalents. The resulting glossary (Latin *glossarium*) was a primitive forerunner of the modern bilingual dictionary. The custom also arose early of appending to the MSS lists which were specialised in subject matter (they might, for example, consist of medical terms). These were also copied out, and a collection constituted a *vocabularium* (vocabulary). This form of classification was the forerunner of the technical dictionary (Osselton 1983). Both types of list met the practical needs of the teacher as well as the scholar: Latin vocabulary was acquired by committing to memory lists of words with their meanings in the mother tongue. Ease of reference to the glossary was later improved by gathering together all words beginning with the same letter ('first-letter order'). The process was carried a stage further by picking out *A*-words beginning with *Aa*-, then those in *Ab*-, etc., to *Az*- ('second-letter order'). Four Old English glossaries of the eighth and ninth centuries preserved in European libraries reflect the development from unordered to second-letter listing, a process which was to lead in time to the fully alphabetical arrangement which is now standard (Meyer 1979). The pre-Conquest glossaries also reflect the growing use of Old English as the glossing language: by the tenth and eleventh centuries they are truly Latin-English.

The primary purpose of these works was of course the elucidation of Latin. Over three centuries were to pass before the compilation of a vocabulary which could serve as an aid to writing. This was the *Promptorium Parvulorum, sive Clericorum* ('Storeroom, or Repository, for Children and Clerics'), the work of Geoffrey the Grammarian, which first appeared about 1440, was printed in 1499, and contained about 12,000 entries with their Latin equivalents (Starnes and Noyes 1946). *Promptorium* was one of a variety of titles used by fifteenth and sixteenth-century compilers (other picturesque examples were *Ortus Vocabulorum*, or 'Garden of Vocables' and *Alvearie*, or 'Beehive'), and indicates the slowness with which the term dictionary came into general use. Although *dictionarius* (literally, a collection of 'dictiones', or sayings) was applied as early as 1225 to a list of Latin words, Sir Thomas Elyot's Latin-English *Dictionary* of 1538 was the first compilation of note to adopt the title. Also evident from bilingual publications within this time-span is the emergence of working methods which were to survive the birth of the monolingual dictionary. In arriving, for example, at an ordered list of English words for the *Abecedarium Anglico-Latinum* of 1552, Richard Howlet (or Huloet) reversed and reordered the entries of an existing Latin-English dictionary (Osselton 1983).

We find, too, that 'dictionary' is not reserved for works with an alphabetical listing of entries. John Withals's *Shorte Dictionarie for Yonge Begynners* of 1553, for instance, the most popular English-Latin work of the sixteenth century, has a topical arrangement (Stein 1986).

Latin was the essential element in all these compilations, either as 'source' or 'target' language. Production of bilingual dictionaries of a modern European language became possible, and desirable, when Latin no longer functioned as the chief means of international communication. The first significant step in this new direction was taken by John Palsgrave, tutor to Mary Tudor, wife of Louis XII. For her, Palsgrave compiled the English-French *Lesclarcissement de la Langue Françoyse* published in 1530. This dealt with pronunciation and grammar as well as vocabulary, and was the earliest dictionary of a modern foreign language compiled in either French or English (Stein 1986). After French, the most significant languages were Spanish and Italian, both for political and trading contacts and as the vehicles of major literatures. Richard Percyvall's Spanish-English *Bibliotheca Hispanica* appeared in 1591, to be followed in 1598 by John Florio's Italian-English *A Worlde of Wordes*, which marked a step forward in another sense. Florio's dictionary included quotations from contemporary Italian authors, thus pre-figuring developments in English lexicography a century and a half later (Frantz 1979). Another merit of Florio's work, and of the French-English dictionary compiled by his contemporary Randall Cotgrave, was the light thrown by their racy English vocabulary – in the absence of any English monolingual dictionary – on the language of Shakespeare (J. Murray 1900).

Towards the end of the sixteenth century, the mounting influx into English of foreign words, and especially of learned borrowings from Greek and Latin – often stigmatised as 'inkhornisms' or 'ink-horn terms' – led schoolmasters such as William Bullokar and Richard Mulcaster to consider the possibility of compiling an English dictionary (Starnes and Noyes 1946). Though there were various transitional works which combined an English list of difficult words with a grammar, the first dictionary in the strict sense was Robert Cawdrey's *A Table Alphabeticall . . . of Hard Usuall English Words* (1604). This compilation was modest enough: it dealt with the spelling and meaning of only about 2,500 terms, of which just under half were copied from Thomas Thomas's Latin-English dictionary of 1587 (Starnes and Noyes 1946). A more substantial work was *The English Dictionarie* of Henry Cockeram (1623), which had separate parts devoted to difficult words and ordinary words. The latter were 'explained' by their hard equivalents – an ingenious method of teaching a learned style. Following the now common practice, Cockeram borrowed heavily from his immediate forerunners and from Thomas (Riddell 1979). The plagiarism was more flagrant in the case of Edward Phillips, whose *New World of English Words* (1658) was greatly dependent on Thomas Blount's

*Glossographia* of 1656, and whose unscrupulous and slipshod methods drew an enraged rebuke from Blount. Like Cockeram, Blount anglicised many Latin words, with the result that a number found their way into later dictionaries and into wider use. Then too, the use of English translations from bilingual dictionaries to pad out word-lists led to the inclusion of many self-explanatory compounds (such as *bread basket*) (Osselton 1983).

Monolingual dictionaries to this point were concerned simply with hard words; the next step was to attempt coverage of the entire vocabulary. In 1665, a committee of the Royal Society set up 'for improving the English language' considered a proposal from the diarist John Evelyn for: 'a Lexicon or Collection of all the pure English Words by themselves', to be gathered in several dictionaries, all to be compiled from actual usage (Riddell 1979, Read 1986). *A New English Dictionary*, published in 1702, and reputedly compiled by John Kersey, was the first to attempt systematic coverage of all English words, though it sought to reject anglicised words not in use, and specialist terms. Kersey's intention was to reach a public which included 'young Beginners and unlearned Persons' (quoted by Starnes and Noyes 1946), a concern which also marked an important shift of emphasis. Nathan Bailey's *Universal Etymological English Dictionary* of 1721, had, as its title suggests, a different fundamental aim. It set out to include all words, not for the sake of completeness itself (it provided the briefest definitions of common words) but for the purpose of explaining derivation. The *Universal* contained cant terms, proverbs and dialect words, and in its 1740 edition was the first dictionary to mark stress position, as for example in the words *descend'*, *descri'be*, *frac'tion* (Landau 1984). Bailey was a major figure of far-reaching influence. In 1730, he published a great folio dictionary, the *Dictionarium Britannicum*, which was to form the working basis of the outstanding lexicographical achievement of the century, the dictionary of Dr Samuel Johnson.

By the middle of the eighteenth century, the tide was running strongly against change and experimentation in language. The need for regulation and clear standards, among men of letters and the socially insecure alike, led to a growth of interest in the normative dictionary, one which, by providing examples from the best authors, might fix the language in its present form and serve as a model for speech and writing. It was now that the dictionary took on the function as a guide to 'correct' usage it is still popularly thought to possess (Osselton 1983). Ideas of compilation were put to Pope, who is said to have drawn up a list of suitable authors (Read 1986); but the first successful initiative was an approach to Samuel Johnson, leading to the signing of a contract with a group of London publishers in 1746, and the drawing up of a *Plan* in the following year. Work was intended to take three years, but Johnson's monumental *Dictionary of the English Language* did not appear until 1755. The 'chief intent' as set out in the *Plan* was to 'preserve the purity . . . of our English idiom', though by the time of publication, eight years later, Johnson seems to have realised that stabilisation of the language was not an attainable goal (Landau 1984). As regards the models chosen to fulfil this aim, the work had a narrowly defined authorial base, reflecting the strong literary preferences of its editor. Thus one third of all quotations came from four authors: Shakespeare, Dryden, Milton and Addison (Osselton 1983). Johnson's editorial methods reveal a degree of scrupulousness which sets him apart from most of his predecessors. Thus, only when he had no quotations did he insert examples from Bailey's dictionary (acknowledged by the use of the label *Dict.*). At the same time, many of the illustrative quotations were supplied from the editor's copious memory; some inaccuracies were thus inevitable.

There is evidence in the *Plan* that Johnson had the historical outlook, though it is now possible to show how far his actual achievement lacked historical fullness and objectivity (Read 1986). The use of quotations is of course no guarantee of a historical treatment: they should be drawn from all sources, without discrimination. After Johnson, lexicographers moved by stages towards this ideal. Priestley was an eighteenth-century herald of the scientific and historical spirit of the nineteenth: he championed the supremacy of usage for determining standards of language (Read 1986). Charles Richardson's *New Dictionary of the English Language*, of 1837, was also significant in foreshadowing the large-scale gathering of quotations that was the essential groundwork to compilation of the *Oxford English Dictionary* (Landau 1984).

Yet much of the inspiration for a major new dictionary on historical lines came from the Continent. In 1812, the German philologist Franz Passow set out the principles by which he believed the new lexicography should be guided. Its aim, he believed, should be to show the origin and successive changes of form and meaning of every word by means of citations arranged in chronological order (K. Murray 1977, Read 1986). The initiative to launch a project along these lines in England was taken by Richard Chevenix Trench, in a paper presented to the Philological Society in 1857. The original intention was to publish a supplement to existing works, but soon this was abandoned and the more ambitious scheme proposed of compiling an entirely new historical dictionary. The plan was to record all words that had been in the language since the middle of the twelfth century, to provide a full perspective of their changing forms and meanings, and to fix as accurately as possible the point of entry of new words and the point of departure of obsolete ones. All this was to be achieved by means of quotations (Merkin 1983). This extraordinarily demanding scheme called not only for a systematic reading programme (undertaken by voluntary helpers), but also for a chief editor of exceptional intellectual powers and moral and physical resilience. This the *Oxford English*

*Dictionary* found in James Murray, 'a lexicographer greater by far than Dr Johnson . . . and greater perhaps than any lexicographer of his own time or since in Britain, the United States or Europe' (Burchfield 1977; ix).

Murray's prodigious achievement (in its completed form the Dictionary was to contain over 400,000 entries and almost two million illustrative quotations) was also a monument to Victorian scholarship, industry and taste. It was the model for several period and regional dictionaries of English, including dictionaries of American and Canadian English, and inspired similar enterprises in other European countries (Merkin 1983). It also gave rise to a series of abridged dictionaries intended for the general reader, of which the best known, the *Concise Oxford Dictionary* (*COD*) appeared before the completion of *OED* itself.

*OED* reflected the overwhelmingly literary, non-scientific, background of its editors and amateur contributors, but in recent years its relatively modest coverage of scientific and technical terms, and popular colloquial usage, has been amply remedied in the four *Supplements* (1972–1986) produced under the general editorship of R.W. Burchfield. On the recent electronic version of this dictionary, see p. 694 below.

## 2. THE THEORY AND PRACTICE OF DICTIONARY MAKING

One eminent practitioner has said of dictionary-making that it is not 'a theoretical exercise to increase the sum of human knowledge but practical work to put together a book that people can understand' (Landau 1984: 121). Certainly it is an activity in which success depends on striking a balance between several conflicting requirements. Central to the dictionary editor's work is of course description, or analysis: the spelling, pronunciation, grammar and meanings of entry-words must be specified precisely, and as extensively or briefly as the dictionary's size and intended readership allow or demand. But at the same time, lexicographers must strive to satisfy the reference needs of the specific user-groups (scientific specialists? school-children? translators?) for whom they are writing, bearing in mind that few users will have a linguistic background, or even a practical training in efficient dictionary use (Hartmann 1983b, Herbst and Stein 1987). There are also commercial pressures. Most projects aimed at producing abridged monolingual or bilingual dictionaries are commercial enterprises, occupying highly qualified staffs for thousands of man-hours and, increasingly, calling for major investment in computer hardware and expertise (Quirk 1982). Editorial staff thus work within very tight constraints of time and space. A dictionary must enter the market on schedule, and be of an acceptable size and price, if it is to compete successfully with rivals in the same field. Such exigencies rule out sudden shifts of editorial policy, or major last-minute revisions (Barnhart 1962, Landau 1984).

In seeking to present information in such a way that the user can get to it rapidly, and grasp it easily, the lexicographer is helped by two well-established and widely understood principles of organisation. The first is of course the principle of alphabetical arrangement. But dictionary-makers in Britain and America are also helped by the fact that, at a level below the academic historical dictionary, that of the one-volume general-purpose dictionary, there is a broad consensus concerning the categories of information that the user needs, and to some extent too the order in which they are to appear. Individual differences of course exist between monolingual dictionaries at this level, and more substantial ones between monolingual and bilingual works, but there is nevertheless a striking degree of uniformity across the entire range (Atkins 1985, Ilson 1986b). This is evident if we compare the current editions of a number of general-purpose English dictionaries compiled for native speakers. Consider, for example, *The Concise Oxford Dictionary* (*COD7* 1982), *Chambers Twentieth Century Dictionary* (*CTCD* 1983), *Webster's Ninth New Collegiate Dictionary* (*W9* 1983), and the *Longman Concise English Dictionary* (*LCED* 1985), a selection representing four publishing traditions, and embracing American as well as British practice. The following categories of information appear in all four, though admittedly in certain of the dictionaries some of the types are not consistently represented:

*Headword.* This is made prominent by bold print and followed in some cases by one or more variant spellings: **forecastle, fo'c'sle** (*LCED*); **mĕ'dallist**, *\*mĕ'dalist* (*COD7*), where the asterisk marks a spelling which is 'chiefly American'.

*Pronunciation.* Usually one recommended form, though sometimes with permitted variants (including, possibly, American pronunciations):
**controversy** /ˈkontrǝˌvuhsi; *also* kǝnˈtrovǝsi/ (*LCED*);
**laboratory**   lǝ-borˈǝtǝ-ri, labˈǝ-rǝ-ǝa-ri (*CTCD*).
Here, both representations include the phonetic symbol 'schwa' /ǝ/, but both otherwise make use of a 'respelling system' (one based on the standard orthography).

*Part of Speech Label.* Indications are given of the word class or classes (noun, verb, adverb, etc.) to which the headword belongs:
**mȳ'riad** *a. & n.* (*COD*); **pong** ... *vi or n* (*LCED*);
**that** ... *demons. pron.* and *demons. adj.* (*CTCD*).

*Irregular Inflected Forms.* Such forms are usually included, sometimes with accompanying pronunciations, as in this example:
'**spring** ... **sprang** /sprang/, **sprung** /sprung/ (*LCED*).

*Usage labels.* These indicate stylistic level (*informal*), specialist register (*physics*), currency (*archaic*), acceptability (*vulgar*), etc.

*Definition(s).*

*Derivatives, compounds and idioms.* Here we are concerned with complex (*slowly*, *slowness*) and compound (*slowcoach*, *slow-worm*) words formed from the headword, with or without their own definitions, and idiomatic phrases containing the headword.

In addition, we find the following categories represented in three of the dictionaries: (*a*) the syntactic function of the headword (thus, verb transitive, attributive adjective); (*b*) example sentences and phrases; (*c*) indications of the kinds of subjects or direct objects which can combine (or 'collocate') with given verbs, and of the prepositions which can follow verbs and nouns; (*d*) a brief etymology.

Limitations of space prevent a full discussion of all these categories or their treatment (cf. Landau 1984, Zgusta 1971, Benson, Benson and Ilson 1986). Some features, too, for example the syntactic properties of headwords, and their capacity to combine with other words (their collocability), are more fully treated in monolingual dictionaries for foreign learners than in comparable works for native speakers. We shall therefore confine ourselves to a number of information categories which are common to monolingual dictionaries of the type already mentioned (though as it happens all can be found in bilingual dictionaries also). These features are the headword, irregular inflected forms, derivatives and examples. The role of translation in bilingual dictionaries, and the treatment of syntax and collocation in learners' dictionaries, will be taken up in later sections.

The components of dictionary structure are entries (or 'articles'), and we can assume to begin with that each entry deals solely or largely with a 'simple' word, that is with a vocabulary item such as *book*, *free* or *finish*, which consists of a single 'base' (Quirk *et al.* 1985). (These examples can be compared with *bookish*, *freedom* and *finisher*, each of which is made up of a single base and a suffix, and is a derivative, or 'complex' word.) Each entry is introduced by the aptly named 'headword', which is one representative form chosen from the set of inflected forms by which the word is realised in writing. In the case of the verb 'finish', the headword is the 'stem' *finish*, the form from which *finishes*, *finished* and *finishing* are obtained by the addition of regular suffixes (Lyons 1977: 512, Dubois 1981: 236, Cowie 1983a: 100). The choice of representative (or 'canonical') form varies from one language to another. While in English dictionaries a verb is represented by its uninflected stem, as already shown, and an adjective by the 'absolute' form (*high*, *low*, *flat*, etc.), in French dictionaries the verb is represented by the infinitive (*aimer*, *finir*, *vouloir*, etc.), and the adjective by the masculine singular: *haut*, *bas*, *plat*, etc. It is of course by their headwords that dictionary entries are alphabetically listed, so that it is by referring to forms that the user gains access to words (Dubois 1981: 236).

Provided the user understands the convention governing the choice of stems as headwords, and knows their spellings, he will have no difficulty in accessing entries for simple words. Normally, too, adult native users of a dictionary will already know the irregular past tense and past participle forms of most verbs which have them, and be able to turn quickly to the entries headed by their stems. All the same, it is standard practice in English (and French) dictionaries of various types to list such forms as separate entries whenever the spelling of the inflected form differs markedly from that of the stem. Such 'dummy' entries consist wholly or largely or morphological information, and explicitly refer the user back to the main entry for the word in question, as in the following entries (Lyons 1977: 513, Cowie 1983a: 101):

**sprang** . . . *pa.t.* of **spring**[1].
**sprung** . . . *pa.t.* and *pa.p.* of **spring**[1]. (*CTCD*)
**bĕ'tter**[1] . . . (*compar.* of GOOD).
**bĕst**[1] . . . (*superl.* of GOOD). (*COD7*)

In dealing with complex words (*quickly, actor, harassments,* etc.) we move on to more difficult ground. Consider the adverb *placidly.* Its meaning can be inferred from the meanings of the base *placid* and the suffix *-ly* (both of which elements should be separately listed in the dictionary), and the process of formation itself (Stein 1985: 38). That being so, *placidly* will be treated not as a main entry but as an undefined 'run-on' – a form in bold print nested within the entry for *placid.* The nouns *placidness* and *placidity,* which are equally 'transparent', can be treated in the same way. Economy dictates that as many derivatives as possible should be entered as run-ons, and as the *COD7* entry for *placid* shows, editors can make further savings by replacing the base with a dash or tilde:

**placid** . . . *adj.* . . . . *-ns.* **placid'ity, plac'idness.** — *adv.* **plac'idly.** (*CTCD*)
**plă'cĭd** *a.* . . . **placĭ'd**ITY *n.,* ~ LY[2] *adv.* (*COD7*)

But adverbs ending in *-ly* and nouns ending in *-ness* are not always straight-forwardly dependent in meaning as well as grammar on the adjectival base (Stein 1985). Some adverbs quite clearly exist as independent words (consider *hardly,* as in *I've hardly ever been there*), and must be treated as main entries. In other cases the adverb or noun may have a meaning or meanings not covered by those of the simple entry-word to which they are appended. In such cases too there are good grounds for listing the adverbs or nouns separately from the adjectives.

As we have seen, illustrative quotations occupy a central place in the large-scale historical dictionary, as they give authoritative support to the lexi-cographer's account of the history of forms and meanings. Opinions differ, however, as to the value of examples, whether actual citations or invented phrases, in smaller-scale monolingual dictionaries. Some abridged monolingual dictionaries (e.g. *CTCD*) provide no examples at all, while others (e.g. *W9*) give a lower priority to them than to definitions or synonyms.

Yet it is undoubtedly true that they are 'a critical part of the dictionary definition and should not be regarded as mere appurtenances' (Landau 1984: 166).

Granted that examples are an essential feature of the dictionary entry, it is a matter of debate whether as a general rule citations are to be preferred to made-up phrases. One advantage of constructed examples is that they can be made to supplement the information given in a definition. For instance, an example can include one or more members of the class denoted by the headword, as in the following entry quoted by Patrick Drysdale (1987: 216) from a Canadian childrens' dictionary

**appliance** . . . *can openers, vacuum cleaners, washing machines, refrigerators, etc. are household appliances.*

An even closer relationship between the definition and the example in its explanatory role is demonstrated by an illustration which combined the headword (or a compound or phrase containing it) and the defining words (the 'definiens') within the same sentence (Drysdale 1987: 222):

**grand**[1] . . . *The* **grand old man** *of British politics is old, experienced, important and probably popular* (*LDOCE* 1978)

However,the usefulness of made-up examples does not stop at clarification of meaning. One advantage claimed for citations is that, for those who need help with writing, they provide authentic models of usage. They also obviate reference to grammatical abbreviations and codes. But the same could be said of many specially constructed examples. Any lexicographer with an eye and ear for natural usage develops skill at devising 'authentic' examples, and where necessary he can adapt these to highlight special features of meaning or function. However, the issue is far from uncontroversial. That the use of citations in dictionaries for the non-specialist (whether native or foreign) still has vigorous advocates is shown by the publication of the *Collins COBUILD English Language Dictionary* (1987), which draws the great bulk of its examples from a computerised store of naturally-occurring texts.

## 2.1 Dictionary typology

Though for ease of discussion we focused in the previous section on one dictionary type in common use, dictionaries are in fact of an extraordinary variety, as is shown by such titles as *Dictionnaire du Français Langue Etrangère* (monolingual, and designed for foreign learners of French), *The Oxford Mini-dictionary of Spelling* (small-scale and a guide to English spelling and word-division) and the *Longman Dictionary of Phrasal Verbs* (dealing with one grammatically circumscribed area of the English vocabulary). These titles illustrate only a few of the variables that can be brought into prominence to meet specific user needs. Well-established sub-categories are indicated in manuals of lexicography by such chapter headings as 'On bilingual dictionaries', 'On dictionaries for special registers', and so on (Hartmann 1983a). However, few attempts have been made to construct an overall scheme of dictionary types, or general typology. Of these, the most elaborate and systematic is that of Malkiel (1962). There is not the space here to explore Malkiel's scheme in detail, but it will be helpful to focus on aspects of two out of the three key variables which he recognises, those of *range*, and *perspective*. One aspect of range is comprehensiveness of coverage, which relates to the distinction drawn in the previous section between unabridged and abridged dictionaries. Another aspect of range concerns the number of languages used in a dictionary (that is, whether it is monolingual, or bilingual or plurilingual) and will be taken up more fully below. Perspective has to do with the compiler's attitude towards his material: with regard to the time axis his view may be diachronic (i.e. historical) or synchronic (limited to one period); with regard to the ordering of items within the overall structure of a work he may opt for a semantic arrangement (as in some of the earliest reference works in English or a modern thesaurus such as *Roget*) or an alphabetical arrangement (as in most of the works discussed in this chapter). Dictionaries which are limited in coverage to one level of language (e.g. spelling, pronunciation) or to one part of the lexicon (e.g. idioms, catchphrases, slang) fall outside Malkiel's typology; yet they clearly form an important grouping, and have been helpfully classified by Zgusta (1971) as restricted (or special) dictionaries. They will be represented here by dictionaries of idioms.

Bilingual dictionaries by definition make use of two languages, one of which is normally the mother tongue ($L_1$) of the user. For quick and painless comprehension of unfamiliar words in the foreign language ($L_2$) the bilingual work has no rival (Tomaszczyk 1979), and it is of course indispensable when a writer is ignorant of, or cannot recall, a specific vocabulary item in the $L_2$ (Moulin 1987). Recent progress in the design of one-volume bilingual dictionaries has been such that an Italian reader of English, say, is now provided not only with Italian equivalents of the headword, but also translations of every run-on derivative or compound, and every example, as in the following entry from Ragazzini's *Dizionario Inglese-Italiano Italiano-Inglese*:

> **incapable** . . . *a*, incapace; inetto: **i. of change**, incapace di cambiare; – **to be i. of telling a lie**, essere incapace di dire una bugia. ￮ **drunk and i.**, ubriaco fradicio. (Ragazzini 1984)

The dictionary from which this extract is taken is bidirectional; it contains two roughly equal parts (Italian-English as well as English-Italian), in each of which words in one language are explained in terms of the other (Landau 1984: 8, Steiner 1984: 173). This is the normal pattern, but it is not the only one. Like the earliest Latin-English glossaries, a bilingual dictionary may consist of a single word-list in a language foreign to its intended users (it may nowadays be based on an existing monolingual dictionary of that language), with translations in the mother tongue incorporated in the single alphabetical list. In the *Oxford Engelsk-Norsk Ordbok* (*OENO* 1983), for example, Norwegian translations appear in place of the original definitions of the monolingual *Oxford Student's Dictionary of Current English* (*OSDCE* 1978), on which *OENO* is based. The exact part played by translations in unidirectional dictionaries of this kind, which are aimed at readers of a foreign language, vary with the estimated needs of the user-group (Reif 1987). In the *Oxford Student's Dictionary for Hebrew Speakers* (*OSDHS* 1985), for example, also based on *OSDCE*, Hebrew glosses accompany the existing definitions.

Let us now return to two-part bilingual dictionaries. Here it will be helpful to draw a further distinction between dictionaries of comprehension, i.e. those which aim simply to help native speakers of each of the two languages to understand items in the other, and the more ambitious dictionaries of communication, which also provide for writing and translation into the foreign language in either direction (Atkins 1985: 15). In practice we seldom find dictionaries which are fully 'communicative' in this sense. As Malcolm Skey, editor of another Italian bilingual work explains, his aim in the English-Italian section is to help the Italian user to 'understand and interpret', and in the Italian-English to help that same user to 'render his thoughts into English' (1977, vii). It is not part of his declared purpose to assist English readers and writers of Italian, however much he may do so in fact.

Indeed it has been claimed that to attempt to include information for 'encoding' (into the L2) and 'decoding' (into the L1) in the same section of a major bilingual dictionary is to invite failure in both endeavours. As Tomaszczyk has argued, the demands made on reference resources by the two types of activity are quite different: 'in active language use a small but exhaustively treated store of vocabulary is quite sufficient, whereas a receptive dictionary [i.e. one for decoding] ought to have a larger store of words' (1981: 291–2). Indeed, various scholars have taken the view that the only satisfactory way of meeting such fundamentally different needs is to provide four dictionaries (two for decoding, two for encoding) for each pair of languages (Snell-Hornby 1987). A partial attempt to implement such a programme has been made in the Soviet Union, where in 1962–3 a series of bilingual dictionaries were produced for English-, French- and German-speaking learners of Russian (Folomkina 1986). For each L1 there was a 'receptive' and a 'productive' dictionary, differences in the information considered necessary for comprehension and use being reflected in the fact that while the receptive volume of the English-Russian pair contained almost three times as many entries as the productive one, both were of approximately the same size (Tomaszczyk 1981).

That progress is still possible within the framework of the more familiar one-volume, two-part dictionary has been demonstrated since the early 1970s, especially in providing for language production. Of fundamental importance to encoding is ease in locating the precise L2 equivalent of a word-meaning in the L1. Where, as in the following excerpt from the *Collins Spanish Dictionary* (*CSD*), the writer or translator is confronted by a list of L2 items, selection is a matter of guesswork.

> **sensibly** . . . *adv* sensatamente; prudentemente; discretamente; . . . (*CSD* 1971).

But elsewhere in *CSD*, and consistently in the *Collins Robert French Dictionary* (*CRFD*), various helpful devices ('sense discriminations') are employed to direct the user to the appropriate translation (Iannucci 1985). One is the provision of a number of synonyms of the headword in its various senses; these are then placed before their translation equivalents in the L2:

> **scrupulousness** . . . (*honesty*) scrupules *mpl*, esprit scrupuleux; (*exactitude*) minutie *f*. . . . (*CRFD* 1978)

Alternatively, or in addition, the dictionary can specify adjectives, nouns, and so on, which typically co-occur (or collocate) with the headword in its distinguishable meanings. These too are an effective aid to narrowing down the search for a suitable equivalent in the L2:

> **noble** . . . *adj* . . . *person, appearance, matter* noble; *soul, sentiment* noble, grand; *monument, edifice* majestueux, imposant. (*CRFD* 1978)

For successful language production in an L2, it is also vital to specify the syntactic properties of entry-words in that language. For foreign writers of English, these include the facts that nouns such as *thirst* or *hunger* are not normally used in the plural form, and that adjectives such as *utter, outright, conscious (of, that), tantamount (to)* have fixed positions relative to the nouns they modify (the first two preceding, the second pair usually following). These restrictions should be noted before the appropriate English translation of the L2 headword, as they are in the following entries from the *Collins German Dictionary* (*CGD*), though not in all comparable ones:

> **Durst** . . . *no pl* . . . thirst
>
> **ausgemacht** . . . *attr* . . . complete, utter
>
> **bewußt** . . . *usu attr* . . . conscious (*CGD* 1981)

Restricted dictionaries are those which deal with a single level of language, like Daniel Jones' *English Pronouncing Dictionary* (*EPD*), or a demarcated area of the vocabulary, like Eric Partridge's equally celebrated *Dictionary of Slang and Unconventional English* (*DSUE*). English does not lack dictionaries of idioms, which fall within the second grouping, but until the mid-1970s British works were in the main small in scale and lacking in depth (e.g. McMordie and Goffin 1954). For larger scholarly treatments the user had to turn to works published outside Britain, and compiled by non-native speakers, such as Ichikawa's *Kenkyusha Dictionary of Current English Idioms* (1964) or Kunin's *English-Russian Phraseological Dictionary* (1955, 4th ed. 1984).

A major project aimed at producing such a dictionary in Britain was not initiated until the late 1950s, when Ronald Mackin began the preparatory work of assembling a body of citations from written sources (Mackin 1978). This project finally came to fruition with the publication of the *Oxford Dictionary of Current Idiomatic English* (*ODCIE*), in two volumes (1975, 1983). Other idiom dictionaries, notably the *Longman Dictionary of English Idioms* (*LDEI* 1979) and the *Longman Dictionary of Phrasal Verbs* (*LDPV* 1983) appeared within the same decade.

The compilation of an up-to-date record of idiomatic expressions, supported by examples of current usage and guided by linguistic principles of analysis, is attended by many difficulties. There is first the problem of structural diversity. English idioms (in the strict sense of semantically opaque combinations of words) occur in a wide range of syntactic patterns (Cowie 1981b). Consider, for example, *a lame duck, call someone's bluff, take someone off, run across someone, paint the town red, be one in the eye for someone.* Part of the dictionary-maker's problem when faced by such diversity is to decide whether at least part of the total spread lends itself to coherent treatment in a separate volume. Idioms consisting of a verb plus adverb (*take someone off*) or verb plus preposition (*run across someone*) form such a grouping that they can be described in terms of a simple framework of related construction-types (and are commonly referred to collectively as 'phrasal verbs'). They were consequently hived off by Oxford and Longman editors alike. There are also editorial difficulties raised by the nature of idiomaticity itself. While the examples quoted earlier are 'petrified' in the sense that their meanings can no longer be explained by reference to those of their parts as used in other contexts (compare *a lame duck* with *a lame excuse,* for instance), there exist very many combinations (such as *a sitting duck* and *burn the midnight oil*) which, while entirely fixed, are nonetheless interpretable as dead metaphors. It is certain that idioms in the strict sense comprise only one of a spectrum of related categories (on which see Chapter 5, above), and that in consequence makers of idiom dictionaries are constantly faced by practical problems of demarcation (Klappenbach 1968).

## 3. THE MONOLINGUAL LEARNER'S DICTIONARY

In recent years, monolingual English dictionaries compiled especially for foreign learners have received a good deal of attention in general discussions of lexicographical theory and practice (Hartmann 1979, 1983a, Ilson 1985, Cowie 1981a, 1987). This is not to say that dictionaries of this type are themselves new. The first work designed specifically for foreign students, the *New Method Dictionary* (*NMD*), appeared as early as 1935, while the better-known *Oxford Advanced Learner's Dictionary* (*ALD*), which in its various editions was later to gain a world-wide reputation among teachers and learners of English, was first published in 1942, in Japan, under the title *Idiomatic and Syntactic English Dictionary* (*ISED*). Nonetheless, it is only in the past ten years or so that the implications for lexicography generally of the design features of the learner's dictionary, reflecting as they do the particular language needs and handicaps of non-native users, have been fully recognised. Various factors have contributed to this sharpening of interest in the EFL model. One is the realisation that in his need for detailed guidance on points of grammar and usage the native language user may not differ all that much from the foreign learner (cf. Ilson 1985: 2). This perception is reflected in the growing practice of addressing to a wider public dictionaries designed chiefly for the foreign learner. So it is that users of the *Longman Dictionary of Contemporary English* (*LDOCE*) first published in 1978, are 'envisaged as predominantly (yet not exclusively) those for whom English is a foreign language' (1978: vii). Another factor leading to increased interest is the difficulty which English users are known to have in interpreting the standard conventions of layout, typography and above all explanation associated with the traditional mother-tongue dictionary. Here again, it is recognised that the older tradition has something to learn from the younger (Ilson 1986a).

Throughout its 50-year history, the learner's dictionary has had a number of central concerns. These have been the development of a controlled vocabulary adequate for precise definition, but at the same time simple enough to be readily understood by the foreign student; the provision of information about syntax and inflection in a detailed, yet succinct and usable form; and the treatment of those word combinations (collocations and idioms) which, though they form part of the common core of the vocabulary, are known to pose special problems for the foreign student (Cowie 1983b, Benson, Benson and Ilson 1986). This movement, at least in its early stages, is inseparable from the careers in English language teaching of three major figures: Michael West, Harold Palmer and A.S. Hornby (Howatt 1984). West's particular contribution, as editor of *NMD*, was in the first of the areas just mentioned. Though Palmer and Hornby were both involved in the so-called vocabulary control movement, it was West alone who made use of a limited vocabulary (of 1490 words) in framing definitions for a learner's dictionary (Cowie 1983b).

Simplified definitions, of course, help mainly with comprehension of a foreign language and translation from it (decoding activities), and research into the uses which foreign students actually make of their monolingual learners' dictionaries show that they employ them predominantly for those purposes (Tomaszcsyk 1979, Béjoint 1981). But students also need to compose in and translate into the foreign language, and the significance of the work of Palmer and Hornby lay in their recognition of the importance of productive (or encoding) needs, and their perception of how these could best be met (Cowie 1983a, 1984).

Practical experience of teaching in Japan had made Palmer and Hornby aware of errors in students' written English caused by extending the rules of sentence construction to individual cases where they did not in fact apply. A foreign student who knew, for example, that an infinitive clause could function as a direct object after such verbs as *intend* and *propose*, as in *I intend to come, I propose to come*, might be led to think that it was also acceptable after *suggest*, as in *\* I suggest to come* (*ISED* 1942:xi). The solution, Palmer and Hornby believed, was to provide a fuller and clearer account of the syntactic patterns in which entry-words could function than was given in the mono-lingual or bilingual works which students normally turned to for guidance.

In 1934 Palmer published a systematic treatment of 'construction patterns', a scheme which set out in an orderly way the principal types of verb comple-mentation found in the simple sentence. Thus, there was one pattern for a transitive verb with noun-phrase object (as in *John caught a fish*), one for a copular verb with adjective complement (as in *Bill is forgetful*), and so on. That this scheme had an essentially practical aim was shown four years later, when Palmer published *A Grammar of English Words* (*GEW*), an alphabetical treatment in some depth of 1000 'core' items of vocabulary, in which an up-dated version of the scheme was a central feature. The pattern information was presented in the verb entries in a strikingly original way. Palmer assigned to each pattern a code number, and inserted the relevant number, or numbers, into the sense-divisions of the entries, at the same time providing a fuller treatment in the Introduction to which the codes could refer.

As it happened, Palmer's system was not to be used in the larger and much more influential *ISED*, published four years after *GEW*. *ISED*'s framework of 25 Verb Patterns was devised by Hornby, and differed from Palmer's in two key respects (Hornby 1938, 1939). First, it organised the patterns into two major groupings, the transitive patterns (Ps 1–19), then the intransitives (Ps 20–25). Palmer's arrangement had been less systematic. Second, though the structural descriptions provided in Hornby's explanatory tables sometimes consisted of clause-functions ('Vb. × Direct Object'), sometimes of constitu-ent classes ('Vb. × Conjunctive × Clause') and sometimes of a blend of both ('Vb. × Object × Adjective'), he was insistent that the fundamental differ-ences between the 25 major patterns should be ones of syntactic function.

By no means all the knowledge needed by the foreign learner for success-ful language production can be accounted for by means of abstract patterns. There are for example within the core vocabulary of English many hundreds of stable word combinations (or collocations) which are enshrined in usage and cannot be generated from scratch by the foreign learner, any more than by the native speaker (Cowie 1978, 1981b, Mackin 1978). Word combinations

686

are of many structural types, but a useful distinction can be drawn between 'grammatical' and 'lexical' collocations (Benson 1985). The former are made up of a major-class word, such as a noun, verb or adjective, and a function word such as a preposition, adverbial particle, or conjunction: thus, *under duress, chatter away* and *responsible for (something)*. Lexical collocations, on the other hand, consist of two major-class words, such as adjective + noun (as in *gloomy foreboding, nice distinction*) or verb + object noun (as in *settle an account, meet a deadline*).

Hornby and Palmer were aware from the early 1930s of the learning problem represented by collocations. They therefore launched an ambitious programme of collection and classification, always with the practical needs of the learner in mind, under the auspices of the Tokyo Institute for Research into English Teaching (Hornby 1933). However, the important distinction between grammatical and lexical collocations was not systematically conveyed in *ISED/ALD1*. Consider, for example, the grammatical collocation *deprive of* (verb + preposition). In *ISED* this is illustrated by means of the example *These misfortunes almost deprived him of his reason.* But examples alone will not indicate the fixed (and entirely predictable) choice of preposition, as compared with the relative openness of choice represented by the nouns *misfortunes* and *reason.* (Cf. *The accident almost deprived him of his sight.*) There is a need for separate highlighting of the preposition, a need which was eventually met in *ALD3* (1974) by the use of bold print, thus:

**deprive** . . . *vt* . . . ~ **of,** . . . *trees that ~ a house of light*

As regards lexical collocations, illustrated by *seize the initiative, a lingering death* or *utterly bewildered*, a convention was already in use in *ISED/ALD1* for representing the lexical choices from which such collocations are formed. This was the use of square brackets to enclose a set of alternatives at the end (less often in the middle) of an example phrase:

*a piece of news [luck, advice, impudence, etc.]*
*a fine piece of work [painting, music, poetry]*

This device had its limitations. It did not, for instance, point up the difference between a range of choice (or 'collocability') which could be extended almost at will (like the second list) and one which contained pitfalls for the learner (like the first: of, *a piece of luck; advice*; *\*a piece of fortune, counsel*). Of course, it would be almost impossible for a general EFL dictionary to indicate such arbitrary restrictions at all satisfactorily. Listing all the acceptable collocations here (and in similar cases) would mean the removal from the dictionary of other information of equal value to the learner. The need can only be fully met by the specialised collocational dictionary, which by excluding material already well handled in the general work, can devote itself to listing all those lexical combinations which present encoding problems for the learner (Hausmann 1979, Cowie 1981b, 1986, Benson 1985).

687

In the thirty-year interval between the publication of the first and third editions of *ALD*, this pioneering work was without a serious rival. The position was to change quite dramatically in the late 1970s with the publication of the *Longman Dictionary of Contemporary English* (*LDOCE* 1978), followed not long afterwards by the more modest but nonetheless praiseworthy *Chambers Universal Learners' Dictionary* (*CULD* 1980). *LDOCE* was remarkable not so much for breaking entirely new ground as for extending imaginatively, and with great professionalism, two of the major lines of development identified earlier in this section: the introduction of a system of syntactic patterns, with a number/letter code, and the use of a controlled defining vocabulary. As regards syntax, the *LDOCE* scheme encoded a wider range of syntactic features than *ALD3*, and at least part of its elaborate system of labels was mnemonic, and thus more 'user-friendly'. As well as treating verb complementation in some detail, *LDOCE* represented by means of codes several subclasses of nouns and adjectives and also the types of phrase and clause construction which could function as their postmodifiers. For instance, U3 stands for an uncountable noun with an infinitive as complement, as in *some reason to believe it*, while F3 indicates a predicative adjective, also with an infinitive construction as complement, as in *eager to please* (Lemmens and Wekker 1986).

Despite the impressively systematic nature of this scheme (number 3, for example, always denotes an infinitive construction, whether it follows a noun, an adjective or a verb) some teacher-critics argued that an increase in the range of encoded information was not altogether in the user's best interests. There is undoubtedly a good deal of consumer resistance to information that is not directly accessible (Béjoint 1981, Heath 1982), and it was with this factor in mind that the compilers of *CULD* decided to use a minimum of grammatical labels and to depend instead on the extensive use of examples to convey syntactic patterns. Note, for example, that though the entry for *recommend* contains no label other than the familiar *vt* (verb transitive), the entry illustrates all the relevant syntactic patterns for the sense 'to advice (someone to do something)':

> *I recommend you take a long holiday, I recommend (that) you take a long holiday, I recommend a long holiday.* (*CULD* 1980)

*LDOCE*'s controlled defining vocabulary (or CV) has attracted as much critical attention as its grammatical scheme, and has been the subject of a number of research projects, including computer studies using an electronic form of the dictionary (Jansen, Mergeai and Vanandroye 1987), so that a brief review of the issues is called for here. A controlled vocabulary, as its name suggests, is one which has been deliberately restricted, according to criteria of frequency, range, learnability, etc., to serve various pedagogical ends. The compilers of *LDOCE* based their selection of approximately 2000 words on earlier frequency lists, referring especially to Michael West's *General Service List* (1953). They also strove to ensure that only the most 'central' meanings of those words were used (*LDOCE* 1978: ix). It is noteworthy too that the CV was employed not simply for framing definitions but also for making up illustrative examples.

The chief advantage claimed for a controlled defining vocabulary is that it facilitates understanding of the foreign vocabulary by ensuring that the more difficult words are defined in terms of words which the learner already knows. The CV devised for *LDOCE* was deployed with skill and ingenuity, though not always with precision (Stein 1979). As for the practical effectiveness of the approach, the (admittedly few) investigations with foreign students which have been carried out have shown that when asked to compare a selected range of *LDOCE* definitions with corresponding definitions from *ALD*, *CULD* and/or a mother-tongue dictionary, students have rated *LDOCE* highest for 'comprehensibility' (Herbst 1986). However, the use of a CV in a pedagogical lexicography often poses severe problems; these have as much to do with the items being defined as with the means used to define them. For example, it may not be possible to define words of high frequency (*go, get, come*, etc.) using only words of higher frequency still (Benson *et al.* 1986), while satisfactory definitions of technical terms such as *dahlia* or *copper* may only be possible by going outside the defining vocabulary altogether (Herbst 1986). Finally, the approach seems to leave out of account certain important aspects of the use of a dictionary as a study aid. It is worth noting, for example, that while developing rapid-reading skills the learner acquires various techniques for guessing word meanings which tend to lessen his dependence on the dictionary (Ilson 1986a, Herbst and Stein 1987). It may indeed be the case that the well-trained student is least dependent on the dictionary for precisely those study activities – reading in and translation from the foreign language – with which the CV was primarily intended to provide help.

## 4. CURRENT TRENDS AND FUTURE DEVELOPMENTS

In the last section we spoke of a growing understanding of ways in which one tradition in dictionary-making can draw profitably on another, and of the increasing importance to dictionary compilers of developments outside lexicography proper. These signs are indicative of the profound changes now taking place in the intellectual, technological and commercial conditions in which lexicographers work (Ilson 1986a). These developments are not localised: to a greater or lesser extent, they affect all countries where lexicography is well rooted. Two related trends can be noted. First, in an occupation noted for its insularity and conservatism, rigid divisions of all kinds are beginning to dissolve: between the academic and the 'commercial' lexicographer, between lexicography proper and the disciplines of linguistics and computer science, between different national traditions. Second, lexicographers are increasingly thinking and behaving as members of a modern academic profession, with an interest in the public discussion of theory and practice, with well-established information channels and with a growing commitment to research and publication (Bailey 1987).

The signs of change were relatively slow to appear in Britain. From the early 1960s, major dictionary projects employing linguists and computer specialists were under way in France (Rey 1977), whilst in the United States the calling of a joint conference of lexicographers and linguists in 1960 was a notable landmark (Householder and Saporta 1962). But by the mid-1970s there were clear indications that established attitudes and practices were being challenged in Britain also. Fresh insights were being brought to bear, though chiefly in bilingual and EFL lexicography, from linguistics and phonetics, and co-operation on major projects was developing between British and American publishers (Quirk 1982). The end of the decade saw the staging in Britain of the first of a series of conferences, which were to be remarkable both for their international character and for the range of professional interests represented (Hartmann 1979, 1983a, 1984, 1986, Ilson 1986, Cowie 1987). This period also witnessed the setting up of two professional bodies, the Dictionary Society of North America (whose journal *Dictionaries* first appeared in 1979), and the European Association for Lexicography. A second journal, *Lexicographica*, the first issue of which was produced in 1985, is published in conjunction with both the DSNA and EURALEX. A third, the *International Journal of Lexicography*, which began publication in 1988, also has links with the two professional bodies.

The opening conference had as its title *Dictionaries and their Users*, and it heralded a period of intense involvement in user-related dictionary studies. (An encouraging trend is the number of postgraduate theses now being devoted to dictionary users and uses.) Hartmann (1987) has provided a valuable survey of research in the field and has distinguished four major perspectives. First, there is research whose chief aim has been to discover the relative importance to dictionary users of individual categories of linguistic information (e.g. meaning, spelling, pronunciation). Second, there are studies (of which Quirk 1973 is a pioneering instance) which aim to provide information about the users themselves – their attitudes, expectations and prejudices. A third type of study investigates the reasons why a user consults a dictionary (his or her reference needs). In one such study (Tomaszczyk 1979) the method was to specify the language-based study activities of the learner (i.e. listening, reading, writing and translation) and then to determine how far the use of the dictionary, and its effectiveness, varied with the type of skill practised. The fourth focus of investigation has been the reference skills which users bring to their use of dictionaries. How effectively can they gain access to the categories of information which their dictionaries contain?

These trends show how, within the past decade, the interests of researchers have broadened to take account not only of what a dictionary contains but of the user's motives in turning to it in the first place. One should be careful, however, not to exaggerate the scale of this research or its practical impact. A guide to dictionary use published under the auspices of the National Extension College (Lewis and Pugmire 1980) probably comes closer to reflecting the attitudes and reference habits of student dictionary users, and their teachers, than do the views of enlightened critics and researchers (for a German view, see Herbst and Stein 1987). The handbook sets out a number of possible uses of a dictionary; but these are based not on an analysis of the reference needs of the learner, but on the various information categories that the dictionary is traditionally expected to contain, i.e. meaning, spelling, grammar, etymology and pronunciation (Hartmann 1987:17). There is no doubt that many users have considerable difficulty in adapting to the substantial changes, linguistic and educational, which have already affected the reference tools at their disposal (Dubois 1981: 248).

We saw in earlier sections that a wide range of dictionary types have long been available to the user: specialisation is an established fact. Yet once one recognises the primacy of user need in determining the content and design of dictionaries, further proliferation of types, differentiated as to the user's language background, occupational field, favoured mode of communication (translation into French? written composition in Russian?) or level of language (pronunciation only? spelling only?) becomes desirable, and also commercially feasible, given the ingenuity already displayed by some publishers in spinning off 'segmental' titles from existing larger works.

The increased availability of specialised dictionaries prompts one to ask at what point in acquiring a foreign language the learner should be encouraged to move from a bilingual to a monolingual target-language dictionary (Folomkina 1986), or the extent to which writers in, or translators into, a foreign language refer to dictionaries of different types (Tomaszczyk 1987). As Hartmann reports, no large-scale research project has yet been mounted to find out which types are actually consulted by given users, and in what proportions (1987: 19). In the meantime, we must depend on small-scale localised but often valuable accounts by teachers for our understanding of how dictionaries are, or can be, used in the classroom. Moulin (1987) has provided a detailed set of guidelines for successful dictionary use when writing in a foreign language, acknowledging the limitations of the dictionary for dealing with highly original uses of language, but more positively emphasising that the learner needs to become familiar with a range of reference works and explaining the usefulness of particular types at various stages of the writing process.

Despite the local efforts of enterprising teachers, however, reports from various countries where English is taught as a foreign language reveal a widespread lack of awareness, in schools and universities, of the usefulness of the dictionary as a learning tool. Several teachers and lexicographers have strongly advocated the provision of systematic training in dictionary use, noting that with each innovation in content or design the gap widens between the sophistication of the monolingual EFL or bilingual dictionary and the quite rudimentary reference skills possessed by the average user (Béjoint 1981, Cowie 1983b, Herbst and Stein 1987).

While encouraging the teaching of reference skills, the lexicographer must provide for the users that he actually has, and it is noticeable that in recent years there has been a marked improvement in the 'user-friendliness' of dictionaries of various kinds. One very clear trend, which owes much to American precedents, is the treatment in separate main entries of the compounds and derivatives, and to some extent the idioms too, of a given base or root, even in cases where the derived items are clearly related in form and meaning to that base (Stein 1979, Cowie 1983b). One can argue that when consulting a dictionary, a user typically confines his attention to the one item that has caused the momentary breakdown in communication, so that rapid access to individual forms, whether simple (*narrow*) or derived (*narrowness*) is at a premium. When moreover the user is decoding, as he is more often than not, he will not need to be reminded, by their proximity within the same entry, that the verb *narrow* can be used by a writer as an alternative to the phrase *become narrow*. This simplifies the argument somewhat, but the argument has followers.

The past twenty years have seen a steadily increasing involvement of the computer at all stages of dictionary production. Several of the computational techniques relevant to lexicography which are now employed or envisaged are of extreme sophistication (for general surveys, see Knowles 1984, Calzolari *et al.* 1987). The present account will be limited to the more modest, yet vital, use of the computer as a kind of electronic amanuensis for the automation of various routine tasks from data-gathering at one end of the dictionary-making process to printing at the other. Chapter 18, section 4.3 above, is relevant here.

We can begin with the question of data-selection, to which two approaches have been adopted, differing in scope and purpose. The first is the setting up of corpora (relatively large bodies of computer-stored material, usually written, occasionally transcribed from speech); the second is the searching of text files originally created for some purpose unconnected with lexicography or lexical analysis (Bailey 1986). As regards the first, two corpora, each of one million words and representative of a range of styles and specialist fields, have for some years been available for general linguistic research. These are the Brown and Lancaster-Oslo-Bergen (LOB) corpora (Sinclair 1982). These relatively small-scale collections meet the needs of analysts of high-frequency 'core' vocabulary, most particularly of grammatical words. They are not, however, well suited to indicating the frequencies and patterns of less frequent 'lexical' words, and are thus of only limited value to lexicographers, even though batches of words supplied from the Brown corpus, with contexts and dates of occurrence, have been found helpful by editors working on the *OED* Supplements (Sherman 1979: 139).

Various steps were taken in the 1960s and 1970s to meet the need for larger bodies of data. French lexicographers were the first to move to practical implementation, and material computerised in the 1960s for the *Trésor de la Langue Française* was of the order of 70 million words (Rey 1977). Clarence Barnhart later proposed a central archive for lexicography in English which should contain 25 to 30 million quotations covering half a million possible items (Barnhart 1973), and at about the same time Laurence Urdang produced a newspaper corpus of 20 million edited words from machine-readable material supplied by publishers (Urdang 1973). Since 1980, a corpus of similar size to Urdang's has been assembled at Birmingham University in collaboration with Collins.

As regards the use by lexicographers of computerised files originally created for non-linguistic purposes, these have ranged from medical reports to mass circulation newspapers and magazines. Such resources permit searches for specific items with the help of specially designed retrieval systems (Bailey 1986: 126), and are already being used by editors of the *New Oxford English Dictionary* to search for words and phrases of special interest. Since many newspapers are now printed with the aid of computer-driven composition systems, it is not difficult to put such texts into machine-readable form.

Where text is not already stored on magnetic tape, the gathering of data can be enormously speeded up by the use of a high-speed optical character reading machine (OCR), which scans written material and transcribes it on to tape (Urdang 1973). A more recent refinement is the Kurzweil Data Entry Machine (KDEM) which can be trained to recognise and interpret not only font styles but most scripts (Knowles 1984).

After data capture by optical scanning, a normal next stage for lexicographers is the automatic construction of a citation file in the form of a KWIC index or concordance (Urdang 1973). In a KWIC concordance the occurrences (tokens) of a given word-form (type) are displayed one above the other for easy access. The individual lines of the display are ordered according to the right-context collocates of the word-form. So *promise that he will return*, for instance, is ranged above *promise to return* (Sherman 1979). An optional further step is lemmatisation. Without special intervention, the computer will treat two or more identical strings of characters as the same, whether they represent different lexical items (*bank* = 'place where money is deposited'; *bank* = 'edge of a river'), different inflected forms of the same lexical item (*put* as 'base' form, *put* as past tense, *put* as past participle), or simply different occurrences of the same form. Using a combination of automatic processes which involve 'morphological segmentation and base form matching' (Venezky 1973: 287), and a data table of 'black list' entries, a lemmatisation program brings together all the inflected forms of a given keyword (thus, *give, gives, giving, gave, given*). Beyond this stage, grammatical tagging programs can be employed to distinguish words which function as different parts of speech (e.g. *matter*, noun, *matter*, verb).

In 1959, Laurence Urdang, then working on the *Random House Dictionary*, designed a database system for 'encoding all the separate elements of the dictionary entries' – i.e. marking them with special symbols or 'flags' (Bailey 1986: 125). This was an important advance, for (*a*) it allowed the extraction of any sub-category of information (e.g. all irregular verb inflections) for checking or intensive editing; (*b*) it made possible the production of, say, technical glossaries by the simple expedient of 'retrieving an appropriately coded sub-set of the lexical data-base' (Knowles 1983: 186-7); and (*c*) not least, it provided for computer-driven typesetting of *RHD* (though in fact this option was not taken up at the time). Work a decade and more later on the *Collins English Dictionary*, on which Urdang was also engaged, shows the degree to which overall management of a project, up to and including printing, was to be transformed by the computer. The headword list of the *CED* was formed into a master file from a data-base of 25 million characters on visual display units (VDUs), which were also used to check and revise data and prepare the phonetic transcription of the headwords. Proof-reading was greatly speeded up by the printing of the proofs in 12-point type, while adjustments to the type-size for the final printing (changing 6-point to 8-point, for instance) could be effected by a single command (Knowles 1983: 186).

The encoded computer-stored text of a major dictionary constitutes a rich and versatile resource for further development and for pure research. The decision to establish the electronic version of the *New Oxford English Dictionary* as a lexical data base, roughly at the same time as the printed dictionary appears, will thus have repercussions far beyond lexicography in the narrow sense (Weiner 1987). The data fields selected will enable the user to enter and retrieve 'the various parts of the entry format that Murray established as the norm for dictionaries on historical principles: head words, pronunciation, form class' (Bailey 1986: 130). But as the questionnaire distributed to potential academic users made clear, it will also be possible for specialists to conduct searches for categories of entry-words delimited according to semantic field, geographical provenance, or period of entry into the language, or to the authorship or period of the works from which they are culled.

## REFERENCES

*List of Dictionaries, 1499 to the Present*

Allen, R.E. (1986) *The Oxford Minidictionary of Spelling*, Clarendon Press, Oxford.

Atkins, B.T. (ed.) (1978) *Collins Robert French Dictionary*, 1st edition, Collins, London and Glasgow (2nd edition, 1987).

Bailey, N. (1721) *Universal Etymological English Dictionary*, E. Bell et al., London.

Bailey, N. (1730) *Dictionarium Britannicum*, T. Cox, London.

Blount, T. (1656) *Glossographia*, T. Newcomb for H. Moseley, London.

Burchfield, R.W. (ed.) (1972–1986) *A Supplement to the Oxford English Dictionary*, Clarendon Press, Oxford.

Cawdrey, R. (1604) *A Table Alphabeticall . . . of Hard Usuall English Words*, I.R. for E. Weaver, London.

Cockeram, H. (1623) *The English Dictionarie*, E. Weaver and N. Butter, London.

Courtney, R. (1983) *Longman Dictionary of Phrasal Verbs*, Longman, Harlow.

Cowie, A.P., Mackin, R. and McCaig, I.R. (1975/1983) *Oxford Dictionary of Current Idiomatic English*, two volumes, Oxford University Press, Oxford.

Dubois, J. with Dubois-Charlier, F. (1978) *Dictionnaire du Français Langue Etrangère, Niveau 1*, Larousse, Paris.

Elyot, T. (1538) *The Dictionary of Sir Thomas Elyot, Knight*, T. Bertheletus, London.

Florio, J. (1598) *A Worlde of Wordes*, A. Hatfield for E. Blount, London.

Geoffrey the Grammarian (1499) *Promptorium Parvulorum, sive Clericorum*, R. Pynson, London.

Hanks, P. (1979) *Collins Dictionary of the English Language*, Collins, London and Glasgow.

Hornby, A.S., Gatenby, E.V. and Wakefield, H. (1942) *Idiomatic and Syntactic English Dictionary*, Kaitakusha, Tokyo.

Hornby, A.S. *et al.* (1948) *The Advanced Learner's Dictionary of Current English*, 1st edition, Oxford University Press, London (2nd edition, 1963).

Hornby, A.S. *et al.* (1974) *The Oxford Advanced Learner's Dictionary of Current English*, 3rd edition, Oxford University Press, London (4th edition, 1989).

Hornby, A.S. and Reif, J.A. (1985) *Oxford Student's Dictionary for Hebrew Speakers*, Kernerman, Jerusalem.

Hornby, A.S. with Ruse, C.A. (1978) *Oxford Student's Dictionary of Current English*, Oxford University Press, Oxford.

Hornby, A.S. and Svenkerud, H. (1983) *Oxford Engelsk-Norsk Ordbok*, J.W. Cappelens, Oslo.

Howlet, R. (1552) *Abecedarium Anglico-Latinum*, Riddel, London.

Ichikawa, S. (1964) *Kenkyusha Dictionary of Current English Idioms*, Kenkyusha, Tokyo.

'J.K.' (1702) *A New English Dictionary*, H. Bonwicke, London.

Johnson, S. (1755) *A Dictionary of the English Language*, W. Stratton for P. Knapton, *et al.*, London.

Jones, D. (1977) *Everyman's English Pronouncing Dictionary*, 14th edition revised by A.C. Gimson, Dent, London.

Kirkpatrick, E.M. (ed.) (1980) *Chamber's Universal Learners' Dictionary*, W. & R. Chambers, Edinburgh.

Kirkpatrick, E.M. (1983) *Chambers 20th Century Dictionary*, W. & R. Chambers, Edinburgh.

Kunin, A.V. (1984) *English-Russian Phraseological Dictionary*, 4th edition, Russian Language Publishers, Moscow.

Long, T.H. and Summers, D. (1979) *Longman Dictionary of English Idioms*, Longman, Harlow.

McMordie, W. and Goffin, R. (1954) *English Idioms*, 3rd edition, Oxford University Press, London.

Mish, F.C. (ed.) (1983) *Webster's Ninth New Collegiate Dictionary*, Merriam, Springfield, Mass.

Murray, J.A.H. *et al.* (eds) (1884.1933) *The Oxford English Dictionary — A New English Dictionary on Historical Principles*, Clarendon Press, Oxford.

Palsgrave, J. (1530) *Lesclarcissement de la Langue Françoyse*, J. Haukyns, London.

Partridge, E. (1970) *A Dictionary of Slang and Unconventional English*, 7th edition, two volumes, Routledge & Kegan Paul, London.

Percyvall, R. (1591) *Bibliotheca Hispanica*, J. Jackson for R. Watkins, London.

Phillips, E. (1658) *The New World of English Words*, E. Tyler for N. Brooke, London.

Procter, P. (ed.) (1978) *Longman Dictionary of Contemporary English*, 1st edition, Longman, Harlow (2nd edition, 1987).

Procter, P. (ed.) (1985) *Longman Concise English Dictionary*, Longman, Harlow.

Ragazzini, G. (1984) *Il Nuovo Ragazzini, Dizionario Inglese-Italiano Italiano-Inglese*, 2nd edition, Zanichelli, Bologna.

Richardson, C. (1835–37) *New Dictionary of the English Language*, Pickering, London.

Sinclair, J. (ed.) (1987) *Collins COBUILD English Language Dictionary*, Collins, London and Glasgow.

Skey, M. (1977) *Dizionario Inglese-Italiano Italiano-Inglese*. Società Editrice Internazionale, Turin.

Smith, C. *et al.* (1971) *Collins Spanish Dictionary*, Collins, London and Glasgow.

Sykes, J. (ed.) (1982) *The Concise Oxford Dictionary of Current English*, 7th edition, Clarendon Press, Oxford.

Terrell, P. *et al.* (1981) *Collins German Dictionary*, Collins, London and Glasgow.

Urdang, L. (ed.) (1966) *Random House Dictionary of the English Language*, Random House, New York.

West, M. (1935) *The New Method English Dictionary*, Longmans Green, London.

Withals, J. (1553) *Shorte Dictionarie for Yonge Begynners*, T. Bertheletus, London.

## REFERENCES TO BOOKS AND ARTICLES

Atkins, B.T. (1985) 'Monolingual and Bilingual Dictionaries: a Comparison', in Ilson (1985): 15–24.

Bailey, R.W. (1986) 'Dictionaries of the Next Century', in Ilson (1986a): 123–37.

Bailey, R.W. (ed.) (1987) *Dictionaries of English: Prospects for the Record of Our Language*, University of Michigan Press, Ann Arbor, Mich.

Barnhart, C.L. (1962) 'Problems in Editing Commercial Monolingual Dictionaries', in Householder and Saporta (1962): 161–81.

Barnhart, C.L. (1973) 'Plan for a Central Archive for Lexicography in English', in McDavid and Duckert (1973): 302–6.

Béjoint, H. (1981) 'The Foreign Student's Use of Monolingual English Dictionaries', *Applied Linguistics*, 2, 3: 207–22.

Benson, M. (1985) 'A Combinatory Dictionary of English', *Dictionaries*, 7: 189–200.

Benson, M., Benson, E. and Ilson, R. (1986) *Lexicographic Description of English*, Benjamins, Amsterdam.

Burchfield, R.W. (1977) 'Preface', in K. Murray (1977): ix–xi.

Calzolari, N., Picchi, E. and Zampolli, A. (1987) 'The Use of Computers in Lexicography', in Cowie (1987): 56–77.

Congleton, J.E., Gates, J.E. and Hobar, D. (eds) (1979) *Papers on Lexicography in Honor of Warren C. Cordell*, Indiana State University, Terre Haute, Ind.

Cowie, A.P. (1978) 'The Place of Illustrative Material and Collocations in the Design of a Learner's Dictionary', in Strevens (1978): 127–39.

Cowie, A.P. (1981a) 'Lexicography and its Pedagogic Applications: an Introduction', *Applied Linguistics*, 2, 3: 203–6.

Cowie, A.P. (1981b) 'The Treatment of Collocations and Idioms in a Learner's Dictionary', *Applied Linguistics*, 2, 3: 223–35.

Cowie, A.P. (1983a) 'On Specifying Grammatical Form and Function', in Hartmann (1983a): 99–107.

Cowie, A.P. (1983b) 'English Dictionaries for the Foreign Learner', in Hartmann (1983a): 135–44.

Cowie, A.P. (1984) 'EFL Dictionaries: Past Achievements and Present Needs', in Hartmann (1984): 155–64.

Cowie, A.P. (1986) 'Collocational Dictionaries, a Comparative View', in Murphy (1986): 61–9.

*Cowie, A.P. (ed.) (1987) *The Dictionary and the Language Learner*, Max Niemeyer Verlag, Tübingen.

Drysdale, P. (1987) 'The Role of Examples in a Learner's Dictionary', in Cowie (1987): 213–23.

Dubois, J. (1981) 'Models of the Dictionary: Evolution in Dictionary Design', *Applied Linguistics*, 2, 3: 236–49.

Folomkina, S.K. (1986) 'Some Linguistic and Pedagogical Aspects of the Foreign Learner's Dictionary', in Murphy (1986): 56–60.

Frantz, D.O. (1979) 'Florio's Use of Contemporary Italian Literature in *A Worlde of Wordes*', *Dictionaries*, 1: 47–56.

Hartmann, R.R.K. (ed.) (1979) *Dictionaries and their Users*, Exeter University Press, Exeter.

*Hartmann, R.R.K. (ed.) (1983a) *Lexicography: Principles and Practice*, Academic Press, London and New York.

Hartmann, R.R.K. (1983b) 'On Theory and Practice', in Hartmann (1983a): 3–11.

Hartmann, R.R.K. (ed.) (1984) *LEXeter '83 Proceedings*, Max Niemeyer Verlag, Tübingen.

*Hartmann, R.R.K. (ed.) (1986) *The History of Lexicography*, Benjamins, Amsterdam.

Hartmann, R.R.K. (1987) 'Four Perspectives on Dictionary Use: a Critical Review of Research Methods', in Cowie (1987): 11–28.

Hausmann, F.J. (1979) 'Un Dictionnaire des Collocations est-il possible?', *Travaux de*

*Linguistique et de Littérature*, 17: 187–95.

Hausmann, F.J. (1985) 'Trois Paysages Dictionnairiques: la Grande Bretagne, la France et l'Allemagne. Comparaisons et Connexions', *Lexicographica*, 1: 24–50.

Heath, D. (1982) 'The Treatment of Grammar and Syntax in Monolingual English Dictionaries for Advanced Learners', *Linguistik und Didaktik*, 49/50: 95–107.

Herbst, T. (1986) 'Defining with a Controlled Defining Vocabulary in Foreign Learners' Dictionaries', *Lexicographica*, 2: 101–19.

Herbst, T. and Stein, G. (1987) 'Dictionary-using Skills: a Plea for a New Orientation in Language Teaching', in Cowie (1987): 115–27.

Hornby, A.S. (1933) *Second Interim Report on Collocations*, Institute for Research into English Teaching, Tokyo.

Hornby, A.S. (1938) 'Report on the Year's Work: Dictionary Problems', *IRET Bulletin*, 148: 20–8.

Hornby, A.S. (1939) 'Editorial: Objects and Objections', *IRET Bulletin*, 155: 147–55.

*Householder, F.W. and Saporta, S. (eds) (1962) *Problems in Lexicography*, Indiana University Press, Bloomington, Ind.

Howatt, A.P.R. (1984) *A History of English Language Teaching*, Oxford University Press, Oxford.

Iannucci, J.E. (1985) 'Sense Discriminations and Translation Complements in Bilingual Dictionaries', *Dictionaries*, 7: 57–65.

Ilson, R.F. (ed.) (1985) *Dictionaries, Lexicography and Language Learning*, Pergamon Press, Oxford.

*Ilson, R.F. (ed.) (1986a) *Lexicography: an Emerging International Profession*, Manchester University Press, Manchester.

Ilson, R.F. (ed.) (1986b) 'British and American Lexicography', in Ilson (1986a): 51–71.

Jansen, J., Mergeai, J.P. and Vanandroye, J. (1987) 'Controlling LDOCE's Controlled Vocabulary', in Cowie (1987): 78–94.

Johansson, S. (ed.) *Computer Corpora in English Language Research*, Norwegian Computing Centre for the Humanities, Bergen.

Klappenbach, R. (1968) 'Probleme der Phraseologie', *Wissenschaftliche Zeitschrift der Karl-Marx-Universität Leipzig*, 17, 2/3: 21–7.

Knowles, F. (1983) 'Towards the Machine Dictionary', in Hartmann (1983): 181–93.

Knowles, F. (1984) 'Dictionaries and Computers', in Hartmann (1984): 301–14.

*Landau, S.I. (1984) *Dictionaries: the Art and Craft of Lexicography*, Charles Scribner's Sons, New York.

Lemmens, M. and Wekker, H. (1986) *Grammar in English Learners' Dictionaries*, Max Niemeyer Verlag, Tübingen.

Lewis, R. and Pugmire, M. (1980) *How to Use Your Dictionary*, National Extension College, Cambridge.

Lyons, J. (1977) *Semantics*, two volumes, Cambridge University Press, Cambridge.

McDavid, R.I. (1979) 'The Social Role of the Dictionary', in Congleton, *et al.* (1979): 17–28.

*McDavid, R.I. and Duckert, A.R. (eds) (1973) *Lexicography in English*, New York Academy of Sciences, New York.

Mackin, R. (1978) 'On Collocations: "Words shall be Known by the Company they Keep"', in Strevens (1978): 149–65.

Malkiel, Y. (1962) 'A Typological Classification of Dictionaries on the Basis of Distinctive Features', in Householder and Saporta (1962): 3–24.

Merkin, R. (1983) 'The Historical/Academic Dictionary', in Hartmann (1983a): 123–33.

Meyer, R.T. (1979) 'The Relation of the *Medulla* to the Earlier English Glossaries', in Congleton *et al.* (1979): 141–50.

Moulin, H. (1987) 'The Dictionary and Encoding Tasks', in Cowie (1987): 105–14.

Murphy, M.G. (ed.) (1986) *Proceedings of the Fourth Joint Anglo-Soviet Seminar on English Studies*, The British Council, London.

Murray, J.A.H. (1900) *The Evolution of English Lexicography*, Clarendon Press, Oxford.

*Murray, K.M.E. (1977) *Caught in the Web of Words*, Yale University Press, New Haven and London.

Osselton, N.E. (1983) 'On the History of Dictionaries', in Hartmann (1983a): 13–21.

Palmer, H.E. (1934) *Specimens of English Construction Patterns*, Institute for Research into English Teaching, Tokyo.

Palmer, H.E. (1938) *A Grammar of English Words*, Longmans Green, London.

Quirk, R. (1973) 'The Social Impact of Dictionaries in the U.K.', in McDavid and Duckert (1973): 76–88.

Quirk, R. (1982) 'Dictionaries', in *Style and Communication in the English Language*, Edward Arnold, London.

Quirk, R., Greenbaum, S., Leech, G. and Svartvik, J. (1985) *A Comprehensive Grammar of the English Language*, Longman, Harlow.

Read, A.W. (1986) 'The History of Lexicography', in Ilson (1986a): 28–50.

Reif, J. (1987) 'The Development of a Dictionary Concept', in Cowie (1987): 147–58.

Rey, A. (1977) *Le Lexique: Images et Modèles: du Dictionnaire à la Lexicologie*, Armand Colin, Paris.

Riddell, J.A. (1979) 'Attitudes towards English Lexicography in the Seventeenth Century', in Congleton, *et al.* (1979): 83–91.

Sherman, D. (1979) 'Retrieving Lexicographic Citations from a Computer Archive of Language Materials', in Hartmann (1979): 136–42.

Sinclair, J. (1982) 'Reflections on Computer Corpora in English Language Research', in Johansson (1982): 1–6.

Snell-Hornby, M. (1987) 'Towards a Learner's Bilingual Dictionary', in Cowie (1987): 159–70.

*Starnes, D.T. and Noyes, G.E. (1946) *The English Dictionary from Cawdrey to Johnson, 1604–1755)*, University of North Carolina Press, Chapel Hill, NC.

Stein, G. (1979) 'The Best of British and American Lexicography, *Dictionaries*, 1: 1–23.

Stein, G. (1985) 'Word-formation in Modern English Dictionaries', in Ilson (1985): 35–44.

Stein, G. (1986) 'Sixteenth-Century English-Vernacular Dictionaries', in Hartmann (1986): 176–84.

Steiner, R.J. (1984) 'Guidelines for Reviewers of Bilingual Dictionaries', *Dictionaries*, 6: 166–181.

Strevens, P. (ed.) (1978) *In Honour of A.S. Hornby*, Oxford University Press, Oxford.

Tomaszczyk, J. (1979) 'Dictionaries: Users and Uses', *Glottodidactica*, 12: 103–19.

Tomaszczyk, J. (1981) 'Issues and Developments in Bilingual Pedagogical Lexicography', *Applied Linguistics*, 2, 3: 287–96.

Tomaszczyk, J. (1987) 'FL Learners' Communication Failure: Implications for Pedagogical Lexicography', in Cowie (1987): 136–45.

Trench, R.C. (1857) 'On some Deficiencies in our English Dictionaries', *Transactions of the Philological Society*, 1–60.

Urdang, L. (1973) 'Technological Potentials', in McDavid and Duckert (1973): 282–6.

Venezky, R.L. (1973) 'Computer Applications in Lexicography', in McDavid and Duckert (1973): 287–92.

Weiner, E.S.C. (1987) 'The *New Oxford English Dictionary*: Progress and Prospects', in Bailey (1987): 30–48.

West, M. (1953) *A General Service List of English Words*, Longman, London.

*Zgusta, L. (1971) *Manual of Lexicography*, Mouton, The Hague.

## FURTHER READING

The items noted with an asterisk in the list above will be found to be especially fruitful for further understanding of this whole topic.

# 20

# LANGUAGE AND WRITING-SYSTEMS

## JOHN MOUNTFORD

## 1. INTRODUCTION

A writing-system is a way of writing a language – in Sampson's terms, 'a given set of written marks together with a particular set of conventions for their use' (1985: 21). The term 'writing-system' is not, however, widely used outside linguistics, nor is it universally used by linguists themselves. Outside linguistics, whether in specialised treatments of this aspect of language (e.g. Diringer 1968, Gelb 1952, to name two of the principal histories of writing) or in ordinary educated discourse, a number of other terms do service for, or get confused with, this central concept. These include *script, spelling, alphabet, language* and *orthography*. This list is not exhaustive (we might have included the term 'character' for instance), but these are the five expressions with which we shall deal in sections 2–6, after a consideration of *writing-system* in section 1.

'Language' appears in this list because, as Sampson (1985: 25) and many others have pointed out, it is common for people to confuse a language and its writing-system ('English has five vowels'). This is a naïve confusion. There are, however, other confusions in this area for which linguists themselves, approaching it from different angles and with certain diffidences, are responsible. Writing was not, like phonetics and phonology, a new domain opened up by a new science, linguistics. Indeed, it was an old domain on which some linguists, perhaps beneficially for the establishment of their own discipline, chose to turn their backs – a position epitomised by Bloomfield in his magnificent and magisterial work *Language* (1935). The result is the unsettled terminology of today, and a still unclear message from linguistics to the man in the street (not to mention the woman in the primary classroom).

'Script' and 'alphabet', in the sense of 'writing-system', both have their home in the older tradition. In popular usage we can pinpoint this sense of 'alphabet' if we recall the experiments made in the 1960s, in British and American schools, with the Initial Teaching Alphabet. 'i.t.a', as it came to be known, was the name of a writing-system, a writing-system for English. Children who learned this 'alphabet' rarely, if ever, learned the i.t.a. letter inventory; what they learned, in the course of learning to read and write, was one way in which English could be written – a writing-system.

But in the 1960s and 1970s, though the term was becoming more current in linguistics, the subject was not. Nevertheless, there have always been linguists deeply concerned in a practical way with writing-systems (see especially Pike 1947, Smalley (ed.) 1964, Fishman (ed.) 1977), and there were descriptions of individual writing-systems (e.g. Haas 1956, Rice 1959). One of these was Albrow's important little study *The English writing system: Notes towards a description* (1972), which we will return to briefly at the end of this article. We mention it here, however, because its title exemplifies a narrow sense of 'writing-system', whereas we shall be using and recommending a wider sense. Albrow's study has nothing to say about, for instance, punctuation; it is devoted entirely to spelling, and does not glance, even prospectively, at any other aspect of written English. Yet punctuation clearly belongs, with spelling, to some greater whole, for which the term 'writing-system' seems perfectly appropriate. The narrow sense was current at the time (e.g. Francis 1967), and has persisted as part of a general terminological, and conceptual, fluidity in this under-cultivated area of linguistics.

As we have said, the term itself, in whatever sense, is not yet firmly established among linguists, let alone in a wider consciousness. In the course of this article we shall refer many times to Sampson's recent book which carries *Writing systems* as its title. The importance of the publication by a leading linguist of a full-length work devoted to this subject, and containing lucid, chapter-length studies of several significant and diverse writing-systems, cannot be exaggerated. Nor should his choice of title be overlooked.

## 2. WRITING-SYSTEM: WHOLE AND PARTS

Spelling and punctuation, we have just suggested, are parts of a larger whole – the writing-system. How big is a writing-system – how many parts does it contain? This section will outline the *scope* of the term, as it will be used in this article.

How wide the scope must be will be evident from the pages of this volume, in which a highly elaborated writing-system is put to highly elaborated use. Very broadly, we can see two kinds of text: the main text, paragraphed and sentenced, which we will call the 'flow' text, and other kinds of text, usually not sentenced, sometimes tabular, typically brief, mostly satellite to the main text, consisting of headings, labels and diagrams, numbers, tables, and so on. Simply to contrast this with 'flow' text, we will call it 'block' text (using 'text' itself very generally).

We can treat the flow text as segmentable, in a largely determinate fashion, by means of a units-within-units scale (Halliday 1985, Chapter 1.1), each unit consisting of at least one member of the unit next below in the scale: e.g. chapter, section, paragraph, sentence, (semi-)colon unit, comma unit, word, eventually to letter, the lowest unit in the scale. Obviously this is a candidate for the term '*grapheme*', and some linguists have equated letters and graphemes; Venezky (1970:50) even discards 'letter' in favour of 'grapheme'. This may have some attraction (though it lacks a common-sense appeal) if one is only concerned with the spelling system. But clearly, in text, there are other minimal elements besides letters; even in the purest literary texts, where numerals are banned from the flow text, there are marks of punctuation. It fits the present purpose of stressing the *scope* of the term 'writing-system' to adopt 'grapheme' as the overall term for the elements by which writing is realised and to distinguish subclasses of grapheme.

The typewriter keyboard displays the graphemes, not systematically, but conveniently. Central on the keyboard, and central to the writing-system, are the letters – central, because, via the spelling system, they realise the verbal component of text. We can call these, as long as we are focused on the writing-system of English, the alphabetic graphemes. Around these are at least three other classes of grapheme. First there are the punctuation graphemes, mentioned first because of their close association with the alphabetic graphemes in servicing flow text. Then there are the figures, the numeric graphemes, which are often integrated into flow text, but can do much more work on their own, being freely combinatorial, as block text of one kind or another, from page-numbers (or, outside books, as e.g. house numbers) to long tables of statistical data. Finally, like the punctuation graphemes in being non-combinatorial, there are a small number of symbolic graphemes, a heterogeneous class, some, such as the pound sign or the dollar sign, having lexical content, and some not, such as the asterisk.

In this way, for a given manifestation of the writing-system, we can arrive at a classified grapheme inventory. But this does not exhaust the resources of the writing-system (see Vachek 1979). There are, in addition, further 'figural' resources, to do with the shapes of the black marks. (Ink is not always black, nor is ink the only medium of marks, but ink epitomises writing in our culture: as Uldall wrote, 'the substance of ink has not received the same attention on the part of linguists that they have so lavishly bestowed on the substance of air' (1944:12).) These further figural resources include the following: the marks can be modified in size and/or in shape and the modifications deployed in single graphemes in text or in stretches of graphemes; in this way we get differentiation devices such as capitals (case contrast), italics (stance contrast), and boldface (weight contrast). Finally there are spatial resources: the arrangement of the black marks in relation to each other, and of groups of black marks in relation to other groups – these spatial arrangements of the graphemic resources giving rise on the large scale to flow text and block text, and on the small scale to identity devices, referral devices, serialisation devices, and so on. Thus footnoting makes use of a certain spatial arrangement of higher and lower on the page (combined, in print but not in typewriting, with a figural difference in size), and it uses small 'raised' numerals as a referral/identity device; in numeric text, higher and lower have a certain significance in fractions (which might be the other way round) and small raised numerals are put to a different purpose. Other writing-systems have used their letters as numerals and have devised other ways of expressing fractions.

Every meaning expressed through a writing-system is expressed by visual means, either figural (shapes) or spatial. A writing-system for one language may use means which it shares with the writing-system of another language or the writing-systems of many languages. This commonalty is an important feature of the global scene: one can point not merely to the massive spread in the past of the Roman alphabet, but to the ongoing penetration of European punctuation and European numerals. This can be regarded as a form of linguistic diffusion, and, where existing practices are abandoned in favour of new by the writing-system of the receiving language, it may be regarded as a form of linguistic convergence. Whatever the degree, however, of such 'graphemic harmonisation', the individuality of the writing-system remains: it resides in the spelling system.

The spelling system is the central system. One advantage of the use we are making of the term 'grapheme' is that, with the notion of the classified grapheme inventory, we can speak of the central class as the 'graphemes of spelling', or 'spelling graphemes'. This is not standard usage. But its adoption does give us a common designation for the letters of alphabetic writing-systems, the syllable symbols of syllabic writing-systems, and the characters of writing-systems like that of Chinese. These are the graphemes that carry the verbal text. We shall have more to say about them in section 4: 'Spelling: the typological component'.

We have taken our bird's-eye view of a writing-system by surveying cursorily and incompletely a grapheme inventory and its subdivisions. But a grapheme inventory, however enlarged, does not, of course, constitute a writing-system. The ways in which the graphemes are spatially arranged and figurally modified to express meanings, whether within their own subsystem or in another (e.g. letters realising words in the spelling system, or serving as identifiers/serialisers outside it) – all these ways are governed by the conventions of the writing-system internalised by literates. These are codified in dictionaries and grammars (though grammars in this century have tended to drop the component 'Orthography', prominent in the past), and in editorial manuals, publishers' stylesheets, and so on. Some of the conventions, especially in spelling, can be stated formally, like rules in phonology; others are more in the nature of principles, which can be weighed against each other, such as are found in pragmatics. Sampson's working definition of a writing-system, with which this article began, includes both 'a set of written marks' and 'a set of conventions'. The term 'writing-system' itself encapsulates these two aspects.

Enough has been said to indicate what is meant by the *scope* of a writing-system (a scope which will be found compatible with recently emerging views of literacy). Before saying more about the conventions governing the relations between graphemes and units of language structure (section 4), we need to talk, in section 3, about the marks.

## 3. SCRIPT: THE VISIBLE MARKS

In the last section, apart from saying that they could vary, we said nothing about the actual shapes of the written marks. These 'actual shapes' are of such wonderful variety and variability that it is not surprising that scholars and practitioners in different cultural traditions have dedicated themselves to the study and cultivation of them. If we speak of 'script' as the surface manifestation of a writing-system, this is not to slight either it or the palaeographers, typographers, calligraphers and others who have explored it so intimately. At no level of language does a specialised linguistic interest preclude other kinds of interest. When Sampson writes, 'In everyday speech the term script is commonly associated with superficial properties of the visual appearance of writing' (1985:20), he is registering a fact about the word which we can take advantage of. (Sampson himself is sensitive to matters of script, as is evident especially in pages 112–19 devoted to the Roman typefaces used in English and other European languages.) What we can do is to capitalise upon this association of 'script' and establish a regular relationship between 'script' and 'writing-system' in the following way. Script is that part of a writing-system by which it becomes visible. It is a necessary part of any writing-system. But there is no necessary connection between any one writing-system and any one script.

In this sense, 'script' must apply to all the visual features of a writing-system, not just to the letters or spelling graphemes. But so that readers can test for themselves the distinction we have just drawn, let us stick to the letters of the English alphabet. Let the reader think up, and write down, twenty-six distinct shapes, none of which resembles any of the standard letter shapes. (This is in itself a salutary exercise, especially if you try giving equally original names to the shapes!) Having done this, readers can assign the twenty-six new shapes randomly to the twenty-six categories which go by the names A, B, C, etc., each one to act as a substitute for a traditional letter. They can then transcribe a text – or compose one – in their 'new alphabet'.

The point is this: only the script will have changed. The spelling system of English will not have changed a jot – not one iota. There are two essential parts to a writing-system: a spelling system and a script; and they are mutually independent. What we have just done (and what schoolchildren and other secret-coders do) is to change the script without changing the spelling system. The converse of this is the course chosen by those English spelling reformers who keep the twenty-six Roman letters: they change the spelling system without changing the script. (On spelling reform, see Haas (ed.) 1969.)

The independence we are according to script must apply, as we have said, to all the resources of the writing-system, not just to the graphemes of the spelling system. All the graphemic shapes can be changed. And not only the graphemes but certain conventions for their arrangement can also be changed, in particular, the conventions which govern their linear continuity in text, in the sense that English, for instance, has rows and Chinese traditionally has columns. What we are referring to here, and including under script, are the features of *orientation*. These are (freak systems apart): *axis*, horizontal or vertical; *direction*, left-to-right/right-to-left or down/up; and '*lining*' (often overlooked), i.e. whether the lines, in a horizontal script, succeed one another downwards or upwards, or, in a vertical script, succeed one another from right to left (as they do in fact in traditional Chinese and Japanese writing) or from left to right. Given book format, in which the hinged side of the pages is vertical, it is direction in horizontal script, and lining in vertical scripts, that determines whether the hinge, before opening, is on the reader's left or right.

People used only to European scripts (Roman, Cyrillic, Greek) or to Indian (Hindi, Bengali, Tamil, etc.), all of which have left-to-right direction, and those used only to Semitic scripts (Arabic, Hebrew), which have right-to-left direction, or to Chinese/Japanese traditional script, which has right-to-left lining, each regard the other as opening the book – or the newspaper – from the back. (Practical considerations of text continuity long antedate the invention of the book: Sumerian clay tablets were columnised and compartmented in standard ways, and were turned over on a horizontal hinge, so to speak, for use on both sides.)

To illustrate once again the contingent nature of script, we might imagine that English was, by fiat, to be written from right to left, or perhaps as the young Benjamin Franklin first encountered written English on his father's printing press: he learned to read initially not only right to left but lining up. Such a change, from an analytical point of view, is a simple change in the script; the rest of the writing-system is unaffected.

But of course, for many languages (a small minority, in fact, if we take the world as a whole), there are profound historical associations between language and script. Put more precisely, this is a matter of association between language and writing-system, with script as an integral part of writing-system. These associations can be equally profound psychologically: hence the need to stress the distinction between language on the one hand and writing-system and script on the other, especially when they go by the same name (see section 6): Hebrew, to cite Sampson's example (1985: 21), becomes identified, in the eyes of user and non-user, with its distinctive square-script written form.

The topic of this section, however, is not the language/writing-system interface, but the writing-system/script interface. To revert to the central system of any writing-system, the spelling system, let us say that the spelling system specifies the graphemes for each spelling, while the actual shapes which manifest these graphemes are a matter of script.

Script is part of writing-system, and a rich field for the linguist to study. Some kind of parallel with phonology has long been recognised by some linguists with the use of terms 'grapheme', 'allograph' and 'graph', to match, in their mutual relationships, 'phoneme', 'allophone' and 'phone'. This fits with the way we are using 'grapheme' here, as long as it is extended to all classes of the grapheme inventory: for numerals have their variant shapes, just as letters do, and so do the graphemes of punctuation and the symbolic graphemes. But the mere fact that we distinguish quite diverse classes of grapheme in this way indicates that there are non-parallels, too, between phoneme and grapheme. 'There are evidently graphemes of a different order', as Stetson put it over fifty years ago in 'The Phoneme and the Grapheme' (1937:356).

The difference arises from the different natures of the two language mediums concerned, speech and writing. Speech is organically integrated with language, making use of internal physiological movements which transmit energy transitorily through air. Writing makes use of external movements which directly or indirectly produce durable modifications to external objects; these modifications of the outer world have no organic relation to language, only a relation by convention; their resources and constraints are very different from those of speech. Writing is manifested as a physical object, or, more precisely, as a two-dimensional array supported by a physical object. This has no analogue in speech; hence the special nature of script.

## 4. SPELLING: THE TYPOLOGICAL COMPONENT

We have said that the two essential parts of a writing-system are a spelling system and a script. Both are essential if the writing-system is to be used in the ordinary way for communication. But the two are separable, as was shown in the last section; and it is possible to discuss one without the other. Scripts without spelling systems are encountered in some dictionaries which print 'foreign alphabets' at the back, sometimes in the form of lists of bare letters, Greek, Hebrew, Cyrillic, etc.; but scripts set out in isolation from spelling systems are also to be found among the working-tools of librarians, archivists, palaeographers and typographers. In this section we shall be talking about the converse of this, about spelling systems in isolation from scripts – though no doubt readers will, in their mind's eye, link scripts (sometimes quite hazy notions of scripts) to the spelling systems mentioned.

Our point of entry can be with the linguist who carries out a phonemic analysis of an unwritten language in need of a writing-system. His analysis complete, he has *still* to select his spelling system. Let us suppose that the syllable structure of the language is very simple, that every syllable consists of a consonant phoneme followed by a vowel phoneme, and that the number of different syllables is quite limited. The linguist might opt for a syllable spelling system, one grapheme to each syllable in the phonology, requiring a syllabary, let us say, of fifty graphemes (like the *kana* syllabary of Japanese). Morphemes in such a language will tend to be two or more syllables long; such morphemes will be spelled with two or more syllabic graphemes or syllabics; morphemes of one syllable will be spelled with one grapheme, one syllabic.

Alternatively the linguist may opt for a phonemic spelling system, one grapheme to each phoneme in the phonology, requiring an alphabet of, let us say, twenty graphemes (Hawaiian requires even fewer). Most morphemes will now be spelled with four or more phonemic graphemes or letters, two to each syllable; morphemes of one syllable will be spelled with two letters; but let us suppose that there are a couple of odd function words consisting of a vowel phoneme only (as there are in English) – these will be spelled with one letter.

Let us assume the linguist chooses the second course. The point of this highly simplified example is to establish that the decision to 'go phonemic' at this point is a decision *about the nature of the spelling-system-to-be*. It is a fundamental decision about that spelling system – that its graphemes will map on to the phonemes. It is *not* a decision about script. Script is still wide open – Roman? Cyrillic? quasi-Arabic? quasi-Chinese? something non-aligned?

(Of course, both spelling system and script may well have been decided long in advance. For 'phonemic plus Roman' as a norm, see Pike's *Phonemics: a technique for reducing languages to writing* (1947).)

After the fundamental decision about the *type* of spelling system, there will be other choices to make, to do with the more detailed structure of the spelling system. Suppose now, instead, that the decision was in favour of a syllabic type, and suppose that the phonology yields fifty different syllables, the product of each of ten consonants pairing with each of five vowels. The syllabary may then consist of fifty graphemes independent of each other (Japanese *kana* are arbitrary in this way). Or the graphemes of phonologically related syllables may themselves be related to each other. The graphemes of the syllables containing the same vowel may be related to each other; or those containing the same consonant may be related to each other; if both sets of phonological relations are respected, we shall have a fully systematic matrix of graphemes. But it is the *spelling system* which acknowledges (or does not acknowledge, as the case may be) the relations existing in the phonology, by the relations it sets up between the graphemes. Of course, these inter-grapheme relations must be made visible by patterns in the graphs which realise the graphemes; but just how they are made visible is a matter of script.

In the heading of this section we have called the spelling system the typo-logical component, and it is now time to deal with the standard typology of writing-systems (see critique in Haas 1976). Of the innumerable ways in which writing-systems can be classified, the most significant structurally concerns how the writing-system carries the verbal text, and this is the job of the spelling system. All spelling systems do this job by representing words (Abercrombie 1965: 87), though they do not all signal word-divisions (the boundaries between words in text). Notably Chinese and Japanese do not do so. But that is incidental. Of much greater interest for our present purpose is the fact that the word-structures of these two languages are very different. Chinese is an 'isolating' language *par excellence*, in which morphemes combine into short polymorphemic words in a limited way, while Japanese forms longer polymorphemic words, like English but mostly by suffixation. In both cases the spelling system represents the words in terms of their morphemic make-up. In the case of Chinese each morpheme is represented directly by a single morphemic grapheme, or 'character', to use the traditional English term. Typically the morphemes function as monomorphemic words, but many can combine into bimorphemic words, with a few bound morphemes functioning only in combination. In the case of Japanese, the morphemes are represented, some by morphemic graphemes – characters or *kanji*, taken over from Chinese – and some by syllabic graphemes, the *kana* graphemes already mentioned.

With morphemic graphemes we complete the three main types of grapheme found in spelling systems, namely morphemic, syllabic and phonemic. Though we referred earlier to the choice between phonemic and syllabic as a fundamental decision in the design of a spelling system, a much more fundamental difference now emerges. In representing morphemes phonemic and syllabic graphemes have this in common: they give information about the phonological realisation of the morphemes. Morphemic graphemes do not. (In principle they do not; in practice, however, they may.) Since there are thousands of morphemes to be represented, each by a distinct grapheme, the inventory of spelling graphemes, instead of being, in round figures, in the order of 15 to 50, as for a phonemic alphabet, or 50 to 500, as for a syllabary, will itself run into thousands. 'Such a spelling system is exemplified, uniquely in the modern world, by the 'character' system of Chinese.

To conclude: The standard typology of writing-systems relates to their spelling systems. Individual spelling systems are largely homogeneous (the mixture found in Japanese is exceptional) and they fall into two main types, for which the simplest labels are 'phonological' and 'non-phonological'. Phonological spelling systems sub-divide into 'phonemic' and 'syllabic'. The labels 'phonological' and 'non-phonological' are open to objection: Sampson (1985: 32) uses 'logographic' for the latter, which is widely accepted, and 'phonographic' for the former. There are may refinements which have to be made to this typology: some relate to the variety of phonographic systems. Sampson, for instance, uses 'segmental' in place of 'phonemic', and since some spelling systems, notably those of Arabic and Hebrew, do not give full phonemic information, this is attractive. Sampson has also suggested a further phonological type, 'featural' (1985: 40), to which would belong the remarkable spelling system of the native Korean writing-system, called Han'gŭl, to which he devotes Chapter 7 of his book. A recent textbook of linguistics has also suggested 'morphophonemic' as a further type, but regards a discussion of it as beyond the scope of an introductory text. In view of the morphophonemic nature of the English spelling system and its accessibility, this judgement may seem surprising. To appreciate the complexity created in writing-systems by the interplay between morphological structure and phonological structure, and between them and the spelling structure (not to mention the effects of lexical structure, the incidence of homonymy, and other factors), the student cannot do better than study Sampson's *Writing Systems*, the last chapter of which, Chapter 10, is sensibly given over to the English spelling system.

## 5. ALPHABET: AN ANCILLARY COMPONENT

Of the three principal types of writing system – logographic, syllabic and phonemic – described in the last section, the term 'alphabet' is most closely associated with the third, the phonemic type. 'Alphabet' and 'letters' are felt to be mutually defining.

We have argued already for the extension of the notion of spelling to writing-systems of all types. In this section we briefly continue that argument and then explore the possible extension of the term 'alphabet'. There may be some reservations about applying the term 'spelling system' to all three types: it fits more comfortably with phonemic writing-systems than with syllabic, and more comfortably with phonological writing-systems than with non-phonological ones. But with the marked growth of interest, in recent years, in the Japanese writing-systems (Seeley (ed.) 1984; Sampson 1985: Ch. 9), it is clear that the term 'spelling' is being readily applied not only to the subsidiary *kana* systems, which are both syllabic, but also to the original *kanji* system which is a morphemic system employing Chinese characters, at least in the mixture of *kanji* and *kana* which constitutes the standard system of today.

The *simplest* argument for extending the application of the term 'spelling' to the Chinese system itself is to say that the one-to-one match of morpheme and grapheme is the decision, so to speak, of the spelling system; what shapes are actually used to realise the graphemes is a matter of script. The fact that it is more complicated than that, that there are similarity relations as well as dissimilarity relations between the graphs realising the graphemes, is a *further* argument for a spelling system – for a more complex spelling system – not an argument for no spelling system at all.

Should the term 'alphabet' be extended in the same direction, and as far? It is not the purpose of this section to propose an answer to this question, but rather by exploring it to illustrate the implications of the wide scope we have given to the term 'writing-system'.

What is clear from the start, just thinking of the English alphabet, is that it is not part of the spelling system: no spelling rules produce the alphabet. But it is part of the writing-system. We can think of it as part of the grapheme inventory, namely the inventory of the 26 graphemes of spelling. Obviously, for every spelling system, the graphemes can be listed. But the order in which to list them is a matter for decision: it might be by graphic make-up (more strictly, by the make-up of the graphs which realise the graphemes), or by the phonological value in the case of phonological writing-systems, or by frequency of occurrence, or by some other systematic method. Or it might be random. And the remarkable thing about the English alphabet is that its order is random. None of the three methods just suggested has any relevance to the standard order of the letters, nor will the reader find any other structural rationale.

This randomly ordered series of letters, institutionalised as the English alphabet, provides the filing system for verbal data on which our social organisation depends. Leaving all machine usage on one side, it works successfully on an enormous scale because English literates, in their millions, commit it to to memory, usually in early childhood. Here the *names* of the letters come into play – names which are habitually treated as marginal words in the language, though they are perfectly respectable words phonologically, and only lose their respectability through their lack of recognised spellings. These names serve two vital functions: they enable us to refer to the letters in speech, and so to communicate spellings and references (and other symbolic uses of the letters) by word of mouth, and they make the alphabet recitable and so memorisable. No doubt it can be learnt solely by eye or by touch, but that is not how normal literates actually learn it.

There are many other special uses, besides their use as an alphabet, to which the letters are put (Malkiel 1965). But we have to extend these remarks beyond the English alphabet to other alphabets, and indeed beyond alphabets, as traditionally understood.

Let us, at least to begin with, adopt the expression 'filing alphabet' for the institutionalised order of spelling graphemes which we find in English and other languages as an ancillary part of the writing-system serving as a principal means of systematic information storage and retrieval. In the case of writing-systems based on the Roman alphabet, it is not necessarily just a sequence of simple, single letters as in English. In Spanish, taking their place in the filing alphabet, we find the digraph *ch* following the single letter *c* and the digraph *ll* following the single letter *l*; in Serbo-Croatian we find that *c* is followed by *č* with a 'diacritic' followed in turn by *ć*, with a different diacritic and *d* is followed by *dž*, a compound of digraph and diacritic. This inter- polation of additional letters exemplifies the sound principle which was recommended, for instance, in a non-European context, by the *Practical Orthography for African Languages* (1962:19), with 'hooked *b*' following ordinary *b*, and so on. But in the Danish filing alphabet we find three additional vowel graphemes tacked on the end after *z*: *æ ø å*, in that order. To eyes conditioned by the Roman letters, these are clearly two A-shapes and an O-shape, and on the interpolation principle they would take their places in the body of the alphabet (the Danish reform of 1948 actually substituted, with a diacritic, *å* for the digraph *aa*, which had come at the beginning of the alphabet before *a* itself). Interpolating has, however, been the rule, rather than appending, in adaptations of the Roman alphabet, so maximising its convergent influence.

This influence is matched in the case of the Cyrillic alphabet. This is also, like the Roman, a generalised stock of letters on which the writing-systems of many languages can be said to draw. Despite its larger size (the Russian version has 33 letters), adaptations of it often require other figurally modified forms, or the use of diacritics especially on vowel letters. (It is, incidentally, useful to have non-language names for these two alphabet stocks. In the last analysis, as we are using them here, 'Roman' and 'Cyrillic' are script names. 'Latin' is widely used instead of 'Roman', but there are advantages in keeping it as a language name. Cyrillic is often misunderstood as 'Russian', which is the modern 'yardstick' alphabet where Cyrillic is concerned, as the English alphabet might be said to be where Roman is concerned.)

The Russian alphabet presents another nuance of institutionalised alphabets. Four of its letters are never word-initial: the 'soft sign', for instance, is a consonantal enclitic among letters, and its function in this respect could be served by a diacritic instead of a segmental graph. This means only that these four letters do not appear as indexical letters in a dictionary; they still have a role in the alphabetisation of entries. Another reflex of their not appearing word-initial is that in listings of the alphabet they are often not assigned 'capital' shapes (though few Russian letters have distinctive capital shapes anyway).

We may note at this point, since it enters into many people's image of what constitutes an alphabet, that case contrast (upper- and lower-case shapes) is confined to writing-systems whose 'alphabeticalness' is unchallenged: which is to say that capitals, and capitalisation of initial letters, are a resource available only in the Roman (including Icelandic and Irish), Cyrillic, Greek and Armenian scripts (though some modern Roman-based writing-systems have been designed without case contrast).

There is little difficulty in extending the term 'alphabet', in the sense of filing alphabet, to syllabic writing. There are three reasons for this. First, outside scholarly controversy, the category 'syllabic' is used quite loosely to cover anything that lies between fully segmental phonemic systems (such as the ones referred to in the last paragraph) and the fully morphemic systems of Chinese. It can include the segmental phonemic systems of Arabic and Hebrew, in which vowels characteristically are not marked at all, or if they are marked, are marked non-segmentally, by diacritics. Both of these writing-systems have reasonably short alphabets consisting, in the case of Hebrew, of 22 letters randomly ordered, and in the case of Arabic, of 28 letters partially, but only partially, ordered by letter-shape. (This, in Arabic script, which is unusual in being always cursive, never letter-divided, means one of two, three or four distinct allographic shapes.) The shortness and the random order are quintessentially alphabetic, despite the absence of vowel-letters, and perfectly good for indexing purposes as Arabic and Hebrew words cannot begin with a vowel.

Second, there is one contemporary writing-system which is sometimes cited as perfectly syllabic (but see Sampson 1985:64), and that is the writing-system of Amharic. (It is the principal writing-system of a small group based on the Ethiopic script.) In this, briefly, the spelling graphemes can be set out in a systematic two-dimensional array, 33 consonants down and 7 vowels across; each consonant graph undergoes the same set of seven differentiations, including zero, to form a set of 231 consonant-plus-vowel graphemes. (The differentiations, except zero, take the form of tiny strokes attached to the body of the consonant graph. Functionally there is nothing to choose between these and unattached differentiations, which would be called diacritics; and since some familiar diacritics are attached ones – cedilla is attached to *c*, and in Danish ø the letter is actually traversed by its oblique diacritic – we can say the Amharic letters carry diacritics too.) Precisely because this matrix is regarded as a syllabary, there may be a reluctance to use the term 'alphabet' in connection with it. But it is based on an institutionalised order for the consonant graphemes which serves as a filing alphabet for the writing-system, and is referred to as an alphabet.

Third, there is the evidence from Devanagari. This is the most widely known script of the huge and diversified family of Indian writing-systems, and it is exemplified by modern Hindi, Marathi, etc., and the ancient but still cultivated Sanskrit. Here again there is a standard phonological array for the graphemes, which serves as the filing alphabet (but, unlike Amharic, there are, in most of the associated writing-systems, additional conjunct graphs for consonant clusters). In this case, however, whatever lack of agreement there may be over the classification of the complex spelling system, which is characterised by consonant graphemes expressing an 'inherent vowel', there is a long and widespread tradition of referring to the Devanagari 'alphabet' and 'letters'.

There is no such tradition when it comes to Chinese characters. There is no collective name for these, in English, corresponding to 'alphabet' and 'syllabary' (unless 'charactery' is revived); and the traditional term 'character' keeps 'letter' at bay. But if we cannot ask what filing *alphabet* Chinese uses, we can ask what filing *system* it uses. The answer is a system based on 214 'radicals', which takes us into the heart of the Chinese spelling system and script.

Script-wise, each character occupies an imaginary square, whether it has few (say five) strokes or many (say fifteen). Spelling-wise, each character is either simplex or complex (though these are not standard terms). This is not a matter of number of strokes, though complex characters will tend to have more strokes than simplex because they consist of *two* constituent characters tucked, in various ways, into one imaginary square. This is a fundamental reason why the system is learnable; the majority of characters are complex characters made up of recognisable parts. One part, one constituent character, will be one of the 214 semantic 'radicals'. These form the basis of the filing system, each complex character being classified by the simplex radical it contains. The 214 radicals are ordered by script – by number of strokes – and the characters listed under each radical are ordered according to the same principle. (In Japanese, *kanji* have the same structure, but the two *kana* syllabaries have standard orders and so provide additional or alternative filing systems.)

We have, in this section, expanded on only one of the subsidiary systems which support or extend the essential components of a writing-system; to give it generality we can call it the filing system, though some may prefer 'indexing system'. It is intimately related to the spelling system, in a way in which the other subsidiary systems – the punctuation system, the numeric system, and the symbolic sub-systems – are not. Hence the typological thread running through this section. Even though they lack this interest, the other systems warrant study on a general scale, across all writing-systems. For present purposes, the filing system must stand as one example only of what must be included in the concept 'writing-system', once its scope is taken to be greater than that of spelling system.

## 6. LANGUAGE – AND SYSTEMS OF WRITING

The danger at the naïve level is that a language and its writing-system will be confused, the language being identified with its writing-system. Sampson in his Introduction (1985:Ch.1:21) points out that this is more liable to occur when language and writing-systems share the same name, instancing, as we said earlier, the use of 'Hebrew' applied without distinction to the language and to its written form. An example nearer home, for English literates, is English itself. The writing-system in which this volume is written has no generally accepted name; English speakers are mass victims of what we might nickname 'the graphetic fallacy'. We shall have a proposal to make in this regard in due course, at the end of the next section, after we have explored from another angle the relationship between language and writing-system. For in these two sections we shall examine the phrase just used, 'a language and its writing-system'. In the present section we shall look at it, so to speak, from above; in section 7, from below.

We have been, up till now, exploring the *scope* of the term 'writing-system'. If we look at the writing-systems in the world today, we see that each one is built round a nucleus of spelling system plus script. These two components might be all there is to an incipient or immature writing-system, but we are concerned here with the hundreds of fully-fledged writing-systems operating in contemporary national states at national or regional level or for more localised communities. Each of these writing-systems also contains a number of subsidiary components, especially a punctuation system, a numeric system, some symbolic subsystems, and on a different, non-textual, dimension, a filing system. This may not be exhaustive, but it serves to emphasise that in describing a writing-system we are describing more than its spelling.

As a unit of description, writing-system has the same inherent attraction as language: hundreds of particular languages, including all the world's standard languages, are well institutionalised and are made objects of attention by linguists and by others concerned, not just with language description, but with language use and maintenance. And the same is true of their writing-systems, the normal relation between the two being perceived as one-to-one. Hence the expression 'a language and its writing-system'. Keeping the language constant, this norm can be diverged from in either direction: there are languages with less than one writing-system – 'unwritten languages', as they are called, typically tribal ones; and there are languages with more than one writing-system. The standard examples of the latter case are Serbo-Croatian with its two scripts, Cyrillic and Roman, which are mutually exclusive, and Japanese with its two spelling systems, mixed *kanji*-plus-*kana*, and *kana* used on their own. *Kana* are syllabic graphemes, recognisable in the normal mixed writing by their simpler recurrent shapes. They are themselves written in two scripts, *katakana* and *hiragana*, which are used for different purposes. In the mixed system *hiragana* typically realise grammatical formatives, namely suffixes and function words, while *katakana* are used to write certain lexical items not easily expressed in *kanji*, such as foreign words (e.g. modern Western loanwords as distinct from the huge stock of Chinese *kanji* borrowed from the seventh century onwards of our era, as the basis of the writing-system).

But the Japanese threefold situation is unique, and the Yugoslavian situation is unusual. One language, one writing-system is regarded as the norm. What is also quite normal is for that one writing-system to be part of a larger pattern of writing-systems sharing a common script. This is what is meant in the title of the section by 'systems of writing'. Cyrillic Serbo-Croatian is on the western edge of a huge Cyrillic alphabet area stretching from Serbia to the Pacific. Roman Serbo-Croatian is on the eastern edge of an even huger Roman alphabet area stretching from Croatia and covering Western Europe, the Americas, most of the Pacific and Oceania, and a great deal of Africa. The rest of the world falls into three other main script areas: the Chinese area – China itself and some adjoining countries, Taiwan, Japan, South Korea; the Indian area, containing a huge family of scripts both within India and beyond; and the Arabic area, stretching from North Africa to Central Asia. As an example of a minor script with a distinct area of its own, we have already mentioned Ethiopic, lying between Roman and Arabic in Africa.

Such a map, of five major script areas, gives a very simple overview of the world's systems of writing. (A version of it will be found on the front endpapers of Nakanishi's *Writing Systems of the World* (1980)). But there are lessons to learn from so simple a picture, which help us to appreciate how writing-systems, despite their diversity, can be, in some respects, a linguistically convergent force rather than the opposite.

In the first place it is possible to imagine a world map of scripts as variegated as the world map of languages. Nothing like that has occurred historically. Writing has spread, and continues to spread, by diffusion. creating as it does certain affinities between language cultures, as every cultural transmission must. These affinities are not merely at the level of script – at the level of visual sameness, resemblance, or derivativeness of grapheme shapes. We said earlier that there is no necessary connection between a script and a writing-system, but only historical associations. We can elaborate on that a little now. There must be quantitative dependencies between scripts and spelling systems, because typologically-different spelling systems require different numbers of graphs to match the numbers of their graphemes (from logographic reckoned in thousands down to phonemic reckoned in tens). Qualitatively, however, the characteristic shapes of any script can, in theory, be used with any writing-system: the twenty-six Roman letters could be replaced by twenty-six 'Chinese' shapes, and Chinese characters could be replaced by complex shapes built up out of Roman letters. What happens in fact, almost universally, is that script is borrowed, and along with script, certain spelling system features are borrowed: the script shapes are borrowed along with their spelling values. Thus Japanese (and Korean) borrowed Chinese characters along with Chinese meanings; in India, language after language derived its script, directly or indirectly, from that used for ancient Sanskrit and Pali, taking over the letters together with their consonantal values and the system of inherent vowel which characterises this family of writing-systems; and in the same way, Arabic, Cyrillic and Roman scripts have all been diffused as scripts allied to distinctive spelling systems, both in general as regards the way the spelling system works, and in particular as regards classes of graphemes (consonants are usually taken over as consonants, vowels as vowels) and as regards the spelling values of individual graphemes, with varying degrees of adaptation and approximation. All this has happened on an enormous scale; we are not talking about a peripheral linguistic phenomenon. It is true that the Roman system of writing has far outstripped the other major systems in geographical spread, in the number of languages to which it has been applied, and in the number of people using it. But the spread of the Cyrillic system, from its birthplace in Moravia or the Balkans (where it now survives in Bulgaria as well as Yugoslavia) to Russia and then eastwards to the furthest boundaries of the Soviet Union – the spread of the Arabic system of writing, to other languages in North Africa and far across Asia, as far as Malay and Borneo (historically into Europe, too: Spanish and Slavonic have both been written in Arabic script) – and the applications of the original Brahmi script to a variety of Indian languages centuries before the expansion of the other two systems – all these transmissions constitute huge chapters of linguistic history, each unfinished today. There have, of course, been retreats as well as advances: systems of writing succeeding one another can be studied in most parts of the world (Arabic retreated long ago in Europe, and quite recently in the Far East), but the succession Arabic-Roman-Cyrillic which some languages have undergone in the Soviet Union is especially instructive. (See Wellisch (1978) Ch.2, the sections on Latinization, Cyrillification, and Arabification.)

In the second place, having in the last paragraph imagined the script map of the world imposed upon a language distribution map and noted the general tendency of languages to belong to areal systems of writing, we may next imagine the language map as one which shows the genetic affiliation of the languages as well as their distribution (see Chapters 24 and 26 below). We then find that each of the major systems of writing has been extended not merely to related languages but to languages of other families of the most diverse kinds. We have mentioned already the case of Chinese and Japanese, which are genetically unrelated languages. Structurally they are poles apart (Inoue 1979:245: 'Chinese is an isolating language, while Japanese is agglutinating;' according to Sampson, Japanese is inflectional as well (1985: 173), making it mixed, like English. The nineteenth-century morphological typology of languages is highly relevant to the structure of spelling systems – unlike the more recent syntactic typology, where again the two languages differ). Phonologically, too, Chinese is a tone language, while Japanese belongs to the other half – the smaller half? – of the world's languages which are not. Yet the Chinese system of writing was borrowed by Japanese. Similarly we can now note that the Indian script embraces (among others) members of two distinct families of languages, Indo-European and Dravidian. The Cyrillic alphabet system has been extended to some sixty languages of various families, and the Roman alphabet to hundreds of languages of all kinds (including many varied languages in the USSR under the Romanisation policy for minority languages in the 1920s and 1930s (Wellisch ibid.; Henze 1977)).

To press home this point of the scale and diversity of script extension, let us glance at the parties to the misalliance, which lasted for several centuries, between a Semitic system of writing, Arabic, and a member of the Turkic family of languages, Turkish, – a combination which had been the administrative language of the Ottoman Empire. In the most celebrated change of writing-system in modern times, these two parted company abruptly in 1928, when the new republic of Turkey switched from Turkish in Arabic script to Turkish in Roman script. As regards Arabic script, we read in Jensen that it has been adapted in its time to write 'the Persian, Turkish, Tartarian, Afghan, Hindustani and Malayan languages, indeed even the Swahili and Haussa languages, besides a few Berber tongues of North Africa' (1970:332). And as regards Turkic languages, we read in Diringer that various members of the family have been written with: (1) the Kok-Turki alphabet (Runes), (2) the

Uighur alphabet, (3) the Arabic alphabet (Diringer enumerates nine other Turkic languages in addition to the Osmanli Turkic of the Ottoman Empire), (4) the Russian or Cyrillic characters (five languages enumerated), (5) the Armenian and (6) the Greek characters used by Armenians and Greeks living in Turkey for writing Turkish, (7) the Hebrew character, and (8) the Roman character (1968:439).

The vintage histories of writing, two of which we have just drawn upon, are works of panoramic scholarship, which trace the diffusion of systems of writing from their earliest beginnings. Jensen in German, Diringer in English and Cohen in French have all been available since the 1950s. They have not been superseded either in compass or in wealth of detail. But, for the final point in this section, arising from the (notional) map of the world's scripts, it is best to refer the reader to Nakanishi's book, mentioned on p. 716 above, which aims to give contemporary information about national, and some regional, writing-systems, illustrating all the main ones with reproductions of the front pages of newspapers.

So far, we have only spoken of the association between script and spelling system and how these jointly contribute to convergence between languages using the same system of writing. But the *scope* of a writing-system extends to its filing system, another feature making for convergence, as discussed in the last section, and to its other subsidiary systems, the punctuational, numeric and symbolic. These also exhibit the convergent influence at work in writing-systems, since they are borrowed too, along with script and system of spelling. But in the contemporary world we find these systems acting convergently between the major systems of writing themselves. The form this takes is one-way: it is the penetration of the writing-systems of other script areas by European punctuation and numerals and by various symbols such as the arithmetical operator signs, copyright sign, dollar sign, and so on. The progressive adoption of European punctuation and numerals is attested for many languages in Nakanishi (1980).

The convergent influence of European mathematical notation must not be underestimated either: wherever it is used, its axis and direction are universally respected. And in this connection, in conclusion, we should not overlook another indication of European penetration at the purely script level, namely the increasing use of horizontal axis, and (usually) left-to-right direction, in the writing-systems of the Chinese script family, all traditionally written vertically. Note that the imaginary square occupied by each character ('equidimensionality' as Martin calls it (1972:85)) lends itself to use on either axis, and, indeed, in either direction: Nakanishi, a mine of information, reports that in Taiwan 'articles in the same newspaper may be written on a horizontal line from left to right and from right to left with no indication' (1980:86)!

## 7. ORTHOGRAPHY – AND THE FUNCTIONAL CLASSIFICATION OF WRITING-SYSTEMS

Up to this point we have avoided using the word 'orthography' except to mention the lost component of grammars which in earlier times (Householder 1971:264) was headed 'De Orthographia' and came first. One reason for not using the term is that it is a synonym of 'spelling'. The two words can be discriminated in a number of ways, but they have a large overlap of meaning, such that we could have chosen, in section 4 above, the grander name 'orthographic system' instead of 'spelling system' (the most substantial linguistic study of the spelling system of English is Venezky (1970) with the title *The structure of English orthography*). There is, however, another role needing to be filled, which 'orthography' fits rather satisfactorily and where 'spelling;' would not do at all. In this section we explain what that role is, and to do so we move from the dimension of *scope* of a writing-system (how big is it? how many parts does it have?) to another dimension, that of the *range* of writing-systems.

In his Introductory Chapter 1, Sampson, in order to prepare the way for his Chapter 7 on the Korean writing-system, illustrates the notion of a featural type of spelling system with an example drawn from much nearer home – Pitman's Shorthand. ('Featural' is Sampson's term, 'spelling system' is ours – see section 4 above.) He explains that this is a phonographic spelling system in which phonetic relations between the phonemes are systematically reflected in the script. Briefly, consonant phonemes are realised by lines, vowel phonemes by separate diacritic dots and small dashes; classes of consonants are systematically distinguished – place of articulation by angle to the horizontal writing-line, manner of articulation by shape (straight lines for stops, curved for fricatives), and voicing by weight (thick strokes for voiced, thin for voiceless), etc. This is only a partial summary, but it is ample evidence that the spelling system of Pitman's Shorthand is quite unlike that of any of the score or so of writing-systems mentioned in the preceding sections, or indeed of any of the hundreds alluded to in the last section – with the exception, as Sampson says, of the writing-system invented for Korean by King Sejong in the fifteenth century.

King Sejong's writing-system, however, was not designed as a shorthand system, i.e. not specially for speed writing. This can be seen from the relative complexity of its script, which contains a unique syllabic clustering convention echoing the rectangular effect of the Chinese script used for Korean prior to Sejong's effort at reform. The script of Pitman's Shorthand, on the other hand, is suited to its purpose of speed in several ways: (1) the graphs that realise the graphemes are simply single strokes – they are shapes that are hardly shapes at all, in that they do not embrace or enclose space as many of our Roman (and King Sejong's) letters do; (2) the number of different distinct shapes required is halved by the thick/thin principle – a different weight realising a different grapheme; (3) the graphs are designed to be written cursively, each attached immediately to its predecessor without any additional joining stroke such as is found in ordinary cursive handwriting; (4) the spelling system exploits the simple line shapes by shortening them to realise certain grapheme sequences; (5) the vowel diacritics can, by convention, be omitted, at the discretion of the writer (who is often the sole reader as well).

From these brief descriptions, first of the spelling system, then of the script, of Pitman's Shorthand, we can see that it is significantly different from our ordinary writing-system. The 'flow' text of the present volume could be written, indeed printed, in Pitman's Shorthand, but few of its intended readership would be able to read it. Even so, the two do share certain basic properties: e.g. both spelling systems are phonological (phonographic), and both scripts have the same orientation – horizontal, left-to-right. More to the point is that they are both writing-systems for English. Yet no-one cites English as an example of a language with more than one writing-system.

This is our starting-point for a quick survey of what we have referred to as the *range* of writing-systems. Just as the existence of punctuation in addition to spelling pointed to a dimension of 'scope' in respect of the structure, or componentry, of writing-systems, so the existence of shorthand, of another writing-system besides 'the ordinary one', points to another dimension which we need to explore. If shorthand is a different kind of writing-system, how many different kinds are there, and what are they?

Shorthand is clearly a specialised kind of writing-system, designed for speed of writing. Early shorthand systems were also used for cryptographic purposes, for secret writing: Samuel Pepys may well have had both aims in view when he wrote his diary in Shelton's Tachygraphy (1635). That gives us two specialised kinds of writing-system, and the start of a systematic nomenclature for further functional kinds. We can distinguish at least the following (Mountford 1973):–

*Stenographies* Function: speed writing. Familiar as 'shorthands', e.g. Pitman's and Gregg's handwritten systems, Palantype machine-written.

*Cryptographies* Function: secret writing. Familiar as private codes or ciphers, or in institutional contexts as part of highly sophisticated information security systems.

*Paedographies* Function: language teaching, i.e. pedagogical. Familiar from 'phonetic transcriptions' in foreign-language teaching, but also used in initial literacy teaching, e.g. i.t.a., mentioned in the Introduction above.

*Technographies* Function: linguistic analysis. Familiar to linguists from various kinds of working text: phonetic field-notes; broad transcriptions; texts, often fragmentary, displaying intonational, grammatical, or other information.

To these may be added (Wellisch 1978: 9):–

*Machinographies* Function: for 'direct and automatic use by machines, such as Morse telegraph keys or print-out devices of computers'. Wellisch contrasts a direct computer print-out of French devoid of all diacritical marks with text produced by 'a properly programmed computer driving a phototypesetting device' displaying 'not only French standard orthography but also different typefaces, indentations, and so forth'.

And, though Wellisch (ibid.: 19) eschews the name:–

*Metagraphies* Function: to convert text from an unfamiliar writing-system into a writing-system with more familiar characteristics without change of language, encountered in foreign names – personal names, place names, trade names – titles of works, institutions, etc., and encountered very often as 'block' text, but also, along with other foreignisms, incorporated into flow text. This form of 'script conversion', as Wellisch calls it, is more familiar under the name 'transliteration'; but if 'transliteration', or 'metagraphy', is taken to mean conversion by means of rules relating only to graphemes, it will, as Wellisch rightly argues, be inadequate, since the spelling values of the graphemes are nearly always involved. Wellisch (1978), *The Conversion of Scripts* – a title which embraces both the large-scale linguistic phenomena of the last Section and the documentary minutiae, no less linguistic, of library science, which is Wellisch's professional domain – is a full-length and very wide-ranging study of writing-systems of this kind.

This set of six specialised kinds of writing-system is not necessarily exhaustive, nor are the functional kinds all mutually exclusive. But the functional classification of writing-systems is incomplete, anyway, until we bring in the most important functional kind of all – the class of 'ordinary writing-systems'. This is the class of writing-system which gets confused with language: this is the kind of writing-system in which this volume is written; this is the kind of writing-system King Sejong designed for Korean: this is the kind of writing-system the earlier Sections of this article were all about, namely:

*Orthographies* Function: general purpose writing-systems serving most of the needs of written communication in a society. Familiar from the standard orthographies of languages with a long tradition of literacy – Chinese, Sanskrit, Greek, Latin, Arabic, English, French, Russian, etc. – but most of the standard orthographies in the world are much younger.

In short, we have here a classification of writing-systems by sociolinguistic function. This classification is, in principle, quite independent of the typological classification by spelling system described in section 4. We can represent it as the genus 'writing-system' subsuming seven species, themselves grouped into one general-purpose species, 'orthography', and six special-purpose species.

That there is a terminological slot waiting to be filled is evident from the various periphrastic expressions which linguists and laymen alike resort to in order to speak about the writing-systems most familiar to them. We have had to do this ourselves in this article, and we find Sampson forced to do the same thing. For instance, King Sejong's writing-system came to be called Han'gŭl in Korean, and in summing up on its systematic design Sampson writes: 'In this respect Han'gŭl is very like Pitman's shorthand, and quite unlike any other script known to me that is used as the ordinary writing-system of a society' (1985:123). It is just that concept, 'the ordinary writing-system of a society', which the term 'standard orthography' can usefully connote. In section 9 we shall note *en passant* that standard orthographies are, as the term implies, a subset of the set of all orthographies.

Before that, we must attend to another nomenclatural promise made at the beginning of section 6. Let us look again for a moment at King Sejong's orthography for Korean. This did not meet, five centuries ago, with immediate approval; traditionalists, Sampson tells us, despised it and clung to Chinese writing – Chinese characters and their lexical values borrowed wholesale into a quite disparate, agglutinating (one is tempted to say Lego) language. In other words, Sejong's orthography did not straightaway become the standard orthography of Korean. The name Han'gŭl, 'great script', was not given to it until early in the present century as part of a movement to improve its image and popularise it. This movement was successful. Han'gŭl is now the Standard Orthography of Korean (see Sampson, or Nakanishi, for differences between North and South Korea). Notice that we now have two proper names for this particular national writing-system, one a proper noun on its own, the other phrasal. On the world scale, the Standard Orthography of Korean (S.O.K.) ranks quite high in terms of populations using it (totalling 50m+ (Malherbe 1983:94); see, however, Wellisch's Chapter 4). But Korean cannot be said to be an influential language nor despite its sudden worldwide visibility during the 1988 Olympic Games, can S.O.K. be said to be an influential writing-system, however interesting it maybe linguistically. Yet the writing-system of another language, the world's most influential language, a writing-system used on a far greater scale than any other in human history, lacks an agreed name of any kind. This is the writing-system in which this volume is written.

Since the language concerned is English, since the kind of writing-system involved is an orthography, and since the particular orthography used is the standard one, we shall for the rest of this article refer to it as the Standard Orthography of English, or S.O.E. for short.

## 8. GRAPHOLOGY: THE LINGUISTIC STUDY OF WRITING-SYSTEMS

Our immediate goal is a sound, conceptually-based terminology for the linguistic study of writing-systems, one which would be, in Lyons's phrase (1963:5), 'materially adequate', in the sense that the meanings assigned to terms should not conflict with their meanings in existing usage. This is what we have tried to do with 'script', 'spelling', 'alphabet' and 'orthography', as well as with 'writing-system' – a term which may puzzle the non-linguist through its unfamiliarity – and with 'language' – a term which puzzles through its very familiarity!

Something will have been achieved if readers recognise that the notion of 'a language and its writing-system' is problematic, that 'it isn't always as simple as that', and that, besides the problem of specifying the language (dealt with elsewhere in this volume), there is also the problem of specifying the writing-system. In many cases, which constitute the norm in our culture, this will be a single writing-system, the standard orthography of the language in question, established by tradition (e.g. in Britain) or by official decree (e.g., classically, in Turkey, but more recently in Malaysia and in many other countries). But the variety of situations is much more extensive than that. There are, as we said earlier, languages with no writing-system at all (these may be pidgins as well as tribal languages); there are languages for which the only writing-system in existence is a linguist's technography, which is likely to be quite unsuitable as an orthographic writing-system; there are languages with unstandardised orthographies and/or competing orthographies (see Garvin's classic case-history of language-planning for Ponapean (1954), and many situations reported in Smalley (ed. 1964), Fishman (ed. 1977); languages with more than one writing-system recognised as constituting a standard orthography within one national state (as in Yugoslavia, and, in a quite different, non-geographical fashion, Japan, – both cited above), and there is the commoner situation of languages which straddle national borders or are otherwise split geographically and so come to possess more than one standard orthography (for example, Korean, Mongolian, Hausa).

But, while we accord to standard orthographies their due importance, their pre-eminence as a general-purpose writing-systems, we must not make the mistake of according no importance to the special-function writing-systems of which we enumerated six different kinds in section 7. We have to consider the *range* of writing-systems which a language may possess. Even in the last paragraph we saw that that range, in respect of a particular language, does not necessarily have the species 'orthography' as its starting-point – it may have the species 'technography'. But, obviously, the special-function writing-systems are normally auxiliary to orthographic systems, and in an account of the writing-systems of a given language would take second place. The point is that they should not be overlooked. This cannot happen if the dimension of range is borne in mind.

Having reached this point where a language can be seen to have, actually or potentially, a plurality of writing-systems, we need a name for that collectivity of writing-systems and for its description and study. Just as the term 'phonology' serves both purposes with regard to sound systems, so the term '*graphology*' offers itself with regard to writing-systems. In fact, this term has been used by some linguists since the 1950s (Mitchell 1958, McIntosh 1961, Halliday *et al.* 1964), and it is admirably suited by its generality and by its parallelism to the term 'phonology' to do the job we require of it.

That job is to cover the totality of the writing-systems of a language. If we imagine an idealised situation (a not unfamiliar move in linguistics), in which a language has a full range of writing-systems, with just one member of each functional kind (one orthography, one stenography, one cryptography, and so on), then the graphology of that language includes all those writing-systems. It is for this reason that the term 'orthography' will not do the job of 'graphology'.

But there is more to 'graphology' than its extensiveness in terms of range. There is its extensiveness in terms of scope – we have to cater not only for all the writing-systems of a language but for all the components of each individual writing-system. The various kinds of writing-system may well show differences in respect of the two essential components, spelling system and script; but these, as we saw in section 2, do not usually account for the whole of any writing-systems. The presence or absence of word-division is not a function of the spelling system *per se*, while the marking of higher syntactic boundaries, whether by differentiated spaces or by actual graphemes, belongs wholly to the punctuation system. Numbers expressed as words belong to the spelling system, but expressed in figures, by numeric graphemes, lie right outside the spelling system. Neither 'spelling' nor 'script' will do the job of 'writing-system', still less the job of 'graphology'.

Bringing together the two dimensions of scope and range enables us to see that the functional kinds of writing-system are likely to differ from each other in respect of these support systems. Let us illustrate this from the graphology of English. Students practising the writing of texts in IPA transcription (technography) have to keep more than the spelling system and script of SOE (orthography) at bay; they must avoid capitalisation, and express all numbers (in the flow text, at least!) as words and not as figures. Cryptographies do well to discard word-division, since the characteristic patterning of function words and content words is a give-away to the cryptanalyst: in SOE, for instance, word-spaces setting off words of one or two letters immediately reveal them as function words. i.t.a., on the other hand, as an initial literacy paedography for English, was designed, while having a simpler spelling system, to look as like SOE possible: its punctuation and (arabic) numeric systems are the same, but it does not have distinctive upper-case shapes, only larger lower-case ones, and it does not have italics. As a stenography, Pitman's shorthand also dispenses with the differentiation resources found in SOE. On the other hand, while SOE has important abbreviatory devices, which play their part in modern word-formation (Adams 1973:136), it does not have the resource which Pitman's has of shortening whole phrases into solid (undivided) phraseograms. As to machinographies, or mechanographies, Wellisch (see section 7 above) gives two examples, Morse and a direct computer print-out, both of which are mechanically produced metagraphies. These too will lack the rich differentiation resources available, typographically, in standard orthographies like SOE or in the standard orthography of French which in our sense of the word will *include* Wellisch's 'different typefaces, indentations, and so forth'). Metagraphies used for bibliographic data, proper names, and so on, are distinct in that they are used for block text rather than flow text. (Metagraphic writing-systems used for economy's sake, e.g. in the romanised texts of Egyptologists, Sanskrit scholars, or students of Mycenean Linear B, are technographies: the texts themselves may be flow text, typical for Sanskrit, or block text, typical for Linear B. As was indicated in connection with stenographies and cryptographies, the functional kinds are not mutually exclusive. Metagraphy has an important part to play in the way in which orthographies handle loanwords and foreignisms.)

Mention of the flow versus block text distinction can serve as a final reminder that graphology is not only concerned with the linear sequence of graphemes in flow text, which has tended to monopolise people's image of writing hitherto. It is also concerned with the figural modification of graphemes and their graphs and with their spatial disposition. We tend to think of the two-dimensional space in which writing operates as a bounded white rectangle waiting for black marks. This is a limited view not only historically, but also contemporarily. Much of the block text people actually see in urban environments is not on or in graphic portabilia, like books and forms and newspapers, but on or in buildings, on hoardings, road-signs and sign-posts, on road vehicles – and on boats, which charmingly carry their names about on them. These environmental texts are remarkable in the variety of their materials and their script shapes – and we must not overlook graffiti, which stand out as hand-produced environmental texts.

Let us conclude this section by pointing out that, in respect of range, environmental texts are in standard orthography (though graffiti may sometimes miss out on standard spelling); this establishes their graphological orientation; and it is orientation which gives certain meanings to block text, whether it is block text on its own or block text in association with flow text.

In SOE, precedence is given to what is above, and precedence is given to what is on the left. These are, to recall Sampson's words with which we began, conventions of the writing-system which govern the use we make of the written marks.

## 9. GRAPHOLOGY, GRAPHETICS, AND GENERAL LINGUISTICS

A single writing-system, of any functional kind (the dimension of range), can be studied, in whole or in part (the dimension of scope), *synchronically* to establish 'how it works' as an on-going system, or *diachronically* to establish how the system changes over time. Two or more writing-systems may be studied *comparatively* (they may be writing-systems for the same language): the comparison may be *genetically orientated*, to establish a historical relationship between writing-systems, or *typologically orientated*, to establish similarities of structure or feature, or indeed similarities of change over time.

Historians of writing have been understandably wary of linguistics in the past, and the genetic classification of the world's writing-systems has been (and continues to be) accomplished by scholars in the various specialised disciplines, typically by those with an interest in ancient writing-systems (e.g. Naveh (1982) on the early history of the alphabet.) But the diversity of disciplines has militated against typological studies, a field which must explicitly make use of general linguistic categories, e.g. (besides spelling systems) the relation of puncuation systems to syntactic units in different writing-systems (punctuation notoriously arouses little enthusiasm, but Catach (1980), Mylne (1979) and Twine (1984) provide valuable correctives).

The need for a unified science of writing has been voiced, by Diringer and by Gelb in particular, as eloquently as linguists' indifference to the subject has been deplored within linguistics by, for a recent example, Feldbusch (1986) (cf. Suzuki 1977). Almost forty years ago, in *A study of writing*, Gelb tried to lay the foundations of a theoretical approach: his 'inner development' of writing corresponds to the (diachronic) study of spelling systems, and his 'outer development' to the (diachronic) study of scripts. This distinction of his can be generalised, on the analogy of phonology/phonetics, to a distinction between *graphology* and *graphetics* (cf. Mitchell 1958: 102).

Part of the theoretical approach inherent in general graphology must be the distinction, drawn in section 3, between the physical marks, which are the objects of highly developed techniques of study in palaeography (including epigraphy) and typography, and their abstract organisation into writing-systems. Graphetics is as capable of receiving a general linguistic framework as graphology is. Applying a more sociolinguistic framework than the traditional 'centrolinguistic' one used just above, we can ask, synchronically, what *variation* or conversely what *uniformity* is to be found in a given script at a given time, and we can ask, diachronically, what *change* or conversely what *maintenance* is to be found in it over time. Palaeographers (manuscripts) and epigraphists (inscriptions) are familiar with such questions, and so are students of modern handwriting and lettering in any of the world's script families.

What masks this field from view in many people's conception of language is the existence of print. But print, too, can be studied synchronically and diachronically in search of variation and change and their opposites, uniformity and maintenance. It is a bad effect of historical periodisation to think that palaeography ends when typography begins. The advent of printing in the modern era, like the development, beside hieroglyphs, of cursive Egyptian scripts in antiquity, is a case of branching, not of linear, variation. The expansion of literacy in 'the age of print' has increased the amount of handwriting, not diminished it. Handwriting is immensely important in the modern world – a visit to any (Western-type) school will convince those who are oblivious to its pervading presence. A general graphetics must bring both kinds of written mark – the hand-made and the machine-made – into a single perspective.

So must graphology. The spelling of English is often cited as an example of a high degree of linguistic uniformity; but the uniformity is confined to the printed manifestation; for variation, go to handwritten English. This contrast has been evident ever since the spelling system of SOE became standardised around 1700. On the history of this variation – and on the operation of social forces on graphology – see Scragg (1974); on standard languages see Haas (ed. 1982); on the mechanisms of change and maintenance see Milroy and Milroy (1985) and Stubbs (1980), (1986) and Chapters 14 and 16 above.

For the sociolinguistics of writing-systems, the next most important book after Stubbs (1980) is Fishman (ed.) (1977). This is full of information on the creation and revision of spelling systems for orthographies and on the social forces affecting acceptance and implementation (many orthographies are designed but few are chosen – hence standard orthographies are a subset of all orthographies). It does not, however, ask a basic sociolinguistic question: Who uses which writing-system to whom for what purpose? – though in a complex society some institutions rely for certain functions on non-orthographic writing-systems, otherwise stenographies and cryptographies would not exist (Gold 1977:358, comes close with a question confined to Yiddish scripts).

The mental processing aspect of literacy is dealt with in Chapter 7 above. But it will not be amiss to mention, under the psycho/socio aspects of writing-systems, a current controversial issue – Goody's 'literacy thesis' (Goody and Watt 1963), which hinges on the cognitive potentialities of alphabetic writing-systems and acknowledges the role of 'block text' beside 'flow text' (our terms). Goody's recent reflections on this will be found in Coulmas and Ehlich (eds 1983), an invaluable collection of articles which testifies to the rapprochement now taking place between linguistics and other disciplines concerned with writing. For a critique of Goody and for a highly critical survey from a social anthropological point of view of how linguists have treated writing, together with a theory of differential literacies (some, for example, orientated to abstraction, others to accountancy), see Street (1985).

Neat refutations of the Bloomfieldian position on writing ('Writing is not language but merely a way of recording language with visible marks' (1935:21, cf. Ch.17)) will be found in Romaine (1982:14–15) and Stubbs (1986:220), both of them accepting the distinction between language and language-medium which underlies this present article (see Abercrombie 1967:Ch.1). Since Bloomfield's book enthroned the phoneme and launched, in its original American edition, the transcription known for a time as the 'linguistic alphabet' in contradistinction to the International Phonetic Alphabet, his cautions against writing may perhaps be regarded rather as cautions against standard orthographies. Or more precisely, we should say they were cautions against the spelling systems of standard orthographies; for the orthographic concept of the sentence as a fundamental grammatical unit remained unassailed (see Halliday: 'a sentence is a constituent of writing, while a clause-complex is a constituent of grammar' (1985:193)).

For the way in which writing, particularly alphabetic writing, has permeated the linguist's (and of course the layman's) language conception, see Linell's (1982) full-length study of linguistic theory and methodology, and also Harris (1986). Harris tackles a linguistic topic hitherto hardly addressed in modern linguistics: the origin of writing. This stimulating exercise in linguistic semiology should be read in conjunction with the archaeological thesis associated with Schmandt-Besserat (1978, 1981), pushing back the earliest origins of writing in Mesopotamia and associating them with clay tokens and their impressions used in primitive systems of accountancy. Harris makes the significant suggestion that 'the human race had to become numerate in order to become literate' (p. 133). This serves as a reminder that the history of spelling systems and of scripts needs to be complemented by a history of what we called 'support systems'. (Rouse and Rouse (1982) and Beaujouan (1982), on aspects of medieval European literacy and numeracy, give a taste of what historical scholarship can uncover.)

We will conclude this section on general graphology with an issue which belongs to general graphetics and is the subject of lively debate: What are the determinants of orientation in writing-systems (see section 3), in particular of direction on a horizontal axis? There is no reason why the notion of graphetics should be confined to the 'scriptal graphetics' suggested above, which corresponds only to acoustic phonetics. Theories about direction make appeal to what we might call 'physiological graphetics' (corresponding to articulatory and auditory phonetics): according to de Kerckhove (1986) direction in fully phonemic writing is determined by the neurophysiology of the reader, while according to Sirtat (1987) direction is determined by the physiology and posture of the writer. Sirat's paper, in particular, valuably illustrates how differently the 'same' activity has been carried out in different cultures, and how it has enjoyed different esteem – high in Egypt and Mesopotamia, low in Greece and Rome.

The case made in this section for the linguistic study of writing is essentially the one argued with great care by McIntosh in 1956 in connection with the analysis of written Middle English (for the terms 'graphology' and 'graphetics', see Mitchell (1958: 102)). As to contemporary English, Nash's study (1983) of 'continentals' residing in Puerto Rico and *inter alia* of the undermining effects of language contact on their control of English spelling and on their language conception, fittingly points the way to the next, and final, section.

## 10. GRAPHOLOGY, ENGLISH SPELLING, AND APPLIED LINGUISTICS

A commonly held view of English spelling is that it is unanalysable. Some teachers, at all levels, hold this view, and so do many other people, including many of the children who are learning SOE at different stages in the school curriculum (we will touch on the EL2 situation shortly). It is an absurd view, but one which linguists have done little to dissipate.

The spelling system of SOE is, of course, as analysable as that of any other writing-system. Belief in its unanalysability is fostered – not actively, but passively – by schools, and does little credit to the education system, since the data for analysis – written words – are abundantly available, freely accessible and easily manipulable. What is lacking is a teaching force with the necessary expertise. That expertise does not have to be acquired via linguistic theory. It might be acquired via engagement with the data of the classroom. We will illustrate this by introducing the notion of 'spelling analysis' – the analysis not of the system as a whole, but of individual words.

We will illustrate, in fact, two kinds of spelling analysis which can be pursued by interested readers. We shall need a notation for this purpose (a graphological technography) but it can be extremely simple. Its essential function is to ensure that we know when we are talking about letters and when we are talking about sounds (for which a suitable phonological technography is needed). Those linguists who do write about writing-systems customarily use diamond brackets to surround graphemes. But for the discussion of SOE spelling, a raised circle or degree sign, to be understood as 'letter', 'letters' or '(standard) spelling' is sufficient: prefixed to letters or to a word it indicates that the focus of attention is on the spelling. In hand-writing, ° is graphetically less cumbersome than ○, especially on blackboards. Distinguishing between letters and sounds is crucial for the first form of spelling analysis, which concerns phonemes ('graphophonemic analysis'); but the emphasis on letters as such matters also for the second form ('junction analysis').

*Graphophonemic analysis.* To spell a word in English – to give the spelling of it – is to name the right letters in the right order. Nothing is expected by way of grouping the letters, which is often done randomly or rhythmically, for instance in pairs – 'S C, H O, O L, "school",' (not attested!). The beginnings of grouping, as a form of spelling analysis, are suggested by the teacher's terms 'digraph' and 'blend', which are used in the early stages of literacy ('reading') and which do not usually pass into the children's vocabulary. A digraph is 'two letters for one sound' (e.g. °ch °oo – either consonantal or vocalic), and a blend is, typically, 'two letters for two sounds', always conson-antal (e.g. °bl °pr, or, syllable-final, °nd). In fact, grouping has begun earlier in the curriculum, with the segmentation of °cat and the establishment of the three correspondences: °c-/k/, °a-/a/ and °t-/t/. There are three essential concepts here: first the mathematical notion, which runs counter to everyday usage, of a group with only one member (important in linguistics); secondly the notion of isolatable sounds (or phonemes – which is simply a general name covering the two subclasses, consonant phonemes and vowel phonemes); and thirdly, the key notion of the 'correspondence', illustrated by those just given (letter č with the phoneme value /k/; °a with the value /a/; °t - /t/).

This area is known to the teacher (the First School or primary teacher) as 'phonics'. We can give it (in keeping with its relevance right through the school years) the rather grander name of 'graphophonemics', relating the graphemes of spelling – the letters – to the phonemes. But once °c, °ch, °a, °oo etc. are recognised as 'graphophonemic symbols' (that is, letter groups belonging to correspondences; °cj would not be a symbol in this sense, nor would °iw), and once °c – /k/ and °ch – /k/ are recognised as 'grapho-phonemic correspondences', the adjective 'graphophonemic' can be waived.

A correspondence is made up of a symbol and a value. (The value, in SOE, is always a single phoneme, except in the case of °x, the spelling behaviour of which has a number of pecularities.) Symbols can be up to four letters long, and can be classified by their leading letter and subclassified by their trailing letters. Thus °c can be a symbol on its own, or it can be the leading letter in °ck or °ch (or freakishly in °cch). A given symbol can have more than one value. The resulting correspondences for that symbol can be ranked as primary, secondary and (multiple) tertiary. For example: for °ch, the primary correspondence is °ch – /tʃ/, as in °chip; the secondary correspondence is °ch – /k/, as in °school; and there is a tertiary correspondence °ch – /ʃ/, as in °machine.

The behaviour of letters can be charted (for example, °c also appears as a trailing letter in the symbol °sc, as in °scene); the structures of symbols can be charted; their ranges of values can be charted; and the correspondences can not only be charted but named. For instance: the graphophonemic analysis of °success (a stumbling-block for some spellers) is °s u c c e ss. We have two values for °c here, both rule-governed: the first °c is followed by a consonant letter (viz. the second °c), and has the value /k/; the second °c is followed by °e, and has the value /s/. The rule is that °c has the value /k/ except before the vowels °e, °i, or °y. (More strictly, we should say that the *symbol* °c is subject to this rule.) Teachers use the expression 'Hard C' and 'Soft C', appropriately enough, with reference to this phenomenon. What is not usually realised is that these are not names of letters, nor names of sounds (phonemes), but names of *correspondences*. Naming can be extended to all correspondences and, like everything else, once named, they become easier to talk about, easier to conceptualise. (For a theoretical approach, see Haas 1970).

Literacy in English, even literacy coupled with 'good spelling', does not imply ability to segment words into symbols (graphophonemic segmentation or analysis). Analysis of °school into °s ch oo l is far from automatic amongst those who can spell the word – to say nothing of the many who cannot. The 'trick' in it is the symbol °ch, with the secondary correspondence °ch – /k/ or Hard CH. Trouble with the spelling of °psychology, sometimes a stumbling-block at tertiary level, can be alleviated if the Hard CH correspondence has been learnt beforehand in its concealed position in °school and in prominent position in °chemistry. (Misspellings of °psychology include *psychycology. Note that in the correspondence °ps – /s/, the leading letter has no phonemic value (= a 'silent' letter); note also that °y has a unique spelling behaviour in that it can be both a consonant symbol and a vowel symbol; spellers who, at primary level, have learned A E I O U as the five vowel letters will often resist recognising the vocalic role of °y at secondary or tertiary level.)

*Junction analysis.* The second form of spelling analysis must be dealt with even more briefly. It concerns, not symbols (graphophonemic units) but morphemes (lexicogrammatical units). In section 4 it was pointed out that, while a subclass of orthographies gives information about the phonological realisation of morphemes, all orthographies represent the morphemes themselves.

Again the starting-point can be simple and familiar. In *they come* we

732

recognise the morpheme *come*, and we recognise the same morpheme in *they are coming*. But in the first case it is represented by °come (four letters), and in the second by °com (three letters). In *they run* we have °run (three letters), and in *they are running* we have °runn (four letters; readers may find the notations °com- and °runn- more comfortable). Nobody seriously suggests that we have a gamut of forms of the suffix -*ing* – °-ing as base-form, with by-forms °ning in °running, °-ting in °getting, °-ping in °stopping, and so on, though that is how typographical tradition in SOE breaks such words at the ends of lines. These phenomena, loss of a letter in °come/coming and gain of a letter in °run/running, together with the change of letter in °try/tried, are the main source of change in morpheme shape in SOE. They are often treated in isolation from each other, yet they can be interestingly linked.

The key concept here is the *spelling junction* (Mountford 1976). The unit of invariant spelling in SOE is the orthographic word. There are no inter-dependencies across word-space, with the exception of °a/an. Between compound lexical morphemes there are no interdependencies in any of the three states of aggregation: *open* °test tube, *hyphened* °test-tube, *solid* °testtube (*testube is a known error, like *lampost). If the same were true in affixation, i.e. at boundaries involving inflectional or derivational morphemes, there would be no need for the notion of spelling junctions. All junctions would be the same simple kind.

But in fact, in SOE, there are 'change' junctions as well as 'no-change' junctions. Obviously when two morphemes are joined, the constituent letters can either remain unaffected or undergo some change. When there is no change, we can notate it as, for example, °jump + ing, °jump + ed, °jump + er, and call these cases *plus-junctions*. Plus-junctions are the commonest kind of spelling junction in SOE, and, of course, the simplest. (To write *sincerly, *likly or *beautifuly is to complicate a very simple spelling procedure.)

Where there is change, we find that a great many of the changes are products of the three kinds of *change junction* exemplified above, which we can notate as °com × ing °run × ing °try × ed. These three are linked. It is in each case the morpheme on the left that undergoes change. The change in each case affects only the lefthand letter at the junction: in °come/coming by subtraction (E-Deletion), in °run/running by addition (Consonant-Doubling), and in °try/tried by substitution (Y-Replacement).

The incidence of plus-junctions and of change-junctions and, within change-junctions, the incidence of these three main types (which are mutually exclusive) are rule-governed and conditioned by the letter cate-gories, consonant-letter and vowel-letter. A fourth major type of change-junction is found at prefix boundaries, similarly conditioned by the letter categories, viz. Consonant-Assimilation, which likewise affects the lefthand letter at the junction, so as to change the shape of the morpheme on the left (e.g. °sub- into °sup- in °suppress, °suc- in °success).

These two kinds of spelling analysis are essentially *ways of talking about English spelling*. One feature of the literate community in English is how *bad* good spellers are at helping poor spellers. One factor in this is the belief, shared by both parties, that English spelling is unanalysable. This can only be an ironic product of the way it is taught, since any spelling system is inherently analytical. Halliday writes: 'In speaking English, we are not normally aware of the internal structure of words; no doubt that is why the constituent morphemes have never come to be marked off from one another in writing' (1985:20). But the morphemes are there to be marked off in SOE, with a little technographical aid which can be converted to paedographical purposes. This is not to say that junction analysis is unproblematical; there are snags enough for the faint-hearted to take refuge in unanalysability.

The same is true of graphophonemic analysis, with the important difference that this requires a phonemic notation. (This is a technography with a spelling system of graphemes in one-to-one correspondence with the phonemes (of some reference pronunciation); the script can be designed to exhibit similarity to SOE rather than general phonetic attributes.) Phonemic notations were popular in the past as paedographies in the teaching of English as L2, used in the teaching of pronunciation. Today, professionally trained teachers of English as L2 are taught a notation as a technography, to enable them to understand aspects of the phonology and grammar and to analyse pronunciation. It is noteworthy that, although this corps of English language teachers is equipped with the necessary phonemic conceptualisation, analysis of the standard spelling system does not figure much in their training: in teaching the spelling system – in contrast to teaching all other levels of the language – reliance is placed upon proficiency (control) and not on proficiency accompanied by expertise (conception).

In the teaching of English as L1, this has always been the case: proficiency (more recently, assumed proficiency) has been enough, without phonemic conceptualisation at all. Even teachers of initial literacy, whose special task it is to initiate learners into, among other things, the sound/symbol correspondences of SOE, are not usually taught a phonemic notation. But it must be borne in mind that in the training of teachers of English within general education, the distinction has not yet been clearly made, at least in the UK, between teachers of English, the language of the curriculum, and teachers of literature. The two expertises are very different, as the world-wide EL2 teaching profession realised in the 1950s.

Applied linguistics has been thought of much more in connection with specialised education, e.g. language teaching to adults, than with general education. Within general education, it has been thought of much more in connection with L2 teaching, e.g. for ethnic community children, than L1

734

teaching, much more, that is to say, in connection with bilingualism than with bimedialism – the creation of a literate linguacy. The centrolinguistic knowledge involved, particularly as regards the structure of SOE, with its high uniformity, is fundamentally the same in all of these fields. It is socio-linguistic and psycholinguistic knowledge which to a certain extent need to vary with the situation – to a certain extent, because general theory apart, one would expect language teachers of all kinds to be concerned with the learner's total linguacy. L2 teaching is more sensitive to the learner's existing proficiency in language than some doctrinaire methods of the past permitted; but L1 teaching, despite earnest endeavours, still teaches literacy at the expense of oracy, or oracy at the expense of literacy. (For 'oracy', the control of language in the medium of speech, see Wilkinson (1965); for 'linguacy', see Mountford (1970).)

Whatever degree of language control it leads to, literacy acquisition in childhood has a massive effect on language conception. This school-acquired language conception is carried through life by the man in the street, and also, unfortunately, by the majority of men and women in the primary and secon-dary school classroom. Some of it may linger, too, in the linguist, who may remain, for example, unsensitised to the orthography of his own language. Albrow is exceptional in having brought linguistic theory to bear upon the spelling system of SOE. The 'polysystemic' approach he adopted, following Firth, led him to set up three systems to account for the data (including, pioneeringly, proper nouns); this may have deterred him from choosing as his title 'The spelling system of English'. Another linguist, Stubbs, has written revealingly of the impact which this account of English spelling had on him: 'I first discovered Albrow's short book on the English writing system some years ago, and for the first time realized tht the English spelling system was (*a*) more interesting than I had thought, and (*b*) not as odd as I had thought. I had in fact never seriously thought about it, never having realized that it could be an interesting subject' (1980: xi).

SOE is an interesting writing-system in itself. It is even more interesting when seen, as general education should enable it to be seen, in its place among the writing-systems of the world as a whole.

This section has concentrated on the spelling system of SOE, something which is taught on a global scale in perhaps the oldest and certainly the largest field of applied linguistics, language (including literacy) teaching. Most of the rest of applied linguistics has to do with language use by literates; orthography design/reform and some parts of language planning have to do specifically with writing-systems. One small new area of concern, which applied linguistics has so far been shy of, is language simplification – e.g. the Plain English Campaign in the UK – and information design (see Steinberg (ed. 1986) on the USA, and Wright (1983)). This area is growing in importance:

and while much of the skill called for lies in clarity of written language (beyond the bounds of this chapter), much also lies in manipulation of the full figural and spatial resources of standard orthographies.

## REFERENCES

Abercrombie, D. (1965) 'Writing systems', in *Studies in phonetics and linguistics*, Oxford University Press, London: 86–91.

Abercrombie, D. (1967) *Elements of general phonetics*, Edinburgh University Press, Edinburgh.

Adams, V. (1973) *An introduction to modern English word-formation*, Longman, London.

Albrow, K.H. (1972) *The English writing system: notes towards a description* (Schools Council Programme in Linguistics and English Teaching Papers Series 2, Volume 2), Longman, London.

Beaujouan, G. (1982) 'The transformation of the quadrivium', in Benson, R.L. and Constable, G. (eds) *Renaissance and renewal in the twelfth century*, Clarendon Press, Oxford: 463–87.

Bloomfield, L. (1935) *Language*, Allen & Unwin, London. (First published: USA 1933).

Catach, N. (ed.) (1980) *La ponctuation, = Langue Française 45.*

Cohen, M. (1958) *La grande invention de l'écriture et son évolution* (3 vols.), Klincksieck, Paris.

Coulmas, F. (1989) *Writing systems of the world*, Blackwell, Oxford.

Coulmas, F. and Ehlich, K. (eds) (1983) *Writing in focus*, Mouton, Berlin.

de Kerckhove, D. (1986) 'Alphabetic literacy and brain processes', *Visible Language*, 20, 3: 274–93.

Diringer, D. (1968) *The Alphabet: a key to the history of mankind* (3rd edition: 2 vols.), Hutchinson, London (first published 1949).

Feldbusch, E. (1986) 'The communicative and cognitive functions of written language', *Written Communication*, 3.1: 81–9.

Fishman, J. (ed.) (1977) *Advances in the creation and revision of writing systems*, Mouton, The Hague.

Francis, W.N. (1967) *The English language: an introduction*, English Universities Press, London.

Garvin, P.L. (1954) 'Literacy as a problem in language and culture', in Mueller, H.J. (ed.) *Report of the 5th Annual Round Table Meeting on Linguistics and Language Teaching*, Georgetown University Press, Washington, DC: 117–29.

Gelb, I.J. (1952) *A study of writing*, University of Chicago Press, Chicago.

Gold, D.L. (1977) 'Successes and failures in the standardization and implementation of Yiddish spelling and romanization', in Fishman (ed.) (1977): 307–70.

Goody, J. (1983) 'Literacy and achievement in the Ancient World', in Coulmas *et al.* (eds): 83–97.

Goody, J. and Watt, I. (1968) 'The consequences of literacy', in Goody, J. (ed.) *Literacy in traditional societies*, Cambridge Universtiy Press, Cambridge: 27–68.

Haas, M.R. (1956) *The Thai system of writing*, American Council of Learned Societies, Washington, DC.

Haas, W. (ed.) (1969) *Alphabets for English*, Manchester University Press, Manchester. (Mont Follick Series, 1.)

Haas, W. (1970) *Phonographic Translation*, Manchester University Press, Manchester (Mont Follick Series, 2).

Haas, W. (1976) 'Writing: the basic options', in Haas (ed.) (1976): 131–208.

Haas, W. (ed.) (1976) *Writing without letters*, Manchester University Press, Manchester (Mont Follick Series, 4).

Haas, W. (ed.) (1982) *Standard languages: spoken and written*, Manchester University Press, Manchester (Mont Follick Series, 5).

Halliday, M.A.K. (1985) *An introduction to functional grammar*, Edward Arnold, London.

Halliday, M.A.K., McIntosh, A. and Strevens, P. (1964) *The linguistic sciences and language teaching*, Longman, London.

Harris, R. (1986) *The origin of writing*, Duckworth, London.

Henze, P.B. (1977) 'Politics and alphabets in Inner Asia', in Fishman (ed.) (1977): 371–420.

Householder, F. (1971) 'The primacy of writing', in *Linguistic speculations*, Cambridge University Press, Cambridge: 244–64.

Inoue, Kyoko (1979) 'Japanese: a story of language and people', in Shopen, T. (ed.) *Languages and their speakers*, Winthrop, Cambridge, Mass.

Jensen, H. (1970) *Sign, symbol and script: an account of man's effort to write*, Allen & Unwin, London. (First published in German, 1958).

Linell, P. (1982) *The written language bias in linguistics*, Dept. of Communication Studies, University of Linköping, Linköping, Sweden.

Lyons, J. (1963) *Structural semantics: an analysis of part of the vocabulary of Plato*, Basil Blackwell, Oxford.

McIntosh, A. (1956) 'The analysis of written Middle English', *Transactions of the Philological Society*: 26–55.

McIntosh, A. (1961) '"Graphology" and meaning', *Archivum Linguisticum*, 13: 107–20.

Malherbe, M. (1983) *Les langages de l'humanité*, Seghers, Paris.

Malkiel, Y. (1965) 'Secondary uses of letters in language', in *Romance Philology* 19.1: 1–27.

Martin, S.E. (1972) 'Nonalphabetic writing systems: some observations', in Kavanagh, J.F. and Mattingly, I.G. (eds) *Language by ear and eye*, MIT Press, Cambridge, Mass.: 81–103.

Milroy, J. and Milroy, L. (1985) *Authority in language: investigating language prescription and standardisation*, Routledge & Kegan Paul, London.

Mitchell, T.F. (1958) 'Syntagmatic relations in linguistic analysis', *Transactions of the Philological Society*: 101–18.

Mountford, J.D. (1970) 'Some psycholinguistic components of initial standard literacy'. *The Journal of Typographic Research/Visible Language*, 4.4: 295–306.

Mountford, J.D. (1973) 'Writing-system: a datum in bibliographical description', in Rawski, C. (ed.) *Toward a theory of librarianship: Papers in honour of Jesse Hauk Shera*, Scarecrow Press, Metuchen, N.J.: 415–49.

Mountford, J.D. (1976) 'Spelling junctions in English', in Nickel, G. (ed.) *Proceedings of the Fourth International Congress of AILA*, Hochschul-Verlag, Stuttgart.

Mylne, V. (1979) 'The punctuation of dialogue in eighteenth-century French and English fiction', *The Library*, 6th series, 1.1: 43–61.

Nakanishi, A. (1980) *Writing systems of the world: alphabets, syllabaries, pictograms*, Tuttle, Tokyo.

737

Nash, R. (1983) 'Pringlish: still more language contact in Puerto Rico', in Kachru, B.B. (ed.) *The other tongue: English across cultures*, Pergamon Press, Oxford: 250–69.

Naveh, J. (1982) *Early history of the alphabet*, Magnes Press, The Hebrew University, Jerusalem.

Pike, K.L. (1947) *Phonemics: a technique for reducing languages to writing*, University of Michigan Press, Ann Arbor.

*Practical orthography of African Languages* (1962) (International African Institute Memorandum 1), Oxford University Press, Oxford.

Rice, F.R. (1959) *The Classical Arabic writing system*, Harvard University Press, Cambridge, Mass.

Romaine, S. (1982) *Socio-historical linguistics: its status and methodology*, Cambridge University Press, Cambridge.

Rouse, R.H. and Rouse, M.A. (1982) '*Statim invenire*: schools, preachers, and new attitudes to the page', in R.L. Benson and G. Constable (eds) *Renaissance and renewal in the twelfth century*, Clarendon Press, Oxford: 201–25.

Sampson, G. (1985) *Writing systems: a linguistic introduction*, Hutchinson, London.

Schmandt-Besserat, D. (1978) 'The earliest precursor of writing', *Scientific American*, June issue: 38–47.

Schmandt-Besserat, D. (1981) 'Tokens: facts and interpretations', *Visible Language*, 20.3: 250–72.

Scragg, D.G. (1974) *A history of English spelling*, Manchester University Press, Manchester (Mont Follick Series, 3).

Seeley C. (ed.) (1984) *Aspects of the Japanese writing system* (special issue) *Visible Language*, 18.3.

Shelton, T. (1635) *Tachygraphy*, Cambridge University Press, Cambridge.

Sirat, C. (1987) 'La morphologie humaine et la direction de l'écriture', Compte-rendus des séances de l'Académie des Inscriptions et Belles-Lettres: (CRAI) 9 janvier 1987.

Smalley, W.A. (ed.) (1964) *Orthography studies: articles on new writing systems*, United Bible Society, London/North-Holland Publishing Co., Amsterdam.

Steinberg, E.R. (1986) *Promoting Plain English*, (special issue) *Visible Language*, 20.2.

Stetson, R.H. (1937) 'The phoneme and the grapheme', in *Mélanges de linguistique et de philologie offerts à Jacques van Ginneken*, Klincksieck, Paris: 353–6.

Street, B.V. (1985) *Literacy in theory and practice*, Cambridge University Press, Cambridge.

Stubbs, M. (1980) *Language and literacy: the sociolinguistics of reading and writing*, Routledge & Kegan Paul, London.

Stubbs, M. (1986) *Educational linguistics*, Basil Blackwell, Oxford.

Suzuki, T. (1977) 'Writing is not language, or is it?', *Journal of Pragmatics*, 1: 407–20.

Twine, N. (1984) 'The adoption of punctuation in Japanese script', *Visible Language*, 18.3: 229–37.

Uldall, H.J. (1944) 'Speech and writing', *Acta Linguistica*, 4: 11–16.

Vachek, J. (1979) 'Some remarks on the stylistics of written language', in Allerton, D.J. *et al.* (eds) *Function and context in linguistic analysis: A Festschrift for William Haas*, Cambridge University Press, Cambridge: 206–15.

Venezky, R.L. (1970) *The structure of English orthography*, Mouton, The Hague.

Wellisch, H.H. (1978) *The conversion of scripts — its nature, history and utilization*, Wiley, New York.

Wilkinson, A. (1965) *Spoken English*, Supplement to *Educational Review*, University of Birmingham, Birmingham.

Wright, P. (1983) 'Technical communication: English for Very Special Purposes', *BAAL Newsletter* No. 18: 24–9.

## FURTHER READING

Butler, E.H. (1951) *The story of British shorthand*, Sir Isaac Pitman & Sons, London.

Chadwick, J. (1958) *The decipherment of Linear B*, Cambridge University Press, Cambridge.

Cutts, M. and Maher, C. (1983) *Small print: The language and layout of consumer contracts* (Report to the National Consumer Council), Plain English Campaign, Stockport.

Downing, J. (1967) *Evaluating the Initial Teaching Alphabet*, Cassell, London.

Gaur, A. (1984) *A history of writing*, British Library, London.

Gray, N. (1960) *Lettering on buildings*, Architectural Press, London.

Gudschinsky, S.C. (1976) *Literacy: the growing influence of linguistics*, Mouton, The Hague.

Henderson, L. (1982) *Orthography and word recognition in reading*, Academic Press, London.

Kahn, D. (1966) *The code-breakers: the story of secret writing*, Weidenfeld & Nicholson, London.

Naveh, J. (1975) *Origins of the Alphabet*, Cassell, London.

Newnham, R. (1971) *About Chinese*, Penguin Books, Harmondsworth.

Ullman, B.L. (1969) *Ancient writing and its influence*, MIT Press, Cambridge, Mass. (First published: Longmans, New York, 1932).

Vachek, J. (1973) *Written language: general problems and problems of English*, Mouton, The Hague.

## JOURNALS

Information Design Journal (1980–)
Visible Language (1967–)
Written Communication (1984–)

# 21

## SIGN LANGUAGE

### BENCIE WOLL

### 1. INTRODUCTION

The term 'sign language' is used here to refer to any one of a large number of languages found among deaf populations throughout the world. These languages are natural, not artificially devised; they are unrelated to the spoken languages about them; they are used for a wide variety of functions; and are learned as first languages. In this chapter, their structures and relationships are presented, together with a discussion of their history and current research.

Sign language-using populations are found throughout the world. Although there are some hearing populations using sign languages for social or cultural reasons – such as the Martha's Vineyard signers of the last century (Groce 1985) and certain aboriginal groups in Australia (Kendon, 1989) – sign languages have largely been found amongst deaf populations, and have been developed by them in place of the spoken languages of hearing populations. The average incidence of pre-lingual deafness in the Western world is between 1 in 1500–2000, so, for example, in Britain, there are about 40,000 pre-lingually deaf persons. This population cannot be considered as being one of handicapped individuals; instead it is more appropriately viewed as a deaf community, parallel in most respects to minority ethnic and cultural groups, sharing a common language and culture. Four main factors have been identified as criteria for inclusion in the American deaf community (Markowicz 1979): self-identification as a member of the deaf community; language use; endogamous marital patterns; membership of social organisations.

These factors are equally relevant in Britain and most other western countries; it should be emphasised, however, that audiometric measures of hearing loss appear to be irrelevant in determining an individual's membership of the deaf community. Rather, membership is marked by the sharing of a common language, common experiences and values, and a common way of communicating with each other and with hearing people. Members of the deaf community have largely shared the experience of special education in schools for the deaf or (more recently) in units attached to ordinary schools. In the past, most education for the deaf was provided in residential schools, where deaf pupils ate, slept, studied and played together, totally isolated from their hearing counterparts. The move in education away from these special schools has been greeted with dismay by members of the deaf community, who recognise the important role of residential schools in initiating young people into the deaf community, particularly as the number of deaf persons with deaf parents is very low (about one in 20). Although for the past 100 years, the education of the deaf has been largely opposed to the use of sign languages, a great deal of signing was of necessity tolerated outside the classroom and, particularly in residential schools, this provided children with substantial opportunities for learning and communicating in sign languages.

Brief mention should be made here of the so-called manual-oral controversy, which has dominated the education of the deaf from the eighteenth century onwards, but which has been fought most fiercely over the past 150 years. Educators have chosen to emphasise the integration of deaf people into hearing society by suppressing sign language, and teaching speech exclusively. There are, of course, many valid reasons for wanting to integrate deaf people into hearing society through speech: 95 per cent of parents of deaf children are hearing; parental aspirations for their children include their integration into hearing society; the native language of teachers of the deaf is English. This emphasis on integration can also be seen in the shift to the use of the term 'hearing-impaired', rather than 'deaf'. Suppression of sign language in schools has been enforced by punishment of children for signing, which has included holding their arms immobile at their sides, making them sit on their hands, wearing placards stating 'I am a monkey', or putting paper bags over their heads. The attempted suppression of sign language has had many justifications: sign language is so easy for deaf children that they will not bother learning spoken language if they are given the opportunity to sign; children's vocal organs will atrophy if they use signing; the use of sign language will restrict deaf children to a deaf 'ghetto'; sign language is not a true language, so children's mental capacities will be impaired if they use it. It is striking how many of these attitudes parallel those towards other minority languages. Some educators of the deaf still express these views:

'It should be noted that not all natural, spoken languages are equally rich as e.g. Dutch

741

or English. There are also simple, less elaborate natural, spoken languages, such as Papiamento . . .; further, certain languages in Africa, India, etc. Consequently these languages are in the first instance not suitable for "higher studies", i.e. education which contains more than the limited cultures in which these languages satisfactorily function.'

(Van Uden 1986)

Other professionals working with the deaf often hold negative attitudes to sign language:

'Signing can cope with everyday chat, but when it is necessary to get down to accurate reporting of specific terminology, signing breaks down. It hasn't the grammar and it hasn't the vocabulary . . . Signing is an aid to comprehension for deaf people, along with hearing aids, lipreading, and the pen and pencil . . . deaf people do not constitute a nation-within-a-nation with their own language, and cannot expect an interpreter to remove all their communication difficulties in the same way as, say, a Frenchman can enjoy interpretation at the United Nations.'

(letter from a social worker in the British Deaf News, January 1987)

## 2. EARLIER APPROACHES TO SIGN LANGUAGE

Knowledge about sign language use among the deaf dates back nearly two thousand years in the western world, and even earlier in Chinese writings. The Mishnah (late second century), a compilation of Jewish oral law, makes several references to the use of signing by deaf people, which although unrevealing as to the form of signing used by the deaf, clearly indicates that it was regarded as a suitable means of communication in law:

'If a man that was a deaf-mute married a woman that was of sound senses, or if a man that was of sound senses married a woman that was a deaf-mute, if he will he may put her away, and if he will he may continue the marriage. Like as he married her by signs so he may put her away by signs.'

(Yeb. 14, 1, Danby 1933: 240).

'A deaf-mute may communicate by signs and be communicated with by signs.'

(Gitt, 5, 7, Danby 1933: 312)

Other sources of the classical period recognised that deaf people used signs for communication, but largely gave no information about the form this communication took. Plato, in the *Cratylus*, refers to significant movements of head, hand and body made by the dumb, and Saint Augustine describes a deaf person who could understand others and express himself by means of gestures.

One reason for the lack of information on sign form is the habitual confusion between signs and gestures. The belief that the deaf possess a universal language is still popular, and information about the enormous variety of sign languages in use is often greeted with surprise and dismay. Indeed, it is only recently that awareness that gestures are not universal has

742

spread. Paget follows a very old tradition in proposing that a sign language 'might be taught . . . to all children . . . If this were done in all countries . . . there would be a very simple international language by which the different races of mankind, including the deaf, might understand one another' (Paget 1953; xvi, cited in Knowlson 1965). In the section below on common myths regarding sign language, these beliefs will be discussed further; one important observation, however, is that the belief in the common universality of sign languages and gestures leads to descriptions of signs as (e.g.) 'the natural gesture of eating', thus providing little data for the linguist.

## 3. ORIGINS OF LANGUAGE AND SIGN LANGUAGE

A major area of concern of philosophers has been the question of how language came into being. Speech as the overt expression of language was believed to be the element of behaviour which made people human; language related directly to man's capacity for thought. The argument over whether thinking could exist without language ran in parallel to the dispute about whether speech or language came first in man. Theories of language origin were regarded so scathingly that by the early nineteenth century, linguistic circles were beginning to refuse to discuss the topic, and disparaging terms, such as 'Heave-Ho', 'Ding-Dong' and 'Pooh-Pooh' were used for language origin theories. In gestural theories of language origins, gestures accompanying actions were claimed to pre-date verbal communication (as they do in ontogenetic development). Alternative theories saw speech developed directly from non-verbal cries, and gesture either as independent or controlled by the meanings expressed in speech.

Probably the best-known philosopher concerning himself with issues of whether speech or gesture was primary was Condillac (1746). His view was that images, which were the basis of thought, were not always representable in speech and were more directly related to gestures. Because sounds had been added to gestures at an early stage, a series of spoken words was often needed to represent what had previously been a single gesture. This then presented a misleading view of thought as existing in sequential sentence-like strings, rather than as global images.

Other writers in the eighteenth and nineteenth centuries were also interested in whether sign languages represented a more primitive language than speech. Diderot (1751) set out a case for considering the sign language of the deaf as a source for learning about the natural order of thought in language. Tylor, a British anthropologist (1874), discussed at length the structure of sign language and its role in the deaf community. He saw sign as a more primitive language form, albeit a very complex one. Stout (1899) considered the relation of language and thought, and following Condillac, believed that signs develop from iconic representations to cognitive symbols which gradually form a language. Like Tylor, he saw sign as a more primitive language form which those who develop speech tend to leave behind. All of these arguments had largely been lost by the beginning of the twentieth century. Saussurean linguistics, with its emphasis on the arbitrariness of the symbol-referent relationship, and the effort made by modern linguistics to force recognition of speech as the primary form of language contributed to the disappearance of interest in sign languages and its replacement by a view of the deaf as living in a world without language. As Hewes (1976) points out:

'Impressed by the apparent arbitrariness of most spoken languages, it has been argued that such arbitrariness is an essential criterion for language or that a high degree of iconicity would interfere with understanding. The sign languages of the deaf are dismissed as crude, rudimentary, and if their users are unable to communicate except in such languages they display various serious cognitive handicaps.' (p. 409)

Bloomfield's dismissal of sign languages as serious objects for study by linguists is a good example of this attitude:

'Some communities have a gesture language which upon occasion they use instead of speech. Such gesture languages have been observed among the lower-class Neapolitans, among Trappist monks (who have made a vow of silence), among the Indians of our western plains . . . and among groups of deaf mutes.

It seems certain that these gesture languages are merely developments of ordinary gestures and that any and all complicated or not immediately intelligible gestures are based on the conventions of ordinary speech. Even such an obvious transference as pointing backward to indicate past time, is probably due to a linguistic habit of using the same word for "in the rear" and "in the past". Whatever may be the origins of the two, gesture has so long played a secondary role under the dominance of language that it has lost all traces of independent character.'

(Bloomfield 1933: 39)

Even more recent textbooks of linguistics have tended to ignore sign languages. The popular introductory text by Akmajian, Demers and Harnish devotes 512 pages to spoken languages, 35 to animal communication, and 5 to a discussion of studies of apes learning American Sign Language. The only references to American Sign Language itself are on page 480, where it is stated that ASL is one of a number of gestural systems; that ASL is used naturally by many people (although deaf people are never mentioned); and that ASL has a structure comparable to that of human spoken languages.

## 4. GESTURE AND SIGN LANGUAGE

The belief in gesture and sign language as being a single universal language first appeared in post-Renaissance texts on rhetoric. The earliest English source (1644) is John Bulwer's 'Chirologia; or the Naturall language of the

Hand. Composed of the Speaking Motions, and Discoursing Gestures thereof. Whereunto is added Chironomia: or the Art of Manuall Rhetoricke etc.'

In Chirologia, Bulwer describes hundreds of gestures of the hands and fingers. He presents the evidence of sign language as proof of the existence of this universal language:

'A notable argument we have of this discoursing facilities of the hand is . . . the wonder of necessity which nature worketh in men that are borne deafe and dumbe; who can argue and dispute rhetorically by signs.' (p. 5)

Bulwer's interest in the deaf led to the publication of his second book, 'Philocophus, or the Deafe and Dumbe Man's Friend by J.B., surnamed the Chirosopher' (London, 1648). This is the first book dedicated to any deaf person, being dedicated to two deaf brothers. In the dedication, Bulwer states:

'What though you cannot express your minds in those verball contrivances of man's invention, yet you want not speeche, who have your whole body for a tongue, having a language more naturall and significant, which is common to you with us, to wit, gesture, the generall and universal language of human nature.

You already can express yourselves so truly by signes, from a habit you have gotten by using always signes, as we do speeche: nature also recompensing your want of speeche, in the invention of signes to express your conceptions.

This language you speak so purely that I who was the first that made it my Darling Study to interpret the naturall richnesse of our discoursing gestures . . . am fully satisfied that you want nothing to be perfectly understood, your mother tongue administering sufficient utterance upon all occasions'.

Twenty-five years earlier, in Spain, Juan Pablo Bonet (1620) had drawn attention to the unique position of gesture as a natural language, and developed a manual alphabet (see below) for educating the deaf. This alphabet, he claimed, was:

'so well adapted to nature that it would seem as if this artificial language had been derived from the language of nature, or that from this, since visible actions are nature's language.'

Dalgarno (1663), a Scottish educator, was also involved in developing a manual alphabet. He was also the first author to state clearly the distance between sign language and spoken language:

'The deaf man has no teacher at all, and though necessity may put him upon continuing and using a few signs, yet those have no affinity to the language by which they that are about him do converse amongst themselves.' (p. 3)

In France, the Abbé de l'Epée, founder of a school for the deaf in the eighteenth century, also believed sign language to be the universal language:

745

'On a souvent désiré une langage universelle, avec le secours de laquelle les hommes de toutes les nations pourraient s'entendre les uns les autres. Il me semble qu'il y a longtemps qu'elle existe, et qu'elle est entendue partout. Cela n'est pas étonnant: c'est une langue naturelle. Je parle de la langue des signes.'

[A universal language has often been wished for, with the help of which men of all nations could understand each other. It seems to me that for a long time such a language has existed. I am speaking of sign language and is everywhere understood. That is not surprising: it is a national language.]

(de l'Epée 1776)

The supposed identity of sign languages in different countries was emphasised well into the twentieth century. An account of the visit of a French deaf man to the school for the deaf in London is a good example:

'As soon as Clerc beheld [the children] his face became animated; he was as agitated as a traveller of sensibility would be on meeting all of a sudden in distant regions a colony of his countrymen . . . Clerc approached them. He made signs and they answered him by signs. This unexpected communication caused a most delicious sensation in them and for us was a scene of expression and sensibility that gave us the most heartfelt satisfaction'.

(de Ladebat 1815)

While all these authors claim that sign language is universal, and identical with gesture, there is often an inherent contradiction in the position of those educators writing about sign language, since they frequently emphasise that the language of the deaf must be learned if the educator is to help the deaf; clearly this would not be necessary if sign language was truly universal. As Knowlson (1965) points out, most universalist claims for gesture are based on the author's observation of actors, mimes or the deaf, rather than on their own attempts to communicate. Often too, authors appear to recognise that signs vary in different countries, but conclude that this represents merely a small degree of variation, rather than evidence against the universalist hypothesis.

In the next section, the linguistics of sign languages will be discussed, with reference, where available, to comparative work on different sign languages.

## 5. THE LINGUISTICS OF SIGN LANGUAGES:

### 5.1 Phonetics and phonology in sign language

At first glance, the use of the terms phonetics and phonology may seem wholly inappropriate in a discussion of sign languages, which, by definition, are not composed of sounds. The terms have been widely used in sign language research, however, because of the similarities in the organisation of sign languages and spoken languages. Other linguists have used the term 'cherology' (from Greek *kheir* – hand).

Arbitrariness, and duality have, since Saussure, been regarded as defining features for all human languages. Before Stokoe (1960), signs had been regarded as unanalysable, unitary gestures, and therefore containing no level analogous to the phonological. His contribution was to recognise that ASL signs could more profitably be viewed as compositional, and thus unlike gestures. He proposed a three-part analysis of signs; unlike the predominantly sequential structure of words, signs were described as consisting of simultaneous bundles of TAB ('tabula': location of a sign in space), DEZ ('designator': the configuration of the hand), and SIG ('signator': movement of the hand in space). This model was generally adopted by researchers on other sign languages (Deuchar 1978; Woll, Kyle and Deuchar 1981; Brennan, Colville and Lawson 1984) with variations relating to whether there was a fourth prime of hand orientation (ORI). For example, the BSL sign RED could be described as consisting of TAB=lips; DEZ=index finger extended from fist; SIG=repeated stroking of the TAB; ORI=palm facing the body, index finger pointing upwards. Stokoe, an American structural linguist, regarded these primes as meaningless elements which combined to form all the signs in a language, in an analogous way to phonemes. In this model, signs form minimal pairs when (e.g.) one DEZ is substituted for another (Figure 29).

Within this model, for any sign language, the repertoire of handshapes or locations is limited, and the available variant articulations for any prime are arbitrarily determined. So, for example, in ASL it is claimed that there is no minimal pair where two signs differ in meaning because one is located at the lips and the other at the chin, but in British Sign Language (BSL) there are such pairs.

The origination of phonological research on signs in structural linguistics led to a concentration in the early years on describing inventories of elements. More recently there has been greater interest in the description of phonological processes.

Even within the inventory approach, two major problems have been noted with the Stokoe phonological model: the first is that the sequentiality of these bundles is not as insignificant as was assumed by Stokoe; and secondly, that there appears to be a relation between at least some of these primes and sign meanings.

## 5.2 Simultaneity or sequentiality

While Stokoe recognised that there was sequential organisation in signs, he claimed that it was not significant at the phonological level of analysis. However, as Liddell and colleagues have observed (Liddell and Johnson 1985), in all three primes there is evidence of sequential organisation. For

*Figure 29* BSL minimal pairs

a. Handshape

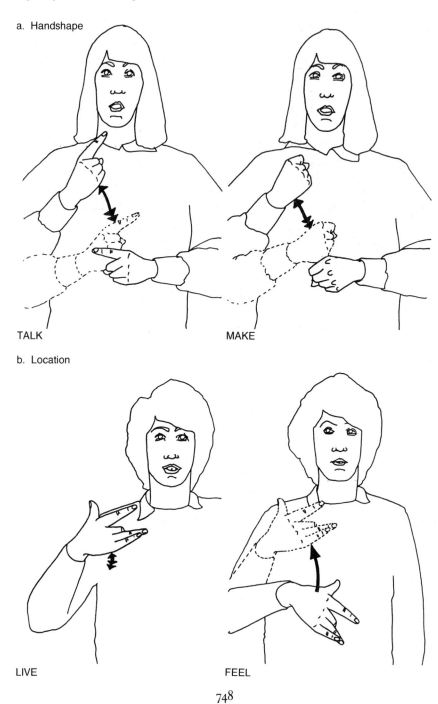

TALK              MAKE

b. Location

LIVE                        FEEL

*Figure 29* (continued)

c. Movement

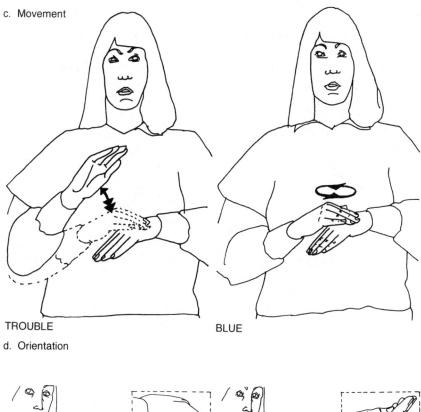

TROUBLE           BLUE

d. Orientation

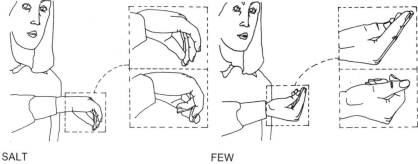

SALT           FEW

*(Figures 29—41, drawings© Bernard Quinn, 1985)*

749

example, the BSL sign SHOWER has a handshape which changes from closed to spread fingers: in MORNING, the location changes from the contralateral side of the chest to the ipsilateral; in the sign TABLE, the hands separate in the first part of the movement; in the second part, the hands move downwards. In contrast with Stokoe's claim, these features do seem to relate to differences in sign meanings. Given that signs have a sequential structure, that structure corresponds to phonological segments contrasting in the same way as in spoken languages, we can thus find minimal pairs of signs distinguished by sequence differences as well as the kind described by Stokoe. The BSL signs SHOWER and COPY (hand closes) can be better described as contrasting only in sequence of movement, rather than as contrasting in handshape and in movement, as would be required in the Stokoe model.

## 5.3 Arbitrariness in phonology

The second issue mentioned in relation to phonological studies of sign language is whether there is meaning at this level. The situation in sign languages is somewhat complex, and will be discussed more fully in the section below on iconicity. Stokoe's model described the elements of sign language phonology as if they were entirely arbitrary. For example, if we look at a number of signs in BSL located at the cheek, such as SWEET, WOMAN, EASY and CRUEL, they have no obvious meanings in common. This is also true of a selection of signs made with a fist handshape such as AGREE, CAR, MY, and STUPID. To claim that there are *no* connections in meaning amongst signs with shared features, however, misrepresents the evidence, as can be seen in the following examples from BSL: signs made with a handshape of little finger extended from the first include: BAD, POISON, ILL, WRONG, END, ARGUE, CURSE, SOUR, EVIL, etc. Signs located at the forehead include: THINK, IMAGINE, DREAM, STUPID, CLEVER, WORRY, UNDERSTAND, etc. In these examples we can see that there appears to be some connection between a given handshape or location and some general meaning. Thus, duality exists, but in a form not identical to that in spoken languages.

## 5.4 Constraints on sign form

Constraints on sign forms arise from two sources: physical limitations, and language-specific restrictions. In the first group are those constraints relating to sign production and reception. It has been noted that all locations on the body are not equally available for signs; unlike gesture and mime, signs are limited to an area bounded by the top of the head, the hips, and the width of extended elbows. Within this space, the greatest number of contrasting locations are found on the face.

*Figure 30* Sequential distinctions in signs

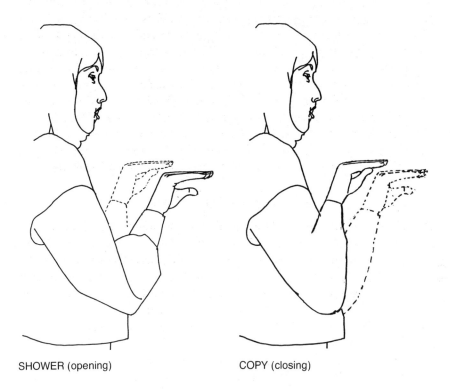

SHOWER (opening)          COPY (closing)

Battison (1978) proposes two constraints on sign form in ASL which also appear to hold for other sign languages. The Symmetry Condition states that if both hands move in a two-handed sign, they must both have the same handshape and the same movement. The Dominance Condition states that when the location of a sign is a passive hand, the handshape of the passive hand must be one of a set of unmarked handshapes. Later research has shown that while this constraint seems to operate in all sign languages, the inventory of unmarked handshapes differs from language to language.

Phonological processes operate on the citation forms of signs; amongst those studied are change of location and deletion of hand. Signs tend to move towards the centre of signing space, and to lose contact with a sign location. It is also common for one hand to be deleted in two-handed signs. (See the section on historical change below for a fuller discussion of these changes.) Liddell and Johnson (1985) discuss at length a whole series of phonological processes in ASL, including movement epenthesis, metathesis, gemination, perseveration and anticipation.

## 5.5 The lexicon: iconicity and arbitrariness in sign form

One of the most striking differences between signs and words is the prevalence of signs which bear some visual relationship to their referents. It is perhaps not surprising that visual languages exhibit more iconicity than auditory languages, in that objects in the external world tend to have more visual than auditory associations. However, because of the importance attached to the concept of arbitrariness in spoken language, the presence of iconicity in sign languages has been considered as making sign languages uniquely different from spoken languages. It is not appropriate here to discuss the role of onomatopoeia or sound symbolism in spoken language, or the extent of non-arbitrariness in syntax, but as Deuchar (1984) points out, it may be more appropriate to speak of conventionality, rather than arbitrariness, as a defining criterion of language.

The presence of iconicity in sign languages has often led to mistaken assumptions. It has been thought that signs could only express concrete and visual meanings, and that the presence of iconicity made sign languages universal. Neither of these beliefs is true. Signs for both concrete entities and abstract ideas often bear no iconic relationship to their referents, and even where there is an iconic origin for a sign, the particular relationship represented is specific to that language. For example, the signs for TREE in different sign languages range from two hands modelling the shape of a tree trunk (Chinese Sign Language) to sketchings of the outline of the shape of a tree (Danish Sign Language) to the forming of the shape of a tree, with the forearm representing the trunk and the fingers the branches (British Sign Language). WOMAN in BSL is signed with the index finger grazing the cheek; in Israeli Sign Language by pinching the earlobe with the thumb and index finger; in Danish Sign Language by indicating the breasts. About 50 per cent of basic sign vocabulary appears to be iconic, at least in the sense that naïve non-signers will agree on the nature of the imagery when told the meaning of a sign (Klima and Bellugi 1979). The presence of iconicity in signs does not appear, however, to affect the learnability of signs or their subjection to regular processes of historical change. For example (Woll and Lawson 1981), the sign for MILK in BSL is derived from a representation of milking a cow by hand. There is no reason to assume that a young child learning this sign will need to know how cows are (or were) milked in order to learn this sign. There is equally no evidence that this sign is being supplanted by another representing an automatic milking machine. There is also an extremely interesting report (Petitto 1985) of a child learning ASL who went through a phase of pronoun reversal of I and YOU, despite what looks like the identity of pointing to oneself and the sign for 'I'. Psycholinguistic research on ASL has also indicated that there is no relationship between

*Figure 31* Iconicity and arbitrariness

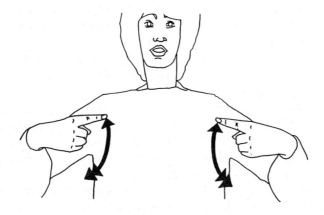

ALLOW (arbitrary relationship to referent)

TREE (iconic relationship to referent)

iconicity and recall of signs; instead, signs are recalled in terms of abstract formational components. It is important therefore not to overemphasise the distinctiveness of iconicity in sign languages. (See Figure 31.)

## 6. HISTORICAL CHANGE IN SIGN FORM

A number of studies of historical change in signs have been undertaken for ASL, French Sign Language and BSL. These studies shed light on the operation of phonological constraints and phonological processes, and also give additional information about the role of iconicity. Woll (1985) has described systematic changes in the phonology of BSL over the past 150 years. When new signs are created, signers often use iconic principles in new sign creation, but these new signs soon begin to alter to assimilate to constraints in the language. For example, the BSL sign MOTORCYCLE has its origin in a representation of holding the handlebars of a motorcycle and turning the accelerator. This violates the Symmetry Condition mentioned earlier, in that only the right hand moves. The sign has therefore changed, so that both hands move, while the direction of the wrist movement has reversed, to match the favoured direction of wrist nodding movement in BSL. The effects of these changes has been to reduce the link with the original mime of operating a motorcycle.

Another common change in BSL is the movement of signs from the periphery to the centre of signing space. This change can be seen taking place in informal conversation: the sign KING, located in citation form on the top of the head is often signed at the side of the head above the ear. This shift has resulted in changes in citation forms. Signs which were formerly located at the top of the head are now signed in the space in front of the body (PERHAPS); signs located on the upper arm have moved to the forearm; signs located at the forearm have moved to the wrist (TROUBLE, POLICE, BLUE).

A third change in signs is reduction from two-handed signs to one-handed signs. Sometimes this has taken place in signs where both hands are active (SCHOOL, FISH, LIVE); it can currently be seen taking place where one hand serves as a passive base for the active hand (TRUE, WRONG).

Assimilation to constraints on sign form can be seen most clearly in compound signs. These are composed of two free morphemes occurring in combination. Research on Swedish Sign Language (Wallin 1983) has distinguished between compounds borrowed from Swedish such as SJUK/HUS from Swedish *sjukhus* 'hospital' and 'genuine' compounds. He lists such compounds (translated into English glosses) as COFFEE/SIGN (cafe), EAT/PECK (hen), SEE/BORROW (imitate), THINK/EMPTY (forget) and THINK/TIRED (absent-minded). The order of elements in compounds is

*Figure 32* Compound signs

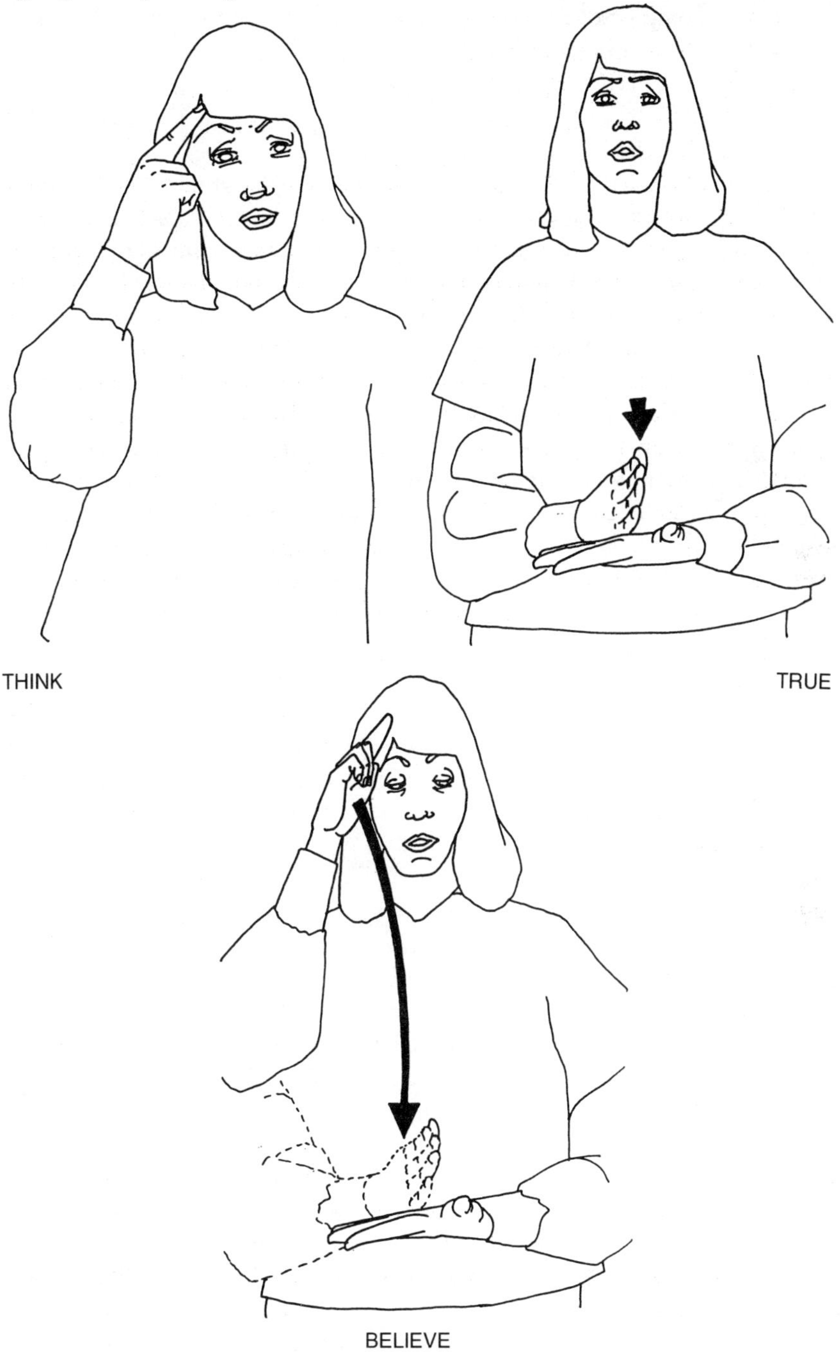

THINK

TRUE

BELIEVE

determined by their height in signing space, with the higher sign preceding the lower. Compounds in BSL most often serve one of two functions: as category terms composed of two exemplars of members of the category (MOTHER/FATHER (parents), TABLE/CHAIR (furniture), MAN/WOMAN (people)) or for certain abstract concepts (THINK/TRUE (believe), SAY/KEEP (promise)). In contrast to the appearance of the two signs when they appear independently, in the compound there are a number of changes reflecting assimilation of movement, handshape and location. Most prominently, the length of time taken for the articulation of the first sign in a compound is greatly reduced compared to the articulation time for the sign occurring alone. (See Figure 32.)

When comparing modern forms of signs with earlier recorded forms, we can see a tendency for compound signs to show assimilation of formational parameters. In some cases, this assimilation has been so great that the modern forms are no longer recognisable as compound forms. The sign NAME, for example, in the earliest illustrations of signs, is a compound of the signs THINK and WRITE. Later illustrations show assimilation of location of the second sign to head height, assimilation of the handshape in THINK to that of WRITE, and loss of the passive left hand in WRITE.

## 7. CONTACT WITH SPOKEN LANGUAGE

All signers live amongst hearing populations using spoken languages, and have some degree of access to the language of the hearing population. This contact is manifested in three areas: fingerspelling, loan-translations, and mouth patterning.

### 7.1 Fingerspelling

Most deaf populations in western countries make use of fingerspelling (often confused by the public with sign language) which represents the standard written language through a series of hand configurations and movements. There are many different manual alphabets (and some syllabaries) in use throughout the world, and are most comparable with other symbol systems derived from written languages such as Morse Code and Braille. Fingerspelling can be used both as a self-contained means of cummunication and as an adjunct to sign language. The amount and function of fingerspelling used by signers is often related to factors such as age, sex, social context and educational background. Fingerspelling is most often used as an adjunct to signing for 'foreign' words such as proper names, place names, and words not translated into sign (often for stylistic purposes, even where there is a sign with the same meaning). (See Table 15.)

Although fingerspelling represents the words of written languages, even an

*Table 15*  British two-handed manual alphabet

utterance articulated entirely in fingerspelling does not have uppercase letters, punctuation or breaks between words, probably because of the relatively slow articulation rate of fingerspelling when compared to speech or signing (only about 60 words per minute). The speeding up and running together of handshapes results in production and perception of fingerspelling largely in terms of an 'envelope' or global pattern, rather than as a series of individual letters. The interaction between fingerspelling and signing can be seen in initialisation, 'loan' signs and initially-modified signs. Loan signs derive from fingerspelled forms, but have so altered to accommodate to constraints on sign articulation that they are often not recognisable as having a fingerspelled origin.

In initialisation, fingerspelling is incorporated into sign language by changing the handshape of a sign to correspond (via fingerspelling) to the first letter of a written word with similar meaning. For example, the ASL signs GROUP, FAMILY and TEAM are distinguished by using the manual-alphabet handshapes G, F and T respectively. This process is found most frequently where a one-handed manual alphabet is in use.

Initial modification is found in languages such as BSL, in signs where additional movements have been attached to fingerspelled letters. For example, in BSL the sign GOLD was originally signed as a repeated G. In the modern sign, the movement is modified so that it resembles the movement of BRIGHT. These initial modifications might be considered to be loan signs, but there is no historical evidence of reduction from fully fingerspelled forms.

## 7.2 Loan signs

Apart from fingerspelled loan signs derived from written words, a few signs are borrowed by translation from spoken words. These are found most frequently in place names and proper names, and are often treated as humorous. Examples include 'Manchester' signed as MAN CHEST, or 'Newcastle' as NEW CASTLE. A variant of this process can be seen in the use of the sign PISTOL for 'Bristol'. Here the mouth pattern in articulating the word 'Bristol' is similar to that in 'pistol'.

## 7.3 Mouth patterns

Because of the exposure of deaf people to spoken language through speech training, many signers use silent mouth patterns while signing. These mouth patterns occasionally serve as the only contrastive element between two signs. In the number system, for example, a series of historical changes have caused the collapse of the contrast between NINE and FOUR. They have identical hand shapes, orientations and movements, and are distinguished solely by the use of associated mouth patterns with each that resemble the articulation patterns of the words 'nine' (lax mouth opens) and 'four' (teeth on lower lip followed by mouth opening). This process is one which seems to be increasing in use amongst younger signers.

## 7.4 Grammatical influences

Certain registers of sign language may make use of grammatical structures borrowed from spoken languages, in such contexts as church services, in combination with extensive use of fingerspelling. Some researchers have seen this as parallel to diglossia (Deuchar 1978).

## 8. SIGN LANGUAGE GRAMMAR

In this section, current research on the grammars of several sign languages will be presented. Most of this will focus on sign language morphology, as this is the area which has received greatest interest to date, but more recent work on sign language syntax will also be discussed.

Because of a number of popular misconceptions, there has been a great deal of misunderstanding about the grammar of sign languages. For those who believe that sign languages are manual representations of spoken languages, there has been little interest in examining their structure; for those who think that sign languages are merely pictorial systems, there has been a tendency to view sign grammar as reflecting 'natural visual logic'. As we have seen at the lexical level, there is a clear effect of use of the visual medium on the grammatical organisation of sign languages. However, appeals to visual imagery as an explanation for structure are insufficient.

Analysis of sign language grammar has also been hampered by the absence of a written form of the language. Sign language data are almost always presented (as in this chapter) by presenting English glosses for signs to make examples understandable to readers unacquainted with sign language notation systems. There are two serious problems with this approach: first, it suggests an equivalence between signs and English words which is often not present; second and more seriously, it obscures the simultaneous occurrence of inflections in signs. As we will see in this section, signs are often heavily inflected. By using English glosses we can either present a string of words for each morpheme, connected by hyphens to indicate simultaneity, or as has been more common, simply provide a single English word for each sign. The use of non-manual components for grammatical purposes also require something other than a linear transcription system.

One theme running through current research on the grammars of sign languages is the relation between modality and grammar. We may regard the function of grammar in a spoken language as organising non-linear meanings into a linear order, and the function of a grammar in a sign language as organising non-linear meanings into both spatial and linear order. Those features common to both signed and spoken languages reflect, in this view, non-modality-specific universals of language.

## 8.1 Morphological typology

American Sign Language has been described by Klima and Bellugi (1979) as an inflecting language like latin. Deuchar has argued cogently that, in terms of Comrie's recent (1981) restatement of the earlier tripartite description of languages as isolating, agglutinating or fusional, BSL and ASL would both be best described as agglutinating (like Turkish) rather than fusional (like Latin), as there is evidence of a one-to-one relationship between inflection and grammatical category. Unlike agglutinating spoken languages, however, sign language inflections occur simultaneously, superimposed one on another:

'The inflectional processes are distinguished from one another exclusively by differ-ences in the global movement changes they impose on classes of uninflected signs. One inflectional process imposes a rapid lax single elongated movement; another inflectional process imposes a smooth circular lax continuous movement; still another imposes a tense iterated movement. Each inflectional process has its own specific properties of movement dimension by which it operates'.

(Klima and Bellugi 1979: 300)

To include sign languages within the class of agglutinating languages, therefore, we would need to alter our definition to permit simultaneous as well as sequential inflection. (See Chapter 9, above.)

## 8.2 Bound forms

In the description of signs so far we have mainly discussed signs which occur as free forms. Bilingual signers can produce citation forms of these signs in response to the question 'What is the sign for x?'. Other signs occur only in bound forms, and a number of these will be discussed briefly.

## 8.3 Negative incorporation

Research on ASL, BSL and French Sign Language has revealed a process in these three languages by which certain verbs are converted to negatives through the addition of a bound form (Deuchar 1987). In ASL and FSL this is an 'outward twisting movement of the moving hand(s) from the place where the sign is made' (Woodward and deSantis 1977); in BSL negative incorpor-

*Figure 33* Verbs in BSL with negative incorporation

DON'T WANT

ation 'involves the modification of the affirmative form of a sign including a movement of upwards rotation of the hand, and change of handshape, if applicable, from a closed to an open handshape' (Deuchar 1987).

There is a striking similarity between those signs and words which accept negative incorporation. It is unlikely that this is the result of contact between, for example, BSL and Old English. (See Figure 33, and Table 16.)

### 8.4 Numeral incorporation

Certain signs in BSL such as YEARS-OLD, POUNDS(£), O'CLOCK, YEARS-AHEAD, YEARS-PAST, DAYS-AHEAD, DAYS-PAST, WEEKS-AHEAD, WEEKS-PAST and WEEKS-DURATION obligatorily incorporate a numeral into the handshape of the sign (Figure 34). Strings such as *FIVE WEEKS-AHEAD or *THREE YEARS-OLD (with the sign for (e.g.) FIVE followed by the uninflected signs WEEKS-AHEAD) are ungrammatical.

Wh-questions in BSL are formed with signs which can be glossed as HOW-OLD, WHO, HOW-MANY, WHEN, WHERE, etc. Several of these have spread fingers and wiggling movement. This handshape and movement are the same as in the sign MANY. The sign WHEN, for example, has the

*Table 16* Negative-incorporating verbs (adapted from Deuchar 1987)

| BSL | ASL | FSL | Latin | Old English | Jamaican Creole |
|---|---|---|---|---|---|
| GOOD NOT-GOOD | GOOD NOT-GOOD | | | | |
| KNOW NOT-KNOW | KNOW NOT-KNOW | KNOW NOT-KNOW | scio nescio | wat nat | |
| WANT NOT-WANT | WANT NOT-WANT | WANT NOT-WANT | volo nolo | wille nille | |
| LIKE NOT-LIKE | LIKE NOT-LIKE | LIKE NOT-LIKE | | | |
| HAVE NOT-HAVE | HAVE NOT-HAVE | HAVE NOT-HAVE | | haebbe naebbe | |
| CAN CAN'T | | | queo nequeo | | kyan kyaan |
| WILL WON'T | | | | | wi wuon |

same location as DAYS-PAST and DAYS-AHEAD; the sign HOW-OLD the same location as YEARS-OLD, and HOW-MANY the same location as cardinal numbers. These forms can therefore consist of the same bound forms as those discussed under numeral incorporation, but with MANY rather than a numeral incorporated.

## 8.5 Plurality

There are three mechanisms for the formation of plurals in BSL: reduplication of movement, reduplication of handshape, and addition of quantity marker. With a few exceptions, most signs can pluralise in only one of these ways.

Reduplication of movement: in pluralisation by reduplicaton of movement, speed of movement is non-significant (in contrast to inflection of verbs) and the movement is repeated with a slight shift of location for each repetition (BOOK, CHILD, BUILDING, IDEA). The structure of the singular form can be expressed as MOVEMENT (+ HOLD); the pluralised form as MOVEMENT + MOVEMENT (+ HOLD).

Reduplication of handshape: in pluralisation by reduplication of handshape, a one-handed sign is pluralised by articulating the sign with both hands (AEROPLANE, CUP). It is possible that there is some distributional meaning attached to this form of reduplication, but this has not yet been investigated. (See Figure 35.)

*Figure 34* Signs in BSL with numeral incorporation

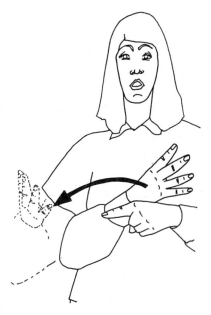

IN-FOUR-WEEKS

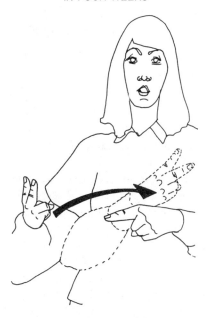

TWO-WEEKS-AGO

*Figure 35* Plural forms of nouns

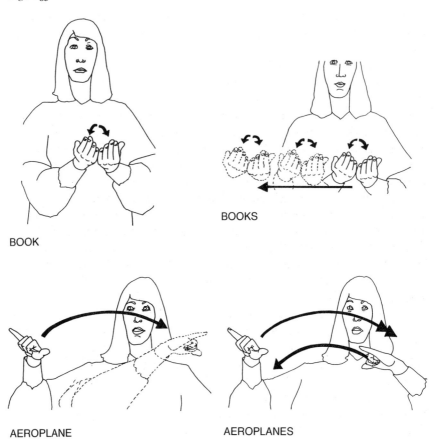

BOOK

BOOKS

AEROPLANE

AEROPLANES

Addition of quantifier: some signs cannot reduplicate either handshape or movement. Plurality in these nouns (MAN, CAR, SHIRT) is expressed by the addition of a postponed quantifier such as MANY or a numeral.

The assignment of signs to one of these three classes is not related to a sign's meaning, but is linked to its derivational origin and to its formational properties. Signs with a repeated movement in citation form tend not to inflect by reduplication: signs with continuous contact between the hand and a body part are less likely to inflect by reduplication than those in neutral space (as signs have moved towards neutral space over the last 100 years, some now reduplicate for plurals which did not do so formerly). Nouns formed by a derivational process from verbs do not take reduplication of movement, even where they are located in neutral space (CAR derived from DRIVE, BROOM derived from SWEEP).

## 8.6  Predicate classifiers

Research on several sign languages (Kyle and Woll 1985, McDonald 1983) has suggested that they exhibit a predicate classifier system, although there is disagreement on the appropriateness of the term 'classifier', some preferring 'Pro-forms'. Like several spoken languages such as Navaho (Young and Morgan 1980), verb stems for movement and location are based on the shape of the involved object, combined with affixes which signal adverbal, pronominal and aspectual information. As well as productive verb affixes and stems in Navaho, there are also a number of frozen forms which have entered the nominal system. McDonald (1983) has argued that in ASL the handshape is the stem of the verb, and is used to signal motion or location of a given class of objects. She has suggested a system like that in Table 17.

As well as the forms which can be described in terms of motion or location, there are a second group which relate to the handling properties of objects. These give us such forms as 'handle a compact or small cylindrical object' (DAGGER, LAWNMOWER (= handle), 'handle a thin, flattish object' (PAPER, CLOTH), 'handle a round object' (KNOB, BALL, LID), 'handle a small object' (COIN, FLOWER), 'handle a small narrow object' (PLUG, SWITCH).

The development of frozen forms, as in Navaho, can produce 'abstract verbs, nouns, or prepositions (ON = flat, wide object). In ASL, the form labelled as 'handle a compact or small cylindrical object' is used in such signs as PRACTICE, MAKE, and WORK. It appears impossible to predict which forms will 'freeze' in which way: BSL WITH derives from the form 'handle a thin, flattish object'; ASL WITH derives from the form 'handle a compact or small cylindrical object'. The ASL sign FALL has the properties *individual, flat, narrow*, but is used with nouns which do not have those properties, such

*Table 17*  Partial table of verb stems in ASL

Motion or location of undifferentiated *whole* versus *individual* objects

Motion or location of *flat* objects versus *curved* objects versus *circular* objects

Motion or location of *narrow* objects versus *wide* objects versus *two-dimensional* objects

| | |
|---|---|
| CUT (with a knife) | whole, flat, narrow |
| SKATEBOARD | whole, flat, wide |
| SCISSORS, LEGS, FALL | individual, flat, narrow |
| SPOON, REFEREE (= whistle) | whole, curved, narrow |
| VAMPIRE (= fangs), KNEEL | individual, curved, narrow |
| DOOR, FEET | whole, flat, wide |
| SCOOP, SNOW PLOW | whole, curved, wide |
| RAINDROPS, BULLET HOLES | whole, circular, two-dimensional |
| TELESCOPE | whole, circular, wide |

*Figure 36* Classifying handshapes

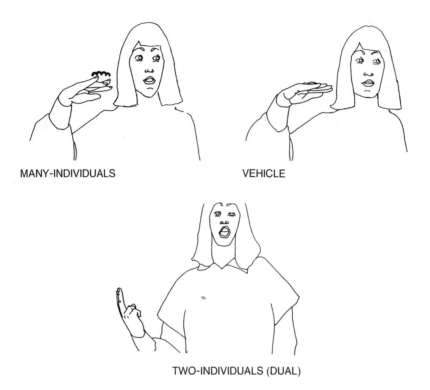

MANY-INDIVIDUALS          VEHICLE

TWO-INDIVIDUALS (DUAL)

as APPLE. The BSL sign CHOOSE, which has the properties *whole, circular, two-dimensional,* can be used with nouns as diverse as DRESS, FRUIT, BOX, etc.

In BSL sentences, stems such as those above can be used in verbs of motion; nouns which do not contain these verb stems are replaced with the appropriate stem (for example, 'The car turns right' is a two-sign utterance, signed as CAR WHOLE-OBJECT-FLAT-WIDE-TURN-RIGHT). Sign language sentence structure will be discussed more fully in the section below on syntax. (See Figure 36.)

### 8.7 Inflection for role

Verbs in BSL can be grouped into three classes: invariant, directional and reversing. Invariant verbs are characterised by showing no inflection for semantic role. Directional verbs obligatorily change the path of their movement to indicate semantic role, but the hand's orientation remains unaltered

*Figure 37* Invariant, directional, reversing verbs

a. Invariant

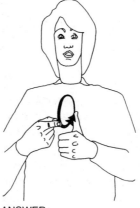

ANSWER

b. Directional

SUPERVISE

c. Reversing

LOOK-AT

767

*Table 18* Invariant, directional, and reversing verbs

| Invariant | Directional | Reversing |
|---|---|---|
| BSL: TELL | SUPERVISE | LOOK-AT |
| PREACH | GIVE | ASK |
| ANSWER | EXPLAIN | TEASE |

throughout these movement changes. Reversing verbs, as well as obligatorily altering the path of their movement, also change their orientation to reflect semantic role. Several examples will make this clearer. (Figure 37).

In directional and reversing verbs the direction of movement is a case marker in an egocentric system. In other words, direction of movement will show the case of the first person. If the first person is agent, there is a movement away from the signer, if the first person is patient, there is a movement toward the signer. Reversing verbs, in addition to these properties, also use orientation to convey semantic role. The unmarked form represents the first person as agent, and orientation of the hands is reversed where the first person is patient.

The initial and final points in the movement in directional and reversing verbs are determined by the assignment of points in space to referents other than first person. Figure 38 shows the location of third and fourth person referents for right-handed signers. Thus the reversing verb LOOK in sentences such as 'He looks at me' would move from point 3 to point 1, with the tips of the extended fingers turning towards point 1; in 'You supervise me' the hand moves from point 2 to point 1, but the orientation of the hand remains unaltered, as SUPERVISE is a directional, not a reversing verb. In the sentence 'I answer you', the verb would remain in its citation orientation and movement, and roles would be indicated pronominally.

## 8.8 Aspectual inflection

The incorporation of aspect affixes into verb stem markers has been mentioned briefly in the section above. In this section, aspect and manner marking will be discussed more fully. Those sign languages studied so far all show complex marking of aspect on the verb. Aspect marking can be grammaticalised, through inclusion in the verb stem, as with a number of sub-categories of imperfective aspect such as duration, habitual and iterative. Perfective aspect in BSL is largely lexicalised, marked by the addition of the verb FINISH as an auxiliary to the main verb of the sentence. (FINISH can also occur on its own as a main verb.) Deuchar's (1984) data includes such sentences as I KILL ALL FINISH (I've killed all (the weeds)), SUGAR PUT-

*Figure 38* Locations for role reference

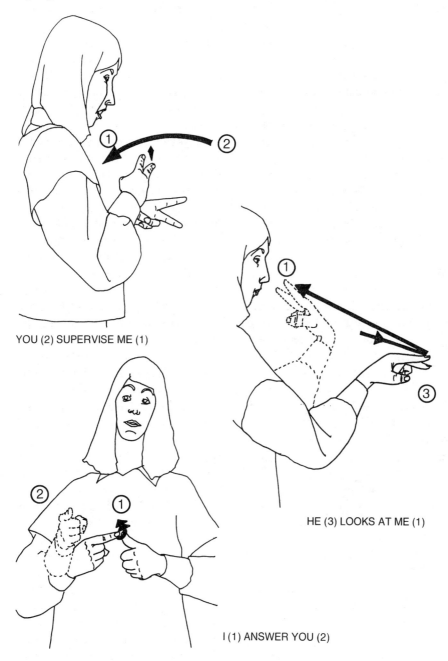

YOU (2) SUPERVISE ME (1)

HE (3) LOOKS AT ME (1)

I (1) ANSWER YOU (2)

IN FINISH (I've put in the sugar) and 3-PERSON SAY YOU ALL READ FINISH (He says, 'Have you finished reading all (of the newspaper)?'). While her data do not include any examples of FINISH co-occurring with present or future time reference (thus suggesting that FINISH might be a tense marker) other researchers have found examples without past time reference such as BUTTONS PUT-IN-A-ROW FINISH, DRAW-SMILE FINISH (he puts the buttons in a row, then draws a smile.) or MUST EGG BEAT FINISH (you must beat the eggs (first)) which confirm her interpretation of FINISH as a perfective aspect marker.

Of the three major categories of morphological process (Matthews 1974:127–9) two, reduplication and modification, are used far more frequently than the other, affixation. Bergman (1983) has focused on five morphological processes in Swedish Sign Language: fast reduplication, slow reduplication, initial stop, doubling and initial hold.

In Figure 39, the verb LOOK-AT is shown in its uninflected form, together with the forms showing fast reduplication and slow reduplication. These terms were first used for ASL by Fischer (1973), and Bergman (1983) has used the same terms for Swedish Sign Language. However, in the BSL the two patterns do not differ so much in actual speed, but in their differing cyclic structures. In slow reduplication, there are pauses between each repetition of the verb; in fast reduplication, there is even movement, with less sense of cycles having intervening pauses. An important observation first made by Supalla and Newport (1978) in describing aspect in ASL verbs, is that reduplication does not apply to the citation form of the sign, but to its underlying form. For example, in BSL the citation form of the sign WALK contains a repeated movement. If this were simply reduplicated we would have four movements. Instead, movement occurs only three times in the reduplicated form. This suggests that reduplication is added to a singly underlying movement rather than the repeated movement of the citation form.

The meanings associated with slow and fast reduplication vary according to the semantics of the verb. With punctual verbs such as JUMP, fast reduplication suggests regularity, repetition of the action or frequency; with durational verbs such as WAIT, fast reduplication suggests habitual action. Slow reduplication of punctual verbs conveys continual action; slow reduplication of durational verbs conveys continuous action. Stative verbs like ANGRY or INTERESTED can undergo slow reduplication only; this is understood as intensifying the verb (VERY-ANGRY, REALLY-INTERESTED).

The combination of inflection for role and aspect results in visually complex configurations as can be seen in Figure 40, where the use of two hands and their orientations indicates reciprocity of action, and the movement pattern indicates inflection for durative aspect.

*Figure 39* Aspectual modification of the verb LOOK-AT

a. SLOW REDUPLICATION: LOOK AT FOR A LONG TIME

b. FAST REDUPLICATION: LOOK AT AGAIN AND AGAIN

*Figure 40* 3rd-person and 4th-person KEEP LOOKING AT ONE ANOTHER

a. LOOK AT EACH OTHER          b. LOOK AT FOR A LONG TIME

c. LOOK AT EACH OTHER FOR A LONG TIME

## 8.9 Pronominalisation

As has already been mentioned, certain verbs use locations in space to identify semantic roles. The locations used by these verbs can also be used for pronouns. BSL has the pronoun signs shown in Table 19 (for right-handed signers).

First and second person pronouns always have a deictic function; third and fourth person pronouns can be either deictic or anaphoric. Anaphoric pronouns can only occur following the localisation of the referent noun in the location assigned to the pronoun. Nouns articulated in the space in front of the body are, for example, moved to third person space; nouns located on a body part would be followed by an indexing of third person space. This assignment of location to a referent then continues through the discourse until it is changed. To indicate anaphoric reference, the signer indexes the location previously assigned to that referent. In an example from Deuchar (1984:97): TWO THREE FOUR HELP HE MARSHAL KNOW IT USED-TO IT (He helps to marshal numbers two, three and four. He knows it, he's used to it), the anaphoric pronoun HE refers to someone named earlier in the discourse. The same person is the subject of the verbs KNOW and USED-TO, so the pronoun can be deleted as the referent of HE has remained unchanged. The pronouns IT in KNOW IT, etc. are not deleted since they are not part of the same topic.

In verbs that inflect for participant role, neither subject nor subject pronouns are required; in invariant verbs, however, where this cannot be read from the pattern of movement, pronouns are normally required. Where the subject is first person, it can be deleted, however. In Figure 41, we can see ANSWER-YOU (I answer you) contrasted with YOU-ANSWER-ME (you answer me). The absence of pronouns in the inflecting verbs can be seen in Figure 37 above.

*Table 19*

| Personal | Possessive | Reflexive |
|---|---|---|
| I | MY | MYSELF |
| YOU (singular) | YOUR (singular) | YOURSELF |
| 3rd PERSON singular | 3rd PERSON'S | 3rd PERSON SELF |
| 4th PERSON singular | 4th PERSON'S | 4th PERSON SELF |
| DUAL | – | – |
| exclusive WE | exclusive OUR | exclusive OURSELVES |
| inclusive WE | inclusive OUR | inclusive OURSELVES |
| THEY | THEIR | THEMSELVES |

*Figure 41* Personal pronouns with verbs

a. I ANSWER YOU

b. YOU ANSWER ME

The operation of anaphora, participant role inflection, classifier and the availability of two articulators can all be seen in the following example 'The woman hits the man'. In this, the sign MAN is articulated with the left hand, followed by the 'person' classifier, located to 4th person space. The left hand remains in the 'person' classifier handshape and 4th person location, while the remainder of the sentence is signed. The sign WOMAN is articulated with the right hand, followed by the 'person' classifier, located to 3rd person space. The verb HIT, a reversing verb, is then articulated, moving on a track from the subject (3rd person) to object (4th person).

left hand: MAN PERSON-CLASSIFIER 4th-PERSON ..........................
sign is held
right hand: WOMAN
PERSON-CLASSIFIER 3rd-PERSON 3rd PERSON HIT 4th-PERSON

## 9. SIGN ORDER

In an early study of ASL, it was suggested that 'the basic word-order in ASL is Subject-Verb-Object' (Fischer 1975: 5). While little work has been undertaken as yet on sign order in other languages there is evidence that in BSL at least, sign order is best described in terms of Topic-Comment Structure (Deuchar 1983), using Li and Thompson's criteria for identifying a topic-prominent language, such as the absence of passive constructions, the absence of dummy subjects such as 'there' and 'there is', and the existence of 'double subject' constructions, with the topic followed by the subject. The example above, 'The woman hits the man', shows typical order in BSL. Deuchar has related this Topic-Comment preference to the status of BSL as a language used mostly for informal conversation. However, a recent experimental study of Italian Sign Language and Swiss-German Sign Language by Boyes-Braem (1987) has indicated that Italian signers show a preference for Subject-Verb-Object ordering, while the Swiss subjects show a Topic-Comment preference.

### 9.1 Simultaneity

The discussion above on sign order obscures the important observation that linear order is not the only available dimension in which syntax can occur. In sign languages, the availability of two articulators moving in visible space offers opportunities for constructions which cannot occur in spoken languages, such as the simultaneous articulation of a noun with one hand and its modifier with the other, as in:

(left hand) BOY    'small boy'    or    (left hand) BORN  'born deaf'
(right hand) SMALL                        (right hand) DEAF

While opportunities for simultaneous modification are limited, because of the necessity of having two one-handed signs, there is a substantial role for non-manual behaviours occurring simultaneously with manual signs in such processes as the marking of questions and negation. This can be seen to parallel prosodic aspects of spoken language such as stress, intonation and tone.

## 9.2 Non-manual question marking

In an earlier section above (8.4), the use of Wh-question signs was discussed. Yes-no questions in BSL are most frequently formed without the use of manual question markers, but with a specific marking of facial expression which occurs simultaneously with the manual part of the sentence. In complex sentences with embedding the non-manual question markers occur only over the duration of the clause being questioned:

hands: WITH PAT GO / PAT STAY THERE    (left hand holds THERE)
                                      (right) YOU RETURN
face:                        Q ..............................................................
(When you go with Pat, will she stay while you come back?)

This facial expression has as its most prominent feature raised eyebrows. Wh-questions are also accompanied by specific facial activity; this normally consists of furrowed eyebrows. This division is not absolute, however, and appears to be related to the information load of the question. Where questions have the function of checking information already received, for example, the brow patterns are reversed.

## 9.3 Non-manual negation

There are a number of signs expressing negation: NEVER, NOTHING, NOT and NOT-YET (which is mainly used as a marker of imperfective aspect), but negation is also frequently accomplished by the use of non-manual activity (headshaking) superimposed on the manual component of the signing:

hands: SIGN TEACH VOICE SOUND
head:                 NEG ................................................................
(I teach signing with no voice and no sound.)

As with question marking, the non-manual sector extends over the portion of the utterance being negated.

## 9.4 Other non-manual activity

Only preliminary investigations on other roles of non-manual activity have been undertaken. Liddell (1980) and Deuchar (1984) suggest that headnods may function as assertion markers in ASL and BSL respectively. Liddell's claim that non-manual marking of restrictive relative clauses takes place in ASL is disputed by Deuchar (1984) and Thompson (1977) who argue that this marking is at discourse level, and identifies material mentioned earlier in the discourse or present in the context, which the signer desires to make prominent.

In other work on non-manual activities Baker and Padden (1978) have studied those which occur at the juncture of 'if' and 'then' clauses and at the relinquishing of a turn by a singer. At the lexical level, Lawson (1983) has examined a small number of signs in BSL which have obligatory and contrastive involvement of mouth position; Vogt-Svendsen (1983) has undertaken a similar study in Norwegian Sign Language.

## 10. SUMMARY

The linguistics of sign languages is an exciting new field. Research on sign languages can help illuminate important issues relating to language universality and the role of medium in language structure, with the aim of answering such questions as:

How arbitrary is language?

How can duality of structure be realised in a language without sound?

How important is simultaneity in language?

Should prosodic and 'para-linguistic' features be incorporated into grammatical description?

NOTE ON THE TRANSCRIPTION OF SIGN LANGUAGES: A number of notation systems have been developed to represent signs. These include pictographic systems (Sutton Sign Writing) and variants of Stokoe notation (Brennan, Colville and Lawson). Glosses also provide convenient access to sign data for readers not familiar with sign notation systems, but it should be remembered that there is no equivalence between a sign form and its gloss. The usual conventions for glossing signs have been followed: signs are presented in upper-case letters; translations into English are indicated with lower case letters and inverted commas.

## APPENDIX: SIGNS FROM BRITISH SIGN LANGUAGE

The notation system used here is a variant of Stokoe notation. Only a subset of the characters have been given, enough to illustrate a small sample of signs.

LOCATION: The first symbol notated for each sign is the LOCATION. This may be the space in front of the body, or a body part. In signs where the location is the non-dominant hand, the configuration of that hand is given as the location

| | |
|---|---|
| neutral space | φ |
| cheek | ᔆ |
| chest | [] |
| forehead | ∩ |

HANDSHAPE: Handshape, whether of the active moving hand, or the passive hand, is notated with alphanumeric symbols. Where two handshapes are given, the first is of the non-dominant hand; a sign notated with a body location and two handshapes is one where both the dominant and non-dominant hands are active. A small superscript 'o' is used to indicate handshape variants with thumb extension.

| | |
|---|---|
| little finger extended from fist | I |
| all fingers extended and spread | 5 |
| index finger and thumb tips touching, other fingers extended and straight | F |
| index finger extended from fist | G |
| clawed hand | E |
| hand flat, fingers extended and together | B |
| index and middle fingers extended from fist and spread | V |
| fist, thumb alongside index finger | A |
| fist, thumb extended | Å |

ORIENTATION: Handshapes, whether of active or passive hands, are followed with one or two subscripts to indicate orientation. Where only one symbol is listed, this represents the orientation of the palm; where two symbols are given, the second represents the orientation of the fingers. For handshapes where the fingers are closed into a fist, the finger orientation is taken by imagining the fingers extended.

| | |
|---|---|
| left | < |
| right | > |

up ∧

down ∨

toward the signer's body T

away from the signer's body ⊥

MOVEMENT: Movement symbols are indicated by superscripts at the right of the notated sign. Where complex movements occur simultaneously, they are written one above the other. Where closing or opening symbols are used, the handshape in brackets is the final handshape.

leftwards movement <

rightwards movement >

upwards movement ∧

downwards movement ∨

movement towards the signer's body T

movement away from the signer's body ⊥

closing movement #

finger wiggle ⌇

up and down movement ~

alternating movement of the two hands ~

interchanging movement of the two hands ⟨⟩

touching X

side to side movement Z

clockwise circling movement ∽

the underlined hand is above the other hand —

the sign is a compound ‖

the movement is repeated ·

The example below illustrates how to read a notated sign. Symbol 1 signifies that the location of the sign is in neutral space in front of the body, and that therefore both the non-dominant and dominant hands are active. Symbol 2 signifies that the handshape of the non-dominant hand consists of the little finger extended from the fist. Symbol 3 signifies that the palm of the non-dominant hand faces the signer's body; symbol 4 that the extended finger points upwards. Symbols 5, 6 and 7 repeat this information for the dominant hand. Symbol 8 indicates that the movement of the sign is up and down; symbol 9 that the up and down movement is performed alternately (one hand moves up while the other moves down).

Example: $\phi I_{T\wedge} I_{T\wedge}\overset{\approx\ ^8_9}{}$  ARGUE
$\qquad\qquad\quad {\scriptstyle 1\ 2\ 3\ 4\ 5\ 6\ 7}$

## SAMPLE LIST OF NOTATED SIGNS

$\phi I_{T\wedge} I_{T\wedge}\overset{\approx}{}$   ARGUE

$\phi I_{\langle\wedge}\overset{\varnothing}{}$   BAD

$\phi 5_{\vee}\overset{\#(F)}{}$   CHOOSE

$\backprime 5_{T\wedge}\overset{\wr}{}$   WHEN

$\phi G_{T\rangle} G_{T\langle}\overset{\sim}{}$   ALLOW

$[]E_T E_T\overset{\approx}{}$   INTERESTED

$B_{\vee}\underline{V}_{\vee}\overset{x}{}$   POLICE

$\cap G_T\overset{\ell}{}$   THINK

$B_{\wedge}\underline{B}_{\langle\perp}\overset{x}{}$   TRUE

$\cap G_{\langle}\overset{\phi}{}\|B_{\wedge}\underline{B}_{\langle\perp}\overset{x}{}$   BELIEVE

$[]G_{\rangle T}\overset{x}{}$   I.

$[]A_T\overset{x}{}$   MY

$[]G_{\rangle\wedge}\overset{\wr}{}$   MYSELF

$\phi \overset{8}{A}_{\rangle}\overset{8}{A}_{\langle}\overset{1}{}$   FINISH

$\cap I_T\overset{\varpi\ \cdot}{}$   EVIL

# REFERENCES

Akmajian, A., Demers, R.A. and Harnish, R.M. (1984) *Linguistics: An introduction to Language and Communication*, The MIT Press, Cambridge, Mass.

Battison, R. (1978) *Lexical Borrowing in American Sign Language*, Linstok Press, Silver Spring.

Bergman, B. (1983) 'Verbs and Adjectives: Morphological Processes in Swedish Sign Language,' in Kyle, J.G. and Woll, B. (eds): 3–9.

Bloomfield, L. (1933) *Language*, Holt, Rinehart & Winston, New York. English edn. 1935, George Allen & Unwin, London.

Bonet, J.P. (1620) *Reduction de las Letras y Arte para Enseñar a ablar los Mudos (Simplification of Sounds and the Art of Teaching the Dumb to Speak)*, Francisco Abarca de Angulo, Madrid.

Boyes-Braem, P. (1987) 'Semantic Roles in Italian Sign Language and in French Swiss Sign Language.' Unpublished paper presented at the 1987 International Pragmatics Conference, Antwerp.

Brennan, M., Colville, M. and Lawson, L. (1984) *Words in Hand*, Moray House Publications, Edinburgh.

Bulwer, J.B. (1644) *Chirologia: or the natural language of the hands*, R. Whitaker, London.

Bulwer, J.B. (1648) *Philocophus: or the deafe and dumbe man's friend*, Humphrey Moseley, London.

Comrie, B. (1981) *Language Universals and Linguistic Typology*, Basil Blackwell, Oxford.

Condillac, F. (1746) *An Essay on the Origin of Human Knowledge*, reprinted 1971, Scholars' Facsimiles and Reprints, Gainesville.

Dalgarno, G. (1661) *Ars signorum, vulgo character universalis et lingua philosophica*, E. Hayes, London.

Danby, H. (ed.) (1933) *The Mishnah*, Oxford University Press, Oxford.

de Ladebat, L. (1815) *A Collection of the Most Remarkable Definitions and Answers of Massieu and Clerc*, Cox and Bayliss, London.

de l'Epée, Abbé (1776) *Instruction of the Deaf and Dumb by Means of Methodical Signs: the True Manner of Instructing the Deaf and Dumb Confirmed by Long Experience*, Le Crozet, Paris.

Deuchar, M. (1978) *Diglossia in British Sign Language*, unpublished Ph.D. dissertation, Stanford University.

Deuchar, M. (1983) 'Is BSL an SVO language?' in Kyle and Woll (eds): 69–76.

*Deuchar, M. (1984) *British Sign Language*, Routledge & Kegan Paul, London.

Deuchar, M. (1987) 'Negative Incorporation in Three Sign Languages', in Kyle, J.G. (ed.) *Sign and School*, Multilingual Matters, Clevedon.

Diderot, J. (1751) 'Letter on the Deaf and Dumb', in Caldwell, R.L. (1971), *Structure de la lettre sur les sourds et muets*. Studies on Voltaire and the 18th Century, No. 84: 109–22.

Fischer, S.D. (1973) 'Two processes of reduplication in the American Sign Language', *Foundations of Language*, 9: 469–80.

Fischer, S.D., (1975) 'Influences on Word Order Change in American Sign Language', in Li, C. (ed.), *Word Order and Word Order Change*, University of Texas Press, Austin: 1–25.

Groce, N. (1986) *Everyone Here Spoke Sign Language*, Harvard University Press, Cambridge, Mass.

Hewes, G.W. (1976) 'The Current Status of the Gestural Theory of Language Origin', in Harnad, S.R., Steklis, H.D. and Lancaster, J. (eds) *Origins and Evolution of Language and Speech*, New York Academy of Science, New York: 485–504.

Kendon, A. (1989) *The Sign Languages of Aboriginal Australia*, Cambridge University Press, Cambridge.

*Klima, E. and Bellugi, U. (1979) *The Signs of Language*, Harvard University Press, Cambridge, Mass.

Knowlson, J.R. (1965) 'The Idea of Gesture as a Universal Language in the XVIIth and XVIIIth Centuries,' *Journal of the History of Ideas*, 4: 495–508.

*Kyle, J.G. and Woll, B. (eds) (1983) *Language in Sign: an International Perspective on Sign Language*, Croom Helm, London.

*Kyle, J.G. and Woll, B. (1985) *Sign Language: the Study of Deaf People and their Language*, Cambridge University Press, Cambridge.

Lawson, L. (1981) 'The Role of Sign in the Structure of the Deaf Community,' in Woll, B., Kyle, J.G. and Deuchar, M. (eds): 166–77.

Lawson, L. (1983) 'Multichannel Signs.' In Kyle, J.G. and Woll, B. (eds): 97–103.

Liddell, S.K. (1978) 'Non-manual Signals and Relative Clauses in American Sign Languages', in Siple, P. (ed.): 60–89.

Liddell, S.K. and Johnson, R. (1985) *Report of the Workshop on Sign Language Notation.* Linguistics Research Institute, Gallaudet University, Washington, DC.

Markowicz, H. (1979) 'Sign Languages and the Maintenance of the Deaf Community,' Unpublished paper presented at NATO Symposium on Sign Language Research , Copenhagen.

Matthews, P.H. (1974) *Morphology: an Introduction to the Theory of Word Structure.* Cambridge University Press, Cambridge.

McDonald, B. (1983) 'Levels of Analysis in Sign Language Research', in Kyle, J.G. and Woll, B. (eds): 32–40.

Petitto, L.S. (1985) 'From Gesture to Symbol: The Relation of Form to Meaning in ASL Personal Pronoun Acquisition,' in Stokoe, W.C. and Volterra, V. (eds), *SLR 83 (Proceedings of the III International Symposium on Sign Language Research)*, Linstok Press, Silver Spring: 55–63.

Siple, P. (ed.) (1978) *Understanding Language through Sign Language Research*, Academic Press, New York.

Stokoe, W.C. (1960) 'Sign Language Structure: an outline of the visual communication system of the American deaf', *Studies in Linguistics, Occasional Paper 8*, University of Buffalo.

Stout, G.F. (1899) *A Manual of Psychology*, University Correspondence College Press, London.

Supalla, E. and Newport,E.L. (1978) 'How many seats in a chair? The Derivation of Nouns and Verbs in American Sign Language,' in Siple, P. (ed.): 91–131.

Thompson, J. (1977) 'The Lack of Subordination in American Sign Language,' in Friedman, L.A. (ed.) *On the Other Hand: New Perspectives on American Sign Language*, Academic Press, New York: 181–96.

Tylor, E.B. (1874) *Researches into the Early History of Mankind*, Murray & Company, London.

van Uden, A. (1986) *Sign Languages of the Deaf and Psycholinguistics: A Critical Evaluation*, Swets & Zeitlinger, Lisse.

Vogt-Svendsen, M. (1983) 'Mouth Position and Mouth Movement in Norwegian Sign Language,' in Kyle, J.G. and Woll, B. (eds): 85–96.

Wallin, L. (1983) 'Compounds in Swedish Sign Language in Historical Perspective,' in Kyle, J.G. and Woll, B. (eds): 56–68.

Woll, B. (1985) 'Change in British Sign Language' *Final Report to the Leverhulme Trust.*

Woll, B. and Lawson, L. (1981) 'British Sign Language', in Haugen, E., McClure, J.D. and Thompson, D. (eds)*Minority Languages Today*, Edinburgh University Press, Edinburgh.

Woll, B., Kyle, J.G. and Deuchar, M. (eds) (1981) *Perspectives on British Sign Language and Deafness*, Croom Helm, London.

Woodward, J. and DeSantis, S. (1977) 'Negative Incorporation in French and American Sign Languages', *Language in Society*, 6: 379–88.

Young, R.A. and Morgan, D. (1980) *The Navaho Language*, University of New Mexico Press, Albuquerque.

## FURTHER READING

The items marked with an asterisk in the list above will be found especially useful for readers who wish to pursue the topic further.

# 22

## LANGUAGE AND ITS STUDENTS: THE HISTORY OF LINGUISTICS

### VIVIEN LAW

### 1. LINGUISTICS AND ITS HISTORY

The history of linguistics is often thought of as a very new discipline; after all, linguistics itself has only been established in its present form for a few decades. But people have been studying language since the invention of writing, and no doubt long before that too. As in many other subjects, the use and then the study of language for practical purposes preceded the reflective process of scholarly study. In ancient India, for example, the need to keep alive the correct pronunciation of ancient religious texts led to the investigation of articulatory phonetics, while in ancient Greece the need for a technical and conceptual vocabulary to use in the logical analysis of propositions resulted in a system of parts of speech which was ultimately elaborated far beyond the immediate requirements of the philosophers who had first felt the need for such categories. Rhetorical training at Rome, the preservation of religious texts in Judaism, the spread of the new proselytising religions of Christianity and Islam, the establishment of vernacular literary traditions in the nation states of Renaissance Europe – all these are contexts in which language, at first a tool, became the focus of study. To achieve a comprehensive picture of how and why language was studied in the past, all these various traditions – and many others – should be taken into account, different as they are from our present-day notions of what is meant by 'linguistics'. Each tradition has its own historians: Bacher on language study among Jews, Sandys on Classical philology, E.J. Dobson (1957) on early work on English pronunciation, H. Pedersen (1931) on comparative philology, and very many others. As linguistics in the post-Saussurean sense has come to be perceived as a discipline distinct from the mainstream of nineteenth-century language study – comparative and historical philology – so it too has found its historians. But whereas most earlier historians concentrated by design on individual, mostly national, traditions of language study, recent historians have defined their field more broadly. If linguistics is the study of language in all its aspects, they reason, then the history of linguistics should encompass all past approaches to the study of language, whatever the methods used or results achieved. This new assumption makes enormous demands upon the individual scholar, ideally a polyglot conversant with all branches of intellectual and cultural history as well as with all aspects of modern linguistics. In practice most scholars have concentrated on one relatively circumscribed area, a congenial doctrine or school. Recent approaches to the history of linguistics – several of them long since abandoned by other branches of intellectual history – include:

1. Revisionist ('palace' or 'Whig') history: the insider's view of the development and historical significance of the school to which he himself belongs. This approach offers a valuable glimpse of a participant's perception of the formation and growth of a new movement, but often overlooks or denigrates the contribution of other scholars – predecessors and contemporaries – to the development of his own school and to the subject at large. Examples include Chapter One of Bloomfield's *Language* (Holt, Rinehart and Winston, New York, 1933), and F.J. Newmeyer's *Linguistic Theory in America* (Academic Press, New York, 1980).

2. Precursorist history: the search for forerunners, direct or indirect, of a modern theory or approach. Although it provides a salutary sense of perspective to those engaged in developing a new theory, from the historian's point of view precursorist historiography has the drawback of distorting the past, singling out some thinkers at the expense of others who were in their time perhaps more influential. It can lead to an anachronistic interpretation of past doctrines, reading into them modern ideas which were never explicitly formulated. A successful and immensely influential specimen of the genre is Chomsky's *Cartesian Linguistics* (Harper and Row, New York, 1966).

3. Disciplinary history: the investigation of the development of a particular branch of modern linguistics. Unquestionably useful in illuminating the present – in showing how a modern discipline reached its present state – disciplinary history has the disadvantage of imposing contemporary cognitive structures – categories like 'phonetics', 'historical linguistics', 'root', 'phoneme' – upon the past. Scholars may be tempted to write the history of linguistics in terms of modern categories and concepts, and may fail to notice the categories in which earlier scholars thought; they may overlook the real interests of earlier linguists as a result. For instance, the modern discipline of phonetics corresponds only in part to ancient *littera* theory. To castigate pre-

Renaissance scholars for failing to develop a full-blown science of phonetics, while at the same time to overlook those branches of *littera* theory which do not correspond to anything in the modern discipline of phonetics, results in an unbalanced picture of the past. The brief historical accounts of the development of the subject which often open textbooks are usually of this type.

4. Contextual history: the study of the linguistic doctrines of the past in their historical and intellectual context. The historian of linguistics with an awareness of the historical, cultural, religious and intellectual circumstances in which a particular teaching arose is in a position to understand the nature and significance of this doctrine in its own time. Aware of the priorities and assumptions of earlier writers, he is less likely to read anachronistic ideas into the past or to condemn earlier preoccupations as worthless. Such a historian should possess not only a background in some area of modern linguistics but also a firm grounding in the cultural history of his chosen epoch and in ancillary disciplines such as paleography, the history of science, and the necessary languages. Roy Andrew Miller's work (1975, 1976) on the linguistic traditions of Tibet and the Far East are outstanding examples of this genre.

The new discipline of historical epistemology, the study of the different modes of thought, outlooks and assumptions that characterise different epochs and different peoples, has brought new insights to the history of linguistics. Historians of linguistics are increasingly prepared to look at the past sympathetically, ready to accept that ideas which to us sound fantastic in their own time made excellent sense. To understand them, to appreciate their contribution to Western culture, we must learn to think away some of the assumptions at the heart of our twentieth-century world-view and instead try to don some of the habits of thought of people of another time. Various aspects of this extremely challenging approach to historiography have been developed within different national traditions. Anglo-American scholars have tended to emphasise the importance of the historical and socio-cultural background, while French work focuses more on linguistic ideas in the context of intellectual history generally. Recent work by German-speaking researchers has shown a tendency to apply the insights of a philosophical training to the history of linguistics. Each approach needs the others: they are complementary, not competing.

Institutionalisation of the discipline of the history of linguistics has proceeded fastest in France and in the English-speaking world. In Paris, members of a CNRS team devoted to the subject ran an international society (Société pour l'Histoire et l'Epistémologie des Sciences du Langage, 1978) and its journal, *Histoire Epistémologie Langage* (1979–). In Canada E.F.K. Koerner runs the journal *Historiographia Linguistica* (1974–) and several series of monographs on the subject; the triennial International Conferences on the

History of the Language Sciences, initiated by Koerner in 1978, bring together several hundred scholars for the discussion of recent research, as do – on a smaller scale – the annual international meetings of the British-based Henry Sweet Society for the History of Linguistic Ideas (1984–). The establishment of a designated lectureship in the history of linguistics at Cambridge University (1984) marks the recognition of the subject in England; but the large numbers of British and North American scholars who regularly attend meetings and publish in the field testify to the broad base of interest in the subject. Interest is growing rapidly in Italy, Spain and the Soviet Union, whilst elsewhere in the world many individual scholars are producing excellent work.

## 2. THE WESTERN TRADITION TO 1900

Western linguistics begins its recorded history at Athens: Plato was the earliest European thinker to ponder the fundamental problems of language. The issues presented in his work are central, an agenda to which the European tradition has returned, consciously or unconsciously, over and over again in the course of its development. Although many ideas have been borrowed from external sources – from the Jewish tradition early in the first millennium AD, from medieval Hebrew and Arab linguistics during the Renaissance, from India around 1800, to name only the most significant – the Western tradition has its own clear pattern of development. Manifestations of a characteristic way of thought, a distinctive world outlook, rather than the accidental product of climate and circumstances, the enduring trends in Western linguistics can be traced in most branches of intellectual enquiry: most markedly in the natural sciences, but also in philosophy, cosmology and the study of man. This has consequences for our narrative, and for linguistic historiography generally, on two planes, the geographic and the temporal.

On the geographic plane, it is futile to attempt to link all the great linguistic traditions in a single chronological sequence, jumping from India, to China, to Greece and Rome, to the Semitic peoples, and back to the West. Each tradition has its own history, and can be explained only out of its own culture and modes of thought. Each has its distinctive contribution to make to man's perception of language. Such a sweeping story of the 'world history of linguistics' in any case has a distorting effect; to place a chapter on linguistics in ancient India before one on linguistics in Greece would inevitably suggest either that Indian work was the progenitor of the Graeco–Roman tradition, or that the later tradition superseded the earlier, both of which would be gross historical misrepresentations. The two traditions developed independently, and cannot be brought into historical relation with one another except in an artificial fashion. They and the other great traditions have continued to

787

develop in parallel to the present day. Ideally, in a survey of the history of linguistics the major traditions would be given equal space. In practice, in a brief sketch written by a Westerner for Western readers, the Western tradition must receive greater prominence; but to redress the balance a little, the three principal non-European traditions – Semitic, Indian, Chinese – will be succinctly characterised in separate sections.

On the temporal plane, in contrast, although some ways of thought remain characteristic of a particular tradition for a long period of time, others succeed one another more or less rapidly with cumulative or cyclical effect. The Western tradition is marked by a major and irreversible change of direction which took place during the fifteenth century. Linguistics, like all other branches of intellectual activity, changed its character fundamentally at the Renaissance. By contrast, the 'transition' from Antiquity to the Middle Ages is so protracted and so difficult to locate that one might well ask whether the time-honoured periodicisation has any inner reality: a division between pre-Renaissance and post-Renaissance linguistics is often more apt. Sub-divisions are necessary for the reader's sake, but are often as arbitrary in the labels attached to them. Greek and Roman linguistics forms a continuum with that of the Middle Ages, the Romans building on and in a limited way developing Greek initiatives, while medieval scholars studied, digested and transformed the Roman version of the ancient linguistic tradition. Some aspects of pre-Renaissance thought, notably etymology and *littera* theory, are more easily handled if ancient and medieval ideas are considered together; for other subjects a chronological discussion will provide an adequate framework.

### 2.1 Greece: language as a tool for understanding reality

The recorded history of Western linguistics begins with a confrontation between two fundamental opposing views of language: language as a source of knowledge, and language as a mere medium of communication. Does language have a direct and essential link with reality, spiritual or physical, or is it purely arbitrary? The implications are considerable: if language in some way contains or mirrors reality, then the study of language is a possible route to knowledge of reality. But if it is arbitrary, then nothing of broader signifi-cance is to be gained from its study: the goal of linguistics will be the under-standing of language and nothing more. Although this is the view – in many cases, the unspoken assumption – of mainstream linguistics today, it has not always been taken for granted. The very earliest Western text on language, Plato's *Cratylus*, addresses just this question.

The atmosphere in the city-state of Athens toward the end of the fifth century BC was one of questioning. In exploring the causes which underlay man's physical and cosmological environment, Presocratic philosophers recognised two vital forces: *phúsis*, nature, the inexorable power ruling the visible world; and *nómos*, a belief, custom or law instituted by divine or human agency. The relative roles of *phúsis* and *nómos* (or *thésis*, convention) in various spheres of human life posed philosophers many difficult problems: did states arise of necessity or by human custom? Were moral laws a natural necessity or merely conventional? In the sphere of language, the Greeks asked whether the connection between words and what they denoted arose out of nature, *phúsei*, or was imposed by convention, *thései*. There were two aspects to the question: first, the nature of the present relationship between words and their denotata, and secondly, how that relationship had come about – the origin of words.

Plato (c. 429-347 BC) devoted one of his dialogues, the *Cratylus*, to this problem. Of the three speakers he depicts, Cratylus maintains that language mirrors the world exactly; Hermogenes defends the contrary position, that language is arbitrary; and Socrates represents a middle stance, pointing out both the strengths and the weaknesses in their arguments, and eventually leading them to a compromise. Hermogenes's opening claim that names are entirely arbitrary and can be imposed at will is refuted by Socrates, who points out that words are tools: just as a misshapen shuttle cannot be used for weaving, so words must have properties which render them appropriate for use. Socrates asks Hermogenes to make two assumptions which hold throughout the dialogue: that words are in some sense right, for otherwise they would not fulfil their function; and that since they originated by convention, they must have been invented by someone, human or divine: the nomothete ('lawgiver'). The natural rightness of names, disputed by Hermogenes, is illustrated by Socrates in a lengthy series of etymologies based on semantic association. For example, the body (*sôma*) is so called because it is the tomb (*sêma*) or the sign (also *sêma*) of the soul, while lightning (*astrapê*) is so called because it turns our eyes upwards (*tà ôpa anastréphei*). Some words, the *prôta onómata*, 'original words', prove not to be susceptible to this kind of semantic analysis. For these, Socrates proposes analysis by means of sound symbolism. If *l*, for example, represents slipping or gliding, words containing this sound can be expected to have some element of slipperiness in their meaning, and this is the case with *liparón* 'sleek', *glukú* 'sweet', *glískhron* 'glutinous'. But counter-examples such as the presence of an *l* in *sklērótēs*, meaning 'hardness', show that mistakes have crept in, or perhaps that some names were wrongly assigned in the first place. Little by little Plato brings the reader to realise that there is an element of truth in both positions. Although many words possess an intrinsic rightness, conforming to *phúsis*, those words in which no such natural structure can be discerned – whether because they were wrongly formed from the outset or corrupted by the passage of time – are nonetheless understood by convention, *thései*. He suggests that the nomothete had access to direct knowledge of reality – the Platonic Forms – but perceived this reality imperfectly. If the nomothete could study reality directly, then so should we, for language is but an imperfect imitation. In short, although language had originally been linked directly with reality, and traces of this connection were still to be found, it was by now a very dubious route to knowledge of reality.

Once it had been accepted that the connection between words and things was not direct but indirect, the precise nature of their relationship remained to be determined. Plato's pupil, Aristotle (384-322 BC), in his *Perì hermēneías* (*De interpretatione*), envisaged a three-tier process: written signs represent spoken signs, spoken signs represent impressions (*pathémata*) in the soul, and the impressions in the soul are the likenesses of actual things. Both impressions and things, Aristotle remarks, are the same for all men, whereas the words which represent the interpretations differ. As his commentators quickly pointed out, this schema raised many difficulties. The Stoics (third and second centuries BC), and many later writers, preferred to add a step between the passive reception of the impression, and speech: the concept, a notion which can be verbalised (Gk. *lektón*, Lat. *dicibile*). Thus, although all men may receive the same impressions of the things they perceive, as Aristotle maintained, nonetheless the concepts they form of them may differ, and it is these that are represented in speech.

According to the Stoics, a concept (*lektón*) was represented in a meaningful utterance, *lógos*. *Lógos* was defined by Diogenes of Babylon (a Stoic of the second century BC whose thought is outlined for us by Diogenes Laertius (third century AD) in his *Lives of the Philosophers*) as 'a meaningful utterance directed by rational thought'. The physical substance of the *lógos* was *phōnē*, 'voice', the utterance considered as mere sound, articulate or inarticulate, without reference to meaning. An utterance (*phōnē*) which could be represented in writing – an articulate utterance – was called a *léxis*. A *léxis* differed from a *lógos* in that whereas meaning was essential to a *lógos*, a *léxis* did not necessarily have meaning. Thus, the English word 'day' is a *léxis* in so far as it is a word of three letters which forms its plural by adding -s; equally, the Greek nonsense-word *blíturi* is a *léxis* in as much as it can be spelt and takes the feminine definite article. Neither 'day' nor *blíturi* is a *lógos*, *blíturi* inherently, in that it is a *léxis asémantos*, a meaningless word-form, and 'day' because it has not yet entered into combination with another word or words to form a meaningful utterance such as 'it is day'. The distinction between *lógos*, the word or utterance viewed as a meaningful entity, and *léxis*, the word viewed as form, is fundamental to Stoic and post-Stoic linguistic thought.

Its effects are seen immediately in the gradual process whereby the utterance was analysed into ever smaller elements, the 'parts of speech'. The

Greek term, *mérē toû lógou*, makes it clear that the starting-point of the analysis was the *lógos*, the utterance seen as meaningful, a fact which explains some of the apparent anomalies in the ancient parts-of-speech system. Philosophers found themselves looking closely at the structure of meaningful utterances. If a proposition was true or false, in which of its parts did its truth or falsity reside? To discuss such problems an appropriate conceptual vocabulary was necessary. In his dialogue *The Sophist* Plato takes the case of an utterance like 'a man learns'. This utterance can be broken down into a name and what is said about it, *ónoma* and *rhêma*. (Outside this context, *ónoma* was the everyday word for 'name' and *rhêma* had the sense of 'word', 'saying', 'proverb'.) The same structure could be found in a sentence like 'Clinias is ignorant', where 'Clinias' occupies a position parallel to that of 'man', and 'is ignorant' parallels 'learns'. In this way *ónoma*, normally 'name', and *rhêma*, 'word', 'phrase', 'saying', come to take on technical meanings corresponding broadly to subject = noun or noun-substitute and predicate = verb or copula plus adjective. The basis of this division is functional and semantic, not formal. From the formal point of view one would not expect that adjectives and verbs should be classed together in a language like Greek, where their inflections are utterly dissimilar; but if only their function is considered it is a natural enough division.

Later philosophers – Plato's pupil Aristotle and the Stoics – looked more closely at the semantic constituents of the utterance. Following the clearer account of the Stoics as reported by Diogenes Laertius, we find that they restricted the term *ónoma*, 'name', to the name proper (or, as it came to be called in traditional grammar, the proper noun), introducing the term *prosēgoría*, 'appellative', for common nouns. *Rhêma* was described as lacking case and signifying something said about someone. Two new categories were identified: the *súndesmos* lacked case and linked the parts of speech, while the *árthron* had case and distinguished the number and gender of nouns.

This system was refined by succeeding generations of scholars. Its fullest development can be seen in a papyrus fragment of the first century AD, P. Yale 1.25 (inv. 446), which preserves the opening sentences of a grammar setting out the definitions of the nine parts of speech. Here, the participle (*metochê*) is characterised as a part of speech which takes articles and cases like the noun, but also tenses like the verb. The pronoun (*antonomasía*, later *antōnumía*) is used instead of a noun, has deictic function, and shows relationships among the persons. The term *súndesmos* is restricted to conjunctions; the preposition (*próthesis*) is defined as a part of speech having only one form, placed before another part of speech and entering into a close relationship with it. The adverb (*epírrhēma*), another part of speech with only one form, is placed before or after a verb but lacks any close syntactic connection with it, and signifies quantity or quality or time or place or denial or agreement or forbidding or exhortation or questioning or a wish or comparison or doubt.

In all these definitions, the overriding importance of meaning is apparent both from the predominantly semantic criteria used to distinguish the parts of speech and from the very categories arrived at. The separation of proper from common noun, the reluctance to recognise the adjective as a separate part of speech – for its substantival function, as in the English expressions 'the good' or 'goods', makes it equivalent in function to a noun – and the classification of the participle as a distinct part of speech, even though to our eyes it is clearly derived from the verb – all these aspects of the definitions of the parts of speech arose from the Greek emphasis on the meaningful rather than the formal aspects of the utterance. Passed on to us in modified form by the Romans, this system has posed later linguists the problem of reconciling a semantically-based word-class system with the frequently incompatible need to accommodate word form.

This same emphasis on the meaningful aspect of speech is apparent in a remarkable treatise on Greek syntax, Apollonius Dyscolus's *Syntax* (*Perì suntáxeōs*), dating from the second century AD. Apollonius draws a parallel between the different levels of language: the same rules of ordering apply to minimal sound-units, syllables, words, and indeed complete utterances. As he says, 'the meaning which subsists in each word form is, in a sense, the minimal unit of the sentence'. Just as the study of orthography can help one to recover the correct form of a misspelt or mispronounced word, so the study of syntax can help one to recover the true structure of a defective sentence. Apollonius devotes himself to showing the rational principles, the inherent regularity, underlying the syntax of the Greek sentence. In so doing, he was almost unique among pre-modern writers in the West; yet his work was only indirectly influential. Between the sixth century and the fifteenth, the Greek language was virtually unknown in the West. Greek writings on grammar, or indeed on any other subject, were quite inaccessible unless they had been translated or adapted into Latin in late Antiquity. Apollonius's syntactic doctrine was applied to Latin by Priscian (c. 500), who modelled the last two books of his great grammar of Latin, the *Institutiones grammaticae*, on Apollonius's *Perì suntáxeōs*, and in this filtered form Apollonius's teachings lived on in the West, giving rise to further work on syntax in the later Middle Ages.

A similar pattern can be observed in the case of morphology. Although it was the Greeks who elaborated the parts of speech system and many of the associated concepts which still play a vital role in modern linguistics, their work passed into the Western tradition not directly, but via the Romans. Greek grammar found its definitive codification in the grammar which travels under the name of the Alexandrian scholar Dionysius Thrax (second century

BC). Only the first five chapters of this work are actually by Dionysius; the rest of the work is now thought to date from a period perhaps as late as the fourth century AD, the culmination rather than the starting-point of a long chain of development. Although often hailed as the source of the Western grammatical tradition, the history of this grammar properly belongs to the Byzantine rather than the Western linguistic tradition. It was the standard textbook in the Greek East, being translated, in whole or in part, into Syriac and Armenian, and providing a focus for numerous Byzantine commentaries and adaptations. In contrast, it was virtually unknown in the West until its first printed edition, in 1727. Instead, it was through the Roman grammarians of late Antiquity that Greek grammatical doctrine, filtered through the medium of the Latin language, was absorbed into the mainstream of the Western tradition.

## 2.2 Rome: codification and transmission

As with most other aspects of their intellectual life, the Romans attributed their introduction to grammar to the Greeks. Suetonius (c. 69–c. 140), in his survey of renowned teachers of grammar and rhetoric (*De grammaticis et rhetoribus*), tells of how the Stoic, Crates of Mallos, broke his leg during a diplomatic mission to Rome in 169 or 168 BC, and whiled away his convalescence by giving lectures on grammar. Although Suetonius records the names of some twenty grammarians between that time and his own, we are remarkably ill-informed about the early history of grammar at Rome. Karl Barwick's suggestion that Stoic doctrine was the prevailing influence at Rome, whereas in the Greek world the Alexandrian school of philology had supplanted the Stoics, is no longer widely accepted.

Nonetheless, Stoic and Pythagorean concerns are visible in the work of the philosopher-historian-antiquarian Marcus Terentius Varro (116–27 BC). Of his more than seventy works only two survive, including six books of the original twenty-five of his great work on the Latin language, *De lingua latina*. After an introductory book, Books II to VII contained an exhaustive discussion of Latin etymology, Books VIII to XIII of inflection, and Books XIV to XXV of the conjoining of words in utterances (presumably syntax). Only Books V through X survive, preserved in a single eleventh-century manuscript from Monte Cassino rediscovered by Boccaccio in 1355; not surprisingly, the work was unknown and quite uninfluential throughout the Middle Ages. In Antiquity its impact was immense. Varro's historical and philosophical leanings gave his work a very different flavour from the other Roman works on language that have come down to us. In the surviving portions of the *De lingua latina* Varro takes up two problematical dichotomies: the role of nature and convention in the origin of words, and that of analogy and anomaly in the regulation of speech. Like Plato, Varro concludes that the original meaning of words, imposed in accordance with nature, has in many cases been obscured with the passage of time, and that etymology can often help to recover the true and original meaning. By *etymologia* Varro understands a semantic kind of explanation, rather than the primarily phonological kind of historical etymology now customary, and he goes some way toward elaborating formal principles useful in its pursuit. Most of Books VI and VII is occupied by a series of etymologies of words arranged according to the fundamental Pythagorean categories of *corpus* 'physical object', *locus* 'place', *tempus* 'time' and *actio* 'action, process'. In Books VIII to X he takes up the issue of the respective roles of analogy and anomaly. Proceeding by means of the *reductio ad absurdum* in a manner not unlike Plato's, he demolishes the need for a controversy over their relative importance, showing that both principles arise out of usage. He draws an important distinction between the underlying, original, nature of language and usage, and between descriptive and prescriptive uses of analogy. As he points out, 'it is one thing to say that it is possible to find analogies in words and another to say that we ought to follow them' (IX 4). His advice is pragmatic: new coinages ought to be guided by analogy, but where an anomalous form is already well-established, it should be allowed to stand. Inflection, *declinatio naturalis*, was an area of language in which analogy could be expected, whereas derivation, *declinatio voluntaria*, often functioned arbitrarily. Varro's importance lies in the clarity with which he formulated and followed through some of the implications of the meaning-form dichotomy, a legacy upon which later generations of Roman grammarians were to build.

Very few grammars survive from the period between Varro and Quintilian (c. 30 BC – c. 100 AD), despite the fact that the first-century grammarians Q. Remmius Palaemon, Valerius Probus and Pansa were heavily cited by later writers. Roman education under the Empire was geared to the training of orators. After learning their letters under the *litterator* or *magister ludi*, children would next study grammar and apply it to the analysis of literary texts under the *grammaticus*, and finally be guided by the *rhetor* in the composition of elegant discourse. Many *grammatici* compiled their own textbooks; most of the surviving ones, dating chiefly from the fourth and fifth centuries, are available in Heinrich Keil's seven-volume edition, the *Grammatici Latini* (Leipzig 1855–80). Apart from works on orthography and on metrics they are of two main types, the *Schulgrammatik* type and the *regulae* type.

The *Schulgrammatik* contained a systematic exposition of grammatical categories exemplified through Latin. Structured like modern reference grammars, that is, consisting of a series of chapters dealing with each topic exhaustively (but with no exercises – a nineteenth century addition – or reading passages), a typical work, Donatus's *Ars maior* (c. 350 AD), was divided into three books: Book I included chapters on *vox* 'voice, sound, phonic substance'; *littera* 'speech-sound, letter'; the syllable; metrical feet; accents; and punctuation. Book II dealt with the parts of speech: noun, pronoun, verb, adverb, participle, conjunction, preposition, interjection; and Book III handled barbarisms (faults in the form of a word), solecisms (faulty collocations of words), other faults, and various rhetorical figures. The emphasis in such works fell, not on the description of the forms of Latin, which the student, a native speaker of Latin, would already know, nor on rules through which to generate them, but on the labelling and classification of known forms. Since the categories elaborated for Greek were to a large extent semantic in nature, they could be transferred to Latin without difficulty. The best-known works of the genre were those by Donatus: the *Ars minor*, a brief introduction to grammar, and the longer *Ars maior*. Other surviving works of the type, attributed to Scaurus, Asper, Dositheus, St Augustine, Audax, Victorinus, and others, were far less influential. No doubt the fact that St Jerome, one of the Fathers of the Church (along with Augustine, Ambrose and Gregory the Great), had been Donatus's student gave his works a doctrinal advantage in an increasingly Christian Empire. As Roman education gradually narrowed its scope, the focus of attention shifted to the grammars themselves, deserting the literary texts they were meant to accompany. Grammarians from the end of the fourth century on (Servius, Sergius, Cledonius, Pompeius) took to writing commentaries upon Donatus's *Ars maior* rather than on Vergil's *Aeneid*, a trend continued in the Middle Ages by scholars trained in biblical exegesis.

The second major grammatical genre was the *regulae* type of grammar, which usually took the form of a reference work designed to help with the identification of Latin forms. Largely by authors working in bilingual parts of the Empire – Priscian, Eutyches, Phocas in the Greek East, as well as Martianus Capella and pseudo-Augustine in Africa – these works permitted the student to look up the ending of a strange noun or verb in an alphabetical list in order to find out what gender, declension or conjugation it might belong to. This genre appears to have been more common outside Italy, particularly in the Greek East, where in late Antiquity people wishing to rise in the imperial administration required fluency in Latin. How they began their studies is uncertain, for apart from some exercises preserved in papyrus scraps, the surviving grammars presuppose an advanced knowledge of Latin. This is particularly true of the best-known grammars from the Greek East, the works of Priscian (Constantinople, c. 500). Three of his works were especially influential in later centuries: the *Institutio de nomine et pronomine et verbo*, a brief survey of the inflectional classes of Latin; the *Partitiones*, a lengthy work which analyses the words of the first line of each of the twelve books of the *Aeneid* in question-and-answer form; and the *Institutiones grammaticae*, an exhaustive reference grammar in eighteen books (nearly 1000 pages). In this work – the one upon which his reputation rests – Priscian combined information of the *Schulgrammatik* type (mostly taken from Donatus) with some of the *regulae* type, thereby constructing a virtually complete (and still useful) description of Latin reinforced with a large number of illustrative quotations from literary authors. Its last two books, on syntax, are heavily based on Apollonius Dyscolus's *Perì suntáxeōs*, and make frequent comparisons between Latin and Greek usage. Priscian's dependence on Greek sources is also apparent in his preference for a modified version of the Greek sequence of the parts of speech: noun, verb, participle, pronoun, preposition, adverb, interjection, conjunction.

✳ ✳ ✳

In many ways, the content of an ancient grammar is not dissimilar to that of a present-day mother-tongue grammar like Nesfield's *Modern English Grammar*, listing and exemplifying categories of a largely semantic nature, and cataloguing morphological irregularities (e.g. irregular plurals). By no means all aspects of ancient linguistics have so close a modern counterpart. Two domains in particular stand out as having developed in a strikingly different direction from anything to which we are accustomed, *littera* theory and etymology. Although the seeds of the modern disciplines of phonetics and morphology are latent in these two important fields of study, they lie dormant throughout Antiquity and the Middle Ages, overshadowed by a very different approach to the study of speech-sounds and words. Before taking up the story of the development of grammar during the Middle Ages, let us survey ancient and medieval views of the *littera* and of the true nature of the word.

### 2.2.1 **Littera** *theory*

Greeks and Romans shared similar conceptions of the nature of the *littera* (Greek *grámma*), the smallest unit of speech (*vox*, Gk. *phōnē*). Two different views were current, often expounded side by side. According to one, the *littera* was the written symbol, the representation of the speech-sound (Lat. *elementum*, Gk. *stoikheîon*). This view, the forerunner of the modern letter–sound dichotomy, was less significant in Antiquity, and indeed, up until shortly after 1800, than the second, more complex view. Both Stoics and Romans described the *littera* as an entity with three properties: its name (*nomen*), its shape or written form (*figura*), and its sound or value (*potestas*). This more flexible view, capable of extension and refinement to a far greater degree than the crude opposition of letter and sound, was the basis for a multifaceted, infinitely varied series of approaches to the *littera* by ancient and still more by medieval scholars.

*Potestas* was the property of the *littera* whose domain came closest to that of the modern subject of phonetics. Plato, Aristotle and the Romans all classified the *litterae* as follows:

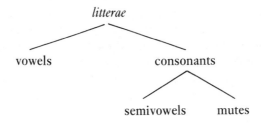

(The category of 'semivowels' included the modern continuants: Donatus lists *f l m n r s x* under this heading.)

Only a few scholars felt the need to go more deeply into articulatory phonetics. Among them were Dionysius of Halicarnassus (fl. 30–8 BC), whose remarkable description of the articulation of the sounds of Greek was unknown in the Latin West until its first edition in 1508 by the great Venetian printer Aldus Manutius, and the metrician Terentianus Maurus (second century), whose verse account of Latin sounds and metres was little read before the Renaissance. In practice, the one-line vignettes offered by Martianus Capella (fifth century) in his allegorical encyclopedia, *The Marriage of Philology and Mercury* (III 261), were the only articulatory descriptions of the sounds of Latin available to most medieval scholars. Such characterisations as 'D arises from the attack of the tongue near the upper teeth' or 'L sounds sweetly with tongue and palate' or 'Appius Claudius detested Z because it imitates the teeth of a corpse' were still being quoted well into the sixteenth century. Not until they became acquainted with the much more detailed articulatory descriptions commonplace in medieval grammars of Hebrew and Arabic did Renaissance Christians begin to take an interest in articulatory phonetics.

In contrast, the properties of *nomen* and *figura* aroused a more active and creative interest among medieval scholars. Collections of exotic alphabets – Greek, Hebrew, 'Chaldee', Gothic, runes, ogam, various codes and ciphers – circulated widely, as did brief tracts on the invention of various scripts. An ancient form of shorthand, Tironian notes, was practised at some monastic centres in the ninth and tenth centuries, while at others scribes added subscriptions in Latin transliterated into Greek characters. A remarkable little treatise from the seventh or eighth century attributed to one Sergilius (an Irishman by the name of Fergil?) describes the movement of the pen in forming each letter, and gives the name of each stroke in Latin, Greek and Hebrew: 'What are the names of the three strokes of the letter A in the three sacred languages? In Hebrew, abst ebst ubst. What are they called in Greek? Albs elbs ulbs. And in Latin? Two oblique lines and a straight one drawn across them.'

But it was not the *littera* as a physically viable or audible unit of speech which interested medieval writers so much as its possible significance in illuminating higher aspects of the world order. One seventh-century author, Virgil the Grammarian, explained: 'Just as man consists of body, soul, and a sort of heavenly fire, so the *littera* is suffused with body – that is, its shape, its function and its pronunciation (its joints and limbs, as it were) – and has its soul in its sense and its spirit in its relation to higher things.' Other authors applied typological and allegorical interpretations to various aspects of the *littera*, most often to its shape. Its sound was of the least importance: that was the earthly part of the *littera*, its 'body'. Only gradually, as the Middle Ages drew to a close, did Western thinkers begin to turn their thoughts to the physical side of speech, even as they started to take seriously the physical manifestations of the natural world. The impetus to do so came, not from within the Western tradition itself, but from outside: first, during the Renaissance, from the Semitic world and later, around 1800, from India.

### 2.2.2 *Etymology*

Ancient and medieval work on the word was characterised by the same reluctance to think about the physical aspect of speech. Morphology, the study of word form, is a branch of linguistics which led a shadowy existence on the edges of language teaching; as a subject of scholarly investigation in its own right, it is a post-Renaissance development. Instead, when ancient and medieval scholars researched the true nature of a word, it was not its original form but its original meaning which they sought. The principles of ancient etymology as formulated by Varro remained influential throughout Antiquity and beyond. Varro acknowledged the Greek distinction between the study of the origin of words, or etymology proper, and the study of what they represented, roughly 'semantics'. He set out four different levels of etymological explanation, ranging from words whose origin was transparent to those which were the seat of a profound mystery. Various factors could obscure the relationship between word origin and word meaning: time, foreign influence, and inaccuracies in the original imposition of names. Changes in word form could take place through various processes: addition, deletion, transposition and change of individual sounds or syllables. Varro and his successors stressed the processes by which change occurred and not the actual sounds involved (although Priscian, the most form-orientated of the grammarians, catalogued the changes undergone by each of the *litterae* in his *Institutiones grammaticae*, 20, 9 – 43, 19). In other words, the resemblance between two word forms (*voces*) was not the significant element; instead, the focus was on the semantic relationship. The types of semantic relationship were catalogues by ancient and medieval writers with as much care as was later lavished on sound changes. One brief but widely-read statement was that included by Isidore of Seville (who died in 636) in his *Etymologiae*, a twenty-book encyclopaedia whose aim was to elucidate the significance of the terminology in every area of human concern. Isidore lists three types of name: those derived from a cause, like *reges* 'kings' from *recte agendo* 'acting rightly', for a king would not be a true king if he did not act rightly (an assumption with drastic political implications developed by medieval political theorists); those which indicate the origin of a thing, like *homo* 'man' from *humus* 'earth', an etymology used by theologians to emphasise man's earthly nature and separation from the divine; and those arising from their opposites, like *lutum* 'mud' from *lavare* 'to wash'. Isidore and his medieval followers thus saw semantic relationships as the key to the true meaning of a word. If finding a connection between *homo* 'man' and *humus* 'earth' could illuminate the true, higher meaning of man and his destiny, then etymology had served its purpose. The origin of the form spelt *homo* was of no concern.

This attitude helps to explain the absence of interest in morphology in ancient and medieval language study. Varro's distinction between *declinatio naturalis*, corresponding to inflectional morphology (noun declensions, verb conjugations and so on), and *declinatio voluntaria*, corresponding to derivational morphology (the formation of new words from existing ones by adding or dropping certain elements) was never followed through completely. Even in the eight century Boniface (later to embark upon his celebrated mission to the Germans) still included nouns formed from verbal bases like *emptio* 'a purchase' and *emptor* 'purchaser' in the paradigm of the verb *emere* 'to purchase'. Neither Varro nor any other ancient grammarian arrived at the concepts of 'root', 'stem' or 'affix': where Varro uses the term *radix* 'root', it is in a non-technical sense. 'Generative' rules of the kind familiar from modern school textbooks – for instance, 'to form the present tense, take the present stem and add the personal endings' – are unknown in ancient and medieval grammars. Instead, grammarians adopted the Word-and-Paradigm model of description: the word was regarded as the minimal unit. Each inflected form was considered distinct and equal. This attitude follows naturally from the primacy of the semantic aspect: how, on the semantic level, can one derive 'you buy' from 'I buy'? Once again, the requisite concepts entered the Western linguistic tradition from outside, from the Semitic and later from the Indian grammatical tradition. Only when these fundamental notions were in circulation was it possible for the modern disciplines of morphology and of historical and comparative philology to appear.

## 2.3 Grammar in the Middle Ages

How, then, did early medieval scholars go about teaching Latin? For Latin, the language of the Western Church, was a foreign language to the new converts of Ireland, England, the German-speaking countries, Scandinavia and Eastern Europe. The semantic and taxonomic orientation of grammars like Donatus's was of little help to these students: the Latin forms which Donatus takes for granted were precisely what they needed to learn. Because 'generative' rules were unknown, paradigms – models setting out every form of the inflected parts of speech in a standard sequence – were essential. At first, teachers simply compiled this information separately, assembling paradigms of countless nouns and verbs with long lists of examples from Christian vocabulary. Every possible subtype – every derivational suffix, every gender, every nominative termination – was exemplified separately; but by dint of experimentation teachers identified morphologically significant subtypes, and restricted their selection of paradigms accordingly. By 700 a fusion of this material with Donatus's *Ars minor* had taken place: in the resulting Insular elementary grammars (so called from their origin in the British Isles) students could find the grammatical concepts taught by Donatus set out along with the paradigms they required if they were to learn to write the language or to understand it fully. These works were the first systematic grammars in the West designed for students of a foreign language – the ancestors of our traditional school grammars. As such, theirs is a major contribution to linguistics – the shift from a primarily semantic and taxonomic grammar to a descriptive, form-based grammar. Slow as Western linguistics was to come to terms with form, the beginnings of the process are to be found here, in the monastic schools of the British Isles in the seventh and eighth centuries.

No less unsuitable than the theoretical orientation of Late Latin grammars was their exemplificatory material. The aim of the young Roman student had been to master the Classical texts most highly esteemed in his day; the young Irish or Anglo-Saxon monk regarded grammar as a tool for the comprehension of the Bible. The examples from Classical literature used by ancient grammarians were replaced to a greater or lesser degree by different teachers: some, like Boniface (c. 675–754), saw no objection to using short extracts from the *Aeneid* next to verses from the Bible, whilst others, like Asporius (c. 600), went so far as to replace Donatus's 'Rome' and 'Tiber' with 'Jerusalem' and 'Jordan'. Few grammarians saw their way to a more thorough-going synthesis of grammar and the Faith. Virgil the Grammarian (c. 650), an enigmatic writer who delighted in stretching the resources of Latin word-formation to accommodate his subtle apperceptions (he invents a verb *vidare*, 'to see with the eyes of the spirit', to contrast with the more usual *videre*, 'to see with the physical eyes'), employed the traditional *ars grammatica* as a framework for showing how scriptural language points *ad sublimiora*, 'towards higher things'. Around 800 Smaragdus, better known for his devotional work *Diadema monachorum*, included in his grammar a survey of the techniques of illocutionary force employed in different scriptural contexts as part of his programme of providing a simultaneous introduction to the comprehension of both grammar and the scriptures.

Under the leadership of Charlemagne and the teachers he assembled at his court in the years around 800, the Carolingian Renaissance brought not only a revival of interest in the literary works of Antiquity, but also a shift in the interests of grammarians. The Insular elementary grammars were discarded, being replaced either by a slightly expanded version of the *Ars minor* or by parsing grammars, textbooks in question-and-answer form, inspired by Priscian's *Partitiones*, which analyse a representative specimen of each part of speech:

What part of speech is the word *codex*?
A noun.
How do you know?
Because it denotes something identifiable and is inflected for case.
Is it proper or common?
Common.
Why?
Because there are many codices.

This remained a popular and productive genre to the end of the Middle Ages: the parsing grammars *Dominus quae pars* and the *Ianua* (*Poeta quae pars*), both printed regularly, were among the commonest grammars in use in the fourteenth and fifteenth centuries, and were the model for political and social satires like *Nummus quae pars*:

What part of speech is 'coin'?
A preposition.
Why?
Because it is pre-posed to all other parts of speech and all branches of knowledge based on them . . .
What number is it?
Both singular and plural.
Why?
Because it is singular among poor men and plural among the rich.

Of equally great significance for later centuries was the rediscovery of another work of Priscian's, the *Institutiones grammaticae*. Far too detailed and cumbersome for classroom use in the seventh and eighth centuries, it was appreciated by the more ambitious scholars of the ninth century. From Alcuin (c. 735–804) on, generations of teachers devoted themselves to the task of making the doctrine of the *Institutiones* more accessible to their students, preparing abbreviated versions, paraphrases, extracts and commentaries, all designed to help the student master its rambling but authoritative doctrine. Its terminology, too, required explanation, bearing a distinct resemblance to that of logic, an as yet unfamiliar area of study.

But logic itself was not entering the curriculum, a potent influence on the development of grammar in the later Middle Ages. Two of Aristotle's works on logic, the *Categories* and the *De interpretatione*, accompanied by Porphyry's *Isagoge* (*Introduction*), entered circulation in Boethius's Latin translation, and were eagerly studied by Alcuin and his circle. The parallel between logical and linguistic categories which is so apparent in these works did not fail to strike their ninth-century readers. One, at the monastery of St Gall in Switzerland, attempted to allocate all the types of common noun listed by Priscian to one or another of the ten Aristotelian categories. Through experiments like this a more thorough-going interpenetration of grammar and dialectic was arrived at. The study of dialectic prompted critical and sweeping questioning of the assumptions of traditional grammar, of which Priscian was taken as the representative *par excellence*. As William of Conches complained at the beginning of the twelfth century, Priscian's 'definitions are obscure and he gives no explanations. And he passes over the reason for the invention of the parts of speech and their properties.' This set the programme for subsequent work. Nonetheless, the encroachment of dialectic into the heart of grammar did not find universal approval. In the middle of the twelfth century the influential grammarian Petrus Helias, lecturing at Paris, deliberately returned to the traditional resources and methods of grammar (greatly enriched, all the same, by its flirtation with dialectic) in his widely-studied commentary on the *Institutiones grammaticae*. Subsequent grammarians followed his lead, and grammar and dialectic entered upon separate paths of development. Grammarians continued to make Priscian the basis of their study, and devoted particular attention to the books on syntax. Given the requirement at universities like Paris and Toulouse that all students hear the *Institutiones grammaticae* expounded a set number of times during their course, an enormous amount of energy went into commentaries and texts taking up detailed points, *quaestiones*.

At a lower level, too, grammarians poured out new elementary and intermediate textbooks, often in verse: among them were Alexander of Villa Dei's *Doctrinale* (1199) and Eberhard Bethune's *Graecismus* (1212), known all across

Catholic Europe, as well as many geographically more restricted works: the grammars of Alexander Neckam, John of Garland, Nicolaus Kempf, Johannes Schlispacher, Johannes Balbi (John of Genoa), Gutolfus de Heiligenkreuz, Thomas of Erfurt's *Fundamentum puerorum*, and many others. Gradually, the grammatical textbook metamorphosed from the tripartite structure of the ancient *Schulgrammatik* to a new four-part structure: *orthographia*, the properties of the *littera*; *prosodia*, the properties of the syllable, such as length and stress; *etymologia*, the eight parts of speech; and *diasynthetica*, syntax. This progressive structure, advancing from the smallest unit to the largest, is the ancestor of the modern hierarchy of phonetics, phonology, morphology and syntax. In these works a narrowing of the scope of grammar can be seen, away from the universal, semantically-orientated concerns of Antiquity to the particular details of one language, Latin. In the circumstances, this narrowing was inevitable: where a widespread need for instruction in the grammar of a particular language exists, then the focus will be on descriptive, 'particular' grammar.

In the latter part of the twelfth century the increasingly conscious restriction of the scope of *grammatica* was counterbalanced by a new impetus to the study of the universal aspect of language. As previously unavailable works of Aristotle's entered circulation from Spain and Sicily in fresh Latin translations from the 1140s on, scholars tried out the new ideas on each one of the traditional branches of knowledge. From the *Metaphysics* and other works they learnt to question the very nature of the traditional disciplines. Aristotle had contrasted speculative, or theoretical, disciplines with practical crafts: 'The goal of theoretical knowledge is truth whereas that of practical knowledge is efficacy' (*Metaphysics* II 993b 21–2). Thus, the architect understands the principles underlying the design of buildings, whereas the builder merely possesses the technical knowledge relating to the mixing of mortar. This dichotomy between theoretical and practical branches of knowledge was extended to language by many writers from Roger Bacon (c. 1214–1292/4) on. *Grammatica speculativa* investigated the universal principles of grammar, while *grammatica positiva* was concerned with the details of a particular language. *Grammatica speculativa* concentrated on the essential and universal, *grammatica positiva* on the accidental and particular. The late medieval practitioners of *grammatica positiva* continued a well-establshed tradition which lived on into the Renaissance; Speculative grammarians, on the other hand, were conscious of the novelty of their enterprise.

The best-known proponents of Speculative grammar were the modistae, a small group of scholars active at the university of Paris between about 1250 and 1320. Martin of Dacia and Michel de Marbais are among the more renowned representatives of the first generation of modistae, Thomas of Erfurt and Siger de Courtrai of the second. Their doctrine was based on the notion of the *modi significandi*, 'ways of signifying', which provided a framework for describing the process of verbalisation. In their view, the real-world object external to human understanding could be grasped as a concept by the understanding, and the concept could be made known by a spoken sign, thereby becoming a signifié, *res significata*. The properties of the *res significata*, its *modi significandi* (directly derived from the real-world properties of the object) served to differentiate semantic units, *dictiones*, grammatically. For example, many different *dictiones* convey the basic idea of grief: *dolor* 'grief', *doleo* 'I grieve', *dolens* 'a grieving one', *dolenter* 'sorrowfully', *heu* 'alas'. They can only be differentiated functionally when the *dictio* becomes part of a complete utterance – a *pars orationis*, 'part of speech' – by the *modi significandi* of the different parts of speech. *Dolor*, the noun 'grief', is distinguished from the verb *doleo* 'I grieve' by having the *modus entis*, the mode of stability and permanence – for grief is a permanent phenomenon existing in the world – whereas the grief inherent in *doleo* may later be succeeded by joy, for *doleo* possesses the *modus esse*, the mode of change and succession.

Modistic syntactic theory, recently the subject of comparison with modern dependency theory, cannot be properly assessed until we know more about non-modistic ideas on syntax such as are preserved in commentaries on the *Institutiones grammaticae*. It may be that the modistae have been credited with ideas which were commonplace in their time. Certainly, it was the cognitive underpinning of their theory, the structure underlying the *modi significandi* themselves, rather than their syntactic theory, which attracted the criticism of their successors. Toward the middle of the fourteenth century modism came under attack from Nominalist philosophers such as William of Ockham (c. 1285–1347/9). He denied the existence of any intrinsic connection between words and reality, the assumption on which the *modi significandi* rested, and pointed out the differences between the properties of mental and spoken language. Language, he concluded, was of no use as a mirror of cognition or of external reality; it would be far better to study thought – or reality – directly than through the treacherous intermediacy of language. In the meantime, however, the doctrine of the *modi significandi* filtered down into lower levels of instruction, particularly in Germany, and some of its terms and concepts – in simplified form – became grammatical commonplaces. Even as late as the Port-Royal *Grammaire générale et raisonée* (1660) the phrase 'manière de signifier' was still heavily used.

## 2.3.1 *Experimentation: medieval vernacular grammars*

It is to the Latin tradition that we must look for the mainstream of medieval linguistic thought, for Latin was the language of all scholarship – the international language linking all literate Christians, as well as the best described language available to the linguist and the philosopher. In theory, Greek and Hebrew possessed the same status as Latin, together revered as the 'three sacred languages' of the inscription on the Cross, but in practice few Westerners before the Renaissance succeeded in mastering more than the alphabet of either Greek or Hebrew. As for the vernaculars, the various spoken languages of Western Europe, only gradually did they come to be written; and only then, when people were used to reading their own language, was there any need for grammars in or of the vernacular.

The term 'medieval vernacular grammar' is often loosely used to denote three very disparate genres: 1) textbooks designed to teach Latin to non-native speakers which use the vernacular as their medium; 2) works written in a vernacular which set out the general principles of grammar – largely those of a semantic and functional nature – and draw their examples from the language in which they are written; 3) works which describe the structure of the vernacular, normally using the vernacular as their medium.

Although most of us today assume that a foreign language is best described through the medium of the mother tongue, this may not be the case in a society where the vernacular is unwritten and lacks the technical vocabulary to deal with grammatical minutiae. Early medieval grammarians retained Latin as the medium of their own textbooks, partly following in Donatus's footsteps (though his grammar, targeted at a Latin-speaking audience, was in its own time of the second type), partly favouring the solution which would most rapidly bring their students to the point of being able to read the Bible in Latin. The first to break away from the well-established tradition was Ælfric, writing in southern England close to the year 1000. Old English by that time had a flourishing literary tradition of its own, and Ælfric could count on an audience of people already capable of reading their native language. For this reason he translated a drastically shortened and rearranged paraphrase of Priscian's *Institutiones grammaticae* into Old English, adding a large number of local touches as he went along. He shows little interest in the grammar of his own language, for that was not his object. He remarks only that both languages have eight parts of speech, that the impersonal is rare in both, and that the assignment of gender to nouns is not always the same. Although Ælfric's grammar was very popular during the eleventh century, the further development of an English grammatical tradition was forestalled by the arrival of the Normans, who brought their own favourite Latin-medium grammars with them. Not until late in the fourteenth century was English again used as the medium for Latin lessons, and by this time the vernacular was claiming its place in grammatical instruction throughout the West.

Grammars which aim to set out general or universal principles of grammar tend to be written in the language of habitual scholarly use of the community for which they are designed. Only where there is an established tradition of vernacular literacy will there be any need for such grammars to be written in the vernacular. Ireland, Iceland and Provence all possessed lively vernacular literary traditions, and in all three areas grammars of this type were written.

The earliest known is the canonical portion of the *Auraicept na nÉces*, 'The Scholar's Primer', a grammar in Old Irish of which the earliest portions may date from the seventh century. Although ultimately modelled on the Roman grammarians of late Antiquity, the doctrine of the *Auraicept* is singularly independent and eccentric. General concepts are mingled with details peculiar to Old Irish; for instance, the concept of case is extended from the six of Latin to include some twenty-eight in Old Irish. Later grammarians in the bardic schools concentrated on the complexities of Irish inflections, word-formation and syntax.

In Iceland, the Old Norse language rapidly extended its domain from the originally oral sagas to scholarly works translated from Latin. Towards the middle of the thirteenth century Óláfr Þórðarson adapted the content of the first and third books of Donatus's *Ars maior* (with much additional doctrine from Priscian and other sources) into Old Norse in the so-called Third and Fourth Grammatical Treatises (named from their order in an important manuscript which contains the four grammatical treatises, the Codex Wormianus (AM 242)). Both the technical vocabulary and the substance of the doctrine are adapted to the very different Icelandic conditions in a remarkably successful manner. Under the heading of *littera*, for example, Þórðarson includes a detailed discussion of runes, while instead of using the traditional excerpts from Latin poets to exemplify the figures of speech, he finds appropriate passages in Norse scaldic and Christian verse.

The better known First Grammatical Treatise, by an anonymous Icelander writing a generation earlier, contains a proposal for the reform of Old Norse orthography which derives much of its inspiration from contemporary runic alphabets. In justifying the numerous symbols he adds to the Roman alphabet used for Norse, the author resorts to the device of minimal pairs to demonstrate the phonemicity of the sounds he wishes to distinguish. Although he occasionally goes too far, admitting several allophones into his alphabet, his procedure is remarkably systematic. This text exemplifies the profoundly utlitiarian nature of most medieval works focusing on a vernacular language, texts of the third type mentioned above. While tackling practical problems like that of orthographical reform, writers like the First Grammarian often stumbled upon techniques which we associate with a highly sophisticated theory; but the resemblance between the First Grammarian's use of minimal pairs and modern phonological analysis is coincidental. It is a commonplace that technology and science develop at different rates and along different paths; similarly, linguistic 'technology' as found in medieval works on orthography, grammars teaching foreign languages, dictionaries and so on, often bears little relation to the concerns of contemporary theoretical linguistics.

The first serious attempts to write a comprehensive grammar of a medieval vernacular took place in thirteenth- and fourteenth-century Provence. The high esteem in which the poetry of the troubadours was held had created a rash of would-be troubadour poets in Italy and Catalonia unfamiliar with the niceties of Provençal usage; later, after the culturally disastrous Albigensian crusade, native Provençal speakers themselves needed instruction in the language of the earliest troubadours. Of the relatively numerous works produced to help this audience, the most remarkable is the *Leys d'Amors*, a treatise on grammar and poetics published in 1356. This is the first systematic description of a medieval European vernacular, and by far the most detailed description of any Western language (apart from Latin and Greek) until well into the sixteenth century. The repertory of grammatical concepts made available by Donatus, Priscian and the modistae provides a sensitively exploited theoretical infrastructure. The author willingly admits that Provençal differs from Latin in lacking a full set of formally indicated cases, although, as he points out, case function can be indicated as clearly in Provençal. Only Provençal usage can be definitive for Provençal, he insists.

The *Leys d'Amors* heralded an ever-increasing degree of interest in the European vernaculars as the fourteenth and fifteenth centuries progressed. Unlike many Renaissance grammars of the vernacular, medieval vernacular grammars belong squarely to the domain of particular grammar rather than universal, practical rather than theoretical or polemical. The attitude of Renaissance scholars to the vernacular was far more ambivalent.

## 2.4 The Renaissance and after: universal and particular

To understand the fundamental difference in character between pre-and post-Renaissance linguistics one must bear in mind the outlook – so foreign to the twentieth-century – of those engaged in intellectual studies in the Middle Ages. People at all times prefer to put their effort into acquiring knowledge which will be true, certain and lasting; yet, paradoxically, the kind of knowledge which satisfies these criteria changes from one epoch to another. Medieval scholars sought such knowledge in the universal and eternal – in the principles which underlie and transcend earthly phenomena rather than in the fleeting phenomena themselves. Thought, sharpened by the study of logic, was to them a more valuable tool than any instrument could be. Once the principles inherent in earthly phenomena such as the life-cycles of living creatures or the movements of heavenly bodies had been stated by a profound thinker like Aristotle, observation served only to exemplify these established principles. That is not to say that medieval scholars were not capable of observation, as Bede's perceptive remarks on the tides show –

merely that it seemed to them to be a less certain route to knowledge than that offered by logic and the mathematical sciences. This attitude extended to language as well, in the distinction between *grammatica speculativa* and *grammatica positiva*. Its implications were at first only partially perceived, and many later medieval grammars, like the *Leys d'Amors*, contain elements of both types. But increasingly these two paths of language study diverged. With growing clarity through the sixteenth century and beyond, one can discern two quite different approaches to language: the 'particular' approach, focusing on the physical phenomena which differentiate languages, which closely parallels the newly-emerging biological sciences in its methods and findings; and the 'universal' approach, which, concentrating on the principles underlying language, continued to derive much of its inspiration and method from philosophy and in particular from logic. Linguistics since the Renaissance is characterised by the constant interplay and alternation of these two approaches, sometimes in the form of open competition between opposing schools, sometimes in subtler form within the work of one individual. The mainstream of scholarly research is normally dominated by one approach; the other, despised by mainstream linguists, goes underground, fostered by 'eccentrics' or by small groups geographically and intellectually distant from the centre. Despite the disadvantages incurred by the lessened continuity of the underground tradition – for many insights are forgotten during this fallow period, and geographical separation often results in isolated scholars duplicating one another's discoveries – it invariably re-emerges as the mainstream. Since about 1500 the focus of linguistic research has alternated between the particular and the universal approach at intervals of approximately one hundred and fifty years. Chronicling the development of linguistics since the Renaissance in century-long chunks would obscure the continuity of each approach. Instead, let us take first the particular and then the universal approach and examine each in turn.

## 2.5 Discovery of the particular

Perhaps the most characteristic feature of Western post-medieval linguistics is the increasingly systematic investigation of the particular in language. Whereas in the later Middle Ages the division between *grammatica speculativa* and *grammatica positiva* corresponded roughly to that between medieval science and technology, this equation no longer holds good from the Renaissance. The medieval view that transitory earthly phenomena contained no perceptible system and were therefore not worthy of study was replaced by the gathering certainty that regularities were inherent even in the superficially arbitrary and irregular phenomena of the physical world. The order of the cosmos was replicated on earth: the system and regularity previously associated only with the non-material heavenly realm were now sought on the physical plane. The growing attention devoted to the natural world as the fifteenth and sixteenth centuries passed is paralleled by the rising interest in the individual and particular in language. Instead of concentrating on what transcended individual languages, scholars began to examine the features which differed from one language to another. The semantic element, assumed to be universal, was increasingly taken for granted as scholars realised the intricacy and diversity in the physical aspects of language – the element in which the meaning was 'incarnated', as medieval scholars had put it. The modern disciplines of phonetics, phonology, morphology, and historical and comparative philology all arose out of this new-found urge to find system in the physical aspects of language.

At the most basic level, descriptive grammars were a pressing need. The Western European vernaculars were encroaching upon the domains once held by Latin: first chronicles and statutes, then popular handbooks and works of entertainment, and eventually even scholarly research were recorded in the local dialect or newly-standardised national language. Once literacy no longer entailed the mastery of Latin, it was a skill accessible to a far broader spectrum of the population, and a sizeable market for spelling manuals and dictionaries of the vernacular grew up during the fifteenth century. Grammars were a less urgent need; the vernacular translations of Donatus's *Ars minor* which proliferated during the fifteenth century were mostly intended to help the young student struggling with his Latin. John Barton's *Donat françois* (c. 1400), the earliest known grammar of French, is a notable exception; but it was intended to help English speakers master correct French. Most late fifteenth- and early-sixteenth-century grammars were, like Barton's work, written for the benefit of foreigners rather than for native speakers. How often do native speakers today consult grammars of their own language, after all?

Occasionally, however, grammars were written with a very different end in view: to demonstrate that (despite allegations to the contrary) the vernaculars were quite as capable of being reduced to rule as the Classical languages. In Italy, for example, many people found it difficult to believe that Classical Latin had ever been the everyday language of the Roman populace. Using the linguistic situation of their own day as a model, they argued that the Latin of Cicero's speeches was a highly complex and artificial language known only to a small group of scholars versed in grammar; at home, Cicero would have used the local vernacular – perhaps, they suggested, Italian itself, or an early form of it – which 'had no rules'. To combat this view the polymath Leon Battista Alberti (among whose numerous writings are works on optics and architecture) wrote a brief grammar of Italian (c. 1450, but not printed until 1973) with the express purpose of showing that Italian too had rules. Likewise, the influential German grammarian Johannes Claius pointed out that his comprehensive grammar (1578), based on Luther's works, would demonstrate the error of the common view that the German language was extremely difficult and not bound by any grammatical rules. Indeed, he deliberately made his rules as similar as he could to those of Latin, in order to make the 'regular' nature of German the more striking. This ambition – by no means restricted to Claius – is one which distinguishes many early modern grammars of the vernacular from their medieval predecessors. Whereas the earlier works were composed with a determinedly practical end in view, and in most cases are remarkably untrammelled by Latin, many Renaissance grammars, whether of European or of more exotic languages, were written with the intention of demonstrating the inherent 'regularity' of that language. The equation of 'regularity' with the rules of Latin became increasingly explicit as the sixteenth century passed, so that later grammars of the vernacular are often more artificially constrained by the Latin model than earlier ones – a case of the universal tradition encroaching upon the particular, to the detriment of the latter.

The new-found linguistic awareness was by no means restricted to the European vernaculars. Greek had hitherto been nearly as inaccessible as the remotest Asiatic language; now, with the arrival in Italy of Greek scholars from Constantinople prepared to teach their language, Plato and the New Testament could at last be studied in the original. Grammars of Greek, at first in Greek, like those of Constantine Lascaris and Manuel Chrysoloras, and then more accessibly in Latin, like Aldus Manutius's, were soon pouring from Italian presses. And what of Hebrew, the third of the 'three sacred languages'? A few eager scholars, ready to brave the opprobrium of the Church, searched for Jews who might be persuaded to teach them Hebrew. The difficulties involved in mastering Hebrew were considerable. Not only was it often impossible to find suitably learned and co-operative teachers – for by no means all fifteenth-century Jews had a good knowledge of Hebrew, and many of those who had were suspicious of the motives of their would-be pupils – but even when a teacher had been found, there were no usable textbooks. The elementary grammars used within Jewish communities were naturally in Hebrew, just as grammars of Latin were usually in Latin, Byzantine grammars of Greek were in Greek, and so on. A Hebrew grammar of this type was quite inaccessible to someone with not the slightest knowledge of the language. One Renaissance Humanist, Conrad Pellican, has left us a vivid description of his struggles to learn Hebrew during the year 1500. He had managed to acquire a copy of the Prophets and the Psalms in Hebrew, and was teaching himself Hebrew by working his way through it comparing the Hebrew text with the Latin translation. Since he knew that in Latin and Greek the verb form of vital importance was the first person singular of the present tense, he searched for first-person forms in the text, but found very few. In despair he turned to a learned visitor to his university, Tübingen, the noted German Humanist and Hebraist Johannes Reuchlin, who told him – with more than a hint of a smile, as Pellican wryly reports – that in Hebrew it is the third person which is crucial, not the first. Pellican had laboured for several months without knowing this elementary fact, one of the very first a beginner nowadays would learn. This and similar anecdotes convey some idea of the difficulties involved in gaining even a smattering of Hebrew, a situation exacerbated by the expulsion of the Jews from many parts of Europe around this time. In the early decades of the sixteenth century a number of Hebrew grammars in Hebrew were printed, foremost among them that of Moshe Qimhi with a commentary by Elias Levita, and various means of making them accessible to complete beginners were tried. One solution was to print a key to the alphabet, and to assume that once the student could decipher the script, he was well on his way to mastering the contents of the book; another was to print a facing Latin translation of the Hebrew text (or, as Sebastian Munster did in his edition and translation of Qimhi's grammar, to print the Latin version in the front half of the volume and the Hebrew original at the back). Only when Reuchlin himself brought out a Hebrew grammar in Latin (*De rudimentis hebraicis*, 1506) – a well-designed and beauti- fully-printed work which closely follows the traditional methods of describing Hebrew developed by Jewish grammarians – did Hebrew become generally accessible. Later grammarians toiled to make Hebrew conform as closely as possible to the familiar Latin mould: Nicolas Clénard's grammar (1529), Reuchlin's successor in popularity, is noticeably more latinate than its pre- decessor.

As the voyages of discovery ventured ever further from home, Europeans encountered a vast number of exotic languages. Reports of the languages of the Near East, then of those of the African coast, the Americas and Asia gradually filtered back as captains and traders returned with phrase books and missionaries sent home grammars and their first translations of the Bible and devotional literature. Whereas at the beginning of the sixteenth century Hebrew was still a rare and difficult acquisition, a century later grammars of Japanese, Tupi, and other previously undreamt-of languages, were in (admit- tedly limited) circulation. Europeans whose work took them to distant places of course needed grammars and dictionaries as practical aids; those at home used these tools, along with the proliferating translations of the Bible, as their linguistic source material. Now that the range of languages had grown beyond the scope of anyone's imagination, chaos prevailed. Who was to restore order? This discovery of Babel, a problem the sixteenth century bequeathed to the seventeenth, met with many attempts at a solution, some from within the particular and some from the universal tradition. Scholars working within the particular tradition tried to come to terms with the languages themselves:

how many languages were there? What were they called? Who spoke them? What script did they use? What was their history? Languages, like plants and animals, lent themselves to succinct characterisation and categorisation. Indeed, it was a naturalist, the Swiss doctor Conrad Gesner, who added a dictionary of languages (*Mithridates*, 1555) to his series of encyclopaedic dictionaries, mostly alphabetically organised, in which he provided potted accounts of all known flora, fauna, rocks and minerals, sea creatures, and so on. In *Mithridates*, so called after the mythical king of Pontus who according to Herodotus could converse with his subjects in each of the twenty-two languages spoken in his kingdom, Gesner gives a brief account of the location and external history of each language, together with any other facts known to him. English, for instance, is described as the most hybrid and corrupt of all languages, owing its origin to a mixture of the ancient British with the Saxon, and lexical borrowings from French merchants and in Gesner's own time from Latin. At the end of the volume was a fold-out table setting out the Lord's Prayer in twenty-two languages. Gesner was the first in a long line of natural scientists to take an interest in the 'particular' aspect of language.

Data-gathering among sixteenth-century linguists often took the form of assembling versions of the Lord's Prayer in as many languages as possible. Gesner's twenty-two versions were all drawn from languages of the Old World, ranging no further afield than Persia and Ethiopia; by 1593 Hieronymus Megiser was able to muster some forty languages, including several Scandinavian and Slavonic languages, one American Indian language, and Chinese. The coverage grew enormously during the seventeenth and eighteenth centuries, culminating in the great collection of more than a thousand published by J.C. Adelung in his *Mithridates* (a conscious echo of Gesner's book) in 1806. Such collections provided would-be historical and comparative linguists with their primary source of data. Brief though it is, the Lord's Prayer contains sufficient vocabulary to permit bold linguists to draw tentative conclusions as to language relationships; but its range of grammatical forms is so limited that it is hardly surprising that systematic morphological comparisons were rarely made until scholars formed the habit of working with longer texts.

Collections of language specimens, and encyclopaedic dictionaries of languages like Gesner's or, early next century, Claude Duret's *Thrésor de l'histoire des langues de cest univers* (1613), signal the new-found enthusiasm for the great variety of languages – a phenomenon previously perceived as a nuisance, a divine punishment, and not worthy of serious attention. It betokens a rise of interest in those features which differentiate one language from another, in form rather than in communicative or epistemological function: a radical shift in perception.

*2.5.1. Form in language: the emergence of phonetics and morphology*

A subtler but no less radical shift was taking place in the way in which language was studied. The semantic element, the 'soul' incarnated in the 'body' of the word, no longer seemed so interesting; first taken for granted by linguists working in the particular tradition, then ignored, it faded into the background, overshadowed by formal aspects of the word.

One area which underwent striking, if sporadic, development from the middle of the sixteenth century was phonetics. Although the basis for an articulatory classification of sounds was available in Priscian's *Institutiones grammaticae*, it had scarcely been noticed during the Middle Ages. Nor is this surprising. Quite apart from the generally low value attached to this most obviously physical part of the word, there was little practical incentive to investigate the sounds of Latin, known only from the written page. Only late in the Middle Ages, with the first descriptions of the vernacular, are sounds systematically described. The desire to record the sounds peculiar to a given vernacular was one impetus; a second was the discovery of the traditional Hebrew classification of the consonants according to their place of articulation: gutturals, palatals, linguals, dentals and labials. Western scholars now experimented with applying these categories to more familiar languages. Sadly, despite the very detailed descriptions of articulation available in grammars of Hebrew like those of Agathius Guidacerius (1529) and Augustus Sebastianus Novzenus (1532), most grammarians never went beyond the fairly routine assignation of each letter to one or another category. Usually it was people with a more practical bent – teachers of deaf-mutes, rather than grammarians – who went deeply into the study of articulation.

Newly available anatomical descriptions of the vocal organs such as that by the Italian anatomist Fabricius ab Aquapendente provided a firm basis for such work. Fabricius published three works with a bearing on phonetics: *De visione, voce, auditu* (1600), containing a detailed description of the structure, movement and function of the larynx; *De locutione et eius instrumentis* ('Speech and its Organs') (1624), a fairly conventional summary of contemporary phonetic doctrine with some articulatory phonetics interspersed; and *De brutorum loquela* (1624), a comparison of the communications systems of animals with human language.

The remarkable work of Fabricius and phoneticians such as the Dane Jacobus Mathiae of Aarhus (*De literis*, 1586) and the Dutchman Petrus Montanus (*De Spreeckonst*, 1635) remained so much outside the mainstream of linguistic research that few of their successors were aware of their insights. With the publication of William Holder's *Elements of Speech* (1669), John Wallis's *Grammatica linguae anglicanae* (1653) and John Wilkins's *Essay towards a Real Character and a Philosophical Language* (1668) an English tradition of phonetics was inaugurated; but even then such basic notions as voicing and nasality continued to baffle many writers until the establishment of phonetics as a recognised discipline, following upon the discovery of Sanskrit and Indian work on phonetics.

Morphology was a formal aspect of language which was pursued with greater confidence. Before the Renaissance the idea that one form could be derived from another was scarcely exploited. Each word was regarded as a semantic unit; there was no question of the isolation of smaller units, as the absence of terms corresponding to 'root', 'stem', 'affix' and so on suggests. Thus there are no generative rules such as the familiar 'to form the Latin imperfect tense, take the present stem, add -*ba*- and the personal endings' in a pre-Renaissance grammar. Instead, the student is expected to observe the pattern set out in paradigms, and to apply the analogy to any verb he might subsequently meet. Renaissance scholars, in contrast, focused more sharply on form. The Spanish Humanist Antonio de Nebrija, author of the first grammar of Spanish (1492), provides an example of this approach in his Latin grammar (1481). Instead of advising the hapless student to memorise pages of verb paradigms, he provides a chapter summarising the formation of the tenses. He starts with the present tense, which, he says, is not formed from any other; rather, the others are formed from it. The imperfect is formed either from the second person singular of the present by dropping -s and adding -bam: amas → ama → amabam, or from the first person, changing the final -o to -e and adding -bam: lego → lege → legebam. Here is a rule which attempts to 'generate' the forms of a Latin verb – a rule of the type that was rarely found in Antiquity and the Middle Ages. And yet Nebrija works only with existing forms (here the first and second persons singular of the present tense), and not, as we might expect, with the root or stem. This remains the case until contact with the Indian notion of root at the start of the nineteenth century. To postulate and work with a form with no independent existence in the language demands a degree of abstraction not yet found in the early modern period. Rules similar to Nebrija's, in principle generative but always based on existing forms, are found in the most widely circulating grammars of this time. And of course many authors continued to rely upon paradigms.

What brought the change in outlook that caused Nebrija and so many others to begin to think about word-forms in terms of these generative rules? Although a few ancient grammarians, notably Diomedes and pseudo-Palaemon, had sporadically used rules of a similar type, the essential tools for the morphological analysis of words were developed outside the Western tradition, among Jewish and Arab scholars. Aware from a much earlier date of word-form (just as in the medical and biological sciences their knowledge of anatomy had been far more advanced), Semitic scholars had devoted much effort to unravelling the morphology of their respective languages. By the tenth century the concept of 'root', an unvarying consonantal core with a stable basic semantic content, had been fully elaborated. For example, the root KTB, containing the notion of 'writing', may by the addition of various affixes become one of several different words: Arabic *KiTaB* 'a book', *maKTaBa* 'a library', *KaTaBtu* 'I wrote', *aKTuBu* 'I shall write', and so on. However, *KTB* by itself is an abstract and unpronounceable consonant cluster with no existence as such in the language. Arab and Jewish scholars early instituted the custom of referring to roots in the simplest verbal form, the third person singular of the past tense: *KaTaBa*. Western grammarians only half understood this convention. They assumed that *KaTaBa* itself was the root, and concluded that verbal roots in any language would be identical with the normal citation form of the word. Thus, *amo* in Latin, *j'aime* in French – the 'theme' or base form – were identified as root forms. The abstract nature of the root in Semitic morphological analysis was thus quite misunderstood. Nonetheless, even this half understood notion permitted a more economical description of the complex morphology of Latin and Greek than had hitherto been possible.

### 2.5.2 *First steps toward historical linguistics: the Indo-Scythian hypothesis and the rise of comparative philology*

Once the basic tools essential to any kind of formal linguistic analysis were available – some rudimentary notions of articulatory phonetics and morphology – they provided the means whereby people could begin to research the historical development and affiliations of languages. With the increasing awareness of the diversity and multiplicity of languages in the world – some of them claiming considerable antiquity – a reassessment of language relationships became urgent. Were all languages descended from Hebrew, as had been assumed throughout the Middle Ages? Or had the original language of mankind been lost at Babel? Speakers of Italian confidently traced their language back through Etruscan to Greek and thence to Hebrew; Europeans north of the Alps were more hesitant. One, Goropius Becanus, demonstrated that the arguments commonly used to prove the primitive, original nature of Hebrew applied rather better to his own language, Flemish (*Hermathena*, 1580). Etymology, focusing increasingly on the comparison of forms rather than of meanings, became a vital tool in proving and disproving one hypothesis after another, and authors boasted of the number of languages they had drawn upon elucidating the vocabulary of their own language. As early as 1597 a few pages of Persian words had been published in Bonaventura Vulcanius's linguistic miscellany, *The Script and Language of the Goths*. On this basis Claudius Salmasius (known to historians for his pamphlet in defence of Charles I, which plunged him into a verbal battle with Milton) elaborated the Indo-Scythian theory, the forerunner of the Indo-European hypothesis. According to this theory, set out in a work on the status of the Greek dialects, *De hellenistica* (1643), Latin, Greek, Persian and the Germanic languages were all descended from a lost common ancestor. To demonstrate this, Salmasius employed techniques familiar to us from nineteenth-century comparative philology: the comparison of cognate forms such as Greek *patér*, German *Vater*, Persian *badar*; phonological correspondences, such as the fact that the Germanic languages regularly have initial h- where Latin has a c- as in Old English *heafod*, Danish *hoffuit*, Dutch *hoofft* for Latin *caput*; and reconstruction, as when he uses a number of cognate forms – Greek *pénte*, *pémpe* and *pénke*, Latin *quinque*, German *fünf*, Old English *fif*, Dutch *vijf*, Persian *bengh* – to reconstruct two possible protoforms, *fenf/fynf* and *fengh*.

Salmasius's work gave rise to a generation of careful historical and comparative studies. Building on Salmasius's findings, the Swedish scholar Georg Stiernhielm set out some vitally important principles for the development of historical linguistics in the preface to his edition of the Gothic Bible (1671): he introduced criteria for defining the relatedness of languages, pointed out that linguistic change is inevitable given either temporal or geographic distance (an assertion which has the drastic implication that there is not the slightest possibility that the original language of mankind could still exist in its original form), and extended Salmasius's list of languages of Scythian stock to include not only Latin, Greek, German, Gothic and Persian, but also what are now called the Romance, Slavonic and Celtic languages, whilst expressly excluding Hungarian, Finnish, Estonian and Lapp.

In Stiernhielm's work the Indo-Scythian hypothesis attained its highest development. By the time it appeared, a reaction against the perhaps exaggerated stress on the similarity of Persian and German had set in, and in any case the attention of the mainstream was shifting back to universal grammar. By the end of the century, Leibniz had reverted to the monogenesis hypothesis, and assumed that linguistic relatedness was contingent upon geographical proximity. Thus, he groups all European ('Japhetic') languages together, disregarding the fundamental dissimilarity – recognised by Stiernhielm – between Finno-Ugrian languages and the Indo-European languages of Europe; and he includes the non-Indo-European Turkish and Tatar amongst the Japhetic languages because they are spoken in Europe, whilst excluding the Asiatic – though Indo-European – Persian. With Leibniz the genetic view of language relationships was giving way to an approach potentially more akin to modern areal typology.

Although it was overshadowed in the latter part of the seventeenth century by universalist tendencies emanating from France, and taken up with special enthusiasm in England, the 'particular' stream continued its development through the seventeenth and eighteenth centuries in various areas: in the increasingly detailed study of phonetics, in the remarkable doctrine of the *Stammwort* or *Wurzelwort* ('stem' or 'root' word) which dominated language study in Germany, and in the continuing study of individual languages and groups of languages, focusing particularly on etymology. Much very careful and sensitive analysis is to be found in vernacular grammars in the seventeenth and eighteenth centuries. Antiquaries took an increasing interest in the discovery and investigation of earlier stages of their own language. Scholars working on individual Germanic languages routinely made use of comparative material from the others. Such study reached its high point in Lambert ten Kate's remarkable work on Dutch, *Aenleiding tot de Kennisse van het Verhevene Deel der Nederduitsche Sprake* ('Introduction to the Elevated Portion of the Low German Language') (Amsterdam 1723). In order to provide a firm theoretical basis for the etymological dictionary of Dutch which occupies much of the second volume he sets out the principles which should in his view underlie *Geregelde Afleiding*, 'principled derivation', which should alone be relied upon for correct etymologies of the Germanic languages, rather than the *Af- en Aen- In- en Uit- en Om-werping van Letters*, the traditional addition, removal, transposition and mutation of letters. He promises not to admit a single change to an 'essential letter', that is, those in stressed syllables, without a convincing rule or indisputable semantic evidence to justify it. His rules consist of lists of phonological correspondences in seven Germanic dialects: Dutch, Gothic, Old Norse, Frankish, Alemannic, Old English, High German.

Ten Kate's exhortation to abandon the techniques of ancient etymology was repeated throughout the century. Charles, President de Brosses, in his widely read *Traité de la formation méchanique des langues, et des principes physiques de l'étymologie* (1765) reiterates his plea and attempts in his turn to arrive at reliable principles for use in etymology. The etymologist is to take into consideration identity of meaning, the spelling (*figure*), which can be a helpful guide when the pronunciation has undergone rapid change, and the sound. Inflectional endings should be disregarded, and in establishing derivations 'la voyelle ne doit presque être comptée pour rien', while consonants of the same place of articulation could be deemed to be interchangeable.

By the second half of the eighteenth century the conceptual resources available since the Renaissance had been tried out in various contexts. Their limitations were being increasingly strongly felt: form-based etymology which relied upon the rudimentary notions of articulatory phonetics current since the Renaissance was arousing the same criticism that the semantic etymology of the ancients was subject to. Historical linguists of the previous century had arrived at startling conclusions which they lacked the technical means to justify; their findings had consequently been displaced by far less penetrating hypotheses. Dissatisfaction with the techniques and assumptions of the time speaks from many a careful scholar's writings at this period.

It was again contact with an alien tradition which brought the requisite stimulus for new development. Through repeated contact with pandits in India, French missionaries and British colonial administrators began to take an interest both in the Sanskrit language and in the native system of grammar. Initially overawed by its complexity – for the familiar paradigms were nowhere to be found, and the student was required to master a complex cumulative series of generative rules – the functionaries of the British administration, most of them well grounded in the traditional analysis of Latin and Greek, soon came to appreciate its precision, and modelled their own grammars of Sanskrit upon it: Carey (1804), Colebrooke (1805), Wilkins (1808) and Forster (1810) all based their works more or less closely upon the Indian grammars from which they themselves had been taught (chiefly native adaptations of Pāṇini's grammar such as the *Mugdhabodha* of Vopadeva). Consequently, scholars at home found these first Western grammars of Sanskrit – when they could obtain them – unfamiliar in their layout and obscure, and, with a few notable exceptions, failed to derive much benefit from them. Not until the appearance of the second generation of grammars – by Yates (1820), Frank (1823) and most influentially Bopp (1824–37) – did Sanskrit, filtered through the familiar Western model of paradigms along with a restricted set of generative rules, become accessible to a large number of scholars. Thus, only a limited number of concepts from the Sanskrit model of grammar made their way into Western linguistics, but those that did were of decisive importance. The much subtler Indian analysis of the sounds of Sanskrit was to begin with only partially understood, but its central notions, the concepts of the horizontal axis of places of articulation (already known from the Semitic tradition) and of the vertical axis of articulatory process (voicing, aspiration, nasality) – vital for an understanding of the *sandhi* assimilations which are a major feature of Sanskrit morphophonology – was rapidly absorbed and integrated into subsequent grammatical and phonetic work. (Later in the century, W.D. Whitney, A.J. Ellis, Henry Sweet and other important phoneticians were to derive inspiration from the study of Sanskrit texts on phonetics, the *prātiśākhyas*). The concept of root was refined in a way which made possible its subsequent role in Indo-European philology. Franz Bopp defined it thus: 'Roots are the primitive elements of words, not themselves found in the language but identifiable from forms derived from them which contain them as a common base or stem'. By stressing their abstract nature and non-equivalence with any existing form, he put the finishing touches to the Semitic notion of root, previously only partially understood, and made possible the kind of etymology towards which Salmasius and his

818

successors had been groping. Bopp's own comparative grammar (*Vergleichende Grammatik des Sanskrit, Zend, Griechischen, Lateinischen, Litthauischen, Gothischen und Deutschen*, Berlin, 1833–54) states the programme for future work:

'In this book I intend to give a comparative description, including everything relevant, of the organism of the languages named in the title, an investigation of their physical and mechanical laws and of the origin of the forms indicating grammatical relationships. We will leave untouched only the secret of roots and the reasons behind the naming of the original concepts; we will not investigate why, for example, the root *I* means "go" and not "stand", or why the sounds *STHA/STA* mean "stand" and not "go".'

The scientific, particular approach had reached its culmination. While the semantic aspect could never be ignored entirely, the focus was now openly and unapologetically on form.

The historical approach to language – the dominant movement in linguistics for most of the nineteenth century – was but one manifestation of the contemporary tendency to look at the world in evolutionary terms. (In this volume it is the subject of Chapter 24 below.) Philologists realised, with some amusement, that they had long taken for granted ideas which both Darwin and his opponents regarded as novel and controversial. The noted Indo-Europeanist, August Schleicher, in his pamphlet *Darwinism tested by the Science of Language* (1863), written in response to Darwin's *Origin of Species* (1859), remarked:

'What Darwin now maintains with regard to the variation of the species in the course of time . . . has been long and generally recognised in its application to the organisms of speech . . . To trace the development of new forms from anterior ones is much easier, and can be executed on a larger scale, in the field of speech than in the organisms of plants and animals . . . The kinship of the different languages may consequently serve . . . as a paradigmatic illustration of the origin of species, for those fields of inquiry which lack, for the present at least, any similar opportunities of observation.'

These parallels raised a further question: if languages, the object of linguistic study, behaved like the objects of scientific study, then was linguistics a science? Or, to pose the question in terms used at the time, was it a historical or a physical science? Max Müller, a German Indo-Europeanist who spent much of his life in England, argued from the nature of the discipline as well as from that of language itself, saying that since the science of language had passed through the same developmental stages – empirical, classificatory and theoretical – as physical sciences like botany and astronomy, the subject must belong to the physical sciences (*Lectures on the Science of Language*, Royal Institution, London, 1861, 1863). But this view of the subject was by no means widely accepted: in 1875 the American scholar W.D. Whitney, renowned equally for his still authoritative grammar of Sanskrit and for his contributions to phonetics and comparative philology, wrote: 'Physical science on the one side, and psychology on the other, are striving to take possession of linguistic science, which in truth belongs to neither' (*Life and Growth of Language*, New York, 1875). This plea for the autonomy of linguistics was to echo on through the twentieth century. (Recent approaches to phonetics, phonology and morphology are discussed in Chaptes 1, 2 and 3 above.)

## 2.6 The universal approach since the Renaissance

The universalist concerns of the modistae, inspired and reinforced by the close study of Aristotelian philosophy, had been supplanted on the philosophical side by Nominalism and on the grammatical side by Humanism. Humanist grammarians like Guarino Veronese, Antonio de Nebrija, Thomas Linacre, Philipp Melanchthon and Lorenzo Valla (to name only a few), preoccupied by the mastery of a clear and elegant prose style, drew heavily upon the late medieval tradition of *grammatica positiva* as well as upon newly-discovered ancient authors such as Quintilian, Varro and various of the Late Latin grammarians. Remarks disparaging the Speculative tendency to mingle dialectic with grammar were commonplace. In contrast, J.C. Scaliger, an Italian scholar who worked in France, whilst insisting on the separateness of the domains of grammar and dialectic, applied the Aristotelian doctrine of the four causes (material, formal, efficient, final) to language in his thorough-going critique of the tenets of contemporary grammar (*De causis linguae latinae*, 1540), and was followed by the scarcely less philosophically-orientated, and vastly influential, *Minerva* (1587) of Franciscus Sanctius (Sanchez) Brocensis. Sanctius's treatment of syntax, a subject which had been virtually ignored by Scaliger, dealt, like that of the English grammarian Thomas Linacre (*De emendata structura latini sermonis*, 1524), with figurative usage, and in particular with ellipsis, a subject covered by many grammarians in the mainstream tradition.

Aristotelianism was by no means the only peephole left for the universalist viewpoint. The growing awareness of the European vernaculars and of the multiplicity of newly-discovered languages outside Europe was counteracted as the seventeenth century began by the uncomfortable awareness that the traditional means for keeping Babel at bay, the Latin language, until then the unquestioned international language, was rapidly losing its efficacy. Challenged by one vernacular after another as the vehicle for scholarly writing, and totally useless outside Western Europe, it was engaged in a hopeless struggle. Faced with the imminent prospect of linguistic fragmentation on a scale unknown in Western Europe since the departure of the Romans, scholars and public alike responded by focusing on the universal aspect of language. Where could a cure for Babel be found? At one end of the spectrum was Jakob Böhme's inspirational account (*De signatura rerum*, 1635) of the *Natursprache*, the original divine language, 'the root or mother of all the languages of the world and the key to a true and perfect knowledge of all things'. Adam, perceiving the workings of the divine creative Word in Nature, had named all the creatures in accord with their own essential qualities, using human language as his medium. This ability to read the language of Nature was lost at Babel. From then on, language was trapped in crude external substance, its words arbitrary and lacking any intrinsic connection with nature. But, like Ramon Lull before him and Rudolf Steiner in the present century, Böhme stressed that the *signaturae rerum*, the indications contained in earthly phenomena as to their true nature, were there to be read by those prepared to undergo the requisite training. At the opposite extreme was the remarkable attempt by John Wilkins to construct an artificial language based on a rational classification of all reality – in essence an Aristotelian system reinforced with empirical input from natural philosophers like the zoologist Francis Willoughby and the botanist John Ray (who was critical of the unrealistic philosophical underpinning of Wilkins's scheme). Such a language, Wilkins hoped, would be at once a clear and unambiguous means of communication and a tool for scientific investigation. This ultimate cure for Babel – to recreate reality, as it were, by imposing arbitrary (or 'conventional') categories upon it and then assigning these categories equally arbitrary labels – died stillborn, received with little enthusiasm by the Royal Society, which had originally commissioned the project. Nonetheless, Wilkins's *Essay Towards a Real Character and a Philosophical Language* (1668) was widely read, on the Continent as well as in England, and provided P.M. Roget – like Wilkins a Fellow (and indeed Secretary) of the Royal Society – with the inspiration for the system used in his *Thesaurus of English Words and Phrases* (1852).

Neither Wilkins nor Böhme, representative though they were of different manifestations of the search for the universal in language, contributed directly to what was to become the mainstream version of universal grammar. The very origin of the Port-Royal *Grammaire générale et raisonnée* (1660) mirrors the conflicting elements at work: the meeting of particular grammar and philosophy. In the course of writing textbooks on Latin, Greek, Spanish and Italian, Claude Lancelot observed the existence of features common to these and (he surmised) all other languages; a philosopher colleague, the embattled Antoine Arnauld, brought inductive confirmation of the cognitive basis of language. Mental operations were made the basis of grammatical distinctions: the three primary operations – forming a concept such as 'round', making a judgement such as 'the earth is round', and reasoning – provided a framework for distinguishing the various parts of speech and for the study of syntax.

Because these operations and their linguistic consequences are universal, they can be exemplified through any language, and French and Latin provide most of the examples. In this way the celebrated analysis of the proposition 'Dieu invisible a créé le monde visible' simply shows how three distinct mental propositions – that God is invisible, that He created the world, and that the world is visible – are included in this one verbal proposition. A distinction between mental language and the verbal language which is the province of grammarians had been part of the theological and philosophical tradition for centuries. That one might seek to derive grammatically analysable sentences from mental propositions was not an enterprise that would have struck someone trained in this tradition as worthwhile. Instead, the analysis of the justification for the parts of speech was of more immediate importance. Having defined the verb as a word whose principal use is to signify affirmation, as in 'the world *is* round', the authors concluded that only in the verb 'to be' was this function realised in its simplest form; other verbs, 'lives', for example, are analysed as consisting of the verb 'to be' plus an attribute: 'is living'. This analysis, found also in the works of the Modistae and elsewhere, is characteristic of the universal tradition – a natural consequence of logical, rather than of grammatical, analysis of the proposition.

The *Grammaire générale et raisonnée* was the acknowledged ancestor of a long series of 'general', 'philosophical', 'universal' or 'speculative' grammars whose authors were concerned to show the pervasiveness of logical principles in language, dissociated from the arbitrary effects of the usage of any particular language. In England James Harris's *Hermes, or a Philosophical Inquiry concerning Universal Grammar* (1751), more explicit in its application of philosophical categories to language than many other works of the genre, and in Germany A.F. Bernhardi's *Anfangsgründe der Sprachwissenschaft* (1805), represent extremes of the development of this genre outside France.

But the philosophical grammar as it developed from the Port-Royal *Grammaire* was not the sole bearer of the universal tradition of language study between 1660 and 1800, although it was an especially widespread and generally acknowledged one. Beginning with Locke, Condillac and the *philosophes* of the French Enlightenment, the question of the origin of language and the nature of its relationship with thought occupied attention. The grammar of exotic languages was studied with increasing attention, for the languages of primitive peoples, the reasoning went, would necessarily throw light on the language of mankind at a correspondingly primitive stage of development. From these beginnings language typology emerged. The problem of the origin of language itself suffered an interesting fate: the prize offered by the Berlin Academy in 1771 for an essay on this subject attracted some 31 entries, and, despite Herder's winning contribution (*Abhandlung über den Ursprung der Sprache*), continued to prompt lively discussion to the end of the century and beyond. That the Société de Linguistique de Paris found it necessary to proscribe contributions on this subject as late as 1866 shows as clearly that popular interest in the subject was still very much alive as that the academic mainstream despaired of ever finding a solution.

But in the meantime an unexpected new element was introduced: the Sanskrit language. The question of language origin was first briefly diverted into the assumption that Sanskrit was the parent language, and then forgotten as energy went into the detailed formal comparison of Sanskrit and cognate languages. A few scholars took advantage of the breadth of perspective afforded by the discovery of Sanskrit and still more exotic languages to formulate far-reaching hypotheses about the nature and role of language. Wilhelm von Humboldt, brother of the scientist and explorer Alexander and a friend of Goethe's, viewed language as the organ of inner existence, the way to understanding – or manifesting – thoughts and feelings (*Über die Verschiedenheit des menschlichen Sprachbaues und ihren Einfluss auf die geistige Entwickelung des Menschengeschlechts*, 1836). The human spirit manifests itself in different forms of civilisation and culture among different peoples, and also in different languages. Each is an attempt, an approximation, a contribution to the universal need to develop a people's intellectual and spiritual powers and to unfold their own mode of relating to the world. Far from representing phenomena directly, each language articulates that speech community's perception of the world around it from its own distinctive point of view. Humboldt's deep interest in the essence of individual differences between languages is found not so much in the mainstream of theoretical linguistics in the twentieth century as in anthropological linguistics, initiated by the work of E. Sapir and B.L. Whorf, and in the work of German scholars from Leo Weisgerber on.

But by the time Humboldt's great work was published (posthumously) the universal aspect of language study was being pushed aside by the newly emerging discipline of comparative philology. Although philologists of the stature of Jakob Grimm, Max Müller, H. Steinthal, and W.D. Whitney concerned themselves with problems like the ultimate origin of language, its relation to thought, and its position among the sciences, their writings on these subjects were eclipsed by the contemporary enthusiasm for historical and comparative work. Thus it was that although the ideas taught by Ferdinand de Saussure in his celebrated lecture course at Geneva (*Cours de linguistique générale*, published posthumously on the basis of his students' lecture notes in 1916) were far from novel, and had been in circulation intermittently during the nineteenth century, in the changed intellectual climate of the post-Great War world they struck the scholarly community as fresh, stimulating, and above all unfamiliar. The consequence was an over-rigid interpretation of ideas presented schematically in the *Cours* which had once been current in subtler and more diversified guises. Such, for instance, has been the case with the doctrine of *l'arbitraire du signe*, the arbitrary nature of the relationship between the linguistic sign and what it denotes. Elevated into a dogma in most branches of linguistics, it contravenes the intuitive feeling of the native speaker (and the literary critic) for the affective value of certain sounds and sound-groups, a fact recognised by von Humboldt (and by Plato long before). The linguistic sign, defined as the union between a concept (*signifié*) and its acoustic representation (*signifiant*), is yet another manifestation of Aristotle's schema, but lacking the refinement of the level of percept. Saussure's distinction between the synchronic and the diachronic approach to language was taken as a charter for the liberation of a synchronic descriptive structural linguistics from historical linguistics, despite Saussure's own awareness of the symbiotic relationship of the two temporal axes. Perhaps the most fruitful of Saussure's insights has been the celebrated *langue—parole* dichotomy – *langue* that aspect of language which is a system of signs existing in the speech community independent of the will of any individual, while *parole* denotes the particular utterances of individual speakers; *langue* is the essential, *parole* the accidental aspect of language.

Saussure's importance lies more in his making explicit the implications of a structuralist approach to language than in the specific tenets of his doctrine, most of which have been modified by both European and American Structuralists – Bloomfield and his followers, Troubetzkoy and other linguists of the Prague School, Hjelmslev and the Copenhagen School, Martinet, Chomsky and the many offshoots of Generative Grammar – who all acknowledge some degree of indebtedness to him. But more important still are the consequences of his work for disciplines on the periphery of linguistics or quite outside it: semiotics, anthropology, history, psychology, philosophy and literary criticism. Particularly among French scholars – Lévi-Strauss, Foucault, Barthes, Derrida – Structuralism has undergone a development which takes it far beyond its original context. Within the linguistic mainstream, attention has recently returned to semantics, and the allied discipline of pragmatics, heavily influenced by logic, has sprung up. The twentieth-century development of these and other branches of Western linguistics is covered in Chapters 5 and 6 of this volume. Rather than duplicate this information, let us now shift the focus of this hitherto Eurocentric account to some equally rich but – to the Westerner – less accessible traditions.

## 3. NON-EUROPEAN TRADITIONS

The Greco–Roman tradition out of which modern Western linguistics has grown is only one of several independent traditions of language study known to have existed in the last three millennia. But it is by no means the most ancient, nor necessarily the most varied or subtle in its understanding of language. The ancient Near East, India and China can all boast of linguistic traditions of greater antiquity, while for richness of insight and comprehensiveness of scope both India and the Arab tradition compete on equal terms with the West. Each of these traditions arose independently of the others and for the most part developed separately, drawing on the resources of the culture within which it grew. Episodes of contact and mutual influence were few but significant: the Arab tradition was repeatedly fertilised by insights derived from the works of Aristotle; Buddhist missionaries took the Indian system of phonetic classification to Tang dynasty China; and Westerners twice received a vital stimulus from alien traditions, from the Semitic tradition around 1500 and from India around 1800. But to understand how each tradition came to take its characteristic shape it is more important to consider people's outlook and way of relating to the world as they are manifested in all areas of culture, than to go source-hunting. In any case, a borrowed piece of doctrine takes on a different significance when transplanted into a alien cultural setting, and the very act of borrowing is itself important.

Although the Arab, the Indian and the Chinese linguistic traditions would each merit discussion on the same scale as the European tradition, space permits of no more than the barest outline. In the circumstances, it has seemed most useful to discuss these traditions with reference to the Western tradition, contrasting the course of their development as well as glancing at those areas of doctrine where contact has taken place. The works mentioned in the suggestions for further reading offer a more comprehensive view of these traditions, as well as ample bibliographical leads.

## 3.1 The Arab world

Apparently arising out of nothing, no venerable Classical tradition stretching behind it, Arab grammatical writing makes its first appearance in the elaborate and detailed form given it by its most renowned exponent, Sībawayhi, a bare 150 years after the death of Muhammad. This extraordinarily rapid codification was followed by an equally speedy and prolific expansion into all areas of language study: phonetics, morphology, syntax, semantics and the philosophy of language. In the space of six centuries linguistics among the Arabs developed in a direction more akin to Western post-Renaissance linguistics than to contemporary medieval work in the West. Yet by 1400 its momentum was gone. Instead of sharing in the intellectual change of direction brought about by the new world outlook of the European Renaissance, Arab writers in all branches of scholarship, scientific as well as linguistic, continued to work out of their old traditions, which had ceased to provide fresh inspiration. By comparison with European linguistics, linguistics in the Arab world reached a technically much more 'modern' level in a remarkably brief space of time – but, like a prematurely blossoming flower, withered away just as its fellows were catching up.

How the study of grammar developed in its very earliest stages in the Arab world is likely to remain a mystery. Two factors played into it, one internal, the other external. Within Islamic culture great importance was attached to the Qur'ān, to the preservation of the text and the exegesis of its contents. As Islam spread to non-Arabic-speaking peoples the need for formal grammatical instruction became urgent, all the more so since the script did not indicate the vowels, nor, in its earliest form, did it distinguish among several of the consonants. Without a thorough knowledge of the language there could be no question of correct oral recitation of the Qur'ān, a vital part of religious ceremony. This was the motivation attributed to the reputed inventor of Arabic grammar, Abū 'l-Aswad ad-Du'alī (who died c. 688). Many of the most noted grammarians of Arabic, starting with Sībawayhi himself, were of non-Arab (often Persian) or mixed descent. Had it been simply a matter of vocalising the text, Arab linguistic scholarship need not have developed further, even as the Massoretes concentrated on the vocalisation of Hebrew and allied problems connected with recitation of the scriptures, but went no further. But the needs of converts speaking unrelated languages, notably Persian, and the possibilities presented by the lively intellectual surroundings at centres such as Nisibis, Jundishapur, and later Baghdad, contributed to the unprecedented speed with which the Arab grammatical tradition emerged. Greek was still used in parts of the Near East in the first centuries of Islam, and much Greek material, including a part of the grammar attributed to Dionysius Thrax, had been translated into Syriac, a Semitic language with widespread currency in the Near East. Although the extent of Greek influence on the foundation of the Arab grammatical tradition is still disputed, the existence of contact between the two traditions is not at issue, and details such as the choice of a model verb meaning 'to beat' in both traditions – *ḍaraba* in Arabic, *túptō* in Grteek – corroborate this. More problematical is the question of dependence at the systemic level. Without parallel in the other major linguistic traditions is the importance of the terminology and concepts of Islamic law in early Arabic grammar.

The earliest grammar to have come down to us from the Arab tradition is the *Kitāb* ('Book') by Sībawayhi (who died in 793). Perhaps its most striking feature to the reader familiar with the Greco-Roman tradition is the minor importance of semantic issues. The introduction begins by setting out the three word classes, names (*ism*), operations/actions (*fʿl*) and words 'directed towards a meaning' which are neither names nor operations (*ḥarf*). Names require no explanation, and are given none; operations take various forms to specify the actions of the names, and indicated what has passed, or what will be but has not yet taken place, or that which is and has not yet finished. Much of the discussion which follows, on *i'rāb*, broadly 'inflection', is form-centred to an extent unknown in the West. Instead of identifying functional, semantic or logical categories such as 'subject' or 'nominative' or 'first person singular', and listing the different forms by which they may be realised, Sībawayhi identifies different formal states and processes, and exemplifies each one as it manifests itself in words of different classes. Thus, 'stabilisation' (or 'taking an -*a(n)* ending') occurs in both the *ism* and the *fi'l*: *ra'aytu Zaydan* 'I saw Zaid' and *lan yaf'ala* 'he will not act'; but 'stretching' (taking an -*i(n)* ending) occurs only in the *ism*, as in *marartu bi-Zaydin* 'I passed Zaid', and 'amputation' (apocope) only in the *fi'l*, as in *lam yaf'al* 'he has not done'. Had a Roman grammarian wanted to work in the same way, he would have decided not to discuss the parts of speech in turn, but instead to treat all the forms ending in the same letter together; those ending in -*a*, for example, would include verbs in the imperative singular, nouns, pronouns, adjectives and participles in the nominative and ablative singular, adverbs and prepositions. Although Sībawayhi works with notions like number, person and gender, they are to a large extent taken for granted: the emphasis is on form.

A natural consequence of a form-orientated linguistics is the handling of syntactic relations in terms of a change in form effected by an operation (*'amil*), whether implicit or explicit. Thus, the sentence *yaqūmu Zaydun* 'Zayd stands' contains two independent elements, neither entailing a relationship of dependency, whereas in *inna Zaydan lan yaqūma* 'truly Zayd will not stand', 'Zayd' is made dependent by *inna* 'truly' and *yaqūma* 'he will stand' by *lan* 'not'. The parallels with modern dependency grammar are more far-reaching than this simple example suggests.

A further manifestation of the Arab preoccupation with linguistic form is the profound interest in articulatory phonetics apparent from the very start of the Arab tradition. Both Sībawayhi and al-Ḥalīl (who died in 791), the compiler of a huge dictionary, provided a classification of the consonantal sounds of Arabic based on the *maḥraǧ*, 'area of emission', a broader notion than the Sanskrit *sthāna* and *karaṇa*, involving the specification of the point in the vocal tract at which the airstream is interrupted. Sībawayhi's list of sixteen *maḥāriǧ* was gradually reduced to five, which passed into the Hebrew and thence into the Western tradition. Recognition of nasality goes back to Sībawayhi himself, who offers the time-honoured test: 'if you hold your nose, the nasals cannot be produced.' Ibn Sīnā, known to the West as Avicenna (980-1037), included among his voluminous writings a treatise on the *ḥurūf* (the Arabic term *ḥarf*, pl. *ḥurūf*, functions like the Latin *littera*) which contained a detailed description of the anatomy and function of the larynx. The lively Islamic tradition of phonetic investigation, represented by a large number of writers from Sībawayhi on, was paralleled by a no less active interest among Hebrew grammarians.

The Arab interest in form and in physical phenomena was a characteristic rooted deeply in their culture, its manifestations visible not only in linguistics but throughout their intellectual life. It was from outside Islam that the impetus came to consider language from other points of view. In the second half of the eighth and during the ninth century many Greek texts were translated into Arabic (sometimes via Syriac), including the Aristotelian corpus. Under their influence, and particularly among grammarians belonging to the Muʿtazilite sect, a more philosophical approach to grammar took root, exemplified in the works of al-Fārābī (who died in 950) and az-Zaǧǧāǧī (who died in 949 or 951). Logic and grammar were compared and their respective domains delimited, and attention was given to such matters as the correct way to frame a definition, at approximately the same time as the assimilation of Aristotelian logic was causing a preliminary reassessment of the role of grammar in the West. Thus, later grammars such as Ibn Ājurrūm's (the famous *Ājurrūmiyya*) define the utterance as having form, composite, informative and conventional: the Aristotelian elements are obvious. (A further parallel with the development of grammar in the West is the popularity in the later Middle Ages of grammars in verse such as the *Alfiyya* by Ibn Mālik.)

The importance attached to the formal aspects of language is a natural consequence of the reasoning that, since language mirrors the world, it must be governed by the same laws. Since all phenomena perceived by the senses could be described in quantitative terms, so too could language. Grammarians sought regularities in language, particularly through observing *qiyās*, 'analogy', while natural philosophers, most notably the Pythagorean-influenced Jābir ibn Ḥayyān, traced the proportions found in natural phenomena in language. Whereas Western pre-Renaissance linguistics stressed those aspects of language which participated in the eternal and spiritual, Islamic scholars devoted equal attention to its earthly side. And yet by the time Western scholars were ready to appreciate the Arab approach, it had lost its impetus. The awakening to form experienced by Renaissance Europeans had nothing new to offer the Arabs. Arab linguists had travelled the same path centuries before; aware of the importance of form from the very start of their tradition, they had exhausted its possibilities. The Renaissance brought them no fresh tools to use. They were the lenders rather than the borrowers, contributing a few fundamental concepts from their rich stock to the founding of the Western disciplines of phonetics and morphology. They had much more to offer, but Western scholars chose to go their own way, arriving at the same insights in their own time, using their own methods.

## 3.2 India

The study of language in India arose out of the needs of religious ritual, and remained closely linked with religion for most of its history. At the most profound level the Vedic hymns acknowledge the mysterious nature and power of speech: 'Speech was divided into four parts known to inspired priests. Three parts, placed in hiding, mortals do not rouse to action; the fourth part of speech they speak' (*Rgveda* I 164.45). And yet, despite their fascination with the spiritual nature of speech, Indians concerned themselves with its physical aspect far earlier than Europeans did. The immediate impetus came from the practical needs of religious ritual. The Vedic hymns and prayers used in Brahmin rituals had been given definitive form near the start of the first millennium BC. Handed down from father to son, the text inevitably began to sound first old-fashioned, and then downright archaic, as the Sanskrit language gradually underwent change. Instead of updating the text, the Brahmins felt it imperative to maintain its traditional form as accurately as possible. To counteract the sloppy pronunciation of the younger generation – the usual response the world over to the effects of language change – they instituted formal training, supported by lists of the legitimate assimilatory features (*sandhi*) found in each collection of Vedic hymns, prefaced (or finished) by a summary of the theoretical notions underlying the practical instruction. Although very brief, usually only three or four pages in length, the outlines contained in these texts (called *prātiśākhyas*) amount to an introduction to the principles of articulatory phonetics. They centre on the Sanskrit alphabet, itself a masterpiece of phonemic analysis and articulatory systematisation:

a ā i ī u ū ṛ ṝ ḷ
e ai o au
k kh g gh ṅ
c ch j jh ñ
ṭ ṭh ḍ ḍh ṇ
t th d dh n
p ph b bh m
y r l v
ś ṣ s h

This order facilitates recognition of four basic categories: vowels (subdivided into monophthongs and diphthongs), plosives + nasals (the 'five groups of five'), glides and fricatives. These categories were described and subdivided with the aid of various subsidiary notions: articulator (*karaṇa*) and place of articulation (*sthāna*), voicing, aspiration, nasality, degree of closure. The systematic nature of Indian phonetic analysis – arrived at somewhere in the first half of the first millennium BC – provided Western scholars from about 1800 with the key to handling features such as voicing and aspiration in an orderly classificatory matrix.

The same attention to the physical aspect of speech is apparent in the oldest and best-known Sanskrit grammar to come down to us, Pāṇini's *Aṣṭādhyāyī* ('Eight Books'), written in the fifth or fourth century BC. The *Aṣṭādhyāyī* is very different from the hierarchically-structured grammars of Greco-Roman Antiquity, or even from Varro's more fluid characterisations. Instead of allowing the structure perceived in the language to dictate the overall shape of the work, as Donatus, for instance, does in beginning with the smallest units of speech and building up to the largest, Pānini attaches overriding importance to the presentation, the outer form, of the doctrine. Economy of expression dominates: not only does he use a large number of technical abbreviations and a telegraphic metalanguage (which has to be mastered by the student at the outset), but he also employs a dittoing procedure which enables him to avoid repeating a rule which applies to many different types of linquistic phenomena – at the expense of assembling together rules which have nothing more in common than being affected by this more powerful rule. Each rule is given equal prominence, down to those which govern a single word; the concept of 'exception', so integral a part of the Western tradition, is absent. Consequently, it is very difficult to form any impression of the structure of Sanskrit from the *Aṣṭādhyāyī* without protracted study. Traditionally, the young child would spend eight years memorising it before being shown how to apply its doctrine, for in order to generate even the simplest verb form, rules from all parts of the work must be applied. Not surprisingly, both commentaries, like Patañjali's huge and detailed *Mahābhāṣya*, (c. 150 BC), and simplified and rearranged versions of the *Aṣṭādhyāyī*, like Śarvavarman's *Kātantra* (before AD 400) and the *Siddhānta Kaumudī* by Bhaṭṭoji Dīkṣita (early seventeenth century), found large numbers of readers.

Underlying Pāṇini's work, and indeed that of all Indian grammarians, is the notion of 'root' as an abstract entity which never – or very rarely – manifests itself in actual speech, but provides the raw material which, after the operation of various phonological changes, becomes a base to which affixes may be added, eventually culminating in the spoken word. So much a part of the linguistic tradition was this that lists of roots were compiled from Pāṇini on. Pāṇini's treatment of morphology is therefore utterly different from that current in the ancient West. He uses no paradigms; instead, he relies on complex sequences of generative rules. To take a somewhat simplified example, to form the third person singular of the present tense of the verb 'go', √*gam*, we have to follow a procedure which involves the addition of a conventional marker indicating a present tense form: *laṭ*. A condition for the addition of *laṭ* to verbs is the insertion of an infix between root and suffix. In the case of roots of the class to which √*gam* belongs, this infix is *-a-*. Replacing the present tense marker with the third person singular ending *-ti* gives *\*gamati*, not yet a Sanskrit word. One further rule, prescribing the change of roots of the √*gam* type when followed by a *laṭ* suffix, remains to be applied, producing the actual Sanskrit form, *gacchati*. Less ponderous – once it has been mastered – than it sounds, this method provides elegant descriptions of much of the luxuriant morphology of Sanskrit. It is rather less appropriate for foreign beginners, however (and it is interesting to note that whereas those European grammarians of Sanskrit who had had the advantage of instruction from a native pandit adhered as closely as they could to the basically Paninian system, scholars based in Europe – notably Frank (1823) and the enormously influential Bopp (1824–37) – abandoned much of the apparatus of the Indian system of description, preferring to adapt the traditional framework of Greek and Latin grammar to accommodate Sanskrit.)

Accompanying Pāṇini's keen sense for the formal structure of language was a precise awareness of the separate domains of form and meaning. One feature of Indo-European languages where their relationship has repeatedly challenged grammarians is that of the nature of case: to what extent can the changes in the form of a noun as it discharges different grammatical functions in a sentence be equated with semantic or real-world categories? In the traditional Western analysis of a pre-sandhi sentence like *Devadattaḥ odanam pacati*, 'Devadatta cooks rice', *Devadattaḥ* is described as the subject of the active verb *pacati*, 'cooks', and therefore has the nominative, or subject, case-form; but in the corresponding passive sentence *odanaḥ Devadattena pacyate*, 'rice is being cooked by Devadatta', *odanaḥ* 'rice', is now in the nominative case, even though its relation to the act of cooking has not changed. Pāṇini circumvents the difficulty by setting up a series of categories, *kārakas*, which, although ultimately based on the syntactic relations through the cases, are semantic notions which can be manifested in many different ways: through a verb (active, passive, in the appropriate mood and tense), a preposition, or by word-formation, as well as by case endings. In our first example, the agent *kāraka* is expressed in the active verb form, *pacati*; the name of the actual agent therefore need not express agency (since a *kāraka* expressed in the verb should not be given double expression), but instead takes the umarked, or default, form, the nominative case. In the second sentence, it is the object *kāraka* which is expressed by the verb *pacyate*, 'is being cooked', and therefore 'rice', *odanaḥ*, is now left unmarked (i.e. nominative); the agent *kāraka*, on the other hand, now has to be expressed explicitly, this time through the instrumental case form, *Devadattena*. Although far more comprehensively elaborated, *kāraka* theory has much in common with the medieval Western doctrine of the *modi significandi*: both attempt to explain how it comes about that the same semantic content can be manifested in different lexical and syntactic structures within a given language. Parallels may be drawn too with Fillmore's 'deep cases' and with Tesnière's dependency syntax. (See Chapter 3, section 5, above).

As in the Western tradition, the problem of sentence meaning was tackled largely by philosophers rather than by grammarians, although occasionally, as in the case of Patañjali and Bhartṛhari, the two provinces coincided in one man. The Vedas again provided the focus: given that their very words were regarded as eternal and uncreated, their nature and status required investigation. The Mīmāṃsā school (third to second century BC) sought a philosophical basis for the Vedas in which linguistic issues played a large part. Its members propounded two opposing views of sentence meaning, both of which took the word as the unit. According to the first theory, sentence meaning was linear and cumulative, based on the word, an autonomous unit of thought and sense. Sentence meaning was simply the sum of the individual word meanings. According to the second, word meaning was defined by sentence meaning. Only when the listener had grasped how 'cow' and 'horse' stood in paradigmatic relation to one another in sentences like 'bring the cow' and 'bring the horse' could he attach any meaning to the isolated words 'cow' and 'horse'. These two views were in time overshadowed by the much more thorough-going work of Bhartṛhari (c. 450–510). In his *Vākyapadīya* he attempted to dislodge his fellow-grammarians from their complacent preoccupation with methodological technicalities by reminding them of the fundamental role of language and of grammar: 'just as all the universals of things depend upon the form of their words for their communication, so is this science the basis of all other sciences' (I 15). No knowledge is possible without the organising, sequential properties of language, so closely linked with memory. Even the child has residual traces of a knowledge of the word from its previous existence, on the basis of which both cognition and the use of the speech organs can arise – neither of them faculties which can be taught. But what is the nature of the words that one utters? 'Just as light has two powers, that of being revealed and that of being the revealer, similarly, all words have two distinct powers' (I 55). A particular relationship obtains between individual sounds and that which is revealed through them, the *sphoṭa*. The speech-essence, the source of the world of reality, goes through three stages in becoming manifest in human speech: the stage of indivisible reality or consciousness without extension in time, in which an idea occurs in a flash, complete; the intermediate stage in which the idea is set out sequentially, becoming a logically-organised linear thought capable of being verbalised (and already possessing certain features characteristic of a particular language); and the stage of producing audible words marked by the individual idiosyncrasies of the speaker. The total meaning of a sentence can no more be explained in terms of its parts than the meaning of a picture can be explained by listing the different colours used in it. 'Just as the meaning of the word is not understood from each sound, in the same way the meaning of the sentence is not understood from each word' (II 60). Meaning itself is indivisible: it bursts forth from the spoken utterance in a flash of intuition. Words, roots, suffixes, individual speech sounds, are an analytical convenience, a grammarian's fiction. By viewing utterance meaning as unitary and primary, and not dependent on individual words, Bhartṛhari provided the basis for a very powerful theory of meaning – one capable of dealing with ungrammatical utterances, with foreigners' grotesque but nevertheless comprehended attempts to communicate, with figurative language, and indeed with the suggestive power of language. Bhartṛhari's successors concentrated on figurative language, applying his teachings and their own to the study of Sanskrit poetry. In the ninth century Ānandavardhana developed a more comprehensive approach to the suggestive power of language in his *Dhvanyāloka*, studying factors such as intonation, emphasis, gesture, tone of voice, and sociocultural elements peculiar to a particular speech community. Traditional Indian semantics is now undergoing lively investigation and development by Indian scholars versed in both Indian and Western semantics.

## 3.3 China

In one respect the ancient Chinese world-view was strikingly similar to that of the pre-modern West, and in another unexpectedly dissimilar; and in each case this is reflected in their views on language. Perhaps the most conspicuous feature of the Chinese outlook is a belief in order. The universe was an ordered system, and everything within it had its place – heaven, the gods, the planets, man, the lower orders. To maintain this highly structured, hierarchical system Chinese society had recourse to the Confucian system of ethics. This system permeated the whole of society: nothing was without its niche, everything had its own meaning and purpose. It was incumbent upon human beings to discover the meaning of the phenomena around them. The second essential trait of the Chinese outlook, one which is visible as clearly in medicine as in linguistics, is a desire to function on two levels: broad, universal principles applicable to every sphere of existence, and individual, particular phenomena. Intermediate levels – generalisations relevant to a particular class of phenomena, for instance – were not investigated. These views naturally had their consequences both in the choice of fields of study and in the way in which they were pursued. If the aim of study is to discover the meaning of a phenomenon, then it will be inappropriate to remain upon the level of the phenomena themselves. Explanations must be sought on a higher level (unless the seeker is to revert to reductionism). Hence, in China as in the medieval West, astronomy merged into astrology and biology into the teleological and moralising remarks of medieval bestiaries. Chinese thinkers observed processes on one level, the physical, but sought explanations on another.

This attitude naturally had implications for the study of language. There was no notion of studying language 'in and for itself'; only those aspects were studied which were compatible with the Chinese world-view. So, for example, there are no comprehensive descriptions of Chinese grammar. Instead, language was used to fortify the ethical bases of Chinese society. For example, Confucius, when asked about the true nature of a government, replied that it was of the essence of a government (*zheng*) to be upright (*zheng*): the semantic connection reinforces the natural order of things, as in the medieval Western association of *reges* with *recte agendo*. Argumentation of this kind plays a large part in early Chinese ethics and philosophy, notably in the works of Confucius and Mencius. Essentially, the question asked was 'what light can language shed on the world?' That part of language most likely to illuminate the world was its meaningful aspect.

Consequently, it was the word which was the focus of Chinese linguistics – the word as the bearer or embodiment of meaning. Levels below the word – morphology and phonetics – could contribute nothing (phonology was a special case which we will consider later), while the study of meaning at a higher level was carried out by literary critics. Syntax was not pursued. Where the word as a meaningful entity is the centre of attention, then linguistic study will tend to focus on word-lists: vocabularies, glossaries, thesauruses, dictionaries. Lexicography and dialect studies, also concentrating on lexis, were the most highly developed branches of linguistics in pre-modern China.

The earliest dictionary, ascribed to a disciple of Confucius, Zi Xia, is the *Er Ya* ('Treasury of Fine Words', between the third and first centuries BC). It is divided into nineteen sections, most of which are semantic categories: names, idioms, difficult words, family relationships, occupations, tools, music, sky (both the calendar and climate), land, hills, mountains, water, plants, trees, insects and reptiles, fish, birds, wild animals, domestic animals. Any semantic classification suffers from certain limitations. Many words do not lend themselves to categorisation on this basis, a problem which the *Er Ya* acknowledged by reserving several sections for miscellaneous terms and words used figuratively. Perhaps more to the point, what of the difficulties faced by the reader of an unfamiliar text who wants to look up a strange character? To be told to look it up in a semantically-classified work puts him a similar plight to that of the Western child who asks how to spell a word and is told to look it up in an alphabetically-ordered dictionary. A path to a solution was suggested by the most famous of all Chinese dictionaries, the *Shuo Wen*

*Jie Zi* ('The Explanation of Simple and Derived Characters') (c. 100 AD). As its name suggests, the focus of classification has shifted from the meanings to the characters. Characters were assigned to one or another of six categories on the basis of their construction – iconic, symbolic, phonetic and phonetic loan, semantic compound, modified – and the semantic common factor, or radical, was isolated and used as the criterion of classification. The original list of 540 radicals was later reduced to 360, and finally to the list of 214 which is still in use today. Dictionaries which rely on radicals as their ordering criterion still have much in common with thesauruses, for all the characters which share the same radical will come together. Thus, all the characters with the 'man' radical come together, ensuring a bunch of words denoting human beings, and similarly words denoting liquids are grouped together because they have in common the 'water' radical, and so on. Under each radical characters are listed in order according to the number of strokes additional to the radical they have, making it possible to locate unfamiliar ones. Only in the present century, under Western influence, have Chinese lexicographers experimented with phonetic principles.

The celebrated distinction between 'full' and 'empty' words, taken over into Western linguistics as a straightforward opposition between words with lexical meaning and words serving only to express grammatical relationships, was in its original context a semantic distinction between words denoting objective concepts or things, and those which were essentially subjective, expressing the feelings and responses of the individual. This category included intensifiers, modal particles and also the verb 'to be' (which has greater assertive force in Chinese than in English).

One problem which Chinese scholars grappled with from very early times was that of indicating pronunciation in a script in which each character represented an entire word. For dialect studies in particular the lack of any means of phonetic representation was a significant handicap. Early works resorted to homophony, saying that character x sounded like character y. Some time before about 600 AD a more satisfactory technique was developed. Called *fanqie*, it involved the analysis of the syllable into two segments, (*a*) the initial vowel or consonant plus (*b*) the rest of the syllable, including the tone. Another syllable beginning with the same initial was found to represent (*a*), and one finishing with the same features as (*b*) to represent the second half. Thus, *dong* could be represented by *de hong*. The system was further refined to permit the indication of suprasegmental phenomena such as palatalisation. The *fanqie* analysis was structural in nature: it works with relationships between entities rather than with the entities in their own right, a procedure also characteristic of Chinese medicine. Not until the basic tenets of Indian teaching reached China with Buddhism, from the seventh century, was a kind of articulatory phonetics elaborated. Initial consonants were divided into five categories according to place of articulation: lips, tongue (=dentals), incisors (= dental affricates), molars (= velars), throat (= laryngeals). Although degrees of voicing were recognised, palatalisation – not catered for by the Indian system – was ignored. Interestingly, although a popular version of Indian grammar was introduced at the same time, it failed to undergo further development. Only with the arrival of Western grammar at the end of the nineteenth century did Chinese scholars give serious consideration to the grammar of their own language. The celebrated product of this meeting was Ma Jian Zhong's *Ma Shi Wen Tong* (1898), a grammar which sought to apply 'universal' (i.e. Latin) categories as closely as possible to Chinese. Only in the present century – when political vicissitudes have permitted – have scholars such as Wang Li attempted to devise a more sensitive grammatical structure for Chinese, a process in which many Western scholars, particularly in America, have joined.

## REFERENCES

Where these are simply evaluated within particular approaches they appear in the text above. Where they are more generally useful they are listed below (with brief references in the text).

## GENERAL REFERENCES AND FURTHER READING

Items are presented in relation to the places and eras surveyed. A reader's further study is best guided by the titles in each section.

### I. General (including works relevant to several sections)

Amirova, T.A., Ol'chovikov, B.A. and V. Roždestvenskij, Ju. (1980) *Abriss der Geschichte der Linguistik*, transl. from the Russian (1975) by Meier, B., VEB Bibliographisches Institut, Leipzig.

Arens, H. (1st ed. 1955, 2nd ed. 1969) *Sprachwissenschaft: Der Gang ihrer Entwicklung von der Antike bis zur Gegenwart* 2 vols., Athenäum Fischer, Frankfurt.

Asher, R.E. and Henderson, E.J.A. (eds) (1981) *Towards a History of Phonetics*, The University Press, Edinburgh.

Auroux, S. *et al.* (1985) *La linguistique fantastique*, Joseph Clims, Paris.

Borst, A. (1957–63) *Der Turmbau von Babel: Geschichte der Meinungen über Ursprung und Vielfalt der Sprachen und Völker* 3 vols., Anton Hiersemann, Stuttgart.

Bynon, T. and Palmer, F.R. (eds) (1986) *Studies in the History of Western Linguistics in Honour of R.H. Robins*, Cambridge University Press, Cambridge.

Foucault, M. (1966) *Les mots et les choses*, Gallimard, Paris, transl. into English as *The Order of Things: An Archaeology of the Human Sciences* (1970), Tavistock, London.

*Histoire Epistémologie Langage* (1979– ).

*Historiographia Linguistica* (1974– ).

Hymes, D. (1974) *Studies in the History of Linguistics: Traditions and Paradigms*, Indiana University Press, Bloomington, Ind.

Koerner, E.F.K. (1978) *Western Histories of Linguistic Thought: An Annotated Chronological Bibliography 1822–1976*, Studies in the History of Linguistics II, Benjamins, Amsterdam.

Parret, H. (1976) *History of Linguistic Thought and Contemporary Linguistics*, Walter de Gruyter, Berlin and New York.

Robins, R.H. (1st ed. 1967, 2nd ed. 1979) *A Short History of Linguistics*, Longman, London.

Schmitter, P. (1982) *Untersuchungen zur Historiographie der Linguistik: Struktur — Methodik — theoretische Fundierung*, Tübinger Beiträge zur Linguistik 181, Gunter Narr, Tübingen.

Sebeok, T.A. (1975) *Current Trends in Linguistics 13: Historiography of Linguistics*, 2 vols., Mouton, The Hague.

Todorov, Ts. (1972) 'Le sense des sons', *Poétique* II: 446–62.

## II. Greco-Roman Antiquity

Allen, W.S. (1981) 'The Greek contribution to the history of phonetics', in Asher and Henderson (1981): 115–22.

Arens, H. (1984) *Aristotle's Theory of Language and its Tradition: Texts from 500 to 1750*, Studies in the History of Linguistics 29, Benjamins, Amsterdam.

Baratin, M. and Desbordes, F. (1981) *L'analyse linguistique dans l'Antiquité classique I. Les théories*, Klincksieck, Paris.

Collart, J. (1954) *Varron grammairien latin*, Publications de la Faculté des Lettres de l'Université de Strasbourg 121, Les Belles Lettres, Paris.

Coseriu, E. (1975) *Die Geschichte der Sprachphilosophie von der Antike bis zur Gegenwart: eine Übersicht, I. Von der Antike bis Leibniz*, 2nd ed., Tübinger Beiträge zur Linguistik II, Gunter Narr, Tübingen.

Derbolav, J. (1972) *Platons Sprachphilosophie im Kratylos und in den späteren Schriften*, Wissenschaftliche Buchgesellschaft, Darmstadt.

Holtz, L. (1981) *Donat et la tradition de l'enseignement grammatical: étude sur l'Ars Donati et sa diffusion (IVe-IXe siècle) et édition critique*, CNRS, Paris.

Householder, F.W. (1981) *The Syntax of Apollonius Dyscolus translated, and with commentary*, Studies in the History of Linguistics 23, Benjamins, Amsterdam.

Hovdhaugen, E. (1982) *Foundations of Western Linguistics: From the Beginning to the End of the First Millennium AD*, Universitetsforlaget, Oslo.

Keil, H. (1855–80) *Grammatici Latini*, 7 vols + suppl., Teubner, Leipzig, repr. 1981, Georg Olms, Hildesheim.

Kemp, A. (1986) 'The *Tekhnē grammatikē* of Dionysius Thrax translated into English', *Historiographia Linguistica*, 13: 343–63.

Law, V. (1986) 'Late Latin grammars in the early Middle Ages: a typological history', *Historiographia Linguistica*, 13: 365–80.

McKeon, R. (1946–7) 'Aristotle's conception of language and the arts of language', *Classical Philology*, 41: 193–206 and 42: 21–50.

Pinborg, J. (1975) 'Classical Greece', in Sebeok, T.A. (1975): 69–126.

Schmidt, R.T. (1979) *Die Grammatik der Stoiker*, transl. from the Latin (1839) by Hülser,

K., bibliography by Egli, U., Schriften zur Linguistik 12, Vieweg, Braunschweig and Wiesbaden.

Steinthal, H. (1st ed. 1863, 2nd ed. 1890–1) *Geschichte der Sprachwissenschaft bei den Griechen und Römern mit besonderer Rücksicht auf die Logik*, Ferdinand Dümmler, Berlin, repr. Georg Olms, Darmstadt 1961.

Uhlig, G. (1883–1910) *Grammatici Graeci*, Teubner, B.G. Leipzig, repr. Georg Olms, Heidelberg (1979).

Wouters, A. (1979) *The Grammatical Papyri from Graeco-Roman Egypt: Contributions to the Study of the 'Ars grammatica' in Antiquity*, Verhandelingen van de Koninklijke Academie voor Wetenschappen, Letteren en Schone Kunsten van België, Klasse der Letteren 41.

## III. The Middle Ages

Ahlqvist, A. (ed.) (1987) *Les premières grammaires des vernaculaires européens* (= *Histoire Epistémologie Langage* 9.1).

Bursill-Hall, G.L. (1975) 'The Middle Ages', in Sebeok, T.A. (1975): 179–230.

Bursill-Hall, G.L. (1981) *A Census of Medieval Latin Grammatical Manuscripts*, Grammatica Speculativa 4, Frommann-Holzboog, Stuttgart-Bad Cannstatt.

Covington, M.A. (1984) *Syntactic Theory in the High Middle Ages: Modistic Models of Sentence Structure*, Cambridge Studies in Linguistics, 39, Cambridge University Press, Cambridge.

Covington, M.A. (1986) 'Grammatical theory in the Middle Ages', in Bynon and Palmer (1986): 23–42.

Hunt, R.W. (1980) *Collected Papers on the History of Grammar in the Middle Ages*, Studies in the History of Linguistics, 5, Benjamins, Amsterdam.

Law, V. (1982) *The Insular Latin Grammarians*, Studies in Celtic History 3, The Boydell Press, Woodbridge.

Law, V. (1985) 'Linguistics in the earlier Middle Ages: the Insular and Carolingian grammarians', *Transactions of the Philological Society*: 171–93.

Pinborg, J. (1967) *Die Entwicklung der Sprachtheorie im Mittelalter*, Aschendorff, Münster and Frost-Hansen, Copenhagen.

Rosier, I. (1983) *La grammaire spéculative des Modistes*, Presses Universitaires de Lille, Lille.

## IV. Since the Renaissance

Aarsleff, H. (1976, repr. with corrections 1983) *The Study of Language in England, 1780–1860* University of Minnesota, Minneapolis and Athlone, London.

Aarsleff, H. (1982) *From Locke to Saussure: Essays on the Study of Language and Intellectual History*, Athlone, London.

Alston, R.C. (1965–73) *A Bibliography of the English Language from the Invention of Printing to the Year 1800*, 11 vols., E.J. Arnold, Leeds and Bradford.

*Anthropological Linguistics* 5.1. (1963): *History of Linguistics*.

Apel, K.O. (1963) *Die Idee der Sprache in der Tradition des Humanismus von Dante bis Vico*, Archiv für Begriffsgeschichte 8, Bouvier, Bonn.

Benfey, Th. (1869) *Geschichte der Sprachwissenschaft und orientalischen Philologie in Deutschland seit dem Anfange des 19. Jahrhunderts mit einem Rückblick auf die früheren Zeiten,* Geschichte der Wissenschaften in Deutschland, Neuere Zeit 8, Cotta, Munich, repr. 1965.

Beyer, A. (1981) *Deutsche Einflüsse auf die englische Sprachwissenschaft im 19. Jahrhundert,* Göppinger Arbeiten zur Germanistik No. 324, Kümmerle, Göppingen.

Brunot, F. (1966– ) *Histoire de la langue française des origines à nos jours,* revised edition, Armand Colin, Paris.

Carvalhâo Buescu, M. (1983) *O estudo das línguas exóticas no século XVI,* Biblioteca breve, Serie pensamento e ciência 71, Lisbon.

Carvalhâo Buescu, M. (1983) *Babel ou a ruptura do signo: a gramática e os gramáticos portugueses do século XVI,* Imprensa Nacional, Lisbon.

Dobson, E.J. (1st ed. 1957, 2nd ed. 1968) *English Pronunciation 1500–1700 I: Survey of the Sources,* Clarendon Press, Oxford.

Droixhe, D. (1978) *La linguistique et l'appel de l'histoire, 1600–1800: rationalisme et révolutions positivistes,* Droz, Geneva.

Dubois, C.-G. (1970) *Mythe et langage au seizième siècle,* Ducros, Bordeaux.

Formigari, L. (1970) *Linguistica ed empirismo nel Seicento inglese,* Laterza, Bari.

Gipper, H. and P. Schmitter (1979) *Sprachwissenschaft und Sprachphilosophie im Zeitalter der Romantik: ein Beitrag zur Historiographie der Linguistik,* Tübinger Beiträge zur Linguistik 123, Gunter Narr, Tübingen (revised version of their article in Sebeok (1975): 481–606).

Hankamer, P. (1927) *Die Sprache, ihr Begriff und ihre Deutung im sechzenhnten und siebzehnten Jahrhundert: ein Beitrag zur Frage der literaturhistorischen Gliederung des Zeitraums,* Bonn, repr. 1965, Georg Olms, Hildesheim.

Hanzeli, V.E. (1969) *Missionary Linguistics in New France: A Study of Seventeenth- and Eighteenth-Century Descriptions of American Indian Languages,* Mouton, The Hague.

Hymes, D. and J. Fought (1981) *American Structuralism,* Mouton, The Hague (revised version of their article in Sebeok (1975): 903–1176).

Jankowsky, K.R. (1972) *The Neogrammarians: A Re-evaluation of their Place in the Development of Linguistic Science,* Mouton, The Hague.

Jellinek, M.H. (1913–14) *Geschichte der neuhochdeutschen Grammatik von den Anfängen bis auf Adelung,* 2 vols., Carl Winter, Heidelberg.

Kayser, W. (1930) 'Böhmes Natursprachenlehre und ihre Grundlagen' *Euphorion,* 31: 521–62, transl. into French by J. Launay, 'La doctrine du langage naturel chez Jacob Boehme et ses sources', *Poétique,* 11 (1972): 337–66.

Knowlson, J. (1975) *Universal Language Schemes in England and France 1600–1800,* University of Toronto Press, Toronto and Buffalo.

Lehmann, W.P. (1967) *A Reader in Nineteenth-Century Historical Indo-European Linguistics,* Indiana University Press, Bloomington, Ind.

Lepschy, G. (1970) *A Survey of Structural Linguistics,* André Deutsch, London.

Lepschy, G. (1986) 'European Linguistics in the twentieth century', in Bynon and Palmer (1986): 189–201.

Michael, I. (1970) *English Grammatical Categories and the Tradition to 1800,* Cambridge University Press, Cambridge.

Muller, J.-C. (1986) 'Early stages of language comparison from Sassetti to Sir William Jones (1786)', *Cratylus* 31: 1–31.

Padley, G.A. (1976) *Grammatical Theory in Western Europe 1500—1700: The Latin Tradition*, Cambridge University Press, Cambridge.

Padley, G.A. (1st ed. 1985, 2nd ed. 1988) *Grammatical Theory in Western Europe 1500—1700: Trends in Vernacular Grammar* I and II, Cambridge University Press, Cambridge.

Pedersen, H. (1931) *The Discovery of Language: Linguistic Science in the Nineteenth Century*, transl. from the Danish (1924) by Spargo, J.W., Harvard University Press, Cambridge, Mass., repr. 1962, Indiana University Press, Bloomington.

Percival, W.K. (1975) 'The grammatical tradition and the rise of the vernaculars', in Sebeok, T.A. (1975): 231–75.

Percival, W.K. (1984) 'The reception of Hebrew in sixteenth-century Europe: the impact of the Cabbala', *Historiographia Linguistica* 11: 21–38.

Ricken, U. (n.d.) *Grammaire et philosophie au siècle des Lumières*, Publications de l'Université de Lille III, Lille.

Rousseau, J. (1984) 'La racine arabe et son traitement par les grammairiens européens (1505–1831)', *Bulletin de la Société de Linguistique de Paris* 79: 285–321.

Salmon, V. (1979) *The Study of Language in 17th-Century England*, Studies in the History of Linguistics 17, Benjamins, Amsterdam.

Salmon, V. (1986) 'Effort and achievement in seventeenth-century British linguistics', in Bynon and Palmer (1986): 69–95.

Stengel, E. (1976) *Chronologisches Verzeichnis französischer Grammatiken vom Ende des 14. bis zum Ausgange des 18. Jahrhunderts, nebst Angabe der bisher ermittelten Fundorte derselben*, new ed. with supplement by H.-J. Niederehe, Studies in the History of Linguistics 8, Benjamins, Amsterdam.

Tavoni, M., ed. (1st ed. 1987, 2nd ed. 1988) *Renaissance Linguistics Archive 1350—1700: A First (Second) Print-Out from the Secondary-Sources Data-Base*, Istituto di Studi Rinascimentali, Ferrara.

Trabalza, C. (1908) *Storia della grammatica italiana*, Ulrico Hoepli, Milan, repr. 1963, Arnaldo Ferrari, Bologna.

Verburg, P.A. (1952) *Taal en Functionaliteit: een historisch-critische studie over de opvattingen aangaande de functies der taal vanaf de prae-humanistische philologie van Orleans tot de rationalistische linguistiek van Bopp*, H. Veenman & Zonen, Wageningen.

Worth, D.S. (1983) *The Origins of Russian Grammar: Notes on the State of Russian Philology before the Advent of Printed Grammars*, Slavica, Columbus, Ohio.

# VI. Non-European Traditions

## *Armenia*

Adontz, N. (1970) *Denys de Thrace et les commentateurs arméniens*, transl. from the Russian (1915) by R. Hotterbeex, Imprimerie Orientaliste, Louvain.

## *Mesopotamia*

Black, J. (1984) *Sumerian Grammar in Babylonian Theory*, Studia Pohl: Series Maior 12, Biblical Institute, Rome.

## Persia

Windfuhr, G.L. (1979) *Persian Grammar: History and State of its Study*, Trends in Linguistics: State-of-the-Art Reports 12, Mouton, The Hague.

## Judaism

Bacher, W. (1975) *Die Angänge der hebräischen Grammatik und Die hebräische Sprachwissenschaft vom 10. bis zum 16. Jahrhundert*, Studies in the History of Linguistics 4, Benjamins, Amsterdam (first published 1895 and 1892).

Hirschfeld, H. (1926) *Literary History of Hebrew Grammarians and Lexicographers Accompanied by Unpublished Texts* Oxford University Press, Oxford.

Swiggers, P. (1979) 'L'histoire de la grammaire hébraïque jusqu'au XVIe siècle, *Orientalia Lovaniensia Periodica* 10: 183–93.

## Islam

Diem, W. (1983) 'Sekundärliteratur zur einheimischen arabischen Grammatikschreibung', in Veersteegh, C.H.M., Koerner, K. and Niederehe, H.-J. (eds), *The History of Linguistics in the Near East*, Studies in the History of Linguistics 28, Benjamins, Amsterdam and Philadelphia: 195–250.

Owens, J. (1988) *The Foundations of Grammar: An Introduction to Medieval Arabic Grammatical Theory*, Studies in the History of the Language Sciences 45, Benjamins, Amsterdam.

Semaan, Kh.I. (1968) *Linguistics in the Middle Ages: Phonetic Studies in Early Islam*, E.J. Brill, Leiden.

Sezgin, F. (1984) *Geschichte des arabischen Schrifttums 9. Grammatik bis c. 430 H.*, E.J. Brill, Leiden.

Versteegh, C.H.M. (1977) *Greek Elements in Arabic Linguistic Thinking*, Studies in Semitic Languages and Linguistics 7, E.J. Brill, Leiden.

## India

Allen, W.S. (1953) *Phonetics in Ancient India*, London Oriental Series 1, Oxford University Press, London.

Cardona, G. (1976) *Pāṇini: A Survey of Research*, Mouton, The Hague.

Nitti-Dolci, L. (1972) *The Prākṛita Grammarians*, translated from the French (1938) by P. Jhā, Motilal Banarsidass, Delhi.

Raja, K. Kunjunni (1963) *Indian Theories of Meaning*, The Adyar Library Series 91, Madras.

Scharfe, H. (1977) *A History of Indian Literature 5.2: Grammatical Literature*, Otto Harrassowitz, Wiesbaden.

Staal, J.F. (1972) *A Reader on the Sanskrit Grammarians*, The MIT Press, Cambridge, Mass. and London.

*The Far East*

Halliday, M.A.K. (1981) 'The origin and early development of Chinese phonological theory', in Asher and Henderson (1981): 123–40.

Miller, R.A. (1975) 'The Far East', in Sebeok, T.A. (1975): 1213–64.

Miller, R.A. (1976) *Studies in the Grammatical Tradition in Tibet*, Studies in the History of Linguistics 6, Benjamins, Amsterdam.

# 23

LANGUAGE ENGINEERING:
SPECIAL LANGUAGES

DONALD C. LAYCOCK and PETER MÜHLHÄUSLER

## 1. INTRODUCTION

Language has been compared variously with either bodily organs such as legs or hands, or else man-made tools like axes and hammers. Related to the view that language is a mental organ is that it is optimally suited to the requirements of human communication and that it is therefore best left alone: given no human interference it will adapt to the communicative purpose it is put to. If language is viewed as a tool, however, there is ample room for the possibility of a misfit between language and the world or its communicative tasks. This constitutes a justification for direct human interference in order to make it a more adequate tool.

As the language metaphors of linguistics change, so do their views on the legitimacy and indeed feasibility of language engineering. What was thought to be inadvisable and impossible within American structuralism, for instance, seems a legitimate concern to those working within the developmental paradigm pioneered by Bailey in the late 1970s.

Our concern here is twofold. First we wish to discuss the theoretical limits within which all human interference with language must take place. Second, we would like to analyse a number of different types of such interference and explore their historical roots. In doing this we have opted to combine recent insights into linguistic naturalness with more traditional terminology.

The parameters of naturalness and artificiality have not always been properly separated in past discussions. In particular, one can observe a tendency to label as 'natural' any solution that draws lexical or grammatical material from an existing linguistic system. It is for this reason that we shall

843

avail ourselves of the widely used distinction between *a priori* and *a posteriori* languages. *A priori* languages are constructed from scratch, their roots being selected on the basis of theoretical philosophical considerations rather than adapted from real human languages. *A posteriori* languages, on the other hand, typically are simplifications or adaptations of one or more existing languages. A number of artificial languages, e.g. Schleyer's Volapük or the proposals made by Comenius, are of a mixed type.

The attraction of *a priori* systems is perceived to be that they offer the possibility of encoding language–independent universal logic. In actual fact, in the absence of such a logic, they tend to be very closely based, in their semantic properties, on the European languages spoken by their inventors and hence turn out to be *a posteriori* languages in disguise. It is not clear to us whether totally language-independent *a priori* languages can be created in principle. The attraction of *a posteriori* languages is often seen to be their 'naturalness'. In practice, the vast majority of special languages have been derived from a very small number of Standard Average European (SAE) languages (principally Romance) and hence reflect the culture-specific semantics of only a small part of the world's population. In this connection, proposals such as Pham Xuan Thai's Frater, an *a posteriori* language based on Latin, Greek, Chinese, Japanese and 'other non-Aryan speech communities' are an interesting exception.

## 2. THEORETICAL CONSIDERATIONS: FORMAL PROPERTIES

Whilst it is possible in principle to add to, subtract from and permutate an existing linguistic structure in an almost infinite number of ways and/or to invent entirely new languages from scratch, in practice many constraints operate if the outcome is to be a communication system which human beings can handle. Further constraints arise if the requirement is to create a language that can be acquired by children and yet others if the requirement is that it should lend itself to acquisition by adults without formal instruction. Quite different limitations obtain when communication between species or with the inhabitants of imagined or real other worlds are at issue. Yet other constraints need to be considered when languages are to be used by and with machines.

Let us explore first the notion of 'possible human language'. It has been characterised either in terms of a set of abstract principles, as in Chomsky's more recent writings, or else in terms of more superficial implicational patterns which lay down the limited possibilities for the combination of surface properties of languages such as word order, the encoding of causatives or the formation of relative clauses. Typologists of the school represented by Greenberg and Comrie note that only a small subset of all mathematically conceivable combinations of features are found in actual languages. Whilst their ultimate aim of discovering those typological features on which the maximum number of other features depends has been achieved only in part, such studies as are available nevertheless tell us a great deal about the highly restricted options of human languages in encoding certain concepts.

Derivations from typological studies include the study of language change, language acquisition, pidginisation and creolisation as well as the notion of 'linguistic naturalness', a gradient concept ranging from the most natural to the most abnatural. The term 'unnatural' is reserved for phenomena that cannot be produced by the human speech organs or handled by the human intellectual apparatus. Examples of unnatural phenomena include sound which can only be produced if the lips are enlarged by wooden plates and the effects of knocking out one or more of the front teeth. However, as natural human languages can be expected to function in conjunction with natural human activities, claims that languages are excessively affected by, for example, the chewing of the areca nut (as has been said of the Santa Cruz language in the Solomon Islands), or by excessive teeth-chattering from the cold (Eskimo), or by extreme heat (African and Pacific Island languages), are nonsense. Languages devised for extraterrestrial communication and computer languages are also unnatural in the technical sense.

'Naturalness' is considered to be a property of human language in general, though the degree to which languages approach the most natural end of the continuum differs. According to Bickerton (1981, 1984), for instance, creoles are maximally natural, whilst old cultural languages such as French or English are located at the other end of the spectrum. Whatever the degree of naturalness in an individual language, the following observations hold for all languages:

(i) The presence of a less natural category implies that of a more natural one. Trial, for instance, implies dual which in turn implies plural (at least with nouns). The reverse is not the case.

(ii) More natural categories are acquired before less natural ones: word final [p] is acquired before [b] and [t] is acquired before [θ] in all positions.

(iii) The maintenance of less natural categories requires more nurture and formal learning than that of more natural ones.

The characterisation of linguistic naturalness is rendered difficult by the presence of two basic requirements to language: that it be produced and that it be perceived. Unless one is dealing with an extremely limited language, e.g. one consisting of only the forms [mama], [pupu] and [dodo], it is inevitable that there is a conflict between optimalisation of production (phonological naturalness) and optimalisation of perception (morphological naturalness).

Generally speaking, what is easier to produce is more difficult to distinguish and vice versa. The requirement of one form = one meaning can cause a high degree of abnaturalness in production. For example, if the English concept 'more than one' was expressed invariably by [s], the resulting plurals of *rat*, *dog* and *rose* would be a rather natural [ræts] next to almost unpronounceable [dogs] and [rœuzs]. The requirement of one form = one meaning has other implications for perception; languages that rank high on the morphological naturalness scale will favour synthesis or polysynthesis such that words consist of many smaller parts, each of them with their fixed meaning. Polysynthesis, as is well known to typologists, virtually excludes fusion and similar natural phonological processes. Language engineers have seldom appealed to such principles in a conscious fashion. Instead, in most instances they seem to have opted unconsciously for strategies optimalising morphological naturalness (*a posteriori* languages such as Esperanto being a good example). This is defensible if languages are to be used among second-language adult speakers. Children, on the other hand, tend to require a considerable amount of phonological naturalness as well and will change languages in the direction of greater pronounceability.

Whereas the understanding of linguistic naturalness among language engineers has been very limited, the notions of simplicity and simplification, the former referring to the end product, the latter to the process leading to it, have played a much more important role. At the most general level simplicity relates to the requirement of expressing the maximum number of distinctions by means of the most economical linguistic apparatus. In practice, any act of engineering which increases the coverage of grammatical rules, removes contextual conditions for their application or eliminates competing rules that do the same job, contributes to the overall simplicity of the resulting system. Above all other things it means that lexical irregularities are replaced, as much as possible, by grammatical regularities.

Technical simplicity is a great virtue for machine languages and in areas of human language, such as scientific terminologies. Human processing skills, limitations on time and other human 'performance' factors impose quite severe limitations on simplicity in languages for human use. Thus, whilst a computer can cope with a convention which expresses the number 17 as two + two + two + two + two + two + two + two + one, human beings cannot. Instead, more number stems are needed. It appears that human languages have only very limited leeway for shifting the boundary between lexicon and grammar. However, this principle is often found to be violated, particularly in *a priori* languages.

In a language imagined by Tyssot de Patot (1710), for example, the numerals are expressed by the successive consonants of the language (*b* is '1', *d* is '2', *p* is '10', and '21' is expressed *dpb*). Even fewer numerical roots are used by John Weilgart, in aUI, his 'language of space' (Weilgart 1968); the first five numerals are expressed by five nasalised vowels, and the next five by the same vowels lengthened (represented in his system by a̠, e̠, i̠, o̠, u̠, A̠, E̠, I̠, O̠, U̠).

Next to violating constraints on the boundary between lexis and grammar in human languages, the promotion of maximum simplicity also clashes with considerations of naturalness within grammar and grammatical components. Thus, from the point of view of simplicity, a system which adds a plural ending every time more than one of an entity is mentioned would seem preferable to one where plural endings occur with some lexical stems only. Applying this principle English should have plural forms such as *traffics, funs, wheats* and pronouns such as *Is, yous* and *hes, shes* and *its*.

From the point of view of naturalness, the most natural environment for plural marking are nouns referring to human beings, followed by animates, countable objects, mass nouns and finally abstract terms. The absence of a form such as *funs* is thus natural, but an irregularity in the technical sense.

Other examples are the Esperanto forms *patro* (stem *patr* + noun marker *-o*) and *patrino* (stem *patr* 'father' + *in* 'feminine' + noun marker *o*). Here we are dealing with a violation of the principle that what is prominent in the perception or experience of speakers of a language should be encoded by simple lexical items. Since the mother tends to be more central to the experience of children than their father, the direction of the derivation should be the reverse of what it is in Esperanto; considerations such as the requirement that languages should be free from sexism, racism and so forth also militate against this Esperanto form.

The principle just mentioned is known as Zipf's Law and it raises another important issue, namely whether languages are in essence iconic or arbitrary. This is not the place to go into detail about the history of this debate. Instead, some areas where iconicity appears to have been regarded as important by language engineers will be briefly illustrated.

Lexical stems can be motivated in two senses, either by being a direct icon of the entities they refer to (onomatopoeia) or else being made up of sound segments that are iconic of aspects of the real world, e.g. [i] for smallness or proximity, [t] for abruptness and so forth. Again, this is the system of Weilgart's aUI, where, for instance, the basic vowels a̠, e̠, i̠, o̠, u̠, represent 'space, movement, light, life, human'; but such a system is proposed as early as 1636 by M. Mersenne, in his *Harmonie universelle*, where the vowels represent the following qualities:

a̠ and o̠= what is great and noble

    e̠= delicate, subtle things, suitable for the representation of sadness and mourning

    i̠= very thin, small things

o͟= the expression of great passion

u͟= dark, hidden things

(Knowlson 1975: 67–8, which see for further examples).

In George Dalgarno's philosophical language, presented in his *Ars signorum* (1661), words tend to have a basic root shape, with the differentiations being expressed by vowels, or by inserted consonants (*r* is 'opposite', *l* 'the mean between two extremes'). Such minimal distinctions are of course totally at odds with the important principle of redundancy in natural language, since the slightest interference in the channel (noise of any kind) will obliterate essential distinctions. Pronouns and demonstratives in Dalgarno's language, for instance, are (using some Greek letters):

*lal* 'I', *hηl* 'thou', *lel* 'he', *lol* 'this',

l υl *'itself'*, *lul* 'who'.

Mishearing the vowel could lead to very serious misunderstanding. Constructing languages entirely out of iconic segments or lexical stems often means having to give up considerations of the next step of iconicity, morphological or constructional iconicity (cf. Mayerthaler 1981). With this type the length and the morphological complexity of a lexical item are related to both the already mentioned cultural prominence and naturalness. Thus, a word referring to great great great grandmother is iconically encoded if it is longer than that for great great grandmother, great grandmother, grandmother and mother, and counter-iconically if it is not. Similarly, plural forms of nouns should be longer or morphologically more complex than singular ones and past tense forms of stative verbs longer than non-past forms. Thus, Esperanto, where equally long and morphologically complex forms are required for all tenses, is not ideally encoded, a problem which does not arise with Volapük where non-present forms are morphologically more complex than present ones.

Little is known about iconicity in word order other than the existence of certain general principles, such as the fact that prominence of a topic should be reflected by its appearance in a syntactically prominent position or sequence of events should be mirrored by sequence of clauses. No examples of conscious attempts to introduce syntactic iconicity are known to the authors.

Attempts to rationalise the pronunciation of artificial languages have been either absent or rudimentary. Thus, highly marked sounds such as [y] and [ø] are found in Volapük, and the distinction between [l] and [r] is found in most of the twentieth-century languages such as Esperanto, Ido, etc. including Frater which is allegedly based on Chinese and Japanese as well as European languages, and complex consonant clusters are encountered in many of them. Much more attention is usually paid to streamlining the writing systems of these languages e.g. by eliminating digraphs or special symbols. This, of course, is in line with the general observation that most artificial languages are derived from a written form of language and designed to facilitate written in preference to oral intercommunication. Whereas some *a priori* languages lend themselves to the former only, artificial languages designed exclusively for oral communication are very rare, a possible example being Schwörer's Kolonialdeutsch (1916), designed for the use of the coloured workforce of a German world empire.

Whereas phonetic or phonological naturalness in the sense of optimalising production is not much in evidence, concern for sound symbolism or onomatopoeic iconicity is encountered frequently, particularly in *a priori* languages. Thus, the idea that the vowel (i) should stand for smallness, (a) for largeness and (o) for roundness or universality is encountered in a number of proposals, though in most instances such iconicity tends to be postulated in an impressionistic manner and be mixed with culture-specific conventions.

The paucity of information in the areas of syntactic and phonetic natural-ness relates to the more general observation that not all levels of language have been equally susceptible to engineering. Deliberate interference with human languages seems to be guided by the following hierarchy:

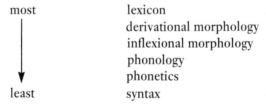

degree of interference

| most | lexicon |
| | derivational morphology |
| | inflexional morphology |
| | phonology |
| | phonetics |
| least | syntax |

Language creation often exploits the principle that there are trade relationships between the levels. Thus, the size of the irregular lexicon is reduced by promoting a more powerful derivational morphology in many *a posteriori* proposals.

At each level a number of operations can be carried out, mainly addition, subtraction, substitution and rearrangement or a combination of these (poly-systemic). Such processes are common in the mechanical alterations of natural languages called 'ludlings' (Laycock 1972), or play-languages of the Pig Latin type. Some examples of each type follow:

| Addition: | you can talk Gree | –yougree cangree talkgree Greegree |
| | you can talk skimono jive | –skyou skcan sktalk skskimono skjive |

| Subtraction: | fabulous | –fab |
| | snake+shark | –snark |
| | sado-masochism | –sadie-maisie |
| Substitution: | Ei, da sitzt 'ne Flieg' an der Wand | –i, di sitzt 'ni Flig' in dir Wind |
| Rearrangement: | look at the old woman | –cool ta the dillow namow |
| | butterfly | –flutterby |
| Polysystemic: | Pig Latin | –Igpay Atinlay |
| | | –withus youvus govus |

Arguably the most important and least heeded property of 'natural' human languages is their versatility. Far from being closed rule-governed systems they are open-ended and only partially governed by rules. The human language ability is rule-changing rather than (as Chomsky and his followers have it) rule-governed creativity. Thus, an important measure for the success of artificial languages should be their adaptive creativity. It can be noted that most invented systems, in particular *a priori* systems, are ill-suited to change. The history of languages such as Esperanto demonstrates that *a posteriori* languages also suffer from this deficiency. Those who are in the business of language elevation (e.g. in the case of Afrikaans, Bahasa Indonesia etc.) have begun to cater for change, though this remains one of the least researched areas.

The uneven coverage of different levels of language is encountered again with rank or size-level. Engineering typically concentrates on the rank of word, maximally the sentence. Very little regard is paid to paragraph or discourse organisation in spite of the fact that languages can differ greatly in their discourse pragmatics; sharing words and grammatical structures is insufficient in bringing about an understanding between different groups.

## 3. THEORETICAL CONSIDERATIONS: FUNCTIONAL PROPERTIES

The study of language functions is still at a pre-theoretical stage and no conclusive findings exist about either the number of functions or the boundaries between them. For the purposes of this section we shall rely on the work of scholars such as Halliday and Jakobson. In Halliday's model (1974), the order in which functions emerge developmentally in child language acquisition is the following:

directive
phatic
expressive
heuristic
metalinguistic
poetic
cognitive

The general principle that awareness about linguistic matters decreases as developmentally earlier phenomena are involved, when applied to the above hierarchy, means that one can expect more deliberate interference with linguistic structures at the cognitive and poetic functional levels.

Any survey of language engineering, both with *a posteriori* languages derived from existing human languages or *a priori* languages designed on the basis of philosophical or theological considerations, will demonstrate the primacy of the cognitive function in man-made systems.

It is interesting to note that in many early examples of language engineering other, non-linguistic, functions were often dominant. Thus, in medieval and postmedieval Europe the creation of a new language was seen as *imitatio dei*, i.e. promoting the creation of a better world. Figures such as Jacob Böhme (1586–1654) insisted that the creation of a perfect language was an urgent necessity in preparing mankind for the imminent second coming of Christ, a view which was also held by many of his contemporaries and successors. Comenius (1592–1670) sketches a three-stage programme for the transition from a pantaglossic via a polyglossic to a monoglossic mankind, the endpoint being reached when all mankind could praise God in a single language.

Similarly abnatural functions of language which emerge again and again are attempts to create codes which could provide access to the secrets of the universe and systems for concealment of information, either for the use of small privileged groups or, in the case of some forms of glossolalia, for individuals only. Such secret languages also emerge 'naturally' in children (e.g. in twin languages such as Spaka – see Diehl *et al.* 1981).

The most important distinction in the area of functions is that between artificial languages designed as replacements of one, many or all human languages and others which are to serve as supplementary interlanguages or languages of special domains. The desirability of a single language was motivated, in many earlier writings, by the argument that the original (pre-Babel) state was one of monolingualism. Later writers, particularly those of the nineteenth and twentieth century emphasise the importance of a single world language for world peace. Thus, Schleyer, the inventor of Volapük, adopted as his motto: '*Menade bal, püki bal*' 'to one human race, one language'; others, such as Baumann, the inventor of Weltdeutsch (1916), saw the use of a single German-derived language of intercommunication as a means of perpetuating German superiority. Whereas single languages, by definition, would have to fulfil all functions of human languages (plus any additional ones which their inventors may wish to promote), auxiliary or supplementary artificial languages can be restricted to a small range of functions and domains.

For the majority of those devising *a priori* languages the main function of language was seen as reflecting the orderliness of creation. It was generally felt that the proper representation of things is taxonomy and that words should be isomorphic with the things they refer to. By bringing about such a fit between language and the world, it was felt that a proper foundation for human cognition was laid.

The expectations of most authors of *a posteriori* languages tended to be less ambitious, though again related to the function of cognition: auxiliary languages were seen as a means of exchanging ideas between members of different communities. Typically, these ideas are those of educated groups (Schuchardt 1928: 371 refers to the exchange of scientific ideas as the most important and most immediate task) which, at the time when most artificial languages were devised, meant the inhabitants of Europe and North America. The demonstration that an artificial language also lent itself to the poetic function was frequently felt to be an important additional virtue. Thus, there has been a stream of poetical work in Esperanto ever since the first volume of poetry appeared in 1893. Distinct from this poetic function is the creation of languages for stylistic or other literary purposes, in order to illustrate how the inhabitants of various utopias and dystopias speak. A survey of these languages (Laycock 1987) draws attention to some salient aspects of such literary creations:

(a) their typological diversity is greater than that of natural human languages, but in quite different ways

(b) unnatural types (e.g. speaking backwards or *a priori* systems) are common among the inhabitants of literary worlds

(c) most *a posteriori* languages are modelled very closely on a small number of European languages, especially in features such as word order (SVO) and nominative-accusative grammar

(d) iconicity is high and regularity paramount

(e) the languages are frequently controlled and regulated by some governing body such as an academy

The desire to bring about a fit between language and the world underlies many literary creations. Thus, to mention some recent examples, the use of Russian and quasi-Russian forms in Burgess's *A Clockwork Orange* has been interpreted as an index of a violent society and the use of numerous West Germanic and Scandinavian roots in Nabokov's Zemblan is appropriate to a country like Zembla, a distant northern land (see Krueger 1967).

The poetic function of artificial languages is manifested not only in 'high' literature but, to an even greater extent and across a wide range of cultures, in verbal play and play languages such as ludlings (those involving regular transformations). Play-languages form part of the linguistic competence of a whole community, but, since their use requires practice, they often serve as virtually 'secret' languages for a particular subgroup in a community, since the other members of the community lack the fluency that comes from constant use. Such a subgroup is frequently composed of adolescents and pre-adolescents, at a stage after children have mastered the basic grammatical norms of the language, and now feel free to experiment, in an environment where their concerns (sexual and individualistic) may already be at odds with those of the adult world.

In view of the fact that language is talked about in terms derived from everyday languages one could expect a concern, on the part of the inventors of artificial languages, for culture-neutral (universal logic) metalanguage. In actual fact, there is little evidence of this among planned and artificial languages other than as part of a wider effort to organise human discourse into taxonomies. Typically, the metalinguistic categories established within the classical tradition are taken over in the construction of languages. Thus, there is an almost universal subdivision into the traditional parts of speech, inflections with verbs (tense rather than aspect) and number indication with plurals. Constructions for which there are no labels at the time of invention, (e.g. ergativity, switch-reference, anti-passives) are not considered by the vast majority of language makers. Linguistic terminology continues to remain unsatisfactory and better attention to metalinguistics, particularly on *a posteriori* sorts of metalinguistics rather than on *a prioristic* systems, remains an urgent task.

Attempts to construct languages appropriate to the expressive function typically relate to religious experience and tend to be restricted to individual needs (as in glossolalia) rather than communication between individuals. In the latter case, as pointed out by Samarin (1976: 6 ff), language creation is geared towards promoting the spiritual cohesion of religious groups as well as the exclusion of outsiders.

Perhaps inevitably, however, such phatic communication is rarely in the form of a fully worked-out language, but is expressed in non-linguistic modes such as glossolalia, which is merely a form of language-babbling, or glosso-mimia, which is the imitation of natural languages in such a way to give the impression that the actual language is being spoken. Glossolalia is common in many of the world's religions – not only charismatic Christianity – and serves to indicate the acceptance by the speaker of a divine spirit. Glosso-mimia, on the other hand, is more common in dramatic representations, where, for instance, an actor may wish to give the impression of being a

German guard in a prison camp; he will speak a nonsensical 'language' with the phonetic qualities of German, and the nature of the role will thereby be established.

The term phatic communication was introduced in the 1920s, i.e. after the majority of *a priori* and *a posteriori* languages under consideration in this paper had already been constructed. Thus, in spite of the importance of phatic communication (i.e. keeping the communication channel open) for harmony in interpersonal relations, little formal planning of language for conflict-avoiding small talk etc. has been produced. Rather, the general assumption has been that the maximum amount of information should be exchanged through planned languages.

Whilst we have so far observed a neglect of the lower non-cognitive functions in artificial languages, there has been considerable activity in connection with the last function to be considered here, the directive function. The idea that it was possible to construct a language for mind control is most closely associated with Orwell's Newspeak (cf. Bolton 1984), where it is argued that, by removing words from the dictionary, the associated concepts and the ability to argue about them is also removed. At the same time, existing words are given new more specific meanings and new terms are coined to suit ideological requirements. Social control through language use (rather than language creation), of course, has a very long tradition and languages constructed with social control as a principal motive also predate literary newspeak. Thus, Schwörer's Kolonialdeutsch of 1916 was designed for purposes such as:

'to increase the regional mobility of native workers, thus increasing their reliability';
'a language for German masters and colonisers to give orders in';
'a symbol of German authority'.

Like Newspeak, Kolonialdeutsch was vastly reduced in its lexical resources, in order to prevent the 'natives' from overhearing their masters' conversations and from 'debating controversial topics among themselves'. Since the German plans for world domination after the First World War did not materialise, this artificial form of German was never implemented, nor were subsequent attempts to revive a similar form of German for use with guest workers. Most current attempts to make language more suited to social control concentrate on small areas of the lexicon rather than large-scale structural revision. Considerable advances have been made in both the language of advertising (e.g. Vestergaard and Schrøder 1985) and politics (Bolinger 1980).

In sum, most language engineering has been carried out with relatively little regard to the functions of language, and a good deal of it with deliberate disregard of functions other than the cognitive one. Whilst cognition is an important aspect of language, its role tends to be overrated by the members of academic institutions. Such progress that has been made in the areas of logic and grammar still needs to be matched by advances in the rhetorical dimensions of language.

## 4. *A PRIORI* LANGUAGES

*A priori* languages exist for the most part as ideational constructs, as, in the sense of being languages that display 'perfection' in all the possible ways – iconicity and total naturalness – they cannot exist as actual languages, or even be constructed to any real degree. Nevertheless, the concept of the ideal *a priori* language has been a common theme throughout all recorded civilisations, and we deal now with some of the principal preoccupations.

The ideal language has been envisaged as the divine language, the primal language, and the philosophical language. For some writers these three are all the same; others may wish to distinguish them. The divine language is that spoken by benevolent superhuman forces such as God or the gods, and angels and other divine messengers; the features are best summarised by Swedenborg (1758, 1958):

'In the entire heaven all have one language . . . Language there is not learned but is implanted by nature with every one, for it flows from their very affection and thought. The tones of their speech correspond to their affection, and the vocal articulations which are words correspond to the ideas of thought that spring from the affection; and because of this correspondence the speech itself is spiritual, for it is affection sounding and thought speaking . . . Because the speech of angels proceeds directly from their affection . . . angels can therefore express in a moment what a man cannot express in half an hour.'

The language, therefore, is immutable, instinctive, iconic, ultra-brief, logical and natural. These qualities are also attributed to the primal language, or supposed original language of mankind, which in most religious systems is considered to be of divine origin.

There are, of course, considerable problems with such a concept, from a linguistic point of view. In such a language it would be impossible to lie, since the complete match between utterance and reality would mean that only true statements could be uttered; moreover, nothing new could be uttered, and all possible statements would already be known to hearers, so that the only choice is between platitudes and silence, or else, as in the imagination of Borges (1970), the uttering of a single word which will in fact substitute for all possible utterances:

'In time, the notion of a divine sentence seemed puerile or blasphemous. A god, I reflected, ought only to utter a single word and in that word absolute fullness. No word uttered by him can be inferior to the universe or less than the sum total of time. Shadows or simulacra of that single word equivalent to a language and to all a language can embrace are the poor and ambitious human words, *all, world, universe.*'

The philosophical language is not usually conceptualised in such an extreme form; it need not be immutable (although change is not easily incorporable into most of the proposed systems), it is capable of being learned (and is therefore not instinctive), and it is not ultra-brief or comprehensive (in the sense of a single utterance being able to stand for much longer utterances in natural languages). Also, as pointed out earlier in this paper, the iconicity and logic of the philosophical language operate in the opposite direction to naturalness.

From about the sixteenth century on (with a few earlier precursors like Ramon Lull) the idea begins to take shape among European scholars that it might be possible to create such a universal philosophical language that would be as non-arbitrary as possible, based on a philosophical categorisation of human experience, and completely regular in morphology and derivation. It is perhaps not coincidental that this idea grows in force with the gradual decline of Latin as the lingua franca of scholarly Europe.

Credit for one of the first serious suggestions for such an *a priori* language is often given to Descartes, in a letter to Père Marin Mersenne (1629). But Descartes admits only grudgingly the possible utility of a multilingual dictionary with an interlingual key, and has few concrete suggestions to make on the construction of a language based on philosophical categories, other than to suggest that the philosophy would have to be correct, and that the morphology should be regular:

' . . car faisant une langue, où il n'y ait qu'une façon de conjuger, de décliner, et de construire les mots, qu'il n'y en ait point de défectifs ni d'irréguliers, qui sont toutes choses venues de la corruption de l'usage, et même que l'inflexion des noms ou des verbes et la construction se fassent par affixes, ou devant ou après les mots primitifs lesquelles affixes soient toutes spécifiées dans le dictionnaire, ce ne sera pas merveille que les esprits vulgaires apprennent en moins de six heures à composer en cette langue avec l'aide du dictionnaire, qui est le sujet de la première proposition.'

Leibniz also toyed with the idea in the third quarter of the seventeenth century, but, as Knowlson (1975) points out, his ideas were only theoretical in nature, and many of his notes on the subject were not accessible to his contemporaries, and have become known only through the work of Couturat (1901, 1903). Credit for one of the most thorough-going attempts to construct such a language must therefore be given to George Dalgarno, who published his *Ars signorum* in 1661.

The complexity to which such philosophical languages can aspire is seen also in a language proposed by Thomas Urquhart in 1953. Urquhart did not create the words of his language, but set down its rules: two hundred and fifty roots, 'eleven genders, ten tenses (occurring with all parts of speech), six moods, four voices, twelve parts of speech – and, more importantly, every letter to have a meaning, and every word generatable in the language will actually occur', so that

92. Two and twentiethly, In this Language the opposite members of a division have usually the same letters in the words which signifie them; the initial and final letter being all one, with a transmutation only in the middle ones.
93. Three and twentiethly, Every word in this Language signifieth as well backward as forward; and however you invert the letters, still shall you fall upon significant words: whereby a wonderful facility is obtained in making of Anagrams.

The whole concept of the *a priori* philosophical language is satirised by Jonathan Swift, in his account (1726) of the philosophers of Laputa, who carried around with them all objects that could conceivably be the subjects of discourse, 'since words are only names for *things*'. The strength of the lampoon lies in the fact that in a short while it would occur to such philosophers that they could carry around *pictures* of the objects talked about, and that it is only a small step from such iconic representation to the iconic representation of objects in words, as envisaged in the philosophical language.

Perhaps because of such satirical comment, it is rare to meet with fully elaborated *a priori* languages later than the eighteenth century. Their direct descendants, however, are the formal language systems described in textbooks of mathematics and formal logic – including the interesting Lincos, a language designed for 'cosmic intercourse' (Freudenthal 1960 and 1974) – and also some computer languages. Mention has also been made of Weilgarth's 'language of space' (1968), which is claimed to be beneficial in imparting concepts to mentally-disturbed children. But such languages also tend to derive a great deal of their structure from *a posteriori* principles, and are therefore not philosophical languages in the strict sense.

Because of the iconic nature of the philosophical language, some attempts have been made to present the language in pictorial form; such 'sign languages' are called pasigraphies. Weilgarth's aUI is one such, since it provides pictorial elements for each of the units of the language, and two other twentieth-century pasigraphies are Leslie Charteris's Paleneo (1972) and 'Blissymbolics' (Bliss 1965). Such systems have their uses in the signs required for communication across many languages at, for example, international airports, but tend, in their detailed elaboration, to be far from transparent, and thus to offer little advantage, if any, over invented languages presented in normal script.

The idea of a pictorial iconic language in general can be traced back to the dawning knowledge, in Europe, of the Chinese language (Frodsham 1964). Chinese was popularly supposed to have a writing system in which whole words, or 'concepts', were expressed by single characters, some of which were analysable as pictorial representations – and were therefore non-arbitrary, along the lines of the philosophical language. In addition, the presence of tones in Chinese, and the concept of music as an 'international language' (a concept which ignores the extremely cultural bases of all music, and also the very limited extent of possible communication) gave rise, from the seventeenth century on, to a large number of 'Utopian' languages based on musical themes. By 'Utopian' languages we mean languages designed to serve Utopian states, and which, like the states themselves, are regulated so as to be, in some way, an 'improvement' on natural languages – whether they are conceived of as merely modified natural languages (*a posteriori* languages), or as philosophical *a priori* languages, or a combination of both.

Although such fictional Utopian languages cannot be considered as serious linguistic engineering, one continuing theme, that of the expression of concepts contradictory in meaning, needs to be singled out, since it resurfaces in the construction of *a posteriori* languages. Since there is a direct logical relation between a word, or concept, and its contradictory, it follows that in an ideal language the contradiction should always be expressed in the same way. In Solresol, an *a priori* language based on the musical scale, and playable on any instrument, proposed in 1818 by Jean-Frédéric Sudre, contrary ideas are expressed by reversing the notes – thus *domisol* is 'God' and *solmido* is 'Satan' - but as Couturat and Léau (1903) point out, the system breaks down with *dosidomi* 'vegetable' and *midosido* 'sacrifice'. A corollary of this regularised negation, so much a feature of the *a posteriori* languages, are the ideas that the same word in a Utopian language can express widely different meanings, even opposites, or that the ambiguity of the spoken language is so high that speech must be accompanied by gesture; such ideas also have their ultimate origin in misconceptions about the nature of Chinese – even the notion of gestures may derive from observation of Chinese signalling written characters in the air. But the Utopian languages of fiction, including science-fiction, are many, and only some of the prevailing themes have been indicated here. (For a comprehensive treatment, see Laycock 1987.)

## 5. *A POSTERIORI* LANGUAGES

*A posteriori* languages are usually defined as deliberately simplified versions of existing human languages or groups of languages. Contrasting with this narrow definition is the broader view which on the one hand studies instances of language engineering leading to more esoteric and more complex languages, and on the other simplified languages (pidgins, koinés and lingue franche) whose simplicity is not the result of deliberate human agency. It is somewhat ironic that perfectly smoothly functioning *a posteriori* languages were used by millions of non-literate speakers in many parts of the world at a time when the academics of central Europe were trying to discover the secret of the optimal language for international communication. It is interesting to note that the majority of these scholars either did not take note of pidgins or else rejected them; as did Jespersen in his Introduction to *An International Language* who argues that 'simplicity does not mean that the language we construct is to be a kind of "Pidgin" incapable of expressing nuances of thought which are necessary to highly cultivated Europeans . . . The inter-language that I am advocating . . . is totally different from such languages through being expressive and efficient, though being extremely simple in its grammatical structure.' One of the few attempts to base an *a priori* language on the structures of the Mediterranean Lingua Franca and other pidgins is Steiner's Pasilingua (1885). Schuchardt, who did intensive research on both pidgins and creoles and international auxiliary languages, also emphasises the importance of the former for the latter and argues that instead of deliberately simplified forms of Latin (such as Nov-Latin or Mondo lingue) one could equally well (1928: 382) 'introduce a creolised version of a Romance language as an international language.'

The originator of the idea of an international auxiliary language is Descartes who, in a letter to Père Mersenne of 1629, outlines proposals for both simplified existing *a posteriori* languages and *a priori* ones, a proposal which met with considerable acceptance in intellectual circles, as the eclipse of Latin and the rise of national languages had made intellectual discourse between scholars from different European nations increasingly difficult. During the seventeenth and first half of the eighteenth century a number of *a priori* languages were constructed (see above) as well as mixed systems such as those of the type proposed by Comenius and Leibniz, the latter (1646–1716) combining a Latin-derived lexicon with universal philosophical semantax. The earliest purely *a posteriori* language is discussed in the *Encyclopédie* of Diderot and d'Alembert in an article by M. Faiguet dated 1765. Whilst only a sketch is provided, a number of principles of simplification are clearly stated which are appealed to over and over again in later examples of *a posteriori* languages. Thus, inflexional morphology is vastly reduced, grammatical accidents such as gender no longer coded and articles disposed of. What little morphology remained was entirely regular.

A complete proposal for an *a posteriori* language based on Latin is that by Carpophorophilus (1734): the Latin lexicon is reduced in size through the elimination of synonyms, the declension is replaced by articles, there is a single plural affix -*im* borrowed from Hebrew and the verbal inflection is regularised.

Numerous similar proposals for *a posteriori* languages follow in the nineteenth century. Most of them were the work of individuals working in isolation and thus never got implemented. The majority of them were based on a few languages spoken in Western Europe, particularly Latin and other Romance languages and, as far as we can see, all of them were conceived as closed systems rather than languages capable of change and adaptation. The first artificial language actually spoken by a significant number of human beings was Volapük, an invention of the German priest Schleyer (1880). As already indicated, Volapük combined elements of both *a posteriori* and *a priori* languages. Thus, part of its lexicon was derived from other languages (mainly English, German and Latin) by regular as well as *ad hoc* processes (e.g. *vola* from English 'world' and *pük* from 'speak'), whilst other items were invented, particularly the bound stems of words such as -*el* 'inhabitant of', as in *Parisel* 'Parisian' or -*af* 'animal' as in *suplaf* 'spider'.

As Volapük was designed eventually to replace all other languages, simplification was restricted to the regularisation of morphological patterns but not the shedding of grammatical categories such as tense, gender or voice. Rather, it was a highly synthetic language, demanding considerable encoding and decoding skills from its users. The following forms chosen from the verbal paradigm of *löfön* 'to love' illustrate this:

*löfob* 'I love'
*älöfob* 'I loved'
*ulöfob* 'I shall have loved'
*löfom* 'he loves'
*löfof* 'she loves'
*löfob-s* 'they (fem) love'
*pe-i-löf-o-f* 'she was always loved'
*löfo-b-seok* 'we love one another'
*no-li-e-löfo-s-la* 'will you not have loved'
*e-löfo-m-la* 'that he has loved'

and about 505,430 possible verb forms.

In spite of such difficulties, Volapük rapidly acquired an international following beyond the wildest dreams of its inventor. An estimated million speakers used this language in 1888 and three international Volapük congresses took place in rapid succession in 1884, 1887 and 1889, the last one with representatives from 13 countries. It is reported that the decision to hold all proceedings in Volapük revealed its deficiencies to the delegates. More important, it appears, was the ideological conflict between Schleyer who wanted to see his invention capable of expressing the full range of semantic distinctions found in other human languages and those who wished to reduce

Volapük to a more modest status of an international auxiliary language. Some of his previous followers (such as the creators of Bopal, Spelin, Dil, Balta, Veltparl and La langue bleue) proposed simplified adaptations, others deserted to the Esperanto movement, which was then gaining impetus.

Esperanto, invented by the Polish oculist Ludwig Zamenhof (1859–1917) is an *a posteriori* language based primarily on Romance and Germanic (Teutonic) lexicon and grammar. A first version published in 1887 and a second version, incorporating many outsiders' suggestions as well as changes by Zamenhof himself, was put forward in 1894.

The spread of Esperanto was slower but more steady than that of Volapük. Its success is due to the more felicitous grammatical structure of the language (considerably less synthetic than Volapük), its flexibility, and possibly political persecution in both Czarist Russia and Nazi Germany which gave the language the status of a progressive liberating anti-language. The equilibrium between an international lexicon and a small set of (about 50) agglutinating inflectional and derivational formatives made it a very easy language to master, particularly for speakers of SAE languages. Some of its structural properties, however, are so typically European (six pronoun system, the distinction between nominative and accusative forms of the noun, the agreement of adjectives with the nouns they modify) or abnatural (the derivation of all feminine forms from a masculine base by affixation or that of polar opposites by means of a prefix *mal-*) that learners from other cultural backgrounds are at a great disadvantage. Another criticism is that a number of widely known international roots (e.g. possible Latin-derived forms such as *anno* 'year' or *skola* 'school' are rejected in favour of less well-known roots such as *jar* (taken from German) or *lernejo* (German root with Esperanto affix).

As in the case of other *a posteriori* languages related to SAE languages, the yardstick for what constitutes a concept and consequently a lexical item is closely modelled on the inventor's own knowledge of languages, in particular German. Thus, there is only one verb translating 'to be', namely, *sein* but two verbs for 'to look after', *flegi* from German *pflegen* for 'look after the sick' and *varti* from German *warten* for 'to look after children'. Speakers of languages other than SAE ones would find such culture-specific lexicalisation a considerable difficulty.

Selecting a single semantic domain, colour terminology, and comparing Esperanto with other artificial languages will illustrate this point. The results of numerous studies on colour systems in human languages (summarised, for instance in Berlin and Kay 1969) show (*a*) that human languages can differ widely in the number of colour distinctions they lexicalise, (*b*) that only a small subset of all mathematically probable combinations of colour terms are permitted in human languages and (*c*) that certain colour distinctions are considerably more basic than others. For constructing a universal auxiliary language this means that one must work from the premise that the only colours one can assume to be readily intelligible to everybody are black, white and possibly red. If one considers concrete proposals, however, one finds a very different picture:

Esperanto (according to Wells 1969) appears to have 12 primary colour terms, including mauve, purple, pink, grey and brown, the latter reflecting Western Germanic predilection for naming dark reddish colours. Unsurprisingly, brown is also one of the colours in Schleyer's Volapük (1885) together with eleven other primary colours including purple, pink, grey and orange. Brown, pink and purple are absent in Henderson's Lingua (1888) where only six basic colours (black, white, red, green, yellow and grey) are found.

The colour brown is absent in Frater (Thai 1957) in spite of the fact that it is a basic colour term in the mother tongue (Vietnamese) of its inventor. The inclusion of another basic colour term in this language, *klor* 'greenish-yellow', may be an instance of hypercorrection or overcompensation for the absence of a blue-green or yellow-gold distinction in Vietnamese.

From such considerations it follows that to call an international auxiliary language La Langue Bleue is not quite felicitous, leaving alone the problem that the sky, which is supposed to have been the limit for this language, tends not to be blue in some tropical parts of the world but has a glaring whitish tone.

However, lexical ethnocentrism was not one of the reasons for the developing rift in the Esperanto movement; rather, as in the case of Volapük, the later fate of Esperanto is characterised by a split between those in favour of the original or a mildly revised language and those advocating radical revisions. The split was triggered by the foundation of the 'Delegation on the adoption of an International Auxiliary Language' in 1900, consisting of a group of competent scholars including the linguist Jespersen. After initial discussion of a larger number of languages (discussed in detail by Jespersen 1921) the choice was narrowed down to Esperanto and Idiom Neutral, a language designed by a group that had left the Volapük movement in 1903. At a later stage Ido, an artificial language derived from Esperanto, was submitted anonymously and received very favourably by the Delegation. The final decision was to recommend Esperanto with a number of reforms along the lines of Ido, a decision unacceptable to many Esperantists. Ido, in turn, received several improvements and changes and a language called Esperantido was proposed by René de Saussure. None of these languages derived from Esperanto could arrest the further spread of the original version which continues to remain the most widely spoken artificial language, and is seen by some as the future language of the Common Market.

The First World War affected the artificial language movement in several ways. First, existing languages, in particular Esperanto, were used in war propaganda by both German and French groups, and second, it promoted the development of *a posteriori* languages derived from single national languages. The need for a language which could bring about international co-operation was felt even more strongly after the war. By then, a number of principles and practices of artificial language-making had crystallised, including:

(*a*) that *a posteriori* languages are preferable to *a priori* ones
(*b*) that naturalness (as yet ill-defined) should be promoted as much as possible
(*c*) that the language should be for the whole world rather than the educated classes of Western Europe
(*d*) that the solution should be the result of teamwork rather than an individual effort
(*e*) that the implementation of the solution should be in the hands of an international authority such as the League of Nations

The first two points are illustrated by an increasing tendency to favour solutions found in actual human languages over invented solutions, even at the cost of reduced regularity. Point (*c*) is not widely applied, however, as the majority of linguists concerned with the improvement or creation of artificial systems continue to be speakers of SAE languages with a very limited experience of languages of other families. Conspicuous by its absence is an understanding of the sociolinguistic mechanisms of cross-linguistic communication. This criticism has been made of virtually all the languages that succeeded Esperanto and Ido, such as Peano's Latino sine flexione (1908) Jespersen's Novial (1928) and Ogden and Richard's Basic English (1931). Among the few exceptions are Hogben's Interglossa of 1943 which combines Greek vocabulary with Chinese syntax, and Thai's Lingua Sistemfrater (Frater) of 1957. Of the above languages Basic English needs to be singled out as a special type since in this reduced form of English, we find that the spelling, pronunciation and grammar of the English language have been left intact, the principal change being a carefully limited lexical inventory of 850 items. This language thus could fulfil the dual functions of international auxiliary language and transitional stage in the acquisition of English as a second language.

The failure of most proposals for auxiliary languages is related to the limited insights and authority of individuals. Thus, decisions of importance tended to be made in international bodies and one of the major present-day proposals, Interlingua, is the work of a team of scholars (including Jespersen, Sapir, Martinet and Swadesh) belonging to the International Auxiliary Language Association.

The problem of implementation is the most difficult in the spread of linguistic innovations of any type. What is needed are i) authority

ii) reasons why innovations should be accepted and iii) considerable financial resources. Esperanto in the days before the outbreak of the First World War had all of these, though the new totalitarianism that followed made its further spread and acceptance difficult. Support from organisations such as the League of Nations and the United Nations for international languages has been very cautious over the years, even more local proposals such as those for a common European language (Eurolengo, Jones 1973) meeting with very little support.

Recent work in sociolinguistics suggests that the acceptance of a language is the consequence of groups of people identifying with one another and with a common means of communication. Another reason why people are willing to learn languages for intercommunication, in particular pidgins or similar lingue franche, is that they expect economic rewards. As long as members of the international community can derive more profit (in various senses of the word) from learning languages such as English or French, the chances of Esperanto, Interlingua or similar systems remain very slender.

## 6. NAÏVE LINGUISTIC ENGINEERING

A form of linguistic engineering is only now being recognised in the languages of small and often illiterate communities: the effect of influential individuals on the speech of the whole community. We can call such linguistic engineering 'naïve' in the sense that it does not proceed from any overall plan, nor is it necessarily aimed at any improvement of the language; mere change is usually sufficient. The principal motives would seem rather to be the need for linguistically differentiating a group from all other groups. The area is little researched; some of what information there is (Laycock 1982a,b) comes from the area of New Guinea, where language groups have the requisite smallness. The maximum size of a community in which an individual can impose linguistic whims, without the assistance of any form of media, would seem to be about 8,000, since this is the largest size that permits of a network in which each speaker is known to every other speaker, or is at least in a specifiable close-kin relation with another known speaker. In such a community the linguistic whims of a chief, or 'big man', or other forceful individual, can 'blanket' an entire community; in larger communities, such innovative language changes spread only in waves, and do not reach the peripheries.

A classical example of such humanly-induced linguistic change would seem to be the metathesised forms of a language like Ririo, in the Solomon Islands (Laycock 1982a), which corresponds to unmetathesised forms in the neighbouring, and closely-related, language of Babatana. The fact that such a difference is not caused by regular linguistic change is seen in the circum-

864

stance that Ririo speakers create new metathesized forms from loanwords that have come into the language only after the metathesis must have already been established – for example, Ririo *kias*, Babatana *kesa*, borrowed from the English word 'cash'.

An even more clear-cut case is provided by the language of Buin, spoken by some 17,000 persons in the North Solomons province of Papua New Guinea. Less than a tenth of the population speak a very distinct dialect called Uisai. The language has several hundreds of grammatical forms (demonstratives, deictics, pronouns) showing a gender distinction between masculine and feminine, through three numbers (singular, dual, plural). In the Uisai dialect, all such forms have reversed polarity – that is, all the forms indicating 'masculine' in the other dialects indicate 'feminine' in Uisai, and vice versa. In such a case, there is no room for normal mechanisms of slow linguistic change, since the change involves a 'flip flop' of two opposing categories, masculine and feminine. Such a change is analogous to the change in Sweden from driving on the left to driving on the right; the change had to be accomplished instantly. The most plausible explanation for such a linguistic change – although this is not subject to direct investigation at the moment – is that some influential person of the Uisai community once announced something like 'As from tomorrow we are not going to speak like other Buin speakers; we are going to say 'he' for 'she', and so on'. Once adopted, the change would be difficult at first for adult speakers, but would soon become natural to younger generations; and within one generation there would be a new group of speakers to whom this was the 'natural' form of speech.

As both the Ririo case and the Buin case involve a single interchange of two elements – reversing final consonant and vowel in the Ririo case, masculine and feminine in the Buin case – it seems reasonable to postulate that one of the major mechanisms in linguistic change, whether conscious or unconscious, may be expressed in terms of interchange of binary opposites. Certainly there is considerable evidence from speech errors, and speech pathology, of interchange of elements, such as initial consonant clusters in spoonerisms (*town drain* for *down train*), or the phenomenon of 'opposite speech' (*black* for *white*) among schizophrenics. Secret languages involving 'opposite speech' are frequently reported, one classic instance being that of the Walbiri (Hale 1971). It is not surprising that naïve linguistic change should exploit a mechanism that appears so close to the surface of our normal linguistic perceptions.

Naïve linguistic engineering is still under investigation, but further research e.g. on taboo and secret languages, may be expected to provide insights into mechanisms of language change, and strategies for language elevation, that will be useful in the study of more sophisticated forms of language engineering.

## 7. LANGUAGE ELEVATION

The term 'language elevation' refers to planning activities that differ in a number of ways from the ones discussed so far including:

(i)  Planning is aimed at actual human languages that either are or, in cases such as Hebrew in present-day Israel, once served as, the language/vernacular of a genuine speech community.
(ii)  Language engineering is usually kept at a very modest level, such *a posteriori* changes as are introduced not greatly affecting intelligibility and continuity.
(iii)  Planning is typically exercised for some functions, domains and media only. The spoken vernacular is not affected to a significant extent.
(iv)  Language elevation typically involves the creation of national languages rather than languages of intercultural or international communication.

Language elevation is manifested in two domains, (*a*) the social domain, where status planning is carried out to enhance the prestige of the vernacular selected for elevation and (*b*) the structural domain, in the form of corpus planning. Corpus planning can be further subdivided into graphisation (development of suitable writing systems), standardisation (regularisation of grammatical patterns and elimination of lectal variability) and modernisation (adapting the language to the needs of a modernised society). Acts of language elevation in the sense used here have their beginnings with technological changes such as printing and political ones such as the development of nation states. The relationship between language and the medium through which it is expressed is roughly as follows:

(*a*)  non-literate societies can tolerate small dialects and considerable dialectal variation,
(*b*)  literate societies with printing tend to favour standardised languages with little dialect variation,
(*c*)  electronic media such as radio and television favour larger languages with little internal variation,
(*d*)  computers call for one large language or a very few such.

Furthermore, the existence of large states does not promote single languages in the absence of strong central governments. Thus, for the empires of antiquity, the existence of many languages within their boundaries made a *divide et impera* policy possible. The emergence of standard written languages in the wake of the invention of printing is illustrated by the example of German where, from the late sixteenth century onwards, a number of language societies promoted first the status of German *vis-à-vis* Latin and subsequently the linguistic purity of the German language itself.

The recognition of a superregional German language was achieved with the publication of Schottel's grammar of 1641. However, the general acceptance and spread of spoken forms of German related to its 'Schriftsprache' did not occur until the nineteenth century, with the introduction of compulsory schooling and the creation of a unified nation. The developments in Italy exhibit striking similarities, as do developments in some of the newer nation states of the Third World such as Malaysia or Indonesia. Numerous longitudinal studies are found in Le Page (1986 ed.), one of the few documents where language elevation is discussed in a diachronic framework. The principal uniting factor is a picture of *ad hoc* decisions, inefficient and costly solutions and lack of methodology. In a large number of instances, language elevation has continued to be carried out in a very haphazard fashion following the whims of politicians and pressure groups rather than the advice of such language planning experts as have established themselves in the recent past. The following sketch of an ideal case of language elevation is hardly a mirror of present-day reality. Nevertheless, it would seem useful to bring together a number of important results from recent work in this field.

The process of language elevation must be seen as consisting of the following four main stages:

(i)   problem identification
(ii)  development of concrete proposals
(iii) evaluation of proposals
(iv)  implementation

Some differences in terminology and emphasis are found. Haugen (1922), for instance, distinguishes the stages of i) norm selection, ii) codification iii) implementation and iv) elaboration. The stage of problem identification involves a diagnosis of what is wrong both with the nationwide patterns of communication and with the structural responses of the vernacular appointed to serve as a national language. The criteria appealed to when evaluating the situation include:

(i)   referential adequacy, i.e. 'the capacity of the language to meet the needs of its users as an instrument of referential meaning' (Haugen 1966: 62);
(ii)  systematic adequacy, i.e. a language should be structured in such a way that its rules are maximally general and natural;
(iii) acceptability, i.e. a form must be adopted or adoptable by the majority of whatever society or sub-society is involved.

Subordinate to these considerations are others, such as euphony, brevity, and symmetry between expression and content, which are listed and discussed by Tauli (1968: 38 ff). Of these, the criterion of acceptability most directly relates to the choice of norm. This choice involves the appointment of one or more

867

vernaculars of a multilingual nation as national languages, and that of a suitable dialect in a linguistically more homogeneous one. In both instances, questions of political power and control are dominant. In principle, the code selectors can adopt one of two strategies: adopt the code associated with the most powerful or most numerous group, or else elevate a vernacular spoken by a small powerless group. Selection of the powerful code is illustrated by the examples such as French (based on the variety spoken around Paris) and Turkish. In both these cases the power was extended, over time, first over non-standard dialects and subsequently other languages spoken within the nation state. Examples of small or non-powerful languages being selected as the basis of a national language are that of Pilipino (or Filipino), the national language based on the central Luzon language Tagalog, and Bislama of Vanuata, a pidgin English which was elevated to a national language after independence. In both instances the choice appears to have found very widespread acceptance. Pidginised forms of vernaculars have also been given official status in the case of Swahili (Tanzania) and Sango (Central African Republic). (For explanation of the terms 'lingua franca', 'pidgin' and 'creole' see the note under the References to Chapter 26, below.)

Code selection can involve more than one language. Thus, a number of the new Pacific nations have designated a number of languages as 'official', typically the former colonial language and one or more regional languages, often assigning to them differential status such as 'official language', 'national language', or 'parliamentary language'. Elevating the status of some languages or varieties tends to promote the status decline of other languages. This is manifested by (*a*) former independent systems becoming subsystems of the standard e.g. Bavarian becoming a dialect of German, (*b*) the functional restriction to private regional matters and (*c*) after a shorter or longer period of inegalitarian bilingualism, eventual language death. The examples of Maori and Hawaiian illustrate that even large majority languages cannot survive in a political climate that offers no adequate status.

The determination of the referential adequacy of languages is made difficult by the observation that languages do not refer to a fixed set of pre-established entities in the real world but rather impose a referential grid on so-called reality. It is therefore not clear for instance how many lexical entries a fully adequate language must have. Moreover, adequacy can only be determined against the background of the functional use speakers make of a language particularly in bi- and multilingual societies. Generally speaking, the adaptation of referential resources to communicative needs is determined by the degree of technological and social change in a given community. The gap between what a language needs to refer to and what it can actually refer to is greatest in times of rapid change or upheaval, such as the westernisation and modernisation of societies. The importance of lexical corpus planning in such a context has been emphasised by a number of researchers (e.g. Tauli 1968 and Wurm, Mühlhäusler and Laycock 1977).

Systematic adequacy refers to the extent to which languages follow regular rules, or, put differently, the relative importance of grammar and lexicon. Old languages, particularly those which have borrowed from other systems or have been used in esoteric functions, tend to be full of exceptions and lexicalisations. Whilst the creation of greater symmetric adequacy is a universal motif in language engineering, there are certain external constraints, in particular the assessment of the relative merits of regular indigenous word formation against borrowing of widely accepted international lexemes (see Rosario 1968). An internal constraint, already raised in the discussion of *a posteriori* languages, is the conflict between linguistic regularity and linguistic naturalness. Generally speaking, those in the business of language elevation have paid insufficient attention to the second aspect.

The development of concrete proposals in the past tended to be the work of single or small groups of self-appointed language reformers, such as Aavik in Estonia or Aasen in Norway. In countries of the Third World, missionaries often carried out language elevation and engineering almost single-handedly. One of the best-known mission lingue franche of New Guinea, the Papuan Language Kâte derives many of its present-day structures from the grammatical and lexical efforts of the German missionary Pilhofer; the standard version of Central African Sango is a similar case. Committees of teachers, linguists and politicians were involved in the elevation of Turkish under Atatürk in 1930 and Greek Katharevousa in the nineteenth century. Teachers and politicians were also the originators of an elevated Bahasa Indonesia.

The area in which the majority of work has been carried out is that of the lexicon, in particular the creation of terminologies and the regularisation of word-formation processes. The simultaneous action of both processes can be seen in the following examples from Pilipino (discussed by Rosario 1968):

| English | Pilipino | Etymology |
|---------|----------|-----------|
| numeral | pamilang | pang- (instrument prefix) + bilang (number) |
| integer | buumbilang | buo (whole) + bilang (number) |
| fraction | bahagimbilang | bahagi (part) + bilang (number) |
| numerator | panakda | pang- (instrument prefix) + takda (schedule) |
| denominator | pamahagi | pang- (instrument prefix) + bahagi (part) |

Another example is afforded by proposals to increase the referential adequacy of Tok Pisin in the area of descriptive adjectives (discussed by Wurm, Mühlhäusler and Laycock 1977). Instead of borrowing adjectives from external languages (e.g. English derived *blain* 'blind' or *hepi* 'happy') it is suggested that an existing word formation mechanism of the language is extended to cover new instances. Thus, the fact that syntactic constructions such as *ai i pas* 'the eye is obstructed' already have corresponding lexical compounds (*aipas* 'blind') is exploited in new forms such as:

| | |
|---|---|
| belgut | 'belly good', happy |
| lekbruk | 'broken legged' |
| belpas | 'constipated' |
| hetgut | 'intelligent' |

The principal task of lexical planners is to anticipate possible explanations, i.e. to speed up the drift that can be determined when such planning is paired with an understanding of the longitudinal developments in the word formation component of the language (as in the case of the above Tok Pisin examples).

Very much the same principles apply to other areas of planning. Understanding the development will direct planners to those solutions that have the least disruptive effect on the system and the greatest chance of being learnable and acceptable to speakers. A discussion of the theoretical desirability of a developmental linguistic foundation for graphisation and other areas of corpus planning is given by Bailey (1975). Bailey's model of ordered variability appears to offer the greatest chance for orderly planning, particularly as it pays close attention to considerations of naturalness. The fact that many language planners, particularly in the past and in some Third World countries, have been educated in a static framework of linguistic description has meant that their efforts were directed towards putative gaps in a static system rather than towards an understanding of natural expansion. The evaluation of proposals is concerned with the considerations just mentioned as well as those mentioned earlier in this section. In practice, evaluation of competing proposals has rarely been made in an orderly manner. Consequently, solutions in almost all areas of all languages that have undergone elevation remain *ad hoc*. The greatest shortcoming appears to be in procedures for evaluating the non-local effect of local changes (e.g. introducing borrowed lexicon may have repercussions outside the lexicon, in phonology and syntax). A developmental Baileyan approach again offers a suitable model, as it is designed to discover implicational relationships between different processes in different parts of grammar.

The implementation of elevation proposals involves considerations of both political power and media control and constraints on the learnability of the suggested system by children. The latter consideration is less important if the language is to be used principally in a written form among an adult educated elite (and many planned languages have been designed for such a group). State control of the education process and the relevant media together with the promotion of the elevated language as an index of upward mobility and power tend to suffice. If, on the other hand, the language is designed for the mass of the adult population and for young children, then considerations of naturalness and considerations of acceptability become important. The lack of success of languages such as Irish Gaelic illustrate this, as do the numerous structural changes which became necessary in modern Hebrew as more and more Israeli children adopted it as their first language.

## 8. CONCLUSIONS

The systematic study of language engineering in its many manifestations is still in its infancy. In spite of the almost universal presence of deliberate human interference in their languages, this factor has been regarded as marginal to the interests of linguistics, both in traditional philology, where languages have been regarded as comparable to other natural organisms, and in more recent frameworks such as Transformational Generative Grammar where 'natural languages' are also at the centre of interest. It is by no means accidental that those linguists who were most interested in artificial languages and language planning, such as Schuchardt, Jespersen, Sapir and, more recently, Bailey and scholars working on variation, are those who rejected the notion that languages were self-contained closed systems and that change was governed by natural laws. Unfortunately, virtually all language engineering has been based on precisely this assumption. The invariance of most *a priori* systems is not greatly relaxed in the majority of *a posteriori* ones, and many instances of language elevation exhibit a noticeable lack of consideration for flexibility and adaptability. Furthermore, the interrelationship between the cognitive and non-cognitive dimensions of human language has tended to be misunderstood or simply ignored in virtually all the cases surveyed in this paper.

Language engineering to date has been, by and large, a haphazard affair, and such success as has been achieved has often been at tremendous cost. Thus, it is by no means clear that the reduction of linguistic heterogeneity has no costs, involving as it does the loss of alternative philosophies and solutions, or that speaking the same language promotes better understanding between people. The importance of the computer in many present-day societies may give a new lease of life to some of the old vices; the languages that computers can cope with are typically closed (rule-governed rather than rule-changing), computer translation assumes a names-for-objects view of the relationship between language and the world and computers are suited to the cognitive functions of language (rather than any other). Of course, language planning for technological purposes, such as that of sublanguages in the Soviet Union (Moskovich 1982) has its place. However, the chess game or computer metaphor offers a fundamentally misleading metaphor of human communication, as does the conduit metaphor which regards communication as an exchange of messages similar to that in telegraphy.

Language engineering for human communication (rather than interstellar, computer or angelic interlocutors) needs to cater for factors such as rule changing creativity, adaptation and accommodation, negotiation of meanings and structures and social indexicality. In other words, if language engineering is to make further progress, it has to turn to the non-cognitive functions and language development. An understanding of how pidgin languages develop may be the most promising point of departure for such an enterprise.

A recurrent motif in language engineering has been, implicitly or explicitly, what Harris (1981: 9ff) describes as the principal constituents of the Western language myth: the telementational fallacy and the determinacy fallacy. Both fallacies go back to Aristotle. The former refers to the view that 'linguistic knowledge is essentially a matter of knowing which words stand for which ideas' (p. 9), the latter that 'all it needs is for men to agree upon some fixed set of correlations between ideas and verbal symbols, in order to provide themselves with a viable system for exchanging thoughts' (p. 10). Under an alternative view, all men are not provided by nature with the same set of concepts. Instead, such realities as they perceive are partially brought into being by the verbal code they employ. According to this view, the aim of replacement of the diversity of present-day languages by a single universal language would result in a dangerous reduction in the range of alternative world-views and philosophies. Moreover, even the more modest aim of creating an auxiliary language which could be used by speakers of all languages with equal facility is likely to run into difficulties. Language engineers are well advised to consider the limitations to their activities.

# REFERENCES

Bailey, Charles-James, N. (1975) 'The New Linguistic Framework and Language Planning', *Linguistics*, 158: 153–7.

Baumann, Adelbert (1916) *Weltdeutsch*, Huber, Munich.

Bausani, Alessandro (1970) *Geheim — und Universalsprachen*, Kohlhammer, Stuttgart.

Berlin, Brent and Kay, Paul (1969) *Basic Color Terms: Their Universality and Evolution*, University of California Press, Berkeley.

Bickerton, Derek (1981) *Roots of Language*, Karoma Press, Ann Arbor.

Bickerton, Derek (1984) 'The language bioprogram hypothesis', *The Behavioural and Brain Sciences*, 7, 2: 173–88.

Blanke, Detlef (1985) *Internationale Plansprachen: Eine Einführung*, Akademie Verlag, Berlin.

Bliss, Charles K. (1965) *Semantography (Blissymbolics): a simple system of 100 logical pictorial symbols*, 2nd enl. ed., Semantography (Blissymbolics) Publications, Sydney, (orig. publ. 1949).

Bodmer, Frederick (1943) *The Loom of Language*, Allen & Unwin, London.

Bolinger, Dwight (1986) *Language — The Loaded Weapon*, Longman, London.

Bolton, W.F. (1984) *The Language of 1984*, Blackwell, Oxford.

Borges, Jorge Luis (1970) *Labyrinths: Selected Stories and Other Writings* trans. from Spanish, ed. Yates, D.A. and Irby, J.E., Penguin, Harmondsworth.

Charteris, Leslie (1972) *Paleneo: a universal sign language*, Interlit A.G., London.

Cobarrubias, J. and Fishman, J.A. (eds) (1983) *Progress in Language Planning*, Mouton, The Hague.

Couturat, Louis (1901) *La logique de Leibniz d'après des documents inédits*, F. Alcan, Paris.

Couturat, Louis (1903) *Opuscules et fragments inédits de Leibniz*, Reprinted Olms, Hildesheim, 1961.

Couturat, Louis and Leopold Leau (1903) *Histoire de la langue universelle*, Hachette, Paris.

Dalgarno, George (1661) *Ars signorum, vulgo character universalis et lingua philosophica . . .*, London (Facsimile ed., Scolar Press, Menston 1968).

Descartes, René (1629) *Lettre à Mersenne*, 20 November 1629, in *Oeuvres et Lettres*: textes présentés par A. Bridoux, Pléiade, Paris, ed. 1953.

Diehl, Randy L. and Kolodzey, Katherine (1981) 'Spaka: A Private Language', *Language*, 57: 2: 406–24.

Freudenthal, Hans (1960) *Lincos: design of a language for cosmic intercourse*, North Holland, Amsterdam.

Freudenthal, H. (1974) 'Cosmic Language', in *Current Trends in Linguistics*, 12: 1019–41.

Frodsham, John D. (1964) '*Chinese and primitive language*: John Webb's contribution to 17th century Sinology', *Asian Studies*, 2/3: 389–408.

*Hale, Kenneth A. (1971) 'A note on a Walbiri tradition of antonymy', in Steinberg, D.D. and Jakobovits, L.A., (eds) *Semantics*, Cambridge University Press, Cambridge: 472–82.

Halliday, Michael A.K. (1974) *Explorations in the functions of language*, Edward Arnold, London.

Harris, Roy (1981) *The Language Myth*, Duckworth, London.

Haugen, Einar (1966) *Linguistics and language planning*, in Bright, W. (ed.) *Sociolinguistics*, Mouton, The Hague: 50–71.

Haugen, Einar (1972) *The Ecology of Language*, Stanford University Press, Stanford.

Henderson, George J. (1888) *Lingua: An International Language*, Tribune & Co, London.

Jacob, H. (1943) *Otto Jespersen: His work for an International Auxiliary Language*, Ido Society of Great Britain, Loughton.

Jacob, H. (1948) *On Language Making*, Dennis Dobson Ltd, London.

Jones, Leslie (1973) *Eurolengo: The language for Europe*, Oriel Press, London.

Kittredge, Richard and Lehrberger, John (eds) (1982) *Sublanguage — Studies in Language in Restricted Semantic Domains*, De Gruyter, Berlin.

Knowlson, James (1975) *Universal Language Schemes in England and France 1600—1800*, University of Toronto Press, Toronto.

Krueger, John R. (1967) 'Nabokov's Zemblan: A constructed Language of Fiction', *Linguistics*, 31: 44–9.

Large, A. (1987) *The artificial language movement*, Blackwell, Oxford.

*Laycock, Donald C. (1972) 'Towards a typology of ludlings, or play-languages',

*Linguistic Communications*, 6: 61–114.

\*Laycock, Donald C. (1982a) 'Metathesis in Austronesian: Ririo and other cases', Pacific Linguistics C-74: 269–81.

Laycock, Donald C. (1982b) 'Melanesian linguistic diversity: a Melanesian choice?' in May, R.J. and Nelson, Hank, (eds) *Melanesia: Beyond Diversity*, Australian National University, Canberra: 33–8.

\*Laycock, Donald C. (1987) 'The languages of Utopia', in Kamenka, Eugene, (ed.) *Utopias: papers from the annual symposium of the Australian Academy of the Humanities*, Oxford University Press, Melbourne: 144–78.

Le Page, R.B. (ed.) (1986) *Abstracts of the proceedings of the Workshop of the International Group for the study of Language Standardization and the Vernacularization of Literacy*, Dept. of Language, University of York, York.

Moskovich, W. (1982) *What is Sublanguage? The notion of Sublanguages in Modern Soviet Linguistics*, in Kittredge and Lehrberger (eds) 1982: 189–205.

Mayerthaler, Willi (1981) *Morphologische Natürlichkeit*, Niemeyer, Tübingen.

Pei, Mario A. (1974) 'Artificial Languages: International (Auxiliary)', in *Current Trends in Linguistics*, 12: 999–1017.

Rónai, Paulo (1969) *Der Kampf gegen Babel*, Ehrenwirth, Munich.

Rosario, Gonsalodel (1968) 'A modernization–standardization plan for the Austronesia–derived languages of South East Asia', in *Asian Studies*, 6/1: 1–18.

Rubin, Joan and Jernudd, Björn H. (eds) (1971) *Can Languages be planned?* University Press of Hawaii, Honolulu.

Samarin, William J. (1976) *Languages in Religious Practice*, Centre for Applied Linguistics, Georgetown.

Schleyer, Johann Martin (1885) *Wörterbuch der Universalsprache Volapük*, Verlag des Zentralburos der Weltsprache, Konstanz.

Schuchardt, Hugo (1928) *Hugo-Schuchardt-Brevier* (edited by Leo Spitzer), Niemeyer, Halle.

Schwörer, E. (1916) *Kolonial-Deutsch: Vorschläge einer künftigen deutschen Kolonialsprache in systematisch-grammatikalischer Darstellung und Begründung*, Huber, Munich.

Slaughter, M.M. (1982) *Universal Languages and Scientific Taxonomy in the 17th century*, Cambridge University Press, Cambridge.

Swedenborg, Emanuel (1758) *De caelo et ejus mirabilibus et de inferno, ex auditis et visis*, John Lewis, London.

Swedenborg, Emanuel (1958) *Heaven and its Wonders and Hell from Things Heard and Seen*, trans. from Latin. New ed., rev. D.H. Hartley, The Swedenborg Society, London.

Swift, Jonathan (1726) *Travels into several remote nations of the world*, Benj. Motte, London.

Tauli, Valter (1968) *Introduction to A Theory of Language Planning*, Almquist & Wiksells, Uppsala.

Tyssot de Patot, Simon (1710) *Voyages et aventures de Jacques Massé*, J. L'Aveugle, Bordeaux.

Urquhart, Thomas (1653) *Logopandecteision, or An Introduction to the Universal Language*, Giles Calvert, London.

Vestergaard, T. and Schröder K. (1985) *The Language of Advertising*, Blackwell, Oxford,

Wells, J.C. (1969) *Esperanto Dictionary*, Teach Yourself Books, London.

Weilgart, John W. (1968) *aUI — the language of space*, Cosmic Communication Company, Decorah (Iowa).

Wurm, Stephen A. (ed.) (1977) *New Guinea Area Languages and Language Study Vol. 3*, Pacific Linguistics C-40, Canberra.

Wurm, S.A., Mühlhäusler, P. and Laycock, D.C. (1977) *Language Planning and Engineering in Papua New Guinea*, in Wurm (ed.) 1977: 1151–78.

Yaguello, Marina (1984) *Les Fous du Langage*, Seuil, Paris.

## FURTHER READING

The items in the above list marked with an asterisk will be found especially helpful for readers keen to probe these topics further.

For computer languages, see Chapter 18, section 1.3, above.

# 24

# LANGUAGE AS IT EVOLVES: TRACING ITS FORMS AND FAMILIES

## N.E. COLLINGE

## 1. INTRODUCTION

Language evolves. Its development in the human animal, in its behavioural, mental and physiological aspects, is a story yet to be fully told; it will not be essayed here. But once language has established itself as the characteristic medium of interaction in the species – and even in its earliest observable forms has achieved an astonishing richness of systems and delicacy of communicative function – then any one manifestation of it splits into different versions and the shape of its elements changes even among a heredity of users. The study known as 'historical-comparative linguistics' (or some similar title according to the researcher's school and language) attempts to trace those splits and detail those changes. Of necessity, it also seeks to establish just what array of forms, at what time, is the datum from which the splits diverge and the changes move. In what follows historical comparativism will be considered in respect of its own history, its methods, its dynamics and its areas of contention.

## 2. THE URGE TO COMPARE, AND TO EXPLORE THE PAST

An inescapable concomitant of living is the awareness that one's own language is inexorably changing and becoming old fashioned. Besides, recourse to literature at once brings acquaintance with earlier forms of the language, whether (for English) as strange as Chaucer's or as reasonably 'normal' as Trollope's. Once that acquaintance is made, interest in old shapes and meanings develops; for some, 'linguistics' never means more than etymology. That curiously fascinating preoccupation has at least this characteristic: etymology is the one aspect of language study which is always and indisputably historical. Moreover, description of current usage and explanation of idiosyncrasies and even defence of spelling conventions can perhaps be made clearer and more acceptable by appeal to what things used to be. So it is enlightening to learn that in *the king was brought wine* the word *king* used to be marked as in the dative case, or that the sounded 'l' in *fault* or the silent 'b' in *doubt* were segments of the Latin words which are the remote origin of the English words, despite a complex history of loss and replacement. But extreme positions have sometimes been taken. For early linguists (say, in the first millennium BC) the historical dimension was only one of several; it tended to exercise the ingenuity more of the occasional amateur than of the committed researcher, for whom the description of language and functional theory were always foremost. So it has usually been, and so it is nowadays. But in relatively recent times, for a period of a little more than a century, a curious fashion of thought prevailed and the 'diachronic' aspect of language was taken to be the only respectable (because the only 'scientific') subject of learned interest. Certainly the result was a body of discoveries of a notably factual kind, even provably true. One language was shown beyond cavil to be the granddaughter of another; a segmental sound in a given context was solidly demonstrated to have evolved into another sound over time and space; formal paradigms of grammar were undoubtedly derived from previous versions – and the bulk of all this work is enormous. The web is constantly unpicked in detail, as will appear; family relationships are rarely entirely agreed for long. But in this sector a thesis succeeds not on the subjective ground of intellectual satisfaction or harmony with the language corpus but according to its power positively to reshape that corpus and to reorganise the data. This it does by calculable proofs (which sometimes find later confirmation in documentary evidence); but, of course, not all historians calculate to the same answer at the same time. Then between roughly 1920 and 1955 the fashionable attitude to historical linguistics became one of amused or irritated condescension to an outmoded and irrelevant pastime. The tide has turned yet again and the value of comparative-historical studies is now seen as, at least, a control on speculative theories of how language operates; hence its own inherent interest is respectable again.

To be historical is not necessarily to be comparative: some concentrate on the history of a single language. The converse is also true and it is commonplace to compare different languages in many aspects (e.g. phonological inventory and tactics, morphological structure, syntactic devices and order of elements in sentences) in order to show where one language is like all others (to establish universals), or like some others (to set it in a typology), or like no others (to vindicate its identity as an idiom). Typology feeds back into 'historical-comparative' study, as will be noted later (section 7.2). But in historical comparativism the aim is to show that various languages are *genetically* related, and to what degree; and here 'comparison' is a technical term to be described shortly. (It is paralleled only in anatomy and physiology. Where other disciplines use the term 'comparative', linguists usually say 'contrastive'.) Individual and family history interlock, and their interaction is shown below (sections 3.3, and 3.4).

The new historicism emphasises 'uniformitarian' evolution (see section 3); it also allows its statements of 'shifts' to seem comfortingly similar to the rules of generative grammarians. But its own preoccupations are at present more with the 'diachrony' – the unfolding story – of grammar and with the social or, anyway, demographic causation of change, noted here in sections 6 and 7.

## 3. THE HISTORY OF HISTORICAL COMPARATIVISM

Interest in language in Europe dates from at least the fifth century BC in India and Greece. The Greeks enthused over the history of words and were attracted to ingenious (and false) etymologies. They moved on to pursue operational analysis (as the Indians always had) and history of forms took a back seat, where it has remained ever since despite some insightful work of the seventeenth century (see Chapter 22, section 2.6.3), being normally regarded as a side-issue which may occasionally illuminate or justify a hypothesis of how some piece of a language system functions and proliferates into different terms. But the epoch between, roughly, 1780 and 1920 was a strange aberration. Then the comparative and historical handling of languages and their 'families' was aggressively in the ascendant and forced description and its associated theory on to the defensive.

### 3.1 The prompters

By the late eighteenth century, long years of discovery of the world's languages had established a rich data base for comparison. There was also a philosophically inspired zeal (largely due to Leibniz) for recognising a general and specific likeness in human behaviour and thinking, and for regarding language as a revealer of understanding. Thus relationship and genealogy were brought into language study. A great survey (after a 1781 monograph), appearing between 1806 and 1817, by J.C. Adelung (1732–1806) displays comparable words in hundreds of languages (see Chapter 22 above) and thus extends the works of earlier compilers and prompts the suggesting of a 'common source' via 'roots' (but with an eye on geography), and with uncritical optimism ushers in the great diachronic industry of the nineteenth century. In some language groupings, considered since the sixteenth century, the relationship was already being made precise; in 1799 S. Gyármathi (1751–1830) grammatically proved the genetic link suggested by Sajnovics in 1770 – and how complex this is may be seen in section 5 below – between various Fennic languages and Hungarian. General historical research and particular discoveries in families were about to occupy centre stage. The last fillip was the often cited programmatic address of 1786 by (Sir William) Jones (1746–94) to the Asiatick Society in Bengal, which he founded (see e.g. Robins 1979: 134, 1987: 1–23). This lawyer, amateur scientist and Indophile proposed that Sanskrit, Greek, Latin, Germanic and Celtic formed the main branches of a family, called Indo-European twenty-seven years later by Thomas Young. Both the languages and the basic idea were already familiar; the novelties are (*a*) the genetic linking of geographically distant languages by appeal to a lost source, and (*b*) the insistence on 'the roots of verbs and the forms of grammar' as the crucial criteria. For half a century there was a tussle between those who adhered to this principle (although once you go beyond a small tally of inflexions and simple affixes, languages which are prime candidates for genetic linking differ drastically and very few valid comparanda turn up with detailed likeness among syntactic structures, even at the phrase level) and those who concentrated on the shared phonological origin of the forms compared. These provided many cogent laws of sound change (but seemed blind to the partial nature of the results and to the morphological justification required for equating the contexts of sounds). Franz Bopp and Rasmus Rask are the respective standard bearers.

## 3.2 The promoters

Functional analysis, typology and the relation of the mind to language did not die out as research objects; and some such early-nineteenth-century thinkers gave ammunition to the new historical army. The statesman Wilhelm von Humboldt (1767–1835) pursued a half philosophical and half anthropological – and essentially creative – approach to language; yet, apart from genetic study of Indonesian, he was among those who wondered whether different forms of grammatical marking (like the isolating, agglutinative and inflecting types) represent stages on an evolutionary path. (He also served the historical cause when he appointed Bopp to his linguistic post in Berlin.) The brothers August Wilhelm and Friedrich von Schlegel (1767-1845, 1772–1829) originated this typology of grammar; moreover, they made the Sanskrit language (known since 1586) and Indian thought familiar in Germany. They pointed to the clear morphology of Sanskrit as both an aid to comparison and a confirmation of the concept of grammar as the unchanging heart of a language. About now 'comparative grammar' emerges as the name for the new study; and comparative anatomy and Linnaean botany made their contribution to the model.

But the empirical current now began to flow in earnest. Franz Bopp ('the factual Bopp', 1791–1867) produced in 1816 the first comparative grammar of the verb in the early IE languages; while Rasmus Rask (1787–1832), required by conditions of a prize essay to seek a known origin for the Scandinavian tongues, notably demonstrated how a pre-Germanic and pre-Greco-Latin source can be found by reconciling changed sound segments within a basic vocabulary. Jakob Grimm (1785–1863) accepted the core of Rask's phonetic findings into a revised version of his own grammar of Germanic of 1822; he thus did much to marry the two lines of research and to harness the in-depth study of one language or a close-knit group for the ultimate cross-linguistic confrontation of forms. Many industriously joined the search, opening up what has been called 'a time of uninspired drudgery'; possibly August Schleicher (1821–68) was the most influential. He purported to set out the sounds and forms of the IE parent language with some precision. He began the convention of marking the purely reconstructed items with an asterisk (so that wags could shake their heads at his 'ill-starred forms'). He declared that sound shifts are the key to history, and that they obey laws (where Grimm had seen only tendencies). And for him language was a natural organism and its study a natural science, even to the point of conformity with Darwinism; hence the genealogical slant. (On Darwin and the linguists, see Chapter 22, section 2.5.2.)

The refinements of method and results provided by e.g. Pott, Schuchardt, Curtius, Ascoli and Whitney may be seen by reference to any of the many reviews of nineteenth-century research (e.g. Pedersen 1924 (1931), Sebeok 1975, Robins 1979, or Bynon and Palmer 1988: Chapters 9–11). But the century closed on a different note. By the early 1870s a group of younger practitioners, a militant tendency, challenged orthodox procedures with calculated impudence. They accepted the unkind label of 'Young grammarians' and claimed to inhabit 'the clear light of day' far from the 'grey theories' of the older scholars. The four central figures were K. Brugmann (1849–1919), B. Delbrück (1842–1922), A. Leskien (1840–1916) and H. Osthoff (1847–1909), and they really represented not all the quite radical thinking of the time (the work of Schmidt or Collitz may be noted) but rather a Leipzig movement consciously at odds with Berlin. But they prompted (by the views noted below, section 4.4.1) a succession of cleansings of the work of Grimm and others, and a series of discoveries leading to comprehensive explanations of the evolutionary facts of Indo-European consonants and vowels (and inter-mediate elements). The discoverers include Thomsen and Verner from Denmark, Ascoli from Italy, Saussure from Switzerland, as well as Brugmann himself – with varying degrees of acceptance of the new revelation. In addition to the rigorous application of sound laws (see below), this included the tenets that Sanskrit is less important as a paradigm of controlled change than are contemporary idioms, that language is not a natural organism except in the sense of reflecting human psychology, and that evolution and its laws are the central issue rather than functional typology or the drawing up of this or that 'family'. At the very least, the movement forced historical linguists to think what they were doing.

### 3.3 Later conrollers and assessors of method

In truth, comparative historical linguistics is a craft based on no theory but on a conscious and careful methodology. In the twentieth century, despite a swing to anti-historicism now succeeded by an interested tolerance between linguists of most kinds, the methodology has been re-examined and even codified. In the 1960s, however, the hypnotic effect of the new fashion of accounting for language structures and forms by users' internalised rules led several scholars to re-write history as so many cases of the losing or moving or generalising of such rules in native speakers' minds (cf. e.g. King 1969). Others saw the inevitable obscuring of the transparent placing and interplay of rules as leading to intolerable opacities which the speakers would cure by more or less radical restructuring of the language. From this comes a school of thought which links change firmly to a theory (or the theorems) of grammar; in its extremer form, it sees change as sudden and catastrophic (so Lightfoot 1979). Others remain convinced that function motivates change, or that re-interpretation of surface forms is the cause, or that a few larger dictates of efficiency entail a multiplicity of smaller shifts (the teleological view). But these are really less part of the history of the comparative-historical school than of the search for the causes of language change and decay, on which see section 6 below.

## 4. THE METHODOLOGY

### 4.1 The basic relationship

Relating languages by family-descent is quite a separate operation from relating them typologically. The latter calculates their likeness in various functional aspects and is always a valid procedure, for in some points any language must be like some others if it is to qualify as a natural language at all. Typological likeness may evolve, but is a matter of parallelism rather than divergence (or convergence). The two relations intersect, except in the very rare cases where no plausible genealogical connections at all can be supposed for a language: Basque is a probable example as is, on a smaller scale,

Burushaski (spoken in the Karakoram range in Pakistan). Other isolated idioms are still undergoing optimistic family placement; Etruscan probably suffers most.

Languages may diverge, in the sense that they split in an amoeba-like fashion and the parts separate widely; or they may converge because their speakers live close together and frequently interact. From time to time fresh pleas are made for an overall convergence theory, and divergence supporters denounce them heartily (so in the 1860s W.D. Whitney against Max Müller). But convergence on some scale is a fact of life. Physical contiguity or trade used to be essential for convergence; modern media, especially television, have made it a global phenomenon. Political or cultural dominance still directs it. The results can be considerable: the Tanzanian language Mbugu has allowed the surrounding Bantu languages to supply its morphosyntax of nouns and verbs – normally the most personal and unchanging part of a language. This second sort of evolution often supervenes on the first; 'areal' effects obscure 'genetic' heredity. (The French respective terms *affinité* and *parenté* are useful.) Indeed, because of the problems caused to linguists by this intersection some prefer to regard languages, descending through time, as permanently many and separate but nudged by physical circumstances into temporary groupings (like the Lucretian theory of the behaviour of atoms). Troubetzkoy in 1939 put this areal-convergence view most trenchantly. Yet examples abound of quite undeniable daughterhood, of which the languages of North (West) India – based on 'Indo-Aryan' – or the Romance group – descended from Latin – are typical. So the genetic-divergence hypothesis is not deposed from its position as the most compelling model, but it may have to be trimmed and qualified.

## 4.2 The model

Genetic relationship suggests a 'family tree'. (Schleicher's notion) still the usual recourse for diagramming what seem, as a rough summary of cumulative evidence, to be the evolutionary interrelations within a group of languages of a presumed common source. It is trivial to object that human genealogies show each child descending from two parents or that their tally of individuals may be less in less fecund lower reaches than in the higher; the true analogy is with the descent of manifold species from ever fewer and simpler genera, orders and phyla. The tree-model is an awkward one, but it is very useful and still fashionable. Figure 42 is a simple example (a corner of the 'Indo-European' field). More such trees are given in section 5 below. This whole biological metaphor is now called 'cladistics' and attracts interdisciplinary

*Figure 42*

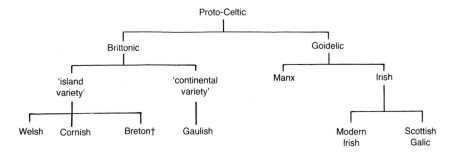

†Breton was transplanted to the mainland of Europe only in the fifth and sixth centuries AD.

*Figure 43*

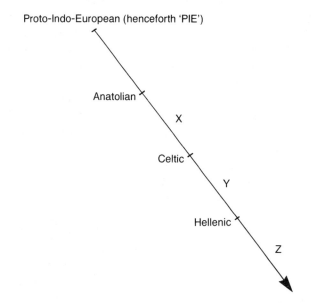

treatment from students of plants, of manuscripts and of languages: see also Chapter 18, section 4.4. above.

One oddity of these inverted trees, in which the lower branches represent the most recent forms of language, is that if one draws them in a slightly different configuration, as in Figure 43, one is denoting the early departure of the Anatolian group from the evolutionary patterns of 'Indo-European', after which it is a marginal and no longer a central witness and its changes, not now paralleled in the other IE languages, are irrelevant to the tree. It branches off before the developments occurring at point $x$ give a revised identity to the continuing tradition (such as perhaps the emergence of feminine gender, or the loss of $w$ as a marker of first person plural in verbs). Celtic is being said to have departed before the events at point $y$, and Hellenic (which has undergone $x$ and $y$) not to have suffered whatever happened at point $z$. Moreover, a later stage of IE (or whatever family is depicted) maintains its claim to true succession precisely by having changed and by differing from PIE (or proto-whatever), and by doing so in just those features in which the marginal languages do not so differ. A strange paradox. But another awkwardness is this, that the decision as to which languages depart at which stage (in this sophisticated tree which puts limits on family centrality) may seem right on one set of diagnostic facts but wrong when another set is considered. For example: it was once canonical (much less so nowadays) to have a major branching between those languages which have a 'k' sound at the beginning of the word for '100' and those which have some sort of sibilant. But traces remain here and there in the 's' group of a verb-formant (a kind of detransitiviser) involving $r$; yet that is most at home in Italic, Celtic and Tocharian which are among the 'k' group. Again, Balto-Slavic and Germanic are both groups in which /ă/ and /ŏ/ have in some way become confused with each other. These two groups are respectively 's' and 'k' types however, but if the vowel treatment is made the criterion for the original branching the absence of verb-forms in $r$ in Germanic is at variance with their sporadic appearance in Balto-Slavic. Greek is a 'k' language and shows an absence of the other two features mentioned; but by its classical period it has regularised a particle *$e$, marking pastness in finite verb forms, into an integral prefix (é-leg-on, 'they were saying'). But this is not a pure Hellenism. The same happens in Indo-Iranian and Armenian, which are within the 's' group – yet there is no sign of this marker in any Baltic or Slavic language in that group any more than in any other language on the 'k' side. Which (ignoring Anatolian and Albanian) leaves the unsatisfactory picture shown in Figure 44. More diagnostics, and more languages, in the tree bring further conflict and endless redrawing. To decide on degrees of 'importance' between features is arbitrary: yet, unless successful, it could produce something as odd as a human genealogy where scattered adventitious matters were included, such as which members of the family were talented or hook-nosed or left-wing. But there are scientific analogues. Bioluminescence (of fireflies, glow-worms, some sea creatures) is very randomly distributed in the animal world; still, it is not a major tool in establishing classes or genera.

Understandably, alternative models have been offered. The best-known is

*Figure 44*

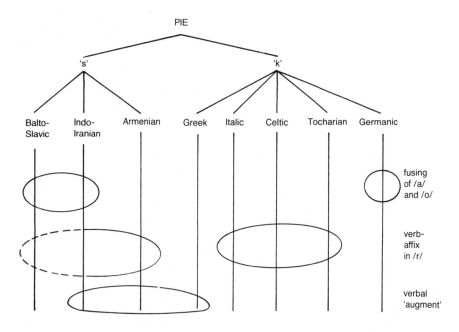

'wave theory', promoted in 1872 by Johannes Schmidt but suggested by Hugo Schuchardt four years earlier. Here attention is directed less to the resultant branching than to the spread of new features themselves. The usual simile is of a series of concentric ripples moving outwards from a stone's impact on a pond – a fair idea of the commonest 'areal' effect on nearer languages. But in a strictly genetic context (which Schmidt's notion does not presuppose) there will have to be a presumption of contiguity of tongues at the right time. Even then the lines of descent would have to cross and regroup in a most complicated way. The analogy can be varied and the lines of descent seen as ridges on a seashore across which a wave has washed and receded, leaving pools in arbitrary places. But some descendants show no sign of such a tide ever having touched them even where known folk-movements have caused regroupings. The tree and wave models can be combined, as in the 'envelope' presentation (invented by Southworth in 1964). In this display those later changes, which actually bring closer some languages which separated at an early stage (and make very distinct others which immediately derive from some comparatively recent 'sub-mother'), may appear as deeper or shallower notches in enclosing envelopes.

So the display (Figure 45) shows that E is a 'sister' of D but has moved closer in observable form to its 'cousin' C'.

*Figure 45 (Adapted from Southworth, 1964)*

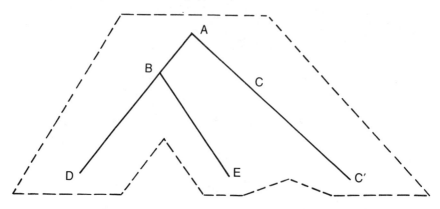

*Figure 46 (Adapted from Southworth, 1964)*

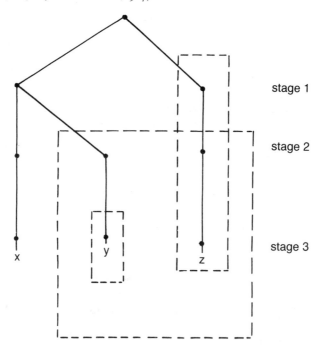

Or, again, chapters of change may be shown, as in Figure 46, where the distant relations Y and Z (which do not share whatever critical change justifies the split at stage 1) share the later innovations at stages 2 and 3, to the exclusion of X.

But this neat notation is defeated by the complexity of the events in a large family and by the operation of universal tendencies. Even close dialects often pursue the same developments in sounds, forms and structures but pursue them at their own speed and in their own order.

The tree, then, with all its faults remains the most illuminating display. The basic configurations deduced from comparing two languages number only three. These are (in the formation of Hoenigswald in 1960, 144-6):

(1)  A/B ≡ A    gives        A
                             |
                             B

(2)  A/B ≡ B  gives          B
                             |
                             A

(3)  A/B ≡ *X gives        where *X is 'neither A nor B', i.e. a
                                               non-extant idiom, reconstructed as a
                                               'proto'-language.

Of course A/B might agree with a known language C, or B/C with A. With three languages the configurations increase to six, and they have interesting implications:

(1)  A/B ≡ A/C ≡ B/C ≡ A gives

(2)  A/B ≡ A but A/C ≡ B/C ≡ *X gives

Once again *X is an explanatory creation: here A/*X, B/*X and C/*X yield the same results and these form *X, a repository of shapes from which the phenomena in A, B and C can all be reasonably and systematically supposed to have evolved.

(3)  A/B ≡ A/C ≡ *X but B/C ≡ *Y  gives

In this case *Y is a 'sub-proto' language, itself a daughter (A/*Y ≡ *X). Even *X may turn out to be a 'sub-proto' when more data (i.e. more languages) are fed in. More will be said on this notion, the extreme case of which will unite all human language in origin.

(4)  A/B ≡ A/C ≡ A but B/C ≡ *Y gives

A surprising but known configuration. In the Romance group A is extant Latin (although a sophisticated register gives us Classical Latin) and *Y is that merely supposed late, regionally different and 'vulgar' variety of it which is reconstructed as 'proto-Romance'.

(5)  A/B ≡ A/C ≡ B/C ≡ *X gives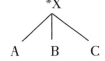

(6)  A/B ≡ A/C ≡ A but B/C ≡ B gives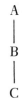

Other apparent shapes merely re-shuffle the A, B, C placings.

    Still, this approach rests on the concept of divergence in time: mothers have daughters and granddaughters, of differing degrees of 'centrality'. But some see convergence as the dominant evolution. Perhaps what we call 'areal' events are really subsets of 'merging' processes such as have (*inter alia*) formed the Indo-European or Afro-Asiatic or Ural-Altaic linguistic families. Perhaps even an *Ursprache* is actually a lingua franca. Yet the opposite view, that divergence is the key and its implications should be followed even to the *prehistoric* point where all languages were one and the same, has been espoused with perhaps the greater fervour (see section 5.3, below).

### 4.3 Systematic comparison

Languages are set up for genetic comparison initially by impression. They seem to have some non-universal elements in common, both as to use and form. These elements will best be found embedded in the formants which convey sub-categories of verbs and nouns and pronouns and will be phonologically traceable, without overdue strain, to a shared origin. The attempt to reconstruct that origin may fail by going beyond the economic or the credible (although you cannot *prove* that two languages are not relatives). The method is hypothetical-inductive, with constraints of naturalness. To reconstruct the original word which arrives in Sanskrit as *aśvaḥ* and in Latin as *equus* will for many reasons turn out to be tricky. But it is within defensible limits to set up, with the help of other relevant languages, something like *\*ek'wos*. Here the 'grammatical' portion, the last two segments, summarises the evidence for the equation of 'form in function' in the really critical sector of language, that where 'inner semantics' is exploited (via number, gender, case) to make sentences possible. To say that is not to equate functions between languages in frequency or importance: the verb-ending +*tum* has the major role of infinitive formant in Sanskrit but plays the minor part of 'supine' in Latin. In lexical sections the difference is even more marked: clearly the numeral 'one' has an Indo-European base-form *\*oi-* with various consonantal additions to give Sanskrit *eka-* (*\*oi+ko-*), Latin *ūnus* (*\*oi+no-*) and so forth, whereas in Greek the numeral derives from a different base (*\*sem*) and *\*oi-* has to be located somewhat out of the limelight, in *\*oi+wo-* in the Homeric adjective *oios*, 'alone', or in *\*oi+n(ā)* in the term (*oinē*) for the 'one-spot' on dice. Again, Albanian *motër* is a more relevant form to compare with English *mother*, German *Mutter*, (West) Greek *mātēr* and so on, than is Albanian *mëmë* – but it is the latter which means 'mother' and the former 'sister'. Once, however, the comparanda have undergone the joint reconstruction process and we have a set of 'original' forms which we may, rather rashly, lump together and call an *Ursprache*, a 'mother', then the systematic nature of the enterprise holds it all together. Given a combination of items separately so reconstructed (e.g. a Proto-Indo-European word built of previously established items), it should be a feasible prediction to say what the shape of the reflex will turn out to be – if it exists there – in Hittite or Sanskrit or Tocharian or Irish or Lithuanian. What the comparativist does was put like this by Jeffrey Ellis (1966: 8:f.) in a statement which has probably not been bettered (although Humboldt said a similar thing in 1828); '(he) observes within one language a number of morphemes or combinations of morphemes each of which from its meaning (lexical or grammatical) has some possibility of being of the same origin (that is, of having had the same meaning originally) as one in another language, and each of which from its phonetic structure has some possibility of being of the same origin (that is, of having had the same phonetic structure originally) as the same one in the other language, and that the latter possibility, and therefore the former possibility, *is raised to an overwhelming probability* when the phonetic developments requiring to be assumed for each are the same for all.' The word 'probability' is a key one here, as will be seen presently.

Thus if several languages of the IE family offer the word 'full' in these forms:
Sanskrit *pūrnaḥ*; Greek *plērēs*; Latin *plēnus*; but Gothic *fulls*; Old Irish *lán*; Welsh *llawn*
the behaviour of the initial segment should be systematically predictable in the word for 'father' once, say, the Sanskrit *pitā* is given: *p*- should be there in Greek and Latin but *f*- in Germanic or nothing (ø) in a Celtic language should replace it. And so it proves: Greek *patēr*; Latin *pater*; but Gothic *fadar*; Old Irish *athir*.

The detailed historical facts covering the whole sequences of segments in these words are very complex (although now very well known). A reconciliation statement will have interesting, even maddening, twists. But the principle is straightforward.

It is important not to confuse **simple** change – as in the pronunciation of what seems to begin in Proto-Indo-European and remain in many languages as a sort of /k/ but becomes eg. *ś* [ʃ] in early Indian – and **implicational** changes, which have the effect of merging segments originally distinct. 'Splits' are interesting but not problematic; often, for instance, speakers come to give a different value to some /k/ sounds, by palatalising those before /e/ or /i/, as the Germans do to the second such sound in *Kirche*, or the Norwegians to the first sound in *kirke* (both from earlier /kyriak-/). But if the new shape becomes identical to the realisation of another segment already functioning in the language it is hard, and very soon impossible, for speakers to recognise its occurrences as a special subset of the tokens of the item with which it has merged. Latin has /r/ and /s/ as does its original mother, but then shifts some of the /s/ set – those occurring between vowels – to /r/; then the set of occurrences of /r/ contains new /r/s, but these are irreversibly merged therein. In *soror*, 'sister', the first *r* is a newcomer and the second an old member, but how to tell? Now, distinctness does not vanish at once. Here some short vowels were lowered before (only) the *new* /r/s. They need not be: *pirum* (? < *(a)piso-*) does not change, nor do forms where an affix-boundary follows the new /ir/ sequences (so *serit* < *si-sit*, but *dir-imō* (< *dis-emō*) remains). But no original /ir/ sequences are affected. So a period in which some of the merging forms were still extricable remains a possibility (and such extrication is often called *Rück(ver)wandlung*). A single exceptional word (*pareiā́* 'cheek') proves indirectly but conclusively enough by its history that when the Ionic group of Ancient Greek dialects fronted and raised /ā/ to a value of about [ɛ:], the speakers of Attic (Athenian) Greek first went along with an across-the-board raising and then reverted to the original value after *r* (and so also, perhaps, after *e* and *i* where the *ā* certainly turns up as the regular reflex). But the irreversible merger, not to be undone because the speakers have lost the power to recover the shape they used to have, is the guarantee of abiding change and of real divergence in evolution. Yet, curiously, this central and critical notion was only recognised in the 1920s (by Polivanov in Russia) and apparently independently in the 1950s (by Hoenigswald in America).

### 4.3.1 Loans

When the historian is poised to perform his comparison and reconstruction there are yet two prior acts of cleansing to be performed on the data. One is internal reconstruction within each language under comparison: more will be said on this important process (section 4.3.2.). The other is the removal of what are quaintly called 'loans'. If one language has taken over a word ready-made from another, that word is not typical and acceptable evidence concerning the borrowing language, at least not entirely. Obvious complications can easily be spotted (some words are made up of parts which are borrowed and parts which are native, and sometimes just the meaning is borrowed and the form 'translated' into the target language). More subtly, there are many shades of integration of loans. The French word *âge* is part of the story of what happened to inherited forms (in this case something like Latin *aetāticium*) and belongs to the systematic history of French; the English loan *age* is, even so, part of English evidence in respect of its new vocalic value [eɪ] and its retention of (medieval French) [dʒ]. Yet *mirage* (apart from some Anglicisation of the /ir/ section) remains a virtual code-switch and should figure entirely in the treatment of French and not at all in English. A pathologist, researching on the likely genetic profile ancestral to an afflicted family, will allow for the smaller effect of those who have married in and discard data from recently adopted children.

### 4.3.2 Internal reconstruction

It is essential not to compare things which merely mislead. Chance identity of meaning or loaned forms may be ignored easily enough, but a subtler source of error may be the failure to use the most historically relevant forms which it is possible to extract from each language under comparison. A language's own history has to be recognised first: to do so is to complete the second major 'cleansing' process on the data. Here the cleansing is partly observational and partly abductive. It is wise to search the documents (including inscriptions, graffiti etc.) for the oldest attested shapes of known forms. For example, by finding that modern English *let* continues two separate earlier verbs, *lǣtan* 'allow' and *lettan*, 'prevent', the historian obviously avoids some fearful mistakes of morphosemantic reconstruction. The second method is called 'internal reconstruction' (IR), and to operate it one needs awareness of the morphology of the given language (even when the results are phonological and rest on careful and credible sound conditioning). A stock example has long been the reconstruction of [raːd] 'wheel' as the older form of the German nominative [raːt], spelt *Rad*, which answers to the genitive [raːdes], spelt *Rades. Rat* [raːt], 'counsel' has the genitive *Rates* [raːtes], whence the pattern is observable. Now the modern nominative [raːt] for 'wheel' can be dismissed: the shift to a voiceless final stop is 'de-evolved'. But the spelling gives it all away anyway, and even a careless researcher who was nose-led by the graphic form would, most unfairly, arrive at the right comparandum. A better instance may be the Latin nominative-genitive relation between *mūs* and *mūris* 'mouse' or *flōs* and *flōris* 'flower' or *honōs* and *honōris* 'honour' or *genus* and *generis* 'kin'. The pattern set by the types *animal – animālis* (or, allowing for final consonant drop, *cor – cordis* or, with a minor vowel shift, *nōmen – nōminis*) predicts an affix + *is* as marking the genitive singular here. Then *amor — amōris, fūr — fūris* follow suit but *\*mūsis, \*flōsis, \*honōsis* are expected but do not surface. But the forms which do occur, taken along with alternations like *amā+re* but *es+se* in verb infinitives, allow a reconstruction of a shifted /s/, becoming /r/ between vowels: so *Lases* preceded *Lares* as the name of local deities. Given, then, that the inhabitants of the town of *Falerii* were called *Falisci*, one deserves no great prize for working out the original form of the town's name – though there is the complication that earlier *\*Falisii* has also suffered the vowel-lowering (*i > e*). Now, how does one react to *serit* 'sows' (noted above)? Add the gains just made to the observation that Latin avoids monosyllabic verbs (e.g. replacing *nat* 'swims' by *natat*) and often does so by reduplication as in *gi-gnit, si-stit*, and one arrives at the form *\*si-sit*, derivative of lost *\*sit*, whose *\*s-* is there in now comparable forms in other idions (as English *sow*, German *säen*). Not only is the Latin reflex returned to a safely presumed prehistorical comparable shape, but other anomalies may be removed. If a short high vowel lowers before this rhotacised /s/, then in the verb 'to be' the future infinitive *fore* or imperfect subjunctive form *forēs* (2sg.) can be returned to *\*fu-se, \*fu-sēs* (cf. *es-se, es-sēs*) and Latin now more helpfully offers only +*se* as infinitive affix and just *es-* and *fu-* as root alternants. The actual sequence of events leading to observable anomalies is often extremely complex and defeats internal reconstruction: again, analogical levelling in paradigms (as when *honōs* gives way to nominative *honor*) often gives a false surface appearance of consistent reflection of a simple inheritance, when in fact tricky alternation was there in the mother language or in the earliest form of our observed language (Hock, 1986: 276f. and 549f., has a good illustration). Moreover, IR must be applied to the surface manifestations of a grammar, even though across categories, and there is no appeal to 'deep' forms.

## 4.4 Comparative reconstruction

Now for the central process of historical-genetic analysis, which is 'comparative reconstruction' (CR). Once the lead-in procedures have been completed the historian sets out the items to be compared between what he presumes to be genetically related languages. The basis of each act of comparison is that the items are more or less the equivalent of one another – and that 'more or less' has been explained above. The aim is a 'reconciliation' form for each sound segment within a morphologically valid structure, whether a grammatical marker (like a verbal inflexion *+*mes* or a derivative noun marker like *+*ment(om)*) or a lexical root. Reconstruction of syntax and its elements is still in its infancy; something will be said about the current fashion in section 7.1 below. Change of shape over time – what happens to an inherited initial /m/ in Celtic, say – is enshrined in shift statements. Such a statement is often given the label of 'So-and-so's law'. This is not because it is of outstanding utility or universal relevance (though some are), but usually because the eponymous hero already had a reputation and enunciated, or just hinted at, a tolerably clear diachronic fact which others find of interest and want to refer to in a convenient if esoteric manner (cf. Collinge 1985).

Let us 'reconcile' some likely Indo-European data, using the accepted symbols of the trade, which are:

>   'is replaced by'
<   'is the historical successor to'
/-   'as placed in the context (environment)'
    (thus /X-Y means 'when following X and preceding Y')
*   'exists only as a putative/reconstructed form'
    (NB: *not* 'impossible' or 'unacceptable'; such items will here be marked †)
+   denotes a morphological boundary
$   denotes a syllable boundary
#   denotes a word boundary (usually)
//   enclose basic phonological segments
()   enclose segments of varying, doubtful or irrelevant occurrence

(1) Sanskrit *sant-*, 'being'; Attic Greek *ont-*, 'being'; Latin *absent-*, 'being away'; *sont-*, 'guilty' (i.e. 'actually being involved'); Old English *sōð* (mod. *sooth*), 'the truth'.

(2) Hittite *a-da-an-zi*, 'they eat'; Sanskrit *dant-*; Attic Greek *odont-*; Latin *dent-*; Gothic *tunþ-*; Old High German *zand-*; and Old English *tōð-* all meaning 'tooth'.

The task is to establish an 'original' word in each case, so that the same processes of sound change may operate in all such sequences on the way to the various attested languages. Then, given the PIE and English forms in case (1) one should be able to predict either, given the other, in case (2). And likewise in all the languages where a reflex is present, of these or similarly structured morphological sequences. Now, clearly, some things are idiosyncratic, like the extra initial vowel in Hittite *adanzi* or Greek *odont-*, or the curious absence of *n* in English, or the variety of vowels (where choice of the PIE version will need a lot of consideration based on much more input). It is reasonable to start from *\*sent-* or *\*sont-* and *\*dent-* or *\*dont-*, and to credit some individual histories with a shift of mid-vowels to /a/. But the history of English presents a typical puzzle, in its loss of *n*. For this, a possible predictive expression of shift could be:

"PIE /n/ > English ø/V-C (#)"

to be read as 'a nasal in PIE is lost in the evolution of English when it occurs between a vowel and a (possibly final) consonant'. This is 'natural' enough. True, the movement of speech organs sometimes induces, or their ease of movement requires, insertion of segments: so the organically 'local' consonants of *Hendry* ( < *Henry*) or Greek *ambro(sia)* etc. ( < *\*a+mro-*) or the added vowels in *Henery* ( < *Henry*) or Spanish *escribir* < Latin *scribere*. But it is more usual for a sound to be lost, especially a nasal as nasality may easily and often be only a superimposed feature of a vowel.

But what of exceptions? Why has English *plinth*? A false alarm: this clear loan word (from Greek *plinthos*, appearing even there in contemporary dialect form as *plithos*, and perhaps an eastern import anyway) will have been struck from the comparanda already, as will e.g. *dent-(al)* etc., from Latin, Now *mouth* (German *Mund*) is as it should be, but what of *month*? But if IR has been performed, Old English *mōnaþ* (cf. Gothic *mēnōþs*) will be the correct datum, obviously irrelevant because of the vowel following the nasal. Very well; but why have we *hound, wound, hundred* and the like? These will cease to be exceptional when the shift's context is made more precise, for they suggest that a constraint is needed on the following consonant: it should not be cited as a stop (in English) but as a 'continuant' with some degree of friction – as when *\*gan+ra* keeps its nasal (*gander*) but *gan+s* (*goose*) loses it before the /s/. The effect of merely apparent exceptions is to falsify and so refine the diachronic statement, a most respectable role.

An important source of such pseudo-exceptions is blindness to the relative chronology of changes. Shifts are to be located in time at least in relation to one another's period of operation. It is crucial that a shift will occupy a certain span of time after it has been accepted and before it ceases to affect items, usually because it has exhausted the range of mutanda. The feminine (nominative) form of the adjective 'all' in Attic Greek started as *pantya and moved to pansa, but did so only after the 'expiry' of another change, of /ns/ to /:n/ /V-V (as when e.g. PIE *ghan+os became khān+os > Attic khēnos); and so it did not pass on to †pāna. Pansa then changed to pāsa in Attic (loss of nasal before friction again), but too late for the loss of /s/ between vowels (noted below) – hence no †pāa or †pā. And its /ā/ developed after Attic had ceased shifting that inherited sound to [ɛ:] – so no †pēa.

A shift may recur, however, even within the same language: so Laconian Greek (spoken in ancient Sparta) lost /s/ between vowels for a second time long after the heyday of that effect (and its finish) in the Mycenaean period. Its form Mōā with genitive plural would be Mō+ān, 'of the Muses' (<*Mōsāom), displaying both instalments; yet the second s vanished with only slight traces at least before 1200 BC while the first went no earlier than the seventh century. Recurrence is predictable if the change is as natural as is this one, the replacement of an aperiodic frictional sound, made by an approximation of organs in the mouth, by the same sort of sound achieved by merely letting air pass from the glottis through and out of the mouth; and this in turn is so unlike other phonic activities in the speech tract that it tends to vanish altogether. Hence, quite commonly, /s/ > /h/ > ø. Similar predictions may be (and have been) made on the basis that deviations from the norm, which is what historical shifts are at first, are more favoured in some cases than elsewhere. Hence the hypothesis of 'drift', or tendency to particular change (cf. Sapir 1921:165f.), which as it happens has seemed easier to apply to morphology and syntax than to phonology. Edward Sapir prophesied the total loss of English whom in favour of who (are we nearly there now?); and he perceived an irresistible trend towards the loss of distinctness between subject and object forms of nouns, and indeed of all inflexions (like case-marking), and a consequent move towards fixed sequential order as the major tool of sentence syntax. Others have elaborated the detailed implications of this idea: Robin Lakoff in 1972 tied together the use of subject-pronouns, articles, prepositions, periphrastic and auxiliary-linked verb-expressions; Vennemann (1975) so explains the whole tendency to favour a central place in the sentence for verbs, subject preceding and object following (see section 6).

As part of 'drift', change may be directed by what are called 'conspiracies'. If a language as it evolves loses final consonants and inserts medial vowels (as in Henery, above) it is worth speculating that these two disparate changes have the common aim of removing sequences like /-CVC#/ or /-CVC$C-/.

That is, they remove 'checked' syllables, i.e. syllables with a closing consonant. Then the alert researcher keeps an eye open for other rearrangements inside syllables which would have the same effect, like the moving of liquids into post-consonantal position where they commonly do not count as full consonants, so that /CVr$C-/, with checking /r/, may be resyllabified as /CrV$C-/. This well-known block of events (the trend to open syllables) actually occurred in early Slavic, ohers of a similar sort elsewhere. (For causes in general, see section 6.)

### 4.4.1 Exceptions

But not all exceptions wilt when historical statements are made more precise. Real, abiding anomalies are frequent. Edgar Sturtevant's famous analogue, the 'Law of Waterloo' (that all Prussian soldiers six foot tall were killed there), applied to the Latin change of /s/ > /r/ /V-V, allows for such false exceptions as Prussians as yet unborn (so we find *causa*, because it did not get that form in time), or naturalised too late (like the import *casa*), or too near to existing corpses – for such seems to be the true analogy – (as when the /s/ in *miser* is kept as it is because of the following /r/), or even in that case when another live Prussian (not in the battle) offsets the effect of the corpse (as when, in *\*swesor* (> *\*sosor*(?)) > *soror*, the initial, (not intervocalic) *s* ensures that the Prussian in the middle does perish, i.e. that /s/ becomes /r/ after all). But after all that, why does *nāsus* 'nose' occur, especially alongside *nārēs* 'nostrils'? Why this sheer and real exception?

In the last quarter of the nineteenth century the *Junggrammatische Richtung* (see section 3 above) took a deliberately overstrong line on this issue. They declared with conscious impudence that a properly stated shift-rule has no real exceptions. This was a policy statement, a 'platform'. It spurred others (and themselves) to increase and widen the cleansing processes and so it put rigour into a profession which was becoming addicted to the *ad hoc*. Still, they recognised that some real exceptions will be present and deserve a sound apologia – and even that at the last there will remain a residue of the unexplained or, anyway, the not yet explained (Jankowsky 1972). This allowed the 'laws' of change to be ultimately probabilistic, which is why such concepts as 'drift' are justified. The kinds of explanation of such real exceptions are, probably, only five in number.

First, elements which are not much integrated into the systems of language (like names) and/or are of high frequency and load (like the simple negator) often disobey the rules. There is an aspirate at the start of the Greek word for 'horse', *hippos*, but in a name like *Leukippos* ('Whitehorse') it is just dropped. The Italian city name *Milano*, deriving from *Mediolan(i)-um*, might have been expected rather to become *\*Medilano* or perhaps *\*Mezzolano*. In Latin there is the heavily used *nōn* (< *\*ne+oeno-*) instead of expected *\*nūn* (cf. *(n)ūllus*). Where French gives a high frequency to derivatives of Latin *senior* or *ambul(āmus)*, they appear as the unusual *sire* and *all(ons)*.

Secondly, special treatment may help to keep apart elements whose conflation would confuse: in some dialects of French a shift of /r/ > /z/ /V-V was favoured and has left the odd vestige in the standard language (so *chaise* < *chaire*). Even Paris was briefly called *Pasys*. But this was even then over-ridden to avoid some homonymy: the distinctness of *oreille*, 'ear' from *oseille*, 'sorrel' was preserved. Fortunately, kin-words are stubborn (cf. *mère* despite *mer*), and they kept *frère* distinct from *fraise*; it seems perverse deliberately to confuse one's brother with a strawberry. But frequently is itself affected: since the two English words *let* conflated in form, one (the 'prevent' one) has become rare and specialised.

Thirdly, shifts may operate over periods which allow overlap with the working of a competing shift, equally applicable to the same input; the successful shift is the more 'intense'. Sometimes a sort of tug-of-war ensues, as in Attic Greek where the central /o/ of *ónoma*, 'name' (< PIE *nom(e)n*) is no doubt attracted upwards by the following labial (as in *anónumos*, 'unnamed') but is hauled back by 'harmony' with the preceding /o/.

Fourthly, there is the phenomenon of 'lexical diffusion'. This term covers the easily documented cases where a shift, usually in sound, does indeed occur in the words of the language which are its defined context but not in all at once. It spreads like treacle across the language, affecting some categories of form quickly, some a little more slowly and some with marked reluctance. Wang and Chen are credited with the recent promotion of this concept (noted by Whitney in 1894) which many now see as the normal pattern, although some regard a progressive weakening in the adverse conditions as being the real point of interest. The slow generalisation may not be arbitrary (as if some words simply attract the change earlier than others) but governed by the differences between classes or sub-classes of word, pronouns perhaps resisting more or less than nouns, interrogatives more or less than demonstratives, and so forth. The picture is not clear, but demographic studies show the varying rates of lexical spread alongside the socially conditioned rates of acceptance by types of speakers. This latter is another, intersecting, factor; for example, when demotic Greek was increasing its domain a few years ago (before its current official and dominant status) conservative minded and/or female speakers showed a much spottier use of its forms (within their 'katherevousa' norm) than male radicals. Hence 'variable rules' may need to be used in description. But that the shift itself is *phonetically* gradual is often demonstrably false (as in the German umlaut move of /a/ from [a] to [e], passing straight 'over' [ε] – cf. King, 1969: 116) or, where steps can be proved, it is trivial. That is, it makes one shift into a succession, which may be true in that instance but is only of interest if a causal sequence is established.

The fifth cause of historical exceptions is analogy. When the neogrammarians insisted on the power of exceptionless shifts they admitted one other force of equal strength, analogy. 'Only these two come into the question' said Leskien. The earlier term was 'false analogy' – as if regular evolution alone were 'true' – but at last the analogical process was understood to be natural, frequent and influential. It might operate lexically: so like meaning begets like form, as when English borrows French *femelle* and then amends it to *female* to match *male*. Numerals become partly like each other, no doubt by acts of counting: '9' gets the initial *d-* of '10' instead of inherited *n-* in Baltic and Slavic languages (cf. Lithuanian *devyni*, Russian *devyat'*); '7' affects '8', and so in late Greek *heptá* changes *oktố* to *hoktố* and in Lithuanian *septyni* gives its ending to *\*aštuo* > *aštuoni* (helped by *devyni*, no doubt). Antonymy works as well: the Latin opposition *pre(he)ndere* vs. *reddere*, 'take' vs. 'give', passes to *prendre* vs. *rendre* in French (English *render*), with equal nasality. Or morphology may be the domain. All persons come to have the same root form *hep-* in the Greek verb 'follow' although *\*hetetai*, *\*hetesthe* would be phonetically 'regular'. The Latin shift of /s/ to /r/ between vowels should leave *honōs* (nom.), *honōris* (gen.); but the former becomes *honor*. Constraints prevent this happening, it is true, e.g. to short-vowel neuters (where *-os* > *-us* /–#/): so *tempus, genus*. But then in that group *robur* 'strength of wood' is an exception just because it is like *arbor* 'tree'; and *arbor* alone of non-neuters spreads its short *ŏ* (regular in final syllables before liquids) to its entire declension (*arbŏris* etc.) – just because *it* is like *robur* in meaning. The new English singular *pea* from supposed 'plural' *peas(e)* rests on the relation of e.g. *flea* to *fleas*; and the old simple pairing of singular *staff*, plural *staves* (cf. *leaf, leaves*) is split into two 'analogical regularities', *staff* – *staffs* and *stave* – *staves*.

It has been claimed that shift laws are regular but make for irregular morphology and that analogy, conversely, is an irregular force promoting levelling. But the truth is more complex. The associative power of lexical linking is not necessarily stronger than that of word class: so adjectives like *unfair, unkind* enforce the *un-* prefix in *unjust, uncivil* despite the pull of the nouns *injustice, incivility*. The clear pattern of weak verbs (*wait – waited, please – pleased*) ought to induce the type to spread (as when children say *goed*). But *wear-weared* gave way to *wear-wore* on the analogy of e.g. *tear-tore*. So clearly a proportion formula (*a : a′ :: b : x*) is at work, as Havet first showed in 1875; but equally clearly *a* and *b* must link up, as when Latin genitive *senātūs* sometimes becomes *senātī* not only because of (1) the nominative:genitive formula *populus : populī :: senātus : senātī* but also (2) the political duality, and the common rime-phrase, *senatus populusque Romanus*. Analogy may keep a pattern intact, as when the Greek aorist (past tense) keeps its formant /+sa/ even after vowels, as *elūsa* (not *†elūa*). But it neither favours not precludes disruptive results; it is an evolutionary factor of mental association and indifferent as to whether its results complicate or simplify morphology.

Between 1947 and 1980 Kuryłowicz and Mańczak elaborated hypotheses as to how forms affect one another, whether different forms with the same function diminish in number, whether marking becomes more or less complex, whether an old form or its analogical usurper will become the 'normal' version, and so forth. These pronouncements are fully exemplified and criticised by Hock (1986: 210–37). They are essentially attempts to show how analogy works and not predictions of when it will or will not occur, for that remains mysterious. Proportion is one factor, usage another, sound-echo a third. Indeed, if all sentence structures are so many expansions of a basic type of 'name + predicate', then all syntax is expansive analogy.

This sort of mental association factor shows that, as was urged against the linguistic Darwinists of last century (see section 3), languages and their forms are not some kind of natural organism. Even so, it is valid and salutary to place one scientific constraint on historical speculation, taken from the natural world and itself a precondition of Darwinism. This is that natural changes, however old, must rest on causes now still seen to be operating, for in an evolutionary situation changes and their causes cannot be absolutely different at different epochs. This conceptual insight is usually credited to the geologist (Sir Charles) Lyell, writing between 1830 and 1833, but James Hutton had the idea in 1789. Not all linguists, however, accept the consequent unlikelihood of merely 'catastrophic' changes. Still, probably nobody will any longer espouse miraculous shifts.

## 5. TREES AND FAMILIES

### 5.1 How a tree is drawn

For those seeking to state familiar relations by applying 'CR', a bench-test (even with fictitious data) may illuminate many matters of method. Given a set of systematically similar forms across several languages, let us build up the genetic tree and encounter some of the commoner historical problems at the same time. Here is such a data-set, offered by six derived languages of an imaginary but possible world (a Ruritania, say), which suggests the reconstruction of a non-extant mother-tongue which once set up may be called 'Proto-Ruritanic' (Table 20).

Clearly, E(rker) and F(rolig) have things in common, like the $\check{c}$- segment in 'wise', the $\acute{s}$ in 'clever' and the $\check{z}$ in 'they speak; and one may fairly suppose that, given E's $\check{c}iryat$ and the $y\bar{a}t/y\bar{a}t\partial$ correspondence, F's absent form for 'he writes' would have been $*\check{c}iryat\partial$. At any rate, no other language seems any more like either E or F than they are like each other. F alone has the common

*Table 20*

|    | Argan     | Burusi  | Copu    | Damuk   | Erker  | Frolig   |               |
|----|-----------|---------|---------|---------|--------|----------|---------------|
| 1. | ʔurate    | ulate   | –       | ulatə   | ulat   | ulatə    | 'he hates'    |
| 2. | iaʔate    | yāte    | yātə    | yātə    | yāt    | yātə     | 'he throws'   |
| 3. | diaki?    | dyaki   | tyakə   | tyakə   | čyak   | čyakə    | 'wise' (fem.) |
| 4. | sapdom    | hapdom  | zabdom  | zaβðom  | zabdon | zaddum   | 'brave' (masc.)|
| 5. | sapdomi?  | hapdomi | zabdomə | zaβðomə | zabdom | zaddumə  | 'brave' (fem.)|
| 6. | kiriate   | keryate | kiryatə | kiryatə | čiryat | –        | 'he writes'   |
| 7. | rapoda    | rapoda  | rabodə  | raβoðə  | rabod  | rabudə   | 'suddenly'    |
| 8. | gosēde    | gohēde  | gozēdə  | gozēðə  | gožēd  | gužidə   | 'they speak'  |
| 9. | lūseti?   | lūheti  | lūsetə  | lūsetə  | lūšet  | lūšitə   | 'clever' (fem.)|

(It may be assumed that the time-depth is greater to the left, smaller to the right, of the columns of forms.)

assimilation of one consonant to another *immediately* following (*bd* > *dd*); this fact could have been established by 'internal reconstruction', had there been such an adverb as *zabuda* (cf. *rabuda*). F also shows raising of mid vowels (e, o, > *i, u*). E alone has dentalised its final nasals (m > *n* / – – #) and noticeably, has lost its final vowels (apocope). Indeed, it must have done those things in the order in which they have been mentioned, and the first change must have stopped happening before the second began: for the forms (cf. the similar C) *zabdom, zabdoma* pass in E via *zabdon, zabdoma* to *zabdon, zabdom*. The other order of events would have given first \**zabdom* and then \**zabdon* for *both* genders: so here is evidence of relative chronology. Undoing the shifts in E and F — 'de-evolving', in fact, as historians do — yields a common, reconstructed set of forms :-

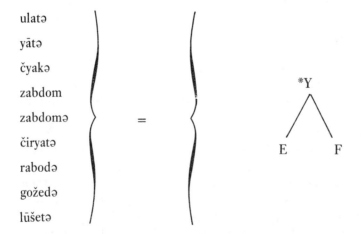

ulatə
yātə
čyakə
zabdom
zabdomə
čiryatə
rabodə
gožedə
lūšetə

Now what status is to be assigned to that set: that is, what is '\*Y'? It must be a theoretical and heuristic construct, for it is not actual: hence it is a 'proto-language'. But if, as may later appear, it is not the ultimate Ruritanic idiom, it is clearly a 'sub-proto'. As such, it enters the evidence as a valid but derived exhibit.

Now to consider D(amuk) and C(opu). The idiosyncrasy of the former is the spirantising of the consonants *b*, *d* but not initial *g*. But now *Y alone offers a palatal-frictional version of voiceless consonants like *t* and *k* (> *č*) if they stand before *i* or *y* (a common occurrence in the world), as well as friction added to *s* or *z* if they stand before *e* (again, a frequent effect of 'front' vowels). If (with an eye on C) these fairly obvious shifts in *Y and D are, once again, all undone and the historical clock thus moved back, both *Y and D become:

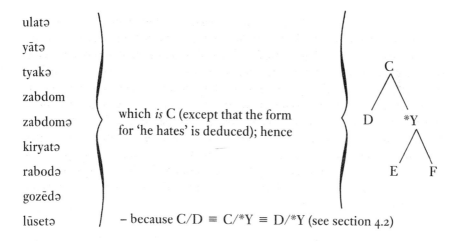

ulatə

yātə

tyakə

zabdom

zabdomə

kiryatə

rabodə

gozēdə

lūsetə

which *is* C (except that the form for 'he hates' is deduced); hence

– because C/D ≡ C/*Y ≡ D/*Y (see section 4.2)

– that is, C is now seen to be the 'mother' of D and *Y. That a known language can be the ancestor of a reconstructed one is not surprising: Latin, thoroughly known in its classical form, is the direct source of that essentially reconstructed immediate mother of French, Spanish, Italian and so on which we call 'proto-Romance'.

As A is so clearly distinct in its forms from the other Ruritanian languages, the next comparison must be between C (which now subsumes D, E and F) and B. Of these, B itself obviously has *h* before vowels where all the other evidence gives *s*, much as Ancient Greek did. Likewise, it seems to have a lowering of vowels (here the vowel *i* to *e*) before *r*, as in *keryate*; again, this is the sort of thing one can find elsewhere in the world. So that B can be tidied up, thus:

ulate

yāte

dyaki

*sapdom

*sapdomi         = 'pre-B'

*kiryate

rapoda

*gosēde

*lūseti

But the branch headed by C has evolved in several more fundamental ways. The simplest shift has been to change all final vowels (evidenced in A and B) into the indistinct 'schwa' (ə). This must be so: it would be much less easy to motivate a change in B from /ə/ into a variety of more distinct vowels (*e, i, a*), *and* into a variety which just happened to be the same as that in A. So 'pre-C' may be 'rewritten' accordingly. More complex is the treatment of stop consonants in C. Where 'pre-B' has *pd, pod, sēd,* C has *bd, bod, zēd,* which means that voicing occurs by assimilation to a following (but not necessarily contiguous) stop. Even more, once *pd* has become *bd* in *\*sabdom,* the sequence *sabd* shifts to *zabd* (a 'cyclic' effect of the shift-rule). Thirdly 'pre-B' has *dyaki* where 'pre-C' now offers *\*tyaki*. This is a trickier problem. Is *y* ignored (as a mere glide)? If so, there has been voice-assimilation in C between the consonants (*d > t* before *k*), but now reversed in effect (*de*-voicing). Or is *y* itself voiceless in this language and equated in assimilatory power with a voiceless stop? Either solution is possible and the evidence may never permit a decision – a frequent fact of life for historical comparativists.

Summarising these adjustments (that is, undoing those shifts which characterise B and C) allows us to reconstruct the original joint shape of 'pre-B' and 'pre-C':

ulate

yāte

dyaki

sapdom

sapdomi

kiryate

rapoda

gosēde

lūseti

– which is *not* the same as any known language tally, and clearly different from A: therefore, once again, this must be a 'sub-proto' idiom – i.e. '*X' (a 'proto' which excludes A).

So that the tree is now

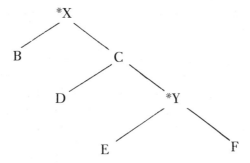

Now we come to the curious A(rgan). It is often impossible to decide whether initially high vowels become glides (i.e. *i* becomes *y*) or the converse: here one or other shift has occurred initially and after consonants. Suppose A represents a very early stage before glides settled into a consonantal version (as in *X and all its descendants): then *idʔate*, *diaki-* and *kiriate* contain original vowel sequences (*ia*). As for the distribution of *r* and *l*, A and *X clearly both had both; but *ʔurate* versus *ulate* has to be explained, and a special effect in A – *l* > *r* between vowels, an accepted context for *r* – is perhaps the simplest solution. These deductions are reasonable, even likely, but far from certain: things may have gone the other way. But A is obviously fuller, in sequences of segments, than are the X-group languages. In 'he throws' -*aʔa*- answers to (later?) -*ā*-, in 'he hates' initial *ʔ*- is balanced by zero in *X, and so is final -*ʔ* in the feminine forms of adjectives. Apparently a glottal occlusion, operating as a phonological (and morphological) segment, has not survived the passage of time between A and *X (or has survived only in the sense that A is very conservative): thus, the shift -*aʔa*- > -*aa*- > -*ā*- within the history of *X is reasonable. This sort of thing is well enough known in Semitic, and most people accept it (with many personal variations as to the details) in early Indo-European, as part of the famous 'laryngeal theory'. (The 'lost' laryngeal has been assigned manifold features, from Saussure's essay of December 1878 to the present day. It may, they say, be one segment or an array of up to twelve different sounds. Many favour three. It may aspirate or voice consonants, lengthen and/or 'colour' vowels, interact with semivowels, and even (e.g. in Hittite) leave consonantal or vocalic 'traces'.)

After all which considerations, the 'de-evolved' versions of A and *X must conflate into:

ʔulate

iaʔate

diakiʔ

sapdom

sapdomiʔ

kiriate

rapoda

gosēde

lūsetiʔ

– and this is at last our 'proto-Ruritanic', so that

etc.

Or it is a defensible array of presumptions, from which we can start to make general statements about much of PR morphology.

Notice that the origin of *ā* in one word in *X is clearly different from that of *ē* and *ū* in others (where we have no evidence that the long vowel was not there all the time). 'Super-tree' building, on wider genetic evidence, might show that *all* long vowels are here actually secondary, even if the process which formed them is prehistoric in Ruritania. Nor do we know just what was going on in the glottis of proto-Ruritanic speakers at the points marked 'ʔ'. The evidence has been milked of all legitimate deductions and from these anybody can set out the *phonological* inventory of the proto-language. More, although we have excluded changes of meaning and ignored the important factor of word-accent and have ordered the data in favour of the least cumbrous solution, it has allowed glimpses of relative timing, cyclic evolution, positional constraints, gaps, phonetic likelihood, and competing explanations of shifts. And it has left a residue of uncertainties. A fairly typical slice of a comparative philologist's on-going experience.

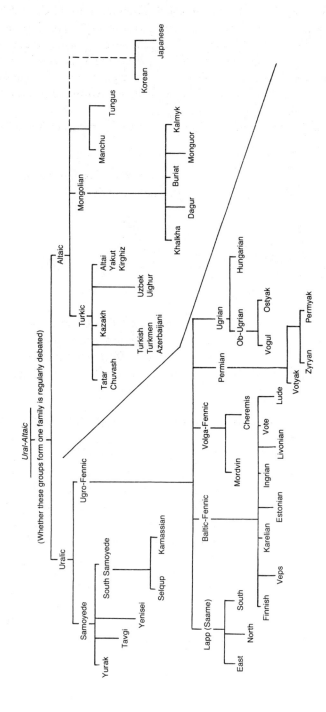

*Figure 47*

The genetic distance between Finnish and Hungarian is worth noting, as is the tenuous link with Turkish. The inclusion and placing of Korean and (even more) of Japanese is still uncertain.

## 5.2 Some known families

Some of the better known actual language families are worth looking at, but nobody should believe that their branchings are matters of general and permanent agreement, or that when a new but related idiom is found it can be placed without argument at its rightful place in the descent. These diagrams (Figures 47–49) are not exhaustive and are, at best, *exempli gratia*.

(A body of now nearly 5,000 tablets found in 1968 and 1974 at Ebla, near Aleppo, shows a previously unknown but very early Semitic language. Some place it on the North-West Semitic branch, specifically as an older form of Canaanite; others are as firm that its morphology is more consistent with its being Old Akkadian, in East Semitic. Not an unusual dissension.)

## 5.3 Larger families

If any proto-language is potentially a sub-proto and may be shown so to be when more evidence comes in, it is not surprising that similarities between

*Figure 48*

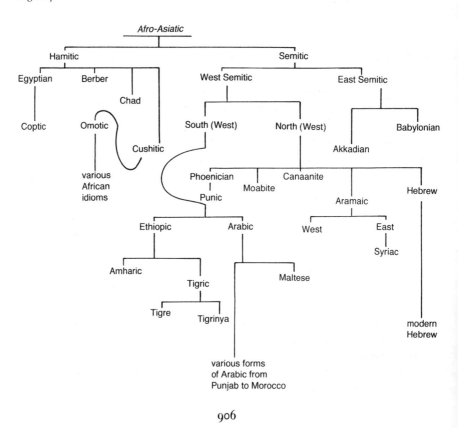

*Figure 49*

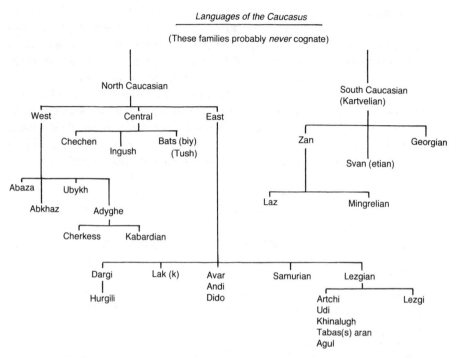

Languages of the Caucasus

(These families probably *never* cognate)

languages of different families have prompted optimists to conflate those whole families and search for a common 'mother'. Indo-European was linked, speculatively, to Semitic by Raumer as early as 1863 or to Finno-Ugric by Thomsen six years later. Fortuitous, non-systematic, similarities are properly discarded. Persian and English are related, but not just because the word *bad* has the same form and meaning in each; after all, unrelated Hungarian has *juh* (like English *ewe* in sound and sense). But a body of regularly cognate forms (especially in the morphological sector where whole syllables or affixes are alike), or demonstrably parallel patterns of syntax, have recently induced some to connect the Indo-European family with the South Caucasian (Kartvelian) group. Others have similarly exploited the lexical likenesses between Indo-European and Semitic. One (Illič-Svityč, 1971 and 1976) reconciled the phonology of Indo-European, Semitic, Kartvelian, Uralic and Dravidian. The 'new-look' given by recent radical analysts to the PIE stop consonant range (see below, section 7.2) has been added to the vocabulary similarities (by Bomhard, 1984) in an attempt to bind the whole Indo-European and Afro-Asiatic families together. Holger Pedersen called all this the search for a 'nostratic' tongue. Nostraticism springs from a belief in 'super-divergence', and is a current fashion.

## 6. THE REASONS FOR CHANGE

The causation of language change is complex and obscure. In 1821 Jakob Bredsdorff listed seven factors of which four were either sporadic or personal (desire for distinctness, mishearing, defective memory and imperfect speech organs); one other was analogy, noted above (section 4.4.1). The last two were laziness (essentially, that speakers keep items distinct by the barest minimum of dissimilarity, and so unneeded features will tend to be discarded) and fresh functional need (leading to actual invention of forms, which is not unknown, as when the poet Milton invented *sensuous* to replace *sensual,* which had developed coarse overtones). The laziness or 'least effort' factor has been elaborated, notably by George Zipf (between 1929 and 1949), into a positive and negative calculus of the stability of speech-sounds. The most frequent segments can afford to jettison features and to reduce articulatory effort, while the intermediate keep them and the least frequent seek to increase them to aid recognition.

The effect of close co-habitation between languages is part of arealism (*affinité*). 'Drift' and 'conspiracies' have been noted already as probabilistic phenomena. The chain-effect of changes, however caused initially, is theoretically trivial (though there has been debate as to whether items in, say, a vowel system 'push' others into a different articulatory position by coming closer to them in kind or 'pull' others into a gap in the system caused by their own move). But more dynamic explanations of change have been offered. They are roughly of three kinds: (1) the rules-and-functions motive; (2) concepts of phonetic strengths: and (3) social motivation.

According to the first view, current mostly between 1969 and 1975 or so, the rules in speakers' mental competence by which forms of words are derived or sound values varied may be shifted in order of application, or lost, or inserted. The result will be a new form of grammar or of phonology in context. Hence shift-statements, properly put, are not to be distinguished from the listed rules of a grammar and the likeness of the two gives respectability to both.

Furthermore, it has been argued that alterations in sequence (or presence) of rules may produce output which renders the statement of rules opaque: a shift may not occur when it is expected because the rule is vacuous or may happen when it 'should' not. After a period in which native speakers tolerate variable degrees of change in the forms of their language or anomalous morphology (or even syntax) arising from varied outputs of current derivational rules, there may come a crisis point at which, in 'catastrophic' fashion, transparency is regained by wholesale change. This concept is akin to that of disruptive change as being the norm; not all see it so. Opacity of a different sort has been suggested as a source of syntactic evolution by those who believe it both possible and fruitful to establish not only the distinction between actors and events (roughly, nouns and verbs) but also that between verbs and 'subjects' and 'objects' in sentences, a very delicate branch of analysis (see below, section 7.1). A more subtle theory, rejecting sharp fractures of that kind, seeks to explains morphosyntactic change – the current challenge – by tracing back the items which enter into the rules of morphology to an earlier existence as more independent elements. Items may start as whole words, subject to semantic linking and rules of lexical structure; they may then suffer a bleaching of meaning, become clitics and then just affixes, of word-class-change (like English *like* > -*ly*) or of past tense or auxiliary status in verbs (like English '*ve*, or Tok Pisin future marker -*b*- from *baimbai*, 'soon'), and so on. Whitney suggested the idea in 1885, Meillet (1912) and Givón (1971) furthered it, and its current name is 'grammaticalisation'. But some argue firmly for cases of the reverse change, from clitics to full words, for example.

The second major type of explanation, a sort of 'natural phonology', originated with Maurice Grammont (1895, 1933) and has led to many phonetic essays on relative 'strength' – that is, the ability of a sound to remain unchanged while changing other nearby sounds in words and phrases. The calculus may be between consonants, vowels and diphthongs or between velars and labials or between stops and spirants, and so forth. There have also been accompanying hypotheses as to just what 'weakening' entails and how it is enhanced – and even how it is demonstrable at a given stage of language rather than being an after-the-event rationalisation of history. Studies of this kind were common in the 1970s; note Foley (1977) and several contributions to Stockwell and Macaulay's anthology of 1972.

Third, some stalwartly insist on a social origin and control for virtually all linguistic change. The 1983 Poznań workshop on sociolinguistics (see Traugott and Romaine 1985) shows an organised approach to history from this angle. Some claim that where speakers have weak ties to particular social groups their language is likely to change with speed (but perhaps less consistency); many have long espoused a notion of imitative change, wherein speakers assimilate their forms to those of individuals or groups which they seek to copy or join. The theorising of William Labov (and various mentors, collaborators and disciples) rests on a belief that in any speech community there is a natural and tolerable amount of heterogeneity, whatever the local causes. The more 'abstract' aspects of language, underlying its grammar and semantic apprehension, will be most uniform; at the lower levels of phonology and phraseology the differences, as long as they do not destroy intelligibility, regularly become changes. Social surveys (especially in Philadelphia in 1980) have helped to establish the constraints on this regularising of the non-regular, and to plot its routes and success and social evaluation and acceptance. Chapter 14 above has some very pertinent observations on this interaction of the present and the past.

# 7. CURRENT CONTENTIOUS ISSUES

Attention will always be directed to those aspects of language history which shape the methods of study; the causes of change and its controls, the role of communicative efficiency, and the divergent and convergent impulses between speech-groups whether regional or social. These have been noted (see above, sections 5 and 6), as has the apparent tendency of individual languages to strip lexical meaning from free words and impress them as new class or category markers in grammar. Still, the following special areas of recent research deserve a separate listing:

## 7.1 History of syntax

Phonology dominated diachronic study last century and even in the earlier years of this century (with some notable exceptions, like the work of Berthold Delbrück). Recently, studies of the syntactic machinery available at various times have extended our understanding of how auxiliary verbs emerge and are exploited, how prepositions develop via adverbial, prenominal, and pre- and post-verbal uses, and so forth. Some cross-linguistic progress was made with the help of such guides as Wackernagel's 'law', which proclaimed that enclitic sentence-connectors (or pronouns or discoursal adverbs) naturally and universally assume second position in a sentence. Theorems based on word order got encouragement from the universals encoded by Joseph Greenberg (1966, cf. 1978 vol. IV) on the basis of the relative placing of Subject and Object noun phrases and main Verbs. SOV and VSO sequences may be claimed to obscure the boundaries between the contiguous noun phrases in different grammatical relations or to rely excessively on case markers or other signalling devices which are vulnerable to decay, whence a shift to another configuration is predicted; and when that happens (e.g. > SVO) subordinated clauses and their verbs may collide with main verbs unless greater separateness is accorded to them by means of relative markers and the like. The structures involved, the historical stages presumed, the linkage of phenomena (e.g. that a verb-final system entails having nominal modifiers to the left of their head nouns, but *post*positions rather than prepositions) – and even the critical assumption that languages will be consistent in harmonising all the implications – all these are constantly called into question on empirical grounds (see Chapter 9, above, and especially Hawkins 1983).

An even more basic distinction between types of syntax is that which sets apart, first of all, the marking of 'active' rather than 'stative' involvement by the subject of discourse in the process mentioned. That is, first in a basic sentence we speak of a nameable entity (which can be said to exist) entering into some predication (of which it can be said whether or not it is true). Then the verb (which conveys the predication) may involve the noun (which conveys the entity) in action (*John runs, John hits Bill*) or in mere state (*John trembles, John resembles you*). Once a second entity enters – as *Bill* and *you* enter, as prime experiencers of the verb's action – then the major thrust of syntax seems to change to distinguishing the roles, or degree of activity and passivity, of the two nuclear noun-phrases. This may be done by specially marking only the source of action (and only when both nouns occur) or by specially marking only the passive (patient) item. These two solutions (and there are several other possibilities and manifold variants actually extant in the world) are respectively called the 'ergative' and the 'accusative' strategies; and that mentioned first above is known as the 'active' type. Here, clearly, is a deal of scope for theories of historical movement between types, especially as the 'active' is rare and vestigial (Guaraní, Lhakota and perhaps Navaho, in various parts of America, and perhaps Acehnese in Sumatra, are among its few recent or contemporary strongholds) and limited in its power to cope with sentence variations of topic or prominence; thus it seems likely to be a relatively early stage. The 'ergative' version (for all its widespread occurrence, from Alaska to North Spain, Georgia to Australia) is scarcely anywhere found in pure form and appears inherently unstable; again, it looks like a point of departure rather than arrival. But there are dissentient voices, and work proceeds.

## 7.2 Appeal to typology

What is universally present in language may concern certain inescapable features (such as ways of marking reference to the speaker as distinct from reference to the hearer) or some formal characteristics of grammar (such as the concept that one form is 'derived' from another, or one item 'governed' by another). For history, these are trivialities. But 'universals' may be of entailment: if a language has feature P (and not Q) it will always have feature X (and not Y). Whether it belongs to the P group or the Q group is part of its typological profile. The most influential spur to historians to think in typological terms was probably a pronouncement (at Oslo in 1957) by Roman Jakobson of this implicational type. He declared that the consonant system traditionally reconstructed for PIE, by including a free aspirate segment and voiced aspirate stop – but no voiceless aspirates – alongside a voiced/voiceless opposition in plain stops, was in typological terms a marked abnormality. No such system is empirically justified (despite some indications that it is not quite unique, turning up in Kelabit, a language of Borneo). The result has been partly an increased sensitivity on the part of historians to the danger of speculative 'retrodiction' (or else a defensive stance against the overrating of typology in setting up 'proto'-languages, which are merely sets of forms of which each is, in its own separate way, the most reasonable start-point for rationalised change into the relevant form of various known languages). But there has been a revising zeal, especially in this very case of the PIE consonants. Here (following suggestions by Haudricourt in 1948 and Martinet in 1953) many scholars have elaborated quite new versions of the system, the common element being (curiously enough) a series of voiceless glottalic-ejective stops (see Chapter 1 above) to replace the traditional plain voiced variety. These stops dislike being close to one another and (it is claimed) usually get voiced. The new vision has been applied by those who work towards a 'nostratic' tongue, by those who recognise some consonant types as markedly 'recessive', by those who puzzle over Indo-European morphology and its odd constraints on consonant incidence, and by some of those who envisage a wide range of glottalic effects in Indo-European of a lost 'laryngeal' consonant. It has also been fiercely opposed by more conservative scholars, although rather in respect of precise sound values encountered and specific remedies hopefully offered for old problems than because the old revelation may not be challenged.

## 7.3 The search for geographical origins

Always an attractive field of enquiry is that of the society and topography of the presumed speakers of the reconstructed mother tongue. Only in the fertile ground of Indo-European has anything newsworthy resulted and even there the main theme has been the location of the original homeland. In 1555 Gesner proposed that all language descended from Hebrew; many subsequent speculators have pursued 'linguistic palaeontology'in the search for roots, and a dozen or so places have been suggested for the original site of PIE. Apart from unfounded guesses (from phonetics) as to the physiology of the old Indo-Europeans, flora and fauna and settlement-types and religious usages have been deduced from widespread lexical roots. Whether the words for beech-tree or salmon really mean one type of tree or species of fish is very doubtful, as are the physical facts behind words for town or land or gods; but the start-point has nevertheless been located in India, Asia, South Russia, Scandinavia, Lithuania, Hungary, North Germany and Africa (ignoring some wilder ideas).

Even the limited search for some area where the Indo-Europeans were for the last time homogeneous, the last pre-dispersal site, had not produced an agreed solution by 1980 or so. The limelight, since 1956, had been on the claim (by Marija Gimbutas) that the pastoral and patriarchal civilisation called the 'Kurgan' culture – the facts of which are known by excavations and the name taken from the Russian word for a burial barrow – dominated all but the most western parts of Europe between the fifth and third millennia BC and contained the specific PIE ethnic group within it. Its source seems to be the Dnieper-Volga basin, its path to include the Pontic (southern Black Sea) area. Its society was patriarchal, its economy pastoral, its homes were small huts, its chief deity a sky god (see also Chapter 13 above). Some saw the true home as a little to the east (North Caucasus-Lower Volga), at least until the fourth millennium BC.

Since 1972 (and more intensely since 1980) the links of language inventory and function as between the Indo-European and the South Caucasian families, and the problem of the long Hittite domination of Central Anatolia and nowhere else, and the domain of certain interlingual lexemes (e.g. 'wine', 'goat', 'land') – all these essentially non-archaeological factors have induced the Soviet scholars Gamkrelidze and Ivanov to propose a dual solution (from 1980; see now 1984, 1985). For them, first, the Pontic-Volga location was a mere leaping-off place for that last wave of diversifying movements which split the later IE stock into Balts, Slavs, Celts, and the Germanic and Italic peoples. Second, these were earlier a single, if secondary, bloc which had had a more southerly fifth or fourth millennium Asiatic home bounded by eastern Turkey, Northern Iraq and the southern Caucasus – a Van-Urmia culture. This area they shared with the Hittites who shifted slightly westward, the Armenians who shifted east, the Indo-Iranians who moved more positively to the south and east, and the Hellenes who flourished thereafter (in successive jerks to the west) in West Central Anatolia, the Asia Minor seaboard, and that Balkan peninsula (with the north Aegean littoral and intervening islands) which we know as Greece. This view rests in part on the new PIE consonant system (noted above) aired in the first volume of Gamkrelidze and Ivanov 1984. Still, as the implications are that both migrant Germanic and more static Armenian are phonologically conservative (and so *both* may be marginal), and that Slavic, Celtic and Italic are equally innovative and central, accepted ideas are thrown into confusion but a new consistency is not gained. Besides, this is not a pan-Soviet theory; I.B. D'iakonov (1982–1985) is the most vocal of doubters and regards *Wörter und Sachen* alike as indicating a Balkan-Carpathian home, somewhere in modern Rumania and Bulgaria. And Gimbutas (1985: 188) is sure that the critical supposed move from Transcaucasia to the northern (Pontic) area 'could have been only the other way round'. The debate continues: Renfrew (1987) believes that archaeology can support a more motivated thesis with (e.g. the Celts or the Greeks as such in their present strongholds, but seen as the products of an expansion of farming people from the start point of agriculture in Eastern Anatolia before 6000 BC. Mallory (1989; especially Chapters 6–8) reviews previous evidence negatively and opts for a large 'Pontic-Caspian' area.

## 7.4 Recent discoveries

As for Indo-European, a useful summary of those sectors where in recent years hypothesis has been rife, and some notably radical revisions have managed to gain a following, is given by Szemerényi (1985). The areas are accentuation (especially in morphological paradigms), noun gender, verbal aspect and tense, and the possibility that PIE was to some extent 'ergative' in syntax. The 'word-order' change (SOV > SVO) has been noted above (section 7.1); it has stimulated many essays on the evolution of syntactic markers and structures. On the other hand, the concept that the absolute date of first divergence of languages can be calculated from their degree of loss of cognate forms for essential items of vocabulary has been disregarded for nearly two decades. This 'glottochronology' is a good example of an idea with a sound scientific analogue (the calculation of age from the amount of reconversion to nitrogen of the 'carbon 14' isotope from the point of an organism's death) which had its period of glamour but proved too hard to plot and too doubtful in its results to retain scholars' enthusiasm. But recent essays have revived it a little, linking it to a variable of spatial distance and sub-grouping, especially in Micronesia.

Other families have been mentioned and each has progress to report; so have the students of the American Indian languages, and of the Dravidian group, of the languages of Africa and of the far East (Sino-Tibetan). They must be sought in their own compilations; the essential principles and methods are those outlined above.

## REFERENCES

The chapter in this volume by Bernard Comrie should be consulted alongside this one.

General guidance on methods will be found in the items asterisked below and in the list of 'Further Reading'.

Bomhard, A.R. (1984) *Toward Proto-nostratic: a new beginning in the reconstruction of Proto-Indo-European*, Current Issues in Linguistic Theory, 27. Benjamins, Amsterdam & Philadelphia.

*Bynon, T. (1977) *Historical Linguistics*, Cambridge University Press, Cambridge.

Bynon, T. and Palmer, F.R. (1986) *Studies in the history of Western linguistics*, Cambridge University Press, Cambridge.

Collinge, N.E. (1985) *The laws of Indo-European*, Current Issues in Linguistic Theory, 35. Benjamins, Amsterdam & Philadelphia.

Ellis, J. (1966) *Towards a general comparative linguistics*, Mouton, The Hague.

Foley, J. (1977) *Foundations of theoretical phonology*, Cambridge University Press, Cambridge.

Gamkrelidze, T.V. and Ivanov, V.V. (1984) *Indoevropejskij jazyk i indo-evropejcy* (2 vols.), Isdatel'stvo Univ., Tbilisi. (English translation by Johanna Nichols expected.)

Gamkrelidze, T.V. and Ivanov, V.V. (1985) Papers on the Indo-European question, in *Journal of Indo-European Studies*, 13: 3–48, 175–84.

Gimbutas, M. (1985) Primary and secondary homeland of the Indo-Europeans, *Journal of Indo-European Studies*, 13: 185–202.

Greenberg, J.H. (ed.) (1966) *Universals of language* (2nd ed.), MIT Press, Cambridge, Mass.

Greenberg, J.H. *et al.* (eds) (1978) *Universals of human language* (4 vols.), Stanford University Press, Stanford.

Hawkins, J.A. (1983) *Word order universals*, Academic Press, New York.

Hoenigswald, H.M. (1960) *Language change and linguistic reconstruction*, Chicago University Press, Chicago.

*Hock, H.H. (1986) *Principles of historical linguistics*, Trends in Linguistics, 34. Mouton de Gruyter, Berlin, New York & Amsterdam.

Illič-Svityč, V.M. (1971/6) *Opyt sravnenija nostratičeskix jazykov* (2 vols.), Academy of Sciences of USSR, Moscow.

Jankowsky, K.R. (1972) *The Neogrammarians*, Mouton, The Hague.

King, R.D. (1969) *Historical linguistics and generative grammar*, Prentice-Hall, Englewood Cliffs, New Jersey.

*Labov, W. (1982) 'Building on empirical foundations', in Lehmann, W.P., and Malkiel, Y. (eds) *Perspectives on historical linguistics*, Current Issues in Linguistic Theory, 24. Benjamins, Amsterdam & Philadelphia: 17–92.

Lakoff, Robin (1972) 'Another look at drift', in Stockwell and Macaulay 1972: 172–98.

Mallory, J.P. (1989) *In search of the Indo-Europeans*, Thames and Hudson, London.

Milroy, J. (forthcoming) *Society and Language Change*, Blackwell, Oxford

*Pedersen, H. (1931) *The discovery of language*. (Translation by J.W. Spargo of original Danish work of 1924.) Reprinted 1962; Indiana University Press, Bloomington.

Renfrew, A.C. (1987) *Archaeology and Language*, Jonathan Cape, London.

Robins, R.H. (1979) *A short history of linguistics* (2nd ed.), Longman, London.

Robins, R.H. (1987) 'The life and work of Sir William Jones', *Transactions of the Philological Society*, (1987): 1–23.

Sapir, E. (1921) *Language*, Harcourt Brace, New York.

*Sebeok, T.A. (ed.) (1973) *Diachronic, areal and typological linguistics . . . .* and

*Sebeok, T.A. (ed.) (1975) *Historiography of linguistics*, (= vols. 11 and 13 of *Current Trends in Linguistics*), Mouton, The Hague.

Southworth, F.C. (1964) 'Family tree diagrams', *Language*, 40: 557–65.

*Stockwell, R.P. and Macaulay, R.K.S. (eds) (1972) *Linguistic change and generative theory*, Indiana University Press, Bloomington.

Szemerényi, O.J.L. (1985) 'Recent developments in Indo-European linguistics,' *Transactions of the Philological Society* (1985); 1–71.

Traugott, E.C. and Romaine, S. (eds) (1985) Papers from the workshop on socio-historical linguistics (1983) – *Folia Linguistica Historica* 6(1).

Vennemann, T. (1975) 'An explanation of drift', in Li, C. (ed.) *Word order and word order change*, University of Texas Press, Austin: 269–305.

Vennemann, T. (1987) *The new sound of Indo-European*, Mouton de Gruyter, Berlin & New York.

Wang, W.S-Y. (1977) *The lexicon in phonological change*, Mouton, The Hague.

# FURTHER READING

The items asterisked above (especially Bynon 1977 and Hock 1986) will give a fuller understanding of historical methods and results. Also worth considering are:

Anttila, R. (1972) *An introduction to historical and comparative linguistics,* Macmillan, New York. (New edn, 1988, Benjamins, Amsterdam.)
Li, C.N. (ed.) (1977) *Mechanisms of linguistic change,* University of Texas Press, Austin.
Palmer, L.R. (1972) *Descriptive and comparative linguistics* (esp. Part II), Faber & Faber, London.

The following volumes, edited by J. Fisiak, report on current approaches to the subject:

(1978) *Recent developments in historical phonology.*
(1980) *Historical morphology.*
(1984) *Historical syntax.*
(1985) *Historical semantics and historical word formation.*
(1988) *Historical dialectology: Regional and Social.*
(all published by Mouton de Gruyter, Berlin.)

as do the successive *Proceedings* of the International Conferences on Historical Linguistics (the *ICHL* Series, the more recent being published by Benjamins in Amsterdam).

# 25

# LANGUAGE AS GEOGRAPHY

## MARTIN DURRELL

## 1. FRONTIERS OF LANGUAGES

### 1.1. Linguistic and national borders

The fact of the geographical diversity of languages is one of the first observations known to have been made about language. The Greeks were aware that there were a number of different mutually comprehensible idioms, which they themselves termed '**dialects**', which could all be designated as 'Greek' and each of which was used in a particular region, cf. Saussure (1973: 262), Haugen (1972: 238) and Hudson (1980: 31). This linguistic and cultural bond served to distinguish them from alien peoples, the 'barbarians', who were defined by the fact that they did not speak Greek.

In the modern world we still use the same terms as the Greeks, i.e. 'language' and 'dialect' and still imagine the relationship between them in much the same way. However, this usage has given rise to many troublesome misconceptions since such a simple model fails to capture the full complexity of the present-day situation. Thus, there is still a tendency to assume that the geographical domain of specific languages coincides exactly with specific geopolitical and cultural units – characteristically nation-states. But when we speak of the 'language' of a modern nation-state, we are commonly using the term in a narrower and more specialised sense, referring not to the totality of related idioms within a particular geographical area, but to a codified '**standard language**'. Such forms have become established for all the major languages of Europe, in a process which has not infrequently lasted centuries. They have gained prestige through their use in 'official' functions and have become accepted as 'national' varieties, concomitantly acquiring symbolic value through their association with the nation, cf. Hudson (1980: 32–4). These

*Figure 50* Linguistic and national frontiers: French and France

normalised forms have come to be identified as 'the' language *per se*, so that when we speak of 'French', 'German' or 'Swedish', for instance, we tend to be referring to this variety alone and not, as would have been the case in ancient Greece, to all the local mutually comprehensible varieties within a particular geographical area. National identity is often associated with the use of a particular language in such a standardised, prestige form within the frontiers of a particular nation-state, cf. Haugen (1972: 262). However, in much of the world, and in many parts of Europe, the relationship between language, nation and state is a difficult issue, fraught with political, cultural and linguistic problems, the full complexity of which is not even wholly comprehended by many linguists, cf. Haarmann (1975). Linguistic, ethnic and political frontiers have grown up over the centuries in quite different ways for quite different reasons, and in practice national borders rarely run together with those of the autochthonous languages. Chapter 26, below, makes many details clear.

We may illustrate the typically complex problems of the relationship between language, people and state by reference to the case of France and contiguous western European countries, which is in no way untypical, cf. Figure 50. Standard French is the 'official', 'national' language of the French republic and is regarded as an essential bond uniting a self-confident and highly centralised cultural community with a long tradition. However, this linguistic and cultural community extends beyond the borders of France, cf. Viatte (1982). The French language also has 'official' status as one of the 'national' languages of Switzerland and Belgium, which are both multilingual states. It should be noted, though, that this does not mean that individual citizens of these countries are necessarily bi- or multilingual. Each of the languages concerned, though accorded equal 'national' status, is, with a few exceptions like the cities of Brussels and Fribourg, restricted to specific areas officially designated as French-, German-, or Dutch-speaking, etc., corresponding fairly closely to the linguistic frontiers, and within the respective areas the native population is essentially monolingual.

Thus, in Switzerland, French is used in a western area, the population of which regards itself as ethnically Swiss, as part of a distinct nation, but equally as part of the wider French cultural community whose language they share. The same is true of the German and Italian-speaking Swiss. In Belgium, on the other hand, a good proportion of the educated population regarded themselves until relatively recently as part of the French cultural community and used standard French even where their native language was a variety of Dutch, i.e. in the northern half of the country. Thus, native Flemings like Verhaeren and Maeterlinck wrote solely in French and are clearly in the mainstream of the French cultural tradition. However, others considered themselves culturally as Netherlandic, and with the success of the Flemish Movement this view has gained almost universal acceptance in northern Belgium, where standard Dutch is now the sole 'official' language in all prestige functions, and French now has 'official' status only in the southern provinces and, together with Dutch, in Brussels, cf. Brachin (1985: 35–42), Donaldson (1983: 20–35), Ter Hoeven (1978) and Willemyns (1977). However, unlike Switzerland, a sense of ethnic identification with a national entity cutting across these linguistic and cultural boundaries is less well established.

Standard French is also a 'national' language in the Grand Duchy of Luxembourg and used in most prestige functions. Standard German is also widely used in less formal contexts, but the first language of the whole population, however, is *Lëtzebuergesch* 'Luxemburgish', cf. Clyne (1984: 19–23), Hoffmann (1979), Knowles (1986), Kramer (1980) and Zimmer (1977). This now has many of the characteristics and fulfils many of the functions of a national language, with a significant degree of codified standardisation. It is thus a clear exclusive mark of ethnic and national identity, even if its speakers feel cultural affinity with the French and German speech areas through the use of both standards as national languages. Nevertheless, the strength of these links is naturally attenuated by the fact that both are languages acquired through education rather than as a mother tongue.

A different situation again obtains in the Italian province of Valle d'Aosta, cf. Viatta (1982: 302). Here the official 'national' language, used in all prestige functions at a supraregional level, is standard Italian. However, the autochthonous language varieties are mainly French (or Franco-Provençal) dialects, and standard French has officially recognised 'regional' status, its use within the province being sanctioned equally with that of Italian. The native population thus belongs to two speech communities, if its ethnic and cultural links are predominantly Italian.

In the Channel Islands, on the other hand, although the autochthonous speech forms are Norman French dialects, neither these nor standard French have any official status whatsoever (cf. Spence 1984), English being used in all prestige functions. Their use has declined markedly since the Second World War, not least because of large-scale immigration from Britain, and is now largely restricted to family situations among the rural population, which lacks any sense of ethnic community with France itself.

Within France itself, standard French is the only language accorded full official recognition. However, for significant portions of the population it is not the first or only language. We find varieties of Dutch in French Flanders and of German in Alsace and northern Lorraine; Breton is spoken in western Brittany, Basque in the western Pyrenees and Catalan in the Roussillon. In much of southern France, the autochthonous dialects are usually referred to as Provençal or Occitan, which is widely regarded as a language distinct from French, if the criteria for such a distinction are not unproblematic, cf. Jochnowitz (1973). However, none of these languages enjoys any significant degree of official recognition (cf. Tabouret-Keller 1981), even where there is a link with larger speech communities, a national or regional standard language and a distinct culture beyond the borders of France. In the main, speakers of these languages consider themselves ethnically and culturally part of the French nation. However, there is equally a sense of belonging to another speech-community besides the French and that this is part of a distinctive regional identity within France.

## 1.2 LINGUISTIC FRONTIERS AND DIALECT CONTINUA

The geographical relationship between language, state, nation and culture may thus be very intricate, with distinct frontiers coinciding in the main only in respect of standard languages and the states (or regions) within which these have some official status. Linguistic, ethnic and political frontiers are quite separate, having arisen in most cases as a result of quite different sets of historical circumstances. It would thus appear useful to distinguish the term 'language' in the sense of a codified standard form (i.e. 'standard language') from 'language' defined as collectivity of related dialects. This wider definition, which was the one understood by the Greeks, presents as yet unresolved difficulties which make the identification of linguistic frontiers extremely problematic in the case of genetically related speech forms. As we have seen, our terminology presupposes a hierarchical structure of different 'dialects' subordinate to a specific 'language'. However, there are no satisfactory objective criteria for assessing the degree of linguistic similarity necessary for two or more dialects to be regarded as belonging to the same 'language'. This problem has been widely discussed: cf. among others, Alinei (1980), Haugen (1972: 237–54), Hudson (1980: 30–7) and Petyt (1980: 11–36), but none of the proposed solutions has met with universal acceptance. From the point of view of geographical extent, it is clear that there may be a well-defined frontier between languages which are totally unrelated, e.g. that between French and Basque or German and Hungarian, or between languages which are only distantly related, e.g. German and Slovene or even German and Danish, but when we are dealing with closely related languages and dialects the problem becomes quite intractable. No objective linguistic criteria are available by which we may measure how dissimilar the grammars of two dialects must be for us to consider them as belonging to distinct 'languages'. Mutual intelligibility provides no operable criterion, indeed, a quite significant degree of comprehensibility is often possible between speakers of what are usually regarded as autonomous (standard) languages, e.g. most of the Western and Eastern Slavonic languages and the Scandinavian languages, cf. Chambers and Trudgill (1980: 6–8) and Haugen (1972: 215–36). On the other hand, many of the major languages of Europe have dialects within the usually accepted borders of their geographical domain which are in no way mutually comprehensible.

In fact, in the conventional designation of a particular geographically determined variety as a 'dialect' of a particular 'language', our definition of 'language' is still based on geopolitical, ethnic or cultural rather than linguistic criteria, as is very clear from the case of Dutch and German, cf. Goossens (1977: 43–50). The geographical domain of both standards coincides with the national frontiers, but from a linguistic point of view this is wholly artificial, as there is no clear linguistic divide between the dialects on both sides of the political borders. The dialects round Xanten on the Lower Rhine and those a few miles away round Nijmegen differ only in quite insignificant detail and the political border does not correlate with the boundary of a single major linguistic feature. Essentially, if we designate the dialects round Nijmegen as 'Dutch' and those round Xanten as 'German' it is because these areas are in the Dutch or German state, the speakers are of Dutch or German nationality and perceive themselves to be speaking 'Dutch' or 'German' respectively. These appellations have, however, no justification on purely linguistic criteria, as linguistically there exists a **continuum** of local speech varieties from the North Sea coast to the Baltic and the Alps. Within this area, geographically adjacent varieties are very similar, whilst those which are separated more widely are much more distinct and may in extreme cases be quite incomprehensible to one another. We shall have occasion to return to the problem of establishing linguistic boundaries in section 3, but, evidently, in selecting features supposedly characteristic of separate languages, geopolitical and cultural considerations tend to be primary and geolinguistic evidence to be used selectively and subjectively in their support. In purely systematic linguistic terms, we can only speak of continua of dialects and the borders of these with unrelated continua.

## 2. AREAL VARIATION IN LANGUAGE

### 2.1 Dialects and accents

Areal variation is a characteristic feature of all languages which have been spoken over a wide area for a significant period of time. Where it does not occur this can be ascribed either to relatively recent settlement, as in the case of North American English west of the Missouri and the Great lakes (cf. Cassidy 1982 and Wells 1982: 467–90) or to special social factors linking a whole speech community over a wide area, as in the case of Icelandic, cf. J. Milroy and L. Milroy (1985: 375–80). In most of Europe, on the other hand, where the same languages have been spoken over a particular area for centuries and social networks have been restricted for the bulk of the population to relatively stable small communities, the result has been an intense fragmentation of the language into local dialects. Prior to the large-scale population movements of the nineteenth and twentieth centuries with increasing industrialisation and urbanisation and the development of mass communications, it was the norm in Europe that in each individual community a form of language was current which was different in some, albeit slight, degree from that of its neighbours. The case of Jersey reported by Spence (1984: 350) is not untypical. Even with a tiny island of some 45 sq. miles regional variation in the Norman French *patois* was so great that 'a language-conscious observer could probably place a speaker within a mile or so of his or her birthplace'. These particular forms played an important role in signalling local and regional network links. The origin of this diversity is ultimately in the differential adoption of linguistic innovations, whether these have arisen in a single area or through parallel developments over a wide region.

The typical geographic fragmentation of long established languages in Europe was the result of social conditions which have changed radically in the last century or so, and in many of the major European countries the use of **traditional dialect** has declined markedly, with these varieties nowadays largely limited to rural speakers, and as often as not to the oldest generation. Such a variety can no longer be taken as exclusively representative of the speech form of a particular locality, cf. Chambers and Trudgill (1980: 15–36); in effect, the study of geographical diversity in language can no longer be seen (if it ever could) in total isolation from the social factors governing the use of regionally restricted forms, as individual communities are no longer homogeneous in their linguistic behaviour. In linguistic terms, the effect has been the abandoning of linguistic features restricted to very small areas in favour of more widely current ones. As often as not, this has meant the adoption of speech forms from prestige supraregional varieties, predominantly, but not exclusively, the 'standard' variety, cf. in particular Trudgill and Foxcroft (1978) and Trudgill (1986: 29–82) who discuss in detail the mechanisms by which such adoption occurs. The result is that we characteristically find now, within any particular locality, a 'vertical' gradient of variation between the traditional dialect, which in many areas, as in much of England, may only be a fragmentary residue, and supraregional forms.

Such variation may take the form of **dialect-switching** or **style-shifting**, cf. Aitken (1979: 86) and Trudgill (1983: 189–91). In the former case speakers alternate between what are perceived as distinct codes with autonomous norms, typically referred to as 'dialect' and 'standard'. This is the characteristic pattern in Italy and in Scotland (cf. Aitken 1984), and is usually held to be the case in Germany, too (cf. Mattheier 1980); although the situation there may be unstable (cf. Barbour 1987). In England it is restricted to areas of the far north and west (cf. Wells 1982), although, as Wakelyn (1977: 155) points out, it was clearly more widespread in former times. In most of England, as indeed in the rest of the English-speaking world, and in other regions such as Denmark, northern France and western Holland where the awareness of traditional dialect as a distinct speech-form has been largely lost, one typically encounters 'style-shifting' between more or less regionally marked forms according to situational or other factors, without there being any consciousness of the existence of more than a single linguistic norm. Such non-standard local varieties are usually referred to as **accents** in contrast to 'traditional dialects'. Whereas the latter are coherent and distinct local varieties, largely autonomous from the standard language, with a different grammar and lexis and a phonological system lacking any systematic correlation to the standard, 'accents' are essentially regionally determined pronunciations of the standard language with relatively little grammatical deviation from it (cf. Petyt 1980: 16–24 and Wells 1982).

The decline of traditional dialect in England has clearly diminished considerably the incidence of geographical variation in the language. Nevertheless, it should not be concluded that all such variation is decreasing and usage converging on standard norms. Numerous studies have found a considerable degree of regionally determined innovative divergence from standard English, particularly among adolescents in urban areas, cf. Cheshire (1982) and Trudgill (1974 and 1983: 191–2).

## 2.2 Examples of variation

### 2.2.1 *Phonology*

Areal variation in phonology is perhaps the most prevalent and widespread type of variation; it has certainly been investigated in the greatest detail for all major language areas. Of all levels, it was the earliest to be the subject of systematic research and this study was evidently the product of nineteenth-century historical linguistics with its emphasis on the description of phonological change and its regularity (cf. Chapter 24), although the oft repeated assertion that the initiator of the first large-scale dialect survey, Georg Wenker in Germany, intended thereby to demonstrate the correctness of the so-called 'Neogrammarian hypothesis', i.e. that sound-laws have no exception, is not strictly true, cf. Bach (1950: 39), Knoop, Putschke and Wiegand (1982) and Wiegand and Harras (1971: 11–25).

The maps of the *Deutscher Sprachatlas* (DSA), which Wenker began, show the geogpraphical extent of numerous historical phonological changes in German. An example which has become classic is that of the areal distribution of the so-called 'Second (or High German) Consonant Shift'. This occurred before the inception of written records and by it, the voiceless plosives of pre-German became fricatives in medial and final position and affricates in initial position or when originally geminate. Wenker's maps clearly showed that the north (or Low) German dialects failed to participate in this change, but also that it was actually not uniform elsewhere (cf. Figure 51). By and large, the shift of all the voiceless plosives to medial and final

*Figure 51* The High German consonant shift (after DSA)

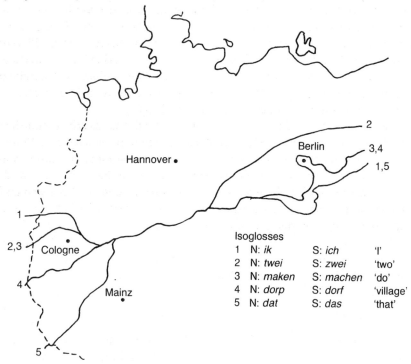

fricatives and that of initial and geminate /t/ to the affricate /ts/ took place over the whole of the High German area, but initial and geminate /p/ only became the affricate /pf/ in the south, and initial and geminate /k/ changed to the affricate /kx/ only in the extreme south. In the development of the modern German standard language the consonant system was adopted from dialects which had the labial affricate /pf/, cf. modern German *Pfund* 'pound' and *Apfel* 'apple', but lacked the velar affricate, cf. German *Kind* /kɪnt/ 'child', but S. Austrian (Tyrol) /kxint/. Furthermore, in the Rhineland, the isoglosses for some individual words deviate significantly from the main isogloss of the consonant-shift (the so-called *Benrath Line*), spreading out from a point near Siegen to form the so-called **Rhenish Fan** (cf. Frings 1956, Kurath 1972: 134–6 Schirmunski 1962: 271–300, Wagner 1927 and Wolf 1983). Thus 'shifted' forms like /ɪç/ 'I,' rather than /ɪk/ are found north of the *Benrath Line*, whilst some 'unshifted' ones, like /dɔrp/ 'village' (cf. German *Dorf*), /ɔp/ 'on' (cf. German *auf*) and /dat/ 'that' (cf. German *das*) extend a considerable distance south. And to the east of the river Elbe, in areas which were not settled by

German speakers until the eleventh and twelfth centuries or later, there is considerable lexical variation in the incidence of 'shifted' forms, with /maxǝn/ 'do' (cf. German *machen*) found as far north as the area round Berlin and /tsvaɪ/ 'two' (cf. German *zwei*), with the dental affricate, in a large area east of Hanover.

Similar phonological variation is naturally also found in the dialects and accents of English. The *Linguistic Atlas of England* (LAE) and the *Atlas of English Sounds* (AES), based on the *Survey of English Dialects* (SED), show the distribution of a number of familiar geographical variants in the English dialects (cf. Figure 52). Thus, in the traditional dialects and also the accents south of a line running approximately from the Severn to the Wash, the vowels of *but* and *butcher* are distinct, as in the RP pronunciations /bʌt/ and /bʊtʃə/, as the result of a phonemic split in the original Middle English short /ʊ/ which took place in the Early Modern English period. By this change, the vowel was unrounded and centralised in many words, but retained unchanged in others. It was, however, not adopted in most dialects and accents of central and

*Figure 52* Vowel isoglosses in English (after LAE and AES)

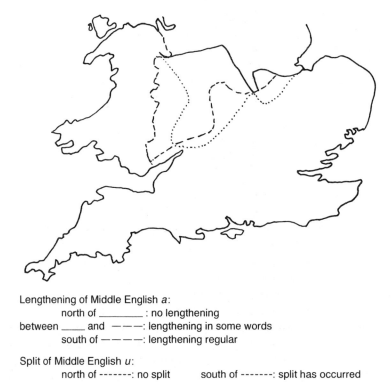

Lengthening of Middle English *a*:
         north of _____ : no lengthening
  between _____ and  ———: lengthening in some words
         south of ————: lengthening regular

Split of Middle English *u*:
         north of -------: no split     south of -------: split has occurred

northern England, where one typically finds the same phoneme, character-istically /ʊ/, in all these words, e.g. /bʊt/ and /bʊtʃə/.

Similarly restricted to the dialects and accents of southern and eastern England is the lengthening of original short /æ/ before fricatives and nasal clusters in some words, e.g. in *grass, laugh* and *grant.* South of the isogloss shown on Figure 52 these and similar words are pronounced with a long vowel, which in RP, which has adopted these forms, is typically a low, back /ɑː/, e.g. grɑːs/, lɑːf/, /grɑːnt/, phonemically distinct from the short /æ/ of, e.g., /gæs/ *gas* or /kænt/ *cant.* This development did not occur in the dialects and accents of the north and midlands, which have retained the original short vowel, usually with a more central quality than is usual in RP, and there /grɑs/, /lɑf/ and /grɑnt/ have the same vowel as /gɑs/ and /kɑnt/. In fact, the situation to the south of this isogloss is not uniform over the whole area. Although in most south-western accents and dialects the vowel of *grass*, etc., is usually long, it is doubtful, as Wells (1982: 345–57, especially 353–5) points out, whether there is a phonemic distinction between this and the vowel, of e.g., *gas*, since it is characteristic of this area that many originally short vowels have been lengthened. However, the border between this region and the area of south-eastern England where there is a clear phonemic opposition between /æ/ and ɑː/ has still to be established since this matter has not yet been investigated in sufficient detail.

In traditional dialect geography, as exemplified by the maps of the DSA and the LAE, and of most other linguistic atlases, phonological variation is thus shown in terms of the differential development of certain historical phonemes as shown in the words elicited through the respective question-naires. What is mapped, in effect, is the variation of isolated sounds in indi-vidual words. This emphasis on isolated phonetic differences seen from a historical perspective was challenged, from the point of view of modern structural linguistics, by Weinreich (1954), although similar ideas had already been voiced by Trubetzkoy (1931), cf. Petyt (1980: 102–7 and 117–31). He suggested that such an atomistic approach was incapable of identifying significant geographical distinctions in a systematic way. What was important were not necessarily differences in phonetic detail, but differences between the phonological structuring in different dialects.

In terms of phonological structure, then, dialects may differ first in the number of phonemic contrasts they draw. Thus, the dialects and accents of northern England are distinguished from those of the south in that, as we saw earlier, they lack a distinction between /ʌ/ and /ʊ/ which is characteristic of the south and thus have one vowel fewer in their phonemic inventory. In Weinreich's view, the important boundary is not that of any individual lexical items, but the one dividing those dialects which possess this phonemic contrast from those which do not. On the other hand, the distinction between

*Figure 53* Front rounded vowels in German dialects (after Wiesinger 1970, 1983b and Kranzmayer 1954)

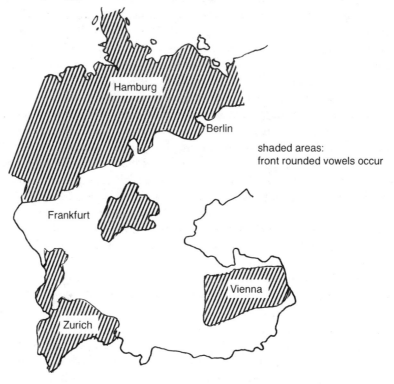

shaded areas:
front rounded vowels occur

long /ɑː/ and short /æ/ in words like *grass* may be considered relatively insignificant, since it does not affect the number of phonemes, but only the incidence of particular phonemes in particular words. Indeed, what now appears significant in terms of phonological structure is the possible lack of such a distinction in the western dialects, about which, as we have seen, the LAE is unable to give us clear information (cf. Trudgill 1983: 36–7).

There may also be significant differences between dialects not simply in respect of the phonemic inventory but also in terms of the types of relevant contrast. Thus, we may distinguish in general terms between those German dialects which have a set of front rounded vowels and those which do not (cf. Figure 53). Furthermore, this distinction is purely synchronic, since these front rounded vowels derive from a number of historical sources, from the very old conditioned fronting process known as *Umlaut,* as in most Low German and Swiss, from the vocalisation of postvocalic /l/, as in Austrian, or from a spontaneous, unconditioned palatalisation of original back vowels, as in Alsace; cf. Keller (1961: 123–30), Lüssy (1983) and Wiesinger (1983b).

Phoneme distribution may also be subject to areal variation. Goossens (1969: 43–5 and 51–2) gives a striking example of this within a relatively small area, showing no fewer than twenty-seven areas with different types of restriction in the occurrence of /ɑ:/ in the dialects of the Belgian province of Limburg, ranging from one where this phoneme is found in all phonetic environments except before /r/ and /j/ to one where it only occurs before /r/, medial /v/ and final /f/.

In the 1960s and 1970s a number of notable attempts were made to account for geographically determined phonological variation in terms of the model of generative phonology, notably Newton (1972) for Greek, Thomas (1967) for Welsh, Vasiliu (1966) for Romanian and Veith (1972) and (1982) for German. They are reviewed in detail by Chambers asnd Trudgill (1980: 5–50), Francis (1983: 171–92) and Petyt (1980: 171–85). Underlying these studies is the assumption that the dialects of the same language could all be considered to possess the same underlying systematic phonemic inventory, and geographical differences could be accounted for in terms of variation in the number, order, scope or form of the rules by which surface forms are derived from these underlying forms (cf. Agard 1971).

A typical example of this approach is provided by the account in Rein (1974) of the vocalisation of the liquids in the Central Bavarian dialects of German. Here, historical /l/ and /r/ in pre-consonantal or final position, as seen in standard German words like *Holz* 'wood', *viel* 'many', *nur* 'only' and *Dorf* 'village', are vocalised to give forms like [hoɪdz̥], [fʊɪ], [nuɐ] and [tɔɐɣ], for instance, in the dialect of Grossberghofen near Munich, cf. Gladiator (1971). There are significant regional variations in the phonetic results of this vocalisation, and Rein shows how, in the case of original /l/, they can be accounted for in terms of variation in the application of seven rules, which occur in seven distinct configuration types within this area. Three rules – to palatalise underlying /l/ to /ʎ/], to round the preceding vowels and to vocalise the [ʎ] to [ɪ] – are common to all the dialects except for some peripheral ones which lack the third of them, the vocalisation rule, and thus form a transitional belt. The other four rules, involving, for example, the unrounding or diphthongisation of the preceding vowel, then differ areally in their application, giving the geographical divisions shown on Figure 54.

A generative phonological approach can show dialect differences in a way which demonstrates their close relationship in a quite explicit way, with the varieties involved differing slightly in the number and type of rules, and in the scope and ordering of them, but not in their underlying structure. However, doubts have been raised regarding its appropriateness in an account of geographical variation in language, cf. Chambers and Trudgill (1980: 47–50), Löffler (1980: 86–8) and Petyt (1980: 182–5). Particular difficulties are caused by 'persistent' rules which present problems of ordering (cf. Newton 1971), by

*Figure 54* Vocalisation of *l* in Bavarian German dialects: dialect areas identified through phonological rules (after Rein 1974)

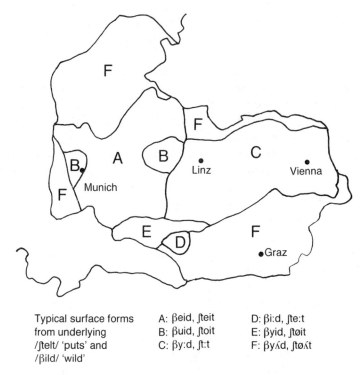

| Typical surface forms | A: βeid, ʃteit | D: βiːd, ʃteːt |
| from underlying | B: βuid, ʃtoit | E: βyid, ʃtøit |
| /ʃtelt/ 'puts' and | C: βyːd, ʃtːt | F: βyʌd, ʃtøʌt |
| /βild/ 'wild' | | |

variations in lexical incidence, as in the case of English /æ/ and /ɑː/, which is not amenable to statement in terms of phonological rules, and by the problems surrounding the establishment and status of the underlying representations. For, despite the insistence by its practitioners that the rules of a generative phonology are actually synchronic, many generative accounts of dialectal variation in terms of differences in the rules by which surface forms are generated from common base forms are in practice indistinguishable from traditional statements of the differential application of historical changes on common ancestral forms; such is indeed the case with Rein's (1974) study of the vocalisation of liquids in Bavarian. However, more recent work, e.g. Glauser (1985), is concerned to evade such problems.

### 2.2.2 *Morphology and syntax*

Morphological variation in language involves geographical differences in the systematic exponence of morpho-syntactic categories. By and large, it has been studied less exhaustively than phonological variation – and variations in derivational morphology have very rarely been investigated, with the exception of relatively simple cases like the diminutive suffix in German: cf. DSA (map 59), Besch *et al.* (eds 1983: II, 1250–5) and Toefenbach (1987). However, most of the major dialect geographical projects provide a certain amount of information, if it is largely restricted to isolated forms which are easily elicited.

An important example of regional variation in the exponence of morpho-syntactic categories is provided by noun plurals in the Romance dialects and this is commonly taken as a diagnostic feature dividing Gallo-Romance (French, Occitan and Rhaetic) from Italo-Romance. In the former, as in Sardinian and some Alpine Italian dialects, plurality is signalled by a suffixed morph -*s*, cf. French *chiens*, Sardinian *canes*, Rhaetic *tgauns* 'dogs'. In Italian, on the other hand, plurality is commonly marked by a change in the final vowel, as in *cani* (sing. *cane*), cf. Devoto and Giacomelli (1974), Posner (1966: 59–63) and Wartburg (1950: 20–31). These differences resulted from alternative directions of analogical levelling when the Latin case system was abandoned. Whilst in Gallo-Romance and Sardinian the original accusative plural suffixes were generalised as a marker of plurality, in Italo-Romance nominative plural forms were selected. It is thus a difference of some antiquity.

Most interest in morphological variation has usually been given to the survival of historical inflectional classes or types no longer current in the relevant standard language. The SED provide numerous examples of this in English, as for instance in the case of the plural marker -*(e)n*, which in standard English is now only found in one lexeme, i.e. *ox* – *oxen*. Regionally, though, a significant number of other words have retained this suffix, e.g. *een* 'eyes' and *shoon* 'shoes' in northern English and Scottish and *housen* 'houses' in the West Midlands and East Anglia, cf. LAE (maps M60–64), Aitken (1984: 104) and Wakelin (1977: 109–11). On the other hand, many dialects have undergone analogical levelling in the paradigms of numerous words which have historical irregularities in standard English. Thus, past tense or past participle forms like *catched* 'caught', *knowed* 'knew/known' and *stealed* 'stole(n)' are widespread in English dialects, cf. LAE (maps M51–55) and Wakelin (1977: 122–4).

Regional variation in the systematic exponence of morpho-syntactic categories tends naturally to involve much larger areas and a greater degree of consistency than, for instance, the geography of isolated forms. Thus, the German dialects vary considerably in the number of case distinctions drawn in nouns and pronouns, cf. Shrier (1965) and Koß (1983). We may illustrate this from the systematic exponence of case in the masculine definite article, where standard German has the four distinct forms, nominative *der*, accusative *den*, dative *dem* and genitive *des*. The genitive has been lost in all German dialects as a morphologically distinct case, but very few dialects, mainly in Swabia and Westphalia, retain distinct forms for the remaining three. In much of the west, including Switzerland, there are two forms, a dative and a common nominative/accusative. The north and east, on the other hand, have a nominative and a common objective case with syncretism between accusative and dative. Finally, a small area near the Dutch border has lost all case distinctions, in common with the dialects of Netherlands and Belgium. However, as Shrier herself makes clear, the exact extent of this important morphosyntactic variation is extremely difficult to ascertain either from the DSA or published dialect surveys, as traditional dialect research has tended to concentrate on individual forms and has rarely been concerned to examine complete grammatical systems. A rare exception to this is the study by Panzer (1972), which gives an account of the geographical structure of the Low German speech area purely on the basis of systematic morphological differences.

Less difficult to isolate are instances where there is variation in the presence or absence of particular morpho-syntactic categories, although, as with the distribution of case systems in German dialects mentioned above, they have not always been fully surveyed. However, it is known that, for example, the dialects of German are bisected roughly at the river Main by an isogloss which marks the southern limit of the simple past tense, cf. DSA (map 79). Whilst the northern and central dialects retain both the simple past and the perfect, as does standard German, e.g. *ich stahl* 'I stole' and *ich habe gestohlen* 'I have stolen', in the south only the perfect is found.

There has been a significant degree of theoretical interest in recent years, within the model of 'Government and Binding' (noted in Chapter 4, section 4), into the nature of 'empty' categories and so-called 'pro-drop' languages. In these latter, unlike in English or French, there is no requirement for an explicit subject in all tensed clauses and the categories of person and number may be fully expressed through verbal inflection rather than through pronominal forms. This is the case in Italian and Spanish, cf. Italian *compriamo* or Spanish *compramos* 'we buy' – and also in the Occitan dialects of southern France by contrast to the northern French dialects and standard French, cf. Jochnowitz (1973: 129–32). It is possible that a study of this areal distinction could provide material of some interest to current syntactic theory, but, as yet, it has not attracted attention.

Indeed, areal syntactic variation has been little investigated in general, although it is by no means unusual. To some extent this is due to the relative neglect of syntax in linguistic theory until fairly recently, but there are also practical problems for the field-worker in eliciting the longer stretches of text or the extensive amount of material necessary for a large-scale systematic

*Figure 55* Direct and indirect objects in English dialects (after Kirk 1985 and LAE)

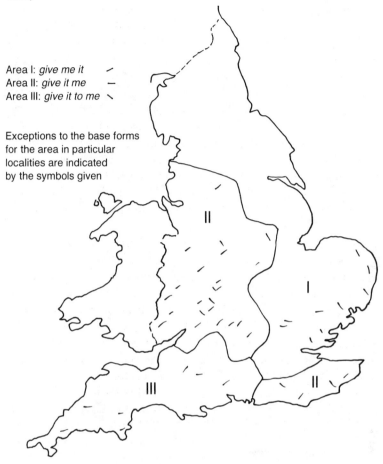

Area I: *give me it*

Area II: *give it me*

Area III: *give it to me*

Exceptions to the base forms for the area in particular localities are indicated by the symbols given

survey of syntactic variants. Nevertheless, as Kirk (1985) has pointed out, there is a not insignificant body of data on regional variation in English syntax in the material of the SED, and he reviews a number of recent studies, many of which, however, are as yet unpublished. As an example of such variation we may cite the differences in English in the order and form of direct and indirect object, where the alternatives *give it to me, give it me* and *give me it* are found in different relatively discrete areas of England: cf. Figure 55, based on LAE (map S1) and Kirk (1985: 131–5), where these forms are discussed in a historical context.

*2.2.3 Lexis*

Geographical variation in the lexis is by contrast relatively well documented for most major linguistic communities. Glossaries of local lexical items were compiled in a number of countries from a relatively early date, cf. the account for England in Wakelin (1977: 43–6) and many modern publications of a popular nature take the form of lists of local words. On a more systematic level, there are numerous large-scale dictionaries of the dialects of larger areas, cf. for Germany the survey of such work in Friebertshäuser (1986), and a number of atlases devoted largely or entirely to word geography, e.g. Kurath (1949) (eastern North America), LAS (Scotland), DWA (Germany), WGE (England) and Thomas (1973) (Wales). Furthermore most atlases covering the Romance language areas, including ALF (France), AIS (Italy) and some of the more recent regional atlases of France like ALMC, together with the RNDA for Dutch, take the form of raw lexical data given in phonetic transcription and are thus primarily orientated towards the presentation of lexical variation.

Of all levels of language, the vocabulary is perhaps most subject to small-scale local variation, since, unlike the phonology, it is not a closed system and words may be adopted, transferred or replaced without major consequences for the linguistic structure or hindrances in communication. Thus, particularly in the field of domestic or agricultural words, which are mainly used exclusively within a relatively small community, traditional dialect may exhibit a great deal of variation in a limited geographical area. A typical instance is seen in the eighty-eight equivalents for 'left-handed' reported in the SED. It should be noted, though, that regional variation is not confined to what might be considered 'traditional' realms of the vocabulary; there is significant variation in the German speech area in the dialect equivalents for relatively recent innovations such as the potato, which was not cultivated widely until the eighteenth century (cf. Martin 1963 and DWA (map XI, 4–5)) and the match, which was not invented until the nineteenth century (cf. DWA (map III, 27)).

Naturally, geographical variation in the lexis, as in other linguistic levels, results from the differential spread of historical change, in this case principally from divergences in the adoption of lexical innovations. In the main, the scholarly study of word geography has tended to concentrate on forms which are historically interesting in some way. Many locally restricted words are archaic survivals in the sense that whilst they are no longer current in the standard language they have been preserved in particular regions, typically in peripheral areas which have resisted innovations from a dominant cultural centre. Thus WGE (map 2) shows that the standard English terms *cow-house* and *cow-shed*, which are both relatively recent formations (cf.

934

*Figure 56* Scandinavian words in English dialects

Words per 100,000 acres:
Area I: more than 20
Area II: between 10 and 20
Area III: fewer than 10

Wakelin 1977: 71–2), are found in the dialects of most of southern and central England, whereas *shippon*, which goes back to an Anglo-Saxon form, is now restricted to two areas, one in the south-west (principally Devon) and one in the north-west (principally Cheshire and Lancashire), from whence it has spread into the English of North Wales (cf. Parry 1985: 58–9). These are clearly the relics of what was once a much more widespread distribution of the word, and older sources suggest that it was once current over a continuous area of western England from most of which it has now been displaced.

By its nature, the vocabulary also reflects innovation due to cultural influence or migrations of population more clearly than, say, the phonology. This is particularly true in the case of lexical loans, as for example in the well-

935

known distribution of Scandinavian words in the English dialects. Although some Scandinavian words, such as *sky*, *take* and the pronouns *they*, *their*, etc., were adopted universally in English, many other Scandinavian words are found characteristically in the local dialects of northern and eastern England, reflecting the density of Scandinavian settlement in this area; cf. Figure 56. The WGE gives maps for a good number of these words, and further information is also to be found in Kolb (1965), Wakelin (1977: 130–8) and Weijnen (1978: 63–8). In some instances, such lexical regionalisms may provide our sole evidence for certain links. In the Bavarian dialects of German we find the words *Ertag* 'Tuesday' and *Pfinztag* 'Thursday', which are commonly assumed to derive ultimately from Greek Areōs (hēmerā) and pemptē (hēmerā). It is now generally, if not universally, accepted that these forms reached the Bavarians through Gothic intermediaries, possibly missionaries, although there is no historical documentation of such contact (cf. Wells 1985: 56).

The study of word geography has concerned itself primarily with identifying the geographical distribution of regional equivalents of isolated lexemes of the relevant standard language. However, this atomistic approach is not wholly satisfactory, as it is now recognised that there is a significant structuring in the lexicon and that regional variation may not consist simply in the use of different words but in differences in how lexical subsets (or 'semantic fields') are structured (see Chapter 5). This was clearly shown in a number of studies based on the material of the DWA, surveyed in Goossens (1969: 70–5) and Reichmann (1983a), as for example in Durrell's (1972) investigation of the equivalents in the German dialects for standard German *warten* 'wait'. Previously, interest in this lexical set had tended to concentrate on the retention of the archaic survival *beiten*, which is the main equivalent in medieval German but which now persists only in a few discontinuous relic areas in Austria and Switzerland. However, in a number of large areas the DWA material reported two or more equivalents with almost equal frequency, e.g. *warten* and *lauern* in the centre and the east and *warten*, *passen* and *belangen* in the southwest. These are in no way alternative synonyms, but reflect the fact that the dialects possess semantic distinctions not found in standard German and thus a different structuring of this lexical subset. Thus, in the southwest, *warten* is a relatively neutral term, whilst *passen* stresses the duration of the activity and *belangen* presupposes a degree of impatience.

Nevertheless, the description of regional variation in the structuring of lexical fields presents extreme difficulty for a number of reasons. Much of the available material has been collected on the assumption of one-to-one semantic correspondences between dialect lexemes and those of the standard language and cannot provide a full view of the structural incongruities which may exist. Furthermore, constructing questionnaires by means of which one might elicit all the relevant material is problematic if one is not fully aware beforehand of what different types of regionally restricted semantic distinction might be present. Given these difficulties and the fact that the systematic investigation of the lexicon is a potentially vast task, it is not surprising that, although it is now widely accepted that the study of regional variation in the lexis must now take account of differences in its structure as well as of differences in the individual lexical items, most work in this area has been confined to small geographical areas, e.g. Zürrer (1975), or to small lexical subsets, as in Durrell (1975), Francis (1983: 22–6), Goossens (1969: 75–114) and Löffler (1980: 110–17).

## 3. THE PROBLEM OF DIALECT BOUNDARIES

One of the major aims of the DSA was to establish the geographical limits of the dialects of German, cf. Wiegand and Harras (1971) and Knoop, Putschke, Wiegand (1982). We saw in section 1 that our inherited terminology is based on a hierarchical model, in that it assumes superordinate 'languages' each divided into a number of 'dialects' which are current in specific and identifiable regions of the territory of the particular 'language'. However, just as it has proved impossible to devise objective linguistic criteria by which one might identify the boundaries of individual 'languages' within a geographical continuum, so there is no agreement on criteria for the determination of boundaries of dialects. As Jochnowitz (1973: 30–1) puts it: 'There has never been a definition of "dialect" that enabled us to determine whether two given idiolects belong to the same dialect, or, for that matter, to the same language'. An unresolved controversy has existed since the beginnings of systematic research into dialects. On the one hand we have those scholars who stand in what we might loosely call the German tradition who assume the existence of discrete dialects and regard it as one of their primary concerns to identify their boundaries, such as Bach (1950: 56–73), Reichmann (1983b), Schirmunski (1962: 132–3) and Wiesinger (1982 and 1983a). On the other, there are those who deny that such boundaries can exist, given that linguistic transitions across space from one region or even village to the next are gradual and imperceptible. This view was expressed as early as 1875 by Paul Meyer and 1888 by Gaston Paris, who was of the opinion that 'il n'y a réellement pas de dialectes . . .' (cf. Bach (1950: 58) and Francis (1983: 50–8), and many scholars have followed them in rejecting entirely the notion of dialects as relatively unified language varieties used by discrete groups within a well defined geographical area, although in some cases the theoretical standpoint may be significantly different, as with Bailey (1973, 1980) and Bickerton (1973).

The crucial problem is that although speakers characteristically make use of regional labels for their particular speech forms and refer to them, for instance, as Venetian, Bavarian, Gascon, etc., and assume that these exist as relatively coherent entities, it has proved inordinately difficult to correlate these designations unambiguously with a discrete set of linguistic features. Ferdinand Wrede, Wenker's successor, proposed a division of the German speech area into major and minor dialect regions and the results were published as map 56 of the DSA (cf. Kurath (1972: 83–6) and Wiesinger (1982)). His method was to base each boundary on a single isogloss, which he took to have the function of a diagnostic indicator. Thus, the boundary of the Bavarian area is given by the geographical limit of the form *enk* 'you' (acc. pl.) as against *euch* or *ui* found in the adjoining regions. Similarly, he divided the Low Saxon area of Low German into West Low Saxon and East Low Saxon on the basis of whether the plural of the present tense of verbs was realised through the morpheme *-(e)t* or *-(e)n*. Wrede used phonological, morphological or (less frequently) lexical isoglosses without distinction and naturally did not take structural considerations into account. Selecting the isogloss of an isolated linguistic feature and ascribing diagnostic significance to it in the definition of linguistic areas may serve for an initial orientation, and Wrede's success in this may be measured by the fact that most handbooks and accounts of German dialects have based their accounts of the German dialect regions on Wrede's subdivisions. Nevertheless, most scholars would now regard this procedure as unsatisfactorily arbitrary. Some of Wrede's underlying assumptions, as, for example, of the relative significance for the subdivision of the German dialects of the isoglosses stemming from the High German consonant shift (cf. Figure 51) are nowhere made fully explicit or justified, and such a procedure will naturally run the risk of making the *a priori* assumption that, say, such an entity as 'Westfalian dialect' exists (perhaps because speakers use such a designation) and then finding an isogloss which most closely corresponds to this assumption. In fact such popular designations will most usually derive not from a perception on the part of speakers of diagnostic linguistic similarities but from the association of the speech form with a particular geographical or political territory. As with languages, the designation of dialects may rely more on political or cultural than primarily linguistic factors.

Furthermore, the selection of a single isogloss to define a linguistic area is highly dubious from a purely linguistic standpoint. As Georg Wenker realised at a very early date (cf. Knoop, Putschke, Wiegand (1982) and Wiegand and Harras (1971)), isoglosses for individual words with the same phonological feature rarely coincide exactly. The isoglosses for the High German Consonant Shift (cf. Figure 51), provide many examples of this, but they are also found in the SED material for the split of Middle English *u* and the lengthening of *a* (cf. Figure 52), where, in the latter case, we see a broad belt where *a* is lengthened in some words only, so that we may find, say, [læst] but [grɑːs] in the data from the same informant. There is thus not a clear division

938

between northern and southern English in respect of these features, but a fairly broad transitional band between 'pure' southern dialects, which have low central /ʌ/ and long /ɑː/ in a relatively uniform number of lexical items, and 'pure' northern dialects, which lack these entirely in the relevant words. Similarly, we also frequently find gradual phonetic transitions from one area to the next. This phenomenon may be illustrated from German-speaking Switzerland, where the SDS (maps I, 15–16) shows short [e] in numerous words in eastern Switzerland which in western Switzerland have [ɛ], so that, for example Zurich [setsə] corresponds to Bernese [sɛtsə], cf. German *setzen* 'to put'. In the central area between these two, intermediate qualities are found, so that there is a gradual progression from a closer to a more open realisation without one being able to identify a clear boundary of any kind.

Isoglosses, then, as lines on a map, may be, as Markey (1979: 103) says, 'highly simplified representations of the geographic demarcation of linguistic differentiation': cf. also Handler and Wiegand (1982). The basic notion of the isogloss as a linguistic boundary is open to doubt, since, as Trudgill (1983: 47–51) clearly points out, they quite erroneously suggest abrupt transitions from one form to another at a particular point in space. That this is not the case is confirmed by the evidence of the DSA and DWA, with their dense network of localities; Bach (1950: 120–1) demonstrates how difficult it was in many cases to draw clear isoglosses from this material, as alternative variants were often current across a broad intermediate area, and Hildebrandt (1967) demonstrates the danger of establishing quite artificial lines in such instances. Many maps of the LAS show similar difficulties in respect of lexical data, with numerous words showing confusingly overlapping distributions. In practice, sudden discrete breaks are rare, and what one finds is a gradual transition from one form to another, whether one is dealing with phonological, grammatical or lexical features. Chambers and Trudgill (1980: 125–42), in an interesting study of the borders between southern English /ʌ/ and northern English /ʊ/ and between southern English long /ɑː/ and northern English short /a/, identified a large region in the East Midlands with complex intermediate stages between 'pure' southern and 'pure' northern dialects. In the case of the low vowels, they found what they termed 'mixed' lects (mainly southern or northern, but with the 'other' vowel occurring at times), 'fudged' lects (with occasional half-long vowels as compromise forms) and 'scrambled' lects (with both 'mixing' and 'fudging'). Although as yet there have been few extensive surveys along the lines suggested by Chambers and Trudgill, it is most likely that many other border areas will exhibit similar phenomena and reward investigation. A recent example, within the generative paradigm, is Glauser (1985).

A traditional solution to the problems posed by the potential arbitrariness of defining dialect areas through the selection of isolated features has been to take all features for which one has data and identify boundaries where numerous isoglosses run together in a so-called 'bundle' of isoglosses. Some of these are extremely well-known, as for instance the border between High German and Low German, where a significant number of other features follow the same course as the isogloss for the High German consonant shift, notably and in the greatest concentration along the mountain ridge of the Rothaargebirge northeast of Siegen (cf. Figure 51). Following this principle, numerous regional dialect studies summarise their data on geographical variation within the area concerned in the form of 'honeycomb' maps, where the difference between the dialects of the individual localities is shown in terms of the size of the bundles of isoglosses between them. Such a quantification of the linguistic distance between localities appears to provide the most objective measure for the identification of dialect boundaries, but, as has been pointed out by many scholars, e.g. by Chambers and Trudgill (1980: 112–20) and Löffler (1980: 134–9), serious problems still remain. There is first the often unremarked fact that such 'honeycomb' maps rarely present clear continuous boundaries. And, of course, the problem of potential arbitrariness, although reduced, may still be present, in that even such bundles will represent a selection of the total number of linguistic features exhibiting variance, as it is scarcely possible to take all into account. Perhaps more seriously, the question must be asked whether the individual isoglosses which are subsumed in such bundles are all of similar real significance, in other words whether some isoglosses ought to be ranked more highly than others, cf. Chambers and Trudgill (1980: 112–20). There is no prima facie reason why, for instance, a single isogloss dividing two localities might not actually be more important than even a large bundle because it marks the boundary of a major linguistic feature, like, for example, the pro-drop/non-pro-drop border between French and Occitan. It is commonly assumed that the isoglosses of single lexical items are less significant than those of such major features, but we lack any widely accepted explicit and well justified metric for grading isoglosses, although there have been many attempts to develop one. Nevertheless, many scholars see quantitative measures as the most objective method for determining the degree of difference between geographical variants, and there has been substantial work again recently which aims at refining these procedures. Such methods, termed **'dialecto-metry'** have been developed primarily within the Romance areas, as by Goebl (1983, 1984 & 1987) and Séguy (1973), but Viereck (1985) has applied them to English and Thomas (1985) has presented work along similar lines on lexical differences within the Welsh dialects. However, the underlying problem that the same significance is thereby ascribed to all isoglosses, of whatever type, has still not been satisfactorily resolved. And, as we have already seen, the underlying assumption of all attempts to identify dialect boundaries on the basis of isoglosses that these represent discrete breaks in the spatial continuum is open to serious challenge.

The problems are not wholly alleviated even if one moves away from the isoglosses of single features as the major criterion for identifying dialect boundaries. When structuralist linguistic theories were first applied to dialectology, it was hoped that these might provide a more objective method for the delimitation of dialect, cf. Ivić (1963) and Stankiewicz (1957). Thus, Catford (1957) showed how the Scottish dialects could be subdivided in terms of the number of vowel phonemes they possessed, with the dialects of the Central Lowlands, for example, having nine (though with variations in the inventory) whereas the peripheral regions of Buchan and Galloway have twelve, cf. also Aitken (1984) for fuller details. In a series of justly celebrated papers using the material of the SDS, Moulton (1960, 1961, 1963 and 1968) presented a survey of divisions in Swiss German dialects on the basis of similarities and differences in parts of their phonological systems, cf. also Goossens (1969: 45–68). Subsequently, numerous other scholars have attempted to delimit dialect areas on the basis of shared aspects of phonological structure rather than on that of the isoglosses of isolated features. Thus, Panzer and Thümmel (1971) attempted to show the internal geographical structure of the Low German and Dutch dialects in terms of the extent to which inherited phonemic contrasts have been retained, and for the dialects of this region Teepe (1973) showed how large dialect areas could be established on the basis of the structural development of the inherited long mid vowels; cf. Niebaum (1980) for further details. Although most attempts to establish dialect divisions on structural criteria have been based on distinctions in phonological systems, Panzer (1972) presented a survey of divisions within the Low German dialects using differences in the inflectional morphology, albeit unfortunately without illustrative maps.

In a rather similar way, linguists working within the generativist paradigm have attempted to establish dialect boundaries on the basis of differences in the rules by which surface phonological forms may be derived from a common underlying base. We have already discussed Rein's account of the subdivisions in the Bavarian dialects which may be identified through their treatment of underlying liquids. Vasiliu (1966) demonstrated how, taking differences in the inventory and ordering of major phonological rules, two major dialect groups may be posited for Romanian, 'Muntenian' (in the north) and 'Moldavian' (in the south), and each of these may be further subdivided according to less prominent differences in rule configuration. It has been claimed, e.g. by Agard (1971), that the generative model can provide us with an explicit method for distinguishing the boundaries of languages from those of dialects. Whilst 'dialects' will merely differ in the constituency, inventory and ordering of rules by which surface phonological forms may be derived from a common underlying systematic phonemic base, as in the example given above, 'languages' will differ in the underlying base itself. Nevertheless, this claim is now widely regarded as too strong. As Francis (1983: 175) points out, given the notorious problem of the lack of theoretical constraints on the abstractness of phonological rules, it would be quite possible to demonstrate that all the modern Romance languages and dialects are 'merely dialects of a common language'. Agard (1971) himself, using the data from Moulton (1962), did indeed suggest that there were two Swiss German 'languages' on the basis of his criteria. More recent generative work, e.g. Glauser (1985), has moved away from these strong claims and been more sensitive to the problems of boundaries and the nature of dialect transitions.

Clearly, divisions based on structural or generative criteria may avoid some of the potential arbitrariness involved in the selection of isoglosses of individual features to determine dialect boundaries, but even so, there is no fully clear theoretical reason why we might be justified in ascribing a greater degree of significance to them as postulated linguistic 'frontiers' than to any individual isoglosses. Nevertheless, many dialectologists still regard Gaston Paris's view as too extreme and remain convinced that there are geographical groups which exhibit such a significant degree of uniformity in their linguistic behaviour as to justify the attempt to identify them. Nevertheless, the precise delimitation of such groups is not possible solely in terms of a particular isogloss or group of isoglosses; rather, one has to be satisfied with establishing areas of relative uniformity on the basis of sets of shared linguistic features which are not necessarily exclusive and distinguishing these from areas which exhibit a lesser degree of coherence. In practice, dialectologists have long followed this insight and spoken of **'focal areas'** ('*Kernlandschaften*') and **'transitional areas'** (*Übergangs-* or *Saumlandschaften*), as Bach (1950: 60–3) and 114–6)) and Petyt (1980: 60–1), but there have rarely been satisfactory attempts to establish these systematically for a large speech-area, perhaps in part at least because of the established tradition of representing geographical variation exclusively through abrupt lines on a map. However, Wiesinger (1983) has proposed a new systematic subdivision of the German dialects on this principle on the basis of a large number of structural phonological and morphological features. There are few clear-cut boundaries, with the exception of the divide between Low German and High German, but he was able, using a uniform methodology and uniform data, to subdivide the whole speech-area into areas of relative homogeneity separated by zones of transition. In many cases, particularly in the west and centre, his results differ significantly from earlier proposals for German, e.g. that by Wrede in the DSA (map 56), which, as we have already seen, were based on assumptions which were not always fully explicit or purely linguistic. The result is an interesting and plausible account which gives us clear insights into the geolinguistic structure of the German-speaking regions without the distortions inherent in divisions based simply on particular selected isoglosses. Similar methods could clearly be used, for example, to establish the divide between southern and northern English, together with the transitional zone in the Midlands, from material such as that presented in Chambers and Trudgill (1980: 125–42) and discussed above.

## 4. ISOGLOSSES: CONFIGURATIONS AND EXPLANATIONS

### 4.1 Isogloss patterns

If geographical variation results from the differential adoption of linguistic changes, then the isoglosses which represent – albeit, as we have seen, in a relatively abstract way – the limits of particular variants reflect the dynamics of change within a speech area. Isoglosses take on particular recurrent patterns through which we are able to identify processes of diffusion of linguistic innovations from 'active' areas, where such innovations have arisen, into 'passive' recipient areas; cf. Bach (1950: 146–57) and Markey (1977: 10–17), if it is not the case that such diffusion necessarily presupposes a single innovating source within the 'active' area, cf. Kurath (1972: 131–6). In the history of particular languages, different regions may have been active and passive in turns at different times, and these fluctuations may all have left their mark on the present-day geography of the language. This is naturally rather the case for, say, German and Italian, where large centralised political entities emerged at a late stage, than for English and French, where the region surrounding the capital cities has for centuries formed the major or only 'active' area.

Isoglosses in the form of a circle present clear instances of diffusion from an innovating centre. These are frequently associated with large urban centres (which are typically 'active') whose linguistic innovations have penetrated the surrounding countryside. Thus, Wiesinger (1970: II, 132, 148) shows the area round Vienna with a monophthong /a/ where other Austro-Bavarian dialects (and standard German) have the diphthong /aɪ/ in words such as *weiß* '(I) know'. In the case of older innovations which have spread more widely, the circle may develop into a more distorted shape as the diffusion proceeds irregularly due to particular factors which for various reasons have restricted or accelerated its progress in certain areas. This is the case with numerous innovations originating in Paris which have been diffused through the northern French dialects, cf. Gluth *et al.* (1982: 489). Over longer periods, the gradual dissemination of such innovations outward from a

943

particular centre may reach the borders of the speech-area, leaving discontinuous **relic areas** on the peripheries or as isolated circles in particular regions which have been 'by-passed', as it were, by the innovation. Thus, Jaberg (1908), using material from the ALF, showed how the original Latin initial /sk/, as in *scala* 'ladder', which in standard French and most French and Occitan dialects has a prothetic vowel, e.g. French *échelle*, lacks such a vowel in six disconnected remote regions, five on the periphery of the speech area and one in a remote region of the *Massif Central*, cf. also Petyt (1980: 61–2). Relic areas of this kind are typically found on the borders of most larger speech-areas; e.g. for Dutch, western Flanders and Limburg, for German, the Alpine regions, and for English, the southwest and the north. Conversely, an isogloss in the form of an isolated circle may be an enclave resulting from the adoption of an innovation from a more distant area. Typically, this occurs in cases where an urban centre has accepted a feature from an 'active' area across intervening rural territory which is more conservative in its speech-form. Thus, the city dialect of Berlin has a number of characteristics which correspond to those of the High German dialects some distance to the south, e.g. *haben* 'to have', whereas the surrounding rural dialects retain Low German forms, e.g. *hebben* (cf. König 1978: 140). Indeed, in the present century, a number of studies in different countries have shown innovations being transmitted solely or principally between urban centres, from each of which they may then be diffused outwards into the surrounding rural areas; see Moser (1954) for Swabia and Trudgill (1983: 64–87) for East Anglia and southern Norway.

There are a number of other recurrent configurations of isoglosses which reflect the irregular adoption of innovations as they have penetrated furthest into areas which, for a variety of reasons, may be more receptive to them. These may be illustrated from Figure 57, which shows how a number of southern features have pushed northwards along the river Rhine, giving wedge-shaped or pipe-shaped patterns in their modern distribution. As Wagner (1927: 59) pointed out, we may draw the general conclusion in respect of such isogloss patterns, which occur repeatedly on the maps of the DSA, that the initial penetration is relatively narrow – in this case along the river valley – but it may subsequently broaden out into a wedge as the innovation is adopted in the lateral regions. Eventually, such a wedge may reach the limits of the speech area, leaving relic areas on each side. Jaberg (1908) shows how this is the case with the northern French form for 'it is necessary' (standard French *il faut*, deriving ultimately from Latin *fallit*) which has penetrated along the Rhone valley as far as the Mediterranean (cf. Petyt 1980: 62–3), with what we may assume to be the original Occitan forms, deriving mainly from Latin *calet* 'it is hot', now restricted to areas to the east or west of the valley and inland from the Côte d'Azur. Wedge-shaped patterns may also arise if an

*Figure 57* Stepped isoglosses along the Rhine (after Bach 1950, König 1978 and DSA)

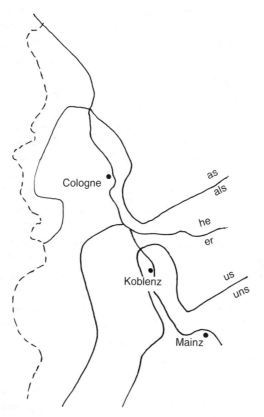

isolated enclave which has adopted an innovation from a more distant region is subsequently joined to it as the innovation spreads across the intervening territory. This typically occurs in cases where the enclave is an important urban area; many isoglosses in the German area show such a configuration round Berlin, which, as we have seen, is in respect of a number of features a High German island within Low German. However, for many other features, including the reflexes of the High German consonant shift in the majority of words, the rural dialects to the southeast of Berlin have subsequently also adopted these features and in this way Berlin is joined to the main body of the High German dialects by a narrow corridor or 'funnel': cf. Figure 51 and Bach (1950: 141–2).

The adoption of numerous innovations from an 'active' area into a 'passive' area over a longer time-scale may result, as we see from Figure 57 for the Rhenish dialects, in isoglosses forming a succession of steps over a broad

945

sweep of territory, and a number of such areas have been identified in Germany (forming what were termed *Staffel-* or *Stufenlandschaften* by German dialectologists), cf. Bach (1950: 144–52) and Schirmunski (1962: 120–2). However, they may be found in other language areas; Fischer (1976) demonstrated very clearly that there is a similar graded progression of isoglosses on the borders of the dialects of southwest England. The most celebrated of such *Stufenlandschaften* is, of course, the 'Rhenish Fan' (cf. Figure 51), but in this case it is still a matter of intense controversy whether it was formed by the differential adoption of a sound-change which progressed from south to north or by the differential implementation of a change which emerged spontaneously and independently, but with local variations, over the whole speech area, cf. Simmler (1981) and Wells (1985: 422–8).

## 4.2 Isoglosses: Explanations

From the beginning of serious dialectological research in Europe scholars have been concerned to identify reasons for the location of linguistic boundaries. Physical, historical, cultural, political and social factors have all been adduced at various times to explain areal linguistic diversity, and schools of dialectologists have often differed markedly in the relative importance they have attributed to one or other of these factors.

Physical geographical features in themselves appear only to influence the distribution of linguistic features in so far as they impede or promote social intercourse or coincide with other borders; few important linguistic boundaries fall precisely together with them. Rivers in particular seldom form significant barriers as they have often been major arteries of communication along which linguistic features may be transmitted, as we have already seen in the case of the Rhine and the Rhône. Mountain ranges could be assumed to be major hindrances to communication and thus to the diffusion of innovations; and indeed the isolation of some such areas has clearly promoted the development of intense linguistic diversity such as we find in the Alps, with its numerous isolated speech islands, the persistence of tiny linguistic communities (such as the pockets of Romansh speech in Switzerland and Italy), and resistance to innovations from outside with a remarkable degree of retention of archaisms; cf. Russ (1981) for the isolated German-speaking village of Bosco-Gurin in Ticino. Equally, though, it is notable that the major watersheds rarely form significant linguistic boundaries, the upper reaches of many valleys having been settled across passes (now often no longer in use). In consequence, the northern frontier of Italian, for example, runs along the middle or ends of the major valleys rather than along the watersheds. Where linguistic borders coincide with mountain ranges, as, for instance, on the Vosges (between French and German) or the Black Forest (between

Alemannic and Swabian dialects of German), this may be rather, in part at least, the consequence of the former dense afforestation of these areas; cf. Bach (1950: 102–3). In the lowlands, marshland has clearly acted as a barrier to the diffusion of linguistic innovation. Fischer (1977) identifies the Somerset levels as a significant linguistic divide in England, whilst in north-west Germany the persistence of a pocket of East Frisian speech in three isolated villages in the Saterland is clearly a result of their geographical situation in a district of swamps and fens; cf. Markey (1981: 254–6).

If linguistic diversity is a result of the differential diffusion of linguistic innovations, then, evidently, linguistic borders may be the result of historical population movements or settlement. Many German dialectologists have assumed that the present-day dialect areas reflected the distribution of tribes which settled these areas during the great migrations. The established names of the major German dialect areas (Swabian, Westphalian, Ripuarian, etc.) reflect this assumption, and major isoglosses, particularly those of the *Rhenish Fan* (cf. Figure 51), were identified with the limits of settlement of individual tribal groups (cf. Knoop *et al.* (1982) and Moser (1952)). Similarly, Wartburg (1950) saw the tripartite division of Gallo-Romance as resulting from the penetration of northern France by Franks and eastern France by Burgundians during the great migrations; cf. also Chaurand (1972: 38–40). Others have attempted to correlate other borders within Romance with different linguistic substrata from the early Roman period, whether Celtic, Etruscan or other, as do Kurath (1972: 88–93 and 150–6) and Weijnen (1978: 31–4).

Clearly, many linguistic divisions do reflect historical settlement patterns and population movements. The modern divisions of Ibero-Romance into Catalan, Castilian and Gallego-Portuguese are evidently the result of the southward expansion of northern Iberian dialects with the *Reconquista*, and these boundaries run across all the major geographical features of the peninsula; cf. Kurath (1972: 96–103) and Wartburg (1950). Similarly, we have seen how the area of Scandinavian settlement in England is mirrored in the present-day dialectal lexis (cf. Figure 56). Nevertheless, the total identification of modern dialect regions with historical settlement areas is clearly impossible. More recent developments have often cut across them, giving boundaries which postdate settlement by centuries, as Wrede realised from the DSA material; cf. Knoop *et al.* (1982: 52) and Schirmunski (1962: 134–9). The same is strikingly the case in England, where, as Martyn Wakelyn has pointed out to me (personal communication), the only Old English dialect boundary which is still identifiable from modern speech-forms is the southern border of Northumbrian from the Ribble to the Humber. Furthermore, our knowledge of historical settlement boundaries is often imprecise, and may even be based – circularly – on evidence from recent dialects; cf. Löffler (1980: 140–4). In a similar way, a correlation between such early settlement boundaries, linguistic areas and ethnographic or cultural regions (identified, for instance, by differences in farming methods or house-building techniques), is difficult to establish with any degree of accuracy. If such links are clearly present and may be understood as deriving from a sense of linguistic and cultural community, the boundaries involved are fluid, with wide transitional zones, just as are those of dialect areas themselves. As Bach (1950: 63) points out, they are sociological rather than geographical constructs; cf. also Chambers and Trudgill (1980: 120–4), Grober-Glück (1982), Jochnowitz (1973: 60–73) and Trudgill (1983).

The problem of identifying linguistic areas unambiguously with historical settlement boundaries, in particular with reference to the *Rhenish Fan*, led a number of German scholars to emphasise the importance of later, medieval and post-medieval, political frontiers to explain the location of linguistic boundaries. Frings (1956, 1957), in particular, showed how the bundles of isoglosses in the Rhineland could be correlated roughly with the borders of medieval states. It is evident that political boundaries may correspond with a sense of social and linguistic community or have presented barriers to social intercourse – particularly where, as is often the case in post-Reformation Germany, they also correspond to confessional divisions. The linguistic frontier running along the political border between Scotland and England is, for instance, one of the most clear-cut in the whole of Europe in terms of the number of isoglosses which can be established for it; cf. Speitel (1969). And even more recent frontiers may be reflected in linguistic diversity remarkably quickly, particularly in the area of the lexis; the German of the GDR has forms like *Plaste* 'plastic' and *Elaste* 'elastic' which are unknown in the Federal Republic, where only *Plastik* and *Elastik* are current; cf. Clyne (1984: 26–42). Nevertheless, the coincidence between the distribution of linguistic features and political boundaries is rarely precise; rather, as the maps in Frings (1956, 1957) show, they run through dialectal transition zones, often in association with other boundaries of types already discussed. Given the fragmentation of Germany before 1806 it may be possible to find historical borders of some kind, whether political, legal or ecclesiastical, corresponding to some degree with the isoglosses of linguistic features, but to assume a necessary causal link in such cases (as was done, at least implicitly, in a number of German investigations) may clearly be *ad hoc*; (cf. Gluth *et al.* (1982) and Goossens (1977: 74–89)), particularly when the boundaries involved are from different periods and of very varied relative importance. Indeed, as Mitzka (1952) pointed out, many important isoglosses do not coincide for any significant portion of their length with any extra-linguistic frontiers and are thus not amenable to explanation in this way. A characteristic example of this is provided by the border of the Early Modern English split of Middle English /ʊ/; cf. Figure 52. The location of this isogloss cannot be accounted for in terms of historical boundaries of any kind. However, as Trudgill (1983: 84–7) points out, it does coincide with an area of relatively low population density between the heavily urbanised areas of the London basin and the Midlands. A London-based innovation thus could be seen as 'petering out' in precisely this region.

In some cases, reasons for the differential distribution of linguistic innovations may be sought in purely linguistic factors; cf. Goossens (1969, 1977: 89–101). The diffusion of a phonological change will, for example, clearly be limited to dialects which possess elements which can feed such a change. Thus, as Schirmunski (1962: 357) suggested, the diphthongisation of the medieval German long high vowels /iː/, /yː/ and /uː/ to /aɪ/, /ɔʏ/ and /aʊ/ failed to spread into areas, such as Alsace or the Siegerland, where these vowels had already been shortened in many environments. Nevertheless, even if one accepts teleological explanations for linguistic change such as are adduced by Goossens (1969) and Moulton (1961), they will frequently only provide reasons for the emergence of a particular development in a specific area, but not for its subsequent distribution.

We thus see that numerous alternative hypotheses have been put forward to explain the location of linguistic borders. All have shortcomings, in part at least because they have often been seen by their protagonists as mutually exclusive. We may recognise that it is rather the case that a multiplicity of factors underlie linguistic diversity (cf. Gluth *et al.* (1982) and Reichmann (1983b)) – or, perhaps, as Trudgill (1983: 54) suggests, that all may be seen as part of more general sociolinguistic mechanisms which are reflected in the desire to be identified, through linguistic behaviour, as belonging to a particular socio-cultural group and not to another, and our present day isogloss patterns result from the various historical stages of such processes. Geographical and historical boundaries have all influenced the diffusion of linguistic innovations and the formation of areas of relative linguistic homogeneity in so far as they have been crucial to the establishment of geographical socio-cultural groupings – or *Verkehrsgemeinschaften* in the sense of Bach (1950: 65–7). As we saw earlier, it is all but impossible to disentangle areal from social factors in the description and explanation of linguistic variation, and the investigation of the interplay of these is likely to provide the most fruitful direction for future studies in linguistic geography.

# REFERENCES

AES: *Atlas of English Sounds* (1979), ed. Kolb, E. *et al.*, Franke, Berne.

Agard, F.B. (1971) 'Language and dialect. Some tentative postulates', *Linguistics*, 65: 1–24.

AIS: *Sprach- und Sachatlas Italiens und der Südschweiz* (1928–43), ed. Jaberg, K. and Jud, J., 8 vols. Ringier, Zofingen.

Aitken, A.J. (1984) 'Scottish accents and dialects', in Trudgill (ed.): 94–114.

Aitken, A.J. and McArthur, T. (eds) (1979) *Languages of Scotland*, Chambers, Edinburgh.

ALF: *Atlas linguistique de la France* (1902–10), ed. Gilliéron, J. and Edmont, E. 13 vols. Champion, Paris.

Alinei, M. (1980) 'Dialect: a dialectical approach', in Göschel, Ivić, Kehr (eds): 11–42.

ALMC: *Atlas linguistique et ethnographique du Massif Central* (1957–63), ed. Nauton, P. *et al.* 4 vols. CNRS, Paris.

Bach, A. (1950) *Deutsche Mundartforschung. Ihre Wege, Ergebnisse und Aufgaben*, Winter, Heidelberg.

Bailey, C.-J.N. (1973) *Variation and Linguistic Theory*, Center for Applied Linguistics, Washington.

Bailey, C.-J.N. (1980) 'Conceptualizing "dialects" as implicational constellations rather than as entities bounded by isoglosses', in Göschel, Ivić, Kehr (eds): 234–72.

*Bailey, R.W. and Görlach, M. (eds) (1982) *English as a World Language*, University of Michigan Press, Ann Arbor.

Barbour, J.S. (1987) 'Dialects and the teaching of a standard language: Some West German work', *Language and Society*, 16: 227–44.

*Besch, W. *et al.* (1982/83) *Dialektologie. Ein Handbuch zur deutschen und allgemeinen Dialektforschung*, 2 vols. de Gruyter, Berlin & New York.

Bickerton, D. (1973) 'The structure of polylectal grammars', in Shuy, R.W. (ed.) *Sociolinguistics: Current Trends and Prospects*, Georgetown University Press, Washington: 17–42.

Brachin, P. (1985) *The Dutch Language. A Survey*, translated by P. Vincent, Stanley Thorne's, Cheltenham.

Cassidy, F.G. (1982) 'Geographical variation of English in the United States', in Bailey and Görlach: 177–209.

Catford, J.C. (1957) 'Vowel systems of Scots dialects', *Transactions of the Philological Society*: 107–17.

*Chambers, J.K. and Trudgill, P. (1980) *Dialectology*, Cambridge University Press, Cambridge.

Chaurand, J. (1972) *Introduction à la dialectologie française*, Bordas, Paris, Bruxelles, Montréal.

*Cheshire, J. (1982) *Variation in an English Dialect*, Cambridge University Press, Cambridge.

*Clyne, M. (1984) *Language and Society in the German-speaking Countries*, Cambridge University Press, Cambridge.

Devoto, G. and Giacomelli, G. (1974) *I dialetti delle regioni d'Italia*, Sausoni, Florence.

DSA: *Deutscher Sprachatlas auf Grund des von Georg Wenker begründeten Sprachatlas des deutschen Reiches* (1927–56), ed. Wrede, F., Martin, B. and Mitzka, W. 23 fascicles, Elwert, Marburg.

DWA: *Deutscher Wortatlas* (1951–80), ed. Mitzka, W. and Schmitt, L.E., 22 vols. Elwert, Marburg.

Donaldson, B. (1983) *A Linguistic History of Holland and Belgium*, Nijhoff, Leiden.

Durrell, M. (1972) *Die semantische Entwicklung der Synonymik für 'warten'. Zur Struktur eines Wortbereiches*, Elwert, Marburg.

Durrell, M. (1975) 'Wortgeographie und semantische Strukturen', *Zeitschrift für Dialektologie und Linguistik. Beihefte, Neue Folge*, 13: 83–105.

Fischer, A. (1976) *Dialects in the South-West of England*, Francke, Berne.

*Francis, W.N. (1983) *Dialectology. An Introduction*, Longman, London & New York.

Friebertshäuser, H. (ed.) (1986) *Lexikographie der Dialekte. Beiträge zu Geschichte, Theorie und Praxis*, Niemeyer, Tübingen.

Frings, T. (1956) *Sprache und Geschichte*, Niemeyer, Halle.

Frings, T. (1957) *Grundlegung einer Geschichte der deutschen Sprache*, 3rd. ed. Niemeyer, Halle.

Gladiator, K. (1971) *Untersuchungen zur Struktur der mittelbairischen Mundart von Großberghofen*, Fink, Munich.

Glauser, B. (1985) 'Linguistic atlases and generative phonology', in Kirk *et al.* (eds): 113–29.

Gluth, K., Lompa, M. and Smolka, H.-H. (1982) 'Verfahren dialektologischer Karteninterpretation und ihre Reichweite', in Besch *et al.* (eds): 485–500.

Goebl, H. (1982) 'Ansätze zu einer computativen Dialektologie', in Besch *et al.* (eds): 778–92.

Goebl, H. (1984) *Dialektometrische Studien*, 3 vols, Niemeyer, Tübingen.

Goebl, H. (1987) 'Points chauds de l'analyse dialectométrique', *Revue de Linguistique Romane*, 51: 63–118.

Goossens, J. (1969) *Strukturelle Sprachgeographie. Eine Einführung in Methodik und Ergebnisse*, Winter, Heidelberg.

Goossens, J. (1977) *Deutsche Dialektgeographie*, de Gruyter, Berlin & New York.

Göschel, J., Ivić, P. and Kehr, K. (eds) (1980) *Dialekt und Dialektologie. Ergebnisse des internationalen Symposiums 'Zur Theorie des Dialekts'*. Steiner, Wiesbaden.

Grober-Glück, G. (1982) 'Die Leistungen der kulturmorphologischen Betrachtungsweise im Rahmen dialektgeographischer Interpretationsverfahren', in Besch *et al.* (eds): 92–113.

Haarmann, H. (1975) *Soziologie und Politik der Sprachen Europas*, dtv, Munich.

Händler, H. and Wiegand, H.E. (1982) 'Das Konzept der Isoglosse: Methodologische und terminologische Probleme', in Besch *et al.* (eds): 501–27.

Haugen, E. (1972) *The Ecology of Language*, ed. Dil, A.S., Stanford University Press, Stanford.

Hildebrandt, R. (1967) 'Deutscher Wortatlas: Probleme der Kartentechnik und Interpretation', *Zeitschrift für Mundartforschung*, 34: 44–54.

Hinderling, R. (ed.) (1986) *Europäische Sprachminderheiten im Vergleich. Deutsch und andere Sprachen*, Steiner, Wiesbaden.

Hoffman, F. (1979) *Sprachen in Luxemburg*, Steiner, Wiesbaden.

Hudson, R.A. (1980) *Sociolinguistics*, Cambridge University Press, Cambridge.

Ivić, P. (1963) 'Importance des charactéristiques structurales pour la description et la classification des dialectes', *Orbis*, 12: 117–31.

Jaberg, K. (1908) *Sprachgeographie*, Sauerländer, Aarau.

951

*Jochnowitz, G (1973), *Dialect Boundaries and the Question of Franco-Provençal, A Methodological Quest*, Mouton, The Hague.

Keller, R.E. (1961) *German Dialects*, Manchester University Press, Manchester.

Kirk, J.M. (1985) 'Linguistic atlases and grammar: The investigation and description of English syntax', in Kirk *et al.* (eds): 130–56.

*Kirk, J.M., Sanderson, S. and Widdowson, J.D.A. (eds) (1985) *Studies in Linguistic Geography*, Croom Helm, London.

Knoop, U., Putschke, H. and Wiegand, H.E. (1982) 'Die Marburger Schule: Entstehung und frühe Entwicklung der Dialektgeographie', in Besch *et al.* (eds): 38–92.

Knowles, J. (1980) 'Multilingualism in Luxembourg', in Nelde (ed.): 355–61.

Kolb, E. (1965) 'Skandinavisches in den nordenglischen Mundarten', *Anglia*, 83: 127–53.

König, W. (1978) *dtv-Atlas zur deutschen Sprache*, dtv, Munich.

Koß, G. (1983) 'Realisierung von Kasusrelationen in den deutschen Dialekten', in Besch *et al.* (eds): 1242–50.

Kramer, J. (1986) 'Gewollte Dreisprachigkeit – Französisch, Deutsch und Lëtzebuergesch im Großherzogtum Luxemburg', in Hinderling (ed.): 229–50.

Kranzmayer, E. (1956) *Historische Lautgeographie des gesamtbairischen Dialektraumes*, Böhlau, Vienna.

Kurath, H. (1949) *A Word Geography of the Eastern United States*, University of Michigan Press, Ann Arbor.

*Kurath, H. (1972) *Studies in Area Linguistics*, Indiana University Press, Bloomington, Ind.

LAE: *The Linguistic Atlas of England* (1978), ed. Orton, H., Sanderson, S. and Widdowson, J., Croom Helm, London.

LAS: *The Linguistic Atlas of Scotland*, (Scots section) (1975– ), ed. Mather, J.Y. and Speitel, H.H. 2 vols. (to date), Croom Helm, London.

Löffler, H. (1980) *Probleme der Dialektologie, Eine Einführung*, 2nd. ed., Wissenschaftliche Buchgesellschaft, Darmstadt.

Lüssy, H. (1983) 'Umlautung in den deutschen Dialekten', in Besch *et al.* (eds): 1083–8.

McArthur, T. (1979) 'The status of English in and furth of Scotland', in Aitken and McArthur (eds): 50–67.

Markey, T.L. (1977) *Prinzipien der Dialektologie. Einführung in die deutsche Dialektforschung*, Hofman, Großen-Linden.

Markey, T.L. (1979) 'A case study in competition', in Gerritsen M. (ed.) *Taalverandering in Nederlandse dialekten*, Coutinho, Muiderberg.

Markey, T.L. (1981) *Frisian*, Mouton, The Hague.

Martin, B. (1963) 'Die Namengebung einiger aus Amerika eingeführter Kulturpflanzen in den deutschen Mundarten', in Schmitt, L.E. (ed.) *Deutsche Wortforschung in europäischen Bezügen*, vol. 2. Schmitz, Gießen.

Mattheier, K.J. (1980) *Pragmatik und Soziologie der Dialekte*, Quelle & Meyer, Heidelberg.

Mattheier, K.J. (ed.) (1983) *Aspekte der Dialekttheorie*, Neimeyer, Tübingen.

Milroy, J. and Milroy, L. (1985) 'Linguistic change, social network and speaker innovation', *Journal of Linguistics*, 21: 339–84.

Mitzka, W. (1952) *Handbuch zum Deutschen Sprachatlas*, Elwert, Marburg.

Moser, H. (1952) 'Stamm und Mundart', *Zeitschrift für Mundartforschung*, 20: 129–45.

Moser, H. (1954) 'Vollschwäbisch, Stadtschwäbisch und Niederalemannisch', *Alemanniches Jahrbuch*: 421–37.

Moulton, W.G. (1960) 'The short vowel systems of northern Switzerland', *Word*, 16: 155–82.

Moulton, W.G. (1961) 'Lautwandel durch innere Kausalität: die ostschweizerische Vokalspaltung', *Zeitschrift für Mundartforschung*, 28: 227–51.

Moulton, W.G. (1963) 'Phonologie und Dialekteinteilung', in Zinsli, P. *et al.* (eds) *Sprachleben der Schweiz*, Franke, Bere: 75–86.

Moulton, W.G. (1968) 'Structural dialectology', *Language*, 44: 451–66.

*Moulton, W.G. (1972) 'Geographical linguists', in Sebeok, T.A. (ed.) *Current Trends in Linguistics*, vol 9: *Linguistics in Western Europe*, Mouton, The Hague: 196–222.

Nelde, P.H. (ed.) (1980) *Sprachkontakt und Sprachkonflikt*, Steiner, Wiesbaden.

Newton, B.E. (1971) 'Ordering paradoxes in phonology', *Journal of Linguistics*, 7: 31–54.

Newton, B.E. (1972) *The Generative Interpretation of Dialect*, Cambridge University Press, Cambridge.

Neibaum, H. (1980) 'Westniederdeutsch', in Althaus, H.P. *et al.* (eds) *Lexikon der germanistischen Linguistik*, 2nd. ed, Niemeyer, Tübingen, vol. 3: 458–64.

*Niebaum, H. (1983) *Dialektologie*, Niemeyer, Tübingen.

Panzer, B. (1972) 'Morphologische Systeme niederdeutscher und niederländischer Mundarten', *Niederdeutsches Wort*, 12: 144–69.

Panzer, B. and Thümmel, W. (1972) *Die Entwicklung der niederdeutschen Mundarten aufgrund der strukturellen Entwicklung des Vokalismus*, Hüber, Munich.

Parry, D. (1985) 'On producing a linguistic atlas: The survey of Anglo-Welsh dialects', in Kirk *et al.* (eds): 51–66.

*Petyt, K.M. (1980) *The Study of Dialect. An Introduction to Dialectology*, André Deutsch, London.

*Pop, S. (1950/51) *La Dialectologie, Aperçu historique et méthodes d'enquêtes linguistiques*, 2 vols, Centre international de dialectologie générale, Louvain.

Posner, R. (1966) *The Romance Languages. A Linguistic Introduction*, Doubleday, New York.

Reichmann, O. (1983a) 'Untersuchungen zur lexikalischen Semantik deutscher Dialekte: Überblick über die theoretischen Grundlagen, über die Sachbereiche und den Stand ihrer arealen Erfassung', in Besch *et al.* (eds): 1295–325.

Reichmann, O. (1983b) 'Theorie des Dialekts: Aussagen und Fragestellungen der germanistischen Forschungsgeschichte', in Mattheier (ed.): 1–26.

Rein, K. (1974) 'Die mittelbairische Liquiden-Vokalisierung', *Zeitschrift für Dialektologie und Linguistik*, 41: 21–37.

RNDA: *Reeks Nederlandse Dialektatlassen* (1930– ), ed. E. Blanquaert and W. Pée, 12 vols. (to date), de Sikkel, Antwerp.

Russ, C.V.J. (1981) 'The Swiss-German dialect of Bosco-Gurin', *Transactions of the Philological Society*: 136–56.

Saussure, F. de (1973) *Cours de linguistique générale*, ed. by T. de Mauro, Payot, Paris.

Schirmunski, V.M. (1962) *Deutsche Mundartkunde*, translated and revised by W. Fleischer, Akademie-Verlag, Berlin.

SDS: *Sprachatlas der deutschen Schweiz* (1962–75), ed. R. Hotzenköcherle, 4 vols, Franke, Berne.

SED: *Survey of English Dialects. The Basic Material* (1962–71), ed. Orton, H. *et al.* 4 vols,

SPECIAL ASPECTS OF LANGUAGE

each of 3 parts, E.J. Arnold, Leeds.

Séguy, J. (1973) 'La dialectométrie dans l'*Atlas linguistique de la Gascogne*', *Revue de Linguistique Romane*, 37: 1–24.

Shrier, M. (1965). 'Case systems in German dialects', *Language*, 41: 420–38.

Simmler, F. (1981) *Graphematische-phonematische Studien zum althochdeutschen Konsonantismus*, Winter, Heidelberg.

Speitel, H.-H. (1969) 'An areal typology of isoglosses near the Scottish-English border', *Zeitschrift für Dialektologie und Linguistik*, 36: 49–66.

Spence, N.C.W. (1984) 'Channel Island French', in Trudgill (ed.): 345–51.

Stankiewicz, E. (1957) 'On discreteness and continuity in structural dialectology', *Word*, 13: 44–59.

*Tabouret-Keller, A. (ed.) (1981) *Regional Languages in France, International Journal of the Sociology of Language*, 29.

Teepe, P. (1973) 'Zur Lautgeographie', in Goossens, J. (ed.) *Niederdeutsch. Sprache und Literatur*, Wachholtz, Neumünster, I: 138–57.

Ter Hoeven, A. (1978) 'The social bases of Flemish Nationalism', *International Journal of the Sociology of Language*, 15: 30–50.

Thomas A.R. (1967) 'Generative phonology in dialectology', *Transactions of the Philological Society*: 179–203.

Thomas, A.R. (1973) *The Linguistic Geography of Wales. A Contribution to Welsh Dialectology*, University of Wales Press, Cardiff.

Thomas, A.R. (1985) 'A differences matrix in areal analysis of dialect data', *Orbis*, 31: 59–71.

Tiefenbach, H. (1987) '-*chen* und -*lein*. Überlegungen zu Problemen des sprachgeographischen Befundes und seiner sprachhistorischen Deutung', *Zeitschrift für Dialektologie und Linguistik*, 54: 2–27.

Trubetzkoy, N.S. (1931) 'Phonologie et géographie linguistique', *Travaux du Cercle Linguistique de Prague*, 4.

Trudgill, P. (1974) *The Social Differentiation of English in Norwich*, Cambridge University Press, Cambridge.

Trudgill, P. (ed.) (1978) *Sociolinguistic Patterns in British English*, Edward Arnold, London.

*Trudgill, P. (1983) *On Dialect*, Blackwell, Oxford.

*Trudgill, P. (ed.) (1984) *Language in the British Isles*, Cambridge University Press, Cambridge.

*Trudgill, P. (1986) *Dialects in Contact*, Blackwell, Oxford.

Trudgill, P. and Foxcroft, T. (1978) 'On the sociolinguistics of vocalic mergers: transfer and appoximation in East Anglia', in Trudgill (ed.): 69–79.

Trudgill, P. and Hannah, J. (1982) *International English*, Edward Arnold, London.

Vasiliu, E. (1966) 'Towards a generative phonology of Daco-Rumanian', *Journal of Linguistics*, 2: 79–98.

Veith, W.H. (1972) *Intersystemare Phonologie. Exemplarisch an diastratisch-diatopischen Differenzierungen im Deutschen*, de Gruyter, Berlin.

Veith, W.H. (1982) 'Theorieansätze einer generativen Dialektologie', in Besch *et al.* (eds): 277–95.

Viatte, A. (1982) 'French outside France', in Green, J.N. and Posner, R. (eds) *Trends in Romance Linguistics and Philology*, Mouton, The Hague: 299–317.

954

Viereck, W. (1985) 'Linguistic atlases and dialectometry: The survey of English dialects', in Kirk *et al.* (eds): 94–112.

Wagner, K. (1927) *Deutsche Sprachlandschaften*, Elwert, Marburg.

*Wakelyn, M. (1977) *English Dialects. An Introduction*, 2nd. rev. ed. Athlone Press, London.

Wartburg, W. von (1950) *Die Ausgliederung der romanischen Sprachräume*, Franke, Berne.

Weijnen, A. (1978) *Outlines for an Interlingual European Dialectology*, van Gorcum, Assen.

Weinreich, U. (1954) 'Is a structural dialectology possible?' *Word*, 10: 388–400.

Wells, C.J. (1985) *German. A Linguistic History to 1945*, Clarendon Press, Oxford.

*Wells, J.C. (1982) *Accents of English* 3 vols. Cambridge University Press, Cambridge.

WGE: *A Word Geography of England* (1974), ed. Orton, H. and Wright, N., Seminar Press, London.

Wiegand, H.E. and Harras, G. (1971) 'Zur wissenschaftshistorischen Einordnung und linguistischen Beurteilung des *Deutschen Wortatlas*', *Germanistische Linguistik*, 1/2: 1–205.

Wiesinger, P. (1970) *Phonetisch-phonologische Untersuchungen zur Vokalentwicklung in den deutschen Dialekten*, 2 vols, de Gruyter, Berlin.

Wiesinger, P. (1982) 'Probleme der Dialektgliederung des Deutschen', *Zeitschrift für Dialektologie und Linguistik 49*: 145–68.

Wiesinger, P. (1983a) 'Die Einteilung der deutschen Dialekte', in Besch *et al.* (eds): 807–900.

Wiesinger, P. (1983b) 'Rundung und Entrundung, Palatalisierung und Entpalatalisierung, Velarisierung und Entvelarisierung in den deutschen Dialekten', in Besch *et al.* (eds): 1101–6.

Willemijns, R. (1977) 'Sprachpolitische und sprachsoziologische Betrachtungen zur Lage des Niederländischen in Belgien', *Osnabrücker Beiträge zur Sprachtheorie*, 4: 6–22.

Wolf, N.R. (1983) 'Durchführung und Verbreitung der zweiten Lautverschiebung in den deutschen Dialekten', in Besch *et al.* (eds): 1116–21.

Zimmer, R. (1977) 'Dialekt, Nationaldialekt, Standardsprache. Vergleichende Betrachtungen zum deutsch-französischen Kontaktbereich in der Schweiz, im Elsaß und in Luxemburg', *Zeitschrift für Dialektologie und Linguistik*, 44: 145–57.

Zürrer, P. (1975) *Wortfelder in der Mundart von Gressoney. Ein Beitrag zur Kenntnis der norditalienischen Walser-Mundarten*, Huber, Frauenfeld.

## FURTHER READING

The items asterisked in the list above will be found especially useful for reading further on this topic.

# 26

## LANGUAGES OF THE WORLD: WHO SPEAKS WHAT

### BERNARD COMRIE

The aim of this chapter is to present an overview of the range of languages spoken in the world today, with occasional glimpses at major historical changes in this distribution. The chapter is divided into sections dealing with particular geographical areas. In addition, a major organisational principle of the chapter is the classification of languages into genetic language families, i.e. groups of languages that descend from a single common ancestor (see Chapter 24 above). Mention is made of all the major language families of the world and of individual languages that either have more than about one million speakers or are the official or national language of an independent country.

No one knows precisely how many languages are spoken in the world today, though a reasonable estimate would be around 5,000. In part this lack of precision is due to inadequate knowledge of the linguistic situation in some of the more remote or otherwise inaccessible parts of the world. Even in other parts of the world, precise statistics on numbers of speakers of languages are often hard to come by, especially where they are not included in official census questionnaires; the figures cited below usually follow either Grimes (1988) or Ruhlen (1987). In part it is due to problems in deciding whether or not two speech varieties constitute distinct languages or are merely two dialects of a single language, a decision that is often made as much on social as on purely linguistic grounds: for instance, Dutch is considered a language distinct from German largely because it corresponds to political entities distinct from Germany (namely, the Netherlands and part of Belgium) and has a distinct cultural-literary tradition; the various mutually unintelligible 'dialects' of Chinese are traditionally considered dialects of the same language because they share the same political, cultural and literary tradition. Finally, there are many languages in different parts of the world that are dying out. It is often difficult to decide precisely when a language dies out, for instance in that the obsolescence process may involve gradual restriction of the language's functions or of the abilities of speakers to use it, rather than the abrupt death of the last speaker; so with many languages it is difficult to reach a definitive decision on whether or not the language is still alive.

The genetic classification of languages that lies at the basis of this chapter is a conservative classification, i.e. relying only on those families where there is consensus or near-consensus that the constituent languages are indeed genetically related. In some instances, where a given geographical area includes a large number of small language families (e.g. the Americas, New Guinea, parts of Siberia), groupings have been used for the sake of convenience but whose genetic validity is explicitly questioned in the text (e.g. Amerind, Papuan, Paleo-Siberian). A more radical classification, with only around 15 major families, is currently being proposed by Joseph H. Greenberg; this is the classification that informs Ruhlen (1987) and some reference is made to it below, though it should be borne in mind that apart from Greenberg's classification of the languages of Africa, his departures from more traditional classifications are highly controversial.

The emphasis of the chapter is on the present-day situation. However, for some parts of the world this gives a distorted picture of the range of linguistic diversity present there. For instance, in virtually every country of the Western Hemisphere, the language spoken by the majority, usually the overwhelming majority, of the population is an Indo-European language. Yet the indigenous languages surviving from before European colonisation represent one of the richest instances of linguistic diversity anywhere in the world, and the section on the Americas therefore concentrates primarily on these indigenous languages. A similar situation obtains in Australia. Even in Europe and the Middle East, at present dominated by Indo-European, Semitic and Turkic languages, the historical record presents us with a more complex earlier picture, one which is at least worthy of mention.

## 1. EUROPE

We will take Europe here in its current geographical sense, i.e. the area bounded to the east by the Ural mountains, the Caspian Sea, the southern Caucasus mountains, the Black Sea and the Bosporus. Even with this broad definition, going beyond the traditional definition of Europe as a cultural area, Europe is dominated by languages of the Indo-European family, with

*Figure 58* Language Families of the World. Based, with the permission of Stanford University Press, on Ruhlen (1987: endpapers), with modifications. (The map does not take account of the colonial expansion of Indo-European and some other languages since 1500.)

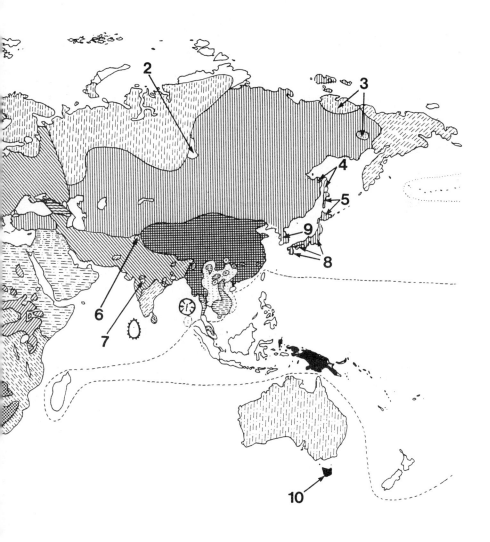

(For legend see p. 960)

959

Legend:

▧ Indo-European

▥ Uralic

▤ Caucasian families

▥ Altaic families

▨ Chukotko-Kamchatkan

▨ Dravidian

▥ Austro-Asiatic

▦ Kam-Tai

⌧ Miao-Yao

▦ Sino-Tibetan

▤ Afroasiatic

▨ Nilo-Saharan

▨ Niger-Kordofanian

⠿ Khoisan

■ Papuan languages

▦ Australian languages

▦ Eskimo-Aleut

▧ Na-Dene languages

▤ American Indian languages, other

1  Basque

2  Ket

3  Yukaghir

4  Nivkh (Gilyak)

5  Ainu

6  Burushaski

7  Nahali

8  Japanese

9  Korean

10 Tasmanian

*Islands*

✹ Indo-European

⟳ Austro-Asiatic

⊕ Andamanese

⟳ Austronesian

⟳ Eskimo-Aleut

other families occupying a peripheral role: Basque, Uralic, Altaic, Caucasian, Afroasiatic.

## 1.1 Indo-European

Today, as at the beginning of the sixteenth century, the Indo-European family covers most of Europe; across the Caucasus (where some Indo-European languages were and are spoken) another block of Indo-European languages starts, covering most of Iran, Afghanistan and the northern and central parts of South Asia, with outliers in Sri Lanka and the Maldives (see section 2.5). The main change since the sixteenth century has been the spread of Indo-European languages to the Americas (English, Spanish, Portuguese, French), to Australia and New Zealand (English) and, to a more limited extent, to southern Africa (English, Afrikaans); English, Spanish and Portuguese now all have far more native speakers in the Americas than in Europe. Even in Africa, where the number of native speakers of Indo-European languages is small, many countries have English or French, in a few cases Portuguese or Spanish, as official language. The Russian colonisation of Siberia has carried that Indo-European language into northern Asia. At present, roughly one person in two in the world is a native speaker of an Indo-European language. This section will concentrate on Indo-European languages spoken in Europe, looking in turn at each of the branches of the Indo-European family.

### 1.1.1 Germanic

Germanic languages are dominant in north-western Europe. Languages with over a million speakers that are also the national or official languages of European countries are: English (Great Britain, Ireland; over 300 million native speakers world-wide, plus millions of second-language speakers), Dutch (Netherlands, Belgium, 20 million), German (Federal Republic of Germany, German Democratic Republic, Austria, most of Switzerland, Liechtenstein, 100 million native speakers world-wide), Danish (Denmark, 5 million), Norwegian (Norway, 5 million), Swedish (Sweden and parts of Finland, 9 million). Among languages with fewer than a million speakers, Icelandic clearly merits mention as the official and national language of Iceland; another Germanic language, Faroese, is the national language of the Faroes, a Danish dependency. Among the many rather divergent dialects of German, one, Luxembourgish, is perhaps both sufficiently distinct structurally and sufficiently developed as a distinct medium to be considered the distinct national language of Luxembourg. Yet another linguistic offshoot of German, Yiddish, is so distinct structurally (largely through the infusion of

Hebrew-Aramaic and Slavonic elements) and so developed as a written medium that it clearly attains the status of a distinct language; once the major language of Central and East European Jews, Yiddish was decimated by the Holocaust, with most of its present 2–3 million speakers in the USA and smaller substantial communities in the USSR and Israel.

Outside Europe, English predominates in most of continental North America, in some Caribbean countries (often in creolised form), in Australia and New Zealand and (sometimes in pidginised form) some other parts of the South Pacific, and as one of the two main languages of the European-descent population of South Africa.

## 1.1.2 Celtic languages

At present, Celtic languages share the fringe of north-western Europe with Germanic languages, but the last two millennia have witnessed a gradual erosion of their position, so that nowadays, Celtic languages are spoken by the minority of the population in Brittany (Breton) and Wales (Welsh) (about ½ million each) and by small minorities in Ireland (Irish) and the Highlands of Scotland (Scots Gaelic). As languages transmitted regularly from native-speaker parents to native-speaker children, Manx died out on the Isle of Man during this century, Cornish in Cornwall around 1800. All can, however, still be regarded as the national languages of their respective countries or areas, in some instances also with some official recognition, especially in the case of Irish, the official language of Ireland. Two thousand years ago, Celtic languages still flourished on Continental Europe, for instance Gaulish in what is now France.

## 1.1.3 Romance languages

The Romance languages are all descendants of Latin, a member of the Italic branch of the Indo-European family. Originally the language spoken only around the city of Rome, the spread of Roman political power led to the virtual elimination of other languages from south-western Europe, including both the other Italic languages, varioius other Indo-European languages (e.g. Gaulish in what is now France), and several non-Indo-European languages (e.g. Etruscan from northern Italy and Iberian from the Iberian peninsula). The Romance languages remain dominant in south-western Europe, with Rumanian as an outlier in south-eastern Europe, but the spread of, especially, Spanish and Portuguese to the Americas means that speakers of Romance languages in Europe are now outnumbered by those in the Americas.

The Romance languages that are also official languages of independent

962

nation-states are: French (France, parts of Belgium, parts of Switzerland, Monaco; 66 million native speakers world-wide, plus several million second-language speakers), Spanish (Spain, 200 million world-wide), Portuguese (Portugal, 130 million world-wide), Italian (Italy, San Marino, 60 million), Rumanian (Rumania, 22 million; the official political spelling is Romania(n)). Catalan and Galician, with about 9 and 3 million speakers respectively, have enhanced their political status with the development of autonomy in, respectively, north-eastern and north-western Spain, while Catalan is also the official language of Andorra. In southern France, perhaps 2 million people regularly use dialects of Occitan (often referred to collectively as Provençal, though this is technically the name of one Occitan dialect group); for many, however, the status of the local variety of Occitan is more akin to that of a dialect of French (see Chapter 25, section 1.1).

Because of important linguistic differences, Sardinian is sometimes regarded, especially by linguists, as a distinct language from Italian. In the USSR, the Moldavian dialect of Rumanian has been elevated to the status of a distinct language, the national language of Moldavia, one of the constituent republics of the USSR; it has rather fewer than 3 million speakers.

Outside Europe, Spanish is the official language of every mainland American country from Mexico to Argentina and Chile, with the exception of Belize, Guyana, Suriname, French Guiana and Brazil, and also of Cuba and the Dominican Republic. A creolised version of Spanish (or possibly of Portuguese with subsequent Spanish influence) called Papiamentu is the national language of Aruba, Bonaire and Curaçao in the Netherlands Antilles, off the Venezuelan coast. Portuguese is the dominant language of Brazil. It is also the official language in the former Portuguese African colonies, with creolised forms of Portuguese being the usual spoken languages of Cape Verde and São Tomé e Príncipe. French is dominant in Quebec and some French territories in the South Pacific and, in creolised form, is the usual medium of communication in Haiti, the French West Indies and on the following Indian Ocean islands: Mauritius, Seychelles, Réunion.

## 1.1.4 Slavonic languages

Along the Germanic and Romance, Slavonic (Slavic) is one of the three branches of Indo-European most widespread in Europe. Speakers of Slavonic languages occupy much of eastern and central Europe and, separated from other Slavonic-language speakers by Hungarian and Rumanian, parts of south-eastern Europe. In the USSR, Russian, though not technically the official language, clearly occupies this position *de facto*; it has over 150 million native speakers and over 60 million second-language speakers. Two other Slavonic languages are the national languages of constituent republics of the USSR: Ukrainian (40 million) and Belorussian (7 million). Polish (35 million) is the official and national language of Poland. Czech (over 10 million) and Slovak (5 million) are the official and national languages of Czechoslovakia. In Yugoslavia, three Slavonic languages are both official and national languages: Serbo-Croatian (17 million), Slovenian (in the north-west, 2 million) and Macedonian (in the south-east, 1 million). Bulgarian (8 million) is the official and national language of Bulgaria.

The major expansion of Slavonic languages outside Europe has been the expansion of Russian to other parts of the USSR, especially northern Asia (see section 2).

### 1.1.5  Other Indo-European branches of Europe

Only two languages of the Baltic branch survive, Lithuanian and Latvian, both national languages of the corresponding constituent republics of the USSR, with about 3 and 1½ million speakers respectively.

Greek is the sole member of the Greek (Hellenic) branch of Indo-European, spoken in Greece and by the majority of the population in Cyprus by about 10 million speakers.

Albanian is another language forming a distinct branch of Indo-European. It is spoken in Albania and neighbouring parts of Yugoslavia, with about 4 million speakers.

Finally, Armenian is another single-language branch of Indo-European, though the two main dialect groups, Eastern Armenian and Western Armenian, are rather different from one another and have distinct written forms. Eastern Armenian is the national language of Armenia, one of the constituent republics of the USSR and located in the Caucasus. Outside Armenia, Armenian-speakers are scattered as a minority across a large number of Middle Eastern and other countries. The total number of Armenian speakers is around 5 million.

### 1.1.6  European representatives of non-European branches of Indo-European

The Indo-Iranian branch of Indo-European is spoken primarily in Asia, but some individual languages are spoken in Europe, though none by numbers approaching a million speakers. The only Indo-Aryan language spoken in Europe (other than as the result of very recent immigration) is Romany, the language of the Gypsies. Some Iranian languages are spoken in the Caucasus.

## 1.2 Uralic

The second major language family of Europe is the Uralic family, sometimes also called Finno-Ugric, though this is properly the name of one (the major) branch of the family (the other being Samoyedic). The major Uralic languages of Europe are Hungarian (Hungary, parts of surrounding countries, 14 million), Finnish (Finland, 5 million) and Estonian (Estonia, one of the constituent republics of the USSR, 1 million); one further language, Mordvin, has rather fewer than 1 million speakers on the middle course of the Volga, living mixed with Russian-speaking populations. Other Uralic languages are spoken in northern Scandinavia (Lappish, now often called Saame) and, usually together with speakers of Russian, in north-eastern European parts of the USSR and north-western Siberia.

## 1.3 Basque

Basque, with some 600,000 speakers in the western Pyrenees, mainly in Spain, though also in France, is a language-isolate, the only survivor from among the non-Indo-European languages that occupied much of south-western Europe before the Indo-European and, more specifically, the Roman expansion.

## 1.4 Caucasian

The Caucasus mountains form a land-bridge between Europe and Asia, and the large number of languages spoken here has gained for the area the name 'mountain of tongues'. Some of the languages spoken in the Caucasus belong to one or other of the major families of the area, in particular Turkic (e.g. Azerbaijani) or Indo-European (Armenian, Iranian languages). However, a number of languages remain as not belonging to any established language family outside the Caucasus; these are the Caucasian languages. Even the question of whether all Caucasian languages form a single family is disputed, with only the following being widely accepted as genetic families: South Caucasian (Kartvelian), North-West Caucasian, North-East Caucasian; and even the unity of North-East Caucasian is open to doubt. Georgian, a South Caucasian language with some 4 million speakers, is the national language of Georgia, one of the constituent republics of the USSR.

## 1.5 European representatives of non-European language families

Around the periphery of Europe, especially in the broad geographical definition used here, there are some representatives of language families that are spoken predominantly outside Europe, especially Asia.

Turning first to Altaic languages, some Turkic languages are spoken on the Volga and in the Caucasus. Of Turkic languages spoken on the Volga, Tatar has some 5½ million speakers, Chuvash about 1½ million. Azerbaijani is the national language of Azerbaidzhan, one of the constituent republics of the USSR in the Caucasus, and is spoken also in north-western Iran, with a total of around 12 million speakers. The geographical definition of Europe includes the western part of Kazakhstan, but Kazakh will be treated in section 2 on Asia. Turkish and closely related Turkic languages are spoken in the Balkans, including not only European Turkey but also substantial minorities in, for instance, Bulgaria. One Mongolian language, Kalmyk, has over 100,000 speakers to the north-west of the Caspian Sea.

Maltese, which is historically an offshoot of Arabic, a member of the Semitic branch of Afroasiatic, is the national and (with English) official language of Malta, with over 300,000 speakers.

## 2 ASIA

Asia divides into a number of cultural areas, and although the organisation of material in this section is by genetic groupings it will be convenient to bear the following cultural division in mind: northern Asia (Siberia), Central Asia, south-western Asia, South Asia ('Indian sub-continent'), East Asia, South-East Asia. The presentation of material will follow roughly this division.

The intrusion of European colonial languages into Asia in terms of native speakers is restricted almost exclusively to northern Asia, where Russian is now the dominant language: even in autonomous administrative units assigned to indigenous peoples, native speakers of Russian are in nearly every instance the majority of the population. In the remainder of the discussion below, Russian will be left out of account.

### 2.1 Uralic Languages

Uralic languages dominate in the sparsely populated western part of northern Asia. For discussion of Uralic languages, see section 1.2.

### 2.2. Altaic Languages

The existence of an Altaic language family, comprising the Turkic, Mongolian and Tungusic languages, is widely, though not universally, accepted. More controversial is the inclusion of yet further languages into this family, in particular Korean and Japanese (see section 2.12).

Turkic languages dominate Central Asia, with the exception of

Tadzhikistan, and several Central Asian Turkic languages have several million speakers: Uzbek (12 million), Kazakh (7 million), Uighur (6 million), Turkmenian (3 million), Kirghiz (2 million); all except Uighur are spoken predominantly in the like-named constituent republics of the USSR, sometimes spreading across to neighbouring countries, while Uighur is spoken predominantly in north-western China. Across the Caspian Sea, in Azerbaidzhan (a constituent republic of the USSR) and north-western Iran we find Azerbaijani (12 million speakers); a few similar Turkic languages are also spoken in other parts of the Caucasus. Separated geographically from the main bulk of Turkic languages is Turkish, spoken in Turkey, parts of Cyprus, also spreading into other Balkan countries, especially Bulgaria; the number of native speakers is over 50 million. Finally, some Turkic languages are spoken on the middle course of the Volga, in particular Tatar (5½ million) and Chuvash (1½ million); native speakers of Tatar stretch well into Siberia as isolated pockets among speakers of other languages, primarily Russian.

The Mongolian languages are spoken primarily in Mongolia, north-central China, and parts of Siberia adjacent to Mongolia, though there are outliers in Afghanistan and even in Europe to the north of the Caucasus (Kalmyk). The language Mongolian, sometimes called Khalkha after its principal dialect, has about 3½ million speakers divided between Mongolia and China.

The Tungusic family includes a number of languages spoken in north-eastern Asia, with numbers of native speakers ranging up to the tens of thousands. The most famous Tungusic language is Manchu, the language of the dynasty that ruled China from 1644 to 1911; nearly all ethnic Manchu are, however, now native speakers of Chinese.

## 2.3 Paleo-Siberian languages

A number of languages remain in northern Asia that are not assigned to the Indo-European, Uralic or Altaic groupings; they are conventionally referred to as Paleo-Siberian (or Paleo-Asiatic). This is simply a label of convenience, and does not imply that the Paleo-Siberian languages are genetically related to one another. All are spoken by at most a couple of tens of thousands of native speakers.

Ket is spoken on the middle course of the Yenisey river and is typologically the most aberrant language of northern Asia; no attempts to relate it closely to other genetic groupings have gained widespread acceptance. Yukaghir is spoken on the northern coast of eastern Siberia; the grouping of Yukaghir with Uralic has gained some acceptance. Nivkh (Gilyak) is spoken at the mouth of the Amur river and on Sakhalin island; it too is widely regarded as a language isolate. Ainu still has a few native speakers on

Hokkaido island (Japan); some scholars believe it to be related to Altaic.

The peninsulas of Chukotka and Kamchatka in the far east of Siberia are occupied by the Chukotko-Kamchatkan family, a well-established genetic grouping. Greenberg's classification would place Chukotko-Kamchatkan in the Eurasiatic family, which would also include the Eskimo-Aleut family, which is represented by Eskimo speakers on the eastern tip of Siberia as well as its more numerous representatives in North America.

## 2.4 Afroasiatic languages

A large part of south-western Asia – Iraq, Syria, Lebanon, Israel, the Arabian peninsula – is dominated almost exclusively by languages of the Semitic branch of Afroasiatic (see section 3.1). Most of the area is dominated by Arabic, with over 100 million speakers world-wide, mainly in south-western Asia and North Africa. Hebrew, a rare example of a dead language revived as a community's normal means of communication, has about 3 million native speakers in Israel.

Before the expansion of Arabic in the later centuries of the first millennium AD, other Semitic languages were dominant in this area. In the immediately preceding period, the dominant language was Aramaic, the native language of Jesus Christ. Going back still earlier to the Assyrian and Babylonian empires, the dominant language was Akkadian. The preceding empire, that of Sumeria, spoke Sumerian, a non-Semitic language and one so far resisting attempts to link it genetically to other languages.

## 2.5 Indo-European Languages

The more easterly part of south-western Asia and the northern part of South Asia are dominated by languages of the Indo-Iranian branch of Indo-European, which also stretches into Central Asia and has outliers in Sri Lanka and the Maldives; the boundary between Iranian languages (to the west) and Indo-Aryan languages (to the east) runs through Pakistan.

The Iranian language with the largest number of native speakers is Persian, the dominant language of Iran. Local varieties of Persian, Dari (in Afghanistan) and Tajik (in the like-named constituent republic of the USSR, in Central Asia), have been elevated to the status of distinct languages. The number of native speakers of Persian excluding Tajik is probably between 20 and 30 million, plus several million second-language speakers, that of Tajik around 4 million. Pashto, the most widely spoken language of Afghanistan and a co-official language with Dari, has about 13 million speakers in Afghanistan and Pakistan. Iranian languages that have large numbers of native speakers but do not correspond to political units are Kurdish (5 million, divided among Turkey, Iraq and Iran), Balochi (2 million, Pakistan), and Luri (3 million), Mazanderani (2 million) and Gilaki (1½ million), the last three spoken in northern Iran.

The precise division of the Indo-Aryan branch into individual languages is controversial; here I follow Ruhlen (1987: 38). The language with most native speakers is Hindi-Urdu (Western Hindi), with over 200 million native speakers in Pakistan and northern India plus several million second-language speakers; the Hindi variant is the official language of India, the Urdu variant that of Pakistan. Bengali has about 140 million speakers, in Bangladesh and the Indian state of West Bengal. Other national languages are Nepali (10 million, Nepal) and Sinhalese (10 million, Sri Lanka); an offshoot of Sinhalese, Divehi, is the language of the Maldives. Other Indo-Aryan languages include the following; those marked with an asterisk are scheduled languages in the Indian Constitution: Lahnda (15 million, primarily Pakistan),*Sindhi (7 million, India and Pakistan), Awadhi (Eastern Hindi, 55 million, India), *Marathi (45 million, India), *Punjabi (40 million, mainly India), Bihari (30 million, India), *Gujarati (30 million, India), *Oriya (20 million, India), *Assamese (16 million, India, Bangladesh), Marwari (13 million, India), *Kashmiri (3 million, mainly India), Bhili (3 million, India), Pahari (2 million, India), Banjari (2 million, India), Garhwali (1 million, India), Kumauni (1 million, India). Mention should also be made of Sanskrit, the classical language of Hindu civilisation, which still claims a few native speakers and is one of the scheduled languages in the Indian Constitution.

## 2.6 Language isolates of South Asia

Burushaski is a language isolate spoken by some 50,000 speakers in northern Pakistan. Nahali, spoken by several hundred people in north-eastern India, is sometimes considered a member of the Austroasiatic family. Andamanese, with about 1,000 speakers, is the indigenous language group of the Andaman Islands; Greenberg's inclusion of Andamanese into Indo-Pacific (see section 4.2) has not gained widespread acceptance.

## 2.7 Dravidian

The Dravidian languages dominate southern India, while one Dravidian language, Tamil, is also spoken in northern Sri Lanka and there are Dravidian outliers further north, in particular Brahui, spoken in Pakistan; these outliers probably reflect an earlier wider dispersion of Dravidian languages before the Indo-Aryan expansion. The four major literary Dravidian languages, all scheduled languages under the Indian Constitution, are: Tamil (over 50 million), Telugu (over 50 million), Kannada (over 25 million), Malayalam (over 25 million). Other Dravidian languages with over 1 million speakers are: Konkani (3 million), Gondi (2 million) and Kurukh (2 million).

## 2.8 Austroasiatic

Recognition of the extent of the Austroasiatic language family, in particular by the inclusion of its most populous language, Vietnamese, has come only recently. Member languages are scattered from north-eastern India to the Malay peninsula, with Cambodia and Vietnam as the only areas that are solidly Austroasiatic-speaking. Vietnamese has about 47 million speakers, mainly in Vietnam, and Khmer about 7 million speakers, mainly in Cambodia. Other Austroasiatic languages with over 1 million speakers are Santali (4 million) and Mundari (1 million), both in India.

Under Greenberg's classification, Austroasiatic would be one branch of a larger Austric phylum, whose other branches would be: Miao-Yao, Daic (Kam-Tai) and Austronesian.

## 2.9 Miao-Yao

The Miao-Yao (Hmong-Mîen) languages are spoken scattered across southern China and neighbouring countries to the south. Miao, now more often referred to as Hmong, has about 5 million speakers, while Mien (Yao) has about 1 million. The broader genetic relations of the Miao-Yao family are uncertain, with attempts being made to link it both to Sino-Tibetan and to Austric.

## 2.10 Sino-Tibetan

Sino-Tibetan is the dominant language family of mainland East Asia, with incursions into South-East Asia and the northern fringe of South Asia. With about 1,000 million speakers (between one-fifth and one quarter of the world's population), it comes second only to Indo-European in terms of number of speakers.

The major genetic division within the family is between Chinese and the rest of Sino-Tibetan. Chinese is the dominant language of China and is spoken by significant numbers of overseas Chinese; Ruhlen (1987: 143) estimates the total number of speakers at 927 million, though this may be an underestimate. Since different regional varieties of Chinese are often mutually unintelligible, some linguists regard the traditional Chinese 'dialects' as constituting rather from five to eight distinct languages, for instance: Mandarin (680 million), Wu (69 million), Yue (Cantonese, 53 million), Southern Min (36 million), Xiang (29 million), Kejia (Hakka, 28 million), Gan (21 million), Northern Min (11 million). Mandarin is also widely used as a second language by native speakers of other varieties of Chinese. Whether one takes Chinese as a whole or just Mandarin, this language has by far the greatest number of native speakers of all the world's languages.

The rest of the family is often referred to as Tibeto-Burman, though since Karen, spoken mainly in south-eastern Burma and adjacent parts of Thailand, is rather divergent from the other non-Chinese Sino-Tibetan languages it is sometimes excluded from Tibeto-Burman. Estimates of the number of Karen speakers and also of the number of distinct languages within Karen vary widely, though Grimes (1988: 441) cites an estimate that S'gaw and Pwo Karen have each over 1 million speakers.

The other Tibeto-Burman languages with large numbers of speakers are Burmese (22 millon, mainly Burma), Tibetan (4 million, mainly Tibet and other adjacent parts of China), and the following languages spoken primarily or exclusively in China: Yi (Lolo, 5½ million), Hani (1 million), Bai (1 million); this last set of figures is from the 1982 census of China as cited in Grimes (1988). One variety of Tibetan, Dzonkha, is the national language of Bhutan.

### 2.11 Kam-Tai

The convention has become established of using Tai as the name of a group of languages and Thai as the name of its principal language, the national language of Thailand. The precise division of Tai into languages is somewhat controversial, though several well-established distinct languages have over a million speakers. Together with Kadai and Kam-Sui, Tai forms the Kam-Tai language family, spoken in Thailand and other parts of South-East Asia and in substantial parts of southern China. Possible genetic relationships to Sino-Tibetan are now generally discounted, more distant relations being sought rather with the Austroasiatic or Austronesian families or both.

Thai proper has about 20 million speakers and Lao about 17 million, though the tendency in Thailand to consider speakers of all Tai languages as native speakers of Thai often leads to larger figures for Thai (up to 44 million) and smaller figures for Lao (down to 3 million) and other Tai languages spoken at least partially in Thailand, such as Northern Tai (6 million), Southern Tai (4 million). The following Tai languages are all spoken in China: Zhuang (13 million), Bouyei (2 million), Zhongjia (2 million), Li (1 million). Shan (2 million) is spoken primarily in Burma. Of the Kam-Sui languages, Dong (Kam) has about 1½ million speakers in southern China.

## 2.12 Japanese and Korean

Whether Japanese and Korean are related to one another or to any other languages remains controversial, though links to Altaic are quite widely accepted. Japanese has some 115 million speakers, primarily in Japan, while Korea has about 55 million speakers, primarily in Korea; both countries are predominantly unilingual.

## 2.13 Austronesian

Although the Austronesian language family has most of its native speakers in the Asian island-nations of Indonesia and the Philippines and in Malaysia, it is convenient to discuss the family as a whole in section 4.1 on Oceania. In Asia, apart from the above mentioned countries, there are small numbers of speakers of Austronesian languages in Taiwan (where the indigenous Austronesian languages are now a tiny minority in comparison with Chinese) and in small areas of coastal mainland South-East Asia.

One Austronesian language, known traditionally as Malay and now officially as Bahasa Malaysia or Bahasa Indonesia, is the official language of Malaysia and Indonesia (and also of Brunei and one of the official languages of Singapore). The number of native speakers is perhaps 20 million, rising to 35 million if one includes more divergent dialects. As the lingua franca of Malaysia and, especially, Indonesia, however, it claims well over 100 million first- and second-language speakers. Other Austronesian languages of Indonesia include: Javanese (50 million, with half as many again second-language speakers), Sundanese (25 million), Madurese (8 million), Minang-kabau (7 million), Balinese (3 million), Buginese (2½ million), Makassarese (2 million), Achinese (Acehnese, 2 million), Toba Batak (2 million), Sasak (1½ million), Lampung (1½ million), Dayak (1 million).

In the Philippines, Tagalog has over 10 million native speakers and at least half as many again second-language speakers, reflecting its adoption as the country's national language. Other Austronesian languages of the Philippines include: Cebuano (12 million), Ilocano (5 million), Hiligaynon (4 million), Bikol (3 million), Samar-Leyte (Waray-Waray, 2 to 3 million), Kapampangan (1½ million), Pangasinan (1 million).

## 3. AFRICA

Within the last few decades, the genetic classification of the languages of Africa has been substantially clarified, primarily through the work of Greenberg (1963). It is now generally recognised that the languages of Africa fall into four major families: Afroasiatic, predominating in the north and spreading into Asia; Nilo-Saharan, predominating in north-central sub-

Saharan Africa; Khoisan, represented mainly in the far south-west of the continent; and Niger-Kordofanian occupying the rest of the continent. The Bantu group of languages, the first to be recognised in sub-Saharan Africa, is now known to be only a relatively low-level sub-grouping within Niger-Kordofanian, even though it occupies almost all of the southern part of the continent. Languages not from these four families occupy a peripheral role in the continent in terms of number of speakers, though most former European colonies in sub-Saharan Africa, faced with a plethora of indigenous languages, have chosen to continue the use of the language of the colonial administration as official language.

## 3.1 Afroasiatic languages

The Afroasiatic family covers most of Africa north of the Sahara and the Sahara itself, dipping down on the eastern side of the continent to include the Horn of Africa too; as noted in section 2, Afroasiatic is also a major language family of south-western Asia. The family has five branches: Semitic, Egyptian, Berber, Cushitic and Chadic. The Omotic (West Cushitic) languages are sufficiently different from other Cushitic languages for some scholars to consider raising Omotic to the level of a separate branch of Afro-asiatic, and even the unity of the rest of Cushitic is not beyond question. The Egyptian branch, comprising the one language Egyptian (i.e. the language of Ancient Egypt) and its medieval descendant Coptic, has been extinct since perhaps the sixteenth century, after serving for millennia as the language of one of the world's earliest and most spectacular civilisations.

### 3.1.1 Semitic languages

Over most of Africa north of the Sahara the dominant language is Arabic, with some 100 million speakers world-wide. The spread of Arabic to North Africa took place initially during the last centuries of the first millennium AD, along with the spread of Islam. Some of the languages spoken earlier in the area have been replaced completely, such as Coptic, while Berber (see section 3.1.2) survives especially in the west of the area. The other part of the continent where Semitic languages predominate is Ethiopia. Amharic, with perhaps 9 million first-language and several million second-language speakers, is the official language of Ethiopia; while another Semitic language of Ethiopia, Tigrinya, has about 3½ million speakers.

### 3.1.2 Berber languages

The precise sub-division of Berber into languages and dialects is particularly difficult. The total number of Berber speakers is probably around 11 million, and several well-defined local variants have over 1 million speakers, e.g. Shilha (3 million), Tamazight (2 million), Kabyle (1 million), Riff (1 million). The main concentration of speakers is in Algeria and, especially, Morocco; in the latter about one third of the population speaks a variety of Berber natively. However, varieties of Berber are spoken as far west as north-western Egypt. In parts of the Sahara, for instance northern Niger, the sparse population is overwhelmingly Berber-speaking. It is probable that the Guanche language of the Canary Islands, long since supplanted by Spanish, was a Berber language.

### 3.1.3 Cushitic languages

The Cushitic languages are spoken in the Horn of Africa. The Cushitic language with the largest number of speakers is Oromo (Galla), with about 9 million speakers. Somali, with about 5 million speakers, is the official and national language of Somalia and is also spoken by about half the population of Djibouti; there are also substantial Somali-speaking populations in Ethiopia and Kenya.

### 3.1.4 Chadic languages

The main concentration of Chadic languages is in northern Nigeria and in adjacent Niger, though there are Hausa-speaking communities as far east as Sudan. The major language of the family is Hausa, with perhaps as many as 25 million divided roughly equally between first- and second-language speakers; it has an established literary language and is the dominant language of northern Nigeria.

### 3.2. Nilo-Saharan Languages

The Nilo-Saharan languages cover a more or less continuous territory including much of Chad (and extending into Libya, Niger, central Sudan, Nigeria and the Central African Republic), southern Sudan, northern Uganda and western Kenya (extending into Ethiopia, Zaire and Tanzania). In addition there are two outliers. One is on the great bend of the Niger River from Mali to north-western Nigeria and includes Dyerma, with over 1 million speakers, nearly all in Niger; the closely related Songhai, spoken in Mali, Bourkina Fasso and Niger, has about a further 500,000 speakers, and the two are perhaps to be considered a single language. The other outlier comprises languages spoken in northern Sudan and Egypt, the main one being Kenuzi-Dongola (Nubian), with perhaps a million speakers. Within the main block of

Nilo-Saharan languages, the following have the largest number of speakers: Kanuri (3½ million, mainly north-eastern Nigeria), Luo (2 million, mainly in Kenya), Dinka (2 million, southern Sudan).

It should be noted that the precise relations of various Nilo-Saharan languages to one another remain in part unclear, likewise the division into languages and dialects. It may turn out that some languages presently classified as Nilo-Saharan do not belong to the family (or to any other established family). On the language/dialect controversy, Dinka, for instance, has been sub-divided into as many as five distinct languages.

### 3.3 Niger-Kordofanian languages

The Niger-Kordofanian family has two branches, Kordofanian, spoken in a small part of central Sudan, and Niger-Congo, covering most of the southern part of the continent. Emphasis here will inevitably be on Niger-Congo. While there is some controversy concerning the precise details of some of the subclassification of Niger-Congo languages, the general picture as set out below is widely accepted, with the following branches: Mende, West Atlantic, Kru, Gur (Voltaic), Kwa, Adamawa-Eastern, Benue-Congo.

Mande languages are spoken in West Africa from Senegal and Mali to Liberia and Ivory Coast, primarily away from the coast. Malinke-Bambara-Dyula, with about 7 million speakers, has a compound name representing its three main dialect groups. The other major language of the group is Mende, with perhaps 1 million speakers, in Sierra Leone.

The West Atlantic languages have a rather scattered distribution, due in large measure to the scattered distribution of the major West Atlantic language, Fula, with perhaps 8 million speakers, ranging from southernmost Mauritania to Cameroon, with major concentrations in Senegal, Guinea, Mali, Bourkina Fasso, Niger, Nigeria and Cameroon. Other major West Atlantic languages are Wolof, with over 1 million native speakers in Senegal, and Temne, with about 1 million speakers in Sierra Leone.

The Kru languages are spoken in south-eastern Liberia and south-western Ivory Coast. The Gur languages are spoken in interior West Africa from northern Ivory Coast to northern Benin; one Gur language, Moore, has about 3½ million native speakers, comprising about one half of the population of Bourkina Fasso.

Kwa languages are spoken along a coastal strip a few hundred miles wide from central Ivory Coast into Cameroon. The group includes several of the major languages of West Africa: Yoruba (15 million speakers, mainly in south-eastern Nigeria), Igbo (12 million, south-eastern Nigeria), Akan (including Twi) Fante (about 4½ million, constituting almost one half of the population of Ghana), Ijo (about 3 million, south-eastern Nigeria), Ewe (over 1½ million speakers, mainly in Ghana, Togo), Edo (about 1 million, Nigeria), Fon (about 1 million speakers, mainly in Benin).

The Adamawa-Eastern group consists of languages spoken from north-eastern Nigeria across to Sudan, often interspersed with Nilo-Saharan languages. One Adamawa-Eastern language, Sango, though having only about 200,000 native speakers, is widely used as a lingua franca in the Central African Republic, with 2 million second-language speakers, i.e. almost the whole population of the country, and official status.

The last major branch of Niger-Congo, Benue-Congo, includes the Bantu languages, which cover almost the whole of the lobe of Africa south of a line drawn from Cameroon to Kenya. The other Benue-Congo languages are spoken in northern and eastern Nigeria and neighbouring areas; most are small in terms of number of speakers, though Ibibio-Efik has about 2 million speakers, Tiv about 1½ million speakers.

Many of the major languages of Africa belong to the Bantu sub-group of Benue-Congo. The best known is Swahili. Although Swahili has perhaps a little over 1 million native speakers, primarily on the coast of East Africa and Zanzibar, it has perhaps as many as 30 million second-language speakers, primarily in East Africa (Tanzania, Kenya, Uganda, parts of Zaire). Other major Bantu languages include the following:

Kikongo (1½ million, Zaire, Angola), Kituba (3 million, Zaire), Lingala (8½ million, including second-language speakers, Zaire, also Congo), Luba-Lulua (Luba-Kasai 4½ million, Zaire), Kinyarwanda (6 million, mainly Rwanda, also sizeable groups in Uganda and Zaire), Kirundi (5 million, mainly Burundi), Kamba (almost 2 million, Kenya), Kikuyu (over 3 million, Kenya), Luyia (over 2 million, Kenya), Sukuma (over 1 million, closer to 2 million if Nyamwezi is included, Tanzania), Luganda (2 million, Uganda), Kimbundu (2 million, Angola), Umbundu (1½ million, Angola), Chibemba (1½ million, about two thirds in Zambia, also Zaire, Tanzania), Nyanja (2½ million, mainly Malawi, also Zambia, Zimbabwe), Makua (3 million, mainly Mozambique, also Tanzania), Thonga (over 2 million, mainly Mozambique, also South Africa), Shona (4 million, mainly Zimbabwe, also Zambia, Mozambique), Tswana (3 million, roughly two thirds in South Africa, most of the remainder in Botswana), Northern Sotho (over 2 million, mainly South Africa), Southern Sotho (3 million, roughly two thirds in South Africa, one third in Lesotho), Swati (over 1 million, rather more in South Africa than in Swaziland), Xhosa (5 million, South Africa), Zulu (6 million, mainly South Africa).

### 3.4 Khoisan languages

Spoken predominantly in south-western Africa (especially Namibia, Botswana, South Africa), these are the languages of the so-called Bushmen and Hottentots. Some Khoisan languages extend into Angola, Zambia and Zimbabwe and there are even two outliers in Tanzania. It is probable that Khoisan languages occupied a much larger part of Africa before the southward expansion of the Bantu languages.

### 3.5 Indo-European Languages

The only part of the African continent where Indo-European languages have gained a foothold in terms of number of native speakers is South Africa, where Afrikaans (an offshoot of Dutch) has perhaps 5 million native speakers, English about 4 million.

Creolised forms of European languages are the dominant means of communication in some of the island states: Portuguese in Cape Verde and São Tomé e Preíncipe; French in Mauritius, Seychelles and the French overseas department of Réunion, giving a total of over 1 million for Indian Ocean French Creole. Spanish is the language of the Canary Islands and of the two Spanish enclaves on the Moroccan coast, Ceuta and Melilla.

### 3.6 Austronesian languages

Malagasy, the language of Madagascar, is the westernmost extension of the Austronesian language family; it has over 8 million speakers.

## 4 OCEANIA

(For explanation of the terms 'lingua franc', 'pidgin' and 'creole' see the note under the References to this chapter.)

With two major exceptions (other than those due to European colonisation), Oceania is dominated by the Austronesian family. The two major exceptions are New Guinea and some surrounding areas, where Austronesian languages are confined to a few coastal areas, and Australia (with Tasmania). European colonisation has resulted in English being by far the dominant language of both Australia and New Zealand, as well as Hawaii at the other end of the Pacific Islands; while French is the dominant language of New Caledonia, spoken natively by over one third of the population. In addition, an English-based pidgin, Tok Pisin, is the dominant language of inter-ethnic communication in Papua New Guinea, spoken as a second language by some 2 million people, over half the total population of the country, and by over 50,000 as a first language.

## 4.1 Austronesian languages

Although some Austronesian languages are spoken on the mainland of South-East Asia and on Taiwan, the primary distribution of Austronesian languages covers the islands from South-East Asia across the Pacific, the northernmost extension being Hawaii and the easternmost Easter Island, with a western outlier in the Malagasy language of Madagascar (see section 3.6). The most populous Austronesian languages are spoken in Indonesia, Malaysia and the Philippines and are covered in section 2.13. None of the Austronesian languages spoken outside this area has more than a few hundred thousand speakers (Samoan and Fijian have around 300,000 each), the majority much less than this. This section will therefore concentrate on the internal relations among Austronesian languages and on mentioning those Pacific Austronesian languages that are official or national languages of independent Pacific states.

Views on the classification of Austronesian languages have not yet stabilised, although it is generally recognised that the most divergent languages genetically are those of Taiwan. The remainder contains two major groups (and perhaps two smaller groups), namely Western Malayo-Polynesian (including the major languages of Indonesia, Malaysia and the Philippines) and Oceanic (including Polynesian, Micronesian and Fijian).

The Pacific island nations listed in this and the following paragraph have an Oceanic language as their national language: Fiji (Fijian, though an influx of Indian indentured labourers in the nineteenth century has left Fiji with slightly more speakers of Hindi than of Fijian). The following are more specifically members of the Polynesian branch of Oceanic: Tonga (Tongan), Western Samoa (Samoan), Tuvalu (Tuvaluan). Mention may also be made of Tahitian, the most widely-spoken language of French Polynesia. Maori and Hawaiian, the indigenous languages of New Zealand and Hawaii respectively, have now almost completely receded before English.

Independent nations with Micronesian national languages are Kiribati (Gilbertese) and Nauru (Nauruan). Micronesian languages are also the main indigenous languages of the Federated States of Micronesia and the Marshall Islands.

## 4.2 Papuan languages

The island of New Guinea, which can be taken linguistically together with some surrounding islands, is the most complex area in the world in terms of the number and variety of languages spoken. Approximately 1,000 languages are spoken by a population of around 5 million. In some coastal areas and on many islands, the local languages are Austronesian, and the Austronesian language Indonesian is also making inroads in the western half of the island,

Irian Jaya (a province of Indonesia), both through the influx of immigrants, primarily from Java, and through its use as the local lingua franca. On most of the mainland of New Guinea, however, languages unrelated to Austronesian are found; they are conventionally called Papuan languages, and scattered Papuan languages are to be found as far west as Alor, Timor and Halmahera in Indonesia and as far east as the Santa Cruz Islands in the eastern Solomon Islands. The term 'Papuan' is primarily a negative designator, indicating languages that are not Austronesian, although the Greenbergian classification includes a proposed Indo-Pacific family that would include all Papuan languages together with Tasmanian and Andamanese, a grouping that has gained relatively little acceptance. In the conservative classification proposed by Foley (1986), there are some 60 distinct families within Papuan, each containing languages about as closely related to one another as the Romance languages; Foley also notes a few plausible higher-level groupings which would incorporate two or three of these families. The more ambitious classification of Wurm (1982) includes 5 major phyla, 6 minor phyla and a small number of isolates. While future work will no doubt lead to the establishment of some higher-level groupings, Foley's conservative classification is closer to what can be reliably claimed at present.

The Papuan languages are all spoken by relatively small speech communities, The largest, Enga, spoken in the Highlands of Papua New Guinea, has about 170,000 speakers.

## 4.3 Australian Aboriginal languages

At the time of European contact, almost exactly 200 years ago, some 200 languages were spoken on the mainland of Australia and offshore islands. At present, perhaps half this number survives, though less than a quarter continue to be transmitted from parents to children; Australian languages are strongest in areas of least European colonisation, such as the Northern Territory, northern Queensland, northern Western Australia and northern South Australia. Dixon (1980) argues that virtually all 200 of these languages form a single family, the only exceptions being Tiwi, spoken off the northern coast, and Djingili, spoken in the centre of the Northern Territory; in the case of Tiwi, it could be that prolonged isolation from other Australian languages has led to the divergence of an originally Australian language. The surviving records of the extinct Tasmanian languages are insufficient to demonstrate whether or not these languages are related to the Australian languages.

The Australian languages with the largest numbers of speakers have around 1–2,000, a number greatly exceeded by some of the pidgins and creoles that have grown up in Aboriginal communities; for instance, Roper

River Kriol has 10,000 native speakers and at least as many again second-language speakers.

## 5 THE AMERICAS

The impact of the expansion of the Indo-European languages since the sixteenth century has manifested itself nowhere more extensively than in the Americas. At present, only three countries of the Western Hemisphere have the majority of their population speaking a non-Indo-European language natively: Greenland (where the majority speak Greenlandic, a variety of Eskimo), Paraguay (where the majority speak Guaraní, a Tupian language) and Bolivia (where Quechua and Aymara together account for more than half the population).

### 5.1. Indo-European languages of the Americas

Over most of the United States and Canada, English is the dominant language, although French is dominant in Quebec, and there are substantial minorities in particular of Spanish-speakers in parts of the United States, especially the south-west, New York and Florida. In most of the rest of the continent Spanish is the dominant language, even where it is not the language of the majority (as in Bolivia and Paraguay), with the significant exception of Brazil (predominantly Portuguese-speaking) and the numerically smaller enclaves of Belize, Guyana, Suriname and French Guiana, which are more conveniently treated with the Caribbean.

Some of the larger Caribbean nations are Spanish-speaking, namely Cuba and the Dominican Republic, also Puerto Rico (a United States territory). In most of the other islands, and also Belize, Guyana, Suriname and French Guiana, one finds creolised forms of English, French or Spanish, though in islands where the official language is the European language which forms the lexical base of the local creole there is typically a 'post-creole continuum', with many inhabitants controlling a range of language varieties between the true creole and the standard metropolitan language. In general, the creole spoken on a given territory is derived from the language of the colonial or ex-colonial power, but there are some exceptions: Sranan, the most widely spoken language of Suriname, a former Dutch colony, is English-based; Papiamentu, the language of Aruba, Bonaire and Curaçao in the Netherlands Antilles, is Spanish-based (or perhaps Portuguese-based with subsequent relexification from Spanish); some of the former British colonies, such as Dominica and St Lucia, have French-based creoles. Special mention should be made of French-based Haitian Creole, the sole language controlled fluently by most of the island's 5½ million inhabitants.

Other European languages have a more marginal hold in the Americas, for instance Danish in Greenland (a Danish dependency) and Dutch as the official language in Suriname and the Netherlands Antilles. While continuing European immigration means that some languages have large numbers of speakers in the Western Hemisphere (e.g. German has over 6 million speakers in the United States, Polish about 2½ million), the prospects for large stable communities speaking these languages are not promising.

## 5.2 Indigenous languages of the Americas

There are probably around six or seven hundred indigenous languages of the Americas, though their position everywhere except Greenland is subservient to that of one or more Indo-European languages; even in Paraguay and Bolivia the official language is Spanish. The total number of speakers is perhaps 18 million. Classifications of the indigenous languages of the Americas run the whole gamut from conservative classifications with around 200 distinct families, to the radical proposal by Greenberg (1987) to recognise only three families in the Americas: Eskimo-Aleut, Na-Dene and Amerind. In the present section, considerations of space mean that only some of the more important languages and well-established language families can be mentioned; only three indigenous languages of the Americas, incidentally, have over 1 million speakers: Quechua, Guaraní and Aymara; to these one might add Nahuatl, if it is considered a single language.

Eskimo-Aleut is an established language family, with possible genetic relationships to languages of northern Asia (see section 2.3). Of its two branches, Aleut is spoken on the Aleutian Islands, Eskimo (Inuktitut) on the coasts and islands from the eastern tip of Siberia through Alaska and Canada to Greenland, where one variety of Eskimo, Greenlandic, is the official language.

Na-Dene is a more controversial genetic unit, but its core is the well-established Athabascan family, spoken over the rest of Alaska and western Canada, but with outliers in the south-western United States, including Navaho with over 100,000 speakers, making it the largest indigenous language north of the Mexican border.

Other important well-established families of North America include Algonquian (north-eastern United States and eastern Canada, though also extending quite far west), Iroquoian (eastern Great Lakes), Siouan (Great Plains), Uto-Aztecan (south-western United States, northern and central Mexico). If Nahuatl, a sub-group of Uto-Aztecan, is considered a single language, then it would have about 1 million speakers; it is the descendant of the language of the pre-Columbian Aztec civilisation. Another major language family of Central America is Mayan, including a number of languages with around half a million speakers (Quiche, Yucatec, Cakchiquel); it includes the language of the pre-Columbian Mayan civilisation.

Three major language families of South America are Arawakan, Cariban and Tupian, the first two spoken predominantly north of the Amazon, the last almost exclusively south of the Amazon. One Tupian language, Guaraní, has about 3 million speakers, nearly all in Paraguay; conversely, almost all Paraguayans speak Guaraní, which has thus attained the status of a national language.

The genetic affiliations of the other two South American languages with the greatest number of speakers, Quechua (7 million) and Aymara (1½ million), are less clear, though the possibility of a genetic link between them (the Quechumaran family) is quite widely accepted. Quechua is spoken primarily in Peru and Bolivia, though it extends northwards into Ecuador and southwards as far as northern Chile; it is the language of the pre-Columbian Inca civilisation. Because of the lack of mutual intelligibility among Quechua dialects, it is often considered a collection of distinct languages rather than of dialects. Aymara is spoken primarily in Boliva and Peru, though extending into Chile and Argentina.

Since the sixteenth century many indigenous languages of the Americas have died out, while others are even now on the verge of extinction. This represents an irretrievable cultural loss to humanity as a whole.

## REFERENCES

Dixon, R.M.W. (1981) *The languages of Australia*, Cambridge University Press, Cambridge.

Foley, William A. (1986) *The Papuan languages of New Guinea*, Cambridge University Press, Cambridge.

Greenberg, Joseph H. (1963) *The languages of Africa*, Mouton, The Hague.

Greenberg, Joseph H. (1987) *Language in the Americas*, Stanford University Press, Stanford.

Grimes, Barbara F. (ed.) (1988) *Languages of the world: Ethnologue*, 11th ed., Summer Institute of Linguistics, Dallas.

Ruhlen, Merritt (1987) *A guide to the world's languages. Vol. 1: Classification*, Stanford University Press, Stanford.

Wurm, Stephen A. (1982) *Papuan languages of Oceania*, Gunter Narr, Tübingen.

(Note: Where a mixed speech community uses a natural language as a convenient general medium it is known as a *lingua franca* (as Latin has often been). Sometimes the medium comprises a mixture of native elements and a simplified variety of an intrusive idiom (like English or French in colonised areas); in that case it is called a *pidgin*. If such a medium is acquired as a natural and native language by new speakers (and undergoes evolution of its own), the term used is *creole*. For a general treatment see:

Todd, L. (1974) *Pidgins and creoles*, Routledge and Kegan Paul, London; Mühlhäusler,

P. (1986) *Pidgin and creole linguistics*, Blackwell, Oxford; Holm, J.A. (1988) *Pidgins and creoles*, 2 vols., Cambridge University Press, Cambridge and for continued serial coverage consult *The Journal of Pidgin and Creole Languages*, Benjamins, Amsterdam (from 1986 onwards).)

# INDEX OF TOPICS AND TECHNICAL TERMS

# INDEX OF NAMES

Note - Page numbers in *italic type* indicate where a reference is printed in full.